Use MyManagementLab to prepare for tests and exams and go to class ready to learn.

Get a Better Grade!

eText

Access the eText while you study—without leaving the online environment!

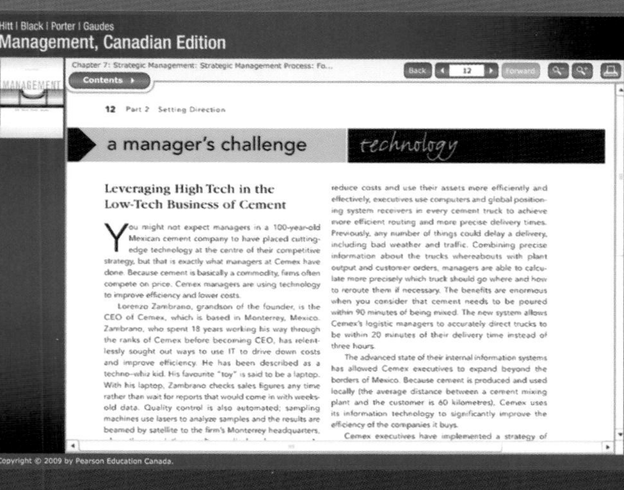

Glossary Flashcards

Use these quick and fun flashcards to study the text's business terms.

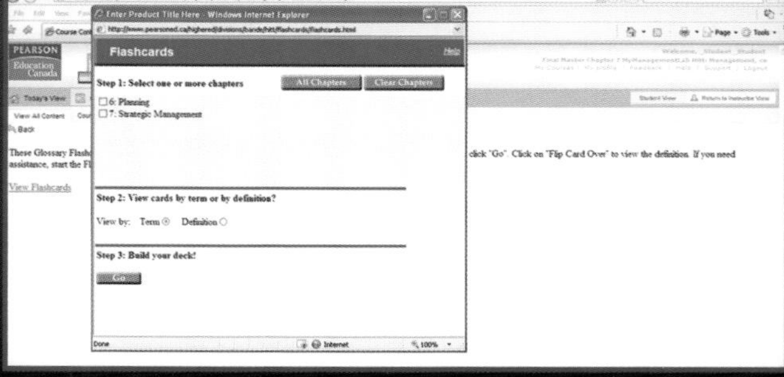

Student PowerPoints

Use these for quick review of key concepts.

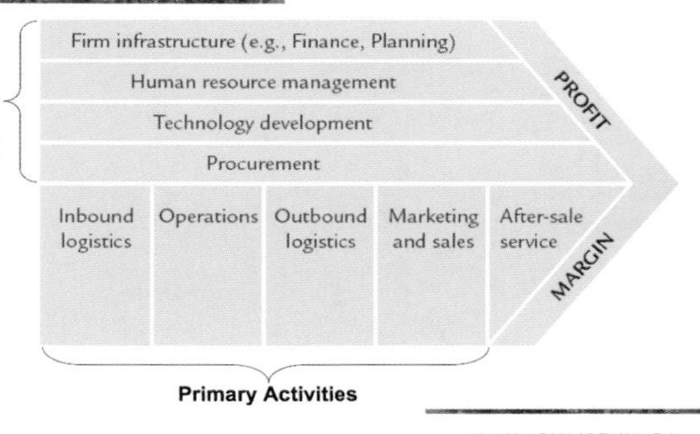

Content and tools to enrich your learning experience and foster interest and mastery of the subject.

PERSONALIZED LEARNING!

Auto-graded Tests and Assignments

MyManagementLab comes with two preloaded Sample Tests per chapter (the Pre-Test and the Post-Test). Work through these diagnostic tests to identify areas you haven't fully understood. The Sample Tests generate a personalized Study Plan, designed specifically to suit your studying needs. Instructors can assign these Sample Tests or create assignments, quizzes, and tests using a mix of publisher-supplied content and their own custom exercises.

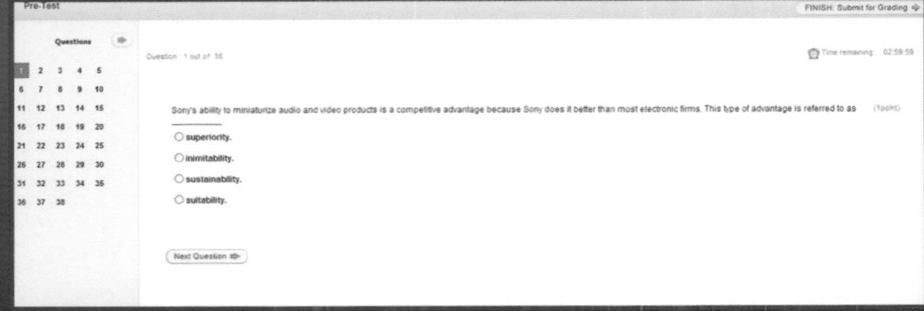

Personalized Study Plan

When you use MyManagementLab, you're treated as an individual with specific learning needs. Because you have limited study time, it's important for you to be as effective as possible during that time. A personalized Study Plan is generated from your results on Sample Tests and instructor assignments. You can clearly see which topics you have mastered and, more importantly, which ones you still need to work on.

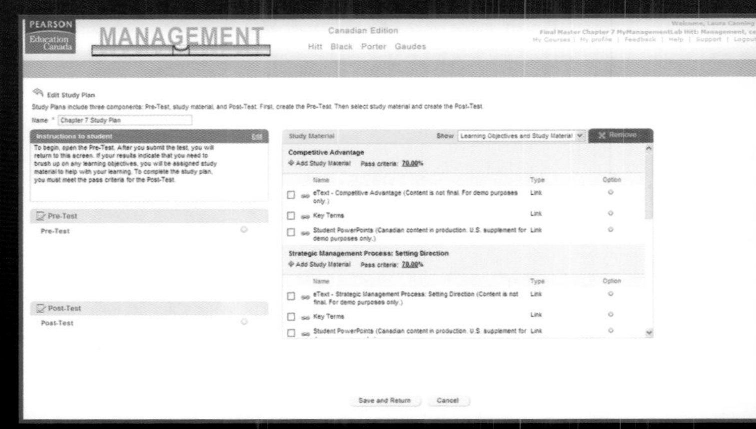

PEARSON

mymanagementlab™

MyManagementLab allows you to gain deeper insight into the world of management.

GAIN DEEPER INSIGHT!

Research Navigator

Four exclusive databases of reliable source content, including the EBSCO Academic Journal and Abstract Database, New York Times Search by Subject Archive, "Best of the Web" Link Library, and Financial Times Article Archive and Company Financials. Research Navigator helps you quickly and efficiently make the most of your research time.

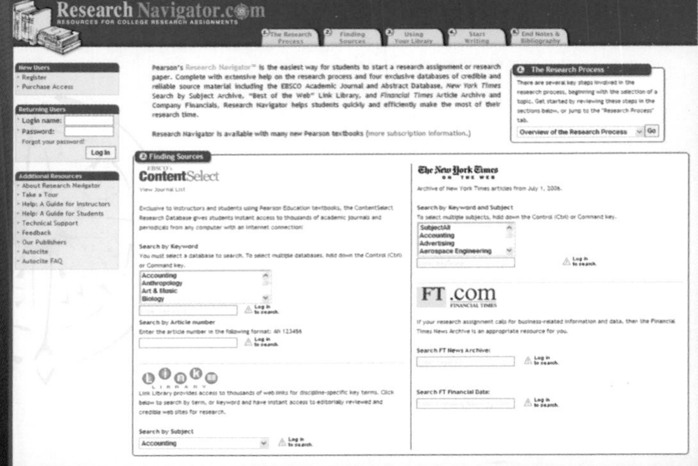

Management in the News

Mini cases developed from current news articles are presented with questions for you to answer. These cases will be updated twice a year, and solutions will be made available to your instructor.

Author Blog and Audio Commentary

Canadian author Andrew Gaudes keeps the text current by updating issues on his author blog. You can listen to audio commentary of chapter overviews and special topics.

www.pearsoned.ca/mymanagementlab

PEARSON

mymanagementlab™

Get a Better Grade!

Personalized Learning!

Gain Deeper Insight!

MyManagementLab includes the following resources:

- Auto-graded Tests and Assignments
- Personalized Study Plan
- Animated text figures
- Student PowerPoint® slides
- Glossary Flashcards
- Research Navigator
- Management in the News
- Multimedia eText
- Author blog
- Author audio commentary
- Links to business news sources
- Video links
- Instructor supplements for each chapter

MyManagementLab is an **online learning system** for principles of management courses. This fun and **easy-to-navigate** site enhances *Management*, Canadian Edition, with a variety of learning resources.

MyManagementLab is found at **www.pearsoned.ca/mymanagementlab**. Follow the simple registration instructions on the Access Code card bound into this text.

PEARSON
Education Canada

MANAGEMENT

Canadian Edition

MANAGEMENT

Michael A. Hitt Texas A&M University

J. Stewart Black University of Michigan

Lyman W. Porter University of California, Irvine

Andrew J. Gaudes University of New Brunswick

Toronto

Library and Archives Canada Cataloguing in Publication

Management/Michael A. Hitt . . . [et al.].—Canadian ed.
Includes bibliographical references and index.
ISBN 978-0-13-205963-3
1. Management—Textbooks. I. Hitt, Michael A.
HD31.M286 2009 658 C2008-900262-8

ISBN-13: 978-0-13-205963-3
ISBN-10: 0-13-205963-0

Vice President, Editorial Director: Gary Bennett
Acquisitions Editor: Karen Elliott
Executive Marketing Manager: Cas Shields
Senior Developmental Editor: Madhu Ranadive
Production Editor: Cheryl Jackson
Copy Editor: Leanne Rancourt
Proofreader: Trish O'Reilly
Production Coordinator: Patricia Ciardullo
Compositor: Integra
Permissions and Photo Researcher: Dawn du Quesnay
Art Director: Julia Hall
Cover and Interior Designer: Geoff Agnew
Cover Image: Veer Incorporated

For permission to reproduce copyrighted material, the publisher gratefully acknowledges the copyright holders listed on page 623, which is considered an extension of this copyright page.

1 2 3 4 5 12 11 10 09 08

Printed and bound in the United States of America.

For my wife and children, Georgine, Adam, David, and Sarah, and the memory of my father, John M. J. Gaudes (1934–2007).

AJG

About the Authors

Michael Hitt

Michael Hitt, Ph.D., is a distinguished professor who holds the Joseph Foster Chair in Business Leadership and the C.W. and Dorothy Conn Chair in New Ventures at Texas A&M University. He received his Ph.D. from the University of Colorado.

Dr. Hitt has authored, or co-authored, several books and book chapters and numerous articles in such journals as the *Academy of Management Journal*, *Academy of Management Review*, *Strategic Management Journal*, *Journal of Applied Psychology*, *Organization Science*, *Organization Studies*, *Journal of Management Studies*, and *Journal of Management*, among others. His publications include numerous trade and textbooks, including *Strategic Management: Competitiveness and Globalization, 6e* and *Competing for Advantage*.

He has served on the editorial review boards of multiple journals including the *Academy of Management Journal*, *Academy of Management Executive*, *Journal of Applied Psychology*, *Journal of Management*, *Journal of World Business*, and *Journal of Applied Behavioral Science*. Furthermore, he has served as consulting editor and editor of the *Academy of Management Journal*. He serves on the board of the Strategic Management Society and is a past president of the Academy of Management. He is a fellow in the Academy of Management and a research fellow in the National Entrepreneurship Consortium. He is a member of the *Academy of Management Journal* Hall of Fame.

Stewart Black

Stewart Black, Ph.D., is co-founder and president of the Global Leadership Institute. He is also executive director of the Asia Pacific Human Resource Partnership for the University of Michigan and a professor of business administration for the Business School.

Prior to beginning his Ph.D. studies, Dr. Black worked for a Japanese consulting firm where he eventually held the position of managing director. Dr. Black returned to the U.S. and received his Ph.D. from the University of California, Irvine. Dr. Black has held faculty positions at Dartmouth and Thunderbird prior to joining the University of Michigan.

Dr. Black is a leading instructor and scholar in strategic change, globalization, leadership, and international human resource management. His research and consulting focus on the areas of change, global leadership, strategic human resource management, international assignments, and cross-cultural management.

He is a co-author of numerous books and articles in the area of international human resource management that have appeared in publications such as *Business Week*, *Wall Street Journal*, and *Fortune*, as well as academic publications including the *Academy of Management Review*, *Academy of Management Journal*, and *Journal of Applied Psychology*.

He is a member of the Academy of Management and has served on the executive committee of the international management division. He has served as editor of the *Journal of International Management* and as an editorial board member of the *Academy of Management Journal*.

Lyman Porter

Lyman Porter, Ph.D., is professor emeritus of organization and strategy, in the Graduate School of Management at the University of California, Irvine, and was formerly dean of that school. Prior to joining UCI in 1967, he served on the faculty of the University of California, Berkeley, and was a visiting professor at Yale University.

Currently, he serves as a member on the board of trustees of the American University of Armenia, and was formerly an external examiner for the National University of Singapore.

Dr. Porter is a past president of the Academy of Management. In 1983, he received that organization's "Scholarly Contributions to Management" Award, and in 1994 its "Distinguished Management Educator" award. He also served as president of the Society of Industrial-Organizational Psychology (SIOP), and in 1989 was the recipient of SIOP's "Distinguished Scientific Contributions" Award.

Dr. Porter's major fields of interest are organizational psychology, management, and management education. He is the author, or co-author, of 11 books and over 80 articles in these fields.

Andrew Gaudes

Dr. Andrew J. Gaudes has a Ph.D. in management, with a major in organization theory and minor in management information systems from the University of Manitoba's I. H. Asper School of Business. He is a tenured associate professor in management and entrepreneurship, and Director of Graduate Studies at the University of New Brunswick's Faculty of Business Administration. In July 2008 he will assume the role of Associate Dean, International Programs.

Dr. Gaudes teaches management of innovation, managerial decision making, managing risk and technology, as well as organizational design. He has also taught courses in management at the University of Manitoba, Sadat Academy of Management Sciences in Cairo, Egypt; the International Institute of Business in Kyiv, Ukraine; University of West Indies (Roytec) in Port of Spain, Trinidad; as well as developed and delivered online courses for Michigan State University's Virtual University.

Dr. Gaudes has authored papers published in peer-reviewed journals, books, and proceedings of national and international scholarly conferences, and has been recognized for his work by an array of fellowships, grants, and contracts. His research interests include specialization strategies of organizations, virtual exchange relationships, and the influence of the physical environment on organizations.

Prior to academia, Dr. Gaudes worked in the area of architecture and interior design. His work experience in this area extended over 13 years in both the private and public sector; as an employee of larger organizations and as an independent consultant in the design, construction, and management of physical environments including restoration, alternative workplace initiatives, disaster recovery planning, and workplace computerization strategies. Dr. Gaudes continues to consult in the area of management.

---

brief contents

contents

Introduction

Part 1
Assessing the Environment 40

CHAPTER 2 ASSESSING EXTERNAL ENVIRONMENTS 40

CHAPTER 4 MANAGING WITHIN CULTURAL CONTEXTS 111

Part 2
Setting Direction 148

CHAPTER 5 INDIVIDUAL AND GROUP DECISION MAKING 148

CHAPTER 6 PLANNING 189

CHAPTER 7 STRATEGIC MANAGEMENT 219

CHAPTER 15 ORGANIZATIONAL DEVELOPMENT AND TRANSFORMATION 516

Preface

Management is an art. Like the artist, the manager observes fine details, but also stands back to view the big picture to ensure a balanced composition. This first Canadian edition of Hitt, Black, Porter, and Gaudes' *Management* introduces students to the art of management. While each chapter has students focus on particular topics in management, it also has them stand back and look at each topic from the larger context; how it influences and is influenced by the organization and its surrounding environment. Quite frankly, this is a very refreshing approach to presenting management to students and it's what makes this text unique.

At the beginning of each chapter we present the topic from a strategic overview, fitting it into the context of the organization and the external environment. As the chapter progresses the reader is brought into more detail on the topic, with the occasional opportunity to stand back to take a look at the bigger picture through the lenses of managers in real organizations. At the end of each chapter we once again provide another opportunity to stand back, but now the reader will also look at the topic from different perspectives. Each perspective allows the reader to consider the topic from a particular point of view. Each perspective will illuminate the topic from a different angle, minimizing areas of darkness and encouraging the full shape of the topic to be realized.

In this edition, we also offer real-world examples that will resonate with a Canadian readership, such as strategic management at CanWest Global, effective management of groups and teams at Edmonton's University of Alberta Hospital, Nellie McClung's pioneering leadership style, motivation at the Royal Canadian Mint, and the challenges of cultural change faced by the Vancouver Organizing Committee for the 2010 Winter Games. Many examples are of Canadian managers in organizations that are large and small, private and public, profit and not-for-profit. Examples retained from the U.S. edition have been updated and some are further infused with a Canadian perspective. We also offer a strong contingent of international examples that will take the reader around the world, fully recognizing the global stage upon which Canadian organizations perform.

Strategic Overview

This text is different from most in that it offers a comprehensive and balanced presentation of strategic management and organizational behaviour concepts. The reality is that practicing managers need to use both in order to address the current challenges they face and to exploit the future opportunities they identify; it is not an "either/or choice." The unique, but interdependent, specialties of four co-authors not only help to balance the treatment of strategic management and organizational behaviour across the chapters, but also to integrate these concepts within chapters. Each chapter begins with a discussion of the strategic importance of the primary concepts within that chapter.

strategic overview

For senior managers to successfully navigate the future threats and opportunities they face, they must have a strategy for how to compete effectively. Although managers have always needed to devise the means to compete (often referred to as competitive strategies), the dramatic increase of competition within many markets in recent years has enhanced the importance of strategy and the strategic management process. While CanWest may be in a market with limited competition, as compared to other sectors, the scale of the operations of both CTV and CBC threatened CanWest's ability to attract advertisers seeking coast-to-coast coverage. In their pursuit of a national presence, CanWest was soon faced with a tremendous amount of debt, which required it to shed assets that were deemed external to their strategic objectives. CanWest management must now ensure that investors are not distanced by the corporation's rapid growth and accumulation of debt. CanWest could be in danger of losing the interest of investors if too much of their revenue goes toward servicing debt. CanWest is a prime example of how important it is to use an effective strategic management process. Without it, an organization's survival may be threatened, even when a firm has only a few competitors and has enjoyed a strong position in the industry.

Another illustration of this increasing competition is provided by the North American automobile market. As recently as 30 years ago, the largest automobile market in the world was dominated by only three major manufacturers: General Motors, Ford, and Chrysler. Chrysler was acquired by DaimlerBenz of Germany in 1998, becoming DaimlerChrysler, and then subsequently sold in August 2007 to Cerberus Capital Management, a firm that specializes in restructuring failing companies. Additionally, the market shares of both GM and Ford have decreased by nearly half in the recent past as foreign competitors, including BMW, Daewoo, Fiat, Honda, Hyundai, Isuzu, Kia, Nissan, Renault, Subaru, Suzuki, Toyota, and others have captured significant market share. In fact, Toyota surpassed GM and became the world's largest automaker in 2007; GM had held the title for 76 years. This provides just one example of how globalization has become a powerful force behind increasing competition. Today, competitors from every corner of the world can converge on markets. Advances in communication and transportation technology add to this competitive intensity.

Never has the need been greater to understand how to develop and implement effective strategies. In recent years, firms like the discount airline Jetsgo filed for bankruptcy and left passengers stranded. Eaton's, a 130-year-old retailer that was once the largest Canadian retailer, went the way of the dodo bird as a result of management's poor understanding of the dramatically shifting retail environment in the 1980s and 1990s. The Office of the Superintendent of Bankruptcy reported that in 2005, 9147 firms filed for bankruptcy in Canada. Andrew Grove, former CEO of Intel, observed that only the paranoid firms survive, primarily because they continuously analyze their external environments and competition, but also because they continuously innovate. Managers who help their firms gain a competitive advantage recognize that it is only temporary; they must constantly innovate and stand ready to change their strategy based on their analysis of the competition and other changes in their environments.[1]

While the principles of strategic management are critical for top managers of a company, the principles are also applicable for managers at various levels of the organization. For example, a lower-level manager may be responsible for a single product line in a company with many products; the principles presented in this chapter can be applied to create a strategy for a product line as well as for an entire company. In addition, even though a company's strategy is developed largely by the top executives, it must be implemented throughout the organization by the other managers and employees. Managers at all levels can do a better job of helping implement a strategy if they understand the strategic management process, how the strategy was developed, and its intended targets.

Chapter Opening Vignette

We open each chapter with a presentation of a management situation in varying types of organizations. The vignettes include international corporations, local Canadian companies, small businesses, and even individuals. The discussions give a practical context to management issues to expose problematic situations and show how effective management can produce positive outcomes.

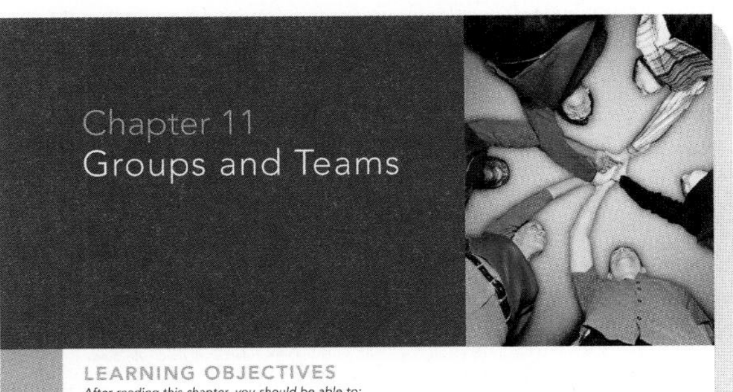

LEARNING OBJECTIVES

After reading this chapter, you should be able to:

1 Describe the similarities and differences between groups and teams.
2 Identify and compare different types of groups.
3 Name the factors that influence group formation and development.
4 Analyze the various structural and behavioural characteristics of groups.
5 Identify the advantages and disadvantages of self-managing, cross-functional, global, and virtual workgroups and teams.
6 Explain the differences in the various types of team competencies.
7 Distinguish between the two major types of group conflict and discuss their causes and consequences.
8 Explain how managers can help their workgroups develop into high-performing teams.

Time for Teams in Health Care

The Canadian health care system has struggled for several years with a lack of professional health care workers to fill the demand placed on it by an aging population. By 2006, medical professionals were being encouraged by the Health Council of Canada, as well as other health care organizations, to collaborate with one another in an attempt to improve the delivery of health care across the country. Professionals, particularly in smaller communities, are being pushed into team-based environments in an effort to compensate for inadequate numbers of medical professionals. Realizing the pressure that is being exerted on health care professionals to work in teams, the federal government started the Enhancing Interdisciplinary Collaboration in Primary Health Care (EICP) initiative to determine the best way to approach this strategy.

The 18-month study demonstrated benefits associated with collaboration in primary health care and concluded that teamwork among health care professionals will be crucial to the sustainability of the health care system. The initiative reported that if primary health care professionals work together, it will not only result in improved care for patients, but will also create a better work environment and support system for over-worked health care professionals. The study argued that medical workers in a team environment would

effectively direct patient care in a timely manner to the appropriate professional and location. A team-based environment would also provide medical professionals with time to promote healthy living to their patients.

A study on collaboration in health care concluded that teamwork among health care professionals will improve care for Canadians. An exceptional case of the benefits of teamwork in health care occurred in May 2007 at University of Alberta Hospital in Edmonton, where a team of health care professionals in collaboration with hundreds of others in the health care field performed 18 organ transplants in 56 hours.

The findings of the initiative also acknowledged that team members require a foundation of understanding to effectively collaborate. To address this, six principles were put forward that form a framework for the future of collaborative health care in Canada. The principles include patient/client engagement, which means allowing patients to participate in decisions related to their health; population health approach, or striving to improve the health of the population as a whole; best possible care and services; access; trust and respect; and effective communication.

In addition to the building principles, the study concluded that the framework requires seven sustaining elements to maintain a vibrant collaborative environment in Canada's health care system: health care specific human resources; funding; liability, which refers to the steps health care professionals must take to insure themselves; regulation; information and communications technology; management and leadership; and planning and evaluation.

The EICP is promoting a health care framework that operates based on these building principles and sustaining elements, and is offering health care providers and policy makers the tools to make it happen on their website (www.eicp-acis.ca).

According to advocates of the recommendations generated by the EICP, increased collaboration among health care professionals will also mean decreased per-patient costs. A collaborative care approach used in British Columbia over a two-year time period, for example, effectively enhanced patient care while reducing per-patient cost by almost $500 per year. More importantly, collaboration among healthcare professionals can save lives. In one exceptional case that occurred in May 2007, a team of health care professionals at Edmonton's University of Alberta Hospital performed 18 organ transplants over the span of 56 hours, giving 15 patients a new chance at life. The marathon session was the result of an unusually high number of donor organs that came available at the same time. Close collaboration among hundreds of people enabled the hospital to perform in a day the same number of operations that are normally undertaken over the course of a month.

Sources: J. Cotter, "Team of Alberta Surgeons Performs 18 Organ Transplants in 56 Hours," June 6, 2007, www.cbc.ca (accessed July 31, 2007); CBC News, "Health Council of Canada Recommends Action to Deal with Chronic Health Problems," March 5, 2007, www.cbc.ca (accessed July 31, 2007); Anonymous, "Interdisciplinary Collaboration in Primary Health Care," *Canadian Pharmacists Journal*, January/February, 2007, p. S5; Canada NewsWire, "Initiative Says the Future of Medicare Is in the Hands of Teams," April 25, 2006, p. 1; Canada NewsWire, "Media Advisory/Interview Opportunity—How Do We Get More Teamwork in Primary Health Care?" February 9, 2006, p. 1; CBC News, "Doctors Told Teamwork the Way of the Future," October 7, 2001, www.cbc.ca (accessed July 31, 2007).

A Manager's Challenge

We worked hard to ground the management knowledge presented in up-to-date research, while at the same time placing this discussion in the context of Canadian practicing managers. To do this, we included examples of managers facing real challenges, in dedicated space several times throughout in a feature called "A Manager's Challenge." The managers discussed in these examples represent all managerial levels in different types of organizations (private profit-oriented and public not-for-profit).

a manager's challenge | *technology*

Not in My Backyard: The Safe Disposal of e-Waste

What do you do when your cell phone no longer works? What do you do with the old Sony Discman players that you find when you clean out your closet? What happens to the VHS recorder that has reached the end of its useful life? How do you get rid of these electronic components when they are no longer needed? Do you bury them in your own backyard? Not likely. Most people walk the items to the curb to get picked up by the local garbage collection. For us, the electronic gadget's life is over, but for the environment, it is the beginning of years of decay and leaching of toxins and heavy metals into the soil and water table.

Canada has a voracious appetite for new technology, and as a result we are accumulating a tremendous amount of unwanted, outdated equipment. By 2010, Canada will be throwing away more than 91 000 metric tonnes of electronic equipment such as PCs, cell phones, and printers every year. In Alberta alone, 362 880 kilograms of lead from electronic equipment ends up in landfills annually. Large organizations that have equipment to dispose of end up having it shipped overseas by way of recycling brokers for disassembly. Between 50 and 80 percent of all tossed electronic equipment, or *e-waste*, finds its way to China, India, or other developing countries for dismantling. The reason old technology is sent abroad for recycling is because it's cheap. For about 5 cents a pound a firm can be rid of hundreds of outdated desktops, printers, and fax machines.

The problem with this option is the great global expense associated with the cost-efficient solution. First, it is often children that strip down the old technology into parts by hand, exposing them to an array of toxic chemicals at the most vulnerable stage of their lives. This could have long-term effects for generations to come. Second, while the parts that can be reused are distributed to plants for refur-

It is often children in developing nations that strip old technology shipped from North America into its various components. Exposure to the toxins in the discarded equipment could affect their physical and mental development.

that is designed to safely shred and separate e-waste. Presently they are processing more than a quarter-million kilograms of e-waste each month, breaking it into five centimetre pieces of plastic and metal and separating it through the use of a magnetic screening process. At 45 cents per pound, however, the safer process is not as cost effective as the offshore option. Companies like Hewlett-Packard are buying into the need for a better way to dispose of technology, and they are willing to pay extra to know that their equipment is safely returned to its basic elements. Still, there are many more firms that would rather pay less for the removal of yesterday's equipment, which makes Noranda a niche player with a customer base that is comparatively small. Management at Noranda anticipated this and they have positioned the firm for the future. They are speculating that it is only a matter of time before legislation is set in place forcing companies to use facilities such as theirs to safely dispose of e-waste.

Another way that the onslaught of e-waste could be man-

Managerial Perspectives Revisited

We have included another unique feature in this text that reflects the fact that the actual challenges managers face do not come in neat packages. In Chapter 1, we explain a set of four general "Managerial Perspectives" that are relevant to all aspects of management. They are (1) managing in an organizational context, (2) managing through people, (3) managing paradoxes, and (4) managing with an entrepreneurial mindset. We subsequently highlight how these perspectives relate to the chapter content at the end of each chapter in a feature called "Managerial Perspectives Revisited."

managerial perspectives revisited

PERSPECTIVE 1: **THE ORGANIZATIONAL CONTEXT** The organizational context is extremely important when it comes to human resource management. In many ways the appropriate HR practices are a function of the organization. Change the context of the organization—its strategy, culture, or industry—and you are likely to need to change the characteristics or capabilities needed in the employees you want to recruit, how you orient them, what training they need, and how you manage their performance or structure their compensation.

PERSPECTIVE 2: **THE HUMAN FACTOR** From one perspective, human resource management is all about working through others; it is about achieving results by attracting, selecting, training, appraising, compensating, and developing others. Because human resource management also typically involves the policies and practices of the company through the human resource department, as a manager, effective HRM will likely also involve working with and through people in your HR department.

PERSPECTIVE 3: **MANAGING PARADOXES** Meeting the HRM challenge creates some important potential paradoxes. On the one hand, individual managers have their own personal views on the effective management of human resources. On the other hand, as managers in an organization, they have to work with, support, and uphold the policies and practices of the company. At times there may be a conflict between the two. In such cases, do managers have an obligation to try to correct company practices that are not in keeping with what their values are or what they believe—or that may be inappropriate or even illegal? This dynamic tension between personal and company standards is one of the principal paradoxes managers face when it comes to managing and motivating the firm's people.

PERSPECTIVE 4: **ENTREPRENEURIAL MINDSET** The entrepreneurial mindset is reflected in the behaviour and actions of a firm's employees. WestJet employees are a good example of workers who hold and display an entrepreneurial mindset. Employees at WestJet are given more latitude in making on-the-spot decisions and exercise a greater interest in the well-being of the customer and, at the same time, the company. Part of this may be attributed to the fact that more than 87 percent of WestJet employees are shareholders, taking part in an employee share purchase plan that the company matches with equal contributions. It may also be the culture of WestJet, where the emphasis is on putting people first. Either way, the approach to managing employees at WestJet is attracting and retaining quality employees that are in turn rewarded for their commitment.

To maintain a company's competitive edge, managers should be committed to constantly improving their human resource management capabilities. While the HR department is designed to support and facilitate the effective management of human resources in the company, it's no substitute for individual managers taking the initiative to engage in key HR activities.

Part-Ending Cases

Even though by necessity we cover specific managerial concepts in separate chapters, the reality for practicing managers is that they often face challenges that are multi-dimensional in nature. As a consequence, at the end of each part, we take the unique step of providing a concise but integrative case, of no more than six pages, that deals with concepts covered in several or all of the chapters in the part. The cases are written by professionals and designed for use in teaching management concepts. While short vignettes used in the chapters are useful in providing illustrations of specific management concepts, the cases at the end of each part provide students and instructors with the opportunity to explore the integrated nature of many challenges practicing managers face.

Introduction integrative case

Clifford Chance—Update

By Callum Campbell

Ten years after Geoffrey Howe gazed from the window of his new offices, Clifford Chance had outgrown its Aldersgate headquarters, and the firm had had to retain additional City of London offices. The current managing partner, Peter Cornell, now surveyed a different firm in a very different legal market.

Throughout the 1990s, Clifford Chance continued to add offices to its network (Prague in 1995, Bangkok in 1996, São Paulo in 1998), and to increase the number of staff in its existing offices. By 2002, Clifford Chance had succeeded in becoming the world's largest law firm, by virtue of both its size (3322 lawyers) and gross revenue ($1 409 032 200). In 1993, 80 percent of the firm's lawyers had been based in its London office. Howe's ambition to globalize the firm had been further realized by the fact that 63 percent of the firm's lawyers were now based outside of London.

The last decade had witnessed wholesale change in the legal industry. Where lawyers once assumed they would stay in the same law firm for life, the aggressive and hostile lateral hire of partners, teams, and the merger of whole firms had become the typical strategies in growing a law firm, strategies which were almost unheard of in 1992. In much of Europe and Asia, City of London–origin firms now dominated the landscape. U.S. firms had made fresh inroads into Europe, many striving to blend into the market as "local players." Global brands had yet to entirely usurp other international strategies. The "best-friends" network established by Slaughter and May in the U.K., Hengeler Mueller in Germany, and Bredin Prat in Paris still won covetable mandates, and remained highly profitable. In each European jurisdiction, independent firms, often outcasts or willing exiles from large mergers, continued to thrive. The most profitable law firms in the world, such as Wachtell Lipton Rosen & Katz, were based almost exclusively in New York. But the number of national firms able to compete for high-end corporate, corporate finance, and banking work was dwindling in step with the expansion of large international networks, like Clifford Chance.

Geoffrey Howe's ambition for his firm in 1993 had taken it to the top of the league tables. But getting there had necessitated a change in strategy. Organic growth could put an office anywhere on the planet, but could not provide critical mass. Nor could it satisfy the firm's aspirations in the key markets of the United States or Germany. On January 1, 2000, Clifford Chance announced the legal industry's most ambitious merger to date, simultaneously joining forces with the 400-lawyer, New York–based law firm Rogers & Wells, and the 260-lawyer, Frankfurt-based firm, Pünder, Volhard, Weber & Axster.

Since the fall of the Berlin Wall, Germany had seen an influx of law firms from both the U.S. and the U.K. Prior to 1990, foreign firms were prevented from merging with German firms or establishing a presence in Germany by vigorously upheld Bar Association restrictions. Liberalization of the industry transformed the market. The three largest firms in Germany, Freshfields Bruckhaus Deringer, Linklaters Oppenhoff & Rädler, and Clifford Chance Pünder, were all the result of Anglo-German mergers, and the majority of the top 15 firms in the country were the offspring of mergers with either U.S. or U.K. firms. Clifford Chance's acquisition of Pünder, Volhard was a bold step that brought it an instant presence with a well-respected, if not top-flight, German firm. It was rumored that the courtship had been competitive, as 15 British firms had been in contact to discuss possible mergers before the firm decided to throw in its lot with Clifford Chance.

The acquisition of Rogers & Wells was more remarkable. A big merger between a U.S. and a U.K. firm had

Callum Campbell (EMBA–Global 2003) prepared this update under the direction of Professor Maury Peiperl from public sources. It is designed as a supplement to the case "Clifford Chance: International Expansion" (© 1993, 1994 INSEAD) from *Managing Change: Cases and Concepts* by Maury Peiperl and Todd Jick (Irwin/McGraw-Hill, 2003). ©2003 by London Business School.

Helpful Pedagogical Features

The book has a full set of other helpful pedagogical devices in each chapter, including learning objectives, key terms, questions to test comprehension, a set of questions focused on applying the knowledge from the chapter, a short exercise for students to practise their managerial capabilities, and an actual case to be analyzed by students to develop their critical thinking skills.

concluding comments

Organizational structures can be thought of as information networks or circuits on a circuit board. The structure influences who talks to whom about what and how often, what information moves through the organization and at what speed. As business and society move from the industrial age to the information age, appropriate organizational structures will be increasingly critical to a firm's success in the marketplace. Likewise, your understanding of and skills at designing effective structures become increasingly critical to your career success. You must be able to quickly and accurately analyze the complexity and dynamism of the internal and external environments.

As the Citicorp example illustrates, the structure has to fit the environment and the organization's objectives. Citicorp's emphasis on brand and costs placed an emphasis on a structure that would centralize brand management and capture economies of scale in other activities.

In addition, to have a successful managerial career, you need to understand the sometimes opposing forces of globalization and localization. Successful organizational structures may require you to find solutions that meet both needs simultaneously, or to organize various functional activities at different points along the continuum from centralized global activities to decentralized local activities.

In general, designing organizational structure can be one of the more complex activities of management. Its critical role in organizational competitiveness virtually guarantees that managers who understand and are skilled at organizational design will be those who are increasingly given more responsible positions.

key terms

boundaryless organization 277
centralized organizations 266
cognitive specialization 258
decentralized organizations 266
flat organizational structure 263
formalization 262
globalization 284
hybrid 274
informal organization 265
integration 259
interdependence 259
liaisons 277
line of authority 262
localization 284
network structures 275
organizational charts 257
organizational design 257
organizational structure 257
outsourcing 275
profit centre 269
span of control 262
specialization 258
tall organizational structure 263
task specialization 258
uncertainty 261
unity of command 262

test your comprehension

1. Define *organizational structure*. How does it differ from organizational design?
2. What is the main purpose of organizational charts?
3. What is *taskspecialization*, and what is its role in organizational design?
4. Why is cognitive specialization important in organizational design?
5. What are the three major types of interdependence among organizational units?
6. In an organization with a relative high level of certainty and low to moderate level of interdependence among business units, would you recommend rules, goals, or values as the principal means for facilitating integration?

closing case DEVELOP YOUR CRITICAL THINKING

Restructuring Skate Canada

Skate Canada is the organization responsible for developing and managing figure skating in Canada. On October 6, 2004, Skate Canada made public its plans for restructuring its national office in Ottawa. Following a study conducted by Deloitte & Touche, the decision to reorganize was made as a means of facilitating each international levels. Employees of this division would be responsible for scouting new athletes, monitoring the progress of the athletes, determining selection criteria for events, choosing athletes who would compete internationally, providing official presence at international events, and developing progress models and teams for athlete enhancement.

The marketing and communications division would

supplements

Supplements for Students

mymanagementlab **MyManagement Lab** This is an online learning system is designed specifically to help you get a better grade in your management course. With loads of practice and study tools correlated to this textbook, as well as a personalized study plan generated from your answers, MyManagementLab puts you in control of your own learning. Everything is available 24 hours a day so you can study where you want, how you want, and when you want. MyManagementLab is found at www.pearsoned.ca/mymanagementlab. Follow the simple registration instructions on the access code card included with new copies of this text.

Author Q&A Video Interviews In this unique resource, we queried faculty from across the country and identified those topics that students find difficult to understand. These brief video clips feature each of our authors speaking in their area of expertise. Some of the topics included are emotional intelligence, transformational leadership, competitive advantage, and core competencies. These videos can be accessed through MyManagementLab.

Supplements for Instructors

All instructor supplements are available on the IRCD described below or can be downloaded by instructors only from the Pearson Canada Higher Education password-protected online catalogue at www.pearsoned.ca.

Instructor's Resource CD-ROM (978-0-13-713189-1) The Instructor's Resource CD-ROM (IRCD) contains everything you need for efficient course preparation. All the supplements on the IRCD have been revised to reflect changes made to the Canadian edition. The IRCD contains the following supplements:

TestGen/MyTest. The test bank contains approximately 100 questions per chapter including multiple-choice, true/false, short-answer, and scenario-based questions. Short-answer questions are questions that can be answered in one-to-five sentences. Scenario-based questions are essay type questions developed around a short scenario. Each question has been referenced by the main topic heading from the chapter.

Instructor's Manual. This instructor's manual offers much more than just the traditional, but limited, chapter outline and answers to the end-of-chapter materials. In addition to these basic items, you will find suggested teaching strategies for 45-, 90-, and 180-minute sessions, chapter coverage suggestions for semester- and quarter-length courses, and modular suggestions for courses focused on general management, strategy, and/or organizational behaviour. The coverage for each chapter includes a variety of resources such as exercises, critical-thinking assignments, debate topics, and research assignments.

PowerPoint® Slides. The PowerPoint® slides are an enhanced, interactive version of the first with video clips and weblinks. The slides include teaching notes and are organized around the main topic headings of each chapter.

Image Library. The image library will contain selected art files from the text.

Videos Two sets of video series are available for students and instructors. The CBC Video series include segments specially selected for readers of *Management*, Canadian Edition, and the Acadia series was developed for all students of management.

CBC/Pearson Education Canada Video Library (DVD 978-0-13-503512-2 and VHS 978-0-13-503511-5). Current information from such CBC series as Venture and The National complement the text and enhance learning by bringing to life practical applications and issues. With the latest news and information on management, these segments provide an excellent vehicle for launching lectures, showing additional examples, and sparking classroom discussion. The CBC Videos are also available for viewing to both students and instructors on Pearson Education Canada's Online Video Central website (accessed through www.pearsoned.ca).

Acadia Video Series. Through the MyManagementLab, students and instructors can watch management interviews from Acadia University's video series. The *Acadia Pearson Business Insider Series* is a user-friendly, multimedia product developed by Acadia University and distributed exclusively by Pearson Education Canada. The web-based database contains video interviews of industry leaders and top executives that are searchable by key terms. The interviews capture insights from business leaders around the world and bring textbooks and lectures to life through a series of questions and answers.

Acknowledgments

The author and Pearson Education Canada wish to thank the following reviewers for their feedback and suggestions during the development of this textbook:

Donna Bentley, North Alberta Institute of Technology
Samuel Clement, Concordia University
David H. J. Delcorde, University of Ottawa
Kay Devine, University of Alberta
Aaron Dresner, Concordia University
Sandra Findlay-Thompson, Mount Saint Vincent University
Denise Ghanam, University of Windsor
Jai Goolsarran, Centennial College
Cheryl Pollmuller, Lethbridge University
Susan Thompson, Trent University
Joe Trubic, Ryerson University
B.E. Williams, University of Lethbridge
Jeffrey D. Young, Mount Saint Vincent University

"Have you ever thought of writing a book?" Peter Luke, my Pearson sales representative at the time, asked me this question in the spring of 2006. I extend my thanks to Peter . . . Really! I also want to extend my sincere gratitude to the selfless commitment of time and energy that Stephanie Ketch provided as an assistant in the research and preparation of vignettes and cases in this text. Her work was excellent, and her enthusiasm and good nature was contagious.

I am indebted to the editorial team at Pearson Education Canada for their tremendous support in writing this book. Karen Elliott, Acquisitions Editor, introduced me to textbook publishing. Her endlessly positive outlook and words of encouragement provided the fuel to keep me going, while the feedback and support I received from Madhu Ranadive, Developmental Editor, instilled confidence that I was heading in the right direction. Cheryl Jackson, Production Editor, was instrumental in ensuring that all parts of the book came together in the end and Leanne Rancourt, Copy Editor, did a wonderful job in ensuring the text was well written and complete. Although the work was at times intense, I can honestly state that the editorial team made writing this book an enjoyable and rewarding experience.

I had the good fortune of meeting the Pearson sales team and am humbled by their energy and drive towards making this book a success—most notably Deborah Merry my local sales representative. Cas Shields, Executive Marketing Manager, has also been very supportive, displaying a commitment to this book that may even rival my own.

I also want to acknowledge the students that I have taught in undergraduate and graduate programs in business over the years at the University of New Brunswick, the University of Manitoba, Michigan State University, the Sadat Academy of Management Sciences (Cairo, Egypt), University of West Indies (Port of Spain, Trinidad), and the International Institute of Business (Kyiv, Ukraine). The shape of this first Canadian edition is largely in response to my experience in the classroom and my students' questions on the topic of management.

In closing, I want to dedicate this book to my family, who supported the project every step of the way. I also dedicate this book to my father, who passed away during the time that I worked on this book. Dad was an artist in every sense of the word. His mastery of oils and watercolours showed me at an early age the art of observation, interpretation . . . and achieving balance.

Andrew Gaudes
January 2008
agaudes@unb.ca

Chapter 1 Introduction

LEARNING OBJECTIVES

After reading this chapter, you should be able to:

1. Answer the question: What is management?
2. Explain why management must be understood within the context of organizations and how organizations affect the practice of management.
3. Describe the role of working with and through people in effective management.
4. Explain managerial paradoxes and how dealing with them lies at the core of management.
5. Specify the nature and extent of commitment required for managerial excellence.
6. Define the term "entrepreneurial mindset" and explain its importance for managers.
7. Describe and compare the different elements of managerial work and the different managerial roles.
8. Discuss the skills necessary to be an effective manager.

Managing: Putting It All Together

As president of The Home Depot Canada and The Home Depot China, Annette Verschuren confronts change, uncertainty, constraints, and the need to make sound decisions on a daily basis. Throughout her career Annette has succeeded in meeting these managerial challenges decisively using skills and insights that she continues to hone.

Verschuren has a background similar to that of many Canadians. She is the middle of five children of parents that immigrated to Canada from the Netherlands in the post–World War II era. Her parents settled on a dairy farm on Cape Breton Island where Annette was born and raised. She studied business administration at St. Francis Xavier

University, and then embarked on a career with the Cape Breton Development Corporation, becoming the director of planning and helping employ displaced coal miners. Verschuren moved to Toronto in 1986 to begin working for the Canada Development Investment Corporation (CDIC), where she was responsible for divesting Crown corporations.

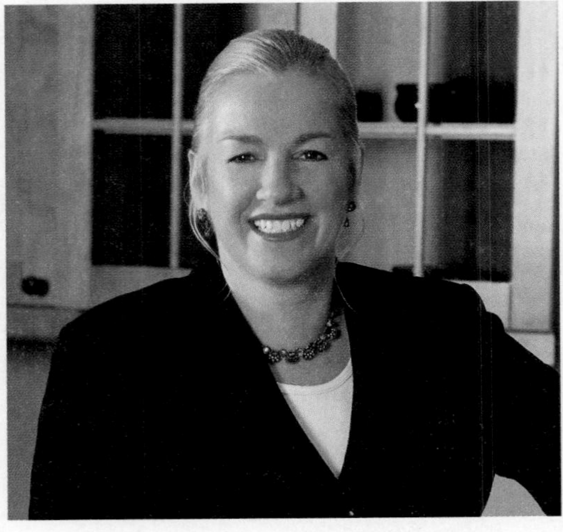

The Home Depot's Annette Verschuren is credited with the success of the company's Canadian retail operations, but she is quick to deflect credit to the hard work of more than 27 000 employees across Canada. She is described as a chameleon, adapting effortlessly from a meeting with corporate executives to a meeting with tradespeople, and is respected by both colleagues and competitors. Verschuren has subsequently been given the lead role in the expansion of The Home Depot into China while still presiding over the Canadian division.

Her first experience with the private sector and retail came in 1989 when she left the CDIC to work for the conglomerate Imasco Ltd. While there, she assumed responsibility for managing Den for Men's 63 Canadian stores. Verschuren later created Verschuren Ventures and convinced Texas-based craft retailer Michaels to expand into Canada. She brought 17 Michaels stores to Canada and employed 1000 people in just over two years, becoming president of Michaels Canada in 1993.

In 1996, Annette received an offer from The Home Depot to take on the role of president of The Home Depot Canada. She would become the first woman and person without home improvement experience to become a president within The Home Depot. When Verschuren entered The Home Depot there were only 19 stores in Canada, and the outlook from corporate head office in Atlanta was that there was only room for 50 Canadian stores. Arthur Blank, co-founder and then CEO of The Home Depot, thought Verschuren was crazy when she forecast that Canada could accommodate 100 stores. Incidentally, there are now 154 stores in Canada, and plans for more.

Annette Verschuren has not completely relied upon the US model in developing The Home Depot Canada. She has instilled new ways of looking at retail home improvement and has, on a number of occasions, demonstrated that the US model can be improved upon. One particular example is Annette's response to a study that showed the large influence women have in home renovation and large purchase decisions. She introduced a more family-friendly store with wider aisles and a cleaner environment, and created in-store departments that handled decorative elements, such as window treatments and wall art.

In order for stores to provide a more local appeal, she also decentralized decision making so that store managers could be more responsive to the demands of local customers, encouraging entrepreneurship at the store level. She also reduced the number of products in stores and scaled down the size of stores slightly to improve upon efficiencies and reduce inventory costs. The net result of Verschuren's adjustments has been a chain of Canadian retail stores that collectively generate sales in excess of $5 billion annually.

While riding the wave of success in Canada, in fall 2006 head office asked Verschuren if she would be interested in leading the expansion of The Home Depot into China. Always in pursuit of new challenges, Verschuren said yes. Meanwhile, she continues to oversee the Canadian operations and fend off competitive advances by Rona and Canadian Tire, as well as entry of the United States number two home improvement retailer, Lowe's. Verschuren has stressed the importance of retaining excellent staff, as it is their contributions that have allowed her to take on the role of fronting the corporation's Chinese expansion.

It is often said that little is certain but change, so Annette Verschuren will undoubtedly continue to face tough challenges ahead. Reflecting on her career to date, Verschuren has explained that she has had to reincarnate herself, changing in order to meet business demands. Given the management expertise she has developed over her career and the skills she has demonstrated in applying it to numerous difficult situations, it appears that the confidence The Home Depot has placed in her is well founded.

Sources: The Home Depot Canada, www.homedepot.ca (accessed July 9, 2007); C. Nuttall-Smith and G. York, "Orange China," *Report on Business*, March 2007, pp. 25–38; C. Green and R. Koci, "An Interview with Annette Verschuren," *Hardware Merchandising*, March/April 2006, pp. 43–48; A. Verschuren, "Business Success: How to Prosper in the New Global Economy," address at the Atlantic Economic Summit, September 28, 2004.

Why feature Annette Verschuren in this opening chapter? The answer is simple: Her career to date—especially how she has approached managerial challenges during her career—will illustrate three key themes that are emphasized in this chapter and throughout the book: The importance of change, technology, and globalization.

Managing Effectively in Today's World: Three Critical Challenges

Change, technology, and globalization: These are undeniably three of the most important challenges that will have an enormous impact on managers in the near future. Consequently, we will be highlighting them in this and every other chapter in this book. We view them as three themes that weave continuously through the different topics that make up this subject called "management."

Change

Change is the most persistent, pervasive, and powerful area of challenge that any manager will have to deal with in any type of organization and in any geographical area. No matter how new or experienced you are as a manager, you will be confronted with both the need and the opportunity to change. Not making any changes at all is unlikely to be an option. As a Greek philosopher once wrote many centuries ago, "Change alone is unchanging,"[1] and that is still as appropriate a statement today as it was then.

Certainly, in her managerial experience so far, Annette Verschuren has had to cope with and master the need to change. She has jumped from staid, well-established organizations to the helm of something new and different. Indeed, her success (so far at least) seems to have come as the direct result of her willingness to risk and embrace change. In her current role with The Home Depot China, she faces daily changes that will occur while entering a completely new market. Doing things the same way day after day would be highly unlikely to lead to progress for her or the organization.

Technology

The other two themes that we emphasize throughout this book, technology and globalization, are nearly as important to any manager as is change. No managers in today's world can ignore the impact of technology and the way it affects their jobs and firms. Technology developments, of course, often force managers to make changes—whether they want to or not. One only needs to point to the internet as a case in point. The internet has had far-reaching effects on how managers do their jobs. Another example is the presence of online retail, which has presented Annette Verschuren with new challenges in addressing the needs of customers through the internet—both its numerous opportunities and its potential threats. The playing field for customers, competitors, and one's own organization has changed.

Globalization

The third theme, or overarching type of challenge, that managers face is globalization, the increasing international and cross-national nature of everything from politics to business. No longer can managers say that "what happens in the rest of the

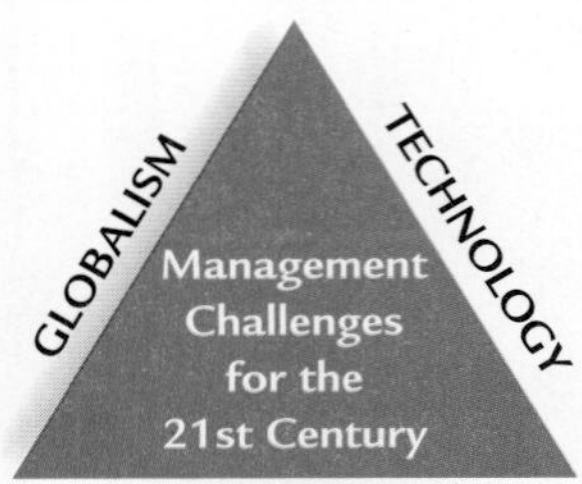

Exhibit 1.1

Critical Management Challenges for the 21st Century

world does not affect me or my organization." It doesn't matter whether you will ever manage a firm outside of your country of origin or not, although it's becoming increasingly likely that you will. Rather, the point is that global events will almost certainly come from outside *into* your organization. They will affect how you set goals, make decisions, and coordinate and lead the work of other people.

Throughout her career, Annette Verschuren has had to engage in managerial activities that went beyond the borders of Canada. Verschuren first brought the Texas-based craft retailer Michaels to Canada, opening 17 stores. She then expanded US retailer The Home Depot from 19 stores in Canada to 154 in just 11 years. Verschuren is now faced with the challenge of expanding the North American home improvement phenomenon to Asia.

While we have discussed the three themes—change, technology, and globalization—separately, these three managerial challenges are often highly interrelated. Both technological and global developments frequently change the direction of organizations and the way they operate. Thus, the three managerial challenges of change, technology, and globalization form an integrated "iron triangle" of exceptionally strong influences on managers and management (as illustrated in Exhibit 1.1).

Managing Strategically to Meet the Challenges

The three major challenges described above combine to create an incredibly complex, dynamic, and competitive landscape in which most managers must operate. To survive and perform well in such an environment, managers throughout the organization are required to manage strategically.[2] Clearly, managers at the top of the organization—like Annette Verschuren—establish goals and formulate a strategy for the firm to achieve those goals. For the goals to be accomplished, the strategy must also be effectively implemented, which requires managers at all levels of the organization to set and accomplish goals that contribute to the organization's ultimate performance.

Increasing globalization and the enhanced use of technology have contributed to greater changes, emphasizing the importance of knowledge to organizational success.[3] The importance placed on the intellectual capital of the organization requires managers to use their portfolio of resources effectively. Of primary importance are intangible resources like the employees and the firm's reputation. Managers are responsible for building an organization's capabilities and then leveraging them through a strategy designed to give it an advantage over its competitors. They usually do this by creating more value for their customers than their competitors do.[4]

Managers are responsible for forming the strategies of the major units within the organization as well. Because the strategy has to be implemented by people in the organization, managers must focus heavily on the human factor. As they implement their strategies they will encounter conflicting conditions. Often this means managing multiple situations simultaneously and remaining flexible to adapt to changing conditions. Additionally, achieving an organization's goals requires that managers commit themselves to always being alert to how strategies can be improved and strengthened in advancing the vision that has been established for the organization. Finally, the dynamic competitive landscape entails substantial change. To adapt to this change, managers are required to be innovative, entrepreneurial, and to continuously search for new opportunities.

Now we turn to a set of basic questions that will be the focus for the remainder of this chapter: (1) What is management? (2) What do managers do? (3) What skills do managers need?

What Is Management?

Before we go any further, it is essential to take time to briefly discuss definitions and terms that will be used throughout this book. So here is how we will be using the following terms as they relate to the overall focus of this book:

Management: This term has several different uses. The primary meaning for the purposes of this book is as an activity or process. More specifically, we define **management** as the process of assembling and using sets of resources in a goal-directed manner to accomplish tasks in an organizational setting. This definition can, in turn, be subdivided into its key parts:

management the process of assembling and using sets of resources in a goal-directed manner to accomplish tasks in an organizational setting

1. Management is a process: It involves a series of activities and operations, such as planning, deciding, and evaluating.
2. Management involves assembling and using sets of resources: It is a process that brings together and puts into use a variety of types of resources: human, financial, material, and information.
3. Management involves acting in a goal-directed manner to accomplish tasks: It does not represent random activity, but rather activity with a purpose and direction. The purpose or direction may be that of the individual, the organization, or usually a combination of the two. It includes efforts to complete activities successfully and to achieve particular levels of desired results.
4. Management involves activities carried out in an organizational setting: It is a process undertaken in **organizations** by people with different functions intentionally structured and coordinated to achieve common purposes.

organizations interconnected sets of individuals and groups who attempt to accomplish common goals through differentiated functions and intended coordination

Management can also have several other meanings in addition to a process or set of activities. The term is sometimes used to designate a particular part of the organization: the set of individuals who carry out management activities. Thus, you may hear the phrase "the management of IBM decided . . . " or "the management of University Hospital developed a new personnel policy. . . . " Often when the term is used this way, it does not necessarily refer to all members of management, but rather to those who occupy the most powerful positions within this set (top management).

Another similar use of the term is to distinguish a category of people (that is, "management") from those who are members of collective bargaining units ("union members" or, more informally, "labour") or those who are not involved in specific managerial activities, whether or not they are union members ("nonmanagement employees" or "rank-and-file employees"). We frequently use the term *member* to refer to any person (any employee) in an organization without regard to that individual's place in the organization. In this book, we use the term "manager" to refer to anyone who has designated responsibilities for carrying out managerial activities, and "managing" to refer to the process of completing those activities.

Let's now consider the question "What is management?" in a different way: by examining four fundamental *perspectives* of management—the organizational context, the human factor, managing paradoxes, and the entrepreneurial mindset. These perspectives cut across the entire managerial process. When you begin a journey, it's helpful to have a broad overview of the terrain you are about to travel *before* learning the details of the different parts of the trip. This overview helps integrate the different perspectives and facilitates your understanding of them to provide a meaningful and powerful adventure. And learning about the complexities of management is, we strongly believe, a journey that adds up to a definite adventure!

The broad perspectives presented here and throughout the book are based on information and ideas from a wide variety of sources: our personal experiences and observations as educators, managers, and consultants; research findings from the scholarly literature; extensive study of the subject; and, particularly, hundreds of conversations and interviews with practising managers over the years. These perspectives represent complementary points of view about management, but they are not mutually exclusive. Rather, each perspective provides a different lens to help you look at the topic and understand its complexities and challenges. These perspectives are presented to provide you with more understanding about what is meant by "management" than you can gain from a single definition. "Management" is too complex a concept to be captured by a definition alone.

In the next few pages, we first state each perspective, followed by typical questions that might be asked about it and our responses to those questions. Thus, the next part of this chapter uses a Q&A approach. The intent of this approach is to encourage you to become more interested in and involved with the material. We hope that it will increase your curiosity about management and stimulate your interest in learning about it.

management occurs in organizations

As you begin the formal study of management, it is important for you to understand that organizations serve as the context for management. And managers, much like the stage, are the constant background for actors in a play. For our purposes in this book, this context can be *any type of organization that employs people*: companies, universities, law firms, hospitals, government agencies, and the like.

Nova Scotia–born Sidney Crosby is a well-known NHL hockey player and is team captain for the Pittsburgh Penguins. Crosby's coach is responsible for managing the team as a whole. Crosby, on the other hand, does not manage the team, but he does provide leadership on and off the ice. Many young hockey players look up to him as a role model. In your opinion, does this make Crosby a manager?

Management Occurs in Organizations; It Does Not Happen in Isolation

Just as water is the necessary environment for fish, or air is for a plane, organizations are the necessary environment for managers to manage. In fact, stated strongly, "management does not exist without organizations."

Q: Can't there be management in nonorganizational settings such as families, political groups, or ad hoc groups?

A: Good question. Managerial activities, such as decision making or communication, can happen in nonorganizational settings such as a family. You can even engage in managerial activities such as planning and goal setting independently, without others being involved. However, these activities in isolation do not constitute management. Management requires integration of all these activities *and* the involvement of other people. This integration only occurs in an organizational context. It is similar to a dialogue taking place only when another person participates in the conversation—otherwise, it's a monologue.

Q: OK, but does the type of organization matter? Does it make a difference whether the organization is small or large, or whether it's for profit or not-for-profit?

A: Certainly the nuances of effective management change depending on the situation and type of organization. Managing in a small company where you know every employee—such as 96 percent of the 3040 businesses in Fredericton, New Brunswick, that have fewer than 50 employees—is not the same as managing in a large organization like RBC Financial Group with over 60 858 employees located in offices in Canada and around the world.[5] Although in this book we consider organizations of all sizes, the premium placed on good managers tends to increase as size and complexity increase. However, the cost of failing to manage effectively is high in all types and sizes of organizations.

Regardless of the fact that some dimensions of effective management are affected by the size and type of organization, the fundamental substance of management does not change. If the basic essence and nature of management changed dramatically from one organizational type to another, we would need a separate textbook for small organization management, large organization management, private company management, public agency management, and so on. In our view, the essentials of management are critical and universal activities in all organizations.

Each Organization Has Its Own Set of Characteristics That Affect Both Managers and Those with Whom They Interact

While it is critical to understand that management occurs in the context of organizations, all organizations are not the same, even those of similar size or complexity. Each organization has its own "personality" (often referred to as the organization's culture), and its own strengths, weaknesses, problems, and opportunities. These various characteristics affect the organization and all who work within it.

Q: What is it about organizations that creates their particular characteristics, and do they influence effective management?

A: Organizations often bring together a variety of people from different backgrounds—different ethnicities and cultures (Asian, African, Arabic, Anglo, Irish, Vietnamese, and so on), different educational levels (high school dropouts,

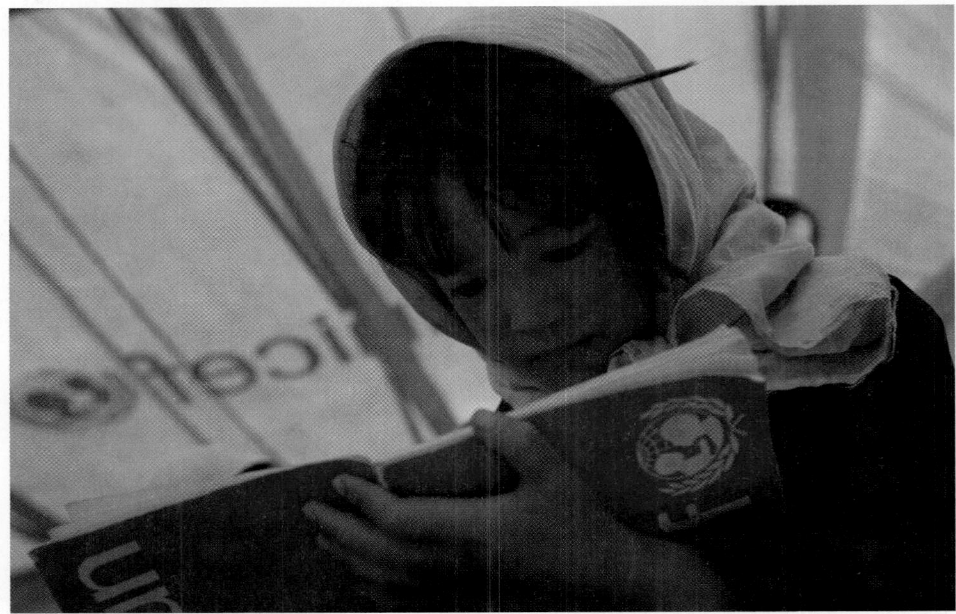

Good managers can make or break all kinds of organizations—large and small, profit and nonprofit. Although the United Nations Children's Fund (UNICEF) is a nonprofit organization, its many members worldwide—both volunteer and paid—make it a complex organization to manage. Large, far-flung organizations make a manager's job harder to accomplish. As a result, organizations such as these place a premium on top managers, and they are generally paid competitively as a result.

college graduates, and MBAs), different technical backgrounds (engineering, digital arts, and accounting), and different socioeconomic levels (from very poor to very privileged)—who must then work together to achieve common objectives. Thus, developing a degree of shared cooperation becomes essential. This can only be accomplished by gaining acceptance of existing ways of working together, using existing structures and processes, or by developing new structures and processes. These behaviours, structures, and processes over time constitute the personality, or culture, of the organization. Whatever one may think or assume about the personality or culture of, say, a typical unit of Imperial Oil Limited, it is likely to be different from that of Radical Entertainment, a video game developer headquartered in Vancouver where shiatsu massage therapy is provided on site and free passes are given out to local ski and snowboarding hills.[6] The basic principles of effective management are relevant in all organizations, but the specific characteristics of an organization affect how those principles are applied.

Q: Does this mean that if I am an effective manager in "Organization A," I will automatically be an effective manager in "Organization B"? Or does this mean that because organizations have different personalities, effective management practices can't be transferred from one organization to another?

A: Sound approaches to management do transfer from one organization to another. This does not mean, however, that your behaviour can be identical and still be equally effective in all organizations. For example, if you learn how to read music, you can apply that knowledge from one piece of music to another, but it does not mean that you can play each piece of music the same way. Furthermore, even if the musical score were the same, it does not mean that you would play the piece exactly the same way for different conductors or with different musical groups. But making these adjustments does not change your fundamental understanding of how to read music and your ability to adapt that knowledge to different circumstances. In the same manner, for example, becoming an experienced and competent decision maker is important in all organizations. However, some organizations may encourage participatory decision making, while others are more directive. No matter what the style, it remains important to develop the skills needed to make good decisions.

Effective management is similar in all organizations, but the challenges differ by organization. For example, an effective manager in a large government bureaucracy like Health Canada, with its rigid rules, can be quite different from one in a start-up, cutting-edge, high-technology business like a new-venture firm, where each experience is new and the rules are developed along the way. Thus, you will need to change how you put management ideas into practice based on the nature of the organization in which you are working. But this fine tuning does not lessen the importance of acquiring a basic understanding of management. In fact, having that understanding allows you to move more easily from one organization to another and still be effective. This does not mean, however—and we want to emphasize this—that you can ignore the differences from one organization to another; you must adapt the way you manage in each new organization. In fact, one of the quickest ways to become an ineffective manager is to remain rigid in how you carry out your managerial functions!

Managers Must Understand Organizations

Because organizations are the context of management, managers must understand how to operate within them. As we stated earlier, organizations are to management what air is to a plane. Yet for a plane to fly effectively, a pilot must possess essential knowledge about the characteristics and composition of air, like how atmospheric density relates to temperature in order to calculate how much lift it can provide. In the hottest days of summer, planes taking off sometimes have to bump passengers when seats are still available on the plane, because as the temperature rises, the air becomes less dense, lift is more difficult to achieve, and the weight with which a plane can safely take off declines.

Q: But what does it really mean to "understand organizations"? I can't possibly know everything about them, so how do I figure out what is more and less important to understand?

A: Just as a pilot does not have to be an astrophysicist or an aeronautical engineer to skilfully fly a plane, you do not need a Ph.D. in organizational science to be an effective manager. However, you do need a solid understanding of some basic features of organizations. Much of what follows in this textbook is designed to provide you with the fundamental knowledge you need in relation to the challenge of managing with skill. Of course, one textbook and one course in management will not provide you with sufficient knowledge. This book, however, will give you the foundation you need to be an effective manager. Without that foundation, you will either learn the hard way from your errors or be an ineffective manager.

Thus, while it is not practical to fully understand all organizations, you need to know how they can affect management practice. The key point is that just as a pilot cannot simply focus on the plane and ignore the conditions of the air, effective managers cannot only focus on management and ignore the organizational context within which it is practised. Clearly, for example, Annette Verschuren knows the difference between what managerial actions are required on the retail sales floor of a Home Depot outlet and what is required in an executive boardroom.

management requires getting things done through people

The act of managing involves an attempt to achieve an objective through the efforts of two, three, ten, a hundred, or even thousands of other people. Somebody acting entirely alone, whether he or she is writing a poem or making a critical investment decision, may be trying to achieve a particular goal, but that person is not managing. Management is, by its very nature, a people-based activity. Managers, no matter how talented, cannot do everything themselves. They need to use their own skills and energies as well as those of other people if they are to be effective. As one high-level executive within a software firm explained:

> *Hard skills, like sales, come easily to me, yet they produce transitory results. Delegating to others, co-creating performance expectations, and trusting people to carry through is not easy. But over the years, I have found that connecting with people one-on-one, and strengthening soft skills, produce meaningful and lasting results.*[7]

The message is clear: If you don't want to work with and through other people, then don't become a manager. You won't like the activity, and you are unlikely to be successful.

Managers Must Be Adept at Assessing Other People's Capabilities

A critical managerial skill, and one that can be developed, is that of assessing other people's capabilities. Knowing the capability of an individual or a group of people to complete one or more tasks, as well as judging what level of performance they might be able to reach with additional instruction, training, and motivation, is essential for building an effective unit.

Q: It sounds difficult to be able to evaluate the capabilities of people and to do it accurately. How do you do it?

A: It's not easy and it takes time, effort, and often experience to develop this kind of managerial skill. However, the important point is that being a manager requires that you do this task well. It's critical to being an effective manager.

Effective Managers Must Be Adept at Matching People's Capabilities with Appropriate Responsibilities

Knowing what a particular individual or particular group is capable of doing is only part of the requirement for successfully getting things done through people. Another equally important requirement is being able to match people with tasks they are best able to perform. In addition to finding the right job for the right person, managers must also ensure that their people have the resources necessary to do the job. Therefore, the manager must be a resource provider (a resource finder and enhancer) as well as a resource coordinator.

Q: That sounds good, but aren't resources always scarce in organizations?

A: Certainly, resources are finite in all organizations. A manager almost always has limited time, equipment, money, and especially people. That is why it is vital to use human resources as skilfully as possible—to be able to connect people and tasks effectively. Often, that process involves forming teams, where the whole is greater than the sum of the parts. Knowing the people in your organization and their capabilities is vital, but it also is essential to fully understand the tasks and the jobs that need to be done. Matching resources and tasks also demands considerable effort to explore whether additional resources are needed. Management is an activity that requires initiative—not passive acceptance of the status quo.

Effective Managers Must Be Adept at Motivating People

The third requirement for successfully getting tasks done through people is motivating them to accomplish the goals. In the current competitive landscape (described earlier in this chapter), formal authority is declining as a useful

All jobs require specific skills and capabilities. The job of managers is to match people with the jobs they are best suited to perform. This requires a considerable amount of evaluation of the job and the person applying for it. For example, a cashier's position usually requires that the employee learn how to operate the cash register, ensure items are properly priced, and be knowledgeable of the different payment methods available. More importantly, cashiers are frequently the customer's sole contact with the firm. What the customer thinks of him or her is likely to be what the customer thinks of the firm.

means for influencing people. Thus, managers must have a good understanding of what people value (what they care about) if they are to be superior motivators.

Q: I don't want to be a psychologist, so how can I understand what each person values and wants out of work?

A: You are not expected to become a psychologist, but it is important that you know some basic approaches to motivate people. In addition, you need to understand how to apply those approaches when it comes to managing specific individuals. That includes not only those who work for you but also your peers and superiors.

Q: But isn't management more than motivating people or getting things done through people?

A: Absolutely. Management is a complex process that requires integration of many different tasks, including planning and organizing what is to be done, developing budgets, and evaluating outcomes. Motivating and leading people are only two components of this overall process. Nevertheless, unless managers can get things done through people, not much will be accomplished. Managers must multiply the effects of their own efforts by influencing and directing the efforts of other people.

management requires simultaneously mastering multiple and potentially conflicting situations

Like most things, if management were easy there wouldn't be such a high premium placed on it. One of the important factors that separates great managers from mediocre managers is the recognition, acceptance, and mastery of managing paradoxes—the ability to cope with forces that pull managers in opposite directions. Great managers do not avoid these tensions but embrace them, harness them, and use them.

Q: Are these opposing forces really trade-offs? If so, managers sometimes have to trade off one opposing force for another. Is this correct?

A: Yes, managers at times have to make decisions about trade-offs. Sometimes they do, in fact, have to go with one set of actions to achieve the desired results—for example, expand the investment in R&D (research and development)—and in the process, forgo another investment and its potential results. That might mean postponing television advertising during *Hockey Night in Canada* for a season. However, great managers do not automatically view competing forces in terms of direct trade-offs; they often recognize that the challenge is to respond to both forces simultaneously in a creative fashion that enables the firm to accomplish both sets of objectives or some portion of them.

Management Is a Complex Process Requiring Integration, Yet Managerial Activities Are Often Fragmented and Do Not Occur in a Logical, Sequential Fashion

Management requires the integration of a variety of activities, such as planning, decision making, communicating, motivating, appraising, and organizing, yet a manager's day is typically fragmented with interruptions, breaks in sequence, and other distractions. In a sense, a manager is like a juggler. The manager may need to keep several balls in the air, simultaneously throwing the balls up and catching them. Rarely does the manager take the time to evaluate the competing "ball" and decide to keep one up while somehow suspending the others in mid-air. All of the balls must be continuously juggled or they will be lost.

Likewise, while managers are constantly confronted with rapidly changing activities and discrete bits or chunks of information, it is the responsibility and challenge of the manager to integrate all of them in a meaningful way. As such, the manager must be capable of seeing patterns of important activities and changes in them, both within the organization and external to it. He or she must then coordinate the resources, people, and activities to achieve the organization's goals.

Q: Although this seems logical, management seems much more simple than you're describing. Isn't the key to simplify management and not make it more complex?

A: Management, as often described by "bestselling" books, may seem simple, and certainly the authors of many of these books would like you to believe that if you just did "X" you would be highly successful. But the reality is that management is complex and requires integration of fragmented actions, information, and resources. Easy solutions may be appealing, but they rarely work. If management were simple, there wouldn't be a new bestseller about it each month—no one would need the new tip of the month.

There may be some value in bestselling management books, but the simple solutions that they offer may work only in a very specific situation; they are unlikely to work in most situations. Solutions that work across a variety of conditions are likely to be more complicated. Effective managers understand that paradoxes—seeming contradictions—lie at the centre of their roles and responsibilities and that one of their key challenges is to deal with those paradoxes effectively.

Management Requires Consistency and Flexibility

Perhaps one of the most important paradoxes is that of simultaneously maintaining consistency and flexibility. Without question, people need some consistency in their organizational lives. Workers could not be expected to perform their jobs well if tasks, or how they were expected to accomplish them, changed each day. Without some consistency, the workplace would be chaotic, and no purposeful organizational objectives could be accomplished. Yet, in the current competitive landscape—with rapidly changing technology, government policies, customer preferences, and competitor capabilities—flexibility, change, and adaptation are essential for survival.

Q: As a manager, how can I be consistent and yet remain flexible at the same time?

A: It is important to understand that as a manager you do not need to make an either/or choice to be consistent all of the time or completely flexible all of the time. For example, your fundamental values and ethical standards need to be fairly stable. People may not agree with your values or ethical standards, but they need to know what they are and that you consistently maintain them. Otherwise, you will appear to be unpredictable and untrustworthy. You also need to exhibit a fair degree of consistency without being overly rigid in your basic approach to dealing with people and problems. People need to perceive that you are open to alternative ideas, but they will have difficulty if you change so often that you seem to be a chameleon.

Managers Must Reflect and Act

Talk to any manager today, and he or she will tell you that one must rapidly deal with often unexpected situations, decisions, problems, and opportunities. One executive put it this way:

> *The fascinating thing about this job is the incredible variability of it . . . It's a never-ending kaleidoscope. I sometimes compare it to playing tennis with an out-of-control tennis-ball serving machine that just keeps shooting balls at you. You've got to keep moving faster and faster to keep up.*[8]

Quick action is often the difference between first and second place or even last place in the competitive marketplace, as Research In Motion has demonstrated with its popular BlackBerry. To some extent, then, capabilities like being able to think and make decisions quickly are admirable managerial qualities.

But there is an inherent problem with focusing on the onslaught of daily activities. This problem is similar to running and focusing on the ground only a metre in front of you. You may notice the stone in the path in time to avoid it, or you may notice a declining or inclining slope in the path and change your pace appropriately. Each individual step you take may be successful, but by focusing on only a metre in front of you, you may not notice that you are running straight toward a wall or cliff. Take, for example, the case of Richard Currie, former president of Loblaw Companies and presently chairman of the board for Bell Canada. Currie is recognized as having turned Loblaw around with innovative products like the "No Name" brand. Under Currie's 25 years of management, Loblaw shares increased 350-fold, becoming the largest private-sector employer in Canada. Two simple dictums that Currie employed through his career have been "don't move too fast" and "no one is as smart as all of us."[9] As this example suggests, taking time to make appropriate decisions and seeking the advice and input from others allows managers to look up and take notice of events beyond their own daily activities.

Q: But how can I deal effectively with all the things I need to each day and still have time to reflect?

A: Management is about activity; it is not about philosophy. But managers cannot know if they are headed in the right direction, if their pace is appropriate, or if their current approach is effective, unless they *take* the time to reflect on these things. Because management is about activity, you are unlikely to *find* time to reflect—you are going to have to *make* time. In fact, many of the insights presented in this chapter have come from managers, as we asked them in our interviews to take time to reflect on management. So, while managers must act and often do so quickly, they must also take time to analyze what they are doing, how they are doing it, and perhaps most importantly, why they are doing it.

Increasingly, Managers Need Global Perspective and Local Understanding of Specific Customers, Governments, Competitors, and Suppliers

International management consultants are fond of saying that in the future there will be two types of CEOs: those who have a global perspective and those who are out of a job. The evidence for the increasing globalization of business is nearly overwhelming, and that is why we make it one of our key themes in this book. It is virtually impossible to read a major magazine or newspaper without finding several stories related to global business in some form—companies entering international markets, competing with foreign competitors, responding to a foreign government's policy change, and so on. This requires a global perspective. However, the paradox is that all business occurs at a local level. The business transactions and the management activities all take place in specific countries with specific employees, government officials, competitors, and suppliers. Roots Canada, for example, has made inroads into the United States and has also been successful in expanding internationally. Roots even got the prestigious role of official outfitter for not only Canada, but the United States, Great Britain, and Barbados for the 2004 Olympics in Athens. The knife cuts both ways however; in early 2004 Roots was faced with closing a Canadian manufacturing facility, locating it offshore because of economic pressures to compete with lower-priced products coming into Canada from American and European firms.[10]

Agreements like the North American Free Trade Agreement (NAFTA) have thrown open doors to customers and firms worldwide. Managers in Toronto cannot assume their products will be as appealing in Miami or Beijing as they are on their home turf. But they also know that their competitors' products won't be either. In recent years, this has made for a broader playing field with make-or-break competitive consequences.

Q: But in a practical sense, how do I "think globally and act locally"?

A: The key is to be able to recognize the drivers behind these competing forces. For many products, it is much cheaper to build one version for the entire world than to have variations for every country. Yet, for many of these products, customers in different countries have different preferences. One compromise is to design the product so it has the widest appeal, recognizing that, as a consequence, it will not appeal to some potential customers. Nevertheless, more sophisticated managers do not trade off global standardization for local appeal or vice versa. Instead, they recognize the inherent challenge in this paradox and seek to standardize aspects of the product that have common appeal and simultaneously customize those features that need to be adapted to local preferences.

For example, McDonald's has a worldwide identity built around the standardization of both its products and its service. The Quarter Pounder and Egg McMuffin are the same product whether you buy them in Charlottetown, Singapore, or Moscow. The company also attempts to standardize managerial styles by requiring managers to learn the company's specific approaches to human resource practices, marketing, inventory management, and quality control. However, McDonald's corporate managers must also learn to adjust their financial and marketing approaches to local conditions. Similarly, McDonald's store managers around the world must learn when to add specialized menu items to suit local tastes—McLobster in New Brunswick, McPoutine in Quebec, the Teriyaki McBurger in Japan, McFalafel in Egypt, and 100 percent kosher beef in Israel.[11]

You might think of this global/local paradox by comparing it to a view of the landscape from a helicopter. Managers often have to "helicopter up" to a level to get a broad perspective of the "forest," or in other words, to obtain a global view. But then they need to come down closer to earth to see the "trees," or the local conditions and marketplace. Managers who can only see what is immediately and directly in front of them risk being ineffective because they can't see "the forest for the trees." At the same time, though, managers who only fly at 20 000 feet risk being ineffective because they miss the small details and nuances that can influence the success or failure of specific decisions or tasks. Thus, effective management is not a matter of having only a broad global perspective or only a knowledge of the specific local situation; it is a matter of being able to develop *both*.

managers must continuously search for and exploit new opportunities

We previously noted that managers must be committed to continuous learning and to creating value for others. However, to survive in the hypercompetitive landscape that exists in the twenty-first century they are required to regularly search for and be open to new opportunities in their current marketplace or to ideas that could create new markets. Entrepreneurship involves identifying new opportunities and exploiting them; thus, managers must be entrepreneurial.

Q: I thought that entrepreneurs developed new businesses and then managers operated them. Are you saying that managers are entrepreneurs?

A: You are correct about what entrepreneurs do, but entrepreneurship is not exclusive of management, especially in the current environment. Entrepreneurial activity is not limited to new, small firms. Managers in large firms need to be entrepreneurial and create new businesses as well. Developing new businesses requires that the lead person and perhaps others take entrepreneurial actions. Given the amount of change and innovation encountered in most industries and countries, businesses cannot survive without being entrepreneurial.[12]

Q: What is required for a manager to be entrepreneurial and be responsible for all of the other activities explained?

A: Managers must develop an entrepreneurial mindset. An entrepreneurial mindset is a way of thinking about businesses that emphasizes actions to take advantage of uncertainty.[13] With an entrepreneurial mindset, managers can sense opportunities and take actions to exploit them. Uncertainty in the environment tends to level the playing field for both large and small organizations and for resource-rich and resource-poor ones. Opportunities can be identified by anyone and exploited to achieve a competitive advantage.

To develop an entrepreneurial mindset, managers must first be alert and open to investing in opportunities today that may provide benefits in the future. They must be amenable to new ideas and to using them to create value for customers.[14]

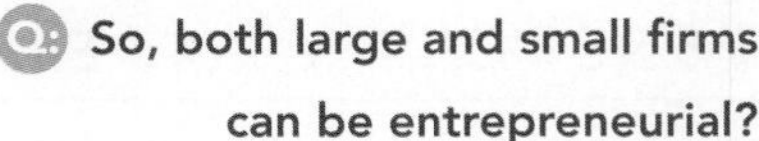

Q: So, both large and small firms can be entrepreneurial?

A: Yes. In fact, large and small firms *and* new and established firms can be entrepreneurial. For reasons described earlier, they not only can be, they must be to survive. Eaton's, once an entrepreneurial company that grew to become one of North America's most influential department stores, no longer exists in part because it lost its entrepreneurial nature when it no longer understood the needs of its customers and was unable to respond to the competitive advances of other retailers in the late 1990s. As a whole, small and new firms tend to be more entrepreneurial, but often lack the ability to sustain this advantage. On the other hand, large, established firms are good at using their size to gain an advantage and in sustaining their strong position as long as new, rival products don't enter the market. However, larger firms have a harder time being entrepreneurial.[15]

An Entrepreneurial Mindset Requires a Commitment to Constantly Learning New Skills and Acquiring New Knowledge

Management is a complex process. It is not just about strategy, or organizing, or decision making, or leadership. It is about all of these activities and more, but it is especially about *integrating them*. To integrate activities, managers require multiple skills (as we discuss later in this chapter): technical, interpersonal, and conceptual. These skills can be learned, or at least greatly improved by learning, if there is a commitment by a manager to such learning. Experience alone does not necessarily provide learning, but the desire for and effort to acquire new knowledge from those experiences often produces learning and the development of new capabilities.

Even the best managers with the most experience must stay abreast of the marketplace because conditions can change rapidly. This means not becoming complacent but committing themselves and their staff to continued learning and improvement to meet new challenges and situations.

Q: But do I really have to keep on learning about how to manage throughout my career?

A: It is dangerous to assume at any point in time that you know all that needs to be known about management. Managers must continuously acquire new knowledge and skills to remain competitive because they constantly confront new situations and challenges. Therefore, a commitment to continuous learning and improvement is vital. Managerial hubris—meaning overbearing pride or self-confidence—has been publicly demonstrated in recent years by the colossal failures of companies such as Enron and WorldCom, which will be better known for the circumstances of their demise than for their products or services. This danger should motivate you to pursue the frontiers of learning and acquire better managerial skills no matter what your level in the organization is.

An Entrepreneurial Mindset Also Requires a Commitment to Adding Value to Other People's Efforts and to Society

At its best, management is not a selfish activity. It should serve others, both in one's own organization and in society at large. This kind of commitment represents a challenge—a challenge to contribute something that benefits people, whether it be employees, customers, shareholders, or others. Meeting this challenge requires not only a sense of obligation and responsibility, but also vision and a burning passion. Otherwise, why be a manager?

What Do Managers Do?

A few years from now when you are getting started on your career, whether in management or some other endeavour, your parents or friends might ask: "What do you actually *do* in your job?" A manager is a manager, right? Well, as we'll see, it's not quite that simple. Just as we tried to provide some different ways of thinking about "what is management?" we will also do the same with respect to the question, "What do managers do?"

Later in this section (see the next two boxes), two managers describe—in their own words—what they do, what they like most about their jobs, and recent changes they've had to cope with in their jobs. These interviews provide a glimpse at some of the flavour and intensity of actual managerial jobs.

There are also other, analytical ways to look at managerial jobs aside from simply asking managers what they do. Over the years, several systems have been developed to classify (a) managerial functions, (b) the roles in which managers operate, and (c) the characteristics and dimensions of managerial jobs. These typologies can provide you with useful ways to examine the extremely varied nature of managerial jobs and responsibilities. In effect, they provide a road map for thinking about what management is.

Managerial Functions

One way to think about the question "What do managers do?" is to analyze the work of managers according to the different functions or processes they carry out. The first such classification system dates back at least 80 years and has sometimes been criticized for not sufficiently characterizing what managers "really do." However, this system is still, after more than eight decades, widely used by management scholars and writers.[16] In fact, as we explain at the end of this chapter, a variation of this traditional typology forms the basis for the general sequencing of the chapters in this book (as well as most other textbooks on the subject of management). The four principal managerial functions that seem most applicable to modern organizations are planning, organizing, directing, and controlling.

planning estimating future conditions and circumstances and making decisions about appropriate courses of action

Planning **Planning** involves estimating future conditions and circumstances and, based on these estimations, making decisions about what work is to be done by the manager and all of those for whom she or he is responsible. This function can be thought of as involving three distinct levels or types: strategic planning, which addresses strategic actions designed to achieve the organization's long-range goals; tactical planning, which translates strategic plans into actions designed to achieve specific and shorter-term goals and objectives; and operational planning, which identifies the actions needed to accomplish the goals of particular units within the organization.

organizing systematically putting resources together

Organizing To carry out managerial work, resources must be put together systematically, and this function is labelled **organizing**. It involves paying attention to the structure of relationships among positions and the people occupying them, and linking that structure to the overall strategic direction of the organization. Since the world today is basically full of uncertainties and ambiguities, the function of organizing is a critical challenge facing managers. At its most basic level, the purpose of this managerial function can be thought of as the attempt to bring order to the organization. Without organizing, it would be a very chaotic environment.

Directing This function has typically had a number of different labels over the years, including *leading*. The latter term obviously does not have the autocratic connotations associated with the word *directing*. Nevertheless, the core of **directing**, or leading, is the process of attempting to influence other people to attain organizational objectives. It heavily involves motivating those for whom you are responsible, interacting with them effectively in group and team situations, and communicating in ways that are highly supportive of their efforts to accomplish their tasks and achieve organizational goals.

directing the process of attempting to influence other people to attain organizational objectives

Controlling In contemporary organizations, the word **controlling** is not entirely satisfactory because it implies, as does the word *directing*, that the activity must be carried out in a dictatorial, autocratic fashion. This, of course, is not the case, although in a particular circumstance a manager might act in this manner. The essence of this function is to regulate the work of those for whom a manager is responsible. Regulation can be done in several different ways, including setting standards of performance in advance, monitoring ongoing (real-time) performance, and, especially, assessing a completed performance. The results of such evaluation are fed back into the planning process. Therefore, it is important to consider these four managerial functions as parts of a reciprocal and recurring process, as illustrated in Exhibit 1.2.

controlling regulating the work of those for whom a manager is responsible

Exhibit 1.2

Managerial Functions

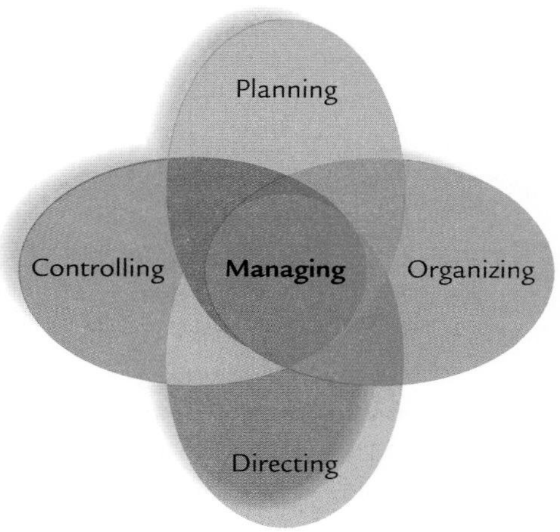

Managerial Roles

An alternative approach to describing managerial work was proposed some years ago by Canadian scholar Henry Mintzberg.[17] He based his classification system on research studies about how managers spend their time at work, and focused on "roles," or what he called "organized sets of behaviours." Although this way of viewing managers' work activities has not replaced the functional approach, it has received a great deal of attention because it provides additional understanding and insights not readily apparent in that more traditional set of categories.

Mintzberg organized his typology of managerial roles into three major categories—interpersonal, informational, and decisional—each of which contains specific roles. Altogether, there are 10 such roles in this system, as shown in Exhibit 1.3 and described in the following sections.

Exhibit 1.3

Types of Managerial Roles

Interpersonal Roles:
- Figurehead
- Leader
- Liaison

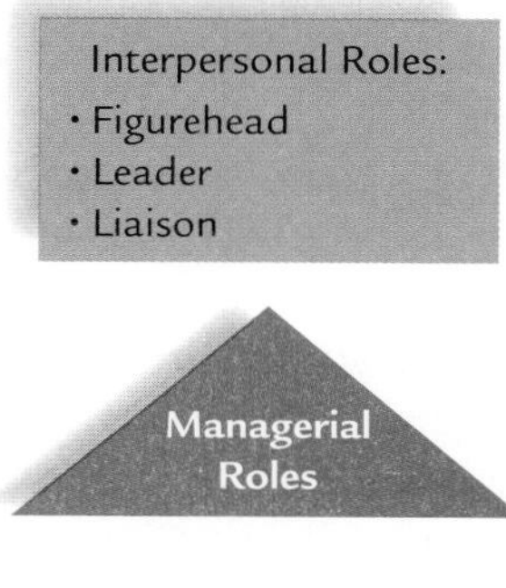

Informational Roles:
- Monitor
- Disseminator
- Spokesperson

Decisional Roles:
- Entrepreneur
- Disturbance Handler
- Resource Allocator
- Negotiator

a week in the managerial life of deb m.

Deb M. is the director of organizational effectiveness for a Canadian oil and gas company.

QUESTION: Describe the type and range of activities you were involved in, as a manager, this past week.

Last week 70 percent of my time was spent in meetings with others. That's a bit high but not totally unusual.

One of the meetings I organized and led. Actually it was a two-day work meeting with HR peers in other parts of the company. We were working on coordinating our HR activities such as recruiting and performance management across the company. We have four separate operating units and each has its own HR department to some extent.

One of the other meetings involved making a presentation to our corporate senior management team regarding our compensation strategy. I was explaining how changes we proposed to make would help us better attract and retain employees with key skills.

I also had a meeting with my boss to review resource needs for my team in order to manage increasing workloads.

I spent several hours interviewing job candidates for a new hire to join my team.

I also conducted an orientation session with a number of our managers to explain our new job evaluation system.

The rest of the time was spent working on several efforts to better integrate and harmonize certain HR practices, such as pay, across the company. This involved both working with my subordinates as well as working on my own.

QUESTION: What do you like best about your job as a manager?

One of the things I like best about my job is that I have the opportunity to influence the decisions and actions that will have a significant impact on the success of the company. Much of our success depends on the people we attract and select into the company and the performance current employees contribute. My job in HR and the work of my subordinates contribute directly to the quality of people we have and how well they perform.

QUESTION: In the past year or so, what is the biggest change you have had to respond to?

We are going through a lot of changes right now. We have changed our strategy and our structure—but most of these changes were planned. The unexpected changes have involved individuals who have either deviated from the agreed-to plan and/or have not shared key pieces of information that would have caused us to plan differently. In the first case, I've had to rely on my interpersonal skills to try and get the person back on track. In the second case, I've had to incorporate the new information and adjust our plans.

Interpersonal Roles Interpersonal roles are composed of three types of behaviour and, according to Mintzberg, are derived directly from the manager's formal authority granted by the organization. They are as follows:

1. *The Figurehead Role:* This set of behaviours involves an emphasis on ceremonial activities, such as attending a social function, welcoming a visiting dignitary, or presiding at a farewell reception for a departing employee. A familiar term for this role of representing the organization, borrowed from the military, is "showing the flag." Although one particular occasion where this behaviour occurs may not be important in and of itself, the activity across a period of time is a necessary component of a manager's job. If you doubt this, just ask any manager you know! For example, the next time you meet the dean of a business school, ask how often she finds it necessary to participate in figurehead activities—think of commencement ceremonies, for instance—and how important this is for the long-term benefit of the school.
2. *The Leader Role:* This role, in Mintzberg's system, is essentially one of influencing or directing others. It is the set of responsibilities people typically associate with a manager's job, since the organization gives the manager formal authority over the work of other people. To the extent

that managers are able to translate this authority into actual influence, they are exercising what would be called leadership behaviour. The leader type of behaviour would be demonstrated when, for example, a newly appointed project team leader gathers his hand-picked team members together and discusses his vision and goals for the team and his ideas as to how to accomplish them.

3. *The Liaison Role:* This role emphasizes the contacts that a manager has with those outside the formal authority chain of command. These contacts include not only other managers within the organization, but also many individuals outside it—for example, customers, suppliers, government officials, and managers from other organizations. It also emphasizes lateral interactions, as contrasted with vertical, interpersonal interactions of a manager, and it highlights the fact that an important part of a manager's job is to serve as a go-between for his or her own unit and other units or groups. The liaison role would apply to the situation where a marketing manager interacts with key customers to learn about their reactions to new product ideas.

Informational Roles This set of roles builds on the interpersonal relationships that a manager establishes, and it underlines the importance of the network of contacts built up and maintained by a manager. The three specific informational roles identified by Mintzberg are as follows:

1. *The Monitor Role:* This type of behaviour involves extensive information-seeking that managers engage in to keep aware of crucial developments that may affect their unit and their own work. Such monitoring, as previously noted, typically deals with spoken and written information and "soft" as well as "hard" facts. A manager attending an industry conference who spends considerable time in informal lobby and lounge conversations to gather data on current developments in the industry would be engaging in this role.
2. *The Disseminator Role:* A manager not only receives information but also sends it. This often includes information that the receiver wants but otherwise has no easy access to without the help of the manager. A supervisor who finds out about reorganization plans affecting his part of the organization and conveys that information to his subordinates would be acting in a disseminator role.
3. *The Spokesperson Role:* A manager is frequently called upon to represent the views of the unit for which he or she is responsible. At lower management levels, this typically involves representing the unit to other individuals or groups within the organization; at higher management levels, this internal spokesperson role could also be supplemented by an external component in which the organization and its activities and concerns often must be represented to the outside world. When the manager of the western region meets with other regional managers and presents the views of his region's sales personnel about how well a proposed new sales incentive plan is likely to work, he is functioning in a spokesperson role.

Decisional Roles The final category of roles in this classification system relates to the decision-making requirements of a managerial position. Four such decisional roles are designated by Mintzberg:

1. *The Entrepreneurial Role:* Managers not only make routine decisions in their jobs, but also frequently engage in activities that explore new

opportunities or start new projects. Such entrepreneurial behaviour within an organization often involves a series of small decisions that permit ongoing assessment about whether to continue or abandon new ventures. This type of role behaviour involves some degree of risk, but that risk is often limited or minimized by the sequence of decisions. Suppose, for example, that a lower-level production manager comes up with an idea for a new organizational sales unit that she discusses with her colleagues and then, based on their reactions, modifies it and presents it to upper-level management. Such a manager would be exhibiting entrepreneurial role behaviour that goes beyond her routine responsibilities.

2. *The Disturbance Handler Role:* Managers initiate actions of their own, but they must also be able to respond to problems or "disturbances." In this role, a manager often acts as a judge, problem solver, or conflict settler. The goal of such actions, of course, is to keep small problems or issues from developing into larger ones. If you, as a manager, were to face a situation where your employees could not agree about who would do a particularly unpleasant but necessary group task, and you then stepped in to settle the matter, you would be functioning as a disturbance handler.
3. *The Resource Allocator Role:* Since resources of all types are always limited in organizations, one of the chief responsibilities of managers is to decide how the resources under their authority will be distributed. Such allocation decisions have a direct effect on the performance of a unit and an indirect effect of communicating certain types of information to members of the unit. The manager of front desk services for a large resort hotel who decides how many and which clerks will be assigned to each shift is operating in a resource allocator role.
4. *The Negotiator Role:* This type of managerial behaviour refers to the fact that a manager is often called upon to make accommodations with other units or other organizations (depending on the level of the management position). The manager, in this decisional situation, is responsible for knowing what resources can or cannot be committed to particular negotiated solutions. Someone who serves on a negotiating team to set up a new joint venture with an outside company would be functioning in the negotiator role.

If nothing else, the collection of roles described in Mintzberg's analysis of managerial work emphasizes the considerable variety of behaviours required in these types of jobs. In considering these 10 roles, it is essential to keep in mind that the extent to which any particular role is important will vary considerably from one managerial job to another. Obviously, where a job fits within the organization will have a great deal to do with which particular role or roles are emphasized. The front-line supervisor of branch-office bank tellers obviously has a different mix of roles from that of the bank's executive vice president. Nevertheless, Mintzberg maintains that the 10 roles form a "gestalt," or whole, and that to understand the total nature of *any* managerial job, *all* of them must be taken into account.

Managerial Job Dimensions

Another extremely useful way to try to gain an understanding of managerial work is to analyze the dimensions of managerial jobs. One particular approach was developed by British researcher Rosemary Stewart.[18] Stewart proposed

a week in the managerial life of greg k.

Greg K. is director of finance and accounting in a large division of a financial services firm.

QUESTION: Describe the type and range of activities you were involved in, as a manager, this past week.

In my managerial job, I have a pretty wide variety of activities that I am involved in—ranging from division project meetings to staff meetings to time to work on my own projects. Here is a brief overview of my activities this past week:

Monday—In the morning I participated in a conference call with various management-level employees to discuss activity at one of our broker/dealers. The remainder of the day was filled with interacting with staff, completing my assignments, and reacting to various inquiries from other departments, divisions, and auditors.

Tuesday—This morning I participated in a biweekly status call with our third-party administrator for one of our products. Following the conference call, I met with one of my direct reports (accounting manager) for our weekly staff meeting. We discussed the status of various department projects, staffing issues, upcoming projects, and current events affecting the division. Later that day I met with our accounting coordinator to discuss the status of a pricing project that she was working on.

Wednesday—This was a light day as far as standing meetings; however, I attended a one-hour training class regarding upcoming new product features that we will be offering.

Thursday—Thursdays are typically busy in the mornings due to a biweekly technology meeting that I participate in and a weekly product meeting that I attend. This typically takes up two to three hours of my morning when both of the meetings occur. This Thursday the head of our department held a monthly staff meeting to discuss general events affecting the department, the division, and the company.

Friday—Today began with a weekly investment meeting in the morning. I represent our division in this meeting that includes other representatives from all divisions of the company. The remainder of the day was spent working on various normal tasks.

Aside from the meetings that I attend throughout the week, the remainder of my work week typically includes other interactions with staff and completion of my other assignments (responsibilities as a "working manager"). I typically interact at least daily (more often than not, multiple times throughout the day) with our department head (VP of finance). We discuss new requests/projects, staffing, status of current projects, etc. I also interact regularly throughout the day with my direct reports (five direct reports) to discuss projects and questions, and provide feedback. I also am responsible for approving all of our sales-force travel and expense reports and approving sales support requests that come from our sales force.

QUESTION: What do you like best about your job as a manager?

I think I need to answer this from two angles, one from the perspective of my direct assignments and one from a managerial perspective:

Regarding my direct assignments, the most rewarding part of my job is contributing to a division project that directly impacts the division with findings and recommendations that are communicated to senior management. Feeling part of the division team is very rewarding.

As a manager, I enjoy problem solving and coaching my direct reports regarding issues that they face. My company offers several management development programs, and one that I found especially useful concerned leadership. I try to apply facets of the class to situations that arise in everyday work.

QUESTION: In the past year or so, what is the biggest change you have had to respond to?

From a management perspective, the most challenging change over the past year was terminating two employees (not my direct reports, but I was very involved in the process) and adjusting accordingly on all fronts of the job. I had not previously been involved in a termination, so it was very challenging. The process included performance concerns, HR concerns, reallocating resources within the department to ensure completion of all assignments, and communication to other employees (a very delicate matter).

that any managerial job (and, in fact, any job anywhere in an organization) can be characterized along three dimensions:

- the demands made on it;
- the constraints placed on it; and
- the choices permitted in it.

Looking at managerial jobs in this way not only provides further understanding of what managers do, but also permits direct comparisons of different jobs; for example, how the position of "manager of information systems" might compare with that of "financial analyst," or the job of "marketing vice president" versus "plant manager."

Demands This dimension of managerial jobs refers to what the holder of a particular position *must* do. Demands are of two types: activities or duties that must be carried out and the standards or levels of minimum performance that must be met. Demands can come from several sources, such as the organization at large, the immediate boss, or the way in which work activities are organized. Typical types of demands would include such behaviour as attending required meetings, adhering to schedule deadlines, following certain procedures, and the like. No doubt, for example, Annette Verschuren has sales and performance targets to meet in her position at The Home Depot Canada.

Constraints Constraints are factors that limit the response of the manager to various demands. One obvious constraint for any manager is the amount of time available for an activity. Other typical constraints include budgets, technology, attitudes of subordinates, and legal regulations. The important point is that any managerial job has a set of constraints, and therefore a key to performing that job effectively is to recognize them and develop a good understanding of how they can be minimized, overcome, or effectively confronted. Someone like Annette Verschuren has had to work within the constraints of deadlines, supplier schedules, customer preferences, and forces in the larger economy she could not control.

Choices This dimension underscores the fact that despite demands and despite constraints, there is always room for some amount of discretionary behaviour in any managerial job. Thus, there are a number of activities that a manager *may* carry out but does not have to. Choices can involve how work is to be done, what work beyond that absolutely required will be done, who will do particular tasks, and what initiatives not otherwise prohibited will be undertaken from almost infinite possibilities. In her present and past managerial positions, Verschuren would have faced a multitude of choices about how to make staffing decisions, how to demonstrate leadership, how to respond to changing market conditions affecting home improvements, and the like.

Exhibit 1.4 illustrates these three job dimensions for two different managerial jobs, that of a project team manager in a manufacturing company and a manager of a medium-sized fast-food restaurant. In these examples, though both jobs are definitely managerial in their nature and how their organizations view them, their demands and constraints are quite different. Some of the types of choices permitted, however, are fairly similar. It's the combination of the specifics of these three dimensions that determines what it would be like to be a manager in these or any other positions.

Exhibit 1.4 Two Managerial Jobs with Different Demands, Constraints, and Choices

	Job A: Project Team Manager	**Job B: Fast-Food Restaurant Manager**
Demands	· Develop new product with strong market appeal · Hold formal weekly progress meeting with boss · Frequent travel to other company sites	· Maintain attractive appearance of restaurant · Keep employee costs as low as possible · Meet standards for speed of service
Constraints	· 12-month deadline for product development · Project budget limit of $1 million · No choice in selecting team members	· Most employees have limited formal education · Few monetary incentives to reward outstanding performance · Federal and provincial health and safety regulations
Choices	· The organizational structure of the project team · Sequencing of project tasks · Budget allocations	· Selection of employee to promote to supervisor · Scheduling of shifts and assignments · Local advertising promotions

What Skills Do Managers Need?

Like any other human activity, managing involves the exercise of skills; that is, highly developed abilities and competencies. Skills emerge through a combination of aptitude, education, training, and experience. Three types have been identified as critical for managerial tasks, particularly for the leadership component of management: technical, interpersonal, and conceptual (see Exhibit 1.5).

Exhibit 1.5

Managers' Skills

Technical	**Interpersonal**	**Conceptual**
· Specialized knowledge (including when and how to use the skills)	· Sensitivity · Persuasiveness · Empathy	· Logical reasoning · Judgment · Analytical ability

Technical Skills Technical skills involve specialized knowledge about procedures, processes, equipment, and the like and include the related abilities of knowing how and when to use that knowledge. Research shows that these skills are especially important early in managerial careers (see Exhibit 1.6) when the leadership of lower-level employees is often part of the role and one of the challenges is to gain the respect of those being led. In addition, technical skills seem to be a particularly critical factor in many successful entrepreneurial start-ups, like that involving Mike Lazaridis and

Exhibit 1.6

Relative Importance of Managerial Skills at Different Organizational Levels

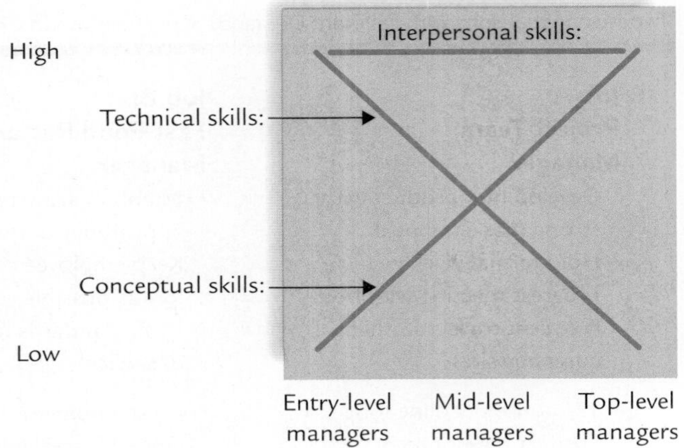

Douglas Fregin, two engineers who founded Research In Motion. Technical skills, whether in an entrepreneurial situation or in a larger organizational setting, are frequently necessary for managing effectively, but usually they are not sufficient in and of themselves. In fact, an over-reliance on technical skills may actually lower overall managerial effectiveness. The first products engineered and designed by Lazaridis and Fregin were generating sales of $500 000, but they realized that they were engineers first and needed someone who understood the business end of an innovation. In 1992, Jim Balsillie, a business school graduate of the University of Toronto and Harvard, joined Research In Motion as co-CEO. Balsillie became the driver behind the organization's corporate strategy and business development, while Lazaridis (president and co-CEO) and Fregin (vice-president of operations) both preside over the technical side of product strategy and research and development.[19]

Interpersonal Skills Interpersonal skills like sensitivity, persuasiveness, and empathy have been shown to be important at all levels of management, although particularly so at lower and middle levels. Exhibit 1.7 summarizes the findings of one study that investigated reasons why some fast-rising executives eventually "derailed" or plateaued in their managerial careers, even when they appeared to start out with acceptable levels of interpersonal skills. As put compellingly by a pair of management researchers, referring to those who have these skills but who lack other capabilities, "The charming but not brilliant find that the job gets too big and the problems too complex to get by on interpersonal skills [alone]."[20]

Conceptual Skills Often called cognitive ability or cognitive complexity, conceptual skills such as logical reasoning, judgment, and analytical abilities are a relatively strong predictor of managerial effectiveness. These skills are often the major factor that determines who reaches the highest levels of the organization. A clear example of someone who was selected for a CEO job precisely because of his conceptual skills is Jack Welch, the well-known former CEO of General Electric. He was appointed to the top position at GE in 1981 and immediately set out to restructure the organization with the objective of making it more globally competitive. His concept of the company included wiping out its bureaucracy to develop a more flexible organization. At the same time, however, he also championed a new corporate culture, one based on greater empowerment of the employee.

Exhibit 1.7 Who Succeeds? Who Doesn't?

Potential managerial leaders share traits early on:	Those who don't quite make it:	Those who succeed:
Bright, with outstanding track records	Have been successful, but generally only in one area or type of job.	Have diverse track records, demonstrated ability in many different situations, and a breadth of knowledge of the business or industry
Have survived stressful situations	Frequently described as moody or volatile. May be able to keep their temper with superiors during crises but are hostile toward peers and subordinates.	Maintain composure in stressful situations, are predictable during crises, are regarded as calm and confident.
Have a few flaws	Cover up problems while trying to fix them. If the problem can't be hidden, they tend to go on the defensive and even blame someone else for it.	Make a few mistakes, but when they do, they admit to them and handle them with poise and grace.
Ambitious and oriented toward problem solving	May attempt to micromanage a position, ignoring future prospects; may staff with the incorrect people or neglect the talents they have; may depend too much on a single mentor, calling their own decision-making ability into question.	While focusing on problem solutions, keep their minds focused on the next position, help develop competent successors, seek advice from many sources.
Good people skills	May be viewed as charming but political or direct but tactless, cold, and arrogant. People don't like to work with them.	Can get along well with different types of people, are outspoken without being offensive, are viewed as direct and diplomatic.

Source: Adapted from M. W. McCall, Jr. and M. M. Lombardo, "Off the Track: Why and How Successful Executives Get Derailed," *Technical Report #21* (Greensboro, NC: Center for Creative Leadership, 1983), pp. 9–11.

Plan of the Book

Now that we have proposed some initial ways to answer the three basic questions of "What is management?" "What do managers do?" and "What skills do managers need?" here in Chapter 1, we want to share with you the overall structure and plan of the remainder of the book. We do this to give you a better understanding of what follows in later chapters. It might even give you some additional insight in answering examination questions that will almost surely come later in the course.

Most books on management, after starting with a set of introductory chapters, group the remaining chapters in clusters around the generally accepted four major functions of management: planning, organizing, directing, and controlling. Our sequence of parts in this book is basically in that order. However, we title the parts in what we consider a more user-friendly and user-useful manner.

The first chapter is under the heading "You as a Manager." This chapter is intended to provide you with an introduction to the subject of the book (Chapter 1).

Part 1 emphasizes the importance of "Assessing the Environment" as a necessary background for considering the various functions of management that are covered later in the book. Chapters 2 and 3 focus on the context for managing in organizations: the outside, or external, environment of management, and the ethical issues that are facing every manager at the start of a new century. Chapter 4 presents the cultural environment. Particularly emphasized in these chapters are the various forces outside and inside the organization that affect how, and how well, a person can carry out managerial responsibilities.

Part 2 focuses on a manager's role in "Setting Direction." Chapter 5 discusses decision making, and Chapter 6 discusses planning for an organization. Chapter 7 raises issues of broad strategy, and Chapter 8 offers an overview of key elements of organization design and structure consistent with strategic directions.

The third part of the book, "Implementing through People," consists of five chapters dealing with this crucial managerial responsibility. It begins with Chapter 9, which discusses the important topic of leadership. Chapter 10 covers the topic of motivation, and especially the necessity for managers to have a framework for understanding how behaviour can be influenced in an organizational context. Chapter 11 turns to the role of groups and teams and how managers can have an impact on improving their processes and performance. In Chapter 12, the topic of communication is explored for its implications in implementing effective leadership in organizations, and Chapter 13 examines the overall issue of managing human resources in the organizational context.

In Part 4, "Monitoring and Renewing," these two necessary managerial activities are addressed from several different perspectives. Chapter 14 reviews some of the basic evaluation and control challenges facing managers. And finally, Chapter 15 addresses the topic of change. Here, and building on issues presented throughout the book, the emphasis is on a manager's proactive role in facilitating organizational renewal and development. That theme—renewal—seems an especially appropriate one on which to conclude the book.

concluding comments

As we conclude this chapter, we again want to emphasize the recurring themes you will be encountering throughout the remainder of this book: Management involves constant attention to, and an embracement of, change; it cannot be carried out without an understanding of the impacts of technology on managerial functions and processes, and it requires a global as well as a local, or "own country," focus. When you combine technology, globalization, and frequent change you create a highly complex and challenging environment in which to manage. Managers throughout any organization must manage strategically to confront these challenges effectively. An organization's strategy should focus on resources that exploit opportunities for competitive advantage and sustain it.

Also, here at the end of Chapter 1, we want to remind you of the four perspectives we stressed earlier: (1) The Organizational Context: Management occurs in organizations; (2) The Human Factor: Management means getting things done through people; (3) Managing Paradoxes: Management involves mastering multiple and potentially conflicting situations simultaneously; and (4) Entrepreneurial Mindset: Managers must continuously search for and exploit new opportunities. The challenge for you as a student is to learn more about the implications of these perspectives; that is, to learn more about the subtleties and complexities of the managerial process. This, of course, requires thought and analysis, but that, really, is only the beginning. Understanding management also requires an ability to synthesize and integrate a diverse array of facts, theories, viewpoints, and examples—in a phrase, as we emphasized earlier, to be able to "put it all together" so that the whole is indeed more than the sum of its parts.

Above all else, however, beyond analysis and synthesis, management requires skill in implementation. This is perhaps one of the most difficult skills to develop—how to put into practice the results of analysis and synthesis and how to make decisions. If there is one skill that senior managers seem most concerned about among new managers, it is that of implementation.[21] Most senior managers believe that the typical business graduate is much better at analysis than at implementation. Obviously, acquiring managerial experience helps considerably in developing the skill to be able to implement effectively, as Annette Verschuren has demonstrated. But experience by itself will not guarantee results. What is also needed is a heightened sensitivity to the importance of developing the skill of implementation. The lack of this skill is analogous to an athletic team formulating a good game plan but then fumbling the ball and dropping passes in the game itself—thus being guilty of "not executing." Therefore, as you read through the remainder of this book, keep in mind the message that management is not just about knowing; it is also, and emphatically so, about *doing*.

key terms

controlling 23
directing 23
management 5
organizations 5
organizing 22
planning 22

test your comprehension

1. What is management? Explain the different parts of the formal definition.
2. What is an organization?
3. Does management occur outside of organizations? Why or why not?
4. What creates the "personality" of an organization?
5. If you are an effective manager in one organization, will you automatically be as effective in all other organizations? Why or why not?
6. Identify three people skills important for managers.
7. What is meant by managing paradoxes?
8. Explain how a manager's life is both fragmented and integrated.
9. Why is it important for a manager to be both consistent and flexible?
10. What is the trade-off between reflection and action?
11. Why do managers need to be able to think globally but act locally?
12. Explain the types of commitment required of an effective manager.
13. What is an entrepreneurial mindset and how does a manager develop and apply it?
14. What are four traditional components (functions) of the overall management process?
15. What is the importance of each of Mintzberg's 10 managerial roles?
16. Describe Stewart's three managerial job dimensions.
17. What are the three major types of skills managers need to develop? Why is each essential to be an effective manager?

apply your understanding

1. Why is it important to examine management from different perspectives? What do you gain from this type of examination? Think of other possible perspectives or metaphors you could use to describe management (e.g., management is a profession; management means "being in charge"). What does your new perspective tell you about management that adds to your understanding?
2. What do you think is the biggest personal reward of being a manager? What is the biggest potential downside of being a manager?
3. Think about two different managerial-type jobs you have personally observed (within your family, as a worker, as a customer, etc.). Compare them using Stewart's concept of job dimensions. Considering each job's content as analyzed by the three dimensions, which one would you choose? Why?
4. This chapter states that effective managers need technical, interpersonal, and conceptual skills. Do all managers need these in the same mix? In other words, would some managers need more of one than of another? Why? Describe the managerial skills you think you need to develop to be an effective manager, and suggest how this might be done.

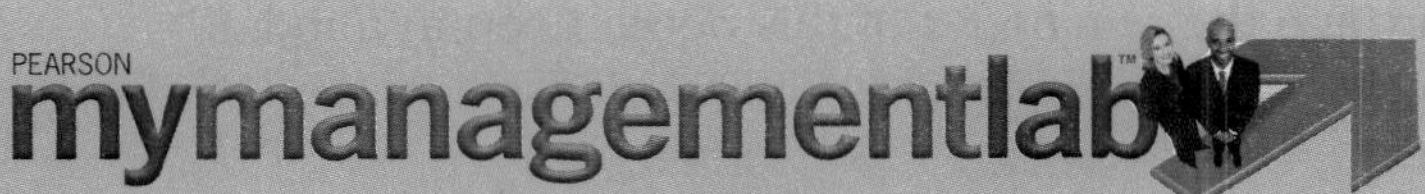

To improve your grade, visit the MyManagementLab website at **www.pearsoned.ca/mymanagementlab**. This online homework and tutorial system allows you to test your understanding and generates a personalized study plan just for you. It provides you with study and practice tools directly related to this chapter's content. MyManagementLab puts you in control of your own learning!

Clifford Chance—Update

London Business School

By Callum Campbell

Ten years after Geoffrey Howe gazed from the window of his new offices, Clifford Chance had outgrown its Aldersgate headquarters, and the firm had had to retain additional City of London offices. The current managing partner, Peter Cornell, now surveyed a different firm in a very different legal market.

Throughout the 1990s, Clifford Chance continued to add offices to its network (Prague in 1995, Bangkok in 1996, São Paulo in 1998), and to increase the number of staff in its existing offices. By 2002, Clifford Chance had succeeded in becoming the world's largest law firm, by virtue of both its size (3322 lawyers) and gross revenue ($1 409 032 200). In 1993, 80 percent of the firm's lawyers had been based in its London office. Howe's ambition to globalize the firm had been further realized by the fact that 63 percent of the firm's lawyers were now based outside of London.

The last decade had witnessed wholesale change in the legal industry. Where lawyers once assumed they would stay in the same law firm for life, the aggressive and hostile lateral hire of partners, teams, and the merger of whole firms had become the typical strategies in growing a law firm, strategies which were almost unheard of in 1992. In much of Europe and Asia, City of London–origin firms now dominated the landscape. U.S. firms had made fresh inroads into Europe, many striving to blend into the market as "local players." Global brands had yet to entirely usurp other international strategies. The "best-friends" network established by Slaughter and May in the U.K., Hengeler Mueller in Germany, and Bredin Prat in Paris still won covetable mandates, and remained highly profitable. In each European jurisdiction, independent firms, often outcasts or willing exiles from large mergers, continued to thrive. The most profitable law firms in the world, such as Wachtell Lipton Rosen & Katz, were based almost exclusively in New York. But the number of national firms able to compete for high-end corporate, corporate finance, and banking work was dwindling in step with the expansion of large international networks, like Clifford Chance.

Geoffrey Howe's ambition for his firm in 1993 had taken it to the top of the league tables. But getting there had necessitated a change in strategy. Organic growth could put an office anywhere on the planet, but could not provide critical mass. Nor could it satisfy the firm's aspirations in the key markets of the United States or Germany. On January 1, 2000, Clifford Chance announced the legal industry's most ambitious merger to date, simultaneously joining forces with the 400-lawyer, New York–based law firm Rogers & Wells, and the 260-lawyer, Frankfurt-based firm, Pünder, Volhard, Weber & Axster.

Since the fall of the Berlin Wall, Germany had seen an influx of law firms from both the U.S. and the U.K. Prior to 1990, foreign firms were prevented from merging with German firms or establishing a presence in Germany by vigorously upheld Bar Association restrictions. Liberalization of the industry transformed the market. The three largest firms in Germany, Freshfields Bruckhaus Deringer, Linklaters Oppenhoff & Rädler, and Clifford Chance Pünder, were all the result of Anglo-German mergers, and the majority of the top 15 firms in the country were the offspring of mergers with either U.S. or U.K. firms. Clifford Chance's acquisition of Pünder, Volhard was a bold step that brought it an instant presence with a well-respected, if not top-flight, German firm. It was rumored that the courtship had been competitive, as 15 British firms had been in contact to discuss possible mergers before the firm decided to throw in its lot with Clifford Chance.

The acquisition of Rogers & Wells was more remarkable. A big merger between a U.S. and a U.K. firm had

Callum Campbell (EMBA–Global 2003) prepared this update under the direction of Professor Maury Peiperl from public sources. It is designed as a supplement to the case "Clifford Chance: International Expansion" (© 1993, 1994 INSEAD) from *Managing Change: Cases and Concepts* by Maury Peiperl and Todd Jick (Irwin/McGraw-Hill, 2003).

long been predicted. The first marriage, observers speculated, would precipitate a flurry of engagements. But no one, it seemed, was anxious to go first.

Rogers & Wells traced its history to 1871 when attorney Walter Carter established an office in the New York Life Building to represent insurance companies bankrupted by the Great Chicago Fire of the same year. Prior to the merger, Rogers & Wells had offices in London, Paris, Frankfurt, and Hong Kong. Forty percent of its work was for foreign clients, or U.S. clients abroad. And it had a healthy turnover: gross revenue the year before the merger was $214 million with profits per partner at $760 000.

But Rogers & Wells was perceived to lack a unified firm culture. The managing partner of one New York firm described it in January 2003 as "more a collection of departments, some very good and some less so." At the time of the merger it could boast a top-of-the-line intellectual property practice representing DuPont, among others, and one of the finest antitrust practices, headed by the phenomenally successful Kevin Arquit. Rogers & Wells did not, however, have the resources or critical mass to compete head to head with firms like Clifford Chance on the global stage.

At the same time, Clifford Chance was starting to cash in on its earlier growth strategy. Gross revenue was up to $709 million. Profits per partner were $904 000. But while it had tried hard to build a successful securities practice in New York, it came up against resistance from the established New York players. When the head of that office, Stephen Hood, met Rogers & Wells' managing partner Laurence Cranch at a San Francisco conference, they jointly perceived a mutual interest. The two firms had complementary corporate finance practices; Rogers & Wells' exemplary antitrust practice would fit nicely with Clifford Chance's corporate capability, and other practice areas—regulatory, IP, litigation—could only be improved by expansions. And they already shared clients, including Chase Manhattan, Citigroup, Merrill Lynch, and Morgan Stanley. Stuart Popham, then head of global finance at Clifford Chance, enthused at the time of the merger: "In Rogers & Wells, we found the perfect fit. We were happy to make a commitment." He later said the marriage was "encouraged by our clients."[1]

Leaving aside the cultural challenges to be faced in the merger, a major sticking point remained—the issue of partner remuneration. Clifford Chance was wedded to a lockstep system—partner compensation was accorded by virtue of seniority and seniority alone. Rogers & Wells, by contrast, operated on an "eat-what-you-kill" basis, with partners rewarded according to the revenue they generated for the firm. The disparity between the firms' compensation spreads was also significant. The lowest-earning partners at Rogers & Wells were taking home only $290 000; high earners, $2.3 million—a compensation spread of 1:8. At Clifford Chance, the spread was no more than 1:2.5. Those at the bottom of the lockstep took home £430 000, but maximum compensation was £1.1 million. Once partners got to the top, their remuneration ceased increasing. In the eyes of high-earners at "eat-what-you-kill" firms, the lockstep system was a barrier to just reward. To its proponents, the lockstep system brought a firm and its partners closer together. The two systems represented two quite different paradigms of professional service firm management.

The merger went ahead as planned on January 1, 2000, without the lockstep issue having been resolved. For the first year and a half, partners at the legacy firms continued as they had before. The eventual solution to the remuneration dilemma involved moving Rogers & Wells' partners into the Clifford Chance lockstep system, using a number of criteria, including but not limited to seniority. For several Rogers & Wells partners, that meant a big reduction in take-home pay. But there were high-earning partners that neither firm wanted to lose. Kevin Arquit and Steve Newborn were seen not just as brilliant practitioners within their own sphere, but crucial to bringing work into the corporate department. To keep them in the fold, they would have to be compensated well above the top of the lockstep. And those partners that were taking home less than the lockstep minimum would continue to do so until they moved up.

The jury was still out on the success of the transatlantic merger. The firm was facing charges that it had "de-equitized" the partners of Rogers & Wells. In a memo reported on the front page of the *Financial Times* in October 2001, the firm's U.S. associates explained why Clifford Chance came last in a survey of U.S. law firms, and further charged that the survey "captured neither the breadth nor the depth of associate anger and frustration." And perhaps the most concrete sign that things had not gone according to plan came in December 2002, when Kevin Arquit announced that he would be leaving Clifford Chance for the New York firm Simpson Thacher & Bartlett, a highly-regarded practice, but without Clifford Chance's global reach. Arquit was on record as having said that one of the attractions of Simpson Thacher was its smaller size.

Elsewhere in the network, there had been challenges to the firm's global management. In early summer 2002, three partners and 26 associates left the firm's Italian offices in a dispute over the firm's attempts to bring Italian management practices in line with the rest of the firm. And in Bangkok, a former partner was suing the firm for $30 million, accusing Clifford Chance of "imperialism" in its approach to its Asian offices.

An article in the U.K. press entitled "Rule Britannia"[2] argued that the London firms that had globalized were failing to reflect this global footprint in their management structure. The table below shows the results of the 2002 management elections and the extent to which Clifford Chance's strategy continued to be run by London-based lawyers.

Clifford Chance had experienced phenomenal success over the previous ten years. But it was not yet clear that Geoffrey Howe's desire to make the firm truly international had yet been realized. Sixty-three percent of the firm's lawyers now worked outside of the U.K., the second-highest percentage of any of the world's 100 largest law firms. But the London office remained *primus inter pares*—with revenues of £412 million, and a 41 percent profit margin. (The firm's worldwide profit margin was 32 percent.)

In its marketing literature Clifford Chance repeatedly referred to itself as "a truly integrated global law firm." The reality was that while Clifford Chance had made extraordinary progress, the results were still mixed, and it had yet to shed its reputation as a London firm.

Callum Campbell (EMBA—Global 2003) prepared this update under the direction of Professor Maury Peiperl from public sources. It is designed as a supplement to the case "Clifford Chance: International Expansion" (© 1993, 1994 INSEAD) from *Managing Change: Cases and Concepts* by Maury Peiperl and Todd Jick (Irwin/McGraw-Hill, 2003). © 2003 by London Business School.

Clifford Chance (from January 1, 2003)

Senior Partner	Stuart Popham	London
Management Committee		
Managing Partner	Peter Cornell	London
London Managing Partner	Peter Charlton	London
Asia Managing Partner	Jim Baird	Hong Kong
U.S. Managing Partner	John Carroll	New York
Continental European Managing Partner	Hans-Josef Schneider	Frankfurt
Finance Director	Chris Merry	London
Executive Partner	Chris Perrin	London
Executive Partner	Phillip Palmer	London
Global Head of Corporate	David Childs	London
Global Head of Litigation	Jim Benedict	New York
Global Head of Finance	Mark Campbell	London
Global Head of Capital Markets	David Dunningham	London
Global Head of Real Estate	Cliff McAuley	London
Global Head of Tax	Douglas French	London

Exhibit 1 Rank of Law Firms by Number of Lawyers

Top law firms by number of lawyers	No. of lawyers	Countries in which firm has offices	Lawyers outside home country
Clifford Chance (U.K.)	**3322**	**19**	**63%**
Baker & McKenzie (U.S.)	3094	37	83%
Freshfields Bruckhaus Deringer (U.K.)	2430	18	61%
Allen & Overy (U.K.)	2197	20	48%
Linklaters (U.K.)	2000	22	52%
Eversheds (U.K.)	1776	6	4%
Skadden, Arps, Slate, Meagher & Flom (U.S.)	1653	12	10%
Jones, Day, Reavis & Pogue (U.S.)	1565	12	18%
Lovells (U.K.)	1432	15	55%
White & Case (U.S.)	1427	24	60%

Source: American Lawyer *Global 100*, November 2002.

Exhibit 2 Rank of Law Firms by Revenues

Rank by revenue	Firm	Gross revenue 2001–2003	Average revenue per lawyer
1	**Clifford Chance**	**$1 409 032 200**	**$424 152**
2	Skadden, Arps, Slate, Meagher & Flom	$1 225 000 000	$765 000
3	Freshfields Bruckhaus Deringer	$1 060 716 000	$436 509
4	Baker & McKenzie	$1 000 000 000	$330 000
5	Linklaters	$ 917 376 000	$458 688
6	Allen & Overy	$ 834 238 800	$379 717
7	Jones, Day, Reavis & Pogue	$ 790 000 000	$535 000
8	Latham & Watkins	$ 769 500 000	$660 000
9	Sidley Austin Brown & Wood	$ 715 000 000	$560 000
10	Shearman & Sterling	$ 619 500 000	$595 000

Source: American Lawyer *Global 100*, November 2002.

Exhibit 3 Clifford Chance Offices Worldwide

Location	Year of Opening	Partners	Other legal advisers	Trainees
Amsterdam	1973	23	117	3
Bangkok	1996	6	26	0
Barcelona	1993	3	18	14
Beijing	1985	1	10	0
Berlin	1990	11	27	0
Brussels	1968	8	48	1
Budapest	1993	4	18	16
Dubai	1976	3	26	3
Düsseldorf	1990	25	104	0
Frankfurt	1949	74	252	4
Hong Kong	1980	31	112	17
Los Angeles	2002	2	10	0
Luxembourg	1982	5	19	8
London	1987	233	880	208
Madrid	1980	19	52	35
Milan	1993	14	60	25
Moscow	1991	5	31	4
Munich	1996	10	34	0
New York	1871	98	380	3
Padua	1997	1	6	5
Palo Alto	2002	2	5	0
Paris	1962	29	172	23
Prague	1995	2	7	11
Rome	1993	6	21	9
San Diego	2002	2	6	0

Exhibit 3 Continued

San Francisco	2002	14	35	0
Shanghai	1993	2	15	1
Singapore	1981	6	15	4
São Paulo	1998	1	11	5
Tokyo	1987	11	38	3
Warsaw	1992	6	13	18
Washington, DC	1949	15	84	0

Personnel Worldwide:

Total number of staff 7500

Total number of legal advisers (of whom 665 were partners) and trainees 3700

(Approximate figures as at December 31, 2002)

Source: Adapted from www.CliffordChance.com.

Chapter 2
Assessing External Environments

LEARNING OBJECTIVES

After reading this chapter, you should be able to:

1 Articulate the role of the external environment in management decisions and effectiveness.

2 Explain the five major dimensions of an organization's general environment.

3 Describe the critical forces in the organization's task environment.

4 Describe the key elements of an organization's global environment.

5 Describe the key considerations in conducting effective environmental scanning.

Russia's Black Gold?

Finding oil and gas reserves hiding beneath thousands of metres of dirt and rock is challenge enough for managers in oil and gas companies. Add to that the challenge of managing operations in locations where political instability, economic turbulence, and social opposition exist—all of which can dramatically affect the organization's performance—and you have a real challenge on your hands. This is the case for oil and gas managers looking at opportunities in the former Soviet Union.

As strange as it might sound, many managers of foreign oil companies long for the old days when permission to explore, drill, extract, transport, or sell oil and gas was tightly controlled by the central oil ministry of the former Soviet Union. But after its fall, if managers wanted to drill in Kazakhstan, for example, and ship crude oil to Italy for refining, they had to negotiate separate agreements with Kazakhstan, Russia, or Georgia, depending on the chosen transportation route. There was no guarantee that the government that signed the agreement one particular day would be the one that was in power the next.

As a result, up until the turn of the century, thousands of wells in Russia lay untapped. The natural pressure pushing the oil to the surface was gone, and the Russians lacked the technology to force the remaining oil out of the ground. Neglect and financial troubles plagued Russia throughout the 1990s and reduced production to an all-time low of 6 million barrels per day in 1996.

But since 1999, a combination of rising world oil prices, the privatization of the market following the Soviet Union's collapse, and increased exports, mostly to Western Europe, have made it more worthwhile than ever to pursue oil and gas production in the former Soviet Union. In 2001, the Russian government proposed changes to the tax code that decreased some of the financing risks that had suppressed investment in oil and gas projects in the past.

Changing societal values about pollution and renewable energy sources have caused some consumers to rethink their SUV purchases and switch to hybrid vehicles or small cars, like the smart fortwo. SUVs remain enormously popular, however, leaving automakers to grapple with the dilemma about the extent to which they should pursue the hybrid market.

Things are so dramatically different, in fact, that today Russia is the world's largest oil and fuel exporter. It has more oil and gas reserves than any other country—nearly 350 billion barrels. That's almost 50 billion more than Saudi Arabia. Russian companies, which are now mostly privatized, have invested billions of dollars and raised production by 40 percent since 1998. They've also watched their stock prices soar as a result. Total revenue for the Russian oil and gas market in 2005 was US$123.5 billion, up 11.7 percent over the previous year. However, the Russian market did not experience the same dramatic growth as Western markets did. This is largely because the Russian market isn't dependent on external suppliers (that is, Russia produces enough oil to satisfy domestic fuel consumption), who have faced wild instability recently because of events like the Iraq war and the crippling effects of Hurricane Katrina in 2005.

In the later part of 2005, the Russian government introduced new restrictions on oil companies that were not majority-owned by Russians. Foreign-owned companies would be prevented from acquiring natural resource rights for Russian oil fields. The move by the Russian government was to ensure that revenues remain in Russia and to reduce the attractiveness of the market to foreign-held companies. As well, the Russian oil and fuel market is not known for ethical practices. Corruption and scandal are rampant, including allegations of bribery and tax evasion and even murder. The richest man in Russia, Mikhail Khodorkovsky, chairman and principal owner of the second-largest oil company, Yukos, was thrown in jail by Russian officials in 2003. The charge laid against Mikhail was tax evasion, and his assets (estimated to be US$15 billion and largely composed of shares in Yukos) were frozen. Many speculate that the Russian government was not pleased with his local influence and ties to the west, so the actions taken were an attempt to silence a potential political rival. Then in 2006, the Yukos Oil Company itself was charged with tax evasion and hit with a tax repayment burden so great (US$27 billion) that it forced the company into bankruptcy and its assets were liquidated.

While the picture in Russia is nonetheless looking brighter than it has in the past, clearly the country's political-legal scenario is still volatile, and other environmental forces continue to pose many risks that managers in the oil and gas industry must confront. Much of the "black gold" available in Russia lies beneath land that is subject to some of the longest and coldest winters in the world. Add to this free-flowing vodka, and workers' living conditions that consist of log cabins and huts without indoor plumbing, and you have an explosive combination. Travellers to the region describe it as similar to the Wild West in the United States back in the 1800s. In Tyumen, things were so wild that many of the elite Black Beret military units were pulled out of Latvia and Estonia and sent to Tyumen to try to keep order.

How does a manager successfully conduct business in such an environment? Most managers of western oil companies don't have much choice but to try. Their efforts to expand production in deep waters offshore have largely failed. Companies such as British Petroleum and ExxonMobil are partnering with Russian players to explore and develop Russian oil fields. Finding the remaining reserves in the rest of the world has become so difficult that many firms are willing to risk the environmental and political turmoil of the former Soviet Union to keep their firms awash in oil.

Sources: BBC News, "Yukos Investor Lawsuit Dismissed," October 26, 2006, news.bbc.co.uk (accessed January 11, 2007); "Oil & Gas in Russia: Industry Profile," *Datamonitor*, May 2006; J. Scott-Joynt, "Khodorkovsky: An Oligarch Undone," May 31, 2005, news.bbc.co.uk (accessed January 11, 2007); *Moscow Times*, "Yukos Told to Work Miracles," January 29, 2004; J. Guyon, "The Game Goes On," *Fortune* (Europe), November 24, 2003, pp. 70–71; B. Powell, "Russia Pumps It Up," *Fortune*, May 13, 2002, pp. 85–91; E. Kreil, "Oil and Gas Joint Ventures in the Former Soviet Union," U.S. Energy Information Agency, www.eia.doe.gov (accessed August 1996); S. Alison, "Russia Sees Second Devaluation as Oil Price Slumps," Reuters Limited, November 23, 1998; A. Konoplyanik, "Special Report—The Russian Oil & Gas Industry: Analysis Raises Questions about Russian Tax Proposal," *Oil & Gas Journal*, August 13, 2001, pp. 54–59; I. Woollen, "Special Report—The Russian Oil & Gas Industry: Central Asian Gas Crucial to Future Russian Gas Supply," *Oil & Gas Journal*, August 13, 2001, pp. 61–65; S. Alexandrovich and R. Morgan, "Special Report—The Russian Oil & Gas Industry: Russian Service Sector Lagging Behind Country's Emerging Oil Boom," *Oil & Gas Journal*, August 13, 2001, pp. 66–71; "Special Report—The Russian Oil & Gas Industry: Russian Oil Firms Mark Dramatic Turnaround in 1999–2000," *Oil & Gas Journal*, August 13, 2001, p. 67; "Special Report—The Russian Oil & Gas Industry: U.S.–Russian JV Entering Second Decade of Operations," *Oil & Gas Journal*, August 13, 2001, pp. 68–69.

strategic overview

Managers in the oil and gas industry who are thinking about doing business in Russia or other former Soviet Union states should carefully analyze the social, technological, economic, political, and global forces in the external environment. Such an analysis would be a critical first step in strategically deciding whether or not to make an investment in the region. Commonly, a firm that wants to enter high-risk foreign markets like Russia forms a strategic partnership with a local firm so that the partner can help guide them through the local political, business, cultural, and other environmental challenges.[1] As noted later in this chapter, however, the institutional and cultural environments often differ across country borders, affecting the strategic decisions made by firms. For example, the institutional environment in Russia has been chaotic as the country has tried to move central control of the economy to a more market-based system. Because local governments have been given the authority to make many of the policy decisions once made by the central government, the "rules of the game" change frequently. As a result, Russian managers tend to make short-term decisions. Alternatively, China (discussed later in this chapter) has been making a more evolutionary shift from central government control of the economy to a market-oriented system. With a more stable institutional environment, Chinese managers tend to focus more on making long-term strategic decisions than do Russian managers.[2] Managers desiring to do business in Russia or China would do well to understand each of their institutional environments and carefully select strategic partners, making sure the potential partners' short-term or long-term orientation is known since it could affect the amount of commitment they are likely to make. Thus, managers charged with the responsibility of entering these markets should thoroughly scan their environments to help them understand the opportunities and pitfalls.

An analysis of the organization's external environments is critical to developing an effective strategy. Analyzing the general and task environments will provide substantial information, enabling managers to identify the opportunities and threats that exist. Managers must develop strategies that take advantage of the opportunities and avoid or overcome the environmental threats.[3] Without a thorough analysis, they are likely to overlook excellent opportunities, leaving them open for competitors to exploit. Likewise, they may be unprepared to counter or deal with a major threat, and the organization's performance may suffer as a result. For example, senior executives at Polaroid did not perceive the major threat to their business from the development of digital technology. As a result, its senior executives were forced to declare bankruptcy.

external environment a set of forces and conditions outside the organization that can potentially influence its performance

task environment forces that have a high potential for affecting the organization on an immediate basis

general environment forces that typically influence the organization's external task environment and thus the organization itself

internal environment key factors and forces inside the organization that affect how it operates

What Does the Business Environment Consist Of?

The **external environment** is a set of forces and conditions outside the organization that can potentially influence its performance. We divide these forces into two related but distinct categories—the external task environment and the external general environment. The **task environment** consists of forces that have a high potential for affecting the organization on an immediate basis. The **general environment** consists of forces that typically influence the organization's external task environment, thus the organization itself. In addition to an external environment, organizations also have internal environments. The organization's **internal environment** consists of key factors and forces inside the organization that affect how the organization operates. Exhibit 2.1 provides a general illustration of these elements. However, for these concepts to be of much relevance to you as a manager, we need to delve into greater detail. To do this, we will start at the general external environment level and work our way in.

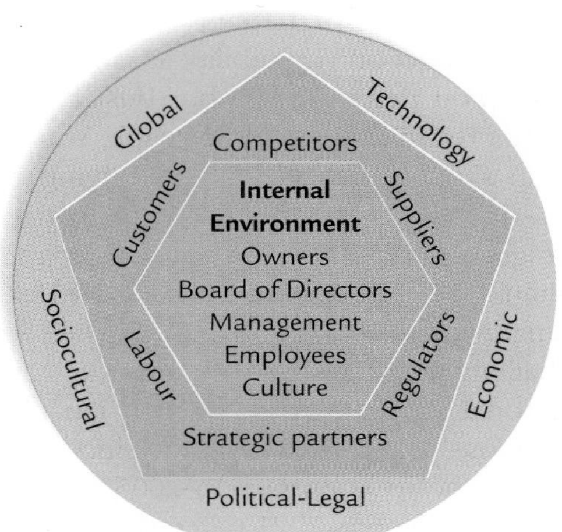

Exhibit 2.1

The Environment of Organizations

General External Environment

A variety of forces in the general environment can influence an organization's task environment and the organization itself. These forces are typically divided into five major categories: sociocultural, technological, economic, political-legal, and global. Clearly, the impact a given general external environment has varies from industry to industry and firm to firm. As a consequence, it is hard to argue for a particular sequence or order of importance for these general-environment forces. The "STEP Global" (i.e., ***S***ociocultural, ***T***echnological, ***E***conomic, ***P***olitical-Legal, and ***G***lobal) sequence we use simply makes remembering the categories much easier.

Sociocultural Forces

The sociocultural forces of the general external environment consist primarily of the demographics as well as the cultural characteristics of the societies in which an organization operates.

Demographics are essentially the descriptive elements of the people in a society, such as average age, birth rate, level of education, literacy rate, and so on. For example, in 1920 the average life expectancy in Canada was 59 years for men and 61 years for women, and in 2004 it was 77.8 years for men and 82.6 years for women.[4] As another example of changing demographics, you have no doubt heard about the baby-boom generation. The baby boom was a phenomenon experienced in four industrialized countries: Australia, Canada, New Zealand, and the United States. The term "baby boom" is appropriate given the explosive birth rate, which averaged as high as four babies per woman in Canada. The boom started around 1946–47 and ended in the mid-1960s, with its termination largely being attributed to oral contraception and the migration of women into the workplace. The 20 years or so of high birth rates led to the baby boomers comprising about one-third of the population of North America.

demographics the descriptive elements of the people in a society, such as average age, level of education, financial status, and so on

But why should you as a manager care about baby boomers or other demographics? It is because demographics can significantly affect both organizational inputs and outcomes. For example, the average level of education and the birth rate in Canada combined can have a significant impact on the supply of workers with a given level of education and training. Specifically, a low birth rate and a modestly increasing level of education could result in a slow-growing or even declining number of technical workers. Clearly, this could have a significant impact on your ability as a manager in a high-tech firm to find the technicians you need to run your business. This is exactly what happened in the 1990s. Technically knowledgeable workers, such as software programmers, were in short supply in Canada, driving up demand for these types of employees. Or consider that people are living longer and that the largest demographic group in Canadian history is fast approaching the age at which health problems begin to increase. This could create unprecedented demands on the Canadian health care system, creating significant opportunities for some and challenges for others.

As an international example, consider that Japan's population in 2005 declined from the previous year for the first time since World War II, with forecasts expecting the decline to continue. In 2005, the number of people in Japan over 65 years of age comprised 21 percent of the population, more than doubling in size in less than a generation. With one of the world's longest life expectancies (85.5 years for women and 78.5 years for men), fewer workers will be supporting Japan's retirees than at any time in the country's history, and many of Japan's retirees will live so long that they are likely to use up their retirement savings before they die if they retire at age 65.[5] This may present unprecedented opportunities for low-cost senior care centres and may mean that younger workers are faced with higher government taxes to support social security programs for seniors.

societal values commonly shared desired end states

Although demographics can give us important statistics about our population, societal values are important translators of those numbers into business implications.[6] **Societal values** are commonly shared desired end states. In practical terms for managers, societal values determine the extent to which an organization's products or services have a market. For example, a switch in values from status to functionality moved firms like Calvin Klein out of the spotlight and L.L.Bean onto centre stage of consumer demand in the early 1990s. This reversed itself in the mid- and late 1990s, as did the fortunes of these two companies. As another example, we can look at the controversy surrounding SUVs (sport utility vehicles) in North America. Throughout the 1990s, SUVs such as the Ford Explorer, Dodge Durango, and Chevy Suburban were the fastest-selling automobiles. However, as concerns about the impact of pollution on global warming increased and fuel prices spiked in 2005 because of the war in Iraq and the devastating hurricane season, people began to create negative sentiment toward SUVs and pressured car companies to make hybrid cars. These hybrids would be powered by both conventional combustion engines and electric motors—cars that, instead of 5 kilometres to the litre, would get 20 or 30 kilometres to the litre. These changing societal values forced managers at major car companies to weigh the demands for and against SUVs in deciding what vehicles to produce and in what volumes. In 2004, managers at Toyota decided to introduce the first hybrid SUV with other manufacturers following their lead. Time will tell if societal values are sufficiently strong for the decision of these manufacturers to be successful.

Astute managers need the ability to combine demographics and societal values to determine important implications for their organizations.[7] To illustrate this, let's take a look at one demographic fact and one shifting societal value. Demographically, the number of 35 to 45 year olds in North America peaked around 2000. Without significant changes in the number of immigrants, that group will decline in number by 15 percent through the year 2015. Demand for workers in this age group is estimated to grow by 30 percent during this same time period. This creates an anticipated labour shortage. Add to this demographic picture a new generation of 35 to 45 year olds who want a better balance between work and home life and you have an interesting situation.[8]

To help bring out the implications of this combination of demographic and societal value facts, imagine that you are a manager trying to recruit an experienced manager from outside into your firm. There is a labour shortage and the highly qualified person you are trying to recruit does not want to travel as much as the job demands. What do you do? Every day that the job goes unfilled costs you money because the results from that position are not being produced. The labour shortage means that every person you turn down because of their desire to not travel lengthens the time the job remains empty and increases the total cost of the vacancy. Failure to understand these external general-environment forces could lead to a poor recruiting plan costing the company money. In contrast, if you recognize and understand these demographic and sociocultural forces, you might anticipate the hiring challenge and create an appropriate plan. For example, you might borrow from what several consulting firms have done lately. Many consulting firms have instituted policies that require consultants to be at client locations on Tuesdays, Wednesdays, and Thursdays, but not Mondays and Fridays. This saves consultants from having to travel on Sundays to get to client locations on Mondays, or travelling on Saturdays to get home from working at client locations on Fridays. As this example illustrates, a full understanding of both demographics and values can help you as a manager make changes and decisions that can help you increase your effectiveness and your organization's performance.

Technology Forces

Technology is another external environment force that can have brilliant or devastating effects on organizations. A specific technological innovation can spell the birth and growth of one firm and the decline and death of another. For example, the invention of the transistor created firms like Texas Instruments and spelled the death of vacuum-tube manufacturers that did not adapt to this technological environment change. While the technological environment can be quite complicated, managers need to keep in touch with two basic aspects of the technology environment—product and process changes.

product technological changes changes that lead to new features and capabilities of existing products or to completely new products

Product Technological Changes **Product technological changes** are those that lead to new features and capabilities of existing products or to completely new products. As a manager, you need to know what product technology changes are occurring, especially in your industry. For example, managers at Xerox were caught flat-footed when new, small personal copiers from Canon were able to produce the volume and quality of copies at half the price of larger Xerox machines. Palm created a new product category with the invention and successful launch of the PalmPilot. This had a serious and negative impact on one of the largest makers of paper day planners at the time—FranklinCovey. Because firms increasingly win or lose as a function of their technological advantages and disadvantages, as a manager you need to have a broad view and keep in touch with technological advances at home and abroad. For example, in the multibillion-dollar global disposable diaper industry, absorbency technology shifted from "fluff pulp" (a paper-based product) to absorbent chemicals. This technological change was important because the absorbent chemicals could absorb more than fluff pulp and do so while making the diaper thinner. Procter & Gamble, maker of Pampers, almost lost its dominant position in the US marketplace because it didn't keep up with the new absorbency technology that emerged from Japan.[9]

process technological changes alterations in how products are made or how enterprises are managed

Process Technological Changes **Process technological changes** typically relate to alterations in how products are made or how enterprises are managed. For example, a new computer colouring technology brought back animated feature films from a steep decline in the late 1980s and early 1990s because it substantially lowered production costs compared with the old, individual frame-by-frame, hand-painted technology.[10] As another example, management information system technology (MIS) like that used by retail giant Wal-Mart allows managers to track merchandise on a daily or hourly basis and thereby know which products are selling and which ones are not. This allows them to effectively order merchandise so that they do not run out of hot-selling items (and miss out on the sales revenues) and can avoid overstocking poor-selling items (and tie up valuable cash in inventory). Interestingly, this process technology has helped Wal-Mart go from US$1 billion in annual sales in 1973 to US$1 billion in weekly sales by 1993 and nearly US$1 billion a day now.[11] Cisco is another firm where technological advances in telecommunications and data transmission have significantly affected the way it operates. For example, in 1995 virtually none of Cisco's revenue came from purchase orders over the internet. By 2000, over 70 percent of its nearly US$20 billion in revenue came from internet sales.

Many North American steel manufacturers were driven into bankruptcy because virtually all of the largest firms were slow to adopt an important new process technology—the electric arch furnace. Most large (or what are called integrated) steel companies made steel by starting with raw iron ore and melting and converting it to large steel slabs that were further rolled and refined. Electric arch furnaces allowed so-called "mini-mills" to start with scrap metal, melt it, and make it into steel products. Starting with scrap metal is significantly cheaper than starting with iron ore. While the metal made in mini-mills cannot be made into such things as beams for skyscrapers, it can be made into sheet metal for making car exteriors, washing machines, toasters, and so on. Dofasco, a steel company in Hamilton, Ontario, was the first, and at the time the only, integrated steel company to add this technology to its traditional steel-making processes. However, although the company now enjoys the benefits of the new electric arch furnace technology, it still took it nearly 10 years to adopt the technology after it was first introduced.[12]

A Manager's Challenge: "Undoing 230 Years of Success" is a great example of the potential impact of the technological environment and the consequences of failing to adequately recognize or respond to technological changes. It briefly documents the rise and fall of one of the oldest and most revered companies—Encyclopaedia Britannica. As you read this example, ask yourself why you think managers at Encyclopaedia Britannica were unable to anticipate the two major technological changes that nearly did the company in. Why did managers respond so slowly to the change? What do you think managers at Britannica should do going forward? Should they fight, ignore, or embrace the latest technology?

a manager's challenge technology

Undoing 230 Years of Success

In 1768, three Scottish printers invented the most famous reference work in the world—the *Encyclopaedia Britannica*. The first was a three-volume edition. It grew from that to a 32-volume edition that children everywhere depended on when it came time to write a report for school. *Encyclopaedia Britannica* became the most authoritative and comprehensive encyclopedia in the business.

In 1920, Sears, Roebuck and Company acquired Britannica. As a consequence, its headquarters moved from Edinburgh to Chicago. It grew under its new owner and became a household name. In 1941, Britannica was sold to William Benton, who continued to build it and then willed it to the Benton Foundation in the early 1970s. Sales continued to grow in the 1970s and 1980s primarily through a direct sales force that called on homes everywhere. The baby-boom generation bought these US$1500 to US$2200 sets for their children in record volume, and by 1990 sales reached a peak of US$650 million and the company had more than 2300 sales representatives.

What happened over the next 10 short years erased over 200 years of success. During this period, Britannica's sales declined by 80 percent. How did this happen? Managers at Britannica dismissed as irrelevant two technological inventions that proved the undoing of the firm's great history.

The first technology they dismissed was the CD-ROM. Managers at Britannica just didn't think that a CD was as attractive or useful as a set of bound (preferably in leather) books. However, their competitors had different ideas. Companies with inferior products such as Encarta, Grolier, and Compton put their encyclopedias on CDs and sold them not for US$1500, but for US$50. Whereas it cost Britannica approximately US$250 to produce an encyclopedia set, it cost only US$1.50 to manufacture a set on a CD. In many cases, however, customers did not even have to pay the US$50 price. Companies like Microsoft found that they could enhance the appeal of their software by bundling these lesser encyclopedias into their main programs free of charge. For a customer, even though the quality of these competitors was not nearly as good as Britannica, the value was better in the minds of many. Why? Customers received lots of information (even if it was less than they would get with Britannica) free. Something for nothing seemed like a better deal to many customers.

As the technological impact of CDs drove Britannica's revenues into a steep dive, executives who at first tried to deny the lasting impact of the technology finally changed their minds and gave in. However, in deciding to put *Encyclopaedia Britannica* on CD, managers encountered two significant problems.

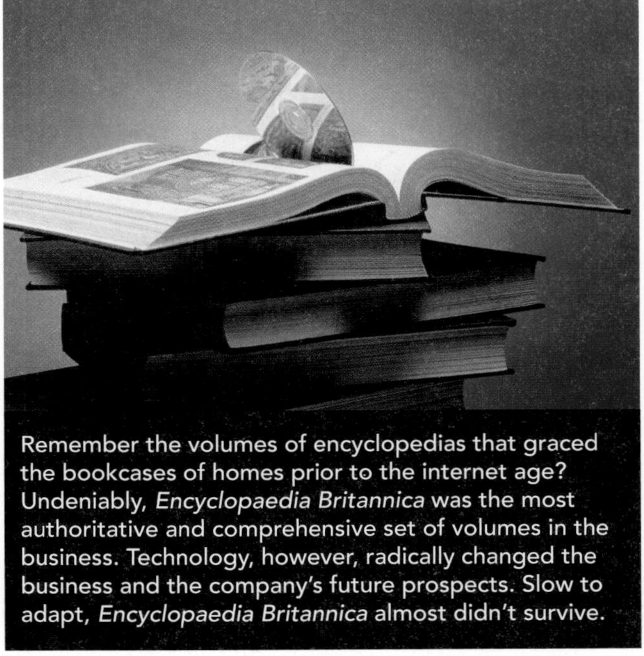

Remember the volumes of encyclopedias that graced the bookcases of homes prior to the internet age? Undeniably, *Encyclopaedia Britannica* was the most authoritative and comprehensive set of volumes in the business. Technology, however, radically changed the business and the company's future prospects. Slow to adapt, *Encyclopaedia Britannica* almost didn't survive.

First, they faced the problem of how to sell the product. Their direct-sales channel would not work for the CDs because there was no way to price the product high enough for salespeople to receive the US$500 commissions per sale that they were used to getting when they sold bound books. Without a substantial commission, salespeople had little incentive to push the new format. Unfortunately, Britannica did not have other distribution or sales channels for its encyclopedia on CD.

Second, and quite ironically, managers at Britannica discovered that the new technology rendered as a weakness what Britannica's executives had always seen as their greatest strength and differentiator—comprehensiveness. Despite the large storage capacity of CDs, the content of Britannica's encyclopedia could not fit on one CD. However, its "inferior" competitors' encyclopedias fit fine on one CD. Unfortunately for Britannica, customers did not want to hassle with three or four CDs, even if there was better content; they wanted to put one CD into their computer, search, and find the information they desired.

With sales declining and problems increasing, Jacob Safra, a nephew of the banking magnate Edmond Safra, bought Britannica in 1996. Although he put a new management team into place, the nature of competition had changed so dramatically that reviving the business was nearly an impossible task at that point. The company was dealt a near-fatal blow with the next technological change—the internet.

With the mass-market introduction of the internet, after 1997 it was increasingly easy to access a free encyclopedia or gain needed information from an ever-growing list of websites and information providers at no cost, as long as you were willing to look at the ads on their sites. Reluctantly, Britannica managers set up their own website for reference material and tried to sell their unrivalled volumes of information through a subscription fee of US$20. Unfortunately, this proved unattractive to customers when information from other sources was free.

Britannica spotted a glimmer of hope, though, when the internet ad market collapsed following the burst of the tech bubble in 2001. The company exploited the turmoil by changing its internet model. Not only must a good search engine find all of the relevant documents, it must put the best 20 or 30 at the top. Britannica does this on their website so internet users don't have to weed through a lot of material to find the "good stuff." It also gives anybody access to its entire site, including the beginnings of all articles, the *Merriam-Webster Collegiate Dictionary*, and articles from many popular and professional magazines. However, it charges a membership fee to read full articles.

To solve its sales commission problem, Britannica set up its first direct-marketing team in 2003. The company's sales are now in the US$200 million range—a fraction of what they once were, but the company is surviving. Moreover, all of its products are available on the internet, CD, and DVD. Britannica is also pursuing joint projects with educational product providers, such as the 2006 deals with ToyQuest and The American Education Corporation to provide products with content. Britannica has also pursued deals to supply mobile platforms such as iPods, PDAs, and smart phones with access to content.

While Britannica struggles to find its place in the digital economy, pressure continues to increase from new players. For example, Britannica has hit yet another major wall in regaining market share from the new and powerful Wikipedia, a free internet encyclopedia. Wikipedia is the brainchild of Jimmy Wales and was launched in 2001 as an open-source compendium of world knowledge where content is entered and edited by anyone. Though Wikipedia is deemed less accurate in its entries (but not by much, as *Nature* magazine discovered in random testing of entries), it is 12 times the size of Britannica, easy to use . . . and it's free.

Sources: Book Publishing Report, "Britannica Takes Content to Ever-Growing Mobile Platforms," May 29, 2006, p. 5; M. Naim, "Megaplayers vs. Megapowers," *Foreign Policy*, Jul/Aug 2006, pp. 6–95; P. Gillin, "Why You Should Care about Wikis," *B to B*, January 16, 2006, p. 13; S. Balmond, "Encyclopaedia Britannica Sets Up Direct Team," *Precision Marketing*, May 23, 2003, p. 1; S. Ellerin, "Three Publishers' Site Search Solutions," *EContent*, February 2003, pp. 44–48; P. Evans and T. Wurster, *Blown to Bits* (Cambridge, MA: Harvard Business School Press, 2000).

Economic Forces

A wide variety of economic forces in the external environment can also significantly influence organizations. Not all economic forces affect all organizations equally, however. The exact nature of the business and industry determines the specific factors that have the strongest influence on an organization. To better understand these economic forces, we group them into three main categories: current conditions, economic cycles, and structural changes.

Current Economic Conditions Current economic conditions are those that exist in the short term within a country. It is relatively easy for most students to imagine how current economic conditions can have important effects on an organization. For example, the current level of inflation can directly affect how quickly costs rise, which in turn might squeeze profits. The current level of unemployment can directly influence how easy or difficult it is to find the type of labour an organization needs. Current interest rates can determine how expensive it is to borrow money or even how much money a firm can borrow to finance activities and expansions. For example, Canadian mortgage rates reached a 40-year low in early 2004. Because the cost of borrowing was so low, many people decided that it was time to either buy a house or refinance their existing home loan with a lower rate and lower their mortgage payment. As a result, home builders and mortgage providers have seen a significant increase in business. With the increased demand for housing, the price of existing homes has also increased throughout much of Canada, with the average price of a home surpassing the $200 000 mark in March 2006 for the first time.

Economic Cycles But economic activity is not static, and current conditions do not necessarily predict future economic conditions. For example, when the Canadian dollar hit a record low of 61.79 cents US on January 21, 2002, few saw this as the onset of a steady increase that would lead to the Canadian dollar reaching parity with the US dollar only 68 months later; a value that had not been seen in over thirty years. Economic activity tends to move in cycles. Although it is difficult to predict exactly when an upturn or downturn in economic conditions will occur, understanding that cycles exist and the key factors that move them is critical for managerial activities like planning. It is also important to understand that specific industry cycles can be more or less pronounced than the general economic cycle of the country. For example, the construction industry tends to have higher peaks and lower valleys than the overall national economy, and the funeral-home business tends to have lower peaks and higher valleys than the overall economy (see Exhibit 2.2). If you were not aware of the impact of economic cycles on your particular industry, you might make poor management decisions. For example, if you were unaware of the exaggerated cycles of the construction industry relative to the peaks and valleys of the general economy, you might not plan for enough labour or materials for the upturn in the cycle and might order more materials than necessary or hire too many people during downturns in the cycle.

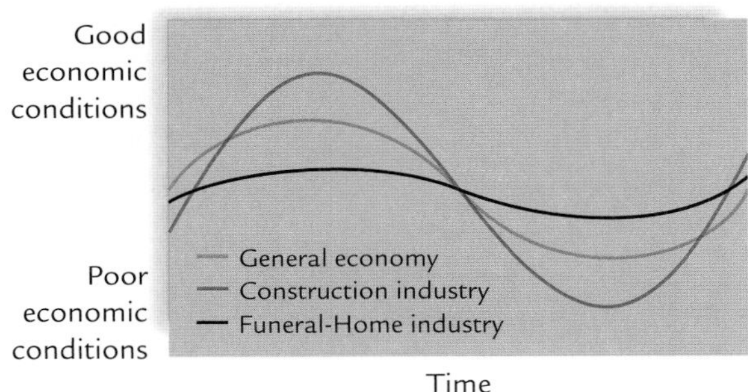

Exhibit 2.2

Overall Economic Cycles and Industry Cycles

Structural Changes Perhaps the hardest yet most critical thing to understand about economic conditions is knowing whether changes in the economy are temporary or whether they represent longer-term structural changes. **Structural changes** are changes that significantly affect the dynamics of economic activity now and into the future. For example, the shift from an agrarian (agricultural) to an industrial economy, and then from an industrial to a service economy, were all structural changes that took place in North America. They affected where people worked, what work they did, the education level they needed to do the work, and so on. If structural changes are taking place and you are unaware of them, you can easily make poor managerial decisions. For example, the structural shift to a more knowledge-based work environment will likely change not only the nature of workers but also what motivates them. In many service companies, such as engineering firms, consulting firms, and law firms, the company's primary assets (its people) walk out the door every day. This is in contrast to industrial companies like car manufacturers, which have millions of dollars in plant and equipment that stay put even when the workers go home. As a consequence, while a car manufacturer may be able to replace a worker

structural changes
changes that significantly affect the dynamics of economic activity

who leaves the assembly line with relative ease and feel only small effects of employee turnover, the same is not true for service companies and for Canada in general, as the structural economic shift from an industrial to an information economy continues.

For example, when a star consultant leaves her firm, she takes with her most of her value to the company—her understanding of client problems and solutions leaves with her. The phone or fax or other hard assets that stay with the company provide comparatively little value. In fact, in some cases the value is so closely tied to the individual that customers leave the company with an individual's departure and redirect their business to wherever the star consultant has gone. Without understanding this structural economic change, you may miss the importance of employee retention and underestimate the role of praising and recognizing the contributions of your star performers so that they stay with your firm. Or you may not see that allowing your employees to travel to client locations on Mondays (instead of Sundays) in the end saves you money because the change in policy helps you retain rather than lose key performers.

Political and Legal Forces

Political and legal forces can also have dramatic impacts on organizations. Laws frame what organizations can and cannot do. As a consequence, they can create both challenges and opportunities. For example, new pollution laws significantly increased the operating costs of coal-burning power plants. At the same time, these laws created new business opportunities for firms like Corning, which developed and sold new filter systems to coal-burning power plants.[13]

Tax laws can also have a profound effect on businesses. In 2005 and 2006, Canadians were exposed to the volatile influence that tax law can have on income trusts. Income trusts allow companies to avoid paying corporate taxes because all income flows directly to the investors, who ultimately pay the income taxes based upon their personal income. Companies were starting to look at becoming income trust organizations rather than corporations to avoid taxes. In November 2005, Minister of Finance Ralph Goodale announced that income trust laws would remain unchanged by the federal government. With the announcement, organizations that had already stated their intent to shift to an income trust organization experienced an increase in value of their shares, and the value of income trust funds that were already in existence also rose. In fall 2006, however, the finance minister of the new government, Jim Flaherty, changed the tax rules governing income trusts to stave off corporations avoiding tax by converting to income trusts: Income trusts will now pay a tax on distributions to shareholders. The results of this new law had an impact on the Toronto Stock Exchange (TSX), where the value of income trust funds dropped by percentages in the double-digits. The value of the Canadian dollar also slipped because of the change in the TSX.[14]

Perhaps one of the most important political aspects of the external general environment is federal government spending. On the one hand, increases or decreases in government spending can have a significant impact on the overall economy. Total government spending at the local, provincial, and federal levels in 2005 and 2006 accounted for between 24.6 percent and 28.6 percent of **gross domestic product**, or GDP (the total dollar value of final goods and services produced by businesses within a nation's borders). The federal government contributed 7.8 percent, the provincial governments 16.8 percent, and the local

gross domestic product the total dollar value of final goods and services produced within a nation's borders

governments between 6 and 10 percent.[15] It's a significant amount, but it should be noted that for more than 10 years the amount that government contributes in spending has been steadily declining. Regardless, increases or decreases in total government spending can have a significant impact on overall business activity. However, even if total spending remains unchanged, if spending moves from one area to another, such as from education to health care, then government spending can still dramatically affect businesses.

More complicated, but perhaps even more important, is whether government spending pushes the deficit up or down. For example, generally, when federal spending pushes the federal deficit up, interest rates also go up. As interest rates go up, money becomes more expensive for firms to borrow, and as a consequence they typically borrow less. As firms borrow less, they expand their business activities at a slower rate or even contract their overall activity. This can push unemployment up, which in turn pushes consumer spending down. In combination this can create a full-fledged economic downturn. So while the political process governing federal spending and the deficit can be quite complicated, managers cannot afford to ignore the effects.

Global Forces

Although all managers should pay attention to the global environment, its importance depends on the organization's size and scope of business. For small organizations, the other general-environment forces may be more important and have a much stronger impact. However, for medium-sized and large firms, the global environment can be as important as or even more important than any of the other general-environment forces we have discussed. This is especially true as the percentage of international sales increases as part of total sales. For example, 70 percent of Coca-Cola's income comes from international sales in over 200 countries; consequently, the global environment is critical to the company's performance. For global firms that operate in multiple countries and try to integrate those operations into an almost borderless enterprise, the line between the other environmental forces and global environments can blur. As an example, for managers at Nokia, a Finnish company that has only 3 percent of sales from inside Finland, the global economic environment *is* the economic environment. In addition, in order to succeed, managers at Nokia must focus on sociocultural changes around the world. They must also take into consideration technological changes in wireless communication in Europe, North America, Latin America, the Middle East, Africa, and Asia Pacific. As a consequence, while we separate global as a distinct general-environment force, the reality for many companies and managers is that the global environment is intimately intertwined with the other environmental forces.

A Manager's Challenge: "Business in China" helps illustrate the challenge of assessing the global environment and then acting on that assessment. While it may seem thousands of kilometres away, China has the world's largest population—1.3 billion people—with the equivalent of Canada's entire population entering the middle class annually. Consequently, Canadian managers envision great trade opportunities with this growing market, but they must also maintain a high respect for human rights. While reading this managerial challenge box, you might ask yourself what industries may be most sensitive to human rights issues. As a manager in Canada, can you afford to ignore this issue?

a manager's challenge *globalization*

Business in China

"How to deal with China as a big economic power—that is the largest issue . . . in the first half of the 21st century," according to Japan's former foreign minister, Yukihiko Ikeda. Many managers would agree—not just in Japan but also in Taiwan, most of Europe, Canada, Australia, and the United States.

The coming expansion of Chinese industry accompanies monumental changes in its economy and its business infrastructure brought about by its entry into the World Trade Organization in November 2001. The combination of expansion and admission to the world's formal trading system creates an unprecedented opening of what may prove to be the world's largest marketplace for nearly every kind of good and service—from cell phones and tractors to DVDs and blue jeans—and the world's largest source of low-cost manufactured goods. For China, "it is a no-going-back, transforming moment," according to Goldman Sachs's CEO, Henry Paulson. Ironically, that economic opportunity also strikes fear into the hearts of many managers.

It is not just fear of investing billions of dollars into China-based enterprises and failing, though that is a very real concern. Many managers, whether bankers, auto manufacturers, or consumer-goods marketers, already know full well the difficulties of finding and choosing the right Chinese business partners, of coping with a protectionist government bureaucracy, of negotiating myriad cultural differences, and of overcoming China's restrictions on building distribution chains and dealer networks. (These rules often leave foreign managers relying on the same distributors their competitors are using inside China.) Add to these risks those that underlie all international trade—language barriers, currency exchange rate fluctuations, changing consumer preferences—and the picture is already daunting.

Many foreign managers, however, also fear that China's own firms, some of which are still state supported, may reap the largest benefits from its steadily growing consumer demand. Despite a rising standard of living, China is still the world's largest low-wage economy, and it may quickly figure out how to produce many goods more cheaply at home rather than import them from abroad. For example, Taiwan-based computer maker Acer held the number-one position in China for years. However, over the last few years, Legend Holdings, domestic maker of Legend PCs, has substantially increased quality while beating Acer on price. The result is that Legend has replaced Acer in the number-one spot within China. As Legend continued to improve quality, it took its cost advantage and expanded internationally to compete with Acer and other computer manufacturers around the world. In 2004, Legend acquired IBM's PC Division and became the third-largest manufacturer in the world. In 2006, Lenovo Group (Legend's parent company) remained number one in China, with its 2005 revenue in excess of US$13 billion.

Boasting more than 1.3 billion people, China presents a huge potential market, both in terms of the low-cost labour opportunities it affords and the amount of goods and services that can be sold there. For example, China's construction output in 2006 was valued at US$151 billion and is expected to grow to become the world's largest with an output of US$700 billion by 2015—a boom spawned by the liberalization of free trade, market reforms, and the country's admission into the World Trade Organization in 2001.

Chinese managers in firms less successful than Legend recognize that if inefficient domestic firms are forced to reform, thousands of Chinese workers will lose their jobs over the next several years. In the agricultural industry, where small farms are still the norm, employment losses may be particularly severe. Offsetting these losses, however, has been the injection of foreign investment to the tune of over US$16 billion for the 2008 Olympic Games. An estimated 434 000 new jobs are expected to be created to develop the Olympic sites. However, there is concern for the quick reduction of jobs immediately following the games. Thus, despite the fact that tariffs and distribution barriers are set to drop, Chinese managers may pressure government officials to resist full-scale foreign competition. The rapid changes in China are taking place within a single generation, and adjustments will be very difficult.

Still, the market remains very attractive. China's technology imports alone were well in excess of US$18 billion in 2006, with an annual growth of 57.5 percent. By October 2006, China's trade surplus had already exceeded the 2005 record-setting surplus of US$102 billion, hitting US$133.6 billion. Its economy grew by 11.3 percent in 2005, and a further 10.5 percent in 2006, with the expectation for future growth to be around 10 percent per year. In all of this explosive activity, Canada's participation remains meagre, with exports to China comprising less than 1 percent of all that China imports annually.

For some, like Zhang Xin, who recently earned a computer science degree from one of the country's most prestigious universities and who will go to work for a cellular-phone-network firm in Beijing, it is a land where life is about to change dramatically. The shift in the social structure of China is creating new issues for the country. Canada has been outspoken in promoting human rights in China as the country emerges into an economic powerhouse. For Canadian managers, figuring out how to do business in China by pursuing business opportunities while maintaining Canadian social values has become a delicate balancing act.

Sources: Canada China Business Forum, "Canada Must Balance Values with Interests in China: CCBC President," December 2006, www.ccbc.com (accessed December 23, 2006); *China Daily*, "China's Economy to Grow 10.5 Percent in 2006," October 16, 2006, www.chinadaily.com (accessed December 23, 2006); *China Daily*, "Monthly Trade Surplus Hits New High," November 8, 2006 (accessed December 23, 2006); J. Lee, "A Look Inside both China and North America's Construction Industries," HomebuilderStocks.com, February 2006 (accessed December 23, 2006); B. Powell, "China's Great Step Forward," *Fortune*, September 17, 2001, pp. 128–142; L. P. Norton, "WTO Blows Tradewinds Between Taiwan and China," *Barron's Online*, interactive.wsj.com/pages/barrons.htm (accessed November 19, 2001); J. Brooke, "Tokyo Fears China May Put an End to 'Made in Japan,'" *New York Times*, November 20, 2001, p. A3; Legend Holdings, www.legendholdings.com (accessed December 23, 2006).

The Special Nature of the Global Environment

As we already mentioned, for many companies the global environment is not separate from the other general-environment forces. As we noted, when managers at Nokia think about the sociocultural external environment or the technological external environment, they generally have to think about it in a global context. So while for the sake of simplicity we have separated the sociocultural, technological, economic, and political-legal general-environment forces from global forces, the reality for many managers is that they are not all that separate. The other reality is that while it is possible and even necessary for many managers to analyze the global environment, as a practical matter they often have to break that analysis down into small pieces. Imagine if you were a manager at Nokia trying to do a global economic analysis across the 100-plus countries in which Nokia operates. As a practical matter this is just too unwieldy, which is why many managers focus their more detailed "global environmental analysis" on one country at a time. This is often called country analysis.[16]

As a manager, how do you assess a country and determine which countries are "good" to do business in and which ones are not? Let's take China, for example. Is it a good country in which to do business? During the early 1980s, China looked like a great place for foreign firms to do business. It had announced an economic liberalization plan and was borrowing billions of dollars to build up its economy and infrastructure. It was a nation rich in natural and human resources. However, China had many millions of people employed in state-owned and inefficient enterprises. These firms were naturally reluctant to see efficient, foreign firms come into the country, fearing that they would produce higher-quality goods at lower prices. Government officials were torn because they saw the need to modernize and yet recognized that they could not have thousands of state-owned firms fail and millions upon millions of workers unemployed. As China's government officials alternately tightened and loosened regulations, many managers saw the country as an economic and political yo-yo.

As the situation in China helps illustrate, most countries have both positive and negative aspects in terms of their eligibility for doing business. In the abstract, this means very little. The key to an effective analysis of the country is relating it to a specific industry or organization and its circumstances. Because industries and businesses operate differently and have different needs, specific policies or government actions pose unequal threats. For example, because KFC can source nearly all of its necessary raw materials within China, changes in import duties do not matter. However, Volkswagen must import many components for the cars it builds in China and therefore cares very much about changes in tariffs.

While managers would certainly examine the sociocultural, technological, economic, political, and legal environmental forces when analyzing a foreign country, there are two additional aspects of the external environment that are typically examined in the context of a foreign country, which are not usually part of a "domestic" general external environment analysis. These are the institutional and physical environmental forces. They are often included in analyses of foreign countries primarily because of the vast differences among countries in terms of institutions and physical characteristics.[17]

Institutional Forces The institutional context involves the key organizations in the country. Although the strength and power of institutions can vary from one country to another, they constitute an important consideration in any environmental analysis.[18] Institutions to assess include the government, labour unions, religious institutions, and business institutions. These organizations are important to analyze in a foreign context because they can be (and often are) dramatically different from those "at home."

Physical Forces Physical features such as infrastructure (e.g., roads, telecommunications, air links, etc.), arable land, deepwater harbours, mineral resources, forests, and climate can have a dramatic impact on existing and potential operations in a country and can be substantially different from those at home. For example, China has vast coal resources deep in its interior, but they are not an attractive business opportunity because of the poor rail and road infrastructure in those regions.

Pulling Together an Analysis of the General Environment

Even though we have tried to provide a number of examples as we moved through the various elements in the external general environment, it can seem a bit overwhelming. While an analysis of the external general environment is not simple, an integrated example may help to pull all of these concepts together. Let's take Coca-Cola as an example. Exhibit 2.3 provides a brief description of key aspects of the general environment, while Exhibit 2.4 pulls that description into a short summary.

While Exhibits 2.3 and 2.4 are by necessity brief and do not paint a full picture of Coca-Cola's external general environment, you can begin to see how a careful analysis of the general environment can provide useful information to managers in such activities as planning and decision making. For example, the sociocultural information may suggest that managers at

Exhibit 2.3 Description of the General Environment of Coca-Cola

Sociocultural

- Demographics
  Baby boomers drinking less soft drinks as they age.
  North American population growth is slowing.
- Values
  Society is increasingly concerned about pollution and recycling.
  Increasing focus on health and the negative aspects of caffeine, carbonation, and sugar.

Technological

- New "canning" technology makes using recycled aluminum easier and cheaper.
- Internet opens up a new means of running promotion contests and activities.

Economic

- Slow economy reduces per-person consumption primarily due to fewer social occasions (parties) at which soft drinks might be served.
- Nearing end of economic downturn and prospects of economic recovery.
- Stricter liability for illness caused by beverage contamination.

Global

- Gradual increase in acceptance of carbonated soft drinks in other countries.
- Widely available electricity and increased ability to afford refrigerators in emerging countries and economies.

Coca-Cola will need to increase their marketing efforts if they are to reach out to ethnic groups who come from countries and cultures in which drinking soft drinks, especially with carbonation, is not common. The information captured in the global dimension of the general external environment may suggest that managers at Coca-Cola should increase their efforts in emerging foreign markets with large populations, like China.

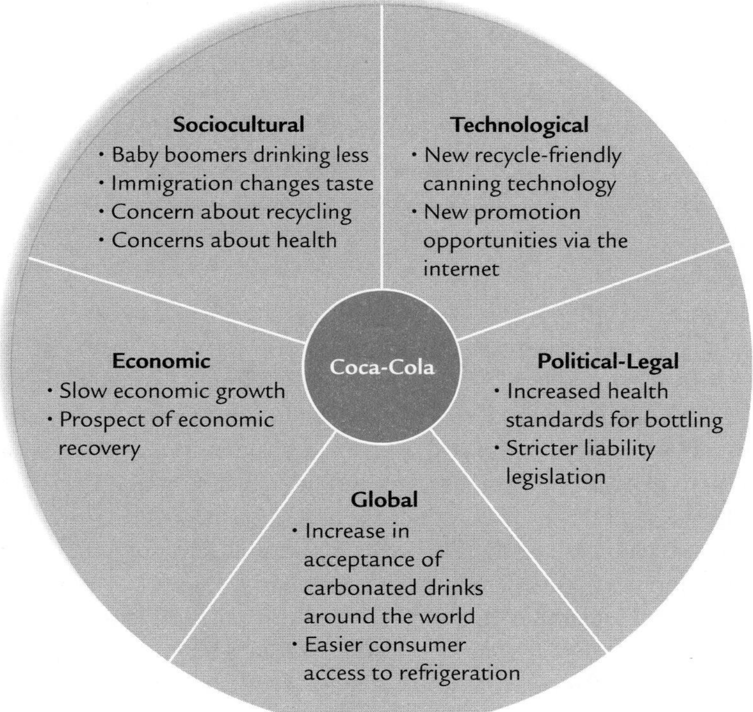

Exhibit 2.4

The General Environment of Coca-Cola

Task Environment

The task environment is the most immediate external environment within which an organization survives and flourishes. It consists of competitors, customers, suppliers, strategic partners, labour, and regulators. Consequently, it typically has the largest influence on the organization, and the fit between the organization and its environment is critical for a manager to understand. Forces in the task environment exert a significant influence on the organization. Because the task environment plays a significant role in the competitive and strategic position of an organization, we will examine certain aspects of these forces in more detail in Chapter 7, when we explore the topic of strategic management.

Porter's Five Forces by Michael Hitt

mymanagementlab

Perhaps the most well-known model of analyzing a firm's task environment was developed by Michael Porter, a professor at the Harvard Business School.[19] This framework conceived of the task environment primarily in terms of five environment forces (Porter's Five Forces) that can significantly influence the performance of organizations in the same industry (see Exhibit 2.5). These forces are examined to analyze the industry. The original research was designed to explain why some industries were more profitable as a whole than others and why some companies within industries were more profitable than other firms in the same industry. In general, research has supported the validity of this model.[20] Three of the five forces (nature of rivalry, new entrants, and substitutes) primarily have to do with the "competitor" category of the task environment. While these three aspects of Porter's framework are related to this one category, we examine each of them separately to provide you with a reasonable presentation of the five forces framework. The other two forces in the framework—customers and suppliers—relate directly to the second and third aspects of the task environment that we listed at the beginning of this section. To these five forces of Porter's framework, we add and will discuss the dimensions of strategic partners, labour, and regulators.

Exhibit 2.5

Profits and Industry Forces

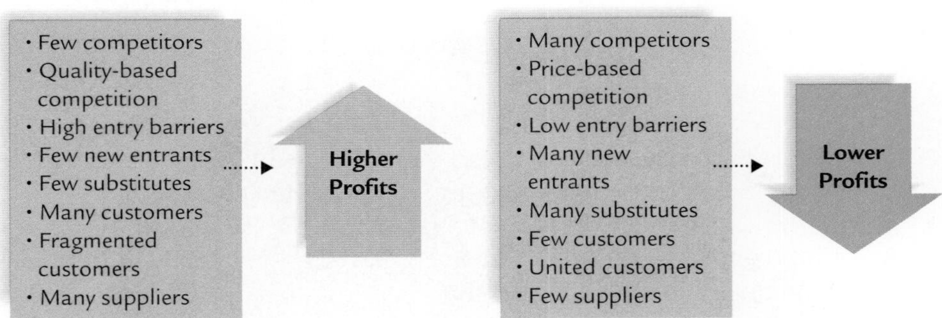

The first aspect of the task environment, according to Porter, is competitors and the nature of competition among them. For example, in analyzing this aspect of the task environment you need to know how big and strong your competitors are relative to you. If you are small and weak relative to your competition, you may choose to stay out of their way and go after business that is less interesting to them. In your analysis of competitors, you also need to know their weaknesses. Those weaknesses may represent opportunities that you can exploit.

Apple Inc. took this view; while Apple had been in computers for nearly 30 years, it was a latecomer to the smart phone industry. Competing products such as Palm's Treo and Research In Motion's BlackBerry were dominating the market when Apple stepped in. But despite the convenience of sending and receiving email as well as phone use, Steve Jobs at Apple found the built-in keyboards and command buttons of the Treo and BlackBerry to be cumbersome. To Jobs, this represented a significant weakness in the smart phone industry and a great opportunity for Apple. So Apple developed a smart phone, called the iPhone, that would not have a built-in keyboard. Instead, the iPhone would have a full-body touch screen that would allow for limitless possibilities in arranging touch-sensitive buttons to suit the needs of the user as mobile applications evolve. On the day that Jobs unveiled the iPhone to the public the value of shares in Palm dropped nearly 6 percent, while Research In Motion fell by nearly 8 percent. In contrast, Apple's shares rose by more than 8 percent, buoyed by the optimism that the iPhone would further increase Apple's sales by US$1 billion.

In addition to understanding your competitors, you also need to consider the nature of competition, or rivalry, in your industry. In general, competition can be based on price or on features of your products or services. Simplified, competitors can try to outdo each other by offering the lowest price to customers or by offering the best product or service. The more competition is based on price, generally the lower the profits. This is primarily because it is easier to lower prices than costs. As prices decline faster than costs, profit margins shrink.

The key for you as a manager is to clearly understand the nature of rivalry in your industry. It is worth noting that in very large industries, like automobile manufacturing, there are quite often different segments. This is important because the nature of rivalry can differ by segment. For example, in the subcompact segment of the auto industry, competition is largely based on price. However, in the luxury automobile segment, competition is primarily based on quality. Issues of safety, engineering, and handling—not price—dominate the ads for Mercedes, Lexus, BMW, and Infiniti. It is only when you have a thorough understanding of this competitive aspect of your industry that you are in a position to combine this information with other data and decide exactly how your company should compete.

New Entrants—Potential New Competitors

The second element of Porter's Five Forces is the extent to which it is easy or difficult for firms to enter the industry. All other elements being equal, new entrants will increase competition. Unless the size of the entire industry pie is expanding, the greater the number of new entrants, the thinner the slice of pie is for each participant. Increased competition (i.e., more entrants) usually leads to lower profit margins because customers have more choices. Unless it is difficult and expensive for customers to switch from one company to another (typically called **switching costs**), companies are forced to pass on greater perceived value to customers when there are more choices. This greater value often presents itself as a reduced price on products to the consumer. For example, if there are five grocery stores within a block of your house, and it costs you very little to go to one store over another, you are likely to go to the store that offers the best deal. As the stores compete for your business, they typically have to lower their profits to offer you a better deal. One grocer may offer shoppers discounts through the use of a loyalty card (the more you purchase at the grocer, the more points you collect, the greater the discount or rewards). This approach attempts to lock in customers by giving them an incentive to shop at one store instead of the others. At the same time, the other grocers may counter this strategy by using their own loyalty cards, or honouring the competitor's loyalty card. One example of this involves gas stations in

switching costs the amount of difficulty and expense involved when customers switch from one company to another

Fredericton, where select Esso stations will accept Canadian Tire 'Money' at face value for the purchase of gasoline.

entry barriers obstacles that make it difficult for firms to get into a business

The factors that keep new entrants out are termed barriers. **Entry barriers** are the obstacles that make it difficult for firms to get into a business. The bigger the barriers, the harder it is to get into the business; the harder it is to get in, the fewer new entrants. For example, the entry barriers in the restaurant business are quite low. Even in major cities, you can be in business for less than $100 000. However, if you wanted to break into the semiconductor business, it would cost you $4 to $6 billion just to build a fabrication plant. This doesn't even take into account the cost of designing or marketing your new chip. Generally, the fewer the new entrants, the fewer the total number of players in the industry. This typically means that each player gets a larger slice of the industry pie. It also means that customers likely have fewer choices, which usually translates into higher profits for the firms already in the industry.

Substitutes

substitutes alternative products or services that can substitute for existing products or services

As a task environmental force, **substitutes** focus on the extent to which alternative products or services can substitute for the existing products or services. Substitution is different from competition. Substitution does not involve a choice of one grocery store over another. Rather, it involves opting for another alternative means of satisfying a customer's need; going to a restaurant instead of the grocery store when you are hungry is an example of a substitute. An example of competition is between local movie theatres; one local movie theatre will obviously consider other local movie theatres as competition. What may not be as obvious, however, is that the nearby bowling alley is a substitute in satisfying the consumer's need. In this case, the bowling alley is competing for the entertainment dollar that could be used to watch a movie on a Friday night. Generally, the fewer the available substitutes, the greater the profits are. For example, if you have no choice in satisfying your hunger except to go to the grocery store for food (i.e., restaurants cannot substitute), grocery stores will make more money. As a manager, this is critical to understand because while competing products are one of the most important defining elements of an industry, you can make poor decisions about strategy, marketing, manufacturing, and so on if you fail to see potential substitutes. For example, as a manager at the movie theatre, you can have more comfortable seating and better sound quality than any other theatre in your neighbourhood, but if bowling becomes a more popular entertainment choice your theatre may still be in a difficult situation.

Customers

All managers in organizations have customers to serve. To the extent that there are relatively few customers and these customers are united, they have more power to demand lower prices, customized products or services, attractive financing terms from producers, and so on. The greater the power of customers, the more value they can extract. Unless you can quickly and significantly lower your costs, the more value customers extract, the lower your profits will be. For example, suppose you work for a diamond mine. To make money, you need to sell the diamonds you extract. For over a century one company, De Beers, has purchased an estimated 80 to 90 percent of the world's diamonds, in part because it owned many of the largest and richest diamond mines in the world.[21] As a diamond mining company, you are *un*likely to make big profits because De Beers basically determines the price it will pay for the diamonds it buys from you. Because there are few if any other buyers for your diamonds, you have little choice but to sell your diamonds to De Beers, and because the company has significant power as a customer, it will pay you a low price. Interestingly, the larger a diamond mine you are, the more this is true. The more diamonds you mine, the less (in relative terms) customers other than De Beers can take, and as a consequence, the more power De Beers will have over you. But things are changing. Both governmental pressure to reduce De Beers's power and several new large diamond discoveries by mining companies not owned by De Beers have made it much more difficult for De Beers to buy up such a large share of the raw diamond market. As its share of annual raw diamond purchases has declined from 80 percent to 65 percent, so has its power over the market.

Strategic Partners

Strategic partners consist of other organizations that work closely with a firm in the pursuit of mutually beneficial goals.[22] The degree of involvement between or among partners can vary from limited engagement to joint ventures in which participating parties hold equity stakes in the partnership. An example of strategic partnering at the low-involvement end of the spectrum is the Star Alliance among many international airlines, including Air Canada, United Airlines, Lufthansa, and All Nippon Airways. These strategic partners' "code-sharing" agreements share the codes (flight numbers) of flying routes so that customers can more easily switch between airlines on a given itinerary. These alliances allow passengers to fly on different partner airlines, but accumulate frequent-flyer points with their main airline. If you were a marketing manager at Air Canada, the Star Alliance would be important to understand in deciding how to market the global travel convenience offered to customers flying on Air Canada or one of its Star Alliance partners. The existence of this alliance would also be important to you as a manager at American Airlines, which is not part of the Star Alliance. In fact, it might be so important and influential that it would cause you to create your own alliance among American Airlines, British Airways, Cathay Pacific Airways, Qantas, and others.

strategic partners organizations that work closely with a firm in the pursuit of mutually beneficial goals

Strategic partnerships can become much more involved, to the point where each member of the partnership owns an equity interest in the partnership itself. Quite often this level of strategic partner involvement manifests itself in joint ventures. For example, KFC and Mitsubishi Real Estate Services Company of Japan formed a joint venture for opening KFC restaurants in Japan. This alliance is not only important to managers within KFC, but to managers within McDonald's as well. In the fast-food industry, the right location is critical to success. A manager at McDonald's has to take into consideration KFC's strategic alliance because Mitsubishi Real Estate Services's long and extensive understanding of the real estate market in Japan makes it more likely that KFC will find and secure ideal locations for new stores. Since the supply of ideal locations is limited, managers at McDonald's have to keep in mind this alliance as they seek out locations for their new restaurants.

Labour

Labour is another important task-environment force. Virtually no organization can operate without people. The balance between supply and demand for types of workers significantly affects a firm's performance. For example, if demand exceeds supply, the imbalance can lead to high labour costs. This can be true at the factory-floor or executive-suite level. Clearly, higher personnel costs could impact a firm's profits unless it can pass these increased costs on to customers. When demand far outstrips supply, you can experience severe labour shortages. You may find that you cannot find the type of workers you need at almost any price. If you are a crew manager of an oil and gas pipeline construction project and you cannot find pipefitters, your business suffers because of either no or slow progress on the pipeline. If you are the manager of a programming group and you cannot find qualified programmers, your product may get substantially delayed or die because a competitor comes out with its product before you and takes the entire market.

Labour unions are another important dimension in the Canadian labour force. While labour unions have declined in Canada over the last several decades, they are still a powerful force in certain industries. For example, about 70 percent of the 61 000 employees in Canada's airline industry are represented by unions.[23] These unions can put powerful pressure on managers to increase wages and offer other desired benefits such as job security, health benefits, or sick days because of the ability of unions to get their members to act in coordination.

Regulators

Regulators consist of both regulatory agencies and interest groups. A regulatory agency is one created by the government to establish and enforce standards and practices, primarily to protect the public's interests. Interest groups are nongovernment organizations (often referred to as NGOs) that are organized to serve the interests of their members. While they have no official regulator or enforcement power, they can exert tremendous influence on organizations.[24]

Regulatory agencies are of special note in an organization's external task environment because of the extent to which they can influence and in some cases dictate organization actions. For example, pharmaceutical companies like Merck cannot introduce new drugs for sale without the approval of Health Canada. The federal regulator also prescribes the standards that new drugs have to meet and the processes of testing and development they must go through to meet those standards. In this context, the regulator determines many of the rules of the competitive game among pharmaceutical companies. Regulatory agencies exist at all levels of government, each having an influence on a particular industry and organizations that operate within it. For example, architects and engineers working on new buildings in Winnipeg would have to comply with federal building codes like the National Fire Code of Canada while also adhering to provincial regulations like the Manitoba Building Code and municipal bylaws dictated by the city's long-range policy plan, Plan Winnipeg 2020.

While young managers may not have much experience with regulatory agencies, experienced managers know that municipal agencies regulating land use and property tax assessment, provincial agencies monitoring workplace health and safety and workers' compensation, and federal agencies enforcing the Goods and Services Tax (GST) and the import and export of goods are just a few of the regulators that exert direct and powerful influences on organizations. Managers must understand these regulators and incorporate their policies into their decisions and actions.

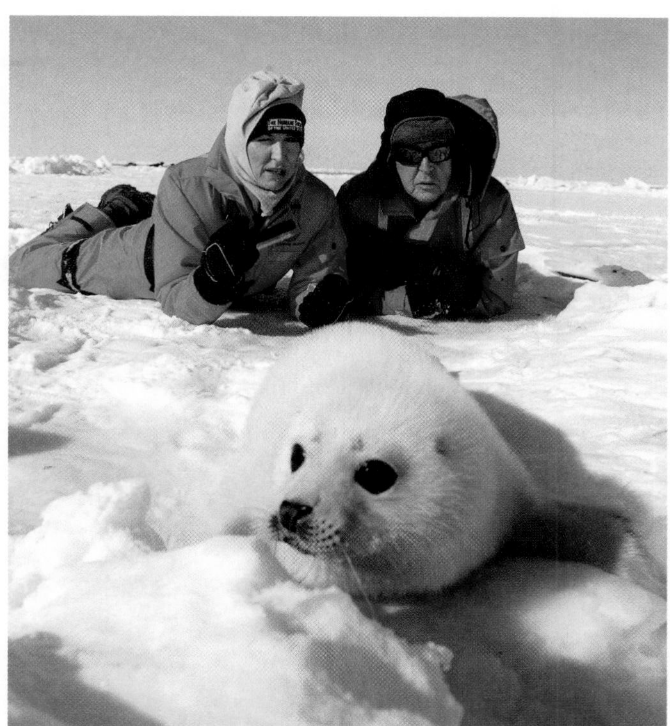

NGOs such as Respect for Animals and the Humane Society apply pressure to governments to ban products that use methods for testing or production that they believe are cruel to animals. Often, NGOs will enlist the services of celebrities to convey the message to government and to sway public opinion. In March 2006, Paul McCartney and his now ex-wife Heather Mills took part in a photo shoot on the ice floes just off the coast of Newfoundland in protest of the annual seal hunt.

Interest groups such as Greenpeace, Amnesty International, the Humane Society, and Mothers Against Drunk Driving (MADD) are often as well recognized by the public as official government agencies. This is primarily because these NGOs have learned that influencing public opinion through the media can have as much influence on organizations as efforts to lobby lawmakers or organizational executives directly. For example, Greenpeace has refined the art of sending small inflatable boats out to try to block shipments they believe are harmful to the environment. They run the boats dangerously close to the cargo ships, creating footage that news stations find hard to resist and that ends up being seen by millions of people.[25]

Task Environment Summary

From this introduction and discussion, it should be fairly clear that these task-environment forces have a powerful influence on organizations and their performance. Task environments are important, but they do not solely determine success or failure. That is, you can position your organization within a task environment and industry so that your organization performs better than your competitors. We mention this because we do not want to create the impression that if you are in an "unattractive" industry (i.e., one in which the task-environment forces are generally aligned to result in lower profits), you are doomed to not do well. Most airlines have lost money because of the nature of the five forces in that industry; however, WestJet has made money. So organizations *can* survive and flourish even in hostile environments. How you can accomplish that is the subject of Chapter 7 on strategic management.

Exhibits 2.6 and 2.7 provide a summary of the task environment for WestJet, an airline founded in 1996 that is known for its low prices and very buoyant flight crew. To make a profit, it maintains a focus on low cost of operations.

Exhibit 2.6 Description of the Task Environment of WestJet

Competitors

- Rivalry
  Primarily based on price, which generally hurts performance.
  Many established and big players.
- New Entrants
  With $35 million anyone can start an airline; however, the frequency of past failure makes it less likely for new entrants.
- Substitutes
  As video conferencing gets better with faster connections, it may substitute for some face-to-face business meetings. It is less likely to substitute for leisure, tourist, or personal visit travel.

Customers

- Business travellers who want convenience.
- Leisure travellers who want low price.

Suppliers

- Boeing supplies all of WestJet's planes.
- Many jet fuel suppliers, such as Imperial Oil.

Strategic Partners

- Currently not a part of any airline alliance.
- Initial partner with satellite TV provider (it later bought the company).

Labour

- Currently not represented by labour unions.
- Ample supply of pilots and flight attendants due to significant downsizing in other airlines.

Regulators

- Transport Canada dictates many standards and regulations.
- Airport authorities determine access and cost of landing slots and gates at airports.

Exhibit 2.7

The Task Environment of WestJet

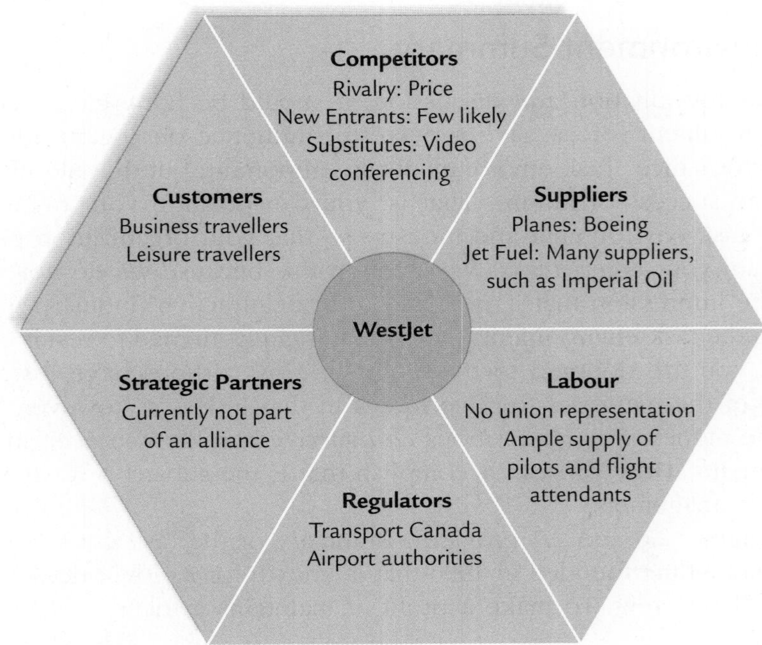

The Internal Environment

Much of this text is about the internal organizational environment, and therefore this section should be considered a very brief introduction. Part of the reason that we introduce the internal organizational environment here is that much of the meaning derived from the external environment can only be found when translated into the organizational context. In addition, much of what should be done or can be done in response to the external environment is a function of the nature of the organization's internal environment.

Owners

Owners have legal rights to the assets of a company. The owner of a company could be an individual or a collection of shareholders. As an example of a diversified group of people and institutions owning a public company, consider that in 2006 Research In Motion had nearly 200 million shares outstanding.[26] The structure and nature of ownership is critical when assessing the relationship between the external and internal environment. For example, if a company is privately held, the owner(s) can determine the general objectives of the organization. The owner might determine that maximizing profits is not the ultimate objective and instead place a strong emphasis on giving back to the community. This is the case with Manitoba firm Peak of the Market.[27] Peak of the Market donates more than 1 million pounds of produce to local food banks and also works with charities and not-for-profit organizations. In 2005, Peak of the Market's president and CEO received the Manitoba Lieutenant Governor's Award for outstanding contribution to the community. This would be quite difficult for a public company like Research In Motion, where the owners include a diversified set of shareholders who, for the most part, want a return on their investment. This brings up the issue of what a company's responsibilities are to shareholders, communities, and others, which we will examine in depth in Chapter 3 when we look at managerial ethics and corporate social responsibility.

Board of Directors

Companies often have a board of directors or a set of individuals elected by shareholders of the company who represent the interests of the shareholders. As such the board of directors has the responsibility of overseeing the general management of the company, but it typically does not run the company. The board can consist of individuals from both inside and outside the company. While boards are not there to run the company, they are not there to simply rubber stamp whatever management wants to do. Boards should understand the nature of the business and its operations and review major decisions to ensure that the interests of shareholders are being protected. In the past several years, boards have come under greater scrutiny for not being as active or involved as perhaps they should have been.[28] This has been primarily driven by large corporate bankruptcies reported in the media like Enron, where it seems that the problems that caused the downfall of the firm could have and should have been known to board members far in advance of when they finally came out.

Employees

Employees are an additional force in the internal environment. To some extent we can use the two dimensions of the sociocultural external general-environment force—demographics and values—as a means of examining key aspects of employees. In terms of demographics, factors such as age and distribution of age, gender, and ethnic diversity can all be important to managers. For example, Dofasco executives commissioned a study in 2000 to better understand their workforce. They found that the average age of workers was 47 with 23 years' experience. This information made management realize that over the next several years, many of its skilled workers would retire. The importance of labour in its external task environment took on special significance when managers within Dofasco realized that the external labour pool was shrinking just at the time it would need to replace its aging internal workforce. In response to their findings, Dofasco managers revitalized an apprenticeship program to get young workers into leadership roles within the organization, reducing the development time frame of a good leader in the organization from ten to fifteen years down to five or six.[29]

Employee values are also important for managers to consider when trying to understand internal environmental forces. In Dofasco's case, employees have a strong value for job security and stability in the tasks they perform. In other words, employees want to know they have a secure job, and they want that job to be largely what it has been in the past. This creates some concern among Dofasco managers when they examine aspects of their general and task environments. In the general environment, economic downturn means that they have to lower their costs to remain profitable. This may require shifting workers from one area of the company to another or even laying some workers off. The shifting steel requirements of customers in its task environment means that Dofasco must be more flexible in the mix of existing products it produces and must be innovative in coming up with new products that meet customer needs. Both of these requirements may mean that employees have to be more flexible in what they do, which is in conflict with the values of many employees. As a consequence, this internal-environment force makes responding to external forces much more challenging.

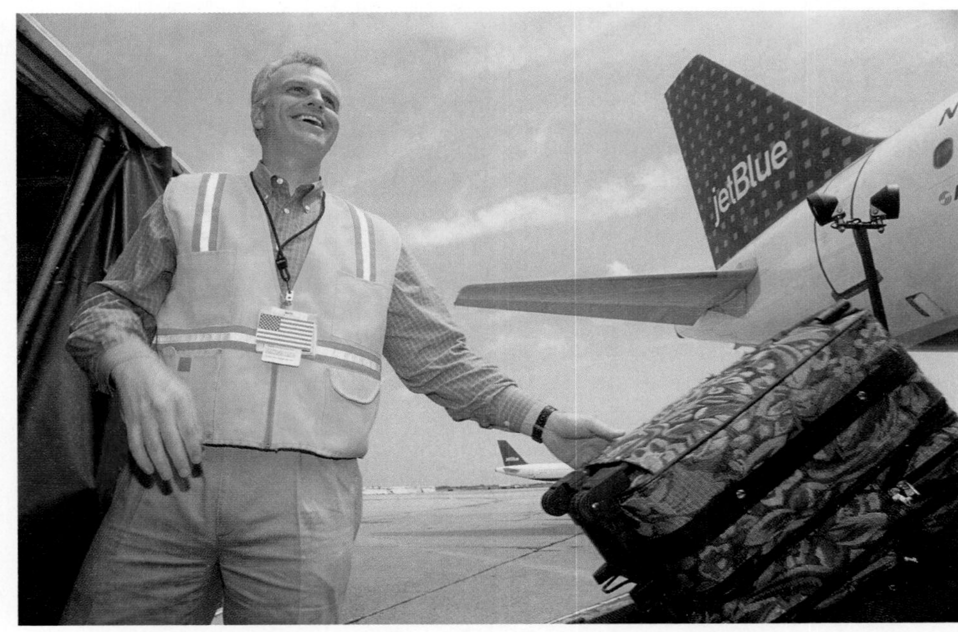

The airline industry in general has been hit hard by profitability problems in recent years. But WestJet, Southwest, JetBlue, Ryanair and other start-up airlines have been successful, in part because of their corporate culture. WestJet employees, who are not unionized, take on different responsibilities when necessary to keep the company's planes in the air and its costs and fares low. Even the CEO of JetBlue, David Neeleman, shown in the photo, would help out where necessary.

Internal and external environmental forces do not necessarily need to be conflicting. They may be complementary. For example, in the case of WestJet, the fact that there was an increasing supply of airline employees in the external labour environment during its start-up and early operations was significant in part because senior managers wanted to have a non-unionized employee base. Given that unions represent the majority of Canadian airline workers, an excess supply of airline employees (due to the increasingly difficult economic times for air carriers through the 1990s, particularly Canadian Airlines) made it easier for WestJet executives to achieve their internal employee objective.

Culture

Culture is such an important and complex topic that we devote all of Chapter 4 to the subject. As a consequence, we will be brief here about the nature of culture and its role in the internal environment. The culture of an organization is a learned set of assumptions, values, and beliefs that have proven successful enough to be taught to newcomers. The culture of an organization can have a significant impact on how the external environment is perceived and what are easy or difficult responses to it.

We can see an illustration of the interplay between internal and external environments if we return to the case of WestJet. For WestJet, an important element of its task environment is price competition. While it is not the only factor, the price of a plane ticket is significant for customers when they decide which carrier to fly with. If executives at WestJet want to attract customers by offering lower prices and at the same time want to make a profit, the company must have significantly lower costs than its competitors. One of the ways to achieve lower costs is by keeping planes in the air longer rather than having them sit unused. This is greatly facilitated by having shorter turnaround times at the gate. (WestJet targets a 30-minute turnaround, while the industry average is over an hour.) This requires pilots, flight attendants, baggage handlers, and cleaning crews to all pitch in and help. Having a culture in which all employees want to do what is necessary to turn the planes around quickly helps achieve the productivity objective, which in turn lowers costs and ultimately contributes to profits even when WestJet's prices are low.

As you can see from these examples, a practical application of environmental analysis requires keeping the dual elements of the external and internal environments in mind and relating the two. This is not an easy task and there is no magic formula for doing it well. Part of the trick, however, is having a systematic understanding of both external and internal organizational environments. The first part of this chapter has provided a fairly comprehensive framework for understanding the external general and task environments of organizations as well as the internal environment.

Environmental Scanning and Response

Given all the elements of the environment that we have covered, it should be clear that effective managers need to scan the environment constantly to monitor changes. This chapter helps that process by pointing out the different critical areas to monitor. Trying to monitor everything would simply be overwhelming. Consequently, the first principle of effective environmental scanning is knowing *what* to scan. Again, the environmental forces we have

Environmental Scanning by Michael Hitt

mymanagementlab

covered constitute a reasonable framework for the "what" when it comes to environmental scanning.

However, even if you know what to scan, you will still need a plan for *how* to scan. What do you look for to provide you with information on economic, sociocultural, legal and political, and technological forces? Where do you look for information on competitors, new entrants, substitutes, customers, and suppliers? Business publications such as *Fortune, Canadian Business, The Economist*, the *Globe and Mail, National Post, Financial Times News*, and *The Wall Street Journal* are probably good starting points. However, for industry-specific information, you will likely need to turn to more specialized trade journals.

An important thing to keep in mind concerning public sources of information is that everyone has equal access to them. Consequently, as a manager you have two basic means of gaining advantage. First, you can work at being superior to others in analyzing publicly available information and anticipating how it relates to your job, company, and industry. Second, you can seek advantage by gaining information from nonpublic sources. This may be as simple as asking people you meet in your business (or even personal) travels about developments in any of the areas mentioned in this chapter. For example, an acquaintance may inform you of rising worker unrest in China that could affect your joint venture there long before word shows up in local or international newspapers. This advance information may help you anticipate and prepare for events rather than just react.

But whether you focus on public or private sources of information, effective scanning has a few basic components (see Exhibit 2.8):

Exhibit 2.8

Environmental Scanning

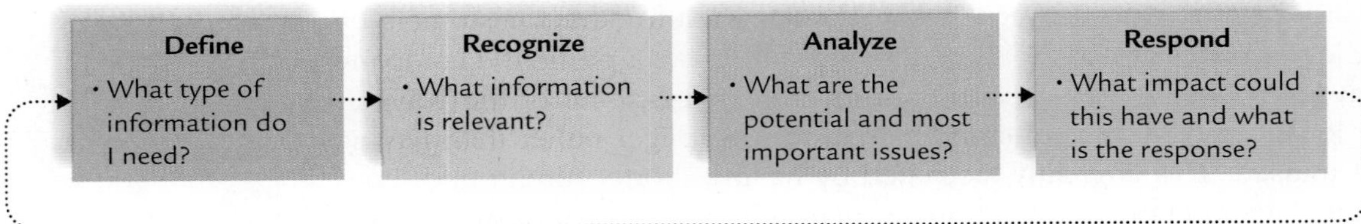

- *Define:* The first step involves determining what type of information you should scan for and where and how you plan to acquire the information.
- *Recognize:* Next you must recognize information as relevant.
- *Analyze:* Once you have recognized information as being relevant, you need to analyze it and determine its implications.
- *Respond:* Finally, the full force of the information lies in its application to your job, company, or industry. Essentially, in this stage you are answering two key questions: What impact will this information have and how can I respond effectively?

Define

Much of this chapter is devoted to addressing this first issue. The categories of the general-environment forces as well as those for the task environment constitute an effective framework for defining what information you need. As we mentioned, both public and private sources should be used in gaining information on all aspects of the external environment.

Recognize

In this digital age, information is not hard to come by. In fact, in many cases you are likely to be overloaded with information even if you use the environmental forces framework from this chapter. As a result, you will need to sift through and determine which information is relevant to your situation. This task is facilitated by asking how specific information you gather might relate to your organization. For example, as we mentioned earlier, even if you know that the economy is currently in a down cycle and is expected to recover within the next 12 months, this information may be more important to a housing construction firm than to a funeral home.

Analyze

Effective analysis has at least two separate but related aspects. First, a good environmental analysis needs to look for and examine the interactive effects of different environmental forces. Second, a good analysis needs to explore the specific implications that environmental forces in isolation and especially in combination likely have for your organization. Interactive effects can be of a complementary or even amplifying nature, or they can be of a mitigating nature. We will examine both through some examples.

To illustrate the importance of examining mitigating interactive effects between or among different environmental forces, let's assume you are a manager in a residential home construction company. During 2000–03, the Canadian economy experienced a slow growth period. Generally, this would cause people to buy fewer homes (new or used) as they worried about their job security and income. However, at the same time interest rates were at 40-year lows. This made owning a home more affordable. Overall, home purchases and mortgage refinancing hit near record highs and continued until the later part of 2006 with much of Canada experiencing unprecedented highs in housing prices. In this case, the low interest rates mitigated and nearly cancelled out what would have normally been a downturn in the economic cycle.

Environmental forces can also serve to reinforce or even amplify each other. For example, the ever-increasing number of retiring university professors in the coming years and the declining number of doctoral students has created a shortfall for nearly every Canadian university. The rise of technology, especially the internet, means that faculty can browse online career search services like chronicle.com and find out the general demand for skills and experience such as theirs and what the market rate is for those skills and experience. In combination, these two forces mean that faculty with valuable and scarce skills have become even harder for universities to hold on to. Add to these two forces the political-legal influence of the North American Free Trade Agreement, which makes it relatively easy for Canadian professors to enter the United States, and you have an even more powerful implication if you are a university administrator charged with attracting and retaining faculty at your school.

Respond

How can organizations respond effectively to changing environmental demands? As we explained at the outset, research as well as experience strongly suggests that responding effectively to changes is key to managerial success over time. As a result, it is impossible and impractical to confine our answer to how organizations can respond effectively to environmental changes to just this section. Still, we can frame many of the general responses in the following four categories: direct influence, strategic response, organizational agility, and information management.

Direct Influence Managers and organizations are not simply at the mercy of environmental changes; they are not passive receptacles that must take whatever the environment dishes out. Managers do and should try to influence the political-legal process when they believe that existing or proposed legal requirements unjustly restrict their activities. For example, in 2004 McCain Foods filed a complaint with Canadian authorities that US producers of fast-rising pizza were "dumping" product into Canada (selling it below cost), which was hurting Canadian producers of fast-rising pizza. The Canadian Border Services Agency investigated and found that US producers were selling pizzas here nearly 40 percent cheaper than at home. Four Canadian importers and two producers (Kraft Foods and Palermo Villa Inc.) were part of the investigation. The findings resulted in a temporary duty being imposed on pizzas entering Canada from the United States. This example illustrates that pursuing political-legal pressure is a strategy that can be used by managers to alter their competitive environment, regardless of whether their allegations hold merit.

Strategic Response But suppose it was found that the producers of the pizza were not dumping their product into the Canadian market. How might producers like McCain Foods respond? In this case they might choose among a number of strategic responses. They might use their own foreign operations or form a joint venture with a foreign company to take advantage of lower costs in that locale to produce the pizzas. Alternatively, they may employ a strategy that highlights the quality of the locally produced pizzas in comparison to the imported pizzas. Canadian firms smaller than McCain Foods may opt for a partnership with other Canadian producers to create economies of scale and reduce production costs. For example, the combined purchasing power of two producers might get them lower costs for materials by leveraging their high purchase volumes for pricing discounts. If the firms merged, they might lower costs by eliminating jobs in common support functions like human resources because they only need 50 percent more HR staff to support twice the number of employees. We will explore more about strategy and strategic response in Chapter 7.

Organizational Agility To the extent that environmental change is frequent and unpredictable, managers might respond by creating a more flexible or agile organization. While we will examine this in greater detail in Chapter 8, managers can structure and design organizations for greater (or lesser) flexibility. For example, rules tend to work best when the environment is fairly stable and does not change much. People can follow the rules, and because the environment doesn't change much, following the rules is likely to produce results that fit the environment. On the other hand, in environments that change often, rules tend to not work well. They lead to rigidity and inflexibility. Having people share common values gives them greater flexibility to respond to the changing environment. Because the needs of customers are seen as changing too quickly, managers at WestJet stress the importance of customer service and responding to the needs of customers as they arise. Seventy percent of WestJet's ad budget is used to promote its customer service. And WestJet's corporate culture is deemed the most admired by 107 business executives polled across Canada.[30]

Information Management If you look back to Exhibit 2.8, you'll notice that the process of environmental scanning is circular, not just linear. In other words, ultimately your response should feed back into your definition. Information management is a specific response that highlights this feedback loop. For example, if you are a manager in a residential-home construction business, you have learned with experience that interest rates are one of the most important forces in the general economic environment. As a consequence, you may develop means of capturing all the indicators and estimators of future interest rates. You may further refine this information management system by determining which indicators or estimators prove to be the most accurate in forecasting future interest rates over time. This information management response actually accelerates and enhances your ability to define, recognize, analyze, and respond to—or perhaps even anticipate—environmental changes.

Summary of Environmental Scanning and Response

By necessity, we have simplified and segmented the discussion of environmental analysis. However, the reality is that one of the greatest challenges you will face as a practising manager is that the environment does not come in nice, segmented pieces. Also, quite often a single event can have an impact across multiple segments of your general and task environment.

One example is the tragic events that took place on September 11, 2001. If you were in any travel-related industry, the potential implications were staggering. Reduction of air travel required cutbacks by airlines, hotels, and resorts. Another example is the 2003 outbreak of severe acute respiratory syndrome (SARS) that killed 800 people around the world, hitting Toronto particularly hard with 44 deaths. The World Health Organization released a travel advisory against nonessential travel to Toronto. The economic impact of the outbreak resulted in an estimated lost revenue of $39 million in April 2003 alone. All gathering places in the Toronto area, such as malls, restaurants, and theatres, had significantly diminished customer traffic. Conferences were cancelled or relocated to other cities and over 800 bus tours were cancelled.[31] Yet another example is the impact of Hurricane Katrina on New Orleans and the Gulf Coast region of the United States in late August 2005. The hurricane is the costliest natural disaster in United States history at an estimated US$150 billion. The cost of oil spiked around the world as available supply diminished because of inaccessible offshore oil rigs in the Gulf, major pipelines being shut down, and damaged refineries. The rising cost of fuel permeated all facets of the Canadian economy, from heating to shipping.

After events like the ones outlined above, managers evaluate and decide upon an appropriate response to the dramatic change in the environment. How will government reaction affect business? How will a manager's customer base be affected? Does this change the customer's propensity to use the products and services offered by the organization? How does a manager respond when her industry is directly affected by the events? How does a manager respond when in a nonrelated industry?

As you can see by just this small set of questions, the analytical task of environmental analysis for managers in situations like this is huge. On the one hand, we presented the task of environmental analysis in an artificially clean and segmented way, but as the three unexpected events above illustrate, actual problems do not present themselves in nice, neat packets. On the other hand, though, imagine trying to analyze the business environment implications without a segmented framework. The task would be overwhelming, to say the least.

managerial perspectives revisited

1 PERSPECTIVE 1: **THE ORGANIZATIONAL CONTEXT** While the external environment is not a deterministic force and inevitably dooms an organization to a predetermined level of performance, it does present important demands, constraints, and opportunities. However, these are not absolutes; they have practical application only in the context of a given organization. For example, an increase in older citizens might create an opportunity for a new pharmaceutical company but present a constraint for a hospital with no room or money for expansion. Consequently, effective managers have to analyze the environment from the perspective of their organization. As we discussed, the ultimate practical value of environmental analysis lies in seeing the implications for your organization and determining the appropriate response. In the absence of the organizational context, external general or task environmental analysis is more of an academic exercise than a managerial activity.

2 PERSPECTIVE 2: **THE HUMAN FACTOR** Hopefully this chapter has helped illustrate how complex an assessment of the external environment can be while providing a few concepts and tools to make that easier. What we haven't stressed during the chapter but should stress here at the end is that it is rare for a manager to conduct a formal assessment of the external environment on his or her own. In fact, the more complex the company and the environment, the more likely it is that several people will be involved in the assessment based on their particular specialty or area of expertise. For example, as a manager, you may need your sales representatives to give you feedback on what their counterparts are doing out in the field. You may need to rely on people in your technology department to keep up with the technological developments of your competitors. You may need people in financial departments to gauge outside forces like interest rates, stock prices, economic outlook, and so on to provide you with information to make good decisions about where and how to spend money in response to these environmental forces. It is because of this that we want to highlight here that one of the distinguishing capabilities of a manager relative to external environment assessments is the ability to work with and through others to gather, analyze, integrate, and then act on the assessment.

3 PERSPECTIVE 3: **MANAGING PARADOXES** One fundamental challenge of environmental assessments is managing to focus on both the near and long terms. Individuals, teams, and companies often have to make changes based on assessments of the current external environment. The present cannot be ignored. But the current economic conditions or state of technology as well as other important aspects of the environment are not likely to remain stable. Consequently, to be effective in assessing the environment and then making strategic, planning, and other decisions, as a manager you will need to be able to manage the paradox of simultaneously considering both the present and the future environmental conditions.

Another potential paradox associated with effective environmental analysis is that of separating and integrating at the same time. On the one hand, you must segment and divide aspects of the environment to analyze and understand the complexities involved. This is precisely why we have divided the external environment into the general and task categories and have further divided each of these into subcategories. However, an environmental analysis of isolated bits and pieces is incomplete. You must also integrate the results of the separate analyses of the various pieces. Effective environmental analysis is not about doing just one or the other, it is about doing both. As stated in this chapter's introduction, the integration of the analyses should help us identify the environmental opportunities and threats that exist. In addition, even though we use the term "environmental analysis," effective management requires both analysis and action. In fact, the practical relevance of the analysis only comes to life with action—organizational response. The actions should be based on the environmental opportunities and threats identified. As a result, as a manager you will need the ability to both think and do; to both conduct an effective environmental analysis and act and react in ways that help you, your subordinates, and the company deal with the external environment.

4

PERSPECTIVE 4: **ENTREPRENEURIAL MINDSET** A critical component of an entrepreneurial mindset is identifying opportunities. Opportunities are most likely to exist in an organization's external environment. Thus, analyzing the external environment is necessary to identify opportunities that the organization can exploit. An organization could identify opportunities afforded by changes in government regulations by analyzing the political-legal environment, for example.

Analyzing changing demographic trends can also provide opportunities. For instance, the aging baby-boomer population in Canada presents many new opportunities for businesses catering to the needs of retiring Canadians. Assessing the environment can broaden managers' knowledge and understanding and allow them to take advantage of entrepreneurial opportunities like this. It also signifies a commitment to acquire new knowledge and skills. Although new knowledge can be tapped from within an organization, the external environment is also an important source. Strategic partnerships can afford access to new knowledge as well.

concluding comments

At this point you can see that while some people might think that the task of external environment analysis is the job of specialized analysts, it is not. It is true that in large organizations entire departments may be dedicated to analyzing the economic or political forces in the environment. Although reports from others inside or outside the company can be valuable, you have to be personally aware of and understand these forces. Without such personal awareness and understanding of critical environmental forces, you might not recognize valuable information even if you had it in your hands. As a manager, you must accurately and systematically identify critical factors in the external environment and understand cause-and-effect relationships. Only then will you be able to anticipate, rather than simply react to, external environmental challenges.

Certainly, effective analysis of all the various forces within the industry, domestic, and international environments is a big challenge. However, two even larger challenges remain. The first is to begin to see links among the various forces within an environment. For example, it is one thing to do a good analysis of the substitution and customer forces within the industry environment; it is quite another to see that the lack of substitutes and the fragmented nature of customers combine to offer an unprecedented opportunity for growth. Only in drawing the connections can you plan effectively and exploit opportunities for growth.

The second major challenge is seeing the connections between a particular business and its industry, domestic, and international environments. Seeing relationships among them is a quality of a truly gifted manager. Think of it in terms of the interactions and relationships found in the natural environment. Finding the right conditions to favour growth and survival is as important to businesses as it is to flowers or trees. Organizations thrive or perish according to their fit with their environments.

Meeting the basic challenge of understanding and analyzing individual environmental forces is a significant accomplishment for a manager. Meeting the challenge of seeing relationships among different forces within an environment is exciting. Meeting the challenge of seeing relationships among different environments is a never-ending challenge—one that makes management an exciting and invigorating profession.

key terms

demographics 43
entry barriers 58
external environment 42
general environment 42
gross domestic product 50
internal environment 42
process technological changes 46
product technological changes 45
societal values 44
strategic partners 59
structural changes 49
substitutes 58
switching costs 57
task environment 42

test your comprehension

1. Define the external environment.
2. What are key differences between the external, general, and task environments?
3. List four examples of important demographics.
4. Why are societal values important to an assessment of the general external environment?
5. What are the key differences between product and process technological changes?
6. Why is an awareness of both types of change critical to an assessment of the technological environment?
7. Why are economic cycles important to consider in addition to current economic conditions?
8. How are structural economic changes different from economic cycles?
9. Why is government spending important to consider when analyzing the legal and political environment?
10. What are the key features of a country's physical environment?
11. Name three key institutions that should be included in an environmental analysis.
12. What are Porter's Five Forces?
13. If the nature of competition or rivalry in an industry is primarily based on price, do profit margins in that industry tend to increase or decrease?
14. What are entry barriers and why do they matter in an analysis of the industry environment?
15. If there are few new entrants to an industry and if entry barriers are large, do profit margins in that industry tend to increase or decrease?
16. What are switching costs?
17. What is the difference between a substitute and a competing product?
18. What are the four steps to effective environmental scanning?
19. Why is there a feedback loop between Respond and Define in the environmental scanning and response model?

apply your understanding

1. What key environmental changes do you think will increasingly force managers to be proficient at conducting environmental analyses?
2. Are there industries that will be more immune to changes in the global environment and as a consequence will be influenced primarily by their domestic external environment? Name at least two and explain why.
3. What are the most difficult environmental analysis skills to develop? What are some possible means of ensuring that you have these valuable skills?
4. Debate the following statement: Computers and news media have made international environmental analysis simpler.
5. Pick a country and go to the library or the internet to find some information about its resources, government, political and legal systems, and physical infrastructure. What type of business would do well in that country? Why?

practise your capabilities

You are the purchasing manager of a specialty retail company that has just over 20 stores in large shopping malls across Canada. These stores specialize in equipment and clothing targeted at "boarders," that is, guys and girls who surf, skateboard, snowboard, and/or wakeboard. Since the 2006 Winter Olympics increased the number of snowboarding events to six, you have seen a steady increase in the popularity of boarding culture, resulting in an increase in customer traffic to your stores.

The president of the company wants you to come up with an initial analysis and recommendation for the coming year regarding whether the company should anticipate an increase or decrease in sales. Last year sales of equipment declined by 9 percent while sales of clothing dropped by 5 percent. In looking toward the future, you decide to do a quick STEP analysis.

Sociocultural

First, you decide you need some information on the demographics of your target customer (i.e., boys and secondarily girls ages 14–24). Is this group growing or shrinking in Canada? Someone mentioned that www.statcan.ca might be a website that could help you find this information.

Second, you determine that you also need to try to get a sense of the values of the boarding culture and how strongly they are supported in your target customer population. Many of your current customers talk about the freedom that boarding represents. The icon of skateboarding is Tony Hawk, so you decide to check out how well his video game is selling. For wakeboards, it's pros like Sunni-Anne Ball and Chad Sharpe that you need to check out. For snowboarding, it's Jasey-Jay Anderson, Matt Morrison, Mercedes Nicoll, and Maëlle Ricker.

Technology

While you don't feel that technology is affecting your clothing lines that much, you wonder if it might be a factor for equipment. Your top equipment brands are Burton for snowboards, Tony Hawk and Hollywood for skateboards, and Neptune and Connelly for wakeboards. So you go to their websites to see if any new technological changes are on the horizon.

Economic

You also want to get a sense of what is happening with the economy. Unemployment, inflation, exchange rates, and consumer spending seem like important facts to research first.

Political-Legal

While no political or legal issues immediately jump to mind as potentially having a big impact on your business, you wonder about insurance laws affecting skateboarding parks or whether helmets or some sort of headgear might be required in the future for snowboarding or wakeboarding. You've seen a few people get rather nasty cuts on their heads when they crashed and the board they were riding hit them, and they required stitches.

1. After gathering information in each of these four areas, which ones seem to point in a positive direction for your business? Which ones seem to point in a negative direction?
2. Currently, your sales are split about 50/50 between equipment and clothing. Does anything in your analysis indicate that this should be changed in the future?
3. What is your overall recommendation? Should purchases increase?
4. On a broader note, should the company think about increasing or decreasing the number of stores it has?

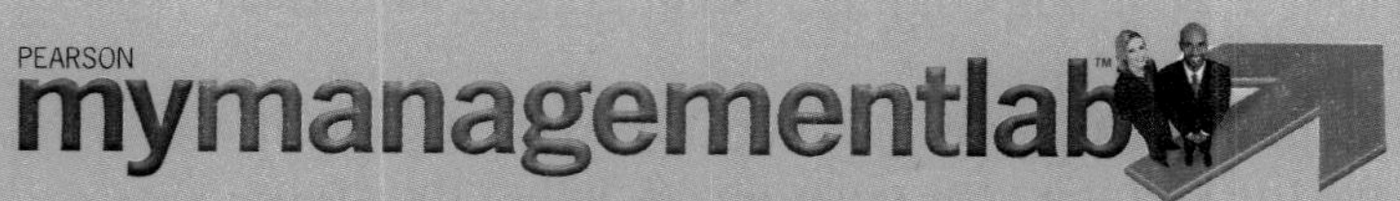

To improve your grade, visit the MyManagementLab website at **www.pearsoned.ca/mymanagementlab**. This online homework and tutorial system allows you to test your understanding and generates a personalized study plan just for you. It provides you with study and practice tools directly related to this chapter's content. MyManagementLab puts you in control of your own learning!

closing case DEVELOP YOUR CRITICAL THINKING

Changing Channels at the Canadian Broadcasting Corporation

With one-quarter of a trillion dollars (US) in annual worldwide broadcasting and cable TV revenue, the Canadian broadcasting market is a very modest player, comprising only 2.2 percent of the world market share. In comparison, the US market commands over half (54 percent) of total world revenues. Canada's small stature is compounded with the fact that growth in the Canadian market to 2010 is forecast to be only three-quarters of what is expected in the United States and global markets. Within the Canadian market, the Canadian Broadcasting Corporation (CBC) is a broadcaster that struggles with the dominating American content pushing its way north into Canadian programming.

Only 40.2 percent of Canadian television viewing time is spent watching Canadian programming. In 2005, total revenue for CBC was $547 million, posting a net loss of $113.7 million. With the CBC's strict mandate to produce and promote Canadian content in its programs in addition to managing the same environmental factors that other Canadian broadcasters face, how can the network survive in this fiercely competitive market?

CBC's broadcasting revenues come from federal funding and advertising, both of which are dependent on a healthy economy. Despite a relatively stable economy, rate of inflation, and the return of public spending in other areas, government funding has continued to decline. Specifically, when adjusted for inflation, the CBC has endured $400 million in funding reductions over the past 15 years, receiving less than $1 billion in federal funding annually. As a result, CBC must rely more on commercial advertising for revenues, like other Canadian broadcasters do, but it must still maintain the burden of producing Canadian content. Presently, it costs five times more to produce a Canadian program than it does to buy the rights to an American program.

The CBC is required by the *Broadcasting Act* to provide 80 percent Canadian content in its programming, whereas other Canadian competitors are only required to provide 50 percent. The imbalance results in the CBC spending significantly more on production than other networks. While the cultural rewards from CBC's production requirements have resulted in distinctly Canadian programs that, if anything, reinforce that we are not American (e.g., *The Red Green Show*, *The Rick Mercer Report*, and *Little Mosque on the Prairie*), the net effect of the financial squeeze results in an increasing threat to the quality and quantity of its programming. In a defensive response, CBC lobbies federal politicians to either increase funding or have the mandate adjusted to fit available resources.

At the same time, broadcasting regulations have changed, opening borders in the television sector and leading to increased competition from US networks. With the changes, Canadian broadcasting is moving toward a more market-driven environment with less government control and financial support. Because of the decreased barriers to entry and unauthorized access to US satellites, American networks have garnered a significant portion of the Canadian television-viewing population.

CBC is heavily impacted by political factors, owing to the fact that its funding is provided each year in the federal budget, which is set by the presiding government. A change in political leadership could mean the loss of funding or the restructuring of the *Broadcasting Act*, which in turn could dissolve the public broadcasting system altogether. CBC currently receives 60–80 percent of the television funding given to Canadian networks through the Canadian Television Fund's Equity Investment Program. Furthermore, since Canada's heritage minister and prime minister appoint the CBC's board of directors and CEO, political debate and scrutiny are often associated with appointments and the direction of the organization. The CBC is regularly criticized whenever they are perceived to be bowing to the party in power. They fall easy prey to anyone that perceives the CBC as acting in a manner that leads to maximizing federal funding. As such, significant decisions regarding programming and major purchases can attract political pressure.

The technological aspect of the environment in which CBC conducts business has also undergone dramatic changes in recent years. Digital technology is quickly becoming the new method of broadcasting. In 2000, the Canadian Radio-television and Telecommunications Commission (CRTC) defined the regulations surrounding licensing for digital and specialty TV services. These new regulations, aimed at bridging the transition from analogue to digital distribution systems, have eroded the barriers to entry for foreign broadcasting suppliers. Canadian private broadcasters have been heavily investing in digital infrastructure, including high definition (HD) television, to stay competitive with US networks. Satellite and digital cable subscriptions between 2000 and 2003 exploded in numbers, increasing by 297.5 and 279.2 percent, respectively.

Yet, because of funding limitations, CBC does not have the available resources to keep up with the digital technology its competitors are turning to. Adoption of this technology would result in an increase in capital expenditures by $50 million per year, with no guarantee of increased revenues. In an effort to resolve this situation, CBC appeared before the CRTC in September 2006 in the first of a series of hearings aimed at establishing a new broadcast policy.

The CBC is recommending a hybrid between high definition and digital cable that ensures the maximum number of Canadians could continue receiving an over-the-air signal. After studying usage patterns, CBC estimates that 98 percent of Canadians would be able to receive the digital signal under this hybrid system.

Online activity is also influencing the viability of the CBC. Currently, 64 percent of Canadian households have internet access and nearly three-quarters of all children have access to the internet at school. Websites with movie and television-program downloads as well as video-sharing sites like YouTube are increasing a viewer's choice for video entertainment. And with the internet's interactive, viewer-based design, it is increasingly becoming a substitute for television. From 1997 to 2003, there was a 23 percent decrease in television viewing among

Canadian children and young adults, the age range that advertisers like to target most. Yet while initial appeal of these sites was limited to the young, techno-savvy teen-to-20s group, the age distribution of online users has grown steadily as content on these sites has expanded to appeal to a wider age spectrum.

As a means of dealing with these numerous pressures, CBC has entered into new media channels—like podcasts—making several of its shows available online and free of charge through its own website, cbc.ca, as well as iTunes. In fact, for nine months in 2006, a CBC podcast on iTunes experienced the most activity out of all Canadian podcasts, logging more than 1 million downloads. CBC has also increased its website's comprehensiveness and ease of use. The cbc.ca website remains the leader in news and media websites for Canadians, ahead of other Canadian broadcasters, CNN, the *Globe and Mail*, and the *New York Times*. To reap benefits from this traffic, CBC has inserted advertising on the site in a manner that does not distract from the content, but results in revenue that has exceeded initial expectations. As well, CBC launched Sirius Satellite Radio Canada to expand into the United States and to reach even the most remote Canadian. The CBC provides six of the ten stations offered by Sirius.

Questions

1. Which do you think are the most important environmental forces for CBC? Why?
2. Are there environmental forces besides those mentioned that you think management at CBC should focus on?
3. How should CBC managers address the issue of the aging baby boomers? What about young viewers?
4. Based on your analysis of the external environment, what changes do you think managers at CBC should make?

Sources: CBC/Radio Canada, "Striking the Right Balance: CBC/Radio Canada Annual Report 2005–2006," October 2006; "Broadcasting and Cable TV in Canada: Industry Report," *Datamonitor*, September 2006; S. A. Andrew, "Free to Be, CBC," *This Magazine* 39, no. 4, pp 16–18; "CBC/Radio-Canada Purposes Future Model for Canadian Television to CRTC," Canada NewsWire, November 27, 2006; "CBC/Radio-Canada Corporate Plan, 2004–2009," www.cbc.radio-canada.ca, accessed on September 28, 2005, pp 30–31; *Broadcasting Act*, laws.justice.gc.ca, accessed on October 1, 2005; "Media Watchdogs Call for End to Patronage Appointments to Top CBC Jobs." Canadian Press NewsWire, September 2004; "CBC Being Starved of Funds for Public Broadcasting," Canadian Press NewsWire, November 8, 2006; G. Dixon, "CBC Makes More Shows Available On-line," *Globe and Mail*, May 4, 2006, p. R4; T. Manera, "The CBC: Looking Ahead," *Media* 11, no. 4, p. 16; www.statcan.ca, accessed October 3–8, 2005; R. Stursberg, "Commentary: CBC Needs Ad Revenues," *Playback: Canada's Broadcast and Production Journal*, July 24, 2006, p. 10.

Chapter 3 Ethics and Social Responsibility

LEARNING OBJECTIVES

After reading this chapter, you should be able to:

1. Describe why an understanding of basic approaches to ethical decision making and corporate social responsibility is important.
2. Explain the basic approaches to ethical decision making.
3. Identify the different implications of each approach in real-life situations.
4. Explain the basic approaches to corporate social responsibility.
5. Develop different implications for each approach to corporate social responsibility.

Confidence in the Japanese Construction Sector Collapses

Scandal broke in the Japanese construction sector in late 2005 when it was revealed that a respected architect admitted to designing and constructing buildings below the minimum Japanese seismic requirements. The story broke on November 17, 2005, when Japan's Ministry of Land, Infrastructure, and Transport reported that architect Hidetsugu Aneha had knowingly designed 20 condominiums and one hotel that were not fit for occupancy. Of the 21 buildings, which were built in Tokyo, Chiba, and Kanagawa, 13 would not withstand an earthquake with a seismic intensity of 5.0 on the Richter scale—and some would not even withstand a moderate earthquake. This revelation shocked many, since the Japanese city of Kobe had suffered a devastating earthquake only a few years earlier in 1995, where more than 6400 people died from a tremor measuring 7.3 on the Richter scale. The day after the announcement was made, Aneha admitted to the allegations. It was later discovered that he had been falsifying reports since 1998. Through further investigation, the ministry found that Aneha actually falsified data on at least 71 of the 208 buildings he had designed.

Aneha blamed pressure from construction firms to design low-cost structural systems for new buildings and a fear that he would not get work if he didn't comply. In a strange twist, Aneha also blamed the inspection companies he used for their lack of diligence in checking his designs. Following the revelations, hundreds of condominium residents were forced to evacuate their homes, leaving them with the burden of finding new accommodation. The owners of four hotels, which Aneha had assisted in designing, decided to suspend operations while they waited for the buildings to be inspected. Some of the buildings are being retrofitted to increase their earthquake resistance, while others are being demolished. Still others remain vacant as all the stakeholders involved decide what to do.

Streamlining of Japan's building-plan review process in 1999 led to systemic corruption within the Japanese construction industry that jeopardized the safety of thousands of building occupants.

The architect's deception was made public after eHomes, a privately owned architectural design inspection firm, admitted that it had failed to detect Aneha's fabrication in his structural reports. A representative of eHomes claims that they did not pick up on the faulty data because Aneha had taken measures to conceal it in the volumes of data regularly submitted for inspection and approval. Aneha also admitted that he used eHomes's inspection services because they regularly approved his fraudulent reports. He continued to use the firm's services, anticipating that his false structural calculations would continue to go undetected.

The inspection of building plans was traditionally undertaken by the Japanese government until 1999 when deregulation efforts led to changes in Japan's Building Standards Law. These changes allowed private firms to certify building designs and thereby streamline the building review process. The changes in the system also meant that architects were free to submit their designs to any inspection company for safety certification. Government officials began to realize that some architects were purposely choosing inspection firms with low standards in an effort to have their designs approved quickly, but problems with the new system surfaced only after the Aneha scandal. The changes to the law did incorporate a safeguard, where Japanese authorities were supposed to perform spontaneous, random audits of the operations of design-review firms each year. However, it was discovered after the Aneha scandal that these audits were not conducted with the initially intended frequency.

There is a growing fear that Aneha's case is only the tip of the iceberg for Japanese architecture. Failures in inspection agencies are thought to be the result of declining standards in investigation firms, and now there is concern that the problem is more widespread. Industry experts have suggested that the deterioration of inspection agencies' standards is related to pressure to complete drawing and structural inspections quickly, thus serving more clients and achieving greater profits. Certain inspection firms have acknowledged that the documentation they examine is often lengthy, making it difficult to check all of the information it contains in the short time frames that the industry demands. Since the Aneha scandal went public, the Japanese government visited 105 of 123 building inspection firms, confirming that 18 had failed to carry out proper screening procedures. In the case of eHomes, it was confirmed that they had not detected data fabrications in 37 out of the 99 projects submitted by Aneha. The firm's inspection licence was immediately revoked by the government, which subsequently led to the firm's demise.

Further evidence of poor government monitoring came from the testimony of the president of eHomes, who claimed that public officials did not take action when he informed them that his firm had detected false data. However, eHomes made the discovery only after a re-examination of Aneha's reports, once they had learned that another inspection firm had detected errors in Aneha's work a year earlier. As a result of the Aneha scandal, the Japanese government has recognized the prevalence of falsified structural data and the need to examine and make changes to the building-safety-inspection system to better detect it.

For his part in the scandal, Hidetsugu Aneha was stripped of his licence as an architect and arrested for breaking the Building Standards Law and the Registered Architects Law; the maximum penalty for these violations is 500 000 yen and 300 000 yen, respectively (approximately CDN$5000 and $3000). On the same day, four other individuals that assisted in designing, approving, and building Aneha's flawed designs were arrested. While none of the individuals faced charges directly related to the data fabrication scandal, police hope to build criminal cases against them. A few weeks later, a fifth individual was arrested for allegedly selling a condominium even though he knew that the building's earthquake-resistance data was inaccurate. Through investigation, the Japanese government hopes to determine where its design certification system failed and follow up with a revision of its laws so that scandals like Aneha's become history.

Sources: BBC News, "Japan Construction Scandal Widens," December 14, 2005, news.bbc.co.uk (accessed November 1, 2006); Japan Real Estate, "Architectural Scandal Deepens," November 25, 2005, jrearticles2.blogspot.com (accessed November 1, 2006); *Japan Times Weekly Online*, "Data Scam on Quake Resistance Shakes the Nation," November 26, 2005, www.japantimes.co.jp (accessed November 1, 2006); *Japan Times Weekly Online*, "Rogue Inspection Dragnet Widens," December 3, 2005 (accessed November 1, 2006); *Japan Times Weekly Online*, "The Depths of Data Fabrication," December 10, 2005 (accessed November 1, 2006); *Japan Times Weekly Online*, "Huser Wanted Disclosure Delayed," January 28, 2006 (accessed November 1, 2006); *Japan Times Weekly Online*, "Aneha to Be Arrested Over Quake-Resistance Data," April 22, 2006 (accessed November 1, 2006); *Japan Times Weekly Online*, "Aneha and Seven Associates in Building Fraud Arrested," May 6, 2006 (accessed November 1, 2006); *Japan Times Weekly Online*, "Trail to the Epicenter of Faulty Math," May 13, 2006 (accessed November 1, 2006); *Japan Times Weekly Online*, "Huser Head Arrested in Building Scam," May 27, 2006 (accessed November 1, 2006); *Japan Times Weekly Online*, "Ehomes Head Admits Faking Papers," July 15, 2006 (accessed November 1, 2006).

strategic overview

Globally, construction is valued at about US$3.2 trillion per year. Corruption in the construction sector is reportedly greater than in any other area in the world economy, and corrupt practices are found in all aspects and stages of the construction process—no area is immune.[1] As the case in Japan illustrates, the design stage plays a dark role in contributing to the scale of corruption in construction. Managers can face pressures that result in ethical and social responsibility issues. Aneha buckled to the pressure of demands for cheaper structural designs with faster completion time frames. As well, once he opened the door to conducting fraudulent practices, he had less reservation in continuing. As Aneha pointed out, the inspectors made it easy for him to continue since their review process was inadequate and didn't catch his false data. What is hard to fathom is the disregard for the safety of thousands by designing and constructing flawed structures, knowing full well that they will collapse when a tremor similar to the Kobe earthquake occurs again.

Should the Japanese government accept partial blame for Aneha's actions and the decay of standards applied in the construction of buildings? How would you feel if you learned that the building you go to school in could collapse under such minimal forces as excessive snow, mild tremors, or heavy rainfall? What if we lost our trust in all that is built, produced, manufactured, or prepared for our consumption? We place a great amount of trust in organizations, assuming that they will conduct themselves in a manner that does not place the public in financial or physical jeopardy, which is why ethics and social responsibility have a powerful role in the discussion of management. Managers in large companies usually act as agents of the owners (as we explain later in this chapter). As such, top executives have an implied obligation to take strategic actions that are in the best interests of the owners or shareholders. If they take actions that help themselves, such as rejecting a takeover bid to keep their jobs, but that may be to the detriment of shareholders, are they acting in an ethical manner? In recent years, numerous executives of top corporations have acted opportunistically, making headlines in the process. Some acted not only unethically but illegally. They harmed both the shareholders and many employees, who lost their jobs when their bosses' misdeeds came to light and the companies went bankrupt.

Both managerial ethics and strategy begin at the top of the organization. For ethical decisions and practices to permeate the firm, top executives must build a culture based on those values. This includes establishing codes of ethics, implementing ethics training for employees, and rewarding ethical behaviour (as discussed later in this chapter). Moreover, it includes behaving in an ethical manner themselves.[2]

An ethical organization is especially important when it comes to implementing the strategies developed by top managers. Managers at the top and throughout the organization along with other employees are likely to face many ethical dilemmas throughout the course of doing business. While the unethical practices that Aneha carried out appear on the grand scale, most organizations face similar pressure situations on a regular basis.

Managers must also grapple with decisions about how to operate their firms efficiently, yet in a socially responsible manner. To do so, top executives may need to establish standards that exceed the requirements of the law. They must also consider the strategic and ethical impact of their decisions on the organization's stakeholders and employees. And their decisions must be perceived to be fair. (We will discuss the various approaches managers can take to organizational "justice" later in this chapter.)

managerial ethics the study of morality and standards of business conduct

corporate social responsibility the obligations that corporations owe to their stakeholders, such as shareholders, employees, customers, and citizens at large

The discussions above coupled with the opening case help to highlight the two key issues of this chapter: managerial ethics and corporate social responsibility. **Managerial ethics** is essentially the study of morality and standards of business conduct. **Corporate social responsibility** is concerned with the obligations that corporations owe to their stakeholders, such as shareholders, employees, customers, and citizens at large.

Relevance to You

You may be wondering, "Why should I care about ethics and social responsibility? Aren't these the types of issues philosophers worry about?" To answer this question, you need only pick up recent newspapers or business magazines. Everything from Bay Street insider trading scandals linked to political announcements, to accounting frauds at CIBC and Nortel,[3] to environmental pollution cover-ups seems to be in the press daily. PricewaterhouseCoopers reported that 45 percent of companies around the world have been victim to some form of economic crime over a two-year period. The average cost to those companies was US$2.1 million.[4] For example, in 2004 WestJet was alleged to have repeatedly accessed Air Canada's internal website over a ten-month period. Beginning in May 2003, a former Air Canada employee's password gave WestJet access to confidential corporate information. WestJet executives were reported to have accessed the secure site more than 240 000 times, retrieving flight and scheduling information. Air Canada launched a $220-million lawsuit against the rival airline only to have WestJet launch a countersuit, accusing Air Canada of hiring private investigators to illegally rummage through recycled materials at the home of a WestJet executive. In the end, both parties dropped their suits. WestJet admitted to accessing Air Canada's website and covered the airline's legal fees of $5.5 million and paid $10 million to a children's charity in the two airlines' names. While the worst was avoided by having the two firms settle out of court, the image that they projected to Canadian consumers will be more difficult to drop.[5]

Clearly, poor managerial ethics and corporate social responsibility can generate much negative publicity, hurt a company's stock price and destroy

South Mountain Company, a US$6 million architecture and construction firm led since 1985 by founder John Abrams, is among the companies honoured for its "Excellence in Ethics" by *Business Ethics* magazine. The company is focused on more than maximum growth and profits. Abrams states that the company is more about workplace democracy and craftsmanship. As a consumer, how important are a company's business ethics to you? Would you be interested in working for a company that did not focus on growth and profit?

shareholder value, or make it difficult for the firm to recruit high-quality employees. In contrast, well-managed ethical behaviour and corporate social responsibility can have significant, positive consequences for employees, customers, shareholders, and communities. Exhibit 3.1 provides a listing of companies honoured for "Excellence in Ethics" by *Business Ethics* magazine. As you read these examples, ask yourself whether you would be more or less likely to work for one of these firms because of its reputation. As a customer, would you be willing to pay a premium price for the product because of the company's reputation?

Exhibit 3.1 Excellence in Business Ethics Award Winners

2005 Winners

Intel (CSR Management Award)
For leadership and excellence in corporate social responsibility management.

South Mountain Company (Workplace Democracy Award)
For using employee ownership as the foundation of life-enchancing company.

New Leaf Paper (Environmental Excellence Award)
For mainstreaming ecological principles into the paper industry.

Weaver Street Cooperative (Living Economy Award)
For its sustainable products, community focus, and democratic governance.

2004 Winners

The Gap (Social Reporting Award)
For taking social reporting a quantum step forward by risking unprecedented honesty in reporting factory conditions.

Chroma Technology Corp. (Living Economy Award)
For exemplifying the living economy with practices of employee ownership, fair wages, and environmental stewardship.

Dell, Inc (Environmental Progress Award)
For responding to stakeholders' concerns with industry-leading computer-recycling initiatives.

Clif Bar Inc. (General Excellence Award)
For its ongoing commitment to environmental sustainability, employee well-being, and community involvement.

King Arthur Flour (Social Legacy Award)
For handing down to employee owners a centuries-old tradition of purity, for both the consumer and the environment.

2003 Winners

Organic Valley (Living Economy Award)
For being an exemplar of the living economy: locally rooted, human scale, stakeholder owned, and life serving.

Baxter Healthcare (Environmental Reporting Award)
For rigour, transparency, and leadership in environmental accounting and reporting.

3M (Environmental Excellence Award)
For sustained commitment, innovation, and substantial impact in three decades of environmental stewardship.

Source: www.business-ethics.com, accessed October 24, 2006.

The Development of Individual Ethics

At this point in your life, do you think you have a fairly well-established set of ethical beliefs and values? If you do, how did you come by them? What role did family, friends, teachers, religion, job experiences, and life experiences have in the development of your ethical beliefs? To explore this issue, think about a situation in which someone made a different ethical judgment from your own. What if you had been born in a different country, raised by a different family, had attended a different school system, experienced different religious influences, had different friends, or held different jobs? Would you hold the same ethical values you do now? Would you reach the identical ethical judgments that you reach now?

There is little debate that family, friends, teachers, religion, job experiences, and life experiences play a significant role in the development of individual ethical values and judgments. What is debated is which factors play the strongest role, because their influence varies from person to person.[6] This debate is unlikely to be resolved soon. Nor is its resolution necessary for our purposes. The primary reason for raising the issue is to realize that to understand how others make decisions, you need to understand something about their backgrounds.[7]

Simply labelling ethical judgments that are different from your own as wrong is likely to foster feelings of mistrust (in both directions) and hurt working relationships. The greater the diversity in the workforce, or more specifically among your set of colleagues and subordinates, the greater is the need for tolerance and understanding. However, as a manager, tolerance does not mean simply allowing subordinates to come to whatever ethical decisions they individually deem right. Because individual decisions can have consequences for the organization, managers often need to shape and influence the ethical thinking, judgment, and decision making of subordinates.

Consider the following real case that was conveyed to us in a recent conversation (we have disguised the names at the manager's request). Imagine you are the marketing manager in a publishing company. Your assistant manager has just recruited a new sales representative, Martha, from a key competitor. Martha worked for your competitor, Dresden, for 11 months after graduating from college. Dresden pays employees a bonus based on performance after the first year of employment. Martha was expecting a $10 000 bonus from Dresden. In discussions with your assistant manager, Martha negotiated for a $10 000 signing bonus if Dresden failed to pay her the performance bonus. Part of the reason your assistant manager agreed to do this is because Martha had been exposed to a number of strategic operations and marketing plans in her first year of employment at Dresden. Given her somewhat junior position in the company, she had not been asked to sign, nor had she signed, a "noncompete" clause that would have prevented her from taking a job with a competitor for a specific time period or disclosing or using the knowledge gained during her time at Dresden. Legally, she was free to take the job with you.

Your assistant manager comes to you and asks if it is okay to try to get Martha to disclose as much as she knows about Dresden's marketing plans. What is your response? Do you think Dresden has an ethical obligation to pay Martha the $10 000 bonus even though she plans to leave only a few days short of completing 12 months of employment? If you were Martha, would you have any ethical misgivings about taking the new job and then relating all you knew about your previous employer's strategic plans? Would Dresden's paying you the end-of-year bonus have any bearing on what you would or would not reveal to your new employer?

Understanding Basic Approaches to Ethics

So how should you make decisions like these? Are there ethical approaches you can look to for guidance? Yes, there are some basic approaches that have been around for a long time. This is in part because the challenge of ethical decision making is not a modern one. **Ethical dilemmas**, or the choice between two competing but arguably valid options, are not new and have confronted people throughout history.

ethical dilemmas having to make a choice between two competing but arguably valid options

In the next section we will describe these basic approaches for two reasons. First, they can be helpful in trying to understand how others approach ethical dilemmas. Second, quite often the lack of a clear approach for making ethical decisions causes **ethical lapses** or decisions that are contrary to an individual's stated beliefs and the policies of the company.

ethical lapses decisions that are contrary to an individual's stated beliefs and the policies of the company

In thinking about the first reason, it is important to keep in mind the increasingly diverse workforce and global business environment. Now more than ever before you are likely to encounter people who use widely different approaches and reach very different conclusions about ethical conduct. This is illustrated in a recent study that examined the extent to which salespeople from the United States, Japan, and Korea viewed a set of actions as posing an ethical issue or not. The study found significant difference among these three nationalities.[8] For example, Korean salespeople did not think that seeking information from a customer on the price quoted by a competitor in order to resubmit a more competitive bid was much of an ethical issue. American and Japanese salespeople saw this as largely unethical behaviour. As a concrete example of this view, in most places in the United States and Canada a real estate broker cannot tell you how much someone else offered on a house you also want to buy. What do you think? Do you think asking a customer for information on the price submitted by your competitors is ethical or not?

Interestingly, from this same international study, researchers found that Korean salespeople did not think that giving free gifts was as much of an ethical issue as American salespeople did. Many organizations across Canada share the American perspective. The issue associated with employees receiving gifts is twofold: First, a free gift may influence an employee to make a decision that may not have otherwise been made. Second, a free gift to select employees within an organization may be perceived by others in the organization as an unfair benefit. Do you think company policies that prohibit the receipt of gifts are appropriate or excessive? How do you feel about restaurant serving staff receiving tips when the cook and cleaning staff do not?

Without understanding how or why others come to different conclusions, it is easy to label people holding the "wrong" beliefs as inferior. For example, in a recent study, Chinese and Australian auditors working for the same multinational accounting firm reached different decisions about proper ethical conduct because of different cultural assumptions. Chinese auditors looked to peers, while Australian auditors looked to themselves in making ethical decisions. This reflects the cultural group orientation of the Chinese and the individual orientation of Australians.[9] If either set of auditors has simply judged the other to be wrong without sensitivity to how culture might influence ethical decisions, imagine how difficult it might be for them to work together on a global audit team. In fact, research has shown that ethnocentricity, or the belief that your perspective is correct and others are inferior, tends to hurt managerial effectiveness, especially in culturally diverse or international contexts.[10] So it is important for new managers to be able to examine the basic approaches to ethical decision making and recognize that individuals' backgrounds, including cultural values, influence ethical decisions and behaviour.

As we stated, the second reason for examining basic approaches to ethical decision making is to avoid ethical lapses. Ethical lapses are more common than you might think. The pressures coming from both the external and internal environment can often be overwhelming. This is especially true if managers lack a systematized and explicit framework for thinking through dilemmas. For example, you may believe that Aneha's actions were blatantly wrong. However, if you were in Aneha's situation, where the pressures from the external and internal environment placed you in a position where you must carry out questionable work practices to acquire a contract, you may not find the choice as clear as when you are an observer.

Basic Approaches to Ethical Decision Making

Several frameworks, or approaches, exist to ethical decision making. We will examine four of the most common: the utilitarian, moral rights, universal, and justice approaches. An understanding of basic approaches to ethical decision making will help you as a manager to examine your own personal ethics and work more effectively with employees whose ethical perspectives are different.

Utilitarian Approach

utilitarian approach an approach to ethical decision making that focuses on the consequences of an action

Utilitarian Approach by Stewart Black

mymanagementlab

The utilitarian approach focuses on the consequences of an action. Simplified, using a **utilitarian approach** results in "the greatest good." Assume you are trying to sell grain to a developing nation and a customs agent demands an extra fee before he will clear your shipment. From a utilitarian perspective, you would try to determine the consequences of the options available to you. For example, you could (1) pay the money, (2) not pay the money and let the grain sit there, or (3) seek intervention from a third party. Which action would result in the greatest good? If there are starving people waiting for the grain, would you argue that the "good" of saving lives outweighs the "bad" of paying an illegal bribe?

Keep in mind when talking about whether an outcome is good or bad, people may see the same outcome differently. In other words, the "goodness" or "badness" of an outcome is often subjective. Factors such as culture, economic circumstances, and religion can all affect those subjective judgments. For example, if you were in Aneha's shoes, would you argue that it was the poor reviewing practices of the private firms and inadequate auditing schedule of the Japanese ministry that should be blamed rather than the actions of one architect?

But many situations are not as clear-cut as to whether they constitute an ethical dilemma or just a business decision. How would you handle a situation in which some members of your staff see an impending decision as strictly business with no ethical implications, while others see it as an ethical dilemma?

For an example of this, take a look at *A Manager's Challenge: "Changing Horses."* In this situation, some members think that a long-term business relationship places certain unwritten obligations on the company to work with a struggling supplier regardless of changes in the business environment. On the other hand, other members of the management team think that the situation is strictly a business-based transaction. They believe that changes in business conditions and performance by the supplier justify changing the relationship. Since the supplier is not meeting its obligations, it's just good business to cut ties with it and move on to a more reliable supplier. If you see this as an ethical dilemma, should you try to influence your co-workers to get them to change their opinions? Or should you change your perspective and simply view it as a business decision like your co-workers do?

a manager's challenge — *change*

Changing Horses

Caren Wheeler was a young purchasing manager at Johannson Wood Products, a 12-year-old company in the Midwest. As the purchasing manager, she was being asked to make a decision about the continued use of a supplier. This represented a big challenge for Caren. Several other managers in the firm viewed the decision in ethical terms, whereas Caren normally didn't think ethics were relevant unless laws were being broken.

Like many innovative mid-sized firms, Johannson Wood Products had formed strong partnerships with a limited number of suppliers to receive supplies on a just-in-time basis and then ship its finished goods in a timely fashion to retail stores. One of those partner suppliers was Creative Applications.

Creative Applications was a small, family-run company that stored and milled Johannson Wood Products' lumber into finished parts. The partnership, negotiated three years ago, had worked well for Creative Applications. Over 60 percent of its revenues came from Johannson Wood Products. In fact, the agreement had come just when Creative Applications was in financial trouble. Although it was not out of the woods yet, the agreement with Johannson Wood Products was critical to Creative Applications' survival.

Recently, however, the partnership had not worked well for Johannson Wood Products. As its sales increased, Creative Applications was having difficulty meeting deadlines. Caren had mentioned this problem to Steve Jackson, Creative Applications' plant manager (and the son of the owner), but no real improvement occurred.

When Caren met with Tom Masters, the president of Johannson Wood Products, and several other managers to discuss the situation, a variety of opinions emerged. Some saw this as an ethical issue and others did not. First the group focused on Steve Jackson's abrasive personality and management style. Many in the meeting felt that he was "a control freak" and could not delegate authority. Consequently, as demand increased, Steve became a bottleneck in Creative Applications' ability to meet delivery deadlines.

One of Johannson Wood Products' managers, who disliked Steve, stated, "I don't think that continuing a relationship with Creative Applications is going to work for us. It's one of those cases where the management capabilities of a small-time operation can't make the transition to a larger producer. We can't afford to keep nursing along a relationship that's not working."

Another manager felt it was unfair to bring personal feelings for or against Steve into the discussion and replied, "We've always told our vendors that if they were there for us, we'd be there for them. For over two years, Creative Applications really performed for us. Are we going to pull out now that they are facing tough times? Remember 18 months ago, when we pressured them to lease an expensive piece of milling equipment because of our increased volume? The equipment dealer would only do it on a three-year lease. Creative did it even though it elevated their costs. If we pull the rug out from under them now, that's not fair, and will hurt their chances of survival—we're still 60 percent of their business. Is it ethical to just pull the plug now?"

A third individual interjected, "I propose that we make an offer to either purchase Creative Applications or start our own in-house capability for milling the products. Here is a proposal that details the capital that would be required for either option and the potential savings that could be generated over a three-year period."

"Caren, what do you recommend?" asked Tom Masters. Several different issues raced through her mind. First, she had not really thought about the situation from an ethical point of view, yet clearly some of the team members felt there were ethical issues involved. In her gut, she felt just dropping Creative Applications was the *wrong* thing to do, but she didn't have any formal ethical justification for her feelings. However, even those who thought it was an ethical issue did not really have any formal ethical argument for their conclusions. Caren wondered if she should change her normal approach and take a careful look at the situation from both an ethical and business point of view. Should she try to get the others to change their approach and also consider the ethical issues? Johannson Wood Products was always stressing loyal partnership relationships. Was it ethical to just sever the relationship with Creative Applications? On the other hand, the delays being caused by Creative Applications were beginning to hurt Johannson Wood Products' ability to meet store orders faster than its competition. What was the right thing to do and what was the right approach to take?

Source: Adapted from Doug Wallace, "Changing Horses," *Business Ethics*, November–December, 1994, p. 34.

Even if you frame the Johannson situation as an ethical dilemma, using the utilitarian approach, what action results in the greatest good and over what time frame? In the short run, continuing to work with Creative Applications will likely hurt your customers, as your products do not arrive as fast as they would like. If this persists, it may enable your competitors to move past you and take market share away to the point that you have to reduce your size and lay off some employees. On the other hand, demonstrating that you are serious about your promise to work with chosen suppliers could lead to an additional commitment from Creative Applications and other suppliers and result in enhanced performance and product deliveries.

Moral Rights Approach

moral rights approach an approach to ethical decision making that focuses on examination of the moral standing of actions independent of their consequences

The **moral rights approach** to ethical decisions focuses on an examination of the moral standing of actions independent of their consequences. According to this approach, some things are just "right" or "wrong," independent of consequences. When two courses of action both have moral standing, then the positive and negative consequences of each should determine which course is more ethical. Using this approach, you should choose the action that is in conformance with moral principles and provides positive consequences. From a moral rights approach, if not honouring unwritten commitments to suppliers is simply wrong (i.e., doesn't have moral standing), then cutting off the supplier to make more money is not justified. The managerial challenge here is that the moral standing of most issues is debatable. For example, you might want to say that it is wrong to lie. But is it wrong to make your competitors think you are about to enter one market when you are really about to enter another so that your company has the element of surprise? Is it just wrong to say you are not working on a particular new technology when you actually are to influence your competitors not to invest in the new technology and thereby have an advantage when you finally perfect it? Again returning to the case of Johannson Wood Products, how would you handle the situation if one employee believes that honouring unwritten, implicit commitments is just right (i.e., has moral standing) and another employee does not? In many companies both explicit policies as well as corporate values often serve a vital role in defining what is right or wrong when there is no universally accepted determination. If the corporate values of Johannson stress honouring not only legal contracts but also implicit promises to suppliers, then should Caren try to get the other managers to change their views and see this as an ethical issue?

Moral Rights Approach by Stewart Black
mymanagementlab

Universal Approach

universal approach an approach to ethical decision making where you choose a course of action that you believe can apply to all people under all situations

Immanuel Kant, perhaps one of the most famous moral philosophers, articulated the best-known ethical imperative, or **universal approach**. Simplified, Kant's moral imperative was "do unto others as you would have them do unto everyone, including yourself." If you follow this approach, you should choose a course of action that you believe can apply to all people under all situations and that you would want applied to yourself. At the heart of universalism is the issue of rights. For Kant, the basis of all rights stemmed from freedom and autonomy. Actions that limit the freedom and autonomy of individuals generally lacked moral justification. If you were in Hidetsugu Ahena's situation and took a universal approach to the situation he was in, it would be unconscionable to knowingly create structures that will not withstand a moderate earthquake. To justify Ahena's choice under the universal approach, you would have to be willing to accept that your residence is destined to collapse in the next earthquake for the gain of the individuals involved in its construction.

Universal Approach by Stewart Black

mymanagementlab

Justice Approach

The **justice approach** focuses on how equitably the costs and benefits of actions are distributed as the principal means of judging ethical behaviour.[11] In general, costs and benefits should be equitably distributed, rules should be impartially applied, and those damaged because of inequity or discrimination should be compensated.

justice approach an approach to ethical decision making that focuses on how equitably the costs and benefits of actions are distributed

Justice Approach by Stewart Black

mymanagementlab

Distributive Justice Managers ascribing to **distributive justice** distribute rewards and punishments equitably based on performance. This does not mean that everyone gets the same or equal rewards or punishments; rather, they receive equitable rewards and punishments as a function of how much they contribute to or detract from the organization's goals. A manager cannot distribute bonuses, promotions, or benefits based on arbitrary characteristics such as age, gender, religion, or race.

distributive justice the equitable distribution of rewards and punishment based on performance

Procedural Justice Managers ascribing to **procedural justice** make sure that people affected by managerial decisions consent to the decision-making process and that the process is administered impartially.[12] Consent means that people are informed about the process and have the freedom to exit the system if they choose. As with distributive justice, the decision-making process cannot systematically discriminate against people because of arbitrary characteristics such as age, gender, religion, or race. Recent research involving employees across multiple countries consistently suggests that perceived justice is positively related to desired outcomes such as job performance, trust, job satisfaction, and organizational commitment, and is negatively related to outcomes like turnover and other counterproductive work behaviour.[13] Procedural justice is generally studied and interpreted within the context of the organization. However, the findings of a recent study show that factors external to the firm may also have strong effects on counterproductive workplace behaviour. In a study contrasting community violence and an organization's procedural justice, violent crime rates in the community where a plant resided predicted workplace aggression in that plant, whereas the plant's procedural justice climate did not.[14]

procedural justice ensuring that those affected by managerial decisions consent to the decision-making process and that the process is administered impartially

Compensatory Justice The main thesis of **compensatory justice** is that if distributive justice and procedural justice fail or are not followed, then those hurt by the inequitable distribution of rewards should be compensated. This compensation often takes the form of money, but it can also take other forms. For example, compensatory justice is at the heart of affirmative action plans. Typically, affirmative action plans ensure that groups that may have been systematically disadvantaged in the past, such as women or minorities, are given every opportunity in the future. For example, special training programs could be instituted for women who were passed over for promotions in the past because they were denied access to certain experience required for promotion.

compensatory justice if distributive and procedural justice fail, those hurt by the inequitable distribution of rewards are compensated

Moral Intensity in Ethical Decision Making

moral intensity the degree to which people see an issue as an ethical one

Exhibit 3.2
Factors of Moral Intensity

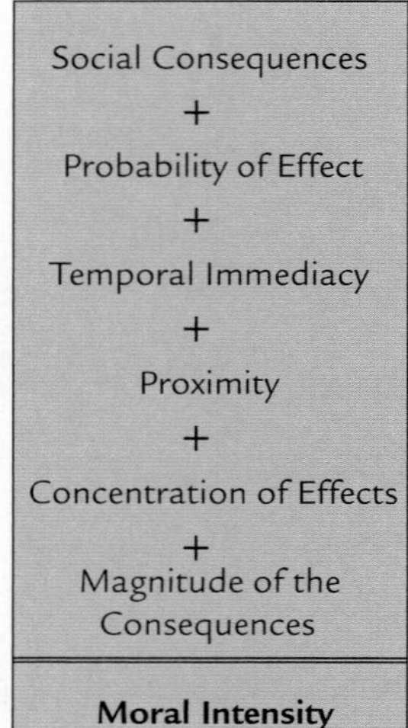

Social Consequences
+
Probability of Effect
+
Temporal Immediacy
+
Proximity
+
Concentration of Effects
+
Magnitude of the Consequences
Moral Intensity

As we have pointed out thus far in this chapter, one of the challenges of ethical decision making for a manager is that for many issues and consequences, people do not have identical perspectives. They differ in whether they see a situation as involving ethics and in how they would determine their course of action. So the practical question is whether managers can help people come to more common views on the moral intensity of issues.[15] **Moral intensity** is the degree to which people see an issue as an ethical one. This is largely a function of the content of the issue. As a manager you can use this framework both to anticipate the moral intensity of an issue and to diagnose the reasons for differing views about the moral intensity of an issue among people.[16] Moral intensity has six components, as illustrated in Exhibit 3.2: (1) magnitude of the consequences, (2) social consensus, (3) probability of effect, (4) temporal immediacy, (5) proximity, and (6) concentration of effect.[17] In other words, the overall moral intensity of a situation is the result of adding each of these components together.

magnitude of the consequences the anticipated level of impact of the outcome of a given action

social consensus the extent to which members of a society agree that an act is either good or bad

The **magnitude of the consequences** associated with the outcome of a given action is the level of impact anticipated. This impact is independent of whether the consequences are positive or negative. For example, laying off 100 employees because of a downturn in the economy has less of an impact than if 1000 employees join the ranks of the unemployed. Many people would judge a 20 percent increase in the price of lawn fertilizer to be of a lower magnitude than 500 people killed or seriously injured because of an explosion in the fertilizer plant caused by poor safety procedures.

Social consensus involves the extent to which members of a society agree that an act is either good or bad. For example, in Canada there is strong social consensus regarding the wrongness of driving drunk. However, the extent of the social consensus across provinces differs when it comes to reviewing laws to prevent impaired driving. In a 2006 review of provincial impaired driving legislation, MADD Canada (Mothers Against Drunk Driving) found a wide variation in the measures taken by provincial jurisdictions to reduce impaired driving. MADD Canada's evaluation ranged from a high score of A– (given to Manitoba for their legislative reforms on impaired driving) to an F (given to Nunavut for their poor performance in the same area). This suggests that while there is a general social consensus regarding the wrongness of drunk driving, the consensus breaks down at the point of legislating laws to reduce the occurrence of drunk driving.[18]

probability of effect the moral intensity of an issue rises and falls depending on how likely people think the consequences are

The third component of moral intensity is **probability of effect**. Even if a particular action could have severe consequences and people agree about the positive or negative nature of that impact, the intensity of the issue rises and falls depending on how likely people think the consequences are. For example, one of the reasons that the advertising and display of cigarettes in stores is heavily restricted in Canada is because of the strong association between smoking and health problems like lung cancer. However, cigarette smoking itself has not been completely outlawed in part because the probability of effect is not 100 percent. The higher the probability of the consequence, the more intense the sense of ethical obligation is. Because people are highly likely to be injured if they are in a car accident, the intensity regarding the moral obligation of auto manufacturers to make safer cars is increasing. Side-impact air bags are now becoming standard in many of the vehicles available in North America. However, because there is no certainty that you will be in an automobile accident, many of the safety features are not required by law.

Temporal immediacy is the fourth component of moral intensity and is a function of the interval between the time the action occurs and the onset of its consequences. The greater the time interval between the action and its consequences, the less intensity people typically feel toward the issue. For example, even if industrial pollution were certain to lead to global warming and result in catastrophic changes to weather patterns, because the consequences are likely to happen 50 years from now, the moral intensity of industrial pollution is much less than if the effects were to happen next year.

temporal immediacy a function of the interval between the time the action occurs and the onset of its consequences

The fifth component is **proximity**. All other factors being equal, the closer the decision maker feels to those affected by the decision the more the decision maker will consider the consequences of the action and feel it has ethical implications. Proximity does not just mean physical closeness. Proximity also involves psychological and emotional closeness and identification. Consequently, an affinity between the decision maker and those affected could be a function of many factors, including nationality, cultural background, ethnic similarity, organizational identification, or socioeconomic similarity. For example, if you feel a psychological and emotional affinity for young people in Africa, then decisions by African managers about laying off workers by seniority (meaning younger workers will get laid off first) will have greater moral intensity for you even if you live thousands of kilometres away. Likewise, a decision to close down a poorly performing but slightly profitable factory that could put your parents and neighbours out of work will also likely have greater moral intensity for you than a factory closure in which the affected workers are unknown to you.

proximity the physical, psychological, and emotional closeness the decision maker feels to those affected by the decision

The last component is the **concentration of effect**, or the extent to which consequences are focused on a few individuals or dispersed across many. For example, even though laying off 100 people has a lower magnitude of effect than laying off 1000 people, laying off 100 people in a town of 5000 has a greater concentration of effect than laying off 1000 people in a city of 2 million.

concentration of effect the extent to which consequences are focused on a few individuals or dispersed across many

The importance of these six facets of moral intensity is twofold. First, as a manager, you can use these facets to anticipate issues that are likely to be seen as significant ethical dilemmas in the workplace.[19] If you can better anticipate issues that are likely to become ethical debates, you have more time to prepare and may be more effective at handling ethical dilemmas. Second, if you are working with a group that is using the same basic ethical approach and still can't agree on the ethical course of action, you can use these facets to determine the source of the disagreement.[20] The disagreement may stem from different perceptions of the situation on one or more of the moral intensity components. For example, your group, like Caren Wheeler's, may be arguing over the ethics of terminating a relationship with a long-time supplier. In examining the source of the disagreement, you may discover a difference in perception as to the concentration of effect. For example, once it is clear that you represent 60 percent of the supplier's business, others who were discounting this factor may change their opinions. This alone may make it easier to reach a decision.

The rock group U2 had to deal with significant negative media coverage regarding their decision to relocate their creative operations outside of Ireland and into the tax haven of the Netherlands (see *A Manager's Challenge: "U2-Faced?"*). Members of the band were both caught off guard by the intensity of the global and domestic public scrutiny and somewhat unprepared to respond at first. If U2 members had used the moral intensity framework, could they have predicted public reaction? If they could, would the framework have helped them make some anticipatory changes in how they manage their operations and present their rationale for the decision to relocate?

a manager's challenge *globalization*

U2-Faced?

Following years of outspoken lobbying on behalf of Africa's poor and sick, the rock group U2 and front man Bono have found themselves recipients of the same criticism that they bestowed upon the wealthy nations of the world. In June 2006, the corporate side of the giant rock group moved operations from their home soil in Ireland to the Netherlands. The decision, as David "Edge" Evans later defended, was based purely on financial grounds: U2 did not want to pay more taxes.

The motivation behind the band's decision to relocate their operations to the Netherlands was that the government of Ireland had decided to change a long-standing leniency on royalty taxes to entertainers in the country. The new tax law requires artists that make more than 500 000 euros (CDN$700 000) to pay tax on half of their creative revenues. U2 was the world's top-grossing band in 2005, bringing in more than 210 million euros (CDN$295 million), with roughly one-third of the band's earnings generated by royalty payments. The Netherlands tax structure for royalties, on the other hand, will result in U2 paying only about 5 percent tax on their royalties. The band members have remained residents of Ireland, as have some of their Irish-based businesses, requiring them to still pay the government of Ireland some taxes based on their income.

Most people wouldn't look twice at such a decision by the typical corporation. However, U2 is not a typical corporation. The tax-saving decision was made by a group that has been active in getting the rich nations of the world to forgive the debt of Africa's poorest nations. Bono, a charismatic figure that has been mentioned as a candidate for the Nobel Peace Prize, has also been a passionate supporter of the Make Poverty History campaign, lobbying nations to increase their financial support to Africa to US$50 billion a year by 2010. Bono has gone so far as to make public pleas while on stage for Ireland's prime minister to increase financial aid from 0.5 percent to 0.7 percent of Ireland's GDP. Bono also pulled no punches when he openly criticized Prime Minister Paul Martin at the outset of the 2005 Canadian federal election campaign for his poor performance in supporting African nations. Bono claimed that he was "crushed" that Canada had not committed to increasing financial aid from 0.3 percent to 0.7 percent of GDP. Bono believed that because Martin was the former finance minister he would be able to "make the numbers work." He also warned Martin that he would feel the impact in the election if he did not increase aid (incidentally, Martin lost the 2005 election).

The rock group U2 decided to relocate their operations to the Netherlands to avoid paying increased taxes in Ireland. The action appeared to many to be in conflict with the band's vocal lobbying of rich nations to increase financial support to Africa.

Many believe that Bono is setting a questionable example by the pursuit of a safe tax haven. To be fair, this is not the first time that super groups have moved operations to pursue tax breaks. For example, the Rolling Stones moved their operations to the Netherlands in the early 1970s. It is no coincidence that one of U2's directors of U2 Limited is the individual behind the Rolling Stones's Netherlands low-tax strategy. Still, most would agree that the image presented by the Rolling Stones and U2 dramatically differ, with the Stones's sex, drugs, and rock 'n' roll attitude being a stark contrast to U2's active social conscience.

On the other hand, some might argue that U2's move to the Netherlands allows them to not only retain their earnings, but also use their tax savings more effectively toward world debt. Traditionally, U2 has provided anonymous donations as well as the royalties of some of their songs toward debt relief and to reduce the spread of AIDS in Africa. By maintaining complete control of their own finances, U2 can allocate funds where they see the greatest benefit rather than giving their funds to government coffers where it is distributed among numerous public bureaucracies that also rely on tax revenues to function.

There are other implications to the band's decision, as well. Countries cannot increase their spending on aid unless they receive revenue from income taxes. It has been reported that well over US$11 trillion has been stuffed into safe-haven mattresses around the world by wealthy individuals. The net result of the redirection of income is a loss of taxes in the range of US$255 billion to governments, which could go a very long way toward solving Africa's debt problem. How are countries supposed to increase aid if their tax base is eroded by tax havens? By avoiding the increased taxes in their home country, U2 is making it more difficult for Ireland to increase its financial commitment to Africa's needy. And what precedent does this set for other individuals with tremendous wealth?

If the members of U2 were to use the moral intensity framework, how would they assess the positive and negative consequences for relocating to the Netherlands? What is the level of social consensus regarding the rightness or wrongness of moving operations to another nation to reduce taxes? How strongly do people feel about corporations avoiding high taxes by locating in safe havens? How likely is it that U2's relocation will affect Ireland's ability to increase its financial aid to Africa? How close or distant will the public feel toward the argument presented by U2 members, or to the plight of poverty-stricken African nations? When the 2010 goal is to provide US$50 billion in annual financial aid to Africa, how concentrated will the effect of U2's pursuit of tax breaks be perceived by the public?

Sources: F. O'Brien, "Bono Criticized at Home for Irish Tax Manoeuvre," *Globe and Mail*, October 17, 2006; O. Bowcott, "Found What You're Looking For? U2 Inspire Irish Ire by Avoiding Tax," *The Guardian*, August 9, 2006; T. Peterkin, "U2 Move Their Assets Out of Ireland," *The Telegraph*, August 8, 2006; CBC Arts, "Bono 'Crushed' PM Hasn't Reached Foreign Aid Goal," November 25, 2005, www.cbc.ca (accessed October 24, 2006).

Making Ethical Decisions

Increasingly, it seems that individuals and organizations are embracing a philosophy of business ethics that was first and perhaps best articulated in 1759 by Adam Smith in his work *The Theory of Moral Sentiments*. Smith's basic thesis was that it is in individuals' and organizations' self-interest to make ethical decisions. Still, a significant challenge remains to you as a manager: How can ethical decisions be fostered and encouraged?

The Manager

As we mentioned at the outset, part of the reason for exploring various approaches to ethical decision making is to help you refine your own approach so that when pressures arise you can make decisions consistent with your ethical framework. To this end, there is perhaps no substitute for taking personal responsibility for ethical decisions. To illustrate this, simply put yourself in Caren Wheeler's position (see *A Manager's Challenge: "Changing Horses"*). If you were Caren, what might the magnitude of consequences be if Creative Applications is dropped as a supplier? How many jobs might be lost? How likely is this? How soon would it happen? If there is some degree of moral intensity to the situation, what approach would you use to come to a decision? Is it right to drop Creative Applications? Caren is expected to provide not only a recommendation but also a rationale for it. What decision would you have made if you were involved in the management of U2's operations? Why?

Even after you have become more comfortable and explicit about how you would resolve ethical dilemmas, the question still remains as to how much you should change your approach to fit in with others or try to change their approach. If you were managing U2's operations, how hard should you work to change the public's perception, persuading them to see the positive benefits of relocating the band's operations to a tax haven? Although it is probably impossible to argue that one of the approaches presented in this chapter is best, applied consistently, each approach does allow a consistent pattern of ethical decision making. This consistency may matter more to those you interact with than whether your decisions are always in agreement with theirs.[21] This is in part because your consistency allows others to better understand your approach and trust you than if they perceive your decision making as random and inconsistent.

The Organization

Just as managers try to foster ethical decisions, organizations have a significant impact on ethical decision making. The overall culture of the company can play a significant role. For example, the emphasis on keeping customers happy and income flowing seemed to contribute to a number of rather lax audits by the accounting firm Arthur Andersen (which subsequently went out of business) for companies like Enron and WorldCom. In contrast, firms can also have a positive impact on ethical decision making and behaviour. In many firms senior managers take explicit and concrete steps to encourage ethical behaviour among their managers. Although there is a variety of ways organizations might accomplish this objective, codes of ethics and whistle-blowing systems are perhaps two of the more visible efforts.

code of ethical conduct a formal statement that outlines types of behaviour that are and are not acceptable

Codes of Ethics Given the ethical dilemmas that managers face and the different approaches for evaluating ethical behaviour, many firms have adopted codes of ethics to guide their managers' decision making. A **code of ethical conduct** is typically a formal statement of one to three pages that primarily outlines types of behaviour that are and are not acceptable. Exhibit 3.3 reprints the Johnson & Johnson credo, that of one of the most respected organizations in the world. The credo was first adopted in 1945 and has been revised four times to its current version.

Exhibit 3.3 Johnson & Johnson Credo

We believe our first responsibility is to the doctors, nurses, and patients, to mothers and all others who use our products and services. In meeting their needs everything we do must be of high quality. We must constantly strive to reduce our costs in order to maintain reasonable prices. Customers' orders must be serviced promptly and accurately. Our suppliers and distributors must have an opportunity to make a fair profit.

We are responsible to our employees: the men and women who work with us throughout the world. Everyone must be considered as an individual. We must respect their dignity and recognize their merit. They must have a sense of security in their jobs. Compensation must be fair and adequate, and working conditions clean, orderly, and safe. Employees must feel free to make suggestions and complaints. There must be equal opportunity for employment, development, and advancement for those qualified. We must provide competent management, and their actions must be just and ethical.

We are responsible to the communities in which we live and work and to the world community as well. We must be good citizens—support good works and charities and bear our fair share of taxes. We must encourage civic improvements and better health and education.

We must maintain in good order the property we are privileged to use, protecting the environment and natural resources.

Our final responsibility is to our stockholders. Business must make a sound profit. We must experiment with new ideas. Research must be carried on, innovative programs developed, and mistakes paid for. New equipment must be purchased, new facilities provided, and new products launched. Reserves must be created to provide for adverse times.

When we operate according to these principles, the stockholders should realize a fair return.

An annual study conducted by the *Financial Times* and Pricewaterhouse-Coopers found that more than half of the top 50 most-respected companies in 2005 were US firms; 13 placed in the top 20 (there were no Canadian companies on the list).[22] A separate examination of 84 codes of ethics in US firms found three specific clusters of issues addressed in these statements.[23] The first cluster included items that focused on being a good "organization citizen" and was divided into nine subcategories. The second cluster included items that guided employee behaviour away from unlawful or improper acts that would harm the organization and was divided into twelve subcategories. The third cluster included items that addressed directives to be good to customers and was divided into three subcategories. Exhibit 3.4 provides a list and description of the clusters and specific categories of issues addressed in these written codes. Most firms did have items in each of the three clusters, though not in all 30 subcategories.

Exhibit 3.4

Categories Found in Corporate Codes of Ethics

Cluster 1

"Be a dependable organization citizen."

1. Demonstrate courtesy, respect, honesty, and fairness in relationships with customers, suppliers, competitors, and other employees.
2. Comply with safety, health, and security regulations.
3. Do not use abusive language or actions.
4. Dress in businesslike attire.
5. Possession of firearms on company premises is prohibited.
6. Follow directives from supervisors.
7. Be reliable in attendance and punctuality.
8. Manage personal finances in a manner consistent with employment by a fiduciary institution.

Unclustered items

1. Exhibit standards of personal integrity and professional conduct.
2. Racial, ethnic, religious, or sexual harassment is prohibited.
3. Report questionable, unethical, or illegal activities to your manager.
4. Seek opportunities to participate in community services and political activities.
5. Conserve resources and protect the quality of the environment in areas where the company operates.
6. Members of the corporation are not to recommend attorneys, accountants, insurance agents, stockbrokers, real estate agents, or similar individuals to customers.

Cluster 2

"Don't do anything unlawful or improper that will harm the organization."

1. Maintain confidentiality of customer, employee, and corporate records and information.
2. Avoid outside activities that conflict with or impair the performance of duties.
3. Make decisions objectively without regard to friendship or personal gain.
4. The acceptance of any form of bribe is prohibited.
5. Payment to any person, business, political organization, or public official for unlawful or unauthorized purposes is prohibited.
6. Conduct personal and business dealings in compliance with all relevant laws, regulations, and policies.
7. Comply fully with antitrust laws and trade regulations.
8. Comply fully with accepted accounting rules and controls.
9. Do not provide false or misleading information to the corporation, its auditors, or a government agency.
10. Do not use company property or resources for personal benefit or any other improper purpose.
11. Each employee is personally accountable for company funds over which he or she has control.
12. Staff members should not have any interest in any competitor or supplier of the company unless such interest has been fully disclosed to the company.

Cluster 3

"Be good to our customers."

1. Strive to provide products and services of the highest quality.
2. Perform assigned duties to the best of your ability and in the best interest of the corporation, its shareholders, and its customers.
3. Convey true claims for products.

Source: D. Robin, M. Giallourakis, F. R. David, and T. E. Moritz, "A Different Look at Codes of Ethics." Reprinted from *Business Horizons* (January–February 1989), Table 1, and p. 68.

A study of codes of ethics for firms in the United Kingdom, France, and Germany found that a higher percentage of German firms had codes of ethics than British or French firms (see Exhibit 3.5).[24] The greater cultural emphasis on explicit communication in Germany may partially explain this finding. Although only about one-third of the European firms in this study had codes of ethics, approximately 85 percent of US firms have formal codes.

Exhibit 3.5
Adoption of Codes of Ethics

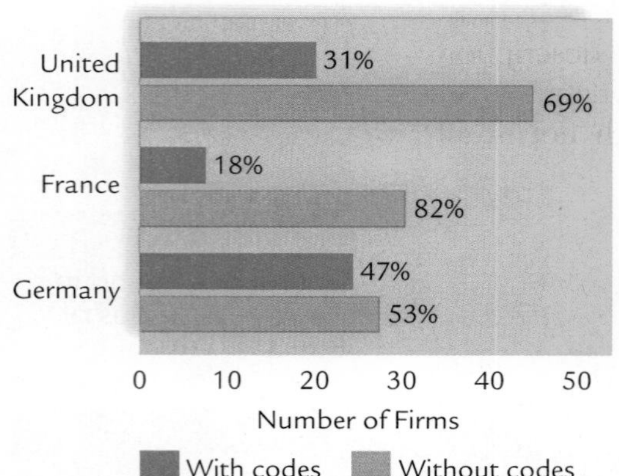

In a separate study, researchers found important differences among firms from what are generally considered more similar than different cultures: Canadian, Australian, and US firms.[25] For example, the codes of ethics differed substantially in terms of explicitly commenting on ethical conduct regarding behaviour concerning domestic government officials (59 percent of Canadian, 24 percent of Australian, and 87 percent of US firms).

Research on codes of ethics indicates that organizations believe codes of ethics to be the most effective means of encouraging ethical behaviour in their employees.[26] Indeed, if a given firm had a code that covered all 30 categories listed in Exhibit 3.4, employees would have a comprehensive guide for behaviour. Unfortunately, the research does not support a strong link between codes of ethics and actual employee behaviour. Firms without formal codes seem to have no higher or lower incidents of unethical behaviour than those with formal codes.[27]

Successfully Implementing Codes of Ethics Establishing a formal, written code of ethical conduct is an important first step for organizations to take to encourage ethical behaviour. However, actions speak much louder than words, and employees are unlikely to conform to the formal code unless other actions taken by the organization reinforce the code and communicate that the company is serious about compliance.[28] In some companies, positions of ethics officer or ombudsman are instituted. These individuals are charged with ensuring that the flow of information is rich in both directions. In other words, they have the responsibility of helping information and policies get out to the employees and also to ensure that employees' concerns, observations of misconduct, and the like can flow up and into senior management levels where action to correct things can be taken.

Communication The first step in effectively implementing a code of ethics is communicating it to all employees. For maximum impact, this communication needs to take a variety of forms and be repeated. It is not enough to simply send out a one-time memo. Rather, the code will need to be communicated in memos, company newsletters, videos, and speeches by senior executives repeatedly over a period of time if people are to take the content of the message seriously.

Training For the code of ethical conduct to be effective, people will likely need training.[29] For maximum impact, the training needs to be engaging. For example, Motorola developed approximately 80 different short cases. Each case presents a situation requiring a manager to make a decision. Individual participants in the training program were asked to decide what they would do and discuss the ethical aspects of the decision. They then compared their decisions to those of senior executives, including the CEO, and what these executives believe is in keeping with the firm's code of ethics.

Lockheed Martin also takes an engaging approach to ethics training with an interesting, innovative twist. In the late 1990s the company developed a board game based on Scott Adams's *Dilbert* character. The game consisted of 50 ethical dilemmas for which players have to decide among four possible responses. Participants rated this approach much higher in satisfaction than traditional ethics training and seemed to recall the learning points more effectively. Later, when the *Dilbert* craze wore off, Lockheed Martin used real business ethics problems as a basis for discussion. The company also has an ethics hotline employees can call if they are experiencing a business dilemma.[30]

Although officials at organizations often think that ethics training programs are effective, current research is less conclusive. What we can say based on research is that the greater the psychological and emotional involvement of participants in the training, the greater their retention of the learning points. This may explain why Lockheed Martin's experience with ethics training has been so positive.

Reward and Recognition In addition to communicating the code to employees and training them, it is critical to make sure that those who comply are recognized and rewarded. Otherwise, employees will simply view the written code as the "formal rhetoric, but not the real deal."

The US oil giant ExxonMobil is a company that recognizes the importance of this principle. It regularly celebrates stories of individuals who have honoured the company's code of conduct even when doing so might have cost the company money. For example, one of its drilling teams was setting up to drill for oil in the jungles of a developing country when a government official came by and stated that before they started the drill they needed to pay for an operating permit. However, the official wanted the payment (approximately US$10 000) paid to him personally in cash. This was against the firm's code, so the team manager refused to pay. The drilling team and their expensive equipment sat idle for more than a week at a cost of over US$1 million. Finally, the government official admitted that all the paperwork and permits were in order and the team was allowed to proceed. ExxonMobil celebrated this incident in its newsletter to reinforce to its employees that the company takes its code of ethical conduct seriously and rewards people who honour it, even if it costs the company money.

Whistle-Blowing A **whistle-blower** is an employee who discloses illegal or unethical conduct on the part of others in the organization. While some firms have implemented programs to encourage whistle-blowing, most have not.[31] As a group, whistle-blowers tend *not* to be disgruntled employees but instead are conscientious, high-performing employees who report illegal or unethical incidents. In general, they report these incidents not for notoriety but because they believe the wrongdoings are so grave that they must be exposed.[32] For example, in 2006 four mechanics employed with Air Canada Jazz made public their concerns regarding economic and scheduling pressures taking priority over flight safety. The employees were concerned that the pressure to cut corners on maintenance was going to affect flight safety. The risk taken by the employees in speaking out was great, since there are no protection laws in place for airline workers in Canada. Air Canada Jazz suspended the workers with pay for two weeks, but they also took steps to address the issues raised by the employees.[33] Research suggests that the more employees know about the internal channels through which they can blow the whistle and the stronger the protection of past whistle-blowers, the more likely they are to initially use those internal channels rather than involving external channels like the media.[34]

whistle-blower an employee who discloses illegal or unethical conduct on the part of others in the organization

In 1998, Joanna Gualtieri, a portfolio manager in Canada's Department of Foreign Affairs, reported billions of dollars spent to support extravagant lifestyles of diplomats, in violation of government laws.

Following the announcement by the Jazz employees, Canadians in support of whistle-blower protection argued that, similar to the United States, airline workers with life-or-death responsibilities should be free to voice safety concerns without penalty. In a 2005 survey, Canadian CEOs believed almost unanimously that there should be laws in place allowing whistle-blowers to sue employers who penalize them for reporting wrongful practices. Nearly two-thirds in the study also believed that third-party whistle-blower hotlines are more effective in persuading employees to come forward than hotlines operated internally.[35] In general, research suggests that the following steps can be effective in encouraging valid whistle-blowing:[36]

- Clearly communicate whistle-blowing procedures to all employees.
- Allow for reporting channels in addition to the chain of command or reporting incidents to one's boss.
- Thoroughly investigate all claims based on a consistent procedure.
- Protect whistle-blowers who make valid claims.
- Provide moderate financial incentives or rewards for valid claims.
- Publicly celebrate employees who make valid claims.

Top Management Example The impact of setting an example is probably no more evident than in the case of ethical conduct.[37] Top management, both in terms of how they behave personally and how they reward, punish, or ignore the actions of others, can severely damage the best intentions and designs of an implementation plan (e.g., communication, training, whistle-blowing, etc.). When it comes to skirting the law or making decisions that fall short when open to public scrutiny, the example of top management is often correlated with the behaviour of middle managers. Managers are rarely persuaded by top executives to "do as I say, not as I do." Leaders at Enron such as Kenneth Lay and Jeffrey Skilling set an example of reporting growth at any price. Standard accounting rules were ignored so that higher revenues and profits could be recorded immediately. Once one rule, law, or policy is ignored by senior officers, who is to say that others shouldn't be? This pattern of illegal and unethical conduct was not confined to Enron but was complemented by the behaviour of senior partners in the accounting firm that was supposed to monitor and certify Enron's accounting practices—Arthur Andersen. In an effort to retain Enron's auditing business and its more lucrative consulting engagements, leaders at Arthur Andersen ignored Enron's accounting irregularities despite its legal and ethical obligation to report them. In the end, leaders even instructed subordinates to destroy and shred documents (against company policy and legal statutes) in an effort to hide wrongdoing on both sides.

The net effect of Lay and Skilling's corruption was the complete collapse of Enron and the 2006 conviction of both men for their part in the scandal. Skilling was sentenced to more than 24 years in prison that same fall. Lay's conviction, however, was extinguished in July 2006 when he died of a heart attack before he was sentenced. As for the accounting firm Arthur Andersen, it went from one of the "Big Five" accounting firms with an employee base of 85 000 in 2001 to surrendering its licences and right to practise accounting in 2002. Only 200 employees remain to handle the lawsuits and dissolution of the firm.

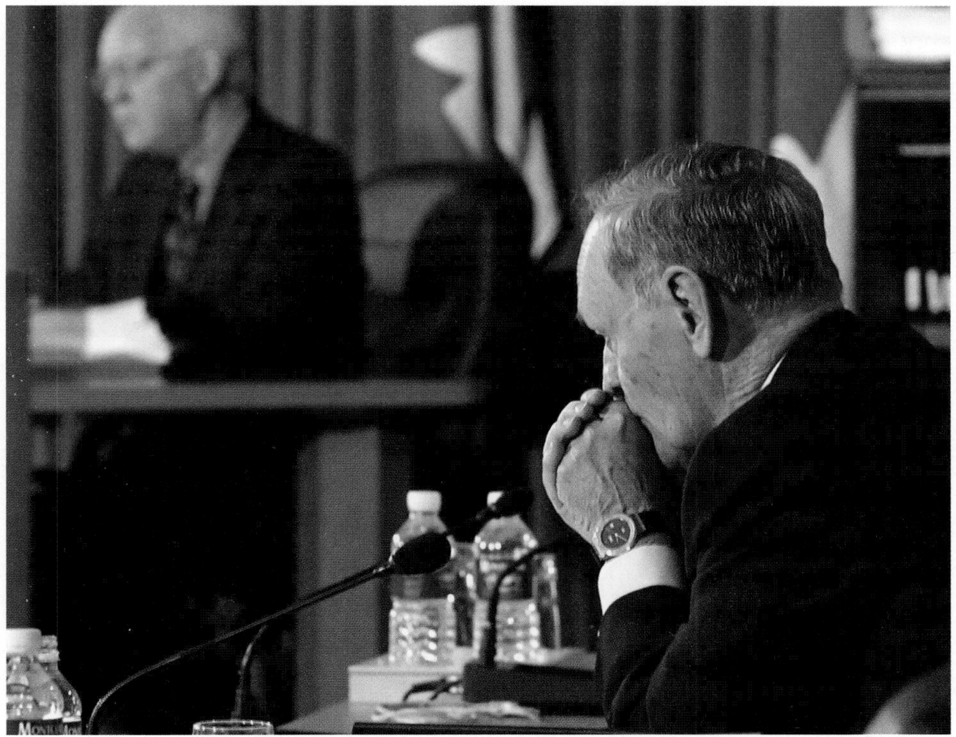

"The fish rots from the top of the head." The saying relates to the fact that people in an organization take their cues from the person leading it. Justice John Gomery, who presided over the enquiry on the 1994–2003 federal sponsorship program, stated in his 2005 report that former Prime Minister Jean Chrétien and Chief of Staff Jean Pelletier should be held responsible for mismanaging the flawed $332 million operation that provided lucrative kickbacks to Liberal supporters. While there was no direct evidence linking the two to the wrongdoings, they both failed in taking the most basic of precautions.

But by following the steps outlined earlier, managers can catch problems before they become national media events and seriously damage the firm's reputation. In addition, new laws are being passed by municipal, provincial, and the federal government to protect whistle-blowers. Employers cannot discharge, threaten, or otherwise discriminate against employees because they report a suspected violation of the law.

The Government

The governments of Canada and many other countries have continued to foster ethical behaviour. For example, the Canadian government has enacted a number of laws and regulations designed to reduce the presence of corruption in government and to encourage whistle-blowing when corrupt practices are found. Yet, the conduct of government officials often speaks louder than words.

Canada has traditionally been respected for its business practices, but a series of high-profile scandals within the government had led to a diminished confidence by business people and analysts. Transparency International prepares a Corruption Perceptions Index (CPI) that ranks countries based on the extent that businesspeople and analysts around the world perceive the presence of corruption in public officials and politicians. In 2001, Canada ranked seventh out of 91 countries in the study, with a CPI score of 8.9 out of a possible 10. By comparison, Australia ranked ninth; the United Kingdom thirteenth; the United States sixteenth, and Germany and Japan were twentieth and twenty-first, respectively. In 2005, however, Canada plummeted to fourteenth place with a CPI of 8.4. Australia remained at ninth; the United Kingdom moved up to eleventh; the United States moved down to seventeenth; Germany moved up to sixteenth; and Japan remained twenty-first.[38]

Clearly, making ethical decisions is not easy. It takes an understanding of various frameworks at the individual level and intervention at the organization and government levels if compliance with particular points of view is to be achieved. It's also clear that making the wrong ethical choice can result in serious negative results for individuals, organizations, and even nations.

While this section has focused on making ethical decisions from the individual point of view, the next section examines the general issues of ethics focusing on the organization. Typically, the issues we cover next are discussed under the general banner of corporate social responsibility.

Social Responsibility

Corporate social responsibility is concerned with the constituencies to which corporations are obligated and the nature and extent of those obligations. As media coverage has increased and organizations such as Greenpeace Canada, the David Suzuki Foundation, and Raging Grannies have put more pressure on organizations, they have increasingly come to terms with the amount of resources they should devote to being socially responsible. Consider the following questions that confront managers daily:

- Should a firm implement environmental standards greater than those required by law?
- Should a firm insist on the same high level of safety standards in all its worldwide operations even if the laws of other countries accept lower standards?
- Do all employees, regardless of nationality or employment location, have the same rights?
- Should managerial actions that are illegal or morally unacceptable in one country be allowed in another country in which they are legal or morally acceptable?
- Should managers consider the interests of employees, customers, or general citizens over those of shareholders?

Questions such as these form the substance of social responsibility debates. Both social responsibility and managerial ethics focus on the "oughts" of conducting business. Although several approaches to corporate social responsibility exist, an examination of two fundamental perspectives will help you reflect on how you personally view the issue and how you might effectively interact with others holding differing perspectives.

The Efficiency Perspective

Perhaps no contemporary person presents the **efficiency perspective** of social responsibility more clearly than the Nobel Prize–winning economist Milton Friedman.[39] Quite simply, according to Friedman, the business of business is business. In other words, a manager's responsibility is to maximize profits for the owners of the business. Adam Smith is perhaps the earliest advocate of this approach. Smith concluded over 200 years ago that the best way to advance the well-being of society is to place resources in the hands of individuals and allow market forces to allocate scarce resources to satisfy society's demands.[40]

efficiency perspective the concept that a manager's responsibility is to maximize profits for the owners of the business

Managers as Owners When a manager of a business is also the owner, the self-interests of the owner are best achieved by serving the needs of society. If society demands that a product be made within certain environmental and safety standards, then it is in the best interests of the owner to produce the product to meet those standards. Otherwise, customers will likely purchase the product from competitors. Customers are more likely to purchase from firms that comply with widely shared and deeply held social values, so it makes sense for businesses to incorporate those values into their operations and products. To the extent that the cost of incorporating society's values is less than the price customers are willing to pay, the owner makes a profit.

Critics of the efficiency perspective, however, argue that quite often customers and society in general come to demand safety, environmental protection, and so on only after firms have caused significant visible damage. For example, society might hold strong values about not polluting the water and causing health problems. However, if the consequences of polluting a river are not visible and people are not immediately hurt, social pressure might not emerge to cause the owner to align his actions with societal values until years after the fact.

Managers as Agents In most large organizations today, the manager is not the owner. The corporate form of organization is characterized by the separation of ownership (shareholders) and control (managers). Managers serve as the agents of the organization's owners. Within this context, Friedman argues that managers should "conduct business in accordance with [owners'] desires, which will generally be to make as much money as possible while conforming to the basic rules of society, both those embodied in law and those embodied in ethical custom."[41] From Friedman's perspective, managers have no obligation to act on behalf of society if doing so does not maximize value for the shareholders. For example, packaging products in recycled paper should be undertaken only if doing so maximizes shareholder wealth. Whether such an action satisfies or benefits a small group of activists is irrelevant. Managers have no responsibility to carry out such programs; in fact, they have a responsibility *not* to undertake such action if it is more costly because it does not maximize shareholder wealth. Similarly, charitable donations are not the responsibility of corporations. Instead, managers should maximize the return to shareholders and then shareholders can decide if and to which charities they want to make contributions.

Simply put, the profits are not the managers' money, so they have no right to decide how or if it should be distributed to charitable causes.

From the efficiency perspective, it is impossible for managers to maximize shareholders' wealth and simultaneously attempt to fulfill all of society's needs. It is the responsibility of governments to impose taxes and determine expenditures to meet society's needs. If managers pursue actions that benefit society but do not benefit shareholders, then they are exercising political power, not managerial authority.

Concerns with the Efficiency Perspective The efficiency perspective assumes that markets are competitive and that competitive forces move firms toward fulfilling societal needs as expressed by consumer demand. Firms that do not respond to consumer demands in terms of products, price, delivery, safety, environmental impact, or any other dimension important to consumers will, through competition, be forced to change or be put out of business. Unfortunately, however, corrective action often occurs after people are injured.

Arnold Dworkin, the owner of Kaufman's Bagel and Delicatessen in Illinois, learned to pay attention to public safety the hard way. On a Wednesday, calls trickled in to the restaurant from customers complaining of vomiting, nausea, and stomach pains, and by Friday the restaurant had to be closed. Customers were suffering from salmonella poisoning, which was traced back to the corned beef being cooked at only 90 degrees rather than the 140 degrees required by local health regulations. Although corrective measures were taken, three weeks later another customer was hospitalized with salmonella poisoning. This time the cause was traced to a leaky floorboard above a basement meat-drying table. Kaufman's lost approximately $250 000 in sales and $10 000 in food, and its insurance company paid out more than $750 000 for individual and class-action suits and hospital claims. Interestingly, because Dworkin dealt with the situation in a straightforward manner by disclosing all the information he had to customers and the media, quickly making every repair, and following all the recommended actions suggested by the safety and health board regardless of cost, his business returned to 90 to 95 percent of its original level within two years.[42]

The other major concern with the efficiency perspective is that corporations can impose indirect consequences that may not be completely understood or anticipated. In economic terms, these unintended consequences are called **externalities**. For example, the British government enticed Nissan to build a new automobile plant there with tax and other incentives. However, the trucks going in and out of the plant created traffic congestion and wear on public roads that were not completely accounted for in the government's proposal. The government had to use tax revenue collected from citizens to repair the roads damaged by Nissan, to which it had given tax breaks. These poor road conditions slowed deliveries to the factory and also created inconveniences for the citizens.

externalities indirect or unintended consequences imposed on society that may not be understood or anticipated

However, even when externalities can be anticipated, consumers often cannot correctly factor in or be willing to pay for the costs. For example, the consequences of poor safety controls at a grass fertilizer plant (explosion, fire, toxic fumes, injury, and death) are understood. As a consumer, can you correctly assess the costs of a chemical disaster and the increased price you should pay to cover the needed safety expenditures? If the answer is "No," this may cause the plant manager to skip necessary safety practices to keep costs low and make a profit. It is not until inadequate safety policies and practices result in a chemical disaster and people are killed or injured that the impact of the externality (i.e., the chemical disaster) is fully appreciated by consumers and therefore appropriately priced in the market.

Social Responsibility Perspective

The social responsibility perspective argues that society grants existence to firms; therefore, firms have responsibilities and obligations to society as a whole, not just shareholders. Thus, while the efficiency perspective states that it is *socially responsible* to maximize the return to the shareholder, the social responsibility perspective states that it is *socially irresponsible* to maximize only shareholder wealth because shareholders are not the only ones responsible for the firm's existence. For instance, creditors of a corporation cannot go beyond the assets of the corporation and seek repayment from the assets of the owners. This protection is termed *limited liability*. This privilege is granted to the corporation by society, not by shareholders.[43] Thus, the existence of the firm is not solely a function of shareholders, and therefore, the responsibilities of the firm cannot be restricted just to shareholders.

Stakeholders In the social responsibility perspective, managers must consider the legitimate concerns of other stakeholders beyond the shareholders. **Stakeholders** are individuals or groups who have an interest in and are affected by the actions of an organization. They include customers, employees, financiers, suppliers, communities, society at large, and shareholders. Customers have a special place within this set of constituencies because they pay the bills with the revenue they provide.[44] Shareholders are also given special status, but in the stakeholder approach, shareholders are viewed as providers of "risk capital" rather than as sole owners. Consequently, shareholders are entitled to *reasonable* return on the capital they put at risk, but they are not entitled to a *maximum* return because they are not solely responsible for the existence of the firm. To maximize the return to shareholders would take away returns owed to the other stakeholders. Thus, managers must make decisions and take actions that provide a reasonable return to shareholders, balanced against the legitimate concerns of customers, employees, financiers, communities, and society at large. While the evidence is not definitive, there is research to suggest that there is a positive relationship between a stakeholder approach and firm performance.[45]

stakeholders individuals or groups who have an interest in and are affected by the actions of an organization

Concerns with the Social Responsibility Perspective One of the key concerns with the social responsibility perspective is that important terms such as "reasonable returns" and "legitimate concerns" cannot be defined adequately. Given that reasonable returns to shareholders and legitimate concerns of other stakeholders could come into conflict, not knowing exactly what is reasonable or legitimate reduces a manager's ability to find the appropriate balance and act in a socially responsible way. This is why from a practical standpoint, even if you believe in the stakeholder framework of corporate social responsibility, making decisions that balance the interests of the different stakeholders is a significant challenge for which there is no magic solution. It is not only possible but also quite likely that customers, employees, financiers, communities, and society at large will have conflicting and competing concerns. Consider the case of a manager in a factory that makes corrugated boxes. His customers want sturdy boxes that can be stacked several levels high. Society increasingly seems to want a higher use of recycled paper. However, boxes made of recycled paper either have higher costs for the same strength or lower strength at the same cost compared to boxes made of nonrecycled paper. In such a case, how would you determine the most socially responsible action? If customers tell you that boxes must meet a certain strength requirement regardless of whether they use recycled paper or not, does this outweigh the desires of the other stakeholders? Should you devote more money to researching and developing stronger recycled boxes even though it takes money away from shareholders by increasing costs and reducing profits?

Comparing the Efficiency and Social Responsibility Perspectives

The efficiency and social responsibility perspectives differ mainly in terms of the constituencies to whom organizations have responsibilities. The two perspectives differ little in their evaluations of actions that either harm or benefit both shareholders and society (see Exhibit 3.6). Their evaluations differ most markedly when actions help one group and harm the other. Actions that benefit shareholders but harm the other legitimate stakeholders would be viewed as managerially responsible from the efficiency perspective, but socially irresponsible from the social responsibility perspective. Actions that harm shareholders but benefit the other legitimate stakeholders would be viewed as managerially irresponsible from the efficiency perspective, but socially responsible from the social responsibility perspective.

Exhibit 3.6
Comparing Efficiency and Social Responsibility Perspectives

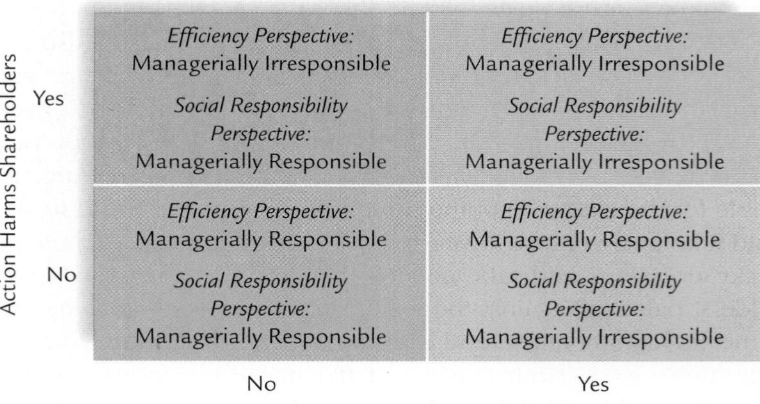

Corporate Responses

How corporations react to the various pressures and constituencies connected to the topic of social responsibility varies widely. These reactions can be simplified and laid out on a continuum that ranges from defensive to proactive, as illustrated in Exhibit 3.7. Although we might imagine that firms adopting the efficiency perspective are more likely to be Defenders, Accommodators, and Reactors, and firms adopting the stakeholder perspective are more likely to be Anticipators, we know of no research that has examined this specific association.

Defenders Companies that might be classified as defenders tend to fight efforts that they see as resulting in greater restriction and regulation of their ability to maximize profits. These firms often operate at the edge of the law and actively seek legal loopholes in conducting their business. Typically, they change only when legally compelled to do so.

Accommodators These companies are less aggressive in fighting restrictions and regulations than Defenders, but they still change only when legally compelled to do so. This type of firm tends to obey the letter of the law but does not make changes that might restrict profits if it is not required to.

Exhibit 3.7 Corporate Responses

	Defenders	Accommodators	Reactors	Anticipators
Belief:	We must fight against efforts to restrict or regulate our activities and profit-making potential.	We will change when legally compelled to do so.	We should respond to significant pressure even if we are not legally required to.	We owe it to society to anticipate and avoid actions with potentionally harmful consequences, even if we are not pressured or legally required to do so.
Focus:	Maximize profits. Find legal loopholes. Fight new restrictions and regulations.	Maximize profits. Abide by the letter of the law. Change when legally compelled to do so.	Protect profits. Abide by the law. React to pressure that could affect business results.	Obtain profits. Abide by the law. Anticipate harmful consequences independent of pressures and laws.

Reactors Reactor firms make changes when they feel that pressure from constituencies is sufficient such that nonresponsiveness could have a negative economic impact on the firm. For example, the firm might change to recycled paper for boxes only when the pressure from customers becomes strong enough that nonresponsiveness would lead customers to boycott its products or simply to choose a competitor's products that use recycled paper.

Anticipators Firms in this category tend to believe that they are obligated to a variety of stakeholders—customers, employees, shareholders, general citizens, and so on—not to harm them, independent of laws or pressures that restrict or regulate their actions. Firms in this category not only abide by the law, but they might take action to avoid harming constituencies, even when the constituencies might not be aware of the potential danger. For example, a firm might take steps to protect employees from harmful chemicals within the workplace even before employees suffer negative side effects sufficient for them to demand work environment changes or before safety laws are passed.

A Manager's Challenge: "Not in My Backyard" helps illustrate some of these corporate responses in the face of advancing and accumulating technology. It focuses on how some firms are responding to the need to plan better methods of disposing of old technology. As you read, you might ask yourself what the motivation seems to be for each of the various firms mentioned in exploring new ways to recycle e-waste. For example, the anticipators: Are they motivated primarily to try to help the environment and reduce the accumulation of toxins in landfills, or are they motivated because they believe their competitive position could be enhanced by already meeting future regulations that might be set in place? What would you do if exceeding current environmental requirements potentially hurt your business? For example, what if the cost of safely recycling your products and old technology meant that you had to charge a price higher than your competition? Or what if your market research suggested that while personal users of your equipment support your recycling policy, commercial users were unlikely to pay the premium price for the safety of proper recycling? Or what if commercial sales accounted for half of your company's total sales? What would you do?

a manager's challenge technology

Not in My Backyard: The Safe Disposal of e-Waste

What do you do when your cell phone no longer works? What do you do with the old Sony Discman players that you find when you clean out your closet? What happens to the VHS recorder that has reached the end of its useful life? How do you get rid of these electronic components when they are no longer needed? Do you bury them in your own backyard? Not likely. Most people walk the items to the curb to get picked up by the local garbage collection. For us, the electronic gadget's life is over, but for the environment, it is the beginning of years of decay and leaching of toxins and heavy metals into the soil and water table.

Canada has a voracious appetite for new technology, and as a result we are accumulating a tremendous amount of unwanted, outdated equipment. By 2010, Canada will be throwing away more than 91 000 metric tonnes of electronic equipment such as PCs, cell phones, and printers every year. In Alberta alone, 362 880 kilograms of lead from electronic equipment ends up in landfills annually. Large organizations that have equipment to dispose of end up having it shipped overseas by way of recycling brokers for disassembly. Between 50 and 80 percent of all tossed electronic equipment, or *e-waste*, finds its way to China, India, or other developing countries for dismantling. The reason old technology is sent abroad for recycling is because it's cheap. For about 5 cents a pound a firm can be rid of hundreds of outdated desktops, printers, and fax machines.

The problem with this option is the great global expense associated with the cost-efficient solution. First, it is often children that strip down the old technology into parts by hand, exposing them to an array of toxic chemicals at the most vulnerable stage of their lives. This could have long-term effects for generations to come. Second, while the parts that can be reused are distributed to plants for refurbishing, there is a hazardous contingent of components that cannot be recycled or reused. These items contain toxins such as mercury, cadmium, lead, and polyvinyl chloride and are left in mounds, seeping into the soil and groundwater in regions where adequate drinking water is already scarce.

How are we going to properly handle the increasing amount of toxic waste being generated because of our consumption of electronic equipment? One method is by safe handling of the recycling process in our own backyard where it can be properly managed and controlled. Noranda has developed an e-waste recycling facility in Brampton, Ontario, that is designed to safely shred and separate e-waste. Presently they are processing more than a quarter-million kilograms of e-waste each month, breaking it into five centimetre pieces of plastic and metal and separating it through the use of a magnetic screening process. At 45 cents per pound, however, the safer process is not as cost effective as the offshore option. Companies like Hewlett-Packard are buying into the need for a better way to dispose of technology, and they are willing to pay extra to know that their equipment is safely returned to its basic elements. Still, there are many more firms that would rather pay less for the removal of yesterday's equipment, which makes Noranda a niche player with a customer base that is comparatively small. Management at Noranda anticipated this and they have positioned the firm for the future. They are speculating that it is only a matter of time before legislation is set in place forcing companies to use facilities such as theirs to safely dispose of e-waste.

It is often children in developing nations that strip old technology shipped from North America into its various components. Exposure to the toxins in the discarded equipment could affect their physical and mental development.

Another way that the onslaught of e-waste could be managed is by building up financial resources to handle the safe disposal of e-waste. Some governments are starting to implement fees at the point of sale for new technology to cover the cost of its disposal when the item is discarded. Alberta has already set in place an environmental fee that is levied against new equipment when purchased. The fee, which ranges from $5 to $45 for new items including cell phones and large-screen televisions, will be used to safely recycle old equipment. The environmental fee should take the financial edge off the cost of safely collecting and processing e-waste. Ontario's government is also looking into a similar program.

However, the best approach by far is eliminating the presence of toxic materials in products in the first place and having manufacturers take back their own products for recycling. Greenpeace has been lobbying all major producers of technology in the hope that they will voluntarily cut back on their use of hazardous materials and initiate free "take-back" programs wherever their products are sold. In an assessment of various high-tech firms, Greenpeace found that Apple lags behind Dell, Hewlett-Packard, Nokia, and Sony. Greenpeace is focusing their polite campaign on having Apple go green in its production of Macs, iPhones, and iPods, stating "it's not about bruising Apple's image, Apple should be an environmental leader." So while Apple celebrated a momentous achievement in April 2007—the sale of 100 million iPods so far—it causes one to wonder where all of them will end up in a few years.

Sources: K. Benedict and G. Richards, "Eco Fee Boosts TV, PC Prices: Program Aims to Keep Toxins Out of Landfills," *Calgary Herald*, February 1, 2005; G. Semmens and S. Myers, "Green Tax Boosts Price of TVs, PCs: Alberta First with e-Cycle Program," *Calgary Herald*, May 7, 2004; D. McLean, "Dead Computer? Make Sure It Gets a Decent Burial," *Globe and Mail*, June 2, 2005; Greenpeace, www.greenpeace.org/apple (accessed November 6, 2006); Apple Computers, www.apple.com (accessed November 6, 2006).

managerial perspectives revisited

PERSPECTIVE 1: **THE ORGANIZATIONAL CONTEXT** When it comes to managerial ethics and corporate social responsibility, the context of the organization is extremely important. While no individual manager will likely win a court case by saying "The devil organization made me do it," it is folly to ignore the tremendous impact that the organization has on individual decisions and behaviours. For example, the company may have a code of ethics, but if its culture is contrary to the code, senior managers should not be surprised when individuals act in ways that go against the code. This is perhaps one of the strongest reasons for a well-established whistler-blower system. Even if the "flow" of the company culture is in one direction, a well-established whistle-blower system can allow conscientious employees to swim against the tide. In addition, managers need to understand the general approach the company takes toward social responsibility. Trying to take an efficiency perspective in a stakeholder-orientated company or vice versa will likely lead to frustration. The match between an individual's ethical and social responsibility orientation and the organizational context is critical. For example, applying the tactics of a Defender in an Anticipator organization or vice versa will likely hurt rather than help one's career. While this does not mean that as an individual manager you cannot or should not try to change others around you or the entire organization, it does mean that ignoring the organizational context is naïve.

PERSPECTIVE 2: **THE HUMAN FACTOR** A manager cannot achieve the desired ethical decisions or approach to social responsibility alone. While personal integrity and ethical decision making is critical for an individual manager, this alone does not satisfy his or her responsibility. Managers are responsible for leading their employees in ways that limit ethical lapses and increase the odds that they behave responsibly. This means, for example, that if your firm has a code of conduct, you have the responsibility of communicating, supporting, and reinforcing the standard with your subordinates. If the firm has a particular orientation toward social responsibility, as a manager you need to help your employees understand what it means and how it applies to the work they do and the decisions they make. Only if managers inculcate the ethical or social responsibility standards of the company in others can it truly have a pervasive impact.

3

PERSPECTIVE 3: **MANAGING PARADOXES** Meeting the challenges required to act ethically and in a socially responsible manner will require managing some important paradoxes. On the one hand, as an individual you may have your own personal standards of integrity, ethics, and social responsibility. On the other hand, as a manager you have a responsibility to uphold the standards of your company. What should you do when there is a conflict between the two? Do you have an obligation to correct inappropriate behaviours or blow the whistle on practices that are not in keeping with company policies or with legal or regulatory standards? The potential paradox between personal and company standards is one of the principal challenges managers face daily regarding ethics and social responsibilities. The other major source of potential paradox is between tolerance and compliance. In diverse cultures encountered by firms that operate globally, differences in ethical values and judgments as well as perspectives on social responsibility are inevitable. Tolerance and understanding of these differences are important. However, at the same time companies are increasingly asking their employees and managers to abide by global standards of conduct and are developing global approaches to social responsibility. As a consequence, managers sometimes face the paradox of balancing tolerance and understanding with integrated standards of conduct.

4

PERSPECTIVE 4: **ENTREPRENEURIAL MINDSET** Although managers need to be alert to identify and exploit opportunities, some especially lucrative opportunities may present ethical dilemmas. Therefore, managers will need to remain vigilant in balancing their personal standards and the organizational standards with the opportunities to earn large returns. They will need to understand fully how their actions will affect others, especially the organization's stakeholders, as revealed in U2's decision to relocate their business to the Netherlands. Establishing a values-based culture should help managers remain committed to ethical practices and social responsibilities while simultaneously remaining alert to opportunities and exploiting them. Whatever decisions are ultimately made by the organization shouldn't require a compromise of managers' personal or organizational standards. In fact, emphasizing ethical practices may actually provide the organization with new opportunities because consumers and other stakeholders value such standards. Most people want to work for or do business with ethical and socially responsible organizations.

concluding comments

There is no universal opinion concerning managerial ethics or the social responsibility of corporations. Grey areas remain, and important questions go unanswered regardless of which fundamental perspective you adopt concerning ethical behaviour or corporate social responsibility. For example, the efficiency approach argues that managers should seek to maximize shareholders' returns but must do so within the laws and ethical norms of society. In today's increasingly global environment, a given firm may operate in a variety of societies. What if the norms of one society are different than those of another? Which societal norms should be honoured?

A social responsibility approach also operates within equally large grey areas. For example, how can you calculate, let alone incorporate, conflicting needs of constituencies across countries? How can a Korean consumer's needs for low price for paper be balanced against the environmental concerns of Indonesian or Brazilian societies where large forests are being cut down to produce the paper? How can all of these concerns be balanced against the potential worldwide concern for the depletion of critical oxygen-providing trees?

In addition to the difficulty of determining the relative weight of different constituencies, managers face the challenge of trying to determine the weights of different groups within one category of constituencies across national borders. How are such determinations made? For example, firms may have employees in many countries, and the concerns of these employees will most likely differ. Employees in Japan may want the firm to maximize job security, while employees in England may want the firm to maximize current wages and be willing to trade off future job security. Similarly, German consumers may want firms to have high environmental standards, whereas Indonesian consumers may have no such concerns. Which standards should be adopted?

The general debates concerning ethics and social responsibility have raged for generations. The purpose of this chapter has not been to resolve the debate but rather to examine the assumptions and rationales of fundamental perspectives. If there were a magic formula for meeting these challenges, there would likely be little need for bright, capable people (we could just turn the problem over to computer algorithms); nor would there be much excitement in being a manager. We hope this examination enables you to evaluate your own views so that you will be prepared when situations arise concerning ethics or social responsibility. Perhaps then the pressure of the moment will be less likely to cause you to take actions that you might later regret. Understanding the general frameworks also helps you to better appreciate others who have differing perspectives and, thereby, interact more effectively with them.

key terms

code of ethical conduct 92
compensatory justice 87
concentration of effect 89
corporate social responsibility 80
distributive justice 87
efficiency perspective 99
ethical dilemmas 83
ethical lapses 83
externalities 100
justice approach 87
magnitude of the consequences 88
managerial ethics 80
moral intensity 88
moral rights approach 86
probability of effect 88
procedural justice 87
proximity 89
social consensus 88
stakeholders 101
temporal immediacy 89
universal approach 86
utilitarian approach 84
whistle-blower 95

test your comprehension

1. Define managerial ethics.
2. What are the key differences between managerial ethics and corporate social responsibility?
3. The utilitarian approach to ethics is often called the "greatest good" approach. What are the key challenges in determining the greatest good?
4. What are the two key elements of the moral rights approach to business ethics?
5. How is the universal approach different from the "golden rule" of do unto others as you would have them do unto you?
6. What are the key elements of distributive, procedural, and compensatory justice and how are the three related to each other?
7. What is moral intensity?
8. What are the six factors that influence moral intensity?

9. How are magnitude of consequences and probability of effect different?
10. Why do temporally immediate consequences usually generate more moral intensity?
11. What are the two types of proximity that can influence moral intensity?
12. According to Adam Smith, it is in the best interests of managers and organizations to make ethical decisions. What is the basis of his argument?
13. What is a code of ethical conduct?
14. What are the most common areas addressed in company codes of conduct?
15. Why do companies without codes of ethical conduct seem to be no worse off than companies with codes of conduct in terms of the number of incidents of ethical wrongdoing?
16. What are five powerful means of enhancing the influence of formal codes of conduct on actual employee behaviour?
17. What is a whistle-blower?
18. What are the key concerns with the efficiency perspective of social responsibility?
19. Who are the major stakeholders to consider from a social responsibility perspective?

apply your understanding

1. How much would you change your ethical values or standards or your view of social responsibility to fit into a company? What if you were sent on assignment to another country where the national standards seemed to differ both from the corporate ones and from your personal standards? How much would you change?
2. Which of the basic approaches to ethical decision making most closely matches your approach for dealing with ethical dilemmas?
3. What is the ethical climate like in your school? What is your school's policy or honour code concerning cheating? What is your ethical responsibility if you see someone cheating?
4. Would you be willing to be a whistle-blower? On what type of issue would you blow the whistle? Inflated overtime submitted on a government contract? Sexual harassment? What organizational and personal factors would you consider?
5. Consider the following scenario: A sales representative from a textbook publisher calls on your professor to try to get him or her to adopt a new textbook. Is it okay for the professor to accept a free lunch from the publisher's sales representative? If it is okay for a professor to accept a free lunch, what about a free game of golf? What about a free set of golf clubs after the game?

practise your capabilities

Your firm has a stated policy that emails constitute company correspondence and therefore are subject to screening. Although the policy explanation is included in the thick orientation document that every new employee receives, most employees aren't aware of the policy. Most of those who are aware of it do not believe that their email or other internet activities are reviewed by the company.

Your boss comes to you with the password to all your subordinates' email accounts and asks you to review them. He has some concern but no hard evidence that one of your subordinates may either be talking with a competitor about coming to work for them or may even be leaking sensitive marketing information to them. He instructs you to not be fooled by what appears in the subject line of the emails because anyone with any smarts would not put the real nature of the email there if they were up to something unethical. Therefore, he wants you to read through all their emails over the last four weeks and monitor them over the next few weeks until the allegation is proven to be true or groundless. He has transferred a small project from you to ensure that you have the time to complete this review over the next week.

1. What would you do? Would you take the assignment?
2. If so, why? If not, why not?

3. If you didn't want to take the assignment, how could you turn it down without hurting your relationship with your boss or potentially damaging your career?
4. Is it ethical to read email that employees may consider private?
5. Is it ethical not to inform employees of what you are about to do?

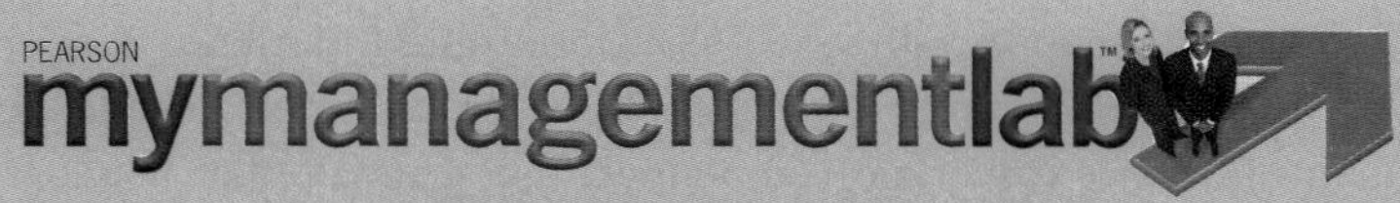

To improve your grade, visit the MyManagementLab website at **www.pearsoned.ca/mymanagementlab**. This online homework and tutorial system allows you to test your understanding and generates a personalized study plan just for you. It provides you with study and practice tools directly related to this chapter's content. MyManagementLab puts you in control of your own learning!

closing case DEVELOP YOUR CRITICAL THINKING

Blowing the Whistle in Canada Is Not for the Timid

In Canada there has been a gradual increase in legislation that protects whistle-blowers. However, the existing legislation is still limited, resulting in retaliation regularly occurring to individuals who voice concern about a misdeed. Often the whistle-blower is punished by his or her employer in the form of job loss or demotion. Even where legislation is in place, seeking restitution almost always involves a lengthy and costly legal battle, and successful prosecutions to date have been difficult. Take for example the case of Dr. Chandra at Memorial University in St. John's, Newfoundland.

Dr. Ranjit Kumar Chandra was recognized worldwide for his research in the area of nutrition and immunology when his research nurse, Marilyn Harvey, informed her employers that he was committing scientific fraud. In the late 1980s Dr. Chandra's research experience was acquired by Ross Pharmaceuticals in the United States to test whether or not their baby formulas could help prevent allergies. Around the same time, both Nestlé and Mead Johnson hired Chandra to conduct similar studies on their formula products. In 1989, Harvey realized that Chandra had published the results of the formula studies before the data had even been collected. Harvey was astonished once again when she discovered a five-year follow-up on the Nestlé study that Chandra was planning to publish. After much deliberation and worrying that she might be wrong, Harvey decided to blow the whistle on Chandra in the early 1990s.

University officials assembled a committee to investigate Harvey's allegations. Despite the committee's conclusion that Chandra had committed fraud, Chandra was not punished for his behaviour and the investigation was halted because he was threatening to sue the university. Harvey was both surprised and disappointed that the investigation had been dropped. By never having to prove the accuracy of his studies or to explain where all of his research funds had gone, Chandra was never held accountable for his fraudulent behaviour.

While blowing the whistle may have meant that Harvey was acting in the public's best interest, this honourable deed was not without its repercussions. In an effort to punish Harvey for her actions, Chandra accused Harvey in July 2000 of stealing data from another one of his studies and brought a lawsuit against her. Chandra terminated the lawsuit a few months later after Harvey proved that his allegations were false. At least one other individual had considered blowing the whistle on Chandra, but decided against it for fear of similar consequences. In 1997, Michael Kramer, a professor at McGill University, wrote a letter to Health Canada suggesting that Chandra was committing fraud. The government ignored the case because it had not funded Chandra's studies. Kramer also got the feeling that Memorial University was not eager to re-open the case. Kramer was further deterred from pursuing the case by the damage that was done to the reputations of others who had reported Chandra. Eventually Kramer decided not to continue with his investigation for fear that it would jeopardize his career.

No doubt that the repercussions to Harvey's career as a result of her reporting Chandra were negative. However, the outcome could have been much worse. Sergeant Jim Cassells, a police officer in Toronto, was faced with criminal charges after alleging cover-ups of corruption within the force. Cassells blew the whistle in May 2006 when he told the media that police had hidden and refused to investigate "cases involving alleged police brutality, public complaints, and internal corruption." Although Cassells's allegations led to a review by a senior officer with the York Region Police, they also resulted in charges being brought against him for discreditable conduct and breach of confidence under the *Police Services Act*.

A worse example still, the result of Dimitri Vrahnos's whistle-blowing was almost fatal. Vrahnos is a Vancouver man whose allegations resulted in a police investigation that led to Glen Clark's resignation as premier of British Columbia in 2001. Back in 1998, Vrahnos told police that his neighbour, Dimitrios Pilarinos, had bribed Clark in exchange for the premier's assistance in getting his application for a casino licence approved. Vrahnos's suspicions were confirmed when Clark testified that Pilarinos had charged him less than he had anticipated for renovations that were done to his home. It became evident during the trial, however, that Clark was unaware that the bill for the renovations did not include a charge for labour, and he was acquitted of accepting a benefit and a breach of trust in August 2002. Pilarinos, however, was convicted on six out of nine criminal charges. Vrahnos's house was set on fire on January 10, 2006, an act that he believes was perpetrated by a member of the Greek community as punishment for tarnishing the reputation of the community.

If the whistle-blower has the tenacity to endure lengthy legal battles, then they have a better chance of prevailing in regions where whistle-blower–protection legislation exists. In 2001, Regina resident Linda Merk began complaining to her employer about the travel expenses of two of her supervisors. Merk also informed the provincial labour standards board of the incident, and eventually she went to the police. Shortly after Merk blew the whistle, she was fired. Merk subsequently pointed out to the courts that the *Labour Standards Act* states that it is illegal for an employer to terminate an employee for reporting wrongdoing to a lawful authority. After a lower court rejected Merk's plea on the grounds that employers are not "lawful authorities," Merk challenged the decision in the Supreme Court of Canada and won, leading to changes in provincial whistle-blower legislation. After taking her case back to the lower court, Merk was awarded compensation of $200 000.

As demonstrated in Merk's case, the consequences of whistle-blowing are not always completely negative; sometimes the scandals that result from whistle-blowing can even bring about reform. In 1998, Marc Hodler, a member of the International Olympic Committee (IOC) since 1963, reported corruption in the bidding for selection of host cities, especially for the 2002 Winter Olympics. Specifically, Hodler claimed that Salt Lake City used bribes to win the 2002 Winter Games. When referring to the public scandal that was unleashed after his allegations, Hodler was quoted as saying "no revolution has been possible without scandal." Following an investigation, a record number of IOC members were eliminated and the IOC enacted a series of reforms, including a ban on visits by members to bidding cities. Despite the positive effects of Hodler blowing the whistle on corruption within the IOC, his allegations were never confirmed.

Questions

1. On your own assessment of the above cases, can you determine how the investigations could have been conducted differently to ensure justice was served?
2. What were the negative consequences that resulted from whistle-blowing? What were the positive consequences? In your responses, consider not only the whistle-blower but also the other parties involved.
3. Who should be assisting the whistle-blower through a period involving the investigation of the claims being made? Does anyone have the obligation to help and defend a whistle-blower?
4. How would you go about developing a whistle-blowing policy for an organization?

Sources: C. Catenacci, "New Brunswick—Another Province with Employment Whistleblower Provisions," www.policypro.ca (accessed October 26, 2006); CBC News, "Regina Whistleblower Wins Compensation," www.cbc.ca (accessed October 26, 2006); CBC News, "Toronto Police Whistleblower Faces Charges," www.cbc.ca (accessed October 26, 2006); N. Hall, "Whistleblower's Home Torched: Dimitri Vrahnos Believes Fire Was 'Payback' for Triggering Glen Clark Probe," www.canada.com (accessed October 26, 2006); C. O'Neill-Yates, "The Secret Life of Dr. Chandra," *The National*, www.cbc.ca (accessed October 26, 2006); S. Wilson, "Olympic Corruption Whistleblower Marc Hodler Dies at 87," CBC Sports, www.cbc.ca (accessed October 26, 2006).

Chapter 4
Managing within Cultural Contexts*

LEARNING OBJECTIVES

After reading this chapter, you should be able to:

1. Explain why a thorough understanding of culture is important for all managers.
2. Explain how culture affects managerial behaviour and practices.
3. Describe the role of fundamental assumptions in corporate, regional, or national cultures.
4. Map aspects of culture in terms of the extent to which they are deeply held and widely shared.
5. Describe the key strategies managers can use to create and change culture.
6. Explain the differences between and describe the implications of high- and low-context cultures.

GE Medical's Sick Patient in France

Senior executives at General Electric (GE), in an effort to increase its global strategic position in medical technology, bought France-based Companie Generale de Radiologie (CGR). CGR was owned by the state and manufactured medical equipment with a specific emphasis on X-ray machines and CAT scanners. When GE acquired CGR, it received US$800 million in cash from state-controlled Thomson S.A. in return for GE's RCA consumer electronics business. At the time, the acquisition of CGR was viewed as a brilliant strategic move. Combined with GE's strong position in medical imaging technology in the United States, the acquisition of CGR gave GE an immediate and significant position in Europe. GE executives projected a US$25 million profit for the first full year of operations. However, things did not turn out as the strategic planners projected.

One of the first things managers responsible for the integration did was to organize a training seminar for the French managers. They left T-shirts with the slogan "Go for Number One" for each of the participants. Although the

*Parts of this chapter have been adapted with permission from a chapter written by J. Stewart Black, appearing in J. S. Black, H. Gregersen, M. Mendenhall, and L. Stroh (Eds.), *Globalizing People through International Assignments* (Reading, MA: Addison-Wesley, 1999).

French managers wore them, many were not happy about it. One manager stated, "It was like Hitler was back forcing us to wear uniforms. It was humiliating."

Soon after the takeover, GE executives from Medical Systems headquarters in the United States sent specialists to France to fix CGR's financial control system. Unfortunately, these specialists knew very little about French accounting or financial reporting requirements. Consequently, they tried to impose a system that was inappropriate for French financial reporting requirements and for the way CGR had traditionally kept records. For example, the two systems differed on what was defined as a cost versus an expense. This cultural conflict (and the working out of an agreeable compromise) took several months and resulted in substantial direct and indirect costs.

When General Electric (GE) purchased France-based Companie Generale de Radiologie (CGR) to bolster its position in Europe, culture clashes between the two companies were legion. Some GE managers believe that the culture clash sounded a wake-up call to GE not only about its employees abroad, but also about foreign consumers and how they differ from their North American counterparts.

GE managers then tried to coordinate and integrate CGR into its Milwaukee-based medical equipment unit in several other ways. For example, because CGR racked up a US$25 million loss instead of the projected US$25 million profit, an executive from Milwaukee was sent to France to turn the operations around. Several cost-cutting measures, including massive layoffs and the closing of roughly half of the 12 CGR plants, shocked the French workforce. Additionally, the profit-hungry culture of GE continued to clash with the state-run, noncompetitive history and culture of CGR. As a consequence, many valuable managers and engineers left the French subsidiary.

GE managers' efforts to integrate CGR into the GE culture through English-language motivational posters, flying GE flags, and other morale boosters were met with considerable resistance by the French employees. One union leader commented, "They came in here bragging, 'We are GE, we're the best and we've got the methods.'" Although GE officials estimated that GE-CGR would produce a profit in the second year, it lost another US$25 million.

Despite these initial cultural blunders, today GE Medical Systems is one of the strongest global competitors in its field. In fact, some managers believe that the culture clashes experienced in France made everyone aware of the important role that national and organizational cultures play in how people see and react to different events. As a consequence, senior GE Medical Systems managers changed their mental maps to recognize that people do not view the world or management the same everywhere. To facilitate this awareness in others, general cross-cultural training, as well as training specifically in the French business environment and culture, was provided for all employees transferred to France. With this greater awareness of organizational and national culture, GE Medical Systems executives were able to leverage the knowledge and alternative perspectives of managers in the French acquisition into a powerful and globally competitive enterprise.

Sources: Personal communication, 2002; J. S. Black, H. Gregersen, M. Mendenhall and L. Stroh (Eds.), *Globalizing People through International Assignments* (Boston: Addison-Wesley, 1999).

strategic overview

As the GE Medical Systems example illustrates, even companies that have strong reputations and many years of experience can run aground on unseen cultural reefs as they navigate in today's complex business waters. Culture is important because it is a significant driver of how people see and interpret events and what actions they take. This is true whether the source of the culture is at the national, organizational, or subgroup level. So understanding what constitutes culture and what makes it so powerful in influencing organizations and their performance is important for all managers.

Many people think culture is something an organization, region, or country has—something you can see, hear, touch, smell, or taste. People who take this view often point to clothing, customs, ceremonies, music, historical landmarks, art, and food as examples of culture. For example, you might notice designated parking spots at a company and infer that the culture of the company places high value on status. You might notice that when you exchange business cards with business associates of a given culture they pay very close attention to the title on your card or education qualifications (such as CA or Ph.D.). Based on this observation, you might infer that people from that country place a high value on hierarchy. However, these cultural markers are only the most visible, and in many ways the least powerful, aspects of culture.

Culture can play a major role in organizations, with direct effects on strategic actions chosen by managers and the performance of the strategies selected. For example, most large and many small organizations now sell their goods and services in markets outside their home countries. They also frequently invest in and manage operations in other countries. To sell products in foreign markets and to establish and operate facilities in other countries requires managers to understand the cultures in those countries. Research has shown that most managers who use a strategy of selling their products in foreign markets first market their goods in countries where the cultures are most similar to their domestic environment. It is easier for managers to enter a market where the culture is similar than one which is quite different.[1] They can better understand the similar culture, requiring less adaptation to the customers and employees in that culture. For example, Canadian organizations entering into international markets may first market their products in the United States or England. If the organization is from Quebec and has a strong French influence, it might also market their products in France. As managers gain experience operating in different cultures, they are likely to expand operations to countries where the culture is less similar and thus may operate in many countries. For example, Siemens sells products in 190 different countries and has established 31 separate websites using 38 different languages.[2] To facilitate movement into new international markets, foreign organizations often develop strategic relationships with local organizations. The local business organizations know the culture in those markets, which helps the managers from the foreign company adapt to that culture.[3] Local organizations have contacts with suppliers and government units, but they also can help the managers of their foreign partner learn about and understand the new culture. Developing a better understanding of the culture will help the foreign managers to sell their products in the new market and will also help them to hire and manage the people that they employ in that new market. Thus, as organizations enter more international markets, managers must learn to manage an increasing amount of cultural diversity. That is, they must understand the different cultural values of their customers and employees, respect those differences, and adapt their products and managerial styles to fit the different cultures. An inability to understand and adapt to the local cultures will ultimately produce failure of the international operations. Therefore, success of an international operation hinges on managers understanding cultural differences before they enter foreign markets and adapting their managerial practices thereafter. It also requires that they integrate and use the cultural diversity to their advantage.

Definition of Culture

culture a learned set of assumptions, values, and behaviours that have been accepted as successful enough to be passed on to newcomers

To appreciate the full importance and impact of culture, we need to take a somewhat complex and broad view of it.[4] Although a team of anthropologists identified over 160 different definitions of culture,[5] we define it as follows: **Culture** is a learned set of assumptions, values, and behaviours that have been accepted as successful enough to be passed on to newcomers. As we mentioned earlier, it is a significant driver of how people see and interpret events and what actions they take.

As the definition suggests, a culture begins when a group of people face a set of challenges. In an organization, the culture might begin to form when the early members face the initial challenges of starting the organization—securing funding, creating products, distributing products to customers, and so on. Early leaders typically have a set of beliefs that guide their behaviours and choices. For example, a leader might believe that tight supervision of employees is best. To the extent that these early decisions and practices work, they typically are retained. This is why early leaders have a significant impact on the exact nature of the company culture.[6] The assumptions, values, and behaviours that are successful are taught to newcomers. In an organization, these newcomers are new hires. In a national culture, newcomers are essentially children born to the group or immigrants who come into the country. So for the newcomers, the culture is learned, not inherited. Culture is taught primarily through symbols and communication, such as stories, speeches, discussions, manuals, novels, poems, art, and so on. Over time, specific assumptions, values, and behaviours come to be shared among the members of the group. However, because circumstances change, what are considered successful responses at one point in time can also evolve and change. As a consequence, culture is adaptive.

With this definition of culture, you can see that the concept potentially can be applied to a group of any size. For example, a large group of people sharing a geographic boundary, such as a country, can have a culture. In fact, many of the studies of culture have used countries as the unit to compare cultural similarities and differences. Within a country, members of the same organization can share an organizational culture. As you might expect, where a smaller group resides within a larger one, such as a company within a country or a work team within a company, research has found that the culture of the smaller group is often influenced by and reflects the culture of the larger group. For example, Japanese companies tend to make decisions by consensus as a reflection of the larger societal cultural value on groups. However, throughout this chapter, whenever we talk about a particular cultural characteristic for a country, region, or company, it is important to keep in mind that there is a distribution of individuals around that characteristic. For example, while Japan as a country tends to have stronger group versus individual orientations, some individuals in Japan are more or less group oriented than the average. Likewise, some Japanese companies may have more or less of a consensus decision-making culture compared to the national culture.

Managerial Relevance of Culture

Before we dive into a deeper understanding of the nature of culture, it may be helpful to first highlight the relevance of culture to you as a manager. Fundamentally, culture is important because it is a strong driver of behaviour. As a consequence, an understanding of culture can be helpful to you in understanding why people behave the way they do and in leveraging culture to help accomplish goals as well as achieve the strategic aims of your organization.

Impact of Culture on Behaviour

As we mentioned, an understanding of culture is critical because culture can dramatically influence important behaviours. For example, culture can influence how people observe and interpret the business world around them.[7] Even when viewing identical situations, culture can influence whether individuals see those situations as opportunities or threats.[8] Culture can lead to different beliefs about the "right" managerial behaviour regarding very specific aspects of management. For example, Swedish managers seldom believe they should have precise answers to most questions subordinates ask, while the vast majority of Japanese managers think they should. Culture can contribute to pre-existing ways of interpreting events, evaluating them, and determining a course of action.[9]

Because culture is not an individual trait but a set of assumptions, values, and beliefs shared by a group, people can and do identify themselves with the culture and the group. To some extent the culture and the group are synonymous in their minds. Research has found that identification with the culture can cause individuals to exert extra effort and make sacrifices to support the culture and the people in it.[10] This means that the greater the extent to which your subordinates identify with the culture of your unit or the company, the harder they are likely to work to make it successful. If culture can significantly influence behaviours, which in turn can influence individual, group, or organizational performance, then it is critical to understand what culture is, how it is formed, and how it can be changed or leveraged.

Cultural Diversity in the Workplace

The impact of culture on perception and behaviour is perhaps more important now than ever before because of the significant increase in cultural diversity you are likely to encounter as a manager. Globalization is a critical factor in this cultural diversity. Even though cultural diversity has always existed among different national, ethnic, regional, and other groups, the globalization of business has increasingly brought that diversity together. As companies globalize and expand operations around the world, they create an increased opportunity and demand for people from different cultures to effectively interact together. One of the key consequences of globalization is that you are much more likely to work with others from a variety of cultural backgrounds. As a result, a thorough understanding of culture—its nature and influence—is a critical component of effective management in these cross-cultural settings.

However, the value of understanding culture is not confined to managers who work in multinational organizations; you do not have to move abroad to encounter cultural diversity. Even if you plan to work in a largely domestic-oriented organization, you will increasingly encounter a culturally diverse workforce and need the ability to understand people with different perspectives and behaviours. To get an idea of the greater cultural diversity you will face, simply consider the following statistics about Canada:[11]

- By 2017, one in five Canadians will be a visible minority (persons other than Aboriginal people that are non-Caucasian in race or non-white in colour), a percentage not seen since the period between 1911 and 1931.
- The highest growth rate for visible minorities will be West Asian, Korean, and Arab, each more than doubling during the period leading up to 2017.

- Nearly half of all visible minorities will be of Chinese and South Asian origin by 2017.
- By the year 2017, young Aboriginal people aged 20 to 29 will increase by 40 percent, which is more than four times the growth rate of the general population of the same age.

These and other statistics point out that as a manager you will encounter an increasingly culturally diverse Canadian workforce. These cultural differences present both challenges and opportunities for managers—challenges that if ignored will have negative consequences for individuals and their organizations, and opportunities that if captured can lead to superior outcomes and organizational competitiveness.

Culture as a Management Tool

Clearly, being an effective manager is not just about understanding others. As we stressed in Chapter 1, managers get paid to accomplish goals with and through other people. Ultimately, as a manager you need to thoroughly understand culture because it can help accomplish your managerial responsibilities. How does culture do this? Since culture is rooted in assumptions and values, once established it guides people's behaviours without overt or constant supervision. For example, as a newcomer to an organization, once you have learned through the words and actions of others that consensus decision making is the "right" way to make decisions in that company, you make decisions that way even if your supervisor is not watching. As we will discuss later in this chapter, while establishing a specific cultural value is not easy, once it is established it serves as a fairly constant guide to and influence on behaviour. An organization's culture can guide what people do and how they do it without you having to monitor and direct your subordinates constantly. This is particularly important with the increasingly complex and geographically dispersed organizations we see today. In many cases, managers may not be present to watch over and direct their people every minute. To the extent that culture can guide behaviour, it can be a powerful management tool.

Canada and its workforce are becoming more diverse, presenting managers with both challenges and opportunities. By the year 2017, for example, more than one in five Canadians will be a visible minority.

Culture can also be a powerful means of directing behaviour and accomplishing organizational objectives like outperforming competitors. A recent study conducted by the Massachusetts Institute of Technology found that firms with strong culture had better and more reliable financial performance than firms with weaker cultures. Another study of 160 companies over a 10-year period found companies that outperformed their industry peers excelled in what are called the four primary management practices: (1) strategy, (2) execution, (3) culture, and (4) structure.[12] However, as a manager, you have to be careful what you instill as the cultural values. Culture is such a strong force in shaping behaviour that the wrong culture can "lead otherwise good people to do bad things." *A Manager's Challenge: "Overly Aggressive Culture Derails Enron"* helps illustrate this problem. In this example, the culture at Enron stressed the value of achieving growth by any means and at almost any cost. As a consequence, many individuals undertook illegal and unethical actions to keep the company growing or at least make it appear to be growing. As you read this case, you might ask yourself if you have ever been part of an organization whose culture pressured you to make decisions and behave in ways that you thought were wrong. Also, you might put yourself in the shoes of an employee at Enron and ask yourself, "Would Enron's culture have influenced my decisions and ethics?"

Levels of Culture

So far we have talked about culture as though it were a single entity. This is not quite accurate. Culture consists of three distinct but related levels.[13] The structure of these elements is like a tree (see Exhibit 4.1). Some elements are visible. These are often termed **artifacts**, or visible manifestations of a culture such as its art, clothing, food, architecture, and customs. At the beginning of this chapter, we gave the example of designated parking spots as a visible manifestation of an organization's emphasis on status. The base of the culture, like the trunk of a tree, is its values. **Values** are essentially the enduring beliefs that specific conduct or end states are personally or socially preferred to others. However, what holds the tree up is invisible. Most of the components of culture lie below the surface and are hard to see unless you make an effort to uncover them. These are the **assumptions** of the culture, or the beliefs about fundamental aspects of life.

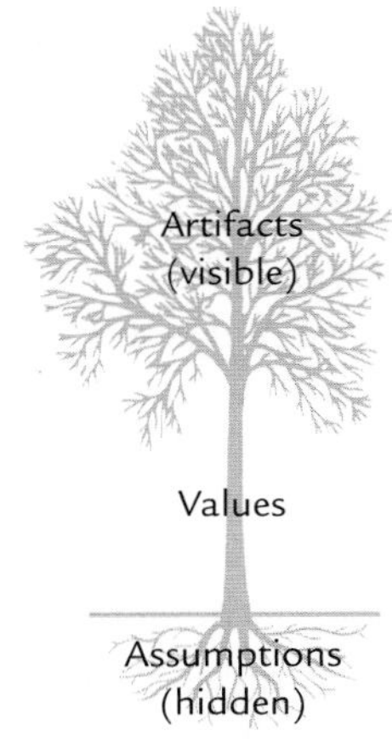

Exhibit 4.1

Levels of Culture

Cultural Assumptions

Understanding cultural assumptions is very relevant and practical for managers. Think of cultural assumptions as the soil in which the overall cultural tree grows. The nature of the soil determines many characteristics of the tree. For example, palm trees need sandy, not clay soil. In contrast, an aspen tree won't grow in the sand. Likewise, certain cultural values and behaviours are only possible with certain underlying cultural assumptions. One of the key implications for managers is that if they understand the fundamental cultural assumptions of a group, they can then begin to understand and even anticipate the values and behaviours of the group. For example, if you know that in the company you just joined hierarchy, or status levels between organization levels, is important, you can anticipate and not be surprised to find that in meetings junior managers (such as yourself) wait for senior managers to speak before sharing their own opinions.

artifacts visible manifestations of a culture such as its art, clothing, food, architecture, and customs

values the enduring beliefs that specific conduct or end states are personally or socially preferred to others

assumptions beliefs about fundamental aspects of life

a manager's challenge

ethics

Overly Aggressive Culture Derails Enron

While growth is the engine that drives shareholder value, pushing the engine too hard can cause things to overheat and then melt down. Enron's leadership did just that—it fostered a hard-charging culture in which some managers cut ethical and legal corners in the unending quest to report ever-higher earnings. Ultimately, the resulting scandal sent Enron into bankruptcy, put thousands of employees out of work, and drove a major accounting firm out of business.

Under CEO Kenneth Lay, the Houston-based company shifted from its beginnings in oil and natural gas production to a fast-growth strategy aimed at making Enron the "world's greatest energy company." Lay publicly announced extremely ambitious financial targets and promised the workforce stock options that would become increasingly valuable as the company's stock price went up. The message and value were clear: Results matter more than means—what you accomplish matters more than how you do it. "You've got someone at the top saying that the stock price is the most important thing, which is driven by earnings," one insider said. "Whoever could provide earnings quickly would be promoted." Managers' goals, performance measures, compensation, and career advancement were all geared to reinforcing a culture of growth at any price.

This culture was reinforced by selecting people from the outside who fit the company's core values. Jeffrey Skilling was one of the more visible examples of this. He joined Enron as a rising star with a strong entrepreneurial spirit. Knowing that utility customers wanted stable gas costs while gas producers wanted to charge higher prices over time, the Enron division he headed arranged long-term contracts to sell gas to utilities from a pool of suppliers. Instead of using the traditional accounting method to record revenues when received, however, Skilling insisted that Enron record all the expected revenue at the start of each contract. Thanks to this controversial approach, the company's earnings looked significantly better than they actually were, and soon Skilling was promoted to president.

Ironically, higher earnings led management to push for more and more deals so Enron could continue to report improved earnings each quarter. Despite some doubts raised by Arthur Andersen, which audited the company's financial statements, senior managers developed elaborate schemes for making earnings look better while making debt look smaller.

Can a corporation's culture be too strong? Many believe this was the case at Enron. Enron employees were pushed by top managers like CEO Ken Lay (shown in the photo at a senate hearing) and rewarded for delivering bottom-line results—even if it meant crossing ethical and legal boundaries.

Managers also fostered a culture that discouraged any internal objections to questionable activities. In fact, says a former Enron executive, "The whole culture at the vice-president level and above just became a yes-man culture." Personnel practices reinforced this. For example, risk-management employees who had to sign off on potential Enron deals were, in turn, rated by the managers whose deals they were examining. Thus, risk-management employees had a built-in incentive to endorse the deals because performance ratings had a big impact on compensation and job security. Twice a year, management rated each employee as an "A," "B," or "C." The "A" employees received much higher bonuses than the "B" employees; the "C" employees got no bonuses at all—and sometimes were forced to leave the company. Small wonder that few were willing to rock the boat. As one employee put it: "Do you stand up and lose your job?"

But losses began to mount within the special corporate entities, and concerns about Enron's accounting pushed the share price lower and lower. Unable to arrange a merger, the company finally filed for bankruptcy in December 2001. And, as mentioned in Chapter 3, Enron collapsed, Arthur Andersen lost its licence to practise accounting, and Skilling and Lay were convicted of fraud, conspiracy, insider trading, and lying to auditors.

Looking back, experts point to Enron's culture as a major factor in the debacle. Even employees and managers who felt uneasy about the company's activities went along to avoid conflict. "It was easy to get into, 'Well, everybody else is doing it, so maybe it isn't so bad,'" remembers one ex-Enron employee. Another says: "You do it once, it works, and you do it again. It doesn't take long for the lines to blur between what's legal and what's not."

Sources: "Egg on Enron Faces," *BusinessWeek*, January 12, 2004, p. 80; M. Langbert, "The Enron Mob," *Fortune*, December 22, 2003, p. 9; "The Talent Myth," *New Yorker*, July 22, 2002; J. E. Barnes, M. Barnett, C. H. Schmitt, and M. Lavelle, "How a Titan Came Undone," *U.S. News & World Report*, March 18, 2002, pp. 26+; J. A. Byrne and M. France, "The Environment Was Ripe for Abuse," *BusinessWeek*, February 25, 2002, pp. 118+; K. P. O'Meara, "Enron Board Accused by U.S. Senate Panel," *Insight*, August 19, 2002, pp. 15–17.

However, we don't want to create the impression that cultural assumptions are deterministic. Even in the natural world different varieties of trees can grow in the same soil. So it is possible for two groups to share the same assumption about hierarchy and exhibit different behaviours. In one group, junior managers only speak after senior managers. In the other group, junior managers never speak in front of senior managers.

Hopefully you can begin to see that although assumptions may seem to be the most abstract level of culture, they are in fact one of the most practical because values and behaviours grow out of assumptions. If you can understand the underlying assumptions, you can begin to understand the types of values and behaviours they support. Without an understanding of assumptions, you might make a number of mistakes in trying to comprehend, change, or even create a new culture. You might mistakenly try to change the existing culture in ways that are not possible because they conflict with the underlying assumptions. For example, if an Australian manager went to Vietnam, she might attempt to reward individual performance, believing it would improve results. However, while Australia has underlying assumptions about the importance of the individual, Vietnam does not. Its cultural assumptions focus on the importance of the group. In fact, in Vietnam, focusing rewards too much on individual performance might actually deliver worse results because people want to fit into the group and not stand out. Without understanding cultural assumptions, you might not recognize that "to change the fruits, you need to change the roots." But we will save a more in-depth discussion of changing culture for later in this chapter.

Most scholars agree that there is a universal category of assumptions represented in all groups.[14] Exhibit 4.2 summarizes these assumptions and provides examples of the specific forms they might take, as well as their management implications.

Humanity's Relationship to the Environment The first set of assumptions concerns those made about the relationship of humanity to nature. For example, in some groups the cultural assumption is that humans should dominate nature and use it for the wealth and benefit of mankind. In other groups the cultural assumption is that humans and nature should coexist harmoniously. The implications of these differing assumptions can be quite significant. The cultural assumption that people should dominate nature is prevalent in North America and can be seen in structures and industry: damming rivers for electricity, mining iron to make steel for automobiles, or logging trees to make homes. However, the implications of this belief may reach beyond these basic activities to strategic planning or management practices in business as well. Groups that assume humans must subjugate themselves to nature often are characterized by strong notions of fate. As a consequence, the idea of having a strategic planning department may run counter to their belief that it is not possible for humans to dominate something as powerful as the environment.

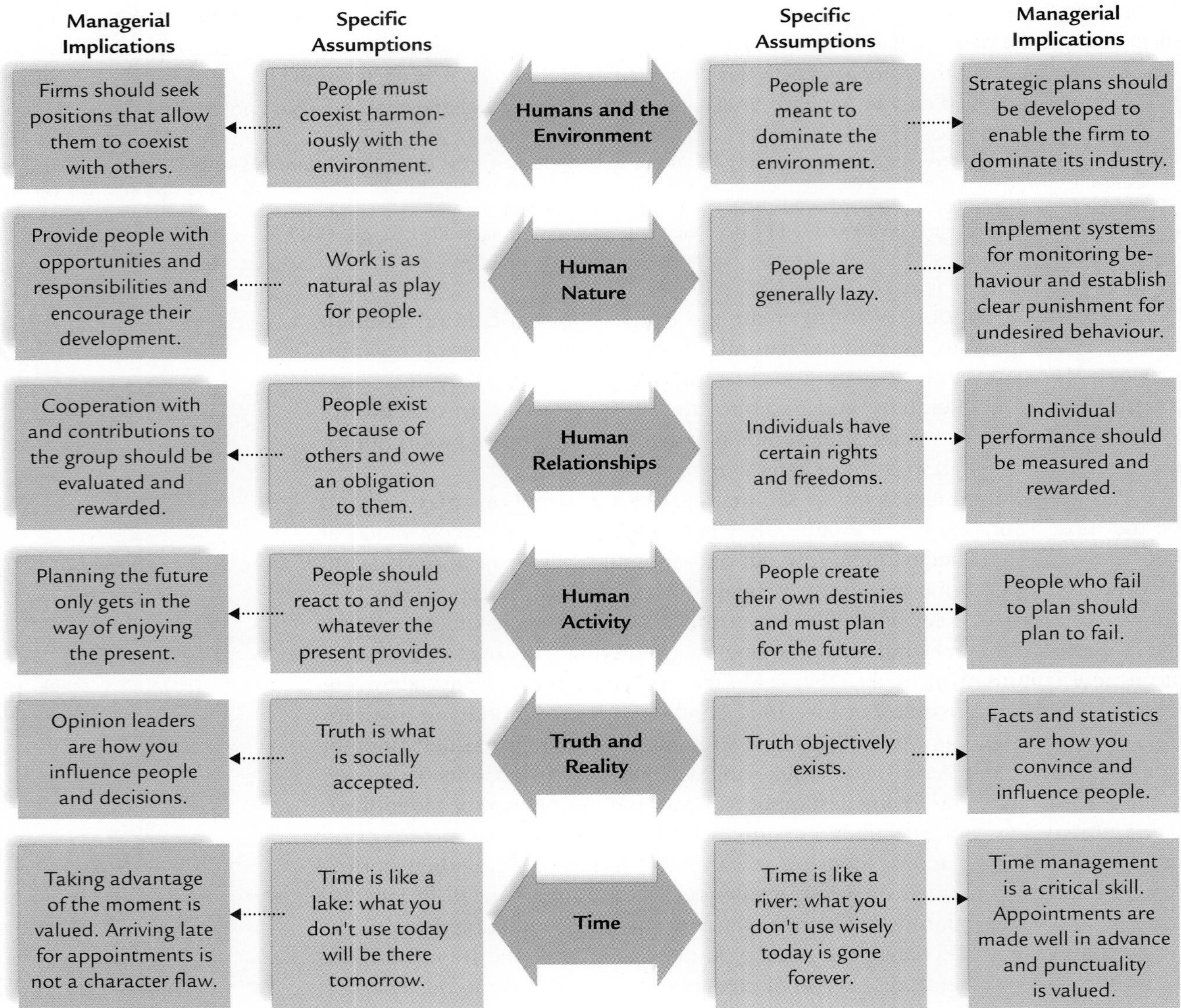

Managerial Implications
Specific Assumptions
Specific Assumptions
Managerial Implications
Firms should seek positions that allow them to coexist with others.
People must coexist harmoniously with the environment.
Humans and the Environment
People are meant to dominate the environment.
Strategic plans should be developed to enable the firm to dominate its industry.
Provide people with opportunities and responsibilities and encourage their development.
Work is as natural as play for people.
Human Nature
People are generally lazy.
Implement systems for monitoring behaviour and establish clear punishment for undesired behaviour.
Cooperation with and contributions to the group should be evaluated and rewarded.
People exist because of others and owe an obligation to them.
Human Relationships
Individuals have certain rights and freedoms.
Individual performance should be measured and rewarded.
Planning the future only gets in the way of enjoying the present.
People should react to and enjoy whatever the present provides.
Human Activity
People create their own destinies and must plan for the future.
People who fail to plan should plan to fail.
Opinion leaders are how you influence people and decisions.
Truth is what is socially accepted.
Truth and Reality
Truth objectively exists.
Facts and statistics are how you convince and influence people.
Taking advantage of the moment is valued. Arriving late for appointments is not a character flaw.
Time is like a lake: what you don't use today will be there tomorrow.
Time
Time is like a river: what you don't use wisely today is gone forever.
Time management is a critical skill. Appointments are made well in advance and punctuality is valued.

Exhibit 4.2

Basic Assumptions and Their Management Implications

Theory X managers assume the average human being has an inherent dislike for work and will avoid it if possible

Theory Y managers assume that work is as natural as play or rest

Human Nature Different groups also make different assumptions about the nature of people. Some cultures assume people are fundamentally good, while others assume they are inherently evil. You can see the direct influence of this category of assumptions in different organizations. Douglas McGregor captured this notion well in his classic book *The Human Side of Enterprise.*[15] McGregor argued that every manager acted on a theory, or set of assumptions, about people. **Theory X managers** assume that the average human being has an inherent dislike for work and will avoid it if possible. Managers accepting this view of people believe that employees must be coerced, controlled, directed, and threatened with punishment to get them to strive toward the achievement of organizational objectives. If enough managers in an organization collectively share these assumptions, the organization will have monitoring systems and detailed manuals on exactly what workers' jobs are and exactly how they are to do them. On the other hand, **Theory Y managers** assume that work is as natural as play or rest. Managers accepting this view of people believe that employees exercise self-direction and self-control to accomplish objectives to which they are committed. Commitment to objectives is a function of the rewards associated with their achievement. Organizations in which Theory Y is the dominant assumption would be more likely to involve workers in decision making or even allow them some autonomy and self-direction in their jobs. Research by the GLOBE project has confirmed this cultural dimension and demonstrated that it affects how leaders manage organizations.[16] For example, Hewlett-Packard (HP) is known as an organization with a culture based on more Theory Y assumptions about human nature.[17]

Human Relationships Assumptions about human relationships really deal with a variety of questions:

- What is the right way for people to deal with each other?
- How much power and authority should one person have over another?
- How much should someone be concerned with him- or herself versus others?

In addressing these and other related questions, Geert Hofstede studied over 100 000 employees within a single firm (IBM) across 40 different countries.[18] He found four dimensions along which individuals in these countries differed in terms of human relationships. One of those four dimensions was the construct of power distance. **Power distance** is the extent to which people accept power and authority differences among people. Power distance is not a measure of the extent to which there are power and status differences in a group—most organizations and most societies have richer and poorer, more and less powerful members. Power distance is not the existence or nonexistence of status and power differentials in a society, but rather the extent to which any differences are *accepted*. In Hofstede's study, people from the Philippines, Venezuela, and Mexico had the highest levels of acceptance of power differences. In contrast, Austria, Israel, and Denmark had the lowest levels of acceptance.

power distance the extent to which people accept power and authority differences among people

Even though North Americans tend to be at the low end of the power distance continuum, the extent to which this assumption exists can vary across organizations. For example, WestJet would be at the lower end of the power distance continuum while Air Canada would be at the higher end. At WestJet, status differentials are minimized while this and other symbols of status are more common and accepted within Air Canada.

A second dimension in Hofstede's study was the extent to which cultures valued individualism or collectivism. **Individualism** can be thought of as the extent to which people base their identities on themselves and are expected to take care of themselves and their immediate families. Hofstede's study found that people from Canada, the United States, Australia, and Great Britain had the highest individual orientations. Individuals from these countries tended to have "I" consciousness and exhibited higher emotional independence from organizations or institutions. They tended to emphasize and reward individual achievement and value individual decisions. **Collectivism** can be thought of as the extent to which identity is a function of the group to which an individual belongs (for example, families, firm members, community members, etc.) and the extent to which group members are expected to look after each other. People from Venezuela, Colombia, and Pakistan had the highest collective orientations. People from these countries tended to have "We" consciousness and exhibited emotional dependence on organizations or institutions to which they

individualism the extent to which people base their identities on themselves and are expected to take care of themselves and their immediate families

collectivism the extent to which identity is a function of the group to which an individual belongs

belonged. They tended to emphasize group membership and value collective, group decisions.

Once again, even within a society, the extent to which people within organizations share the assumption that individuals matter more than the group or that the group matters more than the individual can vary.

masculine societies value activities focused on success, money, and possessions

feminine societies value activities focused on caring for others and enhancing the quality of life

Human Activity Assumptions about human activity concern issues of what is right for people to do and whether they should be active, passive, or fatalistic in these activities. Hofstede's work also addressed this issue. He argued that there were masculine and feminine societies. **Masculine societies** value activities focused on success, money, and possessions. **Feminine societies** value activities focused on caring for others and enhancing the quality of life.

Canada is rated high on the masculine dimension, much like Japan, the United States, and some parts of northern Europe. Workers in these regions believe in phrases such as "people who fail to plan should plan to fail," and "plan the work and work the plan." In other cultures that rated higher on the feminine side, such as Norway and Sweden, emphasis on work is not as great as quality of life and a good work/life balance. Other groups hold the cultural assumption that such preoccupation with planning only gets in the way of enjoying the present.

Truth and Reality Different groups also form differing assumptions about the nature of reality and truth and how they are verified or established. In many societies, truth is assumed to exist and can be discovered through rigorous examination. In other groups, reality is much more subjective and dependent on what people believe it to be. Consequently, opinion leaders or persuasive stories rather than unshakable facts are used to influence people and business decisions in these cultures.

The famous analogy of the three baseball umpires may serve to illustrate the basic assumptions that people can make about reality and truth. The first umpire stated, "There are balls and there are strikes, and I call them as they are." The second umpire stated, "There are balls and there are strikes, and I call them as I see them." The third umpire stated, "There ain't nothing 'till I call it." Clearly, the nature of the game can change dramatically depending on which umpire is calling the pitch. Have you been in an organization in which the assumption of the first umpire dominated the group? Even if you haven't, you can probably imagine what such an organization would be like.

uncertainty avoidance the need for things to be clear rather than ambiguous

Hofstede found that cultures differ in the extent to which they need things to be clear or ambiguous. He labelled this **uncertainty avoidance**. Groups high in uncertainty avoidance can be thought of as most comfortable with a first umpire type of culture and least comfortable with a third umpire type of culture. Groups high in uncertainty avoidance create structures and institutions to reduce uncertainty. Groups low in uncertainty avoidance can be thought of as most comfortable with a second or third umpire type of culture and as disliking a first umpire type culture.

Uncertainty Avoidance by Stewart Black
PEARSON mymanagementlab

Time Different groups also form differing assumptions about the nature of time. Is time viewed as a river or a lake? Those who view time as a river generally hold linear assumptions about time. Like a river, time moves on in a linear fashion: What you do not take advantage of today will be gone tomorrow. This assumption creates a great emphasis on time management, being punctual for appointments, keeping appointment books, and so on. The phenomenal success of Franklin Quest (now FranklinCovey) through the 1990s, a producer of relatively expensive day planners, is testimony to this orientation in North America. Until the advent of electronic day planners, such as the PalmPilot, Franklin grew at a rate several times that of the general economy. It also enjoyed great success when it expanded into Japan and Korea, two other cultures with linear assumptions about time. In contrast, those who view time as a lake generally hold nonlinear assumptions about time: What you do not dip from the lake today will still be there for you to use tomorrow. This has nearly the opposite effect on management behaviours: being late for an appointment is not seen as a character flaw and setting specific day, hour, and minute schedules is seen as unnecessary.

Hofstede's work also addressed this fundamental assumption. Hofstede found that societies could be segmented based on whether they had a **short-term or long-term orientation**. Short-term–oriented societies tend to view time as a river and focus on immediate results and maximizing time management. Long-term–oriented societies tend to view time as a lake and focus on developing relationships, not expecting immediate results or returns on current efforts.

short-term or long-term orientation societies that focus on immediate results and those that focus on developing relationships without expecting immediate results

In spite of its wide acceptance, Hofstede's national culture research has stirred controversy ever since its introduction. Most recently,[19] the underlying assumptions Hofstede made about "culture" as well as the methodology used to collect data and make generalizations have come under scrutiny. Its critics also claim that Hofstede's study erroneously ignores the effects of organizational and occupational culture. Regardless of the criticism and controversy, Hofstede's dimensions of national culture remain widely used and cited in organizational studies.

All groups confront issues represented by these six categories of cultural assumptions. Different organizations can hold differing assumptions; different societies can hold different assumptions. Whether you are trying to understand an organization or a country, you must look at the fundamental assumptions first. In general, this involves asking a general set of questions. Exhibit 4.3

Exhibit 4.3

Questions to Get at Cultural Assumptions

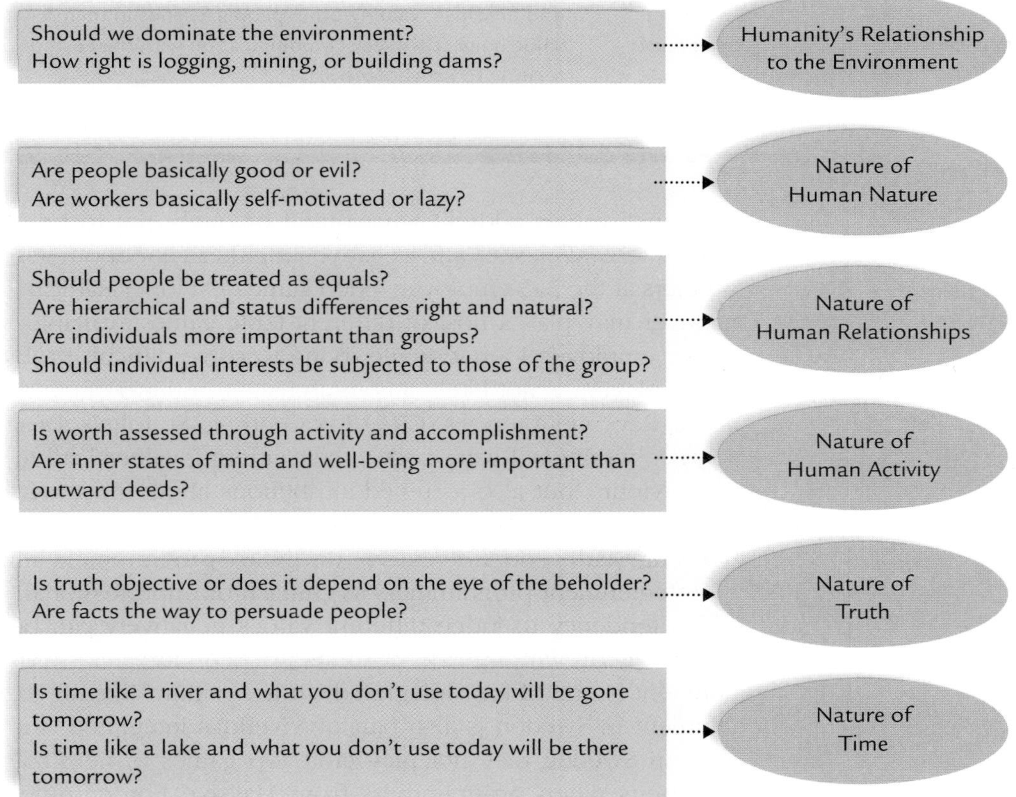

provides illustrative questions for each of the six categories of cultural assumptions. Given that all groups have formed assumptions relative to these six categories, you could use the questions to begin to understand an organization or national culture that is new to you.

Cultural Values

Remember that values are typically defined as enduring beliefs that specific conduct or end states of existence are personally and socially preferred by others.[20] Values are like the trunk of a tree, harder to see than the outline of the branches and leaves from far away but critical to the nourishment and stature of the tree. Fundamentally, values guide behaviour because they define what is good or ought to be and what is bad and ought not to be.

We can view managerial values as enduring beliefs about specific ways of managing and conducting business that have been deemed successful enough to be passed on. Although some comprehensive frameworks have been proposed for values in general (see Exhibit 4.4 for an early classic), no widely accepted framework for organizing managerial beliefs and values exists. It should also be noted that managers can possess more than one classification at the same time.

Exhibit 4.4 Classification of Values

Theoretical people	value the discovery of truth. They are empirical, critical, and rational, aiming to order and systematize their knowledge.
Economic people	value what is useful. They are interested in practical affairs, especially those of business, judging things by their usefulness.
Aesthetic people	value beauty and harmony. They are concerned with grace and symmetry, finding fulfillment in artistic experiences.
Social people	value altruistic and philanthropic love. They are kind, sympathetic, and unselfish, valuing other people as ends in themselves.
Religious people	value unity. They seek communication with the cosmos, mystically relating to its wholeness.

Source: G. W. Allport, P. E. Vernon, and Q. Lindzey, *A Study of Values* (Boston: Houghton Mifflin, 1966).

Because values address what ought or ought not to be, differences in values often lead to clashes and negative judgments about others. For example, programmers at the 245-employee video game developer Radical Entertainment in Vancouver may play a host of different table games available in their 9000-square-foot employee lounge while trying to solve difficult problems. In contrast, game playing is not likely a common sight in the programming offices of the Canada Revenue Agency's (CRA) Tax Centre in St. John's. Despite their similar jobs (i.e., writing software code), their differing values lead to not only different behaviours, but also assumed attributions about those who are not like them. Radical Entertainment programmers might look on CRA programmers as being boring, dull, and uncreative, and CRA programmers might look on Radical Entertainment programmers as childish or unprofessional.

This tendency to judge different values negatively can be problematic for an organization with operations in multiple countries. For example, Radical Entertainment is one of four integrated studios within Vivendi Games. Massive Entertainment in Sweden is also part of Vivendi's integrated studios, but programmers in Sweden may not play table-top games to help solve problems. What happens when programmers from Massive Entertainment in Malmö,

A company's culture can be the source of strengths, weaknesses, and challenges. What passes for the status quo at Radical Entertainment, such as taking time off to play a table-top game or relax in the log cabin located in the 9000-square-foot employee lounge, is likely taboo in the programming offices of the Canada Revenue Agency. The tendency to judge specific values negatively can be especially problematic within a single organization operating in different countries. Cultural differences from country to country can also pose problems for companies seeking to do business internationally.

Sweden, have to work on a project with Radical Entertainment's Vancouver programmers? It could be a barrier to productivity if the two sets of programmers do not understand each other and consequently do not trust each other.

Because values define what is good or bad, right or wrong, they not only guide behaviour but are the source of actions that you can see. In part, this is why archeologists and anthropologists seek out artifacts; they hope to find ones that will help them deduce the values of people who are no longer around to observe. In organizations, this is also why artifacts like stories can provide valuable insights into an organization's culture.

Because values guide behaviour, they are critical for any manager to understand. Not recognizing that values could be different even among employees in the same organization can often lead to unproductive clashes among employees.

Cultural Artifacts and Behaviours

The visible portions of culture are referred to as artifacts and behaviours. In general, the term "*artifact*" is most often associated with physical discoveries that represent an ancient culture and its values, such as buildings, pottery, clothing, tools, food, and art. Archeologists find artifacts when they dig in the jungles and deserts of the world looking for lost civilizations. In modern organizations, important artifacts include such things as office arrangements (individual offices for all versus open offices with no walls), parking arrangements (reserved spaces for some versus open spaces for all), or clothing. Artifacts and behaviours are closely linked. For example, while the clothing worn in an organization or even in a country might be a cultural artifact, wearing a certain style of clothing is a behaviour. But culture can influence behaviours well beyond what to wear. Culture can influence key managerial behaviours, as Exhibit 4.5 illustrates.

Cultural Diversity

As a manager, you will encounter greater diversity in organizations in the future. As we mentioned in the beginning of this chapter, diversity comes from two primary sources: (1) increased international activity of organizations and (2) greater diversity in the cultures of employees.

Exhibit 4.5

Culture and Managerial Behaviours

Culture A
Managerial Activity
Culture B
Plan for every possible contingency. Develop a plan jointly with boss.
Planning
Accept unexpected surprises. Develop a plan and then seek boss's approval.
Structure department strictly by hierarchy. Communicate frequently face to face and rarely use email.
Organizing
Organize department into free-flowing teams. Communicate infrequently face to face and frequently by email.
Inform subordinates of decisions. Intervene when there are disputes.
Leading
Involve subordinates in decision process. Allow subordinates to solve their own problems.
Closely monitor activities and directly guide behaviour. Emphasize financial results in evaluating performance.
Controlling
Evaluate and then reward based on results. Focus on customer satisfaction in evaluations.

For example, the Organisation for Economic Co-operation and Development (OECD) estimates that there were 1.17 million Canadian-born expatriates residing in other OECD member countries in 2001. The Asia Pacific Foundation of Canada includes both Canadian-born and foreign-born Canadian citizens in their estimate of more than 2.7 million Canadians residing in other countries that same year, or nearly 9 percent of the population.[21] As a consequence, managers in any type of organization need to understand culture in general, and specifically the culture of the countries in which they work and operate. With the globalization of business, there is a greater chance that you will have the opportunity to live and work in a foreign country and experience cultural diversity. However, companies are not just sending people out to their foreign operations; they are also bringing employees into their home-country operations from their foreign subsidiaries. This aspect of globalization also increases the need for an understanding of culture and how it affects people's perspectives and behaviours.

Yet the impact of globalization on cultural diversity is not restricted to employees of a company. Globalization means that as a manager you are increasingly likely to encounter and work with suppliers and customers with different cultural backgrounds. If that weren't enough, new technology has added an interesting twist to the impact of globalization on cultural diversity. New technology now allows people of different cultures to be brought together without ever leaving home. For example, teleconferencing and video conferencing capabilities allow people (employees, suppliers, customers, joint-venture partners, etc.) from all around the world to interact. A lack of understanding of culture can make these interactions less effective because when cultural differences manifest themselves, managers can misinterpret, misunderstand, and as a consequence mistrust each other.[22]

Even if you manage in an organization whose primary focus is domestic, supervisors, peers, and subordinates will not be exactly like you. Differences in age, race, ethnicity, gender, physical abilities, and sexual orientation, as well as work background, income, marital status, military experience, religious beliefs, geographic location, parental status, and education, can all influence the assumptions, values, and behaviours of people.[23] Within an organization, such diversity can enhance competitiveness or, if ignored or unmanaged, lower productivity. As

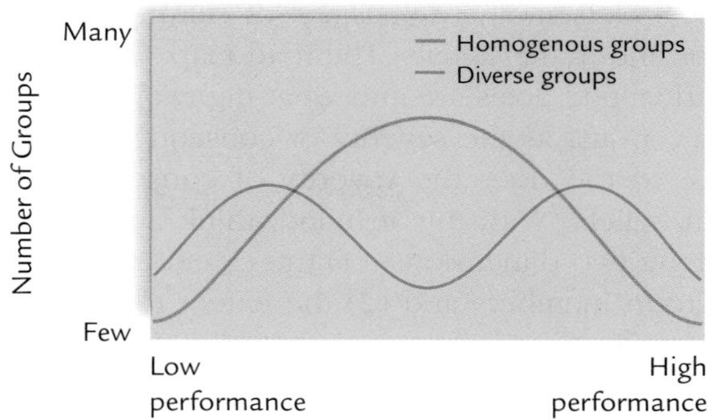

Exhibit 4.6

Effects of Cultural Diversity on Productivity

illustrated in Exhibit 4.6, culturally homogeneous groups in general produce a normal distribution; that is, most groups with culturally similar members produce average results, with a few groups doing quite well and a small minority doing quite poorly. In contrast, most culturally diverse groups either produce significantly worse or superior results with fewer culturally diverse groups producing results in the middle.[24] The culturally diverse teams that did better than culturally similar teams leveraged diverse perspectives, ideas, and innovations into superior performance. The culturally diverse teams that did worse than culturally similar teams were unable to manage the differences among members effectively. This was in part because members of these groups viewed the differences as liabilities rather than assets. Exhibit 4.7 provides a summary of the general arguments for viewing cultural diversity as an asset rather than a liability.

Exhibit 4.7 Managing Cultural Diversity for Competitive Advantage

1. Cost	As organizations become more diverse, the cost of a poor job in integrating workers will increase.
2. Resource Acquisition	Companies with the best reputations for managing diversity will win the competition for the best personnel. As the labour pool shrinks and becomes more diverse, this edge will become increasingly important.
3. Marketing	For multinational organizations, the insight and cultural sensitivity that members with roots in other cultures bring should improve marketing efforts.
4. Creativity	Diversity of perspectives and less emphasis on conformity to norms of the past should improve creativity.
5. Problem Solving	Cultural diversity in decision-making and problem-solving groups potentially produces better decisions through consideration of a wider range of and more thorough critical analysis of issues.
6. System Flexibility	Cultural diversity enables the system to be less determinant, less standardized, and therefore more fluid, which will create more flexibility to react to environmental changes.

Source: T. H. Cox and S. Blake, "Managing Cultural Diversity: Implications for Organizational Competitiveness," *Academy of Management Executive* 5, no. 3 (1991), p. 23.

Strong and Weak Cultures

Culture is not simply the total collection of a group of people's assumptions, values, or artifacts. This is because not all of the assumptions, values, or behaviours are equally influential, nor are they equally shared among members of a group. In other words, their strength varies.

Strong/Weak Culture by Stewart Black

mymanagementlab

To help in understanding this aspect of culture, think of it in terms of mental road maps and traffic signals. The road map, or culture, tells you what the important and valued goals are and what highways or back roads can get you there. However, just as the severity of consequences for assorted traffic violations varies, so too does the severity of consequences for breaching accepted cultural beliefs. With this in mind, think about **strong versus weak cultural values** along two dimensions: (1) the extent to which they are widely shared among group members and (2) the extent to which they are deeply held. This conceptualization is illustrated in Exhibit 4.8.

strong versus weak cultural values the degree to which the cultural values are shared by organization members

Exhibit 4.8

Matrix of Cultural Strength

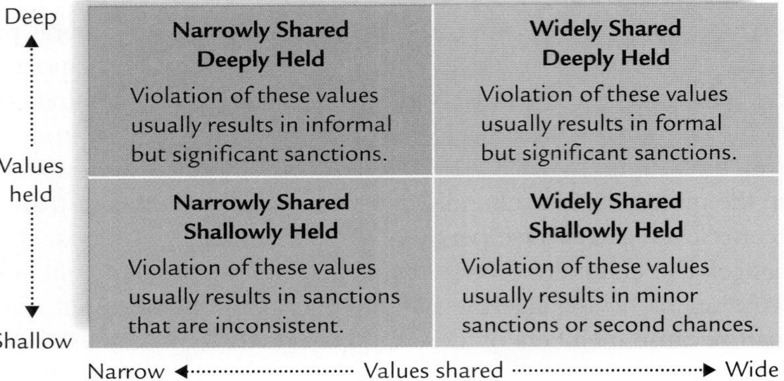

Deep
Values held
Shallow
Narrowly Shared Deeply Held
Violation of these values usually results in informal but significant sanctions.
Widely Shared Deeply Held
Violation of these values usually results in formal but significant sanctions.
Narrowly Shared Shallowly Held
Violation of these values usually results in sanctions that are inconsistent.
Widely Shared Shallowly Held
Violation of these values usually results in minor sanctions or second chances.
Narrow
Values shared
Wide

The assumptions, values, or rules of the culture that are widely shared and deeply held are generally those that are accompanied by substantial rewards or punishments. For example, an organization that deeply values customer service may provide significant rewards or recognition to employees who take steps to satisfy customers even though their actions are not specifically prescribed in a company manual. Such rewards and recognition would demonstrate the strength of customer satisfaction as a value in the organization's culture and further strengthen that value. *A Manager's Challenge: "The Beauty of L'Oréal Is in Its Employees"* illustrates this even further. As you will read, the value placed upon the employees at L'Oréal Canada creates an environment of support and reward for employees that aspire for upward mobility in the organization.

What about cases in which the value is deeply held but not widely shared? This is perhaps the best definition of a **subculture**. Organization-wide cultures may not develop because the needed conditions, such as consistent reinforcement or time, are not present. Consequently, subcultures can be as common, or in some cases more common, than an overall corporate culture, and in a study conducted in Brazilian companies, subcultural groups have been shown to have a stronger impact on performance than overall corporate culture.[25] For example, while managers in many departments within the Swedish company Ericsson might be comfortable with uncertainty, those in the accounting department are not and operate with a much higher expectation of precision. Subcultures can develop within national cultures as well. For example, in the United Kingdom, belching after a meal is considered by some to be a serious violation of proper behaviour, but this view is not held strongly by all. Consequently, you are unlikely to be put in jail for belching, but you might be cut out of particular social circles if you violate that rule. In other cultures, you may offend a host by *not* belching after a meal because it indicates that you were not satisfied with the meal.

subculture where values are deeply held but not widely shared

In the case of widely shared but not deeply held rules, violations of the rules often carry uniform but rather mild punishments. In many cases,

a manager's challenge | change

The Beauty of L'Oréal Is in Its Employees

L'Oréal, a company originally established in France in 1909, has a long history in Canada. Cosmair Canada, a Hamilton-based subsidiary of L'Oréal, began distributing L'Oréal products to Canadians in 1958. Today, L'Oréal Canada is headquartered in Montreal, employing 1200 people across the country, including 850 in Montreal. Now the leader in the Canadian cosmetics industry, L'Oréal Canada manufactures and distributes a wide range of products including cosmetics, skin care, sun protection, hair care, and hair colour products.

L'Oréal Canada reports that their success is due to the passionate, enthusiastic, and dedicated people they employ. The company's culture is centred on employee development and professional growth. In order to mould employees to fit the company culture, L'Oréal regularly hires young university graduates who have not yet adopted a corporate culture radically different from their own. Not only does this facilitate learning, it also allows L'Oréal to invest in developing its employees to advance their careers, thereby creating upward mobility and a sense of loyalty to the company. Movement within the company is strongly encouraged as a means of facilitating professional development, whether it is through a change in divisions, professions, or an international transfer.

New recruits undertake a training process that begins with an integration stage that introduces them to L'Oréal's structure, history, strategy, and activities. This stage also functions as a catalyst for new relationships within the company. On-the-job training, which lasts for approximately six months, begins after the integration stage, and is then followed by technical and sales training. The final stage in the training process is the personal and management development stages, which hone management skills and maximize an employee's potential.

Although training ends, the learning never stops at L'Oréal; the company believes in providing its employees with many opportunities to develop professionally and accelerate their careers. Employees are regularly assessed to pinpoint areas where improvement may be needed and where opportunities for career advancement exist. Additionally, communication and management seminars are held in conjunction with various training programs, tailored to the career aspirations and educational levels of the employees. Training is provided via intranet sites, on-site training, and at various management development centres located around the world. For those interested in pursuing post-secondary education, L'Oréal also offers a tuition reimbursement program, further emphasizing the company's commitment to continuous learning.

L'Oréal is also a strong example of well-integrated diversity in the workforce. Employees come from a wide variety of cultures, age groups, and backgrounds, each bringing a different and valuable perspective to the company. Collaboration is encouraged by enabling diverse team structures, which in turn generates creative ideas. In addition to various employee surveys, L'Oréal publishes two in-house newsletters designed to keep employees current on issues and events. Employees are also kept informed by the company's intranet and electronic news screens located throughout the workplace. The Montreal office also provides employees with a coffee bar where they can relax and exchange ideas before work.

L'Oréal offers its employees a flexible benefits package, allowing them to select a plan that best suits their individual needs. Top-up payments for parents taking parental leave, on-site daycare, and Fridays off through the summer are just some of the options that are offered to cater to the needs of young families. Profit sharing, a foosball table in the corporate headquarters lounge, and a wellness program that includes flu shot clinics and skin protection seminars are just a few of the other perquisites of working for L'Oréal Canada. As the leading cosmetics company in Canada, L'Oréal attracts employees who are motivated by competition and have a desire to remain the market leader. In return, L'Oréal can boast a turnover rate of just 2 percent and sales of $747 million in 2007, up 6 percent from the previous year.

Sources: "At a Glance," L'Oréal Canada, www.en.loreal.ca, accessed June 29, 2007; "Our Culture," L'Oréal Canada, www.en.loreal.ca, accessed June 29, 2007; "Ethics and Values," L'Oréal Canada, www.en.loreal.ca, accessed June 29, 2007; "Training and Development," L'Oréal Canada, www.en.loreal.ca, accessed June 29, 2007; "Career Management," L'Oréal Canada, www.en.loreal.ca, accessed June 29, 2007; "Benefits Package," L'Oréal Canada, www.en.loreal.ca, accessed June 29, 2007; Eluta Inc., "Canada's Top 100 Employers 2007: L'Oréal Canada Inc.," www.eluta.ca, accessed June 29, 2007; S. Dougherty, "L'Oréal Canada Invests Serious Time in Each Employee's Potential: Cosmetics Giant Claims Turnover Rate of Just 2% after 3 Years," *Edmonton Journal,* October 14, 2006, p. 15; S. Whittaker, "Good Morale Is More Than a Cosmetic Exercise," working.canada.com, accessed June 29, 2007; A. Pangarkar and T. Kirkwood, "L'Oréal: Selling Learning Internally," www.clomedia.com, accessed June 29, 2007.

infrequent violation of these rules may carry no punishment at all. We might label this a superficial rule because, while it is widely shared, it does not have deep roots. For example, not interrupting people when they are talking to you is a generally accepted rule of conduct in Canada. However, if one occasionally interrupts it is unlikely that this behaviour will be accompanied by any serious punishment.

The importance of conceptualizing cultural values in terms of their strengths is that you then recognize that not all aspects of a culture are created equal. As we will explore shortly, even when we boil culture down to its most fundamental elements, the number of specific assumptions, values, beliefs, rules, behaviours, and customs is nearly infinite. Consequently, trying to learn about all aspects of a new corporate or country culture can be overwhelming. The simplified matrix presented in Exhibit 4.8 provides some mental economy in trying to understand a new culture. This is likely to be of particular relevance to you as you enter a new organization after graduation.

Imagine your first day on the job. There are a million things to learn about the culture of the company and therefore how others might expect you to act. Where should you start? First and foremost, because rewards and punishments are greatest for those aspects of culture that are widely shared and deeply held, these values and rules are worth learning early. While true mastery of a culture may require understanding all aspects of the culture, focusing first on the widely shared and deeply held values can facilitate early learning and adjustment. In a practical sense, learning these values first can keep you from making costly mistakes and damaging your job performance and reputation. As a simple example, in some companies coming late to work or leaving early is no big deal. What you accomplish rather than the hours you work is what is valued. In other companies, the fastest way to get your career derailed is to come in late or be seen rushing out the door at 5:00 p.m.

What if you want to be a force for change and improvement in the company? Where should you start (or not start)? To the extent that a specific behaviour is widely shared, deeply held, and directly related to one or more of the six fundamental assumptions, the behaviour will be difficult to change. It might be called a **core value**. If you fail to recognize that you are trying to change a core value, you are likely to make the common mistake of directing too few resources and too little effort at the target of change and as a consequence fail. The point here is not that core values should never change but that if they need to change, the resources directed at the change need to match the requirements.[26]

core value a value that is widely shared and deeply held

Understanding the core values of a company can also be important when you are looking for a job. As a newcomer to the organization, you should place a premium on making sure that the organization's core values match your own. You are unlikely to be able to change a company's core values and will not be very happy in an organization with core values that clash with yours.

The simple matrix in Exhibit 4.8 can also be of practical value in international business. A business operating in several countries may have to modify its management approach if it conflicts with core values of a foreign country. For example, in North America, most people strongly believe that rewards should be tied to individual behaviour and that they should not be distributed equally among members of a group regardless of individual performance. This belief is supported by deep-rooted assumptions concerning individualism. The success of a company like Wardrop Engineering in Winnipeg can be attributed in part to the cash bonuses paid, which are based upon individual performance and can sometimes increase an employee's salary by more than 50 percent.[27] Imagine the difficulty a firm from a more collectivist country like Japan might have in expanding operations to an individualist country like Canada. In Japan, bonuses are based almost entirely on company performance—everyone at a given rank receives essentially the same bonus, regardless of individual performance. What if Japanese managers tried to implement this type of group or collectivist reward system in Canada? How successful would it be?

Creating and Changing Organization Culture

Since organization culture can be a mechanism for guiding employee behaviour, it is as important as the company's compensation or performance evaluation systems. In fact, to create and reinforce a particular set of values or corporate culture, alignment between the desired values and other systems in the organization, like the compensation system, needs to exist. *A Manager's Challenge: "One Call; That's All"* illustrates how a manager at FedEx managed the demands for cultural change when new technology was introduced in its call centres. It also helps illustrate how both performance management and rewards had to be changed to change the culture. As you read this case example, what do you see as the role of technology in changing the culture?

Today's organizations face business environments that are more complicated and more dynamic than perhaps at any other point in history. If an organization tried to create specific policies for all possible situations in such a dynamic environment, the resulting manual would be several phone books thick, and consequently of little practical use. Furthermore, by the time it was printed and distributed, the environment probably would have changed enough to make it obsolete. If, on the other hand, employees could be given a set of assumptions and values to use in assessing situations and determining appropriate actions, then the organization could distribute a simple and short booklet on the company's values and let that guide behaviour. Because of this, organizational culture, which many managers originally thought was a "fluffy" topic, is now being seen as a strategic issue that can have a significant impact on the firm's bottom line.

For example, research has found that the similarity or difference between two organizations forming a joint venture (JV) has a significant impact on the success and performance of the joint venture. The greater the organizational cultural differences between the organizations, the more difficulty the JV has. Also, the more different the managers try to make the JV corporate culture from each of the original partners' culture, the more difficulty the JV has. Successful ventures, however, need not necessarily create an "even" blend of corporate cultures. A study of 17 Hungarian–Western cooperative ventures shows that most have successfully adopted the values, practices, and systems of the Western partner.[28]

But what can managers do to create effective cultures or to change cultures that are ineffective to match the environment? There are at least five critical strategies for effectively managing organizational culture (see Exhibit 4.9). In fact, you can think of them as spokes on a wheel. When all five are in place, the wheel of an organization's culture is much easier to push to where you want it to go.

Selection

One way to create or change a culture is to select individuals whose assumptions, values, and behaviours already match those that you desire. Disney uses this mechanism with great success in creating a culture of "guest" service in its theme parks. In fact, former president of Euro Disney (now called Disneyland Paris) Steve Burke attributes some of that park's early problems to poor selection practices and hiring individuals whose attitudes toward friendly

a manager's challenge | technology

One Call; That's All

In 1998, FedEx saw the internet as an important new technology that could change its business. Management felt that if customers could check on the status of their packages any time of day or night, without having to be put on hold when call centres were busy, they would be even more satisfied. By 1999 the company had created a website where customers could log in and determine the status of their packages.

As customers used the internet and the website to answer basic questions, they increasingly phoned the call centres with more sophisticated questions, along with questions specifically about the website. Unfortunately, call centre reps had no access to the website and were trained in very narrow specialties. Consequently, call centre reps would often pass customers along in a series of call transfers to someone they hoped could answer the customer's question. These transfer calls were often dropped, which frustrated customers. Even when calls were not dropped, customers were still frustrated by what seemed like an endless series of handoffs.

The challenge of changing the technology and its use fell to Laurie Tucker, the manager of all customer service centres. To help senior managers see the basic need for change, she created a short video demonstration for the board. It showed a customer calling in while looking at the website, posing a number of questions while the call centre rep apologized because he could not see the site. Senior management subsequently gave approval for what became known as "OneCall." The vision of OneCall was that a customer should be able, in one call, to get the desired information and not be passed on to someone else.

Call centre reps were initially uneasy about the OneCall vision because they had specialized knowledge and wondered how they could possibly answer all questions a customer might ask. Furthermore, most had little or no experience with the company's website. Not only would reps need web access; they would also need training on how to use the company's website and how to walk people through the site. In addition, call reps had to be cross-trained in various tasks so customers did not get passed along in a frustrating series of handoffs.

Once call reps were given the technology and the training, Tucker and her team also had to change how performance was measured to change the culture from one of specialization to one of full service. Previously, call reps were measured and rewarded on call-time objectives. In other words, the more calls you handled in a day, and therefore, the shorter you made each call, the better. This contradicted the vision of OneCall. As a consequence, the old call-time measures and rewards had to be dropped. Reps were rewarded with bonuses based on customer satisfaction, which included a variety of dimensions such as efficiency, accuracy, and friendliness.

The results of achieving this level of belief were significant. In fact, within a few short months one of the early centres to undergo the transformation generated US$10 million in additional sales from delighted customers. Today, of course, the internet is used by so many businesses, it may sound strange that a company like FedEx once struggled to integrate it effectively. The fact is, however, that new technologies are evolving at an ever-quickening pace, so the same sort of learning and adapting process is constantly ongoing.

Source: A. G. Keane, "Relax, It's a FedEx Ad," *Traffic World*, September 15, 2003, p. 33; personal communication, 2002.

customer service were not compatible with Disney's culture. This was also one of the first things Burke changed upon his arrival in France, which he felt contributed to the dramatic turnaround of the park.[29]

Socialization

Even if selection is not perfect, congruent cultural values can be introduced and reinforced in new hires through socialization. These efforts might include early orientation, training, and arranged interactions with experienced organizational members on a group or individual level. But managers should keep in mind that individuals are not just blank sheets upon which the organization can write whatever cultural scripts it desires. Individuals actively seek out information

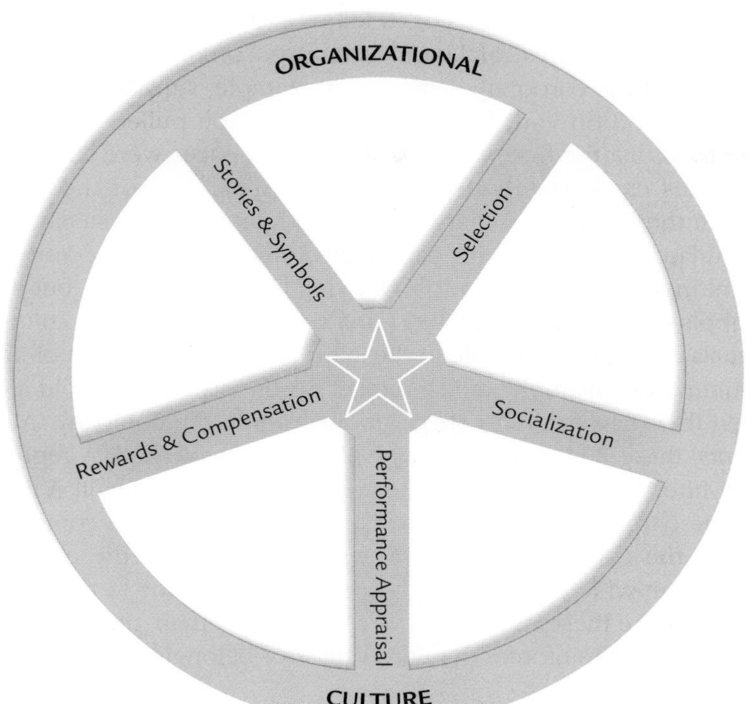

Exhibit 4.9

Strategies to Manage Organizational Culture

and try to learn the organization's culture.[30] Consequently, managers should try to facilitate these efforts and monitor them to ensure that individuals are truly coming to a correct understanding of the organization's culture.

Performance Appraisal

Few things signal what the organization values more clearly to newcomers in an organization than what it measures and evaluates. For example, it would do L'Oréal Canada little good to claim that the organization values customer service but then evaluate employees primarily on punctuality.

Rewards and Compensation

Rewards and compensation may be among the most powerful means of signalling what the organization values and reinforcing desired behaviours in newcomers. If we return to the L'Oréal Canada example, it would do the company little good to talk about customer service as a cultural value and then base bonuses on stockroom inventory control. As we explained earlier in this chapter, the best way to get repeat customers who will purchase most of their cosmetics from you is to serve them better than anyone else. As a manager, it is important to remember that although you may not be able to change the formal reward and compensation system of the organization, you directly control many informal rewards that can significantly affect subordinates (which will be discussed in more detail later in Chapter 10 on motivation). For example, what you praise and recognize people for can significantly influence their values and behaviours.

Stories and Symbols

Organizational culture is also created and reinforced through a variety of symbols and stories, which can be a powerful means of communicating company values. Basically, organizational stories tell employees what to do or what not to do. Symbols like physical layout can also communicate and reinforce specific values of the corporate culture. For example, suppose you were hired by Company X and on your first day at work, as you pulled into the parking lot, you noticed that the first two rows of parking spaces were all reserved and that the spaces closest to the front door were reserved for the most senior executives in the company. What values would you begin to suspect the company held relative to hierarchy or participative decision making? You obviously would want more information before drawing final conclusions, but seemingly small symbols can communicate and reinforce an organization's culture.

rituals symbolic communication of an organization's culture

Rituals also play a key role in the symbolic communication of an organization's culture. For example, in Japan most major corporations hold a common ritual when their newly hired college graduates join the company. Along with their parents, these new hires gather at a large assembly hall. A representative of the new hires pledges loyalty to the company on their behalf. A representative of all the parents then gives a speech in which he or she commends their children into the company's hands. A senior executive of the company then gives a speech in which he vows on behalf of the company to take care of and continue to nurture these new hires. More effectively than any memo or policy statement, this ritual reinforces the core values of belonging and loyalty.

International Contexts and Cultures

All of the basics of culture that we have covered thus far apply to cultures at a national or local level. However, just as it is sometimes difficult to generalize about an organization-wide corporate culture, so too is it difficult to generalize about national cultures. Important subcultures often exist within the boundaries of a nation. Interestingly, Hofstede's study, which has been criticized because it consisted of subjects from within one company, adds important insights precisely *because* all the subjects are members of the same organization. The organization was IBM, which in general is thought to have a rather strong corporate culture. This strong corporate culture might have dampened the differences across national cultures. Yet, in general, Hofstede found greater differences in cultural values between nationalities than within nationalities.

cultural context the degree to which a situation influences behaviour or perception of appropriateness

Perhaps one of the most useful concepts for examining and understanding different cultures is cultural context.[31] **Cultural context** is the degree to which a situation influences behaviour or perception of appropriateness. In high-context cultures, people pay close attention to the situation and its various elements. Key contextual variables are used to determine appropriate and inappropriate behaviour. In low-context cultures, contextual variables have much less impact on the determination of appropriate behaviours. In other words, in low-context cultures the situation may or may not make a difference in what is considered appropriate behaviour, but in high-context cultures the context makes all the difference. For example, in Japan there are five different words for the pronoun "you." The context determines what form of the pronoun "you" would be appropriate in addressing different people. If you are talking to a customer from a large company like Matsushita who holds a significantly higher title than yours and is several years older, you would be expected to use the term *otaku* when addressing the customer. If you were talking to a subordinate who is several years younger than yourself, *kimi* would be the appropriate pronoun. Exhibit 4.10 provides a list of some low- and high-context cultures.

High/Low Context Culture by Stewart Black
mymanagementlab

Exhibit 4.10 Low- and High-Context Cultures

Low-Context Cultures	High-Context Cultures
American	Vietnamese
Canadian	Chinese
German	Japanese
Swiss	Korean
Scandinavian	Arab
English	Greek

Source: Adapted from E. Hall, *Beyond Culture* (Garden City, N.Y.: Doubleday, 1976); S. Rosen and O. Shenkar, "Clustering Countries on Attitudinal Dimensions: A Review and Synthesis," *Academy of Management Review* 10, no. 3 (1985), p. 449.

With this in mind, consider some of the issues in managing people who come together from high- and low-context cultures. For example, imagine a team composed of one person each from Canada, Australia, Korea, and Japan. The team meets to discuss a global production problem and report to a senior executive from a client company. For the two individuals from low-context cultures (Canada and Australia), the phrase "Say what you mean and mean what you say" would not only be familiar but would seem right. Consequently, if the senior executive asked if something could be done and the team had already discussed the impossibility of the task, the two team members from the low-context culture would most likely say "no." To say "yes" when you mean "no" would not be right regardless of the fact that a senior executive from a client is in the room. They would likely view someone who would say "yes" when they meant "no" at best with suspicion and at worst as a liar. Yet for the two team members from high-context cultures, the fact that a senior executive from a client is in the room asking the questions makes all the difference in the appropriate response. For them, in this situation saying "yes" when you mean "no" would be entirely appropriate. To say "no" without consideration of the context would be evidence of someone who is unsophisticated, self-centred, or simply immature. Imagine the consequences if the Canadian replies that what the client is asking for is not possible while the Korean member of the team says it is. Not only would the client be confused, but imagine the attributions that the Canadian and Australian would make about their Japanese and Korean team members and vice versa. Without understanding the influence of cultural context, the trust and effectiveness of the team could break down almost instantly.

From a practical perspective, the key issue is to recognize that neither high-context nor low-context cultures are right or wrong; they are just quite different. These differences can influence a number of important managerial behaviours, including communication, negotiation, decision making, and leadership. While we will examine many of these implications in greater detail in subsequent chapters, *A Manager's Challenge: "When In Rome, How Far Should You Go?"* helps illustrate the concept and some of its implications, by specifically looking at gender stereotypes. It points out that a lack of awareness of this fundamental dimension of cultural differences can lead to misinterpretations, mistaken attributions, mistrust, and ineffectiveness. In contrast, changing yourself and adopting certain behaviours can create goodwill and more effective working relationships. In reading this case, do you think that trying to change oneself and adapt to a new culture can be taken too far? If you were working in a foreign country, which values would be the hardest for you to change?

a manager's challenge | globalization

When In Rome, How Far Should You Go?

Women in business face several challenges stemming from gender stereotypes, particularly when conducting business in foreign cultures. The business world remains predominantly male in many countries around the globe, and the idea that women participate in executive positions within a corporation is rarely accepted elsewhere as it is in North America. For example, 57 percent of Canadian women who export their goods or services report having come up against challenges related to their gender. Cultural differences and a lack of respect as business owners are the two most frequently cited reasons for these difficulties when exporting.

To be successful in conducting business abroad, it is essential to learn about and to adapt to cultural differences. Businesswomen should take steps to learn the customs and business etiquette of the country they will be dealing with; this is particularly important when visiting a culture where women do not usually climb to higher corporate positions. Businesswomen should prepare by reading about the culture of the country they will be travelling to. Other travellers can also serve as an excellent source of advice on international business trips.

Respect for local traditions and customs is second only to competence as a necessary ingredient for success abroad. Although there are far fewer women in managerial positions in countries outside North America, in many countries businesspeople will assume that North American women are competent if they have been sent abroad. Other cultures' opinions of women may sometimes be hard to understand, and might even be offensive, but cultural sensitivity and tolerance should be maintained at all times in an effort to ensure that the business trip is successful.

With careful preparation before departing for a foreign country, there are many ways to break down cultural barriers when conducting business. Greeting a business host in their language is a thoughtful and effective way to show respect during the first meeting. Similarly, distributing business cards with English printed on one side and the host's language printed on the other shows consideration for the other culture while simultaneously communicating rank and position within the company. It should be noted, however, that the appropriate way for handing out and receiving business cards varies significantly between cultures, and

To be successful, managers doing business in another country need not only be competent but also informed about the culture in which they are operating. For example, exchanging business cards is a formal ritual in Asia whereas in North America it's treated more casually.

should therefore be learned before departure. For example, in China and Japan one should use both hands when accepting a card, whereas in certain parts of the Middle East only the right hand should be used, as the left hand is considered unclean.

As is expected in any business setting, clothing attire should be appropriate and modest; in some cultures the colour of clothing has specific significance. In Japan, for example, red is considered too provocative. Food etiquette is also a necessity and varies significantly between cultures. Specifically, one must learn how to decline food in a polite manner to avoid offending the host.

Of particular concern to businesswomen is how to interact with businessmen in other cultures. Women should be aware that in certain countries businessmen may attempt to flirt with or proposition visiting businesswomen. Instead of becoming offended, it is better to answer with an assertive "no." Another safety measure that women should abide by is to never give out her room number, but to plan to meet business contacts in the lobby of the hotel.

All of these recommendations for global businesswomen can be refined down to a few guidelines about working overseas:

1. Learn as much as possible about local and business cultures.
2. Dress conservatively.
3. Be patient.

4. Take cues from those around you.
5. Take advantage of opportunities to socialize.

While all of this advice sounds fine, some women who are faced with conducting business internationally wonder how much they should change and adapt when the local culture is fundamentally different from their own sense of self and from their firm's corporate culture.

Sources: "The Complexities of Women Doing Business Abroad," www.divine.ca, accessed May 17, 2007; Foreign Affairs and International Trade Canada, "Consular Services: Her Own Way: A Woman's Guide to Safe and Successful Travel," August 2006, www.voyage.gc.ca, accessed May 17, 2007, pp. 26–27; R. Bajpai, A. Fung, J. Guyon, P. Hjelt, C. Kano, and R. Tomlinson, "Family Ties," *Fortune*, October 13, 2003, pp. 113–115; S. Taylor, N. Napier Knox, and W. Mayrhofer, "Women in Global Business: Introduction," *International Journal of Human Resource Management*, August 2002, pp. 739–742; K. Melymuka, "Global Woman," *Computerworld*, August 6, 2001, pp. 34–35; Foreign Affairs and International Trade Canada, "Businesswomen in Trade: Research & Stats: Facts and Figures on All Women Exporters," 2002, www.dfait-maeci.gc.ca, accessed May 17, 2007.

managerial perspectives revisited

PERSPECTIVE 1: **THE ORGANIZATIONAL CONTEXT** The context of the organization plays a central role in the management of culture. As we've pointed out, a strong culture can be an effective influence on daily behaviour even when no one is looking. What the content of that culture should be is largely a function of the organization—what its objectives are, what its history has been, and so on. It is virtually impossible to say that certain cultural values should be the core ones for every organization. At one organization customer service may be a core value. At another innovation may be a core value. The context of the organization is especially important when cultural change is needed. How entrenched the old culture is constitutes one of the most important factors to understand when contemplating a cultural change. A cultural value that has existed for a long time and has had a history of success can be one of the most difficult elements of an organization to change. This is also true not just for organizations, but for individuals. For example, if you believe in creativity and innovation for the successful management of programmers, and have achieved this through informal "jam sessions" late at night with pizza and rock music, you may have a hard time changing to the more structured approach of programmers in Germany when you are sent there on a special assignment. In this sense, even in the same company, the context of the organizational unit can make all the difference in how even common objectives like innovation are achieved.

PERSPECTIVE 2: **THE HUMAN FACTOR** Unlike a computer or telephone system, culture only makes a difference with and through people. As a manager, whether you are changing or strengthening a corporate culture, you can only accomplish this by working through people. Part of the challenge is first understanding the different values and beliefs that your employees may have as a function of different family, religious, ethnic, educational, international, or other experiences. If strong organizational cultures are already established then you have to understand where people are today, not just where you want things to be tomorrow. For example, you may want performance to improve, but using individual rewards and recognition may not be the best approach if your subordinates have a strong cultural value regarding groups. In the context

of working with peers, subordinates, and even bosses who have different cultural backgrounds from your own, the ability and desire to understand their values and beliefs is critical to determining where common ground might be or what changes might be required of them or you to work effectively together.

PERSPECTIVE 3: MANAGING PARADOXES Respecting cultural differences while trying to foster cooperation for collective achievement is just one of the many paradoxical challenges related to culture. Clearly, insisting on a common culture without understanding or respecting individual or group differences is unlikely to be effective. At the same time, tolerating differences without ensuring some degree of cooperation when needed is also unlikely to produce desired results. This challenge becomes even more acute when individuals from different nationalities and cultures have to work together within an organization. A common culture can provide unifying direction for cross-cultural teams within a company. However, failure to leverage the cultural diversity of the team members could potentially lead to ineffective team decisions and poor performance. How can you balance the dual objectives of integration while simultaneously tolerating cultural differences? Managers who are uncomfortable with this paradox and don't enjoy working through challenges like this are unlikely to be successful in a business world that is increasingly integrated and diverse.

PERSPECTIVE 4: ENTREPRENEURIAL MINDSET An important part of an entrepreneurial mindset is being open to new ideas, opportunities, and perspectives. While this openness is almost always beneficial, it is particularly beneficial in the context of culture. Managers with an entrepreneurial mindset are more likely to be open to and perceive value in cultural diversity. Diversity in a team setting, for example, should facilitate the development of multiple alternatives and additional opportunities because of the different viewpoints provided by the team's members. An entrepreneurial mindset is also likely to help managers be more open to entering new international markets. This in turn has been shown to provide managers with new technological expertise, which aids them in developing and introducing new products.[32]

Similarly, individuals from different cultures have different behavioural patterns and accomplish tasks differently. This creates other learning opportunities for managers. These learning opportunities can transform managers into innovators and entrepreneurs who will lead their organizations to success. However, absorbing this information and putting it to use requires personal reflection and self-examination. Why? Because understanding people who are different from ourselves, culturally or otherwise, can be challenging.[33] Without a good understanding of your own values and beliefs and why you hold them, the likelihood that you'll realize what others have to offer isn't great.

concluding comments

We hope this chapter has demonstrated that what we wear, how we talk, and when we speak are all heavily influenced by cultural assumptions, values, and beliefs. Groups, whether a department, a company, or a country, typically develop a shared set of mental road maps and traffic signals to effectively interact with each other. The managerial challenge relating to culture is threefold: understanding, changing, and leveraging culture.

In understanding cultures, you should keep in mind that culture consists of assumptions, values, and behaviours and that these elements of a given culture exist because they have been successful in the past. The six basic areas of assumptions that have been presented can facilitate your ability to understand a new culture. This is not to say that every behaviour, custom, or tradition you observe can be traced directly to one of these six categories of assumptions. But many of the fundamental aspects of a culture can be linked to beliefs about humanity's relationship to the environment, human nature, human relationships, human activity, truth and morality, or time. The more widely and deeply the assumptions and values are shared, the stronger the cultural value. The stronger a particular cultural value, the greater the rewards or punishments associated with compliance or noncompliance and the more difficult it is to change.

Changing a culture is always a challenge. Behavioural change and compliance can be achieved with enough monitoring and reinforcement. But doing so will extract a heavy cost of time, energy, and money if the new behaviours are not consistent or compatible with widely shared and strongly held values and assumptions. For example, Japanese executives discontinued wearing traditional kimonos and instead changed to wearing Western clothes in the early 1900s. However, Japanese executives did not adopt Western individualistic values and start wearing all sorts of different styles of business attire. You only need to spend a few moments in any business district in Japan to see that the modern business attire (dark suit, white shirt, modest tie) is as pervasive as traditional kimonos were. Why? Because in Japan people value the group and conforming to it more than individuality. This is a core value, and it has not changed. With this in mind, the challenge in effecting change is to link new desired behaviours to existing values and assumptions. Where this is not possible, old cultural trees—soil, roots, trunk, leaves, and all—must be extracted and replaced with new ones. For most people, this is traumatic, and they usually resist the effort. So to be successful, you must correctly determine not only the behaviour, values, and assumptions that fit with the environmental conditions, but also the change strategy and the amount of *effort needed* to implement it effectively. In addition, the behaviours of those espousing the new culture must be congruent, or in other words, managers must "walk the talk." Employees are quick to pick up on inconsistencies between espoused and actual values and will ignore the "talk" and follow the "walk."[34]

The third challenge lies in using cultural diversity effectively. In today's environment, you will encounter individuals—whether customers, competitors, suppliers, subordinates, bosses, or peers—who have a different cultural background from your own. They will have assumptions, values, beliefs, communication styles, management philosophies, and decision-making processes different from yours. Research suggests that if you simply label those differences as good or bad based on your own assumptions and values, you are not likely to be effective in culturally diverse management situations.[35] If, however, you stop and say, "That's interesting; I wonder why it's that way?" you are more likely to be effective in a diverse environment.

key terms

test your comprehension

1. List three reasons why it is important for you as a manager to have a solid understanding of culture.
2. Define culture.
3. Describe the three levels of culture.
4. What are the key differences between artifacts and assumptions?
5. Describe the six basic assumptions.
6. Do most companies in Canada hold a dominance or harmony assumption regarding humanity's relationship to the environment?
7. What are the key differences between Theory X and Theory Y managers?
8. Define power distance and provide an example of how it affects managerial behaviour.
9. Define individualism and collectivism and provide an example of how they affect managerial behaviour.
10. Would someone from a high-uncertainty-avoidance culture be more likely to believe managers should or should not have precise answers to questions raised by subordinates?
11. Are individuals who believe "time is a river" more or less likely to be late for appointments?
12. Culturally diverse groups often do significantly better or worse than culturally homogeneous groups. What is the key explanation for this?
13. How does the extent to which cultural values are widely shared and/or deeply held affect the strength or weakness of a culture?
14. What is a subculture?
15. What are two practical reasons for identifying the core values in an organization's or country's culture?
16. What strategies can managers use to create or change culture?
17. What are the key differences between high-context and low-context cultures? How do they affect managerial behaviour?

apply your understanding

1. The stronger an organizational culture, the greater the impact it can have on behaviour; however, the stronger the culture, the more difficult it is to *change*. Unfortunately, the environment changes, and values that fit the environment today may be inappropriate tomorrow. What can an organization do to keep the positive aspects of a strong culture and still reduce the risk of becoming extinct by not changing its culture fast enough to accommodate environmental shifts?
2. All organizations have cultures. What are the key cultural aspects of your school? What links are there between key assumptions and values and visible artifacts such as clothing, behaviour, or rituals? Compare your school's culture with that of other schools: How do they differ? How are they the same?

3. If you look forward to working with individuals from a variety of cultural backgrounds, or perhaps even working in foreign countries, what can you do to better prepare yourself for those opportunities?

4. What are the key work values you want in an organization you work for? List at least five. How can you assess the extent to which potential employers have these desired values?

practise your capabilities

John Smith accepted a one-year internship to work in a Japanese company in Tokyo. John had studied some Japanese in university but was not yet proficient in the language. Soon after he arrived in Japan, he received a very thorough orientation to the company, including introductions to all the staff in the department to which he was assigned. His job was primarily to edit and proof English correspondence sent to overseas customers and suppliers.

John quickly settled into his job and felt that he was doing well. Still, he felt that despite his efforts to get to know and be friendly with his colleagues, they always seemed a bit cool and standoffish. Then one night one of the younger workers invited him to a group dinner. The group consisted of several younger staff, the assistant manager, and the department manager.

Dinner was a light affair at a local restaurant. Everyone seemed very relaxed and joked with each other and with John. While people spoke mostly in Japanese, everyone, including the assistant and department managers, was careful to chat with John. After dinner the group went to a nearby karaoke bar where they had drinks and sang songs in English. They loved it when John sang "My Way." By the end of the evening, everyone was laughing and joking nonstop. As John left the group to board his train home, he felt that he had finally broken through and become one of the gang.

The next morning he couldn't wait to get to work and enjoy this new level of friendship and personal relationships. He smiled and tried to joke with several colleagues soon after arriving at work, but was stunned when they acted as if the previous evening had not even happened. They were all back to their "business" selves, especially the two managers. Was last night just a chance for them to poke fun at him? Was it all a sham? Were they embarrassed to be seen as friendly with John (a foreigner) in front of people from other departments? Were they all just two-faced hypocrites who could not be trusted?

1. What explains the change in behaviour toward John?
2. What should John do? Should John confront one of his colleagues at work and ask him or her what is going on? Should he just forget it? Should he try to talk with one of the guys after work? Should he give up on trying to become friends?

closing case DEVELOP YOUR CRITICAL THINKING

Forming the Olympic Spirit: Zero to 100 in Twelve Months

It can take many years to create a culture that is embraced by everyone within an organization. Culture formation can be further complicated when an organization doesn't have the luxury of time for the necessary culture to take root. This is the case for the organizing committee of the Vancouver 2010 Winter Olympics. The planning and preparation for the Games requires hundreds of participants in advance of the event, with its ultimate dissolution shortly after the Olympic flame has been extinguished.

The Vancouver Organizing Committee (VANOC) for the 2010 Winter Games was faced with this challenge when it was established on September 30, 2003. Soon after VANOC was formed, the organization developed a mandate, mission, and vision to guide the organization toward the primary goal of a successful 2010 Winter Games. Unlike most organizations, VANOC was faced with the challenge of rapid employee growth to be followed by a quick disbanding after the 2010 Winter Games. In the span of twelve months (mid-2004 to mid-2005), VANOC went from zero to 100 employees, a number that will continually increase to 1200 by early 2010. An additional 3500 temporary employees will also be hired in 2009 to assist in delivering a quality event. Once the games are over in March 2010, the number of employees will drop to 50, and then close out at zero.

The constant influx of new employees makes it challenging to create and maintain VANOC's organizational culture, particularly when everyone that is employed is faced with certain termination in 2010. The task of developing a strong corporate culture at VANOC is complicated further by the diverse backgrounds of employees as well as the uncharacteristically young age of its workforce. However, to the advantage of VANOC, younger employees are less likely to be concerned with the short-term nature of their employment and are more likely to thrive on the dynamic and autonomous work environment.

John Furlong, CEO of the Vancouver Organizing Committee, must maintain an equilibrium that allows the organization to grow as needed without sacrificing a collective sense of purpose toward a successful event. In an effort to select employees with passion and dedication, VANOC screens its candidates closely. Candidates applying for executive positions are required to complete a personality profile that, among other attributes, measures an individual's ability to deal with ambiguity. Candidates applying for lower-level positions are screened in person by recruiters who are trained to determine whether they will fit in with the value structure being set at VANOC.

Once a candidate is invited to work for the organization, they are introduced to VANOC's corporate culture through an orientation session. The orientation emphasizes the values of teamwork, trust, excellence, sustainability, and creativity. One of the main reasons that employees choose to apply and stay with the organization is the emotional connection to the Games. Knowing this, managers at VANOC leverage the employee's connection to the Games to build a culture and identity over a relatively short period of time. Until the close of the Vancouver 2010 Winter Olympics, the culture will be continually reinforced by all levels of management through regular expression of the organization's values as well as an emphasis on the Olympic spirit.

Questions

1. What actions do you think will have the greatest impact on forming a culture within the Vancouver Organizing Committee?
2. Do you think forming the Vancouver Organizing Committee culture is critical to its improved performance?
3. What outcomes would you want to measure to determine if your actions are working or not?

Sources: P. Brethour, "Torch Passed on to a New Generation," *Globe and Mail*, May 29, 2007, p. B4; P. Brethour, "Shaped by the Crucible of Chaos," *Globe and Mail*, May 28, 2007, p. B3; P. Brethour, "How to Build the Games—in 1,000 Days," *Globe and Mail*, May 26, 2007, p. B4; VANOC, "Information 2010: April 2007," www.vancouver2010.com, accessed June 19, 2007; VANOC, "Our Vision, Mission, Values," www.vancouver2010.com, accessed June 19, 2007; VANOC, "Fact Sheet: The Vancouver Organizing Committee for the 2010 Olympic and Paralympic Winter Games (VANOC)," www.vancouver2010.com, accessed June 19, 2007.

Part One **integrative case**

ICFAI Center for Management Research

Xerox—People Problems

By A. Mukund

"Over the years, they've hyped their HR organization, but it ain't a pretty picture."

—Jim W. Lundy, former Xerox manager, in August 2001

Introduction

In August 2000, Paul Allaire, chairman of the leading document management company Xerox, fired the company's CEO Rick Thoman. Commenting on his decision, Allaire said, "We are grateful for Rick's contributions in leading the company through a period of major repositioning. However, both Rick and the board felt it best for the company to move forward with an experienced Xerox team that will lead Xerox people and efficiently execute the strategy." The move attracted a lot of media attention with analysts commenting how Allaire had himself persuaded Thoman to leave a top position at IBM in 1998 and join Xerox.

Thoman, who was second only to IBM head Lou Gerstner, had also been the senior vice president and general manager of IBM's Personal Systems Group, one of IBM's most troubled operating units, which he helped turn around. Prior to this, he had also been the president and CEO of Nabisco International, president and CEO of American Express International, and chairman and co-CEO of American Express Travel Related Services Co.

However, company observers were not very surprised by Allaire's decision, as from the time Thoman had joined Xerox in May 2000, the company had lost around $20 billion in market value. Thoman was reportedly made to resign for his apparent failure to arrest this massive decline. Allaire made Anne M. Mulcahy the president and chief operating officer and reinstated himself as the CEO, though he was past the company's mandatory retirement age for executives.

Although analysts agreed that Thoman had failed to a certain extent at Xerox, they also argued that he seemed to have been made a scapegoat. Allaire's return as the CEO sparked off a round of heated debates regarding Thoman being blamed for the company's troubles, while Allaire himself was being blamed for being party to the deterioration of Xerox's work culture over the decades.

Background Note

The Xerox story goes back to 1938, when Chester Carlson, a patent attorney and part-time inventor, made the first xerographic image in the United States. Carlson struggled for over five years to sell the invention, as many companies did not believe there was a market for it. Finally, in 1944, the Battelle Memorial Institute in Columbus, Ohio, contracted with Carlson to refine his new process, which Carlson called "electrophotography." Three years later, the Haloid Company, maker of photographic paper, approached Battelle and obtained a license to develop and market a copying machine based on Carlson's technology.

Haloid later obtained all rights to Carlson's invention and registered the "Xerox" trademark in 1948. Buoyed by the success of the Xerox copiers, Haloid changed its name to Haloid Xerox Inc., in 1958, and to The Xerox Corporation in 1961. Xerox was listed on the New York Stock Exchange in 1961 and on the Chicago Stock Exchange in 1990. It is also traded on the Boston, Cincinnati, Pacific Coast, Philadelphia, London, and Switzerland exchanges. The strong demand for Xerox's products led the company from strength to strength and revenues soared from $37 million in 1960 to $268 million in 1965.

Throughout the 1960s, Xerox grew by acquiring many companies including University Microfilms, Micro-Systems, Electro-Optical Systems, Basic Systems, and Ginn and Company. In 1962, Fuji Xerox Co., Ltd., was launched as a joint venture of Xerox and Fuji Photo Film. Xerox acquired a majority stake (51.2%) in Rank Xerox in 1969. During the late 1960s and early 1970s, Xerox diversified into information technology business by acquiring

Scientific Data Systems (makers of time-sharing and scientific computers), Daconics (which made shared logic and word processing systems using minicomputers), and Vesetec (producers of electrostatic printers and plotters).

In 1969, it set up a corporate R&D facility, the Palo Alto Research Center (PARC), to develop in-house technologies. In the 1970s, Xerox focused on introducing new and more efficient models to retain its share of the reprographic market and meet competition from U.S. and Japanese companies. While the company's revenues increased from $698 million in 1966 to $4.4 billion in 1976, profits increased fivefold from $83 million in 1966 to $407 million in 1977.

According to analysts, Xerox management failed in giving a strategic direction to the company as it ignored new entrants (Ricoh, Canon, and Sevin) who were consolidating their positions in the lower-end market and in niche segments. The company's operating costs (and therefore, the prices of its products) were high, and its products were of relatively inferior quality compared to its competitors'. Return on assets soon reduced to less than 8 percent and market share in copiers came down sharply from 86 percent in 1974 to just 17 percent in 1984. Between 1980 and 1984, Xerox's profits decreased from $1.15 billion to $290 million.

In 1982, David T. Kearns took over as the CEO. He discovered that the average cost of Japanese machines was 40 to 50 percent of that of Xerox, which allowed it to undercut Xerox's prices effortlessly. Kearns quickly began emphasizing reduction of manufacturing costs and gave new thrust to the improvement of quality by launching a program that was popularly referred to as "Leadership through Quality." In addition, he initiated major efforts to develop innovative new copiers and related products. He also worked toward re-establishing the entrepreneurial culture at Xerox. Management layers were cut, greater authority was delegated to lower levels, and employees were allowed to participate in decision making.

In the 1980s, Xerox bought Kurzweil, Datacopy, and Ventura—companies that specialized in optical character recognition, scanning and fax machines, and desktop publishing. It also diversified into financial services, insurance, and investment banking. Allaire succeeded Kearns as the new CEO in 1990 and immediately embarked on a major restructuring program to sharpen Xerox's focus on document processing. In 1992, Xerox entered into various tie-ups with Dell Computer Corporation and Microsoft. In the same year, the company announced a worldwide restructuring program including a 10 percent reduction in the workforce. Over the next few years, the company expanded its global network further by setting up/strengthening facilities and research centers in various parts of the world.

In 1993, Xerox announced a companywide initiative to reduce costs drastically and improve productivity. The company indicated that it would reduce the worldwide workforce by more than 10,000 and close or consolidate a number of operations. This restructuring program achieved pre-tax cost savings of approximately $350 million in 1994, $650 million in 1995, and $770 million in 1996. Xerox reinvested a major portion of these cost savings to streamline business processes and support expansion plans in growth markets. As a result, the company's gross margins improved from 40.7 percent in 1994 to 43.6 percent in 1995.

In 1998, Xerox announced another round of worldwide restructuring, including the elimination of 9000 jobs through voluntary reduction, early retirement, and layoffs, and the closing and consolidation of various facilities. Xerox announced another worldwide restructuring program to cut costs, improve productivity, and spur growth. The program included cutting costs by $1 billion, sale of $2 to $4 billion worth of assets, and elimination of 5200 positions worldwide. In the same year, Thoman replaced Allaire as the CEO, though Allaire continued as chairman. Despite these restructuring efforts, poor market conditions resulted in the company reporting a loss of $257 million on revenues of $18.7 billion in 2000.

People Problems—I

In the initial years, Xerox's work culture was reported to be the "envy of the corporate world." The company's chairman, Joseph C. Wilson, and his successor, Kearns, were lauded for forming a positive culture at the company that went on to play a major part in establishing its supremacy in the copier business. A former Xerox HR executive said, "Wilson brought in progressive HR people schooled in HR at outstanding institutions. They helped him build a very people-oriented tradition that became famous for its training, development and sales selection policies."

The strong influence of the HR department on the company's affairs continued when Kearns took over from Wilson. Douglas Reid, who worked as the chief HR executive under Kearns, said, "People came first. There was never any question as senior HR people that people would be treated with respect at all times. We had to make hard decisions, but always treated people fairly and generously. Compensation was designed to be fully competitive. We paid well, attracted quality people, and rewarded people well."

In the 1980s, Xerox faced stiff competition from Canon and Ricoh in the low-end copier business. The company then decided to opt for a total quality movement and cut manufacturing costs. According to analysts, it was the company's strong work culture that helped it fight back effectively as the employees participated wholeheartedly in these programs.

However, things changed when Allaire replaced Kearns as the CEO in 1990. Reid, who had been an integral part of the company's HR function for almost three decades, decided to leave the organization and was replaced by William F. Buehler, who had hardly two years of HR experience.[1] Employees saw Buehler's appointment as an indication of the fact that HR's role in Xerox's corporate setup was on the decline.

Soon after, many HR executives who were part of Reid's team left the company. According to analysts, they did not want to work under Buehler, who lacked a sufficient HR background. One employee said, "An aura of fear has descended on the HR operations, making it difficult for HR to come forward. Earlier in my career, you would lay your body down on the tracks for certain principles. Today it's not being done for anything big. HR has shifted away from being the ombudsman and voice for the employees to being the implementer of management's

Exhibit 1 Xerox—Financial Performance

Year Ended December 31 (in millions, except per-share data)	2000	1999*	1998*
Revenues			
Sales	$10,059	$10,441	$10,668
Service, outsourcing, and rentals	7,718	8,045	7,783
Finance income	924	1,081	1,142
Total Revenues	18,701	19,567	19,593
Costs and Expenses			
Cost of sales	6,197	5,944	5,880
Inventory charges	90	—	113
Cost of service, outsourcing, and rentals	4,813	4,599	4,323
Equipment financing interest	605	547	570
Research and development expenses	1,044	992	1,035
Selling, administrative, and general expenses	5,649	5,292	5,343
Restructuring charge and asset impairments	540	—	1,531
Gain on affiliate's sale of stock	(21)	—	—
Purchased in-process research and development	27	—	—
Gain on sale of China operations	(200)	—	—
Other, net	341	285	219
Total Costs and Expenses	19,085	17,659	19,014
Income (Loss) from Continuing Operations before Income Taxes (Benefits), Equity Income, and Minorities' Interests	(384)	1,908	579
Income taxes (benefits)	(109)	588	145
Income (loss) from Continuing Operations after Income Taxes (Benefits) before Equity Income and Minorities' Interests	(275)	1,320	434
Equity in net income of unconsolidated affiliates	61	68	74
Minorities' interests in earnings of subsidiaries	43	49	45
Income (Loss) from Continuing Operations	(257)	1,339	463
Discontinued operations	—	—	(190)
Net Income (Loss)	$ (257)	$ 1,339	$ 273
Basic Earnings (Loss) per Share			
Continuing operations	$ (0.44)	$ 1.96	$ 0.63
Discontinued operations	—	—	(0.29)
Basic Earnings (Loss) per Share	$ (0.44)	$ 1.96	$ 0.34
Diluted Earnings (Loss) per Share			
Continuing operations	$ (0.44)	$ 1.85	$ 0.62
Discontinued operations	—	—	(0.28)
Diluted Earnings (Loss) per Share	$ (0.44)	$ 1.85	$ 0.34

*Financial Statements for 1999 and 1998 were restated as a result of two separate investigations conducted by the Audit Committee of the Board of Directors. These investigations involved previously disclosed issues in our Mexico operations and a review of our accounting policies and procedures and application thereof. As a result of these investigations, it was determined that certain accounting practices and the application thereof misapplied GAAP and certain accounting errors and irregularities were identified. The company corrected these accounting errors and irregularities in its Consolidated Financial Statements.

Source: www.xerox.com.

policies. The culture that flourished under Reid until 1990—the culture that fostered employee involvement—is disappearing. When I talk to colleagues still there in influential positions, there's a sense of disenfranchisement."

The restructuring moves notwithstanding, the changed work culture at Xerox seemed to have hurt those who mattered the most—the employees. An ex-HR executive at Xerox, Ken Larson, said about the people at Xerox, "They thought they would be there a lifetime; now they have seen their value shrink. They are angry; they feel abandoned. There's a great sense of dissatisfaction with the top leadership. That's pushing the good people out."

The departures were also due to the way employees were being promoted at Xerox after Kearns and Reid left. While the company's policy framework was very clear regarding employee promotion norms, it was reportedly not practiced. Favouritism had become an order of the day—people were promoted on the basis of their relation with the top management. An ex-Xerox executive remarked, "We would gather background and assessment information on all senior managers and sit down with the president and review their potential. The good thing was there was a lot of knowledge shared about the strengths of the executives. But the way people really got promoted was by politicizing with each other. There was always an in-crowd and out-crowd."

Many analysts said that Allaire had decided to treat the HR head position as a "building ground" for preparing

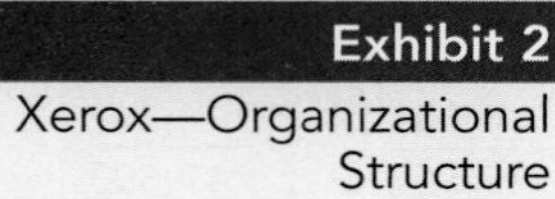

Xerox—Organizational Structure

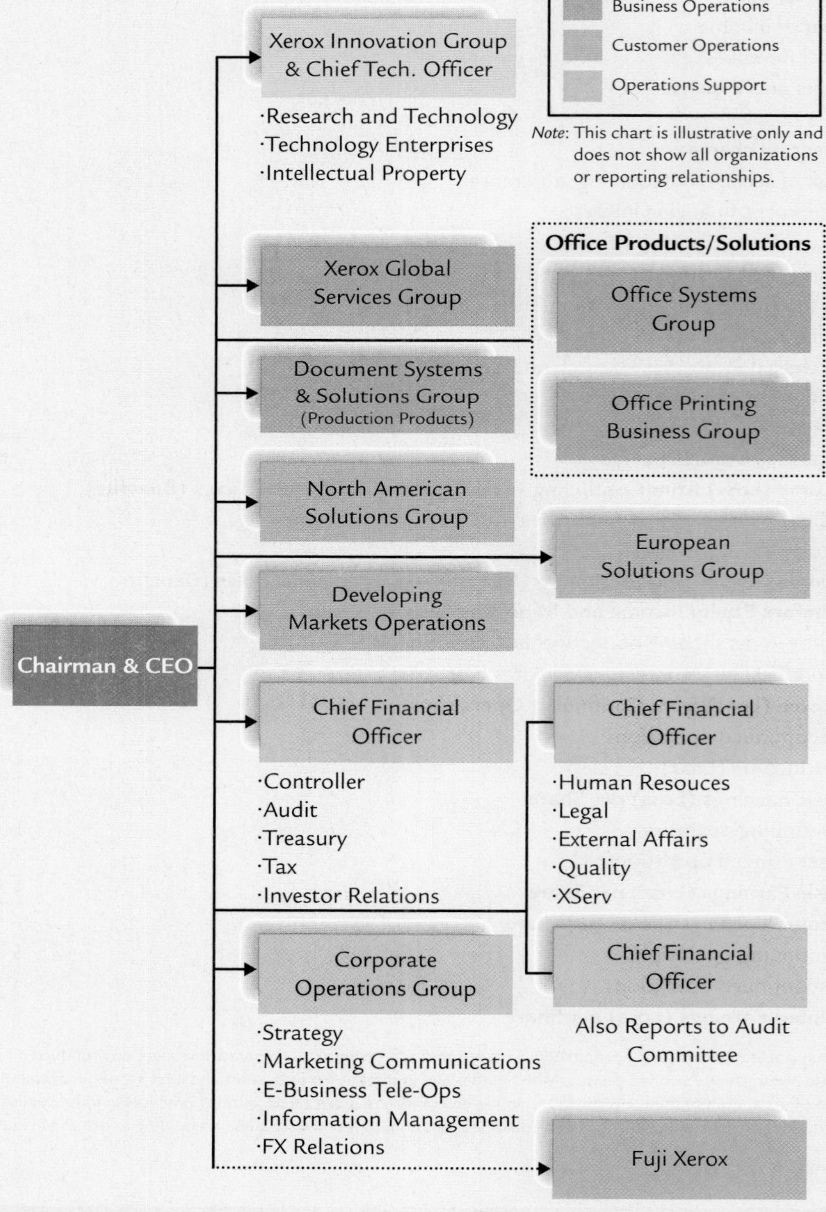

Source: www.xerox.com

promising executives to handle higher positions in the company. This was proved when Buehler was promoted within two years of joining the HR department. Within a short span of time, Xerox began losing its top executives and was reportedly finding it tough to attract new employees as well. Critics of the company's policies said that while in the earlier years, Xerox used to get the best candidates and pay handsome salaries, it was now employing people for the short term and paid only the industry averages.

It was at this point of time that Thoman took control of the company. After joining Xerox, Thoman found severe lapses in the HR control systems of the company. For instance, there were no measures in place to measure per-employee income. In addition, there were a host of problems on the financial management front. Thoman said that he was surprised to realize that the Xerox culture had become all about patronizing the sales force instead of focusing on enhancing customer service.

People Problems—II

Based on his findings, Thoman decided to set things right at Xerox by focusing more strongly on digital equipment rather than the analog ones and by reorganizing the sales force to sell digital solutions instead of copying machines in the existing setup. For the first time in Xerox's history, sales personnel had to focus on industry-based targets (such as the automobile industry customers) instead of individual clients. This also meant that their commissions were reduced significantly.

Much to Thoman's chagrin, the reorganization plan met with severe criticism despite the fact that it had been endorsed by a committee of senior executives. Not only were there hassles in the implementation; Thoman found out that certain instructions he had given regarding the plan had not been followed at all. As sales representatives began losing their accounts, they left Xerox and sales staff attrition increased by almost 100 percent. According to analysts, the company failed in training the sales representatives to make the transition from selling photocopiers to offering long-term solutions.

However, there was more bad news in store. Thoman revealed his decision to carry out large-scale layoffs in two installments of 12 000 and 4500, respectively. The decision was received with unprecedented opposition from various parties concerned. Soon after this, Thoman had to leave Xerox.

Media reports claimed that Thoman's ouster had a lot to do with the fact that Allaire had just not been able to "let go" of the company's control. This was surprising considering the fact that Allaire had invited Thoman to join Xerox, instead of promoting a CEO from within, mainly because he wanted to infuse fresh thoughts into the company. Allaire joined the board after Thoman, which was a typical boardroom move followed in many companies. However, what seemed to have worked to everyone's disadvantage was Allaire's constant interference in Xerox's affairs. For instance, when Thoman wanted to make some changes in the top management, Allaire did not allow him to do so. There were reports that Allaire's "in circle," comprising Mulcahy, Buehler, and others, even threatened to resign if Thoman continued in the company.

Although critics of Thoman's leadership style remarked that he had failed to take into confidence the employees of Xerox for his plans, the debate as to how much he was responsible for the issue continued. Meanwhile, the Mulcahy-Allaire team began working toward putting the company back on track. Mulcahy claimed that her two-decade-long association with Xerox would give her substantial mileage over Thoman.

The Future

Mulcahy's first concern was to put in place "retention programs" to arrest the abnormally high sales force attrition rate. This included increasing their pay and other incentives. Soon, the attrition dropped back to normal levels. The company also decided to offer training and education to the personnel via e-learning. Mulcahy and Allaire got in touch personally with thousands of employees to restore their confidence in the company.

However, Xerox continued to face a fall in its profitability, which indicated that the company would have to keep the options of downsizing, consolidating, and cost-cutting open. The company reported a loss of $384 million for the year 2000. By January 2001, its stock had dropped 72 percent over the previous year. The company was reported to be on the brink of bankruptcy; however a $345 million timely credit from GE Capital helped avoid this. Interestingly enough, brushing off any doubts about the company's future, Mulcahy said, "Paul and I make a great team. We have confidence in each other and support of the board. I have a leadership team that's signed up, is loyal and is participating in the turnaround."

For the fiscal year December 2001, total revenues fell 12 percent to $16.5 billion and net loss rose by 18 percent to $342 million. Company sources attributed this to the global economic meltdown and a higher effective income tax rate. Mulcahy and Allaire indeed seemed to have a tough battle on their hands. According to industry observers, it was all the more important for the duo to pull Xerox out of the various problems it was facing—for this time around, they did not even have Thoman to blame.

Chapter 5
Individual and Group Decision Making*

LEARNING OBJECTIVES

After reading this chapter, you should be able to:

1 Explain the traditional model of decision making.
2 Recognize and account for the limits of rationality in the decision-making process.
3 Identify the traps that individuals regularly fall into when making decisions.
4 Describe the role of risk and uncertainty in decision making.
5 List the conditions when decisions are best made individually and when they are best made collectively.
6 Name the steps to facilitate group participation in decision making.
7 Describe the barriers to effective decision making and ways to overcome them.

Boeing's Dis-Connexion

After weathering the dot.com collapse and struggling through the fallout of 9/11, Boeing decided to terminate their venture into in-flight WiFi service (called Connexion by Boeing) at the end of 2006.

In spring 2000, Boeing announced that they were developing a high-speed data network for passengers and crew members on Boeing-built planes. A similar service had already been created for installation on private business jets, but this was the first-ever foray into online services for passengers on commercial flights. Phil Condit, then chairman and chief executive officer of Boeing, proclaimed that the service would revolutionize the way people travel. Travellers would be able to send and receive email, browse the internet, or watch movies of live sporting events.

The on-board broadband service was expected to be available in 2001 and generate $100 billion over 10 years. However, with the burst of the dot.com bubble in early 2001, skepticism began forming around the habitually over-optimistic projections being offered by e-business analysts. With the forecast flurry of online commerce now in doubt, further skepticism was generated regarding whether or not passengers would latch on to browsing and shopping on the

* Portions of this chapter have been adapted from *Organizational Behavior*, 5th edition, by Richard M. Steers and J. Stewart Black with permission from the authors and the publisher.

internet during flights. Moreover, battery technology of the day gave even the most energy-conscious laptop around three hours of power, so the attraction for many on long flights would be limited to executive seating where power outlets are available, or for the occasional travellers who pack two batteries in their briefcases.

In spite of the uncertainty of internet interest by air travellers, Boeing moved forward and was able to secure an agreement in 2001 with Lufthansa for overseas flights and enter into early discussions on a joint venture with three US carriers . . . all prior to the events of September 11. The entire air travel industry took a massive economic hit following 9/11. Air carriers that did not seek bankruptcy protection were recoiling into conservative management practices, reducing flights, laying off staff, cancelling new hardware, and rethinking the addition of extra services on remaining flights. With the installation costs of the wireless equipment running around $795 000 for each plane, the decision to drop wireless in-flight service was simple for air carriers. This further delayed the expected launch of Boeing's WiFi services.

Companies sometimes have to make decisions and then later reverse them. In these cases the risk of losing consumer and shareholder confidence must be balanced with the prospect of continuing down the wrong path. Boeing took an innovative leap by pursuing broadband services on commercial flights, but the costly venture proved to be too early for widespread adoption by air carriers and passengers and too uncertain in a post-9/11 world. Connexion by Boeing was terminated in 2006.

Unfettered, Boeing continued with the development of Connexion, investing more than $1 billion into the venture. Finally, after three years of delays in rolling out the service, the world's first flight with WiFi-based high-speed internet access on a commercial flight left Munich on May 17, 2004, destined for Los Angeles aboard Lufthansa. The cost for unlimited access for the duration of a flight was set at US$29.95, or US$9.95 for the first thirty minutes and 25 cents for each additional minute.

As consumers began warming up to air travel again, more airlines began acquiring the service: China Airlines, Singapore Airlines, All Nippon Airways, Japan Airlines, and SAS Scandinavian Airlines all signed on. Interestingly, however, no US air carriers installed the service on their planes. By the end of 2004 Connexion had secured 160 corporate accounts where online services would be provided to employees of corporate subscribers. Market watchers started to proclaim Connexion by Boeing as the next big thing in the wireless marketplace. Connexion was being recognized by the mobile network industry and receiving awards for its innovative advances. In 2005 Connexion added even more carriers: Korean Air, Asiana Airlines, and EL AL Israel Airlines. By 2006 more than 170 flights were offering the service every day. On-board broadband was providing all that Boeing had promised in 2000—internet surfing, sending and receiving emails, use of VoIP services like Skype, and even the ability to carry out a video conference—all while travelling at 850 kph 12 000 metres up in the air.

Still, the service was not gaining the interest of enough passengers. The writing was on the wall when Boeing announced a rate change on user fees in early 2006. Connexion was feeling the pressure to make changes to its pricing structure to make the service more attractive and accessible to travellers. Criticism by passengers about the lack of pricing options prompted an announcement by Boeing in January 2006 that they were reducing their rates and offering more pricing options for their in-flight service. Now passengers would be able to get one hour of service for the same price previously charged for thirty minutes. Also, passengers could book two hours for US$14.95, or three hours for US$17.95. As well, passengers could now subscribe to the service for 24 hours, which would cover all connecting flights, for only US$26.95.

The pricing change apparently was not enough to increase passenger use. Just six months after the rate change, with 12 air carriers signed on to the service for a total of 72 long-haul planes, Boeing announced that it was re-evaluating its interest in providing the service. Boeing was going to conduct a market analysis and meet with current clients to determine the future of Connexion. Then, on August 10, 2006, a terrorist plot involving up to 10 transatlantic flights was uncovered in the United Kingdom that led to new restrictions for items allowed on flights. In the UK this included a ban on mobile technology, such as laptops, PDAs, and even MP3 players, for all passengers starting their trip in the UK or transferring from international flights at a UK airport. For the first time, the future use of mobile communications by passengers on flights was in doubt.

One week later Boeing announced that they were exiting the in-flight online market. Management at Boeing doubted that the market would provide the returns necessary to make the venture viable. The cost of shutting down Connexion was projected to be upwards of $368 million over the remainder of the year. However, management anticipated that by not having to invest further into Connexion, nearly half of that amount would be recovered in 2007 alone. The service was slated for termination at the end of 2006, with passengers enjoying free access to the service for the last two months.

In the meantime, Panasonic announced in September 2006 that it was examining the prospect of picking up the service and providing it to the carriers left by Connexion for a lower price. Panasonic would even use the same hardware already installed on the planes by Boeing. For Panasonic, the critical factor was signing on an initial fleet of 500 planes to the service before they decided to enter into the on-board broadband market. In the end, Panasonic announced in July 2007 that they have devised their own business model, which enables them to launch with as few as 50 planes. Some of the first airline clients are expected to be the initial customers of Connexion and will be commencing operations in early 2008.

Sources: J. Wallace, "Connexion Update: Panasonic Says It Is Close to Starting Internet System," *Seattle Post-Intelligencer*, seattlepi.com (accessed October 18, 2007); Boeing News Release, "Boeing Unveils High-Speed Global Communications Service—Live In-Flight Internet, E-Mail, TV; Available Next Year," April 27, 2000; Boeing News Release, "The New Era of In-flight Connectivity Is Here: Connexion by Boeing and Lufthansa Announce the World Premiere of Airborne Internet," May 11, 2004; Boeing News Release, "Connexion by Boeing Achieves Strong Growth in Availability, Partnerships and Customers Served," December 8, 2004; Boeing News Release, "Connexion by Boeing Continues Evolution of Award-Winning High-Speed In-Flight Internet Service," January 11, 2006; Boeing News Release, "Boeing to Discontinue Connexion by Boeing Service," August 17, 2006; D. Gross, "Wi-Fly: Why Boeing Shouldn't Pull the Plug on Connexion," *Slate*, June 23, 2006; Shephard Group, "Panasonic Reaches for the Connexion Torch," September 19, 2006.

strategic overview

In the minds of many, decision making is the most important managerial activity. Management decisions may involve high-profile issues such as acquiring or selling assets, moving into or out of product segments, leaving or entering markets, or launching national or international ad campaigns. Boeing's strategic decision to enter the in-flight broadband market, only to withdraw from it six years later, had a significant impact on the organization. For example, the investment of time and money into nurturing the venture so that it could carry its own takes significant resources away from the core business of Boeing, which is building planes. As well, the decision to abandon the initial investment of more than $1 billion—a decision that will add an additional $368 million of shut-down expenses—is not for the faint of heart.

This illustrates one of the key challenges of managerial decision making at any level—making decisions with uncertainty. Limited information and the presence of inaccurate information and pressure to be responsive can create some of the most powerful challenges in managerial decision making. Consequently, managers need to understand the basic processes of decision making in organizations and the factors that influence them. Several frameworks are available to help explain managerial decision making. Each framework is based on different assumptions about the nature of people at work. So, as an informed manager, you need to understand the models and the assumptions underlying each. The decision by Boeing to terminate Connexion impacts many areas within the organization. Some of the first stakeholders affected by the decision were the employees working at Connexion; Boeing minimized the effect by redeploying staff into other areas within Boeing. The decision also placed Boeing's strategic direction in doubt by investors, since Boeing had already placed significant capital into getting Connexion in the air only to terminate the venture after two years of service. Yet management had to respond to the environment as they saw it. To what extent the terrorist plot in August 2006 played into the decision to pull the plug on Connexion can only be speculated. However, the prospect of having key assumptions (such as passenger use of laptops on flights) thrown out because of increased travel restrictions by a nation with one of the largest air travel hubs in the world would, in all likelihood, not be taken lightly.

Not all managerial decisions are as visible or as important as those described in the Boeing case. Many managerial decisions involve behind-the-scenes issues such as hiring a new employee or changing a production process. In addition, in many situations you must determine the level of involvement of others (e.g., subordinates, peers) in decisions. When are group decisions superior (or inferior) to individual ones? How much participation is realistic in organizations in which managers still assume responsibility for group actions? For example, senior management at Boeing had to decide who to bring into the discussion to terminate Connexion. As a new manager, you might have to decide how many people to involve in a new-hire decision. In making these choices you need to understand how various factors affect the quality of your decisions. Finally, what approaches can managers use to improve decisions in organizations? A knowledge of effective decision making can help you make the most efficient use of your limited time and resources.

Decision-Making Concepts

A characteristic of effective leaders and effective workgroups is their ability to make decisions that are appropriate, timely, and acceptable. If organizational effectiveness is defined as the ability to secure and use resources in the pursuit of organizational goals, then the decision-making processes that determine how these resources are acquired and used is a key building block. For our purposes here, we define **decision making** as a process of specifying the nature of a particular problem or opportunity and selecting among available alternatives how to solve a problem or capture an opportunity. In this sense decision making has two aspects: the act and the process.

decision making a process of specifying the nature of a particular problem or opportunity and selecting among available alternatives to solve a problem or capture an opportunity

The *act* of decision making involves choosing between alternatives. The *process* of decision making involves several steps that can be divided into two distinct phases. The first, **formulation**, involves identifying a problem or opportunity, acquiring information, developing desired performance expectations, and diagnosing the causes and relationships among factors affecting the problem or opportunity. A **problem** exists when a manager detects a gap between existing and desired performance. This is the situation we commonly associate with decision making, and it is the reason that decision making and problem solving are often talked about interchangeably. For example, you may find that your subordinates just have more work than they can get done. To solve this problem, you may decide to hire an additional worker.

formulation a process involving identifying a problem or opportunity, acquiring information, developing desired performance expectations, and diagnosing the causes and relationships among factors affecting the problem or opportunity

problem a gap between existing and desired performance

Although as a manager you will confront lots of problems and have to decide how to solve them, you will also encounter opportunities. An **opportunity** exists when a manager detects a chance to achieve a more desirable state than the current one. For example, for managers at Brunswick Corporation this happened when they decided to buy Baja Boats. At the time of the purchase, Brunswick was already the number-one recreational boat builder in North America, with its Sea Ray, Bayliner, PROCRAFT, and other brands. Buying Baja Boats represented an opportunity to expand into a market niche that executives thought would grow in the future and in which they did not have a significant presence at the time.

opportunity a chance to achieve a more desirable state than the current one

The **solution** phase of the decision-making process involves generating alternatives, selecting the preferred solution, and implementing the decided course of action. Following the implementation of the solution, the manager monitors the situation to determine the extent to which the decision was successful.

solution a process involving generating alternatives, selecting the preferred solution, and implementing the decided course of action

Types of Decisions

Most decisions can be divided into two basic types: programmed or nonprogrammed. A **programmed decision** is a standard response to a simple or routine problem. The nature of the problem is well defined and clearly understood by the decision maker, as is the array of possible solutions. Examples of programmed decisions can be seen in university admission decisions, reimbursement for managers' travel expenses, and promotion decisions with many unionized personnel. In all these decisions, specific criteria can be identified (e.g., grade-point average and test scores for university admission, per diem allowances for expense account reimbursements, or seniority for union promotions). The programmed decision process is characterized by high levels of certainty for both the problem formulation and the problem solution phases, and rules and procedures typically spell out exactly how to respond.

programmed decision a routine response to a simple or regularly occurring problem

nonprogrammed decision a decision about a problem that is either poorly defined or novel

On the other hand, **nonprogrammed decisions** occur in response to problems that are either poorly defined or novel. Nonprogrammed decisions are unique because they are in response to situations that may never have occurred before, or the situation involves a high level of ambiguity. As a result, decision makers must rely upon their own creativity and intuition in formulating a decision. For example, should a university president with limited funds expand the size of the business school to meet growing student demand, or should she expand the university's science facilities to bring in more federal research contracts? No alternative is clearly correct, and past decisions are of little help; instead, the decision maker must weigh the alternatives and their consequences carefully to make a unique decision—a nonprogrammed decision.

Exhibit 5.1

Decision-Maker Level and Type of Decision

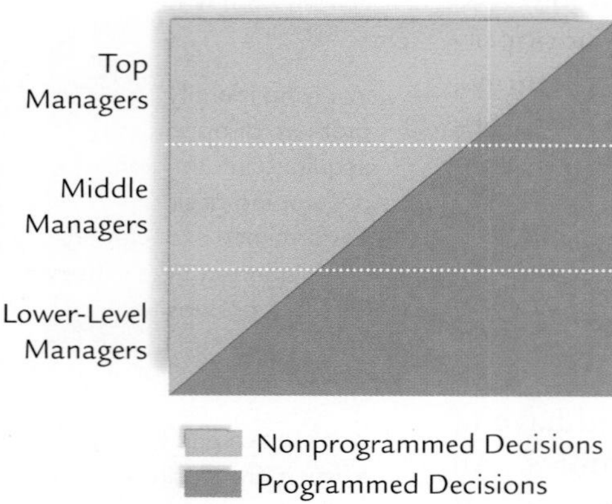

In most organizations, a significant relationship exists between the programmed and nonprogrammed decisions and organizational hierarchy. As shown in Exhibit 5.1, for example, top managers usually face nonprogrammed decisions, as in the case of the university president. On the other hand, university deans or department heads as well as faculty or students seldom need to make such decisions. Furthermore, lower-level managers (such as first-line supervisors) typically encounter mostly programmed, or routine, decisions. Their options and resources, as well as risks, are usually far less than those of top managers. And, as we might expect, middle managers fall somewhere in between.

standard operating procedure (SOP) established procedure for action used for programmed decisions that specifies exactly what should be done

Gresham's law of planning the tendency for managers to let programmed activities overshadow nonprogrammed activities

One final point should be made here concerning the relationship between programmed and nonprogrammed decisions. Programmed decisions are usually made through structured, bureaucratic techniques. For example, **standard operating procedures (SOP)** are often used for programmed decisions. SOPs specify exactly what should be done—the sequence of steps and exactly how each step should be performed. In contrast, nonprogrammed decisions must be made by managers using available information and their own judgment, often under considerable time pressure. The ambiguity of the problem in part contributes to the uncertainty of the outcome, which in turn leads to interesting and important consequences. Managers tend to let programmed activities overshadow nonprogrammed activities. This tendency is called **Gresham's law of planning**.[1] Thus, if a manager has a series of decisions to make, he or she will tend to make those that are routine and repetitive before focusing on those that are unique and require considerable thought. When asked why they do this, many managers reply that they wish to clear their desks so they can concentrate on the really serious problems. Unfortunately, the reality is that managers often don't actually get to the more difficult and perhaps more important decisions. They may just run out of time or continue to occupy their time with the programmed decisions (and their more certain outcomes) than with the nonprogrammed decisions (and their less certain outcomes).

The implications of Gresham's law for managerial decision making are clear. As a manager you must make needed decisions in a timely fashion. As a consequence, you may want to check yourself periodically to see where you are spending your "decision-making time" to see if you are falling prey to Gresham's law of planning. The matrix in Exhibit 5.2 may help you with this assessment.

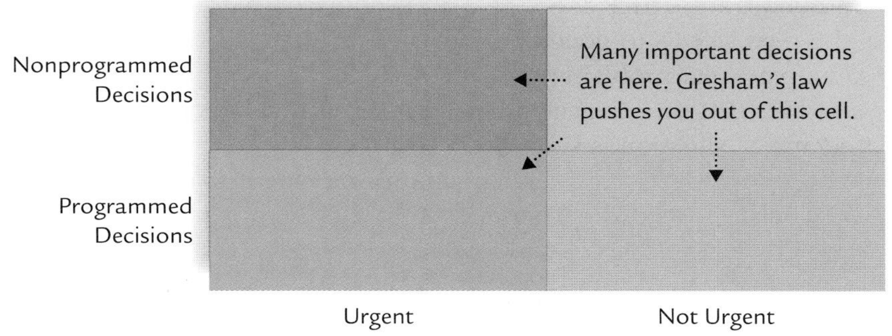

Exhibit 5.2
Gresham's Law and Making Decisions

rational model (classical model) a seven-step model of decision making that represents the earliest attempt to model decision processes

Individual Decision Making

It is no easy task to outline or diagram the details of the decision-making process. Research has been mixed about how individuals and groups make decisions.[2] Even so, at least three attempts to describe the decision-making process are worth noting: (1) the rational/classic model; (2) the administrative, or bounded rationality, model; and (3) the retrospective decision-making model. Each model is useful for understanding the nature of decision processes in organizations. While reading about these models, pay special attention to the assumptions that each makes about the nature of decision makers; also note the differences in focus.

The Rational/Classical Model

The **rational model** (also known as the **classical model**) represents the earliest attempt to model decision processes.[3] It is viewed by some as the classical approach to understanding decision processes. This approach involves seven basic steps (see Exhibit 5.3).

Step 1: Identifying Decision Situations In the classical model, the decision maker begins by recognizing that a decision-making situation exists, that is, that a problem or an opportunity exists.

Step 2: Developing Objectives and Criteria Once you have identified the decision-making situation, the next step is to determine the criteria for selecting alternatives. These criteria essentially represent what is important in the outcome. For example, before you can decide which job applicant to hire as an additional salesperson, you need to determine the important characteristics or outcomes needed. When several criteria are involved, it is often necessary to weigh the various criteria. For example, you might decide that a new hire's sales ability depends on four things: interpersonal skills, motivation, product knowledge, and understanding of the selling process. However, the impact of these factors may not be equal. As a manager, then, you might assign a weight to each criterion: for example, motivation: 30 percent; interpersonal skills: 25 percent; understanding of the selling process: 25 percent; product knowledge: 20 percent.

Exhibit 5.3
Classical Decision-Making Model

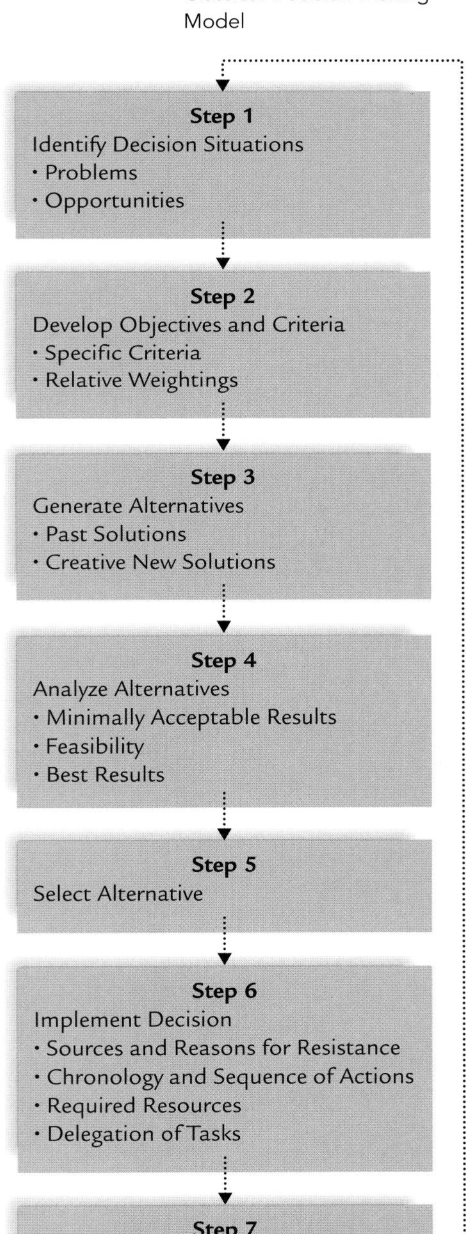

Step 3: Generating Alternatives Once the objectives and criteria are established, the next step is to generate alternatives that achieve the desired result. How can a particular problem be solved or a given opportunity captured? Most of us consider first the alternatives that we have encountered or used in the past. If a current situation is similar to one from the past, past solutions can be effective. However, situations change and to the extent that the current situation is dissimilar to one from the past, or if past solutions have not succeeded, new alternatives must be generated.

Step 4: Analyzing Alternatives The fourth step in the process involves analyzing the alternatives generated. To begin, you need to determine which alternatives would produce minimally acceptable results. Any alternatives that are unlikely to at least achieve the minimally acceptable outcome can be eliminated. Next, you need to examine the feasibility of the remaining alternatives. Returning to our hiring example, you may have found three candidates for your sales position that would likely produce minimally acceptable sales results. But one candidate's salary requirement exceeds your budget; therefore, that person is not feasible. Once infeasible alternatives are eliminated, the next step is to determine which of the remaining alternatives would produce the most satisfactory outcome. Typically, the criteria and weights produced in step two are applied at this point.

Step 5: Selecting Alternatives Selecting an alternative flows naturally out of your analysis. The classical model argues that managers will choose the alternative that maximizes the desired outcome. This idea has often been expressed by the term **subjectively expected utility (SEU) model**. This model asserts that managers choose the alternative that they subjectively believe maximizes the desired outcome. The two key components of this model are the expected outcome produced by a given alternative and the probability that the alternative can be implemented.

subjectively expected utility (SEU) model
a model of decision making that asserts that managers choose the alternative that they subjectively believe maximizes the desired outcome

Step 6: Implementing the Decision In the classical model of decision making, effective decision implementation has four components. First, you assess sources and reasons for potential resistance to the decision. Second, you determine the chronology and sequence of actions designed to overcome resistance to the decision and ensure that the decision is effectively implemented. Setting the chronology and sequence of actions leads naturally into the third step: an assessment of the resources required to implement the decision effectively. Fourth, you need to determine whether you could delegate implementation steps to others and can ensure that those individuals understand and are held accountable for those steps and outcomes.

Step 7: Monitoring and Evaluating Results The final step in the classical model involves monitoring and evaluating the results. To do this, you must gather information and compare results to the objectives and standards you set at the beginning. This is trickier than it may seem. First, you must gather the right information or the evaluation will be distorted at best and meaningless at worst. In addition, the longer the lead time between actions and results, the more important appropriate performance indicators are, even if they are not easy to gather or evaluate. The key point here is the importance of monitoring and evaluating results to detect problems with the original decision and its implementation so that corrective actions can be taken. If the appropriate information is not gathered, the purpose of this final step is defeated.

A Manager's Challenge: "Travel Agencies Find New Technological Paths to Profits" provides a look at two manager/owners of travel agencies and how they weighed their options and decided not to let new technology put them

a manager's challenge *technology*

Travel Agencies Find New Technological Paths to Profits

When Delta Air Lines stopped paying commissions to travel agencies for selling tickets on US routes, the decision came as no surprise to Rita Baron and Barbara Hansen. Baron owns Baron Travel in Atlanta, Georgia, and Hansen and her son own Sunflower Travel in Wichita, Kansas. Both owners had to make critical decisions about whether to toss in the towel or use technology to stay in the travel agency game.

A decade ago, travel agents earned at least a 10 percent commission on any airline tickets they sold, and they enjoyed close relationships with airline sales representatives. Starting in 1994, however, many US airlines cut costs by capping commission levels. At the same time, new software technology allowed people to surf the internet in pursuit of airfare bargains and in this way bypass travel agents. By 2001, the airlines were paying travel agencies just US$20 for selling any ticket (regardless of value) on a domestic flight. By 2002, nearly every US airline had entirely eliminated commissions on domestic flights as a way to boost profitability.

Caught in the ongoing financial squeeze of lower revenues from airlines, more than 6000 travel agencies went out of business. Both Baron Travel and Sunflower Travel decided to pass the loss of revenue from disappearing commissions on to customers via service fees in the range of US$40 per ticket. In implementing this decision, Hansen recognized she had to prove her worth to customers. Thus, she uses her extensive industry contacts to search for the lowest possible fares. Now, says Hansen, "we can often beat the fares customers see on the web." She has taken on the technology of the web with old-fashioned person-to-person networking.

To stay in business, Hansen knew she would have to set Sunflower Travel apart from its local and online competitors. Because of her personal interest in the South Pacific, she decided to focus on selling specialized tours to Australia and New Zealand. Once she developed a relationship with an established tour company operating in those countries, she then decided to use the technology that nearly put her out of business to her advantage. She decided to use the internet to promote her tours. For instance, she linked her site with New Zealand's tourism website and offered online wine retailers special Australian food and wine tours.

In this case, the new technology of the internet and a change in commission policy by airlines presented both Hansen and Baron with a problem. Interestingly, each solved essentially the same problem with a different solution.

Sources: T. Pearson, "Why Use a Travel Agent?" *Travel Agent*, September 29, 2003, p. 20; N. Fonti, "Atlanta Travel Agency Experiences Many Industry Changes," *Atlanta Journal-Constitution*, May 17, 2002, www.ajc.com; P. Thomas, "Case Study: Travel Agency Meets Technology's Threat," *Wall Street Journal*, May 21, 2002, p. B4.

---

out of business. In the end they also decided to use the technology to enhance their business. As you read this case, ask yourself if you see the situation as a problem or an opportunity. What do you think of each manager's solution?

To many, the classical model makes considerable sense. However, it is important to understand the assumptions on which it is built:

- Problems are clear.
- Objectives are clear.
- People agree on criteria and weights.
- All alternatives are known.
- All consequences can be anticipated.
- Decision makers are rational:
  - They are not biased in recognizing problems.
  - They can process all relevant information.
  - They appropriately incorporate immediate and future consequences into decision making.
  - They search for the alternative that maximizes the desired result.

The potential weaknesses of the classical model are easily exposed if you recall your own decision about what university to attend. How clear was the problem or your objectives? Did everyone (you, your parents, your friends, etc.) agree on the criteria and weights for evaluating alternative schools? Did you know or even consider all the possible alternative universities? Could you fully anticipate the consequences associated with attending each school? Were you completely unbiased in your definition of the problem or the opportunity of which school to attend, and did you objectively review all the relevant information? Did you appropriately emphasize short-term and long-term consequences? Did you search for alternatives until you found the one that maximized your desired outcome? If you answered no to some of these questions, you're not alone. A large body of research has shown that people are not as rational as the classical model assumes.[4] In fact, we can identify a series of factors that inhibit people's ability to accurately identify and analyze problems, as shown in Exhibit 5.4.

Exhibit 5.4 Factors That Inhibit Accurate Problem Identification and Analysis

Factor	Description	Illustration
Information Bias	A reluctance to give or receive negative information.	You are favouring Jane as the candidate and dismiss information about a performance problem she had at her last job.
Uncertainty Absorption	A tendency for information to lose its uncertainty as it is passed along.	It is not clear how well Martha did in her previous job, but by the time the feedback gets to you, she is described as a poor performer.
Selective Perception	A tendency to ignore or avoid certain information, especially ambiguous information.	Jane may have several employment alternatives and may even be considering going back to school, but you ignore all this in making her the offer.
Stereotyping	Deciding about an alternative on the basis of characteristics ascribed by others.	Jane graduated from a private high school and went to a highly rated university on a partial scholarship, so you figure she must be a great hire.
Cognitive Complexity	Limits on the amount of information people can process at one time.	You initially have 200 applicants for the position but decide to eliminate anyone with less than three years' sales experience.
Stress	Reduction of people's ability to cope with informational demands.	Your company's market share is slipping because you don't have enough salespeople in the field, so you feel you just can't look at every bit of information on every candidate.

bounded rationality model (administrative man model) a descriptive model of decision making recognizing that people are limited in their capacity to fully assess a problem and usually rely on shortcuts and approximations to arrive at a decision they are comfortable with

Thus, whereas the rational, or classical, model prescribes how decisions *should* be made (i.e., it works as a prescriptive model), it falls short in describing how decisions are *actually* made (i.e., as a descriptive model).

The Bounded Rationality Model

An alternative model, one not constrained by the preceding assumptions, has been presented by Herbert Simon.[5] This model is called the **bounded rationality model** (or the **administrative man model**). The theory of bounded rationality is a descriptive model of decision making that was developed as an alternative to the prescriptive theory of subjective expected utility (SEU) mentioned earlier.[6] The reason behind presenting the model is the realization that there are many instances when decision makers arrive at decisions that would not have been predicted by SEU. The key distinguishing characteristic of bounded rationality from SEU is its recognition that human rationality is limited. It assumes that people, although they may seek the best solution, usually settle for less because the decisions they confront typically demand greater information-processing capabilities than they possess. In short, their rationality is limited, or bounded.

As a result of the great complexities surrounding decisions, people will resort to shortcuts and approximations to arrive at decisions that they are comfortable with, even if they are not fully rational. Limits in rationality come about as a result of complex environments, incomplete and insufficient knowledge, inconsistencies in individual preferences and beliefs, conflicting values between people, and errors in calculation.[7]

The concept of bounded rationality has two key implications for decision making. First, Simon and other scholars have argued that people do not actually identify all possible solutions, assess the costs and benefits, and then select the best alternative. Instead, people will examine solutions that are accessible to them with minimal effort until a satisfactory, but not necessarily optimal, solution is found. As Simon described it, **satisficing** occurs when the first solution that meets their needs, whether or not it maximizes utility, will stop the search for alternatives.

satisficing the tendency for decision makers to accept the first alternative that meets their minimally acceptable requirements rather than pushing them further for an alternative that produces the best results

In addition, the more alternatives that are available to an individual, the higher the aspirations in a satisfactory solution.[8] For example, if you are intent on going to a movie theatre on a Friday night, but there is only one theatre in your area, you may resolve to see the movie regardless of what it is, simply because the movie will satisfy your desire to go to a theatre. However, if you are in an area where there are multiple theatres your aspirations will rise, which may lead you to quickly pass over the movie in the first scenario for another that you find more appealing.

Maximizing Satisficing by Stewart Black
PEARSON mymanagementlab

Second, rather than using explicit criteria and weights to evaluate alternatives, the bounded rationality model argues that people use heuristics. A **heuristic** is a decision-making shortcut that can be based upon pre-set rules, memory, or past experiences. Thus, instead of looking everywhere for possible solutions, you might use a heuristic to arrive at a solution to a problem or for selecting one opportunity over another. The obvious benefit here is the reduction of time and mental energy expended in arriving at a decision. On the other hand, the obvious cost is that the best solution may not be found because of the shortcut that is taken.

heuristic a decision-making shortcut that can be based upon pre-set rules, memory, or past experiences

Based on the above, we can imagine that the decision process will be quite different from the rational model. The process does not involve individuals searching for the best solution; rather, they will look for a solution that is *acceptable*. Also, in contrast to the prescriptive rational model, the bounded rationality model is descriptive; that is, it describes how decision makers actually identify solutions to organizational problems.

A Manager's Challenge: "Gaining a New Perspective on Decisions at UPS" illustrates how United Parcel Service (UPS) tries to give managers experiences that will broaden and diversify their knowledge base. The example illustrates how changes in experience base and emphasis on diversity affect not only managers' perceptions, but also the decisions they make. Do you think having similar experiences would influence your perception of future problems? As a consequence, do you think you might change the way you make decisions?

a manager's challenge — *diversity*

Gaining a New Perspective on Decisions at UPS

Managing diverse perspectives for enhanced decision making is a tough balancing act for managers at United Parcel Service (UPS). On the one hand, UPS has built a successful global delivery business by developing standard procedures for nearly all routine decisions, including how drivers should carry their keys when making deliveries. Yet every year, senior managers send 50 middle managers on a program that is designed to add diversity to the "brown" perspective (that is, the typical UPS perspective) so that these middle managers can make better decisions. The program involves managers spending 30 days in communities far from home that have significant poverty and other problems. UPS founder James Casey initiated the Community Internship Program in 1968. Since then, UPS has invested more than $14 million to send 1100 middle managers through the program, at a cost of $10 000 per participant (plus the manager's regular salary).

Whether managers spend the month cleaning up dilapidated apartments or working with migrant workers, participants say the experience drives home new lessons about diversity. For example, during a month of working with addicts in New York City, division manager Patti Hobbs was impressed by the thoughtful suggestions they offered for keeping teenagers off drugs. Back on the job, she broadened her use of group decision making to involve all staff members in problem-solving discussions rather than only the highest-level managers. "You start to think there's no one person, regardless of position, who has all the answers," she explains. "The answers come from us all."

The program sharpens participants' decision-making skills by taking them out of their comfortable daily work routine. According to Al Demick, UPS's learning and development manager, it "puts people in situations that call on them to use new skills or to use their skills in new ways. Sometimes those are life-and-death situations. People are never quite the same when they come back." Annette Law, a UPS manager from Utah, worked with tenement dwellers in New York City. "I thought I knew all about diversity," she observes. "But what I saw were people just like me, only their opportunities and choices were different." Michael Lockard, a finance and accounting manager, helped inmates in a Chicago prison prepare for release by sharpening their interviewing and job-search skills. The experience shattered Lockard's preconceived notions about inmates and changed the way he approaches decisions at UPS: "I'm much more sensitive to the fact that we must make decisions on a case-by-case basis," he says. "Things are no longer black and white for me."

Because half of all new UPS employees are visible minorities, senior managers believe that the program is an important training ground for the management team. Although executives cannot point to a financial return on this investment, feedback from participants indicates that they not only bring a new perspective to work decisions, but also are inspired to volunteer in their home communities. "We will never really know how many lives we have touched," sums up a recent participant.

Since 1968, UPS has invested more than $14 million to send 1100 middle managers like Flynn Bowen to communities that suffer from poverty and other problems. Initiated by UPS founder James Casey, the Community Internship Program is designed to add diversity to the "brown" perspective.

Sources: K. Pelkey, "Resident Participates in Company's Community Internship Program," *Farmington Valley Post*, July 24, 2003; J. J. Salopek, "Just Like Me: UPS's Unique Intern Program Transforms the Perspectives of Leaders," *T&D*, October 2002, pp. 52+; L. Lavelle, "For UPS Managers, a School of Hard Knocks," *BusinessWeek*, July 22, 2002, pp. 58–59.

The Retrospective Decision Model

A third model focuses on how decision makers attempt to rationalize their choices after they are made. It has been variously referred to as the **retrospective decision model**[9] or the **implicit favourite model**.[10]

retrospective decision model (implicit favourite model) a decision-making model that focuses on how decision makers attempt to rationalize their choices after they are made

One of the most noted contributors to this perspective was MIT professor Peter Soelberg. As Soelberg observed the job-choice processes of graduating business students, he noticed that in many cases the students identified implicit favourites (that is, the alternative they wanted) very early in the recruiting and choice process. For example, one student might identify a manufacturer in Calgary as a favourite. However, students continued their search for additional alternatives and quickly selected the best alternate (or second) candidate, known as the "confirmation candidate." For example, the student might select a high-tech firm in Ottawa as his alternate firm. Next, the students would attempt to develop decision rules that demonstrated unequivocally that the implicit favourite was superior to the confirmation candidate. They did so by **perceptual distortion** of information—that is, highlighting the positive features of the implicit favourite over the alternative. For example, the student might leave out vacation time as a criterion because his favourite firm in Calgary has a very poor vacation policy compared with the alternative firm in Ottawa. However, the student might heavily weight a criterion of the availability of downhill skiing because it is more abundant in the Calgary region, the student's favoured choice. Finally, after deriving a decision rule that clearly favoured the implicit favourite, the student announced the decision and accepted the job in Calgary.

perceptual distortion highlighting the positive features of the implicit favourite over the alternative

Ironically, Soelberg noted, the implicit favourite was typically superior to the confirmation candidate on only one or two dimensions. Even so, decision makers generally characterized their decision rules as being multidimensional. For example, in the case of the two firms in Calgary and Ottawa, the jobs offered were quite similar, and the salary, travel, benefits, and promotion prospects were also nearly identical. Yet the student would claim that the Calgary firm was superior on several counts.

The entire process is designed to justify, through the guise of scientific rigor, a decision that has already been made intuitively. By this means, the individual becomes convinced that he or she is acting rationally and making a logical, reasoned decision on an important topic. Consider how many times you have made a decision in a similar way when looking for clothes, cars, stereo systems, and so on. You start with an item that catches your eye and then spend considerable time convincing yourself and your friends that this is the "best" choice. If your implicit favourite is the cheapest among the competition, you emphasize price; if it is not, you emphasize quality or styling. Ultimately, you end up buying the item you favoured, feeling comfortable that you made the right choice. Here, however, we do not want to create the impression that **intuitive decision making**, or the primarily subconscious process of identifying a decision and selecting a preferred alternative, is bad or wrong. Although some firms often base their decision-making practices on rational analyses,[11] some research has found that not only are intuitive decisions often faster in many situations, but the outcome is also as good as or better than a methodical, rational approach.[12]

intuitive decision making the primarily subconscious process of identifying a decision and selecting a preferred alternative

Influences on Effective Decision Making

From a practical perspective, perhaps the most important question for managers to ask is "What influences effective decision making?" Quite simply, practising managers want to make good decisions. Consequently, it is helpful to briefly

Exhibit 5.5

Influences on the Decision Process

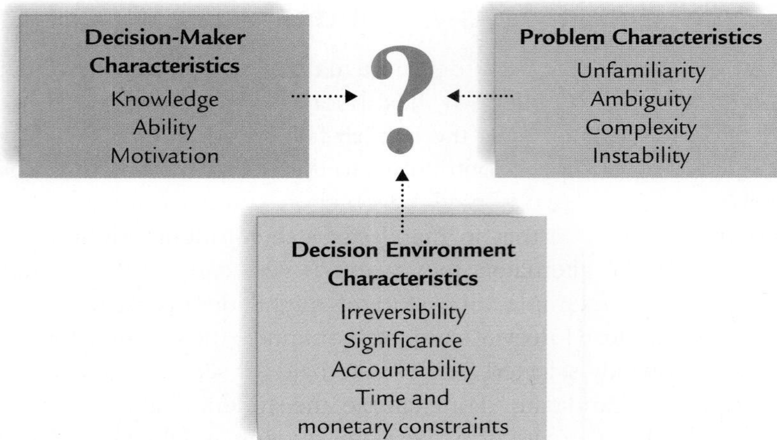

examine the major factors that hurt decision quality and then examine what we can do to enhance individual decision quality. At least three general factors influence decision quality (see Exhibit 5.5).[13]

First, there are the characteristics of the decision maker. Earlier in the chapter we discussed that we may not be as rational as we would like to believe. We can have implicit preferences for alternatives and simply construct rationales for those biases to make it seem as though we are being rational and objective. We can have limitations to our information-processing capabilities and, as a consequence, limit the alternatives we examine. If our motivation is not sufficient, we can easily satisfice and simply accept the first workable solution rather than push to find the best of several workable solutions. If we lack familiarity with the problem or have insufficient knowledge, we can make less than ideal decisions. If we have too much familiarity with the problem, we can be too quick to select solutions that have worked in the past. In the process we might not sufficiently consider what might be different about the past and current situations that might make past solutions inappropriate for the present problem.

Second, the nature of the problem or opportunity itself can influence decision quality. The greater the ambiguity of the problem, the harder it is to be certain of the "right" decision. Also, as we have already discussed, we may shy away from ambiguous problems and, as a consequence, end up with less than ideal outcomes because the needed decisions weren't made soon enough, if at all. The complexity of the problem can also affect the outcome. The more complex the problem is, the more challenging both the decision and its effective implementation are likely to be. The extent to which the problem is stable or volatile can also influence decision effectiveness. Clearly, the more volatile the problem is, the greater the chance that the problem will change and the selected solution won't match the problem.

Third, the environment in which the decision is made influences the decision. Time constraints or any relevant resource constraints (people, money, equipment, etc.) can influence the decision's effectiveness. For example, the more time pressure you are under, the greater the chance that you might "miss" something or become vulnerable to any or all of the bounded rationality limitations we already discussed. If the decision is irreversible and you make the "wrong" decision, you obviously lack the opportunity to modify the decision and correct the results. The importance of the decision can create its own pressures, which in turn can influence the effectiveness of the decision.

Decision-Making Traps

While we all try to make good decisions, we can all fall victim to decision-making traps that lead us away from the optimal solution. Decision-making traps are the result of us searching for shortcuts or using approximations to arrive at a quick conclusion to the tension that goes along with a pending decision. Many of these traps can also be characterized as heuristics that people rely on to make decisions. Four main types of decision-making traps are availability heuristics, the representativeness heuristic, anchoring, and escalation of commitment.[14]

Availability Heuristics We often rely on our memory of past situations to make decisions for current events. The information that remains intact and is best available to our recollection will be most relied upon when drawing from our memory banks. Considering this, it should be apparent that events that are most recent or had a significant impact on us are the events that we will be able to remember most readily, so these are the events we will most likely use in formulating a judgment. The trap here is that the most recent or the most sensational events in our memory are not necessarily an accurate portrayal of the frequency of such events. Nor does it provide all the information necessary to make a decision.

There are three decision-making biases that emanate from the availability heuristic. The first is **ease of recall**; that is, making a judgment based upon the most recent events or the most vivid in our memory. For example, a manager that is conducting an annual evaluation may give an employee a low performance rating because she saw him arrive at work late the previous week, even though the employee's attendance prior to then was unblemished. The second bias is **retrievability**, which refers to the fact that judgments rely on the memory structures of an individual. Our ability to assemble information may be hampered by how we store and later retrieve that information. For example, you would have an easier time assembling a list of all the people you know that have a first name starting with the letter "S" than searching for people that have the letter "A" as the third letter in their first name. The third decision-making bias is **presumed associations**—the assumption that two events are likely to co-occur based on the recollection of similar associations. For example, the number of media reports that link juveniles dressed in black (Goths) to violent outbursts in academic settings creates an environment where individuals presume that all Goths should be watched closely to ensure they do not harm others in schools.

ease of recall making a judgment based upon the most recent events or the most vivid in our memory

retrievability a decision-making bias where judgments rely on the memory structures of an individual

presumed associations the assumption that two events are likely to co-occur based on the recollection of similar associations

Representativeness Heuristic The tendency to judge an event by assessing how closely it relates to a previous similar event is the representativeness heuristic. Individuals will evaluate similarities of current and previous situations using significant or even insignificant features as the basis for a decision. For example, you may see someone that reminds you of another person, possibly because of the way they speak or their facial features, and because of these similarities you may treat the unknown person in the same manner as the person you know.

There are five biases associated with the representativeness heuristic. The first is **insensitivity to base rates**, or the tendency to disregard information that suggests the likelihood of a particular outcome in the presence of other information. For example, if you bought a product that was known to have a 35 percent failure rate, you would likely demand a good warranty or return policy, or simply avoid the product altogether. Yet when you ask most couples engaged to be married if they are preparing a prenuptial agreement they

insensitivity to base rates the tendency to disregard information that suggests the likelihood of a particular outcome in the presence of other information

insensitivity to sample size the tendency to not consider sample size when using information taken from a sample within a given population

misconception of chance the expectation that small sets of randomly assembled objects or sequences should appear random

regression to the mean overlooking the fact that extreme events or characteristics are exceptional cases that will likely revert back to historic averages over time

conjunction fallacy the tendency for people to assume that co-occurring events are more likely to occur than if they were independent of each other or grouped with other events

will answer no, even though the rate of failed marriages in Canada is around 38 percent.[15] Individuals will also demonstrate **insensitivity to sample size**, which refers to the tendency to not consider sample size when using information taken from a sample within a given population. People tend to ignore the fact that larger sample sizes are more likely to represent the full population than small samples. A third bias is the **misconception of chance**—people expect small sets of randomly assembled objects or sequences to appear random. For example, if someone rolled a die three times and each roll was a five, people may anticipate that the fourth roll would not be a five, even though a five has exactly the same odds as any other number appearing—one in six. A fourth tendency that people will fall into is overlooking that extreme events or characteristics will often follow with a **regression to the mean**. If, for example, this year's class of grade four students in a school is on average three inches taller than the previous year's class, the grade four teacher might surmise that, on average, children of the same age are developing earlier. In fact, the next year's class may very well regress to the mean, with the student average height hovering closer to the historic average for students in grade four. A final representativeness bias is the **conjunction fallacy**, or the tendency for people to assume that co-occurring events are more likely to occur than if they were independent of each other or grouped with other events. An example of the conjunction fallacy is the ritual of actions that a hockey goalie will go through in preparation for a game. The goalie believes that if the series of actions are not repeated prior to every game the team will suffer a loss.

anchoring using an initial value received from prior experience or any external information source and giving it disproportionate weight in setting a final value

Anchoring Have you ever bought or sold an item, basing its value on a price you saw listed elsewhere? Of course you have. We regularly determine the value of something based upon someone else's set price for similar items. Where we can falter in this approach, however, is if we regard the first bit of information we receive, regardless of its relevancy, as sufficient for the basis of a final value. **Anchoring** is using an initial value received from prior experience or any external information source and giving it disproportionate weight in setting a final value. For example, you have a friend that works as a waiter on weekends at a local restaurant. He reports to you and another friend that he regularly receives over $100 in tips on Saturday evenings. The other friend is enticed by this, and she decides to take a job as a waitress at another restaurant. In the first few weeks of working at this restaurant your friend has been receiving around $80 in tips each shift, but she is disappointed. Her expectation was that she would receive over $100 in tips each shift. Yet she failed to take into account additional information that would help her determine the expected value of tips, such as the average value of a dinner (which can have a significant effect on tipping), the time of her shift, the number of tables she has to tend to in a shift, the usual value of tips received by other servers in the same restaurant, and so on. Your friend may discover that, compared to other serving staff in the same establishment, her tips are on average greater than others.

escalation of commitment the tendency to exhibit greater levels of commitment to a decision as time passes and investments are made in the decision, even after significant evidence emerges indicating that the original decision was incorrect

Escalation of Commitment The concept of **escalation of commitment** offers an explanation as to why decision makers adhere to a course of action even after they know it is incorrect (that is, why managers "throw good money after bad"). To understand the problem of escalating commitment, consider the following true examples:

- A company overestimated its capability to build an airplane brake that met certain technical specifications at a given cost. Because it won the government contract, the company was forced to invest greater and greater efforts to meet the contract terms. As a result of increasing pressure to meet specifications and deadlines, records and tests of the brake were misrepresented to government officials. Corporate careers and company credibility were increasingly put at stake on the airbrake contract, although many in the firm knew the brake would not work effectively. At the conclusion of the construction period, the government test pilot flew the plane; it skidded off the runway and narrowly missed injuring the pilot.

- An individual purchased a stock at $50 a share, but the price dropped to $20 soon after. Still convinced about the merit of the stock, he bought more shares at the lower price. Soon the price declined further, and the individual was again faced with the decision to buy more, hold what he already had, or sell out entirely.[16]

How do we account for such commitment by individuals and groups to obvious mistakes? At least three explanations are possible. First, we can point to individual limitations in information processing, as first identified by Herbert Simon. People may be limited in both their desire and ability to handle all the information for complex decisions. As a result, errors in judgment may occur. For example, the company in which the stock investor purchased shares may have significant operations in countries where negative changes in exchange rates are occurring or where government regulations have changed. The investor simply may not be able to completely comprehend these issues and how they are hurting the company's performance and subsequent stock price. A second approach is to explain decision errors as a breakdown in rationality because of group dynamics. For example, the stock investor may have received the tip from a trusted friend, or he could be the friend of the company's CEO and therefore has a strong emotional commitment. Although both explanations may help us understand the error, Barry Staw, who has done significant research into escalation of commitment, suggests that they do not go far enough: "A salient feature . . . is that a series of decisions is associated with a course of action rather than an isolated choice."[17]

To help explain such behaviour, Staw turned to the social psychological literature on forced compliance. In studies of forced compliance, individuals are typically made to perform an unpleasant or dissatisfying act (e.g., eating grasshoppers) with no external rewards. In general, after they comply, individuals bias their own attitudes to justify their previous behaviour (e.g., eating grasshoppers is not a bad thing because they are high in protein). This biasing of attitudes is most likely to occur when the individuals feel personally responsible for the negative consequences and when the consequences are difficult to undo.

On the basis of these findings, Staw and his colleagues carried out a series of experiments to find out how willing people would be to continue to commit valued resources to a course of action after it was clear that the original decision had been wrong. They found that decision makers actually allocated more money to company divisions that were showing poor results than to those that were showing good results. Also, decision makers allocated more money to a division when they had been responsible for the original decision to back the division. In short, decision makers were most likely to spend money on projects that had negative consequences when they were responsible.

Exhibit 5.6

Contributing Factors to Escalation of Commitment to Decisions

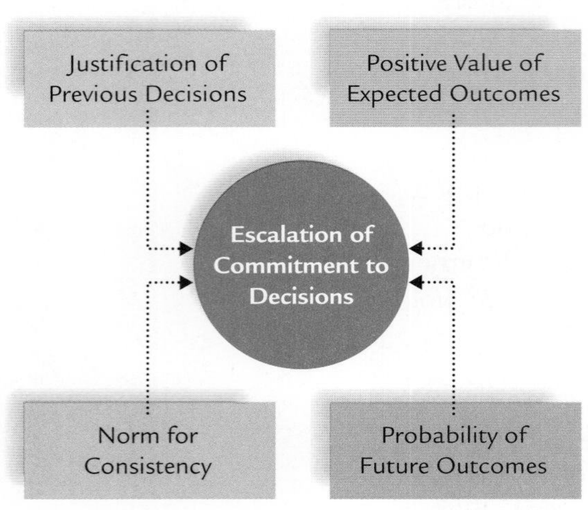

To find out why, Staw suggested a model of escalating commitment (Exhibit 5.6). This abbreviated model shows that four basic elements determine commitment to an action. First, people are likely to remain committed to a course of action (even when it is clearly incorrect) because of a need to justify previous decisions. When people feel responsible for negative consequences and have a need to demonstrate their own competence, they will often stick to a decision to turn it around or "pull a victory out of defeat." This is a form of retrospective rationality; the individual or members of the group seek explanations so that their previous decisions appear rational. For example, banks that loaned billions of dollars to Asian countries in the late 1980s and early 1990s continued to loan more money even after it was clear that the governments would have great difficulty repaying the loans. They continued these loans in part to support their original decision. If they didn't continue the loans, they might be forced to recognize that their original decision was a mistake. This dynamic is not limited to headline decisions, either.[18] It can affect our continued commitment to personal decisions as well. There is a range of examples, from keeping a car that is a lemon, to sticking with a boyfriend or girlfriend long after it is clear that it is not a good match. In each case we try to avoid admitting openly that the original decision was a mistake.

In addition, commitment to a previous decision is influenced by a norm for consistency. That is, managers who are consistent in their actions are often considered better leaders than those who flip-flop from one course of action to another.

Finally, two additional factors—the perceived probability and value of future outcomes—jointly influence what is called prospective rationality. **Prospective rationality** is simply a belief that future courses of action are rational and correct. When people think they can turn a situation around or that "prosperity is just around the corner," and when the goal is highly prized, they exhibit strong commitment to a continued course of action, influenced in part by the feeling that it is the proper thing to do.

prospective rationality a belief that future courses of action are rational and correct

Overcoming Escalation of Commitment. Because escalation of commitment can lead to serious and negative consequences for organizations, we must consider how to minimize its effects.

1. First, as a manager, you should stress in your own mind and to others (superiors, peers, and subordinates) that investments made in the past are sunk costs—that is, they cannot be recovered. All finance theory argues that sunk costs should be ignored in making future decisions, and only future costs and future anticipated benefits should be considered. So when you find yourself in a hole, the first thing to do is stop digging.
2. Second, you must create an atmosphere in which consistency does not dominate. This requires stressing the changing aspects of the competitive, social, cultural, and commercial environment surrounding a business and focusing on the importance of matching current decisions to current and expected future environments rather than to past decisions.
3. Third, you can encourage each member to evaluate the prospects of future outcomes and their expected positive value critically. You can

invite experts from outside the group to challenge members' future expectations, if need be.

4. Finally, as a manager, you can reward processes rather than outcomes. This encourages proper evaluation of projects at key stages where the project can be judged at face value and discourages individuals from undertaking risky heroics to pull a project out of the fire. This would mean celebrating failure if processes were followed and providing unambiguous negative feedback if processes were not followed, even if it led to a successful outcome.

In summary, when we consider effective decision-making processes in organizations, we must remain vigilant in knowing where our weaknesses lie. We need to be aware of our limitations in processing information, what shortcuts and approximations we rely on to make decisions, and our tendency to back a losing venture to avoid criticism and embarrassment.

Making Better Decisions

If all of the factors presented above can influence the effectiveness of decisions, what can you do as a manager to avoid these traps and enhance the probability of making a "good" decision?

Analyze the Situation First, recognizing the decision-making traps is a key factor to success. For example, if you are unaware of Gresham's law or the representativeness heuristic, you have little opportunity to assess whether or not you are falling victim to it. Without this awareness it is almost impossible to deliberately get yourself out of this particular pit if you've fallen into it. As simple as this first step may seem, it is vital. Consequently, one of the first steps to better individual decision making is better decision situation assessment. Exhibit 5.7 provides a simple set of questions related to the three categories of factors diagrammed in Exhibit 5.5 that you can ask yourself to have a clearer picture of the situation and the potential pitfalls.

Exhibit 5.7 Questions Related to the Factors that Influence Decision Quality (see Exhibit 5.5)

Decision-Maker Characteristics

1. Do you have an implicit favourite solution?
2. Do you have a tendency to satisfice and go with the first workable solution?
3. Do you feel overwhelmed by the amount of information you are having to process?
4. Do you feel a lack of knowledge about the problem?
5. Are you particularly unfamiliar or familiar with the problem?

Problem Characteristics

1. Does the problem seem quite ambiguous?
2. Is the problem substantially complex?
3. Does the problem seem stable or volatile?

Decision Environment Characteristics

1. Are you under significant time pressures to make the decision?
2. Do you face substantial resource limitations (e.g., people, money, equipment, etc.) relative to the problem and its solution?
3. Is the decision irreversible?
4. Are the problem and your decision of substantial importance?

Scan the Environment As we discussed, nonprogrammed decisions typically are more ambiguous than routine decisions. As a consequence, there is a greater risk that your decision could be wrong and carry important negative consequences for yourself and others. Going back to our example of the university president who has to choose between expanding the business school or the science facilities, making the wrong decision could be costly, both financially and politically. In fact, her job may depend on making the right decision. If she expands the science facility, there is no guarantee that the added faculty will bring in more contracts and grants. And by doing so, she may be denying admission to a large number of qualified business students. She may also alienate the business faculty and companies that recruit those graduates. In contrast, building the business programs could alienate the science students and faculty, allowing a rival university to get ahead, and possibly prompting many of the university's best scientists to go elsewhere. Clearly, the more complex, ambiguous, and volatile the problem, the more environmental scanning you may want to do prior to making the decision. For example, the university president would want to get as much useful information as she could from outside the organization. In doing so she may discover that a rival school is about to expand its own science complex and wants to hire away the best scientists. On one hand, she may wish to defend what she has, especially if the business school is viewed as less important to the institution's goals. On the other hand, if the provincial legislature has made it clear that they want more business education, she may have to factor this into her decision as well. Overall, environmental scanning may help you gain useful information that can lead to a higher-quality decision.

Think Through the Process As we stated earlier in this chapter, even though the rational approach may not always be descriptive of many decision-making processes, you can and most often should use it to guide your own decision making.

Be Creative Being creative can be an important key to making effective decisions, especially if you discover in doing an analysis of the decision-making situation that you have an "implicit favourite" solution or if you have past experience with a similar but not exactly the same situation. This is also true if the problem is complex or unfamiliar. For example, your problem is how to make a raw egg stand up on the surface of your desk for 10 seconds without assistance and without losing any of the substance inside the egg. In other words, you can't prop it up against something, or use glue, extract the yolk and egg white, and so on. Get creative. Try spinning it. Try balancing it. What works? There is a way to do it.

Know the Right Timing Clearly, you have to be aware of the timeliness of your decisions. Many decisions involve problems or opportunities that have time constraints. For example, deciding to enter a race after it's half over will not generally work out well. At the same time, deciding to run the race before any of the other competitors or spectators show up may not work out well either. Decisions can be made too early or too late. Making a decision sooner than needed can prevent you from creating a full set of alternatives or from examining them thoroughly. Making a decision too late can leave you with a great set of alternatives and a comprehensive analysis but no beneficial results. In popular management literature, this last tendency is often referred to as "analysis paralysis," or the failure to move and make a decision because you are stuck in the process of analyzing the situation, objectives, alternatives, and so on. To avoid poor timing, ask yourself and others when a decision is needed and why. Make sure the timing of the decision is clear and makes sense.

Increase Your Knowledge If you are clear about the timing of the decision, you can help yourself avoid the pitfall of analysis paralysis and still increase your knowledge to make a better decision. The old standby foundation questions that you may have been taught in past creative writing exercises are perhaps the best guide for adding relevant knowledge for better decisions: who, what, where, when, why, and how.

Be Flexible Thankfully, most decisions are not irreversible. As we will explore more fully later in this chapter, much of the sense of irreversibility of decisions comes from the decision maker's desire to seem consistent rather than from the nature of the decision itself. For example, once you jump out of an airplane and start falling, the nature of the decision is irreversible, so you better have a parachute. Consequently, as the rational model of decision making argues, it is important to monitor the outcomes closely and be prepared to modify or even completely change your decision if it seems that the desired outcomes will not materialize.

A Manager's Challenge: "Putting Radio into Orbit" provides an example where managers need to make good decisions in the face of considerable uncertainty. In deciding to launch satellite radio, they must first scan the environment carefully to learn from the actions of others (their successes and mistakes) as well as the nature of the market. In addition, they will need to be creative in coming up with solutions to the problems they face relative to their overall decision to embark on the plan. In reading this case, what is your impression of the industry? Do you think the Canadian market will be as slow to start as the US market was? Do you think the decision to partner with US service providers is the right approach, or should the Canadian providers remain independent?

Group Decision Making

The three models described at the beginning of the chapter (the rational/classical, bounded rationality, and retrospective decision models) attempt to explain certain aspects of individual decision making. However, those models can also illuminate aspects of group decision making. Many of the basic processes remain the same. For instance, using the rational model we can observe that both individuals and groups identify objectives. Both individuals and groups may also attempt to identify all possible outcomes before selecting one and, more than likely, both will fail in that attempt. Both individuals and groups are often observed engaging in satisficing behaviour or using heuristics in the decision process. And both individuals and groups develop implicit favourites and attempt to justify those favourites by procedures that appear to others to be rationalization. Many of the dynamics and processes of groups that relate to decision making as well as other group activities are covered extensively in Chapter 11.

Impact of Groups on Decision Making

What makes group decision making different from individual decision making is the social interaction in the process, which complicates the dynamics. In some situations, group decision making can be an asset, but at other times it

a manager's challenge *technology*

Putting Radio into Orbit

Will Canadian listeners on the go tune in to CD-quality satellite radio? Managers at three Canadian satellite radio providers are planning for a resounding "yes" as they introduce satellite broadcasting, or more specifically, subscription radio (since not all of the digital broadcasting is delivered via satellite) to the Canadian market. Along the way, the managers must make a number of key decisions, despite considerable uncertainty about the level of demand, programming content, competition, and financial backing.

Three prospective Canadian satellite providers (Sirius Satellite Radio Canada, XM Canada, and CHUM Subscription Radio Canada) submitted proposals to the CRTC in 2003 and 2004. Following hearings, all three proposals received approval in June 2005, and by December of that same year Sirius and XM were broadcasting in Canada.

The Canadian managers are learning from the experiences of their American counterparts, XM Satellite Radio Holdings and Sirius Satellite Radio, which are partnering with the Canadian affiliates of the same name. Only CHUM will be 100 percent Canadian. The two US services currently use satellites to beam 100 mostly-commercial-free channels of sports, music, news, children's shows, and entertainment programs to subscribers, who pay between $50 and $500 to buy special receivers and an additional monthly fee ranging from $10 to $15. Managers at XM and Sirius have committed billions of dollars in the expectation that truck drivers, commuters, and others who drive for long periods will pay for clear, continuous reception of specialized radio programming anywhere in the United States.

The US companies had an initial bumpy ride because of slow growth in the number of subscribers and new competition from digital radio technology (which makes ordinary radio signals sound much better without any monthly fee). However, growth has dramatically increased: in spring 2005 Sirius was reporting 1.1 million subscribers while XM reported 3.2 million. By July 2006 Sirius had 4.7 million subscribers and XM boasted 6.9 million.

Watching how US companies cope has helped Canadian managers become more knowledgeable about the nature and complexity of the decisions they face. For example, managers at Sirius and XM had little success selling add-on gadgets that equip existing car radios to receive satellite radio signals, so they finally struck deals with major car manufacturers such as Ford, Chrysler, and Honda to install satellite-ready receivers as an option in new cars. In addition, Canadian satellite radio managers realize that although the Canadian market has many similarities to the US market, there are many critical differences as well. The total number of new cars sold in Canada is less than in the United States, accounting for fewer vehicles equipped with satellite radio receivers. As well, managers will have to adhere to specific CRTC requirements for providing Canadian content within the programming packages offered by their service. There are also significant differences in preferences across Canadian regions for radio programming based on language, sports activities, popular music, and news. So far, though, it seems that satellite radio in Canada is here to stay.

Sources: CBC News "Satellite Radio: FAQs," February 10, 2006, www.cbc.ca/news (accessed October 13, 2006); CNET, "CNET's Quick Guide to Satellite Radio," March 1, 2005, reviews.cnet.com (accessed October 14, 2006); Dow Jones Newswires, "FCC Approves Digital Radio," October 10, 2002, www.wsj.com (accessed October 16, 2006); B. Werth, "Companies Push Satellite Radio While Public Interest Lags," *Herald-Times* (Bloomington, IN), September 10, 2002, www.hoosiertimes.com (accessed October 16, 2006).

can be a liability. The trick for you as a manager is to discover when and how to invite group participation in making decisions. Some assets and liabilities of group decision making are shown in Exhibit 5.8. Going one step further, let's look at what we know about the impact of groups on the decision process itself, especially relative to nonprogrammed decisions:

- In *establishing objectives*, groups are typically superior to individuals in that they bring greater cumulative knowledge to problems.
- In *identifying alternatives*, individual efforts ensure that different and perhaps unique solutions are identified from various functional areas that later can be considered by the group.

- In *evaluating alternatives*, group judgment is often superior to individual judgment because it involves a wider range of viewpoints.
- In *choosing alternatives*, involving group members often leads to greater acceptance of the final outcome.
- In *implementing the choice*, individual responsibility is generally superior to group responsibility. Whether decisions are made individually or collectively, individuals perform better in carrying out the decision than groups do.[19]

Exhibit 5.8 Assets and Liabilities of Group Decision Making

Assets +	Liabilities –
• Groups can accumulate more knowledge and facts. • Groups have a broader perspective and consider more alternatives. • Individuals who participate in group decisions are more satisfied with the decision and are more likely to support it. • Group decision processes serve an important communication function, as well as a useful political function.	• Groups often work more slowly than individuals. • Group decisions involve considerable compromise that may lead to less than optimal decisions. • Groups are often dominated by one individual or a small clique, thereby negating many of the virtues of group processes. • Overreliance on group decision making can inhibit management's ability to act quickly and decisively when necessary.

From the list in Exhibit 5.8, you can see that you cannot conclude that either individual or group decision making is superior. Rather, the situation and the individuals involved should guide the choice of decision technique.

One question about the effects of group participation remains to be asked: Why does it seem to work in many instances? A partial answer to this question has been offered by Ronald Ebert and Terence Mitchell.[20] First, they suggest that participation clarifies more fully what is expected. Second, participation increases the likelihood that employees will work for rewards and outcomes they value. Third, it heightens the effects of social influence on behaviour; that is, peers will monitor and exert pressure on each other to conform to expected performance levels. Finally, it enlarges the amount of control employees have over their work activities. In many cases, participation in decision making can be useful in both organizational goal attainment and personal need satisfaction.[21]

Because participation helps involve employees and increases satisfaction and interaction, it has been an important part of quality improvement efforts. For example, team-based efforts to improve products and processes have always worked best when they included significant participation in decision making.

Contingency Model of Participative Decision Making

A central issue facing managers is the extent to which they should allow employees to participate in decisions affecting their jobs. For example, as work situations, time pressures, and even subordinate capabilities change, does the level of participation in decisions need to change? The short answer is "yes."

Although many advocates of participation emphasize both case examples and even scientific research showing how participation led to improved decision quality, increased commitment of members to decision outcomes, and increased employee satisfaction, participative decision making is not a panacea. A careful review of the research suggests that it is not appropriate for every situation.[22] If participative decision making is not appropriate for all situations, how can you as a manager determine when it will and won't be effective and, therefore, when you should change your decision-making style or approach from one of making the decision on your own to one of involving others in a participative process?

Participative Decision Makers To determine some of the variables that make up good participative decisions, researchers have explored the characteristics of the decision makers. Essentially, researchers have asked the question, "When participative decision making is effective, what do the people involved look like?" First and foremost, research suggests that those participating in the decision-making process must have sufficient knowledge about the content of the decision. Companies such as Ford, Federal Express, Procter & Gamble, and Boeing have put together **cross-functional teams** (consisting of members from marketing, finance, operations, human resources, etc.) for new product launches because each member has unique knowledge that adds value to the overall product launch. In contrast, asking people to become involved in decisions that are completely outside their area of expertise does not lead to either better-quality decisions or more commitment to the decisions and their implementation.

cross-functional teams employees from different departments, such as finance, marketing, operations, and human resources, who work together in problem solving

In addition to content knowledge, members also need to have a general desire to participate. Not everyone wants to become involved in decisions. The desire to participate results from the individuals believing that (1) they have relevant content knowledge, (2) their participation will help bring about change, (3) the resulting change will produce outcomes they value or prefer, and (4) participation is valued by the organization and fits with its goals and objectives. When General Motors first started encouraging more employee involvement in decisions, workers resisted the effort because they did not believe it was "for real." This belief was based on the fact that involvement had not been a part of the company's history; in the past, decisions were made by managers and implemented by employees. As a consequence, it took sustained support from top management before workers believed participation was legitimate.

Participative Decision-Making Process Like individual decision making, participative decision making involves related yet separate processes. Using the classical model of decision making, a participative group moves through the same seven steps, but involvement of group members can vary in each of those steps. Low involvement allows members to communicate their opinions about the problem, alternatives, and solution, but not to influence the final determination. High involvement allows members not only to communicate their opinions, but also to make final determinations. Thus, the degree of involvement could range from high to low on each of the seven elements in the classical decision model. Exhibit 5.9 provides a sample in which a particular group has high involvement in the front end of classical decision making but low involvement on the back end.

Because involvement can vary for each step of the classical decision-making model, a question naturally arises whether any one configuration is better. One study directly examined this question.[23] This study found that high

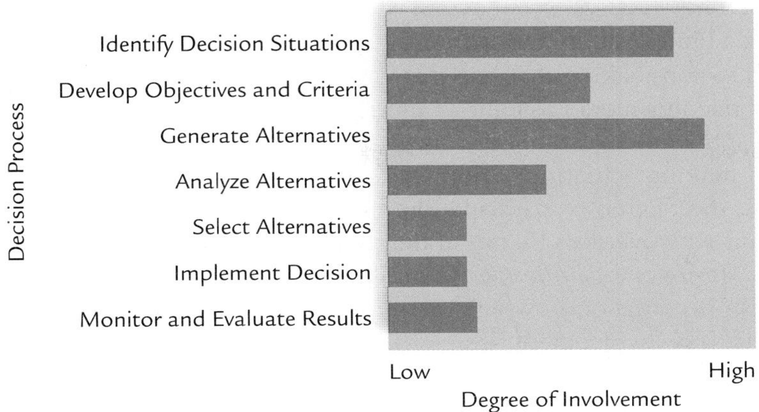

Exhibit 5.9

Sample Configuration of Degree of Involvement and Decision Process

involvement in generating alternatives, planning implementation, and evaluating results was significantly related to higher levels of satisfaction and work-group performance. Involvement in generating alternatives was important because solutions almost always came from the alternatives generated. Involvement in planning the implementation was important because the outcome was affected more by the way a solution was implemented than by the solution itself. And finally, involvement in evaluating results was important because feedback is critical to beginning the decision cycle again.

One of the interesting implications from this line of study is that group members also need to understand group processes for participative decision making to be effective. That is, skills in analysis, communication, and handling conflicts can be as important as knowledge and the desire to participate. For example, one of the critical capabilities in identifying problems is environmental scanning. Not everyone is skilled at scanning the environment and recognizing problems or opportunities, yet it is hard to begin participative decision making without members who can do this. For generating alternatives, a critical capability is creativity. For selecting a solution, a critical capability is managing conflict. It is unlikely that a group can agree on a preferred solution without some conflict, so managing that disagreement effectively is a critical skill. In this sense, much of what is covered in Chapter 11 on groups and teams and their effectiveness applies to effective group decisions.

Exhibit 5.10 provides a summary of the questions a manager should ask in determining whether participative decision making is likely to be effective.

Exhibit 5.10 Contingency Factors for Effective Participative Decision Making

1. Do potential group members have sufficient content knowledge?
2. Do potential members have sufficient process knowledge?
3. Do members have a desire to participate?
4. Do members believe that their participation will result in changes?
5. Do members positively value the expected outcomes?
6. Do members see participation as legitimate and congruent with other aspects of the organization?
7. If the answer to any of the above questions is no, is it possible to change the conditions?

Source: N. Margulies and J. Stewart Black, "Perspectives on the Implementation of Participative Approaches," *Human Resource Management 26*, no. 3 (1987), pp. 385–412.

On the basis of a long-term research project, Victor Vroom and his colleagues Philip Yetton and Arthur Jago also developed a theory of participation in decision making that has clear managerial implications.[24] It is possible to categorize this model as either a model of leadership or a model of decision making. The model not only considers how managers should behave in decision-making situations, but also prescribes correct leader behaviour regarding the degree of participation. Given its orientation toward leadership behaviour, we cover this theory in depth in Chapter 9.

A Manager's Challenge: "Law Firms Change Decision-Making Style" illustrates one situation in which the move from more involvement in decision making to less involvement seems to have been effective. Clearly, when too many people are involved in decisions and when those decisions involve areas of specialization in which the participating members lack expertise, lower levels of participation are more appropriate than higher levels. This is exactly the situation in many law firms that have experienced significant growth. What is your assessment of the situation and the response? Does the changing situation seem to justify less participation in decisions?

Decision Speed and Quality

Have you ever heard of Gavilan Computer? If you own a laptop you should have, but odds are you haven't. In the early 1980s, Gavilan Computer was at the forefront of computer technology and had a virtual monopoly on the developing—and lucrative—laptop computer market. By 1984, however, Gavilan had filed for bankruptcy. Despite a US$31 million stake from venture capitalists, the company experienced long delays and indecision that cost the company its early technological and market advantage. Competitors entered the market and Gavilan failed to exploit its advantage. As one executive observed, "We missed the window."[25] What happened to Gavilan has occurred with alarming frequency in many corporations—especially those involved in high-tech industries—as the indecisive fall by the wayside.

In the early 1980s Gavilan Computer was at the forefront of computer technology. By 1984, Gavilan had filed for bankruptcy.

a manager's challenge change

Law Firms Change Decision-Making Style

Traditionally, all the partners in a law firm participated as a group in making decisions. This system built consensus and commitment and brought diverse backgrounds and opinions to the deliberations. Over time, however, as law firms have merged or added partners, the custom of participative decision making has led to bottlenecks and complications when questions about finance, technology, or other specialized topics appear on the agenda. Not only do the partners need more time to come to an agreement on such issues, but their decisions are also not necessarily better as a result of group participation.

Today law firms face more competition than ever before and feel more pressure to retain and serve corporate clients by keeping up with the faster pace of business. To operate more efficiently and more effectively in such an environment, some large law firms are changing the way they make internal decisions.

For example, Piper Marbury Rudnick & Wolfe is a law firm with 950 attorneys located in offices across the United States. The 300 lawyers at its largest office, located in Chicago, recently changed to a more centralized method of decision making. Instead of bringing all the partners together to vote and then manage the outcome of each decision, the chairperson relies on professional managers who specialize in particular areas of expertise, including marketing, information technology, human resources, and finance. "We realized that because of our size, we had to adopt a corporate model," states the chairperson, Lee I. Miller. "It streamlines our decision making. We are able to react quickly, decisively."

However, partners accustomed to participative decision making may not easily accept the idea of delegating decisions to professional managers without group input. "At times it's a bitter pill," says a partner at the law firm Stellato & Schwartz. "When you ascend to the position of partner, it's based upon your ability to show loyalty, longevity, and business acumen. Inherent in those qualities is a desire to lead. But sometimes that desire has to be set aside for the good of the team." For their part, the managers who make decisions on behalf of law firms must constantly and carefully evaluate how the outcome of each major decision is likely to affect the firm and its partners, even when dealing with support functions such as human resources and finance.

Consider the situation at Wildman, Harrold, Allen & Dixon, an Illinois law firm where John Holthaus is executive director. As an accountant who holds an MBA degree, Holthaus has the technical and managerial background to make the myriad day-to-day decisions that keep the law firm operating smoothly. One way Holthaus proved his worth was by renegotiating the firm's lease to save on rental expenses. "I view my job as that of a hospital administrator who takes care of all the details so the doctors can take care of their patients," he explains. "I'm trying to make it easier for the attorneys to focus on serving their clients." Knowing that Holthaus understands the law firm's objectives and takes care of the tiniest details, the partners have come to rely on him rather than getting bogged down in endless group meetings to make decisions.

Source: Adapted from John T. Slania, "More Firms Mind Their Business: Corporate Model Helps Streamline Decision Making," *Crain's Chicago Business*, January 28, 2002, p. SR10.

In a series of studies of decision making in industries characterized by frequent change and turbulence—so-called high-velocity environments—researchers Kathleen Eisenhardt and L. J. Bourgeois attempted to determine what separates successful decision makers and managers from unsuccessful ones.[26] In high-velocity industries (e.g., microelectronics, medical technology, genetic engineering), high-quality, rapid decision making by executives and their companies is closely related to good corporate performance. In these industries, mistakes are costly; information is often ambiguous, obsolete, or simply incorrect; and recovery from missed opportunities is extremely difficult. In view of the importance of speed for organizational innovation, performance, and survival, how do successful decision makers make high-quality, rapid decisions? And how are those decisions implemented quickly?

Eisenhardt and Bourgeois found that five factors influenced a manager's ability to make fast decisions in high-velocity environments (see Exhibit 5.11). These five characteristics are moderated by three mediating processes that determine the manager's and group's ability to deal with the quantity and quality of information:

1. *Accelerated cognitive processing.* The decision maker must be able to process and analyze great amounts of information quickly and efficiently. Some people—and some groups—can simply process information faster and better than others. Obviously, the faster a manager can process what is presented, the quicker the decision can be made.
2. *Smooth group processes.* To be effective, the manager must work with a group that has smooth, harmonious relations. This is not to say that everyone always agrees. Quite the contrary—members of effective groups often disagree. However, it is the way they disagree and resolve their disagreements that counts. Fast decisions are aided by group members who share a common vision and who are mutually supportive and cohesive.
3. *Confidence to act.* Finally, fast decision-making groups must not be afraid to act. As we already noted, some people are reluctant to make decisions in the face of uncertainty, and they tend to wait until they can reduce the uncertainty. They may fall victim to analysis paralysis. Unfortunately, in high-velocity environments, this uncertainty is never eliminated. Thus, to be effective, fast decision makers must be willing to choose when the appropriate time comes even in the face of uncertainty.

Exhibit 5.11 Factors of Fast Decision Making

1. *Real-time information.* Fast decision makers must have access to and be able to process real-time information—that is, information that describes what is happening right now, not yesterday.
2. *Multiple simultaneous alternatives.* Decision makers examine several possible alternative courses of action simultaneously, not sequentially (e.g., "Let's look at alternatives X, Y, and Z together and see how each looks."). This adds complexity and richness to the analysis and reduces the time involved in information processing.
3. *Two-tiered advice process.* Fast decision makers make use of a two-tiered advisory system, whereby all team members are allowed input but greater weight is given to the more experienced co-workers.
4. *Consensus with qualification.* Fast decision makers attempt to gain widespread consensus on the decision as it is being made, not after it is made.
5. *Decision integration.* Fast decision makers integrate tactical planning and issues of implementation within the decision process itself (e.g., "If we are going to do X, how might we do it?").

Remember that this research is focused on high-velocity environments, not all organizational environments. That is, in businesses that are characterized by relative stability (e.g., the funeral home industry), rapid decisions may prove disastrous. Because stability allows time for more complete data collection and processing, managers in stable environments have less need for immediate action. Thus, as a manager of a team, you need to assess the time factors that characterize your industry. Then you will be able to make decisions appropriate for your industry.

Problems in Group Decision Making

One of the main problems with group decision making has received a lot of attention in recent years—a phenomenon known as **groupthink**. This phenomenon, first discussed by Irving Janis, refers to a mode of thinking in which the pursuit of agreement among members becomes so dominant that it overrides a realistic appraisal of alternative courses of action.[27] The concept emerged from Janis's studies of high-level policy decisions by government leaders. These included decisions by the US government about Vietnam, the Bay of Pigs invasion, and the Korean War. In analyzing the decision process leading up to each action, Janis found indications pointing to the development of group norms that improved morale at the expense of critical thinking. A model of this process is shown in Exhibit 5.12.

groupthink a mode of thinking in which the pursuit of agreement among members becomes so dominant that it overrides a realistic appraisal of alternative courses of action

Groupthink by Stewart Black

mymanagementlab

Exhibit 5.12

The Groupthink Process

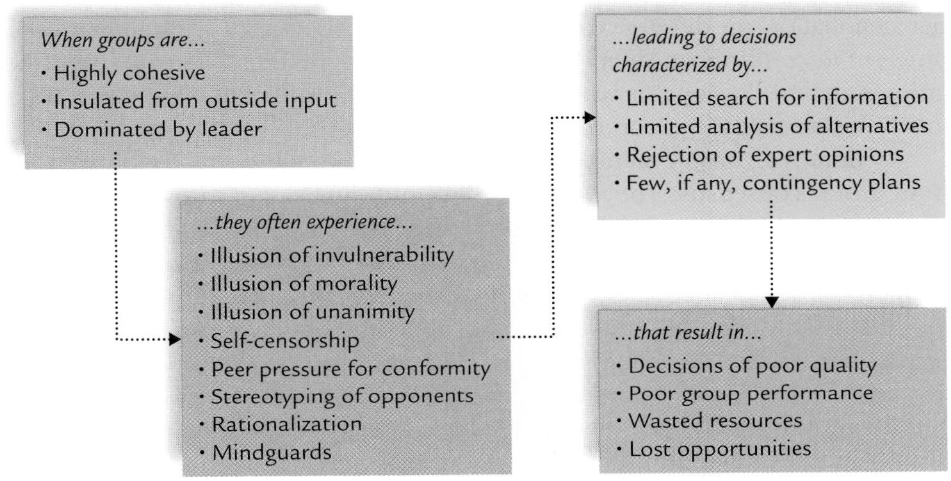

When groups are...
- Highly cohesive
- Insulated from outside input
- Dominated by leader

...they often experience...
- Illusion of invulnerability
- Illusion of morality
- Illusion of unanimity
- Self-censorship
- Peer pressure for conformity
- Stereotyping of opponents
- Rationalization
- Mindguards

...leading to decisions characterized by...
- Limited search for information
- Limited analysis of alternatives
- Rejection of expert opinions
- Few, if any, contingency plans

...that result in...
- Decisions of poor quality
- Poor group performance
- Wasted resources
- Lost opportunities

Source: Adapted from Gregory Moorhead, "Groupthink: Hypothesis in Need of Testing," *Group and Organization Studies* 7, no. 4, December 1982, pp. 429–444. Copyright © 1982 by Sage Publications, Inc. Reprinted by permission of Sage Publications, Inc.

Symptoms of Groupthink In studies of both government and business leaders, Janis identified eight primary symptoms of groupthink. The first is the *illusion of invulnerability*. Group members often reassure themselves about obvious dangers, becoming overly optimistic and thus willing to take extraordinary risks. Members fail to respond to clear warning signals. For instance, in the disastrous Bay of Pigs invasion of Cuba in the 1960s, the United States operated on the false assumption that it could keep its invasion of Cuba a secret. Even after news of the plan had leaked out, government leaders remained convinced of their ability to keep it a secret.

Victims of groupthink also tend to collectively *rationalize* and discount warning signs and other negative feedback that could lead to reconsidering the course of action. For example, Motorola discounted the new competitive potential of Nokia in the early 1990s. After all

- Nokia had a 100-year history in the forest products industry, making products like rubber boots for fishermen, not high-tech mobile phones.
- Europe would not likely adopt a unified digital standard because the various countries had never demonstrated any real ability to coordinate and cooperate.
- Even if they did, the markets of these countries (Germany, France, or Italy) paled in comparison to the size of the US mobile phone market.
- Finland (the home of Nokia) had fewer people than Chicago at the time.

We all know what happened. In 1990 Nokia was not even listed in the top 100 recognized brands, but by 2002 Nokia was number six—ahead of Intel and right behind GE. Motorola's 35 percent global market share of mobile phones was cut in half while Nokia's global share went from virtually nothing to 40 percent at its peak. Today Nokia is the number-one cell phone maker in the world.

Next, group members often believe in the inherent morality of the group. Because of this *illusion of morality*, they ignore the ethical or moral consequences of their decisions. While advertising for tobacco products is illegal in Canada, leading tobacco companies in the United States continue to run advertisements about smoking, ignoring the medical evidence of the hazards involved.

Stereotyping the enemy is another symptom of groupthink. In-group members often stereotype leaders of opposition groups in harsh terms that rule out negotiation on differences of opinion. Often they also place tremendous *pressure to conform* on members who temporarily express doubts about the group's shared illusions or who raise questions about the validity of the arguments supporting the group decisions.

Moreover, group members often use *self-censorship* to avoid deviations from group consensus. They often minimize to themselves the seriousness of their doubts. Partly because of self-censorship, the *illusion of unanimity* forms. Members assume that individuals who remain silent agree with the spoken opinions of others and falsely conclude that everyone holds the same opinion.

Finally, victims of groupthink often appoint themselves as *mindguards* to protect the leader and other members of the group from adverse information that could cause conflict over the correctness of a course of action. The mindguard may tell the dissident that he or she is being disruptive or nonsupportive or may simply isolate the dissident from other group members.

Organizational dynamics like groupthink can lead companies to discount competitive threats. When the Finnish company Nokia—which had traditionally manufactured forest industry products, including rubber boots—entered the US mobile phone market in the 1990s, competitors like Motorola didn't take it seriously.

Consequences of Groupthink Groupthink can have several adverse consequences for the quality of decision making. First, groups plagued by groupthink often limit their search for possible solutions to one or two alternatives rather than all possible alternatives. Second, such groups frequently fail to re-examine their chosen action after new information or events suggest a change in course. Third, group members spend little time considering nonobvious advantages to alternative courses of action. Fourth, such groups often make little or no attempt to seek expert advice either inside or outside their organization. Fifth, members show interest in facts that support their preferred alternative and either ignore or disregard facts that fail to support it. Finally, groups often ignore possible roadblocks to their choice and, as a result, fail to develop contingency plans. This last consequence is similar to retrospective decision making—the decision is made and then data are selected that support the decision. Because peers reinforce the decision, unwillingness to re-examine and change directions is even more powerful in group decisions than individual decisions.

Overcoming Groupthink Because a groupthink mentality poses such serious consequences for organizations, we must consider how to minimize its effects. Janis suggests several strategies. To begin, group leaders can reduce groupthink by encouraging each member to evaluate proposals critically. Leaders can also ensure that the group considers a range of alternatives by not stating their own positions and instead promoting open inquiry.

Other strategies for preventing groupthink involve getting more suggestions for viable solutions. Assigning the same problem to two independent groups can achieve this. Or before the group reaches a decision, members can seek advice from other groups in the organization. Another technique is to invite experts outside of the group to challenge group members' views at meetings.

Groupthink may also be prevented with strategies directed at the group members themselves. For example, for each group meeting a member can be appointed to serve as a **devil's advocate**, a person whose role is to challenge the majority position.[28] Also, after reaching preliminary consensus, the group can schedule a second-chance meeting. This allows group members an opportunity to express doubts and rethink the issue.

devil's advocate a group member whose role is to challenge the majority position

If groups are aware of groupthink, they can use the steps discussed to minimize the likelihood of falling victim to this problem. These steps, which are summarized in Exhibit 5.13, offer advice for leaders, organizations, individuals, and the process itself.

Exhibit 5.13 Guidelines for Overcoming Groupthink

For the company
- Establish several independent groups to examine the same problem.
- Train managers in groupthink prevention techniques.

For the leader
- Assign everyone the role of critical evaluator.
- Use outside experts to challenge the group.
- Assign a devil's advocate role to one member of the group.
- Try to be impartial and refrain from stating your own views.

For group members
- Try to retain your objectivity and be a critical thinker.
- Discuss group deliberations with a trusted outsider and report back to the group.

For the deliberation process
- At times, break the group into subgroups to discuss the problem.
- Take time to study what other companies or groups have done in similar situations.
- Schedule second-chance meetings to provide an opportunity to rethink the issues before making a final decision.

Cultural Dimensions of Decision Making

To this point we have talked about decision making as though it applied the same way the world over. Although we still have much to learn about decision making in different countries and cultures, we can identify several factors that affect how decisions are made. Many stem from the cultural differences we examined in Chapter 4.

One of the factors affecting decision making is the extent to which a culture adopts an individualist or collectivist orientation. For example, in exploring a contingency framework for participative decision making, we cited research suggesting that participation was not effective in all situations and that it should be used when it matches specific elements of a situation. However, it is worth noting that most researchers of participative decision making have come from individualistic cultures such as the United States, Canada, and the United Kingdom. In countries such as Japan, Indonesia, and Korea, managers and employees have a much stronger collectivist orientation. As a consequence, involving others in decision making may not simply be a function of contingency factors, but simply viewed as the "right" thing to do. In collectivist cultures, even when an individual decision maker believes he or she has all the relevant knowledge, a strong collectivist value often leads to the inclusion of others in the decision-making process.

These cultural clashes can often be seen when individuals from opposite cultural orientations must work together. For example, when managers from more individualistic cultures are assigned to work in more collectivist cultures, they quite frequently experience difficulties because they tend to make too many individual decisions and not include others enough.[29]

Basic values concerning hierarchy can also influence decision making across countries.[30] As discussed in Chapter 4, managers in countries such as Malaysia, India, and Thailand have a higher acceptance of hierarchical differences between people (high power distance, in Hofstede's terms), whereas managers in countries such as Israel, Australia, and Denmark do not. Power distance can significantly affect the problem-analysis stage of decision making, especially when it involves group decisions. In low-power-distance cultures, group members tend to openly and directly disagree with each other in discussing the merits or risks of a given alternative. In high-power-distance cultures, such open discussions are less acceptable when individuals of differing ranks are involved. For example, if a lower-ranked individual in Thailand had a significant difference of opinion with his superior, directly raising this during a group meeting would not be acceptable. Rather, the individual would try to find a time, perhaps after work, when he could present his opinion privately to his superior.

On the surface, one might expect organizations in cultures that have high levels of power distance to suffer from problems of groupthink because employees are less willing to voice their concerns or make critical comments, especially when superiors are present. Interestingly, many of these cultures have developed business practices to counterbalance this potential problem. For example, managers in Japan use a technique called *nemawashi*. This term is borrowed from gardening and refers to the process of gradually snipping the roots of a tree or bush that is to be transplanted to reduce the shock to the plant. In business, *nemawashi* translates into many private or semiprivate meetings in which true opinions are shared before a major decision-making meeting. This allows differences of opinion to be stated while still protecting respected hierarchical status. In addition, meeting after work at a bar or restaurant also allows for more direct discussions and disagreements. Both of these practices serve to counteract groupthink fostered by high power distance.

Another factor that can affect decision making is the extent to which cultures differ in their tolerance of risk. In countries with a relatively low tolerance of uncertainty and risk, such as Japan and Germany, nonprogrammed decisions are avoided as much as possible by using standard operating procedures. For example, the operating manual at BMW for how to work through an engineering problem is thick and detailed. Even though the specific engineering problems may vary, BMW executives have tried to make the decisions as programmed as possible. In contrast, managers in countries with a relatively high tolerance of uncertainty and risk, such as Australia, Canada, and the United States, tend to seek out nonprogrammed decisions and to give senior management more responsibility for nonprogrammed decisions. For example, the employee manual at Nordstrom, an upscale department store in the United States, simply states, "Nordstrom Rules: Rule #1: Use your good judgment in all situations. There will be no additional rules. Please feel free to ask your department manager, store manager, or division general manager any question at any time."

Australian, U.S., and Canadian companies like Holt Renfrew are likely to turn to nonprogrammed decision making and give their employees more decision-making latitude.

In addition to cultural values and the way they can affect the decision-making process, social and even corporate cultural values can affect nearly every aspect of decision making. For example, what is seen as a problem, what is viewed as an acceptable or desirable outcome, what criteria are used in assessing various alternatives, how an alternative is chosen (by the highest-ranking member, majority votes, consensus, etc.), or who is involved in planning the implementation of a decision can all be influenced by the underlying organizational or national culture. However, knowing the basic building blocks of decision making helps you ask the right questions and discover important differences in decision making when you work with people from other cultures.

Strategies for Improving Decision Making

Now that we have focused on the problems and processes involved in decision making, and examined several decision-making models, the differences between individual and group decisions, participation in decision making, constraints on effective decision making, and cultural influences, we can consider additional ways of improving the decision-making process. At the beginning of the chapter we mentioned that decisions could be divided into two phases: problem formulation and problem solution. Strategies to improve decision making can also be divided into the same two categories.[31]

Improving Problem Formulation

Problem formulation focuses on identifying the causes for unsatisfactory behaviour and finding new opportunities and challenges. This process is often inhibited by the failure of group members to look beyond the familiar. Groupthink and escalating commitment often limit critical analysis or comprehensive searches for information and solutions. As a result, improvement in problem formulation may require the use of structured debate. **Structured debate** is a process to improve problem formulation through the use of a devil's advocate, multiple advocacy, and dialectical inquiry (see Exhibit 5.14).

structured debate a process to improve problem formulation that includes using a devil's advocate, multiple advocacy, and dialectical inquiry

Exhibit 5.14 Techniques for Improving Decision Making

Structured Debate (Problem Formulation)	Creativity Stimulants (Problem Solution)
Devil's advocate	Brainstorming
Multiple advocacy	Nominal group technique
Dialectical inquiry	Delphi technique

Devil's Advocate As discussed earlier, a devil's advocate is a group member whose role is to disagree with the group. For example, if you asked a group of North American automobile company executives why their sales are down, they might blame Japanese imports. In this case, a devil's advocate would argue that the problem is not with the Japanese, but with the North Americans themselves and their poor product quality. Through this process, the group is forced to justify its position and, as a consequence, develop a more precise and accurate picture of the problem and its underlying causes.

multiple advocacy a process to improve decision making by assigning several group members to represent the opinions of various constituencies that might have an interest in the decision

Multiple Advocacy Multiple advocacy is like the devil's advocate approach except that more than one opposing view is presented. Each group involved in a decision is assigned the responsibility of representing the opinions of its constituents. Thus, if a university is concerned with enhancing racial and cultural diversity on campus, it might establish a commission including Blacks, Hispanics, Asians, women's groups, and so forth. The resulting dialogue should lead to the identification of a useful agenda for discussion.

dialectical inquiry a process to improve decision making by assigning a group member (or members) the role of questioning the underlying assumptions associated with the formulation of a problem

Dialectical Inquiry Dialectical inquiry occurs when a group or individual is assigned the role of questioning the underlying assumptions of problem formulation. It begins by identifying the prevailing view of the problem and its associated assumptions. Next, an individual is asked to develop an alternative problem that is credible but has different assumptions. By doing so, the accuracy of the original assumptions is examined and possibly altered. As a result, group members are forced to "think outside the box" and look at new ways to analyze a problem. These efforts are particularly helpful in overcoming groupthink and escalating commitment because they question the underlying assumptions of group behaviour.

Improving Problem Solution

Problem solution involves developing and evaluating alternative courses of action and then selecting and implementing the preferred alternatives. To improve this process, group members must be as thorough and creative as possible. Stimulation of creativity expands the search for and analysis of possible alternatives. Three such mechanisms are useful: brainstorming, the nominal group technique, and the delphi technique.

Brainstorming The process of **brainstorming** generates many creative solutions without evaluating their merit. It is a frequently used mechanism to provide the maximum number of ideas in a short period of time. A group comes together, is given a specific problem, and is told to propose any ideas that come to mind to solve the problem. In such sessions—at least in the early stages—criticism is minimized so as not to inhibit expression. Once all the ideas are on the table, the group considers the positive and negative aspects of each proposal. Through a process of continual refinement, the best possible solution under the circumstances should emerge.

brainstorming a process of generating many creative solutions without evaluating their merit

Nominal Group Technique The **nominal group technique**, typically referred to as NGT, consists of four phases in group decision making.[32] First, individual members meet as a group, but they begin by sitting silently and independently generating their ideas on a problem in writing. This silent period is followed by a round-robin discussion in which each group member presents an idea to the group. No discussion of the idea is allowed at this time. The ideas are summarized and recorded (perhaps on a whiteboard). After all individuals have presented their ideas, each idea is discussed to clarify and evaluate it. Finally, group members conclude the meeting by silently and independently ranking the various ideas or solutions. The final decision is determined by the pooled outcome of the members' votes.

nominal group technique a process of having group members record their proposed solutions, summarize all proposed solutions, and independently rank solutions until a clearly favoured solution emerges

The NGT allows the group to meet formally, but it does not allow members much discussion; hence the term *nominal* group technique. A chief advantage of this procedure is that everyone independently considers the problem without influence from other group members. As mentioned earlier, this influence represents one of the chief obstacles to open-minded discussions and decision making.

Delphi Technique In contrast to NGT, the **delphi technique** never allows decision participants to meet face to face. Instead, a problem is identified and members are asked through a series of carefully designed questionnaires to provide potential solutions. These questionnaires are completed independently. Results of the first questionnaire are then circulated to all group members (who are still physically separated). After viewing the feedback, members are again asked their opinions (to see if the opinions of others on the first questionnaire caused them to change their own minds). This process may continue through several iterations until group members' opinions begin to show consensus.

delphi technique a decision-making technique that never allows decision participants to meet face to face but identifies a problem and asks for solutions using a questionnaire

The decision-making process includes a variety of problems. Individuals and groups have various biases and personal goals that may lead to suboptimal decisions. Moreover, groups often censor themselves. Even so, techniques such as those discussed here aim to minimize many of these problems by insulating individual participants from the undue influence of others. This allows individuals greater freedom of expression, and the group receives far less filtered or slanted information with which to make its decision. Thus, although not perfect, these techniques can give managers mechanisms to improve both the quality and the timeliness of decisions made in organizations.

The Role of Technology

Much has been said in recent years about the role of technology in decision making at the individual and group level.[33] For routine but complex tasks such as scheduling aircraft, raw materials, and material- and component-flow through a factory, computers and software vastly increase decision-making capabilities. These tools can process amounts of information that would be overwhelming for an individual and at a speed that would be impossible for a human being. For example, despite all the problems and huge losses for commercial airlines in the United States during the 1990s, JetBlue, a US discount airline, became a successful start-up in 1998 and made money when other airlines were losing billions. Part of its success was due to the liberal use of new technology. By putting laptops and software in the hands of pilots, the company did away with the dozens and dozens of people typically required to make decisions about flight paths, scheduling, fuel intake, and so on.[34]

There is also a wide variety of technologies available for helping groups communicate and make decisions without having to get together face to face. Technology that allows group members in different locations to view a common document at the same time and make real-time changes is increasingly being used by design teams in industries like automobile manufacturing. The "virtual" aspects can save considerable travel costs and some have argued that the real-time aspects increase group decision effectiveness. Certainly companies are using technology to conduct virtual meetings and bring teams together from all over the world, but whether the benefits of computer-mediated communication are as great as they were hyped up to be is arguable. One review of recent studies comparing decision making in face-to-face versus computer-mediated communication groups found that computer-mediated communication leads to decreased group effectiveness, increased time required to complete tasks, and decreased member satisfaction compared to face-to-face groups.[35] The study concluded by cautioning about the unbridled rush by organizations to adopt computer-mediated communication as a medium for group decision making.

managerial perspectives revisited

PERSPECTIVE 1: **THE ORGANIZATIONAL CONTEXT** No doubt by this point you see the importance of the organizational context in both individual and group decision making. However, it is worthwhile making the links explicit. For example, time pressures in an organization can significantly affect decision making. On the one hand, the nature of your business may be high velocity and require quick decisions. On the other hand, the culture of your company or just your immediate boss can put pressure on you to make a quick decision when one is not actually needed. Failure to recognize the organizational context could cause you to be late in making a decision in the first situation and unduly early in the second. The cultural diversity of your organization also presents challenges and opportunities. Clearly, when the group and decision-making processes are managed well, cultural diversity can be leveraged for more diverse perspectives regarding the problem or opportunity as well as greater creativity in solving the

problem. At the same time, cultural diversity could present challenges in terms of different levels of comfort with ambiguous problems, desire to participate, or how to confront differences of opinion in a group setting with superiors present. The nature of the organization can also influence the degree to which you face programmed and nonprogrammed decisions. In general, managers working in a railroad company likely face more programmed decisions than those working in the fashion industry. However, even within a given industry the culture of the specific company can influence the degree to which you face programmed or nonprogrammed decisions.

2

PERSPECTIVE 2: **THE HUMAN FACTOR** Even as a manager, you may encounter decisions that you can and should make individually. However, as a manager it is less likely that these individually made decisions can be implemented completely on your own without the involvement of others. Even when facing situations in which you believe the benefits of involving others in decision making outweigh any disadvantages, you will have to decide the extent to which you involve others in the formulation and solution phases. For example, as the complexity and ambiguity of the problems you face and the decisions you have to make increase, so does the likelihood that you will need to involve others in decisions. Will you work through people with higher involvement primarily in the formulation phase, the solution phase, or both? Clearly, to the extent that you involve others in decision making, the decision formulation and implementation success becomes a function of working effectively with and through others.

3

PERSPECTIVE 3: **MANAGING PARADOXES** Managers are likely to encounter paradoxes in decision making. On the one hand, aspiring to follow the rational approach to make and implement decisions can help you avoid common pitfalls of bounded rationality or retrospective decision making. On the other hand, we are limited in our ability to be rational and all too often fall victim to decision-making traps. You will also have to master the potential paradox that is at the heart of Gresham's law. You cannot ignore or simply delegate away all programmed decisions whether they are urgent or not. At the same time, if you allow them to dominate your time and energy, you will be less likely to address nonprogrammed decisions, which often have a bigger impact on your job performance and overall results for the organization. Diversity presents another element of duality. As a manager you get paid in part for your judgment and ability to make decisions. Yet never checking with others as to how they see a situation or never taking into account the diverse perspectives, experience, and capabilities of those around you can lead you to less creative and less effective decisions.

4

PERSPECTIVE 4: **ENTREPRENEURIAL MINDSET** Managers' entrepreneurial mindset is reflected in the decisions that they make and by the degree of their commitment to those decisions and the processes by which they are made. Overall, an entrepreneurial mindset in decision making is reflected by applying one's intuition and being creative along with a willingness to take some risks. A manager can enrich entrepreneurial activities in the organization by searching for new information and encouraging others to express diverse viewpoints. Although escalation of commitment to a prior decision and groupthink (if a group participates in the decision) do not reflect an entrepreneurial mindset, the devil's advocate approach, brainstorming, delphi technique, and the nominal group technique can be used by managers to facilitate a more entrepreneurial approach to decision making. Using such approaches displays managers' commitment to be innovative in continuously searching for new opportunities when they make important decisions.

concluding comments

Decision making is a critical part of any manager's life. You could construe much of what a manager does as decision making. Motivation could be viewed as a decision regarding how to motivate a subordinate. Strategic management could be viewed as deciding what strategy to pursue. Communication could be viewed as a decision about what to say and how to say it. However central decision making may be to managing, to say that it is everything seems a bit much to us.

Still, as a manager you will make many decisions—large and small. As a consequence, you need a reasonably comprehensive but usable framework for guiding your decisions. We have suggested that thinking about decision making in terms of formation and implementation can fit this need. In formulation, it is important to remember that we often select solutions that meet our minimum objectives rather than spending extra time and energy trying to find the solution that maximizes the objectives. However, to appear rational, we often construct objectives and criteria after the fact to justify the decision we have already made. Groups can add a social dynamic to this tendency and make group members feel even more comfortable that they have been rational than individuals might feel alone. After all, if everyone else feels like it's a good decision, it must be. Managed properly, groups can also be an antidote to many of the limitations we described. Consequently, depending on how well the group dynamics are managed, group decision making can render decisions and results that are significantly better or worse than individuals might achieve on their own.

Thus, making a group decision or involving others in decision making is not a panacea to the common pitfalls. The decision of how much to involve others is a function of several factors including the knowledge and motivation of potential participants in the decision, the nature of the problem and decision, the environment in which the problem exists, and the speed with which the decision needs to be made.

Understanding these basics provides a foundation for awareness of how cultural values can influence decision making. This in turn better enables you as a manager to make effective decisions in an increasingly global and culturally diverse environment.

key terms

anchoring **162**
bounded rationality (administrative man) model **156**
brainstorming **181**
conjunction fallacy **162**
cross-functional teams **170**
decision making **151**
delphi technique **181**
devil's advocate **177**
dialectical inquiry **180**
ease of recall **161**

escalation of commitment 162
formulation 151
Gresham's law of planning 152
groupthink 175
heuristic 157
insensitivity to base rates 161
insensitivity to sample size 162
intuitive decision making 159
misconception of chance 162
multiple advocacy 180
nominal group technique 181
nonprogrammed decision 152
opportunity 151
perceptual distortion 159
presumed associations 161
problem 151
programmed decision 151
prospective rationality 164
rational (classical) model 153
regression to the mean 162
retrievability 161
retrospective decision (implicit favourite) model 159
satisficing 157
solution 151
standard operating procedure (SOP) 152
structured debate 180
subjectively expected utility (SEU) model 154

test your comprehension

1. What are the two fundamental stages in decision making?
2. Describe programmed and nonprogrammed decisions.
3. When are SOPs (standard operating procedures) most often used?
4. Describe Gresham's law of planning.
5. How can selective perception influence decision formulation?
6. What is the basic premise of the rational (classical) model of decision making?
7. How does the rational (classical) model of decision making differ from the bounded rationality model?
8. How can biases negatively affect decision quality?
9. How can managers work to overcome the effects of escalation of commitment to past decisions?
10. What are the key advantages to understanding the bounded rationality model of decision making?
11. What is satisficing? How does it differ from satisfying?
12. What is an implicit favourite?
13. How does the retrospective decision model work?
14. Why is analyzing the decision situation a key step in making better decisions?
15. What are the key assets of group decision making?
16. What are the key liabilities of group decision making?
17. When is it appropriate for a manager to be more participative in decision making?
18. Describe the phenomenon of groupthink. What are its symptoms?
19. How can we overcome groupthink?
20. Compare and contrast the nominal group technique and the delphi technique of decision making.
21. How can cultural values affect decision making?

apply your understanding

1. If your subordinates expect you to be consistent in your decision-making style, but you believe that different decision-making styles (e.g., high involvement of others versus low involvement) are appropriate for specific situations, how can you *change* your decision-making approach but not seem inconsistent to your employees?
2. Think of someone you know personally who is an effective decision maker. What key characteristics would you use to describe this person?
3. What are the strengths and weaknesses of a manager with "good instincts" who seems to make effective decisions but whose approach is more like the retrospective than the rational model?
4. Japanese and Korean managers tend to spend considerably more time on and involve more people in the problem formulation stage of decision making than North American managers do. What are the pros and cons you see with this?

practise your capabilities

While sitting in your office, you get a call from the plant supervisor that a request has come in from a major customer that would require you to adjust your product line for a custom run of this client's rush order. The plant supervisor has delegated the decision of whether you should stop your current run and meet the customer's request to you. He needs the decision by tomorrow morning.

Your line is in the middle of an extended standard run that will produce product for five of your mid-sized customers. Your company competes in part by offering both low cost and quality service. The vast majority of your mid-size customers chose you because of your lower prices. You maintain your profitability with these customers through keeping your costs low. Your principal means of achieving this is through running a high volume of standard products through your product line. Many of your large customers appreciate your low price but are willing to pay a premium for customized service and alterations to the products that come off your line.

If you stop the line to make the changes in equipment needed to run the custom order, you will incur both costs and delays to your current standard run. You are about two-thirds of the way through your standard run. It will take approximately three hours to change over to the custom run and two days to run it.

You have made this particular changeover before, but not in the last six months. You know the basics of the changeover but the person most knowledgeable about the details is off sick today. She left you a voice mail saying that she expects to be back to work tomorrow.

In general your team of nine product-line operators is fairly experienced and does not require close supervision, with the exception of two new members to your team. Your team is generally willing to be involved in decisions, but they are also happy to just "do their jobs."

1. Should you make this decision on your own or should you involve the group?
2. Would you stop the current run and change over for the custom run? Why or why not?
3. If you insist that it's impossible to decide based on the information you have, what additional information must you have to make the decision?

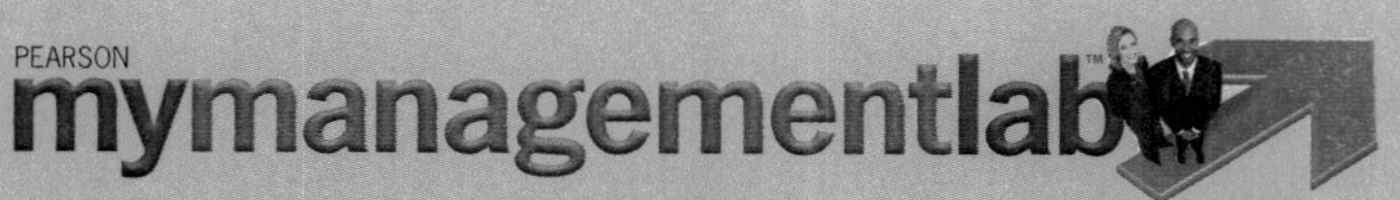

To improve your grade, visit the MyManagementLab website at **www.pearsoned.ca/mymanagementlab**. This online homework and tutorial system allows you to test your understanding and generates a personalized study plan just for you. It provides you with study and practice tools directly related to this chapter's content. MyManagementLab puts you in control of your own learning!

closing case DEVELOP YOUR CRITICAL THINKING

NB Power Fails to Secure Long-Term Supply of Orimulsion

In March 2001, the Province of New Brunswick was faced with the decision of whether or not to pay three-quarters of a billion dollars to convert the Coleson Cove power plant in Saint John from oil to orimulsion. The conversion was required to meet environmental regulations and extend the life of the plant to 2030, which was reportedly necessary before 2005. Orimulsion was considered an attractive alternative to other fuels because it was less expensive and could be stored easily near the plant. Also, it was predicted that an orimulsion plant could produce 450 megawatts of power, whereas a gas plant could only generate anywhere from 270 to 400 megawatts. The orimulsion, a patented mixture of bitumen and water, would be shipped from Venezuela, the world's only supplier.

By mid-January 2002, NB Power had arrived at an agreement with Bitor America (a subsidiary of Petróleos de Venezuela, or PDVSA), the Venezuelan supplier of orimulsion. It was rumoured that the price of the fuel was so low that it made the conversion of Coleson Cove appealing, even though retrofit costs would be enormous. To proceed with the project, NB Power would have to pass an environmental impact assessment and gain approval from the provincial cabinet to spend $747 million on the conversion. After this permission was obtained, construction commenced in December 2002. NB Power reported that it had obtained a 20-year contract for orimulsion, which among other items would obligate Bitor America to compensate NB Power if there were any disruptions in the fuel supply.

Critics of the proposed project felt that there were too many unanswered questions to proceed and that relying on Venezuela for the fuel was risky because of political instability. Then–New Brunswick premier Bernard Lord defended the project, noting that the cost savings from using bitumen would help pay for pollution controls and that the alternative, natural gas, was both expensive and available quantities uncertain. Then in 2003 a general strike in Venezuela prevented shipments of orimulsion from reaching New Brunswick.

Without the orimulsion the plant was forced to burn a more expensive fossil fuel which resulted in a $20 million loss for NB Power over four months. It was at this time that the media began to report that NB Power did not have insurance for a disruption in supply, and in fact had not even secured a signed contract before proceeding with the project. By February 2004, the Coleson Cove plant was well into the $750 million conversion to orimulsion, and speculation surfaced that Premier Lord had approved the retrofit without having obtained a signed contract from Bitor. Representatives for NB Power countered, stating that they had been discussing the fuel situation with the Venezuelan company and did in fact have an orimulsion supply agreement. Despite this and the premier's continued statements, the media onslaught continued, openly questioning whether the supply agreement was a memorandum of understanding rather than a signed contract. If there was no contract with Bitor, the extra cost for an alternate fuel over the next 20 years was projected to be around $2 billion.

Near the end of February 2004, reports surfaced that NB Power was suing the Venezuelan supplier (PDVSA) and its American subsidiary (Bitor America) for $2 billion, stating that they had breached an agreement to supply the fuel. The suit claimed NB Power and Bitor arranged a fuel-supply agreement in July 2001 detailing the terms of supply, the amount and price of the fuel, payment terms, insurance and shipping matters, and taxes and liabilities. Work immediately stopped on construction of the orimulsion delivery system at the port in Saint John, but the retrofit of the plant continued until its completion in December 2004. Finance Minister Jeannot Volpe, who was responsible for NB Power in 2001 when the 20-year agreement was negotiated, claimed that even without a signed contract for the orimulsion the memorandum of understanding with PDVSA was a legal and binding contract.

In March 2004 Premier Lord announced a new president and CEO for NB Power, giving David Hay the responsibility for determining what went wrong with the orimulsion deal. Critics of the Lord government were unswayed by the premier's claims that he was unaware of the risks associated with the deal before announcing the $750 million retrofit. Premier Lord and Ali Rodriguez, president of the Venezuelan supplier, hoped that the issue could be resolved out of court. However, even with continued negotiations, Rodriguez told the press that his company only signed a "generic document" with NB

Power "in which there are no obligations, only the possibility of signing a final contract with no set date." In his discussions he even suggested that the company might demand a higher price for the fuel. Meanwhile, Premier Lord maintained that the agreement with the Venezuelan company was legally enforceable even though no signed contract existed.

Reports in the media soon surfaced that the Venezuelan company no longer wanted to be a supplier of orimulsion; they wanted to focus on producing a more expensive fuel that would result in greater profits. Rodriguez maintained that there was no signed deal with NB Power and so the company had no obligation to supply the province with orimulsion. NB Power said it was entitled to the fuel because the Venezuelan firm's US operations had emailed a fuel-supply agreement the previous May. Yet Bitor argued that it was only a "term sheet" that was signed, and not a legally binding document. Rodriguez had stated that a contract had not been signed because both parties had not agreed on all aspects of the contract. Rodriguez expressed interest in continuing negotiations for the supply of a fuel other than orimulsion, but it was becoming clear to NB Power by mid-March 2004 that PDVSA was not intending to sell orimulsion to the company for the Coleson Cove project.

Further, in March 2004 government reports indicated that Coleson Cove did not require upgrading until 2017, meaning that the $750 million retrofit and the projected $2 billion in extra fuel costs over twenty years could have been avoided. Premier Lord was criticized by the opposition for "reinventing history" to justify the orimulsion deal when his government claimed that the Coleson Cove plant needed to be upgraded by 2005.

Hearings before the Crown corporation's committee investigating what went wrong with the orimulsion deal revealed that certain executives at NB Power had not informed the government about problems with the deal when they arose. David Hay accused three senior officials at NB Power of not telling their board or the government that the deal was in trouble. The committee learned that two officials travelled to Venezuela in May 2003 to sign a fuel agreement with the Venezuelan company, but the trip was unsuccessful as the Venezuelan company was not ready to sign. Although the government knew that no signed contract existed, they were not informed that a signed deal might not be secured in the future because of Venezuela's decision to reduce or even cease production of orimulsion. Stewart MacPherson, former CEO of NB Power and one of the accused officials, contradicted Hay's claims, stating that the government had been informed of concerns about the deal. Government officials, including Lord and the former energy minister, denied these claims, saying that they were unaware of the issues surrounding the deal.

In late June 2004, NB Power announced a net loss because of a $44 million write-off related to the failed orimulsion deal. The loss was for work already carried out on the halted fuel delivery system that would pipe orimulsion from Saint John to Coleson Cove, including site clearing, design, engineering, and environmental impact work. In addition to the losses incurred by the write-off, NB Power also spent over $235 000 to prepare for the legislature committee investigation.

Discussion between the Venezuelan company and NB Power continued into 2005, with Rodriguez still claiming that he wanted to settle the deal outside of court. NB Power CEO David Hay said that while the lawsuit was filed in court, NB Power never served the Venezuelans with the necessary papers. As such, the suit lapsed after six months. NB Power can re-activate the lawsuit at any time.

In the meantime, the people of New Brunswick went to the polls in September 2006 for a provincial election. The orimulsion debacle factored heavily in the opposition campaign and was likely a key factor leading to the defeat of the Lord government to the Liberals and Shawn Graham.

Questions

1. Where are the points in this case where key decisions were made? Do you see the presence of any decision-making traps that led to NB Power's failed deal?
2. How could the orimulsion retrofit and Bitor supply agreement have been carried out differently for a better outcome?
3. What changes should organizations such as NB Power and the Province of New Brunswick make to their decision-making structures to prevent this from happening again?

Sources: K. Bissett, "NB Power Negotiator in Botched Fuel Deal Resigns Suddenly," *Canadian Press NewsWire*, April 27, 2004; *Canadian Press NewsWire*, "NB Generating Station Switching to Venezuelan Fuel to Help Reduce Costs," October 10, 2002; *Canadian Press NewsWire*, "NB Power Utility Suing Venezuela Company Over Fuel Supply Agreement," February 25, 2004; *Canadian Press NewsWire*, "NB Power Confident of Venezuelan Fuel Deal Despite $2-billion Lawsuit," March 9, 2004; *Canadian Press NewsWire*, "More Questions Surround Troubled $2-billion Fuel Supply Deal in NB," March 16, 2004; *Canadian Press NewsWire*, "NB Minister Was Worried About Fuel Deal Six Months Ago, Committee Told," March 28, 2004; *Canadian Press NewsWire*, "NB Power Spent $235,000 Preparing CEO for Hearings on Failed Fuel Deal," July 8, 2004; *Canadian Press NewsWire*, "Venezuelan Energy Minister Hopeful of Out-of-Court Deal with NB Power," February 11, 2005; *Daily Commercial News and Construction Record*, "NB Considers Power Generation Options: Building Orimulsion Plants May Be One Solution," 75(148); C. Morris, "Shaky Deal with Venezuela Political Embarrassment for NB Government," *Canadian Press NewsWire*, February 20, 2004; C. Morris, "NB Government Trusted Advice from Power Officials on Venezuelan Fuel Deal," *Canadian Press NewsWire*, February 26, 2004; C. Morris, "Fears Grow in New Brunswick Over Botched Venezuelan Fuel Deal," *Canadian Press NewsWire*, March 3, 2004; C. Morris, "NB Power Officials Withheld Information that Fuel Deal Was at Risk: President," *Canadian Press NewsWire*, March 25, 2004; C. Morris, "New Brunswick Power Writes Off Delivery System for Venezuelan Fuel," *Canadian Press NewsWire*, June 25, 2004.

Chapter 6
Planning

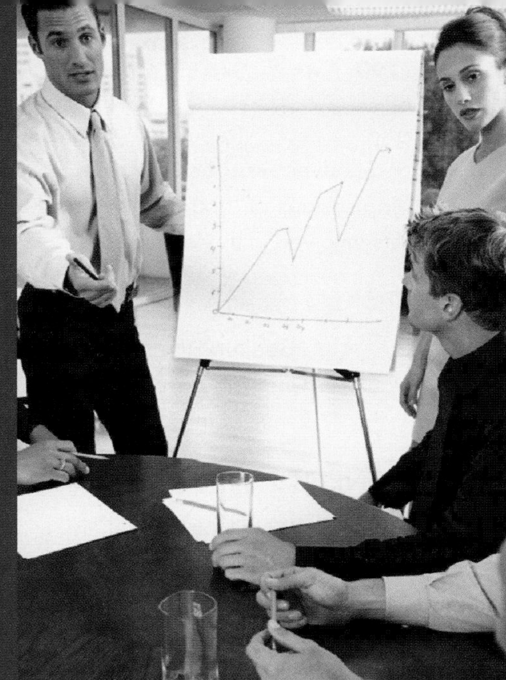

LEARNING OBJECTIVES

After reading this chapter, you should be able to:

1 Define planning and explain its purpose.

2 Differentiate between strategic, operational, and tactical plans.

3 Explain the planning process.

4 Identify key contingency factors in planning.

5 Explain budgeting as a planning tool.

6 Describe an MBO planning system.

7 Describe effective goals.

Procter & Gamble in Eastern Europe

Procter & Gamble (P&G), the maker of Tide, Crest, Swiffer, Vidal Sassoon, and hundreds of other well-known consumer brands, relies heavily on its international markets to sustain long-term growth. Currently P&G markets more than 300 products to more than 5 billion consumers in over 180 countries, and the company has over 100 manufacturing plants in 42 countries. P&G's annual revenue in 2006 was in excess of US$68 billion.

Nearly one-quarter of P&G's total revenues are in Western Europe. So it was only natural that P&G corporate and regional executives had a significant interest in the opening of Eastern Europe in 1989 when the Berlin Wall fell. P&G subsequently entered specific Eastern European countries that had been deprived of quality Western material goods. However, rather than enter rapidly and make mistakes, the regional executives formulated a specific plan for doing so. The steps to this plan included: (1) analyzing the environment, (2) setting objectives and strategies, (3) determining resources, and (4) monitoring outcomes.

1. Analyzing the Environment

Given the instability of the Eastern European countries, P&G executives in Europe took their time to analyze the environment before expanding. In February 1990, company executives from both corporate headquarters and regional operations took a tour of major markets to assess strengths and weaknesses among the countries, including Hungary, the Czech Republic, and Russia. Executives returned with notes and impressions on both the risks and benefits involved in those markets:

RISKS

- Poor infrastructure
- Unstable governments and tense political atmosphere

BENEFITS

- 400 million consumers
- Highly educated and inexpensive workforce
- Movement to a free market system

When the Berlin Wall fell in 1989, it opened up Eastern European markets to Western firms for the first time in decades. Procter & Gamble entered the Eastern European market with a careful, elaborate plan. For example, rather than import Tide to the Czech Republic, which would have been too costly, P&G engineers worked with a Czech plant to produce and manufacture Tide there.

Based on the environmental assessment, the company decided to focus first on Poland, the Czech Republic, and Hungary, and to enter Russia later very cautiously.

2. Setting Objectives and Strategies

P&G executives' next step was to set objectives for its expansion into Eastern Europe. In addition to long- and short-term financial objectives, they had several strategic objectives. Two important objectives were (1) to achieve the lowest cost and best quality sourcing and (2) to achieve superior distribution.

To provide low-cost, high-quality products, executives determined that they would eventually need regional production capacity, because the high cost of importing goods into the region would make them less affordable to consumers. However, the executives wanted to begin operations quickly without too much risk. So the option of building plants was rejected.

The next option was to acquire local manufacturers, although this carried some risk. For example, how could an Eastern European plant manufacture with the same efficiency and quality as a Western plant? Nonetheless, the strategy was less risky than building the plants from scratch. One such acquisition occurred in the Czech Republic where P&G found a company called Rakona. P&G engineers worked with Czech employees at the Rakona plant to conduct test runs of Ariel detergent—the equivalent of Tide detergent in Western Europe. After only a few weeks, the detergent produced in the Czech plant was identical to that produced in Western Europe.

To achieve the highest market share, P&G executives decided that they had to expand rapidly. But they found that distribution channels in Eastern Europe were very poorly developed. Even under favourable circumstances in Russia, it could take three weeks for a case of detergent to be transferred from the Moscow area across Siberia to Vladivostok on the eastern shore.

3. Determining Resources

Once objectives and strategies were set, P&G executives determined what resources were needed. The executives figured that the most critical resource was human—the employees who would build the business in Eastern Europe. Both experienced P&G managers from other parts of the world and local men and women would be needed. And these employees would need both technical and managerial skills to succeed.

4. Monitoring Outcomes

During the implementation of its plan, P&G executives carefully monitored the outcomes, both financial and strategic, in each of the countries they entered. The results have reflected an overall success story in Eastern Europe. After four years of operation, annual sales rose to US$500 million, making the company the largest consumer goods firm in the entire region. Twenty-five brands served the markets, and most were among the top two or three in their product categories. The business also became profitable within the first four years, although it had taken eight years to turn a profit in Western Europe. For Procter & Gamble, the region has now become their most important developing market, surpassing China.

The exclusive distribution arrangements that P&G set in place soon after the opening of Eastern Europe secured for them key markets in Russia and Poland, which made it much more difficult for competitors to get a foothold when they entered later. In Russia, for example, P&G controls around half the laundry detergent sales, shutting out key rival Unilever.

The annual revenue for P&G in Russia alone surpassed the US$1 billion mark in 2004 and has continued to increase.

Today, the company's executives remain optimistic about their long-term business in Eastern Europe. In 2005 P&G acquired Gillette and built the largest production facility for Gillette razor blades in the world in Poland. Because of its careful, thorough planning, the company expects to enjoy high returns over the long term.

Sources: "The Procter & Gamble Company: Company Profile," *Datamonitor*, November, 2006; "From Volatility to Stability," *Soap, Perfumery & Cosmetics*, November 2006; J. Neff, "Entrenched P&G Faces Foes' Inroads," *Advertising Age*, August 28, 2006; "P&G Overhauls Euro Data Strategy," *Precision Marketing*, October 31, 2003, p. 1; Personal communication with John Pepper, 2001; P&G 2001 Annual Report; J. Pepper, "Leading the Change in Eastern Europe," *Business Quarterly*, Autumn 1995, pp. 26–33.

strategic overview

The opening case clearly illustrates the importance of a manager's ability to formulate and implement effective plans. Although planning has been an important managerial activity for some time, it is perhaps more important and perplexing now than ever before. On the one hand, the increase in competition means that if an organization, business unit, or individual manager fails to plan and as a consequence drifts off course or loses momentum, competitors are likely to overtake it. On the other hand, the speed of change and rapid flow of information increasingly require plans that are flexible and dynamic. In today's world, a rigid plan can be as fatal as no plan at all. As important as competition and the rate of change are, both must be viewed within the context of globalization for a manager to be successful today and in the future. Increasingly, as a manager you must not only be aware of local competitors, but also those in other parts of the world. In addition, you must recognize that because information flows throughout the world nearly instantaneously, it can create the need for rapid and dramatic changes in your plans.

Effective planning at all organizational levels can have a significant impact on the firm's performance. Without effective planning, P&G might have failed in its efforts to enter and compete successfully in the Eastern European markets. But the company's activities in these markets turned out to be highly effective, in part because managers had a plan and regularly re-evaluated and changed it. Managers need to continuously analyze and understand their external markets and adjust their plans accordingly. Today, the instantaneous availability of information, rapid changes in economies, markets, and the political environments of countries that firms do business in impact planning continuously. Managers need to be prepared to adapt to changes that occur rapidly, no matter what their plans are—or were.

This requires managers to accurately analyze their internal resources. Managers at P&G, for example, determined that people were the most important component of the plan to enter and succeed in the Eastern European markets. Their conclusion is borne out by current research. In fact, some current research suggests that an organization's human capital is absolutely critical to the successful implementation of a firm's strategic plans.[1]

An analysis of the organization's internal resources and external environment helps a manager determine the company's strengths, like the organization's core competencies, along with its weaknesses and how they might affect its future plans.[2] This analysis can also identify the other resources managers will need to implement their plans and ultimately achieve their goals.

An Overview of Planning

Few activities are more basic to management than deciding where the company is going and how it is going to get there. Organizational **objectives** are the end states or targets that managers aim for, while **plans** are the means by which managers hope to hit the desired targets. **Planning**, then, is essentially a decision-making process that focuses on the future of the organization and how it will achieve its goals. From this perspective, setting organizational objectives has to precede the development of organizational plans. Without objectives or targets, plans make very little sense. Objectives help set direction, focus effort,

objectives the end states or targets that company managers aim for

plans the means by which managers hope to hit the desired targets

planning a decision-making process that focuses on the future of an organization and how it will achieve its goals

guide behaviours, and evaluate progress.[3] Interestingly, managers sometimes spend so much time formulating objectives that they neglect to develop detailed plans that will enable them to achieve their goals. This is akin to making a commitment to graduate from university without any idea of what classes to take or when certain classes need to be taken. It is easy to see why organizational results are significantly influenced not just by objectives but also by the plans for hitting the targets. We will now explore the types of plans that exist, the basic planning process, and the methods for implementing plans effectively.

Types of Plans

Strategic/Tactical/ Operational Plans by Michael Hitt

mymanagementlab

Few organizations today of any size offer just one product or service. As a consequence, they cannot develop a single plan to cover all organizational activities. To understand the planning process for complex organizations, we need to differentiate among three types of plans[4] (see Exhibit 6.1).

Exhibit 6.1 Types of Plans: Key Differences

	Strategic Plans	Tactical Plans	Operational Plans
Time Horizon	Typically 3–5 years	Often focused on 1–2 years in the future	Usually focused on the next 12 months or less
Scope	Broadest; originating with a focus on the entire organization	Rarely broader than a strategic business unit	Narrowest; usually centred on departments or smaller units of the organization
Complexity	The most complex and general, because of the different industries and business potentially covered	Somewhat complex but more specific, because of the more limited domain of application	The least complex, because they usually focus on small, homogenous units
Impact	Have the potential to dramatically impact, both positively and negatively, the fortunes and survival of the organization	Can affect specific businesses but generally not the fortunes or survivability of the entire organization	Impact is usually restricted to specific department or organization unit
Interdependence	High interdependence; must take into account the resources and capabilities of the entire organization and its external environments	Moderate interdependence; must take into account the resources and capabilities of several units within a business	Low interdependence; the plan may be linked to higher-level tactical and strategic plans but is less interdependent with them

strategic plans focus on the broad future of the organization and incorporate both external environmental demands and internal resources into managers' actions

Strategic Plans **Strategic plans** focus on the broad future of the organization and incorporate both external environmental demands and internal resources into the actions managers need to take to achieve long-term goals. There is some evidence that the rigorous use of strategic plans is associated with superior financial performance.[5] As we will examine more thoroughly in Chapter 7, strategic plans cover the major aspects of the organization including its products, services, finances, technology, and human resources. Although the concept of "long term" has no precise definition, most strategic plans focus on how to achieve goals one to five years into the future. For example, after the passage of NAFTA (North American Free Trade Agreement), the Mexican state of Sonora, which borders Arizona, had a strategic plan to revitalize its economy. In evaluating the state's strengths and weaknesses, government officials decided that the most effective way to revitalize its economy was to take advantage of its beautiful beaches and to encourage tourism.

Tactical Plans **Tactical plans** translate strategic plans into specific goals for specific parts of the organization. Consequently, they tend to have somewhat shorter time frames and to be narrower in scope. Instead of focusing on the entire corporation, tactical plans typically affect a single business within an organization. While tactical plans should complement the overall strategic plan, they are often somewhat independent of other tactical plans. For example, the tactical plans of the transportation department for Sonora called for improving the roads leading from the US border to the beach resorts. The tactical plans of the commerce department called for making special low-interest loans available to companies that would build western-style quality hotels in the targeted region. While the tactical plans of the transportation and commerce departments were different, both served to support the overall strategic plan of Sonora. *A Manager's Challenge: "The Bellagio: Using Technology for Effective Tactical Plan Execution"* provides an interesting example of how one company used technology to enhance the execution of an important tactical plan—the hiring of nearly 10 000 workers in five instead of the normal nine to twelve months for a new hotel. As you read this, imagine yourself facing the planning challenge of hiring 10 000 workers in less than half the normal time and still having to ensure that the right people with the right capabilities and characteristics are selected.

tactical plans plans that translate strategic plans into specific goals for specific parts of the organization

Operational Plans **Operational plans** translate tactical plans into specific goals and actions for small units of the organization and focus on the near term. The near term is typically 12 months or less. These plans are the least complex of the three and rarely have a direct impact beyond the department or unit for which the plan was developed. For example, in the case of the Mexican state of Sonora, the purchasing section within the department of transportation created an operational plan that called for the purchase of several new road graders and a new steamroller to facilitate the expansion of the main highway from a two-lane to a four-lane highway.

operational plans plans that translate tactical plans into specific goals and actions for small units of the organization and focus on the near term

As summarized in Exhibit 6.1, strategic, tactical, and operational plans differ from each other on five important dimensions: time horizon, scope, complexity, impact, and interdependence.[6] While these differences matter, the three types of plans should be aligned and integrated with each other. Unfortunately, this type of alignment and integration occurs in only one-third of companies.[7] In addition to types of plans, for a more complete understanding, we need to examine planning at different levels in the organization.

Organizational Levels

In addition to plans that address strategic, tactical, and operational issues of the organization, managers at different levels of the company face different planning challenges. Exhibit 6.2 provides a graphical representation of the three primary levels of a corporation. Managers at each level attempt to address somewhat different questions.

Corporate Level Most corporations of even moderate size have a corporate headquarters. However, complex and large organizations like Bombardier, a world leader in the manufacture of air and rail transportation solutions with more than US$14 billion in annual revenue, often divide the various businesses of the company into large groups. For Bombardier, these groups include aerospace and transportation. The heads of these groups are typically part of the

a manager's challenge

technology

The Bellagio: Using Technology for Effective Tactical Plan Execution

When Mirage Resorts decided to build the Bellagio, one of Las Vegas's most luxurious hotels, it was no small feat. The blueprints called for 3000 rooms, a large gallery to hold a fine-art collection, a glass-domed conservatory, a theatre equipped to hold a new water show by the Montreal entertainment group Cirque du Soleil, an eight-acre replica of Italy's Lake Como—along with the most upscale designer shops and gourmet restaurants. The cost of this, before Bellagio's doors even opened, would run about US$1.6 billion. In addition, Mirage had to find a way to recruit nearly 10 000 workers to staff the hotel. Clearly, the company needed a tactical plan to accomplish this.

As construction got underway, Mirage Resorts's human resource executives began the hiring process. Because of the number of jobs that needed to be filled—by the right people—HR executives at the Mirage had to come up with a plan for receiving and sorting through the anticipated tens of thousands of applications. Even after extracting the best candidates from the applications, managers still had to interview thousands of candidates and to make employment offers.

As part of their plan, executives budgeted US$1 million for a computer software system that would screen as many as 75 000 job candidates. The plan was to complete this screening in three months and to eliminate those who were not suitable and extract those who might be. To recruit the initial applicants, executives planned to run large ads in newspapers announcing that they were hiring employees for the new hotel. The plan called for a toll-free number that applicants would call to make an appointment to fill out an application (not for an interview).

Once the applicants were on file in the computer system and the software program had culled out the inappropriate applicants, the plan called for interviews of an estimated 25 000 to 30 000 candidates at a rate of 700 interviews per day! To do this, executives estimated that they would need to hire and specially train 180 interviewers. In other words, the plan called for hiring people to hire people. The results of the interviews would be entered into a database for later reference.

The plan also called for some low-tech screening mechanisms as well. For example, if a candidate showed up to the interview late without notifying someone, he or she would be dropped from the process. Then–vice-president Arte Nathan explained it this way: "If people didn't show up for their appointments, we figured they'd be no-shows at work, too."

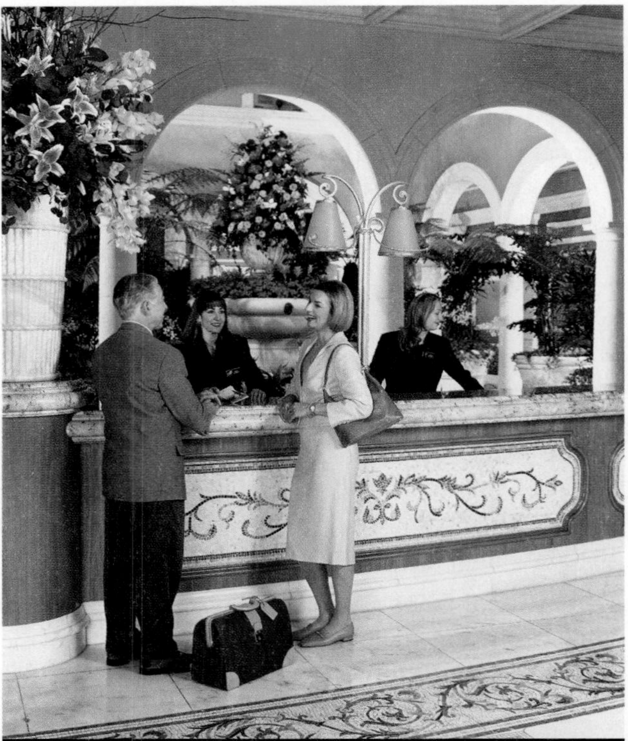

Opening the Bellagio hotel-casino required its owner, Mirage Resorts, Inc., to hire a whopping 10 000 employees in only five months. The task included screening 75 000 applicants and conducting as many as 700 interviews a day to find the best candidates. Similar to building the hotel, it was no small undertaking. Careful and systematic planning, however, made the hiring process a success.

The hiring plan also anticipated the need to conduct as many as 20 000 background checks on candidates that successfully made it through the interviews. This would need to be done in short order—within just a month or two—so the plan was to contract with a professional firm to conduct these background checks on behalf of Mirage Resorts.

This was the plan. So how well did things go? Overall, the plan was well constructed and executed. Instead of the normal nine months it had taken the company to staff a new hotel in the past, this plan resulted in the attracting, screening, and hiring of 10 000 employees in only five months. Arte Nathan also claimed that the process saved the company not only time but direct costs on items such as paper, temporary help, and file space to the tune of US$600 000. Bellagio opened on time and with the right employees trained and in place, in part because of the effective tactical plan for hiring. Since its opening, the Bellagio has become a major attraction for visitors to Las Vegas. Its popularity prompted a further US$375 million expansion to the facility that opened in December 2004.

Sources: MGM Mirage 2005 Annual Report, www.mgmmirage.com, accessed December 17, 2006; "Bellagio," *Meetings & Conventions*, November 2003, p. 4; E. P. Gunn, "How Mirage Resorts Sifted 75,000 Applications to Hire 9,600 in 24 Weeks," *Fortune*, October 12, 1998, p. 195; J. Gurzinksi, "A Raft of Preparation at Bellagio," *Las Vegas Review Journal*, September 30, 1998.

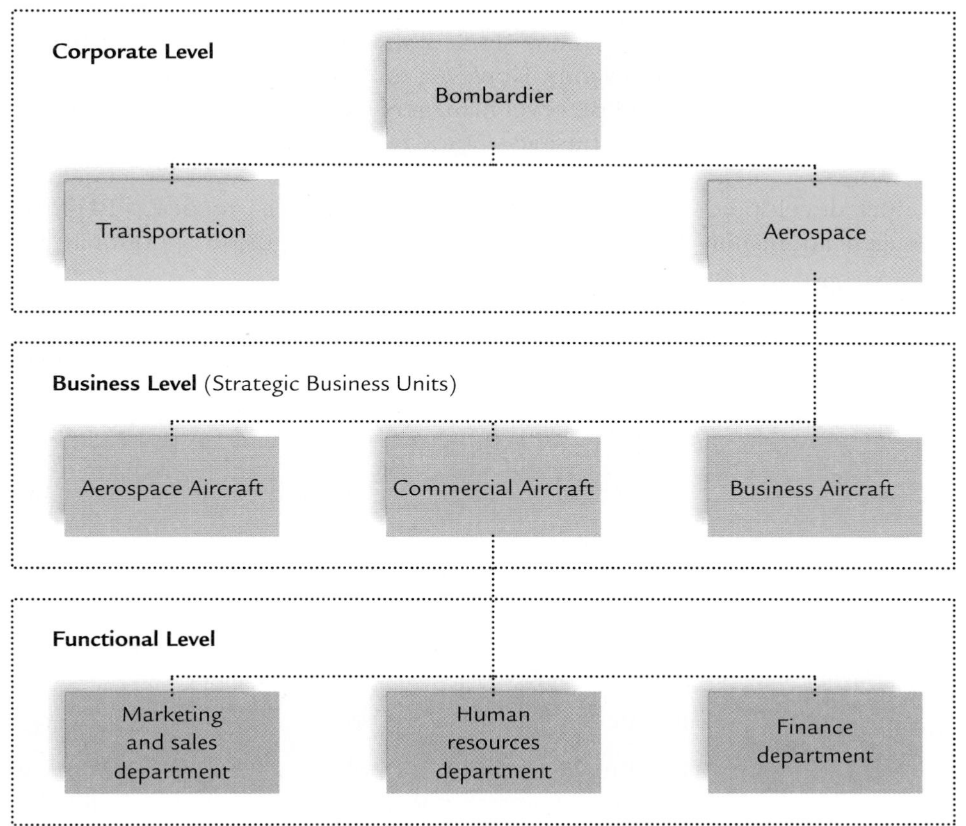

Exhibit 6.2
Organizational Levels

group of senior executives at the corporate headquarters. Executives at the corporate level in large firms would include both those in the headquarters and those heading up the large corporate groups such as finance, human resources, legal, and so on. These corporate-level executives would primarily focus on questions such as the following:

- What industries should we get into or out of?
- What markets should the firm be in? For example, is it time to move aggressively into China? If so, what businesses should move first?
- In which businesses should the corporation invest money?

In the case of Bombardier, if coordination across the aerospace and transportation groups or across businesses within the groups is beneficial, it is the responsibility of corporate-level managers to recognize and capture those opportunities.

Business Level The next level is sometimes referred to as the SBU, or strategic business unit level. At this level managers focus on determining how they are going to compete effectively in the market. For example, within the aerospace area that includes businesses such as amphibious aircraft and commercial aircraft, managers attempt to address questions such as the following:

- Who are our direct competitors?
- What are their strengths and weaknesses?
- What are our strengths and weaknesses?
- What do customers value in the products or services we offer?
- What advantages do we have over competitors?

In Chapter 7 we will examine some of the tools business-level managers can use to answer these questions. However, these questions help you see that the planning questions that SBU-level managers face are more focused on how to compete effectively in the business of today than on what businesses to be in tomorrow. If coordination across different departments (finance, marketing, product development, etc.) or units within the SBU is needed, SBU-level managers are responsible for recognizing and capturing those opportunities.

Functional Level At the functional level, managers focus on how they can facilitate the achievement of the competitive plan of the business. These managers are often heads of departments such as finance, marketing, human resources, or product development. Depending on the SBU's structure, functional managers may include managers responsible for the business within a specific geographic region or managers who are responsible for a specific product like commercial aircraft. Generally, these functional managers attempt to address questions such as the following:

- What activities does my unit need to perform well to meet customer expectations?
- What information about competitors does my unit need to help the business compete effectively?
- What are my unit's strengths and weaknesses?

The main focus of functional managers' planning activities is on how they can support the SBU plan. Functional-level managers are responsible for recognizing and capturing the opportunity, if coordination between individuals within a unit is needed or beneficial.

Interaction between Plan Types and Levels

Strategic plans typically get developed at the corporate level. In fact, strategic planning is arguably the key planning responsibility of corporate managers. Corporate managers, however, tend not to get involved in developing tactical or operational plans. SBU-level managers may be involved in developing strategic plans for their business units and are usually involved in developing tactical plans for their business. However, SBU-level managers typically do not get involved in developing operational plans. In contrast, functional-level managers are not often involved in developing either strategic or tactical plans. Instead, their planning responsibilities tend to focus on the development of operational plans. Exhibit 6.3 illustrates the general pattern of planning responsibility by organizational level. Keep in mind, however, that the specific pattern in any given organization could be different. For example, the size of the organization could affect the pattern. In small organizations, corporate managers might be involved in developing strategic, tactical, *and* operational plans.

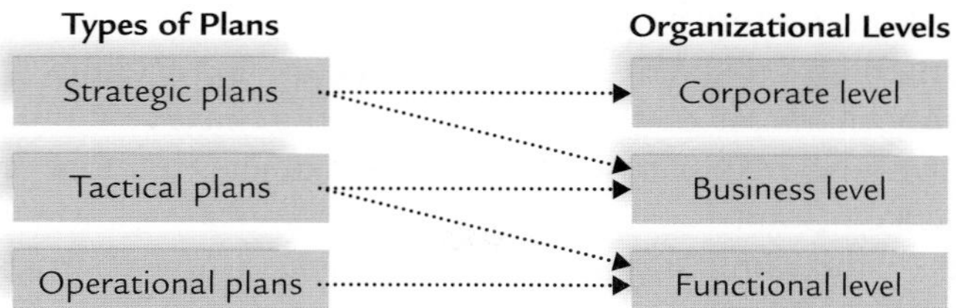

Exhibit 6.3

Interaction between Plans and Levels

The Planning Process

The planning process has seven key elements: environmental analysis, objectives, requirements, resources, actions, implementation, and outcomes (see Exhibit 6.4). In this section, we will examine each of these elements and their role in the overall planning process.

Analyzing the Environment

The first element of the planning process is an assessment of the environment. Managers who formulate or implement plans in the absence of any assessment of the environment may very well fall short of producing the desired results. In contrast, managers who carefully scan the environment and incorporate the information gathered into the planning process can enjoy greater success in the outcomes of the plans they formulate and implement.[8]

Forecasts One of the principal tools managers use in assessing the environment is a forecast. Forecasts are or can be made about virtually every critical element in the environment that managers believe could affect the organization or their area of responsibility.[9] For example, if you were in the residential construction business, interest rate forecasts would be important to you. Generally, as interest rates go up and borrowing money becomes more expensive, fewer people purchase new homes. Those that still purchase new homes necessarily have to purchase less expensive homes than they could if interest rates were lower. Planning for the number of houses to build in the coming year would, as a consequence, be influenced by the interest rate forecast.

Interestingly, there is a cascading effect of forecasts. For example, if you forecast that you will build only 1000 homes instead of 1500 homes over the

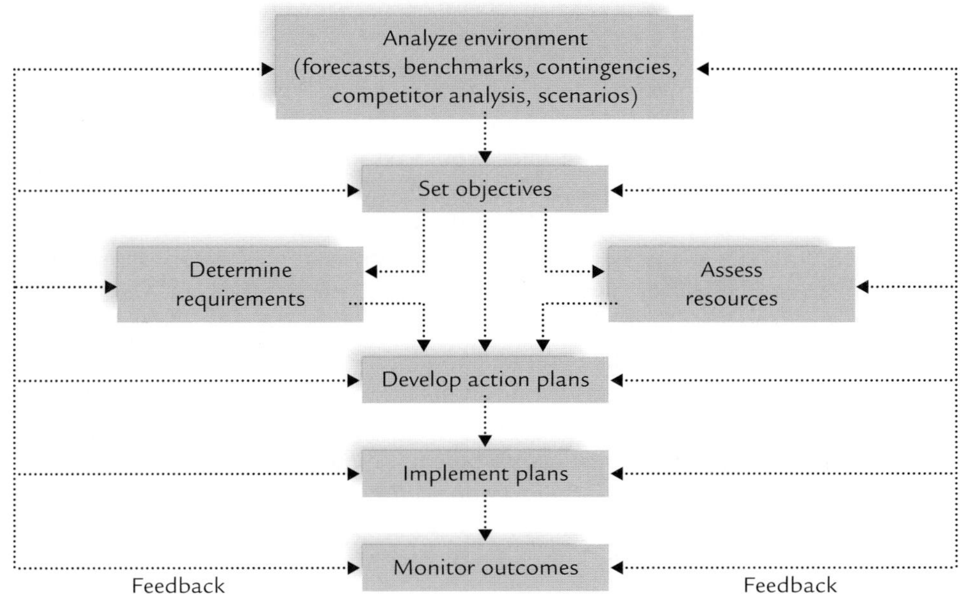

Exhibit 6.4

Planning Process

next year because interest rates are expected to rise from 4.5 percent to 5.5 percent, then you might also forecast a decline in revenues. This may lead the purchasing manager to plan for smaller purchases of lumber and may lead the human resource manager to plan for a smaller number of construction workers. The key point for managers is that it's vital to know what the key forecasts are in the company and to keep track of any changes so that any cascading effects can be recognized earlier rather than later.

Environmental Uncertainty Obviously, forecasting accurately is a tough business. Things frequently change and don't work out the way we anticipate.[10] In Chapter 2, we talked about the key external general and task environmental forces that can change things. In 1988, no one was predicting the fall of the Berlin Wall in 1989. In early 2000, no one was predicting the worst two years of stock market performance that followed in 2002. The key issue for managers and their planning activities is that the greater the environmental uncertainty, the more flexible their plans need to be. In some cases, managers may even develop contingency plans. **Contingency plans** typically identify key factors that could affect the desired results and specify what different actions will be taken if changes in key events occur.[11]

contingency plans plans that identify key factors that could affect the desired results and specify what actions will be taken if key events change

Minnesota Mining & Manufacturing (3M) was founded in 1902 by a lawyer, a doctor, two railroad executives, and a meat-market owner hoping to get rich by mining a superhard material called corundum, used to make grinding wheels. But the soft rock 3M was mining turned out to be an inferior abrasive for wheel grinding, so the company began producing sandpaper instead. Unfortunately, it wasn't a very good product because the humidity in Minnesota kept the paper from drying properly. The company's first breakthrough product, Wetordry sandpaper—developed in response to the humidity problem—didn't come out until 1921.

For example, suppose you were a manager at Boychuk Homes, a home builder in Saskatoon that has built more than 7000 homes over the past 50 years. Clearly, forecasts of future interest rates would be important to you. The forecast might call for interest rates to remain unchanged for the next year. But can you trust the forecast? Rather than just rely on the forecast, you might be better off to develop contingency plans. For instance, what if interest rates go up one point? It is likely that people will buy fewer houses or less expensive houses. Your contingency plan might be to offer reduced financing charges if customers include certain upgrades in their homes like granite countertops. You could perhaps afford to offer buyers this incentive because your profits from the upgrades might be greater than the costs of the finance subsidies. By having this contingency plan in place in advance of the change in interest rates, you can be more prepared to respond.

A Manager's Challenge: "Changing Well-Laid Plans at EMC" provides a great illustration of how dramatically plans may have to change when reality turns out to be different from forecasts. In this case, the forecast of the future

a manager's challenge *change*

Changing Well-Laid Plans at EMC

If you were a shareholder of the telecommunications corporation EMC during the 1990s, and you sold your shares near the end of that decade, you would likely be retired (and not reading this text). During that period, EMC returned a staggering 84 000 percent to shareholders! By the end of 2000, the company controlled 71 percent of the upper-end data storage market. Seventy percent of its US$8.9 billion in revenues and 92 percent of its US$2.3 billion in operating profits were derived from sales of its storage hardware.

But then the bubble burst. Telecom companies and dot.coms that had spent nearly US$2 billion on EMC products in 2000 spent virtually nothing in 2001 as they struggled for survival. In addition, other key customers froze their IT budgets. As a consequence, EMC saw its revenues plunge. If that weren't enough, IBM and Hitachi launched products and a price war aimed at EMC's most lucrative segment of products. In 2001, EMC tried to maintain prices but could not. It saw its market share drop from 71 percent to 57 percent and watched in horror as gross margins dropped by 25 percentage points to 32 percent as they lowered product prices faster than production costs to compete with IBM and Hitachi.

HR managers had staffing plans and compensation plans, sales managers had sales plans, and R&D managers had research plans for 2001 that were based on a growth trajectory and forecast mirroring results in 2000 and years prior. Suddenly, all of those plans had to change—and not just for one year. The troubles of 2001 did not just mark a bad year, but revealed a turning point for EMC.

Prior to 2001, data storage was a mission-critical function of virtually all firms of moderate or larger sizes. Customer information, financial data, inventory, sales, purchasing, and personnel data all needed to be stored, duplicated, and protected. In addition, IBM, Hitachi, and EMC had their own proprietary systems. In other words, an IBM system could not talk to or work with a Hitachi or EMC system or vice versa. In fact, once a customer selected a storage system, it was, in a sense, held hostage by it because it was just too expensive to switch to another system.

Joe Tucci, EMC's new CEO in 2001, announced a bold change in strategy that would change EMC's future. Tucci was going to split EMC into two companies. The first would continue to make "the best storage hardware in the world." The second would focus on software and services with the ultimate objective of creating software that could manage storage requirements regardless of the hardware (IBM, Hitachi, or EMC). In fact, Tucci wanted 50 percent of revenues to come from software and services by 2004.

This had a profound impact on managers throughout the company. For example, HR managers not only had to scrap their hiring and recruiting plans, but they had to develop plans to downsize (terminate) 19 000 people. In addition, they had to revise future recruiting plans to focus on software engineers and others who could help develop the new integrative software that would be needed to achieve Tucci's revenue target of 50 percent.

Sales managers of the new software group had to implement new motivation and incentive plans. EMC hardware products had traditionally cost its customers millions of dollars. Consequently, commissions were very significant to its sales force. In addition, because the products of its three main rivals were incompatible, motivating salespeople to "kill" the competition was the norm. In the new software sales unit, EMC's products would cost only thousands of dollars—not millions. Furthermore, the salespeople found themselves in the awkward position of telling their customers that whatever storage hardware they now chose (IBM, Hitachi, or EMC) didn't matter—even though these same salespeople had spent years telling them that no hardware could match EMC's.

Some of EMC's R&D managers had to completely shift their plans, as well. Whereas in the past they had simply been concerned with developing technologies to enhance the speed, reliability, and performance of EMC's proprietary products, now they would need to focus on competing products and develop technologies and software language that would not only work with those products but enhance their features, too.

And what does Tucci say about all of EMC's prior plans to which it ultimately laid waste? "Companies that are afraid to disrupt themselves almost 100 percent of the time end up being disrupted [by competitors]. I'm doing what our competitors never thought we had the intestinal fortitude to do." The bold shift by Tucci has resulted in positive results for EMC. Gartner Group identified EMC as the 2005 leader in revenue growth among the nine content management software providers and second in market share of total revenue among all the providers. Tucci was also identified by more than 1700 industry analysts and portfolio managers as the top CEO in the IT hardware industry for 2005, and again in 2006, beating out Steve Jobs of Apple (#2) and Mike Hurd of HP (#3).

Sources: EMC website, www.emc.com, accessed December 18, 2006; T. Eid, "Market Share: Enterprise Content Management Software, Worldwide, 2003–2005," *Gartner Dataquest*, May 18, 2006; A. Asaravala, "EMC Is Resolute," *Intelligent Enterprise*, December 10, 2003, p. 8; EMC Annual Report, 2001; D. Roth, "Can EMC Restore Its Glory?" *Fortune*, July 22, 2002, pp. 107–110.

was based on such a successful past that few people anticipated how dramatically and quickly things could change. This past success made the future seem deceptively certain, and so EMC did not have contingency plans to fall back on when it became clear that reality would not match forecasts. Why do you think EMC didn't have any contingency plans? Do you think it would have fared better if it had had some contingency plans?

benchmarking the investigation of the best results among competitors and noncompetitors and the practices that lead to those results

Benchmarking A more recent and popular means of assessing the environment is benchmarking. **Benchmarking** is the investigation of the best results among competitors and noncompetitors and the practices that lead to those results.[12] In terms of results, managers might assess competitors that have the highest revenue-to-employee ratio as a means of assessing productivity. Managers would then compare their own revenue-to-employee ratio to get an idea of where they stand relative to the competition. As part of this assessment, they would also investigate the practices that appear to contribute to high revenue-to-employee ratios. For example, they might find that the firms with the highest ratio tend to have fewer levels of managers because they push decision-making authority down in the organization and have a strong focus on participative management and employee involvement.

These same types of assessments might also be made of noncompetitors. The inclusion of noncompetitors has potential pitfalls and benefits that are different from benchmarking competitors. Clearly, noncompetitors can have underlying business factors that make appropriate comparisons difficult. For example, a telemarketing company that sells relatively inexpensive items over the phone will have a much lower revenue-to-employee ratio than a maker of supercomputers. The telemarketing firm has a relatively labour-intensive business, while the maker of supercomputers has a technology-intensive business. These same problems of comparison and relevance can be present when examining the best practices of noncompetitors. The inventory practices of a service firm may be difficult to apply directly to a manufacturing firm. However, by looking outside one's set of competitors, totally new and significantly better ways of doing things can be found.

Consider the case of Outback Steakhouse. Even though the steel industry was totally different from the franchise restaurant industry, Outback found a motivational practice used by several "mini-mills" in the steel industry that it incorporated with great success. Like any franchise restaurant, Outback makes money as its restaurants make money. The person who makes or breaks a restaurant is the local restaurant manager. In particular, the manager must hire the right people and motivate them effectively to ensure good food and service for the customers. The key for Outback is how to motivate its restaurant managers. The "best practice" that Outback adopted was giving the restaurant managers some ownership in the restaurants they managed. That way if a restaurant made money, so did the manager. The manager felt more like an owner and less like an employee. The adoption of this best practice has had a positive effect on the success of Outback Steakhouse. Thus, even though benchmarking noncompetitors requires some judgment as to what is relevant or appropriate, it can also lead to ideas and practices that put you ahead of the competition.

Benchmarking can be a useful activity even for young managers. For example, suppose you were a sales manager with five salespeople reporting to you. You might want to benchmark outcomes like revenue-per-salesperson as well as processes like goal setting. How were other sales managers setting goals with their subordinates? The key principle in benchmarking is constant curiosity about what others are accomplishing and how they are doing it.

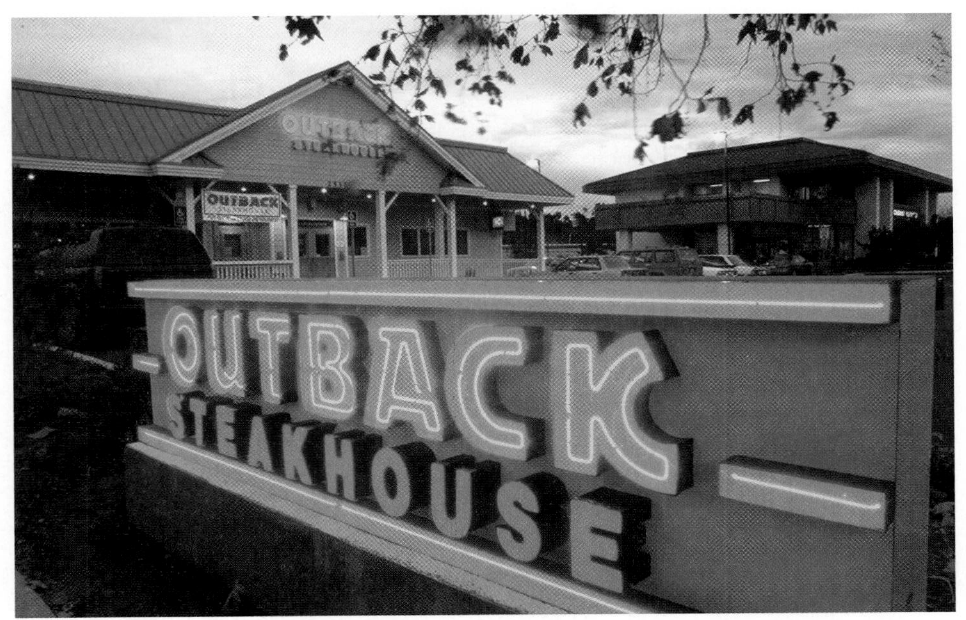

Benchmarking—examining the best practices of one's competitors—can work across industries, too. Outback Steakhouse, an international chain with 13 restaurants in Canada, borrowed an idea used by steel mills to motivate its managers that includes a profit-sharing plan. Outback Steakhouses are managed by a three-person team: a managing partner, manager, and kitchen manager. Because the restaurants are open only for dinner, managers and employees are also able to enjoy a better work–life balance, making Outback an attractive employer.

Setting Objectives

The second element in the planning process is the setting of objectives or desired outcomes. As we mentioned at the beginning of this chapter, it is difficult to establish or implement specific actions without an idea of where those steps are intended to go or what they are expected to achieve.

Priorities and Multiple Objectives One of the first challenges for managers as they set objectives is to determine priorities.[13] Not all objectives are of equal importance or value. Furthermore, some objectives might be important now and less important later. Without a clear understanding of which objectives are most important and temporal priorities, employees may be working at odds with each other or creating unnecessary conflicts.[14]

Consider your own university. Most universities have multiple and sometimes conflicting objectives. For example, on the one hand students feel they pay tuition to learn leading-edge content from the best professors the school has to offer. Universities cannot ignore the expectations of this important set of its constituents. At the same time, though, to generate leading-edge knowledge universities must hire top researchers and fund their research. Without a clear idea of the university's priorities, department heads may find it difficult to determine how best to plan the allocation of the department budget. How much of the budget should go toward activities that help develop the teaching skills of the faculty? How much should go toward funding research?

Similar potential conflicts might exist for a sales manager weighing the objectives of increasing market share and profitability. In many instances, market share can be gained by lowering prices, but this usually hurts profits. The salespeople who work for the manager would have a difficult time knowing exactly where and how to focus their efforts unless she makes her priorities clear. Are they to sacrifice a sale to protect profit margins? Should they offer a small discount to get the sale? At what point would the discount be considered too big to be acceptable? These are the kinds of practical questions that have to be addressed in setting multiple objectives.

There can also be temporal priorities among objectives.[15] For example, suppose you are launching a new product in an established market with well-positioned competitors. You might decide that your current objective is to gain market share and thereby establish a presence in the market. You tell your salespeople to go after 10 percent market share and to offer discounts of up to 20 percent when needed to get the sale. However, once your product is established at, say, a 10 percent market share, you want your salespeople to focus on profitability objectives over increased market share. Without a clear understanding of this sequence in priorities, your salespeople would not be as able to help you achieve your overall objectives. If there are sequences to objectives, spelling them out in advance can help subordinates better understand what is expected of them.

Measuring Objectives Once you've made your organization's objectives clear, how are you going to measure them? For example, you might determine that financial performance is the number-one objective. However, financial performance can be measured in a variety of ways.[16] It can be measured in terms of profits relative to sales or profits relative to assets. For example, a retail shoe store could measure a sales clerk's performance based on sales per hour. This would be in contrast to many other retailers that simply measure net sales. How would this small adjustment make a difference? If your salespeople are measured on net sales, they will likely be motivated to work the greatest number of hours they can. In contrast, your sales-per-hour objective might cause clerks to focus on "sales efficiency," or selling the most in every hour they work, rather than working more hours. The best way to improve sales-per-hour is to sell to repeat customers, because as soon as they walk in the door you know the types of things they like, what their budget is, and so on. Specific measures matter. Even slight differences such as net sales versus sales per hour can have important influences on behaviour.[17]

Determining Requirements

The third element in the planning process is the determination of requirements. Managers essentially address the question, "What will it take to get from here to there?" The "there" is essentially the objectives discussed in the previous section. The "here" requires an assessment or knowledge of where things are today.

To begin the process of determining what is required to get from here to there, you first need to understand the key drivers for the journey. For example, let's suppose you are in the athletic shoe manufacturing business, and your objective is to increase your market share from 10 percent to 15 percent. What is it that drives market share? To drive market share you determine that you need to do two things. First, you need a new line of top-end products since you currently have none. Second, you determine that superior shoe cushion is a key driver of market share for mid-priced running shoes. You discover that running shoe customers make their purchases based on how well a shoe absorbs ground impact. Currently, your cushion technology is not superior. Consequently, it will take new materials to improve the shock absorbency of your shoes.

Assessing Resources

The fourth element in the planning process is an assessment of the required resources and the resources available to you. While this element is closely tied to the identification of requirements, the two are not the same. The easiest way to differentiate the two may be to think of requirements as what is needed to achieve the objectives, and resources as how much is available.

Resources Required Let's return to our athletic shoe example and the key requirement of a new line of products at the top end of the market. Relative to this key requirement, the first critical question is, "What resources are needed to produce a new high-end product?" Let's suppose you determine that it will take three top product-design engineers two months and a budget of $100 000 to produce a prototype. Further, you determine that it will take new equipment at a cost of $500 000 to manufacture the new high-end shoes. Finally, you determine that it will take an advertising and promotion budget of $2 million to effectively launch the new line. These, of course, do not address all the resources required to design, produce, and sell the new high-end product line, but they do illustrate the financial, human, equipment, and technology resources that might be required.

A Manager's Challenge: "Ginch Gonch: Thinking outside the Boxer" helps illustrate the difficulty of assessing required resources when the task is new to the planners. While planning is often presented as a logical and straightforward managerial function, that presentation can be deceptive. When facing new situations, you often "don't know what you don't know" and therefore have difficulty determining what is required, even if you know what you want to do.

Resources Available Knowing what resources are required leads naturally to the next question: "What resources are available?" Clearly, for a plan to be effective it must not only be well formulated but it must be feasible to implement.[18] If the resources required significantly exceed those available, either new resources need to be acquired or the plan must be changed. Changing the plan may require going back and changing the objective. In assessing resources available, managers must ask themselves questions such as the following:

- Do we have the needed human talent to meet the requirements?
- Even if we have the needed talent, is it available? Can we take people off what they are currently working on to put them on the new project?
- If we don't have the necessary talent, can we develop or acquire it within the needed time frame?
- Do we have the financial resources available? Can we get additional funding from the debt or equity markets?
- Do we have the required technology or can we gain access to it at a cost-effective price?

While these are certainly not the only questions managers would need to ask, they provide a reflection of the types of questions that would need to be addressed to determine if there is a gap between the resources required and those available. If there is a gap, managers must determine if it can be bridged or if the objectives and key requirements need to be changed to fit the available resources. For example, when a division of business and technology solutions giant EDS changed its strategy to focus on selling solutions to product development problems and not just computer-aided-design (CAD) products, it found that it needed new salespeople with different skills. Before, when they sold CAD products, salespeople from EDS usually talked to middle-level executives in the engineering and product design areas. In trying to sell more integrated solutions, EDS salespeople needed to talk with more senior executives. In the end, EDS managers trained some of their best existing salespeople and recruited new salespeople as well.

Developing Action Plans

The fifth element in the planning process is the development of specific action plans. The action plans are essentially the marching orders that everyone uses to accomplish the established objectives.

Sequence and Timing A key element of an effective action plan is the sequence and timing of the specific steps or actions that must be taken.[19] One of the common tools used to graphically display the sequence and timing of the specific

a manager's challenge — *globalization*

Ginch Gonch: Thinking outside the Boxer

Jason Sutherland didn't start in the apparel industry. Initially, he was a young award-winning production designer for the film and television industry in Vancouver. Then one day Jason envisioned a new way for men and women to express themselves through their wardrobe, even before they don any outer garments. Jason raised $2 million by selling his home and acquiring investors, and in 2004 he launched Ginch Gonch undergarments. Jason's idea for undergarments was in whimsical protest to the staid line of white, black, and grey underwear offered by companies such as Calvin Klein and The Gap.

Ginch Gonch produces cotton his and hers underwear (briefs, thongs, tanks, and t-shirts) that uses vibrant colours with cartoon-like designs emblazoned on them. The designs hearken back to underwear one may have worn as a kid (i.e., Underoos). The company's mission statement is "Live like a kid," and even the company's name, Ginch Gonch, comes from the Canadian schoolyard slang term for underwear. Ginch Gonch undergarments, however, are not for children. They use premium construction and materials and prints that often have cheeky double meanings. The designer garments are priced in the $25 to $35 range and are marketed primarily to the United States—where consumers spend US$12 billion annually on adult underwear.

Ginch Gonch releases only four design collections a year of finite quantities. When the run is sold out, it is not repeated. Jason likens the limited edition idea to hockey cards, which become collectibles. Jason's vision of adult self-expression through undergarments was a great success. Positive reviews were coming in from influential news and apparel media such as Fashion File, GQ, and Vogue. In less than a year, Ginch Gonch was shipping $150 000 worth of underwear every month. However, a combination of Jason's lack of understanding of supply chain management and the resounding success of the products was about to threaten the long-term viability of the new-found company.

Ginch Gonch was finding it difficult to complete orders, satisfying only 33 percent of the requests coming in. The fear that unreliable order fulfillment would result in retailers dropping the line, which would put the firm into a tailspin, was very real. The initial source of the problem was their choice in garment factory. Jason and the rest of the Ginch Gonch management team were committed to avoiding sweatshops in the production of their garments, but they also knew that they could not afford the costs of production in Canada. After initially working with a factory in Thailand without satisfactory results, Ginch Gonch searched for a manufacturer in China through an agent. Ginch Gonch went with the fifth factory they toured, but the manufacturer turned out to be a bad relationship characterized by delays and flaws that cost Ginch Gonch time and money since they couldn't fulfill orders.

In stark contrast to undergarment leader Calvin Klein, Vancouver's Ginch Gonch produces cotton his and hers underwear that uses vibrant colours with cartoon-like designs emblazoned on them, which are reminiscent of underwear that one may have worn as a kid.

To add to their order-fulfillment problems, Ginch Gonch failed to consider in their plans the growing resentment in the United States toward outsourcing work to China. They were subsequently caught by surprise when the United States government imposed quotas on Chinese-produced textiles. The policy, which was created to safeguard US garment manufacturers, left Ginch Gonch holding onto thousands of units in Vancouver that were initially destined for the US market. Ginch Gonch was in the unenviable position of possessing inventory they could not distribute without cash to fix their production problems.

Sutherland continued to look for an alternate supplier and found a garment factory in El Salvador that had very good working conditions and a solid financial rating, which alleviated any concerns regarding hardship on workers. The El Salvador government had also increased their appeal to North American firms by providing tax breaks and other financial incentives. Still, the transition did not come without more learning. The factory required new equipment and updated technologies to produce the undergarments to Ginch Gonch's specifications, which created more delays in production. Sutherland and the Ginch Gonch management team continued to look for other suppliers, with the likelihood of ending up with multiple sources around the world.

From their early mistakes, Ginch Gonch learned that planning on one supplier for production could lead to a dangerous dependence where they have little or no control on the timeliness or quality of the product, particularly when the operation is as small as theirs. The optimal arrangement, from their experience, is to have multiple sources for different stages of production and distribution. They also learned that when dealing across nations and cultures, it is necessary to have people skilled in formulating deals with the region to assist with everything from language barriers to local laws. So, while Ginch Gonch's mission is to live like a kid, working in a global market requires the experience and wisdom that comes with time.

Sources: "Ginch Gonch," *Venture*, aired October 18, 2006; L. George, "Manties—They're Panties for Men," *Maclean's*, May 8, 2006; G. Babineau, "Unmentionables: An Adventure in Outsourcing Underwear—Globally," *Canadian Apparel*, March/April 2006; K. Nolan, "Intimates Grow Up—for the Young at Heart," *DSN Retailing Today*, January 9, 2006; "Ginch Gonch Flare Wear," *Body*, March 2005.

actions is a Gantt chart (see Exhibit 6.5). Time is typically on the horizontal axis and the tasks to be done are on the vertical axis. The chart shows when actions are to be started and how long they are expected to take for completion. It shows which actions are first, second, or last in the process and whether a preceding action must be completed before a subsequent one can be started or whether there is expected overlap in the timing of specific actions.

In addition to the planned sequence and timing, the actual progress can be charted as well. This allows managers to better assess their progress against the plan and potentially make adjustments. Today, sophisticated computer programs can assist managers in formulating and implementing plans involving literally hundreds of raw materials and components that must be brought together in the right amounts and sequences for the cost-effective production of finished goods.[20]

Exhibit 6.5

Gantt Chart

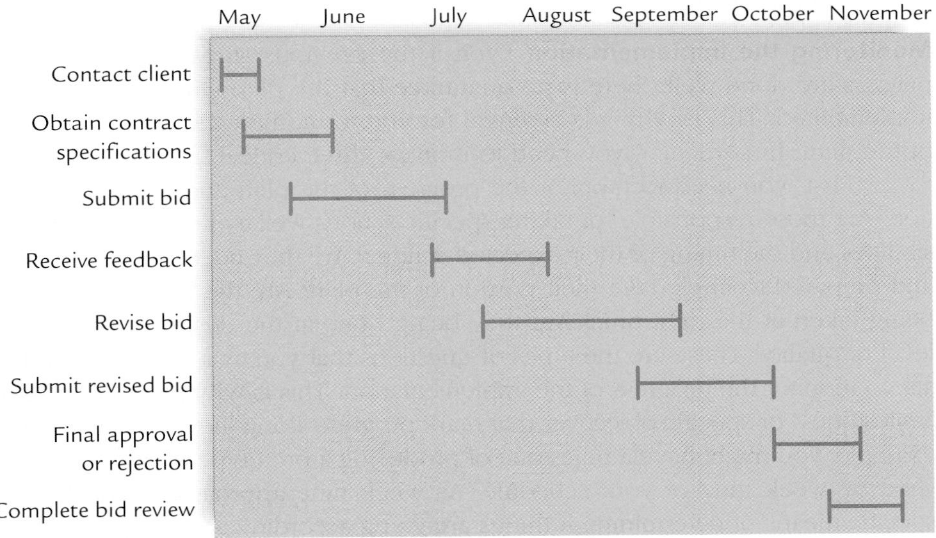

Accountability The second key aspect of effective action plans is a specification of who is accountable for which specific actions. Knowing who is responsible for what can facilitate coordination when more than one person will be executing various actions in the overall plan.[21] Accountability also increases the likelihood that the steps are taken when they should be and done as well as they need to be. Let's go back to our athletic shoe example. You personally take responsibility for hiring the three product-design engineers. You assign one of your subordinates the task of securing space for the designers within the next month. You decide to outsource the manufacturing and assign another subordinate the task of finding reliable contract manufacturers within the next 10 weeks. Finally, you assign another of your subordinates to work with the marketing group to begin generating possible ideas for the promotion and advertising of the launch.

Implementing Plans

Once the action plan has been created, it then needs to be implemented. The quality of the plan implementation can determine the actual results as much as the quality of the plan itself. However, much of the success of the implementation can be assured by doing the previous steps in the planning process well. Plans often fail in the implementation stage because of inadequate assessment of resources required and available. Again let's return to our shoe example. Your subordinate is successful in finding a contract manufacturer with a great reputation. In fact, the company has made shoes for Nike in the past—it even got a good endorsement from Nike when your subordinate checked up on the company. You discover, however, that for your shoes the company will need new sewing machines, and the workers will need training to properly operate the new machines. However, because of the company's poor communication with its workers, the workers mistakenly think the new machines will require fewer workers. As a consequence, they resist the new training for fear they will eventually lose their jobs. Their resistance delays the production of the new shoes, and a critical window of opportunity in the marketplace is lost.

This illustrates in a simple way why plan implementation can be as critical and sometimes more critical than the overall plan objectives. However, no matter how carefully you work out the implementation plan, you will still need to monitor and adjust your implementation efforts because unanticipated events almost always happen.

Monitoring the Implementation Even if the previous steps in the planning process are done well, there is no guarantee that the plan will be successfully implemented. This is why it is essential for you to monitor the implementation of the plan. In particular, you need to monitor three critical factors.

First, you need to monitor the progress of the plan and its implementation. Are those responsible for taking specific actions well aware of their responsibilities and the timing of their expected actions? Are they adequately motivated and prepared to implement their portion of the plan? Are the necessary actions being taken at the right time? Are they being done at the desired or necessary level of quality? These are the types of questions that you as a manager need to ask to monitor the progress of the implementation. This is why plans often have "milestones" or specific objectives that mark progress along the total journey. For example, you might have a milestone of producing a prototype of your high-end shoe by week nine of your schedule. As week nine approaches, you have a specific means of determining if things are going according to plan or not.

Second, as a manager you need to monitor the level of support that the plan receives as it is being implemented.[22] You cannot assume that just because a plan is in place people will support it. You have to constantly assess whether you are providing the required support for the plan's effective implementation. This support might take the form of encouragement, money, or coaching. Few plans of any complexity or duration can be effectively implemented without continuous support. Are the other key supporters providing the encouragement needed? One of your key responsibilities as a manager is to monitor and ensure that the required support is there. For example, in putting your high-end shoe launch plan into effect, you may want to monitor the level of support from those in the marketing department. The marketing department may need to do a number of things in advance of the launch of the new shoe. They may need to talk with reporters working for magazines like *Runner's World* to start creating some "buzz" about the new shoe; they might need to talk with large retailers like Foot Locker to get them excited about not only ordering the shoe but placing it near the front of their stores in a special display. You cannot afford to have this great shoe coming off the factory line with nowhere to go because of poor support from marketing.

Third, as a manager you need to monitor the level of resistance. Many plans and their implementation involve change. To the extent that they do, you should anticipate and monitor resistance to the plan's implementation. We will discuss many of the fundamental reasons for resistance to change later on, in Chapter 15. Still, it deserves a bit of space here because resistance has been the cause of death for many plans. One of the general reasons why people resist change is because they have to do new things and anticipate doing them poorly at first. You can use this principle to help you identify possible sources of resistance.

For example, you might expect the marketing department to be thrilled to have a high-end shoe to promote. However, there are several new activities that will be required of the marketing people that they may not be good at initially. Specifically, the launch of your new shoe requires the marketing people to try to get some endorsements or at least use of the shoe by famous runners. Unfortunately, they have never dealt with celebrities. They don't know how to make contact with celebrity runners or how to pitch them on using your shoe. Because people in the department aren't familiar with the process, they may shy away from it—they may even say they are making progress even though they are not really putting much effort into it. Why are they resisting contacting celebrity runners? Even if they see that it is the right thing to do, they resist because they fear failure at first. You may need to provide extra encouragement or even hire a special consultant to help you make the connections and contacts with the celebrity runners.

Real-Time Adjustment Because we live in a dynamic environment, any plan whose formulation and implementation lasts more than a few days or weeks is likely to need to be adjusted. As the environment changes, what was originally a perfectly acceptable objective may become unrealistic or too easily achieved, and therefore may need to be changed. Likewise, what were perfectly reasonable time frames and required resources at one point may become unreasonable because of sociocultural, technological, economic, or political-legal changes.

This realization has at least two implications. First, it may suggest that as a manager working in a dynamic and changing environment, you need to plan the way a fire department does. A fire department cannot anticipate exactly where or even when fires are likely to break out. Its plans are built upon certain principles of fighting fires and around general categories of fires. If you are a manager in a phone company, one of the key principles is redundancy. If a catastrophic event happens and knocks out your equipment, you have to have a backup system because you won't be able to get new equipment in place fast enough if your original equipment is somehow damaged or destroyed. This lesson is continually reinforced by extreme weather events like Hurricane Juan's devastation in Nova Scotia in September 2003 and the repeated pounding that British Columbia's Vancouver Island and Lower Mainland received from a series of storms in the late fall of 2006. These events prompt managers to ensure that backup equipment and critical replacements are available and ready to roll at a moment's notice. Second, as a manager you need to help your employees recognize and accept the need to adapt plans in real time. You may also need to foster capabilities that enable them to adapt effectively. These capabilities might include skills like good environmental scanning and quick requirement and resource assessment abilities. The key point to remember is that in today's dynamic environment, a fixed and rigid plan may be as dangerous as no plan at all.

Monitoring Outcomes

The final element in the planning process involves monitoring outcomes. If the objectives have been well defined from the outset of the planning process, there should be little question as to what outcomes are to be monitored or how they are to be measured. If the plan was expected to result in increased financial performance and it was to be measured in terms of increased sales, then the outcome should be easy to gauge.

However, most plans also produce unanticipated consequences.[23] The plan and its implementation may produce either negative or positive unanticipated outcomes. Both can be valuable sources of learning. To help illustrate this, let's return once again to our athletic shoe case. Let's suppose that through implementing the plan you discover it takes more advertising money than anticipated to launch your new high-end line of shoes. You find that customers have an image of your firm as a middle-range shoe maker and have difficulty at first believing that you could produce a line of athletic shoes with the technology, quality, and "sizzle" of other makers that are already in the high end of the market. On the unexpected positive side, you also discover that a stitching machine that you bought for your high-end shoes produced a straighter and stronger stitch at a lower price than the machines you were using for your low-end shoes. Using the new machines on both your low-end and high-end shoes will lower your costs, and yet allow you to promote higher quality. This may help you compete with other makers at the lower end of the market who produce lower-quality shoes.

The example above illustrates that managers should capture as much knowledge as they possibly can when monitoring outcomes. There also needs to be a feedback loop so that what they've learned can be used to modify and improve other aspects of the planning process.

Planning Tools

budgets used to quantify and allocate resources to specific activities

capital expenditure budget specifies the amount of money to be spent on specific items that have long-term use and require significant amounts of money to acquire

expense budget includes all primary activities on which a unit or organization plans to spend money and the amount allocated to each for the upcoming year

Managers use a variety of planning tools. For example, earlier in this chapter we referred to Gantt charts as one of the tools managers can use to facilitate the timing and sequencing of actions. In this section we discuss a tool that is also widely used: budgets.

Budgets

Budgets are used to quantify and allocate resources to specific activities. In most organizations, budgets are proposed and set on an annual basis. Budgets might address a variety of issues. For example a **capital expenditure budget** specifies the amount of money that is planned for spending on specific items that have long-term use and require significant amounts of money to acquire. These items might include things such as equipment, land, or buildings.

Another common budget is an expense budget. An **expense budget** typically includes all the primary activities on which the unit or organization plans to spend money and the amount that is allocated for each item for the upcoming year. Virtually all profit and not-for-profit organizations of a moderate or larger size have expense budgets, both for planning and for control purposes.

Most organizations have a two-phased process relative to budgets. The first consists of managers looking ahead and planning their needs. They then put together a budget specifying things like expected capital expenditures or expenses. This **proposed budget** provides a plan of how much money is needed and is submitted to a superior or budget review committee. Once the proposed budget is submitted, it gets reviewed, often in the context of other proposed budgets. An **approved budget** specifies what the manager is actually authorized to spend money on and how much.

proposed budget provides a plan for how much money is needed and is submitted to a superior or budget review committee

approved budget specifies what the manager is actually authorized to spend money on and how much

Regardless of the type of budget, two main approaches to the budgeting process can be taken. The first approach is typically called the **incremental budgeting approach**.[24] In this approach, managers use the approved budget of the previous year and then present arguments for why the upcoming budget should be more or less. This may include particular increases or decreases. Incremental budgeting is efficient because managers do not need to spend significant time justifying the allocation of money toward the same sorts of purchases each year. The principal negative consequence of incremental budgeting is that it can result in "budget momentum." In other words, items that have been given money in the past may be allocated money in the future merely because they have been allocated money in the past. A common frustration with this approach to budgeting is the rampant spending that can occur as a fiscal year approaches its end. In Manitoba, as in many provinces, suppliers of printed material and office equipment saw the provincial government approaching fiscal year end as a boom time for business. Provincial departments would place many orders for supplies and services to be delivered before year end to fully exhaust the current year's budget. If the allocated budget was not fully spent, there was a good chance that departments would receive less money in the subsequent fiscal year. As this example illustrates, incremental budgeting can create a "use it or lose it" mindset, which can in turn lead to the inefficient use of valuable resources and waste, as unnecessary products or services are ordered just to deplete funds.

incremental budgeting approach where managers use the approved budget of the previous year and then present arguments for why the upcoming budget should be more or less

The **zero-based budgeting approach** assumes that all allocations of funds must be justified from zero each year.[25] In other words, the fact that your department was given $100 000 for computer equipment purchases last year does not provide any justification per se for it receiving money for computers this year. Zero-based budgeting requires starting from a base of zero funds and then justifying the resources being requested for each activity. The benefit of this approach to budgeting is that items that cannot be justified on their own current merits (regardless of their past merits and allocated budgets) will not get money. This then leaves the money available for items or activities that can be justified. In general, this can lead to an overall more effective allocation of the organization's financial resources. However, zero-based budgeting takes time because each item must be justified each year. Some items that need money allocated to them may cost more in time and energy trying to justify their proposed funding than they are worth.

zero-based budgeting approach assumes that all allocations of funds must be justified from zero each year

In either approach, budgets are typically used as planning tools by managers to determine priorities, required resources, and keys to implementation. In particular, because money is usually a scarce resource in most organizations—there is almost never as much money available as there are requests for it—allocating money among various activities almost forces a discussion of the relative priority among activities. This is true at all three organization levels. For example, department managers are likely to find they have more demand for money than they have money to allocate. Similarly, corporate officers are likely to find departments and business units requesting more money than the organization has. This leads to a determination of which units and their related activities are of highest priority and should receive budget approval.

In this sense, budgets can be an effective means of integrating and quantifying many aspects of the corporate-, business-, and functional-level plans. While the budgeting process per se does not guarantee that managers will make good decisions about the integration and coordination process, nor that they will make good decisions about priorities, it does raise the likelihood of these key items being discussed and determined.

Goal Setting

Goal setting is a specific planning process for managing performance. Normally we think of it at the individual level, though all of the principles are applicable to setting goals for teams, units, and overall organizations. It is important to examine goals. The research suggests that effective goals can have a significant and positive impact on performance. Much of the research about effective goal setting can be captured in an easy-to-remember and practical acronym—SMART. "Smart" goals have five key characteristics: they are specific, measurable, agreed upon, realistic, and time bound.

Specific As we mentioned relative to organizational objectives in the planning process, goals for firms, units, subordinates, or for oneself should be specific. For example, you may have received feedback from different people or just sensed that "you need to improve your communication skills." Improvement in this area may in fact yield significant benefits; however, as stated it is too vague. To be effective it must be much more specific. Suppose you decide that "communication skills" is too broad and you narrow the scope and make your goal specifically to improve your listening skills. Is this now a good goal? Is it specific enough? The answer is "no." You need to assess what it is you do or don't do that makes you a less-than-effective listener. Perhaps you often interrupt people when they're speaking because you think you know what they are going to say. You determine that your goal is to not interrupt people and wait for them to finish before saying what you have to say. Is this a good goal? Is it specific? While this alone may not make you a great listener, it is a good goal in terms of being specific, and the research strongly suggests that you are more likely to make progress toward a specific goal than a vague goal.

Measured One way to determine whether a goal you have set is specific enough is by whether you think you could measure progress and improvement as well as the ultimate result. Could you measure the number of times you interrupted versus the times you listened and waited for others to finish what they had to say? Clearly you could. Could you measure others' perception of whether you were interrupting or listening and waiting for them to say what they had to say? Clearly you could. But having a goal that is measurable is only part of the battle. In addition, you need to actually measure progress toward the goal. Goal setting is most effective when progress toward the goal is measured and measured often. So how often is often? The research does not provide an absolute answer. What we do know is that once a year is not often enough. In fact, twice a year does not seem to be often enough. Beyond that, it seems that the frequency of measurement needs to be related to the nature of the activities associated with the goal. For example, if you talk with people dozens of times per day and therefore have the opportunity to hit (or miss) your goal of not interrupting many times per day, then assessing your progress once a month is too infrequent.

Daily self-measurement may be appropriate. However, from a practical perspective, you would be unwise to ask others every day how you are doing on listening and not interrupting. This you may want to do weekly or monthly.

Agreed Even if a goal is specific and measurable, if those involved in its achievement do not agree to it, it is unlikely to be met. For organizational goals, this means that a substantial portion of employees must agree to the goal. For unit goals, those in the unit must agree and accept the goal. For subordinate goals, the individual subordinate must accept the goal. Personal goals must be accepted and committed to. Returning to our original example, suppose you lay out the specific goal of not interrupting people and measure progress but do not really accept the goal. (Maybe you don't think interrupting is a bad thing and in fact you believe it saves time in conversations.) In this case, the goal is unlikely to be effective. Obviously, the reverse is true if you accept or are committed to the goal.

Here there is a very practical implication for managers. Because managers are in a position of power, subordinates often say what they believe the manager wants to hear—even when it is not what the subordinates really think. For example, if you say, "Tom, I think this is a challenging but doable goal for you. Don't you?" how is Tom going to reply? A verbal agreement from a subordinate without any real commitment behind the words will likely not result in the goal being achieved. As a consequence, when it comes to the "agreed" part of SMART goals, it is important to listen carefully and invite subordinates to candidly express their commitment to or resistance regarding specific goals. Again, the fundamental objective of this part of SMART goal setting is not superficial agreement but deep commitment.

Realistic Now you have a specific, measured, and agreed upon goal. Will it be effective? Not if it is unrealistic—or if it is too easy. Goals that are too easy are not effective and goals that are too difficult are also not effective. To understand why, let's look at each case in turn. First, goals that are too easy are not effective for two reasons. On the one hand, they are not effective because they do not inspire motivation. In general, people are not motivated to try to achieve things that they perceive as being too easy. Often, they wait until the last minute to put any effort into achieving the goal, believing that a little effort at the last minute will enable them to hit the target. On the other hand, easy goals are not effective because they do not deliver substantial results. First, even if they are achieved, easy goals by their nature do not have a big impact on results—organizational, unit, subordinate, or personal. Ironically, because easy goals are seen as easy, the low motivation they inspire often results in the goals being missed. Goals that are too difficult, though, are also not effective. If a goal is seen as impossible or just highly unlikely to be achieved, people are not motivated to try to hit the target. After all, why waste precious time and energy trying to hit an unachievable target? Thus, effective goals must be challenging but achievable or realistic.

To make this concrete, let's return again to a personal goal of not interrupting others and listening to what they have to say. Assuming you have dozens of opportunities each day to hit or miss this target, is it realistic to set a goal of not interrupting 100 percent of the time, especially at first? If it is a challenging but realistic goal, that is fine. But if you see it as unrealistic, it will not be effective. Perhaps the realistic goal is to not interrupt more than 50 percent of the time during the first week.

Time Bound Even specific, measured, agreed upon, and realistic goals need to be time bound to be effective. In other words, goals need a specific time span within which they are to be achieved. For goals that will take a long period of time to achieve, say a year or more, shorter time intervals are needed. For

The Judy Project, named for the late Toronto businesswoman Judy Elder, is a forum for senior executive women offered at the Rotman School of Management. The goal of the Judy Project is to build stronger business organizations through the advancement of more women into senior leadership positions. The week-long seminar provides participants with skills in networking, career planning, goal setting, and leadership styles. While the seminar is only a week in duration, smaller groups of six to eight participants each will continue meeting regularly as an ongoing personal support group for each other.[26]

example, suppose you think that the right level of listening and not interrupting is 80 percent. In other words, you think that in eight out of ten conversations you should not interrupt but should instead listen and wait until the person has said what he or she has to say. Furthermore, you think that it will take you three months to achieve this goal. The three months becomes the general time boundary within which you plan to achieve the goal. However, as we suggested at the end of the section on making the goal realistic, you may have other time frames that become intermediate milestones for your ultimate goal. You may set a time frame of one week for going from 10 percent listening (90 percent interrupting) to 50 percent listening and not interrupting. You may then set a time frame of one month to get to a level of 70 percent listening and not interrupting.

MBO

Management by Objectives (MBO) is a specific type of goal-setting process, similar to SMART. (Exhibit 6.6 provides a graphic illustration of how MBO works.) Research suggests that MBO systems are most effective if top management demonstrates clear support for and involvement in the system.[27] Most of the general characteristics just described are critical to a successful MBO process. First, specific goals are set. The achievement of these goals should translate into results that support the organization's strategic, tactical, and operational plans and objectives. Goals need to be difficult but achievable. As you would expect, when difficult but achievable goals are accomplished, it has a positive impact on performance.[28] Participation by subordinates in setting their goals tends to lead to difficult but achievable goals. In addition, the goals need to be accepted by subordinates. Goal acceptance has a positive impact on both motivation to perform and actual performance,[29] and participation by subordinates in the goal-setting process increases goal acceptance.[30] MBO goals need specific time frames, and periodic review and evaluation are necessary. Based on these reviews, subordinate performance improves according to the quality of feedback given to subordinates.[31] Individuals need to know if what they are doing is on or off target so that they can retain or adjust their behaviours. Also, feedback can affect the goal-setting process. Specific feedback may indicate that the original goals were too easy, too difficult, or just not directed at appropriate targets.

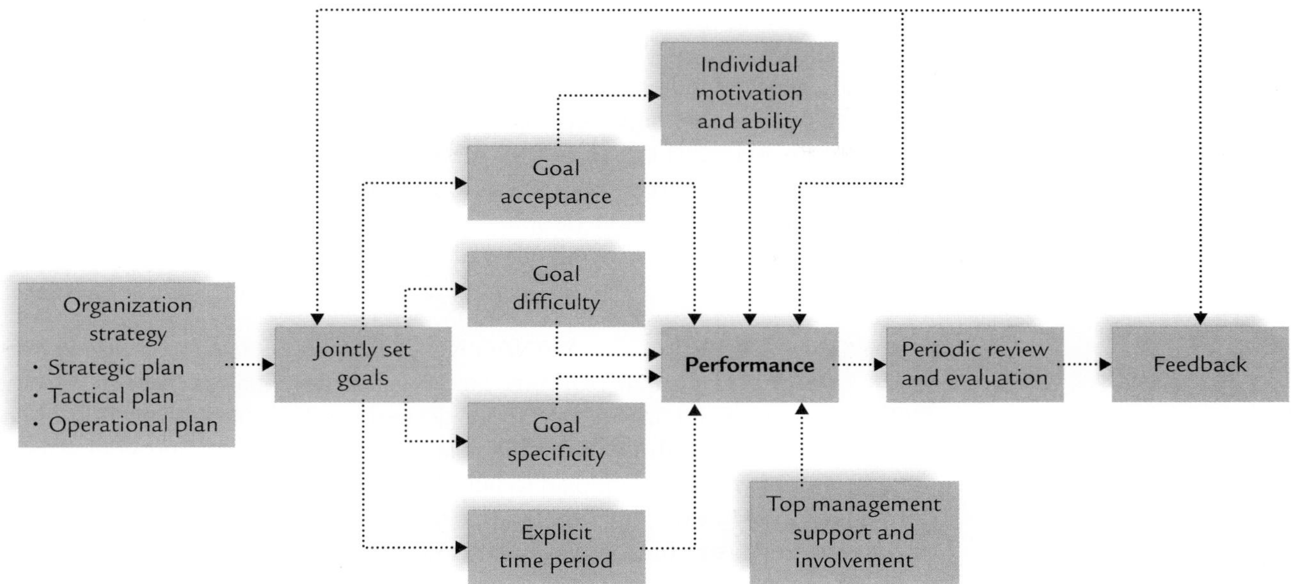

Exhibit 6.6

The Process of MBO

managerial perspectives revisited

PERSPECTIVE 1: **THE ORGANIZATIONAL CONTEXT** Given that we ended this chapter by focusing on goals and used personal goals to illustrate the key concepts, the relevance of the organizational context for goal setting in particular and the planning process in general may not be completely obvious. However, organizational context is critical. Clearly, you could set personal goals and plan your work and projects independent of the organizational context. However, this would likely result in suboptimal personal career and organizational results. At a personal level, we are likely to make greater contributions and gain greater recognition for future advancement if our personal goals are aligned with the strategy and direction of the organization. For example, suppose your company had a low-cost strategy and productivity gains were central to lowering costs in your area of responsibility. How bright would your career prospects be if you were weak at productivity analysis but failed to ever set any improvement goals in that area? The same general principle applies to goals for subordinates, units, and the overall organization. One of the important organizational contexts that we should always consider when setting goals is the strategy of the organization. In addition, the plans that we put in place should consider not only the direction of the company but its culture as well. The details of a plan for change would be different in an organization with a culture that resists change compared to one that embraces it. Thus, many of the details of effective plans have to account for both the direction of the organization and its nature.

PERSPECTIVE 2: **THE HUMAN FACTOR** Goals and plans for organizations, whether the plans are strategic, tactical, or operational, require input from others and their coordinated efforts to accomplish. In fact, a common mistake of those charged with formulating plans for projects or new-product launches is that

they do not think carefully enough about the role that others play in the implementation of the plan. The more complex the plan, the more likely it is that its successful implementation and achievement will depend on multiple people. Managers need to not only develop plans but manage others in the implementation of the plans. This fact is highlighted in the opening case, where P&G determined that the most important resources for successful entry into Eastern European markets were the people—employees and managers—who would ultimately implement its strategy abroad.

PERSPECTIVE 3: **MANAGING PARADOXES** It should be clear by this point that planning has inherent potential paradoxes. On the one hand, failure to achieve desired results is often a function of not having a thoughtful and detailed plan. As the saying goes, "those who fail to plan, plan to fail." On the other hand, in a dynamic world of change where new competitors appear frequently, innovative technology is developed and used unexpectedly, and customer preferences evolve rapidly, managers cannot afford to rigidly maintain even the most well-developed plans; they must be prepared to modify, adapt, or even discard plans as they go. The need to develop thorough plans and be completely committed to their implementation, yet simultaneously flexible if they need to be changed later, presents something of a paradox to managers. Sometimes the challenge of dealing with change tempts managers to not develop thorough plans in the first place. They might reason that some of their efforts will be wasted if the situation were to change. This is faulty reasoning. The environment will always be undergoing changes. The key to responding to these changes is first detecting them. A thorough plan may be one of the best ways to detect signs that the environment is changing and different from what was expected. A thorough plan can serve as an "image projector." When the environment does not reflect back what you have projected, the more detailed the projection, the more specific the discrepancies that can be detected, and the more refined your adjustments and changes to the plan can be.

PERSPECTIVE 4: **ENTREPRENEURIAL MINDSET** As discussed in the introduction to this chapter, the strategic planning process helps to identify opportunities. If managers have an entrepreneurial mindset they will be better able to identify those opportunities when analyzing the environment their companies are attempting to do business in, and they will be more likely to formulate a strategy to exploit those opportunities. The required commitment comes primarily in a disciplined approach to plan formulation and an energetic implementation. Sometimes when you have put so much effort into formulating the plan, you can feel as though the implementation will go well with little further effort. But while poor planning quite often guarantees poor implementation, thorough planning does not guarantee effective implementation. To be effective, managers have to be committed to implement it and even to possibly change it as needed. For example, looking back at the discussion on EMC, even though managers spent considerable time formulating their plan to focus on software, because of the history of the company, even its existing customers could have resisted the new plan. It took considerable commitment to overcome the natural obstacles, implementing the planned actions, and then successfully achieving the goals desired. Yet it is important to emphasize that too much commitment to a particular plan without regard for changes in the environment can be detrimental. An entrepreneurial

mindset is needed to make plans and implement them, and yet remain flexible and open to new environmental opportunities as things change. The planning process itself provides the overall needed discipline for an organization to excel, while an entrepreneurial mindset helps maintain the necessary flexibility.

concluding comments

Planning requires a determination of where the organization wants to go and how it is going to get there. This process includes an assessment of the organization's external and internal environment. Early in their careers, managers typically are more involved in operational plans. Consequently, some organizations or individuals might be tempted to ask why young managers should understand all aspects of the planning process.

The basic answer to this question is twofold. First, lower-level managers are more motivated to implement their specific responsibilities if they know the larger plan. Second, lower-level managers face thousands of specific decisions daily. They cannot make these specific decisions in a way that works toward the organization's overall objectives if they do not understand those objectives. This process would be like facing a series of choices of turning left or right and of slowing down or speeding up without knowing your ultimate destination.

In an ever-globalizing environment, managers are simultaneously faced with three critical planning challenges. First, they must try to learn from the past. Many things that went right or wrong in the past may be helpful in guiding action and shaping plans for the future. Second, managers must keep their ears and eyes closely focused on signals in the current environment—signals from competitors, customers, governments, and so on. The rate of change in the current environment is so fast that too little attention to the present could forfeit the future. Finally, managers must think about and plan for the future. It is the incorporation of three different time perspectives (past, present, and future) that makes planning one of the most challenging managerial activities.

key terms

approved budget 209
benchmarking 199
budgets 208
capital expenditure budget 208
contingency plans 198
expense budget 208
incremental budgeting approach 209
objectives 191
operational plans 193
planning 191
plans 191
proposed budget 209
strategic plans 192
tactical plans 193
zero-based budgeting approach 209

test your comprehension

1. What are the key functions of setting objectives?
2. Define strategic plans.
3. Provide an example of a tactical plan.
4. What are the key elements of operational plans?
5. What are the key differences between strategic, tactical, and operational plans?
6. What impact does organizational level have on managerial planning activities?
7. What are the key issues that managers at the corporate level focus on relative to planning?
8. What type of plans do people at the business level primarily undertake?

9. What are the seven elements in the planning process?
10. Why is forecasting critical to the planning process?
11. Under what conditions are contingency plans most beneficial?
12. What is benchmarking and what role does it play in planning?
13. Why is determining the priority of objectives important?
14. In what ways does measuring objectives influence plan implementation and plan changes?
15. What is the difference between defining requirements and assessing resources in the planning process?
16. How can a Gantt chart facilitate the sequence and timing issues in planning?
17. How can budgeting be used as a planning tool?
18. Describe the two basic approaches to budgeting.
19. What are the strengths and weaknesses of incremental and zero-based budgeting?
20. What is the role of MBO in strategy formulation and implementation?
21. What are the five key elements in effective goal setting?

apply your understanding

1. In your university, professors likely have objectives regarding teaching, research, and service to the university. From your perspective what are the relative priorities of these three objectives? If you could, how would you *change* the priorities and why?
2. Think of an action plan in which you were recently involved. Which elements of the planning process were done well? Which ones were done poorly? What was the impact of these strengths and weaknesses on the outcome?
3. As you look at your own experience and capabilities, where are your strengths and weaknesses relative to the seven elements of the planning process? What is your plan of action for strengthening your planning capabilities?
4. Think about the last goal you set for yourself. How SMART was it?

practise your capabilities

Two months ago you were made manager of a group of six gate agents for Provincial Airlines, Newfoundland's regional airline based in St. John's. One of your subordinates comes to you for advice. The previous manager gave him some rather low marks on his performance evaluation. He wants to make some improvements but feels that he cannot do everything at once. Below are the previous manager's comments about the employee.

Punctuality: Joe is usually on time and rarely misses work without prior notification. However, he never shows up early or stays late to help out during busy times.

Customer Service: In general, Joe does not seem to be a happy person. He is never rude to customers but he does not seem to make them happy either. When problems arise, such as delayed flights, Joe gives customers information and answers their questions in a very matter-of-fact manner. He rarely shows any empathy, and a customer has never complimented him for his service when I have been around.

Check-in Knowledge: Joe has a good understanding of check-in processes. He knows who can get upgrades and what is required. He understands seat assignment policies and executes them with great consistency. However, he fails to notice in advance those customers who have too many bags or whose bags are too large, which simply creates delays and customer frustration when they have to check bags as they are about to board the plane.

Security Procedures: While this is an area that is new to everyone and something that seems to change monthly, Joe is relatively up to date. Soon, airport security personnel will conduct all the "at gate screenings," so this aspect will diminish in importance in the future.

Provincial Airlines has introduced a new strategy that emphasizes customer service. In addition, it is trying to reduce delays and improve its on-time performance.

1. What area(s) would you recommend that Joe try to improve? Why?
2. Create one to three SMART goals and have Joe (a classmate) do the same. Compare the goals. How similar are they? Which goals need to be re-evaluated or changed? Assuming that your assessment of Joe is similar to that of his previous boss and that Joe is typical of the other five subordinates you have, what objectives would you set for your team and what plan would you lay out for achieving them? Even if you don't have all the information you need from the brief description above, what questions would you ask and what information would you need to develop a thorough plan?

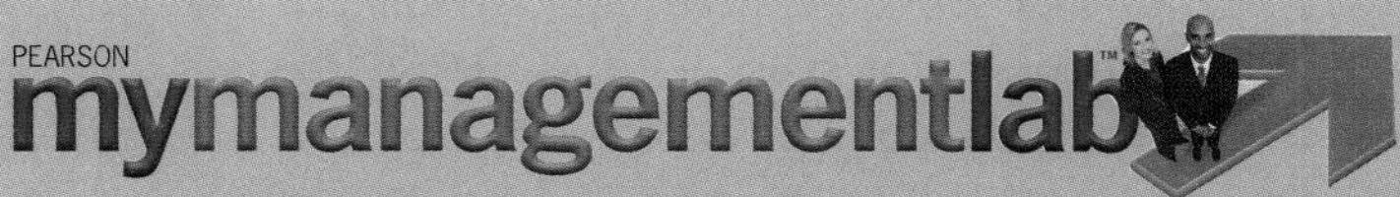

closing case DEVELOP YOUR CRITICAL THINKING

Planning a New Program Launch at LDC

"Pam" (a disguised name but a real person) was director of training at a large training company—Leadership Development Center (LDC). As such, one of her responsibilities was to plan the launch of new training programs. LDC had a reputation for excellent programs targeted at mid-level managers. However, the top executives at LDC felt that the company needed more training for senior executives who were the bosses of these mid-level managers. LDC executives felt that if senior executives personally experienced the quality of LDC training, they would be more likely to recommend and approve training requests for their mid-level managers.

For the new Senior Executive Leadership Program, Pam discussed with her boss and her peers what the program objective ought to be. Some thought the program should be a "loss leader," or in other words, that it should lose money but pay for itself by generating more participants for LDC's mid-level managerial programs. Others thought that the new program should break even financially. Everyone agreed, however, that the program should be of a sufficient quality that participants would have a very favourable impression of LDC. As a result, they would be more likely to encourage their employees to attend LDC programs and approve their requests to do so.

Pam determined that the program's success would be measured in three ways. First, the number of participants in the first program would be measured. Pam calculated that it would take about 18 participants for the program to break even financially. Second, she would survey all participants regarding their satisfaction with the program, its content, materials, facilities, administration, and instructors. Finally, LDC would track the number of mid-level managers from the companies of those attending the senior executive program to see if there was an increased participation level.

In launching the program, Pam looked at the past marketing costs of other new programs. Past new launches had cost about $30 000 in brochure and mailing expenses. She figured that an extra $5000 ought to be enough to launch the new senior executive program.

The current budget did not anticipate the launch of the senior executive program, but another program in marketing had been cancelled, and so there was $20 000 still in the budget for that program, which Pam thought she could spend on the new senior executive program. In addition, she thought she could access $15 000 from the general contingency budget of $30 000.

One of the first things she would need to do would be to talk to various possible instructors and select a "faculty director." This person would design the specific content of the program and coordinate the other instructors and their content. Once the faculty director was chosen, the program would need to be designed, and from the design, a brochure would need to be created. She estimated that the program design would take three weeks and that the design of the brochures would take an additional two weeks. Printing the brochures would take four days, and assembling them for mailing would take another three days. Delivery of the mailed brochures would take about a week. Normally, LDC allowed about 12 weeks between the time people received brochures and when their program applications were due. In general, program applications were due (along with the program fees) three weeks before the start of the program. Two weeks before the program start, all the materials (handouts, notebooks, etc.) would need to be assembled.

Pam had two people who would assist in the implementation of the plan and report directly to her. Tammy would be responsible for contacting the brochure design firm and the printing company and seeing to it that the brochure was ready on time. In addition, she would secure the mailing list and arrange for an outside contractor to stuff the envelopes with brochures for mailing. Dan would be responsible for venue details. LDC had its own training facilities and had contracts with several nearby hotels for lodging arrangements. Dan would also be responsible for the assembly of all the materials, which meant getting handouts and other materials from the instructors on time.

As the plan was put into action, everything seemed to go fine. A faculty member was selected to be the faculty director, and the program design and content were ready in two rather than the anticipated three weeks. The outside design firm quickly produced a brochure that with a few modifications was ready for mailing. Tammy obtained several mailing lists that had the names of senior executives in medium to large companies. The mailing went out about five days early.

Inquiries regarding the program were 100 percent higher than other new programs that LDC had launched in the past. However, as time wore on, the ratio of inquiries to registrations was not good. Typically, one in every ten people who contacted LDC for further information regarding a particular program ended up registering for it. However, with eight weeks to go before the program's start, the inquiry to registration ratio was 100 to 1 (not 10 to 1). With only four weeks to go before the start of the program, only ten participants had signed up. Pam was in a panic as to what to do.

Questions

1. What adjustments would you make at this point? Would you cancel the program or run it at a loss?
2. Draw out a Gantt chart of the sequence and timing of key activities. What insights does this give you regarding the plan and its implementation?
3. What do you think went wrong? What do you see as the strengths and weaknesses of the planning process?
4. LDC seemed to follow a planning process that had worked well for its mid-level managerial programs. Are there differences between senior executives and mid-level managers that might explain why the plan did not work out as anticipated? Could these differences have been anticipated? Should they have been?

Chapter 7 Strategic Management

LEARNING OBJECTIVES

After reading this chapter, you should be able to:

1 Define strategy.

2 Explain the role of environmental analysis in strategy formulation.

3 Explain the strategic planning process.

4 Use strategic planning tools, such as the product life cycle model, portfolio matrix, and SWOT analysis.

5 Describe strategy implementation tools like the Seven S Model.

6 Describe the differences between intended and emergent strategies.

Size Matters: CanWest Global's Pursuit of National Broadcaster Status

Israel (Izzy) Asper, a lawyer by profession, entered the broadcasting business in 1975 when he started CanWest and relocated the Pembina, North Dakota, television station KCND to Winnipeg, Manitoba (renamed as CKND). Asper quickly set out to expand his business, and with the help of other investors soon acquired Global Television Network in Toronto. In 1985, Asper's growth efforts were temporarily halted when he began a legal battle against two of his partners, whom he claimed were preventing him from exercising his stake in the company. Five years later, after winning the dispute, Asper gained control of CanWest Global. Immediately after his victory Asper began to focus on his goal of growing his business and becoming the third Canadian national television broadcaster (next to publicly funded CBC and the privately funded CTV). Gradually, through a series of national and international acquisitions during the 1990s, CanWest Global not only became the most profitable broadcaster in Canada but it also established an international presence.

As part of its national growth effort, CanWest acquired several Canadian broadcasting firms, including U.TV in British Columbia and MiTV in the Maritimes. Around the same time CanWest filed applications with the Canadian Radio-television and Telecommunications Commission (CRTC) for stations in Victoria and various locations in Alberta. In 1993, CanWest expanded its operations in Ontario when it licensed five more re-broadcasters in the province. CanWest succeeded in expanding its operations in Quebec in 1995 when it purchased CKMI-TV, an English station in Quebec City. After extending its signals through Quebec, CanWest was still waiting to gain approval to enter Alberta, which was the final step to achieve Asper's goal of building a third national television broadcaster.

In an effort to gain entry to Alberta, Asper attempted to buy Western International Communications (WIC) for $636 million. The attempt failed, however, because of the majority shareholders' refusal to sell to CanWest. Asper's subsequent attempts to overcome this obstacle by challenging the owners' controlling position in court were also unsuccessful, and CanWest was forced to come up with another plan. Asper refused to give up on his attempts to acquire WIC, knowing that the acquisition would help in gaining the interest of national firms and their advertising dollars, as well as to spread costs over a larger Canadian market. In 1998, CanWest again tried to gain control of WIC by purchasing the shares of Emily Griffiths, a majority shareholder in the company, but she decided to sell to Shaw Communications instead. All along, CanWest continued to buy nonvoting shares in WIC, spending $240 million over a two-year period. Despite the 35 percent ownership in nonvoting shares, Asper remained powerless because of WIC's dual-class share structure.

A lawyer by profession, Izzy Asper became a media mogul by pursuing an aggressive growth strategy that would see his company, CanWest, grow from one television station in Winnipeg to the largest communications company in Canada.

While efforts to acquire WIC were being blocked, CanWest continued to expand in other provinces and in 1997 acquired permission from the CRTC to start a province-wide English broadcasting system in Quebec. In an effort to vertically integrate the firm, CanWest entered the program production and distribution industry in 1998 when it acquired Fireworks Entertainment, a film and television production company. Finally, after pursuing the acquisition of WIC for several years, the CRTC approved the purchase of WIC's television assets from Shaw in 2000. In exchange for $950 million, Asper received 11 TV stations (four in Alberta, three in British Columbia, three in Quebec, and one in Ontario), and two licences for specialty channels. The successful acquisition of WIC resulted in Asper finally achieving his goal of making CanWest Global Canada's third national broadcasting company. To reduce its concentration of stations in key markets after the WIC acquisition, CanWest was required by the CRTC to divest certain stations. In 2001, CanWest sold CKVU-TV in Vancouver to CHUM Ltd. for $125 million; its share in CFCF-TV in Montreal to CTV for around $90 million; and its 50 percent ownership in ROBTv.

Shortly after the WIC deal, CanWest made two other significant acquisitions. The first was that of Netstar Communications for $900 million, including their ownership of TSN and the Discovery Channel. The second acquisition, which was reported as the "biggest media deal in Canadian history," was the purchase of 14 major daily Canadian newspapers, 136 smaller papers, a number of web portals, and a 50 percent share in the *National Post* from Hollinger Inc. The $3.5-billion takeover expanded CanWest into related media markets outside of television and gave them control of nearly every major daily newspaper in the country. This further enhanced CanWest's attractiveness to firms that wanted to advertise across several media formats, increasing its advertising capacity as well as enhancing its news division. The Hollinger deal also made CanWest large enough to increase its power when bidding for US programming. Although broadcasting was still CanWest's core business, acquisition of the newspapers increased its overall size, making it the largest communications company in Canada.

While expanding across Canada, CanWest also extended its reach into international broadcasting markets in Australia, New Zealand, Chile, and Ireland. CanWest looked for stations that were promising but whose operations needed to be "fixed." The first international expansion was in 1991 when it acquired a 20 percent interest in TV3 Television Network in New Zealand. The following year CanWest entered Australia, when it purchased 15 percent of Network Ten, which at the time was operating at a loss. CanWest was successful in making the New Zealand and Australian ventures profitable, but the results were not the same when it entered Chile in May 1994. The difficulty with the Chilean acquisition was that it did not "fit" with CanWest like the company had initially anticipated. Industry analysts suggested that CanWest failed to make the operation profitable because it did not consider the cultural differences of a predominantly Spanish-speaking market. In 1994, CanWest entered the European market for the first time when it acquired a 25 percent interest in Talk Radio Network in the United Kingdom. CanWest further expanded its operations in Europe in 1997 when it made an agreement with an Irish conglomerate to start TV3 Ireland as the first private, national television company.

CanWest continued to focus its strategy on increasing its advertising market share by growing its various businesses. Under the watchful eye of investors, officials at CanWest insisted that the acquisitions were not simply to increase the size of the company. Rather, CanWest expanded to attain synergies among its various strategic business units through combining similar business operations to reduce costs. Essentially, CanWest grew via horizontal integration of various complementary media businesses, claiming that each would be more successful when integrated within the corporation.

As a result of its growth strategy, CanWest's debt load had also grown to around $3.8 billion and was now larger than that of all other Canadian media companies. In 2002 CanWest set out to reduce the corporate debt it had accumulated. The company managed to contribute to this goal by bringing in approximately $500 million from the sale of television stations in Vancouver and Montreal, and by the sale of newspapers in Atlantic Canada and Saskatchewan. In its 2002 annual report, CanWest emphasized its commitment to continue divesting other "nonstrategic assets," including certain community newspapers in Ontario. In July 2003, CanWest sold its share in SBS Broadcasting SA, a European TV and radio company, for $44.1 million.

Even when the company suffered a devastating loss with the sudden passing of Izzy Asper in October 2003, CanWest's strategy didn't change that much. Early in the 2004 fiscal year, CanWest sold its 30 percent ownership in Northern Ireland's Ulster Television for $145 million. As a result of this and similar divestitures, as well as refinancing initiatives and an IPO in New Zealand, CanWest had managed to reduce its debt by over $1.1 billion (to around $3 billion) by the end of 2004. At this point, CanWest officials felt that they had reached a position where they could once again begin to focus their strategic efforts on growth, and therefore began looking for acquisition opportunities, both nationally and internationally. Still, CanWest would continue to look for more opportunities to divest nonstrategic assets in an ongoing debt-reduction effort.

By the end of the 2005 fiscal year, CanWest reported that its debt-reduction efforts had placed the company in a much stronger financial position compared to 2000. Despite its improved financial health, CanWest officials recognized that to pursue their growth strategy they would need an injection of cash via borrowing and several other methods. Once again, CanWest reiterated its intention to occasionally sell off noncore assets and focus on investing in developing economies or segments of the media industry where it could use and transfer its market knowledge and experience.

Sources: D. Berman, "Channel Changer," *Canadian Business*, 98(9), pp. 46–52; D. Berman, "Feeling Oppressed? Call Izzy," *Canadian Business*, 71(7), pp. 48–51; "CanWest Global Milestones," *Broadcaster*, 62(1), p. 10; J. Bugailiskis, "Taking It to the Next Level: Leonard Asper Reveals His Convergence Strategy," *Broadcaster*, 62(1), p. 62; *Today's Story: 2002 Annual Report*, CanWest Global Communications Corp., www.canwestglobal.com (accessed November 23, 2006); *Inform, Enlighten, Entertain: 2003 Annual Report*, CanWest Global Communications Corp., www.canwestglobal.com (accessed November 23, 2006); Investor Day PowerPoint slides from February 7, 2006, www.canwestglobal.com (accessed November 23, 2006); "CanWest to Reduce Debt After Selling Shares of SBS Broadcasting for $44.1," Canadian Press NewsWire, July 9, 2003; CanWest Sells Stake in Ulster Television," CanWest News, June 30, 2004; P. Chard, "Too Many Gringos," *Canadian Business*, 68(9), pp. 48–49; P. Chrisholm, "Tycoon of the Tube," *Maclean's*, 108(48), pp. 36–38; J. Gray, "Izzy's Next Move," *Canadian Business*, 73(15), pp. 47–49; J. Hunter, "Plotting a Takeover," *Maclean's*, 111(3), pp. 46–47; G. Livingston, "CanWest Global 'In No Hurry' to Sell Assets but Aims to Ease $3.8B Debt," Canadian Press NewsWire, January 21, 2003; K. Macklem, "Can the Aspers Do It?" *Maclean's*, 115(14), pp. 48–53; R. Robin, "Mixed-Up Media," *Canadian Business*, 74(19), pp. 65–67; J. Schofield, "Global Domination," *Maclean's*, 111(35), pp. 56–57; R. Sheppard, "Reversal of Fate," *Maclean's*, 113(33), pp. 18–20; P. Waal, "Your Move, Ivan," *Canadian Business*, 71(14), pp. 38–41; J. Wells, "Izzy's Dream," *Maclean's*, 109(8), pp. 40–45; A. Wilson-Smith, "What's Going at Global?" *Maclean's*, 113(9), p. 46.

strategic overview

For senior managers to successfully navigate the future threats and opportunities they face, they must have a strategy for how to compete effectively. Although managers have always needed to devise the means to compete (often referred to as competitive strategies), the dramatic increase of competition within many markets in recent years has enhanced the importance of strategy and the strategic management process. While CanWest may be in a market with limited competition, as compared to other sectors, the scale of the operations of both CTV and CBC threatened CanWest's ability to attract advertisers seeking coast-to-coast coverage. In their pursuit of a national presence, CanWest was soon faced with a tremendous amount of debt, which required it to shed assets that were deemed external to their strategic objectives. CanWest management must now ensure that investors are not distanced by the corporation's rapid growth and accumulation of debt. CanWest could be in danger of losing the interest of investors if too much of their revenue goes toward servicing debt. CanWest is a prime example of how important it is to use an effective strategic management process. Without it, an organization's survival may be threatened, even when a firm has only a few competitors and has enjoyed a strong position in the industry.

Another illustration of this increasing competition is provided by the North American automobile market. As recently as 30 years ago, the largest automobile market in the world was dominated by only three major manufacturers: General Motors, Ford, and Chrysler. Chrysler was acquired by DaimlerBenz of Germany in 1998, becoming DaimlerChrysler, and then subsequently sold in August 2007 to Cerberus Capital Management, a firm that specializes in restructuring failing companies. Additionally, the market shares of both GM and Ford have decreased by nearly half in the recent past as foreign competitors, including BMW, Daewoo, Fiat, Honda, Hyundai, Isuzu, Kia, Nissan, Renault, Subaru, Suzuki, Toyota, and others have captured significant market share. In fact, Toyota surpassed GM and became the world's largest automaker in 2007; GM had held the title for 76 years. This provides just one example of how globalization has become a powerful force behind increasing competition. Today, competitors from every corner of the world can converge on markets. Advances in communication and transportation technology add to this competitive intensity.

Never has the need been greater to understand how to develop and implement effective strategies. In recent years, firms like the discount airline Jetsgo filed for bankruptcy and left passengers stranded. Eaton's, a 130-year-old retailer that was once the largest Canadian retailer, went the way of the dodo bird as a result of management's poor understanding of the dramatically shifting retail environment in the 1980s and 1990s. The Office of the Superintendent of Bankruptcy reported that in 2005, 9147 firms filed for bankruptcy in Canada. Andrew Grove, former CEO of Intel, observed that only the paranoid firms survive, primarily because they continuously analyze their external environments and competition, but also because they continuously innovate. Managers who help their firms gain a competitive advantage recognize that it is only temporary; they must constantly innovate and stand ready to change their strategy based on their analysis of the competition and other changes in their environments.[1]

While the principles of strategic management are critical for top managers of a company, the principles are also applicable for managers at various levels of the organization. For example, a lower-level manager may be responsible for a single product line in a company with many products; the principles presented in this chapter can be applied to create a strategy for a product line as well as for an entire company. In addition, even though a company's strategy is developed largely by the top executives, it must be implemented throughout the organization by the other managers and employees. Managers at all levels can do a better job of helping implement a strategy if they understand the strategic management process, how the strategy was developed, and its intended targets.

Competitive Advantage

competitive advantage
the ability of a firm to win consistently over the long term in a competitive situation

Fundamentally, the objective of strategic management is to determine, create, and maintain competitive advantage. So what is competitive advantage? At its essence, the concept of **competitive advantage** is the ability of a firm to win consistently over the long term in a competitive situation.[2] In the case of for-profit organizations, this means consistently gaining greater profits than competitors. If competitive advantage consists of factors that lead to a consistent winning record, what are these factors?

Competitive Advantage by Michael Hitt

mymanagementlab

Competitive advantage is created through the achievement of five qualities: superiority, inimitability, durability, nonsubstitutability, and appropriability.[3] We will explain and examine each of these qualities later in this chapter, but before we do it is important to stress that all these qualities are built upon one assumption: The product or service a company provides has perceived value in the eyes of the customer. If what is provided to customers has no value in their eyes, then qualities such as superiority or durability have no practical meaning. While perceived customer value may seem like a totally obvious assumption, very well-known companies with bright managers often spend lots of time and money doing things that customers do not value. For example, Hewlett-Packard (HP) is a market leader in printers. Clearly, managers there must be doing something right and providing value in the eyes of customers, or customers wouldn't buy their printers. However, HP was spending a lot of time and money on an aspect of its printers that customers did not value. Prior to 2002, virtually all HP printers were strong enough that a 250-pound person could stand on one and use it for a step stool. In fact, HP printers were some of the strongest on the market in this respect. The key question is, "Do customers value this level of sturdiness to the point that they would pay for it?" It will probably not surprise you to learn that HP managers found that the answer was "No." As a consequence, HP redesigned its printers in 2003 with a lower level of sturdiness, lower costs, and lower prices, which was a huge hit with customers. With the underlying assumption of perceived customer value firmly in mind, let's take a look at each of the five qualities that lead to competitive advantage.

Superiority

The essence of this term and aspect of competitive advantage is straightforward. Are you significantly better than your competitors, and if so at what things? For example, FedEx was one of the first companies to introduce package tracking capability. It created a system for tracking a package all along its route. Thus, it was better than UPS at knowing where a customer's package was. As a student, you no doubt have a comparative advantage at some subjects in school; maybe you are better than most of your classmates at writing or statistics. In the business world, Sony has been able to miniaturize audio and video products (for example, radios, camcorders, and CD players) better than most other electronics firms. Thus, Sony has a superiority advantage at miniaturization of audio and video products. This is sometimes called a comparative advantage because compared to others it is better and has an advantage. It is also sometimes referred to as a distinctive competency because while others may also be good, you are distinctively better.

Inimitability

Superiority alone, however, will not guarantee competitive advantage. In addition, managers must create barriers that make it hard for others to copy their superiority advantages.[4] These barriers can involve a variety of obstacles, from tangible ones like size to more intangible ones like a company's culture.[5] This general concept is easy to understand if you first apply it to yourself. For example, suppose you are better at statistics than most of your classmates; this gives you a superiority advantage. Further, suppose that your superiority in statistics is a function of having taken several math classes in high school and university. For others to become as good as you are at statistics, they would need to take a similar number of classes. The more classes they have to take, the greater the barrier. You can now take the same idea and apply it to companies.

For example, Disney's theme parks are often cited as having a comparative advantage in friendly employees. While today Disney might be superior to other firms when it comes to friendly employees, one of the key questions is, "Is it easy for other firms to replicate this?" If it is, Disney's superiority advantage will soon disappear. But how easy is it to find and keep employees who can smile for hours on end even while being asked where the nearest restroom is for the ten-thousandth time that day? The harder it is for other firms with theme parks to hire, develop, and keep friendly employees, the longer Disney's comparative advantage will persist.

Durability

This brings us directly to the next aspect of competitive advantage. Some advantages are more durable than others. They might last because they are legally protected. Patents, for example, can protect an advantage for years—many scientific patents are 17 to 20 years in length. Advantages like brand recognition can last a long time and may take years to deteriorate. For example, some argue that for nearly two decades after the death of Walt Disney, the Disney "brand" was largely neglected. It nonetheless endured in the minds of children and their parents.[6]

Nonsubstitutability

substitution whether or not the customer's need that you fulfill can be met by alternative means

You would think that if your firm had a superiority advantage that was hard to imitate and lasted, this would be enough to ensure competitive advantage, but it isn't. In addition to these qualities, competitive advantage requires a low possibility of substitution. **Substitution** is concerned with whether or not the customer's need that you fulfill can be met by alternative means. Sometimes students confuse substitution and imitation. It may be easiest to help differentiate the two concepts with a concrete example. Godiva is famous for its chocolates. It has a significant superiority advantage in the taste and smoothness of its chocolate compared to other chocolate makers. Godiva's specialized knowledge makes it difficult for other firms to replicate or imitate the taste and texture of its chocolate. However, if Godiva is to sustain its competitive advantage, customers must find it difficult for a substitute to satisfy the sweet taste and smooth texture that they get when they eat Godiva chocolates. If chocolate lovers find they can satisfy that taste by eating Ben & Jerry's premium ice cream, Godiva's comparative advantage would not sustain its competitive advantage.

To illustrate the difference between imitation and substitution even further, let's return to the case of Encyclopaedia Britannica that we examined in Chapter 2. Encyclopaedia Britannica may have the best encyclopedias in the world, and they may be so good that it is very difficult for any direct competitors to copy or imitate them. However, when the internet made it possible for school children to find information for school reports without having to open one of the 30 bound volumes of *Encyclopaedia Britannica*, the internet

To sustain a competitive advantage, managers must create barriers that make it difficult for others to copy what their firm does well. Chez Cora is a restaurant chain that was started by Cora Tsouflidou in 1987 with one restaurant in Ville Saint-Laurent, Quebec. Today, it boasts 75 restaurants from Manitoba to Nova Scotia. The focus of Cora's is breakfast and lunch, providing a bounty of fruit artistically presented on every plate. To maintain consistency and high standards of quality and to minimize replication by local competitors, all Cora's restaurants are supplied with product from its own central kitchen, Casseroles Cora in Quebec.

became a substitute. As a consequence, Britannica's comparative advantage at making great bound-encyclopedia sets did not help it sustain a competitive advantage in the marketplace.

Appropriability

The final element necessary for competitive advantage is the concept of appropriability. This is a fancy way of asking whether you can actually capture the profits that can be made in the business. For example, even though Nokia had less than 40 percent market share in 1999, it captured roughly 80 percent of the profits made by all mobile phone manufacturers. Scholars talk about this phenomenon in terms of supernormal returns. **Supernormal returns** are the profits that are above the average for a comparable set of firms. These greater-than-average profits are primarily a function of greater-than-average cost-price margins. For example, if the average cost in the industry for a 256 megabyte flash drive is $10 and the average value or price is $15, then the average margin is $5. A supernormal return would be anything above $5 in profit.

supernormal returns the profits that are above the average for a comparable set of firms

At this point it is worth repeating that these elements of competitive advantage are based on the premise of perceived customer value. For example, you may be better at statistics than your classmates, and they may face high barriers to become as good as you. This advantage may be durable because you will not soon forget all the great statistical techniques that you have learned. Furthermore, there may be no real substitutes for analyzing data apart from the statistical techniques you have mastered. However, none of this will necessarily translate into a competitive advantage in the job market unless potential employers value the ability to use statistics. If you are interested in a market research position, then your competencies in statistics could easily translate into a *competitive* advantage in the job market because statistical analysis is a commonly required capability for a market researcher. Similarly, being able to miniaturize audio and video products better than others would lead to few profits for Sony unless the majority of customers wanted smaller radios, camcorders, and CD players, which clearly they do.

While in the rest of this chapter we separately examine specific aspects of the strategic management process, including the formulation and implementation of strategy, it all emanates from this one basic objective—competitive advantage. The various tools and frameworks we will review are those that, in both research and practice, have proven helpful to managers in achieving and sustaining competitive advantage.

Strategic Management Process: Setting Direction

Strategic management is a type of planning process in which managers (1) set the organization's general direction and objectives, (2) formulate a specific strategy, (3) plan and carry out the strategy's implementation, and (4) monitor results and make necessary adjustments. To understand what this means, we need to examine each step in this overall process (see Exhibit 7.1).

Exhibit 7.1

Strategic Management Process

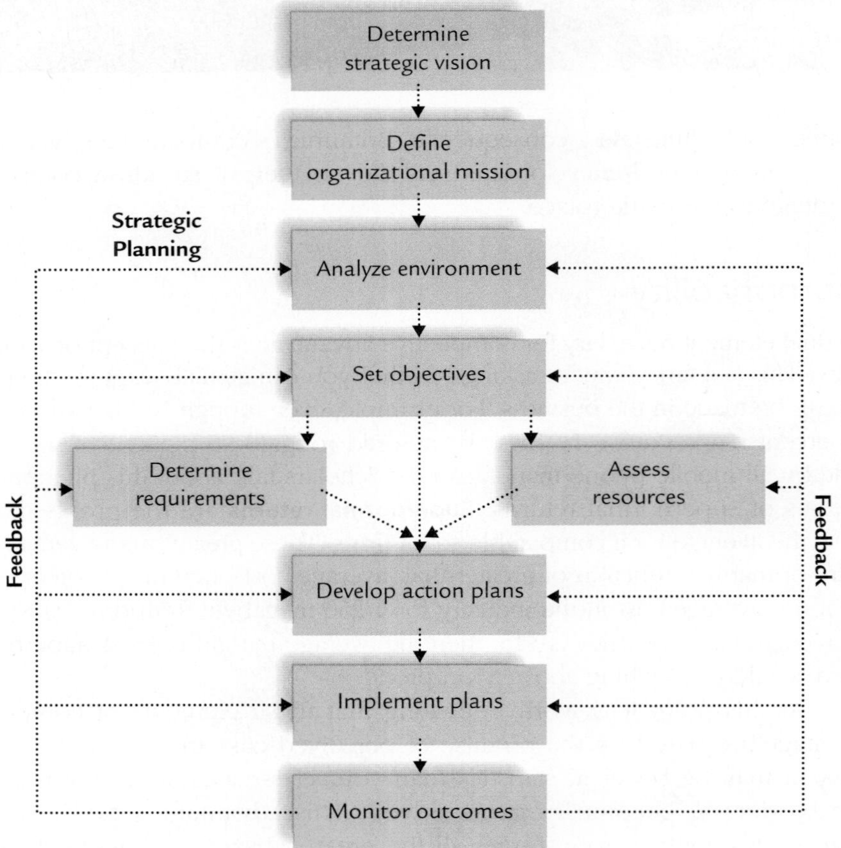

Because a strategy is a plan for the future of the company, many of the key elements in the strategic management process are similar to those we covered in the chapter on planning (Chapter 6). Consequently, we will highlight key similarities in the following sections.

Strategic Vision

strategic vision what an organization ultimately wants to be and do

The first step in the strategic management process is to determine the firm's strategic vision. **Strategic vision** is not easy to define, but it can be thought of as what the organization ultimately wants to be and do.[7] For example, the strategic vision of the Canadian Cancer Society is "creating a world where no Canadian fears cancer." La Senza envisions becoming "the destination specialty lingerie store for all consumers." Xerox Corporation states its strategic vision in simple terms: "The world's document company." The strategic vision of The Co-operators is to be "the Canadian insurance champion and to provide the financial security products and services that Canadians need." As these four examples illustrate, strategic vision captures the general identity, direction, and aspirations of the organization. A key point to keep in mind is that while the other specific elements in the strategic planning process constitute the body of a strategic plan, strategic vision is the heart of the plan.[8] As such, one of its key objectives is to inspire.[9] This is why most vision statements are also statements of "strategic stretch." That is, to live up to the vision, the organization must stretch far beyond where it is today. In practice, an effective statement of strategic vision should paint a general picture of aspiration and create a strong emotional response in just a few words.

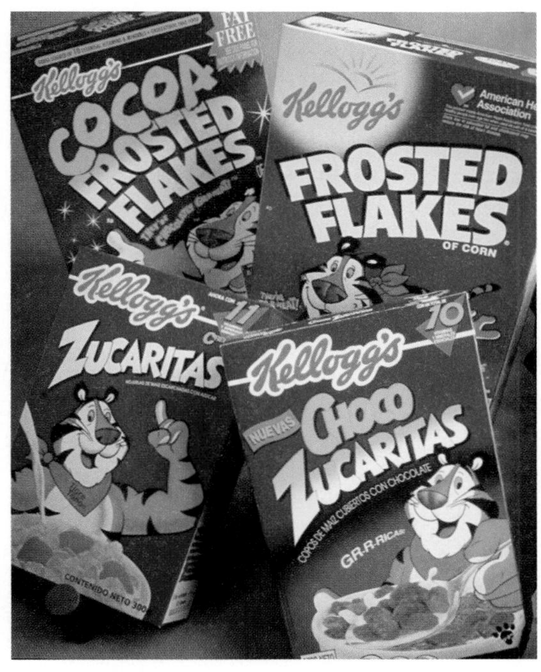

Kellogg, which had sales in excess of US$10 billion in 2005, is the world's leading producer of cereal. They manufacture their products in 17 countries and market them in more than 110 countries. Kellogg's strategic vision is to have the company's cereals on every breakfast table in the world. It's a lofty goal, but it gives the company and its employees something to aim for.

Mission

Although statements of strategic vision are typically only a sentence in length, mission statements are usually much longer. A **mission statement** articulates the fundamental purpose of the organization and often contains several components, including:

mission statement a statement that articulates the fundamental purpose of the organization and often contains several components

- Company philosophy
- Company identity or self-concept
- Principal products or services
- Customers and markets
- Geographic focus
- Obligations to shareholders
- Commitment to employees[10]

Exhibit 7.2

Mission Statement for Famous Players

Famous Players's Mission Statement

At Famous Players it is our passion to provide for our Guests the highest quality of out-of-home film entertainment experience in the ultimate environment.

An example of a mission statement is provided in Exhibit 7.2. As the example illustrates, while mission statements provide more detail concerning the purpose of the organization, they should support and be consistent with its strategic vision. One of the major differences between statements of strategic vision and mission statements is that mission statements tend to be much more specific in terms of stating objectives or values regarding the various components listed above.

Strategic Objectives

strategic objectives objectives that translate the strategic vision and mission of a firm into concrete and measurable goals

Unless an organization's strategic vision and mission are translated into specific performance goals, they are likely to remain statements of good intentions and unrealized achievements. Furthermore, an analysis of the environment is an academic exercise unless the implications find their way into strategic objectives. **Strategic objectives** translate the strategic vision and mission of the firm into concrete and measurable goals. Setting strategic objectives is a critical step in the strategic management process because it facilitates a firm's ability to (1) allocate resources appropriately, (2) reach a shared understanding of priorities, (3) delegate responsibilities, and (4) hold people accountable for results.[11] Specifically, strategic objectives might address any of the following issues:

- Revenue growth
- Profitability
- Customer satisfaction
- Market share
- Financial returns (e.g., return on equity, return on assets)
- Technological leadership
- Cash flow
- Operating efficiency (e.g., costs per unit, expense per employee)

It is important to note that strategic objectives differ from other performance objectives in one fundamental way: Strategic objectives are longer term in nature. They are not yearly objectives or goals. They represent targets for which the company aims over the long term (typically five years or so). Although setting strategic objectives is critical, much of the time managers actually spend on strategic management is taken up in the subsequent steps of the process. These principally involve analyzing the organization's internal environment, formulating a strategy, developing an implementation plan, and monitoring the results.

Strategic Management Process: Formulating a Strategy

In many ways the essence of competitive strategy is determining how the company is going to compete and achieve its strategic objectives, mission, and ultimate strategic vision. However, this also happens to be one of the most complicated aspects of strategic management and one that has caused scholars and practising managers alike to write volumes on the topic. Condensing it down to part of a chapter is not an easy task. By necessity, some ideas and concepts can't be included. As a result, we will first present a set of generic strategies for competitive advantage and then discuss several techniques and tools for formulating a firm's generic and specific strategy.

Generic Strategies for Competitive Advantage

The two most-discussed generic strategies are cost leadership and differentiation.[12] To help illustrate each one, let's return to our flash drive example.

Cost Leadership **Cost leadership** simply involves competing by striving to be the lowest-cost producer of a product or provider of a service and yet charge only slightly less than industry average prices. To the extent a firm has lower costs than its competitors (i.e., cost leadership) and can command prices similar to its competitors, it can achieve above-average profits. For a flash drive manufacturer to obtain supernormal returns through cost leadership, it would need to lower its costs below the industry average (from $10 to, say, $7.50) and still be able to charge near the industry average price (i.e., $15). In this case, the firm would make a profit of $7.50 instead of the industry average of $5. It is important to understand that the cost leadership strategy does not necessarily imply price leadership, meaning offering the lowest price. For example, if the cost leader had costs of $7.50 per flash drive but also charged the lowest price ($12.50), it would earn normal returns (i.e., the industry average of $5).

cost leadership striving to be the lowest-cost producer of a product or provider of a service and yet charge only slightly less than industry average prices

There are a wide variety of ways to achieve cost leadership. You might do it through technology. If you manufacture computer chips, you might invest in the latest technology to reduce defects and increase your "yield" (percentage of good chips) and thereby reduce your average cost per chip. You might achieve cost leadership through economies of scale. You might increase output through your given factories and thereby reduce your per-unit costs. You might achieve it through economies of scope. Amazon does this by pushing more product through its existing sales channel (i.e., its website) and distribution network.

A Manager's Challenge: "Leveraging High Tech in the Low-Tech Business of Cement" helps illustrate how a Mexican company, Cemex, has used technology in a traditionally low-tech business to help it achieve its cost leadership position at home and, increasingly, abroad. While reading the case, ask yourself how durable you think the technological cost advantage is to Cemex. Can others easily copy Cemex and duplicate its results?

Differentiation Managers pursuing a **differentiation** strategy seek to make their product or service different from those of competitors on dimensions highly and widely valued by customers. If they can do so, they can command a premium price. If managers can also keep costs at approximately the industry average, the premium price allows the firm to earn above-average profits. For a flash drive manufacturer to obtain supernormal returns through

differentiation a strategy for making a product or service different from those of competitors

a manager's challenge technology

Leveraging High Tech in the Low-Tech Business of Cement

You might not expect managers in a 100-year-old Mexican cement company to have placed cutting-edge technology at the centre of their competitive strategy, but that is exactly what managers at Cemex have done. Because cement is basically a commodity, firms often compete on price. Cemex managers are using technology to improve efficiency and lower costs.

Lorenzo Zambrano, grandson of the founder, is the CEO of Cemex, which is based in Monterrey, Mexico. Zambrano, who spent 18 years working his way through the ranks of Cemex before becoming CEO, has relentlessly sought out ways to use IT to drive down costs and improve efficiency. He has been described as a techno–whiz kid. His favourite "toy" is said to be a laptop. With his laptop, Zambrano checks sales figures any time rather than wait for reports that would come in with weeks-old data. Quality control is also automated; sampling machines use lasers to analyze samples and the results are beamed by satellite to the firm's Monterrey headquarters, where these and other results are displayed on-screen. As a consequence, Zambrano can check on the real-time kiln temperatures and quality results on the Cemex network. He can then use email to ask managers why their output or quality might not be up to targets rather than wait for quality problems to show up on the customer's job site. In turn, plant managers can now not only track their units' operations, but can also compare them with others and exchange ideas and best practices with managers throughout the Cemex system via email. Overall, quality is up and staff costs are down because it now takes only a handful of people to run one of Cemex's big cement plants.

However, the benefits of information technology are not restricted to just the cement plants or to senior executives. With communication and information sharing—including information about performance—made easier and faster, employees began to look for ways to create improvements in their own departments. The company's distributed IT systems let managers monitor sales figures, for instance, and at the same time allow lower-level employees access to enough information to create healthy rivalries among different units.

Executives at Cemex have used information technology to improve efficiency and performance. To both reduce costs and use their assets more efficiently and effectively, executives use computers and global positioning system receivers in every cement truck to achieve more efficient routing and more precise delivery times. Previously, any number of things could delay a delivery, including bad weather and traffic. Combining precise information about the trucks' whereabouts with plant output and customer orders, managers are able to calculate more precisely which truck should go where and how to reroute them if necessary. The benefits are enormous when you consider that cement needs to be poured within 90 minutes of being mixed. The new system allows Cemex's logistic managers to accurately direct trucks to be within 20 minutes of their delivery time instead of three hours.

The advanced state of their internal information systems has allowed Cemex executives to expand beyond the borders of Mexico. Because cement is produced and used locally (the average distance between a cement mixing plant and the customer is 60 kilometres), Cemex uses its information technology to significantly improve the efficiency of the companies it buys.

Cemex executives have implemented a strategy of expansion into emerging markets such as Spain, Venezuela, Thailand, Egypt, and Puerto Rico. Today they have operations in more than 50 countries. In 2000, Cemex scored a big coup by buying Southdown, the second-largest cement producer in the United States. It was the first time a Mexican firm had bought a US firm. It also made Cemex one of the three largest cement producers in the world.

With each acquisition the company gets better and faster at integrating technical and management methods with those of the parent company. For example, integrating two Spanish acquisitions in 1992 took about 18 months. Armed with laptops and Cemex's information technology system, the integration team reduced that time to under four months in the case of Southdown. The decrease in integration time means real money, because the sooner the benefits of Cemex's technology can be put into the acquisition, the sooner the cost savings can be captured. In 2005 Cemex acquired UK cement giant RMC Group for US$5.8 billion. At the time of acquisition, Cemex forecast US$200 million in cost-saving synergies by 2007, but ended up doubling that within months of concluding the deal. Cemex now has more than US$26.7 billion in assets and earned over US$15.3 billion in 2005. In October 2006 Cemex made a takeover bid for

Australian rival Rinker Group for US$12.8 billion, expecting the cost synergies to be in the neighbourhood of US$130 million by the third year of integration. This has helped make Cemex more profitable than either of its two international rivals, Lafarge, based in France, and the Swiss firm Holcim.

Sources: "Cemex/Rinker," FT.com, October 27, 2006 (accessed November 11, 2006); Cemex, www.cemex.com (accessed November 11, 2006); "Cemex–RMC a Done Deal; Integration Begins Immediately," May 1, 2005, www.cementamericas.com (accessed November 11, 2006); "Cemex Launches E-tail Website, Opens New Customer Service Center," *Caribbean Business*, November 20, 2003, p. 54; Roy Sudip, "Cementing Global Success,"*Direct Investor*, March 2003, pp. 12–14; Julie Watson, "Cemex Buys Puerto Rican Company for Stronger Hold of Caribbean Market," *AP Worldstream*, June 12, 2002; Jenalia Moreno, "Mexican Cement Giant's Deal Laid Solid Foundation for Entering U.S. Market," *Houston Chronicle*, April 10, 2001; "The Cemex Way," *Economist*, June 16, 2001, pp. 75–76.

differentiation leadership, it would need to keep its costs at approximately the industry average, while adding features that would allow it to command a premium price. For example, suppose the firm was able to offer larger memory capacity (1 GB versus 256 MB) without substantially increasing the costs of manufacturing the drives. They could command a premium price (say $17.50 instead of $15) but keep its costs near the industry average of $10. In this case, the firm would make a profit of $7.50 per disk instead of the industry average of $5. Any number of characteristics might provide the basis for differentiation.

For example, the Sony VAIO laptop computer is priced approximately 20 percent higher than comparable laptops from companies like Toshiba. Yet it only costs Sony about 5 percent more to make the laptops. Consequently, it earns supernormal returns. Why do people pay the higher price for a Sony laptop? Primarily for three reasons: first, aesthetics. Sony wanted to create an outward design that looked better ("cooler," in its words) than that of competitors. To many who purchase Sony's laptop, they have succeeded. Second, Sony wanted to make its laptops thinner and lighter. Again, at least to an important segment of customers, this is important and they are willing to pay more for less (less weight, that is). Third, the Sony brand in general represents electronics that are at the leading edge of style and quality. While this third element has cost Sony literally billions to build over the last 50 years, in one sense it costs the company nothing to add this brand value to its laptops.

The key here is that there are a variety of ways and even layers of differentiation that are possible—style, quality, reliability, speed, fashion, durability, and so on. The key is to add differentiation that customers (or at least an important segment of customers) value at a cost that produces a superior margin. In other words, the cost increase to add the differentiation has to be less than the price premium customers will pay for the differentiation. If it costs you 20 percent more to make your product more reliable and customers will only pay 20 percent more for this differentiation, then it will not generate supernormal profits.

In thinking about ways to differentiate, it is important to keep in mind that this can be done via characteristics directly related to the product or service itself, or might be indirectly related through any of the aspects of the firm's activities. Toronto clothing designer Linda Lundström, for example, commands a premium price for her high fashion LAPARKA coats because of the limited run of specialized colours each year and the versatility of being a wind breaker or sub-zero parka—characteristics of the product itself. In contrast, Winnipeg-based Standard Aero, which provides turbine engine maintenance, repair, and overhaul services to aircraft, command a premium prices because they are also able to deliver service to anywhere in the world within

24 hours—a characteristic not of a product but of the firm's extensive customer service network.

When customers highly value a variety of product attributes, competing firms can successfully pursue various differentiation strategies at the same time. For example, Apple Computer might try to differentiate its products based on how easy they are to use, while Dell might try to differentiate its products based on how fast and powerful they are. As long as some customers value ease of use more than speed and other customers have the opposite preferences, Apple and Dell might both be successful in their differentiation strategies. If, on the other hand, customers highly and widely value only one attribute for a given product or service, then firms have fewer options for differentiation strategies. The most successful firm will be the one that is the best at the attribute customers value and that can keep costs low relative to competitors. For example, if customers only value computer speed, then the firm that produces the fastest computer will likely earn the highest profits.

strategic scope the scope of a firm's strategy or breadth of focus

Strategic Scope A firm can limit the scope of its strategy (its **strategic scope**, or breadth of focus), by focusing on a specific segment of customers. Although the restriction reduces the total volume and revenue the firm can obtain from a product, it does not necessarily affect its ability to earn supernormal returns. For example, Ferrari differentiates its product based on style and performance and focuses on a very narrow customer segment. A narrow scope strategy also applies to cost leadership. To the extent that the cost leader can provide products or services sufficiently valuable to command prices near the industry average for some targeted segment of customers, it can achieve above-average profits.

niche strategy a limited scope or breadth of focus

customer segment a group of customers who have similar preferences or place similar value on product features

To succeed when pursuing a limited scope, or **niche strategy**, there must be significant differences among targeted customers or among geographical segments of customers. A **customer segment** is essentially a group of customers who share similar preferences or place similar value on product features. For example, clear segments exist in selling cars. Some people value gas mileage while others value performance. Thus, you can make a high-performance sports car and not really worry about small economy cars taking away your customers. Geographic segments may also exist. First, customers in different locations may prefer different features. If you design and sell suits costing $1000 or more, you need to know that customers in hot and humid climates prefer cotton fabrics while those in drier and cooler climates prefer wool fabrics. If your firm is particularly strong in wool fabrics, you have a clear geographic segment of customers you can pursue with a differentiation, niche strategy. Second, geographic segments also occur when customers have similar preferences but do not have universal access. The most common reason for this is government intervention. For example, a firm might be able to gain access to customers in France but not in Egypt because of government restrictions, even if the Egyptian customers have preferences similar to those in France for a particular product.

Managers pursuing any one of the four generic strategies (see Exhibit 7.3) must remember that in our fast-changing world, today's competitive advantage may be obsolete tomorrow. Managers who help their firms succeed over the long term make old sources of competitive advantage obsolete before their competitors do. Thus, to have sustainable competitive advantage, managers must continually build temporary competitive advantages, replacing old ones with new ones.

Strategy		General	Focused
	Cost Leadership	General player whose product or service features command industry average prices but whose costs are significantly below the industry average. *Example:* Winners	Niche player with average prices and below-average costs that focuses on a segment of customers or a specific geography. *Example:* Tip Top Tailors
	Differentiation	General player whose product or service features command premium prices and whose costs are at the industry average. *Example:* Roots	Niche player with average costs but commanding premium prices that focuses on the high end and customers in a general or specific geography. *Example:* Harry Rosen
		Scope	

Exhibit 7.3

Generic Strategies and Scope

Internal and External Analysis

So how should you determine which of these generic strategies to pursue and what additional specifics should be part of your formulated strategy? This question has been at the centre of a raging discussion, debate, and research agenda for the last 30 years. What we can safely say is that a proper determination of a firm's specific strategy requires an analysis of both its external environment and internal capabilities. This view was first put forward by Kenneth Andrews in the early 1970s.[13] Since then different concepts and tools have been introduced that have focused more heavily on the external environment or the firm's internal capabilities. However, in the final analysis an assessment of both is necessary as well as a judgment about the correspondence between the two.

Environmental Analysis Because we covered the external general and task environments in Chapter 2, we will not review them in any great detail here. Each one of the forces we covered in Chapter 2 can significantly affect the strategy a firm might develop, as well as whether the firm is likely to succeed or fail.[14] As we discussed in Chapter 2, while both general- and task-environment forces are important, often forces in the task environment have a more immediate impact on firm performance. Specifically, the forces associated with competitors are of particular importance when thinking about a company's strategy.[15] As a consequence, the forces related to competitors such as the nature of rivalry, new entrants, and substitution covered in Michael Porter's framework are relevant.

In addition, the tool and concept of customer value proposition is important to examine. A **value proposition** is essentially the ratio of what customers get from a firm to how much they pay relative to alternatives from competitors. Clearly, customers can get many things that they value from a particular product or service. If the product is a car, customers get a certain level of performance, reliability, styling, and so on. For that, they have to pay a price. The key question from a strategic management perspective is, "How much of what the customer really wants do I provide and at what price relative to my competitors?" One of the problems identified in the "dot.com bomb," or the implosion of the internet bubble in 2000, was that many of the companies just did not have a compelling value proposition.[16]

value proposition the ratio of what customers get from a firm to how much they pay relative to alternatives from competitors

To illustrate, let's simplify things a little. Let's say that you are in the automobile business. Further, let's say that what customers really care about is reliability. Assuming we have objective measures of reliability, such as repair expenses per 10 000 kilometres driven, we can actually draw the value propositions by plotting differing reliability levels by the price of the car (see Exhibit 7.4). The diagonal line represents essentially equal value. That is, as you move up the line, you get greater reliability, but you pay for it. The customers who really value reliability are willing to pay a higher price for the car. Those who don't value reliability as highly prefer to pay less. But in terms of value, all points along the line are considered equal. From a strategic management perspective, what you care about is your relative position to competitors within a given customer segment. For the sake of illustration, we have divided customers into three segments: low, medium, and high value placed on reliability.

Exhibit 7.4

Value Proposition for Three Car Companies

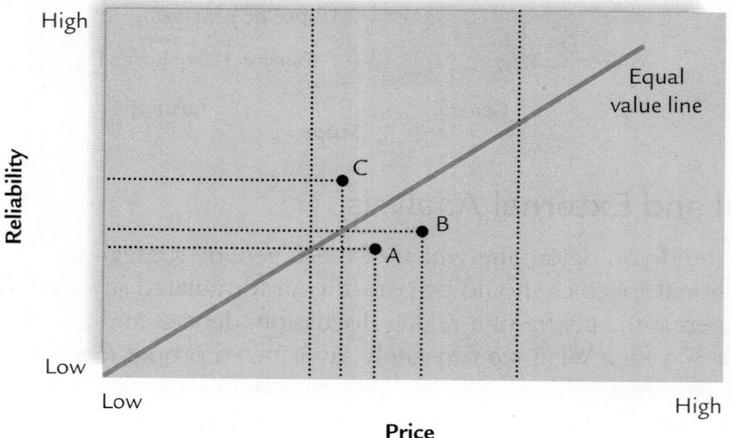

Let's say you produce cars of medium reliability. The attractiveness of the value proposition you present to customers is a function of where you are relative to competitors. In Exhibit 7.4, which company, A, B, or C, represents the best value for the customers? Clearly, it is company C. Company C has a lower price and higher reliability than either companies A or B. Now, of companies A and B, which represents the better value to customers? Actually, their value propositions are quite similar. Company B produces cars with higher reliability than company A, but customers have to pay a higher price for the increase in quality. If you were company B, competing with companies A and C, where would you need to position yourself to offer a more competitive value proposition to your customers? In general, you would have to move up and to the left. In other words, you would have to lower your price and increase your reliability. Specifically, if you matched company C's price and beat it on reliability, you would then offer a superior value proposition, which should enhance your competitive position. You might do this by introducing a new technology that lowered your costs but increased reliability.

The bottom line is that any assessment of the external environment from a strategic management perspective must include an analysis of your competitors and your relative position to them. Although other tools can be used in this process, value proposition has become increasingly widespread because, in the final analysis, it is customers who determine what proposition provides the best value.

value chain a set of key activities that directly produce or support the production of what a firm ultimately offers to customers

Organizational Analysis An analysis of the organization's internal capabilities is equally important to an analysis of its external environment. Of the various tools or frameworks for this purpose, the "value chain" approach proposed by Michael Porter is arguably one of the most cited and widely used.[17] The **value chain** is essentially a set of key activities that directly produce or support the production of what a firm ultimately offers to customers. Porter separates the internal components of a firm into five primary activities and four support activities (see Exhibit 7.5). The **primary activities** are those that are directly involved in the creation of a product or service and getting it into the hands of the customer and keeping it there. As the label suggests, **support activities** facilitate the creation of the product or service and its transfer to the customer. Porter stresses that rather than assessing the cost of these activities, managers must assess the value they add to the product or service to truly understand the firm's ability to compete. The absolute value of a product or service is a function of how much customers are willing to pay and how many customers are willing to purchase the product or service. A firm makes a profit if it can produce something whose value exceeds its costs. To determine where value is added in the firm's internal value chains, managers need to understand each of the nine activities in the chain.

primary activities activities that are directly involved in the creation of a product or service, getting it into the hands of the customer, and keeping it there

support activities activities that facilitate the creation of a product or service and its transfer to the customer

Exhibit 7.5

The Value Chain

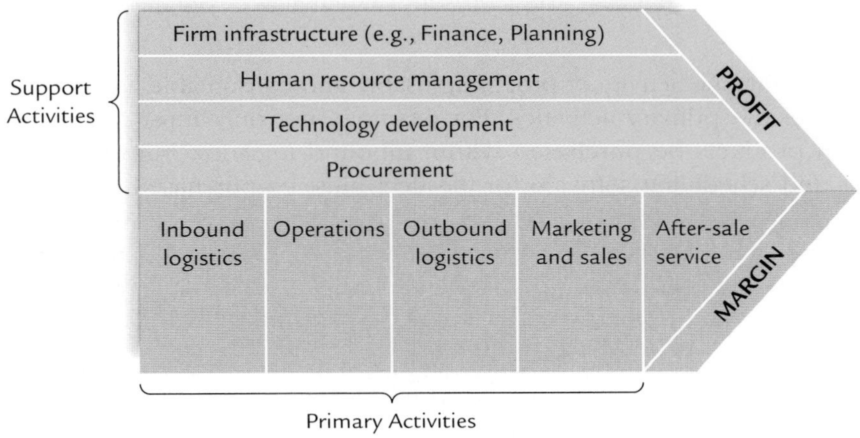

Source: Adapted from Michael Porter, *Competitive Advantage* (New York: Free Press, 1985).

Inbound Logistics This component of the value chain consists of activities that are designed to receive, store, and then disseminate various inputs to the products or services. Raw materials, receiving, transportation, inventory, information, and so on are commonly a part of inbound logistics. In the beer industry, inbound logistics involve getting hops, barley, and malt to various brewing sites.

Operations A wide variety of activities are included within the operations component of the value chain. Activities that transform inputs into the products and services of the firm are at the heart of operations. In addition, activities that keep machines in working order, like maintenance, would also be included in the operations segment of the value chain. In our beer example, operational issues may involve beer recipes for different products and markets as well as the process of bottling and labelling the products.

Outbound Logistics Simply stated, outbound logistics include activities that get the product or service from the firm to the customers. Our beer factory would need to warehouse the finished product, process the orders, schedule delivery trucks, and distribute its products (either directly or through distributors) to get the product delivered to retailers, bars, arenas, restaurants, and other places where it can be sold.

Marketing and Sales Marketing and sales activities are designed to let customers know about the products and services that are available and entice them to purchase what the firm has to offer. The beer manufacturer would need to advertise, promote its products, sell them, and price them.

Service Service activities are designed to keep the product in the hands of the customer after the purchase and increase the probability of a repeat purchase. Service activities may involve repair, supply of parts, installation, or product adjustment.

Each of these primary activities has associated costs. They enhance the firm's industry position and profitability if a customer is willing to pay more for them than they cost. The importance of the various activities changes depending on customer preferences. For example, in the fashion industry, customers often want the latest styles, colours, and fabrics as soon as possible. This places a premium on both inbound and outbound logistics to ensure that what is produced can be delivered quickly to customers.

In addition to the five primary activities, there are four support activities. As illustrated in Exhibit 7.5, these activities cut across all five of the primary activities; that is, elements of a given support activity facilitate each of the five primary activities.

Procurement The activity of procuring usable and consumable assets is found in each of the primary activities. For example, not only must raw materials used in products be purchased within inbound logistics, but also delivery trucks and scheduling software for the fleet must be purchased so that those materials can arrive for processing. The purchases of machinery and replacement parts are examples of specific procurement activities within operations. Firms often have purchasing departments, but procurement may be handled by various people, from purchasing agents to secretaries.

Technology Development Technology development revolves around expertise and the tools or equipment related to the exercise of that expertise. The technology may be as simple as a pencil for manually recording information or as complicated as a computer network and its supporting software. Although technology development is concentrated on product development or process innovation, technology and the means by which it is applied to tasks also has an impact on all five primary activities.

Human Resource Management Given that no activity is completely removed from humans (even automatic processes and equipment are designed, implemented, and maintained by someone), the process of acquiring, training, evaluating, compensating, and developing human resources is present in all five primary activities. Capable and motivated people can have a profound impact on all activities of a firm, so human resource management is a key support activity. In service firms such as law, consulting, or accounting firms, the quality of the people is what customers purchase. Therefore, this component of the value chain is critical to a service firm's fortune or failure.

Firm Infrastructure Although infrastructure usually brings plant, utilities, and equipment to mind, a firm's infrastructure has less to do with brick and mortar than with functions that support all primary activities. Infrastructure consists of planning, finance, accounting, legal, government relations, and other activities and the information supplied by these functions to the various primary activities. For example, legal information concerning worker safety standards may be needed in operations, and legal information on truth in advertising may be needed in marketing and sales.

Just as each primary activity has associated costs, so do the support activities. Support activities enhance the firm's position and profitability to the extent that they assist primary activities and contribute to final products or services that customers value. Like primary activities, the importance of the support activities also changes depending on customer preferences. Returning to our earlier example of the fashion industry, customers' preferences for the latest styles, colours, and fabrics may increase the importance of planning information in the value chain. Planning information that relates forecasting trends, buying seasons, and purchasing cycles to customer preferences would be valuable. Customer preferences might also increase the importance of technology development in support activity. For example, technology that allows clothes to be dyed after they have been knit into a sweater rather than in the yarn stage would add value. This is exactly what Benetton of Italy has done so that the latest colour preferences can be incorporated as late in the manufacturing process as possible. That way there is less time for a mismatch to occur between the changing preferences of customers and the colours delivered by Benetton.

The value chain framework can facilitate your ability to assess what resources you have and how well they are working to deliver value to the customer. One of the benefits of the value chain framework is that it enables you to work through a systematic and reasonably comprehensive analysis without becoming completely overwhelmed. Except for the most simple and small of businesses, it would be easy to miss examining critical aspects of the company.

Leveraging the Value Chain Knowing your firm's value chain is one thing; leveraging it for an advantage in the marketplace is quite another. The first step in managing the value chain for greater profits and performance is to determine where in your value chain you have the potential to add the greatest value. If we return to our beer example, let's say that our German customers value a rich-tasting beer and that they are less sensitive to price. If the flavour of beer is largely determined by the quality of the ingredients and that ingredient quality varies widely, we know we need to concentrate on procurement—we must be sure that we have the highest-quality ingredients. Further, let's suppose that being able to identify high-quality ingredients is primarily a function of experienced buyers who can see, smell, and taste quality differences. Now we know that we must be sure that our human resource management systems are superior in terms of recruiting, selecting, and training these ingredient buyers. The power of the value chain model is that it helps us segment business activities and see the important linkages. However, the model per se does not tell us which specific activities add the most value or which linkages among activities are the most important. That all comes from our analysis.

Recent research has suggested that to fully understand a firm's competitive position and advantage, you need to analyze not only the firm's value chain but also how suppliers, distributors, and other business partners fit into the "value net."[18] Because of the increasingly tight connections between firms and suppliers, distributors, and other business partners, the strengths and weaknesses of partners throughout the entire value network affect the competitive position and advantage of any given firm.[19]

Resource-Based Approach The resource-based approach to strategy acknowledges the importance of the external environment but places emphasis on recognizing and then exploiting the internal strengths of the company.[20] A couple of simple analogies may help illustrate this. Suppose you had a group of gifted orchestra musicians. Even if there were lots of customers for jazz music, the resource-based approach would argue against trying to turn these orchestra musicians into jazz musicians. Likewise, it would not make sense to design a passing-offence strategy in football if you had a great running back but a quarterback with a terrible throwing arm.

But the resource-based approach to strategy does not assume that you are forever stuck where you are.[21] It does argue, however, that the resources you build or add should deliver competitive advantage. In other words, they should be ones at which you are superior (or can become superior); ones that are hard to copy and are durable; ones that cannot be easily substituted; and ones that allow you to capture above-normal profits. Once you have a clear idea of the resources you have, can develop, and have the potential to give you a competitive advantage in the marketplace, then you can begin to formulate a strategic plan as to how to leverage these resources.

Core Competencies by Michael Hitt

mymanagementlab

core competency focusing on an interrelated set of activities that can deliver competitive advantage in the short term and into the future

Core Competencies While the value chain model helps managers analyze activities and discover where the firm creates the greatest value, the concept of **core competency** focuses on an interrelated set of activities that can deliver competitive advantage not just in the short term but into the future as well. Two scholars, Coimbatore Krishna Prahalad and Gary Hamel, argued that competencies that should be considered core would (1) provide access to a wide variety of markets, (2) significantly contribute to perceived customer benefits of the end products or services, and (3) be difficult for competitors to imitate.[22]

As an example, Honda believes that one of its core competencies is the technology behind and the manufacturing of combustion engines. Let's examine this competency in light of these three tests. First, combustion engines have the potential to apply to a wide variety of markets and products. In fact, this has led Honda to produce products that started in motorcycles and now extend to cars, scooters, lawnmowers, snowblowers, and electric generators, among other things. Second, good combustion engine performance results create customer value. For example, better combustion performance can result in significantly better acceleration in cars and motorcycles. Third, combustion technology is hard to imitate. This is partly why Honda moved its engines into various auto-racing leagues, like Formula One racing.

You have no doubt noticed that both the core competency and resource-based approaches share two common elements—value and difficult to imitate. This should not surprise us given that, logically, to have an advantage over competitors you must offer customers what they perceive as value, and to sustain that advantage what you offer must be hard for others to duplicate.

Integrating Internal and External Analyses

Although a variety of tools and techniques can help you integrate your internal and external analyses, in the sections that follow we review three well-known ones: product life cycle, portfolio, and SWOT analyses.

Product Life Cycle Analysis In considering internal resources or external market conditions, it is important to keep in mind that any snapshot you might take internally or externally needs to be placed in the reality of a moving picture of competition. One of the tools that can help place snapshots in context is the product life cycle analysis. Like people, products go through a life cycle that starts with birth and ends with decline (see Exhibit 7.6). When a product is first born, or developed, it is similar to a baby—it needs constant care and does not produce much. During the birth period, most products provide very little revenue and yet require significant investments of time and money. Revenues during this early stage are provided by "early adopters," or consumers who buy products before they are widely accepted in the marketplace. Often these early adopters can provide valuable information on product or service characteristics that can help broaden product acceptance. This in turn enhances the next stage—growth.

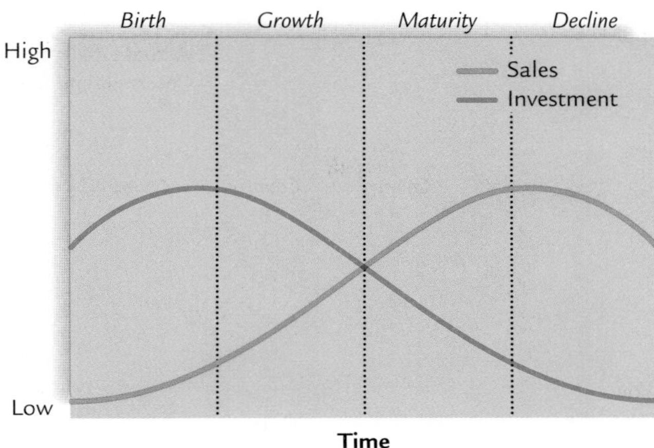

Exhibit 7.6

Product Life Cycle

The steepness and height of the life cycle line during the growth period are primarily a function of how quickly and how widely customers accept the product.[23] The degree to which a firm can exploit economies of scale is one of the most important factors that influences the extent of investment needed during the growth stage.[24] The greater the economies of scale, the relatively less investment required during the growth stage. For example, it takes approximately $2 billion to build a new fabrication plant for a microprocessing chip. However, once that initial investment is made it takes comparatively much less money to produce millions of chips during the growth stage.

The mature stage of the product life cycle occurs when the product or service produces its greatest profits.[25] During this stage, the highest levels of revenues and lowest costs per unit are achieved. This is also the most difficult stage for managers to realize they better have plans for another successful product to offer the market, or expectations to take the current product to other markets to generate new interest elsewhere.

Unless a product is rejuvenated, it typically enters the decline stage because new products or services make it obsolete. The extent to which the new products are "better" (faster, cheaper, more powerful, longer lasting, etc.) is an important factor in how steep the decline curve will be. Switching costs (discussed in Chapter 2) are often another powerful factor. The lower the switching costs, the steeper the decline curve. Obviously, significant new product features and low switching costs could combine to produce a steep and dramatic decline.

One of the most attractive aspects of an international marketplace is that, for a given product, firms can seek out new markets to start the product life cycle all over again (see Exhibit 7.7). A firm can extend the life of a product by taking it international. The key to success for this strategy is managers' abilities to correctly identify countries whose sociocultural, technological, economic, and political conditions match the product and to identify any modifications that could be accomplished economically and would enhance its acceptance in a particular country.[26]

A Manager's Challenge: "Flashback, Flash Forward: The Long-Lived VW Beetle" discusses a product—the original Volkswagen Beetle—that was kept alive for over half a century by the international marketplace. In fact, in this example not only did the international markets keep the VW Beetle alive, but they kept it alive long enough that it was reborn as the New Beetle. While there are clear and intended similarities between the look of the old and new Beetles, everything else (engine, steering, brakes, suspension) is

Exhibit 7.7

International Product Life Cycles

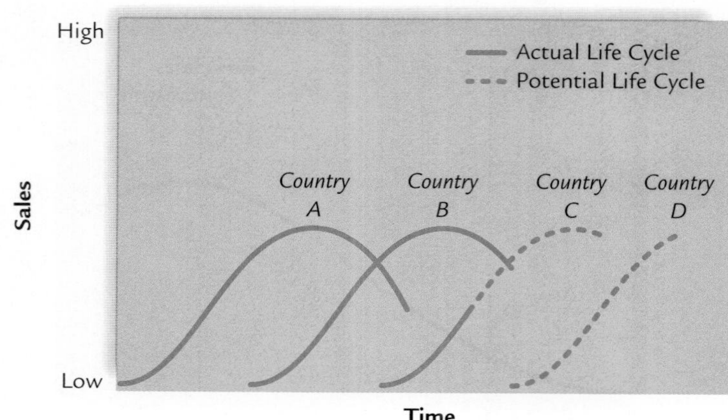

virtually brand new. You might even ask yourself if this rebirth would have been possible without the extended life that international markets gave to the product.

In summary, product life cycle analysis helps you examine the product and how it matches its environment to estimate the likely shape of its life cycle curve. Having an idea of a product's life cycle—the steepness of the curve and how long each stage will last—can significantly enhance your ability to plan properly for increases or decreases in equipment purchases, workforce size, advertising, and distribution.

Portfolio Analysis In many ways, portfolio analysis is an extension of product life cycle concepts. It starts with the assumption that a firm has multiple products and that those products are at different stages of their life cycles. Portfolio analysis has two basic parts. The first is focused on determining where various products currently are in their life cycles. Based on this analysis, the second part is focused on creating corporate strategic plans for where the firm ought to place its investments.

One of the earliest portfolio analysis techniques was the BCG matrix, developed by the Boston Consulting Group. This tool requires managers to assess the market attractiveness of a particular product or business and the attractiveness of its current position in the market, primarily in terms of market share (see Exhibit 7.8).

Exhibit 7.8

BCG Matrix

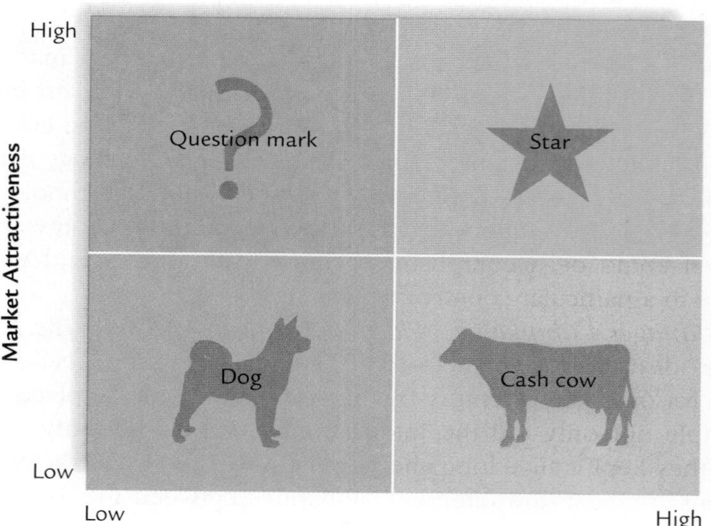

a manager's challenge *globalization*

Flashback, Flash Forward: The Long-Lived VW Beetle

Peace, flower power, and Disney's original version of Herbie the Love Bug were all components of the 1960s. When these things faded from the social scene in the 1970s, it may have been of little consequence to many, but the decline of consumer interest in the Beetle posed a significant problem for Volkswagen. Back in the 1960s, when the Volkswagen Beetle was first introduced, it was one of the best-selling cars of the time: It had an odd but endearing shape; it got good gas mileage and was fairly reliable; when it broke down it was easy to fix. Unfortunately for VW, Japanese manufacturers offered a better value proposition. For nearly the same price, consumers could purchase significantly more reliable cars. These cars caught consumers' eyes, but blindsided Volkswagen.

Because North America was the largest market for the car, VW could have simply accepted the market loss and killed the Beetle. Instead, management looked at the life cycle of the car and other markets. After assessing its options, Volkswagen went to South America and selected Brazil as the next market for the Beetle. Brazil was chosen for several reasons. First, it was a developing country with an automobile market clamouring for affordable but reliable cars. Second, Brazil's roads were not in very good condition, and the four-wheel, independent suspension of the Beetle was ideal for rough roads. (This was one of the reasons the Beetle was a car of choice for off-road races.)

Because the Beetle was well matched to market conditions in Brazil, it achieved popularity there nearly as strong as it had enjoyed in North America 15 years earlier. Volkswagen produced the Beetle in Brazil until the mid-1980s.

When the car's popularity declined in Brazil and production ceased, Volkswagen moved its production to Mexico. Customers there had been purchasing "bugs" since 1964. Producing them in Mexico allowed Volkswagen to capture more of the Mexican market by avoiding import duties and other restrictions.

Surprisingly, Volkswagen re-opened production in Brazil in 1993, with hopes of again marketing the Beetle in North America. However, Volkswagen may have tried to squeeze too much from a product that was in the declining stages of its life cycle. The reintroduction of the Beetle in the United States did not approach the peak of its first appearance. Convinced there was still interest in the original concept, VW undertook a thorough research program to find out how people of all ages, income levels, and lifestyles felt about the car. Based on the results, the company totally redesigned the Beetle. It changed the styling, suspension, and engine, and even moved the trunk from the front to the back.

The reintroduction of the New Beetle in the late 1990s was a huge success, boosting VW sales dramatically over its 1985 levels. The New Beetle pressed the baby boomers' nostalgia buttons, back orders were common, and discounts were nowhere to be found. Disney even released a new version of Herbie the Love Bug. In fact, demand was so strong that some dealers were able to sell Beetles above the suggested list price. The redesigned car rolled away with several coveted awards, including North American Car of the Year, *Motor Trend*'s Import Car of the Year, and *Money Magazine*'s Best Car of the Year, and it was the only car in its class to achieve a five-star safety rating.

In early 2002, Volkswagen unveiled a New Beetle Turbo S, the most powerful and sports-equipped "bug" ever available in the United States. Still, recent years have not been as kind to the New Beetle as it was to the old. Volkswagen's release of the turbo and convertible versions of the bug have helped boost interest and sales, but the initial fervour over the re-release of the Beetle has cooled considerably in the past five years. Relying on nostalgia has not maintained a competitive stance with other competing convertibles that offer more power and extras in the same price range.

Volkswagen's reintroduction of the original Beetle depended on correctly reading the product's life cycle relative to the countries in which it was sold and making the right changes to attract a new segment of the marketplace. But all good things must come to an end, or so the saying goes. In 2003, because of falling demand, Volkswagen ended production of the original Beetle on July 30 in Puebla, Mexico. The last car, painted pink, rolled off the line to the sound of a mariachi band walking behind it. The company's remarkable ability to extend the product's life cycle, however, has allowed the brand to outlive most other car models by decades.

Sources: "2006 Volkswagen Beetle," www.edmunds.com (accessed November 11, 2006); Keith Crain, "Say Goodbye to an Old Friend," *Automotive News*, July 14, 2003, p. 12; Volkswagen press releases, April 4, 2001 and January 4, 2002; David Kelly, *Getting the Bugs Out* (New York: John Wiley & Sons, 2001); Jerry Dubrowski, "VW Unveils New Beetle," Cable News Network online, January 5, 1998; Casey Wian, "Beetle Mania Spreads," Cable News Network online, May 5, 1998; Gregory L. White, "U.S. Car Sales Jumped by 6% in September," *Wall Street Journal*, October 6, 1998, pp. A3, A8; "Volkswagen U.S. September Sales Best Since 1985," *Reuters Limited*, October 2, 1998.

dogs products or SBUs that have relatively low market share in unattractive markets

Products or strategic business units (SBUs are units that are considered strategically important and typically have profit and loss accountability) that have relatively low market share in unattractive markets are classified as **dogs**. These products are often in the decline stage of their life cycle. If a way cannot be found to teach the old dog a new trick, the product or business is often sold or shut down. For example, 5-and-1/4-inch diskettes and drives were made in the millions and made millions in profits during the 1980s, but they were dog products in the 1990s.

question marks products or SBUs that have relatively low market share in attractive markets

Products or SBUs that have relatively low market share in attractive markets are classified as **question marks**. Managers need to find a way to increase their share of the market, be satisfied with a relatively small share, or get out. You may wonder, "If we're in an attractive market, why would we exit?" The answer is typically found in the internal organizational analysis. For example, you would choose to exit an attractive market because you simply do not have the capabilities or resources to be successful, including such things as technology or capital to invest. In the early 1990s, CDs and CD-ROM drives looked like hot markets, but they required different technology and manufacturing capabilities than 5-and-1/4-inch diskettes or disk drives. As a consequence, only a few leading companies, like Sony, were able to readily make a successful transition to the new products.

cash cows products or SBUs that have relatively high market share in markets with unattractive futures

Products or SBUs that have relatively high market share in markets with unattractive futures are classified as **cash cows**. In this case, managers need to feed the cow enough to keep it alive but milk it for all it's worth. Cash cow products or businesses are typically at the maturity stage of their life cycle. Often, the excess cash that is generated is used to fund investments in question marks or promising new products. For example, 3-and-1/2-inch diskettes and disk drives were considered cash cow products for the mid- and late 1990s, and the money was used to fund new products such as read/write CD drives and disks.

stars products that have relatively high market share in markets with attractive futures

Stars are products that have relatively high market share in markets with attractive futures. Typically, stars are in the birth or growth stages of their life cycle. As we discussed in the section on product life cycles, the birth and growth stages usually require the highest investments of time and money. While CDs and CD-ROM drives might have been considered question marks for Sony in the early 1990s, they were considered star products later in the decade. However, the introduction of MP3 players soon followed.

The basic idea behind portfolio analysis is to make sure that the corporation is diversified and does not have too many dogs, does not spend too much time on question marks, and has enough cash cows to fund the future stars. The exact products or businesses that constitute a balanced portfolio change over time. Some stars may mature and become cash cows or even decline and become dogs.

The same basic idea of analyzing market attractiveness and your firm's capabilities and strengths can also be used to construct an international portfolio analysis and plan (see Exhibit 7.9). In constructing a matrix such as in the exhibit, you essentially assess the attractiveness of different countries and your ability to compete in those markets. In this context, dogs are markets that are unattractive, for which you have a low ability to compete successfully. For example, in Exhibit 7.9, Finland and the Philippines are dog markets for our hypothetical company. The strategic planning and management implication here is to avoid dog markets and, if you are in one of these markets, to get out.

Markets that are unattractive but in which you have strong competitive capabilities require some rethinking (United States, Mexico, and Canada in Exhibit 7.9). You need to ask questions such as, "Do those markets have

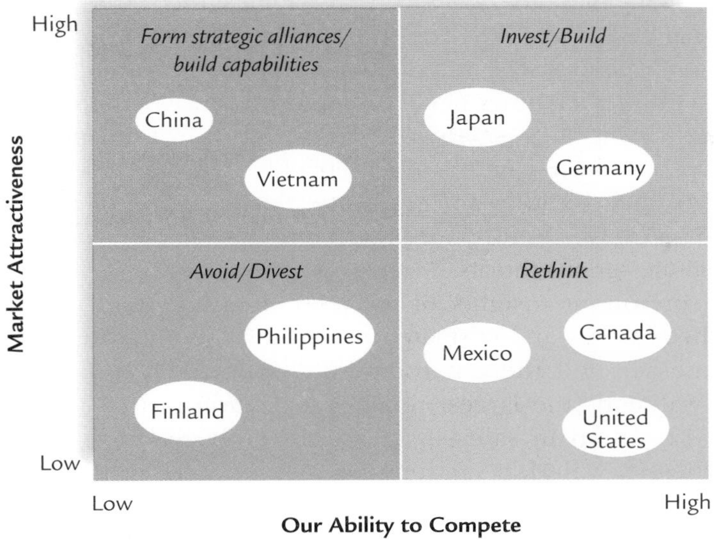

Exhibit 7.9

International Matrix

Market Attractiveness (High / Low) vs. Our Ability to Compete (Low / High)

Form strategic alliances/ build capabilities: China, Vietnam
Invest/Build: Japan, Germany
Avoid/Divest: Philippines, Finland
Rethink: Mexico, Canada, United States

segments that could be attractive? Can we introduce new products that leverage our current strengths?" If nothing can be done to make the market more attractive, the company should milk its current products while preparing to exit the market.

If particular markets are attractive (China and Vietnam in Exhibit 7.9), but you have low competitive capabilities, you have two basic options. First, you can form strategic alliances with partners who have capabilities you lack and who can benefit from those you have. Second, you can take the time and money to build the capabilities you need to compete in the market. For example, China might represent a very attractive market for your new beverage product, but you lack managers who understand the Chinese distribution system. You can take on a partner who has this understanding, or you can train or hire managers with this understanding.

Finally, you should invest and build in markets that are attractive and in which you can be competitive (Japan and Germany in Exhibit 7.9). These "star" markets can provide significant revenues in the future.

In summary, most **portfolio analysis** techniques are designed to assist you in assessing the attractiveness of a market (within a country or across countries) and your current or potential competitive position in that market. Thus, these techniques bring together many of the insights gained from the external and internal analyses discussed in the previous sections.

portfolio analysis techniques designed to assist managers in assessing the attractiveness of a market

SWOT Analysis This approach to competitive analysis requires managers to consider their firm's strengths and weaknesses as well as any opportunities and threats for its continued operation. **SWOT analysis** stands for strengths, weaknesses, opportunities, and threats. SWOT analysis is more a basic framework than a specific strategic planning tool.[27] In conducting a SWOT analysis, you first evaluate your firm's strengths. Next, you evaluate your firm's weaknesses. In doing so, the frameworks of core competencies and resource analysis can be of great help. Alternatively, you might use the value chain framework previously discussed to work through an analysis of your firm's strengths and weaknesses. For example, what parts of the value chain do you do well? Sourcing? Marketing? What do you perform poorly? Customer service? Public relations?

SWOT analysis an analysis that requires managers to consider their firm's Strengths, Weaknesses, Opportunities, and Threats for its continued operation

Once you have considered your firm's internal environment, SWOT analysis requires you to then move to the external environment. First, you ask,

"What are the opportunities facing our firm?" Insights gained from a product life cycle analysis or portfolio analysis can help address this part of the SWOT analysis. For example, what products or businesses are about to enter the growth stage? What countries have conditions conducive to growth of particular products or businesses? Also, insights gained from using Porter's Five Forces discussed in Chapter 2 can help identify not only potential opportunities but also threats within your industry. For example, new products that could become substitutes for your products or new entrants into your markets could constitute serious threats.

The important insights of a SWOT analysis come only after you examine the matches and mismatches between the organization's strengths and weaknesses and the environment's opportunities and threats. For example, Wal-Mart (the largest retail organization in the world, reporting over US$312 billion in sales in 2006) currently has many international opportunities.[28] Wal-Mart's strengths include the ability to get large volumes of products to customers at low prices. However, as a result of its strong focus on the US market, very few Wal-Mart managers have experience or knowledge of foreign markets. Fortunately for Wal-Mart, few competitors can immediately capture these international opportunities; however, Wal-Mart must be careful not to wait too long in pursuing international expansion opportunities because Carrefour, a French discount retailer, is also expanding internationally. This very simple SWOT analysis may explain why Wal-Mart has responded to international opportunities. In 2006 Wal-Mart had more than 6600 stores in 13 countries around the world, employing 1.8 million people. Wal-Mart knows that if an opportunity to make money exists in these foreign markets, a competitor will seek them out. To effectively respond, Wal-Mart has used partners with knowledge of specific international markets, developed managers within Wal-Mart, hired people who can help it expand internationally, and simply bought existing operations in various countries such as Germany, where it bought 21 Wertkauf stores.

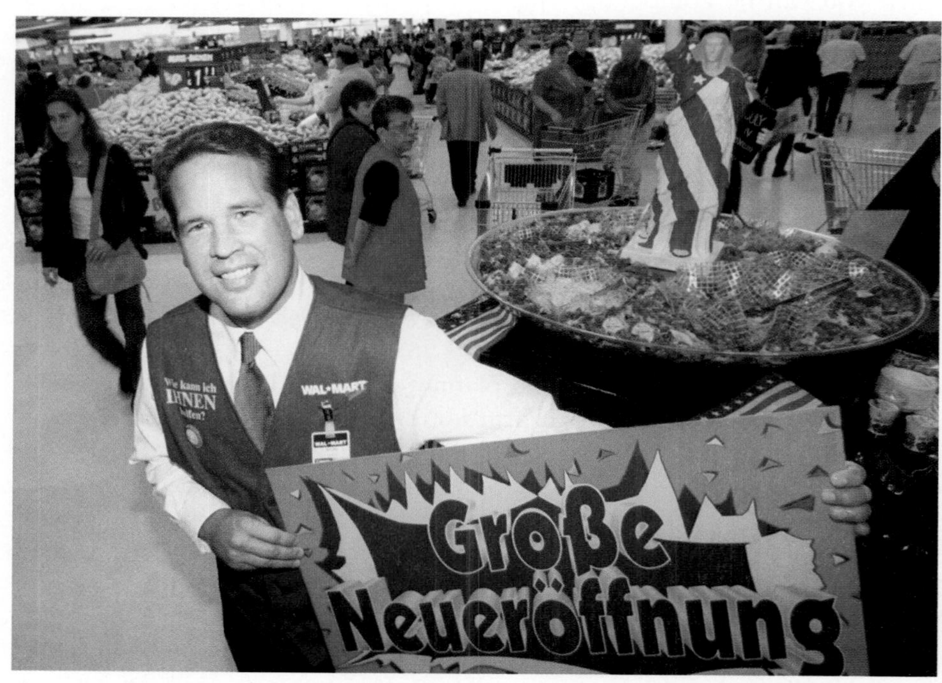

Wal-Mart is the world's largest retailer with over US$312 billion in annual sales—more than the GDP of some countries—giving the company considerable strength in the SWOT paradigm. However, the retail powerhouse faced serious threats from other retailers abroad who were more familiar with the local competitive landscape when it began to expand internationally. To counter that weakness, Wal-Mart formed partnerships with foreign retailers and also acquired established foreign retail chains such as Woolco from Woolworth Canada and Wertkauf stores in Germany.

Strategic Management Process: Strategy Implementation

Once a strategy has been formulated, it must be effectively implemented for desired results to materialize. Some evidence indicates that an average strategy superbly implemented is better than a great strategy poorly implemented.[29] Consequently, strategy implementation is at least as important as strategy formulation. Consider the case of Karen Johnson at Ashworth Consulting (in *A Manager's Challenge: "Changing Strategy at Ashworth Consulting"*). It can be a great strategy to decide to switch from doing lots of small projects for many clients to doing more involved projects for fewer clients. After all, there is a learning curve consultants have to follow regarding a client—its industry, competitors, products, value chain, internal resources, and so on. The further up that curve you go, the higher the mountain a competing consultancy has to climb. To the extent that these greater insights into the client allow you to give better advice, the more value you will provide to the client. Thus, we have some basic ingredients for competitive advantage. However, if key managers like Karen Johnson cannot change their behaviour and translate that strategy into action and get it effectively implemented, in practical terms the strategy is no more valuable than the paper it is printed on. At the same time, this translation has personal implications. Johnson must change aspects of herself as well as her team if she is to be successful. What do you see as the key changes for implementing the new strategy successfully?

Seven S's

Perhaps the most widely used strategy implementation framework is that developed by one of the largest and best-known strategy consulting firms—McKinsey & Company. About 25 years ago, McKinsey discovered that when many of its clients implemented strategic plans that it recommended, things actually got worse for the clients. McKinsey realized that having clients do worse when they follow your advice is not the way to build a successful consulting firm. What emerged from McKinsey's efforts to unravel this mystery was the Seven S framework (see Exhibit 7.10).

Essentially, McKinsey discovered that the reason clients were doing worse when they implemented the new strategies was because the strategies were being implemented within old structures, shared values, systems, skills, styles, and staff. These old aspects of the organization were inconsistent with the new strategy. Like a body that rejects an incompatible new organ, the old aspects of the organization worked against, overwhelmed, and in practical terms rejected the new strategy.

The Seven S McKinsey framework asserts that while each S is important, it is the congruence and fit among them that are critical. For example, IBM has a strategy of leveraging solutions developed for one client, like Bank of Tokyo-Mitsubishi, for other clients in the same industry, like Citibank. This strategy requires significant sharing of information across organizational units. First, to be successful, a structure must facilitate full and timely information exchange. Second, success also requires organizational members who trust each other and who value sharing information. Third, compensation systems must reward people on more than their personal results because the positive effects of their information sharing could easily show up in another unit or even another country. Fourth, effective information sharing also requires data gathering,

a manager's challenge | change

Changing Strategy at Ashworth Consulting

Karen Johnson could hardly believe it had been only five years since she graduated from a university in British Columbia with her business degree and joined Ashworth Consulting, a small firm specializing in strategic consulting. During those five years, she had advanced from research associate to associate consultant to consulting team leader. As team leader, Johnson was now responsible for a team of four people specializing in strategic market entry projects, and she reported directly to one of the five senior partners.

Recently, Johnson and all the other employees in the firm had participated in a two-day company retreat. During those two days, the senior partners had outlined the new strategic vision and plan for the company. In the past, the firm had focused on clients in the Vancouver area and lower region of British Columbia as well as Alberta. Additionally, the firm had somewhat specialized in consulting for firms interested in expanding into Asian markets and helping Asian firms, especially Japanese firms, set up subsidiaries in western provinces. The senior partners believed that the firm needed to broaden its geographical scope beyond the western provinces and Asia and expand its offerings beyond new-market entry.

In the past, the firm's revenues came primarily from doing many small projects for a variety of clients. The new vision called for doing more involved projects and doing more projects for fewer clients. Essentially, the rationale was that Ashworth could add more value, and therefore be harder for competitors to dislodge, if it focused on fewer clients and developed much deeper relationships with them. This involved a shift from short-term project focus to long-term relationship development and management, as well as a shift from specialized projects (i.e., market entry) to more general strategic consulting.

Johnson saw three major challenges related to this change in strategy. First, she would have to translate these general, new strategic directions into concrete goals and activities for her team. Second, she would need to help her team members identify their strengths and weaknesses relative to the requirements of the new strategy and help them with a development plan. Third, if she were to do these first two tasks well, she would also need to change and adapt herself. Johnson's background gave her specialized skills and knowledge in market entry, particularly in Japan. She had lived and worked in Japan and spoke the language. This set of skills had served her well under the old strategy. However, if she did not change, they might become liabilities or at least limitations under the new strategy.

To help translate the general strategy into concrete goals and actions, Johnson held a one-hour meeting with her team members. During the meeting she briefly restated what the old strategy had been and what the new strategy was, as well as the underlying rationale for it. She then asked her team to discuss what implications they saw for themselves as a result of the new strategy. Quickly, several team members mentioned that they would need to broaden their base of competencies from market entry to such areas as joint ventures, alliances, restructuring, and so on.

After the team meeting, Johnson reviewed the team's past clients to look for repeat customers or other indications of potential for deeper client relationships. She identified three firms out of the 15 or so that her team had worked with over the past 24 months.

She next called a meeting with the team to get their ideas about how they might develop deeper relationships with these repeat clients. One of the most promising ideas was to make some unsolicited bids on projects. Several team members had heard of projects the clients were undertaking in the near future on which Ashworth might bid.

After this meeting, Johnson realized that she would need to undertake significant changes in how she managed her team's performance plans as well as her own. It was clear that for the team to succeed in forming stronger relationships with fewer clients across a broader area of strategic consulting, both she and her team members would need to change and develop new competencies. None of this development was currently present in her own or any of her team members' personal performance goals. This needed to change and be corrected.

Still, it would not be possible for her or any of her team members to be equally good at all the required competencies, at least not for a while. Her next big managerial task would be to crystallize her thoughts about what each team member should add to his or her skill set and set her own development priorities. The challenge would be to find the right skills at the intersection of what development areas represented individual interests and strengths and what would serve the strategy and client best. For example, in her own case, Johnson was great at receiving RFPs (request for proposal) from clients and then responding. She was not good at probing for potential consulting opportunities. This was a needed skill if she was to get more work with fewer, focused clients. However, by personality, Johnson enjoyed the more defined and concrete aspects of responding to RFPs compared to the more ambiguous activity of general relationship building and probing for opportunities. Still, she could see that she would need to change if she was to manage herself and her team to success under the new strategy.

Exhibit 7.10

Seven S Model

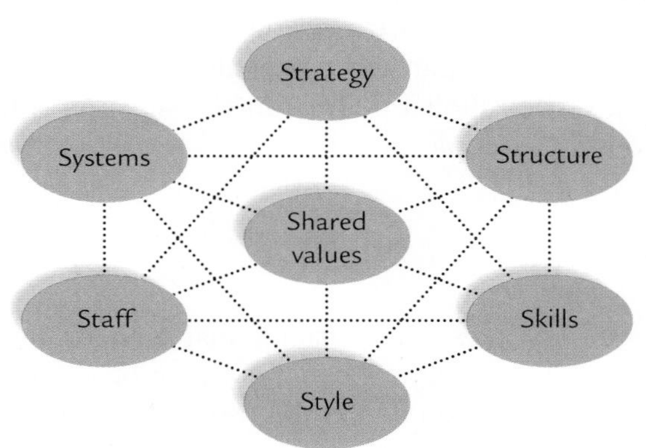

1. **Strategy**—Plan or course of action leading to the allocation of firm's resources to reach identified goals.
2. **Structure**—The ways people and tasks relate to each other. The basic grouping of reporting relationships and activities. The way separate entities of an organization are linked.
3. **Shared Values**—The significant meanings or guiding concepts that give purpose and meaning to the organization.
4. **Systems**—Formal processes and procedures, including management control systems, performance measurement and reward systems, and planning and budgeting systems, and the ways people relate to them.
5. **Skills**—Organizational competencies, including the abilities of individuals as well as management practices, technological abilities, and other capabilities that reside in the organization.
6. **Style**—The leadership style of management and the overall operating style of the organization. A reflection of the norms people act upon and how they work and interact with each other, vendors, and customers.
7. **Staff**—Recruitment, selection, development, socialization, and advancement of people in the organization.

Source: Richard Pascale, *Managing on the Edge* (New York: Simon & Schuster, 1990).

analysis, and dissemination skills. People are not necessarily gifted in all these activities. Fifth, there are key positions where information is generated and transferred. Staff with the highest information skills must be placed in these critical positions. Finally, the leadership style of senior managers must be consistent with the other aspects of the model. This simplified but true example helps illustrate that the key to successful strategy implementation is having an internal organization that is consistent with and supportive of the strategy.

Strategic Management Process: Strategy Evaluation

The final step in the strategic management process is evaluation. Just as evaluation and feedback can improve individual performance, so can they enhance organizational performance. When a small number of managers are responsible for the organization's strategic, tactical, or operational objectives, their individual performance evaluations can often provide a rough indication of how the organization is doing. If the individual's personal objectives are tied directly to operational objectives and they are all meeting or exceeding their goals, the organization as a whole is likely meeting its operational objectives. Most organizations carry out annual or even quarterly organizational performance evaluations. Typically, the strategic results are given to the more senior executives, and the operational results are disseminated principally to lower-level managers. Like individual feedback, organizational performance evaluation is used to reinforce efforts that have contributed to desired results and to correct those that have not.

Strategy as Pattern

Up to this point, we have presented strategic management from the dominant view that it is and should be a rational, conscious plan of action. This perspective is not universally shared, not even in Western firms. As pointed out earlier, many cultures believe that humans do not control their destiny and that strategic management is a vanity born of not knowing one's place in the universe. But even if we do accept the perspective of using planning and strategy as rational, conscious, and purposeful action, we often may not act on that belief. Scholars like Henry Mintzberg at McGill University have argued that strategies often emerge from patterned behaviour rather than from planned and intended actions.[30]

According to Mintzberg, observers often assume that the actions an organization took were planned and intended. Also, journalists often assign a strategy to a corporation based on observed patterns of actions, whether the managers who took those actions had those purposes in mind or not. Mintzberg argues that often the pattern results from a string of actions rather than intentions and explicit plans. That is, certain actions were reinforced by positive consequences, and they were repeated and expanded only as long as positive consequences continued. In turn, these patterns were interpreted by observers as intended. Sometimes even organizational members later interpret these patterns as though they were intended from the outset. Thus, even in firms with managers who believe in planning and strategic management, strategy may come from actions that had positive consequences rather than intentions. Floris A. Maljers, former chairman of the board of Unilever, echoes the view of strategy as pattern:

> *Unilever is often described as one of the foremost transnational companies. Yet our organization of diverse operations around the world is not the outcome of a conscious effort . . . the company has evolved mainly through a Darwinian system of retaining what was useful and rejecting what no longer worked—in other words, through actual practice as a business responding to the marketplace.*[31]

Mintzberg points out that we need to recognize the existence of both *deliberate* strategies and *emergent* strategies. The importance of this distinction is that deliberate strategies focus our attention on analyzing key factors in the domestic and international environment and trying to plan for the future. In contrast, emergent strategies focus our attention on the consequences of past and present actions. An awareness of both influences allows us to focus on the past, present, *and* future and incorporate our own judgments and the environment when we assess what works or doesn't work in the competitive marketplace.

managerial perspectives revisited

PERSPECTIVE 1: **THE ORGANIZATIONAL CONTEXT** While an assessment of the external environment is critical to any formulation of strategy, effective strategy cannot be formulated without consideration of the organization. External environments are influential, but they are not deterministic. In other words, environments are not the sole determinant of successful strategies. From a resource-based or even a core competency approach to strategy, appropriate strategy is derived in part from the advantages within the organization. For example, WestJet is a Canadian airline that has managed to achieve a sustained competitive advantage by pursuing a strategy that provides customers with a high-value product by offering exceptional customer service and low fares. WestJet's strong corporate culture is one of its main competitive advantages; the satisfaction and motivation that this culture fosters in its employees helps to ensure better customer service and a commitment to a low cost structure. Employees are motivated in part by the linking of their success to that of the company through compensation policies like profit sharing. Another of WestJet's strengths results from its plan to improve its product offering through various in-flight upgrades; these improvements will include on-board live satellite television, increased legroom, leather seats, and a food-service program. WestJet's superior low-cost structure has been another significant contributor to the company becoming the leading Canadian low-fare airline. Cost-advantages are achieved by aligning employee goals with company goals; using only one type of aircraft; continually replacing older aircrafts with newer, more fuel-efficient planes; maintaining efficient operations; and investing in technology. In short, WestJet's low cost structure and strong company culture continue to differentiate it from its competitors by contributing to its low fares and exceptional customer service.

PERSPECTIVE 2: **THE HUMAN FACTOR** While it is possible for a strategy to be formulated by a single individual or a small group, it is not possible for it to be implemented except with and through others. Air Canada's senior executive team can decide that the company's new strategy will focus on superior customer service, but until gate agents, flight attendants, reservation agents, and others actually change their behaviour and provide superior service to customers, the strategy has little impact on the financial performance of the company. This is why strategy implementation through others is one of the most critical activities of managers. Sometimes those not involved in the formulation of the strategy fail to recognize the critical role they play in its actual success by implementing it effectively through their subordinates. Imagine Ashworth Consulting's success at changing its strategy if lower-level managers like Karen Johnson are not able to see what the strategy means for her and her team and if she cannot get her team to change their focus and behaviour.

PERSPECTIVE 3: **MANAGING PARADOXES** One concern in formulating strategies that presents a potential paradox to managers is the tension of being committed to a strategy over the long term versus being responsive to changes in the organization's environment. If

management changed strategies too frequently, it is likely that employees (as well as customers, suppliers, and shareholders) would have difficulty achieving a coordinated action. Furthermore, no strategy would be fully realized. It typically takes some time for a strategy to be communicated and implemented by the organization's employees. It also takes time for a strategy to have an effect in the market. As we pointed out with the example of Air Canada, quite often the financial impact of the strategy is not realized until most of the employees change their behaviour to fit with the strategy. On the other hand, aspects of the environment do change. In fact, the current competitive environment for many organizations is highly dynamic. New technologies emerge, new competitors arise, laws and regulations change, and so on. If a strategy becomes too rigid or if management keeps a given strategy too long when the environment is changing rapidly, that inflexibility can threaten the very survival of a company. For example, Polaroid changed too slowly when digital photography technology was introduced, and the company eventually lost the market for its products to new competitors.

PERSPECTIVE 4: **ENTREPRENEURIAL MINDSET** One reason that firms do not change their strategies as needed is because they are not entrepreneurial. That is, they are not continuously searching for new opportunities in the market. Thus, their managers lack an entrepreneurial mindset. Gary Hamel, former scholar and now a prominent strategy consultant, argues that the firms likely to win in the current competitive landscape are bold and innovative in all areas of their business.[32] To respond to this need, others have argued that organizations can engage in strategic entrepreneurship. That is, they can simultaneously search for new opportunities (entrepreneurial) and take actions to gain and sustain competitive advantages (strategic).[33] Strategic entrepreneurship is important for managers and employees. They need to be committed to innovation as a means of gaining or maintaining a competitive advantage. Managers can only master this and other balancing acts if they are committed to developing the required conceptual and practical skills. For many managers the ambiguity associated with entrepreneurial opportunities and the competitive actions in the market necessary to gain a competitive advantage requires additional commitment to become more tolerant of ambiguity. In fact, this ability has been identified in several studies of effective leaders who must both formulate and implement strategies effectively.[34] Perhaps the greatest commitment is that which is required to implement and follow through on a strategic change. Yet, a commitment to strategic change is a part of an entrepreneurial mindset.

concluding comments

Because strategic management is a process of determining where the organization wants to go and how it will successfully compete, it is a critical managerial function. The logic that senior managers must understand the strategic management process is self-evident. Yet it is equally important for entry-level managers to understand the process. Entry-level managers may not be involved in strategy formulation for the entire company, but they must implement the strategy for it to succeed. Furthermore, entry-level managers need to know what the corporate-, business-, or operational-level strategies are to make decisions that support overall strategic objectives. Managers make many daily decisions, and those decisions can have a complementary or conflicting impact on the overall direction and performance of the organization. So it is important that they make informed decisions; it is too costly to monitor all managers to determine whether their decisions and actions are consistent with the overall strategy. Rather, they can be more effective and efficient when they are guided by a clear understanding of strategic management process in general and the strategy of the company in particular. In addition, part of the value you bring to an organization is a function of what it needs as dictated by its strategy. Initially, you need to be able to understand a firm's strategy to assess if and how and where you can add value. However, even if there is a good match at the outset, no strategy lasts forever. To understand what changes you personally may have to make or help others make, you need to be able to understand strategy in general, your firm's strategy in particular, and be able to translate those general elements into concrete implications. This is why strategy and strategic management are not the exclusive property of senior executives but are relevant and vital for all managers.

key terms

cash cows 242
competitive advantage 222
core competency 238
cost leadership 229
customer segment 232
differentiation 229
dogs 242
mission statement 227
niche strategy 232
portfolio analysis 243
primary activities 235
question marks 242
stars 242
strategic objectives 228
strategic scope 232
strategic vision 226
substitution 224
supernormal returns 225
support activities 235
SWOT analysis 243
value chain 234
value proposition 233

test your comprehension

1. What is competitive advantage?
2. What are the five required elements for competitive advantage?
3. What is the difference between the competitive threats of imitation and substitution?
4. What is the purpose of strategic vision?
5. Name five elements that are typically included in a mission statement.
6. Define value proposition.
7. What is a customer segment?
8. What is the purpose of strategic objectives?
9. How can a firm's value chain be used to conduct an organizational analysis?
10. What is the difference between primary activities in the value chain and support activities?
11. What is a niche strategy?
12. What are the three tests of an effective core competency?
13. What are the similarities between core competency and resource-based approaches to strategy?
14. What are the typical stages in a product's life cycle and how can this be used in strategic planning?
15. What is the difference between a dog and a question mark in the BCG portfolio analysis model?
16. What is the typical relationship between cash cows and question marks in the BCG portfolio analysis model?
17. How can a portfolio analysis be used in developing global strategies?
18. What does SWOT stand for?
19. What is the difference between the generic strategies of cost leadership and differentiation?
20. What are the elements of the Seven S model?
21. What is the key principle behind the Seven S model?

apply your understanding

1. Effectively *changing* strategies is often one of the most difficult tasks of management. Why do you think this is the case?
2. How does the articulation of strategic vision affect the strategic planning and management process? Could organizations be just as effective without clear statements of strategic vision?
3. What would a SWOT analysis of your university look like? What are your school's key strengths and weaknesses? What are the major threats in the external environment? What are the opportunities? Make a list of all you can think of.
4. Looking at your life, to what degree do you have an intended versus emergent strategy? Are the classes you're now taking and planning to take in the future more a function of intended steps or of positive and negative consequences encountered as you have pursued your degree?
5. With this assessment in mind, what do you see as the positive and negative aspects of intended and emergent strategies for individuals or for organizations?

practise your capabilities

You are one of the senior managers in a small company that provides software and computer training to the employees of larger companies. Your firm has not really had a concrete strategy (let alone a statement of strategic vision or a mission statement). The company started when a group of friends who did freelance training met and decided to pool their company contacts and hire some additional help to meet the demand that exceeded their collective productivity. The company is now three years old and has a total of 35 employees—most of whom are trainers.

The management team meets to discuss the firm's future and strategy. You suggest that the team conduct a simple SWOT analysis to inform the discussions. The following is the collective group's assessment:

Strengths

- The management team has done a good job of hiring people who have both solid technical capabilities and good skills at teaching others.
- There is a good pool of technical talent from the local university.
- There are strong relationships with a few of the larger companies in the area.

Weaknesses

- There has been some inconsistent pricing of training for clients based on case-by-case negotiations and relationships. Some contracts have high margins and some have low margins.
- Employees have no idea what the value proposition being sold to customers is.
- You do not have a strategy for current or future business.

Opportunities

- Demand seems to be reasonably strong and growing.
- There is potential for expanding geographically as some current customers have offices in other cities and have inquired about providing training in those locations but do not want to pay the travel and lodging costs of your local trainers to go to these other sites.

Threats

- Some of the large "temp" companies (i.e., firms that provide temporary contract employees to other firms, such as Manpower or Kelly Services) who do a lot of training of their temps are beginning to market their training capabilities to their clients. The prices being quoted by these firms are about 15 percent higher than your prices. Customers are somewhat price sensitive.
- The type of training you provide is hard to differentiate. The real difference is not in the content of the training (e.g., everyone covers the same topics when teaching people how to use MS PowerPoint) but in how well trainers do the job and how much the students enjoy the experience and remember what they learned.

1. Based on this general assessment, what is your assessment of the firm's customer value proposition and recommendations for the future?
2. What should the firm's strategy be? Should it try to expand geographically?
3. What additional internal or external assessment is needed for you to make a solid strategy recommendation? Of these additional assessments, what are the top two priorities and why?

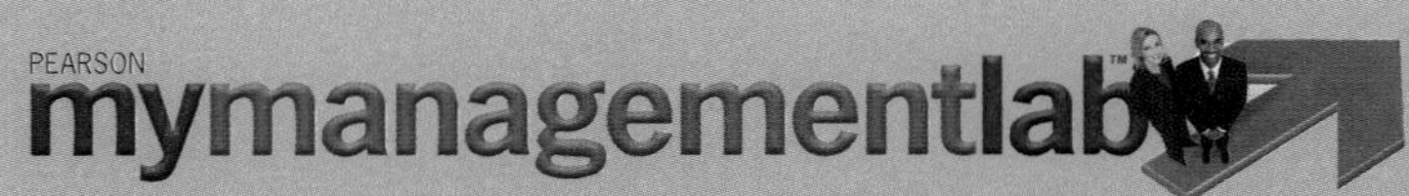

To improve your grade, visit the MyManagementLab website at **www.pearsoned.ca/mymanagementlab**. This online homework and tutorial system allows you to test your understanding and generates a personalized study plan just for you. It provides you with study and practice tools directly related to this chapter's content. MyManagementLab puts you in control of your own learning!

closing case DEVELOP YOUR CRITICAL THINKING

One Region. One Firm: The Atlantic Law Firm of McInnes Cooper

McInnes Cooper is Atlantic Canada's largest law partnership, with offices in all four Atlantic provinces. The McInnes Cooper partnership began in 1859 in Halifax and has been involved in the legal handling of many notable and historic events, including the 1912 sinking of the *Titanic* and the 1917 Halifax explosion. The partnership represents major regional, national, and international interests from its constantly expanding base in Atlantic Canada. In total, there are 200 lawyers located in six Atlantic cities that practise law in myriad areas ranging from asset recovery and insolvency to technology and patent law.

The firm's stated motto is "One Region. One Firm." The intent of this motto is to underscore that the six office locations throughout the Atlantic provinces operate as a single partnership. This provides a unique market position for McInnes Cooper, offering clients a wider pool of expertise and legal resources. While most firms traditionally keep client work in the originating office, thereby localizing revenue, the McInnes Cooper partnership enables sharing of work between offices. This allows client services to provide the appropriate specialization needed by the client while maintaining a high personal focus at the same time. Clients are then able to retain the best lawyer and an unrivalled depth of resources in the Atlantic region to meet their needs, regardless of location. This approach follows the firm's guiding principles of professionalism, integrity, and strong relationships. Like many service-related professions, the senior partners know that a satisfied clientele leads to repeat business and firm growth.

Recently, McInnes Cooper implemented some changes in the firm. One change involved the merger of Patterson Palmer, a large regional law firm located in Halifax, with McInnes Cooper. This merger significantly added to the firm's business law capabilities, giving it the largest concentration of business lawyers in Halifax. It also strengthened the position of McInnes Cooper as the top business law firm in Atlantic Canada.

Every year the Atlantic magazine *Progress* hosts an event known as the Face to Face Conference. This conference provides business leaders with the opportunity to gather and share their experiences and insight. Entrepreneurs have access to a wide array of tools such as turnaround specialists, success stories, and strategic insight. At Face to Face, many opportunities arise such as discovering new business opportunities, meeting new clients, finding new capital for growth, and networking with people who can help strengthen a business.

McInnes Cooper has been a long-time sponsor of Face to Face, yet in recent years there has been some internal concern whether the firm has been maximizing the opportunities present at this conference. For the upcoming conference, management planned to be more aggressive, developing a five-point strategy that would focus on (1) leveraging McInnes Cooper's sponsorship involvement, (2) adding to the momentum around McInnes Cooper's growth, (3) ensuring maximization of peer-to-peer networking, (4) entrenching existing client relationships and partnerships, and (5) scoping out new business development opportunities. The lead partner on the project at McInnes Cooper stated they would have a plan in place long before the McInnes Cooper team arrived at the conference. If played right, the conference would have the potential to be an excellent opportunity to strengthen McInnes Cooper's position as Atlantic Canada's top business law firm.

For McInnes Cooper to achieve its conference objectives, the pre-conference planning team would need to focus on understanding who it was that comprised the target audience and develop key messages that would generate interest in the firm. To do this it was necessary for the planning team to scan the environment and find answers to several questions such as "What industries will be represented at the conference? What are the new and developing trends in these industries? What aspects of McInnes Cooper would delegates from these industries find most appealing?" Once the information was assembled, the planning team then had to determine how McInnes Cooper could personalize key messages that would appeal to participants.

Following the environmental scan, management decided that it was important for participants to leave the conference knowing McInnes Cooper is interested in working with Atlantic-Canadian entrepreneurs and in helping strengthen Atlantic-Canadian businesses. The following key messages were deemed essential to the marketing and positioning strategy:

1. McInnes Cooper is redefining the law landscape in Atlantic Canada.
2. Last summer the firm merged with a respected Halifax office of a regional law firm, ensuring that they are lockstep with the clients' growth and success.
3. As McInnes Cooper moves forward, the partnership sees the powerful benefits that the merger will bring to their clients.
4. The firm's clients are diverse, ranging from small and mid-sized organizations to major international firms. Offices are located in every major city in Atlantic Canada.

These messages were combined with the right information about McInnes Cooper and portrayed on marketing materials. In addition, the pre-conference planning team held a teleconference meeting to ensure each McInnes Cooper delegate was aware of the key messages so that they were conveyed consistently while networking at the conference. The objective was to use the key messages in conjunction with the researched participant information to deliver high-level and relevant information that would spark interest in McInnes Cooper.

Questions

1. Do you think that McInnes Cooper took the right steps in evaluating the external environment to prepare their key messages?
2. In light of the nature of the conference, is the firm's corporate history a strength or a weakness? Why? If it is a strength, are they using it sufficiently in their plan? If it is a weakness, are they effectively drawing the attention of delegates to other firm attributes?
3. Visit the website of McInnes Cooper (www.mcinnescooper.com). Are there any new practice areas that the firm could explore in the current environment?
4. Are there other ways that McInnes Cooper could position itself as the choice for individuals and firms seeking legal services in the Atlantic provinces?

Source: McInnes Cooper website, www.mcinnescooper.com (accessed December 13, 2006); Allison Fillier, *Case Study: McInnes Cooper*, September 2006, University of New Brunswick Faculty of Business Administration.

Chapter 8 Organizational Structure and Design

LEARNING OBJECTIVES

After reading this chapter, you should be able to:

1. Explain the concepts of organizational structure and design.
2. Explain the concepts of specialization and integration and their role in organizational structure and design.
3. Describe mechanisms used to achieve specialization and integration and balance these two structural dimensions.
4. Identify the various structures used by organizations and describe their strengths and weaknesses.
5. List the environmental factors that influence organizational structure.
6. Determine the appropriate organizational structure for a firm given a set of internal and external factors.

BD: Restructuring in Europe

The European Union began in 1996, and 2002 ushered in the most visible sign of the actual integration—the elimination of member country currencies and the mass introduction of the euro. This unification and reshaping of Europe caused many executives to re-examine how they operated and the appropriateness of their companies' structures in the region. Becton, Dickinson and Company (BD), a diversified medical technology company, was one of the firms that needed to rethink the organizational structure it used in its European operations.

BD has revenue in excess of US$5.4 billion with activities in more than 50 countries. However, the integration of Europe caused executives to turn their attention increasingly to Europe. For much of its history, BD was organized primarily by product and divided its products into three major areas. Its *medical surgical systems* unit consisted of product groups such as anaesthesia, infusion therapy, hypodermic products, intravenous catheters, and operating room products. Its *bioscience* unit included product groups such as labware, cell biology, immunology, and cellular analysis. Its *clinical laboratory solutions* unit included product groups such as diagnostic systems, vacutainer systems, and health care consulting. A division president was in charge in each of these product divisions; a separate division president (international division) was responsible for all product sales outside of the United States.

For many years, BD's international division was organized by geography (specifically by country), not by product, as in the United States. For example, BD France carried all the firm's products; the country manager of the French division was then responsible for sales and profits across all BD's product lines within France. The same was true for Germany, the United Kingdom, and so on. This organizational structure worked quite well, because for many years countries in Europe had quite different standards and regulations concerning most of the products BD made and sold. However, the formation of the European Union and its monetary integration reduced the different product standards and made it easier to do business throughout the region.

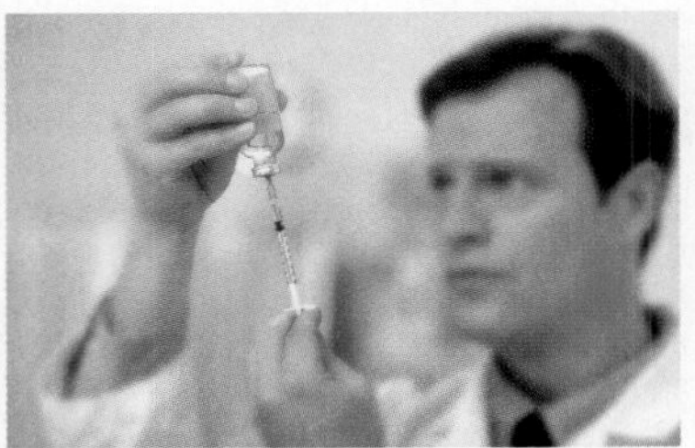

Becton, Dickinson and Company (BD), which has over 25 000 employees in more than 50 countries, is one of the top sellers of syringes in the world. BD also sells a variety of other medical supplies, devices, laboratory equipment, and diagnostic products, including ACE Brand bandages. For years, the company was organized by product line in the United States, and foreign divisions were organized by country. When the European Union was formed, BD had to rethink its structure. Should it reorganize its EU division by product line like in the United States?

The European Union held the promise that BD could make a product to one standard and sell it across all member nations. This would dramatically increase the efficiency of BD's operation in Europe, reduce the per-unit cost, and potentially increase profits. However, with this opportunity came an interesting challenge: How should the company structure its operations in Europe?

One obvious solution was to organize in Europe the same way as in the United States—by products. In this case, within the international division it would form a European hypodermic products group, a European diabetic care products group, and so on. However, no one could say how long it would be before customers in one country, like France, would view products and take actions similar to customers in another country, like Germany. Certainly, the language in which they conducted business would not quickly unify.

Another alternative was to organize the entire company by global product. That is, instead of having an international division, each product division would have worldwide responsibility. If this structure were adopted, the global head of a product such as diabetic care would have responsibility for product sales around the world, including Europe. However, even if all member countries in the European Union adopted similar standards, would those standards be the same as other markets, such as Canada and Japan?

The future structure of the company was further complicated by the nature of some of its most important customers, many of which were hospitals. Hospitals are somewhat different from other customers because they buy products from all of BD's product categories. In other words, one hospital might buy products from the hypodermic, diabetic care, intravenous catheter, operating room, specimen collection, cellular analysis, and tissue culture labware product groups. A product structure in Europe might involve having 10 different sales representatives from 10 different product groups call on each hospital. Wouldn't the customer prefer to have one representative for all of BD's products rather than deal with 10 different sales representatives from the same company?

Other BD competitors were increasingly entering overseas markets, and in North America substantial publicity about rising health care costs was also exerting downward pressures on prices. These external forces meant that BD could not afford to implement the wrong structure. Was it prepared to use a global structure? Would a country structure in Europe be better? Choosing the right organizational structure might make the difference between success and failure in the changing and increasingly competitive environment facing BD.

Sources: "Health Care Equipment & Supplies in France," *Datamonitor*, May 2006; Cinda Becker, "BD Makes IT Moves," *Modern Healthcare*, November 24, 2003, p. 45; BD 2001 Annual Report, BD.com (accessed March 3, 2002).

strategic overview

As the case of BD illustrates, today's complex environment presents a variety of questions about how firms should be structured to survive and prosper. A firm's structure can determine the success or failure of its strategy and its overall performance. The European Union changed the competitive landscape for BD and its competitors. As a result, BD managers had to carefully re-evaluate the structure of their organization to determine if the current one would continue to work or if a new one would be needed for the company to effectively compete.

As we have discussed in previous chapters, a firm's strategy must be carefully implemented for it to be successful. How the strategy gets implemented is largely a question of how managers organize the firm's activities; in other words, what they determine to be the firm's structure.[1] For example, BD had an international division for organizing its activities abroad. In its international division, the heads of each of the geographic units (i.e., country managers) were responsible for the sales of all BD products in their assigned countries. This way, the firm's international strategies could be executed independent of domestic strategy.

Another issue for BD was how much authority each country manager in Europe should have to develop their own strategies differently from those in the rest of the firm. As we will see, the centralization or decentralization of a firm's structure also affects the implementation of its overall strategy and the strategy of its divisions. Sometimes a firm's structure affects the very strategy it should choose.[2]

An increasingly common structure used by organizations today is a network structure (which we discuss in more detail later in this chapter). For example, when a firm decides to outsource its manufacturing operations as Nike and many other athletic shoe makers do, it must establish a network structure allowing it to maintain close contact with the firms to which it is outsourcing the work. The company also might need to maintain close relationships with a number of suppliers to ensure the quality and timely supply of goods. Because organizations often have many alliances, a network structure becomes important for implementing this type of cooperative strategy.[3]

Even if you are several years away from having the responsibility of actually redesigning or restructuring an organization, it is important to understand the fundamentals of organizational design and structure so that you are better prepared to help implement structures to make them effective. There are usually multiple structural options. You must understand common organizational structures and the general advantages and disadvantages of each. This includes the principles linking structure, strategy, and the external environment and the key factors that determine a good fit among these elements. Finally, as a manager, you must be able to apply this knowledge in planning and implementing appropriate organizational structures.

Principles of Organizational Structure

Organizational design is the process of assessing the organization's strategy and environmental demands and then determining the appropriate organizational structure. **Organizational structure** can be defined as the sum of the ways an organization divides its labour into distinct tasks and then coordinates them.[4] Often, organizational structure is talked about in terms of organizational charts. **Organizational charts** illustrate relationships among units and lines of authority among supervisors and subordinates through the use of labelled boxes and connecting lines. For example, Exhibit 8.1 shows the organizational chart of Suncor Energy.

While organizational charts represent important aspects of an organization's structure, they do not equal organizational structure. Just as the structure of someone's physical anatomy is more complex than what is visible, so too is an organization's structure more complex than what can be depicted in a chart. Understanding the principles of organizational structure and design is the key

organizational design the process of assessing the organization's strategy and environmental demands and then determining the appropriate organizational structures

organizational structure the sum of the ways an organization divides its labour into distinct tasks and then coordinates them

organizational charts an illustration of the relationships among units and lines of authority among supervisors and subordinates

Exhibit 8.1

Suncor Energy Organizational Structure

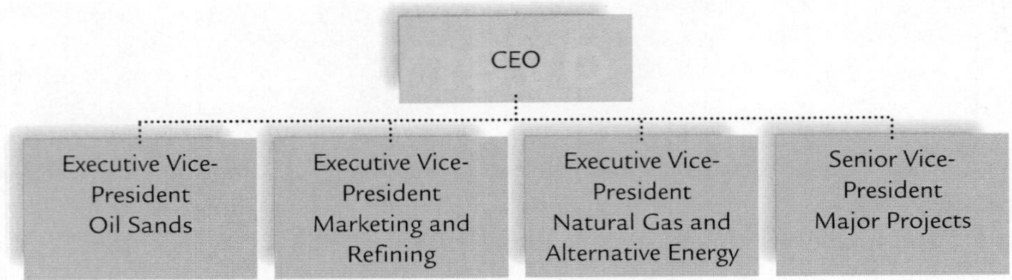

to correctly interpreting the organizational charts that you can see while not losing sight of an organization's structural aspects, which are not so visible but are just as important.

This journey starts with the fundamental dynamic of organization structure and design—the simultaneous separation and pulling together of people and activities.[5] On the one hand, all but the smallest of organizations have to separate people and tasks. In organizations of even moderate size it is not effective for everyone in the organization to do the same thing. At the same time, it is also not effective for any given individual to try to do everything. Some separation and specialization is required to get tasks accomplished, even in a small organization of just a dozen people. On the other hand, if these separate people and tasks are not pulled together, they can veer off in different directions without contributing to the ultimate needs of the customers or objectives of the organization. Consequently, some *integration* or coordinating and bringing together of people and tasks is also necessary. Balancing this pushing of people and tasks apart and pulling them together is the basic challenge of organizational structure and design. Fundamentally, the "right" structure or the right balance of specialization and integration is a function of the demands in the environment and the organization's strategy.

To get at this basic challenge of organizational structure and design, we first examine some of the core elements of organizing and then look at some of the most common organizational structures. With these basics in place, we then explore the challenge of designing structures that fit the changing demands of the environment and the organization's strategy.

Specialization

specialization the extent to which tasks are divided into subtasks and performed by individuals with specialized skills

To understand the organizing process, one of the first elements we need to examine further is specialization. **Specialization** is the extent to which tasks are divided into subtasks and performed by individuals with specialized skills.[6] The main benefit is greater specialization of knowledge and skills. For example, because of the complexity of building a commercial jetliner, Boeing has engineers who specialize in designing wings and others who design airplane doors. Even among those who design airplane doors, some focus primarily on designing the door hinges, while others focus on designing the locking mechanisms that keep the doors sealed at 35 000 feet. This differentiation by what employees do is typically referred to as **task specialization**.

task specialization specialization by what employees do

cognitive specialization the extent to which people in different units within an organization think about different things or about similar things differently

The nature of specialization is not limited just to the tasks people perform, but can also involve employees' thoughts. This is called **cognitive specialization** and is the extent to which people in different units within the organization think about different things and the extent to which people think about similar things differently.[7] For example, accountants typically think about assets and liabilities, while marketing managers think about brand image and market share. However, these two groups might also think about the same thing differently. Accountants might think about organizational performance in terms of financial results, while marketers might think about organizational performance in terms of customer satisfaction.

So why is this important? It is important because while specialization focuses more on individual tasks, it often makes pulling all this specialized capability together to deliver a product or service to the customer a challenge. Suppose both design engineers and manufacturing personnel at Boeing need to work together to make a newly designed 787 Dreamliner door operate properly. Greater separation and specialization make this coordination harder because designers may think about door performance in terms of design sophistication while manufacturing managers may think about door performance in terms of the ease of making and installing the door on the plane. If Boeing ends up with a door that is well designed but difficult and expensive to install, it may suffer any number of undesirable consequences. It may end up with a door that takes away from profits because it is costly to install. Or it may end up with a door that doesn't operate easily or properly because of mismatches between design and assembly.

Integration

In contrast to specialization, **integration** is the extent to which various parts of the organization cooperate and interact with each other.[8] The key benefit of integration is the coordinated movement of different people and activities toward a desired organizational objective. As a consequence, one of the driving forces of integration is interdependence. **Interdependence** is essentially the degree to which one unit, or one person, depends on another to accomplish a required task.

integration the extent to which various parts of an organization cooperate and interact with each other

interdependence the degree to which one unit or person depends on another to accomplish a task

There are three types of interdependence.[9] *Pooled interdependence* occurs when various groups are largely independent in their functions but collectively contribute to a common output. For example, two product groups within the same company, such as office stationery and office furnishings, might send products to the same business to meet the customer's overall needs. *Sequential interdependence* exists when the outputs of one group become the inputs of another group. For example, the raw materials at a manufacturing plant provided by the purchasing department become the inputs for production in the parts department. The parts department then shapes the raw materials into outputs that become inputs in the assembly department. *Reciprocal interdependence* exists when two or more groups depend on one another for inputs. For example, at a high-tech manufacturer, the new-product development department relies on the marketing research department for ideas to investigate, and marketing research relies on new-product development for new products to test on customers. In principle, the greater the interdependence is, the greater the need for cooperation, and thus integration.

A Manager's Challenge: "Restructuring for Growth" illustrates how a new structure and set of interdependencies can create required changes for individual managers. Kevin Nabholz at Suncor Energy discovered that the new company structure put him in a new organizational unit that required managing levels of interdependency that previously had not existed in the organization and with which he personally had little experience. Thus, the change in company structure resulted not only in a structural change for the unit in which he worked, but also what it required of him as a manager to work effectively within the new structure. How big a change does this seem to you? What do you see as the most important changes required of Nabholz as a result of the organizational structure change?

a manager's challenge *change*

Restructuring for Growth

In January 2002, Suncor Energy instituted a new organizational structure that had profound implications for Kevin Nabholz. The new structure called for the creation of a unit called *major projects* that would move many engineering and construction activities in-house that had previously been contracted to outside providers.

Suncor Energy is an integrated energy company; however, unlike most oil companies, Suncor does not drill for oil, it mines oil. It mines tar sand in northern Alberta and extracts the oil from the sand through heat and pressure. It then sells the crude oil to others or refines it internally into products like gasoline and sells it through its retail division, Sunoco.

In recent years, Suncor has become more involved in expanding its oil sands operations. Initially, Suncor was spending close to $1 billion annually on new construction projects. As of 2005, Suncor's capital investment has expanded to the tune of $3.5 billion annually. Suncor executives felt that this level of engineering and construction justified having "in-house" expertise, so they created an organizational unit with the responsibility for managing these projected construction projects.

Kevin Nabholz was put in charge of a new unit consisting of unrivalled engineering and construction complexity, which now had reciprocal interdependence with other business units. For example, the oil sands unit could determine that it needed a new vacuum tower (a construction project that would cost in excess of $100 million). That need would become the input for Nabholz's major projects unit. He would supervise all the engineering and construction (including any use of outside contractors) and then the output from his unit (the new vacuum tower) would become the input for the oil sands unit.

For Nabholz this represented a significant change in the skills required to be successful. In the past, most business units were fairly autonomous and supervised their own construction projects by contracting with outside firms. Now working closely with these internal business units would be the key to success. If effective coordination of project requests, approval, construction, and handover for operation was not achieved, all the desired efficiencies and cost savings of creating this new organizational unit would likely be lost. In addition, whereas before engineering and construction activities were largely contracted to outside firms, now Nabholz would directly supervise employees within Suncor to do much of the project design, estimation, engineering, and supervision of contract construction companies and workers.

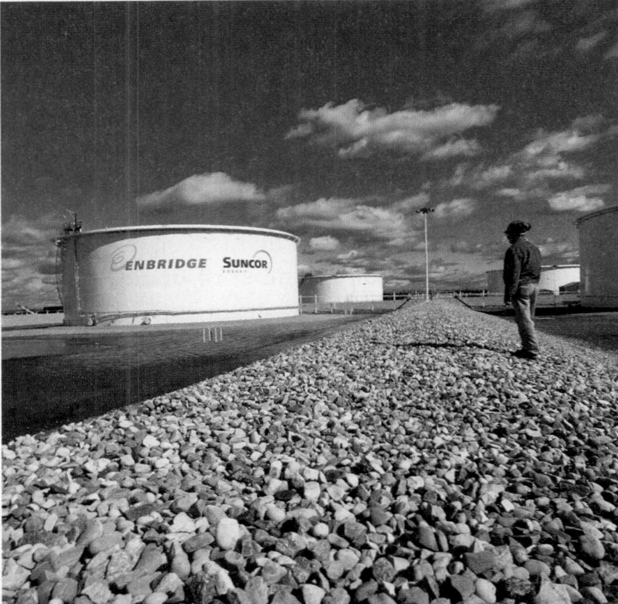

Suncor Energy, based in Calgary, doesn't drill for oil. It extracts oil from sand using heat and pressure, producing light crude oil, diesel fuel, and custom blends—a process it pioneered in 1967. In recent years, the company has been expanding rapidly, going from spending about $1 billion annually on new construction projects to $3.5 billion in 2005. To handle the expansion the company formed a special unit called major projects, headed by manager Kevin Nabholz. Nabholz is shown here inspecting one of Suncor's oil sand tanks near Fort McMurray in northern Alberta.

While some could view the organizational structure change as small, it represented a whole host of required changes and adjustments for Nabholz as the new manager of the unit. Specifically, whereas before there was very little interdependence regarding engineering and construction among units, now there was a significant level of interdependence. Nabholz's success would depend in part on his making the necessary changes and adjustments in his thinking and leadership to ensure that these higher levels of interdependence were well managed and coordinated in the new organizational structure.

Sources: Suncor Energy 2005 Annual Report, www.suncor.com (accessed January 31, 2007); Speech given by Kevin Nabholz, March 14, 2002, Calgary, Alberta.

Another factor that can influence the need for integration is uncertainty. **Uncertainty** for a firm refers to the extent to which future input, throughput, and output factors cannot be forecast accurately. The more difficult it is to accurately forecast these factors, the greater uncertainty the firm faces. And the greater the uncertainty the firm faces, the greater the need for integration and coordination because as events unfold, individuals and organizational units have to coordinate their responses in real time.

uncertainty the extent to which future input, throughput, and output factors cannot be forecast accurately

Integration and coordination can be achieved through a variety of mechanisms.[10] The appropriateness of each mechanism is related to the level and type of interdependence and the extent of uncertainty in the environment.

Rules Rules essentially establish "if-then" guidelines for behaviour and consequence. For example, the rule may be "If you are going to miss class, then you must notify the professor in advance." In a sense, rules are the standard operating procedures (SOP) for the organization. In general, the more task independence, the more useful rules are as an integration mechanism. In contrast, the more task interdependence and uncertainty, the less useful rules are as an integration mechanism. For example, suppose you work as a manager in the promotion department of a record company. Concert cancellations because of weather, travel problems for the band, or any number of other unpredictable factors would likely make coordination and integration through the use of rules ineffective. Rules might work well in the accounting department of your record company, where the environment and requirements are standard and stable, but would likely be less effective in the changing environment of the promotion department.

Goals As task uncertainty and interdependence increase, the probability that preset rules can effectively coordinate tasks declines. Consequently, goals become a more effective coordination mechanism. Instead of specifying what individuals should do, goals specify what outcomes individuals should achieve. Effective goals define quantitative outcomes and often require high levels of effort to achieve. Specifying the outcomes, but not the process, maximizes flexibility in how workers get things done, yet facilitates integration by ensuring that people are working toward the same end. For example, university professors encounter students with a wide variety of needs and situations. Rather than provide professors with set rules, the university typically sets goals in terms of student proficiency. The goals, in terms of learning, ensure that professors are working toward the same end but have the flexibility to respond to specific needs and situations.

Values In cases of high task uncertainty and interdependence, values become an important coordinating mechanism. Values specify what is fundamentally important, like customer satisfaction, but unlike goals they do not specify quantitative outcomes. Values are a better integrating mechanism over goals when there is high uncertainty and high interdependence. Shared values ease coordination under these conditions, because they specify what is important while maintaining flexibility concerning exactly what or how things are accomplished.

Exhibit 8.2 helps illustrate the level of appropriateness of rules, goals, and values in conditions of low to high levels of uncertainty. The exhibit also helps illustrate an important practical matter—overlap. As a matter of practice, it is impossible to specify the line where rules stop being effective and goals start, or where goals stop being effective and values start. Consequently, as a manager you need to understand the principal relationship of rules, goals, and values with different levels of uncertainty. At the same time you will also need to use your judgment. You will have to judge how much of a combination of, say, rules and goals might be appropriate, and exactly when the uncertainty level gets high enough that as a coordination mechanism rules are largely not helpful to you.

Exhibit 8.2

Appropriateness of Rules, Goals, Values

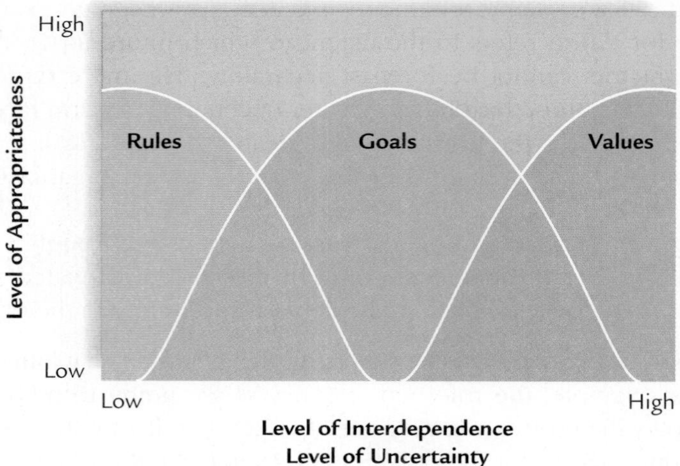

Formalization

formalization the official and defined structures and systems in decision making, communication, and control in an organization

One way to balance both separating and integrating people and activities is through formalization. **Formalization** can be thought of in terms of the official and defined structures and systems in decision making, communication, and control in the organization. These mechanisms can explicitly define where and how people and activities are separated as well as how they are brought together. While all organizations have to manage task specialization and integration, they vary substantially in how much formalization they use to accomplish this.

line of authority specifies who reports to whom

One of the common means of formalization is officially designating what we typically call **line of authority**. Line of authority essentially specifies who reports to whom. It is often called line of authority because in organizational charts a line is typically drawn between subordinates and their boss. If you are part of an organization that strictly adheres to lines of authority, consistently bypassing the lines to get things done could get you labelled as a rebel or as disrespectful. On the other hand, only looking to your boss in an organization that mostly ignores lines of authority might result in people perceiving you as lacking initiative or motivation.

unity of command the notion that an employee should have one and only one boss

More formal organizations also tend to stress **unity of command**. This is simply the notion that an employee should have one and only one boss. If you were working in a highly formal organization with a strong orientation to unity of command, you would only have one boss who would evaluate your new idea and who could direct your work. This does not mean that your boss would necessarily have the authority to approve your new-product idea, but only that you would not report to two different bosses.

span of control the number of employees reporting to a given supervisor

Additionally, more formal systems tend to specify span of control. **Span of control** refers to the number of employees reporting to a given supervisor. More formal organizations tend to have narrow rather than wide spans of control. The logic for this is fairly obvious. Normally, the fewer people you have to supervise, the more closely you can watch and control them. However, several factors can influence the effectiveness of span of control. First, the nature of the task is an important factor. All other things being equal, the more routine subordinates' tasks, the wider the effective span of control can be. In other words, as a manager you can effectively supervise more subordinates if they have predictable and routine tasks. Another factor influencing effective span of control is subordinates' capabilities. Generally, the greater the subordinates' capabilities, the less close supervision they require and the greater can be the effective span of control. Also, your own managerial capabilities influence effective span of control. The greater your managerial capabilities, the wider the span of control you can handle effectively. Putting these three factors together, you can see that if your subordinates are highly skilled and you are a highly capable manager, you can have an effective wide span of control, even with subordinates who have nonroutine jobs. Exhibit 8.3 provides a brief summary of key factors that influence effective span of control.[11]

Exhibit 8.3 Factors That Influence the Span of Control

- *Job complexity*—Jobs that are complicated require more managerial input and involvement and thus the span of control tends to be narrower.
- *Job similarity*—If one manages a group of employees performing similar jobs, the span of control can be considerably wider than if the jobs of subordinates are substantially different.
- *Geographic proximity of supervised employees*—Because employees who work in one location are more easily supervised than employees in dispersed locations, physical proximity to employees tends to allow a wider span of control.
- *Amount of coordination*—A narrower span of control is advisable in firms where management expends much time coordinating tasks performed by subordinates.
- *Abilities of employees*—Supervisors who manage employees who are more knowledgeable and capable can have a wider span of control than supervisors managing less knowledgeable and capable employees. The greater the abilities of employees, the less managerial inputs are required and thus a wider span of control is possible.
- *Degree of employee empowerment*—Because employees who are trusted and empowered to make decisions need less supervision than employees with less autonomy and decision-making discretion, supervisors who empower their employees can have a wider span of control.
- *Ability of management*—More capable managers can manage more employees than less competent managers. The abilities of managers to educate employees and effectively respond to their questions lessen the need for a narrow span of control.
- *Technology*—Communication technology, such as mobile phones, fax, email, and workshare software, can allow managers to effectively supervise employees who are not geographically proximate, have complex and different jobs, and require significant coordination.

Consistent patterns of span of control can affect the overall "shape" of the organization. Narrow span of control throughout the entire organization tends to result in a rather tall **tall organizational structure**, or one that has multiple layers or is high in terms of vertical differentiation. Wide span of control throughout the organization will generally lead to a more **flat organizational structure**. Given similar numbers of employees, a flat organization will have fewer layers in its hierarchy than a tall organization. Exhibit 8.4 shows examples of tall and flat organizational structures, as well as span of control.

tall organizational structure a structure that has multiple layers or is high in terms of vertical differentiation

flat organizational structure a structure that has fewer layers in its hierarchy than a tall organization

The appropriateness of a tall or flat organization is largely affected by the external environment. Tall and formal organizations tend to be slower at making decisions and responding to changes in the business environment. As a result, tall organizations tend to be best suited to stable external environments. Because many organizational environments have become more dynamic, managers often respond by trying to "flatten" their organizational structures—often removing whole levels of hierarchy and people in the

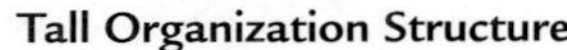

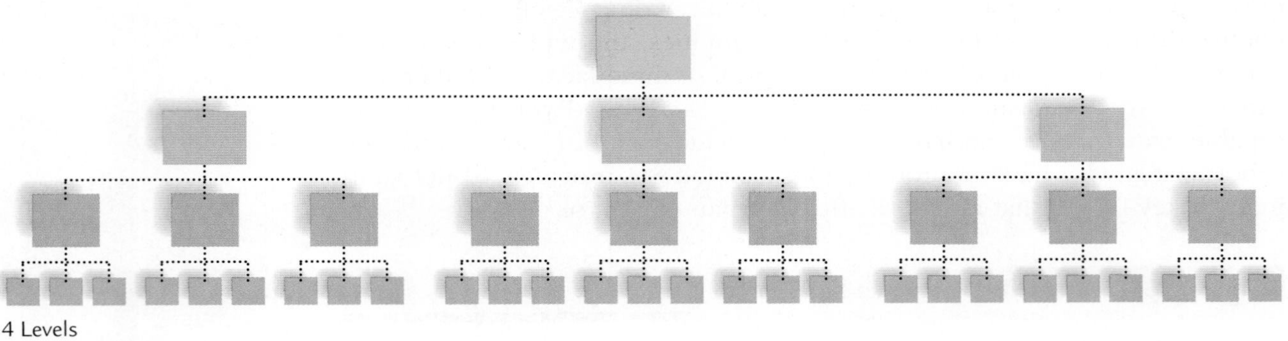

4 Levels
Span of Control = 3
Total Employees = 40

Flat Organization Structure

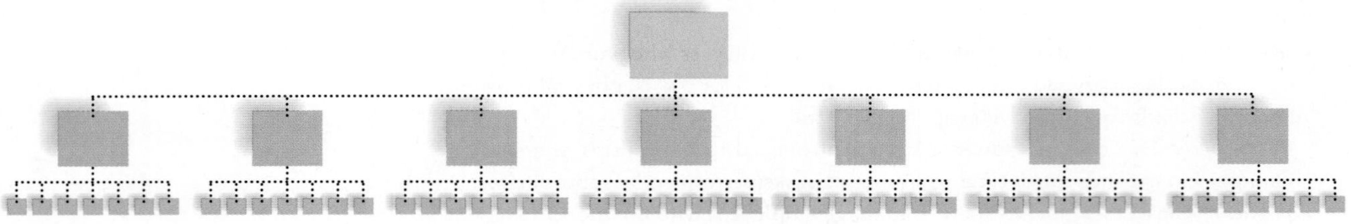

3 Levels
Span of Control = 7
Total Employees = 57

Exhibit 8.4

Tall and Flat Organization Structures

process, which is often called downsizing. They do this so that information does not have to travel as far (from the bottom to the top) for decisions to be made, meaning that they can be implemented faster.[12]

It is important to note some of the managerial challenges that this general movement to flat structures creates. As environmental uncertainty increases for many organizations, managers push toward flatter structures so that information can flow faster and decisions can be made more quickly. However, the environmental uncertainty also tends to result in more nonroutine tasks than routine tasks. This tends to push toward narrow spans of control, which in turn pushes toward taller, not the desired flatter, organizations. So what is the managerial implication and challenge of all this? Flatter organizations and wider spans of control with more nonroutine tasks are only possible if subordinates and managers have higher capabilities. This creates a premium for you as a manager to develop the ability to help your subordinates increase their capabilities and to increase your own managerial competencies.

Today and in the future, technology is arguably one of the most powerful factors influencing effective span of control and helping companies to be flatter. For example, *A Manager's Challenge: "Reach Out and Touch Someone"* describes how technology has enabled a human resource manager to retain his previous span of control despite having subordinates physically spread throughout Asia doing nonroutine work. Do you think the manager could have retained his previous span of control and effectiveness without technology? Does it seem to you that technology will increasingly allow subordinates to reside great distances away and still remain productive?

In summary, formalization mechanisms such as span of control, line of authority, and unity of command work to both separate and integrate people and activities. They do so in an explicit and official way. For example, your line of authority specifies who your boss is and separates you and your tasks

a manager's challenge technology

Reach Out and Touch Someone

Ed is the Asia-region human resource manager for DuPont. Just a few short years ago he and his staff all resided in Singapore—the regional headquarters for the company. Ed had a span of control of about eight people. He had subordinates with specialized responsibilities for training, compensation, recruiting, executive development and succession planning, benefits and pensions, performance management, and organizational development. Each area of specialization had to be coordinated to support the overall strategy and operations of the company in the region as well as the more specific activities of the various business units within specific countries. Ed's subordinates were for the most part experienced and well-trained professionals. Ed himself was an experienced HR executive.

However, as competition grew in the region and costs became an increasingly important factor, senior management looked for ways to both save money and increase the effectiveness of support units like HR. One of the factors that added expense was the firm's practice of bringing specialists who were the best at what they did into the regional headquarters, regardless of their nationality. Unfortunately, this meant that many had to be paid extra for relocating from their home country to Singapore (Ed, for example, was originally from Australia). In addition, while the company had business activities in virtually every country in Asia, the investments in some countries were greater than in others; for example, significant investment was being put into China. The implication for HR was that its support was needed to different degrees in different countries. Because of the company's recent and large investment in China, businesses in that country needed training support at a level several times that of other countries.

Executives wanted to lower costs and increase effectiveness. They lowered costs by placing employees in their home countries where possible. This avoided the extra fees employees were paid for working outside their home countries. They also located HR activities where they were needed most to increase effectiveness. For example, training was located in China where it was needed most. However, Ed relocated back to Australia. He was married and had two boys approaching their teenage years, and therefore was happy to do this. However, the change would mean he would have subordinates not next door to his office but scattered all around the region—a region where it is a 10-hour flight from Sydney to Tokyo.

In addition to Ed's managerial capabilities and the competency of his subordinates, technology played a key role in keeping his span of control about the same, despite a significant increase in physical distance between him and his subordinates. Ed instituted a biweekly staff meeting via conference calls. In many cases, his staff would join via mobile phone as they called in from hotels, airports, and factories around the region. Email also served as a significant means of keeping in touch and sharing documents. Even though it was hard to catch people in their offices because of so much travel, they could all access their email each day or several times a day to keep in touch and stay coordinated. On projects that needed input from several subordinates, Ed used software that enabled everyone to log on to the company's internal system and see the same document at the same time and make and see edits, changes, additions, and so on in real time.

While staying coordinated in such a large region was a challenge, Ed did not think it would have been possible to maintain his previous span of control and be effective were it not for all the technology he had access to. He also felt that in addition to saving money by not relocating so many people, many of his staff (including himself) were much more motivated and happy to be living in their home country because of various family and personal considerations. Thus, technology not only facilitated effective span of control but also increased employee satisfaction.

Source: Personal communication, 2002, 2003.

---

from others who have a different boss. At the same time, the line of authority integrates the other people who report to the same boss that you do.

Informalization

informal organization the unofficial but influential means of communication, decision making, and control that are part of the habitual way things get done in an organization

While virtually all organizations have some degree of formalization, even the most formal organizations also have some degree of informalization. The **informal organization** consists of the unofficial but influential means of communication, decision making, and control that are part of the habitual way things get done in the organization. Informal structures are often not represented in organizational charts, yet they pervade the day-to-day functioning of many organizations. For example, formally you may have only one boss to run your new-product idea by, but informally you may need to chat with a manager in another area to get her opinion on the feasibility of manufacturing the product. Just as the degree of formalization can vary from company to company, so too can the degree of informalization. But it can also vary not just from one company to another but from one country to another. For example, in Japanese companies much of the decision making, communication, and control are accomplished through informal, face-to-face meetings between people who do not have formal reporting relationships. This process is referred to as *nemawasi*. In Japanese organizations, *nemawasi* takes the form of informal conversations in which incremental decisions are made so that by the time an official meeting is held to make the formal decision, the decision has already been made informally.[13]

Centralization and Decentralization

centralized organizations organizations that restrict decision making to fewer individuals, usually at the top of the organization

decentralized organizations organizations that tend to push decision-making authority down to the lowest level possible

In addition to the extent to which the organization's structure is formal or informal, the extent to which it is centralized or decentralized is also important. Centralization and decentralization refer to the level at which decisions are made at the top of the organization or at lower levels. **Centralized organizations** tend to restrict decision making to fewer individuals, usually at the top of the organization. In contrast, **decentralized organizations** tend to push decision-making authority down to the lowest level possible. For instance, European multinational organizations tend to be decentralized and allow units in different countries to make decisions according to local conditions. Often this enables them to adapt to host government demands and different consumer preferences.[14] For many years, Philips, a large multinational electronics firm headquartered in the Netherlands, was viewed as one of the premiere examples of a decentralized international organization. Philips operated in over 60 countries around the world. Many of the larger-country units enjoyed considerable freedom and autonomy. For example, even though the V2000 videocassette recorder (the first VCR) was developed at the company's headquarters, the North American division of Philips refused to purchase and sell the product in Canada and the United States. Instead, North American Philips purchased a VCR made by a Japanese rival and resold it in Canada and the United States under the brand name of Philips.

Japanese firms, on the other hand, exhibit a stronger degree of centralization and tend *not* to delegate decisions as frequently as either European or North American firms.[15] Most Japanese multinational firms operate like centralized hubs into which information flows and from which decisions are announced to foreign subsidiaries. In fact, Japanese firms have encountered increasing complaints from host nationals in local subsidiaries about a "bamboo ceiling." This term refers to the exclusion of host nationals from strategic decision making because nearly all key positions in the subsidiary are occupied by Japanese expatriates sent by headquarters to ensure more centralized control.[16]

Often, students feel that formalization and centralization are essentially the same thing, and that informalization and decentralization are also synonyms. This is not the case (see Exhibit 8.5). You can have a very formal organization that is highly centralized, but you can also have a formal organization that is fairly decentralized. For example, as we illustrated above, Philips is a fairly decentralized company in that decisions are pushed down into the organization. At the same time, Philips is also relatively formalized. Lines of authority, unity of command, official policies, and so on are prevalent. In contrast, the Canadian Armed Forces are both formal and centralized. On the other hand, you can have a highly informal organization that is decentralized or highly centralized. For example, the research we just cited on Japanese firms suggests that on average they are relatively centralized but at the same time function through a high degree of informalization. Likewise, it is quite common for family-owned businesses to be both centralized and informal. That is, the owner makes most of the decisions but informal connections, communication, and control, rather than the formal structure or rules, dictate how things get done. In contrast, Club Med is fairly decentralized and informal. Each general manager of a resort is fairly free to make decisions that meet the needs of his or her unique market. Coordination is achieved through a vast array of informal relationships built up among general managers and corporate managers.

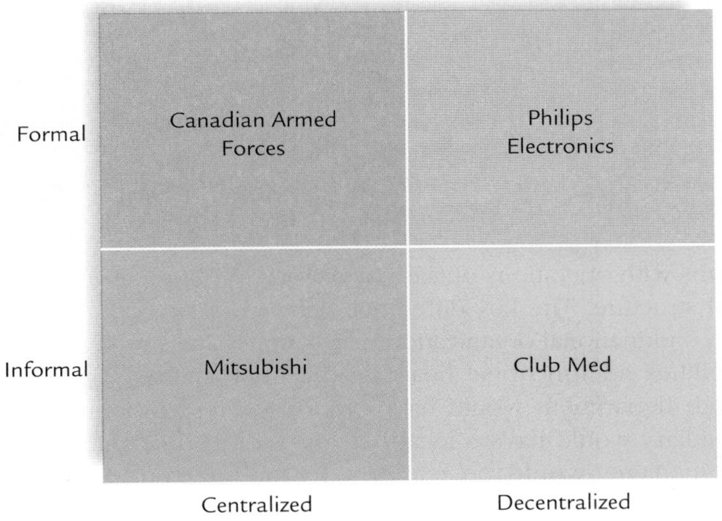

Exhibit 8.5

Combinations of Formal/Informal and Centralized/Decentralized

	Centralized	Decentralized
Formal	Canadian Armed Forces	Philips Electronics
Informal	Mitsubishi	Club Med

Some research suggests the more intense the firm's information needs, the more formal and centralized its structure becomes.[17] The Canadian television broadcasting market can be classified as a business sector that has a high demand for timely and accurate information. In the mid-1990s, CBC/Radio-Canada embarked upon a move to centralize its operations. After successfully implementing a few centralizing initiatives, the broadcaster decided to fully centralize programming in a Montreal location. The facility went fully functional in late 2004. The most immediate benefit to the CBC has been efficiency of resources; even with the expected addition of new stations over time, the need for additional staffing is believed to be minimal.[18]

Common Organizational Structures

Now that we have examined the core elements of organizing, we can explore some of the most common organizational structures. Although a variety of structures exist, six structures represent the most common forms. We examine each of these basic structures, although variations can be obtained by combining more than one form. In reality, most organizations do *not* have pure forms but have hybrids. Once we have reviewed these basic organizational structures and briefly examined their general strengths and weaknesses, we can then move to a more detailed discussion of the conditions that determine which type of structure you as a manager would want to adopt.

Functional Structure

Perhaps the simplest structure is the functional structure (see Exhibit 8.6). The functional structure organizes the firm around traditional functional areas such as accounting, finance, marketing, operations, and so on. This structure is one of the most common organizational structures in part because it separates the specialized knowledge of each functional area through horizontal differentiation and can direct that knowledge toward the firm's key products or services.

Exhibit 8.6

Functional Structure

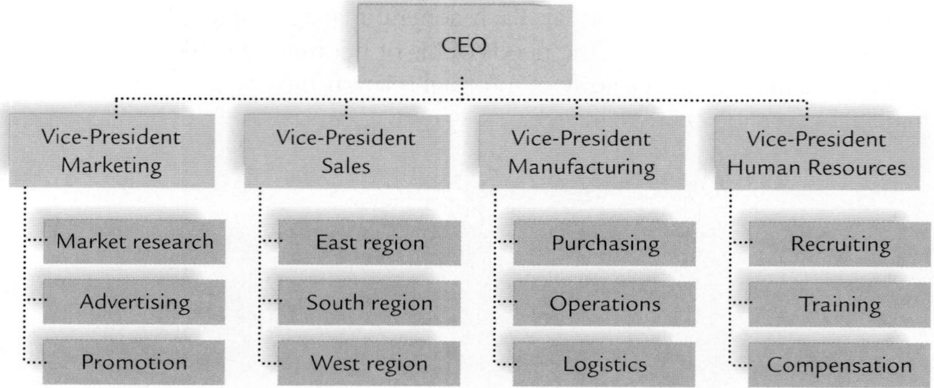

Firms with operations outside their domestic borders might also adopt a functional structure. The key difference between a purely domestic organization and a multinational organization with a functional structure is the scope of responsibilities for functional heads in the multinational firm. In a multinational, each department would have worldwide responsibilities. Thus, while each subsidiary would have a local human resource manager, the top human resource manager would be responsible for directing worldwide human resource activities such as hiring, training, appraising, or rewarding employees. This structure is most common when the technology and products of the firm are similar throughout the world.

The major advantages of this structure include the following:

- Well-suited to small to medium-sized firms with limited product diversification
- Facilitates specialization of functional knowledge and the creation of career paths
- Reduces duplication of functional resources
- Facilitates coordination within functional areas

A global functional structure can also reduce headquarters–subsidiary conflicts because operations throughout the world are integrated into their functional areas, and functional department executives are charged with global responsibility. This, in turn, enhances the overall international orientation of managers. For example, the higher a marketing manager rises in the marketing department, the more that manager needs to think about and understand the firm's global marketing issues.

The primary weaknesses of this structure include the following:

- Often creates problems of coordination across functional groups
- Creates restricted view of overall organizational goals
- Can limit the attention paid to customers as functional groups focus on their specific areas

- Can lead to slower organization response to market changes
- Often burdens chief executives with decisions that involve multiple functions

In an international setting, a functional structure has disadvantages when the firm has a wide variety of products and these products have different environmental demands, such as different government restrictions or standards, customer preferences, or performance qualities. This weakness is exacerbated when different functional departments experience different demands by geographic area. For example, if the accounting practices are similar between the United Kingdom and France but the advertising approaches differ, this will tend to exaggerate coordination difficulties between the accounting and marketing departments.

Product Structure

In a product structure, the firm is organized around specific products or related sets of products (see Exhibit 8.7). (While we use the term "product," it also applies to services.) Typically, each product group contains all the traditional functional departments such as finance, marketing, operations, human resource management, and so on. Each product is generally treated as a **profit centre**; that is, the related expenses are subtracted from the revenues generated by the sales of that product. Most commonly, the heads of the product or services groups are located in the headquarters of the company. However, this is not necessarily the case. For example, the headquarters for Honeywell's commercial and residential control product group is in Minnesota, while the headquarters for its commercial flight instruments product group is in Arizona.

profit centre a unit or product line in which the related expenses are deducted from the revenue generated

Exhibit 8.7

Product Structure

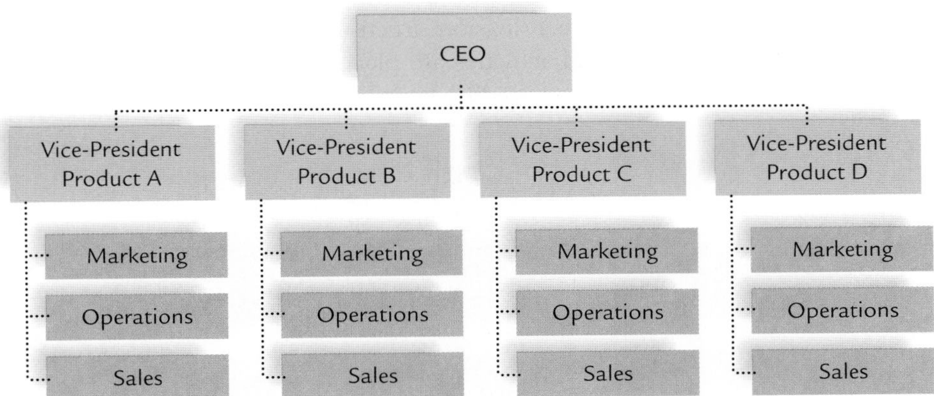

The principal advantages of a product structure include the following:

- Individuals in different functional areas within the product group focus more on the products and customers
- Performance of the product (i.e., profit and loss) is typically easier to evaluate
- There is usually greater product responsiveness to market changes
- It often reduces the burden on top executives in making operating decisions compared to the functional structure

The major disadvantages of the product structure include:

- Duplication and lack of economies of scale for functional areas (for example, IT, finance, human resources, and so on)

- Can create problems for customers who purchase products across multiple product groups
- There can be more conflicts between product group objectives and overall corporate objectives
- There is an increased likelihood of conflict between product groups and greater difficulty coordinating across product groups

Multinational firms also use global product structures. This typically happens when customer needs for a given product are more or less the same the world over. After Becton, Dickinson and Company adopted a global product structure, the head of the biosciences unit became responsible for global strategy formulation and implementation for those products.

Division Structure

The division structure can be viewed as an extension of a product structure. Exhibit 8.8 provides a partial organizational chart of the division structure of BD described at the outset of this chapter. Divisions typically consist of multiple products within a generally related area, though specific products may not necessarily be closely related. At J.D. Irving, a private family-owned company, there are six different business units organized to produce a diversified portfolio of products including forest and products, shipbuilding, retail, transportation, construction, and even food. Within each unit, there are very broad arrays of product groups and specific products. For example, the retail group within Irving consists of 10 different product groups like apparel, tissue products, screen printing and digital graphics, commercial communication, industrial parts and equipment, and products related to office environments. Within each of these groups are numerous specific products. Clearly, it takes a significant size and diversity of products before a division structure is appropriate. Typically in a division structure, all functional activities are placed within each division.

Exhibit 8.8

Division Structure

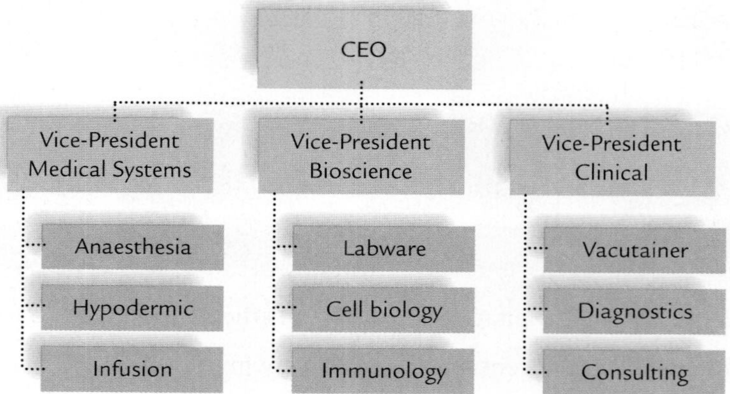

Common strengths of a division structure include:

- Organizing various product families within a division can reduce functional duplication and enhance economies of scale for functional activities
- To the extent that product families within a division serve common customers, customer focus can increase
- Cross-product coordination within the division is easier
- Cross-regional coordination within product families and within the division is often easier

Associated disadvantages include the following:

- Typically only appropriate for diversified, large companies with significant numbers of specific products and product families
- Can inhibit cross-division coordination
- Can create coordination difficulties between division objectives and corporate objectives
- Creates duplication of resources and departments such as human resources and marketing.

Like domestic firms, multinational firms can and do use this structure. In this case, each division is charged with worldwide responsibility. Because division structures are generally extensions of product structure, they have many of the same advantages and disadvantages. For large, diversified multinational firms, the division structure is one of the more common structures.

Customer Structure

As the name implies, customer structures are organized around categories of customers (see Exhibit 8.9). Typically, this structure is used when different categories of customers have separate but broad needs. For example, industrial customers might purchase a different set of products than retail customers.

Exhibit 8.9

Customer Structure

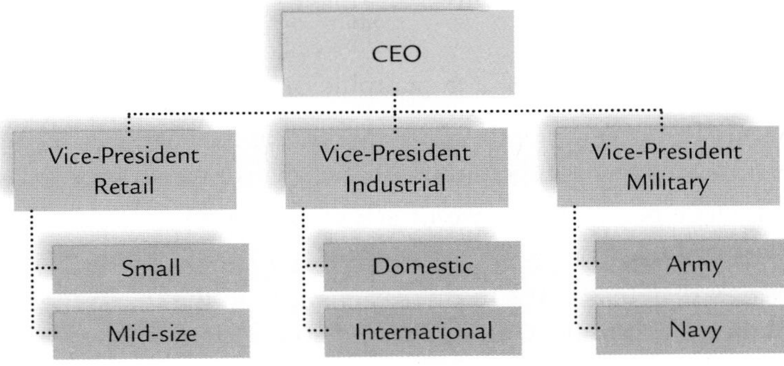

The primary strengths of this organizational structure include the following:

- Facilitates in-depth understanding of specific customers
- Increases responsiveness to changes in customer preferences and needs as well as responsiveness to moves by competitors to better serve customers

The primary weaknesses of the customer structure include the following:

- Typically leads to duplication of functional resources in each of the customer units
- Often creates difficulty in coordinating between customer units and corporate objectives
- Can fail to leverage technology or other strengths in one unit across other units

Many multinational firms find this organizational form difficult to implement because of differences among customers across regions and countries. For example, even though IBM initially had a consulting unit focused on government customers, it found that trying to organize the unit on a global basis yielded more disadvantages than advantages. This was because different governments had different needs and different ways of selecting computing solution providers.

Geographic/Regional Structure

Firms can structure themselves around various geographic areas or regions (see Exhibit 8.10). Within this structure, regional executives are generally responsible for all functional activities and products in their regions. The western regional vice-president might be responsible for all key business activities for British Columbia, Alberta, Saskatchewan, and Manitoba, as well as Yukon and the Northwest Territories. The individual regions are often treated as profit centres. In other words, each region's profitability is measured against the revenues it generates and the expenses it incurs.

Geographic/Regional

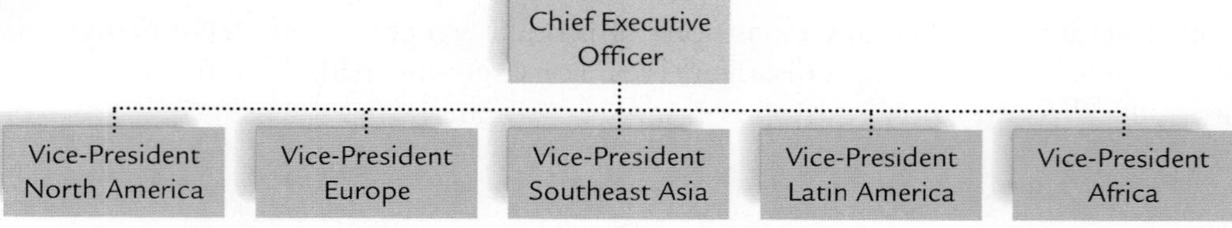

Strengths:

- Facilitates local responsiveness
- Develops in-depth knowledge of specific regions/countries
- Creates accountability by region
- Facilitates cross-functional coordination within regions

Weaknesses:

- Often creates cross-regional coordination difficulties
- Can inhibit ability to capture global scale economies
- Duplicates resources and functions across regions

The major advantages of a geographic or regional structure include:

- Typically leads to in-depth understanding of the market, customers, governments, and competitors within a given geographic area
- Usually fosters a strong sense of accountability for performance in the regional managers
- Increases responsiveness to unique changes in the market, government regulations, economic conditions, and so on for the region

The major disadvantages of a geographic or regional structure include:

- Often inhibits coordination and communication among regions
- Can increase conflict and coordination difficulties between regions and corporate office
- Normally leads to duplication of functional resources across the regions
- Separating production facilities across multiple regions can inhibit economies of scale
- Can foster competitive behaviour among the regions, which is particularly frustrating for customers who have operations across multiple regions

A number of multinational firms employ geographic/regional structures. This is primarily because customers' demands, government regulations, competitive conditions, availability of suppliers, and other factors vary significantly from one region of the world to another. The size or scope of the region is typically a function of the volume of business. For example, in consumer products companies, the Middle East and Africa are often included in the European region (EMEA—Europe, Middle East, and Africa) because the volume of sales in these areas is too small to justify separate regions. On the other hand, for most oil and gas companies with a geographic structure, the Middle East is a separate region all on its own.

Matrix Structure

A matrix structure consists of two organizational structures superimposed on each other (see Exhibit 8.11). A good approach to understanding a matrix structure is to recall from your studies of mathematics that the basic characteristic of any matrix is the presence of rows and columns. In organizational studies, this means that a matrix structure has one departmental structure occupying the rows that run across the organization, such as a project manager overseeing individuals from various departments (research and development, marketing, finance) that are working on the same project, while another structure occupies the columns, such as a manager that oversees individuals in the same department (marketing, for example) that are working on independent projects. As a consequence, for each individual located in the intersecting cells there are dual reporting relationships. That is, one person essentially reports to two bosses. These two structures can be a combination of the general forms already discussed. For example, the matrix structure might consist of product divisions intersecting with functional departments, or geographic regions intersecting with product divisions. This is essentially the structure that Procter & Gamble had for many years. The two overlapping structures are based on the two dominant aspects of an organization's environment.

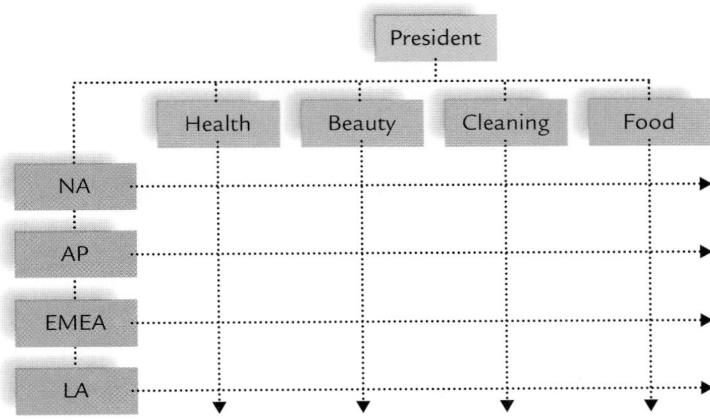

Exhibit 8.11

Matrix Structure

The major strengths of a matrix structure include:

- Typically facilitates information flow throughout the organization
- Can enhance decision quality because before key decisions are made the organization considers the two intersecting perspectives
- Is best suited to a changing and complicated business environment
- Can facilitate the flexible use of human resources

The major disadvantages of a matrix structure include:

- Often increases complexity of performance evaluations because people often have two bosses
- Can diffuse accountability
- Often leads to conflicts as the differing perspectives and objectives of the intersecting units collide

In multinational companies, matrix structures come and go with some frequency. They come into play quite often because while economies of scale for global product, division, or even customer structures are compelling, often regional differences relative to governments, culture, languages, and economies are also strong. This is precisely what has been behind P&G's product and regional matrix. In multinational companies, matrix structures go out because they are difficult to manage. ABB, a large industrial company based in Switzerland, for many years had a division/regional matrix. However, in the late 1990s senior executives determined that the conflicts and difficulties of managing the matrix outweighed the benefits and they changed to a global division structure.

Mixed Organizational Structures (Hybrids)

hybrid a structure that combines one or more organizational structures to gain the advantages and reduce the disadvantages of any particular structure

As we mentioned earlier, although there are pure forms, any combination of the basic organizational structures is possible. The typical objective of a mixed or a **hybrid** organizational structure is to gain the advantages of one structure and reduce its disadvantages by incorporating the strengths of different structures. Because many of these hybrid structures are reflected in contemporary organizational forms, we will explore this issue in more depth in the next section; however, Exhibit 8.12 provides an example of a hybrid functional, product, customer structure.

Exhibit 8.12
Hybrid Structure

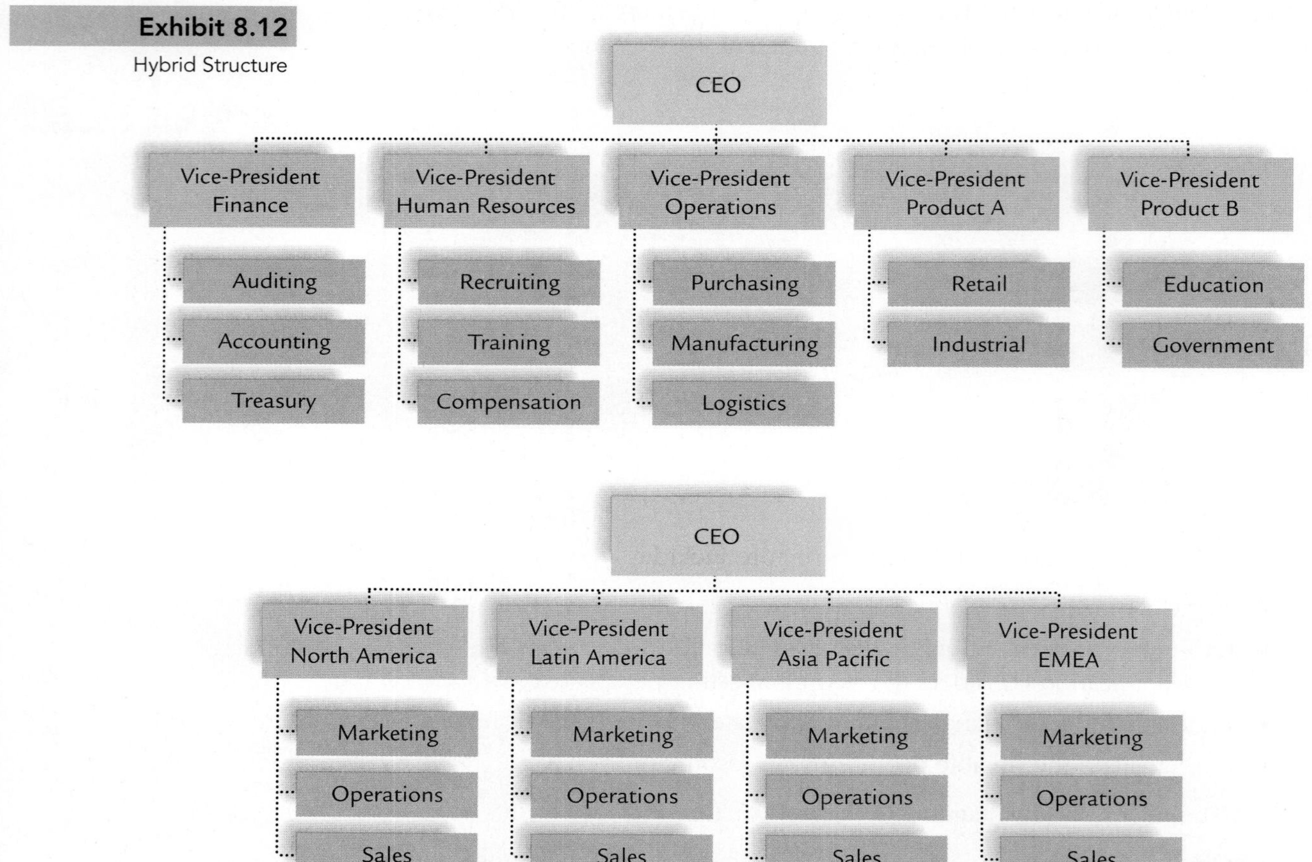

Network Organizational Structures

There are a wide variety of contemporary organizational structures. Many of them do not have common labels or names. This is in part because many of them have their essence not in organizational charts but in the configuration of organizational units and activities. Consequently, one logical way of addressing these forms is by using a concept you were introduced to in the previous chapter—the value chain. Much of what managers are doing in contemporary structures is reconfiguring the firm's value chain in an effort to gain cost savings and specialization benefits and to improve integration and coordination.

While it might be slightly oversimplified, often these contemporary structures are referred to as **network structures**. However, even if we adopt this term, it is too generic to reflect the variety of structures. At a minimum we should not think of one generic network structure. Rather, we should think of a "low networked" to "high networked" continuum. At the low-networked end would be structures in which the quantity and magnitude of externally networked activities is limited. That is, a firm would own and execute most of its primary and support value chain activities and network with outside organizations for only a limited number of more minor value chain activities. At the high-networked end of the spectrum would be structures in which the quantity and magnitude of externally networked activities is nearly unlimited. At the high end of the continuum, the number of externally networked value chain activities would exceed those owned and executed internally.

network structures formal or informal relationships among units or organizations (e.g., along the firm's value chain)

To illustrate this, let's start at the low end of the continuum. One of the simplest ways of taking a value chain activity and networking with an external organization is to outsource that activity. **Outsourcing** is the practice of taking a significant activity within the organization and contracting that activity out to an independent party. For example, Xerox has a multibillion-dollar contract with EDS to perform virtually all of Xerox's IT functions. In fact, a major portion of EDS's revenues comes from performing virtually all the IT functions for a variety of customers (see Exhibit 8.13).

outsourcing the practice of taking a significant activity within the organization and contracting it out to an independent party

Exhibit 8.13

Outsourced Structure

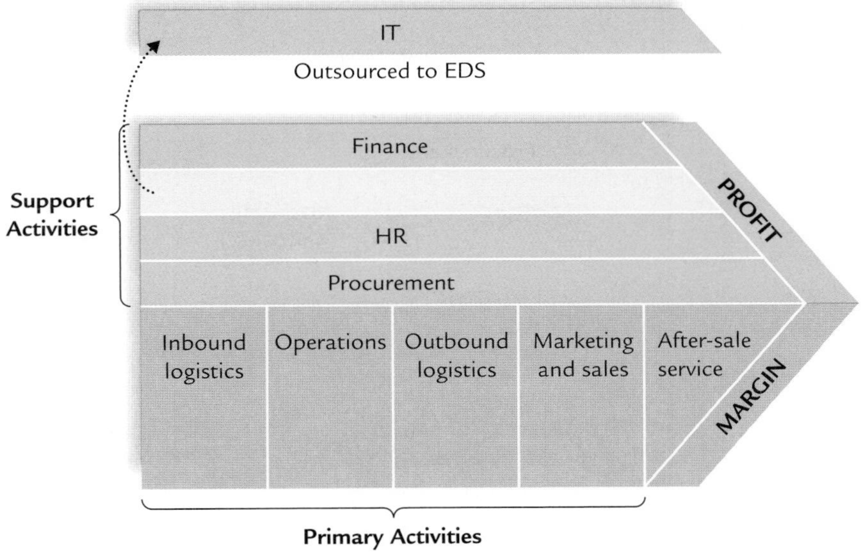

IT
Outsourced to EDS
Support Activities
Finance
HR
Procurement
Inbound logistics
Operations
Outbound logistics
Marketing and sales
After-sale service
PROFIT
MARGIN
Primary Activities

Nike outsources or contracts out essentially all of its shoe manufacturing, or what is essentially the operations segment of the primary activities in its value chain. It is networked or connected to its many contract manufacturers. In fact, it is so tightly connected that it can design a shoe at its Beaverton, Oregon, headquarters, send the blueprints via satellite to one of its contractors, and receive back by courier a prototype shoe from a contract factory all within a week. It is important to note that, increasingly, activities that executives once believed could only be done internally such as IT, human resource administration, design, manufacturing, sales, and customer support, are being outsourced today. Technology has made it possible to network activities together and retain reliability as well as lower costs.

At the high end of the continuum, a firm would have more value chain activities networked to external organizations than owned and executed internally. To illustrate this, suppose that you were better than anyone else at clothing design. Suppose further that in creating your company, you formulated a strategy in which you wanted to compete by having superior design, world-class raw materials, and close relationships with retailers. Based on this strategy, you might want to own and control only a few elements of the entire value chain. In today's environment, you could design an organization in which you performed design, procurement, and sales, but virtually nothing else. You could network with a company such as Kleysen Transport to perform all of your inbound logistics. You could network with various garment manufacturers in Asia to produce your designs. You could network with Canada Post to perform all of your outbound logistics. You could network with CorporaTel (a Canadian customer relationship provider headquartered in the Maritimes) to handle all of your customer service. You could network with MTS Allstream to run your internet and IT functions. You could network with Grant Thornton to run your HR, finance, and tax functions. You could then focus your energies on elements of the value chain (design, procurement, and sales) that you believed would give you a strategic advantage (see Exhibit 8.14).

Exhibit 8.14

Network Structure

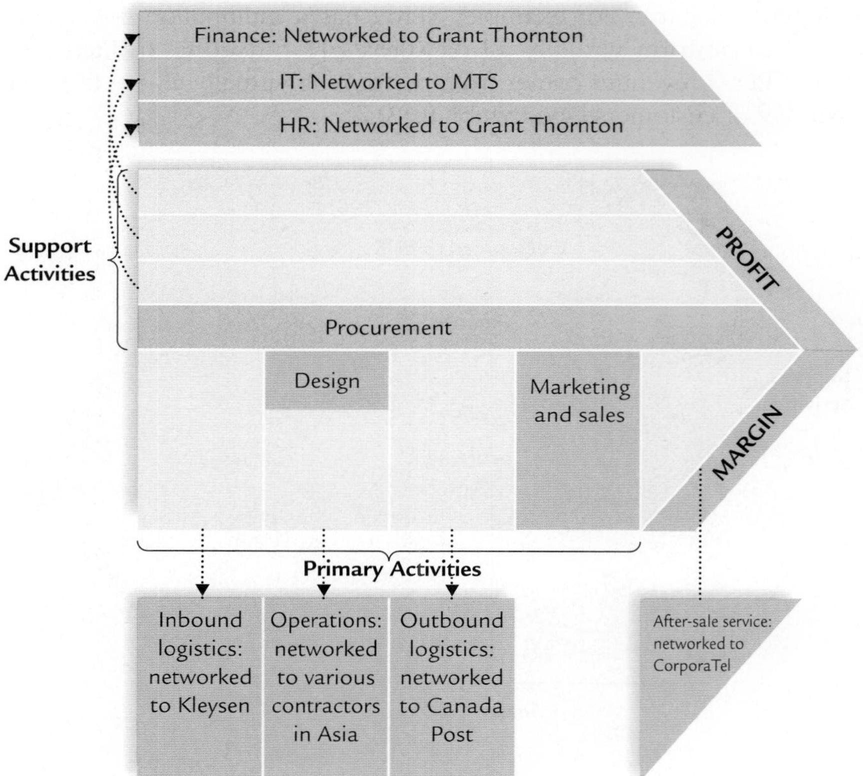

Using the value chain as a tool for understanding contemporary organizational forms, you can see that the potential configurations of value chains in terms of what a company internally owns and controls and what it networks with others to provide are almost infinite. Today you can network to have subelements of any value chain activity performed by others or you can network entire pieces of the overall value chain. For example, National Semiconductor Corporation (NSC) realized substantial savings within its global supply chain by outsourcing its logistics activities. The company, which reported US$2.1 billion in net sales in 2006, distributes semiconductor chips and related products to thousands of customers worldwide. As volume grew and demand for faster delivery increased, NSC decided it needed the expertise of a provider to handle distribution and value-added inventory functions. It outsourced its inventory and distribution activities to FedEx.[19]

Like the more traditional structures, network structures have both advantages and disadvantages. One of the most compelling theoretical advantages was argued to be that networking would allow managers to focus on core competencies or the activities that yield competitive advantage. By concentrating on core activities, managers could do them better. To some extent this is true. However, the "noncore" activities that are networked cannot simply be contracted out and forgotten. The reality is that it takes time, attention, energy, and skill to manage these relationships with external organizations. Even if Xerox determines that IT functions are not core and outsources them to EDS, if EDS does not deliver what Xerox needs, then Xerox's performance suffers. Simplified, network structures can give you greater focus and specialization on specific value chain activities, but they also come with the challenge of coordinating and integrating the organizations that are performing the networked activities.

Summary Observations

As you look back through this section of the chapter and different structures, you may notice an interesting pattern. In general, the advantages and disadvantages of various structures correspond reasonably well to either gaining or losing specialization or integration. This is because when you separate parts of the organization you tend to gain the advantages of specialization. What you get in terms of specialization by functions, products, customers, regions, or value chain activities depends on how you separate or divide units. However, when you separate units you enhance the challenge of integrating their activities. Many of the basic elements of organizing that we discussed at the outset of this chapter are used in part to facilitate more effective integration. For example, rules, objectives, and values can all be used in any of the common structures to facilitate greater integration and coordination.

Many of the more modern and popular concepts regarding organizational structure are designed to help companies maintain the advantages of specialization and overcome or at least reduce the integration and coordination difficulties that naturally occur. For example, GE's former CEO Jack Welch made the term **boundaryless organization** popular. The notion was that the barriers to effective integration that hierarchy, function, geography, and so on cause would be overcome by teams of people who were empowered to work across boundaries. The result is information and skilled employees are able to move across traditional organizational barriers to where they are needed most. However, as modern as this term may sound, it really represents a tool that has been used in organizations for a long time. Teams and committees composed of members from different areas of the company have been around for decades as a means of overcoming integration challenges. Likewise, modern terms such as "quality blackbelts" (i.e., internal experts on quality) or "best practice champions" are contemporary reincarnations of the long-time practice of designating liaisons. **Liaisons** are individuals who are designated to act as a bridge or connection between or among different areas such as quality control, manufacturing process, and so on.

boundaryless organization an organization where barriers to effective integration are overcome by people empowered to work across boundaries

liaisons individuals designated to act as a bridge or connection between different areas of a company

In the end, one of the fundamental dynamics that all managers must understand about organizing is that both specialization and integration are needed. Specialized activities have to be performed, but they must come together in a way that offers competitive value to a customer. Each of the basic

Boundaryless Organization by Michael Hitt

mymanagementlab

structures delivers advantages and disadvantages regarding both specialization and integration. Regardless of the modern buzzwords or legacy lexicon, most managers face a dual challenge. On the one hand, they want to capture the desired advantages of a given structure. However, every structure has its natural disadvantages. As a result, managers also have to use formal or informal mechanisms to reduce or eliminate these natural disadvantages.

Designing Organizations

Fundamentally, in designing organizations managers face the challenge of capturing both specialization and integration advantages while minimizing the often mirror-image disadvantages. This begs the question, "How should they decide to actually structure an organization?" As we have already mentioned, the two main determinants of this decision are the external environment and the strategy of the company. Now we want to go into this in greater detail.

External Environment

As we mentioned earlier, a key factor in determining the match between the environment and organizational structure is environmental uncertainty.[20] While we offered a somewhat simpler description of environmental uncertainty earlier in this chapter, now we want to expand on that description. We do this with two related but separate constructs: the extent to which the environment is (1) complex and (2) dynamic.

Environmental Complexity Let's examine the first element of environmental uncertainty—complexity. Simplified, environmental complexity is fundamentally about the breadth and depth of differences and similarities—complex environments have greater breadth and depth of differences than simple environments. While differences and similarities could be assessed potentially in terms of thousands of dimensions, there are several core categories: products, customers, technology, competitors, suppliers, and geography.

The complexity relative to products can vary widely from firm to firm. For example, a BIC pen is made up of approximately seven parts. Each part is produced with relatively low technology, and the assembly of the parts into the final product also involves relatively low technology. At the other end of the continuum, when Research In Motion puts together a BlackBerry, it has a set of very sensitive high-technology components to assemble. The components range from a simple plastic case and screws to microprocessors and sophisticated circuitry. Thus, Research In Motion has a more complex product environment relative to a BIC pen.

Customers constitute another important category when assessing environmental complexity. For example, McDonald's serves hamburgers to millions of customers each day, but the differences among these customers is relatively small compared to their overall size. In contrast, Toyota serves millions of customers each year but their needs are different enough that key aspects of Toyota cars, such as the suspension systems and emissions, are very different from one region of the world to another.

Technology complexity includes both the diversity of technology required and the level of its sophistication. For example, Research In Motion uses a variety of wireless technologies in its products. The technology involved in the products is of a depth that it requires a high level of understanding In sophisticated communication technology to design and produce.

Competitors also constitute an important category of environmental complexity. The greater the number and diversity of competitors, the more complex the firm's environment is. For example, in terms of television broadcasting, while CanWest Global has a fairly complex product environment, it has a much simpler competitor environment. For all intents and purposes, the only other Canadian competitors are the CBC and CTV. This does not mean that competing against the two is easy but only that its competitor environment is more simple than that of a company like clothing retailer Roots that has literally thousands of clothing manufacturers and labels competing for the same customers.

Like competitors, the greater the number and diversity of suppliers, the more complex the firm's environment is. For example, if we return to CanWest, despite its having a simpler competitor environment, it has a complex supplier environment. CanWest uses broadcast technology and programs that necessitates countless suppliers that provide products ranging from gaffer tape and microwave dishes to episodes of *24*.

The final category, geographic complexity, is included not because it is separate from the previous categories but because it tends to have a significant impact on all the categories above. This is principally because the more geographic regions covered, the greater the probability of differences across the other categories. For example, the greater the number of countries in which a firm operates, the greater the probability of dissimilarities between the countries (their governments, laws, customer preferences, language, etc.). These differences can increase the breadth and depth of differences relative to products, customers, technology, competitors, and suppliers. Consequently, the greater the geographic scope is, the greater the complexity.

Environmental Dynamism The second element to evaluate the overall uncertainty of the environment is the extent to which the environment is static or dynamic.[21] Static environments may have few or many factors, but these factors tend to remain stable over time. For example, the quarrying technology for limestone as well as the component parts has changed little in the past 30 years. In contrast, factors in dynamic environments change rapidly. For example, advancements in areas like television broadcasting technology have changed significantly over the past 30 years. The fashion industry operates in an even more dynamic external environment. Roots faces an environment in which colours, fabric, and styles change not just year to year but season to season.

Firms facing dynamic environments often describe them as "white water" environments, referring to the challenges of navigating a raft down the ever-changing rapids of a river. The rapidly changing external environment typically requires quick internal organization changes. While we emphasize the importance of change in each chapter, we will discuss at length why organizational change is difficult and systematic methods for enhancing success in Chapter 15.

By combining the dimensions of simple–complex and static–dynamic, we can create a four-cell matrix that provides a broad backdrop against which organizational design structures can be placed (see Exhibit 8.15). In general, the more complex and dynamic the environment, the more the organizational structure needs to coordinate different groups' efforts and the greater the speed with which this coordination needs to take place. This means that the more complex and dynamic the firm's environment, the more the structure will need to make use of mechanisms that facilitate coordination and integration, such as values, teams, and liaisons.

Exhibit 8.15
Matrix of Organizational Uncertainty

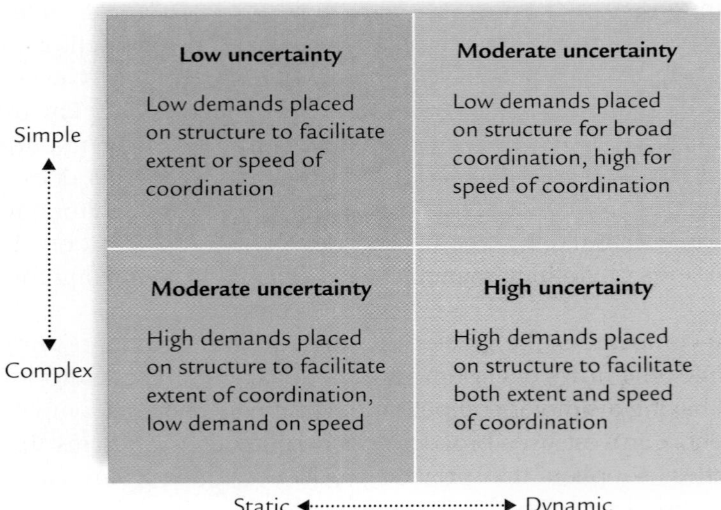

Organization Strategy

The second major element that managers must consider in designing their organization's structure is the company's strategy.[22] Unfortunately, there are no simple rules that we can use to say, "If your company's strategy is X then you should adopt structure Y." However, there are a few principles that can help you understand the relationship between strategy and structure.

The first principle of relating structure to strategy is that the structure should complement and leverage the strategy. But how can we determine this? In reality, this is a hard question to answer because there is no "one way" of formulating strategy. However, we can gain important insights into this principle by examining one of the most common strategy formulation approaches. As we discussed in the previous chapter on strategy, one of the common means of formulating strategy is to determine the company's core competencies or resources that produce value for customers, are hard to imitate, and are scarce. By focusing on these identified competencies or resources, we can more easily evaluate the fit or lack thereof of a proposed structure with the strategy.

A Manager's Challenge: "Restructuring Citicorp Credit Card" provides an effective illustration of how a company changed its structure to fit with its strategy of low cost and brand identity. What role do you think changes in the European Union played in Citicorp restructuring its organization and reconfiguring its value chain? What role do you see transportation as well as telecommunications technology playing in Citicorp Credit Card's new structure?

Moving from Domestic to International Structures

Up to this point, we have mentioned the basic organizational structures in terms of both a domestic and international context. Now we want to take a more focused look at organizational structure in an international context. Very few firms begin as international organizations. Most start in one country and for a period of time focus on the customers within that country. Although international organizations would be easier to understand if they evolved steadily and systematically, they do not. However, there is a general

a manager's challenge | globalization

Restructuring Citicorp Credit Card

In the 1990s, Citicorp Credit Card executives faced the significant challenge of how to restructure their organization to complement the company's strategy. Their strategy called for emphasizing the Citicorp brand and leveraging their global size to capture economies of scale and reduce costs.

As one of the largest banks in the world, Citicorp had global brand recognition. In general, people associated good customer service and stability with the brand. Citicorp executives in the credit card business felt that they could leverage their brand to differentiate their products. Credit card customers valued good customer service and wanted a stable company behind their card. It had taken Citicorp decades to build up its brand recognition and reputation—few competitors would be able to imitate it.

However, the credit card business is one of very thin margins. Since the price of credit cards (that is, the interest charged to customers) is transparent and widely publicized, competing on price by offering lower and lower interest rates is not an attractive way for Citicorp to make money. Controlling costs is really the key to increasing profit margins.

To determine how to leverage the company's brand name and control costs, Citicorp executives examined their value chain. They described their value chain in simple terms. First, they marketed their branded credit card to customers. Then they had to manufacture the "blanks." Blanks are simply the plastic cards without the individual's information printed on it (name, number, expiration date, etc.) or encoded on the magnetic strip. After the blanks were manufactured, they were then "printed." Individual information was printed and encoded onto the card. Once printed, the cards were mailed to the respective customers. The customers then used their cards to make purchases and those transactions were processed. Finally, the customers were billed, money was collected, and customer questions were answered.

Prior to the restructuring, Citicorp Credit Card had what would best be called a geographic structure. That is, all the elements of the value chain were replicated in every major country. While this allowed each country to focus on its customers and respond rapidly to unique competitive situations, it often resulted in different levels of customer service, which hurt the global brand image. The duplicated activities also increased costs.

Given its strategy, how should Citicorp Credit Card restructure itself? One of the first things it did was centralize marketing and brand management. This helped the company standardize and make consistent the company logo, colours, and customer service standards. To capture economies of scale, all manufacturing of blanks for Canada, the United States, and Europe was relocated to the United States. For Canada and the United States, these blanks were then printed in the United States. For all of Europe the blanks were shipped to the Netherlands and printed there. Once printed, all cards for Europe were mailed from the Netherlands. Again to capture economies of scale, virtually all transactions for all of Europe, Canada, and the United States were processed in the United States. Because of different languages and currencies, customer service was kept in each country. However, with the introduction of the euro, regional customer service centres are being established and operated by multilingual customer service agents.

This modern structure defies simple classification. Some activities, like brand management, are centralized, while others, like customer service, are much more decentralized. Yet, the structure complements the strategy. By centralizing brand management, Citicorp has ensured that customers continue to see a consistent image of a stable and customer service–oriented company. By consolidating manufacturing of blanks as well as the printing and mailing of cards, Citicorp significantly lowered the cost per unit. This was especially true for processing transactions. The low cost of sending data internationally allowed Citicorp to consolidate its technicians as well as hardware and software.

The full result of the restructuring will not be known for years, but the preliminary results are positive. Although executives will not disclose specific results, they report that revenues are up and costs are down substantially. This combination means that profits have also increased significantly.

Source: Personal communication, 2003.

relationship between the nature of the firm and its structure. This relationship was first proposed over 30 years ago[23] and has generally been supported,[24] including recently.[25] Simplified, the theory and findings are presented in Exhibit 8.16.

Exhibit 8.16

International Strategy and Structure

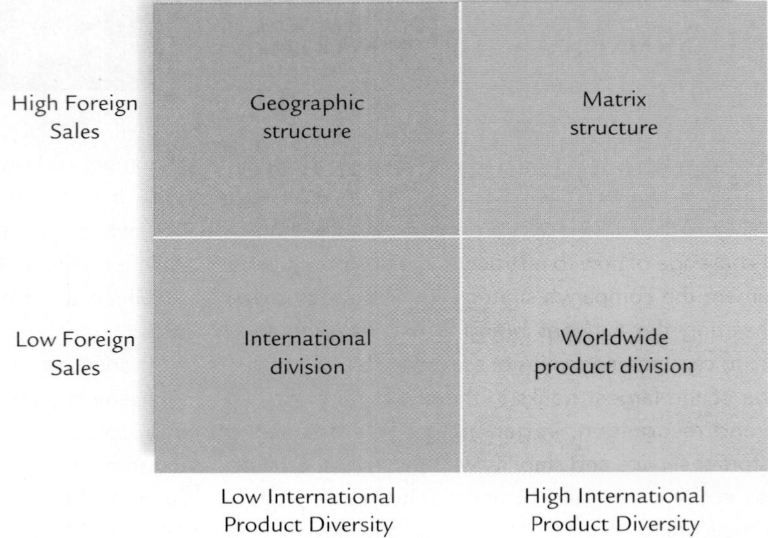

The first dimension of the matrix is the extent of foreign sales. For example, 97 percent of Nokia's sales are made outside of its home country of Finland. The second dimension of the matrix is the extent of product diversification. Product diversification is the extent to which the firm has many different products across many different segments and even industries. For example, Nokia sells primarily mobile phones and network equipment for mobile phone systems. This represents fairly low product diversification. In contrast, GE has many different products across such diversified industries as jet engines, lighting, medical equipment, television and broadcasting, plastics, and power plants.

Low foreign sales and low product diversification generally lead to the formation of an international division to look after international sales. Because there is not that much in foreign sales to look after and because the products are relatively similar, it works to put all the international sales of all products under one roof—the international division. This is what Mississauga's Parker Management Consulting Incorporated (PMC, Inc.) did when it launched PMC International, a separate division that serviced governments and offered private-sector consulting services for international clients.

Low product diversification but high foreign sales usually lead to a geographic structure. This was the case with Nokia. It was divided into five major geographic regions—Europe, Middle East and Africa, North America, Latin America, and Asia Pacific.

Low foreign sales but high product diversification typically leads to global product divisions. In the case of low foreign sales and low product diversification, it makes sense to put all foreign sales under one roof. However, when you have low foreign sales but high product diversification, it makes the most sense to put the foreign sales under the roof of each product.

High foreign sales and high product diversification typically lead to a matrix structure. This was the case for ABB. Like GE, ABB is a large industrial company with a very diversified set of products from train locomotives to power transmission. Because the products are different, the company needed to separate them by product. However, because international sales are a large percentage of overall sales, the company also had a geographic structure. In combination, this formed a product–geography matrix structure.

Thus, while there are some associations between strategy and structure in international firms, there is not a clear sequence of development. At best, it seems that the development of international organizations can be divided into two basic states: initial international structures and advanced international structures. Although most international organizations do not jump directly into advanced international structures, there is no consistent sequence companies follow. Rather, the advanced global structures are determined more by such factors as the size of the organization's international sales, product diversity, size of foreign R&D, and foreign manufacturing.[26]

Domestic Organization with an Export Department As firms venture out from their domestic market to foreign ones, they usually begin with a limited number of products. Typically, the products sold in foreign markets are designed and produced in the domestic market. Consequently, the primary international task is exporting the products to foreign markets. At this stage, most firms simply add an export department to their existing structure to handle the specialized tasks, such as international shipping and customs regulations.

Domestic Organization with an International Division Once the volume of exports exceeds the capabilities of a few specialists, firms commonly establish an international division. International divisions typically are responsible for all functional activities relative to international markets. The international division often has its own small department for accounting, finance, marketing, and sales. However, production activities are not usually part of the international division. Products are produced within the normal domestic organizational structure and then modified or simply turned over as is to the international division. Consequently, the products that tend to be pushed into the international division are those that have broad appeal and for which there are relatively fewer customer differences across countries.

Adding an international division has a number of advantages. First, it is an efficient means of dealing with the international market when a firm has limited experience. The focus on international activities and issues within the division can foster a strong professional identity and career path among its members. It also allows for specialization and training in international activities, which can be valuable later when the firm moves more heavily into the international marketplace and needs individuals with global capabilities. The focus on international markets, competitors, and environments can also facilitate the development of a more effective global strategy. Further, because the top officer of the international division often reports to the CEO (or similar senior executive), international issues often receive high-level corporate consideration and support with this structure.

One major weakness of an international division is its dependence on other divisions for products and support. Because domestic sales of a particular product often make up the largest percentage of the product's overall sales, low priority may be given to international sales. Other parts of the firm that supply products and services to the international division may be unwilling to make modifications that cost them time and money, even if the changes would facilitate greater international sales.

Advanced Global Structures As international sales as a percentage of overall sales increase and as the organization expands into a larger number of countries, it becomes increasingly difficult to maximize the benefits of an international division and minimize the weaknesses. When the organization outgrows its initial international structure, it can choose from among six advanced global structures. As mentioned, there is no particular sequence from one structure to another. These six advanced global structures correspond to the basic functional, geographic/regional, product, division, customer, and matrix structures already discussed, except that they have global rather than domestic scope and reach.

Organizing to Think Globally and Act Locally

globalization the tendency to integrate activities on a coordinated, worldwide basis

Given the increasingly international environment in which organizations compete, it is important to examine one other factor that managers must consider when designing organizational structures—globalization or localization demands.[27] **Globalization** is the tendency to integrate activities on a coordinated, worldwide basis. Firms are pushed in the direction of globalization when benefits gained from worldwide volume, efficiencies, or economies of scale are significant. These benefits could include economies of scale for production, greater leverage of high-cost distribution networks, and greater leverage of expensive research and development activities. In a variety of industries, the minimally efficient production scale is beyond what could be supported in a single market. If we consider the operations at Boeing, for example, the break-even point for a new commercial aircraft is approximately 300 planes, with each plane costing in excess of US$100 million, which requires total sales of US$30 billion. To get an acceptable return on its investment, Boeing has no choice but to try to develop planes that will have global appeal because the US market alone is not large enough. The high level of research and development and scale economies that a company like Boeing experiences pushes many companies toward globalization and to centralization of activities such as product development and manufacturing.

localization the tendency to differentiate activities country by country

By contrast, differences among countries and customer preferences are two key factors that push toward localization. **Localization** is the tendency to differentiate activities country by country. Firms are pushed in the direction of localization when benefits from location-specific specialization and adaptation are significant and factors such as economies of scale are small. Procter & Gamble recently faced the pressures of localization for a laundry detergent it developed. Although P&G wanted to develop one detergent, Visor, for all of Europe and capture the efficiencies of a single development, manufacturing, and marketing effort, it found significant differences between countries. These differences pushed P&G from globalization toward localization. For example, it found that Germans prefer front-loading washers, while the French prefer top-loading washers. This created a problem. The detergent did not get distributed as well among the clothes when poured into a front-loading washer. And as P&G discovered, it is not easy to get an entire nation to change from front-loading to top-loading washers. As this example illustrates, the greater the differences between countries and the more significant these differences are for a product or service, the greater the need for localization.

The P&G example also shows how forces can simultaneously push toward globalization and localization, requiring firms to be globally integrated and locally responsive. In the case of P&G, the manufacturing process pushed for integration because making detergent is basically continuous; that is, like many chemical products, the final product is delivered after a long process of mixing various chemicals in different states and at different temperatures until you get the desired chemical reactions for the final product. This means that the process cannot be stopped at discrete points and finished elsewhere, nor is it economical to alter the process to create different detergents. Both these factors push toward globalization, or the concentration of manufacturing activities without much modification for local market conditions. On the other hand, the significant differences in laundry machines between Germany and France pushed toward localization. P&G solved the problem by developing a plastic ball into which detergent could be poured and that could then be thrown in with the clothes in a front-loading machine.

The plastic ball was designed to dispense the detergent gradually through small holes as the ball bounced around with the clothes while they were being washed.

In general, firms heavily involved in international business face strong pressures for both integration and specialization. For example, they need specialists for marketing to Germans, dealing with French government officials, and complying with Canadian accounting rules. However, they also have greater needs for integration, which can be met in a variety of ways.

Direct Contact Often, direct contact is an important means of integration by sharing information. One of the largest firms in the world, Matsushita, has an interesting way of accomplishing this. Because research and development is vitally important in the consumer electronics industry, Matsushita has a large central research and development lab. To make sure that managers know what is going on in the lab and to ensure that lab scientists know what the market's emerging needs are, Matsushita holds an annual internal trade show. Senior managers throughout Matsushita's worldwide operations gather and examine research results and potential new products. Managers also feed back information about market differences, customer preferences, and competitor positioning to research and development scientists. The result is a massive sharing of information that has helped keep Matsushita ahead of competitors.

Liaison Liaison roles are designed to enhance the links, and therefore information flows, between two or more groups, be they teams, departments, divisions, or subsidiaries. Part of Matsushita's success in the videocassette recorder (VCR) market was due to a purposeful liaison. The vice-president in charge of Matsushita's US subsidiary was also a member of the senior management committee of the parent company in Japan and spent about a third of his time in Japan. This facilitated the link between headquarters and the United States, which was the most important consumer market for VCRs. In addition, the general manager of the US subsidiary's video department had previously worked for many years in the video product division of the production and domestic marketing organization in Japan. This created a strong link between the product division in Japan and the US subsidiary. Also, the assistant product manager in the US subsidiary had spent five years in the central VCR manufacturing plant in Japan. Through these three individuals, Matsushita succeeded in ensuring that vital links at the corporate, product, and factory levels were established between Japan and the United States.

Teams When integration needs arise across a wide set of functional areas, teams can be an effective integration mechanism. Netherlands-based Philips is an example of a firm that uses teams as an integrative mechanism. This may stem from the fact that the firm was founded by two brothers, one an engineer and the other a salesman, who worked together in charting Philips's early strategic course. Whatever the origin, Philips has long had an office of the president as opposed to a single CEO. The office of the president is composed of a technical, commercial, and financial executive. Furthermore, for each product, there is a team of junior managers from commercial and technical functions. These teams integrate various perspectives and information around a single product to ensure that interfunctional differences are resolved early and that necessary design, manufacturing, and marketing issues are integrated from the outset in an effort to increase the success of a product.

McCain Foods is one of many multinational corporations with production facilities in other countries like the one shown here in Strzelin, Poland.

Signs of Poor Structure–Environment Fit

Even if the organization's structure matches the environment at one point in time, it may not be appropriate forever. Environments change and so should organizational structures. Inappropriate organizational structures block needed information sharing, focus attention away from information that needs to be gathered, and consequently hurt decision quality, organizational prosperity, and perhaps even survival. With the wrong structure, managers increasingly make bad decisions, in part because they lack needed information. In the absence of timely, relevant information, effective decisions concerning what products to produce, what quality standards to set, how to reduce costs, how to advertise, or how to position products against competitors decline. Because inappropriate organizational design and structures can severely inhibit organizational effectiveness, being able to recognize the key warning signs of a mismatch is important.

Structure–Environment Fit by Michael Hitt

mymanagementlab

One of the first warning signs is decision makers' inability to anticipate problems. If problems caused by competitors, governments, customers, suppliers, and so on consistently arise without advance notice, this is a warning sign that the organizational structure is inhibiting environmental scanning, data gathering, or information dissemination. If the organization is not designed or structured to correct this problem, decision makers will have to react to rather than anticipate the environment and will be placed at a competitive disadvantage to other organizations.

Another key warning sign is an increase in conflict that prevents effective implementation. This sign, in particular, can indicate that the limits of a functional structure are being stretched and that information exchange mechanisms, such as cross-functional teams, liaisons, or other lateral relations, are needed.

There may also be signs at the individual level. When the number of individuals who do not know what is expected of them or who receive conflicting expectations increase, this is an early warning sign that the organizational structure is not appropriate for the environment.

Recognizing these warning signs allows managers to step back and analyze the external environment and the company's strategy. What has changed in the external environment? Are the changes pushing for a flatter structure? Do they require greater specialization regarding customers, products, or regions? How does the structure need to change to meet the changing demands of the environment? Is the company's strategy still appropriate? If it is, how can the organizational structure and value chain be reconfigured to better meet the needs of the strategy? To answer these and related questions, managers must have a clear and deep understanding of the principles of organizational structure and design.

managerial perspectives revisited

PERSPECTIVE 1: **THE ORGANIZATIONAL CONTEXT** The term "organizational structure" makes it clear that when it comes to designing or applying a structure, it is impossible to do so independently of the organizational context. First and foremost, you need to consider the organizational context of strategy. The structure needs to fit the strategy. If the strategy is one of speed to market and innovation, then a structure with many layers and strong unit boundaries is inappropriate. For example, Nike needs to get new shoe models to market as fast as possible, so it has a very flat structure. You also have to consider the nature of the organization—its culture and strengths and weaknesses. For example, if the new strategy is one of speed to market and the old organizational structure fostered slow, formal, and deliberate decision making, then simply putting in place a new structure on top of old behaviours will not necessarily work. Even if the new structure is the right one for the strategy, its effective implementation has to be considered and planned for in the context of the overall organization.

PERSPECTIVE 2: **THE HUMAN FACTOR** One of the most consistent mistakes made in structuring organizations is to assume that if you change the "boxes and lines"—that is, the organizational chart—that desired new behaviours, flows of information, and so on will automatically follow. They do not. Making an existing or especially a new structure work effectively can only happen by working with and through others. In many cases, to meet the objectives of the structure may require new skills and capabilities of people. If you don't work with your employees to help them acquire the skills and capabilities they need, all the organizational structure and design brilliance in the world will make the new organizational chart only as valuable as the paper it's printed on. As we discussed previously, Suncor created an entirely new unit with its major projects group. However, if manager Kevin Nabholz is unable to help his subordinates learn how to interact effectively with other units in the company, then the projects his group is supposed to design and build are likely to come in late, over budget, or with the wrong operating performance levels.

PERSPECTIVE 3: **MANAGING PARADOXES** Developing an organizational structure that is integrated yet allows for specialization is a potential paradox managers face. Because of the complexity of the competitive marketplace, very few

organizations can afford to choose one over the other. Yet specialization makes integration difficult to achieve, and vice versa. Nonetheless, managers must find an appropriate balance between the two types of structures that matches the strategy adopted by the organization. In Suncor's case, by separating the team working on major projects—specializing it, in other words—the company was able to bring the specialized engineering and construction talents of many different people to each project. On the other hand, if the coordination between the team working on the projects and the business units that ultimately operate the finished equipment is ineffective, the benefits of this specialization are lost. This is also true in the international context. Most firms face pressures both for global integration and local specialization. For example, even though Boeing operates in a global environment, the company must master the challenge of thinking globally but acting locally. It gains economies of scale by keeping the basic structure of the 747 the same regardless of where the customer is located or where the plane will be used, but the sales process is different for customers in different countries, and planes may require minor adaptations. For example, the labels and signs on the various components within the plane, like its exits, restrooms, and instrument panel, might need to be translated into a different language, depending on the primary country in which the plane will be flown. Boeing's organizational structure must enable it to handle both integration and specialization.

4

PERSPECTIVE 4: **ENTREPRENEURIAL MINDSET** In Chapter 1 we explained the importance of an entrepreneurial mindset to innovation and the ultimate survival and success of an organization. The organization's structure can have a major effect on the development and implementation of an entrepreneurial mindset. For example, too much formalization may hinder the flexibility needed to be entrepreneurial and innovative; the overcentralization of authority may lead to the same outcome. But a highly differentiated structure along with strong integration can produce more entrepreneurial activity and innovation. As an example, the geographic differentiation of BD in Europe (discussed in the opening case) exposed the entire firm to many different local and often unique ideas and ways of operating. If the organization of the company is both strong and integrated, these ideas can be communicated to other units and used by them to create more and better products and services. Likewise, a network structure allows the organization to participate in a number of alliances with external partners. Managers can garner knowledge from these partnerships to enhance their own innovations. For example, Dell makes use of its strategic alliances and the knowledge it gains from its partnerships to stay on top of the innovation constantly occurring in its industry.[28]

A commitment not only to the proper design but to the effective implementation of an organization's structure is critical to success. However, changes in structure can occasionally be interpreted by some as threats to power and status of individuals in the organization. Consequently, a commitment to follow through with reorganization efforts is important, given the potential effect it can have on an organization's entrepreneurial activity, ability to innovate, and overall competitiveness.

concluding comments

Organizational structures can be thought of as information networks or circuits on a circuit board. The structure influences who talks to whom about what and how often, what information moves through the organization and at what speed. As business and society move from the industrial age to the information age, appropriate organizational structures will be increasingly critical to a firm's success in the marketplace. Likewise, your understanding of and skills at designing effective structures become increasingly critical to your career success. You must be able to quickly and accurately analyze the complexity and dynamism of the internal and external environments.

As the Citicorp example illustrates, the structure has to fit the environment and the organization's objectives. Citicorp's emphasis on brand and costs placed an emphasis on a structure that would centralize brand management and capture economies of scale in other activities.

In addition, to have a successful managerial career, you need to understand the sometimes opposing forces of globalization and localization. Successful organizational structures may require you to find solutions that meet both needs simultaneously, or to organize various functional activities at different points along the continuum from centralized global activities to decentralized local activities.

In general, designing organizational structure can be one of the more complex activities of management. Its critical role in organizational competitiveness virtually guarantees that managers who understand and are skilled at organizational design will be those who are increasingly given more responsible positions.

key terms

boundaryless organization 277
centralized organizations 266
cognitive specialization 258
decentralized organizations 266
flat organizational structure 263
formalization 262
globalization 284
hybrid 274
informal organization 265
integration 259
interdependence 259
liaisons 277
line of authority 262
localization 284
network structures 275
organizational charts 257
organizational design 257
organizational structure 257
outsourcing 275
profit centre 269
span of control 262
specialization 258
tall organizational structure 263
task specialization 258
uncertainty 261
unity of command 262

test your comprehension

1. Define *organizational structure*. How does it differ from organizational design?
2. What is the main purpose of organizational charts?
3. What is *task specialization*, and what is its role in organizational design?
4. Why is cognitive specialization important in organizational design?
5. What are the three major types of interdependence among organizational units?
6. In an organization with a relative high level of certainty and low to moderate level of interdependence among business units, would you recommend rules, goals, or values as the principal means for facilitating integration?

7. In an organization with a relative low level of certainty and high level of interdependence among business units, would you recommend rules, goals, or values as the principal means for facilitating integration?
8. How is line of authority different from unity of command?
9. How does span of control typically relate to tall and flat organizational structures?
10. What are the pros and cons for both centralization and decentralization in organizational structure?
11. What are the advantages and disadvantages of the functional structure?
12. Why is a matrix structure one of the most difficult to manage effectively?
13. What are the most common advantages and disadvantages of network structures?
14. What are the critical elements of an organization's internal and external environments that a manager should assess in considering a new organizational structure?
15. What are the four basic elements that influence the uncertainty of an organization's external environment?
16. What role does information play in the context of organizational uncertainty?
17. What is the principal role of direct contact, liaisons, and teams in organizational design?
18. How does moving from a purely domestic to an international organization affect organizational structure?
19. What are some of the key warning signs of a poor structure–environment fit?

apply your understanding

1. Universities are typically organized by faculties such as business, biology, engineering, architecture, and so on. Is this an appropriate structure? What aspects of the environment support this structure? Are there any aspects of the internal or external environment that currently or in the near future will push for *changes* in university structures?
2. Organizational design skills are critical to career success, but total organizational design or redesign typically is not put in the hands of newly hired managers. Why then is it important for you to understand early in your career the structure and the specialization and integration mechanisms of the organization you work in?
3. What would be the likely influence of a collectivist culture (refer back to Chapter 4) on the formal or informal aspects of an organization's structure? What would you expect the influence to be of a strong hierarchical cultural value on line of authority or unity of command in a company's structure?

practise your capabilities

A friend calls to ask for your advice. She is being offered the position of brand manager for a new sports drink in a large food and beverage company. Everything about the new position (and pay) sounds great to your friend; however, she's been asked how she wants to structure her unit. Specifically, she has been asked how many people she would be comfortable having report to her. Based on her following description, what span of control would you advise her to take on in her new position?

Most new managers at this level have about four to six subordinates. Your friend indicates that she could have as few as three and as many as thirteen, depending on what she requests and her rationale for the request. Prior to this promotion, your friend has been working on a brand team for three years and acting as the informal team leader for the last 14 months. She was told that part of the reason she was given the promotion is because of how well she seemed to manage her team (three others who were all doing primarily market research work).

The new sports drink has been on the market for six months and has enjoyed a successful launch in Canada, the United States, and Asia. Continued expansion in Europe and Latin America is expected. Your friend emailed you a brief profile of the 13 potential subordinates.

Market researcher: Three different people are currently working on marketing research related to the product. Much of their work was done prior to the launch and now they focus on customer satisfaction and competitive response. Two of the people work in Canada (one in the East and one in the West) and the other works in Japan.

Statistician: There are two statisticians. One is currently based in the corporate headquarters in the east and the other is based in the European regional headquarters in London. Both do essentially the same job of analyzing data and looking for statistical relationships among customer characteristics, product characteristics, marketing/promotion activities, and buying patterns.

Advertising specialist: There are three advertising specialists. One deals primarily with print media; one focuses on broadcast media (principally radio and TV); the third specializes in "alternative advertising" that includes everything from promotional contests to the internet. The print ad and broadcast staff are based in the company's eastern office, while the alternative advertising person telecommutes from his home in Canmore, Alberta. The company's nearest western office is in Calgary.

Administrative assistant: There is one administrative assistant who works for the brand manager that launched the sports drink. This individual acts as secretary, organizer, and general assistant to the brand manager.

Marketing specialist: There are four marketing specialists. Each one resides in a different region (i.e., Canada, Asia, Europe, and Latin America). They are primarily responsible for creating the marketing strategy for their regions. Given that the product has not really launched yet in Europe and Latin America, the two individuals in those regions are currently working on other products and task forces.

Based on this information, your friend presses you for advice.

1. How many total subordinates should she go for? What should be her span of control?
2. If not all 13, which specific subordinates should she ask to have and why?
3. Even while attempting to give your friend some tentative advice on the first two questions, are there other issues you would want to understand, or are there questions you would like to ask your friend before providing a more definitive recommendation? If you could only ask three questions, what would be your top priority questions and why?

closing case DEVELOP YOUR CRITICAL THINKING

Restructuring Skate Canada

Skate Canada is the organization responsible for developing and managing figure skating in Canada. On October 6, 2004, Skate Canada made public its plans for restructuring its national office in Ottawa. Following a study conducted by Deloitte & Touche, the decision to reorganize was made as a means of facilitating each organizational function's efforts toward achieving the long-term strategic goals of the organization. The restructuring involved condensing nine departments into six divisions by combining similar activities, leading to the elimination and reclassification of certain positions and the termination of seven employees. Skate Canada asserted that the seven layoffs were necessary to increase the efficiency and effectiveness of its management structure.

Following the reorganization, the six divisions at the national office included corporate services, membership, skating programs and events, elite athlete development, marketing and communications, and business development. Administration, human resources, orders, finance, and information technology functions were combined in the new corporate services division, which would be responsible for providing the organization with the majority of its support activities.

The membership division remained responsible for the education, development, and services of all Skate Canada members. This would be accomplished by ensuring that all members were aware of and were taking advantage of the resources available to them and that they had sufficient knowledge in their respective areas.

Under the new structure, skating program development and skating event operations were combined in the skating programs and events division. The new division would be responsible for events-related activities such as technical support, on-ice management, and skating family functions. Off-ice event planning would also fall under this division, and would include the managing of accommodations, space requirements, transportation, accreditation, and the coordination of volunteers.

The elite athlete development division would manage athlete activities and services at both the national and international levels. Employees of this division would be responsible for scouting new athletes, monitoring the progress of the athletes, determining selection criteria for events, choosing athletes who would compete internationally, providing official presence at international events, and developing progress models and teams for athlete enhancement.

The marketing and communications division would continue to promote Skate Canada through corporate programming and event promotion, as well as by maintaining and developing the Skate Canada brand. Finally, business development was a new division that would concentrate on generating revenues through sponsorship, licensing, supplier agreements, retail affiliations, ticket sales, and the development of athlete funds.

The organizational changes were anticipated to contribute to sustainable membership, financial growth, and success for Canadian athletes at international competitions, including the Vancouver 2010 Winter Olympics. By 2010, Skate Canada aimed to increase and maintain its membership in several athletic areas while simultaneously providing all of its competitive members with the opportunity to compete nationally or internationally depending on their sport. Additionally, Skate Canada emphasized its commitment to developing its athletes by providing them with an "optimum competitive athlete environment" with an appropriate number of clubs, skating schools, volunteers, officials, and coaches. In terms of competitive achievements, Skate Canada aimed to have 75 percent of its athletes in the top five positions at international competitions. Finally, Skate Canada hoped that Canadian athletes would bring home a total of four medals at the Olympics and World Championships in 2006, and will win another three Olympic medals in 2010.

Questions

1. What do you think prompted Skate Canada to restructure its organization?
2. What type of structure did Skate Canada create in this reformation? What will be some of the drawbacks to such a structure? What will be some of the benefits?

3. How well do you think such a structure might work? What do you perceive would be its advantages and disadvantages?

4. Find out how many medals Canada won in the 2006 Olympics and World Championships. Do you think the changes in organizational structure at Skate Canada had an impact on the number of medals won? Why or why not?

Sources: "Skate Canada Reorganizes National Office," Skate Canada, Press Room: News Releases, October 6, 2004, www.skatecanada.ca (accessed January 26, 2007).

Part Two

integrative case

Paragon Information Systems

Keith Collins, president and chief executive officer of Paragon Information Systems of St. John's, Newfoundland, faced a crisis. On July 19, 1996, four days after his appointment, two vice-presidents resigned to start a new company in direct competition. They recruited away the entire sales force, members of the technical section and support staff. Paragon was reduced from 50 to 36 people by the end of August. Collins needed to respond.

NEWTEL ENTERPRISES LIMITED—CORPORATE STRUCTURE[1]

Paragon was a wholly-owned subsidiary of NewTel Enterprises Limited (NEL), which was itself 55.6 percent owned by BCE Inc. (BCE). NEL was a Newfoundland-based company whose principal operations in the telecommunications and information technology industries were conducted by Paragon and four other subsidiaries:

- NewTel Communications Inc. (formerly Newfoundland Telephone Company Limited), a wholly-owned subsidiary, provided telecommunications and information handling services throughout Newfoundland and Labrador and operated nationally and internationally as a member of Stentor. NewTel Communications was subject to regulation by the Canadian Radio-television and Telecommunications Commission (CRTC).
- NewTel Mobility Limited, a wholly-owned subsidiary, was a provider of wireless communications including cellular telephone, paging and two-way radio in Newfoundland and Labrador.
- NewTel Information Solutions Limited, an 80 percent owned subsidiary, was an information technology integrator with expertise in mainframe systems development and data centre operations, local area network installation, microcomputer systems development and support, wide area network management and information technology planning. Minority owners included Andersen Consulting at 10 percent and Bell Sygma Inc. at 10 percent.
- NewTech Instruments Limited, a wholly-owned subsidiary, was a full service contract manufacturer of electronic, electromechanical and cable assemblies for the telecommunications, marine and defence industries in a global market.

Paragon Information Systems Inc., a wholly-owned subsidiary, was an information technology firm focusing on systems integration, application development and computer networking in the Newfoundland and Labrador market. Through its newcomm division, the company provided Internet access, website development and support to the business market.

Exhibit 1 Consolidated Four-Year Review: Newtel Enterprises Limited (in thousands of dollars, except per share amounts)

	1997	1996	1995	1994
Income Statement Items				
Operating revenues	$ 331,425	324,229	315,401	296,685
Operating expenses	$ 240,175	241,695	238,867	211,810
Extraordinary item	$ (85,480)	–	–	–
Net income (loss)	$ (49,069)	30,550	25,458	32,826
Financial Ratios				
Earnings (loss) per average common share	$ (2.72)	1.70	1.42	1.92
Book value per common share	$ 14.16	18.22	17.88	17.76
Rate of return on average common equity (%)	10.93	9.43	7.97	11.02
Debt to total capital (%)	52.1	45.5	48.0	48.0
Other Statistics				
Capital expenditures	$ 67,016	61,745	83,693	84,484
Salaries and wages	$ 84,749	82,630	86,540	80,574
Number of employees	1,945	1,951	2,004	2,128
Average common shares outstanding (000)	18,018	18,006	17,886	17,138

Source: NewTel Enterprises Limited, op. cit.

The NEL mission statement was

To provide sustained and consistent growth in shareholder value, through primary focus on telecommunications and related businesses in Atlantic Canada. Essential to our success will be exploitation of emerging competitive opportunities, responsive customer service and an effective, action-oriented management team.

Exhibit 1 provides consolidated financial highlights for NEL. Exhibit 2 provides a breakdown of the contributions to revenues and net income by subsidiary.

Exhibit 2 Four-Year Review of Subsidiary Operating Revenues and Net Income

	1997	1996	1995	1994
Operating Revenues				
NewTel Communications	$264,847	$269,433	$263,964	$263,727
NewTel Information Solutions	45,743	40,321	38,340	5,327
NewTel Mobility	20,023	15,556	13,037	9,414
Paragon Information Systems	14,816	12,315	14,860	11,871
NewTech Instruments	11,253	9,820	8,245	6,943
Consolidated Eliminations	(25,257)	(23,216)	(23,045)	(1,911)
Total Consolidated	$331,425	$324,229	$315,401	$296,685
Net Income				
NewTel Communications	$ 31,912	$ 28,226	$ 25,002	$ 32,068
NewTel Information Solutions	3,696	2,080	1,100	–
NewTel Mobility	3,024	2,053	1,509	–
Paragon Information Systems	511	(207)	242	–
NewTech Instruments	776	495	404	–
Consolidated Eliminations	(3,508)	(2,097)	(2,799)	–
Total	36,411	30,550	25,458	–
Extraordinary item	(85,480)	–	–	–
Total consolidated net income (loss)	$(49,069)	$ 30,550	$ 25,458	$ 32,826

Note: All 1995 figures and only the 1994 Total Consolidated Revenues and Total Consolidated Net Income (loss) figures have been adjusted to conform to the NEL 1996 Annual Report presentation.

Source: NewTel Enterprises Limited, op. cit.

Paragon Corporate History

Three entrepreneurs founded Paragon in 1988. The company provided information technology (IT) systems integration, software development, and computer networking products and services to business customers throughout Newfoundland and Labrador, with a main focus on hardware. Total employee count was 50. A second NEL subsidiary, NewTel Information Solutions (NIS), focused more on the services side of the IT business. The latter company was formed by the purchase and privatization of the IT services department of the government of Newfoundland and the subsequent acquisition and consolidation of the IT assets of NewTel Communications. Total employee count was about 250.

In mid-1995, the president of Paragon, one of the three founding executives of the company, was transferred to NIS as the vice-president of marketing. NEL installed a new president at Paragon. However, by the spring of 1996, Paragon's board was dissatisfied with the performance of both the new president and the company. The chairman of Paragon's board—to whom Keith Collins reported at NewTel Communications—approached Collins, advised him that the president of Paragon was about to be removed, and asked if he would take on the job. Collins agreed and subsequently took over as president and chief executive officer on the morning of Monday July 15, 1996.

Cultural Differences

A long-term NEL employee, Collins's background was in telecommunications, not in IT. Aware that switching industries could be difficult, he relished the change and challenge involved. He was also aware that the working relationship between Paragon and the parent company NEL had always been fairly uneasy. Differences stemmed from the backgrounds of the two companies. Paragon had been a relatively free-wheeling entrepreneurial venture under its founding owners. The acquisition by NEL mandated a tighter level of governance, and Paragon became accountable for operating within budgets and for meeting performance targets. Thus, relations between parent and subsidiary were strained at both the leadership and operating levels.

The Crisis Situation

On Friday July 19, 1996, the vice-president of marketing at NIS and two vice-presidents of Paragon, all three of them the founding executives of Paragon, tendered their resignations. They advised Collins that they intended to found a new company in the IT systems space to compete with Paragon. It became apparent to Collins that this move had been under consideration for some time and that his appointment as president had triggered the action, particularly given that he was new to the IT systems business.

The owners of the new company acted quickly to recruit former employees by playing on the past tenuous relationship between Paragon and NEL and by projecting that Paragon would not survive. By the end of August, Paragon experienced a significant drain on its human resource base, shrinking from 50 to 36 employees. In addition to the loss of management expertise, the entire sales force departed along with important technical and support staff. A similar message was played to Paragon's suppliers and clients to undermine its presence in the marketplace. By the end of August 1996, the company found itself in difficult circumstances. A substantial part of Paragon's corporate knowledge resided with the new competitor, and conjecture about the future of Paragon was rampant.

Initial Reaction and Perspective

Faced with the initial onslaught, Collins first reaction was, "Why me"? Very quickly however, he was able to place things in perspective. He had been sent in because the existing processes, strategy and team were not producing the required level of financial performance. The remaining employees were willing to stick with Paragon through the crisis and thus were more open to the fundamental changes required. The disadvantage of the situation was that expertise had been lost from Paragon, leaving it in a weakened condition. This issue was amplified by the fact that the former Paragon management had set up a competitor in Paragon's market space. The advantages of the situation were that the people responsible for Paragon's prior performance were gone, thus making change easier to enact, and Paragon had an established parent company and board of directors to provide support. The board was in fact extremely supportive, having a "whatever you believe you need" attitude, and it assured Collins that there was no intent to close the company down. The need to refocus and restructure the company had always existed. The crisis situation was the catalyst that provided the opportunity.

Reducing Uncertainty

The first major task Collins faced was to reassure employees, suppliers and clients that he had not been sent in to close down Paragon, that the company was in rebuilding mode and would survive and prosper into the future. He met with employees either individually or in small groups, assured them that the company was rebuilding, and solicited their input and advice as to how they could move the company forward. He advised them that he had the backing of the board and the parent company NEL, and they need not be concerned about their employment status.

The same message was conveyed at meetings with clients, i.e., no matter what they had heard from the new entrant to the marketplace or any other players, Paragon was rebuilding. Collins asked for their patience for a few weeks while he rebuilt, and he confirmed that Paragon would honor any previous commitments. On the one hand, clients were willing to co-operate to the extent that they provided copies of proposals and contracts they had entered into with Paragon, given that some of these had disappeared from Paragon's own files. On the other hand, clients were happy that in the future there would be more competition in the marketplace.

Collins flew to meet with Paragon's suppliers and technology partners who had also been advised by the new company that Paragon would be closing down. The suppliers appreciated the fact that Collins made the effort to meet with them and to reassure them that Paragon was both staying in business and intending to grow its business into the future. Thus, knowing that he had support at the corporate level, Collins was able to reassure major stakeholders that the company would remain in business.

The Rebuilding Process

To rebuild the company, Collins needed a new senior management team. Of the previous team, only the controller, the vice-president of software development and the latter's most senior report remained. Collins had two leadership sources: to use people in the organization who had previously been overlooked, and to hire from the outside. He found that the former were well able to rise to most of the challenges presented to them. However, for a job such as the vice-president of sales and marketing, he had to go outside and was able to find a candidate willing to undertake the rebuilding of the department.

Throughout the reshaping process, the underlying strategy was to become more client-focused. However, no attempt was made to immediately restructure the company. The rebuilding process had the impact of stopping the flow of resignations by the end of September. During the rebuilding, it became apparent that Paragon had previously been managed like a personal fiefdom. The "in" employees were favored by previous management and received preferential compensation packages when compared to other equally skilled employees doing the same work at the same level. Thus, Collins and his new team adjusted compensation levels, increasing the overall level of compensation in the company fairly substantially. In some cases salaries increased from 15 percent to 25 percent. Full support was received from the board of directors. The impact was increased stability in the employee group.

Moving Forward

At the end of September, the management team started to look at a new business strategy for the future. They used a SWOT analysis to review company capabilities, opportunities in the marketplace, and which existing activities to continue and abandon. Strategic objectives were set in the areas of marketing, finance, organizational functioning, innovation and abandonment. They found that the company's past strategy focused on the hardware market, yielding margins of eight percent to 10 percent. They determined that, going forward, they should concentrate on adding value by providing services around applications. Typical margins in this area were between 35 percent to 50 percent. The internet was gaining momentum at the time, yet the company had no internet strategy. This presented a substantial opportunity. After two months of activity, the strategic plan and the necessary structure to support it were presented to the board for approval. Immediately thereafter, they were presented to the entire employee body. Management's aim throughout was to "foster an environment in which employees understand their role and value to the organization and are engaged in the strategic process."[2]

The strategic plan and new organizational structure reinforced the gains already made in stabilizing the employee group. By January of 1997, the beneficial impact on corporate culture became evident in the form of a strong sense of participation and ownership throughout the company. On a regular basis, management presented business and financial information to employees at general meetings. An open culture was reinforced. The people who had stayed, and those who had joined, all felt they had endured a difficult set of circumstances, and now they saw a way to improve the company in the future. The following tenet from Paragon's Strategic Direction Statement emphasized the company's approach to its employees: "We will invest in our company so that people will be proud to work here. They will feel supported, recognized and rewarded for their contribution to our shared success."[3] See Exhibits 3, 4, 5 and 6 for an encapsulation of Paragon's new approach.

Exhibit 3 Excerpts from Paragon's 1997 Organizational Functioning Objectives

1. Foster a performance-oriented culture at Paragon that recognizes and supports the contribution of each employee.
2. Implement a new performance-based compensation plan for all groups.
3. Implement a corporate Team Award to recognize and reward the shared success of Paragon's employee group.
4. Establish the optimal organization structure to support Paragon's business objectives.
5. Introduce a new performance management system to provide the framework for individual performance measurement and employee development.

Source: Paragon Information Systems, op. cit.

Exhibit 4 Excerpts from Paragon's Communications Approach

1. Two-way: telling *and* listening.
2. Presented 1997 strategic plan to all staff.
3. Involved managers and cross-section of employees in developing 1998 plan.
4. Regular work group meetings.
5. Regular company information sessions.
6. Monthly reports on financials, sales, etc.
7. Monthly president's information update.
8. Relaxed, 'open door' management style.
9. Regular informal 'team builders.'

Source: Paragon Information Systems, op. cit.

Exhibit 5 Excerpts from Paragon's Compensation Approach

1. Annual study of IT market compensation.
2. Set 'target compensation' for each job, consisting of 'fixed' and 'variable' pay.
3. 'Fixed' pay is base salary expressed in a multi-year scale (e.g., four years to top).
4. Progression up the scale is based on technical certification, demonstrated competence and experience.
5. 'Variable' pay is a per cent of base salary, tied to achieving Paragon's financial and customer service objectives.
6. Sales compensation plan is tied primarily to sales team performance.
7. 'Target compensation' levels are reviewed annually.

Source: Paragon Information Systems, op. cit.

Exhibit 6 Excerpts from Paragon: Learning from the Process

1. A clear business strategy is an essential element to build employee enthusiasm and commitment to corporate goals.
2. Informed, equipped and committed employees can be a company's greatest assets, and are worth investing in.
3. Fostering a culture in which employees feel engaged in the growth process may be a company's strongest contribution to its own success.
4. Compensation is a means to an end, *not* an end in itself.
5. It's impressive what a group of people can accomplish when they don't care who gets the credit.

Source: Paragon Information Systems, op. cit.

Impact on Performance

The new strategy was implemented in 1997. Training was recognized as a priority and investment in this area tripled. Although productivity improvement was neither a stated 1997 objective nor a focus area, financial performance more than doubled that of any previous year in Paragon's history. Revenues were up 17 percent and expenses were down six percent over 1996. The company continued to grow in 1998. Markets expanded beyond the province to the Atlantic region and new technology partners were added. By the end of 1998, the company had 80 employees. The company's portfolio of capabilities expanded to include IT consulting, systems integration, Tier 1 computer systems, computer networking, software development and integration, business internet/electronic commerce, and world-class technology partners.

Part Three | Implementing through People

Chapter 9 Leadership

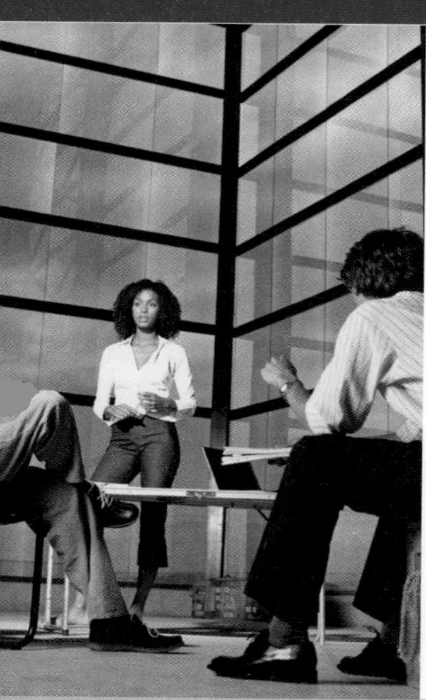

LEARNING OBJECTIVES

After reading this chapter, you should be able to:

1. Identify the different types and sources of power available to a leader.
2. Explain the current view of the importance of leadership traits and skills.
3. Discuss the utility of the two major categories of leader behaviour.
4. Discuss how followers and different situations affect the leadership process.
5. Compare and contrast the various approaches to and theories of leadership.
6. Describe the similarities and differences between leadership and management.
7. Differentiate between charismatic, transformational, and transactional leaders.
8. Analyze the effects of culture on theories of leadership.

Go Nellie

Nellie McClung played a central role in Canada's initial wave of feminism during the first half of the twentieth century. Over the course of her life, McClung was an unrelenting advocate for women's rights, a best-selling writer, a prohibitionist, and a politician. With her humorous, witty speeches and charismatic personality, Nellie was able to influence politicians, lawmakers, and Canadians alike and make them aware of the need to revise Canadian laws to include women.

While McClung was an outspoken activist for many social reform groups, she is most often remembered as a prominent and successful leader in the campaign for female suffrage and women's right to be recognized as "persons" under the *British North America Act* (*BNA Act*). Canadian law in the early 1900s placed women in the same category as criminals and the insane, meaning that they did not have the right to vote or to hold public office. From the perspective of Canadian law, women were not considered persons.

McClung was born in 1873 in Ontario and later settled in Manitoba, becoming a rural teacher and then moving to Winnipeg in 1911 with her husband and five children. In Winnipeg, McClung became increasingly involved in the women's suffrage movement, the campaign to attain voting rights for women. Manitoba's premier Rodmond Roblin was opposed to granting women the right to vote, stating that "nice" women did not want the vote. Roblin's stance only further motivated McClung to mobilize others to petition for the right. In 1914, McClung and fellow "suffragettes" staged a play entitled "The Women's Parliament," in which a role reversal satirized Roblin's baseless arguments by debating the perils of giving men the right to vote. Support for the suffrage movement continued to grow, and in 1915 the Roblin government was defeated. In 1916, the new government under Tobias Norris secured voting rights for women in Manitoba. Later that same year the right was also secured in Saskatchewan, Alberta, and British Columbia.

Manitoba's premier Rodmond Roblin had stated that "nice" women do not want the vote. To this Nellie McClung shot back: "By nice women . . . you probably mean selfish women who have no more thought for the underprivileged, overworked women than a pussycat in a sunny window for the starving kitten in the street. Now in that sense I am not a nice woman, for I do care."

The McClung family moved to Alberta, where McClung entered politics and served one term in the Alberta legislature in 1921 as a member of the Liberal opposition. She used her position in the legislature to continue her fight for social reforms, including allowances for mothers, free medical and dental care for children, as well as liberalized birth control legislation, to name a few.

One of Nellie McClung's greatest accomplishments is her involvement in what is widely known as "The Persons Case." McClung, along with Emily Murphy, Irene Parlby, Louise McKinney, and Henrietta Edwards (known as the "Famous Five") argued to the Supreme Court of Canada that women should be considered persons under the law and should be able to be appointed to the Canadian senate. The Supreme Court's 1928 decision was that the *BNA Act* of 1867 was written at a time when only men were deemed "persons," and was therefore not intended to include women. Undeterred, the women appealed the decision to the highest court overseeing Canadian constitutional law at the time, the Judicial Committee of the Privy Council in England. In October 1929 the committee was unanimous in their decision that the word "person" includes both men and women, stating that any exclusion was "a relic of days more barbarous than ours."

Nellie McClung showed great leadership, opening doors for women in Canada by giving them a voice in policy and laws associated with the family. She was the only female member of the Canadian delegation to the 1938 League of Nations in Geneva, Switzerland, and the first woman member of the Canadian Broadcasting Corporation board of broadcast governors. McClung continued as a tireless champion for women's rights until her death in 1951 in Victoria, British Columbia.

Sources: D. Bramham, "The Last Frontier of Rank Discrimination; Women Had to Fight to be 'Persons,' to Vote, to Share Property. Today, They're Still Second-Class Citizens," *Vancouver Sun*, July 7, 2007, p. C4; Library and Archives Canada, "Nellie Letitia (Mooney) McClung," March 7, 2007, www.collectionscanada.ca (accessed August 1, 2007); "Nellie McClung 1873–1951," www.mta.ca (accessed August 1, 2007); CBC: *Life and Times*, "Nellie McClung: The Sculpting of Angels," January 18, 2000, www.cbc.ca (accessed August 1, 2007); J. L. Granatstein, "Nellie McClung," *Maclean's*, July 1, 1998, pp. 42–43; Timelinks, "Nellie McClung," 1998, timelinks.merlin.mb (accessed August 1, 2007); Patricia Chisholm, "Nervy Nellie—Firing the Heather: The Life and Times of Nellie McClung by Mary Hallett and Marilyn Davis," *Maclean's*, December 6, 1993, p. 68; Mary Nemeth, "The Victory of 'Calamity Nell'," *Maclean's*, July 6, 1992, p. 61.

strategic overview

Over the past decade, the concept of strategic leadership has emerged. Originally, the term was used to refer to people who were members of top management.[1] However, others have argued recently that "strategic leadership" is not a function of position level but rather an emphasis on focus and behaviour. In other words, strategic leadership can be exhibited at any level in the organization, and moreover, for an organization to perform well, effective leaders are actually critical at all organizational levels.

Basically, strategic leadership involves thinking and acting strategically while working with others to create a viable future for the organization.[2] To act strategically in a leadership role, managers or leaders have to anticipate events (analyze the external environment), envision the organization's future (analyze the internal resources and develop a vision for the organization or some unit within it), and remain flexible to adapt to conditions as they change.

Leaders have to exert their power at times but use it effectively to implement the organization's strategies while simultaneously managing and motivating people to do their tasks well, remain committed to the organization, and work to see that the strategic vision is realized. While acting strategically, leaders should also exhibit integrity and build good working relationships (based on trust and equitable treatment) with their followers. The presence of trusting relationships between leaders and their followers is sometimes called "internal social capital." Leaders can use social capital to their strategic advantage (e.g., using human capital to help implement the organization's strategy).[3] In the process of building relationships with followers and implementing the organization's strategy, a leader likely will need to call on technical, interpersonal, and conceptual skills. Additionally, a leader will need to use social and emotional intelligence capabilities and be self-confident to think and act strategically in an effective manner. Similar to the situations confronting Nellie McClung, strategic leadership is highly important to organizations, but also challenging to provide.

However, although acts of leadership in an organization can be widespread and commonplace, often they are not. The central issue, both for organizations and for individual managers, is to turn leadership potential into reality. The very fact that so many articles and books have been and continue to be written on the topic of leadership is a good indication that this challenge is not being met well by either the typical organization or the practising manager.

Leadership is an undeniably critical part of the overall managerial process. It is at the very centre of that part of managing that deals with "Implementing through People" (the title of this part of the book). Without leadership, organizational performance would be minimal. Indeed, it would be difficult if not impossible to talk about the accomplishments of twenty-first–century organizations of all types—whether in business, government, education, or other settings—without referring to the role that leadership played in those successes. So it is a given that leadership is important to organizations, and of course, to society at large. What is not so clear is how to increase its presence and effectiveness. That is the managerial challenge.

Leadership is, above all, a process of influence, as the opening story about Nellie McClung illustrates. As such, leadership can occur *potentially anywhere* in an organization. Leadership is not a set of behaviours limited to the chief executive officer, the executive vice-president, the director of manufacturing, the regional marketing manager, or for that matter, a sports team's coach or its captain. It is a process that can be exhibited by almost anyone, at almost any time, and in almost any circumstance.

In this chapter we will first confront an age-old question, "What is leadership?" and then explore how answers to this question help us understand the relationship between leadership and its close cousins, influence and power. This provides a background for analyzing the nature of the leadership/influence process: the traits and characteristics of people who are most likely to become leaders; the types of behaviours that leaders typically exhibit; the role and influence of followers and the situational circumstances most likely to affect the success of leadership attempts.

Since leadership is more complicated than the popular media would sometimes have us believe, we will also view the process through different lenses or models, emphasizing the point that there is more than one useful way to analyze leadership. Later, we consider some of the current issues that are prominent in both the academic and popular press with the intent of providing a richer picture of how leadership is being enacted in organizations so far in the twenty-first century.

What Is Leadership?

While studying this chapter, it is important to keep in mind that although leadership is a familiar everyday term, it nevertheless is far more complex than we might assume. For that reason, it is an especially interesting and intriguing subject. It is also a topic that is easy to oversimplify and therefore one that often leads to conclusions that are incorrect, misleading, or unjustified. In fact, we could say, "It's not what we don't know about leadership that is the problem; it's what we know that isn't so."

Let's take a look at how organizational scientists have defined the term "leadership." Unfortunately, there is no clear consensus because, as one prominent scholar observed some years ago, "There are almost as many definitions of leadership as there are persons who have attempted to define the concept."[4] Consistent with most definitions, however, we define **organizational leadership** as an interpersonal process involving attempts to influence other people in attaining some goal. This definition, therefore, emphasizes leadership as a social influence process.

organizational leadership an interpersonal process involving attempts to influence other people in attaining some goal

While there is general agreement that leadership is an influence process, there is less agreement on (1) whether the definition must refer only to influence used by those occupying designated leadership positions ("manager," "president," "chairperson," "coach," etc.), (2) whether the influence must be exercised deliberately and for the specific attainment of the group's or organization's goals, and (3) whether compliance of others must be voluntary. Our view on each of these issues follows.

Acts of leadership behaviour *can be exhibited by anyone* in an organization and are not limited only to those holding designated leadership positions. In particular, this means that leadership should not be thought of as occurring only, or even mostly, at the top of the organization—in positions like the one held by Annette Verschuren (refer back to Chapter 1). Thus, leadership behaviour is not confined just to presidents and CEOs of organizations. Leadership can also be seen in the actions of the first-line supervisor who inspires her subordinates to implement safety procedures to avoid production downtime. Leadership is demonstrated by the group member who champions his team's new product and convinces others of its potential. Leadership is shown by the human resource manager who makes sure—without being ordered to—that those in the HR division treat all applicants for positions with the company respectfully and equitably. Leadership is exhibited by workers who set an example for their co-workers by continually seeking ways to improve processes and working conditions.

Ordinarily, however, positions that are labelled managerial or supervisory have more opportunities to exert leadership. Also, leadership behaviour is expected more frequently from supervisors and managers than from people in

Pierre Elliott Trudeau is regarded as having exhibited critical leadership as Canada's prime minister in his ability to repatriate the *British North America Act* in Canada and entrench the *Charter of Rights and Freedoms* into the constitution, which was signed by Queen Elizabeth II in 1982.

other types of roles. Such expectations often profoundly affect the behaviour of both those who hold such positions and those around them. In other words, expectations count!

People act as leaders for many reasons, and their efforts are not necessarily aimed solely at the attainment of a group's or organization's goals. Sometimes leaders' motives can be directed at multiple objectives, including their own as well as, or instead of, the organization's. Motives are seldom pure, but we assume explicitly that effective organizational leadership requires organizationally relevant, goal-directed behaviour, regardless of any other personal objectives.

The use of coercion to gain compliance ("do this or you will be fired" threats) is not typically considered leadership. However, the dividing line between what is and is not coercion is often very difficult to determine. Whether others' responses must be purely voluntary for leadership to occur is not an easy question to answer. When other people comply with someone's attempts at leadership, the reasons may be many and the degree of willingness can range from grudging to enthusiastic. The safest generalization is this: The greater the degree of purely voluntary actions by followers toward the leader's intended direction, the more effective the leadership is.

effective leadership influence that assists a group or an organization to meet its goals and objectives and perform successfully

The preceding discussion raises a further key issue: What is **effective leadership**? Put most simply, it is influence that assists a group or an organization to meet its goals and objectives and perform successfully. This implies that effective leadership is enabling behaviour—that is, it is behaviour that helps other people accomplish more than if there had been no such leadership.[5] Obviously, there are many examples from the past—Louis Riel and Nellie McClung—and the present—Governor General Michaëlle Jean and member of Parliament Steven Fletcher—just to name a few who could be considered leaders. By their actions they have added a leadership ingredient to the sum of the efforts of many people, and thereby helped those people achieve more than they would have otherwise. Again, effective leadership augments and assists by unlocking the potential that resides in a collection of people.

Leadership and Power

It is virtually impossible to consider leadership as a type of social influence without also taking into account the idea of power. **Power** is typically thought of as the capacity or ability to influence. Thus, the greater a person's power is, the greater the potential for influencing others. Power can be used "to change the course of events, to overcome resistance, and to get people to do things that they would not otherwise do."[6] However, the fact that a leader, or anyone else, has power does not guarantee that he or she will use it—or use it well. Possession and use are two different matters.

power the capacity or ability to influence

Whether a leader will use power depends on many factors. One principal reason it is not used is the anticipation of possible undesirable consequences from its use. The use of power is often believed to generate negative reactions. As has been said, "for many people, power is a 'four-letter' word."[7] The famous but somewhat exaggerated statement of this view of power was made more than a century ago in Britain, when Lord Acton wrote to Bishop Mandell Creighton that "power tends to corrupt [and] absolute power corrupts absolutely."[8]

It is not too difficult to think of an organization where power has been used inappropriately by a would-be leader. This was illustrated several years ago when a chief executive officer of a consumer products manufacturer was removed from office, even though he had presided over a major turnaround, bringing the company out of bankruptcy. The reason he was dismissed was because of the way he used his power to intimidate subordinates. On occasion, he even threw objects at them when he was angry. His actions so severely damaged morale at the company that the board of directors had no other option but to find a new CEO.[9]

It would be misleading, however, to regard power only from the perspective of the damage it can do. In many circumstances, a leader's skillful use of power can produce positive outcomes. In fact, frequently the problem in organizations is not that leaders use too much power, but rather that they fail to use the power available to them.[10] This was noted by two behavioural scientists who have studied leadership extensively when they said: "These days power is conspicuous by its absence. Powerlessness in the face of crisis. Powerlessness in the face of complexity. . . ."[11]

Types and Sources of Power

Power, however it is used, does not arise spontaneously or mysteriously; it comes from specific and identifiable sources. The two major types of power, based on their sources, are position powers and personal powers.[12] **Position power** is based on a manager's rank in an organizational structure and is given to the manager by superiors. **Personal power** is based on a person's individual characteristics.

position power power based on an organizational structure

personal power power based on a person's individual characteristics

Clearly, someone who wants to be a leader could have large amounts of both types of power, which should facilitate the exercise of influence. On the other hand, a would-be leader might be low on both, in which case the task of leading obviously would be more difficult. For instance, a lower-level manager who lacks initiative in developing new products or programs and who is a poor communicator with little tact would find it difficult to inspire subordinates to put out extra effort to make changes and reach new goals. This manager lacks personal power and would be unlikely to gain a promotion—thus also failing to increase his position power. In many situations, though, a potential leader who is low on one type of power—for example, occupying a relatively junior-level position—can compensate for that by having very strong personal leadership characteristics that are recognized by other people regardless of the person's formal status in the organization.

To better understand the nature of power in organizations, it is helpful to think about several subtypes of position power and personal power (see Exhibit 9.1).[13]

Exhibit 9.1

Types of Power

Position Powers	Personal Powers
Legitimate—How much authority does the organization give to your position?	**Expert**—Do you have knowledge that others need?
Reward—Are you able to give others the rewards they want?	**Referent**—Do others respect you and want to be like you?
Coercive—Are you able to punish others or withhold rewards?	

Position Powers A person's position in an organization provides a base for the exercise of this type of power. Specifically, the major kinds of power that are attached to a position include legitimate power, reward power, and coercive power.

legitimate power (formal authority) a type of position power granted to a person by the organization

Legitimate Power. Legitimate power is a type of position power granted to a person, say a manager, by the organization. It is sometimes called **formal authority**. In the work setting, such power is intended to give a manager a designated right to expect compliance by his or her employees. Both parties, in effect, agree in advance that requests by the manager are appropriate and within reason, and both parties agree that the subordinates are obligated to respond to those requests.

In today's organizations, with increasing levels of education of the workforce and changing societal norms about what is "legitimate" authority, the effectiveness of this type of power has distinct limits. Often, subordinates will disagree about the scope of a manager's authority; that is, they question the boundaries of what are "appropriate requests." For example, many managers used to expect their secretaries or assistants to make personal appointments for them and perform other nonwork-related services. Today, the relationship between a manager and her assistants has changed, and these types of requests are generally not considered legitimate.

The precise scope of legitimate authority in today's complex organizations is frequently ambiguous, and the resulting agreement between manager and subordinate can typically be more implicit than explicit, leaving room for potential conflict. In addition, the extent of a manager's formal authority is bounded by subordinates' perceptions of that person's credentials. If the basis of a person's selection for a managerial position is questioned, the leverage of legitimate power is somewhat reduced. For example, take a medium-sized firm where the CEO decides to appoint a close relative who has little knowledge of the business to an executive-level position that in the past has been filled by employees who have worked their way up through the ranks. In this case, subordinates may not acknowledge that the relative has a right to the formal power that would normally be associated with the position, and thus they might not respond to requests rapidly and enthusiastically. This would probably be especially true in many North American work situations, but perhaps not as much so in Asian cultures, where family connections are viewed as more appropriate for determining who should occupy high-level positions. In essence, though, in most organizational settings, formal authority represents power, but it definitely is not unlimited power.

Reward Power. One of the strongest sources of position power for any manager is **reward power**, that is, the authority to give out rewards, especially differing amounts of highly valued rewards to different people. In any hierarchy, this power can have significant effects on others' behaviour because it involves dispensing relatively scarce, but desired, resources. Only a few people, at most, can receive plum assignments; only one or two subordinates usually can be given the largest yearly performance bonus; only one person can be awarded the promotion. Because the use of reward power can have such potentially important consequences, a manager needs to be very alert to how his administration of rewards is being perceived. Aside from their direct impact, rewards also have a signalling effect—they let subordinates know, for example, where they stand with the boss.

reward power a type of position power based on a person's authority to give out rewards

However, the use of rewards can also have possible negative effects. Their use can sometimes decrease the motivation of those who do not receive them or receive what they regard to be insufficient amounts. Consequently, managers need to use reward power carefully and skillfully.

Coercive Power. **Coercive power** is the power to administer punishments, either by withholding something that is desired, like a raise, or by giving out something that is not desired, like a letter of reprimand. In typical organizations, such power is used sparingly these days, at least directly and overtly; but it is sometimes used indirectly in the form of implied threats. A manager, for instance, can let it be known that noncompliance with her requests will result in assignment to the least desired projects or committees. A manager in charge of assigning shift work could subtly influence subordinates by assigning those who do not agree with his policies to a series of inconvenient split shifts.

coercive power a type of position power based on a person's authority to administer punishments, either by withholding something that is desired or by giving out something that is not desired

A major problem with the use of coercive power is that it can cause recipients to avoid being detected by disguising their objectionable behaviour rather than motivate them to perform in the desired manner. Furthermore, the use of coercion can generate retaliation. Threatening employees with reduced hours or a pay cut if they don't take on more duties or accept a less-than-generous incentive plan might result in work slowdowns, increased numbers of faulty parts, or complaints to government regulators. Any of these actions would obviously be counterproductive.

It should also be noted that although people with higher-level positions have greater ability to apply coercive power, its use is not confined to managers and supervisors. Potentially, anyone has coercive power. For example, a lower-level employee can harm someone higher up the organizational chart by withholding valuable information or making a situation more difficult than it might otherwise be. This use of coercive power by subordinates may be subtle, but in some cases it may actually be quite effective for that very reason.

Personal Powers Personal powers are attached to a person and thus stay with that individual regardless of the position or the organization. For those who want to be leaders, personal powers are especially valuable because they do not depend directly or only on the actions of others or of the organization. The two major types are expert power and referent power.

Expert Power. **Expert power** is based on specialized knowledge not readily available to many people. It is precisely because many people do not have a

expert power a type of personal power based on specialized knowledge not readily available to many people

particular kind of knowledge that makes expertise a potential source of power. The potential is translated into actual power when other people depend on, or need advice from, those who have that expertise. The best example of expert power in everyday life is the physician–patient relationship. Most people follow their doctors' directives not because of any formal position power but because of the potential negative consequences of ignoring their expertise. Given the increased percentage of knowledge workers (i.e., those who have some special expertise) and the increased use of sophisticated knowledge in many types of contemporary organizations, it is becoming imperative for most managers to have some type of expertise. Having expertise may not necessarily set a manager apart from her subordinates, but not having it may greatly diminish the effectiveness of various forms of position power.

Expert power is not confined to higher organizational levels. Some of the most specialized, and yet most needed, knowledge in an organization can be possessed by lower-level employees.[14] One only needs to observe a boss trying to find a particular document in a file to appreciate the expert power that an administrative assistant often has in certain situations; or to watch the high-level executive waiting impatiently while the technician makes repairs to the computer or fax machine. These examples illustrate the fact that dependencies create an opportunity for expertise to become power, whatever the position a person holds.

referent power a type of personal power gained when people are attracted to, or identify with, that person; this power is gained because people "refer" to that person

Referent Power. When people are attracted to, or identify with, someone, that person acquires what is called **referent power**. This power is gained because other people "refer" to that person; they want to please that person or in some way receive acceptance. Referent power often can be recognized by its subtle occurrences. A subordinate, for example, may begin using gestures similar to those of his superior or even imitating certain aspects of his speech patterns. More importantly, the subordinate may find his opinions on important work issues becoming similar to those of his boss.

For anyone in a leadership position in a work setting, being able to generate referent power is clearly a great asset. It is a cost-free way to influence other people. Referent power makes it possible to lead by example rather than by giving orders. A manager can use her referent power to change work habits, for example. If she comes in early, stays late, takes shorter breaks, and finishes her work rather than putting it off until the next day, her subordinates may model themselves on her behaviour and change their own work habits as well.

A problem with referent power, however, is that it is not obvious how such power can be deliberately and easily developed. There is no formula for how to increase your referent power, and making attempts to get others to like or admire you can frequently cause the opposite reaction. Certain personal attributes, such as honesty and integrity, obviously help. Also, experience and a demonstrated record of success certainly help. The basic lesson seems to be that the referent power of a potential leader is built up over time by consistent actions and behaviour that cause others to develop admiration.

A Manager's Challenge: "Lighting the Way at Amazon.com" describes someone who can employ both types of personal power: expert and referent. He has demonstrated expertise and is using that kind of power to make major organizational changes. He is also likely to take advantage of the opportunity to use and build his referent power.

a manager's challenge change

Lighting the Way at Amazon.com

Thomas J. Szkutak has been using his background in light bulbs and plastics to help the online retailer Amazon.com light the way to lower costs and brighter profits. Before joining Amazon.com as chief financial officer in 2002, he held the same position at GE Lighting, a division of General Electric that makes a wide variety of lighting instruments for home and commercial use. Earlier in his career he was part of the management team for GE Plastic in Europe, Africa, India, and the Middle East. Jeff Bezos, Amazon's CEO, wanted Szkutak to help his company identify and implement changes that would "continue to drive down costs so that we can even further lower prices for customers."

How did Szkutak apply the personal powers and management skills he honed at GE to his current role as CFO of a cutting-edge, internet-based retailer? It didn't hurt that his experience came from GE. GE is a recognized leader in corporate finance training. Every year, 350 university recruits—the best and the brightest of the bunch—go through its prized, two-year financial management program that began in 1919. These "star" graduates walk out of the course with the confidence that people will listen to them. Szkutak was no different.

Moreover, although GE Lighting employs 33 000 around the world and Amazon employs nearly 14 000, the two companies face some similar challenges. Both are battling for global marketshare against formidable competitors and selling products to price-sensitive customers. Yet there are differences, as well—bottom-line differences. Whereas GE Lighting is a mature business that ekes out a relatively small profit margin of 10 percent year after year, Amazon is spending heavily to spur future growth and profits. Lower, big-box-like prices are helping the e-tailer attract consumers interested in buying products other than just books, which has contributed steadily to continued growth and higher profitability for the company. "Lowering prices will go on for years and years, and that's just how we're going to do business," Bezos says.

So why did Bezos choose Szkutak—whose management background is so concentrated in old-line manufacturing companies—for a key leadership position in a fast-paced online business like Amazon? It was precisely because of Szkutak's reputation for cost-cutting at GE, where he and his managers constantly searched for creative ways to contain costs. Since cost-cutting is one of Amazon's major priorities on the path to better profitability, Bezos believed the former GE executive would bring considerable expert power to his duties as CFO at Amazon. Szkutak can also wield referent power because GE's managers and finance executives are admired around the world and he was a senior executive with the company for 20 years.

So has the bet paid off? Yes: 2003 marked Amazon's first full year in the black, and Amazon has maintained this position, reporting an income of US$190 million on net sales of over US$10.7 billion in 2006. Since hiring Szkutak, Amazon has dramatically streamlined its network of product distribution centres, one of its largest and most criticized expenses. Despite a rise in sales, the company has still managed to cut order fulfillment expenses significantly, thanks to better inventory software and smarter storage. It also has honed its order "sorting" process, allowing it to ship roughly one-third more inventory with the same number of people. "They have made incredible progress in operations," said one industry research director.

Sources: Amazon.com 2006 Annual Report, www.amazon.com (accessed August 10, 2007); Mary E. Behr, "If at First You Don't Succeed," *CIO Insight*, November 2003, p. 51; Rob Hoff, "Amazon & Co. Still Floating in Froth," *BusinessWeek* Online, October 23, 2003, www.businessweek.com; Lotte Chow, "All in the Grooming," *CFO Asia*, October 17, 2003; Gene G. Marcial, "Amazon Turns a Page," *BusinessWeek*, October 14, 2002, p. 172; "New CFO at Amazon.com," *Publishers Weekly*, September 9, 2002, p. 12; "Career Journal: Who's News," *Wall Street Journal*, September 3, 2002, p. B10; Monica Soto, "Amazon.com Hires GE Executive as Chief Financial Officer," *Seattle Times*, August 31, 2002.

Leaders and the Leadership Process

We now turn from how leadership is related to power and how the hierarchical structure of organizations influences the uses of different kinds of power, to examining leadership as a process. This process has three fundamental elements in organizations: leaders, followers, and situations. Even though the role of leader typically gets most of the attention, all three factors must be

Exhibit 9.2

Locus of Leadership: Intersection of the Basic Components of the Leadership Process

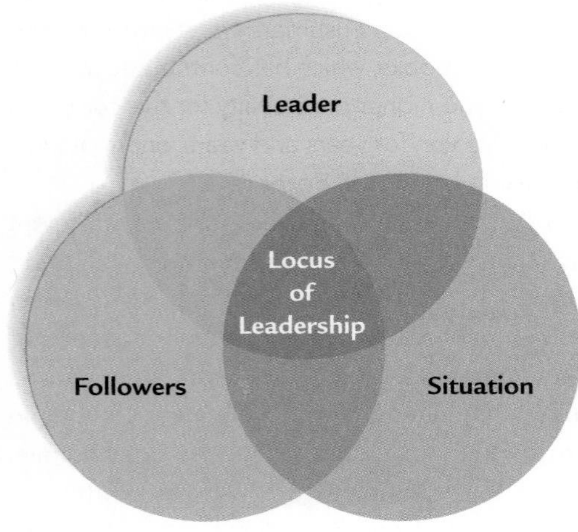

considered to gain a comprehensive understanding of how the process unfolds. As shown in Exhibit 9.2, what has been termed the "locus of leadership" is the intersection of these three variables: where and when the leader with a particular set of characteristics and behaviours interacts with a specific set of followers in a situation with certain identifiable characteristics.[15] Each element influences and is influenced by the other two variables, and a change in any one will alter how the other two factors interact.

The impact of each of these three variables on the basic leadership process will be discussed in more detail in the sections that follow. We begin with the leader: specifically, leaders' traits, skills, and behaviours.

Leaders' Traits

traits relatively enduring characteristics of a person

One critical component of what leaders in managerial roles bring to the work setting is their **traits**, that is, the relatively enduring characteristics of a person. The scientific study of the role of leaders' traits has had a somewhat roller-coaster history. At the beginning of the twentieth century, the "great man"—note that it was *not* the "great person"—view of leadership was in vogue. That is, leaders, almost always thought of as only men, were assumed to have inherited combinations of traits that distinguished them from followers. The notion, then, was that those destined to be leaders were "born" that way, not made. As years passed, however, this theory faded away because of the difficulties of proving that traits were, in fact, inherited. Instead, the focus shifted in the 1920s and 1930s to a search for specific traits or characteristics—such as verbal skills, physical size, dominance, self-esteem—that would unambiguously separate leaders from nonleaders.

The current view is that although specific traits do not invariably determine leadership effectiveness, they can increase its likelihood.[16] As shown in Exhibit 9.3, among the traits that research has indicated are most apt to predict effective leadership are drive, motivation to lead, honesty/integrity, self-confidence, and emotional maturity.[17]

- *Drive:* A high level of energy, effort, and persistence in the pursuit of objectives.
- *Motivation to lead:* A strong desire to influence others, to "be in charge." Such a person is comfortable with the use of power in relating to other people.[18]
- *Honesty/Integrity:* Trustworthiness. Someone with this trait is a person whose word can be relied on consistently and who is highly likely to do what he or she says.[19]
- *Self-confidence:* A strong belief in one's own capabilities.[20] People with this trait set high expectations for themselves and others,[21] and they tend to be optimistic rather than pessimistic about overcoming obstacles and achieving objectives. Obviously, in contrast to honesty/integrity, this is a trait that in the extreme can be a negative. It can result in a sense of infallibility and in an attitude of arrogance that can alienate potential followers. In other words, too much self-confidence can lead to what has been called "the shadow side of success."[22] That is, too much success in leadership, paradoxically, can produce the seeds of later leadership problems. No matter how much confidence

managers have in themselves, their staff, and their employees, nothing substitutes for preparation. The manager who relies on self-confidence at the expense of planning is setting the scene for potential disaster.

- *Emotional maturity:* Remaining even-tempered and calm in the face of stress and pressure. Persons with maturity tend to be accurate in self-awareness about their own strengths and weaknesses; moreover, they are less likely to be self-centred and to be unduly defensive in the face of criticism.[23]

Exhibit 9.3

Leaders' Traits

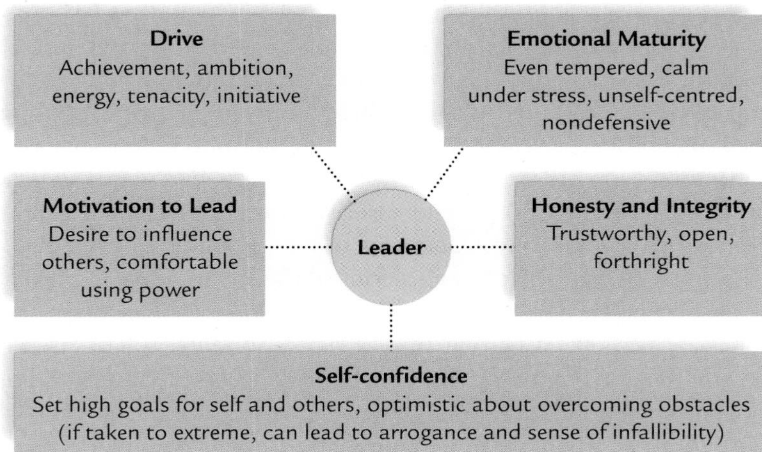

Source: Adapted from S. A. Kirkpatrick and E. A. Locke, "Leadership: Do Traits Matter?" *Academy of Management Executive* 5, no. 2 (1991), pp. 48–60.

Most of the research on traits has involved only, or mostly, men. The extent to which the findings would generalize to both genders remains a subject for further research. Also, it is important to re-emphasize that traits like the ones listed do not guarantee that a person will become a leader or will necessarily lead effectively. Very few people possess every critical trait at an exceptionally high level. However, if a person has one or more of these relatively enduring characteristics, the probabilities for successful leadership are increased. Traits provide potential, but other factors such as skills, attitudes, experience, and opportunities determine whether the potential will be realized.

Finally, most of the research on the relationship of personal traits to the effectiveness of leaders has not considered the impact of culture. It has focused primarily on Western, mostly North American, work environments. Whether traits can universally predict successful leadership is still an open question. It may be that in at least some cultures, other or different traits would be equally or more influential. In fact, the very notion that particular personal qualities or leadership traits are critical to successful influence is open to debate in many non-Western cultures, such as those in Southeast Asia. In countries such as Korea or Malaysia, for example, a person often is in a leadership position by virtue of ownership or family position, and others show respect for that reason rather than because of certain personality features.[24]

Leaders' Skills and Competencies

In Chapter 1 we discussed three types of skills that are important for anyone in a managerial position: technical skills, interpersonal skills, and conceptual skills. As we pointed out in that chapter, early in a managerial career the first two categories of skills—technical and interpersonal—loom especially large in determining whether someone will advance to higher organizational levels. As a person moves up in the organization, the relative importance of technical skills decreases, the importance of interpersonal skills continues to remain strong, and the importance of conceptual skills becomes increasingly critical. Since leadership is a major element in the overall process of management, it should be clear that all three of these types of skills are vital to the leadership function. This is particularly so because leadership involves attempts to influence other people in desired directions. The greater a person's technical, interpersonal, and conceptual skills are, the more likely that person will be able to exert significant amounts of influence.

emotional intelligence an awareness of others' feelings and a sensitivity to one's own emotions and the ability to control them

Emotional Intelligence by Lyman Porter

mymanagementlab

In the past two decades, two other sets of skills or competencies have become increasingly prominent in research relating to influence processes: "emotional intelligence" and "social intelligence." The first of these, **emotional intelligence**, has probably received the most attention to date,[25] with one of its chief proponents even going so far as to say it "is the *sine qua non* [indispensable ingredient] of leadership."[26] The essence of emotional intelligence, as the name implies, involves an awareness of others' feelings and a sensitivity to one's own emotions and the ability to control them.

As shown in Exhibit 9.4,[27] emotional intelligence has been conceived by one of its adherents as having five key components: self-awareness, self-regulation, motivation, empathy, and social skill. Three features of emotional intelligence seem particularly important for a manager to consider: (1) it is distinct from IQ or cognitive intelligence; (2) although in part determined genetically, it probably can be learned or improved by training, coaching, practice, and—especially—effort; and (3) it seems obviously relevant to performing effectively as a leader in an organizational setting.

Exhibit 9.4 Components of Emotional and Social Intelligence

Emotional Intelligence	Social Intelligence
· Self-Awareness	· Social Perceptiveness
· Self-Regulation	· Behavioural Flexibility
· Motivation	· "Savvy"
· Empathy	
· Social Skill	

social intelligence the ability to "read" other people and their intentions and adjust one's own behaviour in response

Although social intelligence shares some similarities with emotional intelligence, the two competencies also differ to an extent. Whereas major components of emotional intelligence involve self-awareness and self-regulation, **social intelligence** is more focused outward on being able to "read" other people and their intentions (see Exhibit 9.4). Thus, social perceptiveness is a principal ingredient. However, so also is what has been called "behavioural flexibility," or the ability and motivation to modify one's own behaviour in response to what is perceived socially. Thus, like emotional intelligence, social intelligence puts a premium on being able to monitor one's own behaviour and adjust that behaviour according to assessment of the social context and circumstances. Again, as with emotional intelligence, social intelligence is both desirable and important for leadership and something that a person can work on and presumably improve. A person who is socially intelligent is someone who has considerable tacit knowledge—knowledge that is not always directly made explicit—or, to use a more everyday term, savvy.

Leaders' Behaviours

For leadership to occur, traits and skills must be transformed into behaviour. Thus, considerable research has focused on leaders' behaviours and their impact on subordinates and followers. As far back as the 1950s, researchers zeroed in on two fundamental types of leader behaviours: those involving assistance in the direct performance of a task, and those involving the interpersonal relationships necessary to support task performance. These two types have been called by different names over the years, but probably the easiest terms to remember are "task behaviours" and "people behaviours." Examples of these behaviours are shown in Exhibit 9.5.

Exhibit 9.5 Leaders' Behaviours

Task Behaviours (Initiating Structure)	**People Behaviours (Consideration)**
· Specifies roles and tasks	· Is friendly
· Plans assignments	· Is supportive
· Schedules work	· Shows trust and confidence in subordinates
· Sets performance standards	· Shows concern for subordinates' welfare
· Develops procedures	· Gives recognition to subordinates for their accomplishments

Task Behaviours The key aspects of **task behaviours**, also termed "initiating structure" behaviours, centre on specifying and identifying the roles and tasks of the leaders themselves and their subordinates. Such behaviours involve planning assignments, scheduling work, setting standards of performance, and devising the procedures to carry out the tasks.

task behaviours behaviours that specify and identify the roles and tasks of leaders and their subordinates, such as planning, scheduling, setting standards, and devising procedures

People Behaviours This dimension of leader behaviours has also been termed "consideration" or "relationship oriented." Essentially, **people behaviours** include being friendly and supportive, showing trust and confidence in subordinates, being concerned about their welfare, and supplying recognition for their accomplishments.

people behaviours behaviours that focus on interaction, such as being friendly and supportive, showing trust and confidence, being concerned about others, and supplying recognition

Because of the consistency with which these two dimensions of leader behaviour have been identified in a wide variety of research studies over the years, you might expect that the most effective leaders would rate high on both dimensions—that is, be both strongly task oriented and strongly people oriented.[28] This has not been conclusively demonstrated, although it has been found that leaders who score highest on people behaviours tend to have the most satisfied subordinates.

Relevant to the issue of the types of leader behaviours is the question of whether female leaders demonstrate different patterns of leader behaviours from those displayed by males. Some research has been said to show that women are more likely than men to exhibit high levels of people skills and that consequently men and women have different leadership styles. However, this issue has been surrounded by considerable controversy. To date, there is insufficient evidence to draw decisive conclusions.[29] What seems clear is that the *individual* differences among women and among men are probably far more important than any relatively small overall average difference between the two gender groups.

Considering all of the research that has been carried out on leader behaviours across the past five decades, the principal message for those in managerial positions would seem to be this: Effective leaders need to focus on *both* structuring the work (task behaviours) *and* supporting and developing good interpersonal relationships with and among subordinates (people behaviours). Looking at leadership in this way is a very useful method for you to use to self-assess your own leadership behaviour: "How am I doing on task behaviours *and* how am I doing on people behaviours?"

Followers and the Leadership Process

We now turn our attention to the second key component of the leadership process: those who *receive* the leadership and influence, namely, followers or subordinates. The amount of research on followers has been considerably less than that on leaders. This is understandable, given the historical emphasis in Western societies on the role of leaders, but it represents a somewhat distorted and probably misleading picture of the complete process.

What Followers Bring to the Process

Followers, of course, have characteristics similar to leaders: personality traits, past experiences, beliefs and attitudes, and skills and abilities. What may be different, though, are the amounts and nature of these characteristics in relation to the leader's. In fact, rarely would they be exactly the same. Also, in a work setting, followers typically have lower position power than the leader. However, in increasingly flatter and less hierarchical contemporary work organizations, the difference is not likely to be as great as in the past. The difference in power is also being decreased by the greater access to information because of internet technology. Such a decrease in the difference between followers' and leaders' formal authority is changing the very nature of the leadership process in today's organizations and presenting new challenges to would-be leaders. In contemporary organizations, leaders cannot assume that they possess more expertise and knowledge than those in follower positions.

Not to be overlooked, moreover, is the fact that almost every leader is also a follower of someone else in the organization. Thus, most people in organizations have to learn how to become good followers as well as good leaders. As a knowledgeable observer has pointed out: "Organizations stand or fall partly on the basis of how well their leaders lead, but partly also on the basis of how well their followers follow."[30]

Effects of Followers' Behaviour

Leaders influence followers, but the reverse is also true: Leaders act, followers respond, and leaders react to those responses. Especially important in these evolving interactions are the followers' perceptions of the leaders—that is, the followers' views of a leader's characteristics and the reasons for the leader's behaviour. It appears that followers often check their perceptions against the traits they think leaders *should* possess and the behaviours they *should* display.[31] In effect, followers seem to develop what have been called "implicit leadership theories," and they tend to judge a leader's actions against particular standards or expectations they already have in mind.[32] When expectations aren't met, followers may blame leaders for a group's or organization's failures; likewise, when expectations are met, leaders typically get the credit. Some theorists argue that leaders in organizations, just like certain stars of athletic teams, frequently get excessive—and sometimes undeserved—credit or blame for outcomes they may not have affected quite so decisively.[33]

Situations and the Leadership Process

The third key element in the analysis of the leadership process is the situation surrounding the process. In addition to followers, the two most important categories of situational variables are the tasks to be performed and the organizational context.

Tasks

The nature of the work to be performed provides a critical component of the situation facing leaders. Change the task, and the leadership process is highly likely to be changed. Research evidence across many studies indicates that several of the most important dimensions of tasks that affect the leadership process include whether they are relatively structured or unstructured and whether they involve high or low levels of worker discretion.[34] For example, a manager of a group of newly trained but relatively inexperienced tax preparers at a firm like H&R Block would probably need to use a fairly high degree of task-oriented leadership to be sure that precise guidelines were being followed in analyzing clients' often complex returns. Alternatively, a project leader in charge of reviewing the work of a group of highly educated scientists doing advanced research in a pharmaceutical company like Alton Pharma Inc. in Oakville, Ontario, would probably be more concerned with ensuring a continuous flow of new scientific information and securing additional funding for the group even when it appears they are not producing immediately useful results. This manager might use a more person-oriented, less directive form of leadership with the research staff.

Organizational Context

The term "organizational context" in this instance means both the immediate work group (those who come in direct face-to-face contact with a leader) and the larger organization (composed of all individuals and groups who do not usually have frequent direct personal contact with a specific leader). A number of features of the organizational context can affect the leadership process. Of particular importance is the fundamental culture of the organization, that is, its history, traditions, and norms. Someone who has come out of a large and comparatively slow-moving company probably would find that the style of leadership he used effectively there is not equally effective in a fast-changing, start-up entrepreneurial firm. The reverse, of course, would be equally true. A leadership style consistent with the fun, informal culture at Radical Entertainment in Vancouver would not necessarily work at a larger and more traditional firm in, say, the banking industry. These may be extreme cases, but they illustrate that an organization's culture is highly likely to determine what forms of leadership will succeed. In addition to culture, other important parts of the organizational context affecting leadership include its structure (Chapter 8) and its pattern of controls (Chapter 14).

This completes our consideration of the basic concepts and processes of leadership. In the next section we review various perspectives or models of leadership and a number of issues that arise in relation to how managerial leadership is demonstrated in organizational contexts.

Different Approaches to Understanding Leadership

The leader. The followers. The situation. Each is essential for telling the story of leadership. But it is the *interactions* of the three variables that determine the outcomes of the leadership process in particular circumstances. Common sense, as well as theories of leadership, would tell us that no specific approach to leadership, regardless of the characteristics of the leader, the followers, and the situation, will work equally well all the time. Thus, since the 1960s or so, a number of different conceptual approaches to leadership have been developed. Each of these has focused on describing combinations of key variables necessary for leadership effectiveness. Several of the most prominent approaches, usually identified by the names of their major proponents, are:

- Blake and Mouton's "managerial grid"
- Hersey and Blanchard's situational leadership model
- Fiedler's leadership contingency theory
- House's path–goal theory
- Vroom and Yetton's normative decision model
- Substitutes for leadership

As you read about each of these different ways of looking at and thinking about leadership, focus on the particular parts of the leader/follower/situation combination that are being emphasized. The relative emphases that the different approaches put on each of these three components of the leadership process are summarized in Exhibit 9.6. None of these theories or approaches has "the" correct way of viewing leadership, but each provides an interesting and helpful window for making sense of leadership complexity.

Exhibit 9.6 Leadership Perspectives: Relative Emphasis on Leader, Follower, and Situation

	EMPHASIS ON:		
Perspective	**Leader**	**Follower**	**Situation**
Blake and Mouton: Managerial Grid	XX		
Hersey and Blanchard: Situational Leadership Model	X	XX	
Fiedler: Contingency Leadership Model	XX		XX
House: Path–Goal Theory	XX	XX	XX
Vroom/Yetton: Normative Decision Model	XX	X	XX
Substitutes for Leadership		XX	

X = Strong Emphasis
XX = Very Strong Emphasis

Blake and Mouton's "Managerial Grid"

This approach, developed by psychologists Robert Blake and Jane Mouton, was one of the earliest to grow out of research on the topic of leadership.[35] Blake and Mouton, using findings from a number of studies, proposed that leaders should view their role as consisting of two primary dimensions: a focus on the tasks to be accomplished and a focus on the people performing them. The term "**managerial grid**" was used because it was proposed that these two dimensions could be thought as going from low (a score of 1) to high (a score of 9). Thus, a graph could be constructed, as shown in Exhibit 9.7, with the x axis being the degree to which a manager was task oriented, and the y axis the degree to which a manager was people oriented. Using this system, managers could be rated on each dimension (by themselves or by others, like subordinates), and their position plotted on the graph (for example: 3 on the x or task-oriented axis, and 7 on the y or people-oriented axis).

managerial grid a method for measuring the degree to which managers are task oriented and people oriented

Exhibit 9.7

Blake and Mouton: The Managerial Grid

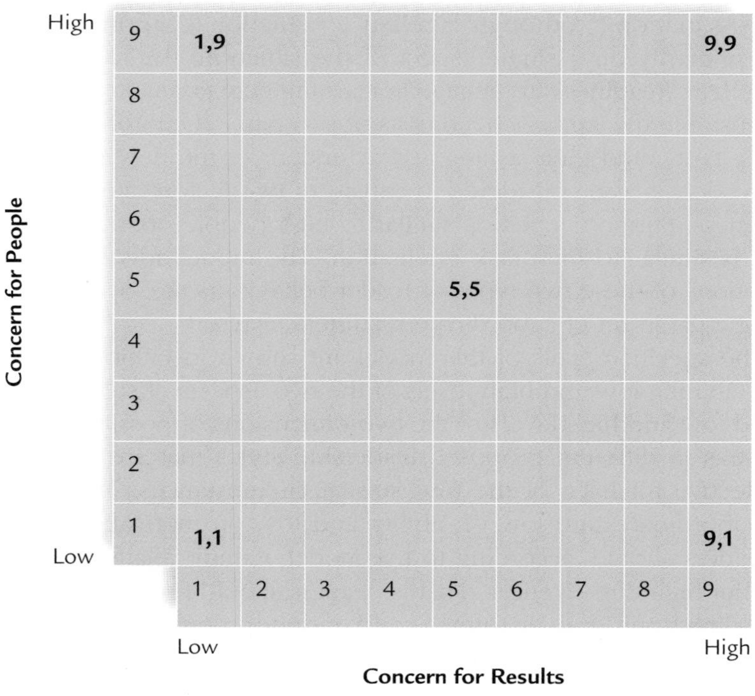

Source: Adapted from R. R. Blake and A. A. McCanse, *Leadership Dilemma—Grid Solutions* (formerly *The Managerial Grid* by R. R. Blake and J. S. Mouton) (Houston: Gulf Publishing Company, 1991), p. 29.

The central theme of the Blake and Mouton approach was that the best managers would be those highest on both dimensions—a high-high leader—or, in terms of the grid, a 9,9. Those who were high on task orientation but low on people concern (9,1), or vice versa (1,9), were viewed as obviously lacking in one or the other of the two critical skills needed for leadership success. Those who were in the middle on both dimensions (5,5) were regarded as average or mediocre leaders, neither highly successful nor definite failures. Note that this approach to leadership puts heavy emphasis on the leader, and gives relatively little attention to the attributes of the followers and, especially, the characteristics of the situation. A high-high leader (or anyone rated close to 9 on both dimensions) was thought to be the best kind of leader, irrespective of who the followers are and what kinds of situations or contexts confront the leader. The managerial grid approach could thus be thought of as a "universal" leadership theory—that is, one that says that there is one absolute best type of leader—one who is high on both a task orientation and a people orientation—under *all* conditions. This approach, developed in the 1960s, was, at least to some extent, anchored in the available scholarly research evidence of the time, and had a simplicity that was highly appealing to practising managers. It helped to highlight two dimensions of leader behaviour that are clearly important. On the other hand, it clearly ignores many important situational variables that affect both how leaders behave and how successful they are. Research has not confirmed that one type of leadership style, whether the so-called high-high style or any other style, is universally appropriate and effective.

Hersey and Blanchard's Situational Leadership Model

situational leadership model a model that states that different types of appropriate leadership are "contingent" on some other variable, in this case "the situation"

The **situational leadership model** is one of the earlier contingency approaches to leadership.[36] It thus is a model that states that different types of appropriate leadership are "contingent" on—or depend on—some other variable, in this case "the situation." Although labelled a "situational" approach, the model focuses primarily on a single aspect of the situation: the followers—specifically, on their "readiness" to engage in learning new tasks. Subordinates' readiness, as used in this approach, consists of two parts: their ability (in relation to a specific task), and their willingness to undertake the new task. The behaviour of leaders is also considered to consist of two factors: supportiveness and directiveness. Supportiveness is similar to high people orientation, and directiveness is similar to high task orientation. The model advocates that certain combinations of these two types of leader behaviours are best or most appropriate for a given set of subordinate readiness levels.

The specific details of this model are shown in Exhibit 9.8. As can be seen, combining low and high levels of the two aspects of subordinates' readiness, and low and high levels of the two dimensions of possible leader behaviour, results in different proposed leadership styles that are presumed to be most effective for each of the four sets of circumstances. Thus, for tasks in which subordinates are low on ability and low on motivation to undertake them, leaders should, according to the model, exhibit relatively low supportiveness but high directiveness. That is, leaders should firmly set goals, provide explicit directions and deadlines, and monitor performance closely. The appropriate leadership style for this combination of circumstances is given the informal label "telling" by Hersey and Blanchard.

Exhibit 9.8

Hersey and Blanchard: Situational Leadership Model

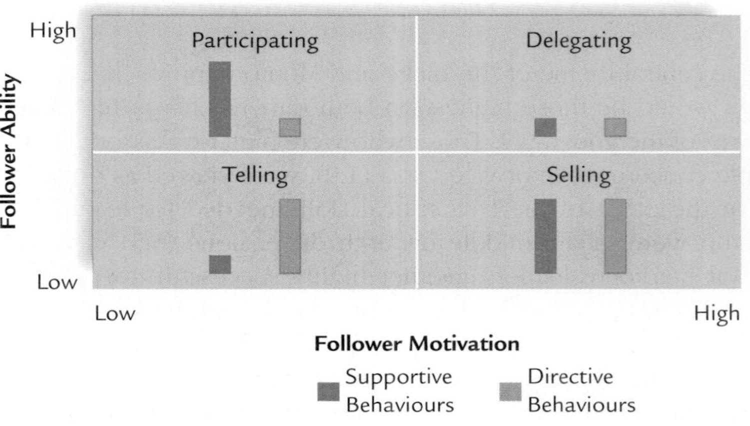

Source: Adapted from P. Hersey, K. H. Blanchard, and D. E. Johnson, *Management of Organizational Behaviour: Leading Human Resources*, 8th ed. (Upper Saddle River, NJ: Prentice Hall, 2001).

When subordinates have low ability for the tasks but high initial motivation to perform them, then leaders should exhibit both strong supportiveness and strong directiveness. Thus, leaders should be highly encouraging, but at the same time should take charge in defining objectives and explaining methods for performing the tasks. This combination of leader behaviour is given the label "selling."

For the third set of subordinates' readiness characteristics—high ability but low motivation—leaders need to use subordinates' ideas and suggestions as much as possible to strengthen their interest in the task and to obtain their commitment; yet they need not be highly directive since the subordinates' capabilities for performing the tasks are already high. The style most appropriate for these conditions is "participating."

The final combination of followers' characteristics, high ability and high willingness to perform, is the appropriate setting, according to the model, for both low supportiveness and low directiveness on the part of the leader. In other words, for this situation, the leader can rely on a high degree of delegation and expect followers to perform well on their own with a minimum of leader involvement. Thus, the recommended style is "delegating."

There is much about the Hersey and Blanchard model that is intuitively appealing. First, as with the Blake and Mouton managerial grid, it is a relatively simple and straightforward model. Second, the summarizing leadership style labels ("telling," etc.) are understandable and easy to remember. Third, like the managerial grid, the model uses research findings to emphasize two important types of leadership behaviours, people oriented ("supportiveness") and task oriented ("directiveness"), that form the four categories of leadership styles.

Despite these positive features of the model, there are some fairly obvious problems with its implementation. Subordinate readiness levels, for example, typically do not come in simple high and low combinations. Often, subordinates will be around the middle on both ability and motivation or willingness, rather than definitely high or definitely low on one or both. Also, the model requires leaders to make an accurate assessment of the two subordinate readiness characteristics, and this is not always easy to do—especially in the case of trying to gauge their "willingness" to perform particular tasks. Probably the most critical deficiency in the Hersey and Blanchard model is that it considers only subordinate readiness as a feature of the task and organizational environment. It essentially ignores other possible major features of the context such as the amount and type of interaction with other individuals or units in the organization, the culture of the group or organization, the history of past events, and the like. Subordinate or follower readiness is important for any leader to consider, but by itself does not determine how leaders should behave nor the success of their efforts.

Fiedler's Leadership Contingency Theory

This theory, also developed several decades ago, grew out of a program of Fred Fiedler's research that centred on leaders' attitudes toward their co-workers. Specifically, leaders were asked to rate on a series of scales (e.g., "pleasant–unpleasant," "supportive–hostile," "open–guarded") the person from their present or past work experience with whom they could work least well. Fiedler called this person their "**least preferred co-worker**" **(LPC)**.[37] Thus, leaders who rated this person relatively harshly received low LPC scores, whereas leaders who rated their least preferred co-worker relatively favourably received high LPC scores. Basically, a leader's LPC score was interpreted to indicate the degree to which a leader was especially task oriented (low LPC score) or person oriented (high LPC score).

LPC (least preferred co-worker) theory a contingency theory of leadership that identifies the types of situations in which task-oriented or person-oriented leaders would be most effective

Fiedler's theory was that leadership effectiveness would be contingent on the type of leader (low or high LPC) *and* the relative degree of favourability of the situation for the leader. According to the theory, a favourable situation for the leader exists when three conditions are present:

- when relations with subordinates are good
- when the task is highly structured
- when the leader has considerable position power

An unfavourable situation would be when these conditions are the opposite. For example, a vice-president of finance who has been assigned the task of preparing the company's annual report, who will be able to work with the same team that produced last year's report, and who also is regarded as excellent by top management would be in a highly favourable situation. In contrast, the leadership situation would be less favourable for a senior manager asked to develop a new product in conjunction with a subordinate who had hoped to be promoted into the position now held by the new manager. The theory predicts, as shown in Exhibit 9.9, that *low* LPC leaders, that is, those most task oriented, are most effective in highly favourable *or* highly unfavourable situations, such as that encountered by the VP of finance in our example. On the other hand, high LPC (high relationship-oriented) leaders will do best in moderately favourable or moderately unfavourable situations. The reasoning, according to the theory, is that task-oriented leaders do not need to be especially sensitive to interpersonal relations in very favourable situations, and in very unfavourable situations a strong task orientation by the leader is the only approach that will work. Conversely, when situations are neither especially favourable nor unfavourable, the theory presumes that leaders more attuned to other people's feelings will do best.

Exhibit 9.9 LPC Theory

SITUATION	
Favourable (for leader)	**Unfavourable (for leader)**
Good subordinate relationships	Poor subordinate relationships
Highly structured task	Unstructured task
Leader with high amount of position power	Leader lacks position power
LEADERS	
Low LPC Perspective	**High LPC Perspective**
Rates least preferred co-worker harshly	Rates least preferred co-worker favourably
Task oriented	Person oriented
Most effective when situation is either highly favourable or highly unfavourable	Most effective when situation is neither highly favourable nor highly unfavourable

Fiedler's theory has been the object of considerable research over the years. Reviews of this theory indicate some support for it, but various details of the theory have been criticized.[38] Probably its chief value is that when it was originated in the 1960s, it highlighted the importance of the nature of the situations leaders face, and it suggested how those situational conditions could make it harder or easier for leaders of particular types to be effective. The theory therefore has a very important implication: It is more difficult for leaders to change their styles than it is for the situation to be changed (or to match leaders with particular types of situations). It also clearly is a contingency theory and not a universal approach in which one type of leadership should work best in all situations.

House's Path–Goal Theory

Robert House and his associates in the 1970s proposed what was termed a **path–goal theory of leadership**.[39] Essentially, this perspective emphasized that the leader's job was to increase subordinate satisfaction and effort by "increasing personal payoffs to subordinates for work-goal attainment and making the path to these payoffs easier to travel by clarifying it, reducing roadblocks and pitfalls, and increasing the opportunities for personal satisfaction en route."[40]

path–goal theory of leadership a contingency theory of leadership that focuses on the leader's role in increasing subordinate satisfaction and effort by increasing personal payoffs for goal attainment and making the path to these payoffs easier

The path–goal analysis of the factors involved in leadership effectiveness draws heavily from expectancy theories of motivation (to be discussed in the next chapter). Thus, it assumes that the leader's role is to influence subordinates' estimated probabilities for being able to convert their efforts into performance that leads to desired rewards. Also, much like several of the other leadership approaches, path–goal theory emphasizes two basic types of leader behaviour: supportive leadership (people oriented) and directive leadership (task oriented). In addition, as with LPC and other contingency theories, path–goal theory assumes that a particular leadership approach will work better in some task situations than in others. As illustrated in Exhibit 9.10, if tasks are frustrating, boring, or highly stressful, supportive leadership behaviour is assumed to help increase subordinate enjoyment and reduce anxiety, thereby raising effort and satisfaction. If tasks are intrinsically enjoyable and interesting, it is assumed that supportive, people-oriented leadership will have little net effect.

Exhibit 9.10

Path–Goal Theory

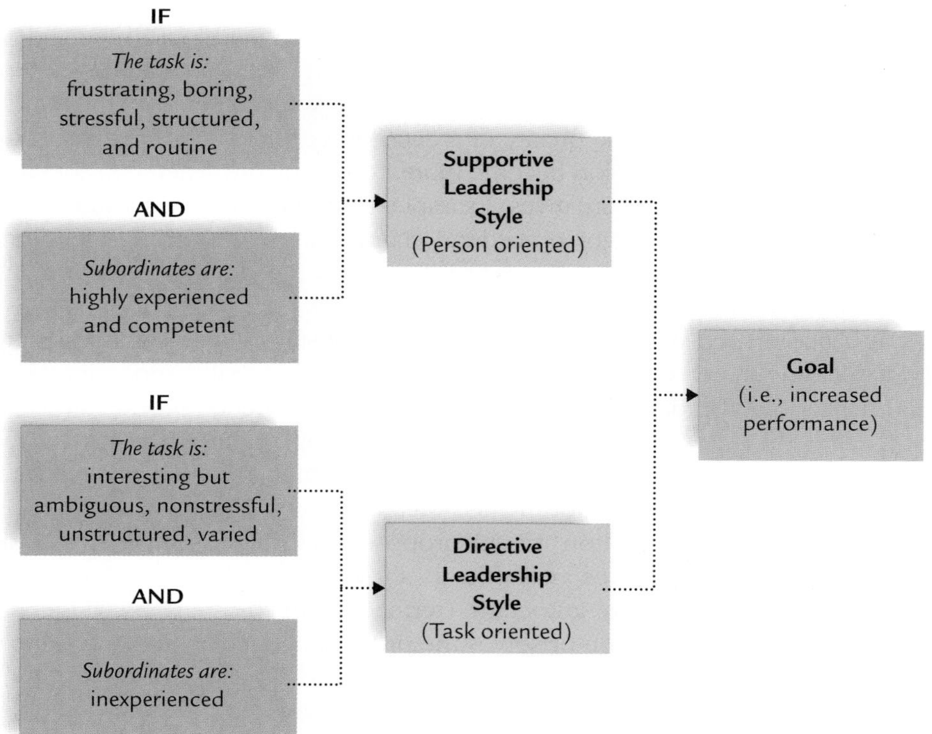

Source: Adapted from R. J. House, "A Path-Goal Theory of Leader Effectiveness," *Administrative Science Quarterly* 16, no. 5 (1971), pp. 321–339.

Directive, task-oriented leadership behaviour, according to the theory, becomes especially important when tasks are varied and unstructured *and* when subordinates are inexperienced. Such directive behaviour is assumed to reduce ambiguities in the situation and to clarify the paths to successful task performance. On the other hand (see Exhibit 9.10), if subordinates are highly experienced and competent *and* tasks are relatively structured, directive leadership behaviour will be superfluous and possibly even resented. In this respect, path–goal theory has similarities to Hersey and Blanchard's situational leadership model.

As with Fiedler's LPC contingency theory, the main contribution of House's path–goal theory has been to provide additional insights into the interactions among leader behaviour, task characteristics, and follower competencies, and to identify which interactions are most likely to result in more productive and satisfying outcomes. It differs from Fiedler's theory in that House assumes leaders can modify their styles to suit the situation rather than having to have the situation changed to fit the leader. The path–goal theory's primary value is in helping potential leaders to think systematically about what types of behaviour on their part might work best in which types of situations.

Vroom and Yetton's Normative Decision Model

normative decision model a contingency model that prescribes standards to determine the extent to which subordinates should be allowed to participate in decision making

Strictly speaking, Victor Vroom and Philip Yetton's **normative decision model** is not a model of leadership.[41] However, it addresses a major issue faced by leaders: the extent to which subordinates should participate in decision making. It is also a contingency model in that it is designed to help leaders determine how much and what type of subordinate participation to use in particular situations. The model is not simply analytical; it also *prescribes* when to use participation as a result of that analysis. Thus, it is called a "normative" model because it provides standards or rules for making such decisions.

The model focuses on two key variables that determine the effectiveness of decisions when measured by group performance: quality and acceptance. Decision quality refers to the merit or degree of excellence of the course of action that is chosen. The quality of a decision becomes more crucial as the consequences of that decision become more important and when considerable variability exists among alternatives. Examples would be when important goals are being set or when major procedural changes are to be made. Decisions about relatively trivial matters, like where to place a piece of office equipment, would not require significant decision quality.

Decision acceptance refers to the amount of subordinate commitment to implementing the chosen alternative. Acceptance is especially important when high levels of subordinate effort and motivation are needed to execute decisions after they are made. If a decision can be implemented directly by the leader without involving followers, for example, then it would not matter a great deal whether decision acceptance was high.

The Vroom and Yetton model proposes that leaders have five basic decision-making procedures available, as shown in Exhibit 9.11. These procedures range from highly autocratic (termed AI in the model), where the manager makes the decision or solves the problem alone, to highly participative (termed G), where the group itself makes the decision. In determining which procedure to use in given situations, a manager could train herself to ask a series of yes–no questions, in a decision-tree style of inquiry, as shown in Exhibit 9.12. As can be seen, the decision tree involves eight components of a situation—the amount of information possessed by the manager and the subordinates, the likelihood that subordinates will accept an autocratic decision, and so forth. By answering this series of questions about the situation, a leader should be able to choose a procedure that will result in effective decisions.

Exhibit 9.11 Normative Decision-Making Model: Decision-Making Styles

Decision Style[a]	Definition
AI	Leader makes the decision alone.
AII	Leader asks for information from team members but makes the decision alone. Team members may or may not be informed what the situation is.
CI	Leader shares situation with each team member and asks for information and evaluation. Team members do not meet as a team, and the leader alone makes the decision.
CII	Leader and team members meet as a team to discuss the situation, but the leader makes the decision.
G	Leader and team members meet as a team to discuss the situation, and the team makes the decision.

[a]A = autocratic C = consultative G = group

Sources: V. H. Vroom and P. W. Yetton, *Leadership and Decision-Making* (Pittsburgh, PA: University of Pittsburgh Press, 1973); V. H. Vroom and A. G. Jago, *The New Leadership: Managing Participation in Organizations* (Englewood Cliffs, NJ: Prentice Hall, 1988).

This model (and later versions of it) has been found to have a fairly high level of validity in predicting successful decisions, and it has been used extensively in management development programs.[42] However, as previously noted, although it is a contingency model that is relevant to leadership, it only deals with a portion of total leadership behaviour: the extent of participation in group decision making.

Substitutes for Leadership

One other important contingency approach needs to be considered. It is not a leadership theory as such, but it raises significant issues for managers to consider—namely, in some circumstances, there can be **substitutes for leadership**.[43] That is, a greater use of leadership behaviours is not always the only, or even the best, solution for some managerial problems. In certain work settings, other approaches can at least partially substitute for the need for leadership or can sometimes overcome poor leadership. Examples of some possible substitutes for leadership are shown in Exhibit 9.13.

substitutes for leadership alternative approaches that can at least partially substitute for the need for leadership or can sometimes overcome poor leadership

Extensive training and experience, for example, can lessen the need for leadership direction in such fast-paced and complex jobs as air traffic controller or police emergency work. The decision speed required in these job situations often would not allow time for intervention by a leader, so prior training substitutes for such influence. Furthermore, in many technical and professional jobs, high levels of formal education reduce the need for close supervision. It is safe to assume that an attorney or scientist or computer programmer working for a company will probably not need the same amount of supervision, and certainly not the same type, as an employee with few skills working in a relatively new position. Too much attempted leadership of such professionals would probably hinder rather than facilitate their performance. Similarly, workers in jobs that supply considerable amounts of intrinsic

Exhibit 9.12

Normative Decision-Making Model for Leaders' Use of Participation: Decision-Tree Questions

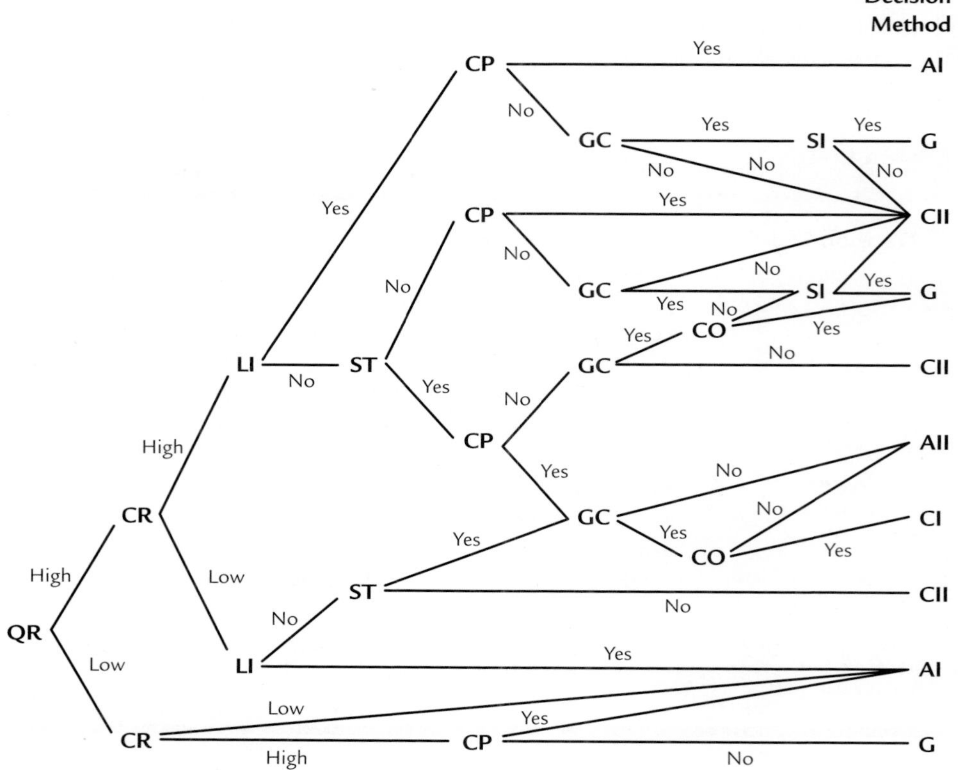

State the Problem

QR How important is the quality of this decision?
CR How important is subordinate commitment to the decision?
LI Do you have sufficient information to make a high-quality decision?
ST Is the problem well-structured?
CP If you were to make the decision by yourself, is it reasonably certain that your subordinates would be committed to it?
GC Do subordinates share the organization goals to be attained in solving this problem?
CO Is conflict among subordinates over preferred solutions likely?
SI Do subordinates have sufficient information to make a high-quality decision?

Source: Adapted and reprinted from *Leadership and Decision-Making* by Victor H. Vroom and Phillip W. Yetton, by permission of the University of Pittsburgh Press. © 1973 by University of Pittsburgh Press.

satisfaction, such as those involving the development of an exciting new product or service, would be unlikely to need leaders to increase their motivation. These examples point to the conclusion that the amount and type of leadership required can vary considerably from situation to situation. Too much attempted leadership, or too much of a particular leadership approach, sometimes can be as dangerous for the organization—and for the would-be leader—as not enough leadership.

neutralizers of leadership aspects of the organization or work situation that can defeat the best efforts of leaders

In addition to substitutes for leadership, there are also "**neutralizers of leadership**," that is, aspects of the organization or work situation that can defeat the best efforts of leaders. Examples would be inflexible organization procedures that do not give leaders sufficient freedom of choice, or an organizational compensation policy that does not allow them to appropriately reward exceptional performance. Thus, neutralizers, like substitutes, emphasize the importance of situational contingencies and how they can impact the effectiveness of leadership. In the case of neutralizers, however, that impact is often dysfunctional.

Exhibit 9.13

Examples of Possible Substitutes for Leadership

Source: Adapted from S. Kerr and J. M. Jermier, "Substitutes for Leadership: Their Meaning and Measurement," *Organizational Behaviour and Human Performance* 22, no. 3 (1978), pp. 375–403.

Contemporary Leadership Issues

In recent years, scholars in the field of leadership have raised several issues that have become increasingly important for management practice. These issues include the similarities and differences between leading and managing; charismatic leadership; transformational leadership; and leadership across different national cultures. Each raises interesting implications for the leadership function of managing.

Leading and Managing: The Same or Different?

Leading and managing are two activities that take place in all organizations, and the two terms are often used interchangeably. The processes appear to be similar in many respects. The question is: Do they completely overlap, or are they distinctly different? The answer depends on how the two terms are defined, especially "managing."

The case for viewing leadership as different from management has been made in recent years by several prominent behavioural science scholars.[44] It focuses on the role of leaders in creating vision for organizations or units, promoting major changes in goals and procedures, setting and communicating new directions, and inspiring subordinates. This set of activities is then contrasted with more mundane, task-oriented "managerial" functions such as dealing with interpersonal conflict, planning and organizing, and in general implementing goals set by others (the leaders).

When leading and managing are defined in these ways, then of course they are different. However, if managing is considered from a broader perspective, as it is throughout this book, then the two activities do not differ as much as might appear on the surface. That is, managing *ought* to involve most of the kinds of activities that are included in the leader's role. Removing such "leading" activities from managing makes an artificial distinction between the two and relegates managing to a routine, almost trivial activity—which it is not.

Exhibit 9.14

The Overlapping Roles of Leaders and Managers

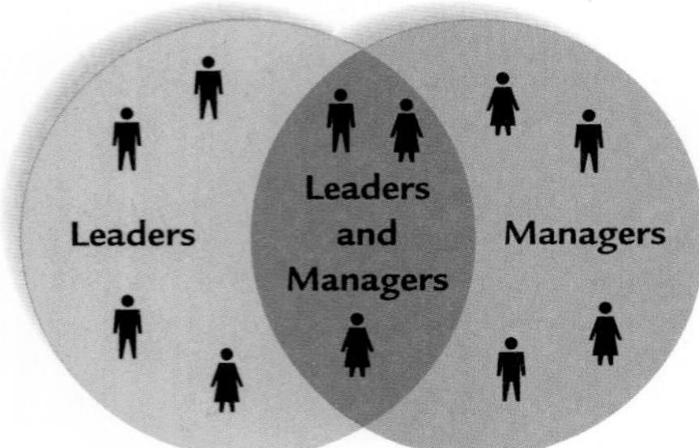

The relation of leading to managing can be illustrated by use of a Venn diagram. Imagine all the leaders from one organization in one circle and all the managers from that same organization in another. The two circles are likely to be partially, but not totally, separate (as shown in Exhibit 9.14). A person can be a leader, and a person can be a manager; but many people are *both* leaders and managers. Leadership is a very important component of management, but management involves more than just leadership. Thus, although not all leaders are managers, and not all managers are leaders, modern organizations need most of their managers to engage in leadership behaviour such as fostering innovation and creativity, finding better ways to achieve or exceed goals, and inspiring other people. Consequently, in this chapter and in this book, we view organizational leadership as a process that should be included as a significant part of the managerial role, but it is definitely not the total role.

Charismatic Leadership

As previously mentioned, when we were reviewing types of personal power, charisma is an especially strong form of referent power. The term "charisma" has a theological origin and comes from the Greek word for "gift." It literally means "divinely conferred gift." Its relevance for organizational settings was first highlighted in the early decades of the twentieth century by sociologist Max Weber.[45] He described the **charismatic leader** as someone who has influence over others based on inspirational qualities of the individual rather than on that person's formal power or position. Thus, followers or subordinates are assumed to identify with that person because of those exceptional qualities. Many people, of course, would like to think they are endowed with charisma, but only relatively few people have these special powers. If they were common, they wouldn't be exceptional.

charismatic leader someone who has influence over others based on individual inspirational qualities rather than formal power

The term "charisma" has been used particularly in the political sphere to describe those who are especially influential with large numbers of people. Examples include historical figures such as Mahatma Gandhi, Nelson Mandela, Winston Churchill, Mother Teresa, Martin Luther King Jr., and Pierre Elliott Trudeau. In the business domain, such people as Izzy Asper, Ted Rogers, and Annette Verschuren come to mind.

It is only in the last couple of decades that the concept of charisma has been used explicitly in scholarly examinations of organizational leadership.[46] One of the first such analyses focused on the specific traits and behaviours of charismatic leaders, such as

- strong needs for power
- high levels of self-confidence
- strong beliefs in their own ideas[47]

In terms of their behaviours, charismatic leaders, more than other types of leaders, are especially likely to

- model desired behaviour
- communicate high expectations for followers' performance
- be concerned with and try to influence the impressions of others
- emphasize ideals, values, and lofty goals

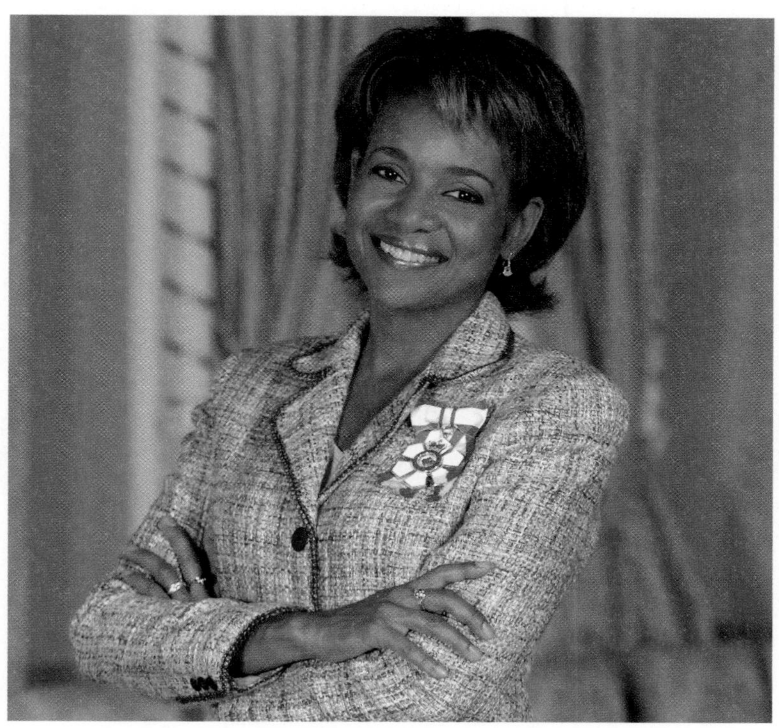

Starting from harsh beginnings in Port au Prince, Haiti, Michaëlle Jean's family immigrated to Canada when she was a child. Her Excellency the Right Honourable Michaëlle Jean, Governor General of Canada since 2005, has openly demonstrated her charismatic approach to the office with emotion and intimacy, while emphasizing her strong commitment to fighting poverty and the abuse of women and children in Canada and abroad.

Another analysis of leadership from a charismatic perspective focuses on particular types of leaders' behaviours that seem to enhance effects on followers.[48] These include:

- emphasizing a vision for the organization that represents a major, but achievable, change
- taking innovative or unorthodox types of actions to achieve goals
- demonstrating self-sacrifices on behalf of the organization

This perspective highlights the idea that anything leaders can do to create follower dissatisfaction with the status quo, to articulate compelling visions, and to offer innovative solutions will increase followers' feelings of collective identity with their leaders and the probability of charisma being attributed to those leaders.[49]

Based on the several scholarly analyses just discussed, Exhibit 9.15 presents a summary set of attributes of charismatic leaders.

Since charisma is a type of "special power" possessed by relatively few people, can a typical manager or leader try to increase his or her charisma? It is clear that people cannot create this type of power simply by assuming they have it, or by asking for it or demanding it. It must be generated or conferred in some fashion. Although few managers have the personality traits to easily or spontaneously produce the levels of charisma that certain renowned business and political leaders have achieved, people in leadership positions can increase the chances that their subordinates will be motivated to follow them and work with and for them. The kinds of behaviour summarized in Exhibit 9.15 are ones that can be developed.

Transformational Leadership

In the past couple of decades, an approach that is quite similar in many ways to charismatic leadership has been studied, and indeed often advocated, by

Exhibit 9.15

Attributes of the Charismatic Leader

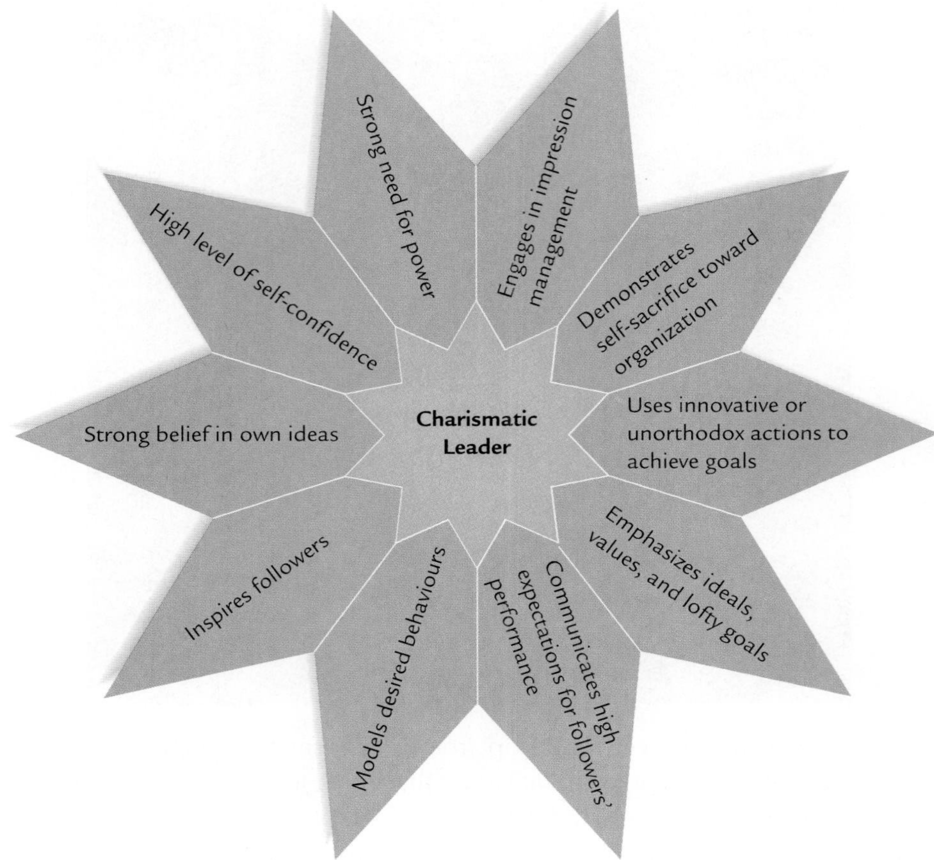

transformational leadership leadership that motivates followers to ignore self-interests and work for the larger good of the organization to achieve significant accomplishments; emphasis is on articulating a vision that will convince subordinates to make major changes

Transformational Leadership by Lyman Porter

mymanagementlab

transactional leadership leadership that focuses on motivating followers' self-interests by exchanging rewards for their compliance; emphasis is on having subordinates implement procedures correctly and make needed, but relatively routine, changes

scholars who write about leadership.[50] That concept is **transformational leadership**. Both ways of looking at leadership involve the notion of being able to motivate followers to make major changes or to achieve at very high levels. Thus, the original concept of transformational leadership, authored by political scientist James M. Burns, was that it was a process in which "leaders and followers raise one another to higher levels of morality and motivation."[51] Later refinements of this approach—by social scientists specifically addressing organizational contexts—emphasized that leaders are transformational, even if they don't necessarily appeal to "higher levels of morality and motivation," as long as they motivate followers to ignore their own self-interests and work for the larger good of the organization.[52] Put another way, attributions of charisma are strongly based on leaders' personal traits and characteristics, but attributions of transformational qualities are largely based on what leaders do as well as what they say.

Transformational leaders, like charismatic leaders, inspire their followers. However, this is done not only through followers' identification with the leader, as in the case of charismatic leadership, but also through the empowerment and coaching of followers. It is in this latter respect that the concept of transformational leadership differs from charismatic leadership. With transformational leadership, followers are not required to be highly dependent on their leaders. Also, whereas instances of charismatic leadership are rare, transformational leadership behaviour is assumed to be potentially possible almost anywhere throughout the organization.[53]

Those who advocate greater transformational leadership in organizations typically contrast it with so-called **transactional leadership**,[54] as shown in Exhibit 9.16. The latter is regarded as leadership that is more passive and that

Steven Fletcher has proven himself a worthy opponent in politics and a leader in representing people with specific health care needs. Elected to the House of Commons in 2004, Fletcher was the first member of Parliament to have a permanent disability, which required improvements in accessibility to the parliament buildings. Fletcher exhibits what many people would regard as classic traits of leadership, including persistence in the pursuit of objectives, a desire to influence others, and a high level of self-confidence.

emphasizes the exchange of rewards or other benefits for compliance by followers. Transformational leadership is seen as an approach that underscores the importance of leaders' appeals to followers' organizational or "common good" interests, whereas transactional leadership is seen as focusing more on leaders' reliance on followers' pursuit of self-interests to motivate their performance. In many respects, however, this distinction is artificial, since individuals often act for both their own interests *and* organizational interests.

Exhibit 9.16 Transformational versus Transactional Leadership

	Transformational Leadership	**Transactional Leadership**
Leader gains subordinates' compliance by:	Inspiring, empowering, and coaching followers	Exchange of rewards and benefits
Appeals focus on:	Organizational and "common good" interests	Self-interest
Type of planned change:	Major organizational change	Routine changes

Another distinction drawn between transformational and transactional leadership by some experts is that the former involves motivating subordinates to make major changes, while the latter involves the implementation of routine changes and procedures. Again, this distinction is not always clear-cut in many organizational situations.

In any event, a transformational perspective does focus on motivating people to attain highly significant, or even unusual, achievements and accomplishments. Several studies have explored how transformational leaders influence their followers to achieve such exceptional results. One study of 12 CEOs, for example, found that transformational leaders (1) recognized the need for major changes, (2) helped subordinates prepare for and accept such changes, and especially, (3) were particularly skillful in persuading subordinates to accept a new way of doing things. That is, they communicated a new vision within the organization. The study indicated that transformational leaders

- viewed themselves as agents of change
- were thoughtful risk-takers
- were sensitive to people's needs
- stated a set of core values to rally around
- were flexible and open to learning
- had good analytical skills
- had considerable confidence in their vision for the organization[55]

Another study of 90 leaders in both the corporate world and the public sector came to similar conclusions:

> *[Transformational leaders] paid attention to what was going on, they determined what parts of events at hand would be important for the future of the organization, they set a new direction, and they concentrated the attention of everyone in the organization on (that new future). This was...as true for orchestra conductors, army generals, football coaches, and school superintendents as for corporate leaders.*[56]

It is clear from these studies that transformational leadership (1) can occur in widely varying circumstances, (2) emphasizes a particular focus on a vision and how to implement it, and (3) requires considerable perseverance and dedication by the leader. Exhibit 9.17 summarizes a set of guidelines for those who aspire to transform their organizations, or their parts of the organization.[57]

Exhibit 9.17 Guidelines for Transformational Leadership

Those Who Want to Be Transformational Leaders Should:
Develop a clear and appealing vision
Develop a strategy for attaining the vision
Articulate and promote the vision
Act confident and optimistic
Express confidence in followers
Use early success in small steps to build confidence
Celebrate successes
Use dramatic, symbolic actions to emphasize key values
Lead by example

Source: Adapted from G. Yuki, *Leadership in Organizations*, 3rd ed. (Upper Saddle River, NJ: Prentice Hall, 1994).

Leadership across Different National Cultures

A final issue with respect to leadership, power, and influence is this: Does leadership differ fundamentally across national cultures, or do the similarities outweigh the differences? The answer is that nobody knows for sure, although researchers are attempting to find answers.[58]

As some observers point out: "*Leadership* is a fairly modern concept. It did not appear in English-language usage until the first half of the 19th century and has been primarily the concern of Anglo-Saxon influenced countries. Prior to that, and in other countries, the notion of *headship* has been more prominent, as in the head of state, chief, or other *ruling* [italics added] position."[59] Or, as another scholar put it, "the universality of leadership [as a part of the managerial role] does not . . . imply a similarity of leadership style throughout the world."[60]

Experts on Southeast Asia, for example, point out two essential cultural features that affect leadership situations and the use of power and influence in that area of the world: requirements for order and compliance and requirements for harmony.[61] The first of these cultural "requirements" involves traditional values that support the acceptance of hierarchies, conformity, and deference to authority. The necessity for the cultural value of harmony involves not only obligations of the subordinate to the superior, but also obligations of the superior to respect the subordinate and care for his or her welfare. Clearly, this is a quite different leadership style than is found in most Western societies. In most Asian cultures, for example, this style can be summarized in the word **paternalism**, where a leader is regarded as the provider "father" who will take care of the subordinate in return for responsible behaviour and performance. This style is also often found in Central and South American countries where there is a strong emphasis on collective as opposed to individual values.[62]

paternalism where a leader is regarded as the provider "father" who will take care of the subordinate in return for responsible behaviour and performance

Despite such differences related to cultural norms and traditions, some similarities in leadership practices—such as greater use of subordinate participation—are beginning to appear with increasing regularity around the world because of the spread of industrialization.[63] Thus, forces for differences in leadership and influence practices because of culture are combating forces for similarities due to industrialization and the increasing levels of education associated with it. Results from the most recent and comprehensive large-scale investigation of attributes of effective leadership across more than 60 different national cultures appear consistent with this conclusion.[64] As Exhibit 9.18 shows, according to the data collected for this study, certain leader attributes, such as "trustworthy" and "decisive," are viewed as positive across all cultures. Likewise, certain other attributes, such as "dictatorial" and "asocial," are universally viewed as negative. The reactions to other leader attributes, however, such as "cautious" and "ambitious," are highly contingent on the particular culture and its values. These characteristics, therefore, are viewed positively in some cultures but distinctly negatively in other cultures.

Sandra Lovelace Nicholas is a Maliseet woman from the Tobique reserve in New Brunswick. She is heralded as playing a major role in the second wave of feminism in Canada. Her successful appeal in 1981 to the Human Rights Committee of the United Nations meant that native women in Canada would no longer lose their status when they marry a non-native man, as set out in the *Indian Act*. Her singular act went against the rule of Canada as well as the male dominant First Nations. Sandra Lovelace Nicholas is now a Canadian senator.

Exhibit 9.18 The Effect of Culture on Attitudes toward Leaders' Attributes

Examples of leader attributes universally viewed as *positive* +	Examples of leader attributes universally viewed as *negative* –	Examples of leader attributes viewed as *positive* or *negative* depending on the culture +/–
+ Trustworthy	– Noncooperative	+/– Ambitious
+ Encouraging	– Irritable	+/– Individualistic
+ Honest	– Dictatorial	+/– Cunning
+ Decisive	– Ruthless	+/– Cautious
+ Communicative	– Egocentric	+/– Class Conscious
+ Dependable	– Asocial	+/– Evasive

Source: R. J. House, "Cultural Influences on Leadership and Organizations: Project GLOBE," in W. Mobley (ed.), *Advances in Global Leadership*, vol. 1 (Stamford, CT: JAI Press, 1998).

Because of expanding industrialization, the need for effective leadership has become a worldwide phenomenon. Precisely *how* that need is being met in specific organizations and in specific countries, however, still appears to be influenced by cultural circumstances and traditions. Nevertheless, the picture of particular leadership styles and practices around the world at the beginning of the twenty-first century may change dramatically during the next few decades.

managerial perspectives revisited

PERSPECTIVE 1: **THE ORGANIZATIONAL CONTEXT** The organizational context provides a significant situational element in determining the success or failure of a manager's leadership efforts. Those efforts, as we have emphasized, can take place not only at the top of the organization, but virtually anywhere within it. For any given manager, however, the organization provides a major resource to support leadership—position power. How managers choose to use that particular source of power will have a lot to do with how effective they will be. A particular aspect of the organizational context that impacts a manager's leadership attempts is the culture of the organization. Culture has the potential to either facilitate or hinder those leadership efforts, and a manager needs to understand the nature of that culture to be effective. Some of the specific issues relating to leadership are directly affected by the organizational context. Take, for example, a manager's attempts to exercise transformational leadership. Think about it: How many transformational leaders can exist within the same organization? How does a higher-level (in the organization) transformational leader affect the efforts of someone lower in the hierarchy who wants to be his or her own transformational leader? These are just some of the knotty leadership issues involved when the organizational context is taken into account as a significant variable.

PERSPECTIVE 2: **THE HUMAN FACTOR** Lester B. Pearson, the fourteenth Canadian prime minister and recipient of the Nobel Peace Prize for his efforts in creating the United Nations peacekeeping forces during the Suez Crisis of 1956, is generally acknowledged

as a great leader. But even he, like any leader, could not have accomplished very much of consequence without being able to work through other people. Pearson could not do everything by himself, and he was masterful in his ability to influence other people, demonstrated by his success at having the Canada Pension Plan and Medicare pass into law while holding only a minority of seats in Parliament. As we have stressed in this chapter, leadership is a social influence process, and Pearson knew how to excel at this. Leadership is also a process of "enabling" the behaviour of other people. Thus, effective leadership helps others to accomplish more than they would have without the leader's influence. Above all, therefore, leadership is a people-intensive and a people-assisting process. Furthermore, almost all of the perspectives and models of leadership that we analyzed in this chapter emphasize the "people" responsibilities of leaders. "Leadership" and "working through people" are inseparable. Any manager who also wants to be a leader has to work through people; there is no other way.

3

PERSPECTIVE 3: **MANAGING PARADOXES** The process of managerial leadership involves dealing with a number of potential paradoxes. One of the most important is the ever-present danger of using too much or too little power. Striking that balance is a challenge for every leader in any type of organization. Leaders also have to decide how much power to share with followers and subordinates and how much to retain. On the surface, it would seem best to increase subordinate empowerment in many situations. With some types of tasks or decisions, however, especially those requiring fast action, managers need to retain their authority and responsibility. Also, not all followers may be up to the challenge of being empowered because of lack of knowledge, skills, or motivation. An additional decision faced by leaders is the relative emphasis to place on task-oriented versus people-oriented behaviours. And further complicating the issue is whether managing and leading are two distinctly different activities, and whether transformational approaches and transactional approaches are mutually exclusive. Both of these issues are often presented as either/or choices, but in fact, they are not. Managers can be leaders and vice versa. Furthermore, leaders often use a style that reflects both transformational and transactional characteristics; they do so because both are necessary to be effective. It should be clear, then, that all-or-nothing approaches to thinking about leadership are seldom helpful in dealing with real-world leadership problems and choices in courses of action.

4

PERSPECTIVE 4: **ENTREPRENEURIAL MINDSET** Recently, some experts have argued that to be entrepreneurial and strategic at the same time, managers need not only an entrepreneurial mindset but also need to exhibit leadership to establish such an entrepreneurial culture within their organizations.[65] Leaders must exhibit an entrepreneurial mindset for followers to do the same. Additionally, leaders play an important role in helping their followers to develop an entrepreneurial mindset and to foster the conditions and incentives for them to use it. For example, leaders can reward risk-taking actions on the part of their subordinates, thereby encouraging their creativity. Finally, leaders face the challenge of how the entrepreneurial skills they foster in their subordinates should ultimately be used. An entrepreneurial mindset means that leaders are committed to being innovative;

they continuously search for opportunities and encourage their employees to be creative. Leaders can facilitate the creative efforts of their employees by fostering an entrepreneurial culture within their organizations. Such a culture results in a set of shared values regarding innovation and enhances the commitment of everyone in the organization to entrepreneurial achievement.[66]

concluding comments

Every manager should also want to be a leader, and an effective leader at that. Every manager has the potential to *become* a more effective leader. But for most people, becoming an effective leader is not an easy or quick task. Most of us, unfortunately, are not endowed with brilliant leadership qualities. Therefore, we don't necessarily begin a managerial job or career with an extremely high degree of referent power. Rather, a managerial position provides us with a certain amount of position power, and we also probably have acquired at least some degree of expertise. From that point on, it is a matter of gaining additional expertise and building our own referent power based on our actions and the example we set. It's also a matter of learning how to diagnose situations where leadership is called for and how to get the most out of whatever resources we have available. Not easy, but doable.

To make accurate diagnoses of leadership situations requires reasonable insight into and an accurate assessment of several key elements: our own personal strengths, the attitudes and capabilities of those we are trying to lead, the nature of the jobs to be done, and the organizational environment. In other words, leadership is not just action. It involves good planning, good observation, and especially, good thinking. Knowing what to look for is half the battle of knowing what to do in a leadership context.

We have also presented a number of potentially useful perspectives on the leadership process that have come from the behavioural and organizational science literature. The important point is to consider how each of them can help you increase your understanding of different aspects of an admittedly complex, and sometimes even baffling, process. No single theory itself provides a foolproof formula for guaranteeing success as a leader. However, the conceptual models and ideas in this chapter can serve to stimulate your thinking about the process of leadership and how you can develop your own distinctive approach to this critical managerial function.

Throughout this chapter we have covered a considerable number of topics relating to leadership in organizations, from the basics of power and influence to the roles of the leader, the followers, and the situation. We continued by reviewing major approaches and models of leadership, and discussing some of the most important current issues relating to leadership. That's a lot about one topic! The challenge is how to put together and, in a sense, to integrate all of this information. There is no easy way to do this. One good way, however, is to think about specific leadership situations you have observed, or perhaps have directly been a part of, and then try to use different parts of the material covered in this chapter to analyze what happened and why it happened. Can you now understand something about leaders and the leadership process that you didn't grasp before? If so, you may be better prepared for the next time you are involved in a leadership opportunity.

key terms

charismatic leader 326
coercive power 307
effective leadership 304
emotional intelligence 312
expert power 307
legitimate power (formal authority) 306
LPC (least preferred co-worker) theory 319
managerial grid 317
neutralizers of leadership 324
normative decision model 322
organizational leadership 303
paternalism 331
path–goal theory of leadership 321
people behaviours 313
personal power 305
position power 305
power 305
referent power 308
reward power 307
situational leadership model 318
social intelligence 312
substitutes for leadership 323
task behaviours 313
traits 310
transactional leadership 328
transformational leadership 328

test your comprehension

1. What is leadership? Why is it characterized as a social influence process?
2. Who can be expected to exhibit leadership in an organization?
3. Differentiate between *position power* and *personal power*.
4. Is the use of coercion to change behaviours an accepted method of leadership?
5. What is referent power, and how can it be developed?
6. What is the "locus of leadership"?
7. What are the three key variables in the leadership process in organizations?
8. According to current views of leadership, what traits are most likely to predict effective leadership?
9. What is emotional intelligence, and how does it differ from social intelligence?
10. How do the two major categories of situational variables affect the leadership process?
11. Why are there so many different approaches to leadership? Do they have anything in common?
12. What are the two dimensions of behaviour in Blake and Mouton's managerial grid?
13. Describe the four types of behaviour identified in Hersey and Blanchard's situational leadership model. What are the components of each?
14. What did Fiedler mean by one's "least preferred co-worker"? What is the major principle involved in Fiedler's theory?
15. According to House's path–goal theory, what is the main responsibility of a leader?
16. What are the key variables and the basic decision-making procedures included in the Vroom and Yetton normative decision model?
17. What is meant by a substitute for leadership? Give an example.
18. Are leadership and management the same? Why or why not?
19. What is a charismatic leader? What are some of the specific traits of such a leader?
20. What is the difference between a transformational and a transactional leader? Is one necessarily better than the other? How does each bring about change?

apply your understanding

1. Think of a specific leader in your work situation, in a friendship group, on a sports team, or in the news. What types of power does he or she appear to use? How does he or she use these different types of power? Would you consider this person to be an effective leader? Why or why not?
2. Do you think people are born leaders? Are there specific traits that can be seen early in a person's life or career that identify that person as a leader? Can someone without these specific traits go on to become a leader?
3. Which of the many approaches to leadership do you think is the best? Defend your reasoning.
4. How would you characterize yourself—as a transformational, transactional, or charismatic leader? Which would you rather be? Can you change your style?

practise your capabilities

A Type of Direction

Ted Willis has been hired as the new supervisor for the parts department of an automobile dealership. On his first day his manager, Linda Dunn, tells him, "You have a tough assignment. In the group you supervise there is an active troublemaker who has managed to keep from getting fired because he is the only employee who knows the inventory system. Three other employees follow his lead in consistently finding things to complain about, and the other four employees stay out of trouble by doing only what they are told." Linda handed the personnel files for the department employees to Ted. "The most important thing," Linda continued, "is that you change the sloppy way work is being done in the department and improve the accuracy in filling parts orders."

After hesitating a moment, Ted asked, "What *was* the former supervisor like?" "Well," replied Linda, "He had semi-retired on the job and let the employees do what they wanted. He was not concerned about accuracy in filling orders or maintaining the inventory. As I said before, it's a tough assignment, especially since all your employees have been with the dealership for more than five years, and most are friends with the owner."

Ted smiled, "I guess I have my work cut out for me."

1. How would you define the leadership problems in this situation?
2. What situational factors should Ted take into account before deciding on what leadership actions to take?
3. Identify the sources and amounts of power available to Ted and his new workgroup. How could they affect Ted's ability to lead this group?

Source: Adapted from J. P. Howell and D. L. Costley, *Understanding Behaviors for Effective Leadership* (Upper Saddle River, NJ: Prentice Hall, 2001).

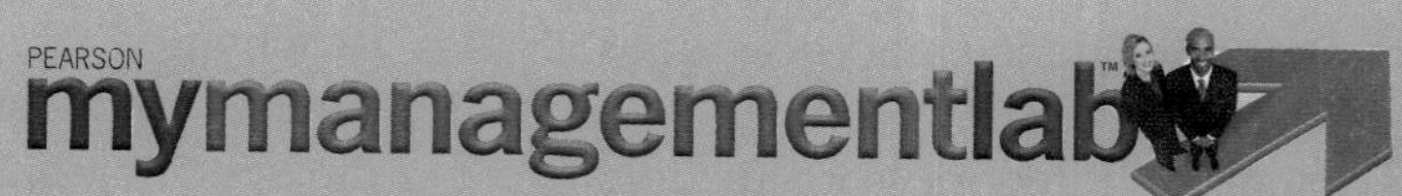

To improve your grade, visit the MyManagementLab website at **www.pearsoned.ca/mymanagementlab**. This online homework and tutorial system allows you to test your understanding and generates a personalized study plan just for you. It provides you with study and practice tools directly related to this chapter's content. MyManagementLab puts you in control of your own learning!

closing case DEVELOP YOUR CRITICAL THINKING

Meet the New Boss (Same as the Old Boss)

Grace Reed had been working at the regional health authority's medical society answering service for 18 months when she received a promotion to shift supervisor. Grace was quite excited. She had worked very hard to develop the technical skills for answering calls and the interpersonal skills for communicating with patients and their doctors. She had also demonstrated her desire for the promotion by volunteering for overtime and holiday work. Finally, it paid off and she had been promoted. However, now she faced problems she had not anticipated. How would she be able to convince her friends to take her seriously in her new role as their boss? How was she going to maintain her friendships and still maintain the discipline needed in the workplace?

The medical society's physicians were extremely disappointed in the level of dedication and care shown by the former answering services, which handled not only physicians but business and private accounts as well. They decided to start their own answering service. Their operators would handle only medical calls, would be better trained to recognize urgent and emergency calls, would receive better benefits, and would be paid at a higher rate than the competing answering services. The doctors believed that by structuring the enterprise in this way, they could attract and retain the best possible workers. They would also have the largest available worker pool from which to choose and would not have to worry about being able to find replacement operators. They hired a professional manager to oversee the day-to-day operations, and each shift had a supervisor whose responsibilities included routine scheduling of workers; recognition of and planning for especially heavy days and shifts; handling complaints from doctors, hospitals, pharmacies, or patients concerning the handling of their calls; learning how to operate new equipment and subsequently training their operators in its use; and maintaining the high level of service required by the physicians. These duties were in addition to working her or his own eight-hour shift.

Grace was the fourth operator hired by the organization, and the first operator promoted from within the ranks to be supervisor. When she was first hired, she was lucky to train with a very experienced, competent operator. She modelled her own skills on those of her trainer and worked diligently to handle the most calls with the fewest mistakes and even fewer complaints. Where the other operators handled only 60 to 70 individual incoming lines, Grace routinely handled 100 to 120 lines, including some of those with the highest volumes of calls. She not only cleared her own calls but frequently assisted other operators in clearing their backlogged messages. When extremely difficult calls came in, such as suicide calls or nuisance calls from patients whom even the doctors did not want to talk to, it was often Grace who was asked to handle them. She rapidly developed excellent relationships with all of "her" doctors, their staff, and even their families. During her first year, she was named operator of the month five times. In her second year, she worked with the existing supervisors to learn how to schedule the workers and received advanced training in other office operations and procedures beyond answering calls.

Although the work was extremely fast paced and required concentration, there was always time for talking with the other operators, joking, and having fun. Strong friendships grew among the operators, who frequently socialized after hours and on their days off. There was a strong feeling of family in the office. The high levels of training and pay led to extremely low turnover rates. There were always waiting lists of applicants for the positions. If an operator wished to leave, he or she had no problem finding work at hospitals or for the phone company. Morale was generally high because of the respect the operators felt they received from "their" doctors for the high-quality work they performed, the higher levels of pay and benefits they received in comparison with operators at other organizations, and the high degree of friendship among operators.

Her friends at the answering service threw Grace a party when she received her promotion. Everyone who wasn't working attended. Everyone was happy for her and sincerely wished her well. They all knew now that you could be promoted from the ranks! Grace was anxious to assume her new responsibilities and even try some new procedures she had been devising.

Within a month, Grace wasn't nearly as happy with her promotion as she had thought she would be. Her friends, who were now her subordinates, didn't seem to pay attention to her suggestions concerning their job performance. They ignored her instructions and frequently treated them as a joke. She worked many hours planning schedules only to have the operators switch shifts, leave early, or arrive late, saying they were sure she wouldn't mind because she understood all of their personal complications with their romantic relationships. She was their friend after all; they knew she would cut them some slack. And her best friends seemed to be some of the worst offenders.

Grace soon realized that her new position was missing one thing—authority to go with her new responsibilities. She had no authority to sanction any of her subordinates: She couldn't dock their pay, make them work overtime, or cut back on their hours. She couldn't shorten their lunch breaks or eliminate their coffee breaks. Any such sanctions could only come from the overall company manager. If she tried to insist that a new procedure be used or that scheduled hours be worked and the operator balked, she had no recourse. If she complained to the manager, she would be viewed as unable to do her job. She couldn't complain to her friends, because they were part of the problem. She tried acting very authoritarian and harshly insisting on the new methods. She was met with hostility, and her friends stopped talking to her. One day she had had enough and berated a group of her friends about how they gave her no respect—they were uncooperative, and they weren't doing their jobs, and she was fed up with it. After all, she didn't ask them to do anything she wasn't willing or able to do herself. Morale was plummeting (hers as well as the other operators') and productivity was falling. Grace felt like a failure at the job she had worked so hard to get, and even beyond that, she felt she was losing her friends.

Grace knew that something was going to have to change. She needed to try something new, to somehow regain the respect of her subordinates and find a new way to inspire improved performance and efficiency and restore morale. And she had to accomplish all this while maintaining her friendships with the other operators.

Questions

1. Which traits, skills, and behaviours associated with successful leaders does Grace possess? Are there characteristics she could enhance to improve her leadership ability?
2. Why did Grace have problems making changes and maintaining discipline when she first was promoted to a position that required leadership?
3. Analyze Grace's leadership situation in terms of her sources of power: Are there types of power she couldn't or shouldn't use? What types of power could she draw on, and how could she use those types to greatest effect?
4. Are there substitutes for leadership present in this situation? What neutralizers must Grace overcome to be an effective leader?

Source: Personal communication to the authors.

Chapter 10
Motivation

LEARNING OBJECTIVES

After reading this chapter, you should be able to:

1 Analyze the motivational forces present in a specific situation.

2 Differentiate between the various content and process theories of motivation and indicate how each can be helpful in analyzing a given motivational situation.

3 Explain how job enrichment can influence an employee's motivation.

4 Compare and contrast the various approaches to reinforcement and describe their relative advantages and disadvantages for use by managers.

5 State how goal setting can affect motivation.

6 Name the major types of social influence on employees' motivation and explain how each type can impact motivation.

7 Describe how values and attitudes toward work can influence motivation.

Motivated to Make Coin

In a period when the value of precious metals increased dramatically and the demand for circulation coins was at its peak, the Royal Canadian Mint was able to keep pace and generate a solid profit at the same time. Established in 1908, the Royal Canadian Mint is a Crown corporation that produces coins in facilities located in Ottawa and Winnipeg. The Ottawa plant specializes in commemorative coins, while the Winnipeg plant produces circulation coins for Canada, as well as numerous countries around the world. While much of the process of making coins is automated, the employees are still a critical component in the design, manufacturing, and distribution of their precious product.

Managers at "the Mint" have long realized that employees are as precious as the more than two billion coins that roll off the line each year. As such, they have brought in programs and benefits that not only keep employees satisfied, but also energize them in their work so that they may fulfill the goals of the organization and contribute in generating the half billion dollars in revenue the Mint generated in 2006 alone. Apart from the free dental, eye care, and prescription plans, the Mint also provides coverage for nutrition planning, massage therapy, physiotherapy, chiropractic care, acupuncture, naturopathy, as well as many other health services. In addition, the on-site physical fitness facility offers free memberships, providing access to treadmills, cycles, rowing machines, weights, a personal trainer, and shower facilities. The full-service cafeteria offers subsidized meals with healthy menu and special diet items, and there is also an internet café on site. Secure bike locations and subsidized auto parking are also provided for commuters.

Management at the Mint also recognizes that there is tremendous personal reward and organizational spinoff benefits in continuous learning. The Mint will subsidize tuition for not only job-related development, but also courses not related to work. Professional membership fees and professional development events are covered by the Mint, as is in-house training in leadership and new languages.

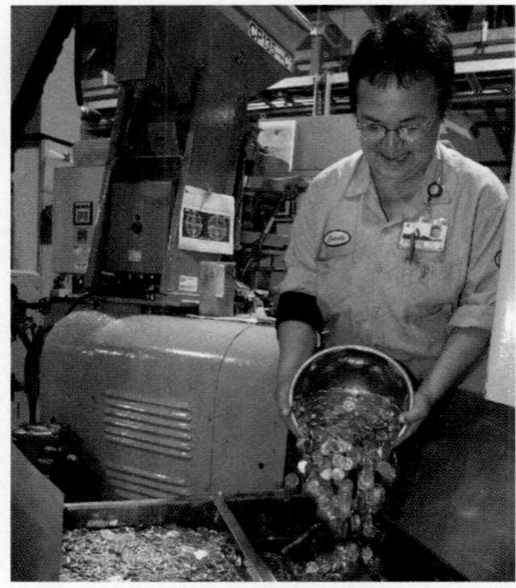

Managers at the Royal Canadian Mint realize that employees are as precious as the coins that roll off the line each year. To keep their employees satisfied and productive, the Mint maintains programs and benefits that have placed them among the top employers in Canada.

In 2006, the Royal Canadian Mint was recognized for its attention to employees with the distinction as one of Canada's Top 100 Employers of the Year by *Maclean's* magazine, and one of the Top 10 Family-Friendly Employers in Canada by *Today's Parent* magazine. The effort has not gone unnoticed by employees or potential recruits either, with employee turnover a scant 1.8 percent across Canada and some 1000 resumes being forwarded to human resource staff each year.

The commitment to the employees paid off substantially in 2006 when the Mint was faced with extraordinary demand for coins in a short period of time. Unexpectedly, Canadian demand for coins increased dramatically because of high retail activity and consumers more often relying on coins rather than electronic transactions for low-value purchases. On a weekly basis, the Mint had to produce up to 87 million coins, which was far in excess of the 50 million required in 2005, or the 43 million in 2004. The employees remained dedicated to the Mint's goals and were pivotal in the success of the organization meeting the demand, resulting in a 28.7 percent increase in net income.

For employees starting families, the Mint provides a top-up on parental benefits to nearly 100 percent of a person's salary for up to one year to new mothers and fathers, including adoptive parents. For employees that already have young children the Mint provides access to nearby daycare facilities. Other family-friendly benefits include flexible hours options such as fewer hours a week or more hours over fewer days. Telecommuting and sabbatical programs are also available to employees that need the flexibility.

Sources: Canada's Top 100 Employers 2007: Royal Canadian Mint, *Eluta Canada*, www.eluta.ca (accessed June 4, 2007); External Forces, Internal Strength: Royal Canadian Mint Annual Report 2006.

strategic overview

A critical issue shown by the opening vignette is the strategic value of motivating employees. The employees working for the Royal Canadian Mint receive greater benefits than the employees may find with other employers. Thus, the Mint's labour costs are higher than the industrial average.

Yet external analysts would argue that the Mint maintains a competitive advantage for several reasons, all related to the highly motivated employees. The employees produce higher-quality products, are more productive, and have lower turnover (that is, fewer employees leave the firm for other jobs). Higher productivity means that they turn out more products for the time worked. So even though they cost more in benefits, they produce more, which reduces the overall cost per product.

As the Royal Canadian Mint example illustrates, organizations and managers who can successfully motivate their employees are rewarded with high performance. However, that is not so easy to accomplish. If it were, every employee would be an outstanding performer. One major obstacle is that conditions beyond a company's or a manager's control can affect employee motivation. Furthermore, these conditions keep changing. The state of the economy, for instance, constantly fluctuates, and this can influence the motivation level of many employees. Also, family and other personal circumstances that arise from outside the organization come into the workplace and affect attitudes about staying or leaving and a willingness to put in extra effort on the job. Understanding these and other forces that impinge on motivation has been a continuing challenge for managers ever since the beginning of the industrial age. However, what we hope to demonstrate in this chapter is that regardless of factors not directly under one's control, the motivation of other people potentially can be influenced by anyone in a managerial position. In other words, managers have many opportunities to affect the motivation of those who work with and for them—especially if they understand some of the basic principles that are involved in the motivational process. If you as a manager want to be able to demonstrate leadership, then you need to develop your capabilities to motivate those around you.

From a motivational perspective, the position taken by the Royal Canadian Mint raises some interesting issues. Perhaps the most important one is whether the Mint's approach to motivating the people who work there would be successful in a wide variety of other organizations and settings. Does the fact that the Mint is in a highly specialized form of manufacturing limit how applicable those approaches are to industries and circumstances that are quite different? Would they work as well in a textile plant situated in Nova Scotia? In a rural area of China? In a Bay Street securities firm? In an architecture firm in Vancouver? Does the fact that the Mint is a Crown corporation make a difference? These are just some of the intriguing questions raised by this opening vignette.

What Is Motivation?

When we use the term "motivation," regardless of the setting, what does it mean? **Motivation** can be thought of as the set of forces that energize, direct, and sustain behaviour. These forces can come from the person, the so-called "push" of internal forces, or they can come from the environment that surrounds the person, the so-called "pull" of external forces. It is therefore essential for managers to recognize the importance of both sets of factors—a major type of duality—when they are analyzing motivational causes of behaviour.

motivation the set of forces that energize, direct, and sustain behaviour

It is important to stress at the outset that an overemphasis on one set of forces (push or pull) to the exclusion of the other can lead to a faulty diagnosis and to actions that do not solve motivational problems. For example, a manager might assume that her subordinate's level of sales calls is low because he is lazy, when in fact appropriate incentives have not been provided that tap his needs or interests. The manager would be assuming the cause to be lack of an internal push force, whereas a more accurate diagnosis in this case would focus on inadequate pull forces. This kind of misreading of motivation, which is easy to do, could lead to the loss of a potentially valuable employee. Likewise, an assumption that a clerical worker is doing an especially good job to please his supervisor would be putting weight on external or pull forces to explain his motivation, while perhaps not giving enough credit to internal push forces. This worker might be a person who is highly motivated no matter what kind of supervision or direction he receives. In both of these examples, a broader view of motivational factors should lead to more valid and useful assessments.

Throughout this chapter, different types of motivational forces will be examined, with particular emphasis on what psychologists and other behavioural scientists have had to say about the content and process of motivation. First, though, we begin with a framework to analyze the sources of motivational forces in the work situation. Following that, several major behavioural theories of motivation are examined. In later sections of the chapter, attention is focused on how reinforcement systems and the social environment of work can affect the strength and direction of motivation.

Sources of Motivation

As shown in Exhibit 10.1, there are three basic categories of variables that determine motivation in the work setting:

- Characteristics of the individual
- Characteristics of the job
- Characteristics of the work situation

Exhibit 10.1 Key Variables That Influence Motivation

INTERNAL (PUSH FORCES)	EXTERNAL (PULL FORCES)	
Characteristics of THE INDIVIDUAL (examples)	**Characteristics of THE JOB (examples)**	**Characteristics of THE WORK SITUATION (examples)**
Needs · For security · For self-esteem · For achievement · For power	Feedback · Amount · Timing	Immediate Social Environment · Supervisor(s) · Workgroup members · Subordinates
Attitudes · About self · About job · About supervisor · About organization	Workload	Organizational Actions · Rewards and compensation · Availability of training · Pressure for high levels of output
Goals · Task completion · Performance level · Career advancement	Tasks · Variety · Scope	
	Discretion · How job is performed	

The first category, the individual's characteristics, is the source of the internal, or push, forces of motivation, that is, what the employee *brings to* the work setting. The individual's contributions to motivational forces consist of three major subsets of variables: (1) needs—such as the need for security, self-esteem, achievement, or power; (2) attitudes—toward self, a job, a supervisor, or the organization; and (3) goals—such as task completion, accomplishment of a certain level of performance, and career advancement.

The second and third categories of basic causal variables refer to the external, or pull, forces of motivation. Characteristics of the job focus on what the person *does* in the work setting. These include how much direct (without the intervention of anyone else) feedback the person receives by performing tasks, the workload, the variety and scope of the tasks that make up the job, and the degree of discretion the person is allowed in meeting the requirements of the job.

The other external category, work situation characteristics, refers to what *happens to* the individual. This category has two sets of variables: the immediate social environment composed of the supervisor(s), members of the workgroup, and subordinates; and various types of organizational actions, such as reward and compensation practices, the availability of training and development, and the amount of pressure applied to achieve high levels of output.

Taken together, the three major categories of variables—individual, job, and work situation—can serve as a useful framework for analyzing the sources of motivation, whether in Bangkok, Lima, or Winnipeg. Focusing on them also forms a good basis for considering the major theories of motivation relevant to managing in organizational settings. These theories are presented next. In addition, it is important to remember that the specifics of any of these sources can change at any time, which in turn can affect an individual's or group's motivation. Therefore, the alert manager watches for such possible changes and re-evaluates, if necessary, his or her approach to motivation.

Motivation Theories Applicable to Work Situations

Several theories of motivation are particularly relevant for work settings. Each of these theories highlights one or more of the variables just discussed (and displayed in Exhibit 10.1). Each theory also provides managers with useful perspectives for understanding motivational challenges and problems and ways to deal with them.

Before examining the basic features of these motivational theories, however, it is important to note that almost all were developed by behavioural scientists situated in North America. Thus, an obvious question is whether these theories apply only in the context of North American culture and society, or whether they are also useful in analyzing motivation in other societies and cultures.[1] Unfortunately, the answer is not clear. Based on the available evidence, the best answer is that some of the theories do have relevance beyond the North American context, but others may have fewer worldwide applications. However, these theories should not be automatically rejected because they originated in a particular cultural context, nor should they be routinely accepted as always applying equally well across different cultures. Their usefulness to the manager resides in providing possible ways of looking at motivational problems and issues, whatever the context.

Psychologists who have studied the topic typically have categorized motivation theories into two types: content theories and process theories, as shown in Exhibit 10.2. The two types together provide us with a deeper understanding of motivation.

Exhibit 10.2 Motivation Theories

	Content Theories	Process Theories
Focus	· Personal needs that workers attempt to satisfy · Features in the work environment that satisfy a worker's needs	· How different variables can combine to influence the amount of effort put forth by employees
Theories	· Maslow's need hierarchy · McClelland's acquired needs theory · Herzberg's two-factor theory	· Equity theory · Expectancy theory

Content Theories

content theories
motivation theories that focus on what needs a person is trying to satisfy and what features of the work environment seem to satisfy those needs

Content theories focus on what needs a person is trying to satisfy and what features of the work environment seem to satisfy those needs. Such theories try to explain motivation by identifying both internal factors, that is, particular needs, and external factors, particular job and work-situation characteristics that are presumed to cause behaviour. Two content theories, need hierarchy and acquired needs, are concerned with identifying internal factors, and one, the two-factor theory, is concerned with identifying external factors.

Need Hierarchy Theories The most prominent need hierarchy theory was developed more than a half century ago by psychologist Abraham Maslow.[2] His theory has had a certain appeal to managers, probably because it is easy to remember and contains five types of needs that are arranged in a hierarchy of strength and influence.

The five needs in Maslow's hierarchy (starting with the most essential or prepotent) are as follows:

- *Physiological:* Needs for the most basic essentials of life, such as air, water, food, shelter, and so on.
- *Security (safety):* The need to feel safe and secure and not to be threatened by circumstances in the surrounding environment that might jeopardize continued existence.
- *Social (belongingness):* The need to be loved, to interact and relate to other people, and to be accepted by them.
- *Esteem:* The need for a sense of one's own worth and competence and for recognition of that worth from other people.
- *Self-actualization:* The need to be personally fulfilled, to feel a sense of achievement and accomplishment, and especially to develop one's own unique capabilities and talents to the highest possible level.

Maslow's need hierarchy
a theory that states people fulfill basic needs, such as physiological and safety needs, before making efforts to satisfy other needs, such as social and belongingness, esteem, and self-actualization needs

An example of a firm that attempts to give attention to virtually all of these needs is provided in *A Manager's Challenge: "SC Johnson: Meeting Employee Needs."*

The essence of **Maslow's need hierarchy** theory is that an individual is motivated to satisfy the most basic needs first (such as physiological needs) and then, if those are satisfied, move to the next level. The benefits and programs available at the Royal Canadian Mint, as described in our opening story,

a manager's challenge *change*

SC Johnson: Meeting Employee Needs

Consideration of employee needs is crucial to developing and maintaining a work environment where employees are motivated to perform. Instead of focusing solely on traditional reward programs related to compensation, employers should also be paying attention to factors such as the continuing development of employees, leadership, communication, and the overall work environment. All of these factors are important since they can all affect employee engagement and retention.

SC Johnson, which operates out of Brantford, Ontario, has been producing cleaning products for Canadian and US markets since 1920. They have found innovative ways to motivate and retain valuable employees and frequently appear on Hewitt Associates's annual "50 Best Employers in Canada" list. True to their branding, "SC Johnson, A Family Company," this organization offers numerous benefits that make the employees feel like family. On-site massage therapy, a recreation facility, and a cottage resort are just some of the many perks of working for SC Johnson. The recreation facility includes a gymnasium, a weight room, and a squash court that family members can also use for free. In terms of traditional compensation, employees are eligible for both bonuses and profit sharing. The payback for these contemporary methods of motivation is that over a quarter of the firm's employees have worked for the company for over 15 years; and not one employee has ever been laid off!

The company also sets itself apart from other employers by maintaining a flexible and informal culture. For instance, employees are offered flexible work hours and the option of telecommuting to maintain a healthy work–life balance. In a similar vein, for a small fee, SC Johnson offers on-site "kid's camps" to employees with children who would otherwise have to find alternative childcare on days when caregivers are unavailable. Finally, SC Johnson offers employees that are experiencing family illness or crises a generous compensation plan that, after one year, includes two weeks of sick leave at full pay and 24 weeks at two-thirds pay; 10 weeks of full pay and 16 weeks of two-thirds pay are offered after an employee has been with the company for five years.

Shirley Harries-Langley, vice-president of human resources at SC Johnson in Canada, recognizes that the company has had great success motivating its employees. In reference to the fact that SC Johnson in Brantford has consistently made Hewitt's list, Harries-Langley has remarked, "We have looked at the feedback received through the employee survey very closely every year and have seen our employee engagement scores continuously improve over time. This has translated into outstanding employee commitment and business results."

Sources: Hewitt Associates, "50 Best Employers in Canada," 2000–2007, http://was7.hewitt.com (accessed May 18, 2007); Claudine Kapel, "Keeping Up with the Total Reward Joneses," *Canadian HR Reporter,* January 29, 2007, pp. 28, 34; Andy Holloway, "S.C. Johnson and Son Ltd.," *Canadian Business,* April 10–23, 2006, pp. 81–82; Canada NewsWire, "Best Employers in Canada Share Five Key Traits, Says Hewitt Associates," December 29, 2003.

illustrate an organization that strives to make sure that its employees' basic needs are satisfied. According to the theory, when those needs have been fulfilled, individuals will be more likely to concentrate their efforts on satisfying higher-level needs. However, if these persons' basic physiological and security needs should become threatened, they would then be likely to revert to focusing on those lower-order needs. They would decrease their efforts to satisfy social, esteem, and achievement needs until the threat has passed.

A good example of this theory occurred a few years ago at a plant of Ahlström Fakop, a Polish subdivision of Finnish paper and power equipment manufacturer A. Ahlström. Managers at the plant were having trouble motivating employees in the formerly state-owned enterprise. Offering incentive pay had not worked. Only when managers let employees know that no one would be laid off if sales targets were reached did employee morale pick up. Many of the employees were more concerned with keeping their job than with their pay level as their country moved from a state-controlled to a market economy.[3]

There are many Canadian firms that know they are no better than the talent of the employees who work for them. They realize that it is their job to motivate them to continue with excellent work: AbeBooks in Victoria provides new employees with three weeks' vacation and tuition subsidies for anyone interested in courses related to their work. The Assiniboine Credit Union in Winnipeg (pictured) provides discounted mortgage rates and $700 towards an employee's health account, which can be applied towards wellness activities such as health club memberships. The Halifax Herald allows employees to take their birthday off with pay and offers scholarships for children pursuing post-secondary studies.

An even more extreme example of this principle occurred in the 1990s in the Los Angeles area. Young Thai nationals were working in garment workshops under conditions that approached slavery. For example, they were not allowed to leave the building in which they lived and worked (for up to 18 hours per day) for months, and in some cases years.[4] Need hierarchy theory clearly would have predicted that the workers would not have been concerned with satisfying higher-order needs like belonging, esteem, and self-actualization when their most basic needs—physiological and safety—were not being met.

The key to understanding a person's motivation, then, from a need hierarchy perspective, is to identify that person's most basic need that is not yet satisfied. For the Thai garment workers in Los Angeles, that level would be the most basic: physiological. Once a need has been satisfied, it ceases to be a motivator unless its fulfillment is threatened again. But if it is threatened, that more basic need becomes the focus of attention, as in the Polish manufacturing plant example.

Many questions can be raised about need hierarchy theory. For example, do the needs occur in the same hierarchical order across all cultures and countries? Probably not. The theory was developed by an American in an American context. There is no convincing evidence that the hierarchy is universal, either from country to country or from one person to the next. As one knowledgeable scholar has argued, based on extensive research findings from a number of countries:

> *Maslow's hierarchy puts self-actualization (achievement) plus esteem above social needs, above security needs. This . . . is a description of a value system, the value system of the U.S. middle class to which the author belonged. I suggest that . . . for (some) countries [such as Greece and Mexico], security needs should rank at the top; for (other) countries [such as Denmark and Sweden] . . . social needs should rank at the top; and (for still other) countries [such as Portugal and Chile], both security and social needs should rank at the top.*[5]

Not only does the hierarchy of needs probably not have the same order across different cultures, it almost assuredly is not ordered the same from one individual to another. Furthermore, different individuals have quite different thresholds for satisfaction of a given need before they try to satisfy the next level. For example, someone who as a child grew up in a family whose financial resources were extremely scarce may go to inordinate lengths to assure current financial security as an adult even though the person is quite well off. Such individual differences in both the order of needs and the threshold for satisfying them clearly adds complexity for managers who attempt to base actions on this theory.

Furthermore, although Maslow's need hierarchy theory is relevant to work situations, it was not developed specifically for that purpose and therefore it has been difficult for researchers to determine its validity or usefulness in predicting behaviour in organizational settings. Probably the greatest value of the theory is that it provides a way of thinking about motivation that highlights the issue of psychological needs and the differing strength of those needs that a person could be trying to satisfy at work.

A somewhat more simplified variation of need hierarchy theory was published by behavioural scientist Clay Alderfer. His alternative version, labelled ERG theory for Existence-Relatedness-Growth, collapsed Maslow's five levels into three and provided a more straightforward way of thinking about need hierarchies. (Exhibit 10.3 provides a graphic comparison of the two classifications of needs.) Although sharing many similarities with Maslow's original theory, ERG theory differs in some respects.[6] For example, it presumes that different levels of needs can be active at the same time and thus a lower level does not have to be completely or even mostly satisfied before higher-level needs can emerge. Also, Alderfer's version suggests that even though a lower-level need has already been satisfied, a person may revert to focusing on that level if he or she is frustrated in trying to satisfy a higher level. Thus, an employee blocked in trying to gain opportunities for increased personal growth because she keeps getting assigned routine tasks may concentrate instead on socializing at work and gain even more satisfaction (than before) of relatedness needs. ERG theory presents an interesting alternative to Maslow's earlier, more complicated version, but the key point is that both theories focus on individuals' attempts to satisfy particular types of needs and on how that can affect the amount and direction of motivation.

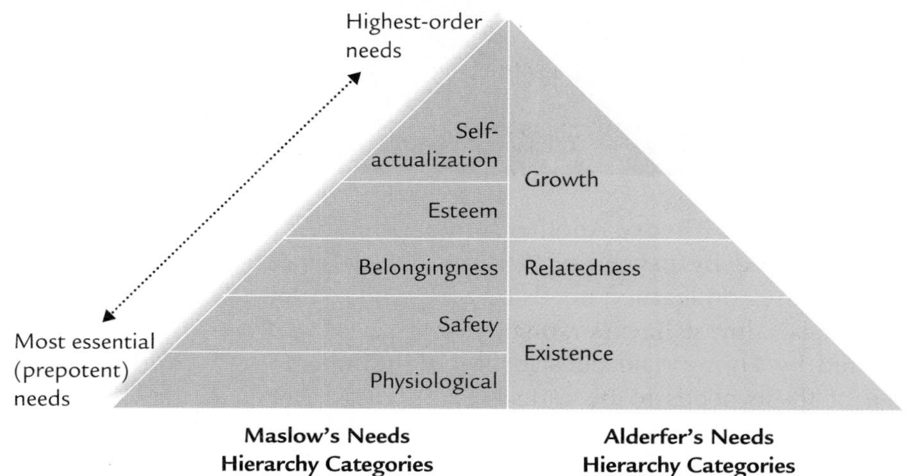

Exhibit 10.3

Maslow's and Alderfer's Needs Hierarchies Categories

From the standpoint of individual managers in an organization, there is probably relatively little they can do personally to affect employees' satisfaction of basic physiological needs. Many managers frequently do, however, have an opportunity to help ensure that employees' safety needs are not threatened and, within the limits of company policy and economic conditions, that security needs are met as much as possible.

With regard to satisfaction of employees' higher-order needs, managers can use their imagination and creativity to play a much more prominent and influential role. Many managerial actions can help employees obtain satisfaction of social, esteem, and even self-actualization needs. For example, at Thrifty Foods in James Bay, the safety committee "reported" on fellow employees. As part of a program called "caught in the act," they rewarded employees that were found undertaking safe work practices.[7] In this example, satisfaction of the needs of both parties is probably increased: self-actualization needs of the initiator for the "selfless" act of taking the time and trouble to write up the good practices of another employee, and esteem needs of the recipient through public recognition.

In recent years a number of companies have provided their employees with an innovative opportunity to satisfy self-actualization needs at the same time that they help others. For instance, some companies sponsor a position where employees work with a volunteer organization such as Canada's United Way/Centraides during their fall fundraising campaign. This type of program allows employees to make a difference in their communities as well as build camaraderie and increase their feelings of self-worth.

Across Canada, United Way/Centraides funds 7000 agencies as well as directs resources to another 10 000 charities. A significant contribution to helping the United Way generate resources is through their *Loaned Representative Program*, which enlists individuals from organizations that are on loan for 16 weeks to help in the fall fundraising campaign.

acquired needs theory
a motivation theory that focuses on learned needs that become enduring predispositions for affiliation, power, and achievement

Acquired Needs Theory Another content theory that is centred on needs was developed by psychologist David McClelland.[8] This **acquired needs theory** focuses on learned needs that become "enduring predispositions" of individuals, almost like personality traits, and that can be stimulated or activated by appropriate cues in the environment. McClelland considered three of these needs to be especially important (which is why his theory is sometimes referred to as the "three-need theory"): affiliation, power, and achievement. However, most of the attention other researchers have given to the theory of acquired needs has concentrated on the need for achievement.

In McClelland's theory, a person who has a high need for achievement is someone who habitually strives for success or attainment of goals in task situations (though not necessarily in other types of settings). The research data collected by McClelland and his associates indicate that high need achievement individuals prefer to

- work on tasks of moderate difficulty
- take moderate risks
- take personal responsibility for their actions
- receive specific and concrete feedback on their performance

In other words, high need achievers want challenges, but realistic challenges, not impossible ones. Especially important from a managerial perspective, McClelland's theory suggests that the need for achievement can be increased by "appropriate" training, that is, by showing people how to recognize and respond to relevant achievement cues. As might be assumed, this feature of the theory has proved to be quite controversial, since many experts doubt the extent to which permanent changes in need for achievement can be brought about by such training.

Is a need for achievement a universal motive? Is it, for example, as prevalent in Brazil as in Canada, or in India as much as in Germany? A study that was carried out across 20 countries appeared to show that achievement, along with power, can be considered a universal motive.[9] Although countries with quite different cultures—for example, very different attitudes toward individuality and collectivism—were included, the study indicated that a high-achieving type of person could be found in each country or culture. The findings suggest that the percentage of high-achieving people varies considerably from country to country, but the critical point is that there are definitely people of this type in every culture that has been studied: "It seems that the primary goal of achievers everywhere is to attain recognition for themselves."[10]

two-factor theory a motivation theory that focuses on the presumed different effects of intrinsic job factors (motivation) and extrinsic situational factors (hygiene factors)

Two-Factor Theory In the early 1960s, Frederick Herzberg, an American psychologist, proposed a motivation theory that came to be called the "two-factor theory."[11] The **two-factor theory** focused on the distinction between factors that can increase job satisfaction ("motivators") versus those that can prevent dissatisfaction but cannot increase satisfaction ("hygiene factors"). As shown in Exhibit 10.4, motivators are "intrinsic" factors directly related to the *doing* of a job, such as the

Exhibit 10.4

Herzberg's Two-Factor Theory: Motivators and Hygiene Factors

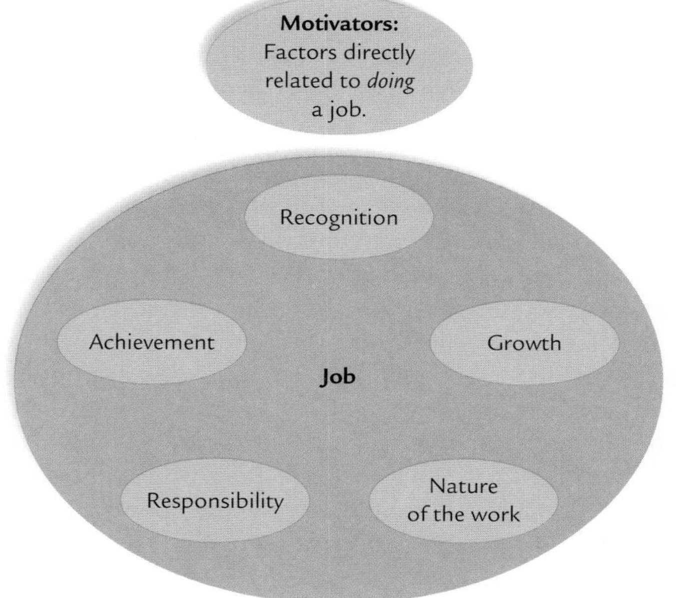

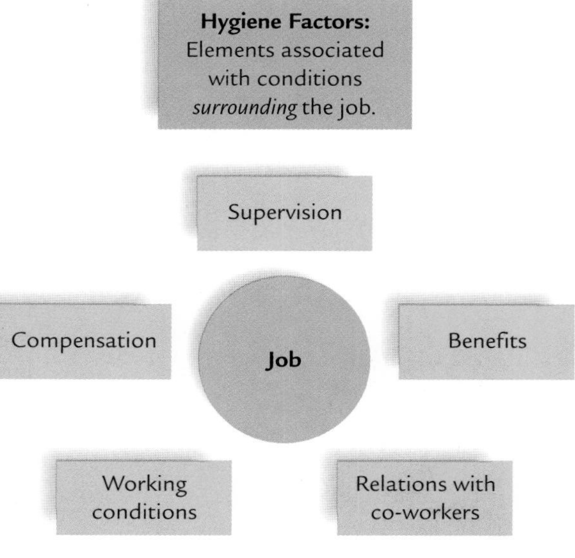

nature of the work itself, responsibility, personal growth, and the sense of achievement and recognition directly received by performing the work. The other factors, "hygiene" factors, are "extrinsic" to directly performing the job. They, instead, are associated with conditions *surrounding* the job. Included in this set are supervision, relations with co-workers, working conditions, and company policies and practices related to benefits and compensation.

Several years ago, General Electric Company, one of the largest companies in the world with over US$157 billion in revenue in 2006, started giving some attention to the distinction between the two types of factors with respect to the motivation of sales personnel. Unlike other areas of the company, such as finance and manufacturing, where there traditionally has been a high level of satisfaction, sales managers tended to have more complaints—about too much paperwork, too many lateral transfers, and too little time to talk directly with their customers. GE executives started by giving attention to hygiene factors, such as cutting down on paperwork and bureaucratic red tape for the sales managers. Then they turned to motivator factors: They instituted new training programs and, in particular, gave the sales managers total responsibility for individual clients rather than having a different manager deal with each product line.[12]

As shown in Exhibit 10.5, the two-factor theory predicts that "motivator" factors actively increase satisfaction, while hygiene factors only decrease dissatisfaction to a state of "neither satisfied nor dissatisfied."

The theory proved an immediate hit with practising managers when it was first proposed some years ago because it contains a relatively simple message: If you want to motivate employees, focus on improving how the job is structured—what they *do*—so that they obtain positive job satisfaction. Simply taking care of the hygiene factors can prevent dissatisfaction, but will have no effect on positive motivation.

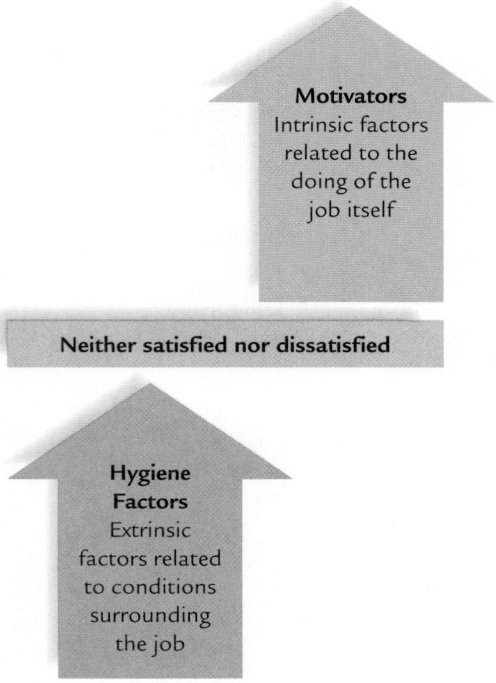

Although intuitively appealing, the two-factor theory has been criticized by many scholars as being overly simplistic. For one thing, research has shown that satisfaction and motivation are not the same thing. Reacting positively to something, like being pleased with doing a more challenging set of tasks, does not necessarily mean that you will have increased motivation or a stronger desire to perform the job better. Therefore, although changing the nature of the work can often lead to an increase in intrinsic satisfaction, it does not necessarily follow that motivation to perform is increased. Critics thus contend that the theory blurs the distinction between satisfaction and motivation. Also, subsequent research has shown that it is not possible to distinguish clearly between variables that only increase satisfaction and those that only decrease dissatisfaction.

Exhibit 10.5

Herzberg's Two-Factor Theory: Differential Effects of Hygiene Factors and Motivators

Motivators
Intrinsic factors related to the doing of the job itself

Neither satisfied nor dissatisfied

Hygiene Factors
Extrinsic factors related to conditions surrounding the job

Implications for Job Design Despite these and other criticisms, the widespread attention given to the two-factor theory has had one very important consequence in the years after it was proposed: an increased emphasis on the design of jobs; that is, on the combinations of specific tasks put together to form particular jobs.[13] If nothing else, the two-factor theory was responsible for influencing both organizational scholars and employers to consider the issue of how the content of jobs affects the motivation to perform those jobs. It highlighted the question of whether it is possible to provide increased opportunities for employees to experience greater feelings of responsibility, accomplishment, and achievement, as described above in the changes made in GE sales managers' jobs. The general approach to designing jobs that try to provide such opportunities is called **job enrichment**.

job enrichment increasing the complexity of a job to provide greater responsibility, accomplishment, and achievement

One of the most comprehensive approaches to the design of enriched jobs with high potential for increased motivation has been labelled the "job characteristics model."[14] Developed by two organizational scientists, J. Richard Hackman and Greg Oldham, the **job characteristics model** emphasizes three components (as shown in Exhibit 10.6):

job characteristics model an approach that focuses on the motivational attributes of jobs through emphasizing three sets of variables: core job characteristics, critical psychological states, and outcomes

- Core job characteristics, such as skill variety and task significance
- Critical psychological states, such as experienced meaningfulness of work and experienced responsibility for outcomes of the work
- Expected outcomes, such as high internal work motivation and high work effectiveness

Exhibit 10.6

Job Characteristics Model

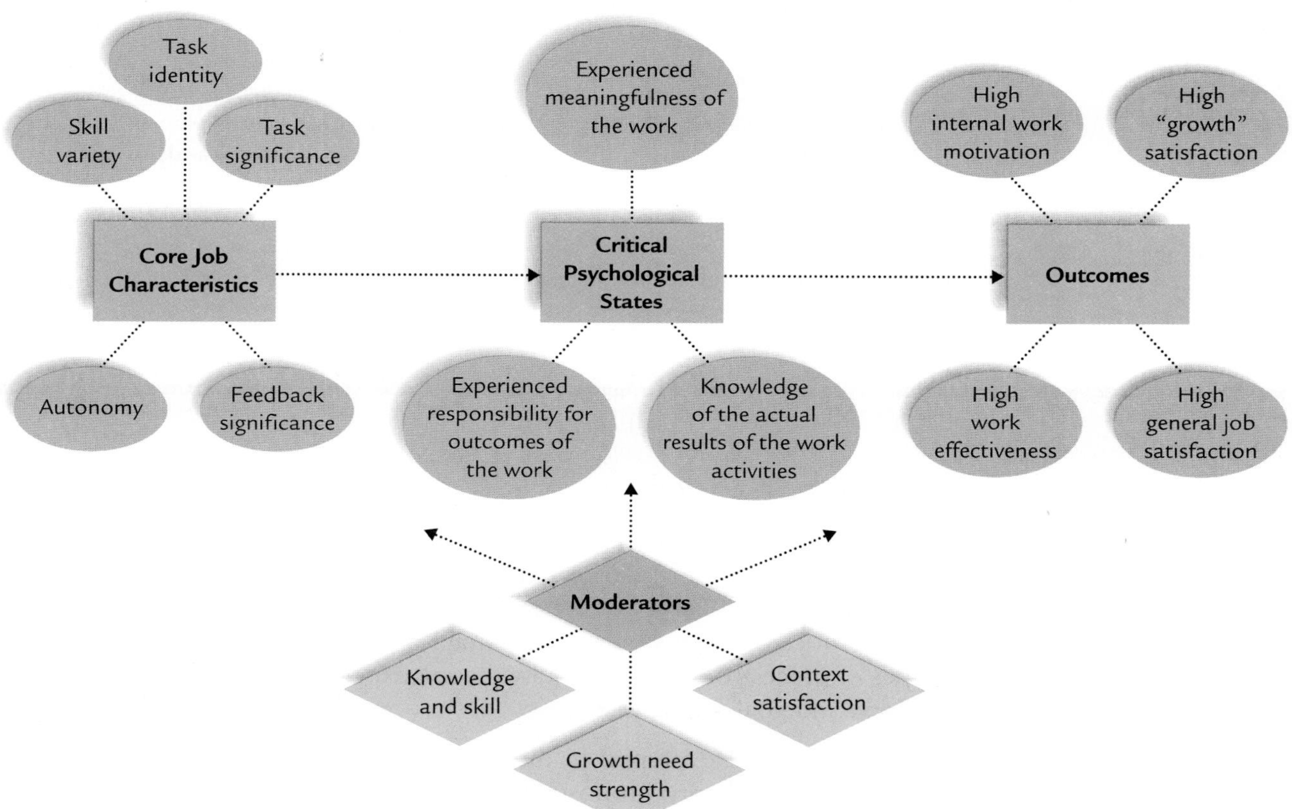

Source: Adapted from J. R. Hackman and G. R. Oldham, *Work Redesign* (Reading, MA: Addison-Wesley, 1980).

The Hackman-Oldham model also includes factors (called "moderators") like individual differences in growth need strength that are presumed to affect the likelihood that enriched jobs will lead to the desired outcomes, although this aspect of the model has not received consistent validation in research studies.[15] Clearly, though, not every employee wants more responsibility, autonomy, and the like—but many do. The message for managers from this model is that if they can create or adjust jobs to include more of the "core characteristics" (see Exhibit 10.7), they may be able to increase the motivation and satisfaction of many of the employees who work in those jobs. Indeed, a useful way for managers, who often have highly enriched jobs themselves, to think about enriching the jobs of their subordinates is to make those jobs more like their own!

Exhibit 10.7 Core Job Characteristics in the Job Characteristics Model

Core Job Characteristics	Definition	Example
Skill variety	The degree to which a job requires a variety of different activities in carrying out the work, involving the use of a number of different skills and talents of the person.	The aerospace engineer must be able to create blueprints, calculate tolerances, provide leadership to the workgroup, and give presentations to upper management.
Task identity	The degree to which a job requires completion of a "whole" and identifiable piece of work, that is, doing a job from beginning to end with a visible outcome.	The event manager handles all the plans for the annual executive retreat, attends the retreat, and receives information on its success from the participants.
Task significance	The degree to which a job has a substantial impact on the lives of other people, whether those people are in the immediate organization or in the world at large.	The finance manager devises a new benefits plan to improve health coverage for all employees.
Autonomy	The degree to which a job provides substantial freedom, independence, and discretion to the individual in scheduling the work and in determining the procedures to be used in carrying it out.	R&D scientists are linked via the company intranet, allowing them to post their ideas, ask questions, and propose solutions at any hour of the day, whether at the office, at home, or on the road.
Feedback from job	The degree to which carrying out the work activities required by the job provides the individual with direct and clear information about the effectiveness of his or her performance.	The lathe operator knows he is cutting his pieces correctly, as very few are rejected by the workers in the next production area.

Source: Adapted from J. Richard Hackman and Greg R. Oldham, *Work Redesign* (Reading, MA: Addison-Wesley, 1980).

Process Theories

process theories motivation theories that deal with the way different variables combine to influence the amount of effort people put forth

Process theories of work motivation deal with the way different variables combine to influence the amount of effort people put forth. In other words, while content theories address the issue of *which* variables affect motivation, process theories focus on the issue of *how* variables affect it. The four most prominent types of process theories are equity theory, expectancy theory, social cognitive theory, and goal-setting theory.

equity theory a motivation theory that focuses on individuals' comparisons of their circumstances with those of others and how such comparisons may motivate certain kinds of behaviour

Equity Theory Developed in the early 1960s by psychologist John Stacey Adams, **equity theory** proposes that individuals will compare their circumstances with those of others and that such comparisons may motivate certain kinds of behaviour.[16] As one observer has pointed out, a particularly vivid example involves professional athletes:

> *(Such) athletes often make the news by demanding that their contracts be torn up before their terms expire. The reason for this apparent lack of respect for contract law usually involves feelings by these athletes that the previously agreed on rates of pay are [now], by some standard [of comparison], not fair.*[17]

Equity theory, as shown in Exhibit 10.8, assumes that people know what kind of effort and skills they put into their jobs and what kinds of outcomes (salary, promotions, etc.) they receive from their employer. The theory also assumes that individuals are likely to compare (1) their *ratios* of inputs to outcomes to (2) the *ratios* of other relevant people such as colleagues or acquaintances (inside or outside their organization). Such comparisons determine whether the individual feels equitably treated. The most important assumption—as in the example of the professional athletes just cited—is that if the comparisons result in feelings of inequity in favour of the other persons, the individual making the observation will be motivated to try to take steps to reduce such feelings. (It should also be pointed out that comparisons can result in feelings of inequity that favour the observer. In that case, the individual could take steps, such as increasing one's own inputs, to reduce the perceived inequity. However, the commonsense assumption is that this kind of situation—where the other comparison person's ratio of outcome to inputs is perceived as being worse than one's own—will occur relatively infrequently.)

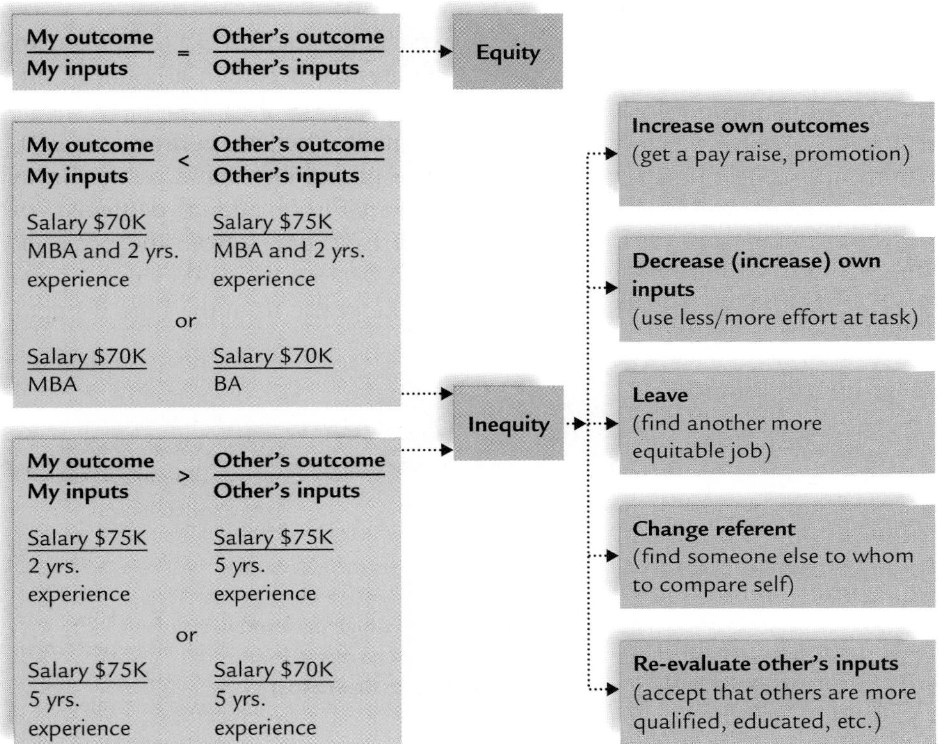

Exhibit 10.8

Equity Theory

Equity theory states that individuals have a number of ways to reduce their feelings that others are "doing better" than they are. One way is to increase their own outcomes, such as getting a salary increase or obtaining a promotion. Another response might be to decrease their inputs; for example, they might try to put less effort into the task and still receive the same level of outcomes, if possible. A third action might be to leave their current situation so that they can obtain a new outcome/input ratio.

If people do not think they are being rewarded equitably—that is, do not believe they are obtaining "distributive justice"[18] (in social scientists' terminology)—they have other ways of dealing with the situation. They might simply change the object of their comparison—that is, they might decide to compare themselves to different people; for example, neighbours instead of work colleagues, whom they think have ratios more similar to their own. This involves no change of behaviour but only a change in the way of looking at a situation. Likewise, people might re-evaluate the inputs and outcomes of those with whom they are comparing themselves, as in "she has more skills than I thought she did," or "his job isn't as good as I thought it was."

Except in limited experimental situations, equity theory has not been very successful in predicting *which* method of dealing with inequity a person will use in a given situation. However, the chief value of this theory is that it highlights the importance of perceived equity and the role of comparisons to others in affecting motivation. In effect, equity theory emphasizes the social nature of motivation.

expectancy theory a motivation theory that focuses on the thought processes people use when they face particular choices among alternatives, especially alternative courses of action

Expectancy Theory Psychologist Victor Vroom formulated a motivation theory applicable to work settings that is based on people's expectations.[19] Although details of the theory can get complicated, the basics are easy to understand and are diagrammed in Exhibit 10.9. **Expectancy theory** focuses on the thought processes people use when they face particular choices among alternatives, particularly alternative courses of action. With reference to the work situation, the theory (in simplified form) proposes that individuals have two kinds of beliefs that can affect the amount of effort they will choose to put forth. One such belief (typically referred to as an "expectancy"), effort (E) to performance (P), symbolized as (E → P), is the probability that a certain amount of effort will lead to a certain level of performance: "If I try to do this, will I succeed?" The other belief (often called an "instrumentality" belief), performance (P) to outcome (O), symbolized as (P → O), is the probability that a particular level of performance will lead to (will be instrumental in obtaining) particular "outcomes" or consequences: "If I succeed, will I get praise from the boss?" The third key variable in the theory is the valence (V) or anticipated value a person attaches to an outcome: "How much will I like praise from the boss if I get it?"

Expectancy Theory by Lyman Porter
mymanagementlab

Exhibit 10.9
Components of Expectancy Theory

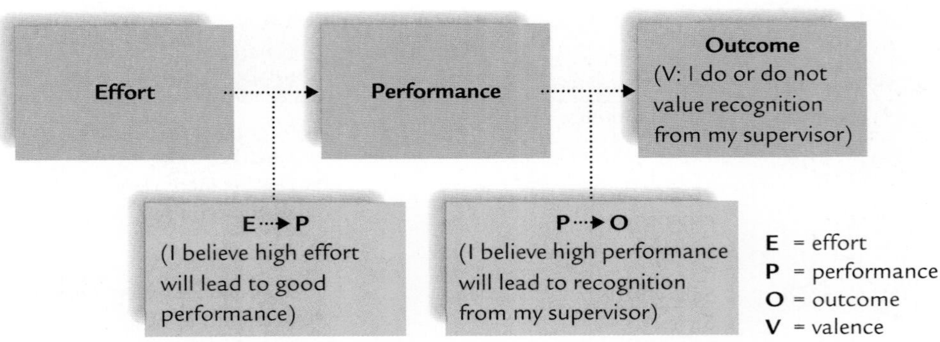

Expectancy theory states that the three key variables interact in a multiplicative, not additive, manner to determine the choice of the amount of effort needed to perform a particular task:

$$\text{Effort} = (E \rightarrow P) \times (P \rightarrow O) \times V$$

Since, according to the theory, these three variables are multiplied to determine level of effort, a low value of any one of the three would lead to the prediction that motivation would be very low. For example, even if a sales representative strongly believes that a certain level of performance (like meeting a sales quota) will lead to a very desirable reward (like positive recognition from her supervisor), her motivation will be low if she does not also have a strong expectation that effort will lead to that level of performance. To restate: Both expectancies and the anticipated value of the outcome must be high for a person to be highly motivated.

A number of implications for managerial practice flow from this theory. For each of the theory's three key variables, managers can take steps to increase employee motivation. The E → P expectancy can be modified by a variety of methods. If a person believes he doesn't have the skills needed to reach a certain level of performance, such self-perceptions can be changed.

His manager can encourage him to get additional training and further practice, and by appropriately guiding and counselling him, build his confidence (thereby influencing his E → P expectancy). Employees who believe they are capable of performing well will be more motivated to achieve their goals.

Additionally, by consistently recognizing accomplishments managers can increase employees' perceptions of the probability of obtaining a desired outcome if they have performed well (thereby influencing the P → O expectancy). How many times, however, do employees perform at a level strongly desired by the organization only to find that, from their perspective, the organization ignores or does not sufficiently recognize their accomplishment? If this happens continually, their level of motivation is certain to decrease.

On the other hand, the reverse is true: If difficult but desired levels of performance are reached and the supervisor or organization recognizes it in an explicit way, future levels of motivation can be increased. Employees are more motivated to perform well when they have a very strong expectation that they will be rewarded.[20] This is the situation at Wardrop Engineering in Winnipeg. At Wardrop, good performance is recognized by offering referral bonuses for employees as well as year-end bonuses that could increase a nonexecutive salary by as much as 50 percent.[21]

The following points sum up, from an expectancy theory perspective, the key ways that managers can potentially influence employees' motivation:

- Identify rewards that are valued
- Strengthen subordinates' beliefs that their efforts will lead to valued rewards
- Clarify subordinates' understanding of exactly where they should direct their efforts
- Make sure that the desired rewards under your control are given directly following particular levels of performance
- Provide levels and amounts of rewards that are consistent with a realistic level of expected rewards

One final issue relating to expectancy theory should be noted: Its application can be affected by cultural circumstances. For instance, in certain countries in the Middle East—where there is a strong emphasis on fate—attempts to change effort → performance (E → P) expectancies might not succeed. Likewise, attempts to single out an individual for public praise in a collectivistic culture, such as in many Asian or Latin American countries, would not likely have as positive an effect on that person's performance as it might in Germany or Australia, where individualism is a stronger characteristic. An approach that considers how individuals calculate the potential personal benefits in pursuing one course of action over another seems more relevant to most Western cultures than to cultures that place less emphasis on personal gain.

Although the psychological processes described in expectancy theory are not necessarily culturally bound, since they can occur anywhere, the frequency with which they occur probably is. For any culture, however, the key point is that expectancy theory is probably most useful in understanding and predicting levels of motivation that involve deliberate choices in the amount of effort to be put forth, rather than routine behaviour that is largely determined by habit.

social cognitive theory (SCT) a theory that focuses on how individuals think about, or "cognitively process," information obtained from their social environment

Social Cognitive Theory A process theory closely related to expectancy theory, and one that has received considerable recent attention among organizational scholars, is **social cognitive theory (SCT)**, developed by social psychologist

self-efficacy an individual's confidence about his or her abilities to mobilize motivation, cognitive resources, and courses of action needed to successfully execute a specific task within a given context

Albert Bandura. For our purposes, we will concentrate on one key component of SCT—**self-efficacy**. The concept of self-efficacy can be defined as "an individual's . . . confidence about his or her abilities to mobilize motivation, cognitive resources, and courses of action needed to successfully execute a specific task within a given context."[22] In other words, self-efficacy is the extent of a person's confidence that he or she can accomplish a given task in a specific situation. Such beliefs have three dimensions: magnitude (how difficult a task can be accomplished), strength (certainty of accomplishment), and generality (extent to which similar but not identical tasks can be accomplished). Research to date appears to show conclusively that when individuals have high self-efficacy beliefs, their work-related performance is better.[23]

From a managerial perspective, you should be asking this question: How can somebody's self-efficacy beliefs be increased? As shown in Exhibit 10.10, social cognitive theory proposes four major determinants:

Exhibit 10.10

Social Cognitive Theory: Methods to Increase an Individual's Feelings of Self-Efficacy

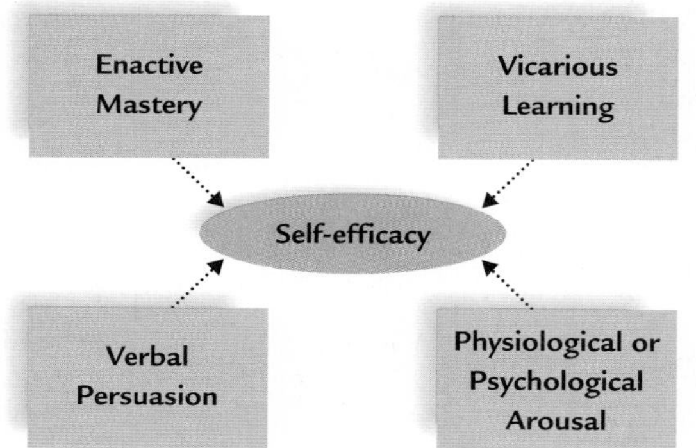

- *Enactive mastery experience:* Succeeding on a similar prior task and attributing that success to one's own capabilities rather than to luck or circumstances. For example, "I have the skill that it takes to succeed on this task," rather than, say, "I was lucky," or "I only did what was expected."
- *Vicarious learning/modelling:* Knowledge gained by observing or learning how others successfully perform a task and then modelling one's own behaviour in a similar manner.
- *Verbal persuasion:* Statements from others that convince a person that he or she can successfully perform the task. For instance, "As your manager, I have full confidence that you have the ability to perform this task quite successfully."
- *Physiological and psychological arousal:* Potential energizing forces that can increase self-efficacy beliefs if the focus is directed to the task. For example, generating expressions of enthusiasm from colleagues can raise the arousal level of an individual. However, if such heightened arousal is focused on one's self—as is often the case, for example, when one is giving a speech—rather than on the task, it can be distracting and thus detrimental to self-efficacy and subsequent performance.

It should be clear that if you are a manager there are several different ways to positively influence the self-efficacy of those who work with and for you. You can create opportunities for them to exhibit enactive mastery by taking on and succeeding in difficult tasks that they may have been initially reluctant to try. You yourself can model successful behaviour for them, or you can arrange working conditions so that they can learn from those employees most experienced and competent at the task. You can, of course, attempt to convince them that they should be able to do a task successfully (but this is not always easy to do). And, of course, you can try to increase their energy level by inspiring them or directing their emotions toward specific task accomplishment. An essential point to keep in mind is that these various approaches to increasing others' self-efficacy are not mutually exclusive. One or more of them can be used together. Findings from research provide convincing evidence that you can motivate others to improve their performance. And, as *A Manager's Challenge: "Sales Potential All Bottled Up"* illustrates, increasing a person's self-efficacy is something that is probably applicable in many different types of cultures.

a manager's challenge — globalization

Sales Potential All Bottled Up

Mark Johnson (a real person whose name we have changed) was in a panic. He was meeting with the Asia-Pacific regional president in less than two weeks, and he would have to explain to him why sales were down 15 percent and profits were down 40 percent in the last six months since Johnson arrived.

Johnson was the managing director of a joint venture (JV) between Pepsi and a formerly state-owned enterprise that made and bottled carbonated cola and noncarbonated fruit beverages in Vietnam. The JV was established to bottle and distribute Pepsi beverages initially in southern Vietnam and eventually throughout the entire country. To everyone's delight, the JV did well during the first couple of years of operation. During that time, the JV management focused on the existing customers of the Vietnamese partner who were other state-owned enterprises. Johnson was sent to the JV in its third year of operation in large part to add a consumer-focused marketing and distribution strategy to the initial institutional base of customers.

Soon after his arrival, sales and profits began to decline. When Johnson asked his sales manager, marketing manager, and sales team why sales and profits were declining, they simply shrugged their shoulders or blamed the rainy season. Johnson was totally frustrated. The sales targets for consumer sales were clear. The commissions that sales personnel would receive if they hit their sales targets were very lucrative by Vietnamese standards. With unemployment at 12 percent, Johnson could not understand why the sales personnel didn't seem to be motivated by the reward system.

In a bit of desperation, Johnson went with a salesman on some sales calls. What he discovered amazed him. First, even though his Vietnamese was not good, he could tell that the salesman was not comfortable with cold calls (calling on a new customer for the first time). Second, it was clear that the distribution and retail industries in Vietnam were significantly more fragmented than in the West. Therefore, to achieve a particular volume of sales, the sales personnel in Vietnam might have to make 10 times as many sales calls. Johnson also discovered that most of the roads outside the main cities of Vietnam were dirt; during the rainy season they became almost impassable for the motorcycles and bicycles that were the primary means of delivering products to retailers.

While the sales team acknowledged the performance expectations and lucrative rewards they would receive for meeting their targets, they were not motivated to try very hard. Why? Because they did not believe they had what it took to be successful. In particular, their past experience in dealing with long-established institutional customers gave them an understanding of managing existing customer relationships and taking orders, but not of making cold calls to small distributors and retailers. Although not the only issue, one of the ways to motivate the sales personnel was to provide them with the information, training, and skills they needed—for example, procedures for making cold calls and how to become more efficient in consumer distribution activities. This increased their beliefs that they could hit their sales targets with these new customers and, consequently, obtain the promised rewards.

Source: Personal communications to author (JSB), 1998–2003.

Goal-Setting Theory A somewhat different type of process theory that has attracted considerable research attention in recent years is **goal-setting theory**.[24] The notion of a goal, a desired end state, highlights the importance of intentions. "Goal setting theory assumes that human action is directed by conscious goals and intentions."[25] Therefore, if managers can influence goals and intentions, they can directly affect performance. The level at which goals are set is a potentially powerful determinant of motivation, and obtaining a person's commitment to particular goals is crucial.[26]

goal-setting theory a theory that assumes human action is directed by conscious goals and intentions

The findings from goal-setting research point to two basic conclusions:

1. More challenging (higher or harder) goals, if accepted, result in higher levels of effort than easier goals.
2. Specific goals result in higher levels of effort than vague goals.[27]

Despite consistent findings supporting a goal-setting approach in a number of well-controlled experiments, one dimension of goal setting has produced inconsistent and often contradictory results. This is the issue of whether goals that are set through a process of participation (by those who will be asked to meet them) result in higher performance than goals that are arbitrarily assigned by someone else, like a supervisor.

There is some research that suggests that cultural factors may be particularly influential in determining whether participation is effective in the goal-setting process.[28] Overall, however, the basic conclusion across accumulated research findings from many studies is that setting goals has consistently positive effects on performance, no matter how those goals are set.

The Role of Reinforcements and Consequences

Actions that occur before behaviour takes place, such as setting goals, are considered antecedents to performance. Such antecedent actions can influence behaviour, especially by clarifying expectations. However, events that happen to the individual *after* behaviour—the consequences of performance—can also have a powerful effect on determining future motivation by reinforcing tendencies to continue or discontinue that behaviour.[29] Consequences can be positive, neutral, or negative and can vary from insignificant to overwhelming. The deliberate application of them, however, provides a manager with a potentially powerful set of tools to influence performance; that is, they are powerful tools *if* the consequences are applied appropriately. As will be clear from the discussion that follows, this is not always easy to do.

Reinforcement Approaches

Analysis of the different reinforcement approaches focuses on whether particular behaviours will likely be repeated or not. The two principal approaches that can be used to increase the probability of behaviour desired by the manager or organization are positive and negative reinforcements.

positive reinforcements desirable consequences that, by being given or applied, increase the likelihood of behaviour being repeated in the future

Positive Reinforcements **Positive reinforcements** are desirable consequences, often referred to as "rewards," that, by being given or applied, increase the likelihood of behaviour being repeated in the future. In many instances, the use of positive reinforcements, like a manager praising an employee for good performance, strengthens the likelihood of that behaviour reoccurring in the future, especially if such praise is not seen by the subordinate as routine or insincere. However, positive consequences also can inadvertently reinforce unwanted behaviour.[30] For example, an employee may take a shortcut at considerable risk to the organization to achieve an important performance goal. The employee's manager congratulates the person for reaching the goal so quickly but does not realize that the risky behaviour is also being reinforced. Other examples of managers' unintended reinforcement of the "wrong" behaviour when trying to make changes that are intended to have positive results are described in *A Manager's Challenge: "Can Motivation Go Wrong?"* It should be fairly obvious that managers need to be more alert to the range of the potential effects of their actions on subordinates' motivation and future behaviour.

a manager's challenge | change

Can Motivation Go Wrong?

The head of a public relations firm gave her staff the task of producing a report on their company's history to celebrate its tenth anniversary. The staff members, who always procrastinated, underestimated the time the project would require and were in danger of falling behind. The deadline could not be put off, however, so the head of the firm allowed them to drop all their other work and even hired temps to help out.

After a chaotic race to the finish line, the project was done, and the head of the company gave the staff a bonus to reward them for their hard work. What lesson did they probably learn about the effects of their procrastinating?

This real example demonstrates how easy it is for managers to mistakenly reinforce the wrong behaviour with the best intentions when making changes. The head of the public relations firm gave her staff several reasons to continue an undesirable behaviour—she lightened their workload, hired extra people to help out, and even gave them a cash bonus at the end. Nearly all the consequences of their poor time management were actually positive!

An insurance company trying to make a change to crack down on the number of overpayments sent to policyholders by mistake also discouraged its employees from doing the research needed to clarify the amounts that were really due. It maintained strict standards that required a certain percentage of claims to be settled within 48 hours, so new hires soon became aware of the norm: "When in doubt, pay it out."

To make matters worse, the company gave 5 percent raises to outstanding workers, 4 percent raises to above-average workers, and 3 percent to all others, even if their work was negligent and irresponsible. In fact, what the company seemed to reward the most was attendance. Those who had three or more separate instances of absence or lateness in any six-month period received no raise at all. So, while workers were highly motivated to show up to gain the 3 percent, they were not well enough rewarded for the quality of what they produced while they were there. Few workers chose to exert themselves enough to win the extra 1 or 2 percent above the minimum.

These examples illustrate that motivation can "go wrong" when managers fail to clarify goals and desired behaviours, especially when trying to make changes. The leaders of organizations need to take the long-term view of results and maintain a "big picture" view of the goals of the total organization. Asking a few key questions can be revealing, too. For instance: Is innovation and risk-taking desired even though rewards go to those who use tried-and-true methods and don't make any mistakes? Are employees' communication skills highly valued, but recognition and praise given only for technical achievements? Is employee empowerment strongly endorsed and advocated in spite of the fact that the organization retains rigid controls over all aspects of its operations and resources?

Sources: C. Sittenfeld, "Great Job! Here's a Seat Belt!," *Fast Company*, January 2004, p. 29; J. L. Komaki, "Reinforcement Theory at Work: Enhancing and Explaining What Employees Do," in L. W. Porter, R. M. Steers, and G. A. Bigley, *Motivation and Work Behaviour*, 7th ed. (New York: McGraw-Hill, 2003); S. Kerr, "On the Folly of Rewarding A, While Hoping for B," *Academy of Management Executive*, February 1995, pp. 7–16.

One of the foremost experts on the use of rewards and reinforcements, Steven Kerr, suggests that for positive reinforcements (rewards) to be effective in motivating behaviour in organizational settings, they should have the following attributes:[31]

- *Equitable:* The size of rewards should be roughly related to the quality and/or quantity of past job-related performance.
- *Efficient:* Rewards must have some capacity for affecting future performance; for example, by making clear that a particular level of future performance will lead to a desired reward.
- *Available (capable of being given):* Managers and organizations should not talk about or offer rewards that are not readily available or are available in such small amounts that they are viewed by recipients as not really rewarding at all. As Kerr states: "Organizations with minuscule

salary increase pools spend hundreds of management hours rating, ranking, and grading employees, only to waste time, raise expectations, and ultimately produce such pitiful increases that everybody is disappointed and embarrassed."

- *Not exclusive:* The possibility of obtaining rewards should not be limited to only a small percentage of employees. The more people that are "ineligible" or excluded from the possibility of obtaining rewards, the less likely a given reward will have a widespread effect.
- *Visible:* To be effective in having more than a very limited impact on the motivation of a number of people, rewards should be visible not only to recipients but also to others who possibly could obtain them in the future.
- *Reversible:* This attribute of effective rewards does not, of course, refer to a reward that can be taken away once given. Rather, it refers to rewards that can be denied or not given in the future, if circumstances warrant. The classic example in modern business organizations is the bonus. Unlike an annual pay raise, a bonus can clearly be a one-time-only reward. It also is a type of reward that can be given again in the future. That feature provides managers with a great deal of flexibility.

negative reinforcements undesirable consequences that, by being removed or avoided, increase the likelihood of a behaviour being repeated in the future

Negative Reinforcements The *removal* of undesirable (i.e., negative) consequences, that is, consequences that a person performing an act does not want, can increase the likelihood of that behaviour being repeated in the future. The removal of such undesirable consequences is called a **negative reinforcement**, just as the addition of desirable consequences is called a positive reinforcement. In both cases, they are reinforcing if they cause behaviour to be maintained or increased. For example, a salesperson working in a sales territory with very difficult and demanding customers finds that, by putting in extra effort, the unpleasant experiences he has been encountering are reduced when he is transferred to a different territory. If he believes the transfer or promotion was a result of his hard work, the removal of the undesirable consequences (the difficult territory with difficult customers) has reinforced the likelihood that he will try hard to please his customers in his new territory. In this instance, both the company and the salesperson benefited from the negative reinforcement.

Negative reinforcements, however, can also work against the best interests of the organization. For example, if a supervisor finds that giving a particular subordinate an "average" rating results in avoiding the unpleasant confrontations with that subordinate that have occurred in the past—when the subordinate was given well-deserved "below-average" ratings—the supervisor's current action is negatively reinforced. However, the subordinate will probably continue with subpar performance, and the organization also will be deprived of accurate information on the subordinate that may be crucial in future promotion decisions.

Both of these reinforcement mechanisms—positive reinforcements and negative reinforcements—maintain or increase particular types of behaviour and performance. Thus, they provide managers with potentially potent ways to increase desired behaviour. However, if care is not taken, their use can lead to continuation or increases in behaviour that is not wanted.

In contrast to these two reinforcement mechanisms for maintaining or enhancing particular behaviours, two other methods involving consequences (discussed next) are methods to *decrease* the probability of particular behaviours.

Punishments Punishments are undesirable consequences that are given following behaviour to decrease the likelihood that it will be repeated. In some organizations, punishments are seen as an effective way to prevent behaviour that is not wanted. In many other organizations, however, punishments are discouraged, often because their use is seen as either inappropriate or ineffective. Also, they can have inadvertent effects of increasing behaviour that is not wanted. For example, an undesired effect of a deliberately applied punishment occurs when a penalty is applied for excessive absenteeism, yet the behaviour that is reinforced is not better attendance but more sophisticated excuses for being absent. This example illustrates that in organizations it is typically quite difficult to make sure that punishments have only the effects intended and no other effects.

punishments undesirable consequences that are applied to decrease the likelihood of behaviour being repeated in the future

There are many examples of unintended punishment, with possible undesirable consequences. These include giving added pressure and responsibilities to someone who has shown that she can handle stress, or giving additional committee assignments to the person who has shown that he is exceptionally responsible in meeting commitments. Unless a manager is highly alert, unintended punishments happen more often than might be expected.

Extinction Another approach used to decrease behaviours is to avoid providing any positive consequences as the result of that behaviour. This process is referred to as **extinction**. It is a well-demonstrated research finding, and a fact of everyday work life, that behaviours that do not lead to positive reinforcements tend not to be repeated, or at least not repeated as much. Managers can use the principle of extinction to their advantage by deliberately not reinforcing employee behaviour that they consider undesirable. For example, managers might refrain from reacting positively to a joke that may be of questionable taste.

extinction the absence of positive consequences for behaviour, lessening the likelihood of that behaviour being repeated in the future

The principle of extinction, however, poses two challenges for managers. One is the inadvertent lack of attention to rewarding behaviour that should be reinforced. A typical example of this often occurs in manufacturing organizations with respect to safety behaviour. Frequently, safe work behaviour is simply taken for granted by supervisors and is not explicitly reinforced. As a result, because safe behaviour usually requires extra time and effort, employees gradually lose motivation to take these extra steps, and eventually an accident occurs. Another common example of unintentional application of the principle of extinction occurs when an employee puts in extra effort on a key project but receives little or no recognition or acknowledgment from the boss. In this type of case, the motivation to behave similarly the next time would not likely be strengthened, not only for the individual involved but also, and even more importantly, for other employees who observe these situations and their outcomes.

The second potential hazard of either the deliberate or unintended use of extinction is that it can leave the interpretation of important situations in the hands of employees rather than under the control of the manager. Explicit reinforcements or punishments provide the recipients with clear, or at least clearer, information regarding what their managers find desirable or undesirable behaviour and performance.

The effects of each of these approaches to the use of reinforcements are summarized in Exhibit 10.11.

Exhibit 10.11 Reinforcement Approaches and Their Effects

Reinforcement Approach	Managerial Action	Effect	Example
Positive reinforcement	Provide desirable consequence	**Increase probability** of behaviour being repeated	Highway construction supervisor receives bonus for each day a project is completed ahead of schedule.
Negative reinforcement	Remove undesirable consequence	**Increase probability** of behaviour being repeated	Management stops raising output quotas each time workers exceed them.
Punishment	Provide undesirable consequence	**Decrease probability** of behaviour being repeated	Habitually tardy crew member is fined the equivalent of one hour's pay each day he is late to work.
Extinction	Remove desirable consequence	**Decrease probability** of behaviour being repeated	Group member stops making unsolicited suggestions when team leader no longer mentions them in group meetings.

Planned Programs of Positive Reinforcement

Organizations often institute programs to systematically apply the principles of reinforcement theory (often called "behaviour modification" or "applied behaviour analysis" programs). These programs involve four basic steps:

1. Specify desired performance precisely. (Example: "Lower and keep the accident rate below 1 percent.")
2. Measure desired behaviours. (Example: "Monitor safety actions A, B, C.")
3. Provide frequent positive consequences for specified behaviours. (Example: "Give semiannual monetary rewards for performing a procedure safely 100 percent of the time.")
4. Evaluate the effectiveness of the program. (Example: "Were accidents kept below 1 percent over the previous six-month period?") Then make progress public knowledge.[32]

Programs of this type have been effective in a wide variety of work settings and in parts of the world as diverse as the Middle East, Europe, and North America.[33] It is important to point out, however, that the effectiveness of the basic principles of reinforcement does not depend on formal company programs for their application. Any person in a managerial position can use these principles. They will be likely to have their greatest effect on the third of the three elements that make up the definition of motivation—the persistence of behaviour.

Social Influences on Motivation

Although the point is sometimes overlooked, understanding motivation involves more than simply analyzing individual behaviour. If our concern is about behaviour in organizational work settings, it is crucial to recognize—as emphasized in Exhibit 10.1 at the beginning of this chapter—the powerful influence of the social context, particularly the individual's immediate workgroup as well as supervisors and subordinates.

Influence of the Immediate Workgroup

The immediate workgroup affects many aspects of a person's behaviour, but one of the strongest effects is on motivation. This is particularly true for organizations operating in cultures and countries that have strong collectivistic tendencies and traditions, such as those in Asia and Latin America.[34] In such cultures, the individual is likely to be heavily influenced by the **in-group**, the group to which the person belongs, but less influenced by others who are not members of the in-group. Although stronger and more prevalent in collectivistic cultures than in some others, group influences on individuals' motivation can occur in almost any culture or organization, given appropriate circumstances.

in-group the group to which a person belongs

What are those circumstances? Primarily, they involve (1) the existence of a group in which an individual is a member, the in-group, and especially (2) the strong desire of the person to be part of that group and to receive that group's approval. When this situation exists, the level of effort or motivation a person exerts almost certainly will be affected by the group's influence.

The direction of social influence on motivation will likely depend on the group's norms—the group's expected standards of behaviour for its individual members. When those norms support the organization's goals, the influence will be to increase levels of motivation. When the norms oppose the organization's objectives, however, the influence will be to decrease levels of motivation to perform. And, as originally demonstrated in a study many years ago, the more cohesive a group is, the more it can affect performance motivation in either direction—up or down.[35] (Group norms will be discussed in detail in Chapter 11.)

A person's workgroup can affect motivational aspects of his or her work behaviour other than just levels of performance. For example, a study of teenage workers in fast-food restaurants demonstrated that when an employee decided to leave the organization, it increased (not decreased) the desire of close friends to continue working at the restaurant. Although such a result might seem unexpected, the researchers explained the finding by hypothesizing that the friends who remained working at the restaurant had to re-examine ("justify") their reasons for staying, which resulted in a stronger determination to do so.[36] Thus, the social influence of the workgroup friends in this study clearly affected motivation of at least one type of behaviour—staying with the organization.

Influence of Supervisors and Subordinates

Supervisors and subordinates, not just workgroup peers, are also part of the immediate social environment that can influence motivation. The impact of supervisors or leaders on the motivation of their employees is linked to their control of powerful rewards and potential punishments, as we discussed earlier. However, it is important to emphasize that the motivational impact of someone in a supervisory position is not the same for all subordinates. In other words, although the person next highest in the organization typically has a strong effect on the motivation of those he or she supervises, that effect is often uneven. The same supervisor can be a source of increased motivation for some employees and a source of dampened motivation for others.[37] Much depends on the one-on-one interpersonal relationships that are developed over time in each supervisor–subordinate pair.

Subordinate employees themselves are not without influence on the motivation of their superiors, especially through their ability to punish behaviour by subtly withholding rewards. Although subordinates typically do not have the same amount of reward leverage over their superiors, as is the reverse case, they are not powerless.[38] For example, they could withhold some expertise that only they have (and that the supervisor may not have) when not pleased with an action of the supervisor. A systems analyst, unhappy with the assignment she has been given, could resist pointing out some key technical details to her boss. Although such subordinate behaviour is unlikely to be overt, it can affect the supervisor's motivation to act in the future in ways that produce these kinds of reactions.

Influence of the Organization's Culture

Not to be overlooked is the impact that the culture of the larger organizational context (beyond the workgroup) can have on employees' motivation. As one management scholar emphasized, "From a management perspective, [corporate] culture in the form of shared expectations may be thought of as a social control system."[39] This influence on motivation is exercised primarily through norms—in this case the organization's expected patterns of appropriate and acceptable behaviour. Just as with a peer group, the more that an individual desires to remain part of an organization, the more he or she will be influenced by that organization's culture. The organization can be considered simply a larger type of group, with its culture often having a less direct influence on motivation than the immediate workgroup, but an influence nonetheless. Organizations that have gone through mergers or acquisitions know only too well that the imposition of unfamiliar cultural features and norms can have potentially devastating effects on the motivation of the "new" entity's members.[40]

Influence of Values and Attitudes toward Work

No analysis of motivation in the work setting can be complete without consideration of the influence of an individual's values and fundamental attitudes toward work. Such values and attitudes are especially sensitive to cultural differences within a country or across countries. Managing in a global context requires attention to these differences if one is to understand work motivation beyond the cultures of a person's own group or country.

Values

Chapter 4 has already provided a general discussion of culture and cultural values. With that as a backdrop, we can look at the role of those values as they specifically affect motivation. As a reminder, values are enduring beliefs that a specific mode of conduct or end state of existence is preferable.[41] As this definition implies, values can be "end state," as in the case of "equality" or "liberty," or they can be "instrumental" and influence means to ends, such as the values of being cooperative, supportive, or competitive. Both kinds of values affect motivation levels because they influence what members of a particular culture consider crucially important. That in turn can influence goals and intentions. Values also affect what kinds of behaviours individuals will find rewarding and satisfying.[42] *A Manager's Challenge: "Money Isn't Everything"* describes how one organization, MBAs Without Borders, is relying heavily on the values of its employees to motivate their willingness to join and stay with an enterprise paying a relatively modest salary.

Attitudes toward Work

Understanding how different groups or cultures view the meaning of work, that is, how much the activity of working is valued, helps us to gain additional insight into motivational differences across cultures. The famous sociologist

a manager's challenge — ethics

Money Isn't Everything

How would you like to work for an organization that finds projects in developing countries within Africa, Asia, Eastern Europe, Latin America, and the Caribbean? You would travel to one of these regions and assist in developing projects that are within five industries: health care, agriculture, finance, income generation, and climate change. You would also be partnering with local and international businesses as well as nongovernmental organizations to develop new businesses. The work will keep you very busy, and it will be rewarding yet challenging; and best of all, the organization exists for just one purpose—to help others. In addition, you must have an MBA. In exchange for your skills and commitment, you will receive paid airfare to your work location, room and board, a laptop, and an approximately $1000-a-month stipend.

While this may sound unappealing in terms of compensation, there are, in fact, a growing number of people that are hoping to work for MBAs Without Borders or similar organizations whose goals satisfy an employee's intrinsic needs. MBAs Without Borders, or MWB, is a not-for-profit organization that sends teams of MBA graduates to developing countries to enable local private enterprises, educate local businesspeople, and engage directly with the local community. The concept was founded in 2004 by McMaster University's DeGroote School of Business MBA graduates Tal Dehtiar and Michael Brown and it has been growing steadily ever since. In 2005 they sent one MBA abroad, and in 2006 ten MBAs were sent to work in 11 countries. In 2007 MWB hopes to send between 20–25 MBAs from various regions around the globe to 15 countries, including India, Pakistan, Zimbabwe, Rwanda, and Ethiopia. The organization has an advisory board, a structure of 15 managing directors, including a marketing director, a communications director, a director of innovation, regional directors, and more than 2500 MBA graduates and 150 MBA student and alumni networks around the world. All are set to embark upon MWB's mission of contributing to the business and social development of upcoming nations through work rotations of MBA professionals. An MBA's dedication to helping develop people and regions is what keeps alive the dream that inspired Dehtiar and Brown to start MBAs Without Borders.

Relying on outside financial backing to help pay its modest managerial salaries, MWB demonstrates how nonfinancial rewards can motivate those whose needs for achievement, affiliation, or self-actualization outweigh their desire for material reward, even if only temporarily. Dehtiar laments that there is not enough credence given to social responsibility within the MBA culture. Dehtiar hopes that MWB will provide a new aura for the graduate business degree.

Sources: MBAs Without Borders website, www.mbaswithoutborders.org (accessed June 5, 2007); A. Holloway, "World of Wonders: A Group Called MBAs Without Borders Is Looking for Dollars," *Canadian Business*, October 25, 2004, p. 138.

Max Weber was one of the first to describe how the meaning attached to work has affected motivation in industrial societies. His contention was that in so-called "Christian countries" of his era (late nineteenth and early twentieth centuries), Protestant religious values emphasized and supported hard work and the accumulation of wealth. This idea led him to coin the well-known phrase "the Protestant work ethic."[43] According to Weber, many people in the United States and in northern European countries were assumed to be guided by such an ethic, whether or not they were literally "Protestants."

A body of scholarly research carried out in the last decades of the twentieth century on the meaning of work focused especially on **work centrality**, defined as "the degree of general importance that working has in the life of an individual at a point in time."[44] To measure work centrality, researchers asked working adult respondents to rate the importance of work to them in relation to other major life roles. The range of agreement by study participants in eight countries to a statement regarding the importance placed on work is shown in Exhibit 10.12. It can be seen that work was relatively more important and more

work centrality the degree of general importance that working has in the life of an individual at a point in time

Exhibit 10.12

Work Centrality: Country Differences

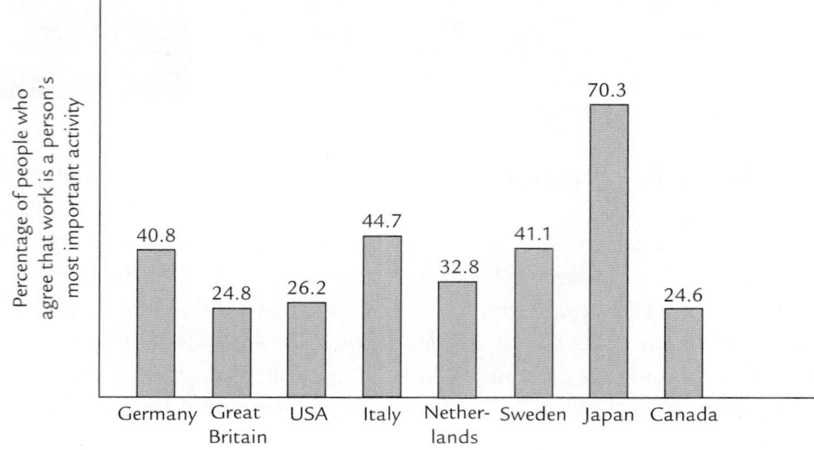

Source: Adapted from T. W. Smith, "A Cross-National Comparison on Attitudes towards Work by Age and Labor Force Status," National Opinion Research Center, University of Chicago, December 2000.

central in life experiences in Japan than it was in the other seven countries, including Canada, which actually rated the importance of work the lowest.[45]

Not all features of the work environment are valued equally by different groups of employees. A recent research study,[46] for example, sheds some light on this issue. The study was carried out on a sample of some 4500 "knowledge workers and managers"—arguably a segment of employees that will be one of the most important to organizations in the future—from 10 large technology-intensive companies (including those in aerospace, software, and pharmaceutical industries) that have major operations in North America, Europe, and Asia. Survey data were collected from this sample and analyzed by age, gender, and geographic region of the respondents. The focus was on what aspects of the work situation are seen as most important. The findings demonstrate that there are differences by age, gender, and region. Factors such as "career advancement" and "professional career development" were rated more important by younger versus older employees. Women at early stages of their careers put more emphasis on job security and less on financial rewards as compared to men. At later stages, women put more importance on career advancement and professional development than did men in the sample. The major difference by region involved "international opportunities" (for career advancement), seen as more important by Asians and Europeans compared to North Americans.

What are the motivational and managerial implications of such research findings that examine the meaning and importance of work, and different features of work, in different cultures and groups? First, they show that since work does not generate the same relative degree of importance among employees, compared with other significant areas of their lives, managers face different motivational challenges relating to different sets of employees or in different cultural contexts. Second, since the meaning of work appears to vary among different categories of employees and in different countries, the findings indicate that specific incentives—such as pay raises, time off, or opportunities for career advancement—will not have the same motivational effect in all situations and with all people. The message is that managers cannot assume that everyone else will value work, and different elements of work, in the same way that they themselves do. A sensitivity to these differences, therefore, can be highly useful in addressing motivational issues and problems.

managerial perspectives revisited

PERSPECTIVE 1: **THE ORGANIZATIONAL CONTEXT** The organization is a major source of influence on motivation. Its culture, policies, routines, formal compensation and reward systems, and other relatively enduring and continuing characteristics all contribute to affecting the efforts of its members to perform well. If you find yourself in a managerial role, it will be important to gain an understanding of these influences and how they impact your own efforts to motivate other people. Often, many features of the organization cannot be easily or quickly changed, so it is up to you, as a manager, to determine how to make those organizational characteristics support your motivational initiatives; in other words, how to make the organizational context a positive motivational force.

PERSPECTIVE 2: **THE HUMAN FACTOR** For any manager, motivation is inherently a *people* process. Of course, as a manager you would be concerned about your own individual level of motivation, but your effectiveness as a managerial leader will depend on your ability to motivate other people. No matter how highly motivated you are yourself, if you can't motivate others you won't be successful. Thus, it is critical that you have some understanding of how you are affecting the motivation of others and what steps you can take to maintain or increase that motivation. A good place to start is to consider how you can increase others' sense of their own self-efficacy for the tasks that make up their jobs, and then how you can generate social influences in the work situation that will reinforce the results of higher levels of self-efficacy.

PERSPECTIVE 3: **MANAGING PARADOXES** The process of motivation is filled with paradoxes. For example: Should you attempt to increase the "push" forces of motivation, or instead concentrate more on the "pull" forces? Should reinforcements be provided, or withheld, if performance is good but not superior? Should the focus be entirely on strengthening the intrinsic job-related factors of motivation, or do the extrinsic factors surrounding the job also deserve attention? Should some of your time be spent on trying to understand individual differences in response to different incentives, or is it better simply to assume that—within limits—most people respond more or less the same to, say, the opportunity for promotion? Likewise, are cultural differences among a set of subordinates to be given major attention, or would motivational efforts be better spent elsewhere?

PERSPECTIVE 4: **ENTREPRENEURIAL MINDSET** An entrepreneurial mindset can affect employee motivation in several ways. First, a manager using an entrepreneurial mindset searches for new opportunities to motivate her employees, and she is willing to try new motivational techniques. Second, if a manager wants her employees to be innovative and develop more effective ways of doing their

jobs or providing service to the firm's customers, she must create an entrepreneurial culture. Additionally, her employees must be motivated to be innovative. As such, managers should reward innovative behaviour in ways that satisfy employees' needs.

Certainly, motivating others in an effective manner can be challenging. Motivating those you are attempting to lead is difficult because so many variables and forces are involved that determine motivation. Managers must be committed to evaluating their employees and the environment in which they work to understand what will motivate them and what won't. Combining this commitment with an entrepreneurial culture can be a powerful motivational force.

concluding comments

Motivation is a topic that interests employers, practising managers, and organizational scholars alike. For companies and other employers, having a highly motivated workforce is often viewed as essential for guaranteeing high levels of organizational success. Having talented employees is not enough if that talent is not coupled with motivation. For managers, a good understanding of the topic provides potentially great leverage in positively influencing the work behaviour and performance of those who work with and for them. For organizational theorists and researchers, the topic represents a major scientific challenge to gain insight and knowledge, especially knowledge that can be transformed into better-performing organizations.

As we emphasized early in this chapter (Exhibit 10.1), thinking about motivation in terms of the three variables—individual, job, and work context—that together determine levels of motivation provides an essential framework for understanding motivational issues and problems. Knowing what the individual brings to the work situation (the internal "push" forces), what the individual does in the situation (part of the external "pull" forces), and what happens to the individual (the other part of the "pull" forces) provides basic clues for making accurate motivational diagnoses.

Armed with this framework, it is possible to make practical use of the several behavioural theories concerning motivation. For the manager, the theories, both those that relate to what motivates people (the content theories) and those that relate to how people become motivated (the process theories), are not ends in themselves. Rather, they should be seen as means or aids to gaining a deeper understanding. They provide multiple ways of gaining insight into the combined effects of a fairly complex set of forces.

Being able to analyze and examine the roles of goals, reinforcements, values, and attitudes provides an additional dimension for those who have to put motivation into practice. Knowing how goals can be used effectively, how the use of various types of reinforcements can create quite different effects, and how the values and attitudes that people bring with them to the work situation (and which are also further developed at work) can shape their responses to motivational initiatives provides additional managerial insights.

Finally, and particularly important, is the necessity for managers of today's multicultural and often multinational workforces not to have a self-centred and ethnocentric view of how to motivate other people. We are all prisoners, to some extent, of the narrow focus of our own particular cultural, ethnic, and socioeconomic backgrounds. But this can get us into more trouble in managing motivation than anything else. It is crucial, therefore, in attempting to become effective motivators, not to assume that everyone else is like us and will react the same way that we would.

key terms

acquired needs theory 348
content theories 344
equity theory 352
expectancy theory 354
extinction 361
goal-setting theory 357
in-group 363
job characteristics model 351
job enrichment 351
Maslow's need hierarchy 344
motivation 341
negative reinforcements 360
positive reinforcements 358
process theories 352
punishments 361
self-efficacy 356
social cognitive theory (SCT) 355
two-factor theory 349
work centrality 365

test your comprehension

1. What is motivation?
2. What is meant by "push" forces and "pull" forces? Give examples of each.
3. What are three major characteristics that determine motivation in organizations? What are some of the variables within each?
4. What is the difference between a content theory and a process theory of motivation?
5. What are the levels in Maslow's need hierarchy? What determines when a person is likely to move from one level to the next?
6. What are some of the characteristics of an individual with a high need for achievement?
7. Can the need for achievement be considered a universal motive?
8. Explain the difference between "motivator" and "hygiene" factors in Herzberg's two-factor theory. What effects are these factors presumed to have on an individual's motivation?
9. How can managers affect motivation by changing job content?
10. What are the components of the job characteristics model?
11. According to equity theory, what might happen if a worker thought he or she was putting in more effort than a co-worker, yet the co-worker received a higher salary or larger bonus?
12. What is the basic equation that represents expectancy theory? Explain what each variable means.
13. According to expectancy theory, what can a manager do to increase an employee's motivation?
14. Give an example of how cultural differences can impact expectancy theory.
15. What is self-efficacy? What are the ways in which it can be increased?
16. What kinds of goals increase motivation? Is it important for managers to help workers set goals?
17. How are antecedents related to consequences and reinforcement?
18. What attributes do positive reinforcements need to have to motivate behaviour?
19. What is the difference between a negative reinforcement and a punishment? Give an example of each.
20. What are the major social influences on work motivation? Give an example of each.
21. Does the effect of values on motivation differ among cultures?
22. What is work centrality? Why is it important for managers to understand this concept when attempting to improve motivation?

apply your understanding

1. You have taken a job as production manager in the electronics plant your company has just bought in Hungary. Your subordinates will be local workers, and your primary goal is to increase their productivity by increasing their motivation. Which motivational theories would you use? Are there any you think would not apply? Why?
2. Is the use of positive reinforcement always the best approach to motivational problems? When might other types of "consequences" be more appropriate?
3. Examine some of your own goals. How did you set them? Were they effective in motivating your performance? If you analyze them in terms of goal-setting theory, how would you change the way you set them in the future?
4. Both equity and expectancy theory suggest that individuals make conscious, reasoned choices concerning their performance. When would a person be most likely to do this? Have you ever seriously analyzed a work situation in the ways suggested by these theories and then changed your behaviour as a result?
5. Which motivational forces are stronger: push or pull? Or are they equal? How might their relative strength change with different circumstances? Why?

practise your capabilities

For 28 years, Jim Preston had been a leading salesman at Maritime Electrical Supply Company. He had constantly qualified for the company's monthly incentive bonuses. Jim was very proud of those bonuses, which not only reflected his high value to the company but also allowed him to provide a higher-than-average standard of living for his family. Some months ago, Maritime was bought out by Fundy Supply, and Sarah Powell was assigned as the new supervisor for the sales force. Although the same incentive system was still in place, Jim had not qualified for a bonus since the buyout and did not even show the same company spirit as before. Sarah, quite worried about Jim's change in attitude and productivity, talked informally with both Jim and his co-workers.

Sarah learned that Jim resented being supervised by a woman, especially one younger than his daughter. She also learned that he was upset with many of the other sales personnel, mostly younger than he, because of their attempt to unionize the office staff. Finally, she discovered that Jim was still receiving and acting on directives from his former boss who had been moved to another part of the company.

Sarah called Jim in for a meeting at which he first stated that he was never told explicitly who his new supervisor was and then blew up at her, yelling, "All of you new brass are the same—always trying to squeeze more out of the little guy. You think you know everything about selling? I was selling electrical parts and supplies before you or any of the other new Fundy supervisors were old enough to know what they are. Now you're telling me how to do my job. Why don't you get off my back? It's my business if I don't earn any bonuses!"

Upon reflection, Sarah decided to try to motivate Jim by adding to the product lines he sold, giving him a larger district, and moving him upstairs to a slightly larger office. Jim, however, didn't respond and seemed focused only on his upcoming retirement. Frustrated, Sarah asked if he would like to take early retirement. When Jim declined the offer, Sarah recommended to her boss that they give Jim a "golden handshake." After all, nothing else seemed to be working.

1. Using the theories presented in this chapter, analyze Jim's behaviour and Sarah's lack of success at motivating him.
2. If you were Sarah and your boss declined the suggestion to release Jim, what would you do next to try to motivate Jim?

Source: Adapted from C. C. Pinder, *Work Motivation: Theory, Issues, and Applications* (Glenview, IL: Scott, Foresman and Company, 1984). Reprinted with permission of Scott, Foresman and Company.

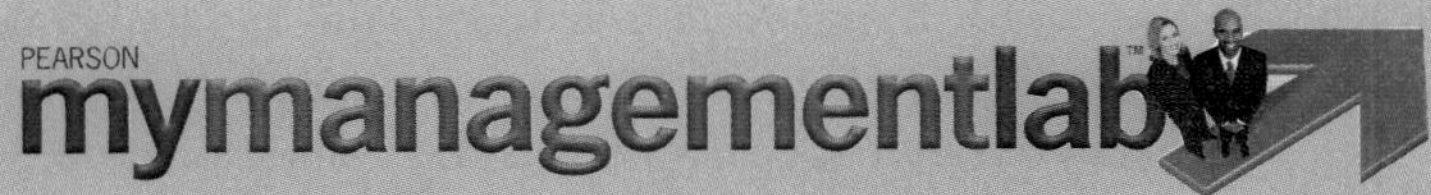

To improve your grade, visit the MyManagementLab website at **www.pearsoned.ca/mymanagementlab.** This online homework and tutorial system allows you to test your understanding and generates a personalized study plan just for you. It provides you with study and practice tools directly related to this chapter's content. MyManagementLab puts you in control of your own learning!

closing case DEVELOP YOUR CRITICAL THINKING

Motivating Leo Henkelman

Despite his bear-like stature, Leo Henkelman was invisible to his employer. To Sandstrom Products, he was nothing more than a strong-backed labourer, a paint mixer who attended to the mill for over a decade. The plant was full of such employees, who came to work each day, did their jobs, complained about the university-educated lab technicians, and collected their paycheques. The money was good and the work was steady, but still Henkelman could not help thinking, "This ain't living." Things would have to change, not only at work but in his personal life.

Henkelman's first job out of high school had been in the slaughterhouse where his father was the foreman. Five days a week, on a shift that began at 3:00 a.m., his task was to stand in the production line and hammer inspection stamps onto the sides of every carcass of beef that passed by. The work was extremely boring, but the pay was decent. He might have stayed at the job longer had he not had a fight with another employee who landed in the hospital. It was his father who fired him.

After a short stint in construction, Henkelman landed a job at Sandstrom Products, a $5.5 million maker of paints, coating, and lubricants. He started as a paint runner, the bottom job at the plant, and spent his days putting paint into cans and putting the cans into boxes. After a year, he was promoted to mill operator and began mixing paints in a blender, following the formulas supplied by the labs. Henkelman's work environment was the plant floor—dark, noisy, and reeking of strong fumes. Adjacent to the plant was the lab, filled with university-educated professionals who wore white shirts and carried business cards. In his work, Henkelman was forced to interact with the lab, particularly if a formula did not work. Time after time, he would suggest solutions to the problem, and the lab basically rejected his ideas. Extremely frustrated, Henkelman realized that the company was not interested in his brain, only in his brawn.

To solve the problems with paint mixing, Henkelman learned to rely less on the formulas supplied by the labs and more on his own experience. Although the mill operators helped each other, the lab mandated that they were to follow the formulas or else. Henkelman admitted that "we did a lot of things under the cover of 'Don't tell nobody that we did this, but we're gonna check this out to see whether it works, because we don't believe the guys in the lab.'" The ongoing feud between the blue-collar plant and the white-collar lab was not only costly and inefficient for the company, but demeaning to all parties involved. As the product quality suffered, customers began to drop off, and Sandstrom saw its profits eroding.

Finding little at work to challenge him, Henkelman sought solace in spending time with friends at bars after work. On many days, he would show up for work with a hangover, only to turn around and return home sick. On other days, he drove around with friends and lost track of time, forgetting to show up for work at all. Once, he was arrested and lost his driver's licence. Realizing that he needed to straighten out his life, Henkelman sought help and slowly began to change his life. Then he underwent back surgery, which caused him to miss three months of work, and his wife threw him out of the house. For a while he lived on the edge of despair, wondering if his life would ever change.

In the meantime, Sandstrom's future was severely threatened. For the past five years the company's net income had been negative. Jim Sandstrom and Rick Hartsock, the company's top executives, knew that they had to make radical changes. Employees were not solving problems as they should, and morale at work was at a record low. Ironically, Rick Hartsock realized that to save the company from failure, he would have to hand the reins to the employees to solve their own problems. It was then that the company decided to experiment with a motivation technique it called "open-book management."

Like many of his colleagues, Leo Henkelman was skeptical. "Just another fad," he thought. What did appeal to him, however, was the focus on results and not on process. Under open-book management, the top brass would provide the objectives and allow employees to figure out how to achieve them through creative problem solving, teamwork, and individual initiative. Hungry for the trust and respect that were offered to him, Henkelman signed up for three teams right away: plant equipment, process control, and merit pay.

The first task for the plant equipment team was a proposal to buy a new $35 000 forklift. The old forklift was over 20 years old and, according to its driver, unreliable and unsafe. The team completed a cost and productivity analysis and presented it to the corporate heads. But management argued that, while it was not a bad idea to buy a new forklift, funds were limited and could be used for something more worthwhile. Henkelman could not help but feel let down and began to feel skeptical again. "Same old story," he thought. However, a few days later, Henkelman and his team were surprised to learn that the forklift expenditure was approved. Spirits boosted, Henkelman said, "It gave me the idea that we can make a difference. It made me feel that we weren't doing all this work for nothing."

As Sandstrom transformed into a company managed by its employees, Henkelman saw the barriers to information begin to fade away. Where the lab had always ruled over the technical manuals, Henkelman and the other plant workers were now allowed to consult them if they wanted to resolve an issue. He eventually even received a password that gave him access to the formulas on the computer, an event unheard of in prior times. No longer paralyzed in a specific job role, he could update the formulas so the process flowed more smoothly. His attitude began to change in his work.

Henkelman's life began to turn around at the same time. He stopped drinking and got an apartment, where he lived alone. With so much spare time, he went into the office and explored the computer, teaching himself about the business. He filled his empty hours, but more importantly, he filled himself with knowledge, with confidence, and with hope. As a virtual new "owner" in the company, he thought it was his duty to understand every aspect of the business. In the old days, he had only learned what he needed to know to do his narrow job well. Now he wanted to understand the entire process, to help grow the business.

Henkelman and the members of the merit pay team took on the challenge of designing an entirely new compensation system. Plant managers had previously used a mixture of seniority and favouritism to compensate their employees, and the subordinates had always been unhappy about this. The workers believed that pay should more closely reflect performance: how useful a worker was on the job, how much a worker knew, and how well tasks were done. These beliefs were not altogether contradictory to that of management; both wanted a highly skilled and effective workforce.

The first proposal drawn up by the team offered plant workers incentives to cross-train in their jobs. However, when management and the team fully analyzed the numbers, they both concluded that the proposal was unrealistic. Rather than dismiss the issue, however, management asked for a proposal that made fiscal sense to almost everyone. Deep in the middle of the analysis, Henkelman came to the realization that he was beginning to think like an owner, not like an hourly employee. The new proposal found a way to pay for the added costs of training but at the expense of some paycheques. Some members of the team quit, but Henkelman was determined to stick it out. After months of hard work—meeting formally, debating with co-workers, striking a balance between paying incentives and maintaining equality among workers—the team came up with an innovative compensation system, which was eventually adopted by the company.

This was a critical turnaround in Henkelman's career. Despite the demands that management made on the team's process, Henkelman felt needed and alive for the first time in his working career: "Because of that I felt and still feel today that I have control of my destiny."

His attitude completely overhauled, Henkelman sought other responsibilities within the company to tap into his strengths. Taking a major promotion, Henkelman was put in charge of scheduling production and even became plant manager for a while. What he found was that neither job suited him. Always a doer, he found it difficult to delegate tasks to others. In a few months, a technician job opened in the lab. Generally, technicians had university degrees in chemistry, and Henkelman had not even taken chemistry in high school. But Bob Sireno, the lab's technical director, wanted Henkelman for the job. He eventually got it.

Henkelman put away his blue-collar shirt and moved to the lab. He would still do what he had always done—make paint—but instead of following orders, he would guide the process from the beginning to the end. His new job allowed him to work with customers, to develop new formulas, and to use his hands-on experience to solve problems where other, less-experienced chemists had failed. Bob Sireno admitted that in a year's time Henkelman had developed skills that had taken university graduates five years to develop. When a complex problem appeared, it was Henkelman who was chosen to solve it—shirt sleeves rolled up and mind determined to make it work.

With a new identity and a new attitude about work, Henkelman remains a valuable team member to Sandstrom Products. Instead of dreading the feuding between departments and the tedium of mixing paint, he now looks forward to each day, wondering what new challenges he will overcome.

Questions

1. Using Maslow's hierarchy of needs, identify the basic needs that Leo Henkelman was attempting to fulfill. How did these needs manifest themselves? How were these needs eventually satisfied?
2. Assess the variables that affected Leo Henkelman's motivation—characteristics of the individual, of the job, and of the work situation.
3. Using the job characteristics model (Exhibit 10.6), analyze Leo Henkelman's motivation: (a) as a worker on the plant floor prior to the introduction of "open-book management"; and (b) as a technician in the laboratory.
4. The company's open-book management approach was designed to get all employees to focus on helping the business make money. What do you think of open-book management as a tool for motivating employees? In what kind of organizational circumstances would it work best? In what kind of circumstances might it be ineffective?

Source: Republished with permission of *Inc.* magazine, Goldhirsh Group, Inc., 38 Commercial Wharf, Boston, MA 02110. "Before and After," David Whitford, June 1995. Reproduced by permission of the publisher via Copyright Clearance Center, Inc.

Chapter 11
Groups and Teams

LEARNING OBJECTIVES

After reading this chapter, you should be able to:

1. Describe the similarities and differences between groups and teams.
2. Identify and compare different types of groups.
3. Name the factors that influence group formation and development.
4. Analyze the various structural and behavioural characteristics of groups.
5. Identify the advantages and disadvantages of self-managing, cross-functional, global, and virtual workgroups and teams.
6. Explain the differences in the various types of team competencies.
7. Distinguish between the two major types of group conflict and discuss their causes and consequences.
8. Explain how managers can help their workgroups develop into high-performing teams.

Time for Teams in Health Care

The Canadian health care system has struggled for several years with a lack of professional health care workers to fill the demand placed on it by an aging population. By 2006, medical professionals were being encouraged by the Health Council of Canada, as well as other health care organizations, to collaborate with one another in an attempt to improve the delivery of health care across the country. Professionals, particularly in smaller communities, are being pushed into team-based environments in an effort to compensate for inadequate numbers of medical professionals. Realizing the pressure that is being exerted on health care professionals to work in teams, the federal government started the Enhancing Interdisciplinary Collaboration in Primary Health Care (EICP) initiative to determine the best way to approach this strategy.

The 18-month study demonstrated benefits associated with collaboration in primary health care and concluded that teamwork among health care professionals will be crucial to the sustainability of the health care system. The initiative reported that if primary health care professionals work together, it not only will result in improved care for patients, but also will create a better work environment and support system for over-worked health care professionals. The study argued that medical workers in a team environment would effectively direct patient care in a timely manner to the appropriate professional and location. A team-based environment would also provide medical professionals with time to promote healthy living to their patients.

A study on collaboration in health care concluded that teamwork among health care professionals will improve care for Canadians. An exceptional case of the benefits of teamwork in health care occurred in May 2007 at University of Alberta Hospital in Edmonton, where a team of health care professionals in collaboration with hundreds of others in the health care field performed 18 organ transplants in 56 hours.

The findings of the initiative also acknowledged that team members require a foundation of understanding to effectively collaborate. To address this, six principles were put forward that form a framework for the future of collaborative health care in Canada. The principles include patient/client engagement, which means allowing patients to participate in decisions related to their health; population health approach, or striving to improve the health of the population as a whole; best possible care and services; access; trust and respect; and effective communication.

In addition to the building principles, the study concluded that the framework requires seven sustaining elements to maintain a vibrant collaborative environment in Canada's health care system: health care specific human resources; funding; liability, which refers to the steps health care professionals must take to insure themselves; regulation; information and communications technology; management and leadership; and planning and evaluation.

The EICP is promoting a health care framework that operates based on these building principles and sustaining elements, and is offering health care providers and policy makers the tools to make it happen on their website (www.eicp-acis.ca).

According to advocates of the recommendations generated by the EICP, increased collaboration among health care professionals will also mean decreased per-patient costs. A collaborative care approach used in British Columbia over a two-year time period, for example, effectively enhanced patient care while reducing per-patient cost by almost $500 per year. More importantly, collaboration among healthcare professionals can save lives. In one exceptional case that occurred in May 2007, a team of health care professionals at Edmonton's University of Alberta Hospital performed 18 organ transplants over the span of 56 hours, giving 15 patients a new chance at life. The marathon session was the result of an unusually high number of donor organs that came available at the same time. Close collaboration among hundreds of people enabled the hospital to perform in a day the same number of operations that are normally undertaken over the course of a month.

Sources: J. Cotter, "Team of Alberta Surgeons Performs 18 Organ Transplants in 56 Hours," June 6, 2007, www.cbc.ca (accessed July 31, 2007); CBC News, "Health Council of Canada Recommends Action to Deal with Chronic Health Problems," March 5, 2007, www.cbc.ca (accessed July 31, 2007); Anonymous, "Interdisciplinary Collaboration in Primary Health Care," *Canadian Pharmacists Journal,* January/February, 2007, p. S5; Canada NewsWire, "Initiative Says the Future of Medicare Is in the Hands of Teams," April 25, 2006, p. 1; Canada NewsWire, "Media Advisory/Interview Opportunity—How Do We Get More Teamwork in Primary Health Care?" February 9, 2006, p. 1; CBC News, "Doctors Told Teamwork the Way of the Future," October 7, 2001, www.cbc.ca (accessed July 31, 2007).

strategic overview

Because so many complex tasks and objectives are beyond the capabilities of a single person, groups and teams rather than individual employees form the fundamental building blocks of twenty-first–century organizations. For example, strategic decisions are generally more effective when made by a team of executives (often called a top management team) than by an individual. That is because most strategic decisions are highly complex, as we learned in Chapter 7. Also, research has shown that these teams make higher-quality strategic decisions if they have diverse functional backgrounds.[1] Diverse teams bring different sets of knowledge, skills, and attitudes to the decision-making process. They also consider a broader range of information and have access to more resources that can help them make more effective decisions. These decisions often lead to stronger competitive actions than decisions made by more homogeneous top management teams.[2] Yet more diverse teams frequently experience greater conflict (as we explain in this chapter) and therefore may take more time to make decisions. Thus, the quality of the resulting decisions has to be balanced against the need for making a rapid decision, like a response to a substantial new and pressing threat in the environment by a major competitor.[3] If these problems of conflict can be overcome, a diverse top management team can also help to implement a complex strategic action by explaining and championing it to different groups within the firm and to separate and distinct constituencies external to the organization (like suppliers, unions, and shareholders). The same sort of diversity can work for other teams within the organization, particularly cross-functional teams.

Groups engage in a diverse set of activities, ranging from developing new products to designing automobiles to constructing budgets to formulating strategic plans. Even those people who are inclined to be independent entrepreneurs eventually face this reality test: If an organization is not based on high-performance groups and teams, it likely will not be able to compete effectively in the current or future competitive landscape. Therefore, it is absolutely crucial that anyone aspiring to a career in management be able to meet two fundamental challenges: how to be an effective *member* in a group or team, and how to be an effective *leader* of a group or team.

The issues in Canada's health care system may seem distant compared to the daily challenges faced by managers in today's work organizations, but they are not. In the flatter and leaner organizations of the early twenty-first century—with their increased emphasis on speed and flexibility—the importance of being able to develop, manage, and operate effectively in groups and teams is even greater than it has been in the past.

Organizations of all types and sizes, whether in business, government, health care, or other settings, are much more likely to use groups and teams now than even a few years ago.[4] This represents a major change in the way organizations function. Consequently, it requires a change in the mindset of both managers and their subordinates. People need to change their attitudes toward group work and emphasize teamwork rather than individual work. Of course, there will always be a place for the brilliant employee working alone who produces a remarkable innovation or creative achievement. Also, not all individuals or cultures adapt equally well to a group-oriented organizational environment.[5] Nevertheless, because they are operating in global markets, organizations now depend more and more on highly networked and interconnected relationships involving groups and teams. Managing such networked relationships requires strong collaborative skills and the ability to work successfully with, and in, groups and teams. These skills are necessary to build social capital within an organization and with groups and companies outside the organization as well. With such skills, managers are in a much better position to be able to lead and gain the acceptance and commitment of others to the important strategic changes common in today's organizations.

It is important to differentiate between groups and teams. They are the same under some circumstances and *not* the same under other circumstances. A **group** is typically defined as a set of people, limited in number (usually from 3 to 20 or so), who have some degree of interaction and shared objectives. A **team**, on the other hand, is a type or form of group. In effect, a team has additional characteristics beyond a mere group: a higher degree of coordinated interaction and, especially, a stronger sense of members' personal responsibility for achieving specified outcomes.[6] Also, groups that become teams typically have created a high level of members' identification with the group. In other words, it matters to members that they are a part of the unit. A useful way to think about the relation between groups and teams is to view it as a continuum, as illustrated in Exhibit 11.1. Individuals are put into—or put themselves into—a group. The group may or may not go on to become a team.

group a set of people, limited in number (usually from 3 to 20), who have some degree of mutual interaction and shared objectives

team a type of group that has additional characteristics: a high degree of interdependent, coordinated interaction and a strong sense of members' personal responsibility for achieving specified outcomes

Put simply, all teams are groups, but not all groups are, or become, teams.[7] A major objective in most of today's organizations is to have workgroups develop and evolve quickly so that they behave more like teams. Although hardly anyone would disagree with this as a goal, the organizational and managerial challenge is to actually make it happen. Such desired results usually cannot be guaranteed without considerable effort, which is a central issue we will return to later.

This chapter begins by briefly identifying the various types of groups that operate in organizational settings. Then we discuss how groups are formed and developed and what some of their most important characteristics are, such as their structure, norms, and degree of cohesiveness. This is followed by an analysis of a critical issue common to many groups—conflict. The chapter concludes with a consideration of the challenges involved in improving group effectiveness.

Exhibit 11.1
Individuals-to-Group-to-Team Continuum

TEAMS demonstrate enhanced:
- Coordinated interaction
- Personal responsibility for group outcomes
- Individual identification with group

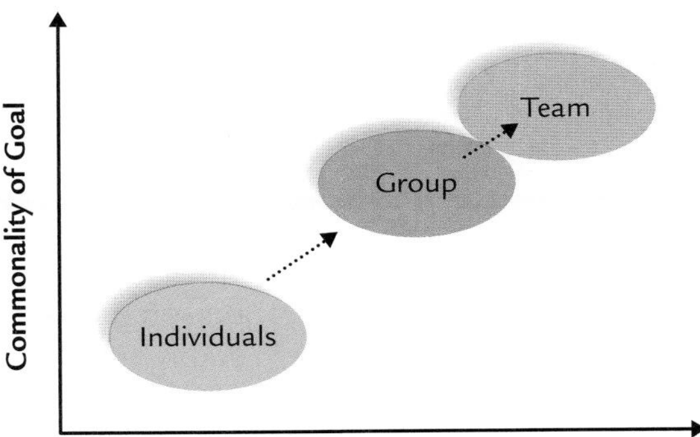

Source: Adapted from M. E. Kossler and K. Kanaga, *Do You Really Need a Team?* (Greensboro, NC: Center for Creative Leadership, 2001).

Basic Types of Groups

Most people who work in organizations are part of at least one group, and often of several different groups. These groups can be of different types, and one major distinction among them is simply whether they are "formal," that is, established by the organization, or "informal," established by particular individuals without direct involvement by the formal organization. Examples of the basic types of groups to which almost all organization members could belong are illustrated in Exhibit 11.2 and described here.

Formal Groups

Within and across almost any kind of organization there are typically three fundamental types of formal groups: command (supervisory), project/task forces, and committees.

Command (Supervisory) Groups A **command (supervisory) group** consists of a supervisor or manager and all those who report to that person; for example, those who report to a particular production supervisor or to a sales manager in a department. Such groups are usually considered to be the basic work units of an organization. Depending on the nature of the tasks assigned to each

command (supervisory) group a group whose members consist of a supervisor or manager and all those who report to that person

Exhibit 11.2 Types of Groups

Type of Group	Features	Examples
Command (Supervisory)	One supervisor with a number of subordinates Relatively enduring Membership changes relatively slowly	Clerical units Manufacturing assembly units Local sales managers reporting to a regional sales manager
Project/Task Force	Temporary Specific limited purpose Group members are aware of temporary nature of group	Product design teams Management information systems teams to develop upgraded computer systems Term project groups in university classes
Committee	Either permanent or ad hoc Meet only periodically Members have different permanent jobs and/or supervisors Membership typically does not represent an employee's highest commitment	Budget committees Safety committees Promotion review committees
Formal	Command (supervisory) Project/Task force Committee	
Informal	Group not originated by the organization Voluntary membership Obvious differences and boundaries between members and nonmembers	Group of employees who lunch together on Fridays Van pool group The "water cooler group"

person, however, the amount of interaction among members may vary considerably from one command group to another. For example, in a clothing manufacturing plant, a group of workers may be assigned to work on a particular style of jeans. They all work to construct the same garment, but because one is sewing the pocket to the leg while another is putting in zippers and yet another is topstitching the waistband, there is very little opportunity for interaction. Contrast this with a marketing team for a toy company, where the members meet frequently to discuss new products, schedule advertising campaigns, and decide on special promotional activities.

Command groups are usually considered relatively enduring, rather than temporary. Also, membership in these groups changes relatively slowly. These factors together affect the nature and quality of the interpersonal interaction among group members. The fact that you know that you will be interacting repeatedly with the same people for an indefinite length of time can have a powerful effect on your relationships with those other members.

project/task force
a temporary group put together by an organization for a particular purpose

Project/Task Forces A **project/task force** is a group put together by an organization for a particular purpose; for example, to design a new product or to work on a particular problem (e.g., how to develop a more rapid and effective response system for customer complaints) that cuts across different organizational units. *A Manager's Challenge: "Making an Elephant Pirouette: Inserting Speed and Agility at IBM"* describes the Speed Team at IBM, which is a perfect example of a project team operating in a technology-rich environment that has been put together to achieve very specific objectives in the absolute minimum amount of time.

a manager's challenge *technology*

Making an Elephant Pirouette: Inserting Speed and Agility at IBM

Managers in all kinds of organizations, large and small, are rediscovering the many uses of teams. Teams can get work done quickly and effectively. They can offer innovative solutions, help others throughout the organization accept and adjust to change, and forge unofficial links and ties that smooth the way for achievements beyond their assigned tasks. Teams can even be formed just to break the rules.

At IBM, the information technology (IT) unit is staggeringly large—100 000 people worldwide. Most teams consist of about 3 to 15 people, but this enormous unit carries a big responsibility—to produce successful software projects for IBM to market to its corporate and consumer markets. To help coordinate the efforts of a unit this size, Steve Ward, IBM's former chief information officer, used to meet regularly with a 200-member leadership council, which is still an unwieldy group. But at one council meeting, Ward decided that speedy action had to become IT's top priority in the months to come, or IBM might be beaten to market by the eager dot.com start-ups that at the time were nipping at its heels.

"One of the things that frustrates me most," he said, "is the length of time between the 'aha' moment and the moment when you actually start changing the organization's direction, getting it to where it needs to be." Ward wasted no time changing direction in this case. The following morning he formed a 21-member ad hoc cadre called the Speed Team and gave them their assignment. It was straightforward: Get the 100 000 members of the IT unit working faster, focusing on web-based applications.

The team got right to work. "I think that we will have failed if the Speed Team is still together three years from now," Jane Harper, the team's co-leader initially said. (In fact, it accomplished its goal in about seven months.) "Our plan, when we started this, was to come together, look at what works, look at why projects get bogged down, create some great recommendations about how to achieve speed, get executive buy-in, and try to make those recommendations part of the fabric of the business."

Speed Team members fanned out across the IT unit and started looking for and dislodging what they called "speed bumps," or barriers to speed. One of the team's first realizations was the fact that time is a tangible resource, just like money or people. Given that, the team focused on two kinds of initiatives for change. "Quick hits" could be accomplished almost immediately and included creating "speed ratings" for performance reviews and getting all IT leaders to better articulate their priorities on the basis of time. Some longer-term projects, those that needed up to 90 days to be accomplished, included coordinating the finance department more closely with IT priorities so funding for new projects wasn't cut when it was time for launch, and establishing how little time it should take for new applications to roll out.

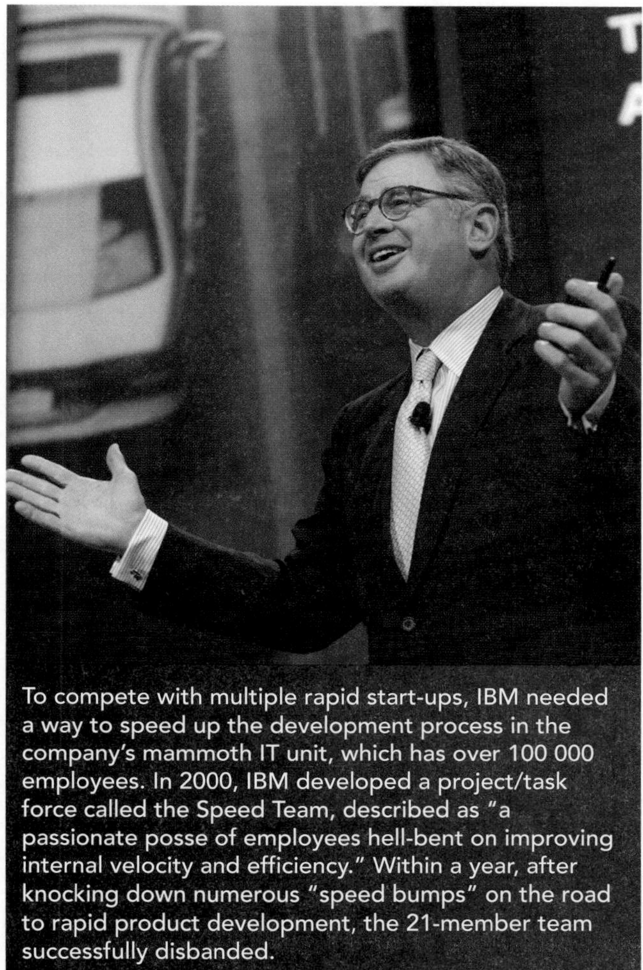

To compete with multiple rapid start-ups, IBM needed a way to speed up the development process in the company's mammoth IT unit, which has over 100 000 employees. In 2000, IBM developed a project/task force called the Speed Team, described as "a passionate posse of employees hell-bent on improving internal velocity and efficiency." Within a year, after knocking down numerous "speed bumps" on the road to rapid product development, the 21-member team successfully disbanded.

Along the way, the Speed Team had time to pick up a few lessons about teams that passed directly into the company's culture. For example, for a team to act swiftly requires a mix of skills, experience, and tenure at the company. Teams also need ultra-clear goals and priorities. According to Ward, "You need to say, 'Our goal is to sell $2 billion a month on the web,' and then work with our team to achieve that goal." Not surprisingly, teams also thrive on fast communications links, such as instant messaging, teleconferencing, and video conferencing. Because information was quickly shared, streamlined communication helped the Speed Team members to work and follow up more effectively, minimize administrative delays, and deal more efficiently with processes that couldn't be eliminated. Going by the spirit of the process rather than the letter of it sometimes helped, too; according to Harper, strict business processes yield high-quality work, but "if you're a smart cook, you don't have to measure every teaspoon of salt; you just take a few pinches."

Ray Blair, Harper's co-leader, wrote the Speed Team's epitaph: "Our evidence of success is that our changes have been adopted by the organization. People have begun to think about the need for speed in their work. We're no longer necessary. Our job was to be catalysts, and catalysts can't linger around."

Even though many dot.coms went bust and IBM's business environment has changed since the Speed Team disbanded, IBM's initiative to instill rapid change in a large organization remains a great example of the use of temporary groups to successfully meet corporate goals. The program has been resurrected and applied as the need dictates across the organization.

Source: L. Meredith, "The iSeries Speed Team—The Next Generation," search400.com (accessed August 3, 2007); A. Layne, "Report from the Past—Jane Harper," *Fast Company*, January 2001; S. Kirsner, "Faster Company," *Fast Company*, May 2000, pp. 162ff.

As the IBM Speed Team example illustrates, project teams and task forces differ from command groups in that they are intended to be temporary. Their members know that the group will likely cease to exist once the project or task is completed. This not only changes members' perceptions and their interactions with one another, but it also changes their relationship to the appointed leader of the project or task-force group. Because of the nature and importance of the goals and objectives set for them, though, task forces constitute some of the most critical group-like activities within, and even across, organizations, and they often involve virtual (non-face-to-face) group situations.

committee a group that is either permanent or temporary (ad hoc) whose members meet only occasionally and otherwise report to different permanent supervisors in an organization's structure

Committees **Committees** can be either permanent or temporary (ad hoc) in terms of the length of their existence. Typically, the most important feature of committees in organizations is that their members meet only occasionally and otherwise report to different permanent supervisors in the organization's structure (Exhibit 11.3). Thus, interaction is episodic, and for most members this is not the formal organizational group to which they have the highest degree of commitment. For instance, a budget committee may meet several times during a company's fiscal year, with the members likely coming from each of the major departments or divisions. The primary jobs of the budget committee members, however, are in their own organizational work units, not serving together on the budget committee. Nevertheless, such a committee's decisions may have critically important implications not only for its members, but also for the larger organization.

Exhibit 11.3 Examples of Committees Present in Many Organizations

· Governance	· Compensation	· Oversight
· Executive	· Finance	· Audit
· Steering	· Safety	· Ethics
· Disaster planning	· Long-range planning	· Public relations

formal group a group that is designated, created, and sanctioned by the organization to carry out its basic work and to fulfill its overall mission

The preceding types of groups are all examples of **formal groups**; that is, groups that are designated, created, and sanctioned by an organization to carry out its basic work and to fulfill its overall mission. However, in many respects informal groups are just as, and sometimes more, important for a manager to pay attention to and understand than formal groups.

Informal Groups

informal group a group whose members interact voluntarily

An **informal group** is one whose members choose to interact voluntarily, not by organizational mandate. A typical example is friendship groups. Although there is no formal joining process, these groups often have fairly obvious boundaries between members and nonmembers. At any given time, people think they know (perhaps incorrectly, from the point of view of others in the group) whether they are a member of a certain group or not. Just observing who eats lunch with whom, or who talks especially frequently to whom, for instance, is often a clear signal of a friendship group's boundaries. Such informal groups can be fairly temporary, but more typically they last for considerable periods of time.

Most important for a manager is the fact that friendship and other informal groups can significantly affect the attitudes and performance of their members in relation to organizational tasks and objectives. A set of employees who were originally strangers, for example, might develop into an informal group after carpooling together over a period of time. If the conversations within this group focus on negative reactions to new organizational policies, then the group could become a source of opposition to those policies. However, informal groups often can provide considerable assistance to managers in dealing with organizational challenges. The key for the manager is whether the group's norms (see discussion later in this chapter) or standards of behaviour can be influenced in the direction of support of organizational and workgroup goals. To do this requires an ability to recognize the existence and membership of important informal groups, to gain an understanding of what the group's current norms are, and to be able to identify where the leadership is within the group. If these steps are taken, then the potential exists for informal groups to become positive forces. Research has shown, in fact, that while "friendship groups do socialize more . . . they also spend more time discussing the task, are more committed and more cooperative [with each other]."[8]

Characteristics of Groups and Teams

All groups have certain characteristics or features that affect the degree and types of influence they have on their members and their level of collective performance. Some of these are structural while others relate to basic features of groups, such as their norms and the degree of cohesion among their members. For all of these characteristics, it is important for leaders and managers to understand their likely effects. Particularly, managers need to be on the lookout for how changes, from both inside and outside the organization, can alter one or more characteristics which in turn can have profound impacts on group functioning and performance.

Structural Characteristics

Just as organizations have structure (as discussed in Chapter 8), so do groups, albeit on a smaller scale. Four of the most essential structural features of groups are size, composition, differentiated roles, and differentiated status.

Size As one review of research on groups stated, "Current literature yields a consistent guideline [for determining the best size for a group]: [use] the smallest number of people who can do the task."[9] Similarly, another review of studies found that member satisfaction decreased as groups got larger, and leaders' behaviours toward members became more task oriented and less people oriented.[10] Likewise, a large-scale study of command group size in 58 offices of a single agency found that organizational productivity per employee decreased with increasing size.[11]

What is an optimal group size? Of course, there is no single answer to this question, since it would vary based on the types of tasks facing the group. However, research shows that with increasing group size, the sense of personal responsibility for a group's output or performance tends to decrease. The phenomenon of reduced effort per person in larger-sized groups has been labelled **social loafing**.[12] Individuals in larger groups apparently are more likely than those in smaller groups to assume that other members will "carry the load." In large groups, also, individual members' specific contributions are less easily identified, and this appears to be a major factor in encouraging such "loafing."[13]

social loafing the phenomenon of reduced effort per person in large groups

There are, however, some approaches that can be used to counter the social loafing tendency. For example, it is possible to structure group tasks to encourage full participation by group members. A key lies in how readily an individual's contribution to the final result can be identified. One experiment using college swim team members found originally that the athletes swam faster in individual time trials than they did at the same distance and with the same stroke during relays. Normally, only the team time was announced at the end of the race, and the times of individual swimmers were not available. When the relay race was structured so that each individual's time was announced aloud at the end of his or her lap, the individuals actually swam faster during the relay than in the individual heats.

Results such as these suggest that managers may be able to encourage higher individual levels of effort on group projects by building in some form of acknowledgment of the contributions made by each member of the group to the final outcome of the project.[14]

Interestingly, additional research seems to indicate that social loafing in groups is less likely to occur in collectivistic cultures (see Chapter 4), such as Asian countries, than in more individualistic cultures such as Canada, the United States, or Australia because of the much stronger group orientation in collectivistic cultures.[15]

The other major reason why group performance per person may decrease as group size increases is simply the increasing costs of coordination, the so-called **process costs**. As groups become larger, the number of person-to-person relationships increases significantly, and coordination becomes more cumbersome. Also, larger size brings additional opportunities for interpersonal conflicts between individuals and among subgroups within the group.

process costs the increasing costs of coordination as group size increases

All of the disadvantages of large group size must be weighed, of course, against the potential advantages of having a more extensive pool of talent, skills, and expertise to boost performance and take on additional problem-solving tasks.[16] Having too few people in a group, especially when tasks are many and complex, defeats the whole purpose of putting together people in the first place. In determining the best size for formal workgroups, managers need to consider the probable losses due to process costs in relation to the likely gains received from larger integrated efforts.

Another managerial challenge relating to group size is that it is not always constant; it can change, sometimes dramatically. The effects are illustrated in the story of a relatively small company called Next Jump, Inc., a provider of rewards and loyalty programs to corporations. It started out as a tiny venture organized by a group of friends. Those friends hired their friends. A "family tree" was even posted, showing the relationships among all of the employees. In just three months the company grew from 30 to 105 employees. As it grew, Charlie Kim, the CEO, tried to maintain the family feeling in the firm. Unfortunately, a victim of its own success, the idea of one large "team" with all members focused on the same goals, working cohesively together, didn't work as the company got larger. Meetings fell apart and confusion and conflict increased. People started quitting. The "family tree" was taken down. Charlie Kim, in his managerial role, was experiencing the effects that a different-sized group can have on its members and on its management.[17]

Composition Groups may be composed of individuals who are very similar or very dissimilar. If the former is the case, we describe the group as homogeneous. If the latter is the case, the composition would be regarded as heterogeneous, or diverse. Most groups these days have some degree of diversity, and many have a great deal. As Exhibit 11.4 shows, there can be different types of diversity within groups, including variations in observable characteristics such as race/ethnicity, gender, and age; and variations in underlying and less immediately obvious attributes such as values, skills, knowledge and information, and length of time (tenure) in the group and in the organization.[18]

Exhibit 11.4 Examples of Diversity within Groups and Potential Consequences

Types of Diversity	Potential Consequences
Observable Attributes	Affective Consequences
· Race	· Satisfaction
· Ethnicity	· Identification with the group
· Gender	· Conflict within the group
· Age	
Underlying Attributes	Cognitive Consequences
· Values	· Innovation
· Skills	· Amount and quality of new ideas
· Knowledge and Information	
· Tenure	Communication-Related Consequences
	· Decreased frequency within group
	· Increased frequency outside of group

Source: Adapted from Frances L. Milliken and Luis L. Martins, "Searching for Common Threads: Understanding the Multiple Effects of Diversity in Organizational Groups," *Academy of Management Review* 21, no. 2 (1996), pp. 402–23.

Some organizations deliberately take advantage of diversity in groups. For example, the MBA curriculum at Queen's University in Kingston, Ontario, uses a team-based learning model where students are formally assigned to teams for the duration of the program. Teams are composed of five or six students and grouped in a manner that maximizes diversity in gender, professional experience, as well as cultural and academic backgrounds.[19]

The key managerial question, of course, is: Does a greater amount of diversity within groups more often help or hinder such outcomes as effective group functioning and performance? Research to date shows that there is no simple answer to this question.[20] Instead, as shown in Exhibit 11.4, we need to look at the effects of group diversity on more specific and immediate consequences, including the following:

- Members' reactions (so-called "affective consequences"), including satisfaction, identification with the group, and conflict within the group
- The output of members' thinking (cognitive consequences), including the number of new ideas or innovations emerging from the group
- Communication effectiveness, both inside and outside the group

Research to date on these kinds of consequences is only suggestive and not conclusive, especially given the fact that, as noted above, there are different kinds of diversity.[21] However, research findings tend to show that increased diversity potentially

- has somewhat negative effects on members' reactions and interactions with each other;
- has somewhat positive effects on increasing the quality of the outputs of members' thinking together as a group, presumably because a wider range of opinions and ideas are discussed; and
- leads to decreased frequency of communication within a group but more communication with those outside a group.

In short, the challenge for you as a manager is to maximize the significant benefits that are possible from having group diversity, and to try to minimize potential disadvantages by anticipating what some of those might be and directly addressing them. One way that seems especially promising in this regard is to give extra attention to developing strong group norms of cooperation; that is, to emphasize the objective of each member viewing and valuing the importance of cooperation within the group.[22] Also, research evidence suggests that it is early in a group's existence that diversity based on members' differences in values and attitudes is most likely to cause difficulties. Therefore, to gain the potential advantages that diversity offers, groups and their leaders need to realize that they should try to work through those initial differences and turn them into advantages rather than obstacles. The encouraging finding is that it appears that the longer a group works together, the more likely it is to find ways to do just that—to succeed in overcoming those initial differences in values and attitudes.[23] Whatever else can be said, though, one thing seems absolutely certain: The use of increasingly diverse work teams, especially—but not only—multinational groups, is becoming commonplace.[24] Therefore, the diversity challenges for managers are growing, not lessening.

Differentiated Roles In groups of any size, different members perform different roles; that is, they occupy different positions with sets of expected behaviour attached to those positions. This is most vividly illustrated in certain athletic teams, where players have specialized roles when the team is on offence and different roles on defence. Roles in workgroups are not always as clear-cut and can range from being fairly general, like performing analytical duties, to being highly specialized with specific task assignments, like monitoring particular pieces of equipment. More and more, however, organizations are attempting to loosen rigid role boundaries in groups to gain greater flexibility in meeting unexpected competitive and environmental challenges.[25]

One obvious type of role that is assigned or emerges in almost all groups is that of leader. In the past, the leadership role in workgroups has tended to be specialized and concentrated in one person, the supervisor. However, the clear trend in today's highly competitive organizations is to attempt to spread the leadership functions of structuring tasks and lending personal support and encouragement as widely as possible among the group's members. This is especially true in so-called self-managing teams, but it is also becoming more common even in typical command-type groups.[26] The principle involved is that if responsibility for leadership functions is more broadly shared and accepted, the group will be able to respond faster and more effectively to rapidly changing pressures and circumstances.

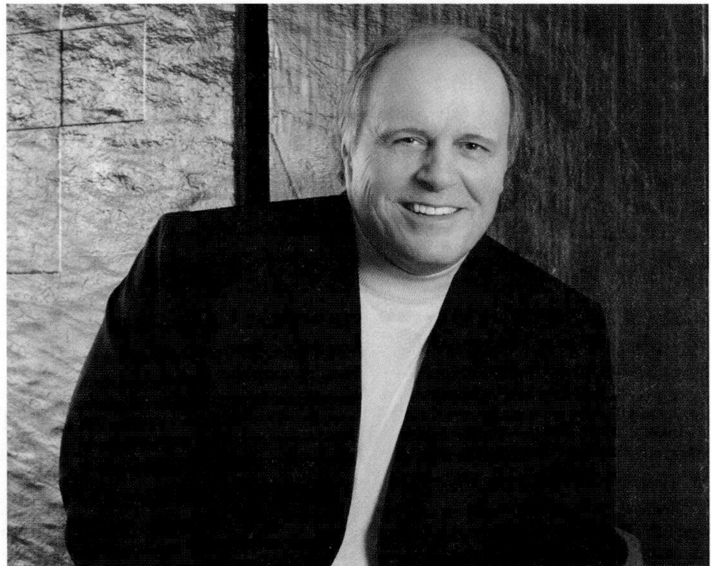

In his first career, John Forzani was a CFL football player. In 1974, Forzani opened a retail sports equipment shop in Calgary and in 1994 acquired Sports Experts, becoming the largest sports retailer in Canada. Forzani discovered that business is much like football: In the game, only a select few get the ball, which means the remainder of the players have to do their job to ensure the ones with the ball are able to move down the field. In business, individuals carry out specific tasks that, together, lead to positive results.[27]

Two particular issues that groups face with respect to roles—and that you yourself have probably faced in your own group experiences—are role ambiguity and role conflict. **Role ambiguity** refers to a situation in which the expected behaviours for a group member are not clearly defined, which can increase the stress level for that person. **Role conflict** emerges when a member has to fulfill two or more contrasting sets of expectations, such as taking time to be friendly with customers versus meeting a certain quota of customers to be served during a work period. In such a situation, a manager has to make choices that are often very difficult.

role ambiguity a situation in which the expected behaviours for a group member are not clearly defined

role conflict a situation in which a member of a group faces two or more contrasting sets of expectations

Differentiated Status Not only do members have different roles in groups, they also often have different levels of status or rank. **Status** is the standing or prestige that a person has in a group, and it can be based on a number of factors such as perceived leadership abilities, seniority, or special skills, among others.

Role Ambiguity by Lyman Porter

PEARSON mymanagementlab

status the standing or prestige that a person has in a group

Research has shown that status differences can strongly influence interactions within the group.[28] For example, higher-status members tend to receive more communications than do lower-status members, and lower-status members tend to defer to higher-status members when groups are making decisions.[29] Such effects might be especially strong, of course, in high–power-distance cultures, such as those in South America and Asia. However, in cultures with low or medium power distance, effective communication and decision making are likely to be inhibited in groups if status differences and their effects are too extreme. Relevant information would be less likely to be widely shared and thus not be given sufficient attention.

Behavioural Characteristics

There are two chief features of groups and teams that involve behavioural-type characteristics: namely, the norms that develop in groups and the degree to which groups are cohesive.

Norms

norms a group's shared standards that guide the behaviour of its individual members

Norms, as we indicated in our earlier discussion on informal groups, are a group's shared standards that guide the behaviour of its individual members.

For example, when members of a group behave similarly toward supervisors or outsiders, like stopping nontask conversations when they enter the room, they are demonstrating the effect of group norms. It would be very difficult, if not impossible, for groups to function if they did not have norms.[30] Each person's behaviour would be too unpredictable for coordinated action to take place. Norms also help to reduce ambiguity; thus, they provide members with cues and useful guidelines about how to behave. Such normative information is particularly important for new members of a group who need to learn what is going on in the work situation as rapidly as possible.

Characteristics of Group Norms. An understanding of norms and their significance can be gained by reviewing several of their main features:

- Norms are usually established for the more important issues of concern to the group; for example, rates of minimally acceptable output or performance.
- Norms do not necessarily apply to all members of the group; some apply only to certain members (like the leader), usually based on the status or particular role of those members. For example, it may be acceptable for a senior member of a group, but not for a junior member, to arrive late for meetings.
- Norms vary in the degree of their acceptance by group members; some norms are accepted and endorsed by virtually all members, others by only a majority. For instance, norms regarding how to deal with work problems might be accepted by everyone, but norms regarding desirable attire might be endorsed by only certain members.
- Norms vary in how much deviation members are permitted in following them; in other words, some norms are very loose and permit a great deal of leeway in behaviour, while other norms, especially those regarding key group issues, are much more restrictive on members' behaviour.[31] For example, a member of a group who talks to outsiders about the group's internal problems might receive severe censure from fellow group members, whereas someone who talks louder than normal during meetings might be tolerated (up to a degree, at least) by group colleagues.

Development of Group Norms. Norms do not suddenly and magically appear in groups. They seldom, if ever, develop in a purely spontaneous way. Rather, they arise out of interaction among group members. An example of a typical norm development process is shown in Exhibit 11.5. Key factors that often have a major influence on the process include the following:[32]

- *Early behaviours:* Typically, initial behaviours, especially in newly formed groups, establish standards for subsequent behaviour. In committees, for example, the first few meetings help establish norms about how candid, or how indirect, discussion of sensitive issues is likely to be. Such quickly established norms are often difficult to reshape or change later.
- *Imported behaviours:* Members of a group often bring with them standards of behaviour that were prominent in their former groups. "When in doubt, stay with the familiar" seems to be the (sometimes incorrect) watchword of many people in organizations. When a high-status member imports a norm, as in the case of those with acknowledged expertise or high power, the prominence of that norm is likely to be

strong. A new chief executive officer, for example, may believe in a norm of communication "only through channels" regarding suggestions and input from members of the organization, even though this may run counter to the previous norm of openness fostered by the former CEO. However, because the new CEO has high status, few are likely to challenge this imported norm.

- *Critical events:* A sudden challenge to the group, like criticism from another group, can create specific and vivid responses that form the basis for how members should be expected to respond in the future. A time of crisis makes people particularly alert to cues in their environment and thus tends to reinforce norms that emerge from that period. In a corporation that has announced layoffs, for example, new norms regarding the overt display of diligent work habits may emerge.
- *Explicitly stated standards:* Not to be overlooked is the fact that leaders or high-status members of a group may simply assert that "this is how we will do it around here!" Newly appointed supervisors and athletic coaches, for example, frequently use this approach with their groups or teams.

Exhibit 11.5

Example of the Development of Group Norms

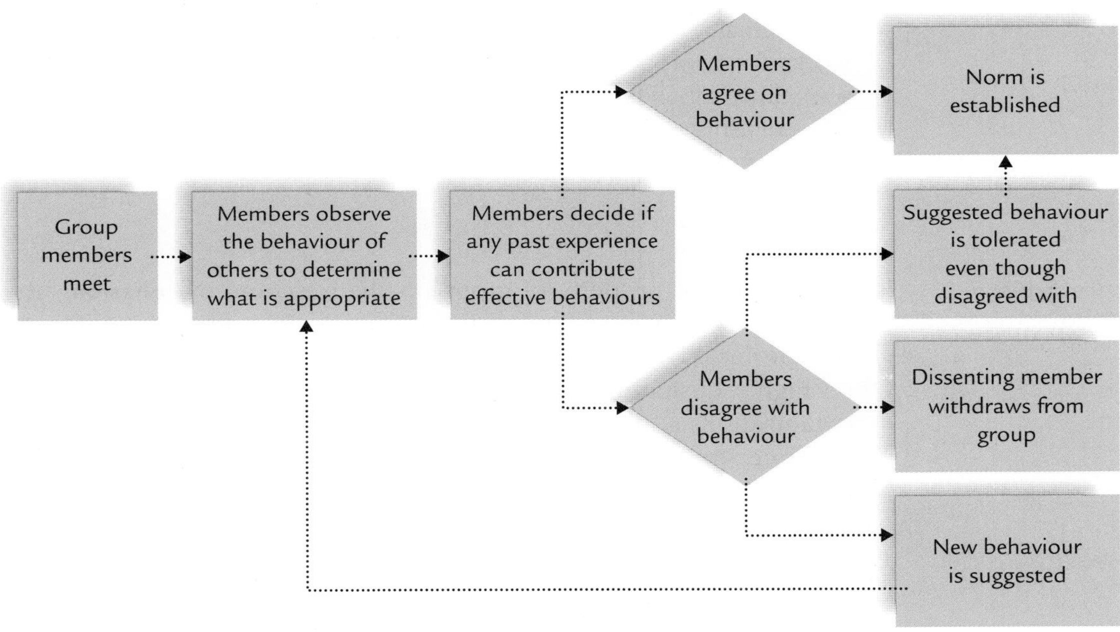

Source: K. Bettenhausen and J. K. Murnighan, "The Emergence of Norms in Competitive Decision Making Groups," *Administrative Science Quarterly*, 30 (1985), pp. 350–372.

Effects of Group Norms. Since norms are, essentially, accepted standards, their primary effect is to shape or influence the behaviour of individual members of a group. Thus, norms can be thought of as constraining or reducing the variability of actions and attitudes across a set of group members. That is, the existence of strong norms tends to narrow individual differences in behaviour and beliefs. This results in a certain degree of **conformity**, or close adherence to the group's norms by the individual members.

conformity close adherence to the group's norms by individual members

Whether such conformity is "good" or "bad" depends on the perspective of the viewer. If the norms support a manager's goals for a group—for example, that everyone should look for opportunities to make creative suggestions to improve the group's effectiveness—then the manager would regard conformity as very helpful. Take, for example, Kingfisher Oceanside Resort & Spa, in Courtenay, British Columbia. The management at Kingfisher created the "Angel Fish Fund." The fund provides financial support to employees that may have fallen on some financial hard times, such as an unexpected dental bill or an accident. Thirty percent of the 188 employees voluntarily contribute by way of a payroll deduction to the fund, which generates about $1500 bi-weekly toward the support of a few monthly anonymous nominations. The average assistance given to staff in need is $350. The initiative at Kingfisher has instilled a "good" norm where people want to help other people, and at the same time, do their job well.[33]

If norms conflict with the objectives a manager is trying to achieve, then greater conformity would be regarded as negative. The obvious implication for you as manager is that you should be as concerned about the content or direction of group norms as about the amount of conformity to them.

From the point of view of an individual member of a group, norms can sometimes be too constraining. In that case, the individual may deviate from the group's expected attitudes and behaviour. Such divergent actions or expressed views are potentially troubling to others in the group because they can threaten the group's solidarity and, perhaps in extreme cases, even its existence. Therefore, the group sometimes imposes sanctions on the deviant in an attempt to bring about greater conformity. The classic case in certain Western work situations, particularly at the hourly worker level, is the individual who works faster or slower than the group thinks he or she should. Such persons, sometimes labelled "rate busters" or "slackers," are often subjected to ridicule or ostracism to persuade or force them to work at a rate more in line with the group's norms for production effort.

Cohesion

cohesion the degree to which members are motivated to remain in the group

Another major property of groups is their amount of **cohesion**, "the degree to which members are motivated to remain in a group," to *want* to stay in it.[34] Group cohesion is usually considered to have many advantages and to be highly desirable if it can be developed.[35] Indeed, when managers and organizations attempt to turn groups into teams, they are, in effect, trying to generate stronger group cohesion. However, as will be discussed later, high levels of group cohesion may not always result in positive outcomes.[36]

Development of Group Cohesion. There are no sure-fire ways for you as a manager to build strong cohesion in groups that you lead or in which you are a member. However, the available research suggests three factors that can be potentially important in developing greater group cohesion:[37]

1. Strengthening interpersonal attraction among group members;
2. Generating a record of high performance and past success of the group; and
3. Fostering competition with other groups.

The most consistently important of these factors appears to be the first, namely, whether members of the group think they have something in common with other members and tend to like being with them; that is, whether they feel like they belong to a true team. The evidence for the other two factors in bringing about cohesion is not as clear-cut, but both past group success and current or anticipated conflict with other groups seem to unite groups and increase their cohesion, especially if strong interpersonal attraction among members is already present. Obviously, a group whose members don't especially like being with each other may disintegrate when faced with competition from external groups, rather than develop greater cohesion, which again places a premium on developing interpersonal bonds.

Effects of Group Cohesion. Increased cohesiveness of groups can have a number of potential advantages.[38] Chief among these is an increase in the quantity and quality of group interaction.[39] A second potential advantage of greater group cohesion is that the group has stronger influence on each member to conform to the group's standards or norms. Assuming—and this is a critical assumption—that those norms are positive from the manager's perspective, then this is a significant advantage. A third possible advantage is that cohesive groups appear to be more effective in achieving goals that group members accept, although research on this point is not totally consistent. A final possible advantage of higher group cohesion is that members tend to have greater satisfaction with the group.

As positive as these potential advantages might seem, high group cohesion sometimes can be a mixed blessing from a manager's point of view (see Exhibit 11.6). First, if the group has norms that do not support the organization's goals, then greater cohesion is definitely a minus. Individuals may be more influenced in the "wrong" direction—as when, for example, a group of workers tolerates sexual harassment—than if there is little cohesion. Another possible disadvantage of strong group cohesion is that deviance from group norms may not be handled effectively. Highly cohesive groups are more likely to reject any deviance, even if it represents creative ideas that could ultimately be useful to the group. Related to this is the danger that groupthink[40] (previously discussed in Chapter 5) may be accentuated in highly cohesive groups. Dissenting viewpoints, as expressed in the phrase "devil's advocate," often can be quite useful to a group in causing it to critically test its opinion or decisions.

Exhibit 11.6

Effects of High Levels of Group Cohesion

Positive effects	Negative effects
• Increased quality and quantity of group interactions • Strengthened adherence to group norms • Increased effectiveness in achieving group goals • Augmented individual satisfaction with group membership	• Counterproductive norms may be emphasized • Useful or creative ideas may be ignored if they deviate from established norms or values • Increased probability of developing groupthink • Potential decrease in intergroup cooperation

Still another potential disadvantage of high within-group cohesion, but one that is frequently overlooked, is that between-group cooperation may be adversely affected. Most organizations have many workgroups; some have hundreds or more. The challenge for higher-level managers is to have these groups and teams work together and interact smoothly and reliably. So it is a concern if higher within-group cohesion hinders intergroup cooperation. For example, in developing and marketing a new product, problems may develop among the production, marketing, and sales departments. If the production group is highly cohesive and has a norm of never allowing outsiders to know they have problems, they may be reluctant to notify other units that a key piece of equipment is not functioning correctly. Without this information, the marketing department might generate unrealistic expectations for the release date, and the sales teams would then promise higher numbers of the product to customers than would actually be available.

This example illustrates that the active promotion of strong within-group (team) cohesion by managers could decrease rather than increase overall functioning of the organization because of the potential for increased fragmentation. This situation is sometimes encountered in highly decentralized organizations, where employees show extremely strong loyalty to their own unit, for example, marketing, but considerably less concern for the welfare of other units, say, production, and the need to coordinate with them. Thus, in this case, intra-unit cohesion may gain greater autonomy for the unit, but it can hinder the achievement of integrated organization-wide objectives.

Formation and Development of Groups and Teams

Groups in organizations form for many reasons and in many ways. Most often, of course, the company or organization deliberately puts groups together to serve stated organizational purposes. Informal groups, however, are another matter. They form more or less spontaneously on the basis of actions by their members and to serve those members' self-interests, which may or may not coincide with those of the organization.

Influences on the Formation of Groups and Teams

The most important factors influencing the formation of groups in organizations are the goals of the organization, the opportunities for interaction and sharing mutual knowledge, and the psychological needs of potential group members.

Organizational Goals The goals and purposes of the larger organization directly affect the nature of its formal groups. The organization creates new groups, whether command, task forces, or committees, based on its judgment that needs are not being met adequately by existing groups. New groups may arise because of organizational growth, changes in the products or services the organization offers, or simply perceptions by key managers that greater efficiency and effectiveness can be gained by adding to, altering, or combining existing groups.

A key issue for organizations and managers when new groups are formed is whether they will be given adequate resources to accomplish their specific goals.[41] If you are a member of a new group put together by the organization, you are likely to have a number of questions, such as

- Why am I, rather than someone else, in the group?
- What are the real reasons why the group was put together?
- What are my new responsibilities going to be?
- Are the stated objectives for the group realistic and are they the actual goals that will be measured?

Such questions naturally occur to anyone who becomes part of a new group, but they don't always get asked directly or openly. Managers who form groups must therefore anticipate questions such as these, whether or not they are raised explicitly, and must be prepared to provide necessary information and explanations. If you become responsible for putting together a new organizational group, you need to recognize that, as discussed earlier, the formation of a new group does not necessarily mean that a new team has been created. You may have the hope that your new group will develop into a team with a strong sense of shared responsibility for the group's performance and output, but cohesiveness and cooperation are not something that you can decree. Managers cannot simply declare new groups to be "teams" and expect that they will operate that way. Team development depends on managerial skills and follow-up actions to elicit true teamwork in more than name only.[42]

Opportunities for Interaction and Sharing Mutual Knowledge In the formation of groups and their possible development into teams, physical proximity is obviously a helpful factor. When people have the opportunity to work together closely, it can facilitate learning about similarities of interests and experiences. These similarities can provide a basis for the development of friendships that can assist the work of the group.

However, in this age of electronic communication, groups are often highly dispersed geographically and cannot use the advantage of close physical proximity. In such circumstances, it becomes even more critical to increase opportunities for interaction, even if that is only via electronic messages. In other words, in dispersed "virtual" groups, it is essential to take steps to develop mutual knowledge—to find "common ground"—among members.[43] These could include such actions as attempting if at all possible to have at least one face-to-face meeting, arranging possible visits by one or more team members to other members' local sites, encouraging members to share information about their particular work context (time constraints, other task demands, local customs, etc.), and especially, to take extra efforts to make sure that members have access to all relevant information.[44]

Psychological Factors There are many personal reasons that motivate organizational members to form closer relationships in groups, especially basic human needs for security, social support, self-esteem, and status. By belonging to groups, even virtual ones, employees are often able to fulfill needs that may not be well satisfied by the work itself. Thus, the feeling of belonging to a group at work can be highly rewarding for many individuals. It can be, in effect, a significant way for individuals to achieve a distinct social identity that is meaningful both for themselves and for others who interact with them.[45]

Stages of Group Development

Whether groups are formed by the organization or by voluntary actions of individuals, they tend to move through distinct or identifiable developmental stages as they mature.[46] One popular early statement on this issue uses an easy-to-remember set of terms for such stages: "forming" (getting acquainted), "storming" (expressing differences of opinion), "norming" (building consensus on basic issues), and "performing" (carrying out cooperative group actions).[47] Although this model has considerable appeal as a way to think about phases of group development across time, it does not apply universally to all groups. As one set of management scholars has noted, "It seems unlikely that a single sequence can describe the development of all kinds of teams [and groups]."[48]

Despite this fact, several identifiable stages do show up with some regularity in organizational contexts (see Exhibit 11.7).

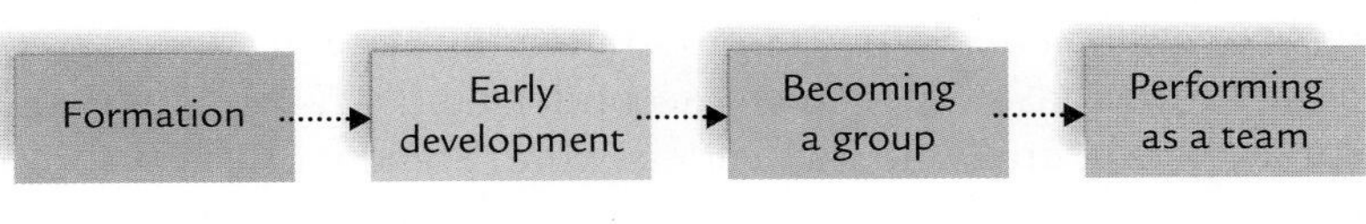

Exhibit 11.7
Stages of Group Development

Formation If you are forming a new group, you will face some unique challenges. One kind of challenge is presented when potential team members are not used to a group-oriented approach to work. If they have been comfortable in working within a prevailing individual-based organizational culture, they are obviously facing a significant change.

Another kind of challenge in the formation stages is that the group's members will have lots of questions, whether they ask them openly or not. For example, they will want to know who is in the group and why they are there, who is leading the group, and where each person is "coming from" in terms of his or her existing attitudes and viewpoints. Nearly all new groups go through this "getting to know you" stage. Teams can do many things to build team camaraderie quickly, including having T-shirts made with a logo designed by the group, and drafting their own mission statements, charters, and project plans.

Early Development Following a group's formation and initial interactions, an early development stage settles in that may last for some time, depending on the nature of the group and its tasks. In this stage, members learn what is expected of them, what is acceptable behaviour, and how well they relate to each other. Typically, members cautiously exchange, and sometimes jealously guard, information. If you are the group's leader it is an important time for learning about how opinions within the group overlap or differ on key matters. Often, conflicts over group goals or the means to reach them may emerge in this stage. An analogy to adolescence in human development might be apt for helping you understand this stage of group development.

Becoming a Group In this stage, at least a minimum amount of consensus about group issues begins to appear, as well as a degree of individual identity with the group and its goals. How much cohesion and group identity will actually emerge will vary widely from group to group at this stage. A critical factor will be how well the group is meeting each member's needs and how well members think the group is being led. In this stage particularly, if you are in a leadership role you can have considerable impact on the group's development and help it to become a true team.

Performing as a Team In this stage, a group is able to perform like a team and take actions as a coherent entity and not just as a set of loosely affiliated individuals. Internally, this means that the group is able to influence members' attitudes and behaviour on matters of importance to the group, and externally it means that others in or outside the organization are being affected by its actions.

Each of the preceding four stages can be illustrated by the following story of a project group that was put together in a large consumer products company:

- *Formation:* During a re-engineering effort at this company, eight managers from various functions were asked to work together to take on the project of analyzing the company's effectiveness in a number of areas and making performance-enhancing recommendations. In the early group meetings, most people were uncomfortable and unsure. Some were quiet, offering no input and waiting for others to move the meetings along. Some bonded in immediate alliances, and yet others jumped right in and began trying to perform the team's tasks.
- *Early Development:* Soon the group members began to understand the scope of their task. They began to understand who among them really had influence, and who the leaders were. Some work was accomplished, and while the members' relationships and confidence improved, overall the group's performance was very low.

The 2006 Canadian Olympic men's curling team, led by Brad Gushue, made member changes to their team just prior to the Canadian Olympic trials, adding two-time world champion skip Russ Howard to the roster as team second. The team collectively realized that the young group (their oldest member was 25 at the time) would have a much greater chance of winning with Howard (then 50 years old) than without him. It turned out they were right. Team Gushue won the gold medal in Torino, Italy—the first time that Canada had ever won Olympic gold in men's curling.

- *Becoming a Group:* Next, the group began to focus on encouraging group, rather than individual, behaviour. They began listening to each other and assessing suggestions in terms of the group's goals rather than as a display of each individual member's goals. They found ways to resolve conflicts and established standards of group conduct.
- *Performing as a Team:* The group now regarded themselves as a team. The next hurdle was learning that they did not always have to agree with each other—that they could disagree and still accomplish their task. They began evaluating all parts of suggestions, coping with divergent opinions, and creatively managing their conflicts. Their effectiveness and performance steadily continued to improve.
- *Outcome:* Over the 15 weeks of the team's existence, they analyzed the order taking, product scheduling, sales reporting, and pricing processes in their company. They identified and recommended several cost reduction and process improvement plans, with their recommendations resulting in savings of $2.5 million to their company.[49]

Returning to the general issue of stages in group development, whether a team's actions across these stages are continuously effective or not is debatable. Events internal or external to the group could still cause it to revert to an earlier stage of development, where it might need to re-form and attempt to become a "performing group" all over again. However, if a group has no specified ending point, that is, an "adjourning" phase, there is no inherent reason why the performing stage cannot last indefinitely. To keep a group or team in this stage continually is a clear managerial and leadership challenge.

Examples of Prominent Groups and Teams in Today's Organizations

Now that we have examined some of the basic characteristics of groups and teams and how they form and develop, we are ready to look at some examples of particular kinds of groups and teams that are becoming increasingly prominent in today's organizations (see Exhibit 11.8). Not every organization will have each of these groups, but where they do exist they present some special managerial challenges.

Exhibit 11.8 Prominent Groups and Teams in Today's Organizations

Type	Potential Advantages	Potential Disadvantages
Self-Managing	More team-like behaviour	Not all employees want to manage themselves
Cross-Functional/ New Product	Increased creativity Dispersed knowledge Speed to market	Increased group conflict
Global	Increased creativity from diversity of backgrounds	Paralysis Inaction Failure
Virtual	Increased speed of communication Decreased costs	Increased misinterpretation Lack of trust Difficult to manage

Self-Managing Workgroups (Teams)

self-managing (autonomous) workgroup a group that has no formally appointed supervisor but is similar to command groups in that the members coordinate their organizational work as if they all reported to the same formally appointed supervisor; members usually appoint their own informal team leader

A relatively recent, but increasingly important, variant of a command workgroup is the **self-managing**, or so-called autonomous, group—a workgroup that has no formally appointed supervisor. These groups are similar to command groups in that the members coordinate their organizational work as if they all reported to the same formally appointed supervisor. However, the group manages itself on behalf of the organization's objectives, and its members usually appoint their own informal team leaders.[50] The group is made up of a number of members with diverse skills that can be applied to the group's task. It generally is responsible for decisions concerning how to accomplish the work—which members will perform which tasks and in which order.

The idea of group self-management, however good it appears in principle, may not appeal to all employees. Furthermore, it cannot be assumed to fit into all types of cultures.[51] Therefore, managers and organizations who want to establish such groups need to consider potential pitfalls and resistance as well as the possible advantages.

Cross-Functional New Products (Services) Groups

Groups that draw their membership from distinctly different types of units within an organization, such as R&D and marketing, have been around for many years. However, their number and importance have increased markedly in recent years. A primary objective for such groups or teams is to bring to bear on the task as much creativity and dispersed knowledge as possible. A good example of a cross-functional team operating in a very basic industry is one put together by the Golden West Bakery plant in Greater Manchester, England. The plant makes buns for McDonald's hamburgers. A cross-functional team composed of members from both production and maintenance was put together with the dual goals of improving productivity and reducing waste. The team managed a complete overhaul of both the maintenance and production processes that was so successful that the company decided to restructure to take greater advantage of an increased use of teams of all types.[52]

Other major objectives of cross-functional teams, especially in high-technology firms, are to speed the products to market while at the same time controlling or minimizing costs. The principle of cross-functional teams sounds good, but the reality is often that the outcomes are less favourable than expected because of the inherent potential for increased conflicts in groups composed of members with widely varying initial perspectives.[53] To deal with this basic issue, research results suggest approaches (indicated below) that managers can use to try to increase the following attributes of effective cross-functional groups:[54]

- Members' feelings of "ownership" ("at-stakeness") of the group's decisions. Approach: Work to see that each member believes that he or she has the opportunity to influence the group's decision making.[55]
- Transparency or openness regarding members' motivations, expectations, and personal agendas. Approach: Try to make sure that such differences brought into the group are freely discussed and shared.
- "Mindfulness" or, essentially, reaching high-quality decisions. Approach: Ensure that all divergent points of view are explicitly recognized and examined.
- High levels of synergy and mutual cooperation ("synergy"). Approach: Facilitate the building of as much trust as possible within the group so that no one feels that someone else will try to take advantage of them.

Global Teams

Another type of group that is becoming increasingly prominent, especially in larger organizations, is the multinational group (almost always referred to as a "multinational team"). It is usually a highly diverse group, whether representing one or several functional areas, because members are often from very different cultural backgrounds. For reasons that we have already discussed, diverse teams potentially offer major advantages for organizations. However, reality is not always quite so rosy. All too frequently, the efforts of such groups end up in paralysis, inaction, or even outright failure.

One set of researchers divided up multinational teams into three general types: the destroyers, the equalizers, and the creators.[56] "Destroyers" are groups that turn out to be utter disasters; they channel their members' efforts and attention into unproductive conflicts and interpersonal attacks. For example, one member of a European destroyer team described the team environment candidly: "Those Brits on our team are too serious; the Germans are so stuck-up about engineering that they don't think anyone else has a brain; and the French couldn't care less about production quotas." "Equalizer" types of teams are those that think they are doing well and have little apparent conflict, yet seem unable to produce anything better than mediocre results. Essentially, equalizers are underperforming teams that fail to take advantage of their cross-national diversity. "Creator" teams are those that directly accept and build on their differences and use them to enhance their creativity.

Virtual Teams

As mentioned earlier in this chapter, organizations are increasingly establishing **virtual teams**, or groups composed of individuals who do not work together in close physical proximity. Members of virtual teams are often geographically dispersed, cross-organizationally or cross-nationally. As their name implies, such

virtual team a group composed of individuals who do not work together in close physical proximity

groups rarely, if ever, meet in person and instead conduct most or all of their business via electronic communication. Such virtual teams are used, for example, by T4G, an IT firm specializing in web and software development that is located in Vancouver, Toronto, Saint John, and Halifax. While all 200 employees have their own designated desk, employees spend less than half their time in the office, working mostly from client's places or from home. The employees are used to working on virtual teams to get their work done. From Paul Barter's perspective (the vice-president of strategy), it's more about getting the work done rather than where the work is performed. The major benefit of the virtual team initiative at T4G has been retaining good staff. It's a competitive market to acquire and retain quality staff, yet T4G has been able to double in size over two years. Barter attributes this to the attractive work environment that they maintain for employees.[57]

Increased speed of communication and decreased costs are obvious advantages of virtual groups. Nevertheless, as can be imagined, virtual teams also have their own associated set of potential problems. First, communication, though fast and sometimes nearly instantaneous, can be incomplete and easily subject to misinterpretation by the receiver. Second, trust among group members may be very difficult to develop because of the absence of the typical getting-to-know-you socialization process that occurs with nonvirtual groups that meet face to face. Third, managerial supervision may be more difficult than in a typical group. Issues that can crop up in any group, such as role ambiguity and social loafing, for example, may be intensified in virtual groups.

Building and Managing Groups and Teams

Throughout this chapter we have mentioned some of the steps that you as a manager can take to increase the quality of group functioning and the satisfaction of group members. In this section we focus on three issues that are particularly critical in building and managing groups and turning them into true teams: developing team competencies, dealing with team conflict, and improving group and team effectiveness.

Developing Team Competencies

As we have emphasized throughout this chapter, working with, and in, a group is different from simply doing your own individual job well. It is the interaction with other people, whether face to face or by electronic and other indirect means, that makes the difference. Therefore, to be able to perform effectively in a group, it is important that you develop competencies in teamwork. To be a competent team member is not necessarily the same thing as being a competent individual performer. A very useful way to think about what is required from you in a team situation is to consider three basic areas of teamwork competencies: **k**nowledge, **s**kills, and **a**ttitudes (KSAs).[58] Specific examples of team competencies in these three areas are shown in Exhibit 11.9.

Knowledge (K) in the group context refers to the necessary understanding of facts, concepts, relations, and underlying relevant information necessary to perform team tasks. As shown in Exhibit 11.9, examples of the kinds of specific knowledge that are especially useful in team situations include knowledge about the team's mission and goals, the sequencing of tasks faced by the team, fellow team members' roles and responsibilities, and teammate characteristics.

Skills (S) refer to highly developed behavioural and cognitive capabilities that are necessary to carry out team tasks and meet team goals. These include (as shown in Exhibit 11.9) such competencies as adaptability and flexibility in

Exhibit 11.9 Examples of Specific Team Competencies in Three Areas

Knowledge	Skills	Attitudes
· Knowledge of team mission, objectives, norms · Task sequencing · Team role interaction patterns · Understanding team work skills · Teammate characteristics	· Adaptability and flexibility · Mutual performance monitoring and feedback, self-correction · Coordination and task integration · Communication · Decision making and problem solving	· Team orientation · Shared vision · Team cohesion · Mutual trust · Importance of teamwork

Sources: Adapted from J. A. Cannon-Bowers and E. Salas, "A Framework for Developing Team Performance Measures in Training," in M. T. Brannick, E. Salas, and C. Prince (eds.), *Team Performance Assessment and Measurement: Theory, Methods, and Applications* (Mahwah, NJ: Lawrence Erlbaum Associates, 1997), p. 47.

relation to accomplishing team tasks; being able to monitor one's own and fellow team members' performance; communication; being able to accept and give criticism; and being able to assume leadership responsibilities within the group.

Attitudes (A) involve relatively stable feelings and beliefs about something. In other words, our attitudes, generally speaking, indicate how we view important parts of our environment. In a group-work situation, these important attitudes would include (see Exhibit 11.9) those toward the concepts of teams and teamwork, the need for team cohesion, assessment of a team's capabilities, and the level and importance of trust within a group.[59]

A helpful way to analyze required team competencies in the areas of knowledge, skills, and attitudes was developed a few years ago by a group of organizational psychologists[60] and is displayed in Exhibit 11.10. This system of analysis categorizes the types of team competencies needed using two variables: (1) whether a needed competency is specific to a given task, or applies to all kinds of tasks; and (2) whether a needed competency is specific to a given team, or applies to all kinds of teams. The resulting categorization scheme organized along these two dimensions can be summarized in a 2 × 2 table, as shown in Exhibit 11.10.

Relation to Team \ Relation to Task	Specific	Generic
Specific	Context driven	Team contingent
Generic	Task contingent	Transportable

Exhibit 11.10

Types of Team Competencies

Source: Adapted from J. A. Cannon-Bowers, S. I. Tannenbaum, E. Salas, and C. E. Volpe, "Defining Competencies and Establishing Team Training Requirements," in R. A. Guzzo, E. Salas and Associates (eds.), *Team Effectiveness and Decision Making in Organizations* (San Francisco: Jossey-Bass Publishers, 1995), p. 339.

transportable competencies competencies that can be used in any situation

By far, the most important type of competency in this classification system for you as a potential manager is represented in the bottom right of Exhibit 11.10: "transportable team competencies." **Transportable competencies** are those that can be used in *any* situation. They are helpful for anyone who works with a variety of teams and with teams that face a wide variety of tasks. Therefore, transportable KSAs are the most essential group competencies for any manager or team member to develop. A knowledge of what is required to work together in teams of any type is crucial and highly transferable. Interpersonal, communication, and team-building capabilities are the hallmark of transportable team skill competencies. An especially important attitude would be an appreciation for the value and usefulness of teamwork. In short, it is clearly worth your time and effort to acquire and improve team competencies that are portable.

team-contingent competencies competencies that are specific to the particular team, but applicable across a wide range of tasks

In the upper-right corner of Exhibit 11.10 are **team-contingent competencies**—competencies that are specific to the particular team, but applicable across a wide range of tasks. Many typical command (supervisor-led) groups would be examples of teams that need these types of competencies. Such groups require a high level of team-member knowledge of each other—each member needs to know what each other member's skill and expertise is. Members also need to have a clear understanding of how their group coordinates with the larger organization. In these kinds of group circumstances, the composition of the group's membership is particularly important. This can be seen when there is a change in that composition (addition or loss of a member) that usually reduces the team's effectiveness until a new member can be brought up to speed. Skills needed in this team-dependent category include skills that apply to a wide variety of tasks, such as leadership, communication, and conflict resolution skills. Also, since the composition of the team is so crucial, the perception of strong team cohesion would be an important attitude.

context-driven competencies competencies that are specific to both the unique nature of the particular tasks and the particular composition of the team

In the upper-left corner of Exhibit 11.10 are "**context-driven**" competencies. As the category name implies, the particular circumstances—relating to both task and team—in which the group is performing are crucial to the competencies that are needed. They are competencies that would be specific to both the unique nature of the particular tasks and the particular composition of teams. The task-specific/team-specific kinds of knowledge needed would, for example, include a shared understanding of the different parts of the specific overall task, information about other team members' habits and tendencies, and an understanding of the team's norms. The kinds of teams that would benefit from such context-driven competencies would include surgery teams, military combat teams, and sports teams. An example from the sports world illustrates the need for both task-specific *and* team-specific knowledge. Many professional sports' leagues have mid-season all-star games, where the best individual players from each team (or at least from most teams) in one part of the league come together to play the best players from the other part. Thus, all of the players are experts at their own tasks. They have high task-specific knowledge and skills. However, they lack the high level of team-specific knowledge they have regarding their own teams. The consequence of this situation is that the performance of players on all-star teams typically turns out to be lower than the performance of those same players when playing on their own regular teams. The problem is the relative lack of team-specific knowledge.

Examples of skills needed in this category would include the ability to reallocate duties among members under changing circumstances and the ability to develop a common understanding of overall task requirements. In the area of attitudes, a task-specific/team-specific type of competency would be the development of a collective sense of team strengths and weaknesses.

Task-contingent competencies (lower-left corner of Exhibit 11.10) are needed in teams that perform a specific and recurring set of tasks but have varying sets of members. In the knowledge area, team members in this category of teams would need expertise regarding the specific task characteristics they would encounter on a regular basis. Skills needed would be those that are highly related to the particular set of tasks involved. An attitude that would be helpful in this kind of situation would be a positive view of working as part of a team, regardless of who the other team members are. Examples of teams that need these kinds of competencies among their members would be many aircraft crews, firefighting teams, and the like. For this task-driven set of conditions, it doesn't matter who is on the team on a given day, just that members are competent in performing their particular tasks. Members of the team have to trust the other members to do their jobs, *even if* they have never met each other before. As long as the pilot knows how to take off and land, and the navigator knows how to navigate, the flight team is okay.

task-contingent competencies competencies that are needed in teams that perform a specific and recurring set of tasks but have varying sets of members

Dealing with Team Conflict

When people work together in groups, there is always the potential for conflict. Disagreement or opposition between or among group members can occur for a number of reasons and can have a variety of consequences. Although the effects of group conflict, such as a marked decrease in cohesion within the group, often can be negative, that is not always so. In fact, some types of conflict, particularly task or substantive conflict (discussed next), can have positive effects. One senior executive viewed it this way:

> *We can agree our way into horrendous decisions. But when people are allowed to express their opinions, no matter how disagreeable, magic can occur. More ideas are put on the table, which can lead to more discovery, which can lead to quantum leaps in improvement and innovation. . . . When marketing and engineering disagree violently about something, you've got a wonderful opportunity to figure out how to make improvements by meeting both [of their] objectives.*[61]

The important point to remember is that conflict among members within groups is fairly common, and it is not always something to be avoided. In fact, the absence of any conflict at all can be a sign that the group is not openly generating a variety of viewpoints and potential approaches for solving problems and making good decisions.

Types of Group Conflict Researchers have generally distinguished two basic types of group conflict: task conflict and relationship conflict. **Task conflict** is conflict that focuses on differences in ideas and courses of action in addressing the issues facing a group. It is also sometimes called cognitive (thinking) or substantive conflict.[62] Research indicates that at least some amount of task conflict often can be beneficial to the group,[63] especially for less routine and more complex tasks.[64]

task (substantive) conflict conflict that focuses on differences in ideas and courses of action in addressing the issues facing a group

The other major type of conflict that can occur in groups, relationship conflict, is usually found to be almost always dysfunctional. **Relationship conflict** focuses on interpersonal differences and is sometimes called affective or emotional conflict. It is usually a negative type of conflict for groups because it distracts focus from tasks and ideas.[65] It discourages rather than encourages consideration of multiple points of view and the open discussion of ideas and solutions.

relationship (affective) conflict interpersonal differences among group members

Causes of Group Conflict There are many potential causes of group conflict, but they can usually be linked to one of the two types of conflict. The causes of task conflict, for example, include:

- Ambiguities regarding the task
- Differences in goals, objectives, and perspectives (e.g., stemming from differences in functional backgrounds among group members)[66]
- Scarcity (actual or perceived) of resources to accomplish group goals

Possible causes of relationship conflict are as follows:

- Dissimilarities in the composition of the membership of the group, including demographic diversity (in age, ethnic/cultural background, gender, etc.) and status/power differences[67]
- Differences in interpersonal styles of individual members
- Differences in values[68]

Several of the potential causes of group conflict can occur together; for example, when a very diverse group that includes several people with distinctive interpersonal styles or quite different values encounters a highly ambiguous task. When there are such multiple causes, finding ways to deal with the conflict becomes even more difficult, of course.

Managing Group Conflict If you are put in the position of leading a group, what can you do to help your group deal with conflict? Probably the most important managerial guideline for dealing with group conflict is to try to increase the ratio of substantive to relationship conflict.[69] This would mean, for example, strongly encouraging a culture of openness to express differences of opinion about task methods and objectives, and also being especially receptive to novel or creative approaches to coping with task requirements.[70] In this way, maximum amounts of relevant information can be brought to bear on the issues faced by the group,[71] and unintended groupthink tendencies can be minimized. In addition, you should help to clarify and reduce task ambiguities and try to get the group to focus on larger goals beyond individual member interests—goals, in other words, that emphasize the common interests of all the group members. Also, there is evidence to suggest that active attempts that are taken to avoid relationship conflicts may be the best way to eliminate or at least reduce their harmful effects on group members' satisfaction and performance.[72]

Demographic differences, differences in interpersonal styles, and differences in values can lend a group strength. However, the same differences can also become the source of intragroup conflict. Managers should actively emphasize the common interests of members and discourage personal conflicts among them.

Most of what we have been talking about so far applies to conflict *within* groups (**intragroup conflict**). In organizational settings, of course, conflict *between* or among groups—**intergroup conflict**—can also occur frequently. Strategies for managing intragroup conflict apply equally well to intergroup conflict. Therefore, managers should look for opportunities to reduce unnecessary relational conflicts in those intergroup interaction situations and increase the focus on substantive differences. Also, emphasizing larger, more organization-wide goals can help increase cooperation and thus performance.[73] So, for example, if sales and production can concentrate on the issue of improving customer satisfaction—to elevate it to the highest priority—then their differences on how many variations of a product to make and market can be minimized or resolved. As with intragroup conflict, the potential exists for positive effects from intergroup conflict.

intragroup conflict differences that occur within groups

intergroup conflict differences that occur between groups

Improving Group and Team Effectiveness

Teams and groups are not static parts of organizations. They come into existence, go out of existence, and change over time. Additionally, and most importantly, their effectiveness and performance can be changed and improved. As a leader of a group, however, this is not necessarily easy to do. There is no magic formula to bring this about. Nevertheless, there are some useful approaches to consider that have the potential for helping to improve a group's performance in organizational settings.[74]

Assessing the Effectiveness of Groups What exactly do we mean by group effectiveness? What distinguishes highly effective groups from less effective groups? A survey of 61 companies revealed that about two-thirds used objective, quantifiable criteria to measure group effectiveness; these included measures of production output, quality improvements, cost reductions, and turnaround times. A number of the companies also used more subjective criteria including member participation, cooperation, and involvement.[75]

How can we tell when a group is performing especially well? Analyses of research findings by one of the foremost experts on group effectiveness, Richard Hackman, suggest three major indicators (see Exhibit 11.11):[76]

1. Whether the group's outputs—products, services, or decisions—are valued by those who receive or use them. Are a committee's recommendations implemented? Does a product development group's creation ever get put into production? Is upper management satisfied with the performance of a customer service unit?
2. Whether the group's capacity for further cooperation among its members is maintained or increased.

Exhibit 11.11 Characteristics of Highly Effective Groups

- Any product or service they develop is highly desired and valued by customers.
- Increased cooperation among members is encouraged and achieved.
- Group membership increases individual members' feelings of satisfaction, personal growth, and overall well-being.

Source: J. R. Hackman (ed.), *Groups That Work (and Those That Don't): Creating Conditions for Effective Teamwork* (San Francisco: Jossey-Bass, 1990).

3. Whether members gain satisfaction and a sense of growth and well-being from being part of the group. A group or team is unlikely to be regarded by outsiders as effective if its own members do not seem satisfied and are not experiencing feelings of accomplishment by being part of the group.

Most observers would probably say that the first of these criteria of effectiveness—acceptance of the group's outputs by others—is the most important one in organizational settings. However, if neither of the other two indicators can be achieved by a group, it is highly unlikely that it will be able over time to produce valued output. Thus, all three are important components of group effectiveness and need attention from anyone who wants to improve groups. *A Manager's Challenge: "A Tale of Two Teams"* provides a vivid example of two groups where there was no difficulty in assessing their effectiveness. Although operating in the same external cultural environment and with certain other similarities, the groups went in opposite directions in building effectiveness.

Ingredients Necessary for Group Effectiveness For a group to perform effectively, it must be able to do three things especially well:

1. Exert enough effort to accomplish its tasks at acceptable levels of quantity and quality;
2. Obtain sufficient knowledge and skills to carry out its work;
3. Use appropriate strategies to apply its effort, knowledge, and skills effectively.[77]

These three bases for achieving high levels of group effectiveness sound simple, but they are major challenges for leaders of groups. To ensure that these components are actually in place consistently, managers need to address several issues.

Develop Appropriate Group Structures To be effective, groups need clearly defined tasks and objectives that can motivate their members. Groups also need to be sized appropriately for their tasks, and they need a membership with a sufficient mix of skills and expertise. This means that if a group leader has the option of choosing the members, those selection choices will often make a large difference in how well a group performs initially and what its capacity is to improve.

Develop Appropriate Support from the Organization[78] Groups operating within companies and organizations need support from their surrounding environment, such as rewards for effective collaboration among members,[79] education and technical training for performing critical group tasks,[80] relief from other duties, and access to necessary information.

Obtain Appropriate Coaching and Consultation Assistance In the day-to-day world of work, most groups need outside help (whether from inside or outside the larger organization) to reduce potential conflicts, increase coordination in dealing with problems within the group, and provide strategies for approaching the group's tasks. Increased collaboration is an important objective,[81] and the message here is that it is often the case that a group should not try to go it alone. It should not hesitate to seek assistance from wherever seems most appropriate—especially assistance that can be relatively objective and "with no axes to grind."

a manager's challenge — *globalization*

A Tale of Two Teams

The country of Israel was the setting for a study of two teams that ended up with quite different effectiveness results. The two teams—both operating in the public sector—had the same timetable, budget, and project scope, but were established to complete two very different tasks in the late 1990s. One project was an immediate success; the other languished throughout months of bickering among team members. What made the difference?

The Center for Business Promotion (CBP) was an arm of Israel's Ministry of Trade and Commerce. It was staffed by a small team of seven or eight professional members with one or two secretaries and a pair of student interns. Its charter was to attract foreign investors and tourists to Jerusalem through the creation of accurate and accessible databases available through special websites. With economic renewal via tourism a top priority in the mayor's office, the CBP team went right to work on the website project as an informal workgroup, despite having responsibilities for many other diplomatic, media, and economic duties.

Its first step was to jettison the ministry's outdated sources and send the two interns out to collect fresh data by scanning newspapers and attending venture capital and professional conferences looking for likely entrants to the data bank. The team also carefully avoided ministry interference, hired a consultant to help them find contractors to build and update the website, and within six months delivered to foreign investors diskettes of current data about Israeli companies that were later replaced by the internet site.

Meanwhile, the City of Jerusalem put together an Internet Committee to build a similar site for attracting foreign tourists. The site was to offer easy access to a valuable data bank of hotels, restaurants, and attractions and allow the option to make reservations online. Team members spent an unproductive year arguing over who would own the website, even though in the meantime they had to hire an outside company to actually construct the site.

Although the outside company had many ties to the municipal government and its key computer systems, it failed over and over to develop online information systems for residents of Jerusalem and made several costly mistakes. A year after the Internet Committee was formed, work on the site had not even begun. With pressure mounting to complete the project and to integrate the website with government tourist offices, a second Internet Committee was formed. Turf battles broke out as committee members tried to use the project to benefit their own departments, ranging from engineering to culture to treasury.

Months later, after a reorganization of the committee into two separate units and the creation of a second proposal, the City of Jerusalem finally had an internet site, though its content had little to do with the original purpose.

Sources: A. Peled, "Outsourcing and Political Power: Bureaucrats, Consultants, Vendors and Public Information Technology," *Public Personnel Management*, Winter 2001, 20 pp.; A. Peled, "Creating Winning Information Technology Project Teams in the Public Sector," *Team Performance Management*, 2000, pp. 6–14.

Exhibit 11.12 provides a summary of the preceding points and shows how the manager's attention to the group's structure, support from the organizational context, and relevant coaching and consultation can help increase each of the three ingredients necessary for group effectiveness: high levels of effort, sufficient knowledge and skills, and appropriate strategies for applying effort and skills. The points presented and summarized in the exhibit do not provide a cookbook for group or team success. Rather, they are useful guidelines for managers and organizations to consider in approaching *their* task of helping groups to improve performance for themselves and for those who rely on the outputs of their work. Likewise, Exhibit 11.13, based on extensive research,[82] provides a helpful checklist for those who assume leadership positions in groups and teams to measure how well they are fulfilling that role in their groups. If team members concur that their leader is in fact doing a good job in these various areas of the role, then it is likely that the group (and not just the leader) will perform well.

Exhibit 11.12 Enhancing Group Effectiveness

	POINTS OF LEVERAGE		
Necessary Processes	**Group Structure**	**Organizational Context**	**Coaching and Consultation**
Apply ample effort	Motivational structure of group task	Organizational reward system	Remedying coordination problems and building group commitment
Acquire sufficient knowledge and skill	Group composition	Organizational education/ training system	Remedying inappropriate "weighting" of member inputs and fostering cross-training
Develop task-appropriate performance strategies	Group norms that regulate member behaviour and foster scanning and planning	Organizational information system	Remedying implementation problems and fostering creativity in strategy development

Source: Adapted from J. R. Hackman (ed.), *Groups That Work (and Those That Don't): Creating Conditions for Effective Teamwork* (San Francisco: Jossey-Bass, 1990), p. 13.

Exhibit 11.13 A Checklist for Leaders of Groups

How well do you:

- ❑ Encourage members to learn from each other?
- ❑ Recognize and praise members for their contributions?
- ❑ Keep key people outside the [group] informed about its accomplishments?
- ❑ Promptly inform members about major developments that [may] affect them?
- ❑ Give [group] members authority to make [at least some] important decisions?
- ❑ Openly accept and respond to feedback from [group] members?
- ❑ Review the [group's] performance at the end of major tasks?
- ❑ Offer specific and concrete suggestions for how members can improve?
- ❑ Understand what motivates members to work hard?

Source: Adapted from G. L. Hallam, "Seven Common Beliefs about Teams: Are They True?" *Leadership in Action* 17, no. 3 (1997), pp. 1–4.

managerial perspectives revisited

PERSPECTIVE 1: **THE ORGANIZATIONAL CONTEXT** Organizations are increasing their reliance on groups and teams, compared to years past. It also seems irrefutable that any given group or team is strongly affected by the organizational context that surrounds it. Thus, as a manager or leader of a group you will have to look both inward toward the group and its members and outward toward the organizational environment if you are to be effective. In a way, the larger organization can be considered as a sort of group of groups. It will be up to you to gain an understanding of the resources and constraints that are provided by those "other groups" and how that knowledge can assist you in developing a high-performing *team*.

PERSPECTIVE 2: **THE HUMAN FACTOR** The building blocks of groups and teams are, of course, its people. Managers need to find ways to meld the talents of individual persons into a coherent and functioning unit. This means that you will need insight into how to assign individual members to the particular tasks and jobs that make up the group's work, and then, especially, how to encourage their maximum efforts to cooperate and coordinate with each other. It also means that it will be a challenge to stimulate each person's creativity in contributing to the overall set of group tasks without at the same time triggering unacceptable levels of relationship conflict among team members.

PERSPECTIVE 3: **MANAGING PARADOXES** Managers frequently find themselves simultaneously being both members of groups and leading their own groups. This requires nimbly shifting roles, and often doing so quickly. However, at times these roles may create a paradox for the manager. He or she may have to deal with other paradoxes related to groups as well. For example, diverse groups tend to make better decisions but are more difficult to manage and are likely to experience greater conflict than more homogeneous groups. Too much diversity can result in excessive conflict, and too much homogeneity can lead to insufficient innovation and creative problem solving.

PERSPECTIVE 4: **ENTREPRENEURIAL MINDSET** Individuals may have entrepreneurial mindsets, but as we have explained in previous chapters, this mindset can also apply to an organization or groups and teams within an organization. This is important because research has shown that teams can be more creative than individuals because of the different ideas and shared knowledge of the individuals that comprise them. Of course, individuals are unlikely to bring their ideas to the table unless creativity and innovation are encouraged. Thus, having an entrepreneurial mindset within the organization is needed to motivate groups and teams to innovate.[83] Today, a number of large corporations have R&D teams to develop and design new products. Commonly, these teams are cross-functional with design engineers, scientists, manufacturing engineers, and marketing specialists all working to develop the same product. Each member brings his or her valuable knowledge and skill sets to the process. Not only can teams be more creative, if managed appropriately, they can also develop better-quality products with the features consumers want. However, the innovation process must begin with the organization making a commitment to having an entrepreneurial mindset and encouraging groups and teams to do likewise.

concluding comments

Groups are becoming increasingly vital parts of contemporary organizations operating in a world of accelerated change and competition. Consequently, if you aspire to become an effective manager or executive in an organization, you will need to be able to (1) understand different types of groups and how they function and (2) know how to lead them effectively. These are fundamental challenges, but they can be met.

Many people who carry out their own individual work exceedingly well, and who interact very comfortably in one-on-one relationships, often run into difficulties when called on to manage group activity. Groups multiply the number of interpersonal relationships involved, which in turn creates a level of complexity that needs to be assessed and mastered.

To be able to manage groups successfully is a skill that can be learned. It requires deliberate effort to be perceptive and to notice many subtle nuances as well as the more obvious aspects of interpersonal relationships occurring inside groups. Are certain norms forming, and if so, what are the directions of these norms? Is a group developing cohesion, and does it lend support to the organization's larger goals or only to the narrow self-interests of the immediate group? Is there conflict within the group, and is it focused on better problem solving or only on potentially destructive personal relationships? Attention to these and similar issues will provide a solid base for leading productive groups.

Successful management of groups also requires constant awareness of how the conditions surrounding groups are changing and how that evolving context will affect what groups do and how they perform. Two of those major changes occurring in the environment in which groups operate are the rapidly increasing use of technology to facilitate interactions among group members and the expanding global activities of many organizations. Both of these trends carry with them the potential for many positive improvements. However, they also can present particular challenges to leaders of groups to be able to use technology effectively and to take advantage of global opportunities. These and other features of the organizational context outside of a group are nearly as important as the interactions that take place inside it in determining how effectively it performs.

Finally, as we noted early in this chapter, there is strong pressure in many of today's organizations for managers to develop their groups so that they become real "teams," with all that that term implies. Groups that turn into teams have the potential to vastly magnify the productivity and quality of a set of individuals. But true teamwork must be created and nurtured by skilful management.

key terms

cohesion 388
command (supervisory) group 377
committee 380
conformity 387
context-driven competencies 398
formal group 380
group 377
informal group 381
intergroup conflict 401
intragroup conflict 401
norms 385
process costs 382
project/task force 378
relationship (affective) conflict 399
role ambiguity 385
role conflict 385
self-managing (autonomous) workgroup 394
social loafing 382
status 385
task (substantive) conflict 399
task-contingent competencies 399
team 377
team-contingent competencies 398
transportable competencies 398
virtual team 395

test your comprehension

1. What are the similarities and differences between a group and a team?
2. What are the major types of groups found in organizations? Give examples of each.
3. What is the fundamental difference between a formal and an informal group?
4. How do organizational goals affect the formation of groups?

5. What are some of the concerns of new group members?
6. How is proximity related to the formation of informal groups?
7. What personal needs may be satisfied by group membership?
8. What are the four stages of group formation? What are the important features of each?
9. What are the structural characteristics of groups? Why is each important?
10. Is there an optimum group size? Why or why not?
11. What is "social loafing"? Can managers do anything to minimize or eliminate it?
12. To what extent is social loafing likely to be equally prevalent in all cultures?
13. How do heterogeneous groups differ from homogeneous ones?
14. What are some of the types of diversity found within groups? What effects can diversity have on group members and on group functioning?
15. Provide examples of role conflict and role ambiguity that illustrate the difference between the two terms.
16. Why are norms important to groups?
17. What are some of the key factors that often have major influences on the development of norms?
18. Is it always good to have a high level of conformity within a group?
19. Can managers affect the level of conformity within a group? Why or why not?
20. What is meant by group cohesion? How does it develop? Are high levels of group cohesion always desirable?
21. How does a self-managing (autonomous) workgroup differ from a typical command group?
22. What are the advantages and disadvantages of virtual teams?
23. Why is there an increased usage of cross-functional workgroups in organizations today? How can managers increase the effectiveness of these groups?
24. What are KSAs and how are they related to team competencies?
25. What are the causes of the two basic types of group conflict?
26. Can managers eliminate group conflict? Should they try?
27. What are three major indicators that can be used to identify high-performance groups?
28. What kinds of issues must managers address when attempting to improve group effectiveness?

apply your understanding

1. As a manager, would you rather work with highly diversified teams or with more homogeneous teams? Why? Which types would be best for which types of situations?
2. Think about a group in which you have been involved at work, at school, or perhaps while playing a sport. What were the structural characteristics of the group? What were some of its norms? Would you characterize it as a group or as a team? Why?
3. Some students groan and complain when told they must participate in a group project. Why do you think this is? What is it about group work that irritates some students so much? After reading this chapter, can you think of ways to structure and lead a group to gain these individuals' cooperation and motivation?
4. As a manager, if your workgroup is demonstrating considerable intragroup conflict, what would you do?
5. Which type of team—self-managing, cross-functional, global, or virtual—do you think is the most difficult to manage? Why?
6. How would you characterize your own level of group competency? What do you think are the most important KSAs relevant to groups and teams that you should master next?

practise your capabilities

It is 3:00 p.m. on the afternoon before your team project is due in your management class. You are about to meet with your team to put the finishing touches on your paper. Each member had originally agreed to provide two pages of material on disk, with a hard copy for editing. As your group members arrive for the meeting you find out that some don't have even one page prepared and that almost all are handwritten. You realize there is a lot to do if this paper is going to be in shape by tomorrow. The parts must be integrated, typed, edited, proofread, polished, and exhibits must be made.

There are six of you on the team. The varsity athlete has been grateful when meetings have been postponed or cancelled to accommodate practice. Unfortunately, today she must attend a mandatory practice from 4:00 to 9:00 p.m. The international student, who has good oral but poor written English, would like to help and has strong ideas. However, this student always feels resented by you. The two of you just don't get along. The fraternity president was aware that tonight's formal dance would provide a conflict for this meeting. However, he had spent a lot of time polishing and editing part of the paper and provided hard and disk copies of it. Another member has just gotten the lead in the school play and has absolutely no interest anymore in this class project. Frustrated by past missed deadlines, willing to settle for a so-so paper, and unwilling to miss tonight's rehearsal, the actor has provided a handwritten rough draft. The last member has airline reservations for 4:30 this afternoon, just finished scribbling down some ideas, doesn't care who writes the paper, so long as it gets done, and is willing to lend the team a laptop computer.

As the team leader, you wonder how things could possibly have gone so wrong and what you are going to do now, keeping in mind that this group is going to have to work together again next week to develop a presentation to give to the class.

1. What type(s) of conflict exist in this group? How has it affected the group's productivity?

2. Keeping in mind issues discussed in this chapter, what would you, as team leader, do now?

Source: Adapted from S. B. Wolff and J. W. Wohlberg, *OB in Action: Cases and Exercises*, 6th ed. (Boston: Houghton Mifflin, 2001), pp. 205–206.

closing case DEVELOP YOUR CRITICAL THINKING

The Team That Wasn't

As the new director of strategy at FireArt, Inc., a regional glass manufacturer, Eric Holt spent all his time trying to get his new team to make it through a meeting without the tension level becoming unbearable. Six of the top-level managers involved seemed determined to turn the company around, but the seventh seemed equally determined to sabotage the process. Forget camaraderie. It was not like Eric was unfamiliar with leading teams, having come to FireArt from a vice-president position with a consulting firm where he managed three teams of manufacturing specialists. Yet, since his arrival at FireArt, there had been three team meetings, and Eric has still been unable to get everyone on the same side of an issue.

Eric checked the clock in his apartment: Only three more hours before he had to watch as Randy Louderback, FireArt's charismatic director of sales and marketing, either dominated the group's discussion or withdrew entirely, tapping his pen on the table to indicate his boredom. Sometimes he withheld information vital to the group's debate; other times he coolly denigrated people's comments. Still, Eric realized, Randy held the group in such thrall because of his dynamic personality, his almost legendary past, and his close relationship with FireArt's CEO that could not be ignored. And at least once during each meeting, he offered an insight about the industry or the company that was so perceptive that Eric knew he *shouldn't* be ignored.

As he prepared to leave for the office, Eric felt the familiar frustration that had started building during the team's first meeting a month earlier. It was then that Randy had first insinuated, with what sounded like a joke, that he wasn't cut out to be a team player. "Leaders lead, followers . . . please pipe down!" had been his exact words, although he had smiled winningly as he spoke, and the rest of the group had laughed heartily in response. No one in the group was laughing now, though, least of all Eric.

FireArt, Inc., was in trouble—not deep trouble, but enough for its CEO, Jack Derry, to make strategic repositioning Eric's top and only task. The company, a family-owned maker of wine goblets, beer steins, ashtrays, and other glass novelties, had succeeded for nearly 80 years as a high-quality, high-price producer, catering to hundreds of midwestern clients. It traditionally did big business every football season, selling commemorative knick-knacks and memorabilia to team fans. In the spring there was always a rush of demand for graduation items—champagne goblets emblazoned with a school's name or beer mugs with a school's crest, for example. Fraternities and sororities were also steady customers. Year after year, FireArt showed respectable increases at the top and bottom lines, posting $86 million in earnings three years before Eric arrived.

In the last 18 months, though, sales and earnings had flattened. Jack, a grandnephew of the company's founder, thought he knew what was happening. Until recently, large national glass companies had been able to make money only through mass production. Now, however, thanks to new technologies in the glass-making industry, those companies could execute short runs profitably. They had begun to enter FireArt's niche, Jack had told Eric, and with their superior resources, it was just a matter of time before they would own it.

"You have one responsibility as FireArt's new director of strategy," Jack had said to Eric on his first day. "That's to put together a team of our top people, one person from each division, and have a comprehensive plan for the company's strategic realignment up, running, and winning within six months."

Eric had immediately compiled a list of the senior managers from human resources, manufacturing, finance, distribution, design, and marketing, and had set a date for the first meeting. Then, drawing on his years as a consultant who had worked almost solely in team environments, Eric had carefully prepared a structure and guidelines for the group's discussions, disagreements, and decisions, which he planned to propose to the members for their input before they began working together.

Successful groups are part art, part science, Eric knew, but he also believed that with every member's full commitment, a team proved the adage that the whole is greater than the sum of its parts. Knowing that managers at FireArt were unaccustomed to the team process, however, Eric imagined he might get some resistance from one or two members.

For one, he had been worried about Ray LaPierre of manufacturing. Ray was a giant of a man who had run the furnaces for some 35 years, following in his father's footsteps. Although he was a former high school football star who was known among workers in the factory for his hearty laugh and his love of practical jokes, Ray usually didn't say much around FireArt's executives, citing his lack of higher education as the reason. Eric had thought the team atmosphere might intimidate him.

Eric had also anticipated a bit of a fight from Maureen Turner of the design division, who was known to complain that FireArt didn't appreciate its six artists. Eric had suspected that Maureen might have a chip on her shoulder about collaborating with people who didn't understand the design process.

Ironically, both those fears had proved groundless, but another, more difficult problem had arisen. The wild card had turned out to be Randy. Eric had met Randy once before the team started its work and had found him to be enormously intelligent, energetic, and good-humoured. What's more, Jack Derry had confirmed his impressions, telling him that Randy "had the best mind" at FireArt. It was also from Jack that Eric had first learned of Randy's difficult yet inspirational personal history.

Poor as a child, he had worked as a security guard and short-order cook to put himself through college, from which he graduated with top honours. Soon after, he started his own advertising and market research firm, and within the decade, he had built it into a company employing 50 people to service some of the region's most prestigious accounts. His success brought with it a measure of fame: articles in the local media, invitations to government functions, even an honourary degree from the local business school. But in the late 1980s, Randy's firm suffered the same fate as many other advertising shops, and he was forced to declare bankruptcy. FireArt considered it a coup when it landed him as director of marketing, since he had let it be known that he was offered at least two dozen other jobs. "Randy is the future of this company," Jack Derry had told Eric. "If he can't help you, no one can. I look forward to hearing what a team with his kind of horsepower can come up with to steer us away from the mess we're in."

Those words echoed in Eric's mind as he sat, with increasing anxiety, through the team's first and second meetings. Although Eric had planned an agenda for each meeting and tried to keep the discussions on track, Randy always seemed to find a way to disrupt the process. Time and time again, he shot down other people's ideas, or he simply didn't pay attention. He also answered most questions put to him with maddening vagueness. "I'll have my assistant look into it when he gets a moment," he replied, when one team member asked him to list FireArt's five largest customers. "Some days you eat the bear, and other days the bear eats you," he joked another time, when asked why sales to fraternities had recently nose-dived.

Randy's negativism, however, was countered by occasional comments so insightful that they stopped the conversation cold or turned it around entirely—comments that demonstrated extraordinary knowledge about competitors or glass technology or customers' buying patterns. The help wouldn't last, though; Randy would quickly revert to his role as team renegade.

The third meeting, last week, had ended in chaos. Ray LaPierre, Maureen Turner, and the distribution director, Carl Simmons, had each planned to present cost-cutting proposals, and at first it looked as though they were making good progress.

Ray opened the meeting, proposing a plan for FireArt to cut throughput time by 3 percent and raw-materials costs by 2 percent, thereby positioning the company to compete better on price. It was obvious from his detailed presentation that he had put a lot of thought into his comments, and it was evident that he was fighting a certain amount of nervousness as he made them.

"I know I don't have the book smarts of most of you in this room," he had begun, "but here goes anyway." During his presentation, Ray stopped several times to answer questions from the team, and as he went on, his nervousness transformed into his usual ebullience. "That wasn't so bad!" he laughed to himself as he sat down at the end, flashing a grin at Eric. "Maybe we can turn this old ship around."

Maureen Turner had followed Ray. While not disagreeing with him—she praised his comments, in fact—she argued that FireArt also needed to invest in new artists, pitching its competitive advantage in better design and wider variety. Unlike Ray, Maureen had made this case to FireArt's top executives many times, only to be rebuffed, and some of her frustration seeped through as she explained her reasoning yet again. At one point, her voice almost broke as she described how hard she had worked in her first 10 years at FireArt, hoping that someone in management would recognize the creativity of her designs. "But no one did," she recalled with a sad shake of her head. "That's why when I was made director of the department, I made sure all the artists were respected for what they are—artists, not worker ants. There's a difference, you know." However, just as with Ray LaPierre, Maureen's comments lost their defensiveness as the group members, with the exception of Randy, who remained impassive, greeted her words with nods of encouragement.

By the time Carl Simmons of distribution started to speak, the mood in the room was approaching buoyant. Carl, a quiet and meticulous man, jumped from his seat and practically paced the room as he described his ideas. FireArt, he said, should play to its strength as a service-oriented company and restructure its trucking system to increase the speed of delivery. He described how a similar strategy had been adopted with excellent results at his last job at a ceramics plant. Carl had joined FireArt just six months earlier. It was when Carl began to describe those results in detail that Randy brought the meeting to an unpleasant halt by letting out a loud groan. "Let's just do *everything*, why don't we, including redesign the kitchen sink!" he cried with mock enthusiasm. That remark sent Carl back quickly to his seat, where he half-heartedly summed up his comments. A few minutes later, he excused himself, saying he had another meeting. Soon the others made excuses to leave, too, and the room became empty.

No wonder Eric was apprehensive about the fourth meeting. He was therefore surprised when he entered the room and found the whole group, save Randy, already assembled.

Ten minutes passed in awkward small talk, and looking from face to face, Eric could see his own frustration reflected. He also detected an edge of panic—just what he had hoped to avoid. He decided he had to raise the topic of Randy's attitude openly, but just as he started, Randy ambled into the room, smiling. "Sorry, folks," he said lightly, holding up a cup of coffee as if it were explanation enough for his tardiness.

"Randy, I'm glad you're here," Eric began, "because I think today we should begin by talking about the group itself . . ."

Randy cut Eric off with a small, sarcastic laugh. "Uh—I knew this was going to happen," he said.

Before Eric could answer, Ray LaPierre stood up and walked over to Randy, bending over to look him in the eye.

"You just don't care, do you?" he began, his voice so angry it startled everyone in the room.

Everyone except Randy. "Quite the contrary—I care very much," he answered breezily. "I just don't believe this is how change should be made. A brilliant idea never came out of a team. Brilliant ideas come from brilliant individuals, who then inspire others in the organization to implement them."

"That's a lot of bull," Ray shot back. "You just want all the credit for the success, and you don't want to share it with anyone."

"That's absurd," Randy laughed again. "I'm not trying to impress anyone here at FireArt. I don't need to. I want this company to succeed as much as you do, but I believe, and I believe passionately, that groups are useless. Consensus means mediocrity. I'm sorry, but it does."

"But you haven't even *tried* to reach consensus with us," Maureen interjected. "It's as if you don't care what we all have to say. We can't work alone for a solution—we need to understand each other. Don't you see that?"

The room was silent as Randy shrugged his shoulders noncommittally. He stared at the table, a blank expression on his face.

It was Eric who broke the silence. "Randy, this is a team. You are part of it," he said, trying to catch Randy's eye without success. "Perhaps we should start again . . ." Randy stopped him by holding up his cup, as if making a toast. "Okay, look, I'll behave from now on," he said. The words held promise, but he was smirking as he spoke them—something no one at the table missed. Eric took a deep breath before he answered; as much as he wanted and needed Randy Louderback's help, he was suddenly struck by the thought that perhaps Randy's personality and his past experiences simply made it impossible for him to participate in the delicate process of ego surrender that any kind of teamwork requires.

"Listen, everyone, I know this is a challenge," Eric began, but he was cut short by Randy's pencil-tapping on the table. A moment later, Ray LaPierre was standing again.

"Forget it. This is never going to work. It's just a waste of time for all of us," he said, more resigned than gruff. "We're all in this together, or there's no point." He headed for the door, and before Eric could stop him, two others were at his heels.

Questions

1. In what stage of development is FireArt's strategy team? What characteristics of the team point to this stage of development?
2. Do you believe Eric Holt is an effective team leader? Why or why not? What could he do to improve the effectiveness of the team?
3. What is the underlying attitude behind Randy Louderback's behaviour? Why may he be trying to undermine the success of the team?
4. Categorize the type of conflict this group is experiencing. (That is, is it related to a task or to personality?) How could the conflict be resolved? Do you think Eric can change the behaviour of group members?

Source: Suzy Wetlaufer, "The Team That Wasn't," *Harvard Business Review*, November–December 1994, pp. 22–26. Reprinted by permission.

Chapter 12 Communication and Negotiation

LEARNING OBJECTIVES

After reading this chapter, you should be able to:

1 Explain why communication is vital for effective management.
2 Describe the basic process of communication.
3 Explain how culture can influence communication.
4 Identify key barriers to effective communication.
5 Describe approaches to overcoming communication barriers.
6 Describe the basic process of negotiation.

A Communication Collision

It was a car lover's dream. Two brothers, Jack and John Goudy, left their desk jobs to open their own auto repair shop. At first, just the two brothers did brake jobs and replaced exhaust systems. Then, as business grew, they hired a few workers and moved to a larger shop. Within a decade, Two J's Auto Repair was cranking in sales of half a million dollars per year, but then those sales reached a plateau and gradually began to decline. So John, who was in charge of sales and accounting, searched for a new way to improve business. He found it by using technology. John began integrating cutting-edge technology into the shop operations. But he had to convince his workers, including Jack (who spent more time in the shop than in the office), that his strategy for rebuilding Two J's would be successful.

John convened a staff meeting to communicate his new strategy to the employees. Armed with graphs and charts, he talked about profit sharing, employee involvement, and state-of-the-art technology. "From today on, we're a completely different business," he predicted. He did not know how prophetic that statement would prove to be. John's audience did not share his enthusiasm; in fact, they did not understand his message at all because they had received no previous training in the areas of finance, human resources, or the use of technology. They didn't understand the vocabulary he used or the ideas he was presenting. "It was a sea of blank faces with an occasional mutter here and there," John recalls. Thus, the flow of miscommunication at Two J's began.

John purchased a new computer, which reduced the amount of paper communication generated by the office. But employees eventually discovered that the original estimates and the final invoices did not match each other, which caused them to believe that he was withholding work hours—and pay. He installed a closed-circuit TV in the shop so that, when customers phoned to inquire about the status of their repairs, he could glance quickly at the monitor and answer them. Unfortunately, shop workers believed that John had installed the TV as a surveillance tool to monitor them, and they resented what they perceived to be a lack of trust.

When Jack and John Goudy left their desk jobs to open their auto repair shop, it seemed like a car lover's dream. But poor communication between the two and their staff members turned the one-time dream into a nightmare. Fortunately, they realized their "failure to communicate" and were able to improve the situation.

Although John had provided his employees with an elaborate explanation of the profit-sharing plan (which they did not understand), they were skeptical of it because of mixed messages he sent: John often groaned about poor profits but would suddenly arrive at work driving a new sports car. Sensing declining morale, John started to hold daily "release meetings," designed to let employees voice their frustrations and concerns. But even these backfired. "John talked about working together like a football team," says one employee. But the meetings quickly dissolved into lectures. "John talked, we listened." Another employee observes, "It was clear John didn't care much about what we thought. He was too excited about his big ideas."

Jack, meanwhile, tried to serve as a go-between for John and the workers. "John wasn't working in the shop anymore," he explains. "Unfortunately, he dismissed their ideas when they offered suggestions." Eventually, even Jack and John could be heard fighting in the office. "They routinely got into yelling matches, one threatening to walk out on the other," says one veteran Two J's worker.

Finally, despite John's efforts to attract new customers and provide better, faster repairs through technology, workers began to leave the shop for jobs with other companies. At first, he did not understand what had gone so wrong; he had not realized how gruelling running his own business could be. He also knew that he was not a strong communicator. "Every day there were questions," he comments. "After a while, they just ground me down." When the company hit rock bottom, John started to get the message. He began to recognize the importance of communication—not only with customers, but also with his own workers—and proceeded to make small changes. "Now [when I attend staff meetings], I bring a yellow pad, scribble, and listen."

This chapter is about the importance of communication—whether it takes place via yellow pad or computer—throughout an organization.

Source: Elizabeth Conlin, "Company Profile: Collision Course," *Inc.* 14, no. 13 (December 1992), pp. 132–142.

strategic overview

Effective communication is crucial for managers in formulating a successful strategy and implementing it. Strategy formulation requires a substantial amount of communication. To identify a potentially successful strategy, managers must analyze their external environment, such as their competitors, their markets, industry forces, and government regulations. This first requires them to absorb and evaluate a large amount of information communicated to them before taking action based on it. Taking action to support the strategy then means communicating the relevant information to others in the organization, convincing them of your strategy, and explaining what they have to do to implement it.

In the opening case example, John's strategy for Two J's Auto Repair was to use technology to give customers better service by making faster repairs and providing them with more information about the repairs in progress. However, his strategy failed because of poor communication. First, he developed the strategy alone, which means he may not have gathered and evaluated enough information from his employees. Second, the implementation of the strategy was unsuccessful because he communicated it poorly, to them and his brother.

For example, Two J's employees did not understand the reason why the new technology was being implemented, and John didn't listen effectively to them. Besides needing better listening and receiving skills, it appeared there were interpersonal barriers between him and his employees that he needed to overcome before any new strategy could be successfully implemented. Without doing these three things—gathering adequate amounts of information, including information from his employees; properly listening and communicating his goals to them; and using good communication skills to foster better interpersonal relations, the strategy John designed for Two J's predictably failed.

communication the process of transferring information, meaning, and understanding from sender to receiver

Most of us take communication for granted because we do it every day. Communicating effectively, however, is not easy.[1] Accurate and persuasive communication within and between organizations, person to person, person to group, or group to group, is frequently, and sometimes unexpectedly, difficult, as the opening case example demonstrates. Receivers often do not have a complete understanding of what senders mean. But the heart of **communication** is exactly that: the process of transferring information, meaning, and understanding from sender to receiver. And carrying out that process convincingly and proficiently is absolutely essential for a manager to exercise leadership. In fact, leadership is unlikely to be successful in the absence of excellent communication skills. The first step for a manager to become an outstanding leader, therefore, is to become an outstanding communicator.

In this chapter, we start with an overview of the basic communication process, followed by an examination of the modes and media of communication. These topics provide a background for the next section on the organizational context of the communication process as it affects managers. Although the organization can facilitate managerial communication, it also can be one of the key barriers to communication—interpersonal, organizational, and cultural—which are discussed in the following section. This section in turn is followed by one that, appropriately, highlights some of the steps that managers can take to reduce or overcome these barriers.

The final parts of this chapter focus on one particular area of communication that is especially critical for managers—negotiation. In those sections, we discuss the impact of cultural influences on negotiation strategies and on the negotiation process itself. Throughout this chapter we need to keep in mind a basic perspective: Although communication is a universal human activity, successful communication is not habitual. It requires motivation, skill, and knowledge.

Basic Model of Communication

How do people communicate? How do they send and receive messages? What factors can disrupt communication? Let's look first at the basic model of the communication process (Exhibit 12.1).[2]

Exhibit 12.1
Basic Communication Model

All communication involves four actions and five components. The four actions are encoding, sending, receiving, and decoding. The five components are sender, message, medium, noise, and receiver. The actions and components combine to transfer meaning from the sender to the receiver. The sender originates the message by **encoding** it, that is, by constructing the message. The message is the content of the communication. The sender then transmits the message through a **medium**. A medium is the method or means of transmission, not the message itself. Examples of media are spoken words, video, written memos, faxes, and emails. The receiver acquires, or receives, the message by hearing it, reading it, or having it appear on a fax or computer. The receiver then begins **decoding** the message, that is, interpreting it. Sometimes distractions interfere with the message; these interferences are called **noise**. Noise contributes to misinterpretations of the original message, and it is only through feedback, or verification of the original message, that communication problems may be located and corrected.

encoding the act of constructing a message

medium the mode or form of transmission of a message

decoding the act of interpreting a message

noise potential interference with the transmission or decoding of a message

The basic model of communication is fundamental and universal; that is, it occurs whenever communication takes place, regardless of the culture or organization. However, while the basic acts and components of the communication process are the same everywhere, how the acts are carried out and the nature of the components are deeply influenced by cultural, organizational, and even personal contexts.[3] Who can send messages to whom, what kinds and what volumes of messages are sent, what medium is used to transmit messages, what sort of interference or noise is likely to occur, and what cues are available for decoding messages are just some of the many examples of the types of communication issues that can vary from manager to manager, from organization to organization, and from country to country.

Modes of Communication

Communication can occur in either a verbal mode or a nonverbal mode, as shown in Exhibit 12.2. Each mode has particular characteristics and issues that an effective manager must understand.

Verbal Communication

Most of us think of spoken words when we think of verbal communication. The key, however, is not that the words are spoken but that words—language—are

Exhibit 12.2 Modes of Communication

	VERBAL MODE (LANGUAGE USED TO CONVEY MEANING)		NONVERBAL MODE
	Oral	**Written**	
Examples	· Conversation · Speeches · Telephone calls · Video conferences	· Letters · Memos · Reports · Email · Fax	· Dress · Speech intonation · Gestures · Facial expressions
Advantages	· Vivid · Stimulating · Commands attention · Difficult to ignore · Flexible · Adaptive	· Decreased misinterpretation · Precise	· Effectiveness of communication increases with congruence to oral presentation · Can emphasize meaning
Disadvantages	· Transitory · Subject to misinterpretation	· Precision loss in translation · Inflexible · Easier to ignore	· Meanings of nonverbal communication not universal

used to convey meaning. Consequently, when we talk about verbal communication, we mean *both* oral and written communication.

Oral Communication The spoken word has the potential advantages of being vivid, stimulating, and of commanding attention. In most organizational situations, it is difficult for receivers—the listeners—to ignore either the speaker or the words spoken. Just think about the last time someone spoke to you directly. Even if you weren't interested in what the person had to say, wouldn't it have been difficult to simply ignore the person, turn, and walk away?

Also, oral communication is exceptionally flexible for both the sender and receiver. While you are speaking, you may try to make a point a certain way, but along the way change your words for the listener to understand you. Because oral communication is generally interactive, it can be quite responsive and adaptive to circumstances. However, this mode of communication has the major disadvantages of being transitory (unless recorded) and subject to considerable misinterpretation. Even when individuals use the same language, the subtle nuances of the spoken word may be missed or incorrect meaning may be attached to them. Oral communication between those whose first languages differ, as in many management situations today, simply multiplies the chances of intended meaning going awry.

Written Communication When messages are put in writing, as in letters, memos, email, and the like, the opportunity for misunderstanding the words of the sender are decreased. The receiver may still misinterpret the intended message, of course, but there is no uncertainty about exactly what words the sender has used. In that sense, written communication has precision. However, not everyone writes well, and so greater precision does not necessarily lead to greater understanding. This is further complicated when the words need translation from one language to another. For example, North Americans often write "at your earliest convenience" when requesting action, meaning that the request is somewhat urgent, but Europeans frequently interpret it to mean they can respond whenever they want. Because the writer/sender does not know immediately how well or poorly the message is getting across, written communication has the disadvantage of not being very flexible. In addition, it is often not as vivid or compelling as oral communication. Although you might find it difficult to ignore someone speaking to you, it would probably be much easier to ignore an email you received.

Nonverbal Communication

In direct interpersonal communication, nonverbal actions and behaviours often constitute significant messages. A whole range of actions, or lack of them, has the potential for communicating. Body language, posture, the way you dress, speak words, use gestures, handle utensils, exhibit facial expressions, and set the physical distance to the receiver are just some of the many forms of nonverbal communication.

As a manager, keep in mind that when verbal and nonverbal messages are contradictory, receivers often give more weight to the nonverbal signals than to the words used. For example, you may say to employees, "I have an open-door policy. Come and talk to me whenever you need to." However, if you never seem to be able to find the time to see them or rarely look up from your work when employees enter, they will soon come to believe the nonverbal message, "I'm busy," rather than the verbal message, "I encourage you to talk with me."

Of course, when nonverbal messages are consistent with the spoken message, the odds of effective communication taking place are increased. For example, suppose that in addition to saying you had an open-door policy you looked up when employees entered, made eye contact with them, smiled, and turned away from your computer and the report on which you were working. In combination, what sort of message do you think you would be sending?

The problem for managers in many of today's organizations where they work with employees from different cultural backgrounds and often work across international borders is that there are no universal meanings to the various nonverbal actions. For example, the traditional "OK" sign in North America is a gesture for money in Japan and is a rather rude gesture in Brazil. You might think that just toning down your nonverbal gestures would be a good way to avoid inadvertent wrong messages. Such an effort would be fine in Finland, but someone in Italy or Greece might infer from your subdued nonverbal cues that you are uninterested in the discussion. Because there is no simple answer, you should learn about the nonverbal cues and gestures of countries and cultures you deal with the most.

Media of Communication

The means of communication, or, in other words, *how* or by what methods information is transmitted from sender to receiver, are typically referred to as communication media (or, in the singular, medium). In organizations, there are basically a limited number of types of media that can be used. These range from the very personal and direct face-to-face interaction to the very impersonal and indirect posted notice or bulletin board that is frequently used in organizational settings. In between are telephone conversations, electronic messages, letters, memos, and reports.

It is obvious that these different media have different sets of characteristics, such as the following:

- Personal–impersonal nature
- Speed in sending and receiving
- Availability of multiple cues to assist receivers in acquiring accurate meaning from the messages
- Opportunity to receive immediate and continuing feedback from the receiver

media richness different media are classified as rich or lean based on their capacity to facilitate shared meaning

The term that has been used to summarize the nature of these characteristics of different media is called "**media richness**."[4] Different media are classified as rich or lean based on their "capacity to facilitate shared meaning."[5] (See Exhibit 12.3.) Thus, interpersonal, face-to-face interactions, for example, would be regarded as rich because they provide several types of information and multiple ways to obtain mutual understanding between sender and receiver, whereas a general email message sent to a number of receivers would be regarded as leaner because it lacks some of the features listed above. The general principle here is that the more ambiguous the message to be communicated and the more complex the issue, the richer the medium of communication should be.

Exhibit 12.3

Factors Contributing to Media Richness

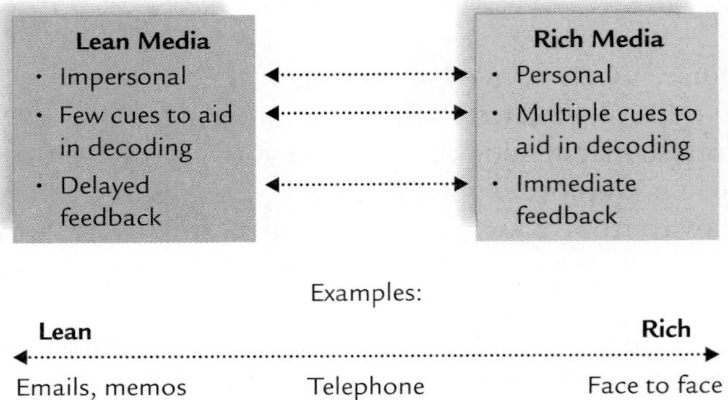

The concept of media richness has important implications for managers when they communicate. It serves to emphasize that different media have different capabilities for conveying meaning, and that managers therefore should be sensitive to matching message with medium. Using face-to-face meetings to convey simple, straightforward information, such as the time of a meeting next week, would be an unnecessary waste of a rich medium. That is, it would involve too much time and effort of both sender and receivers to obtain shared meaning of a relatively unambiguous message. On the other hand, using a memo, for example, rather than a face-to-face meeting, would probably be a poor choice for settling a serious disagreement with subordinates. The medium would be too lean to enable the manager to resolve a complicated, highly ambiguous matter.

Often, of course, time pressures and distance may make it relatively costly for a manager to use a richer rather than a leaner medium. That is why, in recent years, technological advances in such communication media as instant messaging (see *A Manager's Challenge: "Staying Connected through Instant Messaging and VoIP"*) or video conferencing often provide acceptable trade-offs between an ideally rich, face-to-face medium for resolving complex issues, on the one hand, and an ideally low-cost written memo (whether sent via email or otherwise), on the other hand.[6] The key point, if you are a

a manager's challenge — technology

Staying Connected through Instant Messaging and VoIP

A growing number of managers are using instant messaging (IM) and voice over internet protocol (VoIP) technology to stay in touch with colleagues and subordinates located in the same office or even thousands of miles away. With instant messaging, sales representatives who need immediate answers to clinch a deal simply bring up the IM software and send the boss a brief, to-the-point question that automatically appears in a box on his screen. In turn, the manager can type a quick response to suggest a particular strategy or approve a special discount. If personal discussion is required, the sales rep can go to the VoIP software to engage in a conversation from her computer—with or without a video image. No waiting for answers to email messages, no small talk—just instant communication to keep the business running smoothly and productively.

With IM and VoIP applications users can tell at a glance whether a particular person is online and available to receive a message. If necessary, they can type messages and exchange files or engage in a conference call with several people at one time, essentially convening online meetings. Clearly, IM and VoIP, with their live interaction and support for mobile employees, are helping companies keep their workforces connected at a fraction of the cost (in terms of both time and money) of conventional phone calls and letters.

Despite the benefits, not everyone is a fan of IM and VoIP communication. Why? Because, by and large, IM and VoIP initially came into the corporate world through the back door. Many employees downloaded free IM and VoIP software from sites such as Skype, Yahoo! and AOL onto company computers without permission from top managers, who tend to view it as a new tool for goofing off and chatting with one's friends. However, the new methods of communicating are becoming legitimized by firms such as Telus and Bell, who are offering VoIP business solutions across sectors such as finance, government, and education. Doctors and nurses at Toronto's Mount Sinai Hospital are now using a VoIP network to better serve their patients.

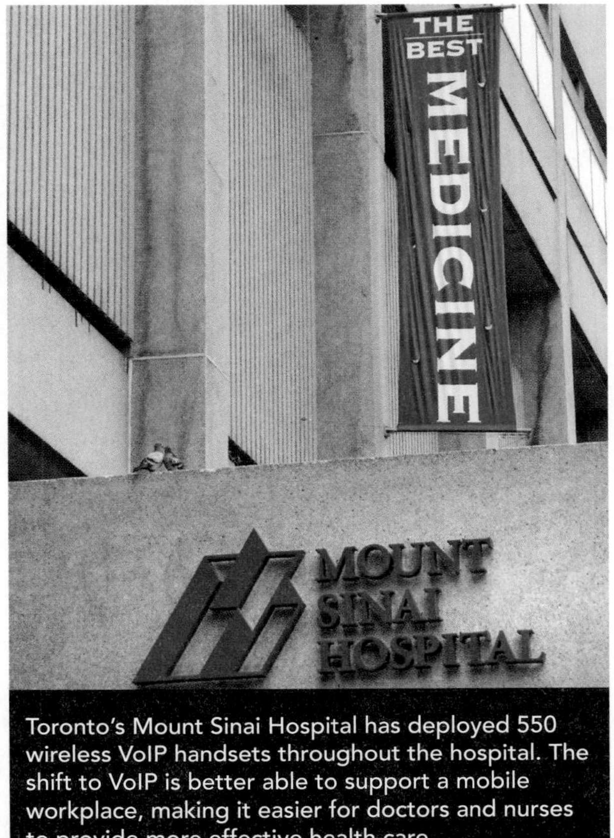

Toronto's Mount Sinai Hospital has deployed 550 wireless VoIP handsets throughout the hospital. The shift to VoIP is better able to support a mobile workplace, making it easier for doctors and nurses to provide more effective health care.

Even when IM and VoIP are used for legitimate managerial business purposes, some managers say they have difficulty staying focused on tasks like writing reports when messages suddenly appear on the computer screen. Others feel pressure to stay close to their computers, even late into the evening, in case colleagues in other time zones have questions or need decisions made. Moreover, free downloadable software creates security holes because the messages and files being shared never pass through a server. That means they can't be scanned for viruses, nor can they be monitored by management or archived.

Nonetheless, these new communications technologies are coming into their own in the business workplace as software developers devise industrial-strength versions with security and auditing features.

Sources: V. Ho, "VoIP Faces Challenges in Healthcare," *itworldcanada.com*, accessed May 28, 2007; "VoIP Right for Businesses of All Shapes and Sizes," *Globe and Mail*, April 13, 2005, p. B11; D. Robb, "Instant Messaging: A Portal to Online Threats?" *Government Procurement*, December 2003, pp. 10–13; M. Sarrell, "Corporate IM," *PC Magazine*, November 11, 2003, p. 132; Y. Bhattacharjee, "A Swarm of Little Notes," *Time*, September 16, 2002, pp. A4+; A. Stuart, "IM Is Here. RU Ready 2 Try It?" *Inc.*, July 1, 2002, pp. 76–81.

Air traffic controllers communicate with pilots of aircraft, providing instruction, information, and clearances during their flight. Controllers will also hand off aircraft from one area control centre (ACC) to another. Clear communication is imperative between the controllers and pilots to prevent accidents.

manager, is to choose a medium that best suits the degree of potential ambiguity in the message, consistent with the constraints of circumstances and the resources of you and your organization. The choice of an appropriate medium should not be left to chance.

The Organizational Context of Communication

Managers do not deal with communication in the abstract, but rather within an organizational context. The structure and processes of organizations powerfully shape the nature and effectiveness of communication that takes place within and between them.[7] Organizations, whether businesses, hospitals, or government agencies, have a set of defining characteristics, all of which affect communication in one way or another.[8] Thus, organizations

- are composed of individuals and groups;
- are oriented toward goals;
- have differentiated functions;
- have intended coordination; and
- have continuity through time.

Organizations of any size, regardless of country, are not simply a random set of individuals who by chance come together for a brief period with no purpose. The fact that they have goal orientations, structures, and coordination greatly influences the nature and amount of communication that takes place. This influence can be analyzed in terms of directions, channels, and patterns of communication.

Directions of Communication within Organizations

Because organizations of any degree of complexity have both differentiated functions and more than one level of positions with more or less responsibility, the directions of communication within them can be classified according to the level for which they are intended:

- **Downward communication** is sent from higher organizational levels to lower levels; for example, from the organization's top executives to its employees, or from supervisors to subordinates.
- **Upward communication** is sent from lower organizational levels to higher levels; for example, from nonmanagement employees to their supervisors, or from a manager to her boss.
- **Lateral communication** is sent across essentially equivalent levels of an organization; for example, from one clerical assistant to another, from the manager of Product A to the manager of Product B, or from the marketing department to the engineering design department.

downward communication messages sent from higher organizational levels to lower levels

upward communication messages sent from lower organizational levels to higher levels

lateral communication messages sent across essentially equivalent levels of an organization

The contents of communications within organizations usually vary according to the direction of the communication activity. As shown in Exhibit 12.4, downward communication typically involves such matters as goals, objectives, directions, decisions, and feedback. Upward communication commonly focuses on information, suggestions, questions, problems, and requests for clarification. Lateral communication is oriented toward exchanges of information—both formal and informal—that assist or affect coordination and joint problem solving.

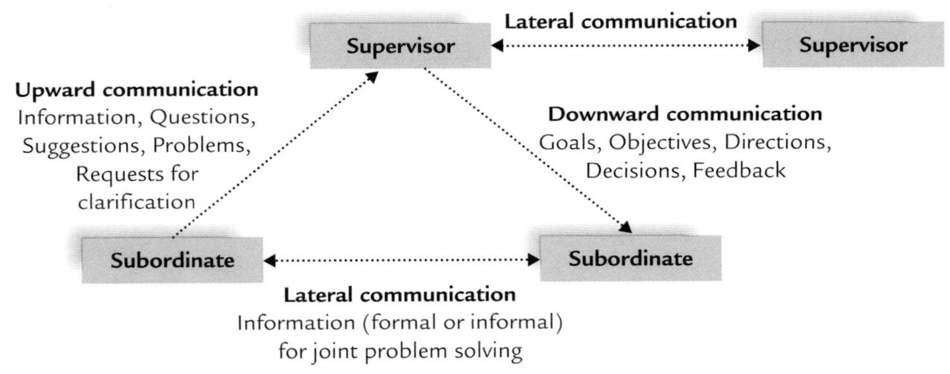

Exhibit 12.4
Directions of Communication within Organizations

While the subject matter of communication in a particular direction tends to be fairly similar in most medium-sized to large organizations, the culture of the organization (or the culture of the country in which the organization operates) can affect the process. For example, in an organization in which authority and hierarchy are stressed, upward communication might be more formal than in an organization with a more egalitarian culture. As a simple illustration, in a strongly hierarchical organization, a conversation might start with the subordinate addressing a superior several levels above as Mr. or Ms. Jones. In many countries, such as Korea, the conversation might start by addressing the superior by his or her title, such as Director Park. In organizations with less emphasis on hierarchy, the conversation might start by addressing the superior by his or her first name. Likewise, organizational or country culture can influence the frequency and flavour of upward communications. For example, in organizations with strong hierarchical values, upward communication tends to be less frequent.

In summary, organizational communications flow upward, downward, and laterally. The direction of the communication has a significant impact on the type of communication that is likely to take place. In addition, the culture of the organization and the region or country in which the organization is located can further determine the exact form that communication will have and even the frequency of each direction of communication.

Channels of Communication within Organizations

Organizational channels, or routes of communication, consist of two fundamental types: formal and informal. Both types are essential for organizational functioning, and neither type can easily substitute for the other.

formal communication channels routes that are authorized, planned, and regulated by the organization and that are directly connected to its official structure

Formal communication channels are those that are authorized, planned, and regulated by the organization and that are directly connected to its official structure. Thus, the organization's designated structure indicates the normal paths for downward, upward, and lateral formal communication. Formal communication channels (shown in Exhibit 12.5) are like highlighted roads on a road map. They specify organizational members who are responsible for tasks and communicating information to levels above and below them and back and forth to adjacent units. Also, formal channels indicate the persons or positions to whom work-related messages should be sent. Formal channels can be modified, and thus they have some flexibility, but they can seldom be disregarded.

Exhibit 12.5

Formal and Informal Channels of Communication in Organizations

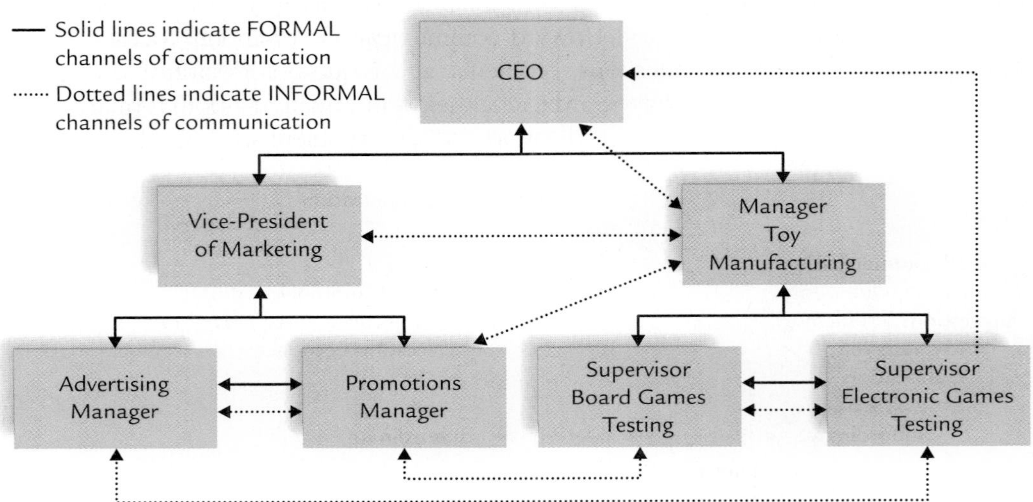

informal communication channels routes that are not pre-specified by the organization but that develop through typical and customary activities of people at work

Informal communication channels are communication routes that are not pre-specified by the organization but that develop through typical interpersonal activities of people at work. Channels can come into existence and change or disappear rapidly, depending on circumstances. However, they may also endure in many work situations, especially where individuals have been working together over a period of time. If a specific pattern becomes well-established, it would ordinarily be called a "network" (to be discussed later).

Several important features of informal communication channels should be noted:

- They tend to operate more often in the lateral than in the vertical direction compared to formal channels (see Exhibit 12.6) because they are not designated by the organization and its top officials.
- Information flowing through informal channels often moves extremely fast, mainly because senders are highly motivated to pass on information. The so-called "grapevine," a term applied to an informal network that supports the exchange of rumours or gossip between people, is a classic example of entrenched methods supporting rapid transmission of messages through informal channels.[9] In recent years, the communication capabilities of the internet have facilitated the emergence of large-scale, word-of-mouth networks. Some researchers propose that

these mechanisms are poised to have a significant impact on informal information flow in organizations.[10]

- Informal channels carry work-related as well as nonwork information. The fact that channels are informal does not mean that only gossip and other messages unrelated to jobs and tasks are carried by them. In fact, crucial work-related information is frequently communicated in this way. Of course, some of the messages passed through informal channels may contain inaccuracies or be negative, and thus are seen by some managers as a source of problems. However—and this is important to emphasize—few organizations could exist for very long if they had to rely only on formal communication channels!

Exhibit 12.6 Characteristics of Formal and Informal Communication Channels

Formal Communication Channels	Informal Communication Channels
· Authorized, planned, and regulated by the organization · Reflect the organization's formal structure · Define who has responsibility for information dissemination and indicate the proper recipients of work-related information · May be modified by the organization · Minor to severe consequences for ignoring them	· Develop through interpersonal activities of organization members · Not specified by the organization · May be short lived or long lasting · Are more often lateral than vertical · Information flow can be very fast · Used for both work-related and nonwork information

Patterns of Organizational Communication

Identifiable patterns of communication that occur with some regularity within and between organizations, whether using formal or informal channels, are typically called **communication networks**. Put another way, communication networks are stable systems of interconnections. Thus, networks involve consistent linkages between particular sets of senders and receivers. For example, as shown in Exhibit 12.7, a middle-level divisional marketing manager in Calgary might have a particular network that involves her boss in Montreal, three key managers in other departments in the Montreal headquarters, her seven subordinates located in major western cities, and two outside vendors of market research data. Another network for the same manager might involve two lower-level managers in other units in the Calgary office and her former colleague and old friend who is now a sales supervisor in Winnipeg and who has access to inside information on how well new marketing approaches are working in that region.

communication networks identifiable patterns of communication within and between organizations, whether using formal or informal channels

An example of a larger, more organization-wide network would be McCain Foods's worldwide pattern of communication relationships between its headquarters in Florenceville, New Brunswick, and its production plants. Of course, networks can also be formed across organizations as well as within. This is what often happens when sets of managers from two companies, such as BASF South East Asia and Shell Eastern Petroleum Ltd., for example, have to work together on issues that arise in an international joint venture, in this case the Ellba Eastern plant on Jurong Island, Singapore.[11] A particular challenge in

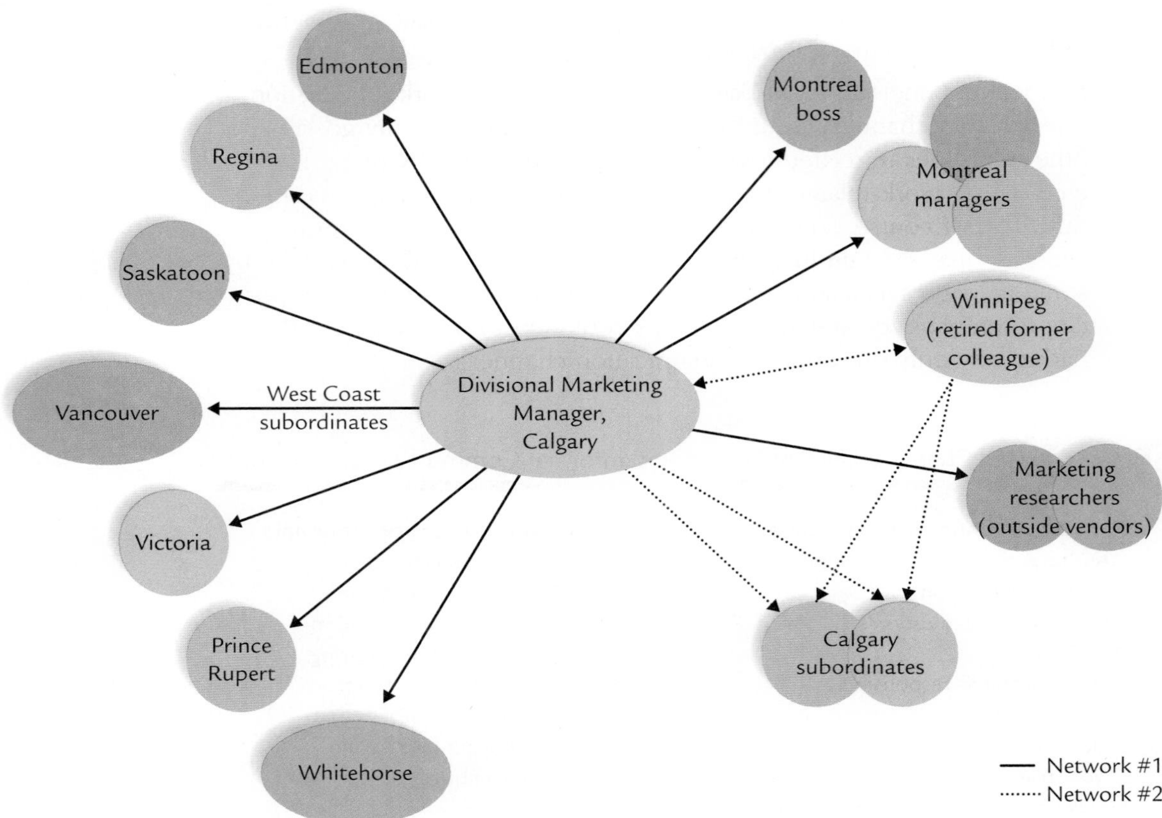

Exhibit 12.7

Examples of Two Organizational Communication Networks

building an effective network for a project that was to last for a number of months and which involved a number of participants from different organizations is illustrated in *A Manager's Challenge, "Communication Is Secret Weapon for Change."* The challenge here was to change the way communication had been carried out in the past—and thus to develop more effective networking processes—on this type of large, complex project that has many sources of senders and receivers.

The importance of communication networks to managers is that they can provide significant and regular sources of information, both of the formal and informal type, that might otherwise take a much longer time to obtain if the various links had to be set up from scratch each time some new topic or problem came up. Also, when managers are members of established networks, it can make it easier for them to influence the other people or groups involved in the networks. Consequently, for both of these reasons, managers need to pay particular attention to what networks they can and want to be a part of, and to the composition of those networks. It is no accident that the term **networking** has come to signify a process that has the potential for gaining advantages for a manager (or anyone for that matter) by having one or more sets of individuals or groups with which one can interact easily and regularly, and with whom one can communicate a sense of confidence and trust.

networking a process of developing regular patterns of communication with particular individuals or groups to send and receive information

In traditional Western organizations, it has always been relatively easy for males in management positions to establish various networks with other males (thus providing the basis for the phrase "old boys' network"). However, at least until very recently, it has been much harder for women and members of underrepresented ethnic groups to establish similar helpful networks in their organizations. Research suggests, in fact, that organizational networks involving individuals from these groups are different in terms of both composition and relationships

a manager's challenge | change

Communication Is Secret Weapon for Change

Imagine the complications of managing communication among the workforces of several competitors who must work on the same government project. Increasingly, after intensive bidding battles to win contracts for complex systems of equipment, managers at major manufacturing firms must face this situation when they have to collaborate with the very competitors they have just outbid.

Consider what happened when BAE Systems, one of Europe's largest aerospace and defence companies, won a multimillion-dollar contract. As a condition of being designated the prime contractor by the UK Ministry of Defence to design a very large and sophisticated new product, BAE was required to work with a number of companies to finish on schedule and within budget. "With products as complex as [this one], the days of single-source suppliers are over," and "we had to become more collaborative," said Ian Haddleton, BAE's integrated systems solutions manager. As many as 1000 people from BAE and other firms were going to participate in the months-long redesign project. Therefore, in preparation, management decided to foster closer collaboration by making major changes in the company's approach to communication in carrying out such a complicated endeavour.

To start, BAE managers "agreed on a set of values with our customer that is now the guideline and principle for anyone working on the project," Haddleton explained. Based on these values, all project participants would be able to determine what information was important and with whom it should be shared. As an example, employees of BAE and other collaborating companies agreed to air concerns early in the project so they could be adequately analyzed and addressed before key design decisions were locked in place.

Next, BAE managers set up a web-based data exchange system to support collaborative communication among the hundreds of project participants. "With a project of this size and the number of companies involved, it's always difficult to know who is responsible for what, and whom to ask when needing advice or information," Haddleton noted. The data exchange system stored the latest information about each participant's role and responsibility. It also allowed participants to upload project-related data (such as proposed design specifications) so that others could post comments, questions, and suggested changes for all to review. And because the system was web-based, BAE could control access and not have to ask other companies to replace their proprietary communications systems.

Changing their approach to communication helped BAE's managers become more effective in keeping the product's design on course month after month. "Now, more than ever before, it's much easier for us to function as an extended team," summarized Haddleton. "The way we work today is certainly an improvement over the way things used to be done."

Sources: S. Windsor-Lewis, "Communicating to Avert Industrial Action at BAE Systems," *Strategic Communication Management*, December 2003–January 2004, pp. 18–22; "Product Development's Secret Weapon: Communication," *Design News*, June 17, 2002, pp. S1+; "BAE Systems Strengthens AMS after MBDA Missile Merger," *Defense Daily*, May 1, 2001; F. Tusa, "The Rise of European EW," *Journal of Electronic Defense*, June 2001, pp. 54+.

from the old Western networks that were composed primarily of Caucasian males.[12] It does not make such networks any less important or useful to managers from these groups, but it does serve to emphasize that network patterns of communication in organizations can vary based on a number of different situational circumstances, including the age, gender, and ethnicity of the individuals involved.

Barriers to Communication

Although the organizational context provides numerous opportunities for effective and productive communication, it likewise can present many barriers that interfere with the communication process. Such barriers can arise from several different sources, including interpersonal, organizational, and cultural (see Exhibit 12.8).

Exhibit 12.8 Barriers to Communication

Level	Origin of Barrier	Affects Communication Between:
Interpersonal	· Selective perception · Frame of reference · Individual differences · Emotion · Language · Nonverbal cues	· Individuals or groups
Organizational	· Hierarchical (barriers resulting from formal structure) · Functional (barriers resulting from differences between functional departments)	· Individuals and/or groups within an organization · Individuals and/or groups in different organizations
Cultural	· Language · High/low-context culture · Stereotyping · Ethnocentrism · Cultural distance	· Individuals or groups in different organizations with different national cultures · Individuals or groups from different organizational cultures · Individuals or groups from diverse cultural backgrounds within an organization

Interpersonal Barriers

Obstacles to interpersonal communication can occur with either the sender or the receiver. The burden is simultaneously on both the sender and the receiver to ensure accurate communication. It is, however, the sender's obligation to choose the language and words—that is, to encode the message—carefully to carry the greatest precision of meaning. Precision is especially important if the sender is trying to persuade the receiver to do something in a language or communication style different from what the receiver prefers. For example, if you are trying to convince your boss to authorize a new project and you use an informal style and choice of words, your boss may not be receptive if she prefers a more formal approach. You will probably need to adjust your style for the communication to be effective.

selective perception the process of screening out some parts of an intended message because they contradict our beliefs or desires

frames of reference existing sets of attitudes that provide quick ways of interpreting complex messages

The receiver, of course, is often the source of communication breakdowns. For example, the receiver might have a **selective perception** problem.[13] That is, the receiver may unintentionally screen out some parts of the intended message because they contradict his beliefs or desires. For example, you might stress the increased productivity that would result from a proposed project, but your boss is focusing on the estimated cost of the project. Although selective perception is a natural human tendency, it hinders accurate communication, especially when sensitive or highly important topics are being discussed. Another way to state this point is that individuals tend to adopt **frames of reference**, or simplified ways of interpreting messages, that help them make sense of complex communications. These shortcuts, however, may prevent the intended message from being received.[14]

Selective Perception by Lyman Porter
mymanagementlab

Individual differences between senders and receivers in terms of such basic characteristics as their age, gender, ethnicity, or level of education sometimes can be the source of communication barriers. In general, it would be reasonable to assume that the fewer the differences between the two parties on these kinds of attributes, the lower the communication barriers. Even where these kinds of differences exist, however, such as a difference in gender between sender and receiver, the research evidence tends not to find consistently serious impediments to effective communication related to that characteristic.[15] It is more a matter of a manager being very alert to the *possibility* that individual differences in sender and receiver characteristics could impose a significant obstacle to good communication in a specific instance, rather than assuming it will never be a barrier or, conversely, will always be a barrier.

Emotions can be another barrier.[16] How the receiver feels at the time can influence what gets heard or how it gets interpreted. You certainly have had the experience of feeling that someone was "touchy" or overly sensitive when responding to your message. As a consequence, comments that normally would be taken as mere statements get interpreted as criticisms.

Language can also be a barrier. Even for people who speak the same language, a given word or set of words can mean different things to different people.[17] For example, the word "cool" has been applied not only to denote something that is cold, but for large sums of money, someone who is calm, or something that is fashionable.

Nonverbal cues can also be barriers to effective communication in two basic ways. First, people can send nonverbal signals without being aware of them, and therefore create unintentional consequences.[18] For example, you might make minimal eye contact with your boss while trying to convince her to approve your proposed project, and yet be unaware that you are doing so. Your boss might think the project has merit but interprets your low level of eye contact as an indication that you are hiding something. Your boss could then reject a project that she might otherwise have authorized. Second, as we have already touched on, nonverbal cues can mean different things to different people.[19] A weak handshake might indicate politeness in Indonesia but communicate lack of confidence in Alberta.

Organizational Barriers

Just as interpersonal barriers can limit communication, so can organizational barriers. Such barriers can interfere with communication between individuals or groups within the same organization, between individuals or groups from two different organizations, or between entire organizations. The basis of these barriers lies within the hierarchical structure of organizations. All organizations of any complexity have specialized functions and more than one level of authority. This specialization creates a situation that is ripe for communication difficulties. For example, one person might come from marketing and the other from research and development. The person in marketing might think nothing of exaggerating while the person from research and development always understates her points. Consequently, the marketer might see the R&D scientist as unimaginative and boring, while the scientist might view the marketer as superficial and careless. In addition, the two parties might come from different levels in the organization. The differences between responsibility and level of authority could cause a senior executive to expect an explanation of the broad impacts of a proposed project on the entire organization, and a junior technical expert to focus on the detailed schedule of the project.

Cultural Barriers

Communication and culture are tightly intertwined. Culture cannot exist without communication, and human communication only occurs within a cultural context. Since the act of communicating is so closely connected to the surrounding environment, culture can ease or hinder it. Thus, similarity in cultures between senders and receivers facilitates successful communication—the intended meaning has a higher probability of getting transferred. Differences in culture hinder the process. The greater the cultural differences between sender and receiver, the greater the expected difficulty in communicating. Therefore, other things being equal, it should be easier, for example, for a Canadian manager to communicate with an Australian subordinate than with a Greek subordinate.

Organizational cultures can also differ. The industry of an organization, for example, can influence its internal culture, as we pointed out in Chapter 4. Therefore, it is more likely that an executive at CanWest Global could communicate successfully with an executive at CBC than with an executive at Imperial Oil. It is not that extreme cultural differences prevent good communication; rather, the possibilities for breakdowns in communication increase in proportion to the degree of differences in the background and customs of the two parties.

The extent to which a sender and receiver differ in a high-context or low-context communication style also significantly influences the effectiveness of the communication. As we discussed in Chapter 4, individuals in high-context cultures tend to pay great attention to the situational factors surrounding the communication process and as a consequence substantially alter what they say and how they say it based on the context.[20] (See Exhibit 12.9.) Individuals in low-context cultures tend to pay less attention to the context and so make fewer and smaller adjustments from situation to situation.[21] Although the greatest differences in high- and low-context cultures occur across countries, there are also such differences across organizations. For example, Japan is a high-context culture that has three distinct levels of language that a

Exhibit 12.9

Communication Differences in High-and Low-Context Cultures

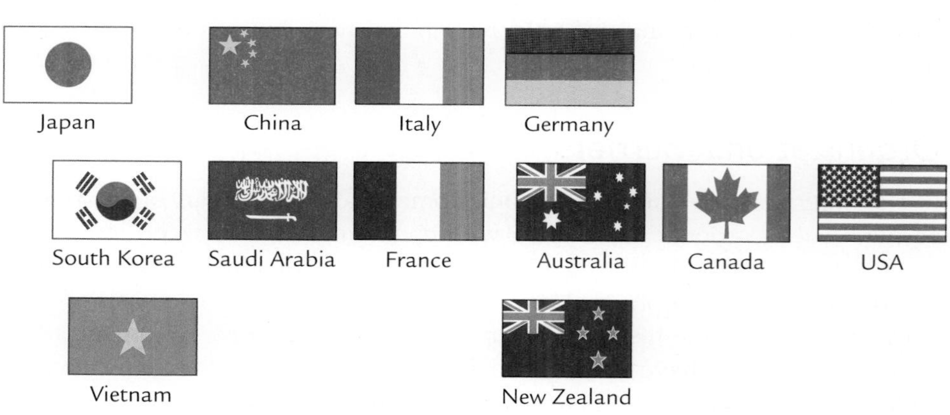

High-Context Cultures

- More and greater adjustments in messages
- Rank of receiver will probably affect message and medium
- Nonverbal communication cues may be very important
- Medium may be as important as message

Low-Context Cultures

- Fewer and smaller adjustments in messages
- Rank of receiver may or may not affect message or medium
- Nonverbal communication cues not as important
- Message is more important than medium

Source: www.crwflags.com/fotw/flags.

speaker uses, depending on his or her status compared with that of the listener. Thus, there are actually five different words for "you" that are used, depending on relative rank and status. However, even within Japan, communication is much more high context at Mitsubishi Heavy Industries than at Nintendo.

What is most problematic when individuals from high- and low-context cultures communicate is that each often forms negative interpretations about the other's communication approach. Individuals from low-context cultures tend to interpret the wide swings in words and style indicative of people from high-context cultures as evidence of insincerity, hypocrisy, and even instability. These interpretations make trust difficult and at the extreme can make effective communication impossible. On the other hand, individuals from high-context cultures view the lack of change in communication style of individuals from low-context cultures as evidence of immaturity, selfishness, or lack of sophistication.

In Japanese culture, managers are taught that to communicate effectively, you should "say what you mean, and mean what you say."[22] Vague directives and instructions are seen as a sign of poor communication skills. The assumption, therefore, is that the burden of proof for effective communication is on the speaker. In contrast, in cultures such as those in Arabic countries and in Latin America, the assumption is that both the speaker and the listener share the burden for communicating effectively. In cultures like these, chances of unpleasant encounters and direct confrontations and disagreements tend to decrease.

Probably the greatest single cultural barrier that can affect communication across different departmental, organizational, regional, or national cultures is ethnocentrism.[23] **Ethnocentrism** is the belief in the superiority of one's own group and the related tendency to view others in terms of the values of one's own group. Ethnocentrism leads individuals to divide their interpersonal worlds into in-groups and out-groups. As we discussed in Chapter 11, in-groups are groups of people with whom you identify and about whom you care.[24] Members of the in-group tend to be trusted, listened to, and have information shared with them. Members of out-groups tend to be viewed with skepticism, if not suspicion, and are not given full information. This type of behaviour exists in organizations as well as in interpersonal interactions. When British European Airways merged with British Overseas Airways Corporation some years ago to form British Airways, the ethnocentric orientation of each side almost led to the bankruptcy of the merged unit, which lost nearly US$1 billion before the communication barriers were overcome.

ethnocentrism the belief in the superiority and importance of one's own group

Ethnocentrism by Lyman Porter

PEARSON mymanagementlab

Another cross-cultural barrier to communication closely related to ethnocentrism is **stereotyping**, the tendency to oversimplify and generalize about groups of people. The more firmly held the stereotype by a communicator, the harder it is to overcome preconceived expectations and focus on the specifics of the message that is being sent or received. Stereotyping occurs both within and between cultures and thus it affects communication in virtually all organizational settings. For example, suppose you are a technical service manager in a software company and the president has a definite stereotype of people in your position. Generally, the president sees technical service managers as focused on details and unable to see the big picture. With a strong stereotype of this sort, the president may not recognize that you understand and are considering the competitive implications (not just the technical ones) of a new software tool.

stereotyping the tendency to oversimplify and generalize about groups of people

Cross-cultural communication problems can stem from language differences, but more subtle problems occur because of cultural differences and biases such as *stereotyping* (the tendency to oversimplify and generalize about groups of people) and *ethnocentrism* (the belief that one's own culture or group is superior).

cultural distance the overall difference between two cultures' basic characteristics such as language, level of economic development, and traditions and customs

Another major cultural barrier to communication can be labelled **cultural distance**.[25] This concept refers to the overall difference between two cultures' basic characteristics such as language, level of economic development, and entrenched traditions and customs. Cultural distance was illustrated by a study that gathered 21 senior executives from major corporations in Japan, the United States, Brazil, the United Kingdom, and India for a five-week period of cultural explorations. The executives attended lectures and seminars, built rafts and climbed cliffs together, and even travelled in fact-finding teams to the countries represented. Nevertheless, observers reported that communication remained a problem the entire five weeks.[26] Although much of the difficulty came from obvious language differences, a more subtle difficulty came from cultural differences. Many of the Japanese managers, attempting to fit in, adopted American nicknames, but they actually hated being called by them. The Americans couldn't understand why the Japanese were so quiet, not realizing that they felt that it was unwise to speak first at a meeting. The more senior the Japanese executive, the more he listens, and the executives on this trip were quite senior. Similarly, a development project undertaken by Alcan Aluminum of Canada and the National Nonferrous Corporation of China brought together managers from both firms to learn more about each other's culture. Even though a set of managers from China spent a whole year in Canada studying North American business methods, effective communication remained an elusive goal throughout the period for both sides.[27] Such examples emphasize that the degree of cultural distance between organizational employees from different nationalities represents a potentially very difficult communication barrier to overcome. The severity of the problem should not be underestimated.

Improving Communication

The various barriers discussed in the preceding section can interfere with effective communication, but there are ways to deal with—or overcome—them and improve your communication capabilities. How important is it for you to have a commitment to developing good communication skills? Consider this: "In the *Wall Street Journal*/Harris Interactive survey, recruiters rated [business] school graduates on a variety of attributes—and then rated the attributes in terms of how important they are in a job candidate. Topping the list of 24 attributes are communication and interpersonal skills."[28] As the *Wall Street Journal* article went on to say: "Interpersonal communication . . . skills are what corporate recruiters crave most but find most elusive in MBA graduates."

Given the obvious importance of this topic, in the remainder of this section we discuss some of the most essential approaches that are necessary for you to consider in improving your communication abilities as a manager in organizations.

Improving Listening Skills

When the subject is improving communication skills, most people first think of improving their speaking or writing skills. However, contrary to popular belief, probably the single best thing you can do to enhance your communication skills is to focus on improving your receiving rather than sending skills.

Be More Open-Minded Stereotyping, ethnocentricity, rigid frames of reference, and selective listening can all become barriers to comprehending the intended message of a sender, so one of the first things to do to enhance listening skills is to spend time developing a greater awareness of your personal tendencies in the direction of any of these problems. Once you have a better awareness of these tendencies, you can monitor and control them during conversations. Part of the reason for direct and conscious attention to this area is that most people speak at about 120 words per minute and yet can listen at a rate of about 1000 words per minute.[29] This creates the opportunity for our minds to wander or make judgments about what we are hearing. These tendencies can distort what is heard and how it is interpreted.

Develop Empathy Once personal tendencies have been examined, the next step is to develop empathy. **Empathy** is identifying with and understanding the other person's feelings, situation, and motives. To some extent, this requires thinking about the situation of other people. What are their feelings relative to the topic at hand? What are their motivations? Why are they talking about this particular subject? These and other questions can help you enhance your understanding of the personal context of the message being sent.

empathy the ability to put yourself in someone else's place and to understand his or her feelings, situation, and motives

Listen Actively The next step to improving communication is to take actions to ensure that you—the receiver—hear and understand what the sender is trying to communicate. In conversations, making eye contact is a good way to help speakers feel comfortable and convinced that you are sincerely interested in understanding what they have to say. It is important to focus on the content of the message being sent regardless of the style of its delivery. Even if people are not choosing the best words or are making grammatical errors, they may have something quite valuable to communicate. Focusing on style over substance can cause the value of the message to be missed. To make sure you understand what is being said, ask clarifying questions. Also, even when you think you have understood the message, it is a good idea to paraphrase, that is, restate what you think the message is. This can be put in the form of a question or statement. For example, you could ask, "So are you saying that . . . ?" Or you could say something like, "What I understand you to be saying is. . . ."

Observe Nonverbal Cues As we discussed earlier in this chapter, nonverbal cues are critical to effective communication.[30] Listening more open-mindedly and actively to the words is only part of the task. You also need to concentrate on observing nonverbal cues. In cross-cultural settings, this means that you need to remember that a nonverbal cue or gesture can have different meanings in different cultures. There is little substitute for learning about the nonverbal cues and gestures of the culture of those with whom you will be interacting.

Improving Sending Skills

There are many situations in which you will be the sender of a message. Effective communication can be enhanced by developing better sending skills.

Simplify Your Language One of the first things a sender can do to enhance communication is to simplify the language in the message. Clearly, what is simple will vary, depending on the audience. Simplifying may involve eliminating jargon that might not be familiar to all members of the audience. It may also involve choosing more succinct and active words and shorter sentences. Perhaps the best clue for spotting complicated and passive language is excessive use of prepositions. The more prepositions in a sentence, the higher the likelihood that the language could be simplified and the message could be stated more directly.

Organize Your Writing Executives consistently complain about the poor writing skills of new managers.[31] Their complaints lie not in spelling or grammar mistakes, though clearly these should be eliminated, but in the lack of logical thought processes. As a manager, you are likely to write more reports and memos than you may want, and the effectiveness of those written communications will have an important impact on your career. Consequently, developing good writing skills is vital to being an effective manager. Nothing substitutes for practice.

Understand Your Audience Perhaps the single best thing a sender can do to enhance the effectiveness of communications is to understand the audience.[32] For example, consider the following questions, which come from the material we have covered thus far in this chapter:

- What is the direction of the communication (up, lateral, or down), and does the receiver have any expectations concerning this type of communication?
- Is the communication formal or informal, and how should it be structured to have the intended impact on the receiver?
- Are there expectations from the receiver about the explicitness or implicitness of the message you want to send?
- Does the receiver have any biases for or against certain modes of communication (e.g., for or against email, face-to-face conversations, and so on)?

If you do not understand the person or persons to whom you are sending a message, it is almost impossible to answer these questions. Knowing your audience (i.e., the receiver or receivers) is critical to improving your sending skills. Knowledge of the audience is particularly important in cross-cultural settings. Exhibit 12.10 lists some ways to improve cross-cultural communication.

Organization-Level Improvements in Communication

Organizations can take steps to change their policies and methods for how and when managers should communicate. Unfortunately, guidelines for this more structural approach are not as well developed as those for individual managers.

Exhibit 12.10 Tips on Being a More Effective Cross-Cultural Communicator

1. Study general principles that apply to all types of intercultural communication.
2. Learn about the fundamental characteristics of the other cultures with which you will be working.
3. For high-context cultures, learn as many details in advance about the target organization(s) and their specific individual representatives.
4. For high-context cultures, use at least a few words or phrases in the listener's language.
5. For high-context cultures, be especially careful about body language and tone of voice.
6. For low-context cultures, organize written communications so that the major points are immediately and directly stated.
7. Study and respect communicators' preferences for greater degrees of formality, especially compared with the typical North American approach of casual informality.

A study of research and development laboratories within 14 large multinational firms, however, provides some suggestions.[33] The study produced strong evidence for the importance of **gatekeepers**, or so-called "boundary-spanning" individuals who are at the communication interface between separate organizations or between units within an organization. Large companies especially need to be able to structure the activities of gatekeepers to maximize their usefulness to the communication process and to make sure that the most critical information is both sent and received. Findings from the study indicated that communication could be improved by implementing rules and procedures that increased formal communication, replacing some face-to-face communication with electronic communication, developing particular communication networks, and even creating a centralized office to manage communication activities.

gatekeepers individuals who are at the communication interface between separate organizations or between different units within an organization

Communication and Negotiation

In the last sections of this chapter, we focus on one particular type of communication that is especially crucial for a manager—negotiation. **Negotiation** can be thought of as the process of conferring to arrive at an agreement between two or more parties, each with their own interests and preferences. The purpose of negotiation is to see whether the parties can arrive at an agreement that serves their mutual interests. Since reaching an agreement inherently involves communication, negotiation and communication are inseparably linked. Thus, the negotiation process can be considered a special part of the general communication process.

negotiation the process of conferring to arrive at an agreement between different parties, each with their own interests and preferences

The Importance of Negotiation to Managers

Today's managers often find themselves in the role of negotiator. This can occur in different types of situations. One type is during the ongoing, day-to-day activities of the manager's organizational unit, where there is a need to negotiate a settlement or resolution of some kind of disagreement. This could be a disagreement between the manager and his own boss, between the manager and another manager from a different unit, or between the manager and one or more of his subordinates. Disagreements could also occur between subordinates or between entire departments. Typically, in these kinds of circumstances, the manager would function as an individual negotiator.

The other basic type of negotiation situation in which managers could find themselves would be where they are part of a formally appointed negotiating team representing their unit or organization in discussions with representatives from another unit or organization. In either kind of negotiating situation, managers are taking on the role of facilitator—attempting to ensure that all parties can agree on a common course of action. Also, regardless of the specific features of the situation, the principles of effective approaches to negotiation can help settle any kind of disagreement a manager might encounter—inside or outside an organization.

Achieving More Effective Negotiations

Managers have available several potentially helpful approaches to increasing their chances of achieving successful negotiation outcomes (see Exhibit 12.11). One especially useful principle to keep in mind when serving as a negotiator is to focus on the parties' *interests*, not their positions.[34] Each side to a dispute has interests, whether or not they enter into negotiations with fixed positions. **Interests** are a party's concerns and desires—what they want, in other words. **Positions**, on the other hand, are a party's stance regarding those interests. An example of an interest would be the desire by a subordinate to receive a specific challenging new assignment. A position in this example would be a statement by the subordinate that "I am the one who should receive this new sales territory because. . . ." It is easier to get agreement on interests than on positions because (1) for a given interest there are probably several possible positions that could satisfy it, and (2) behind two opposed positions there are likely to be at least some interests that are shared rather than in direct conflict.[35] Thus, if such mutually compatible interests can be identified, the chances of reaching an acceptable conclusion to the negotiations are increased. In the example above, even though the boss is not able to give the desired new sales territory to this particular subordinate, a common interest may be identified—such as the desire of both parties to see that the subordinate's good performance in the past is rewarded with some other kind of challenging new assignment in the future—even though it can't be this particular assignment now.

interests in negotiation, a party's concerns and desires—in other words, what they want

positions in negotiation, a party's stance regarding their interests

Exhibit 12.11

Improving Effectiveness of Negotiations

Less effective	More effective
• Positions	• Interests
• People Involved	• Problem/Issue
• Maintaining/Increasing Competition (Win/Lose Focus)	• Decreasing/Lessening Competition (Collaborative Focus)

A second sound principle for negotiations (again, see Exhibit 12.11) is to focus on the problem or issue rather than on the people involved, as we discussed in the section on conflict in Chapter 11. The key point here is that a negotiator should endeavour to concentrate on the substance of the disagreement rather than on who is doing the disagreeing or what they are like as people. This principle is well summarized in the advice to negotiators to "be hard on the problem, soft on the people."[36]

Another helpful principle for managers who are involved in negotiations is to try to lessen the competition between the two parties (an "I win, you lose" situation) by establishing an atmosphere of collaboration (a "we all win" situation). **Collaboration** is an attempt to get both parties to attack a problem and solve it together, rather than have one party defeat the other, as in a

collaboration a part of negotiation in which parties work together to attack and solve a problem

win–lose athletic contest. Thus, both parties should be encouraged to develop creative solutions that increase the total amount of resources available to be shared or divided by the two parties.

Finally, if managers find that negotiations are extremely complex and the parties seem emotionally invested in the outcome, they can often request intervention by a neutral third party. Sometimes disinterested managers within the organization may be asked to serve in this role. The third-party negotiator can serve the role of judge, mediator, or devil's advocate. In the role of a judge, the manager handles negotiations and decides on the best possible course of action, which the parties then agree to follow. In mediation, the manager controls the negotiation process, but someone else makes the final decision based on the arguments presented—possibly a senior executive in the organization. As we have discussed in other chapters, a devil's advocate asks questions that may oppose the positions of both parties. The attempt here is for all parties to think about positions that they may not originally have considered.

Key Factors in Cross-National Negotiations

As noted earlier, as a manager you may find yourself a member of negotiating teams. With the greater frequency of international assignments, this may particularly be the case when working in situations that require negotiations across national borders. Because of the advances in transportation and communication technologies, along with expanding capital flows worldwide, organizations are engaging in ever-larger amounts of foreign trade and international business partnerships. Together, all of this activity increases the importance of your being able to negotiate successfully in cross-national circumstances as well as in your own organization or country.

Analysis has shown that there are three principal variables that determine the outcome of negotiations in general, and especially in these kinds of cross-national situations: (1) the people involved, (2) the situation, and (3) the process itself.[37] Research from an array of internationally oriented studies also indicates that each of these variables is strongly influenced by cultural differences.[38]

People Although there are some cultural differences in preferred negotiator characteristics, there seem to be some traits and abilities that are fairly universal for the task of negotiation. They include good listening skills, strong orientation toward people, and high self-esteem, among others.[39] In addition, an ability to be influential in the home organization appears to be a commonly preferred personal attribute.

Research has also found that negotiators will modify or adapt their behaviour when working in cross-cultural negotiations. However, there were differences found in the extent that negotiators will adjust their approach to accommodate individuals from another country. American negotiators were found to be the most tenacious in their behaviour across cultures, making minimal adjustments, while Japanese negotiators were found to be more accommodating, tending to make more adjustments. The same study also compared intracultural negotiations (negotiations with differing cultural groups within a country) between anglophone and francophone Canadians. The study found that francophone Canadians were much more accommodating with anglophone Canadians than with cross-cultural negotiators (negotiations with differing cultural groups outside of Canada), and anglophone negotiators enjoyed more joint profits across teams when negotiating with francophones than with cross-cultural negotiators.[40]

Situations of Negotiations The second major variable affecting negotiation outcomes is the set of situational circumstances. Probably the most important are the location of the negotiations, the physical arrangements, the emphasis on speed and time, and the composition of the negotiating teams.

Location. Typically, there is a strong tendency to want to negotiate on your own turf or at neutral sites, especially for critical negotiations. The so-called "home court advantage" seems to be universal; everyone feels more comfortable and confident and has greater access to information and resources when negotiating at home. For international negotiations, negotiations conducted in a manager's own offices or even in his or her home country can be a psychological advantage.

Characteristics of locations, however, can vary by culture. For example, in North America negotiations regularly occur in a formal setting, such as an office or conference room. In contrast, in Japan and Mexico, where relationship building is crucial, major parts of the process are likely to occur in an informal or nonwork setting, such as a restaurant or golf course. In Korea, the final contract produced from the negotiations is likely to be signed in a formal and public setting rather than in someone's office.

Physical Arrangements. The usual North American approach to setting up a room for negotiations is to place the parties on opposite sides of a table facing each other, which has the obvious effect of emphasizing competing interests. Other arrangements are possible, including seating the parties at right angles or along the same side "facing the problem," or at a round table where all are part of the total problem-solving effort.[41]

Emphasis on Speed and Time. North Americans typically avoid wasting time. They want to "get right to the point" or "get down to business." Other cultures differ from that viewpoint. In Mexico or China, for example, the norm is to invest considerable time in relationship building and other activities not directly related to the central negotiation process. Consequently, in such cultures speed is sacrificed and the effectiveness and efficiency of subsequent negotiations often hinge on how well relationships have been developed.

Composition of the Negotiating Teams. The composition and size of teams representing the parties can also influence negotiations. For example, the more people involved at the negotiation table, the more preparation that needs to be done to ensure that the team presents a united front. The composition of the team in terms of decision-making authority is also important. If individuals at the table have authority to make binding decisions, the negotiations are generally more efficient than if they do not.

Team composition can vary significantly by culture. In countries that are sensitive to status differences and ranks (for example, Singapore, India, Venezuela, Japan), having similar status, position, age, and authority between the negotiating teams is much more important than in other countries (like New Zealand, Canada, United States). The size of negotiating teams also can differ markedly by culture. In the North American individualistic-oriented culture, team size is ordinarily much smaller than in more collectivist-oriented cultures such as those of Taiwan, China, and Japan. The resulting mismatch in size can communicate unintended messages. Taiwanese, for example, might interpret a single negotiator or a small team as a sign that the other party does not consider the negotiations to be important. Similarly, someone from North America might interpret the presence of a large team from a Taiwanese firm as an attempt to intimidate them with numbers.

The Negotiation Process The third—and probably most crucial—variable determining the outcome of negotiations is the negotiating process itself. The five common stages in this process, which are basically the same across all cultures,[42] are described below and shown in Exhibit 12.12.

Exhibit 12.12

The Five Stages in the Negotiating Process

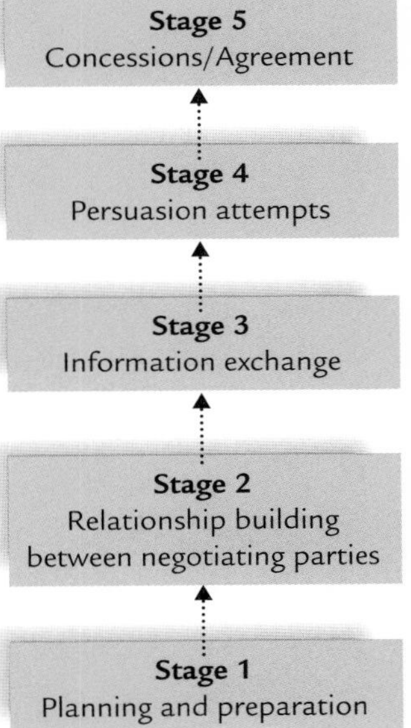

Stage 1: Planning and Preparation. This stage involves laying the foundations through advance planning and analysis prior to any face-to-face interactions. At this stage, individuals or teams conduct background research, gather relevant information, and plan their strategy and tactics. In addition, preliminary decisions are made about what the objectives will be and what can and cannot be conceded during the course of the negotiations.

Stage 2: Relationship Building between Negotiating Parties. This stage is commonly referred to as "nontask time," in which each side attempts to establish comfortable working relationships with the other side. North Americans are generally inclined to make this stage briefer and believe such activities are relatively unimportant. On the other hand, negotiators from some other cultures such as Latin America, the Middle East, and Asia believe exactly the opposite. Research suggests three behavioural elements emerge during this stage: developing trust, developing personal rapport, and establishing long-term association.[43]

Stage 3: Information Exchange. In this stage, each party attempts to learn about the needs and demands of its counterparts. North American managers often attempt to hurry through these activities with an attitude of "you tell me what you want, and I will tell you what I want."[44] In contrast, managers from Asian cultures take a much more indirect, more drawn out, and more thorough approach to acquiring and exchanging information. Arabic and Latin American managers appear to follow a similar approach, except that the latter are even more leisurely in their use of time at this stage.[45]

Stage 4: Persuasion Attempts. This stage focuses on attempts to modify the position of the other party and to influence that side to accept the negotiator's desired set of exchanges (for example, an exchange of a certain price for a certain quantity or quality of goods or services). North American managers usually treat this as the most important stage, with assertive and straightforward efforts to obtain a desired conclusion. Such persuasion can sometimes involve the use of warnings or threats to try to force the other party to agree.[46] Managers from Arabic countries tend to show tactics similar to those of North Americans at the persuasion stage, but they are less inclined to hurry. Negotiators from Asian cultures take a slow, careful approach but do not tend to use direct assertiveness in persuasion until later in the negotiations. As reported in one research study, "when not sure of the offer, they frequently resort to the tactics of 'pretending to lack authority' or 'deliberately delaying [a] counter offer'."[47] Managers from Latin American cultures tend to use a mixture of approaches during this stage by showing a moderate degree of assertiveness but also a willingness to use the tactic of "calculated delay" when this seems advisable.[48]

Stage 5: Concessions/Agreement. At this final point, if reasonable progress has been made, compromises and concessions are made that permit each party to take away something of value. Since North American managers tend to begin the negotiation process with positions fairly close to what they will finally accept, they do not have much leeway for concessions.[49] Managers from Arabic and Latin American countries seem to open negotiations from more extreme positions, which permit them to offer concessions late in the process. Managers from Asian countries often employ "normative appeals" (such as "it's your obligation") to try to get the other party to offer concessions.[50]

managerial perspectives revisited

PERSPECTIVE 1: **THE ORGANIZATIONAL CONTEXT** Almost all types and forms of managerial communication are affected by the organizational context. The structure and characteristics of organizations can facilitate or impede effective communication. The policies and procedures of the organization likewise can help or hinder a manager's attempts to send and receive information and meaning to and from different sources. Particularly affected by the organizational context is the direction of communication. The meaning of transmitted information varies considerably depending on whether it is being sent or received upward, downward, or laterally. The organizational context also presents major challenges and opportunities to build powerful communication networks.

PERSPECTIVE 2: **THE HUMAN FACTOR** The very phrase "interpersonal communication" suggests the centrality of the people aspects of communication. As we discussed earlier in this chapter, among the chief barriers to successful communication are the interpersonal ones. Managers who can gain insight into this kind of potential barrier and how such processes as selective perception and frames of reference can affect communication will increase their chances of becoming more effective communicators. We also observed in the latter part of the chapter how certain characteristics of people help determine the likelihood of constructive outcomes of negotiations in cross-cultural circumstances.

PERSPECTIVE 3: **MANAGING PARADOXES** Communication can be a source of paradoxes to be managed. For example, a manager has to be alert to how both verbal and nonverbal modes of communicating affect potential receivers. A verbal message may convey one meaning, but a nonverbal message may convey another. Oral and written communication can also present paradoxes. Managers often attempt to reinforce their intended messages by sending them by both modes of communication, but this does not guarantee successful communication. In other words, being effective at communicating in one mode is not the same thing as being effective in the other. If they are ineffective at one or both, their messages can be misunderstood, causing more confusion rather than more collaboration among their employees. Therefore, it is critical for most managers to hone both forms. In the area of negotiations, another paradox to be managed is the necessity to pay attention to the differences between "interests" and "positions."

PERSPECTIVE 4: **ENTREPRENEURIAL MINDSET** As we have said, a key component of being entrepreneurial is identifying opportunities. To identify opportunities, managers have to gather substantial amounts of information and analyze them. They must remain alert to unique trends and changes in markets and customer needs. Gathering this information requires managers to communicate with many people and engage in active listening. Furthermore, exploiting opportunities requires them to communicate their ideas and strategies effectively to others in the organization.

The other relevant observation that can be made here is that communication is an area (as with leadership in general) where people can develop and definitely improve their skills if they have sufficient desire to do so. Those with an entrepreneurial mindset are more likely to try. The same is true for becoming a more skilled negotiator: A commitment to improving can result in positive benefits.

concluding comments

As emphasized at the beginning of this chapter, being a good communicator and knowing how the communication process works is essential for becoming an effective manager and leader. In fact, most experienced managers will tell you that communication skills are vital to career success, and a variety of studies emphatically support this claim. Of course, the first step is to understand the nuances of the basic communication process. But that is only a starting point. Although the process seems simple enough, the major challenge is to be able to implement that process successfully on a regular and consistent basis. That, in turn, requires applying your knowledge about the nature of organizations and some of the other key functions of managing (such as planning, organizing, and leading) that have already been discussed in previous chapters.

If good communication were easy, then everyone would be able to do it well most of the time. However, in any organizational context, there are always barriers and obstacles that interfere with effective communication. It is critically important, therefore, to be very aware of these potential obstructions so you can take steps to overcome and deal with them. Communication is an excellent example of a management activity where there is a great cost to naïveté and inexperience and a great benefit to be gained by awareness and analytical insight. Very few people are naturally superb communicators, but there is ample opportunity to become a much better communicator if you focus on developing that awareness and insight.

It also will be especially helpful in your management career if you can add some understanding of the process of negotiation to your repertoire of communication skills. As we noted in this chapter, negotiation is a particular type or form of communication because of the up-front recognition and acknowledgment of different interests and preferences as the starting point for the process. Various factors, like cultural differences, can increase the difficulty and complexity of the process. Again, however, like communication in general, being able to become a better negotiator is a capability that can be honed. Gaining negotiation experience is especially helpful, particularly if that experience is followed by careful analysis and attention to what was learned from the process.

key terms

collaboration 434
communication 414
communication networks 423
cultural distance 430
decoding 415
downward communication 421
empathy 431
encoding 415
ethnocentrism 429
formal communication channels 422
frames of reference 426
gatekeepers 433

informal communication channels 422
interests 434
lateral communication 421
media richness 418
medium 415
negotiation 433
networking 424
noise 415
positions 434
selective perception 426
stereotyping 429
upward communication 421

test your comprehension

1. What is communication?
2. What are the parts of the communication model?
3. What is noise? How does it affect the communication process?
4. Why is oral communication usually more compelling than written communication?
5. Which mode of communication is the most flexible? The least flexible? Why?
6. Why is it important for nonverbal cues to be consistent with verbal cues? What happens if they are not?
7. What is meant by "media richness"?
8. What are some of the characteristics of media that you should consider when deciding which one to use for a given message?
9. What are the typical differences in content of upward, downward, and lateral communication within organizations?
10. What are the differences between formal and informal communication channels? When would you use each?
11. What is a communication network?
12. Why is networking important?
13. What are the three types of barriers to effective communication?
14. How are selective perception and frames of reference related?
15. In what way can emotions become a barrier to effective communication?
16. What are the principal differences between high-context and low-context cultures relative to communication?
17. What is ethnocentrism, and how does it impair effective communication?
18. What is cultural distance?
19. What are the two basic methods for improving your communication ability?
20. Discuss the four ways to improve your listening skills.
21. What are some of the methods used to improve your sending skills?
22. What can organizations do to improve communication within them?
23. In negotiation, what is the difference between an "interest" and a "position"?
24. What are four helpful principles for effective negotiation?
25. What are the key factors in cross-national negotiations?
26. Describe each of the five stages of negotiations and how they can contribute to the overall outcome.

apply your understanding

1. Despite the considerable emphasis that most companies and other types of organizations put on communication, why do you think that many employees feel there is inadequate communication with and from their managers?
2. Assume that you are now working in the first, truly management position in your career. What is likely to be the most important communication issue/problem you will face in the first few months in that position?
3. Will the continued increase in electronic communication within and between organizations be likely to increase or decrease the communication issues/problems faced by the typical manager? Explain the reasoning behind your answer.
4. How can knowledge of the basics of negotiation assist managers in doing their day-to-day activities, especially in regard to exercising leadership and influence? Can you provide examples?

practise your capabilities

When Chris Barnes was promoted to manager in the production department at Telmark Plastics, sales had been increasing for three years and productivity and morale in the department were high. Lately, however, orders have been slowing down. Some days there haven't been enough orders to keep all of the workers busy. And it isn't just in Chris's department. An economic downturn has sent the entire company into a tailspin. The CEO has instructed all managers to find ways to cut costs by 22 percent immediately.

Feeling very pressured and too busy to talk to any of the workers right away to get their opinions, on Tuesday Chris sent the following short memo to the production department employees:

> *TO: Production Workers:*
> *I have been instructed to cut costs by 22 percent. This means we will need to make some tough decisions. We will have a meeting to discuss alternatives on Friday afternoon at 5:00 p.m.*

Through the rest of the week, Chris noticed clusters of workers having intense conversations that stopped whenever he approached. Productivity was slipping. There was more absenteeism than normal. Every member of the department appeared angry, depressed, and worried.

On Friday afternoon, as soon as Chris entered the meeting room the yelling started. The entire evening shift seemed to think they would probably all be laid off. The day shift had somehow come to the conclusion that they were going to have to take significant pay cuts or maybe be replaced by less expensive workers. Chris finally managed to calm everybody down and told them that the meeting wasn't to announce layoffs or pay cuts, but to discuss any other ways they could think of to cut costs. Didn't they read the memo?

Chris had expected everyone to show up with creative ideas on how to cut costs, not expectations of being laid off! What had gone wrong?

1. Comment on Chris's choice of media for (a) the announcement and (b) the meeting. Would you have made the same choices?
2. Identify any barriers to communication in this situation. How could they have been reduced?
3. If you were Chris, what would you do following the meeting to improve the communication between yourself and your workers?

closing case DEVELOP YOUR CRITICAL THINKING

How One Company Tackled Major Communication Problems

Since 1946, when Paul Iams founded The Iams Company in Dayton, Ohio, to raise the nutritional level of packaged pet food, the product category has grown into a US$7 billion business. Procter & Gamble saw so much profit potential in pet food that it bought Iams in 1999. Iams-branded dog and cat food products are sold through supermarkets, drug stores, pet stores, feed outlets, and other retail locations. A second Iams brand, Eukanuba, is sold only through veterinary offices and pet specialty stores.

In 1982, Clay Mathile, an Iams employee since 1970, bought the company from the founder. Within three years, Iams—still a private company—was ringing up US$50 million in annual sales with a 200-person workforce. Then human resource managers decided to conduct the company's first survey of employee attitudes. The employees reported generally positive attitudes. However, management was troubled by the unexpectedly strong response to a question asking whether employees agreed with the statement: "We do not get enough information about how well our workgroup and company are doing."

Digging deeper into the survey results, Mathile and his managers realized that Iams employees were asking for more frequent and more detailed communication regarding both their particular facility's performance and the company's performance overall. Even though Iams was not publicly held, employees were paid bonuses based on sales and profits and were therefore keenly interested in following the company's progress. As a result, Mathile and his team began thinking about a formal process to share key information more often with employees, supervisors, and plant managers, addressing these internal audiences as if they owned company shares. Just as important, the process had to allow information to flow upward as well as downward so managers could take the pulse of the organization and, at the most basic level, determine whether the employee audience understood the messages.

Taking a cue from the quarterly reports that public companies issue to shareholders, senior managers began travelling to meet with groups of employees every three months. Each Iams factory or office shuts down for a few hours during the quarter so that the employees and supervisors can hear top managers talk about the company's current financial situation as well as safety accomplishments and future plans. In addition, senior managers make a point of welcoming new employees and explaining Iams's mission and strategy. Then, each facility's top managers discuss local goals and results and acknowledge promotions and other achievements. Finally, a manager from headquarters reports on developments in one department, such as new employee benefits or upcoming product introductions. At the end of each meeting, senior managers and local facility managers stand in front of the room and field audience questions.

Managers in certain departments also use technology to share information with a far-flung employee base. For instance, managers used to bring the North American sales force together for twice-yearly new-product briefings. In between, they scheduled telephone conference calls as needed to discuss upcoming product introductions. With the advent of video conferencing technology, however, sales managers can now see and talk with the entire sales team at any time. Moreover, with online chats, email, and other web-based tools, managers can assess what the sales force needs to know and reinforce key data when necessary.

Another contributing factor to Iams's success over the years has been its efforts to communicate its dedication to the well-being of animals to pet owners everywhere. Such public relations efforts have included cause-related marketing events such as the Iams Be Kind to Animals Week in 2005 and the Iams "See the Difference, Make a Difference" campaign in 2006. Both of these campaigns were run in support of the Canadian Federation of Humane Societies (CFHS), a not-for-profit organization that endorses Iams's research policies.

In 2007, Iams was forced to put its knowledge of public relations to the test in an effort to protect the company's reputation as a quality pet-food provider. On March 16, Menu Foods, a pet-food producer in Mississauga, Ontario, issued a recall on some of its products, including certain batches of Iams and Eukanuba brands. The recall was made in response to over 8000 complaints of pet illness made to the Food and Drug

Administration (FDA) in the United States. After receiving word of the recall by this supplier, Procter & Gamble promptly issued its own voluntary recall of specific packages of wet dog and cat foods.

In the wake of the pet-food contamination debacle, managers at both Procter & Gamble and Iams began a series of communications with the public. The public was continuously reminded that "the health and well-being of pets is paramount in the mission of Iams and Eukanuba" and that no dry food products were affected by the recall. Furthermore, in early April, a full-page, letter-style ad was placed in 59 major North American newspapers expressing the company's regret by stating that employees were "heartsick any of our products were involved [in the recall]."

As consumers continued to report renal failure and deaths to the media, P&G Pet Care was careful to mitigate public anxiety by announcing that production of all wet pet foods at the affected Menu Foods plant had been terminated. In addition, an independent task force of veterinary health professionals was formed to review P&G Pet Care's participation in the recall. After conducting its review, the task force commended the company for its involvement in the recall and its willingness to share information with consumers, veterinarians, and regulatory authorities. Details of the task force report were made available to the public on the Iams website.

Dan Rajczak, general manager for the Iams and Eukanuba brands in North America, acknowledged the public's concerns and the importance of keeping stakeholders informed. He commented that "it was important for Iams and Eukanuba employees to communicate directly to pet owners and be as helpful as we can in explaining what's really happening." Iams has been doing its best to maintain a positive image of the company by maintaining constant communication with the public amid growing anxiety and confusion. But it is still too soon to know how sales will be affected in the long term.

Questions

1. What effects, if any, is Iams's emphasis on quarterly meetings of employees with senior-level managers likely to have on the quality and extent of day-to-day communication between lower-level managers and their immediate subordinates? How will it help or hinder that communication?
2. How has the richness of the media used by Iams managers changed over the years? How do you think these changes have affected senders and receivers?
3. Do the communication benefits of holding companywide quarterly meetings outweigh the costs of halting operations so employees can attend and having executives travel in person to different locations for the meetings? Explain the basis for your answer.
4. Was the communication strategy used by Iams regarding the contaminated dog and cat food the right strategy? Explain your answer.
5. Does this case suggest any linkages between the type and extent of managerial communication and employee as well as consumer trust in company management?

Sources: J. Neff, "Pet-Food Crisis a Boon to Organic Players: Companies Specializing in Natural Products Thrive as P&G, Others Scramble," *Advertising Age*, April 8, 2007, pp. 3–4; "Iams and Eukanuba Employees Publish Open Letter Today to Reassure Pet Owners," Canada NewsWire, April 3, 2007; "P&G Pet Care (NYSE: PG) Position Statement in Response to Today's Announcement by the Food & Drug Administration," Canada NewsWire, March 30, 2007; "P&G Pet Care Announces Voluntary Participation in Menu Foods' Nationwide U.S. and Canadian Recall of Specific Canned and Small Foil Pouch 'Wet' Cat and Dog Foods," Canada NewsWire, March 16, 2007; 'Shining' Examples of Iams-Fed Pets Add Up to Thousands of Dollars for Canadian Federation of Humane Societies," Canada NewsWire, May 16, 2006; Canada NewsWire, "First-Ever Iams® Friends for Life™ Designer Charm Bracelet Raises Money for the Canadian Federation of Humane Societies," Canada NewsWire, April 29, 2005; J. Neff, "P&G Claims Iams Is Top Dog in Pet Food," *Advertising Age*, March 10, 2003, pp. 4–5; J. Meyer, "Strategic Communication Enhances Organizational Performance," *Human Resource Planning*, June 2002, pp. 7+; J. Neff, "It's a Dog-Eat-Dog World," *Food Processing*, June 2001, pp. 49+; E. Goodridge, "Users Tap Collaborative Functions of E-Learning Apps," *InformationWeek*, December 10, 2001, p. 34.

Chapter 13 Managing Human Resources

LEARNING OBJECTIVES

After reading this chapter, you should be able to:

1. Explain how the management of human resources is a role both for the human resource management department and for all managers.
2. Describe the key means by which companies find job candidates.
3. Explain how companies select job candidates.
4. Highlight the keys to effective socialization and training.
5. Describe the common methods of managing performance.
6. Discuss the various compensation and reward systems commonly used.
7. Explain how various laws affect core HR activities.

HRM at HOK Toronto

The Canadian building industry has enjoyed a significant period of growth over the last decade or so. For the past 11 years, the value of building permits issued in Canada has steadily increased, reaching a value of more than $66 billion in 2006. Architectural design firms have also benefited from this dramatic growth. However, growth has come with the burden of searching for the right design personnel that can both emulate the character of the firm and cover the demand for work that is arriving at the design firm's door.

A growing market was not always the case for the building industry in Canada. During the declining economy of the late 1980s and early 1990s the building industry experienced a flat period, with few large projects and not enough work to go around. Architecture firms were forced to cut back on the number of employees, letting go architects, technologists, and office support that, at the time, were only contributing to the overhead of the firm and putting the company further into the red with every passing month. It was a period of low morale; job stability was foremost in an employee's mind, stifling creativity and affecting innovation and production.

This cycle is common to the building industry and architecture profession, since construction activity and demand for design professionals has traditionally fluctuated with the economy—periods of dramatic growth offset by periods of stagnation and decline. What is particularly difficult for the architectural design sector of the building industry is that when design professionals are let go, all too often they leave the industry altogether, which results in a declining number of professionals available to reinsert into positions when the economy is in an upswing.

The boom/bust cycle is common to the building industry and architecture profession, since construction activity and demand for design professionals has traditionally fluctuated with the economy. HOK in Toronto is an architectural firm that is applying a multifaceted strategy to address the challenge of acquiring and keeping good people.

While the current extended growth in the building sector has been long enough to have people enter architecture schools and graduate into entry positions in firms, the recent bust-to-boom cycle has created a new challenge for human resources specific to the current generation: Managers must contend with a gap that exists between older senior designers and younger entry-level designers, which is a joint result of economic cycles and the baby-boom generation. Many designers who would have comprised the middle set of professionals in architecture firms today were laid off in the 1990s, as they were the junior designers at that time. The length of the downturn led to many designers deciding to leave the profession.

The personnel that remained in design firms eventually moved into senior roles in their organizations, and as the economy strengthened a new younger cohort entered the field. The net effect of the lost middle cohort is that design firms are largely composed of two groups: a cohort of experienced senior designers that are poised to retire, and a junior cohort that is, by and large, too inexperienced to assume the role of senior designers. Given the current conditions, the next 10 years could prove to be the most challenging as key people leave the industry and create a void of experience and networks.

Some design firms are initiating human resource management strategies with the hope of increasing recruiting and strengthening retention, as well as preparing for future economic cycles. HOK is a multidisciplinary architecture and design firm with 26 global offices that is applying a multifaceted strategy to address the challenges of acquiring and keeping good people. HOK's Toronto office has 290 employees. The objective of management is to ensure that HOK Toronto can maintain a medley of creative employees across all ages and levels of experience who can pour their innovation into new projects for the firm.

Given the nature of the industry, personnel have a particular sensitivity to their surroundings. HOK in Toronto has designed an innovative workplace environment with great consideration for comfort. The office has been designed to be bright and airy, including abundant natural light and fresh air with ergonomically designed workspaces and windows that employees can open.

HOK also accommodates employees' personal lives with customizable work hours that may involve alternative arrangements such as a four-day workweek, unpaid leave that protects the employee's position, or even sabbatical arrangements where an employee can work four years with a fifth year off. Guaranteed access to daycare in downtown Toronto has proven to be a high-value benefit, given the scarcity of spaces available to professionals with young children in the Toronto area. A similar benefit is provided for employees that have infirm parents, where elder care is available on a back-up basis when care requirements and work demands conflict.

Another facet to HOK's strategy is providing internal development to move staff up through the ranks via mentorship and coaching, as well as offering lateral moves to different projects, which is particularly appealing for design professionals searching for variety. Forty hours of paid time for study and exam writing toward professional designations in architecture and interior design is also offered to employees.

Although the above programs are already in place, the management at HOK continues to look for new ways to further enhance the appeal of their firm to new and existing employees at all levels.

Sources: "Dealing with the Labour Shortage," *Canadian HR Reporter* 20, no. 15 (September 10, 2007), p. 11; HOK Toronto website, www.hok.com (accessed October 7, 2007); "Country Profile, Canada: Construction," *Economist Intelligence Unit*, 2007, p. 50.

strategic overview

Historically, many organizations have promoted the idea that people are their most important asset. Unfortunately, their actions didn't support their claims. For example, when the economy enters a recession and organizations encounter reduced demand for their goods and services, they cut costs by laying off employees. Recently, organizations have begun to reassess the importance of their employees. One of the reasons for this change is the realization that employees generally possess the knowledge that enables the firm to compete effectively in the marketplace. In fact, much of the knowledge in a firm is held by its employees, making employees critical assets. The firm's employees are also its most unique resource and cannot be easily imitated by competitors. Firms that have greater knowledge about technology, customers, manufacturing processes, and the products and services consumers want can win competitive battles. But it is predicated on the ability of the organization to learn, innovate, and change its processes.[1] To do these things effectively requires human talent.[2]

As a result, human resource management has evolved in recent years, particularly the strategic aspects of it.[3] In this chapter, we underscore the importance of this link. As the opening case on HOK Toronto suggests, organizations must have adequate amounts of human capital to implement a strategy of any value. However, the company must also have quality human capital, especially among its managers. As such, the company's human resource efforts should be aimed at identifying and selecting employees who have the knowledge, skills, and capabilities the organization needs to compete, and fostering and retaining those employees with good compensation and reward systems.

In general, human resource management (HRM) encompasses the activities of acquiring, maintaining, and developing the organization's people—its human resources. The traditional view of these activities focuses on planning for staffing needs, recruiting and selecting employees, orienting and training staff, appraising their performance, providing compensation and benefits, and managing their career movement and development. From this perspective, HRM involves both the activities of the human resource department and its specialized staff as well as all managers. While the HR department likely sets policies and practices for hiring people, for example, managers are quite often involved in selecting employees because once hired, the new employees are going to go to work for them. Similarly, while the HR department may set up the exact performance appraisal forms and processes, managers are the ones who actually assess employee performance. Thus, while it is important for you to understand the role of a company's human resource department, it is even more important for you as a future manager to understand your role in managing human resources. How can you manage your human resources effectively? In general, you need the following capabilities:

- The ability to recruit and select the right people.
- The ability to effectively socialize and train people in your unit.
- The ability to effectively evaluate their performance.
- The ability to determine reward systems that will motivate high performance.
- To know what additional experience or education your subordinates need to develop to advance in their careers.

One of the most enlightening studies on the importance of effective human resource management and career success looked at cases of career derailment. The study found that the number-one reason for managerial career derailment (in other words, the number-one reason why managers who got on were subsequently bumped off the upwardly mobile career track) was their inability to successfully carry out the activities associated with effective human resource management.[4] Consequently, managers who gain a competitive advantage at human resource management activities place themselves squarely in a superior position for upward movement and greater opportunities and responsibilities. While the bulk of this chapter focuses on the key elements of effective human resource management, the actual practices in HR are heavily influenced by laws and regulations. Managers need to be familiar with these laws and regulations and how they affect different HR activities. Consequently, a summary of them appears at the end of the chapter.

The employment challenges at HOK Toronto illustrate two key issues: (1) a firm's ability to survive and prosper in the future is increasingly a function of the human resources they have, and (2) as a manager, your own career success or failure may depend on how well you manage human resources during both good economic times and bad. We can all think of firms whose success seems tied to products, technology, or strategy, but not people. Where would Apple be without the Macintosh, iMac, or iPod? Would Research In Motion (RIM) be an important competitor in mobile communications without the BlackBerry? Clearly, these and other "golden eggs" seem to lie at the heart of certain firms' fortunes. But the real key to any golden egg is the goose that laid it. Such valuable resources do not just materialize. Without bright, capable, and motivated people, Apple would not have developed the Macintosh or iMac. Without people who recognized the growing need for data transmission and email communication, RIM would not have seized the advantage in this arena. In short, people invent and use technology; people gather, analyze, and disseminate information; people formulate and implement strategy. Thus, HOK Toronto's dependence on people for its future success is not unique or even uncommon. Both the quality of a firm's strategy and the success of its implementation depend on getting the right people and maximizing their performance and potential.

The Strategic Role of Human Resource Management

As we discussed in the chapter on strategic management, competitive advantage comes through creating and leveraging products that provide value to customers but are hard for competitors to imitate. Since people are behind every product or idea that a company generates, having a human resource strategy in place is essential. For example, WestJet has moved its way up to the second-largest air carrier in Canada, becoming one of the most admired corporate cultures in the country. In an industry that is more known for losses and bankruptcies than success stories, what has WestJet accomplished that so many before failed to do? Senior management at WestJet believe that it is the people that work for them and the company's commitment to putting people first. This type of human resource strategy creates happy employees, who in turn treat customers better, which ultimately leads to a better bottom line.

HR and Strategy Formulation

While the traditional view of HR as a function has not involved strategy formulation, it is a perspective that is changing.[5] Increasingly, executives are looking at their people and their present and future capabilities to determine what the company's competitive strategy ought to be.[6] As one executive put it, "In football, if you have a quarterback with a great arm, does it make sense to design an offense built upon the run?" Recall from our discussion of competitive advantage in the strategic management chapter that competitive advantage comes largely from creating value for customers through resources that are hard for competitors to copy. The capabilities employees possess are often hard for competitors to copy. To the extent that these capabilities also create value for customers, they become a source of competitive advantage and can therefore play a role in what the company's competitive strategy ought to be.

HR and Strategy Implementation

Exhibit 13.1

General Framework of HRM

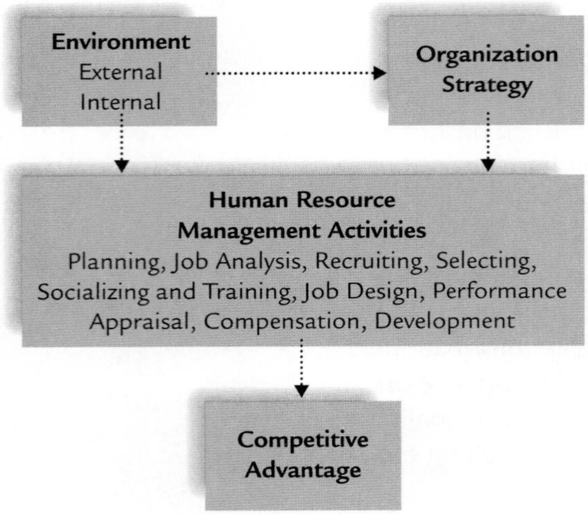

Clearly, not every strategy is or should be driven by a firm's human resources. However, it is hard to think of a strategy that can be effectively implemented without the proper management of its human resources. Consequently, both executives in charge of the HR function and managers throughout an organization need to manage their human resources in a way that supports and helps implement the strategy.[7]

Exhibit 13.1 incorporates these various perspectives into a strategic framework of human resource management (HRM). As the figure illustrates, specific human resource activities (planning, job analysis, recruiting, selecting, socializing and training, job design, performance appraisal, compensation, and development) exist within the context of the firm's strategy and environment. The fit of these human resource activities with the strategy and environment leads to competitive advantage for the organization and for the individual manager.[8]

Human Resource Management Activities That Get the Right People

To this point, we have explored the link between competitive advantage and human resource management and have also briefly examined the importance of the fit between HRM practices and the firm's strategy. We now outline the key HRM activities listed in Exhibit 13.1.

Simplified, there are two main HRM goals: (1) getting the right people and (2) maximizing their performance and potential. Although there are a number of activities related to these two general categories, all managers need to get the right people into the right place at the right time and then help them maximize their performance and future potential. For example, a brilliantly creative person might be right for a firm that competes through product innovation, like Research In Motion, but might be wrong for an organization that competes via cost leadership and low fares, like WestJet.

Getting the right people cannot be accomplished without understanding and aligning HRM activities with the corporate strategy. Although it is necessary to discuss each of these activities separately, you should not forget that they are related and that success or failure in one activity can significantly influence the success or failure of another.

Planning

Human resource planning is concerned with assessing the future human resource needs (demand), determining the availability of the type of people needed (supply), and creating plans for how to meet the need (fulfillment). At the organizational level, HR planning is sometimes a shared responsibility among HR specialists and executives in other functional areas like accounting, finance, marketing, and operations.

Forecasting Demand The key objective is to determine how many and what type of employees the firm needs at a point in the future, say, one or five years hence, considering the firm's strategy and the general business and economic environment. For example, many Japanese electronics firms estimated in the mid-1990s that the product segments of music and games would increase at double-digit rates for 20 years. Much of the assembly work of putting together the various components of the music- and game-playing machines would require relative low-skilled and low-cost labour.

Assessing Supply At the time, much of what these firms produced for export to other countries was assembled in Japan. As they looked at the future labour supply in Japan, however, two key facts emerged. First, based on demographic trends, it was clear that the population of Japan in the age range of 19 to 35 (the most common age of assembly workers) was going to shrink. Second, based on economic growth expectations, many of these companies forecast that labour costs were going to increase significantly. Thus, many of the managers in electronics firms in Japan determined that the demand for low-cost and low-skilled labour for product assembly would outstrip the supply of these types of workers in Japan.

Formulating Fulfillment Plans The firms determined that demand would outstrip supply by approximately 2 to 3 million people by the turn of the century. To address this shortfall, many of these senior executives and government officials examined the possibility of allowing immigrants into Japan to fill the labour shortage and lower the labour costs. However, this approach generally lacked political and popular support. As a consequence, many executives of these electronics firms decided to automate some aspects of component manufacturing and also examined the automation of final assembly. However, while some components could be manufactured cost-effectively through automation, automating final assembly looked to be too costly. As a consequence, most of the executives in these firms decided to aggressively move final assembly operations offshore to countries with a good supply of semi-skilled and low-cost labour, such as China, Vietnam, and Indonesia.

Even though the human resource management department might be specially charged with looking at HR planning, individual managers must also be skilled planners as well. As a manager you will want to be able to determine the number and types of employees you will need in your units, assess the supply in the marketplace, and develop a plan to get the right people. Just as with the organization, as a manager you cannot distinguish between a "right" and "wrong" employee without thoughtful consideration of your firm's strategy. For example, after his first departure from Apple, Steve Jobs started a company called NeXT to compete in the high-end computer and work station market. Within just a few years, Jobs decided to shift the firm's strategic orientation from hardware to software. For managers in product development, this meant that they needed more programmers than engineers and that they initially needed fewer employees overall. Because the market for software programmers was tight, NeXT managers focused their efforts on attracting dissatisfied programmers at other companies and highlighted the exciting things that they were doing at NeXT.

To fulfill your employment needs, you may need to consider the use of *part-time* or *temporary* employees. This can give you the flexibility to meet significant but temporary increased demand for employees. It allows you to reduce your workforce more easily if demand falls, as well as to try out employees before hiring them permanently if demand remains strong.

You may decide to *outsource* specific workforce demands.[9] For example, many companies now outsource their call centre jobs involving customer service or telemarketing to other companies like Blue Ocean Contact Centers.

In a sense, this offloads the fluctuations in demand for call centre representatives to another company that specializes in these tasks and has concentrated capabilities in hiring and training people for these jobs.

Job Analysis

job analysis determination of the scope and depth of jobs and the requisite skills, abilities, and knowledge that people need to perform their jobs successfully

Job analysis is a critical but often overlooked human resource activity. **Job analysis** is concerned primarily with determining the scope and depth of jobs and the requisite skills, abilities, and knowledge that people need to perform their jobs successfully.

The data and insights that come from a job analysis are typically used to create a *job description*, or a list of duties and capabilities required for the job. Typically, this leads to a *job specification*, or a statement that describes the skills, experience, and education that a candidate should have to perform the job.

Recruiting

Recruiting is primarily concerned with determining what the desired candidate pool consists of and attracting those candidates to specific positions within the organization. As with the other activities we have already discussed, the desired pool of candidates cannot be determined without considering the firm's strategy. Whom you want is a function of whom you need—whether you can get the type of person you want is a different story. Can you offer them what they want? Can your competitor offer them more?

Let's consider the first question. The key to knowing whether you can offer people what they want is to actually find out what they do want. Consider the case of UPS in Germany. When UPS expanded into Germany, managers had a difficult time selecting good drivers because they simply were not attracting high-quality applicants. Several factors contributed to this, most notably the fact that the brown UPS uniforms were the same colour as those of the Nazi youth group during World War II. UPS was not offering what high-quality prospective drivers wanted and was, in fact, offering something (brown uniforms) they did not want.

The second question is not simply a matter of whether you can offer candidates more money than your competitors. People are not motivated only by money (see Chapter 10). Rather, it is important to consider the work environment, the nature of the work, the flexibility of the benefits, and the opportunity for advancement as factors that could attract candidates to your organization.

Once you have assessed these two questions, a variety of approaches can be used to generate job candidates. Each one has its strengths and weaknesses and, as a consequence, should be used as the situation dictates. Some companies try to persuade firms and their managers to go "high-tech" to select their candidates. These companies use tools like skills tests, psychological tests, and even artificial intelligence to make candidate selection faster, cheaper, and better. After reading *A Manager's Challenge: "Guru's Gamble on a High-Tech Selection System,"* what do you think? Would you be inclined to use such a service?

job posting an internal recruiting method whereby a job, its pay, level, description, and qualifications are posted or announced to all current employees

Job Posting **Job posting** is a popular internal recruiting method whereby a job, its pay, level, description, and qualifications are posted or announced to all current employees. Increasingly, posting is done electronically through email. Job postings help ensure that all qualified employees have an opportunity to apply for a particular job. Job posting can also help current employees have a better idea of the types of jobs available and the qualifications needed to be successful in those

a manager's challenge *technology*

Guru's Gamble on a High-Tech Selection System

How can managers seeking to fill an open position determine which candidate represents the best match with their company's needs and work style? Former Guru.com founder and one of the most influential people in the recruiting industry, Ray Marcy, thought he had a high-tech answer to this perennial challenge. Marcy realized that managers who post job openings often receive hundreds of responses. Then they have to spend hours (perhaps even days) wading through each applicant's credentials to narrow the field and select the most qualified candidates.

Marcy proposed a radically different approach to the selection process. He believed that Guru could use artificial intelligence (AI) software to sift through candidates for open positions and identify a handful of highly qualified finalists from which client companies could select. As a result, managers seeking to hire a new employee would invest far less time in the selection process, but wind up with a far better match between the candidate, the job, and the company.

To implement this approach at Guru, Marcy hired an industrial psychologist to develop psychological tests that would show what companies were actually seeking in job candidates. In addition, he hired an AI expert to create the technology that would electronically evaluate candidates for posted jobs. Despite this high-tech emphasis, Marcy also recognized the importance of maintaining human contact during the selection process.

If you were a manager posting an open job on the website, a Guru "talent agent" would immediately call to learn more about the position's requirements and the company's work style. The agent would ask you if you are seeking to hire someone who is independent, accommodating, risk-taking, creative, or has other work-style traits. Next, the talent agent uses the AI system to identify qualified candidates from among those in Guru's database and other job-search databases. Using Guru's online system, these candidates complete a work-style assessment test so the talent agent can compare their styles with the styles desired by the hiring manager. Finally, the talent agent sends the hiring manager information on the three candidates whose background and work styles most closely match what you are seeking. The entire process, from the time you submit an open position to the time you receive a listing of matching candidates, takes 48 hours or less.

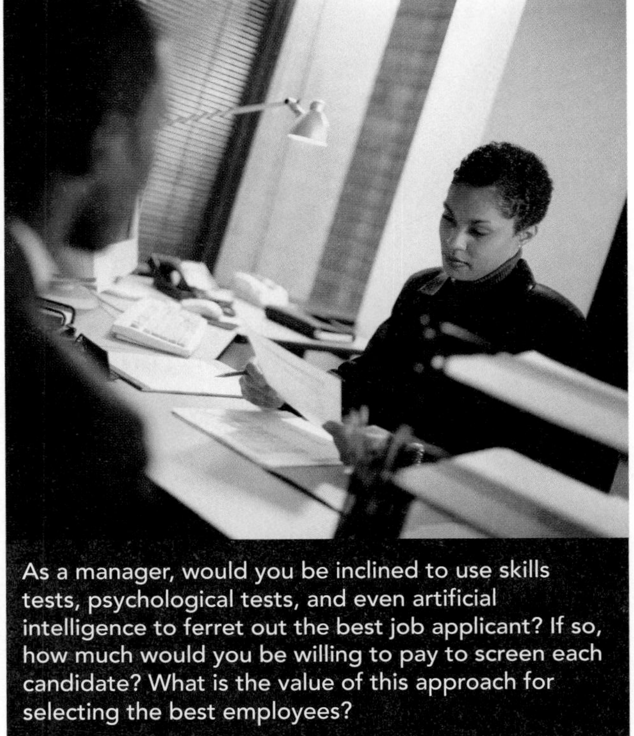

As a manager, would you be inclined to use skills tests, psychological tests, and even artificial intelligence to ferret out the best job applicant? If so, how much would you be willing to pay to screen each candidate? What is the value of this approach for selecting the best employees?

Guru's fee for screening and recommending candidates was US$7500, about one-third of the cost of using a traditional search firm to fill an open position. However, some techno-savvy companies have built their own internal systems to help their managers select candidates for open positions, and other online job sites have similar tools.

Moreover, before Guru could fully capitalize on the artificial intelligence screening system, the marketplace changed dramatically. Tech firms laid off thousands of workers following a crash in the economy's tech sector, and employers found themselves less willing to pay high fees to hire them. As the firm took shape, assessment did not become the core activity of Guru.com's business—hiring freelancers did. Today, Guru.com is the world's largest online market for freelance talent with more than 600 000 active professionals in over 160 categories listed. Over time, many placement firms applied similar elaborate automated screening methods to minimize time in reviewing candidates.

Source: Guru.com Facts, www.guru.com (accessed October 4, 2007); S. Fister Gale, "Putting Job Candidates to the Test," *Workforce Management, 2003 Vender Directory* 82, no. 11, p. 90; S. Clifford, "Guru's Gamble," *Business 2.0*, July 2002, pp. 92–93.

jobs. This can allow them to plan their careers. On the negative side, job postings can generate unqualified applicants who need to receive explanations about why they were unqualified and did not get the job. Without adequate explanation, they are likely to wonder whether the job was really "open" when it was posted. If employees begin to doubt the process of posting jobs, it can generate skepticism and limit candidates and therefore also the posting's effectiveness.

Advertisements Advertisements in general or specialized publications can also be an effective means of generating job candidates. National business newspapers such as the *Globe and Mail* and the *National Post* cast a wide net. Professional magazines such as *Canadian HR Reporter* cast a very specialized net. Regional or local publications, such as your city newspaper, focus on the local labour pool. Increasingly, the internet is being used as a source of advertising job openings. As use of the internet matures, it is likely to develop regional and industrial segments that will facilitate a more targeted advertising of jobs.[10] The major downside of advertisements is the time and expense of screening out and rejecting unqualified candidates.

Employment Agencies Employment agencies can also be effective in generating job candidates in some fields. The agency's effectiveness is largely a function of how well it understands your organization and the requirements of the specific job. Agencies tend to be expensive and usually not cost effective for low-level and low-paying jobs. In contrast, most openings at the senior management level use executive search firms as part of their recruiting efforts. As their fee for finding an acceptable candidate, these firms typically charge at least one-third of the successful candidate's first-year compensation.

Employee Referrals Managers may find current employees a great source for job candidates. Current employees with tenure in the organization understand the organization, its culture, and often the particular job that needs to be filled. They usually know something about an applicant as well: work history, educational background, skills and abilities, personal characteristics, and so on. Given that their recommendation puts their own reputation on the line to some degree, current employees tend to recommend individuals whom they believe will do well. Their personal relationship with the recommended candidate allows employees not to just sell the company on the individual but to sell the individual on the company. In general, research suggests that current employee referrals are one of the most effective recruiting methods. Employee referrals are less effective when the firm is looking for a different type of employee than it currently has. Current employees tend to recommend people like themselves. So a company pushing into international activities or new technology may find that its employees don't know people in these new areas to refer.

School Placement Centres School placement centres are also a popular source of job candidates. Placement centre offices can range from those found in high schools, technical schools, and colleges to universities and advanced degree programs. If given adequate time and clear job specifications and requirements, school placement centres can do much of the pre-screening, filtering out unqualified candidates. This can save the firm significant time and money in the recruiting process. Schools are increasingly using video conferencing capabilities to set up "virtual" interviews and online job fairs. Technology helps firms broaden the field, allowing them to reach places to which they may not be able to travel physically. The weakness of school placement centres is that they often deal with so many companies and students that they might not know enough about either to conduct ideal screening.

The Internet Companies are discovering that the internet is a powerful recruiting tool. Most major companies use their corporate websites to list jobs and attract candidates. In addition to using their own sites, companies are increasingly using sites like Monster.ca. Monster.ca now has over 2 million resumés and 25 000 posted positions in its database and is part of the even larger Monster Worldwide network. Workopolis.com and Canjobs.com are two other sites where companies frequently post ads for Canadian positions.

Selecting

Successful selection is a function of effective planning, analyzing, and recruiting, as well as applying appropriate selection techniques.[11] Even if you get the right set of candidates before you, you need to be able to determine which one is best for the job. For example, international banks have no trouble attracting people to overseas positions, because international experience is important in the increasingly global banking industry. However, managers selected for overseas assignments sometimes fail and have to return home early at a significant cost to the employer. The early returns not only cost the company but also hurt employees' careers. These failures are partly a function of poor specification of the characteristics that predicted success in an overseas assignment and limited use of effective selection techniques.[12]

One of the key points to keep in mind relative to any selection technique is that if legally challenged, the organization must be able to demonstrate that the selection technique is valid. A **valid selection technique** is one that can differentiate between those who would be more successful in the job and those who would be less successful. For example, educational background is often used in selecting new hires because knowledge typically has a proven relationship with job performance. That is, it is hard to perform well in a job for which you do not have the requisite education and knowledge. There are a variety of selection techniques; each has its own strengths and weaknesses.

valid selection technique a screening process that differentiates those who would be successful in a job from those who would not

Valid Selection Techniques by Stewart Black

mymanagementlab

Interviews The most widely used selection technique is the interview. In most cases, the interview is unstructured. An **unstructured interview** is one in which interviewers have a general idea of the types of questions they might ask but do not have a standard set. As a consequence, interviewers might ask different candidates different questions. With different questions and responses, comparing candidates can be like comparing apples and oranges. Not surprisingly, a major weakness of unstructured interviews is that they tend to have low levels of validity.[13] In contrast, **structured interviews**, in which interviewers ask a standard set of questions of all candidates about qualifications and capabilities related to job performance, can be quite valid. Validity can be further enhanced by carefully recording interviewee responses on a standardized form and taking approximately the same time in each interview. Exhibit 13.2 provides tips for interviewers and Exhibit 13.3 provides tips for interviewees.[14]

unstructured interview an interview in which interviewers have a general idea of the questions they might ask but do not have a standard set

structured interview an interview in which interviewers ask a standard set of questions of all candidates about qualifications and capabilities related to job performance

Work Sampling There are a variety of techniques that could be classified as work sampling. Essentially, all these techniques attempt to simulate or exactly duplicate the job the person would be doing if hired. The underlying rationale is straightforward: If you perform poorly or well in the work sample, you would likely perform similarly in the real job. In general, the main strength of work sampling techniques is that they make a reasonably accurate prediction of how an individual will do in a job. The main drawback is that they tend to be time and cost intensive. Research supports the validity of work sampling techniques.

Exhibit 13.2 Tips for Interviewers

1. Plan the interview by reviewing the candidate and the job specifications.
2. Establish rapport with a friendly greeting and start the interview with a nonjob question.
3. Follow a structured set of questions.
4. Avoid questions that require or solicit a simple *yes* or *no* response.
5. Try not to telegraph, or give cues for, the desired answer.
6. Make sure the candidate has plenty of time to answer—do not monopolize the conversation.
7. Listen carefully and paraphrase key candidate answers to be sure you understand what they meant to say.
8. Ask for specific, not general, examples of the candidate's experience and accomplishments.
9. Leave time at the end of the interview to answer questions from the candidate.
10. At the close make sure the candidate knows what the next steps are and approximate timing.
11. After the candidate leaves, review your notes and highlight important points while they are fresh in your mind.

Exhibit 13.3 Tips for Interviewees

- Prepare for the interview by researching the company through articles and its own website.
- Smile and provide a warm greeting and firm handshake if the interviewer extends his or her hand.
- Make sure that your overall appearance (hair style, clothing, makeup, and so on) match the nature of the business and culture of the company.
- Watch your nonverbal behaviour to ensure that you maintain good eye contact and convey enthusiasm without being overly expressive with your hands or other body movements.
- Try to solicit the interviewer's needs early in the interview.
- Early in the interview be sure to get a complete picture of the job through questions like "Can you tell me about what has led people to succeed in this job in the past?"
- Explicitly relate yourself and your capabilities to the interviewer's needs through statements like "You mentioned that one of the keys to this position is the ability to motivate others. In my experience at XYZ. . . ."
- Take your time before answering; you do not need to begin talking the instant the interviewer asks a question.
- Conclude the interview by thanking the person for the opportunity and expressing your interest in the company and the position.

assessment centres a work sampling technique in which candidates perform a number of exercises, each one designed to capture one or more key aspects of the job

Assessment Centres Assessment centres use work sampling techniques. Typically, candidates are required to go through a number of exercises, and each exercise is designed to capture one or more key aspects of the job. For example, a supervisor's job might require good prioritization skills. The assessment centre might have an "in-basket" exercise to assess this skill. The exercise consists of an in-basket filled with letters, memos, and reports that the candidate must read and then prioritize. The individual's ability to recognize and respond to high-priority items comes out during the exercise. In general, research supports assessment centres as an effective selection method for new hires as well as for individuals moving up in a firm.[15]

Work Simulation **Work simulation** techniques typically involve situations in which job candidates perform work that they would do if hired, or work that closely simulates the tasks they would perform. Work simulation can also be an effective training technique. An example of this can be found at Atomic Energy of Canada Limited (AECL). AECL is in the business of designing, building, and maintaining nuclear reactors in Canada and around the world. They use simulation technology to train employees in areas where they would otherwise be exposed to hazardous materials. This approach allows the employees to gain the experience without being unnecessarily exposed to environmental hazards.

work simulation situations in which job candidates perform work they would do if hired or work that closely simulates the tasks they would perform

Written Tests Written tests are also widely used to select job candidates. This is due in part to the fact that the tests can be administered cost effectively to a large number of job candidates. Cognitive ability and intelligence tests measure an individual's general cognitive complexity and intellectual ability. Although the validity of these tests has been mixed, they do seem to be acceptable predictors for supervisory and management jobs. Personality tests are more controversial. While they can be reasonably good predictors of people's ability to work well with other particular personalities, they have not been good overall predictors of job performance.[16] Integrity tests are a more recent development. These tests try to assess the general level of a person's honesty. In general, they seem to be of debatable validity.[17] Written tests have the advantage of being inexpensive to administer, but the results are more valid regarding general performance and success than for success in a specific job.

Background and Reference Checks Background checks attempt to verify factual information that applicants provide. Service Canada has found that up to 60 percent of applicants use misleading information. As a consequence, checking to make sure applicants graduated with the degrees they claim, from the schools they cite, and held the jobs with the responsibilities they describe can be quite valuable. The objective of reference checks is to get candid evaluations from those who have worked with the job candidate. It is important that managers not only ask applicants for three references, but that they also check the references to confirm that what the applicant has stated in his or her resumé or during an interview is true.

Physical Examinations Companies that require physical examinations as part of the selecting process typically do so because the job has high physical demands. In addition to helping them select physically qualified candidates, physical exams also protect firms. First, the physical exam information may help firms reduce insurance claims. Second, it may help protect the firm from lawsuits by identifying high-risk applicants, like someone who might experience a heart attack from the physical strains of the job. However, managers must be careful to ensure that the physical requirements being screened in the examination are in fact related to job performance and are not sources for discrimination.[18] Physical examinations can also be used for screening out people who are inappropriate for the physical demands of the job. Drug testing is another screening mechanism companies use to ensure that employees' judgment and capabilities are not impaired while on the job.

Human Resource Management Activities That Maximize Performance

Once the right people are in the right positions, the organization needs to ensure that they are performing well. What constitutes maximum performance and potential is largely a function of the organization's strategy. For example,

3M Canada chooses to compete on new-product innovation and strives to have the majority of its revenue come from products that are less than five years old, such as FireStrap. FireStrap is a product designed to contain a fire by not permitting it to pass through walls. For this level of innovation, 3M needs employees like Larry Whitty, the developer of FireStrap, who can think of and test new ideas. For 3M, maximum performance and potential are largely defined in terms of employee innovations. Based on this, 3M undertakes a variety of activities to maximize employee creativity. Five specific categories of activities can significantly influence employee performance and potential.

Socialization and Training

Just as early life experiences can shape the general character, personality, and behaviour of people, so too can early training and socialization experiences shape important aspects of employees' performance.[19] For example, early training and socialization affects (1) the probability that new hires will stay with the firm, (2) the extent to which they will perform well, and (3) the degree to which they will develop to their full potential.[20]

Managers can use a variety of training methods to enhance the performance and potential of employees. We cover several here. Although early career training is important, in today's changing environment, training and learning are likely to become career-long endeavours.

Orientation One of the first opportunities for an organization to shape the expectations and behaviour of new employees is during orientation programs.[21] Typically, these programs provide a broad overview of the industry, the company and its business activities, its key competitors, and general information about working in the company (such as key policies, pay procedures, and fringe benefits). Work-unit orientation sessions are typically more narrow and are generally designed to help the new employee get up to speed on the new job, co-workers, work-unit policies and procedures, and expectations. To maximize the effectiveness of orientation programs, managers should consider the following recommendations:[22]

- Keep paperwork to a minimum to avoid information overload. Do include paperwork that must be completed immediately.
- Include an informal meeting with the individual's immediate supervisor.
- Alternate heavy information, such as that related to benefits and insurance, with lighter live or video presentations from corporate officers.
- Provide a glossary of terms unique to the organization.
- Match each new employee with a "buddy" (that is, an experienced worker) based more on personality compatibility than similarity of jobs.

On-the-Job Training Techniques On-the-job training (OJT) is the most widely used training technique in organizations. As Exhibit 13.4 illustrates, there are a wide variety of techniques that a manager can use to train employees. Over your career, you will likely be exposed to most, if not all, of these approaches.

Off-the-Job Training Techniques Off-the-job training can also be used with positive effect. The most common off-the-job training approach is the classroom-based program. The program may be only an hour, or it may be several weeks in length. It may be conducted by in-house experts (employees of the company) or by outside experts from the industry or the education field, such as university professors. The program may involve lectures, case studies, discussions, videos,

Exhibit 13.4 On-the-Job Training Techniques

1. *Expanded Responsibilities.* This training technique expands the job duties, assignments, and responsibilities of an individual.
2. *Job Rotation.* Also called *cross-training,* this practice moves individuals to various types of jobs within the organization at the same level or next-immediate-higher level for periods of time from an hour or two to as long as a year.
3. *Staff Development Meetings.* Meetings are usually held offsite to discuss facts of each individual's job and to develop ideas for improving job performance.
4. *"Assistant to" Positions.* Promising employees serve as staff assistants to higher-skill-level jobs for a specified period of time (often one to three months) to become more familiar with the higher-skilled positions in the organization.
5. *Problem-Solving Conferences.* Conferences are held to solve a specific problem being experienced by a group or the organization as a whole. It involves brainstorming and other creative means to come up with solutions to the basic problems.
6. *Mentoring.* A guide or knowledgeable person higher up in the organization helps a new employee "learn the ropes" of the organization and provides other advice.
7. *Special Assignments.* Special tasks or responsibilities are given to an individual for a specified period of time. The assignment may be writing up a report, investigating the feasibility for a new project, process, service, or product, preparing a newsletter, or evaluating a company policy or procedure.
8. *Company Trainers.* Special programs can cover such topics as safety, new personnel procedures, new products or services, affirmative action, and technical programs.
9. *Outside Consultants.* Recognized experts are brought to the company to conduct training on such topics as goal setting, communications, assessment techniques, safety, and other current topics of importance. They often supplement training done by company trainers.
10. *Consultant Advisory Reviews.* Experts in specialized fields meet with various managers and employee groups to investigate and help solve particular problems. The emphasis is on problem solving rather than training.
11. *Reading Matter.* A formal program is created to circulate books, journals, selected articles, new business material, and so on to selected employees. An effective program also includes periodic scheduled meetings to discuss the material.
12. *Apprenticeship.* Training is provided through working under a journeyman or master in a craft. The apprentice works alongside a person skilled in the craft and is taught by that person. Apprenticeship programs also often include some classroom work.

Source: Adapted from W. P. Anthony, D. L. Perrewé, and K. M. Kacmar, *Strategic Human Resource Management* (Fort Worth, TX: Harcourt Brace Jovanovich, 1993).

or simulations. Individual-based programs are also increasingly popular. Formal correspondence courses are sometimes used when employees have different learning speeds and motivations but the learning objectives are clear. Computer-assisted programs are also used when employees have different learning speeds and motivations. Current technology now allows for text, graphics, and a variety of visual displays as well as interaction. Many programs now adjust content and difficulty level in real time based on how well the individual is doing.

Training Objectives Orientation and training programs can have a variety of objectives. However, at a fundamental level, these programs are intended to address employee technical, interpersonal, or conceptual abilities. Technical skills can range from being able to read and perform simple math to being able to program a supercomputer.

Because very few employees work in isolation, improved interpersonal abilities are the target of a wide variety of training programs. Programs might address skills such as effective listening, conflict resolution, negotiation, and coaching. In a recent study, executives cited poor interpersonal skills as one of the biggest problems in new university or MBA graduates.[23]

The final category is conceptual abilities. This category includes a variety of skills and abilities, such as problem solving, decision making, planning, and organizing. A given training program might be designed to address just one of these categories, two, or all four.

Regardless of the category the program is designed to target, most successful programs provide participants with several things:

- An understanding of what is and is not the correct behaviour.
- A clear knowledge of why certain behaviours are correct or incorrect.
- Sufficient opportunities to practise the desired behaviours.
- Feedback on performance with further opportunities to practise and improve.

An important part of well-designed training is an evaluation of its effectiveness.[24] Perhaps the simplest means of assessing training is what is often called the "smile index," or the satisfaction of participants with the training. This is quite often gathered just after the training is finished via a questionnaire. Clearly, it is unlikely that any aspect of the training that participants do not like will be retained by them and have a positive impact on their knowledge or behaviours. However, the fact that participants enjoyed the training or thought it was useful does not guarantee that it will have the intended impact. A more rigorous assessment of training would involve a pre-training and post-training assessment. For example, if the training were primarily intended to convey knowledge, then a "pre and post" assessment design would involve assessing the knowledge level of participants before the training and at some point afterward. These basics would also apply to an assessment of the skills they learned. In addition, if the training is intended to improve job performance, like quality, you might assess the impact of the training by comparing important metrics, such as defects per 1000 before and after the training.

While a reduction in defects might tell you if the training had the intended effect, it does not tell you if the training was cost effective. Determining this is much more complicated. In general you have to assess both the direct (the cost of trainers) and indirect costs (the productivity lost while workers were in training instead of on the job). You then have to compare these costs to the benefits, such as the savings from fewer returns because of higher quality. However, one key challenge is determining the period over which to add up the benefits. For example, if higher quality is saving you $100 per day in returns, should you estimate the total value of these savings over a week, a month, a year, or several years? Your answer dramatically influences the total benefit quantification and therefore the final determination of whether the training costs are exceeded by the benefits, and if so by how much.

Job Design

job design the structuring or restructuring of key job components

Job design is focused on the structuring or restructuring of key job components. A job design typically includes the responsibilities. Thus, while job analysis focuses on what the components of a job are, job design is the process of determining which components ought to be put together and how they should be arranged to enhance performance.[25] For example, does an assembly-line worker work in isolation and repetitively attach a given part to a product, or does he work in a team with others building an entire unit?

In some texts, job design would be much earlier in the sequence than we have placed it. In general, for a brand new job that has never been filled before, job design does take place early in the sequence. Also, jobs were traditionally designed and then appropriate people were selected to fit into the jobs. The reality of today's dynamic environment has changed that approach. In some cases, it is possible and appropriate to design jobs and then try to match people to them, but in other cases jobs might need to be designed or redesigned to fit the available people. There are also situations that require a combination of both fitting the person to the job and fitting the job to the person. For example, **job sharing** involves two people working part time in the same job. Effective job sharing requires two individuals who can coordinate well and have similar capabilities. It has become popular with working mothers who are faced with balancing family and economic and professional demands. Increasingly, technology is allowing managers to design and redesign jobs in ways not possible before.

job sharing a situation in which two people share the same job by each working part time

During the early and mid-1990s, re-engineering became a popular concept regarding the design or redesign of work. **Re-engineering** is the fundamental rethinking and radical redesign of business processes to achieve dramatic improvements in critical, contemporary measures of performance, such as cost, quality, service, or speed.[26] Computer and information technology advancements have allowed organizations to design more enriched, satisfying, and productive jobs. Increasingly, organizations are looking at ways to give employees more flexibility in the way their work is accomplished. Technology is one way to provide that flexibility. Maximizing subordinates' performance and your unit's performance is your goal as a manager regarding effective job design.

re-engineering the fundamental rethinking and radical redesign of business processes to achieve dramatic improvements in critical, contemporary measures of performance

Performance Appraisal

Before organizations or managers can encourage or correct the actions of employees, they must know how the employees are doing. Performance appraisal is concerned with (1) establishing performance objectives and standards, (2) measuring performance against those standards, and (3) providing feedback to employees concerning that measurement and evaluation.[27] As we stated before, the objectives of the job and the standards against which performance is measured must be driven by the strategy of the firm.

For most managers, performance appraisal is perhaps the most important, yet most difficult, human resource activity. This difficulty is not only because of the complexity of evaluating past performance and setting future performance targets, but because performance appraisals involve communicating to employees how they are doing relative to established targets. Often employees are not quite measuring up to established standards and require feedback for corrective action; however, few people like to give or receive negative feedback. Still, without this feedback, neither individuals nor organizations can maximize performance. As a consequence, all managers need to understand the key factors that drive effective performance appraisal systems and be skilled at implementing them.

Graphic Rating Scales Perhaps the most popular method of providing performance feedback is through graphic rating scales (see Exhibit 13.5 for an example). A graphic rating scale typically lists a set of qualities on which the employee is evaluated. The level of performance on each of these items is then rated in terms of a graduated scale. The scale typically ranges from 1 to 5. The degree of specificity concerning the definition of each point on the scale

Exhibit 13.5
Graphic Rating Scale

Employee name: ____________ **Dept.** ____________

	Excellent	Good	Average	Fair	Poor
1. Quality of work	☐	☐	☐	☐	☐
2. Quantity of work	☐	☐	☐	☐	☐
3. Cooperation	☐	☐	☐	☐	☐
4. Dependability	☐	☐	☐	☐	☐
5. Initiative	☐	☐	☐	☐	☐
6. Job knowledge	☐	☐	☐	☐	☐
7. Attitude	☐	☐	☐	☐	☐

can range from one-word descriptors (e.g., 1 = poor) to complete sentences (e.g., 1 = Does not meet the minimum standards).

The popularity of graphic ratings is due to two main factors. First, they are relatively quick and easy for managers to complete. Given that most managers have many employees whom they must evaluate and that managers typically are not rewarded for writing up high-quality evaluations, they have a natural incentive to complete the evaluations as quickly as possible. Second, because the evaluation items and the rating scale are common across all employees, it is easy to quantify the results and compare employees' performance ratings.

However, there are two key limitations that as a manager you should keep in mind relative to graphic rating scales. First, the characteristics being evaluated may not be clearly defined; thus they are left to individual interpretation. Consequently, one manager might focus her interpretation of "interpersonal skills" on conflict resolution abilities, while another manager might focus his interpretation on listening skills. Given the two different interpretations, it is difficult to compare the employees evaluated by the two different managers. Furthermore, the two different managers might have different interpretations of the rating scale. One manager might only allow the top 5 percent of employees to receive a high rating of "5 = excellent." Another manager might interpret a "5" as applicable to the top 20 percent of employees. Once again, the different interpretations would make comparing employees rated by different managers difficult.[28] This incomparability is important because over 85 percent of firms use performance appraisals to determine merit increases, bonuses, and promotions.

behaviourally anchored rating scales (BARS)
a performance appraisal system in which the rater places detailed employee characteristics on a rating scale

Behaviourally Anchored Rating Scales **Behaviourally anchored rating scales (BARS)** are designed to keep many of the advantages of the graphic rating scales and reduce the disadvantages. The general design of BARS is similar to graphic rating scales in that managers rate employee characteristics using a quantitative scale. However, the characteristics are specified in greater detail and described in terms of behaviours rather than abstract qualities. Likewise, the scales are much more tied to descriptions of specific behaviours rather than ambiguous terms (see Exhibit 13.6 for an example). The greater specificity and link to behaviours reduces, but does not eliminate, the potential for noncomparability of ratings across different evaluators.[29] However, some potential for manager bias remains.[30]

Behaviourally Anchored Rating Scales by Stewart Black
mymanagementlab

360-Degree Feedback The primary rationale behind 360-degree feedback appraisal systems is that an individual's performance should be viewed from

Position: __________

Job dimensions: __________

Plans work and organizes time carefully so as to maximize resources and meet commitments.	9	
	8	Even though this associate has a report due on another project, he or she would be well prepared for the assigned discussion on your project.
	7	This associate would keep a calendar or schedule on which deadlines and activities are carefully noted, and which would be consulted before making new commitments.
	6	As program chief, this associate would manage arrangements for enlisting resources for a special project reasonably well, but would probably omit one or two details that would have to be handled by improvisation.
Plans and organizes time and effort primarily for large segments of a task. Usually meets commitments, but may overlook what are considered secondary details.	5	This associate would meet a deadline in handing in a report, but the report might be below usual standard if other deadlines occur on the same day the report is due.
	4	This associate's evaluations are likely not to reflect abilities because of overcommitments in other activities.
	3	This associate would plan more by enthusiasm than by timetable and frequently have to work late the night before an assignment is due, although it would be completed on time.
	2	This associate would often be late for meetings, although others in similar circumstances do not seem to find it difficult to be on time.
Appears to do little planning. May perform effectively, despite what seems to be a disorganized approach, by concerted effort, although deadlines may be missed.	1	This associate never makes a deadline, even with sufficient notice.

Source: Table from *Strategic Human Resource Management* by William P. Anthony, Pamela L. Perrewé, and K. Michele Kacmar, p. 456. Copyright © 1993 by Harcourt Brace & Company, reproduced by permission of the publisher.

Exhibit 13.6

Behaviourally Anchored Rating Scale

360-degree feedback a performance appraisal system in which information is gathered from supervisors, co-workers, subordinates, and sometimes suppliers and customers

multiple perspectives.[31] Most **360-degree feedback** systems involve collecting appraisal evaluations from an individual's boss, peers, and subordinates. In some companies, evaluations are also collected from suppliers and customers, depending on the nature of interaction the employee has with these constituencies. The positive aspect of 360-degree feedback is that because data are gathered from multiple sources, employees are encouraged to focus on all key constituencies. This reduces the tendency, for example, to simply cozy up to the boss and work poorly with peers or subordinates. The major drawback is the time and energy it takes to collect, process, and effectively feed the data back to the individual. In addition, a recent study shows that 360-degree feedback might not have the validity attributed to it. Lowest-performing employees sometimes give themselves the highest ratings. These individuals were relatively easy to spot because their supervisor ratings were significantly lower. However, a problem occurs for "modest" employees, or employees who underrate themselves. This research suggests that more modest feedback recipients might be underrated by their supervisors. The study also found that peers often overestimated the performance of poor performers.[32]

critical incidents recording of specific incidents in which the employee's behaviour and performance were above or below expectations

Effective Performance Feedback Regardless of the system of evaluating employee performance, the results of the evaluation need to be fed back effectively to employees to make a positive difference in their performance. There are two important points to keep in mind. First, if expectations concerning unacceptable, acceptable, or superior performance were not clear to the employee prior to the appraisal, negative assessments will not likely influence motivation or performance. Consequently, performance expectations must be clear and acceptable to the employee from the beginning. Second, if the employee believes that, as the manager, you are biased in your observations, your assessment will not have the effect you desire. This is why recording both positive and negative **critical incidents** is important. This simply involves the recording of important, specific incidents in which the employee's behaviour and performance were above or below expectations. This record then allows you to avoid remembering only the most recent events and also facilitates your ability to talk about specifics in the appraisal interview.[33] This brings us to a brief list of recommendations for an effective performance appraisal interview:

1. Review key work objectives, goals, or standards against which the employee's performance is measured.
2. Summarize the employee's overall performance by reviewing specific positive and negative incidents.
3. Discuss causes of weak performance and listen carefully to the employee's explanation.
4. Discuss alternative means of improving future performance and encourage employee input.
5. Establish an agreed approach, timetable, and review process for future improvement.
6. Establish key objectives, timetables, and standards for the upcoming performance period.
7. Leave the meeting on an encouraging and positive note.

These may seem like simple steps, but they can go a long way to improving the effectiveness of one of the most difficult yet important human resource challenges you face as a manager.

Compensation

Although rewards and compensation can be instrumental in getting the right people, their primary function is retaining and maximizing the performance of employees once they have entered the organization. Rewards by their nature are designed to encourage desired behaviours. As already discussed, desired behaviours must be linked to the firm's strategy. Thus, reward systems must also be linked to the firm's strategy.

Unfortunately, employees are often rewarded for doing one thing and yet expected to do another. For example, most stockbrokers at retail brokerage firms are rewarded with bonuses based on the volume of transactions they complete. This leads many brokers to "churn" individual investors' accounts. That is, brokers buy and sell shares to generate commissions even though the investment objectives of the investors did not justify such frequent transactions.

As a consequence of this churning and the associated fees charged to customers, investors often take their accounts to competing brokerage firms. In the end, the reward structures encourage churning, but churning ultimately hurts firm revenue and broker commissions because customers leave.

Pay Most firms establish a pay structure based on level in the company and type of position. A **pay structure** establishes a range of pay for a particular position or classification of positions. Traditionally, pay structures have been hierarchical and segmented. Most companies are now moving to **broadband systems** in which the range of pay is large and covers a wide variety of jobs.[34] Exhibit 13.7 provides a graphic illustration of a traditional pay structure and a more modern broadband system. The major advantage to a broadband system is the greater flexibility it gives organizations to match pay to individual value and changing labour market conditions.

pay structure a range of pay for a particular position or classification of positions

broadband systems pay structures in which the range of pay is large and covers a wide variety of jobs

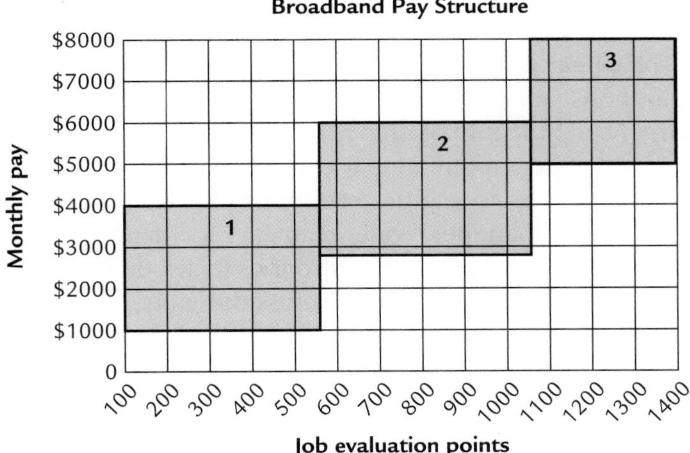

Exhibit 13.7

Traditional and Contemporary Pay Structures

Another important pay trend is the movement away from an individual's total compensation package being primarily composed of salary and toward a greater portion of compensation being at risk.[35] **At-risk compensation** is simply pay that varies depending on specified conditions. These conditions might include the general profitability of the company; hitting particular budget, revenue, or cost savings targets for a unit; or meeting specific individual performance targets. Increasingly, companies are placing a higher portion of total compensation "at risk." This is primarily because if total compensation is made up of salary and if salaries are raised at a level comparable to inflation, inflation

at-risk compensation pay that varies depending on specified conditions, including the profitability of the company; hitting particular budget, revenue, or cost savings targets for a unit; or meeting specified individual performance targets

and subsequent salary increases can add significantly to company costs. On the other hand, if a higher percentage of compensation is tied to performance, higher compensation costs only occur with higher performance. Consequently, **incentive plans**, or approaches that tie some compensation to performance, are increasingly being spread throughout the organization, whereas traditionally they were reserved for only the most senior managers.

incentive plans systems that tie some compensation to performance

Benefits Traditional benefit plans include items such as medical, dental, and life insurance. In the past, companies used to compete for employees and retain them in part through offering attractive benefit plans. However, as companies added more and more features to the plans to make them attractive to a broader base of employees with differing needs, companies found themselves paying 20 to 40 percent of salary in benefits. To reduce the soaring benefit costs and still meet differing employee needs, companies began to offer **cafeteria-style plans**, in which employees had a set number of "benefit dollars" that they could use to purchase the specific benefits that fit their particular needs.

cafeteria-style plans benefit plans in which employees have a set number of "benefit dollars" that they can use to purchase benefits that fit their particular needs

Rewards and Motivation Although much of the responsibility for reward and compensation systems is placed on the human resource department, effective rewards are more than the dollars paid out in salaries and bonuses or the dollars tied up in health care and other benefits. And though individual managers can influence pay increases and the like, they also have the greatest control over equally powerful rewards such as recognition and praise. Consequently, it is important for you to understand the broad range of rewards and how they influence the performance of your employees.

Career Systems and Development

One of the most powerful motivators for people to join organizations and to perform is the opportunity to grow and develop.[36] Career and employee development systems are designed to respond to that particular motivation and to ensure that the human capabilities needed in the organization are being developed. The **career paths** (i.e., a set and sequence of positions and experiences) organizations want employees to have to prepare for certain responsibilities is largely a function of the firm's strategy. For example, Sony is simultaneously trying to capture global efficiencies and respond to local market conditions. Sony tries to capture economic efficiencies by manufacturing nearly all of its small, handheld video cameras for markets throughout the world at a single factory in Japan. Yet it also tries to sell these cameras in a way that appeals to the different local tastes across the globe. Consequently, Sony places a high premium on international experience for career paths that lead to the top of the organization. Sony also competes on integrated team design. That is, individuals from various functional areas such as market research, engineering, sales, and finance work together at the outset of a new product development. Therefore, Sony places a premium on employees' working in several functional areas over the course of their careers, or what is referred to as **cross-functional job rotation**.[37]

career paths sets and sequences of positions and experiences

cross-functional job rotation opportunities for employees to work in different functional areas and gain additional expertise

While responsibility for organizational career and development systems is often that of the human resource function, individual managers are those most knowledgeable about the development needs of specific employees and are often those to whom individual employees go in search of career guidance. In addition, managers develop reputations as being effective or ineffective at employee development, and these reputations influence the quality of subordinates managers attract, which in turn affects the performance of their units.

Thus, while some may view employee career pathing and development as an activity for which the HR department is responsible, it is actually a critical activity at which all managers must be skilled.

Promotion Employees can and should expand and improve their capabilities in their jobs, and development need not involve promotion. However, for a large percentage of an organization's employees, job development is the means to gain promotion to positions of greater responsibility and pay. In large companies promotions often involve relocations as well. With the increasing percentage of couples who both work, these relocations, especially international relocations, can be challenging.[38] **Dual-career couples**, or couples in which both partners work full time in professional, managerial, or administrative jobs, frequently do not want to be separated, and yet finding a job for the other partner, especially in a foreign country, can be a serious obstacle to an individual's accepting a promotion and transfer. Furthermore, work visa restrictions may prevent employment of the spouse in a foreign country even if a transfer or interim job can be located. To cope with this challenge, companies are expanding their spouse relocation assistance programs and are also forming informal associations so employees interested in relocating can exchange information about transfers and job opportunities to help each other out.[39]

dual-career couples couples in which both partners work full time in professional, managerial, or administrative jobs

Termination Despite your best efforts to recruit, hire, train, compensate, and manage the performance of your employees, you may find that you have to terminate or fire an employee. Firing for cause usually involves the termination of an employee for criminal behaviour like theft of company property, or violation of company policies like sharing confidential information with competitors. Most companies have detailed and written policies about the criteria for "cause terminations" and the steps that a manager must follow to fire an employee who meets these conditions. An employee can also be fired for *failure to perform*. Again, most companies have detailed policies about what must be done first before an employee can be fired for poor performance. Often these policies involve the following:

1. Informing the employee of the performance standards.
2. Formally and specifically documenting incidents of poor performance.
3. Informing the employee of these performance failures, reiterating the standards, and setting time frames and actions for performance improvement.
4. Formally informing the employee of the consequences of failure to meet the standards and time frame established for performance improvement.

If the employee's performance does not improve sufficiently subsequent to taking these measures, many companies require his or her manager to work with a specialist in the HR department to actually fire the employee.

Layoffs Layoffs involve the termination of groups of employees because of economic or business reasons and are not a function of the employees' performance per se. Research has demonstrated that companies suffer in their ability to attract and retain good employees in the future if they do not conduct layoffs in a *reasonable* manner. Clearly, "reasonable" is open to interpretation, but practices that seem to be perceived as reasonable include outplacement aids such as resumé-writing assistance, career counselling, office space access, secretarial help, and job-hunting assistance. Often these activities are outsourced to companies that specialize in helping laid-off workers find employment.

Labour Relations

Labour relations come into play when employees are represented by formal unions who negotiate on their behalf regarding wages, benefits, and other terms of their employment. Some industries, like the airlines, have a large proportion of employees represented by unions. For example, in the airline industry not only are some of the lower-paid employees, like baggage handlers, represented by unions, but highly paid employees, like pilots, are also represented by unions. Managers must find a balance between meeting the needs of the unionized employees on such core issues as compensation, benefits, and job security, and meeting the needs of the business including controlling costs, remaining flexible to respond to a changing environment, and sustaining a reputation that allows the company to attract and retain needed employees now and in the future.

Laws and Regulations Affecting HRM

Perhaps more than any other area of management, laws and regulations affect human resource management. Exhibit 13.8 provides a summary of areas where major developments in labour legislation in employee standards occurred in Canadian jurisdictions over a one-year period (September 2005 to August 2006). The basic intent of such legislation has been to ensure that equal opportunity is provided for both job applicants and current employees. Because the laws were intended to correct past inequalities, many organizations have voluntarily implemented or been pressured by employees and other constituencies to

Exhibit 13.8 Major Developments in Canadian Labour Legislation on Employment Standards in 2005–2006

Type of Legislation	Jurisdiction
Compassionate Care Leave and Benefits	Canada, British Columbia
Parental Insurance	Quebec
Emergency Leave and Related Matters	Ontario
Minimum Wages	Manitoba, New Brunswick, Prince Edward Island, Quebec, Yukon
Prohibited Wage Deductions	Prince Edward Island
Banking Industry and Commission-Paid Salespeople Hours of Work	Canada
Construction Industry Workers	Manitoba, Yukon, Nova Scotia
Garment Industry Minimum Wages	Quebec
Recorded Visual and Audio Visual Entertainment Production Industry	Ontario
Apprentices of Defined Trades	Manitoba
Retail Establishments and Hours of Operation	Nova Scotia
Administration and Enforcement of *Employment Standards Act*	British Columbia, Ontario, Saskatchewan, Yukon
Wage Earner Protection Program	Canada
Human Rights in the Workplace	Ontario, Newfoundland and Labrador
Mandatory Retirement	Ontario, Newfoundland and Labrador
Pay Equity	Quebec
Whistle-Blower Protection	Canada, Manitoba

Source: Human Resources and Social Development Canada website www.hrsdc.gc.ca (accessed September 30, 2007).

implement **affirmative action programs** to ensure that organizational changes are made. These programs may involve such things as taking extra effort to inform minority candidates about job opportunities, providing special training programs for disadvantaged candidates, or paying special attention to the racial or gender mix of employees who are promoted.

affirmative action programs hiring and training programs intended to correct past inequalities for certain categories of people based on gender, race and ethnicity, age, or religion

As businesses globalize, laws within Canada can have an impact on how Canadian businesses operate in other countries. Countries to which managers might be sent for development opportunities only complicate the situation. For example, Japan is Canada's second-largest export market and the fifth greatest source of investment in Canada. Therefore, Canadian firms are likely to send **expatriate employees**—employees sent overseas on lengthy, but temporary assignments—to operations in Japan. However, in Japan, less than 3 percent of senior management are women. This may suggest that in a traditionally male-dominated society, female expatriate managers from Canada may face a severe **glass ceiling**—an invisible barrier that prevents women from being promoted to the highest executive ranks. Yet Canada's *Employment Equity Act* of 1995 states that the gender of Canadian employees cannot be a barrier to employment opportunities.[40]

expatriate employees employees sent overseas on lengthy, but temporary, assignments

glass ceiling an invisible barrier that prevents women from promotion to the highest executive ranks

Keep in mind that the intent of most of the legislation and regulation in Canada and the United States is designed to provide equal opportunity. This, however, does not prevent organizations from using certain criteria that you might think of as discriminatory, if it can be demonstrated that the criteria are **bona fide occupational qualifications (BFOQ)**, or qualifications that have a direct and material impact on job performance and outcomes.[41] For example, you might think that not hiring male employees who have a mustache or beard (or requiring them to shave them before being hired) would constitute discrimination. However, Disney has such a policy for its theme park workers and has prevailed when taken to court. Disney was able to retain the policy despite legal challenges because the company was able to demonstrate statistically that customers reacted better to and were more satisfied with clean-shaven park employees than those with beards and mustaches. In Disney's case, being clean shaven is a BFOQ.

bona fide occupational qualifications (BFOQ) qualifications that have a direct and material impact on job performance and outcomes

Sexual Harassment

Sexual harassment is a major workplace issue, given the devastating impact it can have on people who are victims of harassment, the negative impact it has on an organization's workplace and reputation, and the significant financial penalties that can be assessed against organizations that allow it to occur. Sexual harassment takes two basic forms. The first is sometimes called *quid pro quo* and involves requests or implied suggestions that sexual relations are required in exchange for continued employment or benefits like promotion. The second form involves actions that create a "hostile environment." A hostile environment can be created through jokes, touching, comments, pictures, and other means of communicating unwanted sexual innuendo. Sexual harassment suits have increased dramatically over the last several years. As a consequence of the judgments (which are often several hundred thousand dollars), companies are increasingly offering training programs to try to help managers understand the law and avoid such incidents.

Workforce Diversity

Effective management of workforce diversity is a growing managerial challenge. Historically, diversity was defined in terms of differences along traditional racial categories. Today, most organizations think of workforce diversity in terms of a wide range of factors, including age, gender, race, religion, cultural background, education, and mental and physical disabilities. Eight percent of the Canadian workforce are visible minorities, 1 percent are Aboriginal Peoples, 60 percent are women, and 5 percent are persons with disabilities.[42] The diversity of backgrounds raises a variety of human resource management questions. For example, with the need to reach out to such a diverse group of potential employees, what types of recruiting efforts will be effective and avoid unintended discrimination? How can the diverse backgrounds, perspectives, and talents of employees be effectively managed?

Canada Council for the Arts is an arm's length federal agency providing services and grants to Canadian artists and arts organizations and is a leader in recruiting traditionally underrepresented groups. The agency currently meets or exceeds average Canadian levels of diversity in the workforce, with 11% of their workforce composed of visible minorities, 6% Aboriginal Peoples, 73% women, and 5% persons with disabilities.[43]

Managing Workforce Diversity While there are ethical arguments for why organizations should embrace diversity, efforts to effectively manage workforce diversity typically are justified in terms of business reasons:

- Need to attract enough capable workers to meet turnover and growth demands of the business
- Enhanced creativity and innovation when solving problems
- Knowledge and understanding of the diverse marketplace and customers

The experience of most organizations, however, is that these advantages are hard to obtain. Just as multiple perspectives, values, and ways of thinking can bring new insights and creativity to a problem, they can also create a significant management challenge. Diverse workgroups often encounter the following problems:

- Communication problems and misunderstandings
- Mistrust
- Conflict and incompatible approaches to resolving the conflict
- Lower group cohesiveness and greater subgroup formation based on elements of diversity such as language, race, or gender

Given the potential benefits and the significant challenges of effectively managing workforce diversity, we review some general guidelines for you as a manager to follow:

- *Know yourself.* How much exposure have you had to people with ethnic, racial, religious, educational, or cultural backgrounds different from your own? How tolerant and understanding of the differences have you been? How comfortable were you? How curious were you?
- *Prepare yourself and your employees.* How skilled are you and your employees at listening, conflict resolution, negotiation, and communication?
- *Provide support.* To what extent are there support groups for employees with minority backgrounds to keep them from feeling unappreciated and wanting to leave the organization? To what extent do minority employees have mentors who can help them understand and become an effective part of the organization?
- *Guide behaviour.* To what extent do you monitor the behaviour of your subordinates and peers? How consistent are you in providing positive reinforcement of behaviours that foster tolerance of and effective use of diversity? To what extent do you privately provide negative feedback to individuals who display intolerance or other problem behaviours?

From both a domestic and international perspective, workforce diversity is only going to increase. One of the ways you can distinguish yourself from others and add value to your organization is through your ability to work effectively with subordinates, peers, customers, and suppliers with diverse backgrounds. *A Manager's Challenge: "Marriott Provides a Step Up"* profiles one company in which senior managers have changed how they help middle managers successfully meet the diversity challenge. As you read the box, you might ask yourself which HR practices you would find most helpful to you if you were a manager in the Marriott company.

Globalization

Globalization also poses a significant challenge to human resource management. Many argue that the world is getting smaller. However, from a human resource perspective, the world is getting larger! If you look at the history of almost any multinational corporation (MNC), at its beginning the firm operated in one or a very limited number of countries. As it grew, it expanded into more and more countries. Telecommunication and transportation technologies in particular have facilitated this expansion. Now companies like McCain Foods operate in more than 110 countries around the world. For McCain, that translates into employees speaking a multitude of languages and practising a variety of religions, dealing with 110 different governments, and coping with hundreds of different customs, holidays, and traditions. As companies expand into new countries and cultures, the world for them gets larger and more complicated.

As firms expand outside their home countries, they will confront a variety of HRM challenges. For example, do the selection techniques that work in one country also work in another? Can one performance appraisal form be applied in all operations around the globe? Must reward systems be adapted and changed from one country to the next? If they must be adapted, how can a firm avoid the risk of employees perceiving these differences as inequitable? What must a firm do to ensure that it provides development opportunities for employees in all its

a manager's challenge | change

Marriott Provides a Step Up

For managers at Marriott International, maintaining a core of workers to handle entry-level jobs and provide excellent service is critical to supporting its competitive position and continued growth. Moreover, nearly one-third of Marriott's managers started in hourly wage positions, another reason why this group is vital to the company's success. However, given the changing composition and nature of the entry-level workforce, Marriott managers have come to recognize that compensation alone will not attract, motivate, or help retain the workers they need. Managing a diverse workforce who speak some 50 languages can be a real human resource challenge.

To learn more about the changes in its workforce, Marriott managers conducted a study and learned that about one-quarter of the workers had literacy problems. In response, Marriott initiated an on-site English as a second language (ESL) program during work hours. The business reason? Workers who speak English can better serve English-speaking hotel guests.

However, managers were still busy offering advice about family conflicts and childcare solutions and sometimes lending money to employees for urgent bills. Instead of dealing with customers, some managers were spending too much time doing social work. As a result, Marriott managers changed their approach to human resource management. They added programs such as the Associate Resource Line, a confidential service that counsels employees across a broad spectrum of personal matters. They also started up social services referrals and childcare referrals to attract and motivate hourly workers—and keep turnover lower than that of competitors.

More than 50 languages are spoken among Marriott's 151 000 employees in 67 countries around the world. The hotel chain has been honoured for its work–life practices by many organizations, including *Diversity, Inc.*, *Working Mother*, and *Latina Style* magazines. In an industry where the hourly employee turnover rate is 80 to 90 percent, Marriott's 35 percent turnover rate is exceptionally low.

By responding to the changing composition and needs of the entry-level workforce, managers help sustain Marriott's competitive position and its reputation for exceptional service. The company's continued growth has delivered even more opportunities for employee personal and professional growth, which managers highlight to attract and retain employees.

Sources: Marriott International, Inc 2006 Annual Report, www.marriott.com (accessed October 8, 2007); Adapted from A. Wheat, "The Anatomy of a Great Workplace," *Fortune*, February 4, 2002, pp. 75+; J. Hickman, "America's 50 Best Companies for Minorities," *Fortune*, July 8, 2002, pp. 110+; "America's 50 Best Companies for Minorities," *Fortune*, July 9, 2001, pp. 122+; J. Gordon, "The New Paternalism," *Forbes*, November 2, 1998; "Best Companies for Asians, Blacks, and Hispanics," *Fortune*, August 2, 1998.

operations? How does any global firm ensure that it finds and develops the best possible talent wherever in its worldwide operations that talent might be located? When a firm needs to send employees outside their native countries as a means of developing their international skills and abilities, how does it effectively select these individuals? How should these employees be trained prior to their international assignments? How can these individuals be effectively evaluated when factors such as real changes in exchange rates, government price controls, and other external factors significantly influence bottom-line results of overseas operations? These are just a sampling of the questions and human resource management challenges raised by today's increasingly global environment.

managerial perspectives revisited

1 PERSPECTIVE 1: **THE ORGANIZATIONAL CONTEXT** The organizational context is extremely important when it comes to human resource management. In many ways the appropriate HR practices are a function of the organization. Change the context of the organization—its strategy, culture, or industry—and you are likely to need to change the characteristics or capabilities needed in the employees you want to recruit, how you orient them, what training they need, and how you manage their performance or structure their compensation.

2 PERSPECTIVE 2: **THE HUMAN FACTOR** From one perspective, human resource management is all about working through others; it is about achieving results by attracting, selecting, training, appraising, compensating, and developing others. Because human resource management also typically involves the policies and practices of the company through the human resource department, as a manager, effective HRM will likely also involve working with and through people in your HR department.

3 PERSPECTIVE 3: **MANAGING PARADOXES** Meeting the HRM challenge creates some important potential paradoxes. On the one hand, individual managers have their own personal views on the effective management of human resources. On the other hand, as managers in an organization, they have to work with, support, and uphold the policies and practices of the company. At times there may be a conflict between the two. In such cases, do managers have an obligation to try to correct company practices that are not in keeping with what their values are or what they believe—or that may be inappropriate or even illegal? This dynamic tension between personal and company standards is one of the principal paradoxes managers face when it comes to managing and motivating the firm's people.

4 PERSPECTIVE 4: **ENTREPRENEURIAL MINDSET** The entrepreneurial mindset is reflected in the behaviour and actions of a firm's employees. WestJet employees are a good example of workers who hold and display an entrepreneurial mindset. Employees at WestJet are given more latitude in making on-the-spot decisions and exercise a greater interest in the well-being of the customer and, at the same time, the company. Part of this may be attributed to the fact that more than 87 percent of WestJet employees are shareholders, taking part in an employee share purchase plan that the company matches with equal contributions. It may also be the culture of WestJet, where the emphasis is on putting people first. Either way, the approach to managing employees at WestJet is attracting and retaining quality employees that are in turn rewarded for their commitment.

To maintain a company's competitive edge, managers should be committed to constantly improving their human resource management capabilities. While the HR department is designed to support and facilitate the effective management of human resources in the company, it's no substitute for individual managers taking the initiative to engage in key HR activities.

concluding comments

In this chapter, we presented human resource management as a set of activities performed by all managers rather than a set of functions locked within a human resource department. A company's human resources are its most fundamental source of competitive advantage. In addition, individual managers can create competitive advantages for themselves in their careers through superior management of human resources. In particular, managers who can match their management of human resources with the strategy of the organization may find themselves in a superior position relative to their peers.

As a manager, it is unlikely that you will want to leave activities such as recruitment, selection, training, or development of your employees entirely to the human resource department. While human resource departments in most companies play a formal role in all the activities we have covered in this chapter, if you want to get the right people and maximize their performance, you will need to be involved in and skilled at these activities as well.

Relegating HR activities to a specific department is an old school of thought and not reflective of today's environment. As business continues to push toward being knowledge based, the effective management of intelligent employees becomes increasingly important. As an executive of an engineering service firm said to us, "I watch the company's assets walk out the door at the close of business each day." From that perspective, effective human resource management becomes a central component of every manager's job.

key terms

affirmative action programs 467
assessment centres 454
at-risk compensation 463
behaviourally anchored rating scales (BARS) 460
bona fide occupational qualifications (BFOQ) 467
broadband systems 463
cafeteria-style plans 464
career paths 464
critical incidents 462
cross-functional job rotation 464
dual-career couples 465
expatriate employees 467
glass ceiling 467
incentive plans 464
job analysis 450
job design 458
job posting 450
job sharing 459
pay structure 463
re-engineering 459
structured interview 453
360-degree feedback 461
unstructured interview 453
valid selection technique 453
work simulation 455

test your comprehension

1. What are the key human resource activities at which a manager must be skilled?
2. Why is it important to keep the firm's strategy in mind when engaged in HR activities like selection?
3. What are two advantages of part-time or temporary employees in meeting a firm's workforce needs?
4. What are the principal aspects of job analysis?
5. How can job posting help a firm with its internal management of human resources?
6. Describe five effective means of recruiting new employees.
7. What does it mean for a selection technique to be valid?
8. What is the primary difference between structured and unstructured interviews and what effect does this difference have?

9. What is the basic rationale for work sampling as a selection method?
10. Identify three written tests used in selection and describe their validity.
11. Why are reference checks of little use in selection?
12. List the five things that can be done to make orientation programs more effective.
13. Define *re-engineering* and explain its use in organizations.
14. What are the key differences between graphic rating scales and behaviourally anchored rating scales?
15. List seven steps that can be taken to make performance appraisal sessions more effective.
16. Why are organizations moving away from traditional pay structures to more broadband pay structures?
17. What is a cafeteria-style benefit plan?
18. What does it mean to fire someone for cause?
19. What is the purpose of affirmative action programs?
20. What is a BFOQ?
21. What is the difference between quid pro quo and a hostile environment in cases of sexual harassment?
22. Describe three things you can do to improve your capability to manage greater diversity in the workforce.

apply your understanding

1. What do you think will change most dramatically in the future in terms of what it will take to attract young people to companies?
2. Think about the best and worst bosses you've ever had. To what extent did human resource management skills differentiate the two? In particular, which skills?
3. As you look forward to a future management position, what HRM strengths and weaknesses do you feel you have?
4. If you look at your university, what HR activities does it perform well? What are needed improvements?
5. What do you think will be the most challenging HR activities in the future?

practise your capabilities

You are the captain of a firefighting squad consisting of two trucks and 12 firefighters. You have two females in your squad. As firefighters your squad is on duty for 24 hours and then off duty for 24 hours at a time. When on duty you all live together in the firehouse where you eat, sleep, train, relax, and hang out together. Some days are so intense with calls that you do not have time for anything else. Other days by comparison are quite slow.

The effectiveness of your team is a function of skill and trust. The techniques of suppressing a fire or evacuating people from a burning building may be lost on the average person, but the depth of these required skills are vital. A significant amount of trust is also required to be effective. For example, if you were injured in a burning building, you would want to know that your team members would be able to get you out.

In most firehouses, including yours, the addition of women has happened only recently. All women firefighters have to pass the same physical and skill tests given to the men. However, firehouses have traditionally had a strong flavour of male-oriented conversation, humour, and activities such as lifting weights as a means of helping the team bond.

One of your newest female recruits has come to you complaining of a sexually hostile work environment. She complained that the jokes she overhears are full of offensive humour and that several of the guys have offensive pictures inside their lockers. Because the firehouse is an older one, there are not separate locker rooms or showers. Although separate shower times have been scheduled, the recruit also complained that some of the guys had "accidentally" walked in when she was showering because they "forgot" the schedule.

The other female member of the squad, who has been in the unit for nearly a year, disagrees with the description of the environment as sexually hostile, but would not really go into any details or specifics.

1. What actions would you take?
2. Suppose, in talking individually with the guys in the squad, some say that they can see that a couple of the younger, single guys might be a bit "macho" in their conversations among themselves. What would you do if these younger guys report that they feel the new female recruit is simply eavesdropping on private conversations?
3. How would the fact that the new female recruit seems to be as physically strong and more skilled than two of the younger "macho" guys in the squad affect your actions? What would you do differently if she were not a good performer?

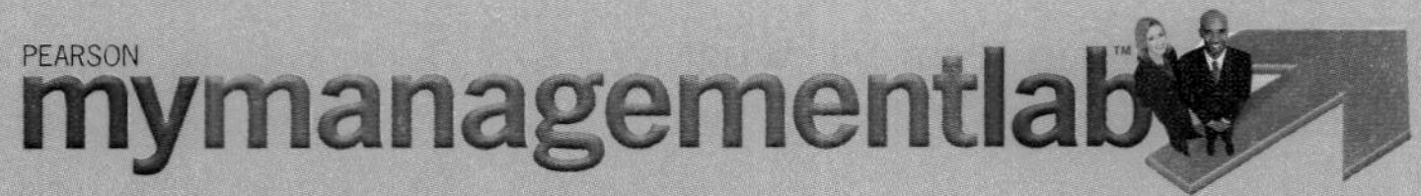

To improve your grade, visit the MyManagementLab website at **www.pearsoned.ca/mymanagementlab**. This online homework and tutorial system allows you to test your understanding and generates a personalized study plan just for you. It provides you with study and practice tools directly related to this chapter's content. MyManagementLab puts you in control of your own learning!

closing case DEVELOP YOUR CRITICAL THINKING

HSBC Bank Canada's Unique Advantage

As the Canadian workforce grows older and more diverse in composition, managers face new challenges in attracting, retaining, and managing skilled workers at all organizational levels. As a result of cultural shifts, demographics, and immigration, the labour pool is composed of more women, older workers, and visible minorities than ever before. Some companies have been slow to adjust to the increasing diversity, while others—like HSBC Bank Canada—have embraced it wholeheartedly.

HSBC is one of the largest banking and financial services in the world. It provides its services from 10 000 offices in 82 countries and territories. HSBC Bank Canada is the seventh-largest bank in Canada with 130 branches and a net income of $274 million in the first six months of 2007. In 1992, the Canadian operations created the Valuing Diversity Council, which is composed of employees across departments, geography, and levels within the bank.

The Valuing Diversity Council advises senior managers on ways to improve the workplace environment for individuals covered by the federal government's *Employment Equity Act* of 1986, which includes women, visible minorities, Aboriginal people, and people with disabilities. The council also participates in developing, implementing, and monitoring diversity programs within HSBC. The initiative has been very successful in raising the level of awareness among staff and management in HSBC. Senior executives within the organization have incorporated the diversity initiatives into HSBC's business priorities and actively demonstrate their commitment by advocating employee cooperation and buy-in at all levels.

An example of how the council has raised awareness and understanding of diversity within HSBC is their production of a series of modules on diversity that have been integrated into internal training programs at HSBC. The modules help in improving the knowledge and skills of employees and managers on the subject of diversity. The topics covered in the modules aid in short-circuiting potentially destructive perceptions such as stereotyping and discrimination of other employees and customers. The modules also assist in improving an employee's ability to manage others with training on empathizing and communicating with people from a variety of backgrounds.

The steps that HSBC Bank Canada has taken to promote diversity are innovative in two ways. First, rather than make the human resource department solely responsible for diversity, senior managers have demonstrated their active support and involvement. Second, the diverse composition of the Valuing Diversity Council helped these groups address diversity on a larger scale. Now every department and unit within HSBC supports diversity, and the company's long-term commitment to diversity will allow every employee to make valuable contributions to growth in the coming years.

The net effect of HSBC Bank Canada's diversity initiatives has been a more creative, innovative workforce that is more adept in teamwork situations, which in turn has led to an increase in productivity. The culture at HSBC today is that all customers and employees should expect fair and respectful treatment. HSBC has been recognized as a Canadian leader in workplace diversity—exemplified by retail branches composed of 40 employees that may speak as many as 15 different languages—and has regularly been identified as one of the best companies to work for in Canada. However, HSBC and the Valuing Diversity Council have not slowed in its efforts to widen what they consider to be a unique advantage. They want to increase currently underrepresented groups, such as people of Aboriginal descent as well as people with disabilities, and have launched targeted outreach initiatives to reach their goal.

Questions

1. Why is HSBC Bank Canada so committed to diversity? How will this benefit the company?
2. Do you believe the company is forcing the issue of diversity? Is it necessary to have diversity training as part of their internal training programs? Explain your answer.
3. Independent surveys suggest that companies cannot easily quantify the effects of diversity. How would you suggest that HSBC Bank Canada measure the effects of a diverse workforce? If a company ignored workforce diversity, how might it be affected?

Sources: "Valuing Diversity," HSBC Bank Canada, www.hsbc.ca (accessed October 8, 2007); "Fact Sheet," HSBC Bank Canada, www.hsbc.ca (accessed October 8, 2007); "Corporate Profiles: HSBC Bank Canada," Human Resources and Social Development Canada, www.hrsdc.gc.ca (accessed October 8, 2007); "Canada's Top 100 Employers," www.canadastop100.com (accessed October 9, 2007).

Part Three **integrative case**

Ste. Basil Hotel–Moscow: Struggling with Values in a Post-Communist State

By Charles A. Rarick, Barry University ©2003, CA Rarick, Barry University, Miami, Florida, USA.

Abstract

This case profiles the difficulties experienced by an American expatriate operating a luxury hotel in Russia. The American general manager is confronted with problems of employee motivation, poor customer service, corruption, and the possible loss of the hotel to its Russian partner.

It was a typical October day in Moscow as Greg Hill looked out the window of his office in the Ste. Basil Hotel. As he saw the snow begin to fall he realized that it was going to be a very long, cold winter in Russia and he longed for the sunshine and warmth of his previous assignment in Miami Beach. While the move to Moscow had been a difficult experience, he and his wife had adjusted reasonably well, and Greg believed that the move would position him for advancement in his American company. He felt that the hardship of living in Russia would be offset by advancement opportunity but he was now very concerned about his future. A deeply religious man, Greg began to pray for a solution to his problems.

The Ste. Basil Hotel in Moscow is a four-star hotel located in Red Square. The idea for a luxury hotel was conceived by Louis Cunningham, CEO of LCC Properties. LCC owned a number of luxurious hotel properties in the United States, Canada, South America, and Japan. Cunningham developed the idea for a luxury hotel after a visit to Russia in 1994 in which he and his wife toured the former communist state. Cunningham noticed that the quality of hotels in the country was poor, most being old Soviet style in appearance and operations. Cunningham knew that a number of American and European businesspeople were traveling to Russia, and that an opportunity existed for a hotel that matched the level of quality found in the West. On subsequent visits, Cunningham spotted an abandoned construction site near St. Basil Cathedral and decided that it would be a prime location for a luxury hotel. The site was owned by the Russian government, which agreed to provide the site if LCC would invest the necessary $50 million to develop it into a four-star property. The Russian government also insisted that LCC create a partnership with the state-owned airline that would take 51 percent of the operation. Although Cunningham didn't like the idea of minority interest in the project, he was excited about the location, and even more excited about the prospect of being a pioneering capitalist in a former communist country.

With the fall of the Soviet Union in 1991, Western businesses began to take an interest in the former communist state. The reform movement begun by Mikhail Gorbachev would eventually result in the collapse of the Soviet Union, and the satellite states would gain their independence. The early reform movement of *glasnost*, or "openness," resulted in the lifting of censorship, the release of dissidents, and greater tolerance for religious freedom. Glasnost was followed by *perestroika* or "restructuring," in which the economy was decentralized and privatized. Military spending was cut and free elections were held. As the former communist superpower turned toward capitalism, Western businesses looked for opportunities.

A Luxury Hotel in Moscow

Louis Cunningham was one of those seeking this new opportunity. Although Cunningham was extremely excited about the project and had a particular interest in seeing a capitalist spirit come to Russia, he was forced to delegate most of the responsibilities for the new venture, due to the failing health of his wife. The new hotel was named the Ste. Basil because of its proximity to St. Basil Cathedral. Cunningham chose the abbreviation

"Ste." because he thought it would "add class" and provide the luxury image the hotel sought to project. Cunningham selected Greg Hill to be the general manager of the new hotel and to oversee completion of the construction of the facility. Greg Hill was a 47-year-old general manager of a luxury hotel in Miami Beach, Florida. He had worked for LCC since graduating from a small college in the Midwest with a degree in hospitality administration. Hill and his wife, who were raised in St. Louis, Missouri, had moved a number of times as Greg gained increasingly responsible positions with LCC. With their two children away at college, the Hills felt that moving abroad would be less difficult than it had been when the children were younger. They did enjoy living in Miami and hoped to retire to south Florida at a later date. The opportunity to build and manage a new hotel in a former communist country was an offer that Greg felt he could not turn down. He believed that success in this project could move him into the ranks of upper management at LCC. Mrs. Hill was a teacher in Miami and enjoyed other cultures. She looked forward to living in a foreign country, and in fact often felt that moving to Miami was like living in a different country. The Hills were friendly people, and although not considered worldly, they were open to new experiences and adjusted to new situations well.

The move to Moscow and the completion of the hotel's construction provided many unforeseen difficulties, but the Russian partners were helpful in overcoming most obstacles. Greg Hill developed the Ste. Basil into a fine hotel. It stood out in great contrast to the poorly equipped and managed hotels which were remnants of the Soviet era. The Ste. Basil provided its guests with an outstanding restaurant and café, an indoor pool, an exercise facility, a dry cleaning service, satellite television, modem/data portals, conference rooms, currency exchange, a gift shop, and concierge services. The rooms were clean, modern, and spacious. The hotel catered to foreign businesspeople from the United States and Europe and was one of the highest priced hotels in Moscow. Room rates ranged from $215 to $450US per night. Conference facilities could also be rented and the hotel provided a catering service to conference participants. With increasing business between Russia and the West it was believed that the Ste. Basil would be the obvious choice among business travelers.

Recruitment of Employees

The Ste. Basil would have to fill all positions, with the exception of general manager, with local labor. Since Greg Hill was the only American expatriate, he felt that he should be actively involved in the recruitment and selection process. With the help of his Russian partners, Hill placed an advertisement in the *Moscow Times* for all hotel positions. The advertisement was in English since it had been decided that all employees should be proficient in the English language. Response to the advertisement was overwhelming. Thousands of people arrived to apply for the positions. Many of the people who sought employment at the Ste. Basil were educated beyond job requirements. The Ste. Basil received applications from scientists, attorneys, doctors, professors, writers, as well as recent university graduates. Greg was told that the applicants could make much more money working for an American company than continuing in their present professions.

Greg was assisted in applicant screening by his assistant general manager. Victor Popov was appointed by the Russian partners to act not only as the assistant general manager, but also to help Greg with his assimilation and understanding of Russian culture. Victor had at one time been employed in the airline industry as an engineer. He held degrees in engineering, including a master's degree in radio engineering from the St. Petersburg Electrotechnical University. Victor's great-grandfather had been a pioneer in the development of radio and the family name was well respected in Russia. Victor spoke fluent English and German, in addition to his native Russian. His hotel experience was limited to a short assignment in an East German hotel, and it was never clear to Greg what his responsibilities were in that assignment. Greg and Victor went through each application and began eliminating individuals who were clearly not qualified. Anyone who had previous hotel experience was eliminated from further consideration. It was thought that these employees had acquired bad habits working for state-owned hotels and it would be very difficult to retrain them. The only exceptions would be for critical positions such as chef, which required previous experience. Victor strongly suggested that older applicants (over 35 years of age) should also not be selected. Greg was not sure about this request, but he deferred to Victor's judgment. Greg, however, refused to follow Victor's advice and eliminate all female applicants with small children. Greg did eliminate anyone who had an advanced degree such as an attorney, scientist, or physician, feeling that such a person would become quickly dissatisfied with the position.

After the initial screening, applicants were invited for an interview. This proved difficult since many of the applicants did not have a telephone and could not be reached except by mail. Greg decided to eliminate those candidates since the applicant pool was more than sufficient. When word got out that the hotel was interviewing, some of the applicants without telephones walked in and requested interviews. Victor granted some of these applicants interview appointments. The interviewing and selection process took two weeks and included structured and unstructured questions, questions asking applicants to provide their recommendations to hypothetical problems they might experience on the job, a written test of English ability, and a short intelligence test (in English). For the most part Greg was discouraged by the responses of the applicants, especially the responses to the unstructured and situational questions. Many of the applicants provided very short answers or were unable to answer at all. These applicants were eliminated from further consideration. In the end, however, Greg and Victor were able to assemble a workforce which both felt would be satisfactory.

Orientation and Training

A mandatory three-day orientation session was conducted for all employees. The orientation program provided employees with information on LCC Enterprises such as its history and mission; basic training on the importance of customer service; grooming; manners; and company policy. After the three-day orientation program, specific job training was provided. Greg was assisted at this point by a team of six expatriates from LCC who were brought in for the short-term training assignment.

Greg had expected that the employees would be very motivated to learn their jobs since their compensation was considerably more than most had previously received in their careers in Russia, and working at a luxury American hotel provided a degree of status. He was disappointed by the responses to the training program. Many of the new employees seemed more interested in asking about compensation, benefits, and how the hotel would benefit them, than specific questions concerning their responsibilities. Greg noticed some of the employees dozing off during the orientation program. In addition, Greg was discouraged by the reactions he received from some of the employees to a gift the hotel gave on the first day of orientation. The hotel provided, as a welcoming gift to each employee, a large basket of toiletries wrapped with a large red ribbon. Some of the employees wanted two or three of the baskets and some asked for money instead. Although this disappointed Greg, many employees appeared grateful for the opportunity to work and seemed motivated to do a good job. Greg was pleased that with the exception of two people, all employees were able to successfully complete their job-specific training. With the employees selected and trained, the Ste. Basil Hotel was ready to begin welcoming guests.

A Slow Start

During the first few weeks of operation Greg spent most of his time with external relations. He was busy dealing with suppliers, government officials, and travel industry representatives. Greg delegated much of the day-to-day operations to Victor, who would consult with him if a problem arose which he could not handle. Occupancy was very low, as expected, yet the restaurant and café did a brisk business from the start. The low level of occupancy was somewhat beneficial in that it allowed the staff time to continue to learn their duties on-the-job. The American trainers had returned home, and with Greg busy with other matters, Victor made decisions and answered questions from the staff.

Although Greg did not have much contact with many of the employees during this time he did notice that in general the employees did not seem to present the warm, hospitable atmosphere that the hotel sought. The employees infrequently smiled and often seemed to be in a bad mood. Greg mentioned this point to Victor who told him that it was "the Russian nature," but that he would ask the employees to try harder. Greg decided that while he was too busy to intervene, he would try to "catch someone doing it right" and reward him or her with positive reinforcement. On several occasions when he found an employee smiling or presenting the proper attitude he would give them an "O.K." sign (thumb and forefinger closed in a circle) as a show of approval. Much to his surprise this provoked a negative reaction in the employees. Greg was also surprised by the frequent use of the Russian word "nyet"; in fact, it seemed to Greg that the "no" word was almost an automatic response to any request.

Trouble with Victor

As time went on, Greg was able to devote more of his attention to internal operations. He was beginning to become concerned about Victor's approach with employees. While Victor was a handsome and confident man, and appeared to be well liked by the hotel's customers, his approach to employee relations was unattractive. In one particular case a desk clerk was fired in a loud outburst in front of several guests. It was particularly troubling in that the clerk, Svetlana, was a favorite of Greg's. Svetlana was a divorced mother of two young girls who had been struggling to provide the sole support for her family after her husband left. Svetlana was a devout member of the Russian Orthodox Church and Greg considered her to be an honest, conscientious, and faithful employee. Victor informed Greg that he had terminated her for excessive time off. Victor explained that Svetlana had asked for two days off to care for one of her children who was sick and she did not return to work for a week. Victor explained that he had assumed that she had quit, and so he was surprised to see her behind the front desk working. Her attitude was poor, according to

Victor, and she insulted him, so he lost his temper and fired her in front of all parties present. As Greg probed further he was told by Victor that there is an old Russian proverb—"A dog is wiser than a woman. It never barks at its master." It was clear to Greg that Victor had a low opinion of women and that he was engaging in behavior which was inconsistent with LCC company policy. Greg informed Victor that he was going to contact Svetlana and hear her side of the story.

With some difficulty, Greg was finally able to contact Svetlana and he asked her to come in to the hotel to discuss the matter. Svetlana told Greg that she did request two days off but that her other child had also become ill and she needed to care for her too. She was fearful to let Victor know that she would not be able to come in for the additional days. Greg was sympathetic and told her that he would reinstate her. When Victor was told of Greg's decision he just shook his head and said "nyekulturny" and walked away. Greg was not sure what this meant but he was sure it wasn't favorable. Greg decided that all decisions concerning employee discipline would first have to be approved by him and he issued a memo stating the policy. Victor took the memo very seriously and proceeded to consult Greg on all personnel matters. He did seem genuine in his actions (although Greg was not completely sure of this) but the constant requests for Greg's approval became a nuisance.

Additional difficulties continued to arise with Victor. It concerned Greg that Victor began spending a lot of time in the hotel restaurant with a small group of Russian men. They didn't appear to ever eat a meal, they only smoked and drank vodka and gave disapproving stares at anyone who came near them. The group appeared to Greg to be a bit rough and not the type of clientele that the hotel sought to attract. After a few weeks Greg decided that it was time to investigate. He began by checking into the amount of money the group was spending in the restaurant and he was shocked to discover that Victor was providing the drinks free of charge to the group. When questioned about this, Victor replied that these men were important to the success of the hotel and that the money for their drinks was money well spent. Greg was confused by the response and continued to ask about the men. Victor finally stated in a firm tone—"Trust me General Manager, I know what I am doing." Greg felt that he had better let the issue go for now but that he should keep an eye on the situation.

Attempt at Improvement in Customer Service

With the issues concerning Victor still in his mind, Greg decided that he must begin to address the issue of customer service, and he would probably need to do it without Victor's assistance. Although business was beginning to increase, customer feedback indicated that many guests felt that the hotel staff was not on par with what was expected from a four-star hotel. Guests commented that the staff was "unhelpful," "uncaring," "cold," and "went out of their way to avoid work." These frequent comments were an embarrassment to Greg and LCC Properties, so he decided that he should ask for help from the corporate staff to bring the hotel up to standard.

With the arrival of two customer service trainers from the United States an ambitious training program was instituted. Every employee, including supervisory staff, would be required to complete 20 hours of additional training. The trainers repeated the initial training in guest relations which the employees had experienced when they were first hired, and additional training was conducted in handling problem guests and seeking continuous improvement in customer relations. An incentive program was designed by the trainers where each guest would be given a card on which they could recommend an employee for recognition for their good service. At the end of each week the hotel would reward the employee who had accumulated the most recommendations with a certificate for a free meal for two in the hotel restaurant. In addition, the employee would have his or her picture placed at the front desk with the caption "Employee of the Week." In the next few weeks it did appear that customer service was improving; however, Greg worried that the improvement might be short-lived and that the Ste. Basil would not be able to match the level of service found in other LCC properties. He had heard that some of the employees resented the competitive nature of the incentive.

A Visit by the Krysha

During the following months business improved at the Ste. Basil. As Greg was in his office reviewing the hotel's revenues and expenses for the past six months, a smile grew on his face. While there were still some problems with customer service, employee punctuality, and employees showing initiative, Greg felt that LCC would be pleased with the operating results of the hotel. The hotel continued to show strong gains in occupancy. The restaurant and café were doing well, but the conference facilities were still underutilized, in Greg's opinion.

Greg's thoughts were interrupted by a knock on the door. Victor entered and asked if he could speak with him for a moment about a "very important matter." Greg welcomed Victor in and was surprised to see that he was not alone. Behind him were four men that Greg had seen previously in the hotel's restaurant with Victor. Greg introduced himself and the men remained silent. Victor seemed very uncomfortable as he explained that the men had requested that the hotel hire them for their services. Greg was not sure what Victor meant, but he was developing an uneasy feeling that something was wrong. Victor explained that the men were needed for "security purposes." Greg realized that Victor did not mean to imply that they were asking for security guard positions and so he asked that the men please step outside the office for a moment. As they did, Victor began to explain that these men were members of the Russian mafia and that they wanted protection money. Victor explained that it was quite common in Russia to pay for such a service, but Greg was adamant in his refusal to pay. Greg berated Victor for even bringing the men into his office and questioned why he was meeting with them in the hotel restaurant. Victor stated that he was protecting Greg and the hotel from problems, and that Greg should consider the fact that an American was recently murdered in Moscow by the Russian mafia. Greg told Victor to leave the office and to inform the men that the Ste. Basil did not need their services.

THE RUSSIAN COLD

As Victor left the office, Greg's telephone rang. It was Dmitry Puzankov, attorney for the Russian partners. Dmitry explained to Greg that the partners wanted to meet with him to discuss some contract matters. When pressed for an explanation, Dmitry explained that the partners wanted to negotiate the profit distribution of the agreement and some "other changes" including their request that Victor be made "Executive General Manager." Upon ending the conversation with Dmitry, Greg telephoned down to the front desk as he wanted to meet with Svetlana and he knew that she was scheduled to be working. Greg had come to rely on Svetlana for advice on Russian culture. He was informed that Svetlana had not reported to work due to illness of one of her children. As Greg watched the snow fall upon the Moscow streets below he wondered about the security of his present position, the personal safety of himself and his wife, and his future with LCC Properties. It seemed to Greg that the temperature of his office had suddenly dropped as a cold chill ran throughout his body.

Part Four | Monitoring and Renewing

Chapter 14 Control

LEARNING OBJECTIVES

After reading this chapter, you should be able to:

1 Discuss the effects of too much or too little control in an organization.

2 Describe the four basic elements of the control process and the issues involved in each.

3 Differentiate between the different levels of control and compare their implications for managers.

4 Explain the concept of standards and why they are so important in organizations.

5 Compare bureaucratic and clan controls.

6 Identify the important qualities required for information to be useful in the control process.

How Much Control Is Enough?

Can a single individual topple an entire multinational corporation? The answer is, surprisingly, yes. The lack of control at Barings Bank sank the 233-year-old British bank and rocked the financial world. In early 1995, a 28-year-old trader caused one of the most spectacular collapses in modern financial history. When the dust finally settled, Barings had suffered trading losses in excess of US$1 billion. Ironically, just two years earlier, Peter Baring, the company's CEO, had stated in a speech, "[Financial] derivatives need to be well controlled and understood, but we believe we do that well here."

Baring Brothers was one of the oldest and most prestigious banks in Great Britain, and was even a bank to the House of Windsor. Barings's money helped to keep British armies in the field during the Napoleonic Wars. The Baring family had run the firm for 233 years, and Peter Baring was carrying on the tradition.

In 1992, Barings sent Nick Leeson to assume a post as the chief trader of Baring Futures in Singapore. Leeson traded futures contracts on the Nikkei 225, Japan's version of the Dow Jones index. His job was to exploit the small differences in the buying and selling of these contracts, otherwise known as arbitrage. The trading of futures was considered a relatively safe bet because they generally only resulted in small profits or losses at one time. But Leeson became more sophisticated in his trading knowledge, and he became more "bullish" (that is, he took greater risks).

On January 17, 1995, a massive earthquake devastated Kobe, Japan, and the Nikkei responded with uncertainty. Later that month, the Nikkei plunged more than 1000 points. For Barings and for Leeson, this natural disaster turned into a financial disaster. The traders in the Far East panicked, Leeson in particular.

Leeson made huge investments, betting on the rebound of the Nikkei. While traders at other investment banks cut their losses, Leeson proceeded to put Barings's money into billions of dollars worth of futures contracts that would only make money if the Nikkei rose. Traders in Tokyo and Singapore watched, but they figured that the bets that Barings was making were offset by hedges in other areas. However, this turned out not to be the case. For every percentage point that the Nikkei slipped, Barings lost tens of millions of dollars. Eventually, the losses exceeded Barings's net worth.

Workers are shown exiting the Barings Bank building in London, after it was purchased by Dutch financial group ING for only 1£. Some parts of Barings were integrated into ING while other parts were sold or shut down. Barings had been one of the oldest and most prestigious banks in Great Britain before employee Nick Leeson bankrupted it by speculating in the Nikkei 225 (Japan's version of the Dow Jones index).

Whether senior management really knew what was going on in Singapore is not clear. Someone at the London headquarters knew—because Leeson had made the investments with borrowed funds, a common practice. As Leeson's bets lost, Barings in London funnelled US$900 million to Singapore to offset the losses. By late February, the Nikkei had not bounced back, and Leeson and his wife skipped town.

Barings went bankrupt on February 26, 1995. As British regulators took control of the bank, Interpol, the international intelligence agency, sent out an alert to all governments in neighbouring countries to find Leeson. A few days after the bank's collapse, the "rogue trader" walked into the arms of police at Germany's Frankfurt airport. Leeson was convicted of fraud and sentenced to six and a half years in a Singapore prison, but served only four years, being released in 1999. While in prison he wrote a book entitled *Rogue Trader,* which is an account of his fraudulent acts. A *New York Times* review of the book was not very complimentary, but it did state that the book should be read by "banking managers and auditors everywhere," suggesting that there are lessons to be learned in the lack of control employed by Barings at the time of Leeson's reckless endeavours.

Sources: P. Dwyer, "Descent into the Abyss," *BusinessWeek*, July 1, 1996, pp. 28–29; F. Norris, "Upper-Class Twits Made Me Do It," *New York Times*, March 31, 1996; S. D. Kaye, "Ripples from a Fallen Bank," *U.S. News & World Report*, March 13, 1995, pp. 68–72; B. Powell, D. Pedersen, and M. Elliott, "Busted!" *Newsweek*, March 13, 1995, pp. 36–43.

strategic overview

As shown in the opening case on Barings, control is a critically important component of management activities in organizations, and it can play an important role in how an organization's strategy is developed and implemented and in the evaluation of its success. Oftentimes, control is exercised based on the financial outcomes of a strategy, like an organization's profits. However, control is sometimes focused on the type of strategy selected and the manner in which it is implemented. While controls focused on strategy (as opposed to financial outcomes) are difficult to develop and apply, they are crucial to ensuring that the organization remains innovative. Financial controls often focus on achieving short-term results like meeting the firm's profit goals for a quarter or a year. But when the focus is on strategy, managers must look toward longer-term results, like investing in the development of innovative new products. In fact, the types of controls implemented can affect the formulation of future strategies. Research has shown that when managers use controls focused on strategy, they are better able to focus on the long term and develop more effective organizational strategies.[1]

The type of control can also affect both the formulation and implementation of strategies by managers. Bureaucratic controls tend to focus on controlling behaviour in organizations with rules and regulations. Universities often employ bureaucratic controls because of the large number of students, faculty, and employees whose behaviour they must oversee. However, these controls are frequently tight and may constrain the types of strategies that can be pursued. For this reason, universities often make major changes only very slowly. Alternatively, controls based on the organization's culture (called "clan controls," and explained later in this chapter) better ensure that the strategies chosen fit well with the values of the organization. For example, WestJet has a unique culture and uses it to select new employees who share the organization's values. This same culture, or clan control, governs the behaviour of both managers and employees, who then have the same vision for the organization. Because all of the employees understand WestJet's culture and "buy into it," managers are better able to develop effective strategies that match the firm's values and implement them.

Regardless of the types of controls used, managers shouldn't feel so controlled or constrained that they can't respond to environmental changes such as challenges from competitors and the prospect of innovative products being introduced to the market. Many organizations now employ the balanced scorecard approach (explained later in this chapter) to ensure that managers are able to balance controls and needed flexibility to continue to learn, innovate, and change.

Probably the most critical part of that challenge, for individual managers as well as for organizations, is where to draw the line between too much control and too little control. Most of us can think of examples from our own work or other group experiences where we have encountered the downside of excessive control by individuals or supervisors or the organization itself through its rules and regulations. At the extreme, overcontrol conjures up images of "Big Brother," where you cannot make a move without first obtaining permission from someone higher up in the organizational structure.[2] More typically, too much control can result in resentment and limited motivation.

At the other extreme, too little control, as illustrated in the opening example, can expose an organization and its managers to very costly risks. Take, for example, the opening case in Chapter 3 where Japanese architect Hidetsugu Aneha was able to falsify structural documents because of the infrequent auditing undertaken by the Japanese government on privatized plan inspectors. In milder forms, undercontrol contributes to sloppy operations and failure to use resources efficiently and effectively. Errors or mistakes can increase, and the organization may not know where or when problems are occurring and, most importantly, how to fix them. In severe cases, the potential consequences can be catastrophic for the organization, as they were for Barings, or for the public, as they could have been for the occupants of the under-designed buildings in Japan.

Exercising control, then, presents not only major challenges for managers but also difficult dilemmas. The issue gets further complicated by the fact that, as we will discuss later, there are different types of control. A certain type of control may be quite effective in one situation but very ineffective or even damaging in different circumstances. The bottom line is that managers, no matter where they are in an organization or at what level, will have to deal with fundamental questions of control.

Managerial control problems occur in sophisticated organizations and in all countries. The example in the opening paragraphs makes this abundantly clear. If a major multinational corporation like Barings can have difficulties with control, so can smaller organizations with fewer resources and less sophisticated systems. Likewise, if these kinds of problems can develop within a firm headquartered in the United Kingdom and doing business across the globe, they can occur in any location or culture where managerial activity takes place. Exercising effective control is a universal and exceedingly important managerial challenge.

To explore the issue of control, we first look at the role that control plays in organizations and the way it relates to other managerial functions such as strategy and planning. Next, the four basic elements of the control process—establishing standards, measuring performance, comparing performance against standards, and evaluating results (and, if necessary, taking action)—are reviewed. Following this is a discussion of the different levels of control (strategic, tactical, and operational) and the various forms of control. This chapter concludes with an examination of factors that can influence the effectiveness of controls, such as their focus, amount, and the cost of implementing them. How consideration of these factors leads to crucial managerial choices is also explored.

The Control Function in Management

On the face of it, the word "control" sounds negative. It can mean restraints, constraints, or checks. This clearly connotes restricted freedom of action—an idea that many people, especially in some cultures, may find troublesome. Certainly, within the context of organizations, **control** involves regulation of activities and behaviours (see Exhibit 14.1). To control in an organizational setting means to adjust or bring conformity to specifications or objectives. In this sense, then, the control responsibilities of managers are bound to restrict someone's freedom. A manager cannot control without restricting. However, whether this is good or bad for the individual or group that is being controlled, for the manager who determines the amount and type of control, or for the organization at large depends on the consequences of the control and whose perspectives are being considered.

control the regulation of activities and behaviours within organizations; adjustment or conformity to specifications or objectives

Exhibit 14.1

The Control Function in Management

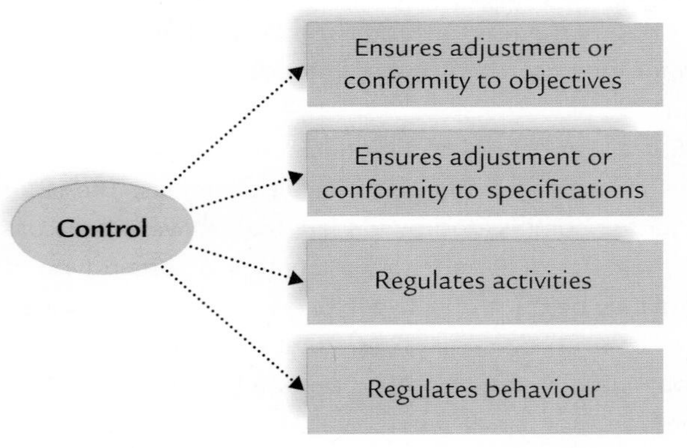

Some amount of control in organizations is unavoidable. The very essence of organizations is that individuals give up total independence so that common goals and objectives can be accomplished. As one organizational scholar put it, "The coordination and order created out of the diverse interests and potentially diverse behaviours of members is largely a function of control."[3] Thus, control is a fundamental characteristic of organized activity. Managers should always keep in mind, however, that control is a means for achieving a goal and is not the goal itself (as is well demonstrated in *A Manager's Challenge: "The Keg"*).

The managerial function of control comes at the end of a chain of the other major functions of planning, organizing, and leading. (Indeed, that is why a chapter on control is almost always found toward the end of most management textbooks.) If those prior functions are carried out well, generating positive responses to controls will be much easier. Conversely, if major

a manager's challenge *change*

The Keg

For fine restaurants, cooking is an art, not a science. The reputation of the food at these restaurants is usually a function of the chef's creativity. So the ideas of standardization and tight control are generally alien to upscale restaurants.

This is not the case with The Keg Steakhouse & Bar, a company that operates over 90 steakhouses across North America. Since the first Keg restaurant opened in North Vancouver in 1971, the company has continued to expand, making it the largest casual-restaurant brand and one of the most popular steakhouses in Canada. The Keg was originally created as a private company and later became public, trading on the Vancouver and Toronto Stock Exchanges.

As a result of a few changes in ownership since its establishment in 1971, The Keg has operated a number of non-steak restaurant concepts including The Old Spaghetti Factory, Brandy's Cocktail Lounges, Crock & Block, and others. After it was purchased by Canadian entrepreneur David Aisenstat in 1997, The Keg began to focus once again on its "core steakhouse and bar concept." With this change in focus, The Keg became increasingly dedicated to providing its consumers with steaks of the highest quality. To accomplish this goal, steaks are aged to ensure tenderness, and are then seasoned with a "special blend of seasonings" to give the steaks a distinct flavour. Steaks are not the only menu items for which preparation is carefully controlled to ensure consistent quality across all Keg locations; all desserts are made by its dessert supplier in Toronto.

Over the years, The Keg has experienced several challenges because of changes in the external environment. A particularly difficult year for the restaurant industry was 2003, with the SARS scare, continued terrorism threats, hurricanes, the increasing value of the Canadian dollar, and the mad cow disease scare. Despite these pressures in its operating environment, The Keg managed to increase its sales to $292 million from $277 million the previous year. In 2004, while the amount of money spent at Canadian steakhouses declined 13 percent from the previous year, The Keg's sales continued to climb. According to the company's 2006 annual report, The Keg reached a sales record of more than $372 million, which was an increase of $46 million, or 14.4 percent, from 2005.

The Keg has managed to survive periods of difficulty and has continued to grow and prosper by continually enforcing specific controls. The entrees are consistent between locations, as cooks are instructed to follow head office's precise preparation instructions, which are sent to each restaurant on DVD. The Keg has very few suppliers, which are "monitored almost fanatically" in an effort to ensure that all food meets the company's "detailed and so-specific" quality requirements. The result of these controls is a consistent atmosphere and a dependable menu that creates loyal customers.

Sources: The Keg Steakhouse & Bar, "The Keg History," www.kegincomefund.com (accessed April 25, 2007); Annual Report 2006, www.kegincomefund.com (accessed April 25, 2007); The Keg Steakhouse & Bar, "News 2005: Keg Chews Up the Competition Even As Industry Sales Drop," www.kegincomefund.com (accessed April 25, 2007); K. Wells, "The Keg: A Rare Treat," *The Telegram,* May 3, 2005, p. B1; R. Harris, "Consistency Pays Off," *Marketing,* September 6, 2004, p. 4; W. Hanley, "Keg Boss Gives Street Steak, Sizzle," *National Post,* October 25, 2003, p. IN1; W. Chow, "Well Done! The Keg at 30: Steakhouse Mogul David Aisenstat Celebrates with Ambitious Expansion," *Vancouver Sun,* September 21, 2001, p. F10.

problems exist in planning, organizing, or leading, almost no amount of attention to control is likely to work very well. In this sense, effective control is a managerial function that depends heavily on the other functions that precede it. When these preceding functions work well, control tends to work well. When they don't, control can become a major headache for a manager.

Control can also be thought of as a "causal" variable because the results of control efforts can inform and improve the planning process of the organization. Control is thus part of a feedback loop into planning and organizing (see Exhibit 14.2) that can help managers adapt to changing circumstances and conditions. When either the internal or external organizational environment changes, good control systems let managers know if the current ways of operating are still meeting the organization's objectives.

Exhibit 14.2

Control's Feedback Loop

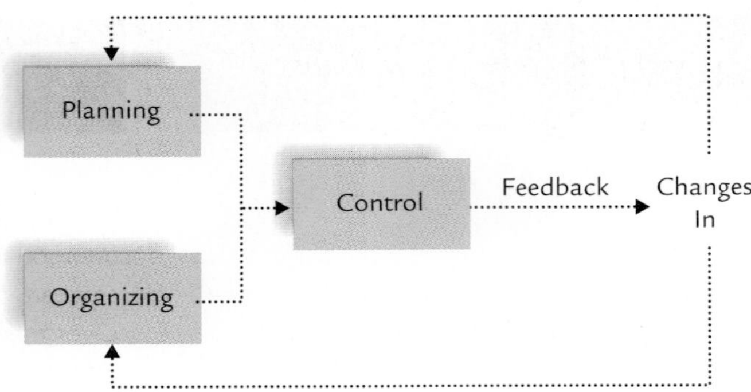

Exhibit 14.3

The Basic Elements in the Control Process

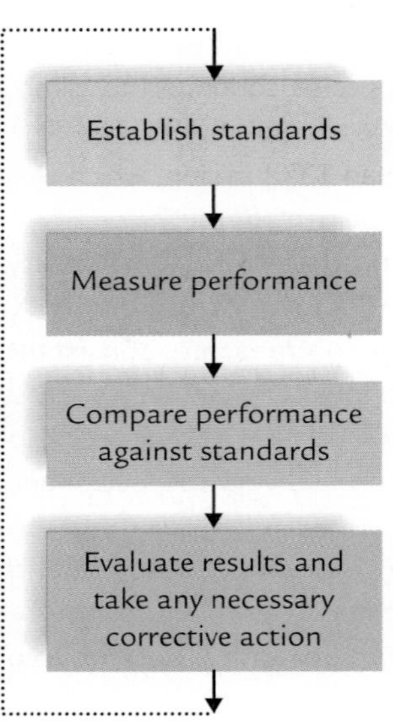

The Basic Control Process

The basic elements of the control process in an organizational setting are simple and straightforward (see Exhibit 14.3):

1. Establish standards
2. Measure performance
3. Compare performance against standards
4. Evaluate results (of the comparison) and, if necessary, take action

Each of these basic components involves important managerial attention and decisions.

Establish Standards

standards targets of performance

Specifying what management expects is absolutely critical at each step of the control process. This starts at the top of the organization and, ideally, should eventually involve every level of employee. First and foremost, those at the highest levels should be able to articulate a vision and formulate broad strategic goals for the organization. For instance, part of the vision of the Royal Canadian Mint is to be "a world-class brand that exceeds expectations with outstanding products and services."[4] From this example, it is easy to see how particular **standards**, or targets of performance, might be developed. Without a strategic vision and goals for the overall organization, managers in various parts of the organization find it difficult to develop meaningful and agreed-upon performance yardsticks.

The establishment of standards—wherever they exist throughout the organization—requires as much specificity as possible. The reason for this is that measuring performance against standards cannot readily be accomplished if the standards are vague. A standard of "efficiently respond to customer complaints," for example, does not provide usable guidelines for determining whether the standard has been met. A standard of "responds, on average, to three customer complaints per hour" would permit an objective measurement of performance.

However, for some aspects of performance, especially in higher-level and more complex jobs like those in research laboratories, it is often not possible nor even desirable to set up easily quantified standards (like number of discoveries per year). In these kinds of positions, the most important elements of performance may be the most difficult to measure, like the probable long-term impact of a given discovery. Moreover, as in the example in the preceding paragraph, the *quality* of response to customer complaints may be more

If anyone knows how to put on the "ritz," it's the Ritz-Carlton's 32 000 employees located at its 63 hotels worldwide in 21 countries. Each Ritz employee gets over 100 hours of customer service training annually. A daily "SQI" (service quality indicator) in every hotel is displayed on TV screens for hotel personnel to see. The SQI monitors production and guest service processes up to the minute so service problems are apparent and can be immediately remedied.

important than the *rate* of response. However, quality is often more difficult to measure. As shown in Exhibit 14.4, the more abstract the standard, the greater the possibility of confusion in measuring performance, and the greater the problem of gaining the acceptance of those measurements by members whose performance is being assessed.

Exhibit 14.4

The Effect of Specificity of Standards on Performance Measurement

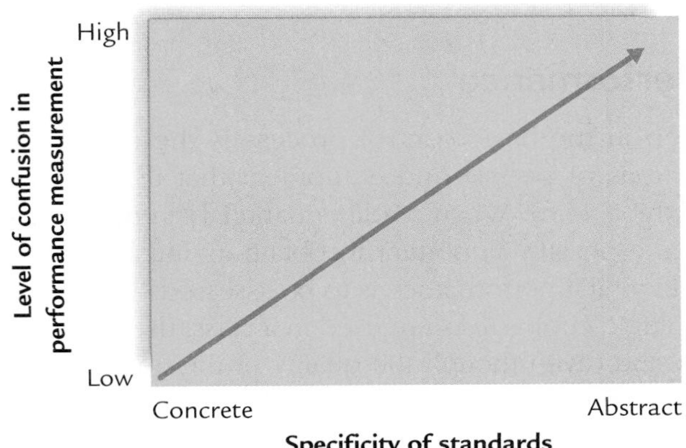

Other issues also can arise in the establishment of standards (see Exhibit 14.5). One revolves around the decision regarding who should set the standards. In general, research has shown that in setting standards, participation by those who will be affected is beneficial in two respects.[5] First, because they have had some opportunity to influence the standards being set, those affected are more likely to be committed to meeting them. Second, involving those who have to meet the standards often results in a useful exchange of information and expertise that, in turn, results in more appropriate standards. At Siemens AG's top-notch medical solutions plant in Forchheim, Germany, for example, managers are striving to achieve a cost-savings goal of 10 percent per year while at the same time improving quality manufacturing performance. To do so, they have involved all of the workgroups in the control process, and each group meets weekly with their manager to examine the past week's performance and set goals for the following week. The initiative led to a shortening of delivery time by 90 percent (from 22 weeks to 2 weeks) and substantial improvements in reliability.[6]

Exhibit 14.5

Issues in Establishing Standards

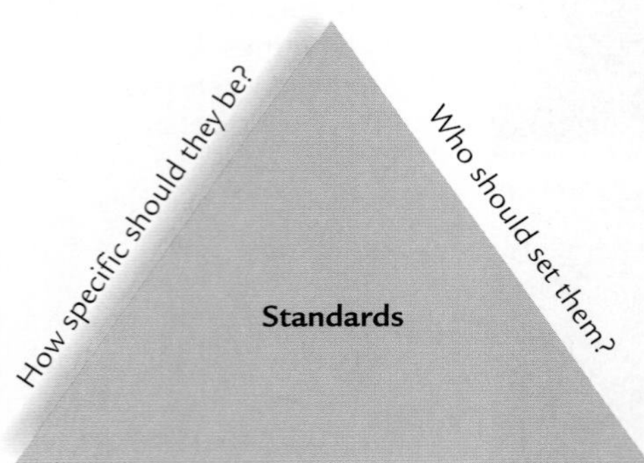

Another issue is the degree of difficulty of the standards themselves. As we saw in the chapter on motivation, the research on goal setting points to the conclusion that difficult but achievable goals seem to result in the highest levels of performance.[7] Similar views have been expressed regarding goals in the budgetary process. Thus, "the ideal budget is one that is challenging but attainable."[8] Achievable budget standards are regarded as desirable because they reduce the motivation to manipulate data or to focus only on short-term actions at the expense of long-term objectives. Achievable budgets also have the potential for increasing morale and generating a "winning atmosphere."[9] This assumes, as noted, that the budgetary targets are not only attainable, but also reasonably difficult. Here, again, where to draw the line between goals that are too challenging and those that are not challenging enough is itself another managerial challenge.

An interesting side note on the topic of budgets is that some companies have rejected the use of budgets and the wrangling over what the data indicate. In the absence of budgets, they use alternative financial and nonfinancial goals and measures. Companies that have rejected budgets require employees to measure themselves against the performance of competitors and against internal peer groups. Since employees do not know whether they have succeeded until they can look back on the results of a given period, they must make sure that they beat the competition. A key feature of many companies that have rejected budgets is the use of rolling forecasts, which are created every few months and typically cover five to eight quarters.[10]

Measure Performance

The second step in the basic control process is the measurement of performance—the actions of people and equipment that the organization wants to monitor (see Exhibit 14.6). When readily quantifiable criteria do not exist, however, it becomes especially important to obtain as much consensus as possible about the way in which performance is to be assessed. To use an analogy, when true/false or multiple-choice tests are used in a class, the score a student receives is seldom contested (even though the quality of the questions often is). On the other hand, the score given to the answers on a test composed of essay questions

Exhibit 14.6

Issues in the Measurement of Performance

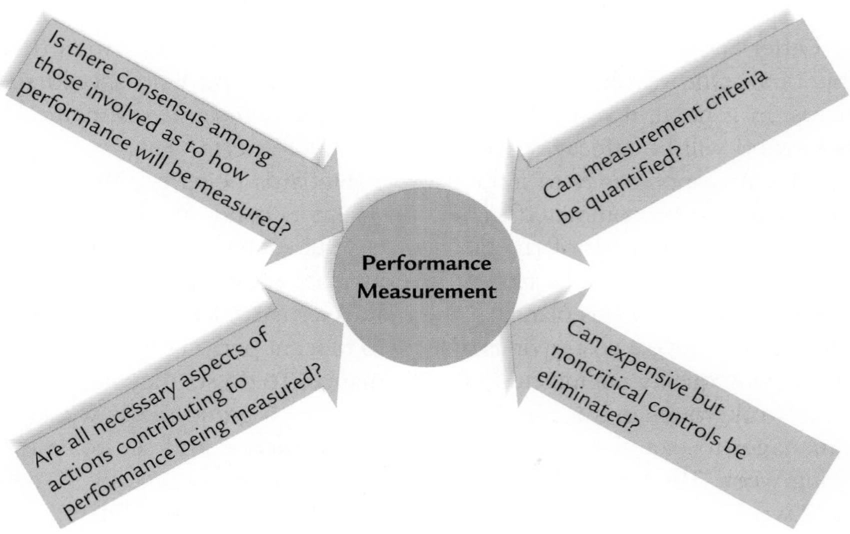

is frequently disputed between student and teacher. The more the instructor and the class members can agree in advance about the qualities of good answers and on how the essay questions will be graded, the more likely the measurement process will be accepted. This occurs even though that process is clearly subjective. Similarly, in work situations, gaining up-front commitment to the performance measurement methods will reduce later complaints about what those measurements show and what they mean to individuals and to the organization.

Since performance in many jobs involves multiple activities, it is important for measurement to be comprehensive. If only some aspects of performance are measured, results can be misleading; they can skew the data that are used for the next two steps in the control process, especially taking action to change performance. The Royal Bank of Canada, Kodak, Motorola, and Hydro-Québec are just a few of the more than 73 percent of North American companies that use a comprehensive control technology called the "Stage-Gate" process throughout the life of a project. The Stage-Gate was developed by Dr. Robert G. Cooper, a marketing professor at McMaster University's DeGroote School of Business. Each project is divided into several stages with "gates" between them. Collectively, the gates act as comprehensive quality control checks that have to be passed before the gate will open, allowing the project to move on to the next stage. This allows management to review the progress of the project at each gate and decide whether it merits continued funding.[11] A potential danger, of course, is that promising new products might be killed too soon by overeager, stage-gate keepers.

Finally, even though measurement should be comprehensive, not everything that possibly could be measured should be measured. Measurement has a cost, and the usefulness of the information obtained may not justify the costs. The issue here is one of criticality, that is, what is measured should be highly relevant to the goals of the organization. Activities that are necessary but do not provide relevant indicators of progress toward goals do not justify the expense to measure them. What is easy to measure may not be what is most important to control. Furthermore, from the perspective of many managers in operations, what gets measured in an organization is often what gets done.

Compare Performance against Standards

Comparing performance results against previously set standards is the third step in the control process. Just as performance measurement is strongly influenced by the standards, so are comparisons affected by the kinds of measurements available. If key measurements have not already been built into the system, it is usually not possible to go back and reconstruct them for purposes of comparison. Sometimes managers realize too late that appropriate comparisons cannot be made.

When several dimensions of performance have been measured, this step in the process can involve multiple comparisons. If those comparisons all point in the same direction, interpretation is relatively straightforward. However, the picture of performance that emerges from a set of comparisons may be inconsistent or contradictory. That is, some comparisons may show good adherence to standards and targets, and others may reveal problems. So managers need to know how to interpret the patterns of comparisons and to draw appropriate conclusions. A single negative comparison may outweigh a number of positive comparisons, or vice versa.

For example, after a major restructuring, Safeway found that its sales per grocery store had nearly tripled and its sales per employee had also risen by 70 percent. Overall profits were up, but customer satisfaction scores were down. What were managers to make of this? In Safeway's case, sales per store and per employee as well as overall profits were up because it had sold off or closed its least profitable stores (many of which were operating at a loss). All of this might paint a very positive picture. However, the fact that customer satisfaction was down was potentially a bad sign. Grocery stores make money through volume. Therefore, if dissatisfied customers were to start spending less at Safeway and more at competitors, the positive results could deteriorate rapidly. Consequently, placing too much emphasis on per-store sales compared with customer satisfaction would be a control mistake.

In this third control step, managers need to compare expected performance with actual performance. These comparisons often involve both subjective estimates as well as objective ones. However, even if the comparison involves only objective, quantitative numbers, judgment is still needed. For example, suppose Safeway's customer satisfaction numbers were down from 5.5 to 5.2. Anyone can calculate that customer satisfaction had declined by 0.3 points. However, the key question is whether this drop is significant. The answer to this question requires managerial judgment.

Evaluate Results and Take Action

The fourth step, evaluating results and taking action, is arguably the most difficult managerial task in the entire control process. The results that emerge from the performance comparisons may or may not require action. Managers need to consider whether any single comparison or a pattern of comparisons requires action to be taken. If actual performance deviates from expected performance, how much of a difference is required before something is done about that difference? That question has no single answer. It requires evaluation of the importance and magnitude of the deviation.

An analogy illustrates what is involved in this type of judgment. In industrialized countries, the directors of the national banking system—in Canada, the board of directors and governor of the Bank of Canada—periodically receive the most current data about the national economy; for example, the unemployment rate, the consumer price index, the index of consumer confidence, the rate of new starts in home building, and the like. These data are compared against predetermined benchmarks to make a decision about whether to take action (for example, to increase interest rates). The problem for the board, as for any manager in an organization, is to determine which data are most important and how much of a change is significant. However, the issue is even more complicated than that. Managers must determine whether a slight change in the same direction for all of the indicators is more or less important than a major change in just one indicator. As any macroeconomist would testify regarding the national economy, this type of judgment is not easy.

The other basic judgment that must be made in this fourth step is what action to take if the pattern and size of deviations from expected performance are determined to be significant. Managers need knowledge about the causes of the deviation as well as about the potential actions that are possible.

Clearly, the evaluation and action step of control requires managers to have strong diagnostic skills as well as a certain level of expertise. Sometimes, the causes of a problem may be easily recognized, but the decisions about which actions to take to correct them may be extremely difficult. Conversely, the most effective actions may be well known, if only the causes could be clearly identified.

If a manager discovers major negative differences between performance and standards, some type of action is clearly needed because failure to act can lead to more severe problems in the future. However, if the deviations are major but positive, the necessity for action is usually much less (see Exhibit 14.7). Such positive differences, though, may in fact provide valuable insights about unexpected opportunities that should be pursued. For example, a major maker of baby food discovered stronger-than-expected sales of its new line of toddler foods in Florida, which has a higher-than-average percentage of elderly residents. Further investigation revealed that the increased sales were not because of a higher-than-expected number of toddlers; rather, they were due to older customers with teeth problems who bought the product because it was easier to chew. This led to a whole new line of packaged foods targeted at this particular consumer segment.

To help maintain positive performance, employees who are doing better than expected can be given increased recognition and rewards to reinforce their excellent performance. Likewise, sales that exceed their forecast may mean that production should be increased or the product line should be extended. Costs that are below target may suggest an efficient practice that could be duplicated for other employees to follow, to reduce the costs even further. In short, it is as important to evaluate surprises on the upside as it is on the downside.

Exhibit 14.7

Outcomes of Performance Measurement

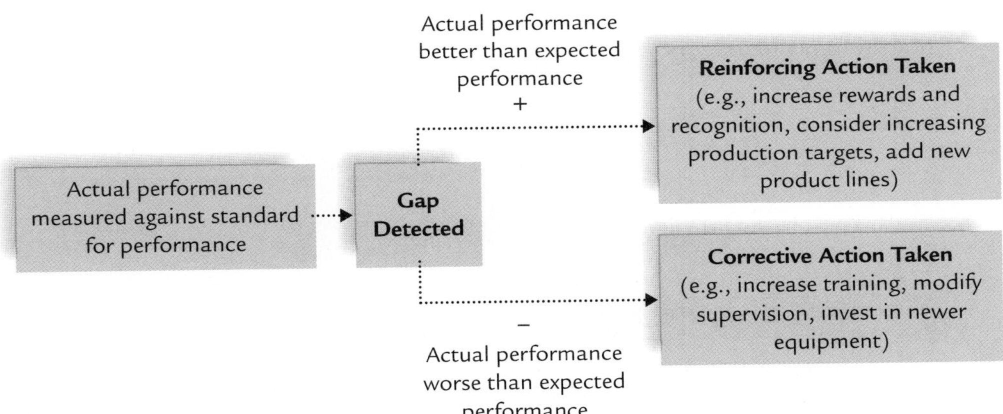

One other issue is involved in determining what action managers should take in the case of significant deviations from standards (whether in the positive or negative direction). This is the judgment about whether the standards are correct and the performance is the problem, or whether the performance is appropriate but the standards are too difficult or too easy. That is why a broken-line feedback arrow is shown from "Evaluate Results" to "Establish Standards" in Exhibit 14.3, indicating that the standards may need to be adjusted. Over time, standards are sometimes modified as experience is gained and the feasibility of existing standards is better understood. If a great deal of effort and care has been used in setting the standards and participation in setting them was broad, then the issue is probably likely to be one of performance. If, however, the standards have been set hastily or without appropriate input from the relevant parties, then performance may not be the problem. This kind of issue points out once again the tight interconnection of the four basic steps of the control process.

Scope of Control in the Organization

Even though the four steps of the control process are similar wherever they occur in organizations, the scope of what is being controlled can vary widely. This, in turn, affects how the steps are actually put into use. A bank provides a simple illustration. The bank manager may need to assess whether she has an adequate level of deposits relative to outstanding loans. The scope is quite broad because the outcome of this assessment could affect the entire organization. If the ratio is too low, the bank may need to reduce its level of lending or try to get more deposits. On the other hand, the manager may also need to evaluate the ratio of human bank tellers to automatic teller machines at each branch. In this case, the scope is much narrower because the issue only involves a small part of the bank's total set of activities. In the former instance we would label the scope as "strategic," and in the latter instance it would be regarded as an "operational" control issue. These represent two of the three major categories of control scope. The third and intermediate level, between strategic and operational, is a category typically called "tactical." (Refer back to Chapter 6, "Planning," for a discussion of the three categories of "strategic," "tactical," and "operational.")

Strategic, Tactical, and Operational Control Systems by Michael Hitt

mymanagementlab

In the remainder of this section, we look at the issues involved in each of these three types of control classified by the breadth of their scope. However, it is useful to remember that no hard-and-fast boundaries separate the three types (see Exhibit 14.8). The differences between strategic and tactical control issues are often blurred, and likewise, it is not always clear whether a control issue should be considered tactical or operational. Nevertheless, the three categories help remind managers where they should focus their attention.

Exhibit 14.8

Types and Scope of Control

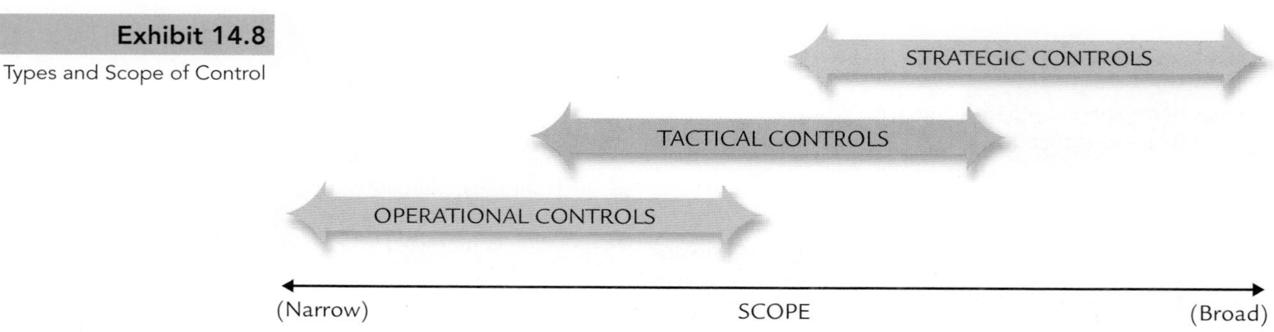

Strategic Control

strategic control
assessment and regulation of how the organization as a whole fits its external environment and meets its long-range objectives and goals

As discussed in Chapter 7, strategy refers to the direction for the organization as a whole. It is linked to the mission of the organization and to the basic plans for achieving that mission. Thus, **strategic control** is focused on how the organization as a whole fits its external environment and meets its long-range objectives and goals. Strategic control systems, where they exist, are designed to determine how well those types of objectives and goals are being met.

A particular challenge in formulating strategic controls is the fact that strategic goals are broad and, especially, long term. This means that such goals typically are more abstract than goals for particular units. Consequently, setting strategic standards and measuring strategic performance can be especially challenging. For this reason, research has shown that only a relatively small number of firms in both Europe and North America have set what could be termed strategic control systems.[12] The numbers will undoubtedly increase in the future, but important obstacles interfere with establishing such systems.

A significant factor that affects whether strategic control systems can be set up and whether they will be effective is the unpredictability of the external environments in which many organizations operate and from which they obtain resources. This also makes it difficult to develop standards and measures that are relevant for more than short periods of time. In fact, it is particularly difficult for firms to develop useful criteria for assessing the long-term performance of individual managers.[13]

Environmental conditions for large companies affect how much leeway each division or unit is given in determining its own competitive strategies for dealing with its particular markets.[14] The issue is essentially one of how much strategic control systems should be centralized versus decentralized, and how much variation should be allowed by unit. Such a decision involves not only matters of strategy but also of organizational structure (Chapter 8). Sometimes, in fact, because of changes in the external environment, companies find they have to reverse course on their overall strategic approach to controls. Thus, McDonald's has restructured its US operations to reinstate controls it had abandoned in the mid-1990s. Why? Because it was experiencing a decreased earnings trend. To deal with this, it is controlling not only its ingredients but also the experience customers have in its restaurants. It has gone back to more inspections of every store and the use of mystery shoppers. It is also making more use of extensive customer surveys.[15]

Research indicates, however, that "the efficiencies of managing through centralized control may be greater . . . when the operating environments of divisions in multidivisional organizations are relatively stable and predictable" (see Exhibit 14.9).[16] When there is more uncertainty in the environment, centralized control becomes less efficient. In other words, in relatively turbulent environments, it is difficult for centralized strategic control systems to keep up with events, and consequently, more responsibility for control must be delegated to major units. When the environment is changing rapidly, as it is for many companies these days, too much reliance on organization-wide strategic goals and standards of performance that are set too far in advance can interfere with the needed speed and flexibility of the various operating units to respond effectively to the environment, especially in complex organizations with many types of units.[17]

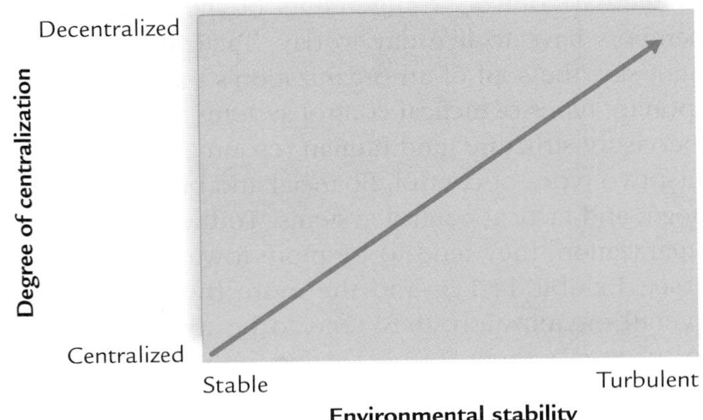

Exhibit 14.9

Degree of Centralization of Control in Relation to Environmental Stability

As shown in Exhibit 14.10, both the degree to which it is possible to precisely measure how well performance conforms with strategic goals and the degree of turbulence or uncertainty in the environment can affect the value of having strategic control systems.[18] They are most likely to be useful when measurement is easy and operating environments are relatively calm, as in the case of the cement industry, for example. Although this industry basically follows the ups and downs of the construction industry, the factors that significantly affect these movements are relatively well-known. For instance, changes in interest rates have a significant impact on building booms and busts. As rates go down and money is cheaper to borrow, construction increases. As rates go up and money becomes more expensive to borrow, construction decreases. Thus, for a cement firm, strategic controls like being number one in sales in a region can be relatively useful. Conversely, strategic controls are probably least useful when exact measurement is difficult and the environment is fluctuating rapidly.

Exhibit 14.10

Approaches to Strategic Control

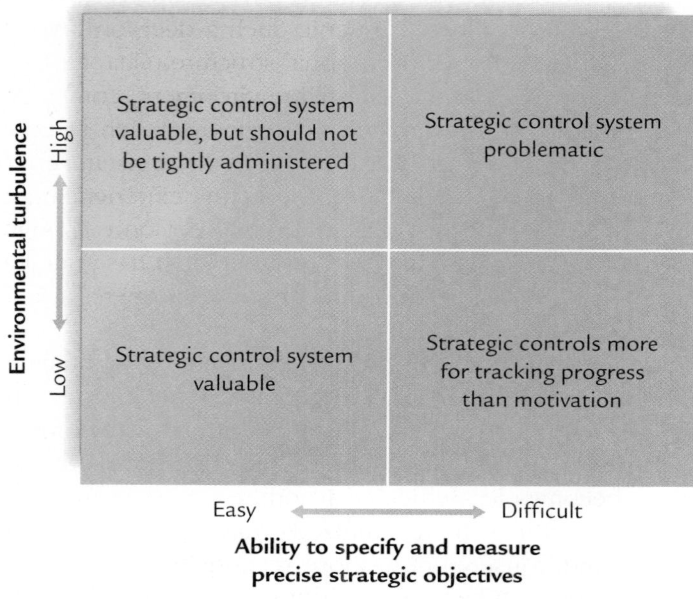

Source: M. Goold and J. J. Quinn, "The Paradox of Strategic Controls," *Strategic Management Journal* 11, no. 1 (1990), pp. 43–57 (p. 55).

Tactical Control

tactical control the assessment and regulation of the day-to-day functions of the organization and its major units in the implementation of its strategy

Tactical control focuses on the implementation of strategy. Thus, this level covers the fundamental control arrangements of the organization, those with which its members have to live day to day. Tactical control forms the heart and, one might say, the soul of an organization's total set of controls. Four of the most important types of tactical control systems are financial controls, budgets, the supervisory structure, and human resource policies and procedures.

The first two types of control, financial and budgetary, contain elements of both strategic and tactical control systems. To the extent that they focus on the entire organization, they tend to be more toward the strategic end of the continuum (see Exhibit 14.11), and the more they focus on specific units within an overall organization, they tend to be toward the tactical end. We have chosen to discuss them in this section since they most often focus on organizational units, but keep in mind that they, especially financial controls, can also be used for some strategic control considerations.

Financial Controls Financial controls include several important quantitative ratios involving key financial statistics. Although such financial data are always generated at the overall organizational level as well as at the organizational-unit level, they are especially useful at the unit level as a form of tactical control.

Exhibit 14.11

Characteristics of Strategic and Tactical Controls

Tactical Controls	Strategic Controls
Time Frame	
Limited	Long, unspecific
Objective	
Controls relate to specific, functional areas	Controls relate to organization as a whole
Types of Comparisons	
Comparisons made within organization	Comparisons made to other organizations
Focus	
Implementation of strategy	Determination of overall organizational strategy

The data used for the most important financial controls involve a basic cost-benefit analysis. For example, ratios relevant to the **profitability** of a given unit are constructed from revenue data (benefit) in relation to given amounts of investment (cost). The ratio is called **ROI** (**return on investment**, or alternatively, **ROE**, **return on equity**) and compares the amount of net profit before taxes (the numerator of the ratio) to the total amount of assets invested (the denominator). Thus, a unit that has a profit of $500 000 for a given year from invested assets of $10 million would have an ROI of 0.05 for that year. If another unit generated that same amount of profit on invested assets of only $5 million, its ROI would be 0.10 and would thus be considered to have had superior financial performance since it generated equal benefit for less cost.

profitability the ratio of cost to benefit

ROI (return on investment) a measure of profitability obtained by dividing net income by the total amount of assets invested

ROE (return on equity) an alternative term for ROI

Other financial ratios that are commonly used to assess unit performance include those related to **liquidity** (current assets in relation to current liabilities), which provides an indication of how well the unit can meet its short-term cash requirements; **leverage** (total debt to total assets), which provides an indication of ability to meet long-term financial obligations; and **efficiency** or **activity** (for example, the amount of sales in a given period relative to the cost of inventory used to generate those sales), measuring how efficiently assets are used.

liquidity a measure of how well a unit can meet its short-term cash requirements

leverage the ratio of total debt to total assets

efficiency (activity) the ratio of amount of sales to total cost of inventory

Examples of these four types of ratios for two organizations in the retail industry for the year 2006 are shown in Exhibit 14.12. It can be seen from the exhibit that West 49 had a lower ROI than Le Château that year, somewhat less liquidity, a slightly less favourable leverage ratio, and a less efficient use of inventory. Thus, if these had been two units within the same organization, one would say that for this year Le Château as a unit was doing better overall insofar as financial performance was concerned.

The important point here is not the detailed steps that need to be taken to calculate the ratios. Rather, it is that when the ratios are calculated, they can be used to compare one organization, or one unit, to another. Thus, it is the comparative nature of the ratios that provides managers with information needed to take action during control. The numbers used to calculate a ratio, such as inventory turnover, for example, will show whether the ratio is relatively unfavourable, and if so, an examination of the two components used in the ratio will also indicate whether the problem seems to be in the amount of

Exhibit 14.12 Examples of Company Financial Ratios

Ratio	Formula	Company			
		Le Château, 2006		West 49, 2006	
		In $ millions		In $ millions	
PROFIT					
Return on Investment	Net Profit before Taxes / Total Assets	38.4 / 185.7	0.207	6.9 / 102.1	0.067
LIQUIDITY					
Current Ratio	Current Assets / Current Liabilities	107.1 / 61.6	1.74	33.2 / 26.9	1.23
LEVERAGE					
Debt to Assets	Total Debt / Total Assets	77.5 / 185.7	0.417	43.3 / 102.1	0.424
ACTIVITY					
Inventory Turnover	Sales / Inventory	303.9 / 41.0	7.41	195.3 / 24.0	8.14

sales (too low) or in the amount of inventory (too high) or both. In other words, financial ratios can provide a very useful diagnostic tool for managers to determine where to take control action to improve situations.

break-even point (B-E P) the amount of a product that must be sold to cover a firm's fixed and variable costs

Another financial measure, the **break-even point (B-E P)**, is sometimes used for control purposes in business organizations. Essentially, a B-E P analysis is a quantitative formula used to determine what volume of some product or service must be sold before a firm's fixed and variable costs are covered by the next sale. That is, the break-even point is where the selling price of a unit of a product (or service) minus its variable costs exceeds the fixed costs for that unit. Clearly, the lower the fixed costs are, the fewer the units of goods or services that need to be sold for a break-even point to be reached. Likewise, the lower the variable costs, the higher the profit per unit and therefore the fewer the units that need to be sold to reach that point. Break-even analysis, then, provides a way for managers to gauge whether new products or services have a potential to turn a profit. Managers can therefore exercise control *before* new ventures are undertaken. Even more important for ongoing operations, a break-even analysis focuses managers' attention on reducing or controlling the two categories of costs—fixed and variable—to take the pressure off the need to sell larger volumes.

An example of where a break-even analysis can illustrate comparisons between two organizations or business units is provided by the airline industry. Many of the larger airlines have set up separate subsidiary airlines to handle short-haul commuter routes, for example, Jazz, which is a part of Air Canada. These commuter airlines can operate on relatively small volumes of passenger traffic because their costs—like lower wage bases for their pilots—produce lower break-even points. Similarly, certain independent airlines—if they are especially efficient—can charge very low fares on many of their routes and still make a profit. Canadian air carrier WestJet replicated the model applied by US discount air carrier Southwest Airlines, which uses a flexible point-to-point route system instead of the hub-and-spoke system of most other airlines and avoided the cost of meals by serving only snacks long before other airlines did.[19]

Although a B-E P analysis can provide extremely useful information for managers for control purposes, such an analysis also has limitations. Looking strictly at the numbers of a B-E P analysis may discourage certain decisions that could ultimately result in very profitable activities that do not initially appear to be profitable. Also, it is not always easy to allocate costs between fixed and variable categories, and it is sometimes difficult to project costs accurately, especially variable costs. Like other financial controls, a B-E P analysis can be an aid to exercising effective control, but it is not by itself a guarantee of wise decisions. What it does do, however, is highlight the potential advantages to be gained by controlling specific types of costs.

Budgetary Controls Budgets are used in almost every organization (as we discussed in Chapter 6 on planning), and like financial controls can sometimes be considered elements of a strategic system. **Budgetary controls**, however, are more usefully viewed as a significant tactical control because they focus on how well strategies are being implemented. In contrast to purely strategic control, budgetary controls

budgetary control a type of tactical control based on responsibility for meeting financial targets and evaluating how well those targets have been met

- typically cover a relatively limited time frame (usually twelve-month or three-month periods)
- focus exclusively on one type of objective (financial)
- usually cannot be used to compare a total organization's progress relative to its competitors[20]

Anyone occupying a managerial position is controlled by budgets and uses budgets to control others. A budget is a commitment to a forecast to make an agreed-upon outcome happen.[21] Thus, it is more than a forecast, which is simply a prediction. A budget is designed to influence behaviour so that forecasts or plans for expenditures and (where relevant) revenues can be achieved. It "controls" by assigning responsibility for meeting financial targets and for evaluating how well those targets have been met. It would be difficult indeed to maintain an organization if none of its members were held accountable for limits on expenditures.

When using budgets as a form of control, managers face several important issues, as shown in Exhibit 14.13. One is the question of whether to use a fixed budget for a specific period, usually 12 months, and stick with those numbers, or to revise it midway during the period based on changes in operating conditions. Ace Hardware, for example, now uses a rolling planning and budgetary process. With the old annual type of process, the conditions on which Ace's budget were based were frequently out of date by the time the budget was finalized. In the middle of a recent year, however, the company's sales were within 5 percent of the expected amount and closely tracked the budget. "We haven't had sales so close to budget at this point in the year in five years," said the company's manager of financial planning and analysis.[22] A rolling budgetary process with relatively frequent revisions has the advantage of being more current and therefore more accurate; however, it also can take more managerial time and effort.

Another budget issue is whether compensation bonuses should be based on the achievement of budgetary targets. This sounds good, but it has the great disadvantage of encouraging budget game-playing, because the person being evaluated has an incentive to provide high-cost and low-revenue estimates. This way, by creating "budgetary slack" with relatively easy targets, the person has a higher probability of hitting the targets and earning a bonus. Thus, managers who supervise the preparation of budgets need to be alert to how a bonus

Exhibit 14.13 Issues in Budgetary Control

Issue	Questions
Rolling budgets and revision	Should the budget period be for 12 months followed by another 12-month budget a year later, or should a calendar quarter be added each time a new calendar quarter begins? Should the budget remain fixed for the budget period or should it be revised periodically during the period?
Fixed or flexible budgets	Should performance be evaluated against the original budget or against a budget that incorporates the actual activity level of the business?
Bonuses based on budgets	Should incentive compensation, if any, be based on actual versus budgeted performance, or on actual performance against some other standard?
Evaluation criteria	Should the budget used to evaluate performance include only those items over which the evaluated manager has control, or should it include all unit costs and revenues appropriate to the managerial unit?
Tightness of the budget	What degree of "stretch" should there be in the budget?

Source: Adapted from N. C. Churchill, "Budget Choices: Planning vs. Control," *Harvard Business Review* 62, no. 4 (1984), pp. 150–64 (p. 151).

system of this type can distort estimates and undermine control. Managers also need to make sure that they don't inadvertently create a short-term focus on the part of subordinates attempting to meet budgetary targets at the expense of achievement of more important, longer-term organizational goals.[23]

A third budgetary control issue involves the question of whether those responsible for meeting specified targets should be evaluated only on expenditures and revenues over which they have direct control, or whether they should be evaluated on a final "net" figure based on all costs and revenues for a given unit. The former results in a more direct link between managerial behaviour and budgetary responsibility, but the latter is the ultimate "bottom line," especially for publicly held corporations. For example, as a manager of a sales unit, you might have strong control over the revenues that your unit generates and the money spent on travel expenses. When these travel expenses are subtracted from sales, your unit might look very good. However, if your unit also uses marketing and promotion materials to get these sales, they may need to be factored into the overall assessment. Otherwise, you may overspend on marketing and promotion activities.

The final and perhaps most important managerial control issue regarding budgets is how tight or loose to make them. Should a budget require those charged with meeting it to make an extra "stretch"? As we have said before, research indicates that the best performance results come from goals that are challenging but achievable. Since budgets represent goals, this conclusion seems highly relevant to the issue of budgetary control.

supervisory structure a type of tactical control based on reporting levels in an organization

Supervisory Structure Controls The basic **supervisory structure** of an organization is probably the most widespread tactical control system that a typical organizational member encounters. The amount and form of such control varies considerably from organization to organization, but almost always exists in some form. In organizations of any size, there is always someone or some group to which an employee or manager reports. (Recall the discussion of span of control in Chapter 8.) Even the most collegial and least bureaucratic types of work organizations, such as research laboratories and not-for-profit enterprises, have some sort of reporting structure that regulates the activities of each member.

Human Resource Controls **Human resource policies and procedures** are a fourth major type of tactical control that affects everyone working in an organization. They provide a number of different opportunities for control (see Exhibit 14.14):

human resource policies and procedures a type of tactical control based on the organization's overall approach to using its human resources

- Selection procedures can specify the range of abilities that will be brought into the organization.
- Training can improve skills and elevate performance to meet standards.
- Appraisal and evaluation methods can reinforce desired behaviour and discourage undesirable levels of performance.
- Compensation can be used to motivate employees and increase their efforts in particular directions.

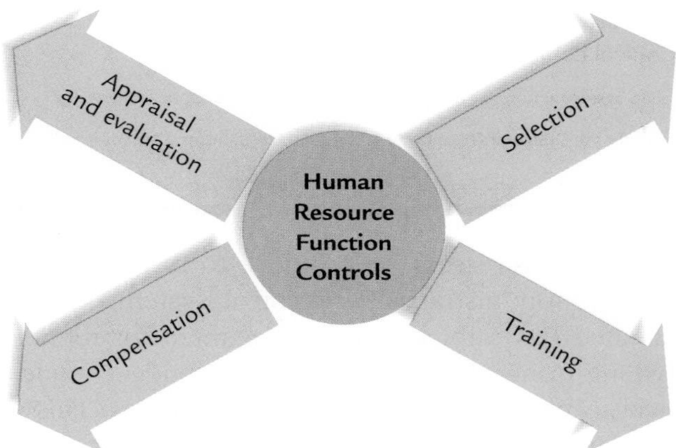

Exhibit 14.14

Opportunities for Control in the Human Resource Function

An example of using human resource procedures to reinforce desired behaviour occurred when Standard Life of Scotland, one of the largest insurance companies in Europe, changed its performance evaluation and reward systems to a "contribution management system." The new system focused on the importance (not just the number) of an employee's accomplishments, the effort to develop the competencies to accomplish critical tasks, and the employee's contribution to customer satisfaction and the overall performance of the business. The change in approach required employees to be highly involved in goal setting, training plans, and reward determinations. As a result of these changes in HR procedures, the company has gone from being one of the lowest-ranked on performance and customer satisfaction to one of the highest within the United Kingdom. It was also voted "Company of the Year" five years running in its industry.[24]

Because the effects of human resource policies and procedures are so extensive, they are very powerful means of control. When used with skill and deftness, they are a significant aid to the achievement of organizational objectives, as in the above Standard Life example. When used ineptly and with heavy-handedness, however, they can hinder organizational progress.

Contrasting Approaches to Using Tactical Controls The ways in which tactical control systems are implemented say a great deal about an organization (what it is like to work there and how effective the control is). These control systems characterize an organization and are a critical part of its identity. For these reasons, it is important to specify and discuss the two fundamental approaches to tactical control: (1) imposed, or bureaucratic, control and (2) elicited, or commitment or clan, control (see Exhibit 14.15).[25] Most organizations use a combination of these two approaches, but also tend to emphasize one over the other.

Exhibit 14.15 Control in Bureaucracy and Clan Structures

Type of Control	Social Requirements[a]	Control Approach	Informational Requirements
Bureaucracy	· Norm of reciprocity · Legitimate authority	· Adherence to rules and regulations · Formal and impersonal · Emphasis on detecting deviance · Imposed on the individual	· Rules
Clan	· Norm of reciprocity · Legitimate authority · Shared values, beliefs	· Stresses group consensus on goals and their measurement · Mutual assistance in meeting performance standards · Uses deviations as guidelines in diagnosing problems · Control comes from the individuals or groups	· Traditions

[a]Social requirements are the basic agreements between people that, at a minimum, are necessary for a form of control to be employed.

Source: Adapted from William G. Ouchi, "A Conceptual Framework for the Design of Organizational Control Mechanisms," *Management Science* 25, no. 9 (1980), pp. 833–87 (p. 838).

bureaucratic control an approach to tactical control that stresses adherence to rules and regulations and is imposed by others

commitment (clan) control an approach to tactical control that emphasizes consensus and shared responsibility for meeting goals

Bureaucratic control stresses adherence to rules and regulations and a formal, impersonal administration of control systems. Thus, for instance, Imperial Oil Limited has a thick operating manual for refinery managers. It specifies everything from which types of capital budget requests need which type of approval to equipment maintenance schedules. This approach highlights rational planning and orderliness. It heavily emphasizes detecting deviance from standards. But its foremost feature, in a control sense, is that control is *imposed* on the person, group, or activity. From an employee's perspective, "others" do the controlling.

Commitment, or clan, control stresses obtaining consensus on what goals should be pursued and then developing a shared sense of responsibility for achieving those goals. It is called a "clan" approach to control because of the emphasis on generating shared values, as in a set of close relatives, and on mutual assistance in meeting performance standards. Clan control is consistent with strong cultures where values are widely shared and deeply held (see Chapter 4). A firm using a clan approach may, for example, emphasize care in the employee selection process to make sure that those coming into the organization have values similar to those that are prominent in its culture. The firm may have no real policy manual, and employees may be given general goals and basic budgets within which they need to work rather than specific constraints. A clan-based firm would rely on the employees' understanding of and commitment to the organizational objectives as the primary means of control. Unlike the bureaucratic approach, the clan approach tends to treat deviations from standards more as a basis for diagnosis than for corrective action. Its foremost feature, in a control sense, is that control is viewed as being *elicited from* rather than imposed on the person, group, or activity. From an employee's perspective, the employee or his or her group, rather than others, does the controlling.

You might wonder why every organization doesn't use a commitment approach. It sounds as if it would function better for both the organization and those who work in it. However, things are not that simple. Creating a genuine clan-like atmosphere among employees, especially in large organizations, is extremely difficult. It takes time and also considerable managerial effort. It may not succeed, or more likely, will succeed only partially. If a true clan-like, high-commitment culture is not created, an organization cannot rely on self-control by individuals or groups to exercise sufficient control. However distasteful it may sound, some amount of bureaucratic managerial control seems necessary for most complex organizations.

Even from the perspective of the organization's members or employees, self-imposed clan control may not be as satisfying as it would seem at first glance. A detailed study of a small manufacturing company illustrates the point.[26] This company converted its traditional hierarchical structure, which emphasized a high degree of supervisory control, to a structure that was built around self-managed work teams. In the first phase of the transition, the teams spent a good deal of time developing consensus on what constituted, both collectively and individually, good work and good patterns of behaviour. In the second phase, the teams developed strong norms regarding expected behaviour. Experienced team members expected new workers to buy into the teams' values and act according to their norms.

Under the old system, supervisors tolerated some slackness among the workers. But in the team system, the members exercised their newfound authority with much less patience. In converting to a clan approach to control, the teams' norms tended to become formalized—that is, they became self-imposed rules. As one team member said, "If we can just get our code of conduct in writing, then everyone will know what to do. We won't have so many problems . . . if we can just get it written down." The researcher studying this company stated, "The teams had now created, in effect, a nearly perfect form of control . . . an essentially total system of control almost impossible to resist. . . . The team members had become their own masters and their own slaves." Such clan control had developed into (in the researcher's term) an "iron cage."

The previous example serves to emphasize the point that no single approach to managerial control will work well in all situations. It also shows that whatever approach is chosen will have its own unique problems as well as advantages.

Operational Control

operational control the assessment and regulation of the specific activities and methods an organization uses to produce goods and services

Operational control, as the name implies, regulates the activities or methods an organization uses to produce the goods and services it supplies to customers and clients. It is control applied in the core and support processes toward the transformation of inputs into outputs, such as the actions that produce a car, administer therapy to an ill patient, cook and serve a restaurant meal, send a satellite into the sky, or write computer software. In short, operational control "is where the rubber meets the road."

pre-control a type of operational control that focuses on the quality, quantity, and characteristics of the inputs into the production process

concurrent control a type of operational control that evaluates the conversion of inputs to outputs while it is happening

post-control a type of operational control that checks quality after production of goods or services outputs

The overall management of operations involves a number of critical and often technical issues. Here we focus specifically on an overview of the control process relating to operations. Operational control can be analyzed by relating it to the three basic elements involved in any type of service or goods production: inputs, transformation, and outputs (Exhibit 14.16).[27] These three elements can be related to the location of control in the production process: before transformation occurs, or **pre-control** (also known as feedforward); during transformation, or **concurrent control**; and after transformation takes place, or **post-control** (also known as feedback).

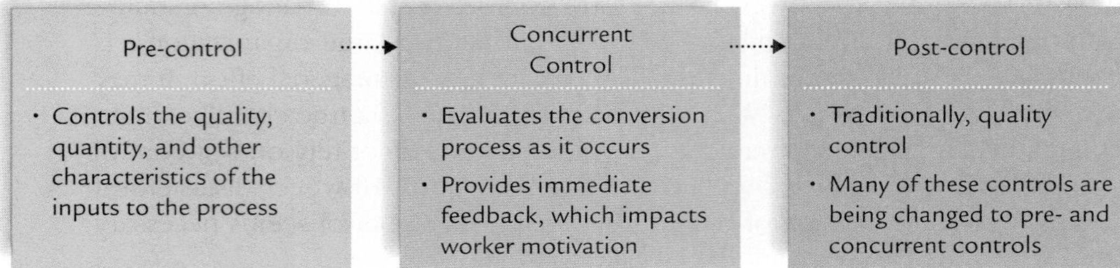

Pre-control
• Controls the quality, quantity, and other characteristics of the inputs to the process
Concurrent Control
• Evaluates the conversion process as it occurs
• Provides immediate feedback, which impacts worker motivation
Post-control
• Traditionally, quality control
• Many of these controls are being changed to pre- and concurrent controls

Exhibit 14.16

Operational Controls

Pre-control of Operations This form of operational control focuses on the quality, quantity, and characteristics of the inputs into the production process—for example, the purity of steel, the grade of beef, the number of passengers, the age of patients, the test scores of entering students, the aptitudes of job applicants.

The more stringent the control over the quality of inputs, the less need for control at the later two stages. The higher the quality of recruits to the Royal Canadian Mounted Police, for example, the easier it is to train them to be competent police officers. However, there is a cost involved in exacting pre-control standards. Higher-quality inputs typically cost more, and the effort to ensure that the quality is high also increases costs. Nevertheless, in many cases those costs will be well justified by what is saved in the later control steps and by the positive evaluation of the eventual goods and services. In other words, customers may be willing to pay more for better products and services.

Concurrent Control of Operations Concurrent control involves real-time assessment of the quality of the transformation process; that is, evaluating the conversion of inputs to outputs while it is happening. For example, eVineyard, a US internet wine retailer, created its business plan based on having a virtual, concurrent control of inventory. Because of the regulatory complexities of

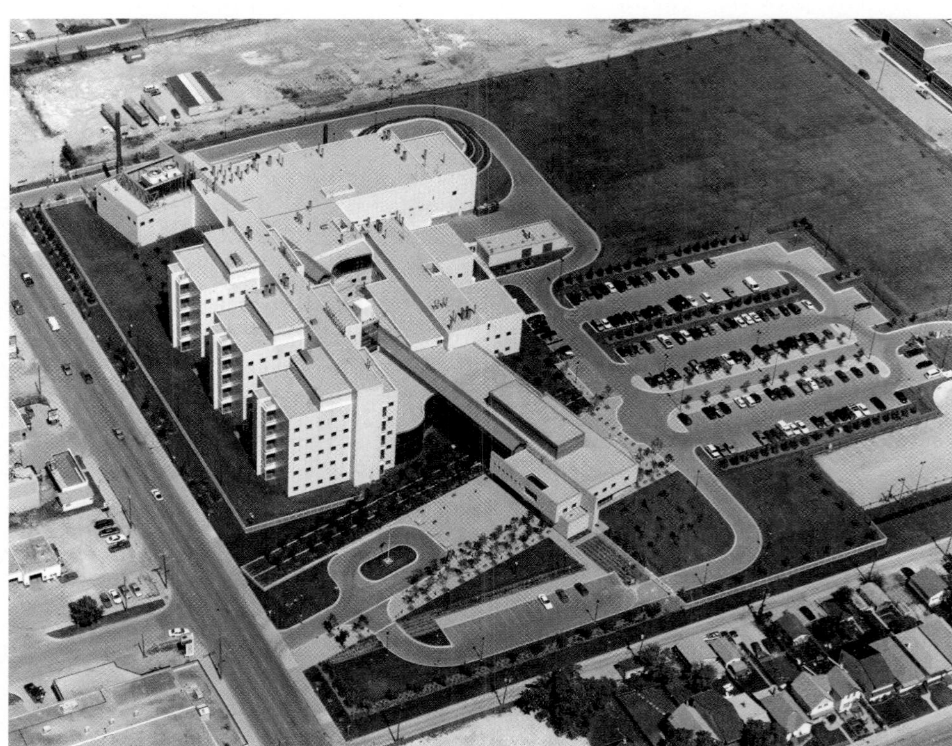

Because of the potentially disastrous effects a lethal virus could have if it began to spread in a city, the design, construction, and management of a high-containment laboratory require a great deal of pre-, concurrent, and post-control. The Canadian Science Centre for Human and Animal Health in Winnipeg is Canada's only Level-4 lab—one of approximately 15 in the world—and is capable of housing the world's deadliest pathogens, such as Ebola and Junin. The lab took 10 years and $172 million to design and build. Part of the pre-control process in the opening of the lab was allowing poured concrete, initially for the foundation and later for walls in high-containment areas, to cure for 12 full months, as well as covering such walls with an epoxy coating. In June 1999 the lab opened and in 2000 it received its first cargo of six of the world's most deadly viruses. Since opening, the lab has been pivotal in Canada's battle against diseases such as SARS, bird flu, and Mad Cow.

distributing liquor products for interstate sales, wine has to be passed through a local wholesaler and retailer before it gets shipped to the consumer. eVineyard set up local retail "shops" next door to local wholesalers and paid cash for daily shipments. "We don't buy wine until we have an order, so we don't have inventory cost," explained one of the company's marketing managers. In fact, eVineyard takes possession of bottles just long enough to package and ship them to buyers. This type of concurrent control enabled the company to hold down its costs and prices and survive the dot.com crash as well as to take over competitors wine.com and wineshopper.com. eVineyard has since adopted the name wine.com for its internet presence.[28]

Other typical examples of concurrent control are the monitoring of a customer service representative's performance while handling a telephone inquiry or the inspection of fruit while a batch is proceeding along a conveyer belt to the canning machinery. This type of control is designed to provide immediate feedback so that operations can be changed rapidly to decrease errors or increase quality. To have effective concurrent control procedures, however, managers must give considerable attention in advance to how such systems are designed and implemented. Also, managers need to be aware that this kind of control can have strong impacts on the motivation of those carrying out the operations, since the feedback is so immediate and often very direct.

Post-control of Operations Post-control was the traditional form of control in manufacturing—checking quality *after* a product (TV sets, shoes, furniture, etc.) was produced. Thus, companies typically have had quality control inspectors or whole departments that checked the rate of defective products and then decided what to do if those rates were too high. For example, Toyota inspects each car coming off the assembly line against a basic list of criteria. It also randomly inspects cars based on a significantly longer and more detailed list of quality criteria. In recent years, quality control at many companies has been greatly diminished in favour of pre- and concurrent controls. The adage has been "*Build* quality into the product, rather than inspect quality into the product."[29] Also, the more contemporary approach to operational control has been to shift control responsibilities to operations personnel and away from separate evaluators at the end of the process.

Factors in Control Effectiveness

Regardless of good intentions, control systems in organizations may break down completely, as illustrated in the opening case of this chapter, or they may not work very well. There can be many reasons for this, but alert managers can take the initiative to reduce these possibilities. The effectiveness of control is very much under the control of managers. Again, there are no automatic prescriptions or heuristics for managing the control process well. Instead, managers can use certain potential sources of influence to increase the probabilities of success. In this section, we look at some of the key factors that determine the effectiveness of controls (see Exhibit 14.17).

Focus of Control

The decision of where to focus control in an organization involves critical choices based on what actions and outcomes should receive the greatest attention. The guiding principle for focusing control is that it should be closely linked

Exhibit 14.17 Key Factors in Determining the Effectiveness of Controls

Key Factor	Concerns
Focus of control	· What will be controlled? · Where should controls be located in the organizational structure? · Who is responsible for which controls?
Amount of control	· Is there a balance between over- and undercontrol?
Quality of information collected by the controls	· Is the information useful? · Is the information accurate? · Is the information timely? · Is the information objective?
Flexibility of controls	· Are the controls able to respond to varying conditions?
Favourable cost–benefit ratio	· Is the information being gathered worth the cost of gathering it?
Source of control	· Is control imposed by others? · Is control decided by those who are affected?

to the strategic goals and, particularly, the planning process of the organization. For example, the Royal Bank of Canada placed a strategic focus on customer service. As a consequence, while the company would probably not be wise to ignore other controls, the focus would need to be on how to address the needs of customers and maintain a high level of customer satisfaction.

To be most effective, planning should be part of the control process, and control should be part of the planning process. Priorities should be set to select what is to be intensely monitored and controlled and what is to be given less attention. As software firms have found out, for example, little is to be gained from requiring star programmers to come to work on a precise schedule, given that the real objective is to produce innovative software. It is worth considerable control effort in that kind of organization, however, to make sure that the software that is written is as absolutely error-free as possible. Conversely, it is extremely important for restaurants to have their serving personnel be on time so that service is given promptly, whereas an occasional small mistake in taking a customer's order could be tolerated.

balanced scorecard an integrated and "balanced" set of measures for four critical areas or perspectives: financial, customers, internal business, and innovation and learning

One approach to determining the focus of control that has become popular in the last decade or so is the "**balanced scorecard**." Essentially, the advocates of this approach argue that historically—since the early years of the twentieth century—there has been an overfocus on financial measurements such as ratios and budgetary control procedures and a corresponding neglect of other important areas of measurement of a company's performance.[30] To remedy this, the developers of the balanced scorecard approach proposed an integrated and "balanced" set of measures for four critical areas ("perspectives," as they called them):[31]

Balanced Scorecard by Michael Hitt

mymanagementlab

- The (traditional) financial perspective: How do shareholders perceive the company?
- The customer perspective: How do customers perceive the company?
- The internal business perspective: How well is the company doing in excelling in internal business operations and procedures?
- The innovation and learning perspective: How well is the company doing at innovating, improving, and creating value?

It is also argued by the originators of this approach that the financial perspective primarily pays attention to the past, while the other three categories are much more future oriented. In effect, a presumed advantage of the balanced scorecard is that it requires managers to link measures of organizational success more closely to strategic objectives and to assess whether success in one area may be coming at the expense of poor performance in another area. It is intended, therefore, to bring greater focus and concentration on a total set of the most important areas of evaluation and control.

Many organizations are adopting some form of a balanced scorecard approach. Carleton University, Nova Scotia Power, and St. Michael's Hospital in Toronto, for example, use the balanced scorecard to help improve organizational performance. However, only 17.3 percent of Canadian organizations are using the management tool.[32]

As might be expected, however, some issues have been raised about the details of the balanced scorecard approach. One is whether these are the "correct" areas to measure and whether there are only four. A missing area, for example, is how employees perceive the organization and whether it is doing a good job of attracting and retaining talent. Another issue is whether each and every organization needs balance across all four areas or whether companies should concentrate on only one or two of the areas or some other sort of mix.[33] Still another issue—which is common to any system or overall approach to control measurement—concerns the degree of difficulty in designing and implementing the types of measures called for in this comprehensive approach.[34] Regardless of these issues, however, it is clear that the balanced scorecard has introduced a fresh and needed approach to focusing control on more than just financial numbers.

Focus of control refers not only to what should be controlled, but also to where control should be located in the organizational structure. This means paying careful attention to which people or positions in the structure have responsibility for different types and areas of control and how broad or narrow their scope of responsibility is. Control responsibility that is too diffuse can lead to omissions, and responsibility that is too concentrated can result in bottlenecks and decision delays. For example, if too many different people are assigned responsibility for quality control of a complex set of equipment, each may assume that one of the others has taken care of a particular problem, and as a consequence, some aspect of control gets left undone. On the other hand, if only one person is charged with inspecting all the pieces of equipment, that person may get overloaded, with the result that some critical detail gets inadvertently overlooked. Either way, effective control could be compromised.

Amount of Control

As we discussed at the beginning of this chapter, one of the greatest control challenges for any organization or manager is to determine the appropriate amount of control. To complicate the matter further, not all organizations need to employ the same level of control, as illustrated in *A Manager's Challenge: "Control: Too Much or Too Little?"*

Effective control involves finding a balance between overcontrol and undercontrol. Often, less-experienced managers tend to apply more control than is necessary in their eagerness to demonstrate that they are "in charge." This in turn can produce unintended resentment and resistance. Thus, new managers need to be aware of this tendency and moderate it.

a manager's challenge — technology

Control: Too Much or Too Little?

Controls that are too tight can keep an organization from functioning at its best; however, controls that appear too restrictive for one organization may be just right for another. Consider the fast-food giant McDonald's, which began as a "mom and pop" shop in San Bernardino, California, in 1954 and has since grown into a successful multinational corporation. McDonald's position as a leader in fast food can be attributed in part by the systemization of its operations. Every element of the supply chain is standardized and streamlined, from employee job descriptions to equipment and materials. The replication of predetermined policies and procedures across all restaurants facilitates training and results in consistent performance.

The strict controls that McDonald's imposes on all aspects of its operations are in place to achieve its goal of consistency in product and meeting or exceeding industry and government standards. Whether you are in Tokyo, Cairo, Stockholm, or Yellowknife, a Big Mac should look and taste the same. Quality and safety inspections are critical in maintaining these high standards, which is why McDonald's and its suppliers follow strict safety protocols and test products thousands of times before they are sold to consumers.

McDonald's imposes strict requirements from its suppliers to maintain consistency across stores. To provide burgers with consistent tastes and textures, all of McDonald's burger suppliers are required to test cook patties using the same grills as McDonald's before they are shipped. Once food products reach the various locations, McDonald's uses specialized equipment, such as rapid bun toasters, video display systems, and heated preparation tables, to ensure consistent food preparation. Employees are trained on how to prepare the different menu items and how to handle food safely, while supervisors and "mystery shoppers" monitor their compliance with these procedures.

In contrast to McDonald's, The Cabin Restaurant is a fast-food restaurant with far less stringent controls. The small, one-room restaurant in Fredericton, New Brunswick, has remained the only location since its establishment, also in 1954. A 1950s-style diner with burgundy booths, chrome-plated stools at a soda counter, and a miniature jukebox at every booth, The Cabin's atmosphere has remained relatively unchanged.

The Cabin offers its clientele simple, homemade recipes that are prepared without following specific cooking instructions or measuring the ingredients. Unlike McDonald's, meals at the Cabin are not mass produced by suppliers; they are traditional recipes that are made from base ingredients on site. Many of The Cabin's recipes simply could not be mass produced without losing the homemade taste that has kept some customers coming back for more than 40 years. Current owners David Halfyard and Linda Beardall point out that many customers enjoy old-fashioned recipes that remind them of the meals they ate growing up. Every Thursday, many regular patrons make sure they stop by the restaurant, knowing that this is the day that employee Jude Sampson makes her famous bread pudding from a secret family recipe.

Despite several changes in ownership and fewer controls than gigantic competitors like McDonald's, The Cabin Restaurant remains a successful business, with many regular customers who would prefer the cozy, one-of-a-kind atmosphere to a multinational franchise any day.

Sources: L. Stewart, "Aaah . . . The Comfort of Comfort Food; They're Our Favourite Foods—the Ones That Soothe Us When We Need It the Most," *The Daily Gleaner*, January 19, 2007, p. C1; P. Nelson, "A Step Back in Time: The Cabin in Fredericton Has Been Serving Homecooked Meals to Its Loyal Patrons for at Least 50 Years," *New Brunswick Telegraph-Journal*, April 12, 2003; S. Biggs, "'McDonald-ize' Your Shop," *Bodyshop* 32, no. 3 (2002), p. 30; McDonald's Canada, "FAQs," "Commitment to Quality," "Food Safety," "Our Beef Story," "Our Potato Story," "Food Freshness," 2006, www.mcdonalds.ca (accessed June 14, 2007); McDonald's Corporation, "Fact Sheet: Food Safety at McDonald's," "Fact Sheet: Food Quality at McDonald's," 2006, www.mcdonalds.com (accessed June 14, 2007).

If this were not a big enough challenge in itself, it is compounded in multinational corporations. In those organizations, perceptions of what is too much control can vary considerably from one country and culture to another. For example, tight monitoring of a manager's time and movements is more accepted in countries like Thailand; however, managers in Australia are likely to react quite strongly and negatively to tight monitoring.

When managers have more experience, they have a better basis for gauging the minimum levels of control that will get the job done without incurring unjustified risks. Even seasoned managers often find it difficult to correctly judge the degree of control required, and problems of undercontrol can crop up where least expected. No predetermined "right" amounts of control apply to all work situations. The best guideline for a manager to follow is to view the amount of control as something that, within limits, can be adjusted. Additionally, the undesirable consequences of excessive control and the dangers of too little control need to be made part of careful assessments of performance requirements and not inadvertently or casually overlooked. As we have already mentioned, involving those who will be directly influenced by the control measures in setting the amount of control increases the chances that an appropriate level of control is set from the outset. Furthermore, if adjustments need to be made, this initial involvement will likely reduce the resistance to these changes.

Quality of Information

Effective control requires knowledge based on data—that is, it requires good information. Four characteristics that determine the quality of information are usefulness, accuracy, timeliness, and objectivity.

Usefulness Not all data collected for control purposes are equally useful in managerial operations and decisions. Sometimes data that were once useful continue to be collected, even though the original purposes for obtaining that information have disappeared. Such a situation was discovered several years ago in a division of BorgWarner Incorporated. BorgWarner is a US$4.6 billion company that develops engine and powertrain products for the automotive industry. It has plants and offices located around the world, including Simcoe, Ontario. Because of major changes in the operating environment at an automotive transmission unit, the company decided to find out which accounting reports, if any, were actually helpful to managers. Did the information contained in the reports actually assist managers to do their jobs better? The answer was a resounding "no." Investigation indicated that the accounting department thought it was gathering data that two separate groups could use: corporate managers and plant managers. Yet it turned out that the information being disseminated was of assistance only to the first group. As a result, the accounting department worked with operations managers in the plants to develop control reports that would help them do their particular jobs more effectively.[35]

Accuracy Data or numbers that are inaccurate or misleading not only fail to provide a good basis for control steps, but also breed cynicism among those whose performance is being measured. Since control actions, especially those designed to change behaviour that does not meet agreed-upon standards, can have such powerful effects, it is vital that substantial effort be put into obtaining data that are absolutely valid; no information is better than inaccurate information.

Timeliness Even accurate data, if they arrive too late, are not useful. This is true for any organizational actions, but especially so for purposes of control. In the fast-paced world of global business, data that are out of date are of virtually no use. For effective control, information must arrive on time to those who can take action and make any required changes. In everyday life, for example, information that reaches truck drivers 10 minutes after the wrong route has been taken is not very useful. Effective control systems require speed.

Objectivity Objectivity, especially as it relates to control, can be a double-edged sword. Almost everyone would agree that objective facts are better than subjective, and possibly biased, opinions. However, for some kinds of performances, objective data may not be possible to obtain or may even be misleading. In diving competitions, for example, objective measurement of the exact height that a diver jumps off a springboard may be much less important than the subjective opinion of an experienced judge on the form of the dive. Similarly, in organizations, some of the most easily measured activities, and therefore the most easily controlled, may be relatively insignificant for the achievement of major, strategic goals. All other factors being equal, objective information would be preferred, but in many situations those other factors may not be equal and thoughtful judgments rather than unimportant "facts" may provide the best basis for action decisions.

For example, in a customer service call centre, it is relatively easy to gather objective data on the length of time a customer service agent spends on the phone with each caller. However, comparing the number of callers served by each agent may not tell you the most important thing—how well each customer was served. In fact, if the number of calls answered becomes the key performance measure, customer service agents may begin to provide poor service to get customers off the phone quickly and move on to the next customer, thereby maximizing the number of calls they take in a day. In this case, it is clear that the objective data (the number of calls taken) may not be the most important data (that is, how well the customer is served). Measuring customer service effectively may require having a supervisor randomly listen in on service calls or going to the cost and effort of trying to measure customer satisfaction by polling customers who have called in to the service centre.

Flexibility

For control to be effective, its procedures must respond to changing conditions. Organizations and managers become accustomed to control procedures that are already in place; it is a human tendency to stay the course when things appear to be going well. But that tendency can defeat effective control. Well-designed control systems should be able to account for changing circumstances and adjust accordingly. Rigidity of control systems is not usually a feature to be prized—flexibility is.[36]

Favourable Cost–Benefit Ratio

The designs of some control systems look good on paper, but they prove to be impractical or costly to use. To be effective, the benefits of controls must outweigh both the direct financial costs and the indirect costs of inconvenience and awkwardness in implementation. Elaborate, complicated control systems immediately raise the issue of whether they will be worth the expense involved. Sometimes, the simplest systems are nearly as effective. Consider again our customer service call centre example. While objective customer satisfaction data may be preferable to subjective supervisor evaluations, obtaining satisfaction ratings directly from customers may cost significantly more and not provide much better information than well-trained supervisors.

Of course, some situations may call for intricate controls because of the extremely high costs that would occur from unacceptable performance. Organizations that must carry out certain activities associated with high levels of hazard—such as hospitals, virology laboratories, nuclear power plants, and air traffic control agencies—need to invest heavily in control systems that ensure an exceedingly high degree of reliability. Consequently, they have to make costly investments—for example, in continual training, backup staffing, and very expensive equipment—to control operations and reduce the possibility of a catastrophic accident to absolute minimum levels.[37] In such cases, high control costs are obviously justified.

Sources

The source of control often affects the willingness of organization members to work cooperatively with the system. As we discussed earlier, in recent years many organizations have changed from bureaucratic control to control that relies more on members' monitoring their own or their team's performance. Thus, the source of control has shifted, and the change may increase positive reactions because employees have more trust in a process over which they have some influence.

Similarly, controls that provide information from equipment or instruments often seem less resented and more fair than controls involving what can be viewed as the sometimes arbitrary actions of supervisors. This principle was illustrated at Unum Insurance Company, a leading provider of income protection that started in the United Kingdom in 1970 and now has offices in North America. Several years ago it installed an elaborate information system (involving a more-than-US$30 000 investment in hardware and software per employee) to help improve the performance of the company's information-systems professionals by measuring the amount of work to be done, identifying errors as they occur, and assisting in correcting those errors. The affected employees accepted the errors identified by the new system more readily than they had from supervisors because the system had no personal "axe to grind."[38] For any type of control, the source has a great deal to do with the acceptability of the system. Acceptability, in turn, affects how well control systems work in practice and not just in theory.

managerial perspectives revisited

1

PERSPECTIVE 1: **THE ORGANIZATIONAL CONTEXT** Organizations could not function as organizations without control. It's as simple as that. It is not a question of whether to have control or not have control. Instead, the basic issues involve how much and what type. Early in the chapter we emphasized that control as an organizational and managerial process is closely connected to other major organizational processes, such as planning, organizing, and leading. Control is affected by these processes, but in turn control also affects them. Thus, control is integral to an organization's entire set of activities.

2

PERSPECTIVE 2: **THE HUMAN FACTOR** Within any organizational setting, for the process of control to work effectively it needs the cooperation of the people who are affected by it. Many aspects of control, as we pointed out, are impersonal in nature, as when instruments provide information on whether some product or process is within quality boundaries. However, it ultimately is up to people at some level, or several levels, to take action based on that information. If the people affected by managerial control activities are working to defeat and impede control, eventually the quality and quantity of organizational performance are affected. On the other hand, if they are supportive, performance can be enhanced. Often the reactions of the people affected by control are a good barometer of whether the organization is heading in the right direction in its other activities.

3

PERSPECTIVE 3: **MANAGING PARADOXES** There are two major potential paradoxes for managers to consider with respect to the topic of control. First, managers need to make sure that they and their associates view control as a "means" and not as an "end." Sometimes managers get so obsessed with the necessity and importance of control that they send the unintended message that it is in fact *the* objective, rather than simply being a way to assist in meeting organizational goals. Second, managers need to determine where the most appropriate balance is between overcontrol and undercontrol. Either condition, if not detected and modified, can lead to unfortunate consequences.

4

PERSPECTIVE 4: **ENTREPRENEURIAL MINDSET** If managers adopt an entrepreneurial mindset they are more likely to develop balanced controls—controls that meet both the firm's financial and strategic objectives. These managers understand the importance of adhering to financial budgets and constraints, but they aren't blinded to entrepreneurial opportunities that may exist and require money to develop. Moreover, the *types* of control used depend on a manager's entrepreneurial mindset. On the one hand, a strong managerial emphasis on financial control has been found to produce less innovation, while a managerial emphasis on strategic control tends to facilitate innovation within an organization.[39] Why? Financial controls tend to cause managers to focus on short-term gains rather than long-term opportunities.

In addition, the use of clan control versus bureaucratic control by a manager is likely to help him or her take a long-term perspective and be more innovative—especially when these values are inculcated within the organization's culture. When this occurs, members of the organization are highly committed and share a strong set of mutually agreed-upon values. Such a commitment may be easier to obtain in a smaller organization, but many larger organizations can nonetheless benefit from clan control because they have more committed members whose efforts they can mobilize than do their competitors of similar size and complexity.

concluding comments

Control is a crucial, albeit many times difficult and sometimes even unpleasant, managerial function. As we have emphasized repeatedly throughout this chapter, the challenge for managers is to make wise decisions about how much and where control needs to be used, and then how to apply that control. Control is essential, but many a manager and even many an organization have run into severe difficulties because the control process has not been well handled.

Knowing the basic elements of the control process is a helpful start in gaining perspective about how to exercise appropriate control. Understanding some of the pitfalls and obstacles that can interfere at each of these steps provides a basis for avoiding unnecessary "rookie" mistakes. Not many managers would have the aspiration to be a great "controller," but likewise, most would not like to be known as excessively naïve about the need for control. Keeping in mind the factors that influence control effectiveness—such as the focus, amount, and degree of flexibility—is a way to reduce the chances of unintended control blunders and improve the probabilities of success.

Clearly, control is a matter of both science and art. On the one hand, there are a variety of quantitative measures available to assess individual, group, and organizational performance. Particular areas, such as finance and operations, tend to use many quantitative control measures because they deal with things that are easy to count (money, products, defects, etc.). However, the fact that something can be easily measured doesn't mean it should be. Likewise, the fact that something is hard to measure doesn't mean it shouldn't be. The key to managerial success relative to control is making good judgments and *then* good measurements. Without good judgment concerning what, how, and when to measure something, the measurements are of little value. Control can add real value to an organization, but that outcome is not guaranteed unless managers with judgment make it happen.

key terms

balanced scorecard 504
break-even point (B-E P) 496
budgetary control 497
bureaucratic control 500
commitment (clan) control 500
concurrent control 501
control 484
efficiency (activity) 495
human resource policies and procedures 499
leverage 495
liquidity 495
operational control 501
post-control 501
pre-control 501
profitability 495
ROE (return on equity) 495
ROI (return on investment) 495
standards 486
strategic control 492
supervisory structure 498
tactical control 494

test your comprehension

1. What is meant by "control" in organizations?
2. How is the control function linked to other managerial functions?
3. What is meant when control is described as a causal variable, as well as being a dependent variable?
4. What are the four elements of the control process?
5. Who is responsible for setting standards?
6. What are standards and how are they used in organizations?
7. What are the key issues managers must consider when establishing standards?
8. When measuring performance, can nonquantifiable data be helpful? How?
9. What is the limiting factor in comparing performance against standards?
10. Which is the most difficult managerial task in the control process? Why?
11. What happens when a gap is detected between expected performance and actual performance?
12. What is the difference between "reinforcing action" and "corrective action"? When would you use each?
13. Compare strategic, tactical, and operational control. Why are the boundaries between each not always clear?
14. When are strategic controls more useful? Less useful?
15. What is the relationship of the external organizational environment to the development of strategic controls?
16. Contrast budgetary control with strategic control.
17. What is the main focus of tactical control?
18. List and discuss four types of tactical controls.
19. Describe four managerial control issues involving budgets.
20. What is the fundamental difference between bureaucratic control and commitment (clan) control?
21. Define operational control.

22. What is the relationship between pre-, concurrent, and post-controls of operations? Which type is best?
23. What are the seven factors of control effectiveness?
24. What are the advantages and the problems involved in using a balanced scorecard approach?
25. What factors determine the usefulness of information to the control process?

apply your understanding

1. Do you think it is possible for an international firm to have a common control system even for a single activity, like manufacturing, when it has plants in countries such as India, Australia, Japan, Canada, and Germany? Explain your answer.
2. If you were the manager of your university's control system for exams, would you tighten or loosen the amount of control? What signals would you look for to determine whether your adjustments were appropriate?
3. In general, do you think that people respond to control systems or that control systems respond to people? In other words, will people generally conform to the tightness or looseness of a control system, or should the tightness or looseness of the control system depend on the nature of the people involved?
4. If you were a worker and management wanted to tighten controls over your job, what would they need to do to get you to go along with the tighter controls?

practise your capabilities

Charlie had begun her career at one of Le Château's retail stores as a sales clerk during high school. She loved it there. Le Château stocked cutting-edge fashions with stock changing as rapidly as the customers' styles. It was a high-energy, fast-changing environment in which to work. An internship during college helped her gain her first entry-level management job in the chain after graduation. Promotions had been steady, and two months ago Charlie began her new job as assistant store manager. If she performed well in this position, the next step would be to manage her own store. She had decided that she would impress upper management by controlling costs and improving the efficiency of the store. Her predecessor in the assistant manager position—who had received a promotion—had been, in her opinion, far too easygoing. He had allowed the sales and stock personnel to perform their jobs more or less as they saw fit, within broad limits. When Charlie took over as the new assistant manager, however, she decided to "tighten things up."

Charlie's first action was to make a thorough review of the company rules and procedures for stock and sales personnel. For three weeks, she made daily inspections of the stock rooms to make sure all of the boxes were stacked properly and neatly, and that all boxes that were opened were immediately unpacked and the merchandise put away. She noted every example of incorrect storage. On the sales floor, she inspected every garment display, sometimes even rearranging them. She watched each move the sales clerks made, and once or twice noted the specific amount of time spent in conversation between employees and compared it to the time they spent with customers. She timed lunches and rest breaks and reviewed everyone's time cards. After three weeks of review and inspections, she called a meeting for Monday morning, before customers arrived, to announce the changes she would be making.

"I really want our store to shine! We need to impress top management with our efficiency and level of sales. Remember, there are bonuses available for increases in sales above the company average, for cost containment in the stock rooms, and even for low absenteeism and tardiness. So, from now on, this store is going to run like clockwork. There will be no more skirting the rules. We will be working according to the letter of the law. I am issuing a copy of the company policy manual to each of you along with the rules you will be following in implementing these policies. I have several ideas on how we can improve the operation of this store and help us all qualify for those bonuses." Charlie then went on to tell the store personnel about all of the new forms she was having printed that would detail each task with signature lines where each employee would sign off whenever he or she finished a specific task. Arrival, departure, and break times would be much more closely monitored than before. Additionally, sales personnel would constantly be walking the sales floor looking for customers to increase sales. There should be very little time for idle conversation. There were so many new rules to explain that the meeting took over two hours. Charlie ended the meeting by saying: "Let's have the best, most efficient, store in the chain! I know you can do it."

1. How do you think the store personnel are going to respond to Charlie's new rules and regulations, in light of the fact that they should have increased opportunities to earn bonuses? Why?
2. Using the concepts in this chapter, analyze the types of control that Charlie is using.

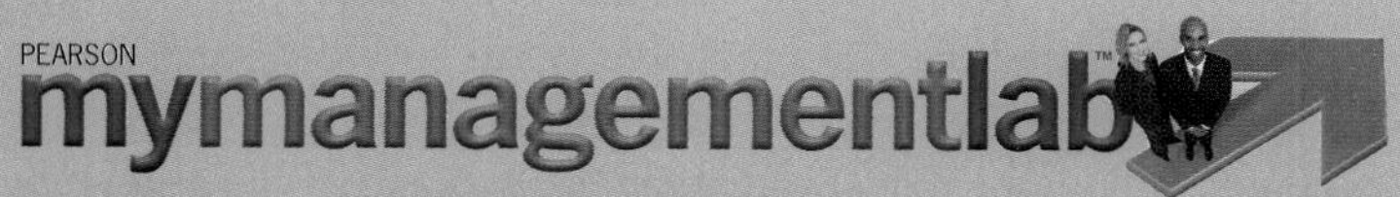

To improve your grade, visit the MyManagementLab website at **www.pearsoned.ca/mymanagementlab**. This online homework and tutorial system allows you to test your understanding and generates a personalized study plan just for you. It provides you with study and practice tools directly related to this chapter's content. MyManagementLab puts you in control of your own learning!

closing case DEVELOP YOUR CRITICAL THINKING

Ford Slams the Brakes on Costs

Top managers at Ford Motor Company had good reason to wonder whether Ford would live to celebrate its centennial in 2003. The company had overcome tough times during the 1940s, when Henry Ford II brought it back from the financial brink. Starting in the 1970s, Ford and its domestic rivals began feeling the pressure from foreign automakers with highly efficient designs, streamlined production methods, and better quality controls.

By the time William Clay Ford Jr. (nephew of Henry Ford II and great-grandson of the founder) became CEO in 2001, costs at the number-two North American carmaker had spun out of control and quality concerns were mounting.

The new CEO was keenly aware of how far the company had fallen in just a few years. Consider that in 1999, Ford reported record profits topping US$7 billion. In 1996, it was even poised to unseat number one, General Motors. Yet by 2001, under former CEO Jacques Nasser, the company was losing US$5.5 billion. Nearly all its US$15 billion cash hoard had been spent acquiring Volvo's car operations and the Land Rover business plus starting several fruitless e-commerce initiatives. Meanwhile, price-sensitive and quality-conscious customers were choosing foreign-made cars and trucks. This trend drove Ford's North American market share down to just 25 percent.

Furthermore, Ford's costs were considerably higher than those of GM and other automakers, which severely damaged its profit situation. In the late 1990s, the company was earning an average of nearly US$2000 on every vehicle sold in North America. But costs kept creeping up, in part because car designers and engineers were not held to strict standards for the price of parts or for costly production changes to make the new models. For example, purchasing managers were instructed to buy 126 different fuel caps and 150 different radios for installation in the vehicles rolling off Ford's assembly lines. Such seemingly small inefficiencies repeated over and over added up to a major cost disadvantage within a few years. Soon the company was losing nearly US$200 per vehicle sold.

Trouble was also brewing in the company's credit division. Ford Credit's managers wanted to fuel vehicle sales, so they set looser guidelines that allowed more customers to qualify for low-interest and no-interest loans—including a higher number of customers with below-average creditworthiness. As the economy faltered, more borrowers fell behind on their payments, and Ford repossessed more vehicles than planned. Losses at the credit unit ended up contributing to even higher losses for Ford overall in 2001.

On becoming CEO, Bill Ford's top priority was reasserting control from the top down at Ford. He changed senior managers at Ford Credit, appointed the former CEO of Ford Europe to oversee international purchasing, named a new chief operating officer, and brought back Ford's retired chief financial officer to tighten the reins on corporate finance. This new management team helped Ford develop a comprehensive plan to slash costs by US$4.5 billion and more in the years to come. The plan called for laying off 35 000 workers to drastically reduce payroll costs, axing four vehicle models to simplify the manufacturing process, closing factories to boost efficiency, and standardizing vehicle parts to reduce the number of different parts purchased. Additionally, the plan called for fine-tuning production to raise quality levels and lower recall and warranty claim costs, imposing higher creditworthiness thresholds to reduce credit losses, and revamping both rebates and low-interest-rate loans to improve profitability. After one of a dozen inside efficiency teams found out most personnel were getting their news online, Ford even cancelled company-paid magazine and newspaper subscriptions. "We're still trying to put the brakes on a freight train," commented the CEO, whose personal sacrifice included downsizing to a smaller corporate jet. "We've got to stop it before we can turn it around."

Supporting the turnaround, Ford management pushed to speed up new-product development and vehicle introductions to generate more cash more quickly and—just as important—to generate excitement among dealers and customers. Although the company was relying heavily on budgets, schedules, and other formal methods to enforce the controls, the CEO personally visited numerous Ford plants and offices to pump up workforce commitment. "I'm asking you to work hard," he told employees. "Keep the big picture in mind. Think about what really matters. Do that and nothing else."

However, some parts of Ford had difficulty adjusting to the new controls. Managers in the luxury car division, for instance, could not meet a speedy launch schedule for a new Jaguar aluminum-chassis model; without the new model, the division fell short of its revenue and profit goals. In addition, managers working on a new Mustang model tried to get Bill Ford to approve a development plan that failed to meet the company's profit goals. Although they assured the CEO that they soon would resolve the profit-sapping issues, Bill Ford refused to authorize any plan that did not explicitly meet the goals. Similarly, he sent engineers trying to improve the fuel economy of Ford's SUVs back to the drawing board until they could produce a plan to meet the target of boosting fuel efficiency by 25 percent within three years. In all these cases, rather than second-guess Ford managers, the CEO set clear limits and asked specific questions to steer his subordinates in the right direction.

Still, the new controls were already having an effect in other key areas. By concentrating on producing fewer vehicles of better quality, Ford's manufacturing units helped lower warranty claims and recall fewer vehicles. And higher quality gave the company higher marks in customer surveys. Working with their counterparts in purchasing and engineering to standardize parts and arrange better deals with global suppliers, production managers also squeezed US$240 from the cost of every vehicle produced. In all, Ford managers have made enough cuts to lower costs by US$6 billion so far. Ford reported a modest profit of US$36 million in 2005, but this was in stark contrast to the US$626 million in losses the year before. All the same, Toyota still managed to overtake Ford as the world's second-largest auto manufacturer in 2006, and market share in North America had slipped from 25 percent to 18 percent that same year. In 2007, Toyota became the largest auto manufacturer in the world and Ford slipped to fourth place.

Setting and meeting standards to achieve the tough financial goals as well as all the other goals needed to support a turnaround will be neither fast nor easy. "What keeps me up at night is that we're not moving fast enough," the CEO says. "Yes, we are making progress, but are we making it fast enough?" Bill Ford knows that the company's future depends on how well he and his managers continue putting the brakes on costs while hitting the accelerator on quality and sales. In 2006, Ford announced that they would reduce their workforce by 30 000 employees over six years, cutting their manufacturing capacity by 26 percent in North America, but losses continued to plague the company. In September 2006, Bill Ford stepped down as CEO and Alan Mulally, a former executive at Boeing, took the helm. In January Ford posted a net loss of US$12.7 billion for 2006, the largest reported loss in company history.

Questions

1. Discuss Bill Ford's actions using the steps of the basic control process as a model. Did he follow this process? What did he do in each step? Did he leave out any important steps?
2. Can Ford's turnaround plan be characterized as tactical or strategic controls? Why? How are the actions and decisions of lower-level managers likely to be influenced by the plan?
3. How does the amount of control used by Ford Credit's managers affect control and performance in other areas of the parent company?
4. Thinking in terms of focus of control and amount of control, what caused the problems at Ford in the first place?

Sources: C. Isadore, "Ford: Biggest Loss Ever," CNNMoney, January 25, 2007, money.cnn.com (accessed October 22, 2007); G. Wong, "Ford's Net Loss Widens to $5.8 B," CNNMoney, October 23, 2006, money.cnn.com (accessed June 14, 2007); D. Usborne, "Ford to Slash 30,000 Jobs and Close 14 Plants in North America," *The Independent*, January 24, 2006; J. Halliday, "Pedal to the Metal," *Advertising Age*, November 17, 2003, p. 4; A. Wilson and B. Wernle, "Ford Share Slides Toward 75-Year Low," *Automotive News*, October 6, 2003, p. 8; B. Morris, "Can Ford Save Ford?" *Fortune*, November 18, 2002, pp. 52+; S. Milles, "Ford Speeds Cost Cutting," *Wall Street Journal*, September 23, 2002; D. Hakim, "A New-Model Ford on a Risky Track," *New York Times*, September 29, 2002, sec. 3, pp. 1, 12; K. Kerwin, "Bill Ford's Long, Hard Road," *BusinessWeek*, October 7, 2002, pp. 88–92.

Chapter 15 Organizational Development and Transformation

LEARNING OBJECTIVES

After reading this chapter, you should be able to:

1 Describe the general process of change.

2 Identify the internal and external forces for change in an organization.

3 Discuss the technological, cultural, strategic, structural, and systems dimensions of change.

4 Analyze the process managers should use in evaluating the need for change.

5 Describe the process of organizational change.

6 Diagnose the causes of resistance to change and discuss possible approaches to dealing with such resistance.

7 Describe three approaches to planned comprehensive organizational change and compare their similarities and differences.

Leading Change at LSP

Leading Signal Processing (LSP—a disguised name but a real company) produces diagnostic instruments primarily for the health care industry. For most of its history, its leading-edge products, based on state-of-the-art analogue signal technology, were used by scientific and hospital researchers in diagnostic tests and cellular and blood chemical analysis.

After years of success, the CEO noticed digital signal processing emerging as a competing technological platform, though initially it seemed unable to rival LSP's analogue technology in performance. He also recognized a shift in customers and end users. In the past, MDs and Ph.D.s had performed diagnostics and analyses in research labs and hospitals; now technicians in clinics were increasingly performing these tests. Many of LSP's largest customers were slow to make this transition, but mid-size and small customers were quickly changing over to save money. In addition, the market was moving away from separate tests and analyses and toward integrated systems and analyses.

While LSP's CEO recognized that these environmental shifts would require organizational changes to retain the company's competitive edge in the marketplace, many of the firm's scientists—analogue technology experts—resisted, seeing digital technology as a threat to their jobs. The more the CEO talked about environmental shifts, the harder these scientists worked on customized analogue products for customers, especially big customers.

The CEO also realized that the trend toward integrated systems would require LSP's workforce to collaborate using both cross-product and cross-functional teams composed of employees from research, development, marketing, and manufacturing. Such teamwork was rare at LSP.

As competitors brought new digital products to market, LSP's research scientists scoffed at their initially lower reliability and inferior performance. To help his subordinates see the urgent need for change, the R&D manager applied his "80/20 rule," a guideline suggesting that 20 percent of the problem accounted for 80 percent of the solution. He thought he could achieve most of the needed changes if his subordinates recognized the changes in customers and end users—the core 20 percent of the problem. So he hired a new employee who represented the new users: a clinical technician who held an associate's degree, sported purple hair and a nose ring, had grown up on video games, and preferred intuitive, graphic user interfaces to the complicated text interfaces of LSP's current products. The scientists soon noticed the contrast between the old users and the new and accepted the need for switching to digital technology and a more user-friendly product for less-sophisticated customers.

Medical and biotechnology companies face rapid do-or-die changes. Managers can't just seek to move the organization itself to the forefront; they also have to be prepared to help and persuade the people to personally embrace change. Not doing so can be fatal to the organization.

Implementing the needed changes was even more difficult. Because LSP's scientists had never worked on cross-functional teams, they lacked the communication skills to work with nonscientists, and had poor group decision-making and conflict resolution skills. In addition, the R&D manager had to change his management methods. Instead of holding mainly technical discussions with subordinates, he now had to manage their interpersonal interactions. Thus, what started as a vital business change expanded to require personal changes among LSP's managers as well as changes in how these managers supervised their employees.

strategic overview

Many managers find themselves in situations similar to that of the CEO at LSP, in which they face the development of new technology and products. The CEO at LSP had to change the firm's strategy to match its competitors and retain its customers. However, he was slow to do so. He recognized early on that changes in the technology were occurring, but he failed to react, falling victim to some of the forces of failure explained later in this chapter.

Even after the CEO recognized the need for change, he could not easily implement it. The researchers and scientists in LSP's R&D unit resisted change efforts. They were relying on more traditional "mental maps." It is likely that the inability to overcome these problems early cost LSP some of its customers. What's worse is that now it may be difficult to win them back.

As a manager you will not only have opportunities to manage change at the organizational level, but you will increasingly have to manage change at a more micro level—managing team change, individual change in subordinates, and personal changes in yourself.[1] Failure to adapt personally, to help other individuals change, or to effectively lead change in a team can all have devastating effects not only for the individuals involved but for the organization overall. After all, how effective would LSP's CEO's effort to transform the company have been if the R&D manager was unwilling or unable to change himself or others?

A major driver of organizational change is the external environment in which the organization exists. Changes in many of these external forces mean that managers must alter their organizations' strategies. For example, when competitors implement a successful strategic action, like introducing a popular new product to the market, the organization may have to respond to protect its share of the market. The development of new technologies, the introduction of new industry regulations, and changes in the demographic composition of society will also frequently result in the need for new strategies to respond to the opportunities or threats these environmental changes pose.[2]

Organizations never stay the same because the world around them never stays the same. From ancient times forward, all organizations have had to build the capacity to change into their structures.[3] Making changes and managing that process have been essential to the vitality of all organizations throughout time and especially today. However, managing the change process is no easy task. While the need to change is often obvious, making successful changes presents formidable managerial challenges. As most managers discover, sooner or later, there are fundamental issues of change that need to be confronted. For example:

- How much change is enough?
- How fast should change take place?
- How should the need for continual changes be balanced against the need for a minimum level of stability and continuity?
- Who should be the major players in change processes, and what should their roles be?
- Who, exactly, is likely to benefit and who could be harmed by particular changes?

How these and other similar questions are answered will determine the fate of attempted changes in any organization.

Throughout this book, we have emphasized understanding *change* as a major theme because it is so critical to managerial success. In this final chapter we focus specifically on bringing about change in organizational settings, and we address specific means and methods used in changing the overall organization as well as units within it. The present chapter presumes a basic knowledge of the other topics covered in this book. This knowledge will be helpful in analyzing the significant issues involved in organizational development and transformation.

Organizational contexts, because of their complexity, provide many opportunities as well as many challenges for making changes. Some of these changes are unplanned and reactive, often involving unpleasant consequences for those who work in organizations. A sudden layoff of a large number of employees to reduce expenses quickly is one familiar example. Other changes involve more planning and often have the intent of transforming the entire organization or at least major parts of it so that sudden, drastic changes, like major reductions in personnel, will not be necessary. When a change is planned, comprehensive, and apt to modify important characteristics of the organization, the terms "organizational development" or "organizational transformation" are applicable. (We also discuss a special use of the term "organizational development" later in this chapter.)

The first parts of this chapter examine general issues and principles relating to organizational development and transformation. We first review why organizations change—focusing on the forces that can cause changes. Particular attention is given to analyzing external and internal forces of change, and on recognizing and diagnosing those forces as they affect the need for change. We also look at some of the reasons why change initiatives fail so often and some keys managers can use to ensure their change efforts are successful. Specific areas of the focus of changes are considered next: technology, shared values and culture, strategy, structure, systems, and staff. These sections in turn provide a background for an examination of managerial choices regarding the preparation, implementation, and evaluation of the change process.

The chapter concludes with an analysis of three major, typically organization-wide, approaches to planned change frequently used in contemporary organizations. These include the organizational development (OD) approach, process redesign (also known as re-engineering), and the development of the learning organization. We will look at how these approaches are used and at their relative strengths and weaknesses.

Importance of Understanding Change

It is important to recognize that organizational change not only involves revising strategies, structures, or technology; it often requires changes at a more personal level. A change in strategy is not possible without individuals in the organization changing. As the opening case illustrates, changing the strategy and products at LSP requires employees from both R&D and marketing to change many of the ways they currently perform their jobs. For example, cross-functional teams are necessary to develop the new in-house technology and products to use it. To effectively implement cross-functional teams, the R&D managers must sometimes focus on managing the interpersonal relationships of team members rather than the technical aspects of the project they normally focus on. The managers may have to change how they motivate their subordinates, how they resolve conflicts, or their negotiation style to support the new strategy. Clearly, change is a fact of organizational life that can affect all aspects of a manager's responsibilities.

Failure of Change Efforts

The first evidence that change is a subject worthy of extra focus is how often it fails (the forces behind change failure will be discussed in more depth later in this chapter). Obtaining accurate data on the frequency of failure is challenging, but one well-known authority states that between 50 and 70 percent of strategic change efforts fail to meet their objectives.[4]

Nature of Change

The nature of change may give us some insight into why it seems to fail so often and why dealing with it today and in the future is so challenging. Clearly, not all change is equal. Some change we can see coming and other change catches us totally by surprise. All other factors being equal, it is easier to deal with predictable change than unpredictable change. With predictable change not only can you see what is coming but you have the opportunity to prepare for the event in advance. Exhibit 15.1 shows the results of a survey of executives concerning how they perceive the predictability of the change they face. As you can see, the vast majority of executives feel that most of the change they face is highly unpredictable.

Some scholars have argued that to the extent that change is increasingly unpredictable, we may have to personally and organizationally change how we deal with it.[5] Instead of having concrete plans for how to respond to anticipated changes, we may have to be more flexible. For example, airline pilots do make flight plans, but they know they may encounter turbulence that will likely alter their flight plans. However, they do not try to specify in advance exactly how they will respond to changing conditions. For example, if they run into unexpected turbulence, they do not specify in advance that they will increase or decrease altitude by a specific amount, but they know that changing altitude is one of the key means they have of dealing with unpredicted changes in their environment.

Exhibit 15.1

Predictability of Change

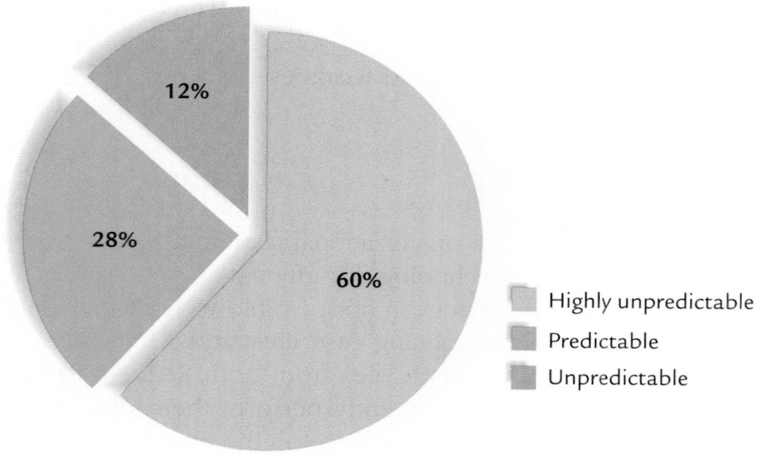

Source: Canadian Conference Board, 2001.

While it is impossible to plan the details of anticipated change, researchers have found that the planning process for a major change effort can impact employee attitudes, which may ultimately have performance implications. Surveys conducted at two electric power generating plants operating in the challenging and turbulent environment of deregulation show that when employees feel that management is dealing with the change process in a procedurally just manner, trust in management increases.[6]

Rate of Change

Another factor that makes change worthy of special focus is the rate of change. Even if most change is unpredictable, if the rate of change is steady or declining, we might be more effective in dealing with it. While objective measures of the rate of change are somewhat hard to come by, the same survey of executives as in Exhibit 15.1 asked about the perceived rate of change. The vast majority of executives felt that the rate of change was increasing (see Exhibit 15.2).

In combination, Exhibits 15.1 and 15.2 offer some intriguing implications. If the rate of change is increasing, then we may benefit by increasing our ability to anticipate change. However, given that much of the change we face is somewhat unpredictable, we may benefit from increasing our ability to respond

Exhibit 15.2

Rate of Change

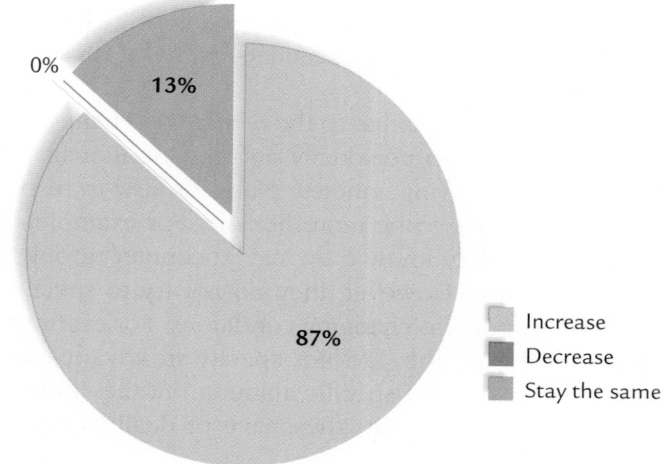

quickly to changes when we unexpectedly encounter them.[7] Enhancing both these abilities can help us perform better as managers. For example, suppose a new technology allows you to work on an engineering project simultaneously across several time zones with a team of individuals spread out geographically around the world. Further suppose that this in turn helps you respond to changes faster than other managers in your company. This might give you cost savings (e.g., from lower travel costs) and productivity gains (e.g., from faster project completion) that would help you stand out among managers in your company.

Managerial Competency for Leading Change

If we can safely assume that managing change is going to become more important for companies and managers,[8] then it might be instructive to know how good executives believe their managers are at this task. After all, even in the workplace, the rules of supply and demand apply. If the demand for effective leaders of change is high and increasing while the supply is low, then that places a premium price on those who can manage change effectively. That premium price may translate into rewards such as higher pay, more opportunities, or faster rates of promotions for managers who can distinguish themselves at this critical managerial activity.

Exhibit 15.3 suggests that senior executives in the same survey do not see an ample supply of capable leaders of change. Other studies have found that change management is consistently regarded as one of the most important capabilities for future leaders, and at the same time is one that most managers need to improve on.[9] In one study, more than 80 percent of senior executives surveyed and interviewed identified "change management" as one of the most important capabilities for future leaders. Interestingly, in this same study a majority of leaders expressed dissatisfaction with the current level of change management capabilities among even their high-potential managers.[10] This suggests that the demand for effective managers of change far outstrips supply, which creates a premium for this managerial capability. It also creates a need and justification for special focus on this topic.

Ability to Manage Change by Michael Hitt

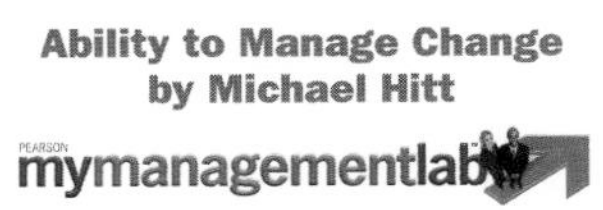

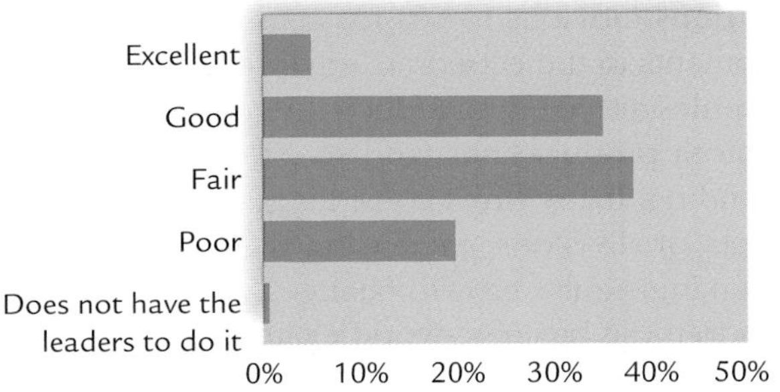

Exhibit 15.3
Prevalence of Change Management Capability

Forces for Change

The causes of organizational change originate from both external and internal forces, and a manager must be alert to all of them (see Exhibit 15.4). Sometimes those causes arise almost totally from factors outside the organization, such as economic or business conditions, technological developments, demographic shifts, and the like. At other times, the forces are mostly from inside the organization. Internal forces include such factors as managerial decisions to make changes and employee pressures for urgent changes. Often, of course, the total set of causes of change represents a combination of both external and internal reasons.

Exhibit 15.4
Forces for Change

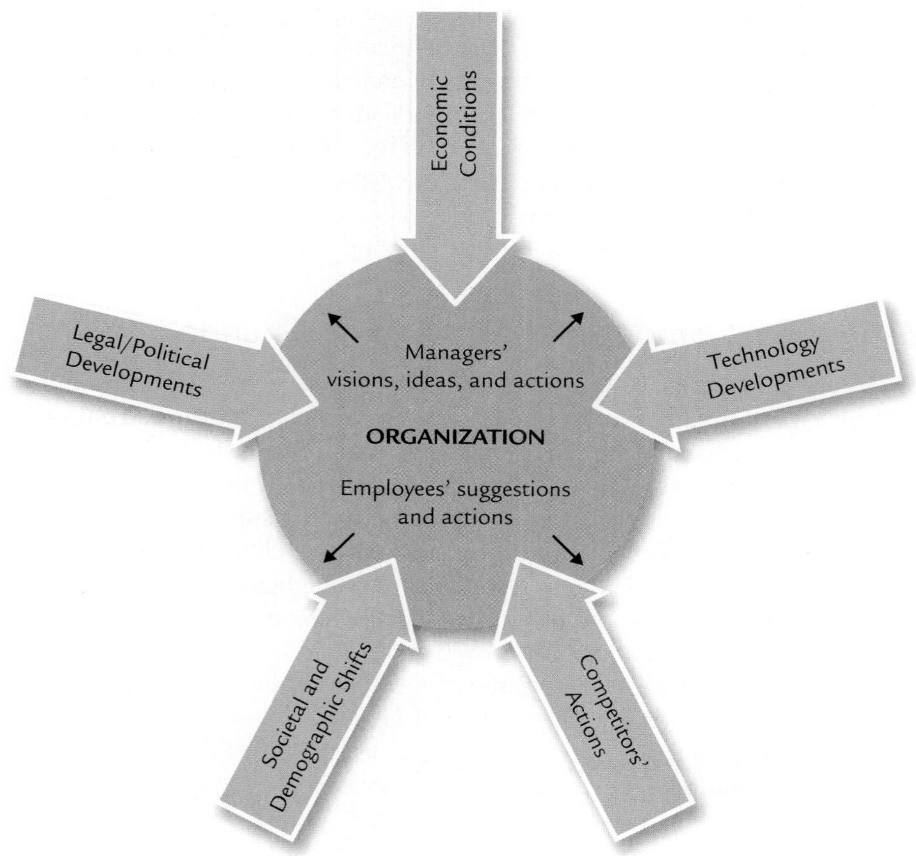

Forces Outside the Organization

A whole host of forces outside the organization, as discussed earlier in Chapter 2 on the external environment, can bring about changes inside it. Here we mention again several of the most important.

Economic Conditions Obvious forces for change affecting business organizations are developments in the economic environment. If the economy is weak, then many companies are likely to reduce their workforces or at least limit hiring, prune low-profit product lines, and so on. Conversely, if the economy is vibrant and expanding, many firms consider adding new services or products, creating new units or divisions, increasing their geographic areas of operations, and undertaking similar growth changes.

Analogous to these business-world examples, many nonbusiness organizations, especially government agencies, contract or expand in relation to economic conditions because their budgets are directly impacted by those forces.

Competitors' Actions Regardless of the state of the economy, most businesses and many other organizations are likely to be extremely sensitive to moves made by their direct competitors, especially those in response to changes in the market or customers' preferences. The actions of other significant players in the immediate environment can often trigger changes inside a given organization, even when that organization would prefer not to make any changes at that time.

Technology Developments Changes in technology developed outside an organization frequently require it to respond, whether it wants to or not.

Technological advances offer both opportunity and threat to organizations, but if they are major breakthroughs and relate directly to an organization's core activities, managers have little choice but to make corresponding changes. Several years ago, for example, the technological advancements provided by the internet persuaded a traditional face-to-face personnel recruiting company to make major changes in how it does business, to the extent that it not only changed its corporate name but it also became an innovator in its non–high-tech industry by using the internet to allow job applicants to post short, streaming video commercials of themselves.[11]

Legal/Political Developments When governments make new laws or courts issue new interpretations of those laws, managers need to respond, even when the solutions or types of changes that should be made are not obvious. *A Manager's Challenge: "MediPlan's Poison Pill"* illustrates how MediPlan's success and ultimate demise were the result of the political environment in both Canada and the United States.

Societal and Demographic Shifts Other types of external forces for change can take longer to develop and be more subtle and difficult to detect, such as changing societal attitudes toward various products, services, and practices. Many employers around North America, as well as many restaurants and bars, for example, have had to change their practices regarding letting employees and customers smoke in indoor settings. In response to both tighter legal restrictions and changing levels of customer tolerance to smoking in confined areas, these organizations have had to pay attention to an area of employee/customer behaviour they had long ignored.[12]

Shifting demographic patterns, such as the aging population in North America and Japan, are another type of slow-moving external force. For example, within the last few years, Statistics Canada has projected that between 2006 and 2026, the number of people in Canada over age 65 will grow at a faster rate than all other age groups, nearly doubling from 4.3 million to 8 million, and will comprise 21.2 percent of all Canadians.[13] Such alterations in the age makeup of society will, for example, challenge retailing and other consumer-oriented firms to change product mixes and take new approaches to sales and marketing. These kinds of demographic shifts do not take place overnight, of course, but they can exert a powerful force nevertheless.

a manager's challenge *change*

MediPlan's Poison Pill

In most cases, retail prices in Canada are higher than in the United Sates. However, the pharmaceutical industry doesn't follow this typical pattern. On average, prescription drugs are significantly cheaper in Canada than in the United States. This role reversal can be largely attributed to two main influences. First, Canada's federal government negotiates with pharmaceutical companies to obtain lower drug prices for Canadian citizens. Second, pharmaceuticals are not permitted to market their products directly to Canadian customers, which reduces marketing costs. In the United States, drug companies are allowed to spend vast amounts of money on marketing, the cost of which is ultimately passed on to customers at the cash register.

Canada has long been a very attractive source for retail prescription drugs for American consumers. Residents in northern States, particularly seniors on a fixed income, would regularly travel to Canadian border communities to fill prescriptions. Bus tour companies would embark on junkets, transporting a busload of American seniors to Canada with the primary purpose of acquiring prescription drugs at a fraction of the price listed in the United States.

At the turn of the new millennium, as the internet became more reliable for commerce, Canadian pharmacists saw the price disparity and a strong US dollar (around CDN$1.50 for US$1.00) as a great online opportunity that would fill a need. Pharmacists started online dispensaries to facilitate cross-border trade in prescription drugs. The new channel extended the reach of Canadian pharmacies into the United States and soon grew into a half-billion-dollar industry. Within Canada, Manitoba was the primary location for internet pharmacies, owing to abundant, inexpensive warehouse space, the central location for time zones and transport, and more lenient rules for issuing prescriptions over the phone.

In 2001, MediPlan Pharmacy in Minnedosa, Manitoba, was one of the first Canadian pharmacies to launch online sales of prescription medication. It soon became a market leader. MediPlan was founded by two husband and wife teams in their 20s, Andrew and Catherine Stempler, and Mark and Chantelle Rzepka, and it immediately marketed aggressively in the United States, taking out full-page ads in US dailies with large circulation, like *The New York Times*. The company operated by advertising and listing product on the internet and having customers or their physicians place prescription orders by mail or fax. A local doctor, for a nominal fee, would review and co-sign the prescription prior to it being filled. A typical day would see 300 packages shipped to customers.

As business increased and online pharmacies received more attention, the medical community learned of the practice and became more vocal in disagreement. Changes in MediPlan's external environment began in 2002, when the College of Physicians and Surgeons of Manitoba advised doctors against co-signing prescriptions for internet orders. Around the same time, the Canadian Medical Protective Association, which provides malpractice insurance, informed its members that they would not be eligible for coverage if they were ever sued "over problems arising from internet prescriptions."

Problems for MediPlan escalated when US officials began to worry about safety issues such as quality control and unregulated or counterfeit drugs crossing the border from Canada. In addition to this, US drug manufacturers intensified lobbying efforts to prevent Canadian companies from selling pharmaceuticals to US consumers.

In October 2004, Alan Bell, a terrorism expert, was hired by the US pharmaceutical industry to conduct an investigation into its rival, Canadian internet pharmacies.

After completing his investigation, Bell voiced his concern over the business practices of 15 of the 18 pharmacies that he had studied and concluded that internet pharmacies were a terrorism threat. Shortly after Bell's investigation, US Customs and Border Protection began to impose stricter controls on prescription drugs being imported from Canada by confiscating more and more shipments. Although shipping drugs to the United States from Canada is technically illegal, in the past the FDA had not seized small shipments that were bought for personal use. Needless to say, MediPlan was severely impacted by these drug confiscations.

On August 30, 2006, the US Food and Drug Administration (FDA) issued a warning to American citizens that advised them not to purchase prescription drugs from websites that have orders filled by MediPlan, alleging that MediPlan had been selling counterfeit drugs to US consumers. In the same news release, the FDA suggested that US consumers use caution when purchasing drugs from online pharmacies, alleging that 85 percent of supposedly Canadian drugs were really coming from "unreliable sources" in 27 other countries around the world. MediPlan stated that these allegations were "completely false" and politically motivated and that MediPlan tested its drugs on a regular basis to ensure that they were safe. Nonetheless, the warning proved to be MediPlan's poison pill.

In September 2006, following the FDA's accusations and the pressures from American pharmaceutical companies, the owners of MediPlan decided to shut down its distribution centre in Minnedosa, putting 15 of its 89 employees out of work. Distributions were moved to CanadaDrugs.com, a much larger firm in Winnipeg, so that MediPlan drugs would continue to reach their consumers. By December, MediPlan owners were tired of fighting, and weren't prepared to make changes to the organization to fit the model that the pharmaceuticals, College of Physicians, and insurance carriers would accept. MediPlan was sold to CanadaDrugs.com in an effort to exit the business with as much profit as possible.

Sources: "Internet Pharmacy Not Prescribed by Doctors' Organizations," CBC News, January 15, 2002, www.cbc.ca (accessed January 12, 2007); G. Smith, "Was Big Pharma Caught in Its Own Web of Spin?" *Globe and Mail*, October 24, 2004, www.globerisk.com (accessed January 12, 2007); "Cross-Border Rx," CBC News Indepth, January 17, 2006, www.cbc.ca (accessed January 12, 2007); "U.S. Customs Cracks Down on Prescription Drug Shipments," CBC News, February 9, 2006, www.cbc.ca (accessed January 12, 2007); "FDA Warns Consumers Not to Buy or Use Prescription Drugs from Various Canadian Websites that Apparently Sell Counterfeit Products," FDA News, August 30, 2006, www.fda.gov (accessed January 12, 2007); "FDA Targets Canadian Websites for Counterfeit Drugs," CBC News, August 30, 2006, www.cbc.ca (accessed January 12, 2007); "Internet Pharmacy Moves Part of Operation Out of Minnedosa," CBC News, September 27, 2006, www.cbc.ca (accessed January 12, 2007); "Online Drug Pioneers Sell Business, MediPlan Closing in Minnedosa; CanadaDrugs.com Buys Operation," *Winnipeg Free Press* Live, December 29, 2006, www.winnipegfreepress.com (accessed January 12, 2007).

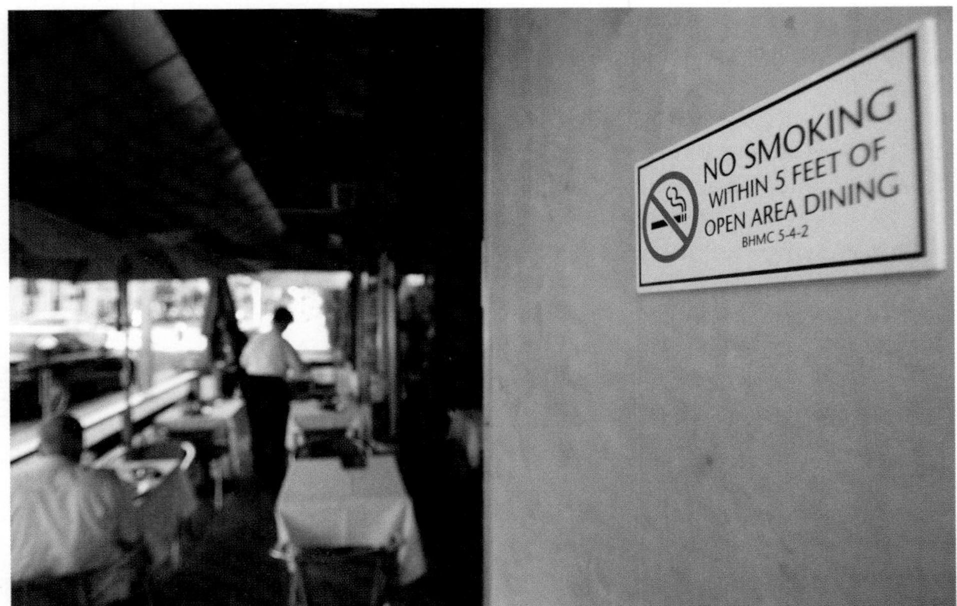

Nonsmoking restaurants are evidence of new societal values in Canada, leading many business owners to fear for their profits in the face of legal bans on smoking in public places.

Forces Inside the Organization

As with external factors, many potential forces inside the organization can cause change to take place. Two of the most important are (1) managerial decisions and (2) employee preferences and pressures.

Managerial Decisions Managers at any level of an organization operate under certain constraints that limit their freedom of action. However, in many instances they have considerable authority to make changes in their particular parts of the enterprise. Generally, of course, even in this age of flatter organizational structures, the higher up that managers are in an organization, the more leeway and the more power they have to institute change. Managers are often reluctant, though, to use their power for this purpose. Indeed, as pointed out in Chapter 9, some authorities would argue that managers tend to *underutilize* their power to make changes, rather than use too much power.[14] The risk, obviously, is that an attempted change will be unsuccessful, and the manager may end up with less power than before. Therefore, as will be discussed in the next section, one of the most critical leadership issues facing you as a manager is accurately evaluating the need for change. When managers do make decisions to change, though, those decisions can affect the status quo in significant ways.

Employee Preferences and Suggestions Managerial decisions are not the only source of change inside organizations. Lower-level employees often are an excellent source of innovative suggestions for change. The challenge for managers in obtaining employee preferences and suggestions, of course, is to sort out the creative proposals and hunches that have potential for increased performance and improved work climate from those that would be ineffective or unworkable if implemented.

In extreme instances, of course, employees may exert overt pressure for change, resulting in work-to-rule campaigns or strikes. Managers need to distinguish employee pressures that address legitimate needs for change from pressures that attempt to obstruct or intimidate. Making such judgments wisely and responding appropriately are essential managerial skills, as discussed later in this chapter. Regardless of the extent to which managers have that skill, however, employees can be a stimulus for change that frequently cannot, and should not, be ignored.

The key here is to simply recognize that the forces for change are enormous in number and in power. The practical implication is that change will be an inescapable issue for you as a manager. Consequently, it is important to have an understanding of (1) the general process of change, (2) the general forces for change failure, and (3) keys for successful change.

Process of Change

The fact that effective change management seems to be in high demand but short supply suggests that managing change is not an easy process. If it were easy and simple, we would certainly expect many more managers to have mastered it by now. After all, the demand for change management at any level (personal, team, or organizational) is not new. Consider this quote made 500 years ago by Niccolo Machiavelli:[15]

> *There is nothing more difficult to carry out, nor more doubtful of success, nor more dangerous to handle than to initiate a new order of things. For the reformer has enemies in all those who profit by the old order, and only lukewarm defenders by all those who could profit by the new order. This lukewarmness arises from the incredulity of mankind who do not truly believe in anything new until they have had actual experience with it.*

Thus, while the intensity and rate of change may be greater today than in the past, the basic demand for change management has been around for a very long time. Given that managing change is an important and challenging aspect of life for any manager, it is important to have an understanding of the basic process of change.

One of the most enduring, simple, and yet comprehensive frameworks of the change process was proposed by psychologist Kurt Lewin over 50 years ago.[16] He argued that change, including personal change, went through three distinctive phases: unfreezing, movement, and refreezing.

Phase 1—Unfreezing

As individuals we all develop habits. A habit is a patterned way of doing something that has been successful and therefore reinforced to the point that we exhibit the behaviour without really thinking about it. For example, you may have a habit of turning right at a certain intersection to go home. This habit may become so strong that you find yourself turning right at that intersection even when you really need to go left to go to someplace other than home.

We can think of this general process of forming habits in terms of simple and discrete behaviours, like turning right to go home, or in terms of more complex behaviour patterns. For example, when confronted with a conflict, we might develop the pattern of taking steps to fight for our point of view, or we might develop a pattern of trying to avoid the conflict and confrontation.

Similarly, just as we can develop behavioural habits, we can develop cognitive habits or ways of seeing and interpreting events around us. Quite often the cognitive and behavioural patterns are linked. For example, if we form the pattern of viewing conflict as bad, then we might easily form the behavioural pattern of trying to avoid conflict when it appears.[17]

In some cases, cognitive and behavioural traits may allow individuals or teams to better adapt to change, and therefore affect performance. In a recent study, researchers found that after an unforeseen change in the task environment, teams whose members had higher cognitive abilities were more achievement oriented and generally more open, and were able to adapt to their new roles better, resulting in higher performance.[18]

Lewin argued that unless we undo or unfreeze these old patterns, it is difficult to change to something new. To better appreciate Lewin's theory, you might think about an ice sculpture. Suppose you wanted to change an ice sculpture of a bird into a fish. You could try to chip away at the old and fashion the new, but it's a difficult process. Instead, what would happen if you unfroze, or melted, the bird sculpture? You could then use the water to create a new block of ice from which you could carve a fish. Trying to simply carve a fish out of the original bird sculpture is perhaps possible, but not very efficient or effective. In other words, from Lewin's perspective, changing to something new requires undoing or **unfreezing** something old.

unfreezing undoing old patterns

Phase 2—Movement

Once old tricks are unfrozen, then you are in a position to actually move, to make the needed changes. As a manager, **movement** may involve changing your perceptions, decision-making approach, communication style, and so on. Research has demonstrated that one of the biggest determinants of movement is the level of certainty or uncertainty associated with the change.[19] Generally, the greater the uncertainty of what will happen, the greater the resistance to the change and the less likely that there will be any movement in the desired direction of the change. The context in which the decision to change is made can also influence managers' perceptions of certainty or uncertainty.

movement changing perceptions based on the level of certainty or uncertainty associated with the change

In general, there is a relationship between the magnitude of the change and the level of uncertainty.[20] For example, the uncertainty of success associated with trying to jump across Niagara Falls is much greater than that of trying to jump across a one-foot-wide ditch. As a result, you are more likely to try to jump across the ditch than Niagara Falls. While this may seem obvious, this general principle is of great practical value to you as a manager. It means that as the level of uncertainty associated with a desired change increases, so will the likely level of resistance, and therefore, the more effort you will have to put into planning and preparation to make the change a success.

Phase 3—Refreezing

But suppose you see the need for change and to unfreeze the past and that you actually make the initial change. Are you confident that the change will last? What percentage of people who start a new diet or exercise program stick with it? It is less than one in four. Lewin contended that the "pull" of old habits is strong and that simply making the move from old to new is not enough to ensure lasting success.[21] This is in part because, whatever it is, the "old" pattern exists in the first place because it has been rewarded with success. In other words, most people have the communication patterns, leadership style, decision-making approach, and so on because these patterns have worked in the past. In this sense, you can think of old habits and patterns as having a kind of gravity that will pull us back to them unless a greater force is in place to keep us moving forward.

Thus, Lewin talked about "refreezing" after the movement phase. When most people hear the term "refreezing," they usually get images of things frozen solid and unmovable. But Lewin did not mean that the new state should be static with no movement. Instead, the term was designed to reflect the notion that after a change is made, forces need to be put in place to keep people and behaviours from giving in to the gravitational pull of the past and reverting back to old patterns. As a consequence, **refreezing** involves monitoring the change to see if it is producing the anticipated and desired results. To the extent the change is succeeding, the refreezing phase should involve reinforcing the change so that it becomes more established.[22]

refreezing the process of reinforcing change so that it becomes established

For most students and managers, Lewin's model of change makes intuitive sense. It can even make change seem simple. However, we all know that change is not easy. This naturally raises the question: "What gets in the way of successful change and how can we overcome these barriers?"

Forces for Failure

As we mentioned near the beginning of this chapter, most change initiatives fail. Successful change is uncommon since there are powerful forces that work against change. To help illustrate the forces for failure, we integrate Lewin's model with a more recent framework that draws on the same principles but illustrates them in a visual way.[23] Exhibit 15.5 illustrates the basics of this framework.

Exhibit 15.5

Change Failure Framework

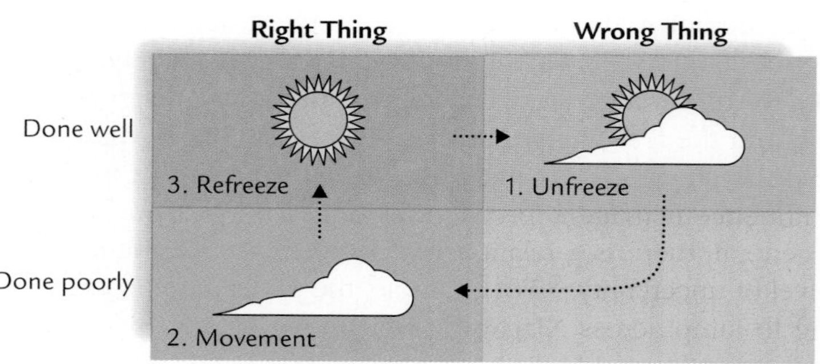

Resistance to Change by Michael Hitt

mymanagementlab

Most change is preceded by something. Usually, it is preceded by success. In other words, people usually have a history of doing the right thing and doing it well. Then something changes in the external or internal environment and the right thing becomes the wrong thing. For example, suppose you, as a manager, had the habit of making decisions on your own without seeking input from subordinates. This pattern worked for many years, in part because the decisions you faced were fairly simple. You had all the knowledge you needed to make the decisions without seeking the input of others; your individual decision-making approach was right and you were good at it. Then something happened. The nature of your company's customers changed. They now require much more sophisticated products. These new products involve technologies that are new to you. You now need to involve others in decision making because you don't have all the information or answers on your own. The environment has shifted and what used to be the right thing—individual decision making—is now the wrong thing. However, you are still very good at it.

Starting the change process requires the recognition that what was right for the past is wrong for the future. This is the unfreezing process. If you fail to recognize that the change in customer requirements demands a change in your decision-making approach, the whole change process never even gets started. However, even if you begin to notice that your old approach is not working so well, you also need to recognize not just that individual decision making is now wrong, but that a more participative approach is the new "right" or required approach.

Unfortunately, even if we accept that the old right thing (e.g., individual decision making) is now the wrong thing, and even if we accept that participative decision making is the new right thing, we do not typically become instantly good at it. As Exhibit 15.5 illustrates, we often have to go from doing the wrong thing well to doing the right thing poorly. For example, if you have made decisions on an individual basis for many years, even if you recognize the need to make decisions in a more participative manner now, you are not likely to be great at it at first. Few of us expect to be instantly proficient at something new, even if we believe that we must make the change. Unless people are confident that they can go from doing the new right thing poorly to doing it well, they fail to move.[24]

Once you start to move toward the new right thing, the gravity of the old starts exerting its force and pulling you back from the change. Once they become proficient enough, natural positive consequences follow the new behaviours and reinforce or refreeze them. However, failure often happens during the refreezing phase because many managers don't sufficiently monitor or reinforce the new behaviours. As a result people fail to finish.

Now that we have an overall framework, let's look more specifically at the three failures—failure to see, failure to move, and failure to finish—to better understand the dynamics of these change failures so that we can discuss how to overcome them and effectively manage change in ourselves, in our subordinates, and in teams that we may have to lead.

Unfreezing: The Failure to See

As we mentioned earlier, if people fail to see the need for change, then change cannot get started. So the natural question is, "What keeps people from seeing the need to change?"

The Power of Past Mental Maps To answer this question, we must revisit the issue of how we develop certain cognitive or behavioural patterns in the first place. To help with this analysis, we might think of these habitual cognitive patterns as mental maps.[25] Like physical maps, mental maps guide us. We use them to interpret landmarks and decide where we are and how to get to where we want to go. Imagine having a city map that showed a park where there wasn't one, that had a street turning left when it really turned right, or that did not show an intersection where one existed. What would you do with that map? On the other hand, suppose you had a map that was successful at helping you navigate the city, that helped you effectively get where you wanted to go. What would you do with that map? No doubt you would throw out the first and hang on to the second map. Like physical maps, we tend to retain the **mental maps** that have proven successful in the past and throw out those that have not.

mental map habitual cognitive patterns

For example, suppose you had a cognitive map that led you to believe that conflict was bad, and you followed that map by avoiding conflict when it emerged. You would tend to continue this pattern or hold on to the mental map only if it worked. In other words, if avoiding conflict usually kept you out of uncomfortable confrontations, and if these conflicts you avoided subsequently just disappeared, you would likely hang on to this "conflict avoidance" map. On the other hand, if your attempts to avoid conflicts consistently allowed the conflicts to grow in intensity and later emerge as unavoidable and larger confrontations, you would likely throw out your "conflict avoidance" mental map.

In general, the longer a given mental map has proven itself successful in the past, the harder it will be to give up.[26] In one sense, we can view this as a positive and natural "self-preservation" mechanism. After all, what would happen if we randomly held on to or jettisoned mental maps and their associated patterns of behaviour? We would randomly "live and die" as our behaviours did and didn't fit the environment. As conscious creatures, humans tend to have an aversion to random survival.

Overly Simplistic View of the Past and Future Thus, past success is one of the forces that keep us from seeing the need for change and even starting the unfreezing process. Even when our past maps begin to falter, past successes simply outnumber and overwhelm the current failures. However, to better understand this phenomenon, we need to dig a little deeper. Part of the reason that current failures do not easily override past success and easily jumpstart the unfreezing process of change is because we often take a somewhat simplistic perspective of the past, present, and future.

As an example, suppose you had a pattern of leading subordinates by telling them exactly what to do, when to do it, and how to do it (what is often referred to in the popular press as "micromanagement"). Suppose this approach worked for you nine times in a row. On the tenth time, this approach didn't work and you got a bad result. Would you likely change your leadership style when you face your eleventh situation? Based on 10 past incidents, it can seem as though you have a 90 percent chance that your directive leadership style will work in the future.

However, this is true only if the future environment or context is the same as the past in which your leadership style worked. For example, your directive leadership style may have worked in the past because the tasks your subordinates faced were simple and well-understood by you, or because your subordinates were not very knowledgeable about the tasks. Consequently, you could tell them what to do and they were willing to accept your direction. If the current and future environment involves tasks that are significantly more complex, the complexity may exceed your ability to direct your subordinates' every move. Furthermore, if your subordinates are more capable than they were in the past, they may not need or want your micromanagement.

Unless you see the difference in the context, you are unlikely to see the need to change your leadership style. In fact, if you do not see the difference in context, it is quite likely that it will take a big disaster or a number of smaller failures before you even begin to question the robustness of your past directive leadership style for the future. After all, one failure in light of nine successes is not very convincing that your style needs to change. However, five failures in light of nine successes may begin to cause you to question the appropriateness of your directive leadership style for the future. While it is natural for people to wait until the number of failures mounts before they change, it can often be quite expensive. Failures are not usually free; they typically have costs (financial, reputational, etc.) associated with them.

Thus, one of the strongest forces for failure to see the need to change is failure to look at and recognize differences between the past and current (as well as future) context. Until we can overcome this force for failure in ourselves and others, it is unlikely that unfreezing will occur and that the change process will even get started.

Maintaining Equilibrium Unfortunately, research and experience have shown that people have an almost automatic or instinctive resistance to unfreezing attempts and an inherent desire to maintain equilibrium.[27] When presented with a force of change, people will often push back with an equal, opposing force.

In summary, there are three key forces that keep the unfreezing part of the change process from even getting started. First, what is to be changed or unfrozen is most likely there for good reason. Whatever the cognitive and associated behavioural pattern, it likely exists because it worked in the past. Second, we often fail to look at and recognize differences in context between the past and present (as well as the future). As a consequence, we typically discount current incidents of failure and weight more heavily the past incidents of success. Thus, we fail to recognize the need for change. Third, there seems to be a natural tendency for people to resist pressures to change to maintain equilibrium. Consequently, quite often the more pressure that is applied to unfreeze things, the greater the resistance.

Movement: Failure to Move

As we mentioned earlier, even if people see the need for change, they still may not make the desired changes. You might be wondering, "Why would people fail to move if they see the need?" Much of the answer to this question lies in the nature of the desired change. As we mentioned earlier, typically the larger the desired change the greater the associated uncertainty. However, change uncertainty is not a generic phenomenon. It has at least three critical dimensions.[28] Understanding each dimension enables you as a manager to better plan and prepare for the needed steps to achieve the desired movement.

Change Uncertainty The first aspect of change uncertainty is centred in the change itself. As we already mentioned, people's current mental maps and behavioural patterns exist because they have proven successful in the past. As the environment changes and what worked before begins to fail, people do begin to question the validity of their past maps and behavioural patterns for the future. However, research has found that if all people have is evidence that their old map is wrong but they do not have a clear idea about what new map would be right, they tend to stay with what they know—that is, they tend to keep using the old map even though they are aware that it has faults. In other words, something (even if it is flawed) is better than nothing.

To help illustrate this principle in a more concrete fashion, let's return to the example of leadership style. Suppose you find that your old directive way of leading is just not quite as successful today as it was in the past. Further, suppose that you recognize this and see that there is a need for change. What would you do if it were not clear to you what new leadership style you should move toward? You might venture off into the unknown and randomly try some new leadership style. You might . . . but most people don't. People often keep doing what they do well, even when they recognize that it has become irrelevant, if the new direction that they should go is not clear. Even if they recognize that there is a need to change because things are not working as well as before, if they lack a clear alternative they quite often intensify their efforts at doing what they know.

Outcome Uncertainty People also fail to move because of uncertainty regarding the outcomes of the change. In other words, people ask themselves the question: "Even if I know where I'm going, how clear is it that good things (or bad things) will happen when I get there?" For example, what results will you achieve if you switch from a directive to a coaching leadership style? The less clear the answers are to these sorts of questions, the less likely you are to change.

Requirement Uncertainty The third aspect of change uncertainty has to do with the requirements for the change. In other words, how clear is it that those that have to make the change have what it takes? Do they believe they have the knowledge, skills, tools, and so on to make the change? If the answer is "no," they are unlikely to make the change, even though a great reward awaits them if they do.

Refreezing: Failure to Finish

This final stage of Lewin's change framework is important because he recognized, and research has confirmed, that without reinforcement people will return to past habits and patterns.[29] This is especially true if the results from the change are slow in coming. This is in part why people have difficulty changing their diet or exercise habits. They want the envisioned changes in their fitness or appearance, but when those results are slow in coming, they often return to the old habits.

To better understand the forces that lead to failure to finish, we have to keep in mind that part of the gravitational pull of past patterns is the past positive consequences they generated. For example, if you had the pattern of sleeping in late and eating cheesecake, it was in part because there were positive consequences for these behaviours. It felt good to sleep in and cheesecake tastes so great. Even if you decide to change and exercise each day and eat more broccoli, if positive consequences of the new behaviour are slow in coming, the positive consequences of sleeping in and eating cheesecake become more powerful and pull you back.

The truth is that most significant change does not produce instant, positive consequences. The lack of reinforcement of the new behaviours allows the gravitational forces of the old to pull us back. There are two key reasons why most people trying to change revert back to doing things the old way.

First, in many cases the change involves something new—new behaviours, new thinking, new skills, and so on. Most people are not instantly good at things they have not done before. Because they are not instantly good, it is only natural that they do not instantly generate good consequences.

The second reason that change fails to stick is because, even if one persists in the new behaviour and incrementally gets better at it, the long process of improvement often makes people feel lost. They don't know where they are in the process and are not sure how much progress they are truly making. When people feel lost, they tend to give up and quit trying to move forward. They fail to finish. After all, what good does it do, they ask themselves, to keep moving when you are not sure that the effort you are expending is doing any good? Anyone who has studied a foreign language can easily appreciate this phenomenon. Often, you study and study and practice and practice, but you are not sure what progress you are really making. Because the progress is small and incremental, it is hard to notice. Without a sense of progress, you give up.

Keys to Successful Change

With the overall framework of unfreeze, move, and refreeze, and the related common failures of not seeing, moving, or finishing, practising managers want to know how they can overcome the common failures and successfully lead and manage change in themselves and others. That's precisely what the next three sections address.

Overcoming the Failure to See

If people are blind to the need for change, how can you help them see? If people could see the environmental shifts and therefore the needed changes on their own without your help, they probably would. To better understand why we fail to see the need to change and how we can overcome this failure, we can gain some insights from physical sight. To see physical objects, we need contrast in shape, light, colour, and so on.[30] We also see best those objects that are directly in front of us rather than off to the side in our peripheral vision. Even though in the context of change we are not talking about seeing physical objects, the two factors that help us see physical objects—contrast and confrontation—also apply to helping people see the need for change.

Contrast As we mentioned, **contrast** is one of the key means by which the human eye distinguishes different objects. In combination, differences in shape, brightness, and colour give us contrast. In complex personal, team, or organizational settings, there are so many things to look at that people can (and do) selectively focus on elements from the past and present that are similar rather than different. In effect, they can choose to ignore key contrasts and thereby avoid looking at why what worked in the past might not work in the future. This brings us to the second part of the answer to overcoming the failure to see—**confrontation**.

contrast a means by which people perceive differences

confrontation a means of helping people perceive contrasts by providing an inescapable experience

Confrontation It is precisely because the organizational and business realities we face are complex that people are able to ignore or literally be blind to the "obvious" differences between the past and present. This is why they do not see the reasons that strategies, structures, cultural values, processes, technologies, and so on must change. The fact that most people do not easily see these contrasts is clear and compelling evidence that they cannot be left on their own to visualize them. Managers often have to confront their people with the key contrasts between the past, present, and future.

Combining Contrast and Confrontation: An Example One of Hewlett-Packard's (HP) most important businesses is printers, which account for about two-thirds of its profits. However, for a period of time that extended over several years, HP managers saw their strong position slip away, especially in the low-end range of their product line. Lexmark introduced good-quality printers for under $100 and saw its share of the market double to 14 percent. In response to this change in the environment, the head of HP's printer unit, Vyomesh Joshi, determined that HP had to change. It had to build a new line of printers, including a printer that was $49, or $30 cheaper than its least expensive printer at the time. He also challenged his group to go from "concept to shelf" (from the idea to putting the printer on retailers' shelves) in three years rather than the normal four.

Most HP managers said they thought building a printer for $49 instead of $79 was impossible. Tom Alexander, a key project manager, knew he needed to "explode their complacency." In a team meeting he created a high-contrast and highly confrontational experience that helped people get past the failure to see. After listening to people say how impossible the task was, Alexander grabbed an HP printer, put it on the floor, and stood on it—all 200 pounds of him. In that instant, the people in the room broke through the failure to see barrier and got the message. HP printers did not need to be engineered and constructed as stepping stools. And more importantly, as long as they were it would be impossible to bring down the cost.

In the end, HP managers delivered a line of 14 inkjet printers and 7 "all-in-one" printers based on just two cost-efficient platforms. The new line came in on time and at the desired cost, including a printer for $49. Following their introduction, HP sold US$5.6 billion worth of the new printers (a 12 percent year-over-year increase) at a profit margin of 16.5 percent (a 14 percent increase in profitability). HP took 70 percent of the market share, most of which was taken from Lexmark.[31]

80/20 rule a "rule" that suggests that 80 percent of the desired outcome is provided by 20 percent of the contributing factors

Creating High Contrast One of the first keys in creating effective and high contrast is focusing people's attention on key differences. In general, this is often referred to as the **80/20 rule**.[32] In general, this "rule" suggests that 80 percent of the desired outcome is provided by 20 percent of the contributing factors. For example, quite often 80 percent of a company's revenues are accounted for by 20 percent of its customers. We also see cases in team sports where 80 percent of the points are provided by 20 percent of the players. While there may be many differences or contrasts that explain 100 percent of the need for change, pointing them all out can often overwhelm or confuse people. This is why it is effective to focus on the core contrasts. At HP, much of a printer's cost came from the materials and construction, which were stronger than needed. Customers needed printers to print, not stand on. Tom Alexander helped his team see that, and the team lowered the new line of printers' cost by changing the design to use less plastic in the case and by using thinner and cheaper plastic. While you can no longer stand on HP printers, you can buy a high-quality one for under $50.

In addition to focusing on the core contrasts, you also want to help people see and remember those key differences. Research has clearly demonstrated that the more you create images in people's minds, the more clearly they can recall the associated messages. There is a reason the old adage says that "a picture is worth a thousand words." Thus, two keys to successfully creating effective contrasts are to first focus on the critical differences and to create images (versus just presenting numbers or words) in people's minds. The image of Tom Alexander standing on the old HP printer was worth more in changing people's minds than all the numbers about how Lexmark was taking market share away from them.

Creating Confrontation Clearly pointing out the contrasts between the old and new is a critical first step. However, pointing these contrasts out once is usually not enough. Even twice is not enough. To ensure a high level of confrontation, you will likely have to present the contrasts repeatedly so employees will not view them as "one-time passing parades" that they can simply ignore. Repetition is a powerful means of ensuring high confrontation. However, it is not the only means. An additional means is employing what we might call "inescapable experiences." These experiences need to be of such a nature that they are not easily avoided and that they involve as many of the senses—touch, smell, sight, sound, taste—as possible. We know from a wide body of scientific literature that the more senses involved and the deeper their involvement, the higher the impact of the experience and the more that is learned and retained.

Overcoming the Failure to Move

Simplified, some of the most practical and powerful steps in ensuring change success involve overcoming the three sources of uncertainty described earlier in this chapter. Consequently, even after people see that the old way is not working any more and recognize the need for change, they need to see clearly and believe in an alternative. One of the first means of overcoming the failure to move is to educate people as to what the desired change is. If you want to change from an individual decision-making style, you need to not only recognize the need to change, but you have to be able to see the new approach; you may have to get a clear picture of what it looks like to involve others in making decisions, or you may have to educate yourself as to how you can effectively involve others in gathering and processing information. Until the new destination is clear, you are likely to stay where you are.

Overcoming the Failure to Finish

As we mentioned, the pull of past patterns and the lack of early positive consequences often causes change not to last. Refreezing is not an instant process because instant expertise in the new behaviour is almost never possible. Many authors and studies of change have addressed the importance of early and consistent positive reinforcement of desired change. In the popular literature on change, this theoretically important notion is often referred to as ensuring **early wins**. Whether this or another popular term is used, the concept and the theory behind it are the same. When people engage in change, they need early and consistent reinforcement to overcome the gravitational pull of past patterns and build momentum in moving toward establishing new patterns.[33]

early wins early and consistent positive reinforcement of desired change

It is important to provide feedback on progress so that employees gain a sense of movement and progression. This feedback should first and foremost focus on their personal progress. Often, this requires managers to sit down with subordinates in a face-to-face conversation where managers point out those areas where subordinates have made progress. As we have stated, the more complicated or long the change, the harder it can be for individuals to have a clear sense of personal progress. Just as important, in cases where the change is not just individual but involves others, people benefit from knowing how the group is progressing collectively.

Focus of Organizational Changes

When managers decide that change is needed, or when they realize that they have no choice but to make changes, one of the first issues they face is: What do I change? To help us answer that question it is useful to refer back to Chapter 7 ("Strategic Management") and the discussion of the McKinsey Seven S model of strategy implementation. Here, we will highlight five of those Ss that are particularly relevant for this section. In addition, however, we will also include a sixth focus—technology (see Exhibit 15.6). Any change will almost certainly involve at least one of these areas of focus, and most changes will involve several. Especially complex and comprehensive changes—"transformational changes"—will involve all six.

Technology

For many organizations, the most obvious and most frequent object of change is technology (see Exhibit 15.7). This has always been the case in manufacturing and capital-intensive companies, where replacing and upgrading equipment and technology have been the keys to organizational survival and an

Exhibit 15.6

Focus of Organizational Changes

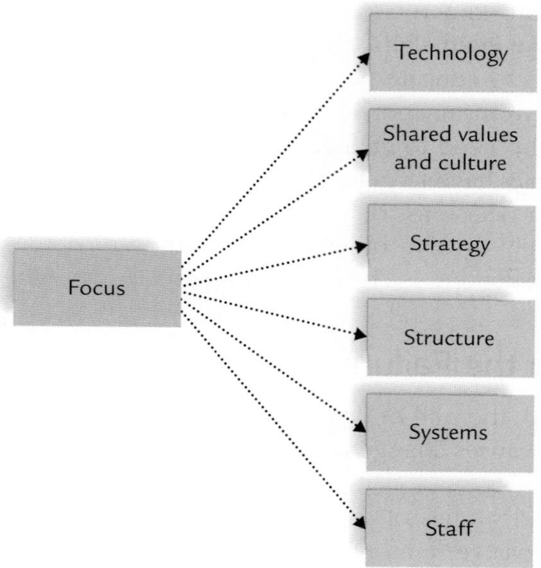

ability to keep ahead of the competition. In recent years, however, virtually all types of firms, government agencies, and nonbusiness organizations have been giving increasing attention to improving and expanding their information technology.[34]

Thus, for almost any organization at the beginning of the twenty-first century, from the corner dry cleaner to the largest multinational, making changes in technology becomes a prime and nearly continual focal point. The critical issues for managers, however, involve the significant and often unexpected spillover effects of changes in technology on other areas such as structure, systems, and staff. New equipment, for example, can result in entirely different patterns of work relationships among employees, which can create considerable confusion. Such effects, if they are major or last a long time, can dilute or even cancel the positive effects of the improvements. A focus on technology is, therefore, a frequent starting point of changes, but it is not necessarily a good indicator of where major problems may occur.

Exhibit 15.7 Some Specific Examples of Focus of Change

Focus	Examples
Technology	· Update computer systems · Use holography in product design
Shared Values and Culture	· Implement diversity awareness program · Institute participatory decision making throughout organization
Strategy	· Change from niche market to general market focus · Change focus from individual customer to large corporate customer
Structure	· Change from a geographic to a customer structure · Implement an international division
Systems	· Replace batch with continuous-flow manufacturing · Change from last-in/first-out to first-in/first-out inventory valuation
Staff	· Encourage cooperation through cross-training programs · Increase number and availability of training workshops for lower-level employees

Shared Values and Culture

The shared values and culture of the organization, as discussed in Chapter 4, are a second potential focus for change in organizations (see Exhibit 15.7). In its way, changing an organization's culture can be as potent in its consequences as making major changes in technology systems. In fact, if it were easy to make changes in the culture of an organization, managers likely would try to do so more often. Despite such powerful potential, however, the embedded traditions and accepted ways of doing things that constitute an organization's culture can be extremely difficult to change successfully. For example, when China Development Industrial Bank bought Grand Cathay brokerage of Taiwan, over 100 of Grand Cathay's key employees left within the first year as a result of the new culture that had been imposed. As one departing employee put it, "Grand Cathay had a very democratic culture. When policies were made, we were always invited to give feedback. Our opinions mattered. But the new management has a very autocratic style."[35]

A key to changing an organization's culture is to start by trying to change its values, since what is valued is the underlying essence of the culture. Substituting new shared values for old values is hardly a simple process, though. The assertion of new values in a mission statement is easy. Getting them accepted and, as social scientists would say, "institutionalized," so that they become part of the basic fabric of the organization, is exceedingly difficult. Changing a culture, by whatever means, may take a long time and not achieve necessary changes quickly enough. More likely than not, it is easier and less costly for managers to attempt to change other factors, such as strategy or structure. Nevertheless, culture does represent a significant, if difficult, target for fundamental changes.

The underlying culture at Chapters is that it is not only a place to buy books, but also a place where customers can eat, read, and socialize with others. The firm has developed its stores in a way to encourage people to linger and enjoy their time while there.

Strategy

Because an organization's overall strategy, along with its basic mission statement and espoused values, provides major directions for its activities, it can serve as another potent focus of managerial change efforts (see Exhibit 15.7).[36] In contrast to its culture, an organization's strategy or set of strategies may be less difficult for managers to change. Top management typically is more in control of determining strategy than the other characteristics of the organization and, in fact, is expected to do so. Thus, by announcing strategic changes, which may occur after extensive consultation with managers throughout the organization, managers at the highest levels can strongly influence change.[37] Of course, whether strategic changes are then implemented effectively is another matter entirely.

Structure

Changing the structural makeup of organizations is sometimes one of the most valuable tools managers have to create other desired changes, such as improved productivity or more creative problem solving (see Exhibit 15.7). Many structural changes, such as reorganizing on a product basis rather than a geographic one or consolidating major divisions, can be made at the macro, or total organization, level. Nokia, which has offices on multiple continents, had initially been organized on a geographic basis but later reorganized by product. Now each division operates with its own strategy and profit and loss responsibility.[38]

Other structural changes can be made at the intermediate level, involving such actions as combining or dividing departments or changing locations and reporting relationships within or among units. Still other structural changes can be made at very micro levels, such as forming new project groups or altering the composition of particular jobs or positions.

As with changes in strategy, changes in structure are not especially difficult to pull off initially, but making them work to generate the desired effects can be particularly challenging for managers. Research shows that almost no other events in organizations can create as much political manoeuvring as potential, or rumoured, reorganization.[39] The ambiguity of the effects of such changes, coupled with their potential importance for the jobs of those who may be directly affected, causes high levels of anxiety and frequent political activity.

Systems

Another major object of change can be the systems of formal processes or procedures used in and by an organization (see Exhibit 15.7). Such changes involve attention to the sequence and manner in which work activities and operations are carried out. For example, Intel changed its procedure for opening new plants. To avoid problems with small differences from one plant to another, its new procedural system for opening plants is to "copy exactly," even down to the colour of the workers' gloves.[40]

Changes in processes and procedures often come about because of prior changes in technology or structure. In this sense, modifications of the way work is performed, whether by individuals or groups, can be considered residual changes. The purchase of new equipment, for instance, would be a primary change, and the adoption of new procedures because of this equipment would be the secondary change.

Staff

Finally, people—both individuals and groups—can be the focus of major changes (see Exhibit 15.7). Essentially, changes that focus on people involve one or more of four elements:

- Who the people are
- What their attitudes and expectations are

- How they interact interpersonally
- How they are trained or developed

In the first instance, change can be brought about by adding, subtracting, or interchanging people. Bringing in a new supervisor or transferring a difficult employee from one unit to another are examples of change focusing on the selection and placement of people.

The second element, attitudes and expectations, often can be an important focus because people act on the basis of them, and they sometimes can be modified without excessive effort or cost by the manager. Providing people with new information or a new way to look at problems, issues, or events has the potential—but no certainty—of creating significant change in their behaviour.[41]

Attempts to alter the way staff relate to each other—such as by being more cooperative with and more supportive of each other—represent a third people-oriented change focus.

The fourth and often most lasting people-change approach involves direct enhancement of their knowledge, skills, and abilities—typically through education, training, and personal development activities. Such change can improve the performance of individuals, groups, and even larger units, regardless of any other changes a manager might initiate.

As with other types of changes, however, efforts to change people can be costly. Managers need to weigh the costs of managerial time and effort, and frequently significant budgetary expenditures, against potential benefits such as a more capable workforce, increased creativity and innovation, better morale, and perhaps, decreased turnover.

Evaluating the Need for Change

Is change always necessary? To answer that question, you should undertake two critical steps. One is to recognize the possible need for change and to correctly assess the strength of that need. The other is to accurately diagnose the problems and issues that the change or changes should address. Misjudgments at either step can lead to severe problems, if not outright disaster.[42] Jumping in to make changes before taking *both* these steps is a recipe for almost certain failure.

Recognizing and Assessing the Need for Change

As we have stressed earlier, making changes is definitely not a cost-free activity (see Exhibit 15.8). This puts a premium on not making changes where the costs will outweigh the potential benefits. It also means that it is crucial to make an accurate assessment of the strength of forces behind the need for change.

Proactive Recognition Effective managers, no matter where they are in the organization's structure, are those who can recognize needs for change at the earliest possible time. This is because they should have systems and methods in place to monitor the environment in which they and their units operate, and these systems should be capable of detecting clues that may not have become obvious warning signs yet.[43] This kind of planned, proactive assessment of the need for change is intended to provide advance notice so that changes can be made sooner, with better planning and potentially with less

Exhibit 15.8

Relative Cost of Change

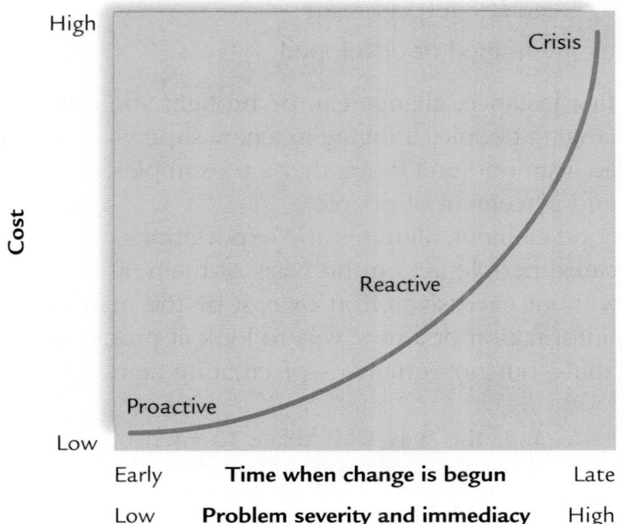

cost. Methods can range, for instance, from elaborate and sophisticated information systems to more mundane activities such as trendspotting of anomalies in sales reports and actively seeking out the views of clients, customers, and employees.

Reactive Recognition Not *all* needs for change can be identified in advance, regardless of how much proactive recognition is attempted. Invariably, some developments in the internal or external environment will take place so quickly, or reach critical mass so unexpectedly, that managers must *react* to them rather than *plan* for them in advance. In such instances, the forces for change become too large to ignore, and the issue becomes one of how and when to react rather than whether or not to react.[44]

Diagnosing Problems

The recognition that change needs to take place is only a starting point. Much like a physician identifying the source of a symptom in a patient, the next step is to make an accurate diagnosis of what is causing the problem or issue so that changes can be made to deal with it effectively. Initiating changes that do not address the underlying causes is sometimes worse than making no changes at all. Thus, managers need to avoid premature conclusions about causes. Instead, they should obtain information from a variety of sources, if possible; compare those sets of information to uncover consistent patterns or trends; and, especially, attempt to determine what are the most likely causes. The end result of a comprehensive analysis of this type should be an accurate, valid diagnosis of what, and who, needs to change.

The Change Process

So far in this chapter, we have focused on the background and context of change in organizations: the forces for change, the reasons why change often fails, the types of change possible, and especially, managers' roles in understanding, assessing, and evaluating the need for change. Now we turn to the change process itself: planning and preparing for it, implementing it, dealing with resistance to it, and evaluating its outcomes (see Exhibit 15.9).

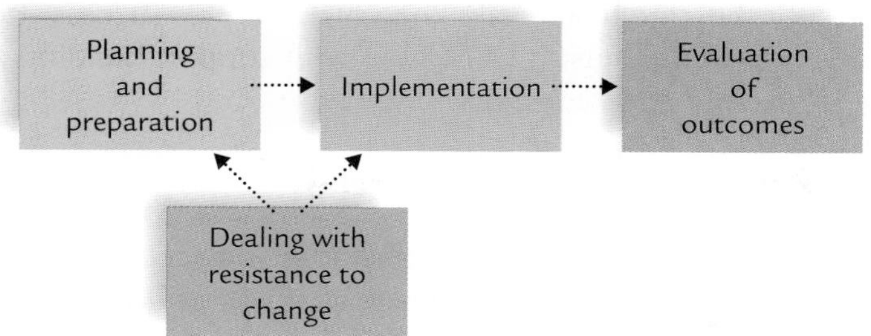

Exhibit 15.9

The Change Process

Planning and Preparation for Change

Once a manager or a group of managers has been convinced that change is necessary and that an accurate diagnosis has been made of the causes requiring change, preparation for the changes can begin. As shown in Exhibit 15.10, such planning calls for attention to several important issues.

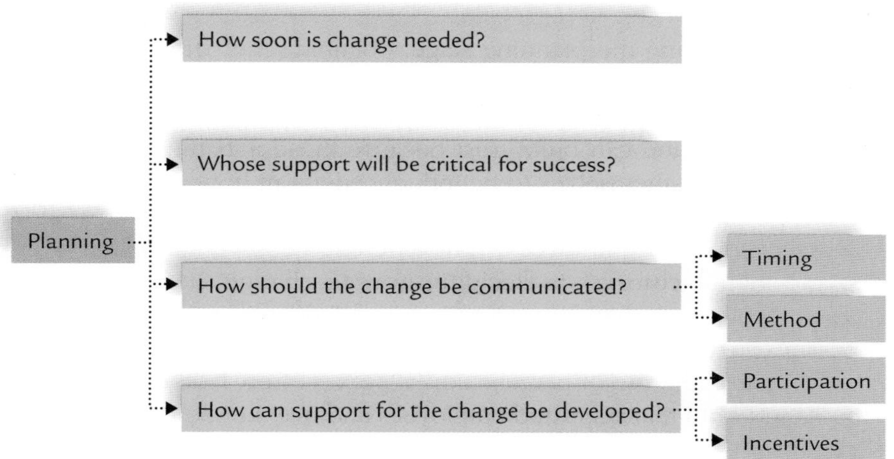

Exhibit 15.10

Planning Choices for Change

Timing Managers are often tempted to initiate something quickly, especially if the need for change seems exceptionally strong. Whether rapid implementation is a good idea or not represents a difficult judgment call. Acting too quickly can lead to changes that are not well-planned and that often fail because they lack sufficient support. On the other hand, waiting too long to make necessary changes can also be a recipe for failure. In the summer of 1997, Gilbert Amelio, then-CEO of Apple Computer, was ousted by the company's board of directors precisely because, according to knowledgeable observers in the industry—and "many of Apple's own employees"—he did not move "quickly enough to help return the company to profitability" and failed to "act with a sense of urgency."[45] It is clear that the timing of changes can be critical to their success. Visionary Steve Jobs returned to Apple and was reinstituted as CEO. Since his return, Apple has introduced consumers to the successful iMac line of desktop and laptop computers, as well as the global phenomenon iPod and its supporting online music store iTunes. The most recent Apple innovation, the iPhone, is yet another huge success.

Building Support One of the best guarantees for successful implementation of a change initiative is to build support for it in advance. Developing this foundation requires especially careful consideration of who will be affected by the changes and how they will likely react. This means that managers need to have a clear understanding of the situation and circumstances in which the changes will take place if they are to increase the probability of success. It also means that this kind of analysis must be followed with support-building activities by the manager. Several of these are discussed here.

Communication. A key step in building support for major changes is to talk about them in advance to those who will be affected. Cooperation is likely to be enhanced the more that people understand (1) the reasons for the changes and especially, (2) the ways in which those changes are likely to impact them. Seldom do changes fail because of too much communication, but they are likely to encounter difficulty when too little information is provided.

Particularly important in using communication to build support for proposed changes is to provide a compelling rationale for those changes. Those to be affected need to know the specific objectives of the changes and how those relate to the larger goals and values of the unit or total organization. It is also important in communication to focus special attention on those who are likely to be influential in shaping the attitudes of their colleagues. In other words, extra effort spent on communication with opinion leaders can be a good investment.

Participation. During the planning stage, obtaining the participation of those to be affected by changes can help build later support for those changes. Plans can often be improved and commitment gained through such participation. In addition, participation can build trust because those initiating the changes, in effect, are allowing themselves to be influenced about how and when to make the changes. An example of effective use of participation is Toyota's efforts to involve a wide set of employees from different areas—engineering, logistics, sales, and manufacturing—in deciding how to change the way the Corolla model is made. The change suggestions involved not only design, but also other issues such as cost cutting and quality enhancements.[46]

Of course, the use of participation is not cost free. It takes time and effort on the part of both managers and employees and may not be feasible if speed is essential or if it is not easy to arrange for effective participation. Also, participation may backfire if participants' suggestions and requests diverge widely from managers' goals. Furthermore, if those asked to participate sense that their input is not really wanted and that a manager is only "going through the motions," this can quickly lead to a feeling of being "manipulated." In such cases, participation has eroded rather than built support for change. Nevertheless, participation should at least be considered as a viable approach. The real issue is whether the failure to use participation makes change more difficult to implement than using participation. The answer is often "yes."

Incentives. One other factor that can help build support for change is to emphasize incentives for those who will be affected. Simply communicating how the change itself will directly affect them in a positive way can often increase support. Examples are the installation of new equipment to make working easier, or reorganization to provide clearer direction, or additional training to add to an employee's repertoire of skills. At other times, providing incentives may involve conferring benefits directly to those affected. This could include, for example, either nonmonetary incentives like more desirable working conditions, or the use of some form of monetary incentives like increased compensation for increased responsibilities. Of course, in some circumstances, providing explicit incentives is often not practical. However, offering something tangible in return for support of changes that may cause extensive adaptation and even stress on the part of those affected may be appropriate and may directly encourage stronger support.

Managers should consider some important cautions, however, when weighing the possibility of using incentives to generate support for change. One is that providing incentives to those likely to be most affected may make them feel that they are being "bought off." Thus, the use of incentives for change, especially monetary incentives, can potentially boomerang by increasing skepticism and cynicism about managers' motives and thus increase rather than decrease resistance to the changes. Furthermore, offering explicit incentives one time for a change may increase the probability that those affected will expect incentives any time a new change is made in the future. Therefore, introducing incentives as a way of building support for change is not something that should be done lightly and without consideration of possible serious, though unintended, side effects.

Implementation Choices

Where planning for change leaves off and implementation of change begins is often difficult to specify because the process is, or should be, more or less continuous. Regardless of where that boundary is, however, implementing change involves several critical choices for managers (see Exhibit 15.11). Four of the most important are discussed here.

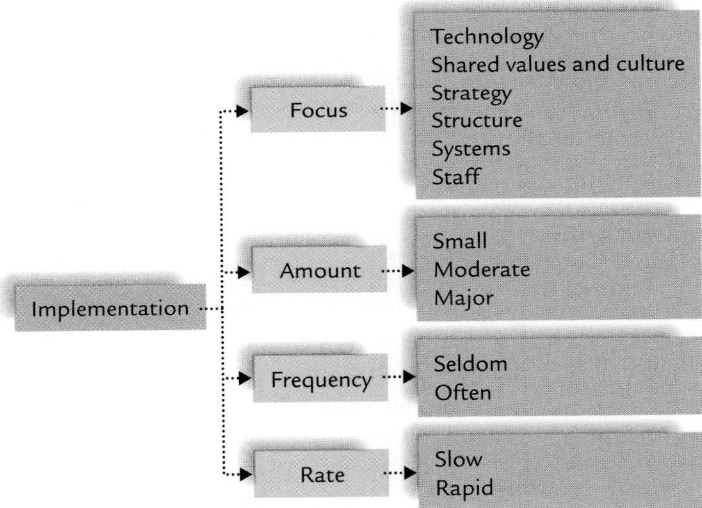

Exhibit 15.11
Implementation Choices

Choice of Focus Earlier in this chapter we identified six types, or focuses, of change: technology, shared values and culture, strategy, structure, systems, and staff (see Exhibit 15.6). To initiate the change process, one or more of these focuses need to be selected. The choice depends in large part on the objectives to be accomplished, which in turn are linked to the problems identified in the assessment of the need to change. If the major problem is outdated equipment, then obviously, changing the technology will be the focus of choice. However, if the problem is one of sluggish growth in sales compared to competitors, then the choice of focus is not so self-evident. It could be that the organization is not sufficiently market oriented, which could indicate a need for change in the culture of the organization.

Often, the problems uncovered in the assessments of the need to change require attention to several simultaneous areas of focus, such as a new strategic direction for the organization *and* a major modification of its culture and structure that more closely fits the new strategy.

Choice of Amount Even after managers have decided what approaches to take and have started to implement those choices, they must also confront another related set of issues: How much change should take place? That is, how comprehensive should the change be, and what parts of the unit or the whole organization should be affected? These questions have no easy answers.

When change is too little, the benefits are not likely to outweigh the costs involved. For example, 3M Corporation tried for several years to fix its magnetic data storage business problems through minor cost-cutting changes. After 10 years of escalating losses, it finally divested itself of this part of the company.[47] Even modest changes can take a great amount of effort and cause disruptions that are almost as great as if the change were much more sizable. Thus, managers must decide whether implementing minimal changes is worth these costs, or whether they should simply wait until the problems are large enough to justify the substantial investments that will be required. The argument in favour of making minimal changes, however, is that even though the immediate cost–benefit ratio may not be favourable, changes postponed until later will be much more expensive; therefore, the longer-term benefits can easily prove the worth of making small changes early. The old adage of "pay me now or pay me later" comes to mind here.

Changes can be too massive as well as too small. Although managers may be tempted to make big changes once they decide to make changes, they often overlook the potential costs. Of course, very large changes are sometimes called for, especially when major changes are occurring in the unit's or organization's environment. Major changes also can have the positive side effect of "galvanizing the troops" so that organization members support the changes because they are necessary and are inspired to give their best efforts. However, as we will discuss later, any change can cause resistance, and big changes can cause immense resistance. Thus, too great a change, in effect, can create more chaos and more problems than were there initially. When this happens, no change at all would have been better than the change that was made.

The lesson for managers is that great care must be taken in deciding how much change should be implemented.[48] Potential problems exist in making changes so small that they either don't justify the costs or they produce minimal effects. Similarly, there can be other kinds of dangers in making changes that are too large. In particular instances, however, one of these extremes may in fact be the best alternative. The general guideline, therefore, is that the amount of change should fit the severity of the problems, and this should be determined by a sound analysis of the strength of the need for change. *A Manager's Challenge: "Ownership Changes Prompt Internal Changes at Avaya Ireland"* illustrates a company that, as a result of fierce international competition, made a choice to implement large, major changes that resulted in a significant award for the quality of its products.

Choice of Frequency Another aspect of change that needs to be considered is the frequency of changes. In these times of competitive pressures and relative turbulence in many organizational environments, change must be implemented much more often than in the past. In some sense, change is a more or less constant condition. However, if specific changes, especially those of at least moderate size, are made continually, organization members can get mentally and physically exhausted. Imagine, for example, that you are a member of a sales department in a large, geographically dispersed company. First, management decides that sales data should be centralized and installs a

a manager's challenge *globalization*

Ownership Changes Prompt Internal Changes at Avaya Ireland

Avaya Ireland (AI) has been challenged to change throughout most of its history. The company was founded in 1961 as Telectron to make telephone networking equipment for businesses in Ireland. During the early 1980s, it was purchased by AT&T; during the mid-1990s, it was spun off by AT&T as part of Lucent Technologies; and in 2000, it was spun off by Lucent as part of Avaya, Inc. Each of these ownership changes forced AI's management to re-evaluate the company's people, strategy, structure, and processes in the context of global competition.

While AI was part of AT&T, for example, technology began evolving away from the current product line, a recession dampened sales, and costs crept upward. Entrenched in an insular structure organized by function, managers focused on their own areas rather than paying close attention to the external environment and tackling companywide strategies. AI's executives had no consistent process for setting objectives, developing plans, and communicating with staff. Worse, they had no mechanism for recording and responding to customer complaints or measuring customer satisfaction.

Under Telectron's management, the workforce had not feared for their jobs. But AT&T operated internationally and had to contain costs to stay competitive. When AT&T laid off workers to cut costs, morale plummeted. An internal survey conducted shortly afterward revealed that, compared with AT&T's workforce in Europe, Africa, and the Middle East, the workforce in Ireland was significantly less satisfied with the corporation's values, leadership, working relationships, and empowerment. At the same time, AI's managers were acutely aware that AT&T's management could adjust to difficult conditions in one country or unit by shifting operations to another. Thus, AI was unlikely to survive within AT&T without making profound changes to become more responsive and market oriented.

AI's management started by planning to revamp the structure for more flexibility, collaboration, and empowerment. Experts helped management train employees in teamwork and team leadership principles in preparation for a transition away from a functional hierarchy to a team structure. Next, they set up an off-premises meeting so representatives of each department could take a fresh look at the company's situation away from the pressures of the daily work routine. This meeting identified four problem areas: (1) lack of teamwork, (2) inadequate training, (3) poor communication, and (4) insufficiently defined roles for managers and employees. Rather than address only these areas, AI's top management decided to strive for a higher level of excellence by challenging the company to win the European Foundation for Quality Management (EFQM) Excellence Award.

To do this, they defined targets for product development and seven other internal processes tied to the award's standards. Then they assigned cross-functional teams to assess AI's capabilities and determine what changes in skills, attitudes, and actions would be needed to hit those targets and qualify for the award. The teams returned with numerous ideas that management implemented, such as analyzing and eliminating outdated products and wasteful procedures. AI's executives also created a Customer Solutions Centre to encourage interaction with customers and impress them with the company's technical strength. Finally, they established a process for aligning individual and team goals with the company's strategic objectives so the workforce would understand where the organization was headed, how it would get there, how performance would be measured, and what was in it for them.

These decade-long changes transformed AI from a company fighting for survival in Ireland to a world-class winner of the EFQM Excellence Award, an astounding accomplishment since some of the best companies in Europe vie for this honour. In winning, AI also proved how implementing changes beyond the obvious fixes can propel a company to new heights. Moreover, in internal surveys, AI's employees say they are more customer focused and concerned about quality and innovation. Among those innovations is VoIP, which can slash corporate phone bills. Demand for VoIP is expanding exponentially, and Avaya's leading switchboard product integrates the new technology without a company having to replace its entire system, including its phones.

Today Avaya Inc.'s future is looking brighter than ever, and its financial viability is coming across loud and clear. Revenue has steadily increased year-over-year since 2003, with 2006 revenues in excess of US$5.1 billion—not bad for a firm once considered to be just an old telephone-equipment company fighting to survive.

Sources: Avaya 2006 Annual Report, www.avaya.com (accessed September 15, 2007); P. Galarza, S. Gandel, and L. Gibbs, "Best Investments," *Money*, January 2004, p. 64; P. Hochmuth, "Avaya Looks to Reinvent Itself," *Network World*, November 11, 2002, pp. 25+; G. Dwyer and C. Doyle, "Award-Winning Results from Implementing Strategic Change at Avaya Ireland," *Journal of Organizational Excellence*, Winter 2002, pp. 29–41.

new data information system linking all the regions. Next, management reorganizes the structure of the department by geographic region rather than by type of product. Next, management institutes a team structure linking sales with marketing and research and development personnel for new projects. Each of these changes, by itself, may improve customer satisfaction and employee performance. However, if they all occur within a short space of time, you might not have time to adjust to any one change before finding yourself in the midst of a new change. Therefore, the frequency of changes must be considered along with their size to gauge the effects on those who will have to respond.

Choice of Rate Just as the amount and frequency of change represent important choices in making changes, so does the rate of change. If the pace of change is too slow, conditions that created the need for it in the first place may again shift significantly so that the wrong problems are being dealt with by the end of the entire change process. Also, change that is too slow can frustrate many people who want to see at least some early and tangible results in return for their efforts. For instance, suppose a company spent several months putting together new work teams and training employees in decision-making techniques, group processes, conflict resolution techniques, and use of computerized performance tracking. Then suppose it delayed installing the new equipment and software. Employees would likely be frustrated by not being able to put their new knowledge and skills to immediate use.

Change that is too rapid can also cause major problems. Whether the change is primarily technological, structural, procedural, or some other focus, people need to adapt to the rate. Rates that are excessively fast can exceed the typical person's ability to cope and increase resentment and resistance. It has even been suggested that in situations of rapid change, the work experience may be so stressful and so damaging to a person's self-identity as to trigger violent behaviour.[49]

Of course, managers sometimes deliberately and appropriately make rapid changes. One obvious case is when the forces for change are so overwhelming that swift change is essential. Furthermore, managers sometimes institute a fast rate of change precisely to determine who can keep up and who cannot. In such circumstances, a rapid rate may be a viable change tactic—if the manager has carefully considered what is to be accomplished and what the potential negative consequences or costs might be. In many other cases, however, managers have not adequately assessed the possible costs and benefits and may have simply implemented an abrupt change because of their eagerness to see results quickly.

As with choices about the amount of change, managers often face clear options about the rate of change they can choose. However, there is one major difference. When dealing with the rate of change, managers can make mid-course corrections more easily than they can when it comes to the amount of change. (It is very difficult, for example, to suddenly convert a large change into a small change.) If the initial pace has started slowly, managers can increase it if this appears desirable. Likewise, a change that has started out rapidly can be slowed, allowing for adaptation to catch up with events. Thus, just as the rate of speed of a car can be increased or decreased depending on road conditions, so can the rate of change in organizational settings. Of course, just as in a car, if the rate is changed too often or too drastically, it can be very uncomfortable for those required to adapt. This in turn can reduce confidence in the person responsible for the changes.

Resistance to Change

Those who lead organizations tend to be favourably disposed toward change. From their perspective it is easy to see the necessity for change and believe it is best for the organization. Consequently, although almost any change carries with it the seeds of resistance, managers are often surprised and frequently disappointed by resistance. They should not be. Some degree of resistance may be inevitable in organizational changes, and in some cases resistance may actually be positive in that it highlights important issues that may need more careful consideration.[50] In this section we examine some of the reasons for resistance to change and some general approaches for dealing with it.

Reasons for Resistance The basic reason people resist change can be summed up in an old saying (slightly restated) that is applicable to many organizational circumstances: "The devil people know is preferred to the devil they don't know." Change embodies potential risks and threats for those affected. They think they know how to size up those risks and threats in their present situation, but they are uncertain what they will be in the changed situation. Thus, the "known" present will be preferred to the "unknown" future, and therefore change is likely to be resisted. Within this overall context, some more specific reasons for resisting change can be identified.

- *Inertia*. People in organizations get comfortable with their present way of doing things. Even if they perceive no increase in risks, people simply find it easier to do things the way they always have rather than to operate or behave differently. Ingrained and overlearned habits die hard.
- *Mistrust*. Even if those proposing change emphasize positive future consequences, people often doubt that they will actually occur. Such skepticism is especially magnified if change occurs in an existing climate of mistrust or if previous change efforts have failed.
- *Lack of Information*. A third contributing factor to resistance to change can be a lack of adequate information about both the need for the change and what its effects are likely to be. Even a seemingly small change like a minor reorganization of a specific unit can produce opposition, often of a subtle nature, simply because basic information is not provided.
- *Lack of Capabilities*. A powerful cause of resistance to change is the perceived lack of capabilities on the part of those who will be expected to implement the change. If people feel threatened by changes they think will require skills and abilities they do not presently have, then resistance is almost guaranteed.
- *Anticipated Consequences*. Another reason for resistance can be straightforward assessments of expected gains and losses by those affected; in other words, employees determine what is best for protection of their self-interests. Those affected by the change may consider possible loss of status or influence, which may be ignored or underestimated by the managers who are instigating the change. Calculations of whether a change is "good" and should be supported, or is "bad" and should be resisted can be quite different from the viewpoint of those initiating the change and those who receive it. The two sides' self-interests, often defined by each party as "better for the organization," may be diametrically opposed.[51]

Dealing with Resistance to Change Resistance to change typically involves more than one of the preceding factors. As a result, from a manager's perspective, there is probably no "quick fix" to reduce or eliminate resistance. However, this does not mean that resistance cannot be minimized. Therefore, having a framework for analyzing the resistance can be helpful. Some ways to analyze and deal with resistance are discussed next.

force field analysis uses the concept of equilibrium, a condition that occurs when the forces for change, the "driving forces," are balanced by forces opposing change, the "restraining forces," and results in a relatively steady state

- *Force Field Analysis.* One very useful way of looking at the problem of resistance is what is called a "**force field analysis**," which was first proposed some years ago by psychologist Kurt Lewin. This analysis, as depicted in Exhibit 15.12, uses the concept of equilibrium, a condition that occurs when the forces for change, the "driving forces," are roughly balanced by forces opposing change, the "restraining forces." Such a condition results in a relatively steady state that is disrupted only when the driving forces for innovation become stronger than the restraining forces for inertia (the two forces that some have called the "in" forces[52]). If we apply this analysis to typical organizational changes, we see that managers basically have two choices: Add more force for change, like putting more pressure on subordinates to conform to new procedures, or reduce the resistance forces, like convincing informal leaders that they will benefit from the change. The basic problem with increasing the driving forces is that this often results in increasing the opposing forces. Therefore, Lewin's analysis suggests that weakening restraints may be the more effective way to bring about change. (This is similar to the old Aesop fable about the contrasting strategies of the wind and the sun who compete to get persons to take off their coats. The sun won.)

Exhibit 15.12

Force Field Analysis

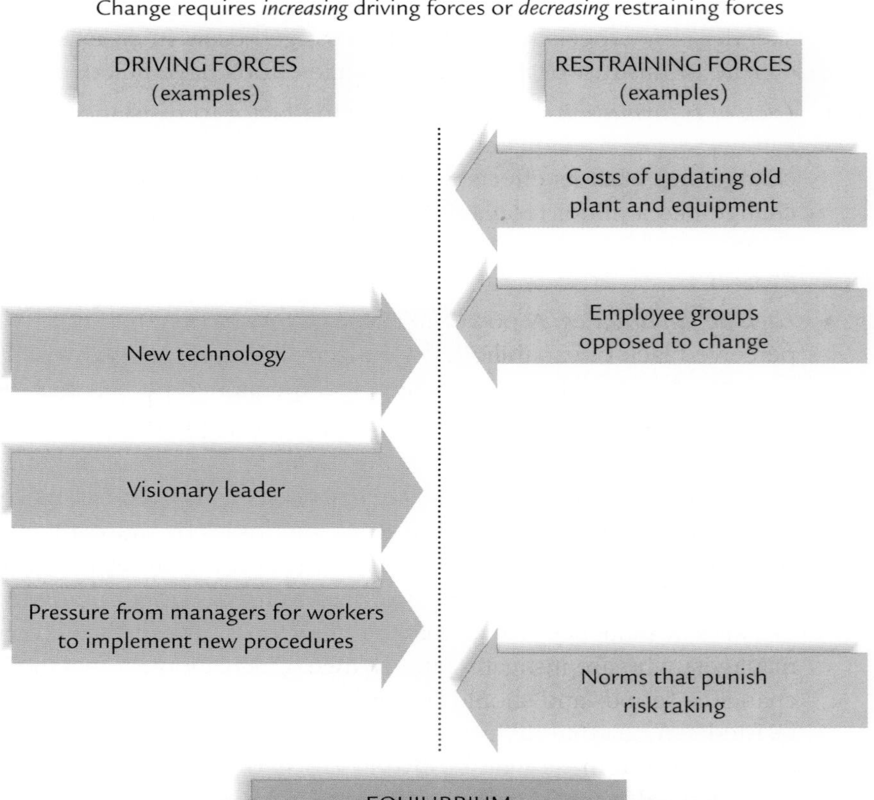

What are some ways to reduce resistance to change? Several approaches are the same as those discussed in the section on "Planning and Preparation for Change," since it is in the planning stages that potential resistance can first be anticipated and steps taken to address it. However, not all forms of resistance can be foreseen or dealt with in advance, so various other approaches are also needed in this stage. A set of such approaches, with their associated advantages and disadvantages, is shown in Exhibit 15.13. Particularly important in this exhibit is the column showing the circumstances in which a particular approach is most likely to be effective. The message here is that not all approaches will work in all situations, and a manager must be selective in choosing when and where to use a particular method. Several factors are especially critical in making these choices:

- Timing of use of approach
- Cost in managers' and employees' time
- Cost in financial and other resources
- Degree of risk involved

Exhibit 15.13 Possible Methods for Dealing with Resistance to Change

Approach	Commonly Used In Situations—	Advantages	Disadvantages
Negotiation and Agreement (e.g., use formal or informal processes to gain advanced agreement to change before implementation)	In which someone or some group will clearly lose out in a change, and in which that group has considerable power to resist	Sometimes major resistance can be reduced or avoided	Can be expensive in many cases if it alerts other groups to want to negotiate too
Participation and Involvement (e.g., involve affected employees in planning the change)	In which the initiators do not have all the information they need to design the change, and in which others have considerable power to resist	People who participate are more likely to be committed to implementing change, and any relevant information they have will be integrated into the change plan	Can be both time consuming and awkward if participants design an inappropriate change
Communication and Education (e.g., provide increased information to employees concerning the short- and long-term effects of the change)	In which there is a lack of information or inaccurate information and analysis	Once persuaded, people will often help with the implementation of the change	Can be very time consuming if many people are involved
Facilitation and Support (e.g., offer seminars in stress management, personal development, anger resolution, etc.)	In which people are resisting because of problems in adjusting to the changes	No other approach works as well with problems of adapting to changes	Can be expensive, and still fail
Explicit and Implicit Coercion (e.g., use position power to order change)	In which speed is essential, and the change initiators possess considerable power	It is speedy and can overcome many kinds of resistance	Can be risky if it leaves people angry at the initiators and lowers trust in them

Source: Adapted and reprinted by permission of *Harvard Business Review*. An exhibit from "Methods for Dealing with Resistance to Change" by John P. Kotter and Leonard A. Schlesinger (March/April 1979), p. 111.

- Importance of the issues involved
- *Participation.* Participation may be very effective in defusing some resistance, or even identifying valid reasons why the change might not work, but it can be a costly use of everyone's time and can be risky for managers because the outcomes are hard to predict. For example, in a setting in which past change efforts have failed or have hurt employees (for example, through layoffs), asking for people's participation may not seem legitimate.
- *Communication.* Communication can be relatively inexpensive, but if it comes too late it may not have much effect. For example, communicating and emphasizing to employees that a firm's profits have dropped sharply, after layoffs have already been announced, may seem like an after-the-fact attempt to justify the layoffs and may only result in increased levels of mistrust and resistance in the future.
- *Facilitation.* Facilitation and support would probably be welcomed by those who might not want to go along with the changes, but the costs can be substantial, especially if outside consultants are used.
- *Coercion.* Coercion, such as threatening transfers or denying future promotions, is risky and not designed to lessen resistance, but it may overcome resistance in the short term. For this to work, management must have the power to follow through with threats, and the threats must be of sufficient magnitude to motivate compliance on the part of employees. In extreme situations managers may have no other choice, but if this option is chosen, they need to recognize that it will likely increase mistrust and resistance to change efforts in the future.

A final point to be made about dealing with resistance to change is that managers should recognize that the amount and nature of resistance may be very useful diagnostic tools to gauge whether the change is appropriate and will actually bring about desired results if implemented. To put this another way, managers need to *listen* to resistance and determine whether they have accurately assessed the need for change and the process of implementation. The fact that resistance arises certainly does not mean that the proposed change must be abandoned or postponed. On the other hand, it may be a very important signal that managers ignore at their peril, as illustrated in the following example of an actual situation.

The owner of a small tire store bought three major new power tools for his tire replacement mechanics. The owner believed that the power tools would improve the performance and satisfaction of his employees since less time and less muscle power would be required. However, within one month, all three tools were out of commission—one had been left in the trunk of a customer's car, one had been run over by a truck, and one had been dropped from a hoist. When the owner probed the reasons for the losses, he found that they were not purely accidental. The employees, who had worked together for over 12 years, could not talk to each other over the noise of the power tools, and they had always enjoyed the camaraderie on the job. Without the opportunity to explain their opposition to the change, they became dissatisfied with their new working conditions and, in effect, sabotaged the new tools.[53] Had the owner appreciated why the employees might resist, he could have considered other, perhaps superior, alternatives.

Evaluation of Change Outcomes

Once change has been carried out, whether throughout the entire organization or within a single unit, managers need to evaluate the outcomes. If the effects of changes are not appraised in some manner, managers have no way of knowing whether additional changes are needed and also whether the particular approaches implemented should be used again in similar circumstances. To carry out the evaluation process, three basic steps are required: data collection, comparison of results against goals, and feedback of results to those affected by the changes (see Exhibit 15.14).

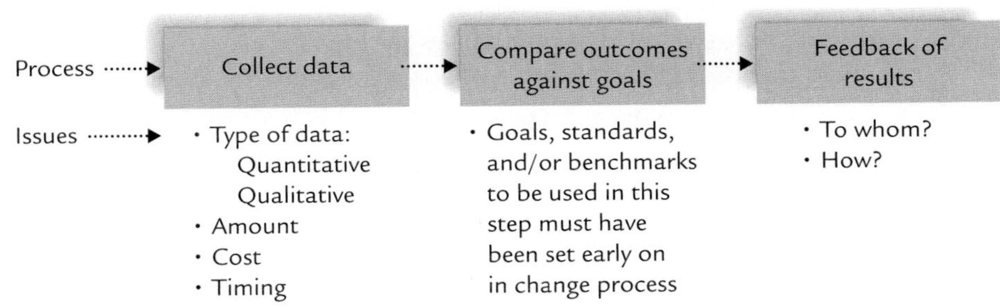

Exhibit 15.14
Evaluating Change Outcomes

Data Collection The data that can be collected to evaluate the outcomes of change essentially come in two forms: objective (quantitative) data and subjective (attitude) data. Both types can be useful to the manager who has implemented change, and often it will be necessary to tap several sources of each type. For example, after introducing major new information technology, a manager could evaluate by measuring changes in output per employee, speed of response to customers, accuracy in reports, attitudes of employee users within the organization, and attitudes of clients who deal with employees using the new technology.

It is important to keep in mind that the collection of different sets of data (such as these) to measure change outcomes may well require significant costs. Therefore, not every type of data that could be collected should be collected. As with other organizational actions, the benefits should be weighed against the costs. The point, though, is that significant sources of data should not be overlooked, and the more types of data that can be collected, the more likely the analysis will be informative. Also, in most cases, data should be collected at periodic intervals to measure the lasting power of the change. A recent survey showed that two-thirds of companies are using some form of scorecard software to measure everything from financial progress to customer satisfaction. These scorecards can be customized to reflect only the measures the company wishes to track. Then, by targeting the distribution of this kind of data, a company can ensure, for example, that managers from marketing, finance, and research and development are all discussing the same measures in meetings.[54]

Comparison of Outcomes against Goals Collection of data is only a first step in evaluating outcomes. The crucial next step is the comparison of those outcomes against the goals and various benchmarks or standards set in advance of the change. Without those goals and standards, interpretation of the data will be almost meaningless. To know that sales increased by 3 percent is interesting but lacks meaning unless it can be compared with some explicit objective, such as a 5 percent increase. Likewise, to know that employees' job satisfaction after the change averages 3.5 on a 5-point scale doesn't tell a manager much unless that can be measured against a goal of "at least 3.0." In other words, absolute results are not as informative as relative results. Goals and benchmarks that have been specified in advance of change efforts provide the basis for making meaningful relative comparisons.

Feedback of Results A final step in evaluating change outcomes is communication of the findings to those who are involved with or affected by the change. Managers seldom, if ever, neglect to provide this information to interested superiors. However, when it comes to subordinates, this step is frequently overlooked or seen as desirable but not mandatory. This may be short sighted. Failure to provide feedback can leave subordinates and other employees with a sense of frustration, and they may even question a manager's motives for not supplying it. It also can produce an element of distrust, making it even harder to carry out successful changes in the future.

Managers can provide feedback to both superiors and subordinates in a variety of ways, including written reports, direct oral reports and briefings, discussions with small groups, and so on. No one method is more effective than others. The key point is that in nearly all cases, some feedback about the effects of changes is better than no communication at all.

Specific Approaches to Planned Change

Throughout the earlier parts of this chapter we have presented general issues and principles relating to organizational change and renewal. Here, in this final section, we look at three specific, usually organization-wide, approaches to planned change. The first is *organizational development*, which is an approach with a strong behavioural and people orientation. The second is the more engineering-based approach called *process redesign* (or *re-engineering*). The final part of this section describes what is almost more a particular framework or perspective than a change approach as such—*organizational* learning.

The Organizational Development (OD) Approach to Change

organizational development (OD) an approach to organizational change that has a strong behavioural and people orientation, emphasizing planned, strategic, long-range efforts focusing on people and their interrelationships in organizations

T-groups groups of individuals participating in organizational development sessions away from the workplace; also called basic-skills training groups

Organizational Development by Michael Hitt

mymanagementlab

The essence of an **organizational development (OD)** approach to change is its emphasis on planned, strategic, long-range efforts focusing on people and their interrelationships in organizations.[55] While "organizational development" may seem like a general term that could be applied to almost any aspect of the topic of organizational change, as we noted at the beginning of this chapter, it in fact refers to a specific approach to bringing change to organizations. It grew out of behavioural science research aimed at improving the communication and quality of interactions among individuals in groups. Researchers put together groups of individuals in sessions away from the workplace in what were termed basic-skills training groups, or, as they came to be called for short, **T-groups**.[56] The T-group orientation over time broadened into a focus on interpersonal relationships throughout the larger organization, and hence the attention to *organizational*, not just group, development.

Values and Assumptions The early formulation of what eventually evolved into the OD approach placed particular importance on certain values and assumptions, and they have remained at the heart of this approach to this day.[57] First and foremost is the assumption that "people are the cornerstone of success in any organizational endeavor."[58] A second value or assumption is that most people desire opportunities for personal growth and enhancement of their capabilities.

Another basic belief about people that underlies this approach to change is that their emotions are as important as their rational thoughts. Therefore, the open expression of these emotions can be critical in facilitating real change.

The fundamental assumption about organizations in the OD approach is that they are systems composed of interdependent parts, and thus, a change in any one part can have major effects on other parts.[59] Another assumption is that the way organizations are designed and structured will influence the interpersonal relationships among the people within them. In other words, the behaviour of people in organizational settings is at least partly caused by the conditions they encounter there—and these conditions can be changed.

Basic Approach to the Process of Change The basic OD approach to organizational change, as already described, involves the three fundamental steps of unfreezing, movement (changing), and refreezing.[60] Thus, in an OD approach to change, the initial challenge is to critically examine existing behavioural patterns by getting people not to take them for granted but to question them and look at their effects.

In the traditional OD approach, both the first and second steps—unfreezing and movement—will benefit from the use of **change agents**, individuals specifically responsible for managing change efforts.[61] These people can be either internal change agents, that is, from inside the organization (often from the human resource area) or they can be external change agents. In either case, the OD change agent is someone who is not a member of the particular groups or units directly involved. Frequently, this person is a consultant, someone with presumed expertise in helping groups see the need for change and in making changes.

change agents individuals who are responsible for implementing change efforts; they can be either internal or external to the organization

The changes themselves are achieved by the use of one or more **interventions**, that is, "sets of structured activities," or action steps, designed to improve the organization.[62] Some of these interventions, like fact finding, begin in the unfreezing stage, and others, such as team building and coaching/counselling, take place in the changing stage. Several of the more common types of interventions are shown in Exhibit 15.15.

interventions sets of structured activities, or action steps, designed to improve organizations

The priority in the second change stage is on exploring new forms of behaviour and relationships. Particularly important at this point is an emphasis on behavioural processes, such as leader–group relations, decision making, intergroup cooperation, and the like. This **behavioural process orientation** is a key distinguishing feature of the OD approach to organizational change.

behavioural process orientation a key distinguishing feature of the OD approach to organizational change that focuses on new forms of behaviour and new relationships

Merely engaging in new and different ways of behaving, relating, and interacting is not enough for changes to have lasting effects. This is the reason for the third stage, refreezing. As we saw earlier, the intent of this third stage is to make sure that the changes "stick" and that behaviour and relationships don't easily return to their former—less effective—states. However, since the time of the original formulation of the three-stage change process many years ago, the goal of refreezing has been broadened into the objective of **organizational renewal**. The idea behind organizational renewal recognizes that in a fast-changing, competitive world, new habits and patterns rapidly become outdated themselves and may need to be replaced after relatively short periods of time. Therefore, the emphasis has shifted from simply locking changes into place and instead to developing a capacity for renewal, a goal that incorporates flexibility and the ability to change more or less continually.

organizational renewal a concept of organizational change that proposes a goal of flexibility and capability for continual change

In recent years, the OD approach to change, which formerly was almost a rigid set of procedures that required specific behavioural science expertise in the form of an experienced change agent, has evolved into a more general approach that places more emphasis on the direct use of line managers as

Exhibit 15.15 Types of OD Interventions

Intervention	Objective	Examples
Diagnostic Activities	To determine the current state of the organization or the parameters of a problem	Interviews Questionnaires Surveys Meetings
Individual Enhancement Activities	To improve understanding of and relationships with others in the organization	Sensitivity training (T-groups) Behaviour modelling Life and career planning
Team Building	To improve team operation, abilities, cohesiveness	Diagnostic meetings Role analysis Responsibility charting
Intergroup Activities	To improve cooperation between groups	Intergroup team building
Technostructural or Structural Activities	To find solutions to problems through the application of technological and structural changes	Job enrichment Management by objective New technology introduction
Process Consultation	To disseminate information concerning the future diagnosis and management of human processes in organizations including communication, leadership, problem solving and decision making, and intra- and intergroup relationships	Agenda setting Feedback and observation Coaching and counselling Structural change suggestions

Source: Adapted from Wendell L. French and Cecil H. Bell Jr., *Organization Development: Behavioral Science Interventions for Organizational Improvement*, 5th ed. (Upper Saddle River, NJ: Prentice Hall, 1995), p. 165.

potential change agents. Also, many of its intervention methods, like team building, have become day-to-day, mainstream organizational activities. The OD legacy survives in various forms in many organizations today, but other comprehensive approaches to organizational change have attracted increasing attention from many managers in the last decade or so. Two of these are process redesign and organizational learning.

Process Redesign (Re-engineering)

process redesign (re-engineering) involves a fundamental redesign of business processes to achieve dramatic improvements

Process redesign, often simply called "**re-engineering**," involves a fundamental redesign of business processes to achieve (intended) dramatic improvements.[63] Technology, especially information technology, usually plays a central role in such re-engineering efforts. However, the human and managerial issues related to process redesign are also extremely crucial to its success in organizations (see Exhibit 15.16).

Exhibit 15.16 Issues in Process Redesign

Objectives	Coverage	Potential Drawbacks
· Reduce Costs · Shorten Cycle Times · Improve Quality	· Breadth · Depth	· Requires high level of persistence and involvement of top management · Effort may be greater than results · High chaos factor · High levels of resistance

This approach to comprehensive organizational change first appeared in the late 1980s, and seemed to peak in popularity in the mid-1990s.[64] In one form or another it is still in use today, although clearly less so than a decade ago. The approach is based on two key principles: (1) Many companies have business processes for meeting customer needs that are inefficient and outdated, and (2) many organizations have structures that involve more people than are necessary for efficient operations. The objectives of this approach are to reduce costs, shorten cycle times, and improve quality.[65] For example, one of the early applications of this approach was financial services in retail banking, where the credit approval process was shortened from several days to almost instantaneous with the support of IT and a reduced reliance upon management and staff.

Those process redesign efforts that appeared to achieve the most success had both breadth and depth.[66] Breadth of re-engineering means change in terms of the redesign of a set of processes across a complete business unit rather than a change in a single, limited process. Depth of re-engineering means change in a related set of core organizational elements such as roles and responsibilities, structure, incentives, shared values, and so on rather than any one or two of these elements.

Adequate breadth and depth by themselves, however, are not enough for process redesign to succeed. Implementation has turned out to be exceedingly difficult. A major commitment must come from the top of the organization, that is, from key executives (of the overall organization or its major units) who can supply the necessary resources to implement these activities and who can take the time to demonstrate personal involvement in the entire redesign process. Like any comprehensive change approach, for re-engineering to be successful, enormous energy, planning, coordinated effort, persistence, and attention to detail are required. Without substantial backing, it is likely to fail.

Even under the best of circumstances, however, re-engineering does not always produce effective change, and this has caused some disillusionment after the early enthusiasm for it.[67] For one thing, the amount of effort required has not always seemed commensurate with the results obtained. One European commercial bank, for example, saw its re-engineering effort yield only a 5 percent cost reduction rather than the anticipated 23 percent reduction.[68] Because of less-than-expected effects, some managers and organizations simply decide not to continue with re-engineering projects.

A second reason that some managers have become disenchanted with process re-engineering, regardless of any positive benefits like increased efficiency, is that it can cause more or less constant disorder and considerable resistance, or as some managers have called it, "mass chaos."[69]

As the history of companies' attempts to implement process redesign illustrates, it is an approach to organizational renewal that is not exactly embraced by many of those who have to take part in it. In fact, one of the co-authors (Hammer) of the book that was most influential in popularizing this approach has stated that the people aspects of re-engineering were not always given enough attention: "I was insufficiently appreciative of the human dimension. I've learned that's critical."[70] Nevertheless, despite its problems, at least some CEOs and other corporate leaders appear to remain positive about the potential of this comprehensive approach to change.

Organizational Learning

organizational learning exhibited by an organization that is skilled at creating, acquiring, and transferring knowledge, and at modifying its behaviour to reflect new knowledge and insights

Although the concept has been around for some time, it is only relatively recently that **organizational learning** has become a major focus in approaches to organizational change and renewal.[71] To date there is limited evidence regarding its impact on overall corporate performance, but the evidence that is available appears to support a positive relationship between a firm's use of the organizational learning concept and its financial performance.[72]

By way of definition, an organization that is good at this process is said to be "skilled at creating, acquiring, and transferring knowledge, and at modifying its behavior to reflect new knowledge and insights."[73] Such an organization, in fact, would be called a *learning organization*. The central idea is that organizations that emphasize this perspective are (1) attempting to change and improve continuously, not just periodically, and especially, (2) basing these improvements on a foundation of new knowledge they have acquired.

Several factors have been shown to facilitate learning by organizations:

- Existing and well-developed central, core competencies of current personnel.
- An organizational culture that supports continuous improvement.
- The availability of organizational capabilities (like managerial expertise) to be able to implement the necessary changes.[74]

Clearly, managers and organizations cannot simply decide or declare that learning should take place. The elements listed above need to be in place as a starting point if organizational learning is going to lead to any real benefits. Then a number of activities need to take place to fully implement an ongoing learning process in organizations. Five of the more important are explained here.[75]

Systematic, Organized, and Consistent Approach to Problem Solving A learning process in organizations requires the continual collection of factual data, rather than reliance on assumptions or guesswork, to aid problem solving and decision making.

Experimentation to Obtain New Knowledge Learning organizations do not simply solve current problems. They experiment with new methods and procedures to expand their knowledge and gain fresh insights. They engage in a steady series of small experiments to keep acquiring new knowledge consistently and to help employees become accustomed to change. For example, such major manufacturing companies as Standard Aero, Alcan Aluminum, and Bombardier constantly try new methods and processes to see whether they can improve their productivity. As they become experienced with learning and experimenting, they become less resistant to change in general. Learning organizations also invest in bolder, one-of-a-kind experiments such as substantial demonstrations or pilot projects.

Drawing Lessons from Past Experiences Enterprises with strong learning cultures pay particular attention to lessons from both past failures and past successes. They exemplify the old maxim: "It is not having had the experience that is important; it's what you learn from the experience that's important." To do this requires managers and the organization to draw conclusions and not leave such learning to hit-or-miss chance.

Learning from the Best Practices and Ideas of Others Organizations and their managers that are strongly committed to learning are also humble in a certain respect. They do not assume that they already know how to do everything better than other organizations, whether they are competitors, enterprises outside their own industry or sphere of operations, or customers. They consistently spend resources to scan their environments to gain information and knowledge from a variety of external sources. One increasingly common form of this is **benchmarking**, where the best practices of competitors are identified, analyzed, and compared against one's own practices (refer back to Chapter 6). Thus, for example, the world's leading petroleum producers use reports from Environmental Information Service to benchmark against their competitors in terms of compliance with and involvement in environmental issues.[76] Exhibit 15.17 is a list compiled by The Benchmarking Exchange (TBE), which has more than 38 000 member firms from 91 countries. The list shows the top ten business processes that are being benchmarked around the world. Exhibit 15.18, also compiled by TBE, shows the major organizations that are currently most active in their use of the benchmarking approach.[77]

benchmarking identification, analysis, and comparison of the best practices of competitors against an organization's own practices

Exhibit 15.17 Top Ten Business Processes Being Benchmarked

Rank	Business Processes Being Benchmarked
1.	Information Systems/Technology
2.	Benchmarking
3.	Environment/Health/Sustainability/Safe
4.	Billing
5.	Call Centres/Help Desks
6.	Customer Service/Satisfaction
7.	Employee Development/Training
8.	Human Resources
9.	Maintenance/Refurbish/Repair
10.	Quality

Source: www.benchnet.com (accessed September 14, 2007).

Exhibit 15.18 Major US Organizations Using Benchmarking

Rank	Organization
1.	Xerox
2.	TRW
3.	Automotive U.S Department of Veterans Affairs
4.	U.S. Army
5.	Saudi Aramco
6.	Internal Revenue Service
7.	Corning
8.	American Ordnance LLC
9.	Battelle
10.	Ergon Energy

Source: www.benchnet.com (accessed September 14, 2007).

Other ways of generating this kind of learning include putting together **focus groups** of customers that spend time in small groups for intense discussions of the positive and negative features of products or services. The objective in using these and similar methods is to gain knowledge that would be difficult, if not impossible, to get only from people and available data inside the organization. In other words, learning organizations work hard at not being parochial and insular.

focus groups small groups involved in intense discussions of the positive and negative features of products or services

Transferring and Sharing Knowledge Another core activity of an organizational learning approach is to make sure that the new knowledge that is gained is actually disseminated widely throughout relevant units of the organization. This requires that managers be alert to both the need for information sharing and ways to do it. The latter would include such activities as distributing reports, developing demonstration projects, initiating training and education programs, and rotating or transferring those with the knowledge.

As an approach to change, an organizational learning perspective has much to offer. It emphasizes paying constant attention to the possible need for changes, and it embodies the goal of renewal—of pushing organizations to continually reinvent themselves through the purposeful and persistent acquisition of new knowledge. The implementation of active organizational learning directly confronts the fundamental issue stated at the beginning of this chapter: Since environments never stay the same, successful organizations can never stay the same. One of the best ways to both keep up with changing environments and keep ahead of them is for managers to focus intently on instilling a learning culture in their areas of responsibility.

managerial perspectives revisited

PERSPECTIVE 1: **THE ORGANIZATIONAL CONTEXT** The context of the particular organization you work in is critical to change. The more changes in the environment outside the organization, the higher the likelihood that changes will occur inside the organization. If it is hard to change oneself, it is even harder to change other people! Nevertheless, in the organizational environments of today and the foreseeable future, the need for organizations to keep changing and renewing will always be present. However, the ease or difficulty of carrying out changes and renewal will be strongly affected by the particular conditions—structure and culture—existing in an organization. In general, the more responsive the overall organization, the greater you are compelled to make changes. As a result, you have to be tuned in to what is going on around your organization and to the level of responsiveness and expectations of change inside your organization.

PERSPECTIVE 2: **THE HUMAN FACTOR** Obviously, personal changes that you need to make in your managerial capabilities and approach will be done primarily by you. However, as a manager you can only get team changes made through others— you cannot make the changes for others. People can be either the great facilitators or the great roadblocks of change. People, as a variable in the process, are more than just responders or recipients of change, however. They also potentially can be a great source of ideas about what changes need to be made, how changes should be carried out, and whether or not changes are working the way they were intended.

PERSPECTIVE 3: **MANAGING PARADOXES** Potential paradoxes are at the heart of many organizational changes and transformations. Reinforcing and retaining some current mental maps and behaviours while at the same time unfreezing, changing, and refreezing new mental maps and behaviours is critical to managerial success. For

example, managers must weigh change versus stability. Making major changes is difficult because people resist changes, especially major ones. Moreover, while changes may be needed quickly, rapid change can produce organizational chaos if implemented incorrectly. Take, for example, the rapid changes in Russia's economic system in the late 1980s. The changes appeared to be a move in the right direction, but the Russian government didn't have the necessary infrastructure to support and implement many of them. Of course, the changes in Russia were massive. Smaller-scale changes within companies trying to transform their organizations can, nonetheless, be a major undertaking.

Managers are constantly confronted with potential paradoxes like this when deciding on the kinds of changes to make and their timing and implementation. Those managers who have the greatest understanding of the tradeoffs facing them—pros and cons—will have the best chances of achieving success and renewing their units or organizations.

4

PERSPECTIVE 4: **ENTREPRENEURIAL MINDSET** In organizations where managers have adopted an entrepreneurial mindset and diffused it throughout the organization, changes are easier to implement. An entrepreneurial mindset makes the organization and the people in it more flexible. On the other hand, many organizations have to make major changes because they have not been entrepreneurial in the past and therefore have lost their competitive advantage to other, more entrepreneurial organizations. These organizations may need to develop and introduce new products in the market to compete with organizations that have outpaced them. However, in developing substantially new products, organizations may require a change in their culture to encourage more creativity and risk-taking by their employees. In other words, these firms will need to develop an entrepreneurial mindset, which itself can be difficult to do. Consequently, unless managers who are responsible for particular organizational development and transformation initiatives are themselves committed to the changes—and demonstrate their commitment to them—employees aren't likely to follow. Above all, managers need to be committed to the goal of constant organizational renewal and improvement. Commitment to the status quo is the antithesis of managing effectively in organizations. Adopting an entrepreneurial mindset will help managers make this type of commitment.

concluding comments

Clearly, change in organizations is often necessary—but hardly ever easy. What may seem like an obvious need for change from the point of view of the person in charge, the manager, may not seem that way at all to those who have to adapt and carry out the change. People resist change for a variety of reasons, many of them valid. In general, if people do not *feel* or *believe* in the need for change, they are likely, at best, to be apathetic supporters of change and, at worst, to be active resisters. Therefore, creating a shared feeling of the need for change and a belief in its necessity is one of the first and most critical steps in achieving successful change.

As we have discussed in this chapter, producing effective change requires an analysis of the likely sources and reasons for resistance and a consideration of the most effective possible approaches for overcoming that resistance. Once people are "unfrozen," they need a new "state" to move toward. In other words, as a manager, you will need to persuade people not only that the place where they are currently is untenable, but also that the place where you want them to go is better. In addition, they will need from you a clear sense of *how* they are going to get from where they are now to the new place you want them to go.

Simplified, change is about helping people you manage answer three basic questions: (1) What's wrong with just staying put? (2) Where do we want to go instead? (3) How are we going to get there? Without convincing answers to these essential questions, most people are unlikely to change. The stimulating thing about managing change, however, is that no two situations are identical, nor are the people who are involved in or affected by the change.

In the final analysis, organizations and managers need to view the condition of "things as they are" with extreme skepticism. Like the principle in physics that says "nature abhors a vacuum," the status quo in organizations should be regarded almost as abhorrent. It is fraught with dangers, many of which are subtle and hard to recognize. Consequently, managers need to be ever alert against becoming prisoners of their own success and just sticking with what has worked in the past. Being able to make meaningful changes that lead to organizational renewal in a way that adds value is one of the premier managerial challenges of our times.

key terms

behavioural process orientation 553
benchmarking 557
change agents 553
confrontation 533
contrast 533
early wins 535
80/20 rule 534
focus groups 557
force field analysis 548
interventions 553
mental map 529
movement 527
organizational development (OD) 552
organizational learning 555
organizational renewal 553
process redesign (re-engineering) 554
refreezing 528
T-groups 552
unfreezing 527

test your comprehension

1. List the forces that act from outside an organization to bring about change within it.
2. What are an organization's internal forces for change?
3. What components within an organization can be changed? (*Hint:* This chapter discusses six of them.)
4. Explain the notion of unfreezing as described by Lewin.
5. Why do people fail to move or change when there is uncertainty about the required change?
6. Why is refreezing an important part of the change process?
7. What is meant by proactive and reactive change?
8. What are the four major steps in the change process?
9. What are some of the considerations managers face when planning change?
10. Why is it important to involve those who will ultimately be affected by a change in the planning process?
11. List the drawbacks to using incentives to gain cooperation during a change.
12. Why is it important to be careful in choosing the amount and rate of change? What are the benefits and drawbacks involved in large- and small-scale change? In rapid or slow change?
13. Why do employees resist change?
14. What are some of the ways managers can overcome employees' resistance to change?
15. What is meant by "force field analysis"?

16. In evaluating the outcome of planned change, what types of data are used?
17. What are the three steps in evaluating the outcome of a planned change?
18. What is the emphasis of the OD approach to change?
19. What are the key steps in the OD approach to change?
20. What is a change agent? Where do they come from?
21. What is the difference between the breadth and the depth of re-engineering?
22. Describe a "learning organization."
23. How can you tell when you encounter a learning organization?

apply your understanding

1. Think of the last organizational change that affected you. Maybe your university, for example, recently changed some policy on major curriculum requirements or something similar. Were you a supporter of or resister to the change? What mistakes did the organization make? What could it have done differently to facilitate the change?
2. The exact outcomes of change programs are often not evaluated. Why do you think this is the case?
3. Changes in strategy are generally not effective without changes in other aspects of the organization. Why do you think this is the case?
4. Crisis change is more common but more costly than anticipatory change. What do you think the keys are to effective anticipatory change?
5. How easy or difficult is it to convert a traditional organization to a learning organization?

practise your capabilities

Two years ago, GenCom gave its production review committee responsibility for developing and implementing procedures to improve manufacturing productivity. Jerry, the manager of the engineering department, is the co-chair of the committee along with Gene, the production manager. They and the three other committee members have joint responsibility for deciding on any major changes intended to improve productivity. This month's regular meeting of the production review committee had already started when Gene hurried in. "Have you seen these production figures? Have you? They are incredible—just look at the increase in productivity in this department!" Jerry was surprised at Gene's enthusiasm and said, "Wait a minute, slow down. Just what are you talking about that has you so excited?" At this, Gene realized the other members of the committee hadn't yet seen the new report and quickly handed around copies. He then took a deep breath and started explaining.

"Several months ago, I ran into Kim, the manager of extract processing, and said that I was somewhat disappointed by the latest productivity figures and wished someone could figure out a way to improve them. I didn't think about that statement until just this morning when Kim walked into my office and handed me this report. It seems she has had her team working on the problem for the last four months. They collected information on productivity levels at other similar companies and carefully studied the procedures of the most successful. They worked with several of the ideas in their group, testing the ideas separately and in combination and with new additions until they found a method that seemed to work. Wow! I'll say it seems to work. Just look at those figures. I think we ought to immediately implement their idea in all of the production units. Just think of the profit improvements that would result from across-the-board performance improvements matching these."

Jerry and the other members of the committee were pleased with the report and decided to accept Gene's recommendation for a companywide application of the new procedures developed by Kim's team. They had all been anxious to find a new initiative that would really work, since their last two change attempts had been unsuccessful. In fact, both previous initiatives had been scrapped rather quickly. The first one had not worked because the plant didn't have the right type of equipment and infrastructure to support it. The second had failed because of high levels of resistance from employees. However, after discussion, the committee members were convinced that this new approach would definitely work, and they decided to implement it throughout all relevant units. After all, it had worked out exceedingly well in Kim's department.

1. Analyze the forces for and focus of change in this situation.
2. What problems might you anticipate with the committee's decision to implement Kim's procedures companywide? How would you try to deal with those possible problems?

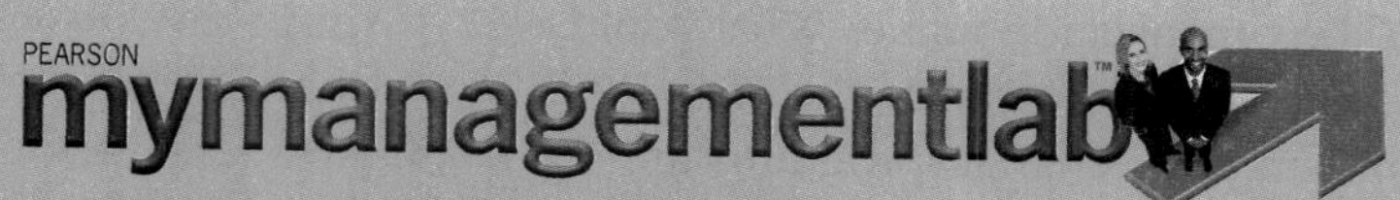

To improve your grade, visit the MyManagementLab website at **www.pearsoned.ca/mymanagementlab**. This online homework and tutorial system allows you to test your understanding and generates a personalized study plan just for you. It provides you with study and practice tools directly related to this chapter's content. MyManagementLab puts you in control of your own learning!

closing case DEVELOP YOUR CRITICAL THINKING

Telefónica Calls for Change

The pace of change within the global telecommunications industry has quickened as more countries eliminate monopolies and encourage competition through deregulation and privatization. Spain cleared the way for competition starting in 1998, allowing British Telecommunications and other rivals to challenge Telefónica, which formerly held a monopoly position as the nation's largest telephone company. By then, Telefónica was ready to compete in a deregulated market. Ten years earlier, its top managers had anticipated deregulation and planned a comprehensive program of change to prepare itself for the new environment. Since deregulation, Telefónica has continued to change by expanding into other countries and other offerings beyond traditional dial-up phone service.

Prior to deregulation, Telefónica was a slow-moving, government-owned bureaucracy with more than 100 000 employees who were virtually guaranteed lifelong employment. Prices were high and customers with questions or problems could contact the company only during a five-hour daily window. The wait for a new phone line could go on for weeks. And when customers lost service, the outages lasted 150 minutes on average.

Looking ahead, however, Telefónica's managers realized that competition and emerging technological developments would give customers new choices and new power. They realized that the company risked losing its market leadership position if changes were not made. Therefore, they decided on a new mission: to become the "favourite provider of telecommunications, voice, data, sound, and image services" to current and potential customers. The new mission pointed the way toward a more customer-oriented future for Telefónica.

At this point, management looked toward one division as a model for change throughout the organization. The Alicante unit in eastern Spain, with a workforce of more than 1200, was one of the company's most profitable and fastest-growing units. Eyeing the opportunity for additional growth in Alicante, Telefónica's top management decided to invest heavily in new equipment and networks there. Yet new technology alone would not boost revenues without customer service improvements that could only occur by making structure, culture, strategy, process, and people changes.

Alicante's managers decided to get rid of the existing bureaucratic controls and the hierarchical rigidity that facilitated downward communication while preventing communication between departments. They also recognized the need to make customer service a priority for middle managers, front-line managers, and employees, which required a cultural shift from a monopoly mindset to a competitive mindset. Moreover, they wanted the entire staff to have the training and motivation to participate in problem solving and improvements to support the new goals and mission. Finally, they wanted to change employee attitudes by reinstilling a sense of pride in working for Telefónica. Yet change could not be so rapid that it would alienate the staff, nor so slow that it would have little effect on performance.

In consultation with middle management, Alicante's senior managers drafted a plan outlining the basic processes, technologies, training, and communications that would be needed to achieve specific annual goals for service improvements. They gathered broad-based support by circulating this document among lower-level managers and employees for comments and suggestions. Nearly all of these changes were incorporated into the plan, which was submitted to headquarters for review in the context of the overall corporate strategy. After the plan was communicated to all employees of Telefónica, the Alicante division began implementation.

First, senior and middle managers formed teams to study the division's current practices, identify tasks that did not deliver customer value, and design new processes and procedures to achieve the service goals. Second, they set up a training program to educate the entire staff about the goals, the new practices, and the standards to be used in measuring progress. Third, as milestones were achieved, management put together a best-practices manual to document and share the most effective procedures within the corporation.

Once this plan was underway, the next step for Alicante's top managers was to design an educational program to build the management skills, teamwork capabilities, and commitment of middle managers. In designing this program, they asked middle managers to describe the factors that might cause Telefónica to succeed or fail in a competitive environment. They also asked middle managers about their self-image as leaders and the characteristics that Telefónica managers would need to help fulfill the company's goals and mission. The middle managers identified advanced technology, new services, and responsiveness to customer needs as main factors in making Telefónica more customer oriented in a competitive market. They noted that failure could occur as a result of poor planning, lack of workforce commitment, excessive hierarchical levels, and inability to adapt to market realities.

Further, the managers felt like they were under intense pressure from senior managers as well as from the need to follow rules and achieve results. They believed they were bearing the burden of moving the company forward, yet lacked sufficient connections with each other; and they did not have an opportunity to effectively plan because they were constantly solving unexpected problems. According to the middle managers, the ideal Telefónica manager would be strongly committed to the firm, open to change, a team player, ready to listen, an inspiration to others, and willing and able to delegate to others. Alicante's senior managers asked the managers what skills and knowledge they needed to become an ideal manager. The managers responded by asking for training in goal setting, teamwork, organizational skills, problem solving, motivation, and communication.

Not only did the managers receive training in these six areas, Alicante's executives invited them to participate in drawing up a year-long development plan to spread what they called the "new management style" through better communication, training, employee empowerment, and processes. For example, the unit began issuing a monthly newsletter to reinforce customer-oriented goals and values. It also distributed a quarterly report to educate all employees about new services available for customers and publicly recognized employees and managers who proactively came up with creative solutions to problems. At the end of the year, all managers were surveyed to assess their progress in changing their management style. The response showed that 75 percent were satisfied with the results; 92 percent said that top management had provided the support needed for managers to make the change.

Alicante's progress prompted Telefónica to extend this change process throughout the company as it made the transition to a deregulated, private company (with a small ownership stake retained by the Spanish government). Soon the internal changes prompted external changes appreciated by customers. Telefónica reduced rates, offered 24-hour customer service, installed new phone lines within 24 hours, and cut the length of service outages by 20 percent. It also moved aggressively into South American markets, becoming one of the continent's largest providers of wireless services, and added new technologies and services like internet access. To reward performance, management offered stock options to the entire workforce.

Today, Telefónica is a global leader in telecommunications with one of the most advanced telecom networks in the world. Telefónica competes head-to-head with Vodafone in Spain for wireless communication supremacy, and is currently the leader in providing fixed-line telecommunications as well as internet services. Reported revenue from operations in 2006 was in excess of 52 billion euros (CDN$81 billion), reflecting an increase of 41.5 percent over 2005 revenue.

Questions

1. Analyze the process that Telefónica's management used to create change within the company.
2. What factors reduced the amount of resistance to this change by managers and employees?
3. Once the change was successful in Alicante, what problems might management have faced in instituting this change throughout Telefónica?
4. Would you consider Telefónica a learning organization? Explain your answer.
5. Could other highly bureaucratic companies change their cultures and processes as radically as Telefónica did, or were there particular circumstances here that would limit this kind of change to this specific organization?

Sources: "Internet Access in Spain: Industry Profile," *Datamonitor*, June 2007; "Fixed Link Telecoms in Spain: Industry Profile," *Datamonitor*, June 2006; "Wireless Telecommunication Services in Spain: Industry Profile," *Datamonitor*, June 2006; Telefonica Financial Report, www.telefonica.es (accessed September 14, 2007); J. Bright, "The Rain in Spain Falls Mainly on New Entrants," *Total Telecom Magazine*, October 2003, pp. 16–18; "Spain: Phone Company to Sell Shares," *New York Times*, September 3, 2002, p. C8; S. Kapner, "Telecom Giants Retrench in Europe," *New York Times*, July 26, 2002, p. W1; E. Claver, J. L. Gasco, J. Llopis, and R. Gonzalez, "The Strategic Process of a Cultural Change to Implement Total Quality Management: A Case Study," *Total Quality Management*, July 2001, pp. 469+; S. Baker, "Takeover Escape Artist," *BusinessWeek*, April 10, 2000, pp. 20+; E. Claver, J. L. Gasco, J. Llopis, and E. A. Lopez, "Analysis of a Cultural Change in a Spanish Telecommunications Firm," *Business Process Management Journal* 6, no. 4 (2000): pp. 342+; P. Heywood, "Spain's PTT Shapes Up," *Data* Communications, August 1998, p. 36.

Part Four integrative case

HR Restructuring—The Coca-Cola & Dabur Way

By A. Mukund

> *"We had grown but we hadn't structured our growth."*
>
> —*Dabur sources in 1998.*

> *"Three major strands have emerged in Coke's mistakes. It never managed its infrastructure, it never managed its crate of 10 brands, and it never managed its people."*
>
> —*Businessworld in 2000.*

The Leader Humbled

It all began with Coca-Cola India's (Coca-Cola) realization that something was surely amiss. Four CEOs within seven years, arch-rival Pepsi surging ahead, heavy employee exodus, and negative media reports indicated that the leader had gone wrong big time. The problems eventually led to Coca-Cola reporting a huge loss of US$52 million in 1999, attributed largely to the heavy investments in India and Japan. Coca-Cola had spent Rs 1500 crore for acquiring bottlers, who were paid Rs 8 per case as against the normal Rs 3 (1 crore = 10 million). The losses were also attributed to management extravagance such as accommodations in farmhouses for executives and foreign trips for bottlers.

Following the loss, Coca-Cola had to write off its assets in India worth US$405 million in 2000. Apart from the mounting losses, the write-off was necessitated by Coca-Cola's overestimation of volumes in the Indian market. This assumption was based on the expected reduction in excise duties, which did not happen, which further delayed the company's break-even targets by some more years.

Changes were required to be put in place soon. With a renewed focus and energy, Coca-Cola took various measures to come out of the mess it had landed itself in.

The Sleeping Giant Awakes

In 1998, the 114-year-old ayurvedic and pharmaceutical products major Dabur found itself at the crossroads. In fiscal 1998, 75 percent of Dabur's turnover had come from fast-moving consumer goods (FMCGs). Buoyed by this, the Burman family (promoters and owners of a majority stake in Dabur) formulated a new vision in 1999 with an aim to make Dabur India's best FMCG company by 2004. In the same year, Dabur revealed plans to increase the group turnover to Rs 20 billion by the year 2003–2004.

To achieve the goal, Dabur benchmarked itself against other FMCG majors, such as Nestlé, Colgate-Palmolive, and P&G. Dabur found itself significantly lacking in some critical areas. While Dabur's price-to-earnings (P/E) ratio[1] was less than 24, for most of the others it was more than 40. The net working capital of Dabur was a whopping Rs 2.2 billion whereas it was less than half of this figure for the others. There were other indicators of an inherently inefficient organization, including Dabur's operating profit margins of 12 percent as compared to Colgate's 16 percent and P&G's 18 percent. Even the return on net worth was around 24 percent for Dabur as against HLL's 52 percent and Colgate's 34 percent.

The Burmans realized that major changes were needed on all organizational fronts. However, media reports questioned the company's capability to shake off its family-oriented work culture.

Restructuring the Mess the Coca-Cola Way

In 1999, following the merger of Coca-Cola's four bottling operations (Hindustan Coca-Cola Bottling North West, Hindustan Coca-Cola Bottling South West, Bharat Coca-Cola North East, and Bharat Coca-Cola South

East), human resources issues gained significance at the company. Two new companies, Coca-Cola India, the corporate and marketing office, and Coca-Cola Beverages were the result of the merger. The merger brought with it over 10,000 employees to Coca-Cola, doubling the number of employees it had in 1998.

Coca-Cola had to go in for a massive restructuring exercise focusing on the company's human resources to ensure a smooth acceptance of the merger. The first task was to put in place a new organizational structure that vested profit and loss accounting at the area level, by renaming each plant-in-charge as a profit center head. The country was divided into six regions as against the initial three, based on consumer preferences. Each region had a separate head (Regional General Manager), who had the regional functional managers reporting to him. All the regional general managers reported to VP (Operations) Sanjiv Gupta, who reported directly to CEO Alexander Von Bohr (Bohr). The 37 bottling plants of Coca-Cola, on an average six in each region, had an Area General Manager as the head, vested with profit-center responsibility. All the functional heads reported to the area general manager. Coca-Cola also declared VRS at the bottling plants, which was used by about 1,100 employees.

The merger carried forward employees from different work cultures and work value systems. This move toward regionalization caused dilution of several central jobs, with as many as 1,500 employees retiring at the bottling plants. The new line of control strengthened entry- and middle-level jobs at the regions and downgraded many at the center. This led to unrest among the employees and about 40 junior- and middle-level managers and some senior personnel including Ravi Deoi, Head (Capability Services) and Sunil Sawhney, Head (Northern Operations), left the company.

As part of the restructuring plan, Coca-Cola made a strategy-level decision to turn itself into a people-driven company. The company introduced a detailed career planning system for over 530 managers in the new set-up. The system included talent development meetings at regional and functional levels, following which recommendations were made to the HR Council.

The council then approved and implemented the process through a central HR team. Coca-Cola also decided that the regional general managers would meet the top management twice a year to identify fast-track people and train them for more responsible positions. Efficient management trainees were to be sent to the overseas office for a three-week internship. To inculcate a feeling of belonging, the company gave flowers and cards on the birthdays of the employees and major festivals.

Coca-Cola also undertook a cost-reduction drive on the human resources front. Many executives who were provided accommodation in farmhouses were asked to shift to less expensive apartments. The company also decided not to buy or hire new cars, as it felt that the existing fleet of cars was not being used efficiently. In the drive for "optimum utilization of existing resources," Coca-Cola decided against buying a Rs 50 crore property in Gurgaon and it also surrendered a substantial part of its rented office space in Gurgaon, near Delhi. Company officials felt that this was justified because a lot of officials had moved out of the Delhi headquarters due to the localization. Moreover, this was necessitated by the resignations and sackings. Salaries were also restructured as part of this cost-reduction drive. Coca-Cola began benchmarking itself with other major Indian companies, whereas it was offering pay packages in line with international standards. Coca-Cola also realigned some jobs based on the employee's talent and potential.

However, the company's problems were far from over. In March 2000, Coca-Cola received reports of wrongdoing in its North India operations. The company decided to take action after the summer season.[2] In July 2000, Coca-Cola appointed Arthur Andersen to inspect the accounts of the North India operations for a fee of Rs 1 crore. The team inspected all offices, godowns, bottling plants, and depots of Jammu, Kanpur, Najibabbad, Varanasi, and Jaipur. The findings revealed that the North Indian team had violated discounting terms and the credit policy, apart from being unfair in cash dealings. The team was giving discounts that were five times higher than those given in the other regions of the country. There were also unexplained cancellations and re-appointments of dealerships.

In light of the above findings by Arthur Andersen's team, Coca-Cola carried out a performance appraisal exercise for 560 managers. This led to resignations en masse. Around 40 managers resigned between July and November 2000. Coca-Cola also sacked some employees in its drive to overhaul the HR functioning. By January 2001, the company had shed 70 managers, accounting for 12 percent of the management. Bohr said, "I had to make some tough decisions because the buck stops here. We needed to weed out certain practices. That's an important message sent out—that we'll take action if we can't work on principles of integrity. The investigation was the right thing. The business is healthier now."

However, media reports revealed a different side of the picture altogether. The managers who had quit voiced their thoughts vociferously against Coca-Cola, claiming that the whole performance appraisal exercise was farcical and that the management had already decided on the people to get rid of. They termed the issue as Coca-Cola's "witch-hunt" in India. Reacting to the management's comments regarding discount norm violations, one former employee commented, "All discounts were cleared by the top management. They always pushed for higher volumes and said profitability is not your problem. So, we got volumes at whatever costs. Nobody told us this was an unacceptable practice." This seemed to be substantiated by the fact that in the Delhi region, which consumed only 6,000–8,000 cases per day, the sales team received a target of pushing 25,000 cases a day. It was commented that this was done so as to "make things look good" when the company sent its financials to the global headquarters. It was also reported that the performance appraisals and the subsequent dismissals were carried out in a very "inhuman" and "blunt" manner.

Worried by such adverse comments about the company, Alexander decided to take steps to ensure a smooth relationship with the new people in the company. He personally met the finance heads in every territory and made the company's credit policy clear to them. Coca-Cola also standardized the discounting limits and best practices irrespective of market compulsions. The company launched a major IT initiative as well, to make the functioning of the entire organization transparent at the touch of a button. Things seemed to have stabilized to some extent after this. Justifying the decision to let go of certain personnel, Alexander said, "We don't mind those quitting who were just okay. We told them where they could hope to be, based on their performance. Some who have left may not have had a good career with Coke."

The Dabur Way

Dabur's restructuring efforts began in April 1997, when the company hired consultants McKinsey & Co., at a cost of Rs 80 million. McKinsey's threefold recommendations were: to concentrate on a few businesses; to improve the supply chain and procurement processes; and to reorganize the appraisal and compensation systems. Following these recommendations, many radical changes were introduced. The most important was the Burmans' decision to take a back seat. The day-to-day management was handed over to a group of professional managers for the first time in Dabur's history, while the promoters confined themselves to strategic decision making.

Dabur decided to revamp the organizational structure and appoint a CEO to head the management. All business unit heads and functional heads were to report directly to the CEO.

In November 1998, Dabur appointed Ninu Khanna as the CEO. The appointment was the first incident of

Exhibit 1

Organizational Structure (Before Restructuring)

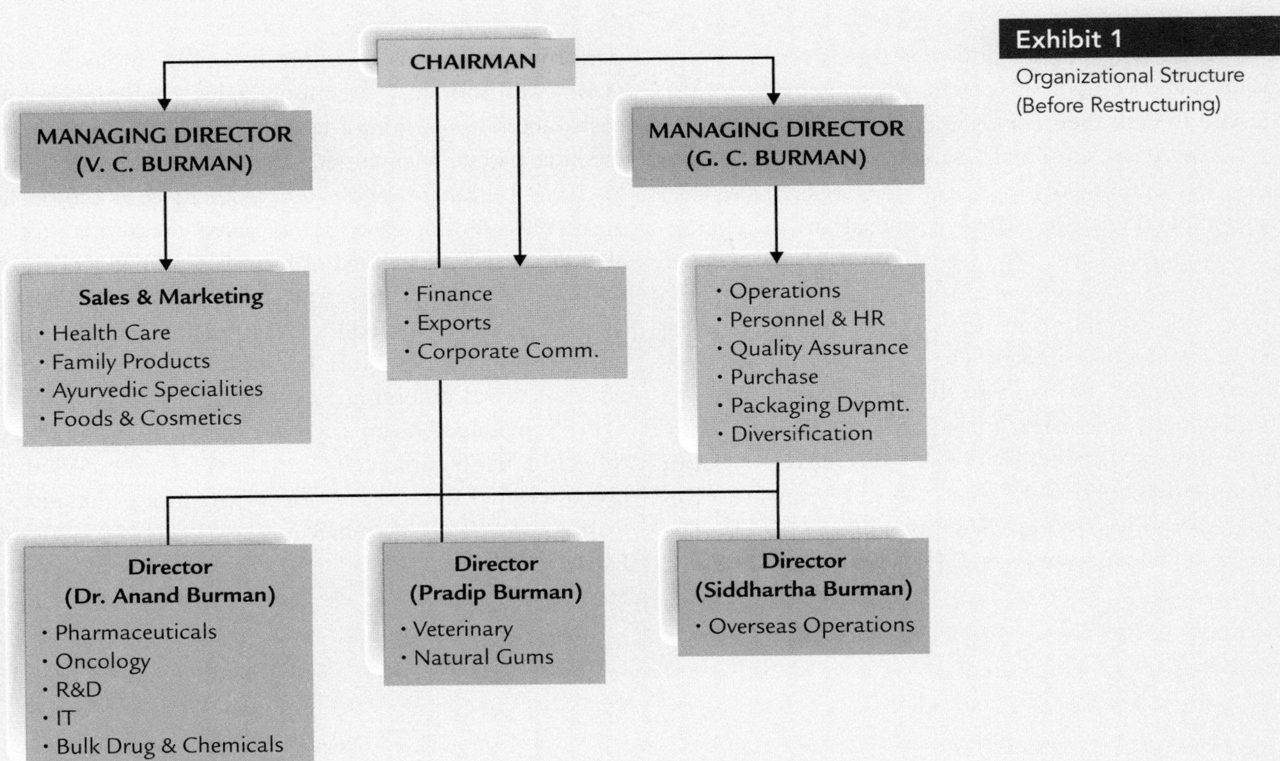

Source: Company Annual Report.

an outside professional being appointed after the restructuring was put in place. Ninu Khanna, who had previously worked with Procter & Gamble and Colgate-Palmolive, was roped in to give Dabur the much-needed FMCG focus. Dabur had also appointed Cadbury India's Deepak Sethi as Vice President–Sales and Marketing–Health Care Products division; Godrej Pilsbury's Ravi Sivaraman as Vice President–Finance, and ABB's Yogi Sriram as Vice President–HRD.

Dabur made performance appraisals more objective by including many more measurable criteria. Concepts such as customer satisfaction, increased sales and reduced costs, cycle-time efficiency, return on investment, and shareholder value were all introduced as yardsticks for performance appraisals. Harish Tandon, general manager, HR, Dabur, remarked, "Now Dabur is working toward making compensation more performance oriented, and the performance evaluation system is being worked on. Today, performance in terms of target achievement is the main factor followed by other criteria such as sincerity and longevity of service." The focus of appraisals thus shifted to what a person had achieved, as much as on what he or she was capable of.

Dabur's employee-friendly initiatives included annual sales conferences at places like Mauritius and Kathmandu. These conferences, attended by over 100 sales executives of the company, combined both "work-and-play" aspects for better employee morale and performance. Dabur also gave cash incentives to junior-level sales officers and representatives upon successful achievement of targets. Employees were also allowed to club their leaves and enjoy a vacation.

To increase employee satisfaction levels, Dabur identified certain key performance areas (KPAs) for each employee. Performance appraisal and compensation planning were now based on KPAs. Employee training was also given a renewed focus. To help employees communicate effectively with each other and for better dissemination of news and information, Dabur brought out a quarterly newsletter, "Contact." The interactive newsletter worked as a two-way communication channel between the employees. Dabur also commissioned consultants Nobel & Hewitt to formulate an Employee Stock Option Plan (ESOP). The scheme, effective from fiscal 2000, was initially reserved for very senior personnel. Dabur planned to extend the scheme throughout the organization in the future.

The After Effects

Both Coca-Cola and Dabur had to accept the fact that a major change on the human resources front was inevitable, although the changes in the two were necessitated by radically different circumstances. More importantly, the restructuring seemed to have been extremely beneficial for them. Besides improved morale and reduced employee turnover figures, the strategic, structural, and operational changes on the HR front led to an overall "feel-good" sentiment in the companies.

In 1999, Coca-Cola reported an increase in case-volume of 9 percent after restructuring. Volumes increased by 14 percent and market share increased by 1 percent after the regionalization drive. The company's improving prospects were further reflected with the 18 percent rise in sales in the second quarter of 2000. However, in spite of all the moves, Coca-Cola's workforce was still large. Given the scale of its investments, the future was far from "smooth sailing" for the company. With the newfound focus and a streamlined human resources front, Coca-Cola hoped to break even by the end of fiscal 2001.

At Dabur, with the restructuring moves in place by the late 1990s, the company's future business prospects were termed excellent by analysts. The new structure, the performance-oriented compensation, and the new performance appraisal system increased employee efficiency and morale. The annual sales conferences and cash incentives to junior-level sales officers helped in meeting higher sales targets. Dabur's sales increased to Rs 10.37 billion in 1990–2000 from Rs 9.14 billion in 1998–1999—an increase of 13.5 percent. Dabur's profits also increased by 53 percent from 501 million to Rs 770 million. The year was a milestone in Dabur's history as the company crossed the Rs 10 billion mark in sales turnover for the first time. Even in early 2001, Dabur's efforts toward emerging as a competitive and professionally managed company were yet to be completely reflected in its financials. Analysts commented that given its track record and the restructuring initiatives, Dabur was all set to reach its target of becoming an FMCG major.

Exhibit 2

Organizational Structure (After Restructuring)

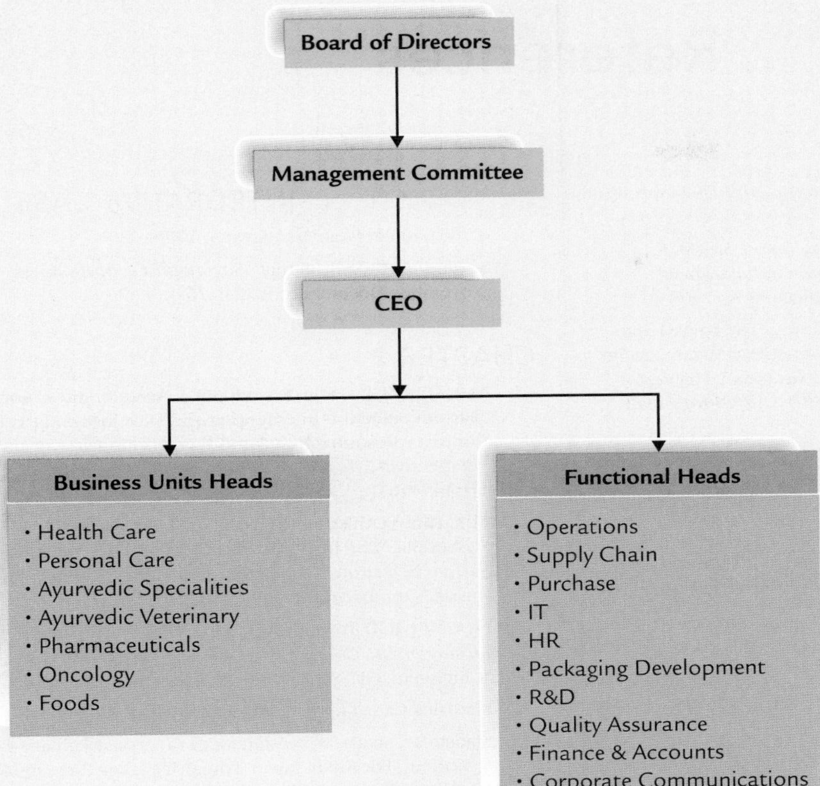

Source: Company Annual Report.

References

CHAPTER 1

1. G. Davenport (trans. 1976). *Herakleitos and Diogenes.* Pt. 1, Fragment 23.
2. M.A. Hitt, R. D. Ireland, and R. E. Hoskisson, *Strategic Management: Competitiveness and Globalization* (Cincinnati, OH: Southwestern Publishing Co., 2003).
3. A. S. DeNisi, M.A. Hitt, and S. E. Jackson, "The Knowledge-Based Approach to Sustainable Competitive Advantage," in S. E. Jackson, M.A. Hitt, and A. S. DeNisi (eds.), *Managing Knowledge for Sustained Competitive Advantage* (San Francisco, CA: Jossey-Bass, 2003).
4. D.A. Sirmon, M.A. Hitt, and R. D. Ireland, "Managing the Firm's Resources in Order to Achieve and Maintain a Competitive Advantage." Paper presented at the Academy of Management Conference, August, 2003.
5. Team Fredericton, www.teamfredericton.com (accessed July 7, 2007); RBC Financial Group, www.rbc.com (accessed July 7, 2007).
6. Radical Entertainment, www.radical.ca (accessed July 8, 2007).
7. R. E. Mueller, "The Inadvertent Entrepreneur: Accepting Change Is a Shortcut to Success," February 15, 1995, *Success* 47, no. 11 (2000), p. 22.
8. S. Martin, "Thoughts on a Long Ride: An Interview with Ray Fowler," *Monitor on Psychology* 33, no. 11 (2002), p. 37.
9. Z. Olijnyk, "Richard Currie," *Canadian Business*, April 11, 2005, pp. 78-79; S. Howland, "Richard Currie Named Chancellor of the University of New Brunswick," www.unb.ca (accessed July 7, 2007).
10. Roots Canada, www.roots.ca (accessed July 8, 2007).
11. McDonald's, www.mcdonalds.com/countries/index.html (accessed July 5, 2007); IAmFood.com, www.iamfood.com (accessed July 5, 2007); A Japanese Exchange Program, japan.lisd.k12.mi.us (accessed July 5, 2007).
12. M.A. Hitt, R. D. Ireland, S. M. Camp, and D. S. Sexton, *Strategic Entrepreneurship: Creating a New Mindset* (Oxford, UK: Blackwell Publishing, 2000).
13. R. McGrath and I. MacMillan, *The Entrepreneurial Mindset* (Boston: Harvard Business School Press, 2000).
14. R. D. Ireland, M.A. Hitt, and D. G. Sirmon, "A Model of Strategic Entrepreneurship: The Construct and Its Dimensions," *Journal of Management* 29: 963-989.
15. Ibid.
16. S. J. Carroll and D. J. Gillen, "Are Classical Management Functions Useful in Describing Managerial Jobs and Behavior?" *Academy of Management Review* 12 (1987), pp. 39-51.
17. H. Mintzberg, "The Manager's Job: Folklore and Fact," *Harvard Business Review* 5, no. 4 (1975), pp. 49-61.
18. R. Stewart, "A Model for Understanding Managerial Jobs and Behavior," *Academy of Management Review* 7 (1982), pp. 7-13.
19. C. Gagné, "The Other RIM Guy," *Canadian Business,* December 5, 2005, www.canadianbusiness.com (accessed July 7, 2007); Research in Motion, www.rim.net (accessed July 7, 2007).
20. M.W. McCall and M. M. Lombardo, *Off the Track* (Greensboro, NC: Center for Creative Leadership, 1983).
21. L.W. Porter and L. E. McKibbin, *Management Education and Development: Drift or Thrust into the 21st Century?* (New York: McGraw-Hill, 1988).

INTRODUCTORY INTEGRATIVE CASE

1. *Time* Online, Monday, August 9, 1999.
2. V. Pawsey, "Rule Britannia," *European Legal Business* November/December 2002, p. 26.

CHAPTER 2

1. M.A. Hitt, M.T. Dacin, E. Levitas, J.-L. Arregle, and A. Borza, "Partner Selection in Emerging and Developed Market Contexts: Resource-Based and Organizational Learning Perspectives," *Academy of Management Journal* 43 (2000), pp. 449-467.
2. M.A. Hitt, D. Ahlstrom, M.T. Dacin, E. Levitas, and L. Svobodina, "The Institutional Effects on Strategic Alliance Partner Selection in Transition Economies: China Versus Russia," *Organization Science*, in press.
3. M.A. Hitt, R. D. Ireland, and R. E. Hoskisson, *Strategic Management: Competitiveness and Globalization* (Cincinnati, OH: South-Western Publishing Co., 2005).
4. Statistics Canada, www.statcan.ca (accessed January 4, 2007).
5. Statistics Canada, www.statcan.ca (accessed January 4, 2007); S. Moffett, "For Ailing Japan, Longevity Takes Bite Out of Economy," *Wall Street Journal*, February 11, 2003, p. 1.
6. A. Sagie and Z. Aycan, "A Cross-Cultural Analysis of Participative Decision-Making in Organizations," *Human Relations* 56, no. 4 (2003), pp. 453-473.
7. S. P. Seithi and P. Steidlmeier, "The Evolution of Business' Role in Society," *Business and Society Review* 94 (Summer 1995), pp. 9-12; L. L. Martins, K.A. Eddleston, and J. F. Veiga, "Moderators of the Relationship between Work-Family Conflict and Career Satisfaction," *Academy of Management Journal* 45, no. 2 (2002), pp. 399-409.
8. S. Gelsi, "Class for the Masses," *Brandweek* 38, no. 13 (1997), pp. 23-33.
9. J. Lawrence, "P&G Losing Ground in Product Innovation," *Advertising Age* 64, no. 48 (1993), p. 44; J. Lawrence, "It's Diaper D-Day with P&G Rollout," *Advertising Age* 64, no. 39 (1993), pp. 1, 60; J. Lawrence, "Kimberly, P&G Rev Up to Market Latest Twist in Disposable Diapers," *Advertising Age* 63, no. 26 (1992), pp. 3, 51.
10. B. Johnstone, "Rainbow Warriors," *Far Eastern Economic Review* 147, no. 7 (1999), p. 90.
11. Wal-Mart Annual Report, "2006 Annual Report: Building Smiles."
12. Personal communication with Dofasco senior management, 2003.
13. "Glass Fibers Make Smokestacks Cleaner," *Machine Design* 67, no. 18 (1995), p. 123.
14. CBC News, "Flaherty Imposes New Tax on Income Trusts," November 1, 2006, www.cbcnews.ca (accessed January 4, 2007).
15. Government of Canada, "Making Sense Out of Dollars 2005-2006," Government of Canada, www.admfincs.forces.gc.ca (accessed December 21, 2006).
16. A. K. Sundaram and J. S. Black, *The International Business Environment* (Upper Saddle River, NJ: Prentice Hall, 1995).
17. J. E. Oxley and B. Yeung, "E-Commerce Readiness: Institutional Environment and International Competitiveness," *Journal of*

International Business Studies 32, no. 4 (2001), pp. 705–723.

18. C.M. Lau, D. K. Tse, and N. Zhou, "Institutional Forces and Organizational Culture in China: Effects on Change Schemas, Firm Commitment and Job Satisfaction," *Journal of International Business Studies* 33, no. 3 (2002), pp. 533–550.
19. M. Porter, *Competitive Strategy: Techniques for Analyzing Industries and Competitors* (New York: Free Press, 1980).
20. S. Slater and E. Olson, "A Fresh Look at Industry and Market Analysis," *Business Horizons* 45, no. 1 (2002), pp. 15–22.
21. N. Stein, "The De Beers Story: A New Cut on an Old Monopoly," *Fortune*, February 19, 2001, pp. 186–206; "Glass with Attitude," *Economist* 345, no. 8048 (1997), pp. 113–115.
22. R. D. Ireland, M. A. Hitt, and D. Vaidyanath, "Alliance Management as a Source of Competitive Advantage," *Journal of Management* 28, no. 3 (2002), pp. 413–446; B. R. Koka and J. E. Prescott, "Strategic Alliances as Social Capital: A Multidimensional View," *Strategic Management Journal* 23, no. 9 (2002), pp. 795–816; D. Rigby and C. Zook, "Open-Market Innovation," *Harvard Business Review* 80, no. 10 (2002), pp. 80–89.
23. Canadian Auto Workers Union, www.caw.ca (accessed December 24, 2006).
24. D. Martin, "Gilded and Gelded: Hard-Won Lessons from the PR Wars," *Harvard Business Review* 81, no. 10 (2003), pp. 44–54; P. Christmann and G. Taylor, "Globalization and the Environment: Strategies for International Voluntary Environmental Initiatives," *Academy of Management Executive* 16, no. 3 (2002), pp. 121–135.
25. Greenpeace, www.greenpeace.org (accessed March 1, 2003).
26. Research in Motion, www.rim.net.on (accessed January 4, 2007).
27. Peak of the Market, www.peakmarket.com (accessed on January 4, 2007).
28. S. Finkelstein and A. C. Mooney, "Not the Usual Suspects: How to Use Board Process to Make Boards Better," *Academy of Management Executive* 17, no. 2 (2003), pp. 101–113; J. M. Ivancevich, T. N. Duening, J. A. Gilbert, and R. Konopaske, "Deterring White-Collar Crime," *Academy of Management Executive* 17, no. 2 (2003), pp. 114–127.
29. www.swlearning.com (accessed January 4, 2007).
30. Natalie Williams, "Why It's (Still) Good to Be WestJet," *Strategy*, November 2005, www.strategymag.com (accessed January 4, 2007).
31. CBC News, "In Depth Report on SARS," www.cbc.ca (accessed January 4, 2007).

CHAPTER 3

1. "Transparency International Corruption Perceptions Index 2005," Transparency International, 2005, www.transparency.org (accessed November 4, 2006).
2. M. A. Hitt, R. D. Ireland, and R. E. Hoskisson, *Strategic Management: Competitiveness and Globalization* (Cincinnati, OH: South-Western Publishing, 2005).
3. Canadian Imperial Bank of Commerce was charged with and later settled on aiding and abetting the Enron Corporation in accounting fraud. CBC News, "CIBC Agrees to $80 Million US Penalty over Enron Accounting Fraud," December 23, 2003, www.cbcnews.ca (accessed January 13, 2007). Nortel Networks was found to have committed accounting fraud to get out of the slump following the dot.com bubble burst. CBC News, "In Depth: Canada's Tech Giant," December 1, 2006, www.cbcnews.ca (accessed January 13, 2007).
4. PricewaterhouseCoopers, "Global Economics Crime Survey 2005," www.pwc.com (accessed October 24, 2006).
5. CBC News, "WestJet Countersues Air Canada," June 30, 2004, www.cbcnews.ca (accessed October 25, 2006); CBC News "Air Canada Seeking $220 Million in Suit Against WestJet," July 22, 2004, www.cbcnews.ca (accessed October 25, 2006); CBC News, "Air Canada Settles Spying Lawsuit," May 30, 2006, www.cbcnews.ca (accessed October 25, 2006).
6. D. Peterson, A. Rhoads, and B. C. Vaught, "Ethical Beliefs of Business Professionals: A Study of Gender, Age, and External Factors," *Journal of Business Ethics* 31, no. 3 (2001), pp. 225–232; E. Marnburg, "The Questionable Use of Moral Development Theory in Studies of Business Ethics: Discussion and Empirical Findings," *Journal of Business Ethics* 32, no. 4 (2001), pp. 275–283.
7. J. Tsalikis, B. Seaton, and P. Tomaras, "A New Perspective on Cross-Cultural Ethical Evaluations: The Use of Conjoint Analysis," *Journal of Business Ethics* 35, no. 4 (2002), pp. 281–292; L. Thorne and S. B. Saunders, "The Socio-Cultural Embeddedness of Individuals' Ethical Reasoning in Organizations (Cross-Cultural Ethics)," *Journal of Business Ethics* 35, no. 1 (2002), pp. 1–14; J. B. Hamilton III and S. B. Knouse, "Multinational Enterprise Decision Principles for Dealing with Cross-Cultural Ethical Conflicts," *Journal of Business Ethics* 31, no. 1 (2001), pp. 77–94; C. J. Robertson and W. F. Crittenden, "Mapping Moral Philosophies: Strategic Implications for Multinational Firms," *Strategic Management Journal* 24, no. 4 (2003), pp. 385–392.
8. A. J. Dubinsky, M. A. Jolson, M. Kotabe, and C. U. Lim, "A Cross-National Investigation of Industrial Salespeople's Ethical Perceptions," *Journal of International Business Studies*, Fourth Quarter 1991, pp. 651–669; J. K. Giacobbe-Miller, D. J. Miller, W. Zhang, and V. I. Victorov, "Country and Organization-Level Adaptation to Foreign Workplace Ideologies: A Comparative Study of Distributive Justice Values in China, Russia and the United States," *Journal of International Business Studies* 34, no. 4 (2003), pp. 389–406.
9. A. Kolk and R. Van Tulder, "Ethics in International Business," *Journal of World Business,* February 2004, pp. 49–61; J. Tsui and C. Windsor, "Some Cross-Cultural Evidence of Ethical Reasoning," *Journal of Business Ethics* 31 (2001), pp. 143–150; C. J. Robertson and W. F. Crittenden, "Mapping Moral Philosophies: Strategic Implications for Multinational Firms," *Strategic Management Journal* 24, no. 4 (2003), pp. 385–392.
10. J. S. Black, H. B. Gregersen, and M. E. Mendenhall, *Global Assignments* (San Francisco, CA: Jossey-Bass, 1992).
11. J. Rawls, *A Theory of Justice* (Cambridge, MA: Harvard University Press, 1971); J. Greenberg, "A Taxonomy of Organizational Justice Theories," *Academy of Management Review* 12 (1987), pp. 9–22; Giacobbe-Miller et al., "Country and Organization-Level Adaptation to Foreign Workplace Ideologies," pp. 389–406.
12. T. Donaldson and T. W. Dunfee, "Toward a Unified Conception of Business Ethics," *Academy of Management Review* 19 (1994), pp. 252–284; J. A. Colquitt, R. A. Noe, and C. L. Jackson, "Justice in Teams: Antecedents and Consequences of Procedural Justice Climate," *Personnel Psychology* 55, no. 1 (2002), pp. 83–109.
13. R. Pillai, E. Williams, and J. J. Tan, "Are the Scales Tipped in Favor of Procedural or Distributive Justice? An Investigation of the U.S., India, Germany, and Hong Kong (China)," *International Journal of Conflict Management* 12, no. 4 (2001), pp. 312–332; D. Fields, M. Pang, and C. Chiu, "Distributive and Procedural Justice as Predictors of Employee Outcomes in Hong Kong," *Journal of Organizational Behavior* 21, no. 5 (2000), pp. 547–562; Y. Cohen-Charash and P. E. Spector, "The Role of Justice in Organizations: A Meta-analysis," *Organizational Behavior and Human Decision Processes* 86, no. 2 (2001), pp. 278–321; J. A. Colquitt, D. E. Conlon, M. J. Wesson, C. Porter, and Y. K. Ng,

"Justice at the Millennium: A Meta-analytic Review of 25 Years of Organizational Justice Research," *Journal of Applied Psychology* 86, no. 3 (2001), pp. 424–445; S. L. Blader, C. C. Chang, and T. R. Tyler, "Procedural Justice and Retaliation in Organizations: Comparing Cross-Nationally the Importance of Fair Group Processes," *International Journal of Conflict Management* 12, no. 4 (2001), pp. 295–311; J. Greenberg, "Who Stole the Money, and When? Individual and Situational Determinants of Employee Theft," *Organizational Behavior and Human Decision Processes* 89, no. 1 (2002), pp. 985–1003; B. J. Tepper and E. C. Taylor, "Relationships among Supervisors' and Subordinates' Procedural Justice Perceptions and Organizational Citizenship Behaviors," *Academy of Management Journal* 46, no. 1 (2003), pp. 97–105.

14. J. Dietz, S. L. Robinson, R. Folger, R. A. Baron, and M. Schultz, "The Impact of Community Violence and an Organization's Procedural Justice Climate on Workplace Aggression," *Academy of Management Journal* 46, no. 3 (2003), pp. 317–326.
15. J. M. Jones, "Ethical Decision Making by Individuals in Organizations: An Issue-Contingent Model," *Academy of Management Review* 16 (1991), pp. 366–395.
16. J. Paolillo and S. J. Vitell, "An Empirical Investigation of the Influence of Selected Personal, Organizational and Moral Intensity Factors on Ethical Decision Making," *Journal of Business Ethics* 35, no. 1 (2002), pp. 65–74.
17. Ibid.
18. Mothers Against Drunk Driving, www.madd.ca (accessed October 25, 2006).
19. A. Chia and L. S. Mee, "The Effects of Issue Characteristics on the Recognition of Moral Issues," *Journal of Business Ethics* 27 (2000), pp. 255–269.
20. D. Carlson, K. M. Kacmar, and L. L. Wadsworth, "The Impact of Moral Intensity Dimensions on Ethical Decision Making: Assessing the Relevance of Orientation," *Journal of Managerial Issues* 14, no. 1 (2002), pp. 15–30; J. M. Dukerich, M. J. Waller, E. George, and G. P. Huber, "Moral Intensity and Managerial Problem Solving," *Journal of Business Ethics* 24, no. 1 (2000), pp. 29–38.
21. P. S. Ring and A. Van De Ven, "Developmental Process of Cooperative Interorganizational Relationships," *Academy of Management Review* 19 (1994), pp. 90–118.
22. "World's Most Respected Companies 2005," Finfacts Ireland, www.finfacts.com (accessed October 25, 2006).
23. D. Robin, M. Giallourakis, F. R. David, and T. Moritz, "A Different Look at Codes of Ethics," *Business Horizons*, January–February 1989, pp. 66–73.
24. C. C. Langlois and B. B. Schlegelmilch, "Do Corporate Codes of Ethics Reflect National Character? Evidence from Europe and the United States," *Journal of International Business Studies*, Fourth Quarter 1991, pp. 519–539.
25. G. Wood, "A Cross-Cultural Comparison of the Content of Codes of Ethics: USA, Canada, and Australia," *Journal of Business Ethics* 25, no. 4 (2000), pp. 281–298.
26. Robin et al., "A Different Look at Codes of Ethics."
27. Ibid.
28. L. P. White and L. W. Lam, "A Proposed Infrastructural Model for the Establishment of Organizational Ethical Systems," *Journal of Business Ethics* 28, no. 1 (2000), pp. 35–42; S. A. DiPiazza, "Ethics in Action," *Executive Excellence* 19, no. 1 (2002), pp. 15–16.
29. C. Verschoor, "To Talk about Ethics, We Must Train on Ethics," *Strategic Finance* 81, no. 10 (2000), pp. 24, 26; T. Donaldson, "Editor's Comments: Taking Ethics Seriously—A Mission Now More Possible," *Academy of Management Review* 28, no. 3 (2003), pp. 363–366
30. "Stronger Than Ever," *LM Today*, January 2004, p. 8; K. Shelton, "The Dilbert Dilemma," *Executive Excellence*, November 2003, p. 2; R. Carey, "The Ethics Challenge," *Successful Meetings* 47, no. 5 (1998), pp. 57–58.
31. M. McClearn, "A Snitch in Time," *Canadian Business*, June 18, 2004, pp. 60–67; M. P. Miceli and J. P. Near, *Blowing the Whistle* (Lexington, MA: Lexington Books, 1992).
32. Miceli and Near, *Blowing the Whistle*.
33. "Pearson Four Suspended: Whistle-Blowing Jazz Mechanics Cited Safety Concerns," *Hamilton Spectator*, www.hamiltonspectator.com (accessed August 25, 2006).
34. M. P. Miceli and J. P. Near, "The Relationships among Beliefs, Organizational Position, and Whistle-Blowing Status: A Discriminant Analysis," *Academy of Management Journal* 27 (1984), pp. 687–705.
35. BDO Dunwoody/Chamber Weekly CEO/Business Leader Poll by Compas Inc., "Whistleblowing," *Financial Post*, May 30, 2005, www.bdo.ca (accessed October 24, 2006).
36. Miceli and Near, *Blowing the Whistle*.
37. R. Sims and J. Brinkmann, "Leaders as Moral Role Models: The Case of John Gutfreund at Salomon Brothers," *Journal of Business Ethics* 35, no. 4 (2002), pp. 327–339; R. Galford and A. S. Drapeau, "The Enemies of Trust," *Harvard Business Review* 81, no. 2 (2003), pp. 88–95; L. R. Offermann and A. B. Malamut, "When Leaders Harass: The Impact of Target Perceptions of Organizational Leadership and Climate on Harassment Reporting and Outcomes," *Journal of Applied Psychology* 87, no. 5 (2002), pp. 885–893.
38. "Transparency International Corruption Perceptions Index 2001," Transparency International, 2001, www.transparency.org (accessed October 25, 2006); "Transparency International Corruption Perceptions Index 2005," Transparency International, 2005, www.transparency.org (accessed October 25, 2006).
39. M. Friedman, "The Social Responsibility of Business Is to Increase Its Profits," *New York Magazine*, September 13, 1970, pp. 32–33, 122, 126.
40. A. Smith, *An Inquiry into the Nature and Causes of the Wealth of Nations*, ed. R. H. Campbell and A. S. Skinner (Oxford, UK: Clarendon Press, 1976).
41. Friedman, "The Social Responsibility of Business Is to Increase Its Profits," p. 32; C. E. Bagley, "The Ethical Leader's Decision Tree," *Harvard Business Review* 81, no. 2 (2003), pp. 18–19.
42. M. Rothman, "Nightmare at Kaufman's," *Business Ethics*, November–December 1994, pp. 15–16.
43. J. Joha, L. Serbet, and A. Sundaram, "Cross-Border Liability of Multinational Enterprises: Border Taxes and Capital Structure," *Financial Management*, Winter 1991, pp. 54–67; C. Handy, "What's a Business For?" *Harvard Business Review* 80, no. 12 (2002), pp. 49–55.
44. Joha, Serbet, and Sundaram, "Cross-Border Liability of Multinational Enterprises: Border Taxes and Capital Structure."
45. B. Ruf, K. Muralidhar, R. Brown, J. Janney, and K. Paul, "An Empirical Investigation of the Relationship between Change in Corporate Social Performance and Financial Performance: A Stakeholder Theory Perspective," *Journal of Business Ethics* 32, no. 2 (2001), pp. 143–156; C. Sanchez, "Value Shift: Why Companies Must Merge Social and Financial Imperatives to Achieve Superior Performance," *Academy of Management Executive* 17, no. 2 (2003), pp. 142–144.

CHAPTER 4

1. A. K. Gupta and V. G. Govindarajan, "Converting Global Presence into Global Competitive Advantage," *Academy of Management Executive* 15, no. 2 (2001), pp. 45–57.

2. M. A. Hitt, R. D. Ireland, and R. E. Hoskisson, *Strategic Management: Competitiveness and Globalization* (Cincinnati, OH: South-Western Publishing, 2005).
3. M. Koza and A. Lewin, "Managing Partnerships and Strategic Alliances: Raising the Odds of Success," *European Management Journal* 18, no. 2 (2000), pp. 146–151; M. Peng, "The Resource-Based View and International Business," *Journal of Management* 27 (2001), pp. 803–829.
4. E. Schein, "Coming to a New Awareness of Organizational Culture," *Sloan Management Review*, Winter (1984), pp. 3–16.
5. A. L. Kroeber and C. Kluckhohn, *Culture: A Critical Review of Concepts and Definitions* (Cambridge, MA: Harvard University Press, 1952).
6. Schein, "Coming to a New Awareness of Organizational Culture."
7. A. L. Wilkins and W. Ouchi, "Efficient Cultures: Exploring the Relationship between Culture and Organizational Effectiveness," *Administrative Science Quarterly* 28 (1983), pp. 468–481; K. A. Wade-Benzoni, T. Okumura, J. M. Brett, and D. A. Moore, "Cognitions and Behavior in Asymmetric Social Dilemmas: A Comparison of Two Cultures," *Journal of Applied Psychology* 87, no. 1 (2002), pp. 87–95; M. J. Gelfand, M. Higgins, L. H. Nishii, and J. L. Raver, "Culture and Egocentric Perceptions of Fairness in Conflict and Negotiation," *Journal of Applied Psychology* 87, no. 5 (2002), pp. 833–845.
8. J. E. Dutton and S. Jackson, "Categorizing Strategic Issues: Links to Organizational Actions," *Academy of Management Review* 12 (1987), pp. 76–90; Gelfand et al., "Culture and Egocentric Perceptions of Fairness in Conflict and Negotiation."
9. R. G. Eord and R. J. Foti, "Schema Theories, Information Processing, and Organizational Behavior," *The Thinking Organization,* ed. H. P. Simes and D. A. Gioia (San Francisco: Jossey-Bass, 1986); Wilkins and Ouchi, "Efficient Cultures"; Gelfand et al., "Culture and Egocentric Perceptions of Fairness in Conflict and Negotiation."
10. D. Druckman, "Nationalism, Patriotism, and Group Loyalty: A Social-Psychological Perspective," *Merson International Studies Review* (1994), pp. 43–68.
11. Statistics Canada, www.statscan.ca (accessed July 2, 2007); A. Belanger and E. C. Malenfant, "Ethnocultural Diversity in Canada: Prospects for 2017," *Canadian Social Trends*, Winter 2005, pp. 18–21.
12. A. Zuckerman, "Strong Corporate Cultures and Firm Performance: Are There Tradeoffs?" *Academy of Management Executive* 16, no. 4 (2002), pp. 158–160; N. Nohria, W. Joyce, and B. Robertson, "What Really Works," *Harvard Business Review* 81, no. 7 (2003), pp. 42–52.
13. Schein, "Coming to a New Awareness of Organizational Culture."
14. Ibid.
15. D. McGregor, *The Human Side of Enterprise* (New York: McGraw-Hill, 1960).
16. R. J. House, "Cultural Influences on Leaders and Organizations," in *Advances in Global Leadership*, vol. 1, pp. 171–233 (JAI Press, 1999); J. C. Kennedy, "Leadership in Malaysia: Traditional Values, International Outlook," *Academy of Management Executive* 16, no. 3 (2002), pp. 15–26.
17. J. Foley, "Hewlett-Packard Reaches a Cultural Crossroads," *Information Week*, July 23, 2001, p. 47.
18. G. Hofstede, *Culture's Consequences* (Beverly Hills, CA: Sage, 1980); G. Hofstede, "Dimensions Do Not Exist: A Reply to Brendan McSweeney," *Human Relations* 55, no. 11 (2002), pp. 1355–1631; A. Sagie and Z. Aycan, "A Cross-Cultural Analysis of Participative Decision-Making in Organizations," *Human Relations* 56, no. 4 (2003), pp. 453–473; D. Williamson, "Foreword from a Critique of Hofstede's Model of National Culture," *Human Relations* 55, no. 11 (2002), pp. 1373–1395.
19. B. McSweeney, "Hofstede's Model of National Cultural Differences and Their Consequences: A Triumph of Faith—A Failure of Analysis," *Human Relations* 55, no. 1 (2002), pp. 89–118.
20. J. Rokeach, *The Nature of Human Values* (New York: Free Press, 1973); T. Lenartowicz and J. P. Johnson, "A Cross-National Assessment of the Values of Latin American Managers: Contrasting Hues or Shades of Gray?" *Journal of International Business Studies* 34, no. 3 (2003), p. 266.
21. Kenny Zhang, "Recognizing the Canadian Diaspora," *Canada Asia* 41, March 2006.
22. N. Adler, *International Dimensions of Organizational Behavior* (Boston, MA: Kent Publishing, 1994).
23. "Delphi Makes Another Investment in China," *Automotive News*, December 22, 2003, p. 25; M. Loden and J. Rosener, *Workforce America! Managing Employee Diversity as a Vital Resource* (New York: Irwin, 1991).
24. Adler, *International Dimensions of Organizational Behavior*.
25. M. K. Kozan, "Subcultures and Conflict Management Style," *Management International Review* 42, no. 1 (2002), pp. 89–105; C. M. Byles, "Brazil's Distinct Subcultures: Do They Matter to Business Performance?" *Academy of Management Executive* 16, no. 2 (2002), pp. 165–166.
26. S. Black and H. Gregersen, *Leading Strategic Change* (Upper Saddle River, NJ: Prentice Hall, 2002); M. Cortsjens and J. Merrihue, "Optimal Marketing," *Harvard Business Review* 81, no. 10 (2003), pp. 114–122.
27. R. Yerema, "Every Company Likes to Say They Treat Their Staff like Valued Assets. Here Are the Very Best That Are Actually Doing It." *Maclean's,* October 13, 2006, www.mcleans.ca (accessed July 2, 2007).
28. V. Pothukuchi, F. Damanpour, J. Choi, C. Chen, C. Chao, and S. H. Park, "National and Organizational Culture Differences and International Joint Venture Performance," *Journal of International Business Studies* 33, no. 2 (2002), pp. 243–265; C. Fey and P. W. Beamish, "Organizational Climate Similarity and Performance: International Joint Ventures in Russia," *Organization Studies* 22, no. 5 (2001), pp. 853–882; W. M. Danis and A. Parkhe, "Hungarian-Western Partnerships: A Grounded Theoretical Model of Integration Processes and Outcomes," *Journal of International Business Studies* 33, no. 3 (2002), pp. 423–455.
29. Personal communication, 1998.
30. V. D. Miller and F. M. Jablin, "Information Seeking during Organizational Entry: Influences, Tactics, and a Model of the Process," *Academy of Management Review* 16 (1991), pp. 92–120; R. M. Kramer, "When Paranoia Makes Sense," *Harvard Business Review* 80, no. 7 (2002), pp. 62–69; R. Galford and A. S. Drapeau, "The Enemies of Trust," *Harvard Business Review* 81, no. 2 (2003), pp. 88–95.
31. E. Hall, *Beyond Culture* (Garden City, NY: Doubleday, 1976).
32. S. A. Zahra, R. D. Ireland, and M. A. Hitt, "International Expansion by New Venture Firms: International Diversity, Mode of Entry, Technological Learning and Performance," *Academy of Management Journal* 43 (2000), pp. 925–950.
33. S. Black, H. Gregersen, M. Mendenhall, and L. Stroh, *Globalizing People through International Assignments* (Reading, MA: Addison-Wesley, 1999); J. L. Graham and N. M. Lam, "The Chinese Negotiation," *Harvard Business Review* 81, no. 10 (2003), pp. 82–91.
34. M. Murphy and K. M. Davey, "Ambiguity, Ambivalence and Indifference in Organizational Values," *Human Resource Management Journal* 12, no. 1 (2002), pp. 17–32; Galford and Drapeau, "The Enemies of Trust."
35. Black et al., *Globalizing People through International Assignments*; Graham and Lam, "The Chinese Negotiation."

PART 1 INTEGRATIVE CASE

1. He was with sales and marketing at AT&T.

CHAPTER 5

1. H. A. Simon, *The New Science of Management Decisions* (Upper Saddle River, NJ: Prentice Hall, 1977).
2. G. R. Ungson and D. N. Braunstein, *Decision Making* (Boston: Kent, 1982).
3. D. Miller and M. Star, *The Structure of Human Decisions* (Upper Saddle River, NJ: Prentice Hall, 1967).
4. Simon, *The New Science of Management Decisions*; J. Parking, "Organizational Decision Making and the Project Manager," *International Journal of Project Management* 14, no. 5 (1996), pp. 257–263.
5. H. A. Simon, *Administrative Behavior* (New York: The Free Press, 1957).
6. H. A. Simon, G. B. Dantzig, R. Hogarth, C. R. Plott, H. Raiffa, T. C. Schelling, K. A. Shepsle, R. Thaler, A. Tversky, and S. Winter, "Decision Making and Problem Solving," *Interfaces* 17, no. 5 (1987), pp. 11–31.
7. H. A. Simon, "Rational Decision Making in Business Organizations," *The American Economic Review* 69, no. 4 (1979), pp. 493–513.
8. J. G. March and H. A. Simon, *Organizations* (New York: Wiley, 1958) pp. 140–141.
9. F. Phillips, "The Distortion of Criteria after Decision Making," *Organizational Behavior and Human Decision Processes* 88, no. 2 (2002), pp. 768–784.
10. P. Soelberg, "Unprogrammed Decision Making," *Industrial Management* (1967), pp. 19–29; D. Cray, G. H. Haines, and G. R. Mallory, "Programmed Strategic Decision Making," *British Journal of Management* 5, no. 3 (1994), pp. 191–204.
11. G. Loveman, "Diamonds in the Data Mine," *Harvard Business Review* 81, no. 5 (2003), pp. 109–113; E. Bonabeau, "Don't Trust Your Gut," *Harvard Business Review* 81, no. 5 (2003), pp. 116–123.
12. J. Johnson, et al. "Vigilant and Hypervigilant Decision Making," *Journal of Applied Psychology* 82, no. 4, pp. 614–622; E. Bonabeau, "Don't Trust Your Gut."
13. T. R. Mitchell and J. R. Larson, *People in Organizations* (New York: McGraw-Hill, 1987).
14. M. Bazerman, *Judgment in Managerial Decision Making,* Sixth Edition (New York: Wiley, 2005).
15. "Divorces," *The Daily*, March 9, 2005, Statistics Canada, www.statcan.ca (accessed January 7, 2007).
16. B. M. Staw, "The Escalation of Commitment to a Course of Action," *Academy of Management Review* 6 (1981), pp. 577–587; G. Whyte, A. M. Saks, and S. Hook, "When Success Breeds Failure," *Journal of Organizational Behavior* 18, no. 5 (1997), pp. 415–432; D. R. Bobocel and J. P. Meyer, "Escalating Commitment to a Failing Course of Action," *Journal of Applied Psychology* 79, no. 3 (1994), pp. 360–363; J. Ross and M. Straw, "Organizational Escalation and Exit: Lessons from the Shoreham Nuclear Power Plant," *Academy of Management Journal* 36, no. 4 (1993), pp. 701–732.
17. Staw, "The Escalation of Commitment to a Course of Action," p. 578.
18. G. McNamara, H. Moon, and P. Bromiley, "Banking on Commitment: Intended and Unintended Consequences of an Organization's Attempt to Attenuate Escalation of Commitment," *Academy of Management Journal* 45, no. 2 (2002), pp. 443–452.
19. E. Harrison, *The Managerial Decision Making Process* (Boston: Houghton Mifflin, 1975); J. R. Hough and M. A. White, "Environmental Dynamism and Strategic Decision-Making Rationality: An Examination at the Decision Level," *Strategic Management Journal* 24, no. 5 (2003), pp. 481–489.
20. R. Ebert and T. Mitchell, *Organizational Decision Processes: Concepts and Analysis* (New York: Crane, Russak, 1975).
21. S. S. K. Lam, X. P. Chen, and J. Schaubroeck, "Participative Decision Making and Employee Performance in Different Cultures: The Moderating Effects of Allocentrism/ Idiocentrism and Efficacy," *Academy of Management Journal* 45, no. 5 (2002), pp. 905–914.
22. N. Margulies and J. S. Black, "Perspectives on the Implementation of Participative Approaches," *Human Resource Management* 26, no. 3 (1987), pp. 385–412.
23. J. S. Black and H. B. Gregersen, "Participative Decision Making: An Integration of Multiple Perspectives," *Human Relations* 50 (1997), pp. 859–878.
24. V. Vroom and P. Yetton, *Leadership and Decision Making* (Pittsburgh: University of Pittsburgh Press, 1973); V. Vroom and A. Jago, *The New Leadership: Managing Participation in Organizations* (Upper Saddle River, NJ: Prentice Hall, 1988).
25. R. Hof, "Why Once-Ambitious Computer Firm Quit," *Peninsula Times Tribune*, September 29, 1984, p. B1.
26. K. Eisenhardt and L. J. Bourgeois, "Making Fast Strategic Decisions in High-Velocity Environments," *Academy of Management Journal* 32 (1989), pp. 543–576; Hough and White, "Environmental Dynamism and Strategic Decision-Making Rationality."
27. I. Janis, *Victims of Groupthink* (Boston: Houghton Mifflin, 1972); M. E. Turner and A. R. Pratkamis, "Twenty-Five Years of Groupthink Theory and Research: Lessons from the Evaluation of a Theory," *Organizational Behavior and Human Decision Processes* 73, nos. 2, 3 (1998), pp. 105–115; J. K. Esser, "Alive and Well after 25 Years: A Review of Groupthink Research," *Organizational Behavior and Human Decision Processes* 73, nos. 2, 3 (1998), pp. 116–141.
28. S. Schulz-Hardt, M. Jochims, and D. Frey, "Productive Conflict in Group Decision Making: Genuine and Contrived Dissent as Strategies to Counteract Biased Information Seeking," *Organizational Behavior and Human Decision Processes* 88, no. 2 (2002), pp. 563–586.
29. J. S. Black, H. B. Gregersen, and M. E. Mendenhall, *Global Assignments* (San Francisco: Jossey-Bass, 1992).
30. K. Y. Ng and L. Van Dyne, "Individualism-Collectivism as a Boundary Condition for Effectiveness of Minority Influence in Decision Making," *Organizational Behavior and Human Decision Processes* 84, no. 2 (2001), pp. 198–225.
31. C. Schwenk and H. Thomas, "Formulating the Mess: The Role of Decision Aids in Problem Formulation," *Omega* 11 (1983), pp. 239–252.
32. A. Van De Ven and A. Delbecq, "The Effectiveness of Nominal, Delphi, and Interacting Group Decision-Making Processes," *Academy of Management Journal* 17 (1974), pp. 607–626.
33. B. B. Baltes, M. W. Dickson, M. P. Sherman, C. C. Bauer, and J. S. LaGanke "Computer-Mediated Communication and Group Decision Making: A Meta-Analysis," *Organizational Behavior and Human Decision Processes* 87, no. 1 (2002), pp. 156–179; Bonabeau, "Don't Trust Your Gut."
34. J. Levere, "Low-Fare Airline Aims to Build on Attitude and Hostility," *New York Times*, December 1, 2000.
35. Baltes et al., "Computer-Mediated Communication and Group Decision Making: A Meta-Analysis."

CHAPTER 6

1. M. A. Hitt, L. Bierman, K. Shimizu, and R. Kochhar, "Direct and Moderating Effects of Human Capital on Strategy and Performance in Human Service Firms: A Resource-Based

Perspective," *Academy of Management Journal* 44 (2001), pp. 13–28.

2. M.A. Hitt, R. D. Ireland, and R. E. Hoskisson, *Strategic Management: Competitiveness and Globalization* (Cincinnati, OH: South-Western Publishing Co., 2005).
3. J.A. Pearce, K. Robbins, and R. Robinson, "The Impact of Grand Planning Formality on Financial Performance," *Strategic Management Journal*, March–April 1987, pp. 125–134.
4. R. Van Wingerden, "Managing Change," *International Journal of Technology Management* 21, nos. 5/6 (2001), pp. 487–495.
5. D. Rheault, "Freshening Up Strategic Planning: More than Fill-in the Blanks," *Journal of Business Strategy* 24, no. 6 (2003), pp. 33–38; B. Walters, I. Clarke, S. Henley, and M. Shandiz, "Strategic Decision-Making among Top Executives in Acute-Care Hospitals," *Health Marketing Quarterly* 19, no. 1 (2001), pp. 43–59.
6. J. Camillus, "Reinventing Strategic Planning," *Strategy and Leadership*, May–June 1996, pp. 6–12; L. Olson, "Strategic Lessons," *Association Management* 44, no. 6 (1992), pp. 35–39; J. J. Murphy, "Identifying Strategic Issues," *Long Range Planning* 22, no. 2 (1989), pp. 101–105.
7. "The Times that Try Men's Souls," *Journal of Business Strategy*, January/February 1999, p. 4.
8. C. Ngamkroeckjoti and L. Johri, "Management of Environmental Scanning Processes in Large Companies in Thailand," *Business Process Management Journal* 6, no. 4 (2000), p. 331; M. A. Peteraf and M. E. Bergen, "Scanning Dynamic Competitive Landscapes: A Market-Based and Resource-Based Framework," *Strategic Management Journal* 24, no. 10 (2003), pp. 1027–1041; M. D. Watkins and M. H. Bazerman, "Predictable Surprises: The Disasters You Should Have Seen Coming," *Harvard Business Review* 81, no. 3 (2003), pp. 72–80.
9. C. Jain, "Forecasting Process at Wyeth Ayerst Global Pharmaceuticals," *Journal of Business Forecasting Methods & Systems*, Winter 2001/2002, pp. 3–6; E. A. Boyd and I. O. Bilegan, "Revenue Management and E-commerce," *Management Science* 49, no. 10 (2003), pp. 1363–1386; M. Spann and B. Skiera, "Internet-Based Virtual Stock Markets for Business Forecasting," *Management Science* 49, no. 10 (2003), pp. 1310–1326.
10. G. Vastag, S. Kerekes, and D. Rondinelli, "Evolution of Corporate Environmental Management Approaches: A Framework and Application," *International Journal of Production Economics* 43, nos. 2/3 (1996), pp. 193–211; B. Boyd and J. Faulk, "Executive Scanning and Perceived Uncertainty: A Multidimensional Model," *Journal of Management* 22, no. 1 (1996), pp. 1–21; D. Lane and R. Maxfield, "Strategy under Complexity: Fostering Generative Relationships," *Long Range Planning* 29, no. 2 (1996), pp. 215–231; Watkins and Bazerman, "Predictable Surprises."
11. Michael J. Hileman, "Future Operations Planning Will Measure Plan Achievability," *Oil and Gas Journal*, March 18, 2002, pp. 84–87; L. Rouleau and F. Segui, "Strategy and Organization Theories: Common Forms of Discourse," *Journal of Management Studies* 32, no. 1 (1995), pp. 101–117.
12. "Benchmarking Strategies," *Brand Strategy*, December/January 2004, p. 3; A. Kouzmin, E. Loffler, H. Klages, and N. Korac-Kakabadse, "Benchmarking and Performance Measurement in Public Sectors: Toward Learning for Agency Effectiveness," *International Journal of Public Sector Management* 12, no. 2 (1999), p. 121; R. Bergstrom, "Benchmarking," *Automotive Production* 108, no. 9 (1996), pp. 63–65; J. Vezmar, "Competitive Intelligence at Xerox," *Competitive Intelligence Review* 1, no. 3 (1996), pp. 15–19; David J. Smith, Y. Hwang, B. K. W. Pei, and J. H. Reneau, "The Performance Effects of Congruence between Product Competitive Strategies and Purchasing Management Design," *Management Science* 48, no. 7 (2002), pp. 866–885.
13. C. Barker, C. Thunhurst, and D. Ross, "An Approach to Setting Priorities in Health Planning," *Journal of Management in Medicine* 12, no. 2 (1998), p. 92; A. Bhid, "The Questions Every Entrepreneur Must Ask," *Harvard Business Review* 74, no. 6, pp. 120–130.
14. E. A. Locke and G. P. Latham, *A Theory of Goal Setting and Task Performance* (Upper Saddle River, NJ: Prentice Hall, 1990); A. Lederer and A. Mendelow, "Information Systems Planning and the Challenge of Shifting Priorities," *Information and Management* 24, no. 6 (1993), pp. 319–328.
15. D. Federa and T. Miller, "Capital Allocation Techniques," *Topics in Health Care Financing* 19, no. 1 (1992), pp. 68–78.
16. F. Sunderland and M. Kane, "Measuring Productivity on a Value Basis," *National Productivity Review* 15, no. 4 (1996), pp. 57–76; S. D. Pugh, J. Dietz, J. W. Wiley, and S. M. Brooks, "Driving Service Effectiveness through Employee–Customer Linkages," *Academy of Management Executive* 16, no. 4 (2002), pp. 73–84.
17. J. P. Morgan, "EVA Measures Competitiveness," *Purchasing*, September 4, 2003, pp.16–18; K. Lehn and A. Makhiji, "EVA and MVA: As Performance Measures and Signals for Strategic Change," *Strategy and Leadership* 24, no. 3 (1996), pp. 34–38; R. Kaplan and D. Norton, "Strategic Learning and the Balanced Score Card," *Strategy and Leadership* 24, no. 5 (1996), pp. 18–24; I. Morgan and J. Rao, "Aligning Service Strategy through Super-Measure Management," *Academy of Management Executive* 16, no. 4 (2002), pp. 121–131; L. Aiman-Smith and S. G. Green, "Implementing New Manufacturing Technology: The Related Effects of Technology Characteristics and User Learning Activities," *Academy of Management Journal* 45, no. 2 (2002), pp. 421–430; L. G. Love, R. L. Priem, and G. T. Lumpkin, "Explicitly Articulated Strategy and Firm Performance under Alternative Levels of Centralization," *Journal of Management* 28, no. 5 (2002), pp. 611–627.
18. Bhid, "The Questions Every Entrepreneur Must Ask."
19. L. Rivenbark and M. Frost, "Strategic Planning for Success," *HR Magazine*, July 2003, pp. 120–121; L. Kempfer, "Planning for Success," *Computer-Aided Engineering* 13, no. 4 (1994), pp. 18–22; P. Sweet, "A Planner's Best Friend?" *Accountancy* 113, no. 1206 (1994), pp. 56–58; J. Rakos, "The Virtues of the Time-Bar Chart," *Computing Canada* 18, no. 17 (1992), p. 32.
20. S. Mallya, S. Banerjee, and W. G. Bistline, "A Decision Support System for Production/Distribution Planning in Continuous Manufacturing," *Decision Sciences*, Summer 2001, pp. 545–556; P. Cowling and M. Johansson, "Using Real Time Information for Effective Dynamic Scheduling," *European Journal of Operational Research*, June 1, 2002, pp. 230–244; S. G. Taylor, "Finite Capacity Scheduling Alternatives," *Production and Inventory Management Journal*, Third Quarter 2001, pp. 70–74.
21. F. Harrison, "Strategic Control at the CEO Level," *Long Range Planning* 24, no. 6 (1991), pp. 78–87; A. Di Primo, "When Turnaround Management Works," *Journal of Business Strategy* 9, no. 1 (1988), pp. 61–64.
22. W. R. Guffey and B. J. Nienhaus, "Determinants of Employee Support for the Strategic Plan of a Business Unit," *S.A.M. Advanced Management Journal*, Spring 2002, pp. 23–30.
23. M. Ishman, "Commitment–Compliance: Counterforces in Implementing Production and Inventory Control Systems," *Production and Inventory Management Journal* 36, no. 1 (1995), pp. 33–37.
24. J. White, "Almost Nothing New under the Sun: Why the Work of Budgeting Remains Incremental," *Public Budgeting and Finance* 14, no. 1 (1994), pp. 113–134.
25. W. Llewellyn, "A Review of the Budgeting System," *Assessment* 1, no. 5 (1994), pp. 47–50.

26. L. Bogomolny, "Melting the Glass Ceiling," *Canadian Business*, 79, no. 9, pp. 11–12.
27. H. Weihrich, *Management Excellence: Productivity through MBO* (New York: McGraw-Hill, 1985); H. Levinson, "Management by Whose Objectives?" *Harvard Business Review* 81, no. 1 (2003), pp. 107–116.
28. G. P. Latham and L. M. Saari, "The Effects of Holding Goal Difficulty Constant on Assigned and Participatively Set Goals," *Academy of Management Journal*, March 1979, pp. 163–168; A. Drach-Zahavy and M. Erez, "Challenge versus Threat Effects on the Goal-Performance Relationship," *Organizational Behavior and Human Decision Processes* 88, no. 2 (2002), pp. 667–682.
29. M. Erez, P. C. Earley, and C. L. Hulin, "The Impact of Participation on Goal Acceptance and Performance: A Two-Step Model," *Academy of Management Journal*, March 1985, pp. 50–66.
30. Locke and Latham, *A Theory of Goal Setting and Task Performance*.
31. P. Mali, *MBO Update* (New York: Wiley, 1986); J. M. Jackman and M. H. Strober, "Fear of Feedback," *Harvard Business Review* 81, no. 4 (2003), pp. 101–107; R. E. Kaplan, "Know Your Strengths," *Harvard Business Review* 80, no. 3 (2002), pp. 20–21.

CHAPTER 7

1. M. A. Hitt, R. D. Ireland, and R. E. Hoskisson, *Strategic Management: Competitiveness and Globalization* (Cincinnati, OH: South-Western Publishing Company, 2005).
2. M. E. Porter, "Towards a Dynamic Theory of Strategy," *Strategic Management Journal* 12 (1991), pp. 95–117; R. Durand, "Competitive Advantages Exist: A Critique of Powell," *Strategic Management Journal* 23, no. 9 (2002), pp. 867–872; D. Miller, "An Asymmetry-Based View of Advantage: Towards an Attainable Sustainability," *Strategic Management Journal* 24, no. 10 (2003), pp. 961–976; N. G. Carr, "IT Doesn't Matter," *Harvard Business Review* 81, no. 5 (2003), pp. 41–49; R. R. Wiggins and T. W. Ruefli, "Sustained Competitive Advantage: Temporal Dynamics and the Incidence and Persistence of Superior Economic Performance," *Organization Science* 13, no. 1 (2002), pp. 82–105.
3. B. Wernerfelt, "A Resource-Based View of the Firm," *Strategic Management Journal*, September–October 1984, p. 171; J. Barney, "Firm Resources and Sustained Competitive Advantage," *Journal of Management* 17, no. 1 (1991), pp. 99–120; R. Amit and P. J. H. Schoemaker, "Strategic Assets and Organizational Rent," *Strategic Management Journal*, January 1993, p. 3; K. R. Conner, "A Historical Comparison of Resource-Based Theory and Five Schools of Thought within Industrial Organization Economics: Do We Have a New Theory of the Firm?" *Journal of Management*, March 1991, p. 121; M. E. Porter, *Competitive Advantage* (New York: Free Press, 1986).
4. D. Bunch and R. Smiley, "Who Deters Entry?" *Review of Economics and Statistics* 74, no. 3 (1992), pp. 509–521; D. M. De Carolis, "Competencies and Imitability in the Pharmaceutical Industry: An Analysis of Their Relationship with Firm Performance," *Journal of Management* 29, no. 1 (2003), pp. 27–78.
5. S. K. McEvily and B. Chakravarthy, "The Persistence of Knowledge-Based Advantage: An Empirical Test for Product Performance and Technological Knowledge," *Strategic Management Journal* 23, no. 4 (2002), pp. 285–305; A. Andal and G. S. Yip, "Advantage Amnesia," *Business Strategy Review* 13, no. 1 (2002), pp. 1–11; A. Afuah, "Mapping Technological Capabilities into Product Markets and Competitive Advantage: The Case of Cholesterol Drugs," *Strategic Management Journal* 23, no. 2 (2002), pp. 171–181.
6. D. J. Collis and C. A Montgomery, "Competing on Resources: Strategy in the 1990s," *Harvard Business Review*, July–August 1995, pp. 119–128.
7. G. Hamel and C. K. Prahalad, *Competing for the Future* (Boston, MA: Harvard Business Press, 1994).
8. R. Emmerich, "What's in a Vision?" *CMA Management* 75, no. 8 (2001), p. 10.
9. O. Harari, "Three Vital Little Words," *Management Review* 84, no. 11 (1995), pp. 25–27; G. Hamel and C. K. Prahalad, "Strategy as Stretch and Leverage," *Harvard Business Review* 71, no. 2 (1993), pp. 75–84.
10. J. Collins and J. Porras, "Building Your Company's Vision," *Harvard Business Review* 74, no. 5 (1996), pp. 65–77; C. Rarick and J. Vitton, "Mission Statements Make Sense," *Journal of Business Strategy* 16, no. 1 (1995), pp. 11–12.
11. J. Younker, "Organization Direction-Setting," *Tapping the Network Journal* 2, no. 2 (1991), pp. 20–23; W. Schiemann, "Strategy, Culture, Communication: Three Keys to Success," *Executive Excellence* 6, no. 8 (1989), pp. 11–12.
12. Porter, *Competitive Advantage*; M. Partridge and L. Perren, "Developing Strategic Direction: Can Generic Strategies Help?" *Management Accounting—London* 72, no. 5 (1994), pp. 28–29.
13. K. Andrews, *The Concept of Corporate Strategy* (Homewood, IL: Richard Irwin, 1971); J. A. Aragon-Correa and S. Sharma, "A Contingent Resource-Based View of Proactive Corporate Environmental Strategy," *Academy of Management Review* 28, no. 1 (2003), pp. 71–88; S. A. Zahra and A. P. Nielsen, "Sources of Capabilities, Integration and Technology Commercialization," *Strategic Management Journal* 23, no. 5 (2002), pp. 377–398; V. K. Garg, B. K. Walters, and R. L. Priem, "Chief Executive Scanning Emphases, Environmental Dynamism, and Manufacturing Firm Performance," *Strategic Management Journal* 24, no. 8 (2003), pp. 725–744.
14. E. Zajac, M. S. Kraatz, and R. Bresser, "Modeling the Dynamics of Strategic Fit: A Normative Approach to Strategic Change," *Strategic Management Journal* 21, no. 4 (2000), pp. 429–453.
15. Porter, *Competitive Advantage*.
16. R. W. Oliver, "Is It the Beginning, or Is It the End?" *Journal of Business Strategy* 22, no. 1 (2001), pp. 7–9.
17. Porter, *Competitive Advantage*.
18. D. Bovet and J. Martha, "From Supply Chain to Value Net," *Journal of Business Strategy* 21, no. 4 (2000), pp. 24–28; D. Bovet and J. Martha, "Value Nets: Reinventing the Rusty Supply Chain for Competitive Advantage," *Strategy and Leadership* 28, no. 4 (2000), pp. 21–26; A. Afuah, "How Much Do Your Competitors' Capabilities Matter in the Face of Technological Change?" *Strategic Management Journal* 21, no. 3 (2000), pp. 387–404.
19. Afuah, "How Much Do Your Competitors' Capabilities Matter"; J. Stock, T. Speh, and H. Shear, "Many Happy (Product) Returns," *Harvard Business Review* 80, no. 7 (2002), pp. 16–17; J. Hagel III, "Leveraged Growth: Expanding Sales without Sacrificing Profits," *Harvard Business Review* 80, no. 10 (2002), pp. 68–77; V. Shankar and B. L. Bayus, "Network Effects and Competition: An Empirical Analysis of the Home Video Game Industry," *Strategic Management Journal* 24, no. 4 (2003), pp. 375–384.
20. J. Barney, "Looking Inside for Competitive Advantage," *Academy of Management Executive* 9, no. 4 (1995), pp. 49–61; W. Dyer and V. Sighn, "The Relational View: Cooperative Strategy and Sources of Interorganizational Competitive Advantage," *Academy of Management Review* 23, no. 4 (October 1998), pp. 660–679; B. S. Teng and J. L. Cummings, "Trade-Offs in Managing Resources and Capabilities," *Academy of Management Executive* 16, no. 2 (2002), pp. 81–91; M. A. Peteraf and M. E. Bergen, "Scanning Dynamic Competitive Landscapes: A Market-Based and

Resource-Based Framework," *Strategic Management Journal* 24, no. 10 (2003), pp. 1027–1041; A. M. Rugman and A. Verbeke, "Edith Penrose's Contribution to the Resource-Based View of Strategic Management," *Strategic Management Journal* 23, no. 8 (2002), pp. 769–780; D. G. Hoopes, T. L. Madsen, and G. Walker, "Guest Editors' Introduction to the Special Issue: Why Is There a Resource-Based View? Toward a Theory of Competitive Heterogeneity," *Strategic Management Journal* 24, no. 10 (2003), pp. 889–902.

21. K. Eisenhardt and J. Martin, "Dynamic Capabilities: What Are They?" *Strategic Management Journal* 21, nos. 10/11 (2000), pp. 1105–1121; R. Adner and C. E. Helfat, "Corporate Effects and Dynamic Managerial Capabilities," *Strategic Management Journal* 24, no. 10 (2003), pp. 1011–1025.
22. C. K. Prahalad and G. Hamel, "The Core Competence of the Corporation," *Harvard Business Review* 68, no. 3 (1990), pp. 79–91.
23. M. Gort and R. Wall, "The Evolution of Technologies and Investment in Innovation," *Economic Journal* 96, no. 383 (1986), pp. 741–757.
24. C. Anderson and C. Zeithaml, "Stage of the Product Life Cycle, Business Strategy, and Business Performance," *Academy of Management Journal* 27, no. 1 (1984), pp. 5–24; P. Ghemawat, "The Forgotten Strategy," *Harvard Business Review* 81, no. 11 (2003), pp. 76–84; M. Zeng and P. J. Williamson, "The Hidden Dragons," *Harvard Business Review* 81, no. 10 (2003), pp. 92–99; G. P. Cachon and P. T. Barker, "Competition and Outsourcing with Scale Economies," *Management Science* 48, no. 10 (2003), pp. 1314–1333.
25. E. Comiskey and C. Mulford, "Anticipating Trends in Operating Profits and Cash Flow," *Commercial Lending Review* 8, no. 2 (1993), pp. 38–48.
26. J. Cantwell, "The Globalization of Technology: What Remains of the Product Life Cycle Model?" *Cambridge Journal of Economics* 19, no. 1 (1995), pp. 155–174; T. Tyebjee, "Globalization Challenges Facing Fast Growing Companies," *Journal of Business and Industrial Marketing* 8, no. 3 (1993), pp. 58–64; D. Kelly, *Getting the Bugs Out* (New York: John Wiley & Sons, 2001).
27. J. Barney, "Looking Inside for Competitive Advantage," *Academy of Management Executive* 9, no. 4 (1995), pp. 49–61.
28. J. Kahn, "Wal-Mart Goes Shopping in Europe," *Fortune*, June 7, 1999, pp. 105–110; "How Well Does Wal-Mart Travel?" *BusinessWeek*, September 3, 2001, pp. 61–62.
29. B. Quinn, *Intelligent Enterprise* (New York: Free Press, 1992); C. B. Dobni and G. Luffman, "Determining the Scope and Impact of Market Orientation Profiles on Strategy Implementation and Performance," *Strategic Management Journal* 24, no. 6 (2003), pp. 577+; L. G. Love, R. L. Priem, and G. T. Lumpkin, "Explicitly Articulated Strategy and Firm Performance under Alternative Levels of Centralization," *Journal of Management* 28, no. 5 (2002), pp. 611–627.
30. H. Mintzberg, "The Strategy Concept I: Five Ps for Strategy," *California Management Review*, Fall 1987, pp. 11–24.
31. F. A. Maljers, "Inside Unilever: The Evolving Transnational Company," *Harvard Business Review*, September–October 1992, p. 2.
32. G. Hamel, "Innovate Now!" *Fast Company*, December 2002, www.fastcompany.com.
33. M. A. Hitt, R. D. Ireland, S. M. Camp, and D. L. Sexton, *Strategic Entrepreneurship: Integrating a New Mindset* (Oxford, UK: Blackwell Publishing).
34. S. Black, A. Morrison, and H. Gregersen, *Global Explorers: The Next Generation of Leaders* (New York: Routledge, 1999); K. M. Sutcliffe and K. Weber, "The High Cost of Accurate Knowledge," *Harvard Business Review* 81, no. 5 (2003), pp. 74–82.

CHAPTER 8

1. C. W. L. Hill, M. A. Hitt, and R. E. Hoskisson, "Cooperative versus Competitive Structures in Related and Unrelated Diversified Firms," *Organization Science* 3 (1992), pp. 501–521.
2. B. W. Keats and M. A. Hitt, "A Causal Model of Linkages among Environmental Dimensions, Macro Organizational Characteristics and Performance," *Academy of Management Journal* 31 (1988), pp. 570–598.
3. M. A. Hitt, R. D. Ireland, and R. E. Hoskisson, *Strategic Management: Competitiveness and Globalization* (Cincinnati, OH: South-Western Publishing Co., 2005).
4. H. Mintzberg, *The Structuring of Organizations* (Upper Saddle River, NJ: Prentice Hall, 1979).
5. P. Lawrence and J. Lorsch, *Organization and Environment* (Boston: Harvard University Press, 1967); J. Galbraith, *Designing Complex Organizations* (Reading, MA: Addison-Wesley, 1977).
6. Ibid.
7. D. Miller and C. Droge, "Psychological and Traditional Determinants of Structure," *Administrative Science Quarterly* 31 (1986), pp. 539–560; L. L. Levesque, J. Wilson, and R. Douglas, "Cognitive Divergence and Shared Mental Models in Software Development Project Teams," *Journal of Organizational Behavior*, March 2001, pp. 135–144.
8. Lawrence and Lorsch, *Organization and Environment*; Galbraith, *Designing Complex Organizations*; M. A. Schilling and H. K. Steensma, "The Use of Modular Organizational Forms: An Industry-Level Analysis," *Academy of Management Journal* 44, no. 6 (2001), pp. 1149–1168; O. Sorenson, "Interdependence and Adaptability: Organizational Learning and the Long-Term Effect of Integration," *Management Science* 49, no. 4 (2003), pp. 446–463.
9. R. Steers and J. S. Black, *Organizational Behavior* (New York: HarperCollins, 1993); R. H. Hall, *Organizations: Structures, Process, and Outcomes*, 5th ed. (Upper Saddle River, NJ: Prentice Hall, 1991); Sorenson, "Interdependence and Adaptability."
10. R. Cyert and J. March, *The Behavioral Theory of the Firm* (Upper Saddle River, NJ: Prentice Hall, 1963); J. R. Galbraith, "Organization Design: An Information Processing View," *Interfaces* 4, no. 3 (1974), pp. 28–36; Hall, *Organizations*; J. Birkinshaw, R. Nobel, and J. Ridderstrale, "Knowledge as a Contingency Variable: Do the Characteristics of Knowledge Predict Organization Structure?" *Organization Science* 13, no. 3 (2002), pp. 274–289; R. J. Trent and R. M. Monczka, "Pursuing Competitive Advantage through Integrated Global Sourcing," *Academy of Management Executive* 16, no. 2 (2002), pp. 66–80.
11. E. E. Klein, "Using Information Technology to Eliminate Layers of Bureaucracy," *National Public Accountant*, June 2001, pp. 46–48.
12. D. Nadler and M. Tushman, *Competing by Design: The Power of Organizational Architecture* (New York: Oxford University Press, 1997).
13. Y. Rhy-song and T. Sagafi-nejad, "Organizational Characteristics of American and Japanese Firms in Taiwan," *National Academy of Management Proceedings*, 1987, pp. 111–115.
14. C. A. Bartlett and S. Ghoshal, "Organizing for Worldwide Effectiveness: The Transnational Solution," *California Management Review*, Fall 1988, pp. 54–74; D. H. Doty, W. H. Glick, and G. P. Huber, "Fit, Effectiveness, and Equifinality: A Test of Two Configurational Theories," *Academy of Management Journal* 36 (1993), pp. 1196–1250.
15. J. R. Lincoln, M. Hanada, and K. McBride, "Organizational Structures in Japanese and U.S. Manufacturing," *Administrative Science Quarterly* 31 (1986), pp. 338–364.

16. J. Schachter, "When Hope Turns to Frustration: The Americanization of Mitsubishi Has Had Little Success," *Los Angeles Times*, July 10, 1988, p. 1.
17. E. Wang, "Linking Organizational Context with Structure," *Omega* 29 (2001), pp. 429–443.
18. "CBC/Radio-Canada's Move to Centralcasting," Broadcast Engineering, October 1, 2005, www.broadcastengineering.com (accessed January 31, 2007).
19. A. Coia, "Leaving Logistics in Capable Hands," *World Trade* 15, no. 7 (2002), p. 26.
20. R. Duncan, "What Is the Right Organizational Structure?" *Organizational Dynamics*, Winter 1979, pp. 59–79; Hall, *Organizations*; Y. Luo, "Market-Seeking MNEs in an Emerging Market: How Parent–Subsidiary Links Shape Overseas Success," *Journal of International Business Studies* 34, no. 3 (2003), pp. 290+.
21. M. Badri, D. Davis, and D. Davis, "Operations Strategy, Environmental Uncertainty and Performance: A Path Analytic Model of Industries in Developing Countries," *Omega* 28, no. 2 (2000), pp. 155–173; M. Van Gelderen, M. Frese, and R. Thurik, "Strategies, Uncertainty and Performance of Small Business Startups," *Small Business Economics* 15, no. 3 (2000), pp. 165–181; V. K. Garg, B. A. Walters, and R. L. Priem, "Chief Executive Scanning Emphases, Environmental Dynamism, and Manufacturing Firm Performance," *Strategic Management Journal* 24, no. 8 (2003), pp. 725–744.
22. R. Engdahl, R. Keating, and K. Aupperle, "Strategy and Structure: Chicken or Egg? (Reconsideration of Chandler's Paradigm for Economic Success)," *Organization Development Journal* 18, no. 4 (2000), pp. 21–33; D. E. W. Marginson, "Management Control Systems and Their Effects on Strategy Formation at Middle-Management Levels: Evidence from a U.K. Organization," *Strategic Management Journal* 23, no. 11 (2002), pp. 1019–1031; J. Smith David, Y. Hwang, B. K. W. Pei, and J. H. Reneau, "The Performance Effects of Congruence between Product Competitive Strategies and Purchasing Management Design," *Management Science* 48, no. 7 (2002), pp. 866–885; M. Goold and A. Campbell, "Do You Have a Well-Designed Organization?" *Harvard Business Review* 80, no. 3 (2002), pp. 117–124.
23. J. Stopford and L. Wells, *Managing the Multination Enterprise* (New York: Basic Books, 1972).
24. J. Daniels, R. Pitts, and M. Tretter, "Strategy and Structure of U.S. Multinationals: An Exploratory Study," *Academy of Management Journal* 27 (1984), pp. 292–307.
25. J. Wolf and W. Egelhoff, "Reexamination and Extension of International Strategy–Structure Theory," *Strategic Management Journal* 23 (2002), pp. 181–189.
26. Ibid.
27. C. Bartlett and S. Ghoshal, *Managing across Borders* (Boston: Harvard Business School Press, 1989); P. Ghemawat, "The Forgotten Strategy," *Harvard Business Review* 81, no. 11 (2003), pp. 76–84.
28. M. Dell, "Collaboration Equals Innovation," *InformationWeek*, January 27, 2003; pp. 24–26.

PART 2 INTEGRATIVE CASE

1. NewTel Enterprises Limited 1996 Annual Report, supplemented as necessary by the reports for years 1994, 1995, 1997, and 1998.
2. Paragon Information Systems presentation to the Newfoundland and Labrador Employers' Council Fall Conference: November 13, 1997.
3. Paragon, op. cit.

CHAPTER 9

1. S. Finkelstein and D. C. Hambrick, *Strategic Leadership: Top Executives and Their Effects on Organizations* (St. Paul, MN: West Publishing Company, 1996).
2. R. D. Ireland and M. A. Hitt, "Achieving and Maintaining Strategic Competitiveness in the 21st Century: The Role of Strategic Leadership," *Academy of Management Executive* 13, no. 1 (1999), pp. 43–57.
3. M. A. Hitt and R. D. Ireland, "The Essence of Strategic Leadership: Managing Human and Social Capital," *Journal of Leadership and Organizational Studies* 9 (2002), pp. 3–14.
4. R. M. Stogdill, "Historical Trends in Leadership Theory and Research," *Journal of Contemporary Business*, no. 4 (1974), pp. 1–17 (p. 2).
5. D. Katz and R. L. Kahn, *The Social Psychology of Organizations*, 2nd ed. (New York: Wiley, 1978); S. D. Dionne, F. J. Yammarino, L. E. Atwater, and L. R. James, "Neutralizing Substitutes for Leadership Theory: Leadership Effects and Common-Source Bias," *Journal of Applied Psychology* 87, no. 3 (2002), pp. 454–464.
6. J. Pfeffer, *Managing with Power: Politics and Influence in Organizations* (Boston: Harvard Business School Press, 1992), p. 45.
7. D. A. Whetten and K. S. Cameron, *Developing Management Skills*, 4th ed. (Reading, MA: Addison-Wesley, 1998), p. 229.
8. G. E. G. Catlin, *Systematic Politics* (Toronto: University of Toronto Press, 1962), p. 71.
9. M. Davids, "Where Style Meets Substance," *Journal of Business Strategy* 16 (1995), pp. 48–52+.
10. Pfeffer, *Managing with Power*.
11. W. G. Bennis and B. Nanus, *Leaders: The Strategies for Taking Charge* (New York: Harper & Row, 1985), p. 6.
12. B. M. Bass, *Leadership, Psychology, and Organizational Behavior* (New York: Harper, 1960); A. Etzioni, *A Comparative Analysis of Complex Organizations: On Power, Involvement, and Their Correlates* (New York: Free Press of Glencoe, 1961); G. A. Yukl, *Leadership in Organizations,* 3rd ed. (Upper Saddle River, NJ: Prentice Hall, 1994).
13. J. R. P. French and B. Raven, *The Bases of Social Power*, in D. Cartwright (ed.), *Studies in Social Power* (Ann Arbor, MI: Institute for Social Research, 1959), pp. 150–167.
14. D. Mechanic, "Sources of Power of Lower Participants in Complex Organizations," *Administrative Science Quarterly* 7 (1962), pp. 349–364.
15. R. M. Stogdill, "Personal Factors Associated with Leadership: A Survey of the Literature," *Journal of Psychology* 25 (1948), pp. 35–71.
16. R. G. Lord, C. L. De Vader, and G. M. Alliger, "A Meta-Analysis of the Relation between Personality Traits and Leadership Perceptions: An Application of Validity Generalization Procedures," *Journal of Applied Psychology* 71 (1986), pp. 402–441; S. A. Kirkpatrick and E. A. Locke, "Leadership: Do Traits Matter?" *Academy of Management Executive* 5, no. 2 (1991), pp. 48–60; Yukl, *Leadership in Organizations*; R. M. Kramer, "The Harder They Fall," *Harvard Business Review* 81, no. 10 (2003), pp. 58–66.
17. Kirkpatrick and Locke, "Leadership: Do Traits Matter?"; Yukl, *Leadership in Organizations*; D. V. Day, D. J. Schleicher, A. L. Unckless, and N. J. Hiller, "Research Reports—Self-Monitoring Personality at Work: A Meta-Analytic Investigation of Construct Validity," *Journal of Applied Psychology* 87, no. 2 (2002), pp. 390–401.
18. J. B. Miner, "Twenty Years of Research on Role-Motivation Theory of Managerial Effectiveness," *Personnel Psychology*

31 (1978), pp. 739–760; F. E. Berman and J. B. Miner, "Motivation to Manage at the Top Executive Level: A Test of the Hierarchic Role-Motivation Theory," *Personnel Psychology* 38 (1985), pp. 377–391.

19. Bennis and Nanus, *Leaders: The Strategies for Taking Charge*; J. M. Kouzes and B. Z. Posner, *The Leadership Challenge: How to Get Extraordinary Things Done in Organizations* (San Francisco: Jossey-Bass, 1987).

20. A. Bandura, *Social Foundations of Thought and Action: A Social Cognitive Theory* (Upper Saddle River, NJ: Prentice Hall, 1986); B. M. Bass, *Handbook of Leadership: A Survey of Theory and Research* (New York: Free Press, 1990); D. C. McClelland and R. E. Boyatzis, "Leadership Motive Pattern and Long-Term Success in Management," *Journal of Applied Psychology* 67 (1982), pp. 737–743; A. Howard and D. W. Bray, *Managerial Lives in Transition: Advancing Age and Changing Times* (New York: Guilford Press, 1988).

21. Kouzes and Posner, *The Leadership Challenge*.

22. J. R. O'Neil, *The Paradox of Success: When Winning at Work Means Losing at Life: A Book of Renewal for Leaders* (New York: G. P. Putnam & Sons, 1994); M. Maccoby, "Narcissistic Leaders: The Incredible Pros, the Inevitable Cons," *Harvard Business Review* 82, no. 1 (2004), pp. 92–100.

23. Bass, *Handbook of Leadership*; Bennis and Nanus, *Leaders: The Strategies for Taking Charge*; Howard and Bray, *Managerial Lives in Transition*; C. D. McCauley and M. M. Lombardo, "Benchmarks: An Instrument for Diagnosing Managerial Strengths and Weaknesses," in K. E. Clark and M. B. Clark (eds.), *Measures of Leadership* (West Orange, NJ: Leadership Library of America, Inc., 1990), pp. 535–545; D. Goleman, R. Boyatzis, and A. McKee, *Primal Leadership: Realizing the Power of Emotional Intelligence* (Boston: Harvard Business School Press, 2002); D. L. Coutu, "Putting Leaders on the Couch: A Conversation with Manfred F. R. Kets de Vries," *Harvard Business Review* 82, no. 1 (2004), pp. 64–71.

24. R. I. Westwood and A. Chan, "Headship and Leadership," in R. I. Westwood (ed.), *Organizational Behavior: Southeast Asian Perspectives* (Hong Kong: Longman, 1992), pp. 118–143.

25. Goleman, Boyatzis, and McKee, *Primal Leadership*; D. Goleman, "What Makes a Leader?" *Harvard Business Review* 7, nos. 5, 6 (1998), pp. 92–103; J. D. Mayer and P. Salovey, "Emotional Intelligence and the Construction and Regulation of Feelings," *Applied and Preventive Psychology* 4 (1995), pp. 197–208; J. D. Mayer et al., "Leading by Feel," *Harvard Business Review* 82, no. 1 (2004), pp. 27–37; J. E. Dutton, P. J. Frost, M. C. Worline, J. M. Lilius, and J. M. Kanov, "Leading in Times of Trauma," *Harvard Business Review* 80, no. 1 (2002), pp. 54–61.

26. Goleman, "What Makes a Leader?"

27. D. Goleman, *Emotional Intelligence* (New York: Bantam Books, 1995).

28. J. Misumi and M. E. Peterson, "The Performance–Maintenance (PM) Theory of Leadership: Review of a Japanese Research Program," *Administrative Science Quarterly* 30 (1985), pp. 198–223; R. T. Lewis, "New York Times Company President and Chief Executive Officer Russell Lewis on 'The CEO's Lot Is Not a Happy One . . .' (with Apologies to Gilbert and Sullivan)," *Academy of Management Executive* 16, no. 4 (2002), pp. 37–42.

29. E. A. Eagly and B. T. Johnson, "Gender and Leadership Style: A Meta-Analysis," *Psychological Bulletin* 108 (1990), pp. 235–256; J. B. Rosener, "Ways Women Lead," *Harvard Business Review* 68, no. 6 (1990), pp. 119–225; G. N. Powell, "One More Time: Do Female and Male Managers Differ?" *Academy of Management Executive* 4, no. 3 (1990), pp. 68–75; D. J. Campbell, W. Bommer, and E. Yeo, "Perceptions of Appropriate Leadership Style: Participation versus Consultation across Two Cultures," *Asia Pacific Journal of Management* 10, no. 1 (1993), pp. 1–9; G. Morse, "The Emancipated Organization," *Harvard Business Review* 80, no. 9 (2002), pp. 20–21.

30. R. E. Kelly, "In Praise of Followers," *Harvard Business Review* 66, no. 6 (1988), pp. 142–149.

31. R. G. Lord and K. H. Maher, "Alternative Information-Processing Models and Their Implications for Theory, Research, and Practice," *Academy of Management Review* 15 (1990), pp. 9–28.

32. B. J. Calder, "An Attribution Theory of Leadership," in B. M. Staw and G. R. Salancik (eds.), *New Directions in Organizational Behavior* (Chicago: St. Clair, 1997); R. G. Lord, C. L. Devader, and G. M. Alliger, "A Meta-Analysis of the Relation between Personality Traits and Leadership Perceptions," *Journal of Applied Psychology*, 71 (1986), pp. 402–410; A. C. Edmondson and S. E. Cha, "When Company Values Backfire," *Harvard Business Review* 80, no. 11 (2002), pp. 18–19.

33. Calder, "An Attribution Theory of Leadership"; J. Pfeffer, "The Ambiguity of Leadership," *Academy of Management Review* 2 (1977), pp. 104–112.

34. A. N. Turner and P. R. Lawrence, *Industrial Jobs and the Worker: An Investigation of Response to Task Attributes* (Boston: Harvard University, Division of Research, Graduate School of Business Administration, 1965); R. W. Griffin, *Task Design: An Integrative Approach* (Glenview, IL: Scott, Foresman, 1982); J. R. Hackman and G. R. Oldham, *Work Redesign* (Reading, MA: Addison-Wesley, 1980).

35. R. R. Blake and J. S. Mouton, *The Managerial Grid* (Houston: Gulf Publishing, 1964).

36. P. Hersey, *Situational Selling* (Escondido, CA: Center for Leadership Studies, 1985); P. Hersey, K. H. Blanchard, and D. Johnson, *Management of Organizational Behavior: Leading Human Resources*, 8th ed. (Upper Saddle River, NJ: Prentice Hall, 2001).

37. L. R. Anderson and F. E. Fiedler, "The Effect of Participatory and Supervisory Leadership on Group Creativity," *Journal of Applied Psychology* 48 (1964), pp. 227–236; F. E. Fiedler, *A Theory of Leadership Effectiveness* (New York: McGraw-Hill, 1967); M. M. Chemers and F. E. Fiedler, "The Effectiveness of Leadership Training: A Reply to Argyris," *American Psychologist* 33 (1978), pp. 391–394.

38. M. J. Strube and J. E. Garcia, "A Meta-Analytic Investigation of Fiedler's Contingency Model of Leadership Effectiveness," *Psychological Bulletin* 90 (1981), pp. 307–321; L. H. Peters, D. D. Hartke, and J. T. Pohlmann, "Fiedler's Contingency Theory of Leadership: An Application of the Meta-Analysis Procedures of Schmidt and Hunter," *Psychological Bulletin* 7 (1985), pp. 274–285.

39. M. G. Evans, "The Effects of Supervisory Behavior on the Path–Goal Relationship," *Organizational Behavior and Human Performance* 5 (1970), pp. 277–298; R. J. House, "A Path–Goal Theory of Leader Effectiveness," *Administrative Science Quarterly* 16 (1971), pp. 321–329; R. J. House and G. Dessler, "The Path–Goal Theory of Leadership: Some Post Hoc and A Priori Tests," in J. Hunt and L. Larson (eds.), *Contingency Approaches to Leadership* (Carbondale, IL: Southern Illinois Press, 1974), pp. 81–87; R. J. House and T. R. Mitchell, "Path–Goal Theory of Leadership," *Journal of Contemporary Business* 3, no. 4 (1974), pp. 81–97.

40. House, "A Path–Goal Theory of Leader Effectiveness," p. 324.

41. V. H. Vroom and P. W. Yetton, *Leadership and Decision-Making* (Pittsburgh, PA: University of Pittsburgh Press, 1973); B. H. Vroom and A. G. Jago, *The New Leadership: Managing Participation in Organizations* (Upper Saddle River, NJ: Prentice Hall, 1988).

42. Vroom and Jago, *The New Leadership.*

43. S. Kerr and J. M. Jermier, "Substitutes for Leadership: Their Meaning and Measurement," *Organizational Behavior and Human Performance* 22 (1978), pp. 375–403; J. P. Howell, D. E. Bowen, P. W. Dorfman, S. Kerr, and P. M. Podsakoff, "Substitutes for Leadership: Effective Alternatives to Ineffective Leadership," *Organizational Dynamics* 19 (1990), pp. 20–38; J. P. Howell and P.W. Dorfmann, "Substitutes for Leadership: Test of a Construct," *Academy of Management Journal* 24 (1981), pp. 714–728; P. M. Podsakoff, S. B. MacKenzie, and W. H. Bommer, "Transformational Leader Behaviors and Substitutes for Leadership as Determinants of Employee Satisfaction, Commitment, Trust, and Organizational Citizenship Behaviors," *Journal of Management* 22 (1996), pp. 259–298; S. B. MacKenzie, P. M. Podsakoff, and R. Fetter, "The Impact of Organizational Citizenship Behavior on Evaluations of Salesperson Performance," *Journal of Marketing* 57 (1993), pp. 70–80; P. M. Podsakoff, B. P. Nichoff, S. B. MacKenzie, and M. L. Williams, "Do Substitutes for Leadership Really Substitute for Leadership? An Empirical Examination of Kerr and Jermier's Situational Leadership Model," *Organizational Behavior and Human Decision Processes* 54 (1993), pp. 1–44.

44. S. Finkelstein, "Seven Habits of Spectacularly Unsuccessful People," *Strategy Review* 14, no. 4 (2003), pp. 39–51; N. Nohria, W. Joyce, and B. Roberson, "What Really Works," *Harvard Business Review* 81, no. 7 (2003), pp. 42–52; Bennis and Nanus, *Leaders: The Strategies for Taking Charge*; J. P. Kotter, "What Leaders Really Do," *Harvard Business Review* 68, no. 3 (1990), pp. 103–211; A. Zaleznik, "Managers and Leaders: Are They Different?" *Harvard Business Review* 70, no. 2 (1992), pp. 126–135.

45. M. Weber, *The Theory of Social and Economic Organization*, A. M. Henderson and T. Parson, trans.; edited with an introduction by T. Parsons (New York: Free Press, 1948).

46. S. Callan, "Charismatic Leadership in Contemporary Management Debates," *Journal of General Management* 29, no. 1, pp. 1–14; M. Frese, S. Beimel, and S. Schoenborn, "Action Training for Charismatic Leadership: Two Evaluations of Studies of a Commercial Training Module on Inspirational Communication of a Vision," *Personnel Psychology* 56, no. 3 (2003), pp. 671–697; R. Khurana, "The Curse of the Superstar CEO," *Harvard Business Review* 80, no. 9 (2002), pp. 60–66; S. W. Tester, B. M. Meglino, and M. A. Korsgaard, "The Antecedents and Consequences of Group Potency: A Longitudinal Investigation of Newly Formed Work Groups," *Academy of Management Journal* 45, no. 2 (2002), pp. 352–368; D. De Cremer and D. van Knippenberg, "How Do Leaders Promote Cooperation? The Effects of Charisma and Procedural Fairness," *Journal of Applied Psychology* 87, no. 5 (2002), pp. 858+; J-C. Pastor, J. R. Meindl, and M. C. Mayo, "A Network Effects Model of Charisma Attributions," *Academy of Management Journal* 45, no. 2 (2002) pp. 410–420; O. Behling and J. M. McFillen, "A Syncretical Model of Charismatic/Transformation Leadership," *Group and Organizational Management* 21 (1996), pp. 163–191; J. A. Conger, *The Charismatic Leader: Beyond the Mystique of Exceptional Leadership* (San Francisco: Jossey-Bass, 1989); J. A. Conger, R. N. Kanungo, S. T. Menon, and P. Mathur, "Measuring Charisma: Dimensionality and Validity of the Conger-Kanungo Scale of Charismatic Leadership," *Canadian Journal of Administrative Sciences* 14 (1997), pp. 290–302; R. J. House, "A 1976 Theory of Charismatic Leadership," in J. G. Hunt (ed.), *Leadership: The Cutting Edge* (Carbondale, IL: Southern Illinois Press, 1977); R. J. House, W. D. Spangler, and J. Woycke, "Personality and Charisma in the U.S. Presidency: A Psychological Theory of Leader Effectiveness," *Administrative Science Quarterly* 36 (1991), pp. 364–396.

47. House, "A 1976 Theory of Charismatic Leadership."

48. Conger, *The Charismatic Leader*; J. A. Conger and R. N. Kanungo, "Toward a Behavioral Theory of Charismatic Leadership in Organizational Setting," *Academy of Management Review* 12 (1987), pp. 637–647.

49. C. G. Emrich, "Images in Words: Presidential Rhetoric, Charisma, and Greatness," *Administrative Science Quarterly* 46 (2001), pp. 527–561; J. A. Conger, R. N. Kanungo, and S. T. Menon, "Charismatic Leadership and Follower Effects," *Journal of Organizational Behavior* 21 (2000), pp. 747–767.

50. D. Tourish and A. Pinnington, "Transformational Leadership, Corporate Cultism, and the Spirituality Paradigm: An Unholy Trinity in the Workplace?" *Human Relations* 55, no. 2 (2002), pp. 147–172; R. Kark, B. Shamir, and G. Chen, "The Two Faces of Transformational Leadership: Empowerment and Dependency," *Journal of Applied Psychology* 88, no. 2 (2003), pp. 246–255; T. Dvir, D. Eden, B. J. Avolio, and B. Shamir, "Impact of Transformational Leadership on Follower Development and Performance: A Field Experiment," *Academy of Management Journal* 45, no. 4 (2002), pp. 735–744; J. Barling, C. Loughlin, and E. K. Kelloway, "Development and Test of a Model Linking Safety-Specific Transformational Leadership and Occupational Safety," *Journal of Applied Psychology* 87, no. 3 (2002), pp. 488–496; B. M. Bass, D. I. Jung, B. J. Avolio, and Y. Berson, "Predicting Unit Performance by Assessing Transformational and Transactional Leadership," *Journal of Applied Psychology* 88, no. 2 (2003), pp. 207–218; J. M. Burns, *Leadership* (New York: Harper & Row, 1978).

51. Burns, *Leadership*.

52. B. M. Bass, "Leadership: Good, Better, Best," *Organizational Dynamics* 13, no. 3 (1985), pp. 26–40; B. M. Bass and B. J. Avolio, "Developing Transformational Leadership: 1992 and Beyond," *Journal of European Industrial Training* 14, no. 5 (1992), pp. 21–27.

53. Bass, *Leadership, Psychology, and Organizational Behavior.*

54. Bass, Jung, Avolio, and Berson, "Predicting Unit Performance"; B. J. Avolio, "Re-Examining the Components of Transformational and Transactional Leadership Using the Multifactor Leadership Questionnaire," *Journal of Occupational and Organizational Psychology* 72 (1999), pp. 441–463.

55. C. L. Hoyt and J. Blascovich, "Transformational and Transactional Leadership in Virtual and Physical Environments," *Small Group Research* 34, no. 6 (2003), pp. 678–716; N. M. Tichy and M. A. Devanna, "The Transformational Leader," *Training and Development* 40, no. 7 (1986), pp. 27–32; Yukl, *Leadership in Organizations*.

56. Bennis and Nanus, *Leaders: The Strategies for Taking Charge*.

57. Yukl, *Leadership in Organizations*.

58. R. J. House et al., "Cultural Influences on Leadership and Organizations: Project GLOBE," in W. Mobley (ed.), *Advances in Global Leadership*, vol. 1 (Stamford, CT: JAI Press, 1998).

59. R. I. Westwood and A. Chan, "Headship and Leadership," in R. I. Westwood (ed.), *Organizational Behavior: Southeast Asian Perspectives* (Hong Kong: Longman, 1992).

60. S. Ronen, *Comparative and Multinational Management* (New York: Wiley, 1986).

61. Westwood and Chan, "Headship and Leadership."

62. E. Ogliastri et al., "Cultura y Liderazgo Organizacional en America Latina: El Estudio Globe" (Culture and Organizational Leadership in Latin America: The Globe Study), *Revista Latinoamericana de Administración*, 1999.

63. M. Dickson, D. N. Den Hartog, and J. K. Mitchelson, "Research on Leadership in a Cross-Cultural Context: Making Progress, and Raising New Questions," *Leadership Quarterly* 14, no. 6 (2003), pp. 729–769; P. W. Dorfman and J. P. Howell, "Leadership in Western and Asian Countries: Commonalities and Differences in Effective Leadership Processes across Cultures," *Leadership Quarterly* 8 (1997), pp. 233–274.

64. House et al., "Cultural Influences on Leadership and Organizations."

65. R. D. Ireland, M. A. Hitt, and D. G. Sirmon, "A Model of Strategic Entrepreneurship: The Construct and Its Dimensions," *Journal of Management* 29 (2003), pp. 963–989.

66. M. A. Hitt, R. D. Ireland, and R. E. Hoskisson, *Strategic Management: Competitiveness and Globalization* (Cincinnati, OH: South-Western Publishing Co., 2005).

CHAPTER 10

1. G. Hofstede, "Culture and Organizations," *International Studies of Management and Organization* 70, no. 4 (1980), pp. 15–41; C. Sue-Chan and M. Ong, "Goal Assignment and Performance: Assessing the Mediating Roles of Goal Commitment and Self-Efficacy and the Moderating Role of Power Distance," *Organizational Behavior and Human Decision Processes* 89, no. 2 (2002), pp. 1140–1161; P. E. Spector, C. L. Cooper, J. I. Sanchez, M. O'Driscoll, and K. Sparks, "Locus of Control and Well-Being at Work: How Generalizable Are Western Findings," *Academy of Management Journal* 45, no. 2 (2002), pp. 453–466.

2. A. H. Maslow, *Motivation and Personality*, 2nd ed. (New York: Harper & Row, 1970).

3. R. Jacob, "Secure Jobs Trump Higher Pay," *Fortune*, 1995, p. 24.

4. K. Schoenberger, P. J. McDonnell, and S. Hubler, "Thais Found in Sweatshop Are Released," *Los Angeles Times*, August 21, 1995, pp. A1+.

5. Hofstede, *Culture and Organizations*, pp. 55–56 and Figure 7.

6. C. P. Alderfer, "An Empirical Test of a New Theory of Human Needs," *Organizational Behavior and Human Performance* 4 (1969), pp. 142–175; C. P. Alderfer, *Existence, Relatedness and Growth: Human Need in Organizational Settings* (New York: The Free Press, 1997); H. Levinson, "Management by Whose Objectives?" *Harvard Business Review* 81, no. 1 (2003), pp. 107–116.

7. WorkSafeBC, www.worksafebc.com (accessed June 4, 2007).

8. D. C. McClelland, *Human Motivation* (Glenview, IL: Scott, Foresman, 1985); D. C. McClelland and R. E. Boyatzis, "Leadership Motive Pattern and Long-Term Success in Management," *Journal of Applied Psychology* 67 (1982), pp. 734–743; D. C. McClelland and D. G. Winter, *Motivating Economic Achievement* (New York: The Free Press, 1969).

9. S. H. Schwartz and W. Blisky, "Toward a Universal Psychological Structure of Human Values," *Journal of Personality and Social Psychology* 53 (1987), pp. 550–562; S. H. Schwartz and W. T. Bilsky, "Toward a Theory of the Universal Content and Structure of Values: Extensions and Cross-Cultural Replications," *Journal of Personality and Social Psychology* 58 (1990), pp. 878–881.

10. M. Erez and P. C. Earley, *Culture, Self-Identity, and Work* (New York: Oxford University Press, 1993), p. 102.

11. F. Herzberg, *Work and the Nature of Man* (Cleveland, OH: Worth Publishing, 1966); F. Herzberg, "One More Time: How Do You Motivate Employees?" *Harvard Business Review* 46 (1968), pp. 54–62; F. Herzberg, B. Mausner, and B. B. Snyderman, *The Motivation to Work* (New York: Wiley, 1959).

12. M. Murray, "Giant Task: GE's Immelt Starts Renovations on the House that Jack Built—Under Intense Spotlight, CEO Focuses on Core Operations that Welch Had Trimmed, Opening the Books a Bit Wider," *Wall Street Journal*, February 6, 2003, p. A1.

13. R. W. Griffin, *Task Design: An Integrative Approach* (Glenview, IL: Scott, Foresman, 1982); J. L. Pierce and R. B. Dunham, "Task Design: A Literature Review," *Academy of Management Review* 1 (1976), pp. 83–97.

14. J. R. Hackman and G. R. Oldham, *Work Redesign* (Reading, MA: Addison-Wesley, 1980).

15. R. B. Tiegs, L. E. Tetrick, and Y. Fried, "Growth Need Strength and Context Satisfaction as Moderators of the Relations of the Job Characteristics Model," *Journal of Management* 18 (1992), pp. 575–593; X. Huang and E. Van De Viert, "Where Intrinsic Job Satisfaction Fails to Work: National Moderators on Intrinsic Motivation," *Journal of Organizational Behavior* 24, no. 2 (2003), pp. 159–180; S. Friday and E. Friday, "Racioethnic Perceptions of Job Characteristics and Job Satisfaction," *Journal of Management Development* 22, nos. 5, 6 (2003), pp. 426–442.

16. J. S. Adams, "Towards an Understanding of Inequity," *Journal of Abnormal and Social Psychology* 67 (1963), pp. 422–436; J. S. Adams, "Inequity in Social Exchange," in L. Berkowitz (ed.), *Advances in Experimental Social Psychology*, vol. 2 (New York: Academic Press, 1965), pp. 267–299; R. T. Mowday, "Equity Theory Predictions of Behavior in Organizations," in R. M. Steers, L. W. Porter, and G. A Bigley (eds.), *Motivation and Leadership at Work*, 6th ed. (New York: McGraw-Hill, 1996); J. D. Shaw, N. Gupta, and J. E. Delery, "Pay Dispersion and Workforce Performance: Moderating Effects of Incentives and Interdependence," *Strategic Management Journal* 23, no. 6 (2002), pp. 491–512; C. C. Chen, J. Choi, and S-C. Chi, "Making Justice Sense of Local-Expatriate Compensation Disparity: Mitigation by Local Referents, Ideological Explanations, and Interpersonal Sensitivity in China Foreign Joint Ventures," *Academy of Management Journal* 45, no. 5 (2003), pp. 807–817.

17. C. C. Pinder, *Work Motivation in Organizational Behavior* (Upper Saddle River, NJ: Prentice Hall, 1998), p. 287.

18. L. W. Porter, G. A. Bigley, and R. M. Steers, *Motivation and Work Behavior*, 7th ed. (New York: McGraw-Hill, 2003), p. 47; L. K. Scheer, N. Kumar, J-B. E. M. Steenkamp, "Reactions to Perceived Inequity in U.S. and Dutch Interorganizational Relationships," *Academy of Management Journal* 46, no. 3 (2003), pp. 303–316.

19. V. H. Vroom, *Work and Motivation* (New York: Wiley, 1964).

20. J. Caisson, "Jump Start Motivation," *Incentive* 775, no. 5 (2001), pp. 77, 88; A. Erez and M. A. Isen, "The Influence of Positive Affect on the Components of Expectancy Motivation," *Journal of Applied Psychology* 87, no. 6 (2002), pp. 1055–1067.

21. R. W. Yerema, *Canada's Top 100 Employers* (Toronto, ON: Mediacorp Canada Inc., 2007).

22. A. D. Stajkovic and F. Luthans, "Social Cognitive Theory and Self-Efficacy: Going Beyond Traditional Motivational and Behavioral Approaches," *Organizational Dynamics* 26, no. 4 (1998), pp. 62–74; T. A. Wright, "What Every Manager Should Know: Does Personality Help Drive Employee Motivation?" *Academy of Management Executive* 17, no. 2 (2003), pp. 131–133.

23. A. D. Stajkovic and F. Luthans, "Social Cognitive Theory and Self-Efficacy: Implications for Motivation Theory and Practice," in L. W. Porter, G. A. Bigley, and R. M. Steers (eds.), *Motivation and Work Behavior*, 7th ed. (New York: McGraw-Hill, 2003); A. Bandura and E. A. Locke, "Negative Self-Efficacy and Goal Effects Revisited," *Journal of Applied Psychology* 88, no. 1 (2003), pp. 87–99.

24. M. Erez, "Goal Setting," in N. Nicholson (ed.), *Blackwell Encyclopedic Dictionary of Organizational Behavior* (Cambridge, MA: Blackwell Business Publishing, 1995), pp. 193–194; E. A. Locke, "The Motivation Sequence, the Motivation Hub, and the Motivation Core," *Organizational Behavior and Human Decision Processes* 50 (1991), pp. 288–299; E. A. Locke and G. P. Latham, *A Theory of Goal Setting and Task Performance* (Upper Saddle River, NJ: Prentice Hall, 1990); W. Q. Judge, G. E. Fryxell, and R. S. Dooley, "The New Task of R&D Management: Creating

Goal-Directed Communities for Innovation," *California Management Review* 39, no. 3 (1997), pp. 72–85; Wright, "What Every Manager Should Know."

25. E. A. Locke and G. P. Latham, "Goal Setting Theory: An Introduction," in R. M. Steers, L. W. Porter, and G. A. Bigley (eds.) *Motivation and Leadership at Work*, 6th ed. (New York: McGraw-Hill, 1996).
26. Erez, *Goal Setting*; A. Drach-Zachavy and M. Erez, "Challenge versus Threat Effects on the Goal-Performance Relationship," *Organizational Behavior and Human Decision Processes* 88, no. 2 (2002), pp. 667–682; T. W. Britt, "Black Hawk Down at Work," *Harvard Business Review* 81, no. 1 (2003), pp. 16+; N. Nicholson, "How to Motivate Your Problem People," *Harvard Business Review* 81, no. 1 (2003), pp. 56–58.
27. Ibid.
28. M. Erez and P. C. Earley, "Comparative Analysis of Goal-Setting Strategies across Cultures," *Journal of Applied Psychology* 72 (1987), pp. 658–665; S. S. K. Lam, X-P. Chen, and J. Schaunbroeck, "Participative Decision Making and Employee Performance in Different Cultures: The Moderating Effects of Allocentrism/Idiocentrism and Efficacy," *Academy of Management Journal* 45, no. 5 (2002), pp. 905–914.
29. J. E. Komaki, T. Coombs, and S. Schepman, "Motivational Implications of Reinforcement Theory," in R. M. Steers, L. W. Porter, and G. A. Bigley (eds.), *Motivation and Leadership at Work,* 6th ed. (New York: McGraw-Hill, 1996).
30. S. Kerr, "On the Folly of Rewarding A While Hoping for B," *Academy of Management Journal* 18 (1975), pp. 769–783.
31. S. Kerr, *Ultimate Rewards* (Boston: Harvard Business School Press, 1997).
32. Komaki, Coombs, and Schepman, "Motivational Implications of Reinforcement Theory."
33. Ibid.
34. H. C. Triandis, "Collectivism vs. Individualism: A Reconceptualization of a Basic Concept in Cross-Cultural Social Psychology," in G. K. Verma and Y. C. Bagley (eds.), *Cross-Cultural Studies of Personality, Attitudes, and Cognition* (London: Macmillan, 1988), pp. 60–95; Erez and Earley, *Culture, Self-Identity, and Work*.
35. S. E. Seashore, *Group Cohesiveness in the Industrial Work Group* (Ann Arbor, MI: Survey Research Center, Institute for Social Research, University of Michigan, 1954).
36. D. Krackhardt and L. W. Porter, "When Friends Leave: A Structural Analysis of the Relationship between Turnover and Stayers' Attitudes," *Administrative Science Quarterly* 30 (1985), pp. 242–261.
37. F. Dansereau Jr., G. Graen, and W. J. Haga, "A Vertical Dyad Linkage Approach to Leadership within Formal Organizations: A Longitudinal Investigation of the Role Making Process," *Organizational Behavior and Human Performance* 13 (1975), pp. 46–78; G. B. Graen and J. F. Cashman, "A Role Making Model of Leadership in Formal Organizations: A Developmental Approach," in J. G. Hunt and L. L. Larson (eds.), *Leadership Frontiers* (Kent, OH: Kent State University Press, 1975), pp. 143–165; M. Mongeau, "Moving Mountains," *Harvard Business Review* 81, no. 1 (2003), pp. 41–47.
38. D. Mechanic, *Students under Stress: A Study in the Social Psychology of Adaptation* (New York: Free Press, 1962).
39. C. O'Reilly, "Corporations, Culture, and Commitment: Motivation and Social Control in Organizations," *California Management Review* 31, no. 4 (1989), p. 12.
40. E. Schonfeld, "Have the Urge to Merge? You'd Better Think Twice," *Fortune* 135, 1997, pp. 114–116.
41. M. Rokeach, *The Nature of Human Values* (New York: Free Press, 1973).
42. Erez and Earley, *Culture, Self-Identity, and Work*; Locke, "The Motivation Sequence, the Motivation Hub, and the Motivation Core."
43. M. Weber, *The Protestant Work Ethic and the Spirit of Capitalism* (T. Parsons, trans.) (New York: Scribner's, 1958); R. Wuthnow, "Religion and Economic Life," in N. J. Smelser and R. Swedbert (eds.), *The Handbook of Economic Sociology* (Princeton: Princeton University Press, 1994), pp. 620–646.
44. G. W. England and I. Harpaz, "Some Methodological and Analytic Considerations in Cross-National Comparative Research," *Journal of International Business Studies* 14, no. 2 (1983), pp. 49–59.
45. Tom W. Smith, "A Cross-National Comparison on Attitudes toward Work by Age and Labor Force Status," National Opinion Research Center, University of Chicago, December 2000.
46. D. Finegold and S. Mohrman, "What Do Employees Really Want: The Perception vs. the Reality." Paper presented at the World Economics Forum Annual Meeting, Davos, Switzerland, 2001.

CHAPTER 11

1. J. Bunderson, "Team Member Functional Background and Involvement in Management Teams: Direct Effects and the Moderating Role of Power and Centralization," *Academy of Management Journal* 46 (2003), pp. 458–474; S. Finkelstein and D. Hambrick, *Strategic Leadership* (St. Paul, MN: West Publishing Company, 1996).
2. M. A. Hitt, R. D. Ireland, and R. E. Hoskisson, *Strategic Management: Competitiveness and Globalization* (Cincinnati, OH: South-Western Publishing, 2005).
3. S. Barsade, A. Ward, J. Turner, and J. Sonnenfeld, "To Your Heart's Content: A Model of Affective Diversity in Top Management Teams," *Administrative Science Quarterly* 45 (2000), pp. 802–836.
4. H. J. Leavitt, "The Old Days, Hot Groups, and Managers' Lib," *Administrative Science Quarterly* 41 (1996), pp. 288–300; L. I. Glassop, "The Organizational Benefit of Teams," *Human Relations* 55, no. 2 (2002), pp. 225–249.
5. B. I. Kirkman and D. L. Shapiro, "The Impact of Cultural Values on Employee Resistance to Teams: Toward a Model of Globalized Self-Managing Work Team Effectiveness," *Academy of Management Review* 22 (1997), pp. 730–757; S. S. K. Lam, X-P. Chen, and J. Schaubroeck, "Participative Decision Making and Employee Performance in Different Cultures: The Moderating Effects of Allocentrism/Idiocentrism and Efficacy," *Academy of Management Journal* 45, no. 5 (2002), pp. 905–914; D. C. Thomas and K. Au, "The Effect of Cultural Differences on Behavioral Responses to Low Job Satisfaction," *Journal of International Business Studies* 33, no. 2 (2002), pp. 309–326.
6. E. Sundstrom, K. P. de Meuse, and D. Futrell, "Work Teams: Applications and Effectiveness," *American Psychologist* 45, no. 2 (1990), pp. 120–133.
7. M. Cotrill, "Give Your Work Teams Time and Training," *Academy of Management Executive* 11, no. 3 (1997), pp. 87–89; R. D. Banker, J. M. Field, R. G. Schroeder, K. K. Y. Sinha, "Impact of Work Teams on Manufacturing Performance: A Longitudinal Field Study," *Academy of Management Journal* 39 (1996), pp. 867–890.
8. K. A. Jehn and P. P. Shah, "Interpersonal Relationships and Task Performance: An Examination of Mediation Processes in Friendship and Acquaintance Groups," *Journal of Personality and Social Psychology* 71 (1997), pp. 775–790; Anonymous, "Friends Make Good Teammates," *Quality* 36, no. 1 (1997), p. 12; K. A. Mollica, B. Gray, and L. K. Trevino, "Racial Homophily and Its Persistence in Newcomers' Social Networks," *Organization Science* 14, no. 2 (2003), pp. 123–136.

9. Sundstrom et al., "Work Teams," p. 126; B. B. Baltes, M. W. Dickson, M. P. Sherman, C. C. Bauer, and J. S. LaGanke, "Computer-Mediated Communication and Group Decision Making: A Meta-Analysis," *Organizational Behavior and Human Decision Processes* 87, no. 1 (2002), pp. 156–179.

10. B. Mullen, C. Symons, L. Hu, and E. Salas, "Group Size, Leadership Behavior, and Subordinate Satisfaction," *Journal of General Psychology* 116, no. 2 (1989), pp. 155–170.

11. B. Mullen, D. A. Johnson, and S. D. Drake, "Organizational Productivity as a Function of Group Composition: A Self-Attention Perspective," *Journal of Social Psychology* 127 (1987), pp. 143–150.

12. B. Latane, K. Williams, and S. Markings, "Social Loafing," *Psychology Today* 13, no. 5 (1979), pp. 104–110; P. C. Barley, "Social Loafing and Collectivism: A Comparison of the United States and the People's Republic of China," *Administrative Science Quarterly* 34 (1989), pp. 565–581; S. M. Murphy, S. J. Wayne, R. C. Liden, and B. Erdogan, "Understanding Social Loafing: The Role of Justice Perceptions and Exchange Relationships," *Human Relations* 56, no. 1 (2003), pp. 61–84; X-P. Chen and D. G. Bachrach, "Tolerance of Free-Riding: The Effects of Defection Size, Defection Pattern, and Social Orientation in a Repeated Public Goods Dilemma," *Organizational Behavior and Human Decision Processes* 90, no. 1 (2003), pp. 139–147; H. Goren, R. Kurzban, and A. Rapoport, "Social Loafing vs. Social Enhancement: Public Goods Provisioning in Real-Time with Irrevocable Commitments," *Organizational Behavior and Human Decision Processes* 90, no. 2 (2003), pp. 277–290.

13. K. L. Bettenhausen, "Five Years of Group Research: What We Have Learned and What Needs to Be Addressed," *Journal of Management* 17 (1991), pp. 345–381.

14. K. D. Williams, S. A. Nica, L. D. Baca, and B. Latane, "Social Loafing and Swimming: Effects of Identifiability on Individual and Relay Performance of Intercollegiate Swimmers," *Basic and Applied Social Psychology* 70 (1989), pp. 73–81.

15. W. K. Gabrenya, Y. Wang, and B. Latane, "Social Loafing on an Optimizing Task: Cross-Cultural Differences among Chinese and Americans," *Journal of Cross-Cultural Psychology* 16 (1985), pp. 223–242.

16. M. E. Shaw, *Group Dynamics: The Psychology of Small Group Behavior*, 3rd ed. (New York: McGraw-Hill, 1981).

17. R. E. Silverman, "For Charlie Kim, Company of Friends Proves a Lonely Place," *Wall Street Journal*, pp. A1+.

18. L. H. Pelled, "Demographic Diversity, Conflict, and Work Group Outcomes: An Intervening Process Theory," *Administrative Science Quarterly* 7 (1996), pp. 615–631; L. H. Pelled, K. M. Eisenhardt, and K. R. Xin, "Exploring the Black Box: An Analysis of Work Group Diversity, Conflict, and Performance," *Administrative Science Quarterly* 44 (1999), pp. 1–28; K. Jehn, G. B. Northcraft, and M. A. Neale, "Why Differences Make a Difference: A Field Study of Diversity, Conflict, and Performance in Workgroups," *Administrative Science Quarterly* 44 (1999), pp. 741–763.

19. Queen's University, www.business.queensu.ca/mba_programs (accessed July 16, 2007).

20. S. G. Cohen, "What Makes Teams Work: Group Effectiveness Research from the Shop Floor to the Executive Suite," *Journal of Management* 23 (1997), pp. 239–290; J. T. Polzer, L. P. Milton, and W. B. Swann Jr., "Capitalizing on Diversity: Interpersonal Congruence in Small Work Groups," *Administrative Science Quarterly* 47, no. 2 (2002), pp. 296–324; G. S. Van der Vegt and O. Janssen, "Joint Impact of Interdependence and Group Diversity on Innovation," *Journal of Management* 29, no. 5 (2003), pp. 729–751.

21. Pelled, "Demographic Diversity, Conflict, and Work Group Outcomes," Pelled et al., "Exploring the Black Box"; J. A. Chatman and F. J. Flynn, "The Influence of Demographic Heterogeneity on the Emergence and Consequences of Cooperative Norms in Work Teams," *Academy of Management Journal* 44 (2001), pp. 956–974; D. A. Harrison, K. H. Price, and M. P. Bell, "Beyond Relational Demography: Time and the Effects of Surface- and Deep-Level Diversity on Work Group Cohesion," *Academy of Management Journal* 41 (1998), pp. 96–107; Jehn et al., "Why Differences Make a Difference"; J. S. Bunderson and K. M. Sutcliffe, "Comparing Alternative Conceptualizations of Functional Diversity in Management Teams: Process and Performance Effects," *Academy of Management Journal* 45, no. 5 (2002), pp. 875–893; Harrison et al., "Time, Teams, and Task Performance," pp. 1029–1045.

22. Chatman and Flynn, "The Influence of Demographic Heterogeneity."

23. Harrison et al., "Beyond Relational Demography."

24. J. Gordon et al., "Workplace Blues," *Training* 35, no. 2 (1996), p. 16.

25. M. S. Abramson, "First Teams," *Government Executive* 18, no. 5 (1996), pp. 53–58; L. F. Brajkovich, "Executive Commentary," *Academy of Management Executive* 17, no. 1 (2003), pp. 110–111; L. Thompson, "Improving the Creativity of Organizational Work Groups," *Academy of Management Executive* 17, no. 1 (2003), pp. 96–97; Van der Vegt and Janssen, "Joint Impact of Interdependence and Group Diversity"; R. Sethi, D. C. Smith, and C. W. Park, "How to Kill a Team's Creativity," *Harvard Business Review* 80, no. 8 (2002), pp. 16–17.

26. C. C. Manz and H. P. Sims Jr., "Leading Workers to Lead Themselves: The External Leadership of Self-Managing Work Teams," *Administrative Science Quarterly* 32 (1987), pp. 106–129.

27. C. Noronha, "Ask the Legends: John Forzani," *Canadian Business* Online, www.canadianbusiness.com (accessed July 16, 2007).

28. Shaw, *Group Dynamics*; M. C. Thomas-Hunt, T. Y. Ogden, and M. A. Neale, "Who's Really Sharing? Effects of Social and Expert Status on Knowledge Exchange within Groups," *Management Science* 49, no. 4 (2003), pp. 464–477; T. R. Tyler and S. L. Blader, "Autonomous vs. Comparative Status: Must We Be Better than Others to Feel Good about Ourselves?" *Organizational Behavior and Human Decision Processes* 89, no. 1 (2002), pp. 813–838; P. M. Valcour, "Managerial Behavior in a Multiplex Role System," *Human Relations* 55, no. 10 (2002), pp. 1163–1188.

29. J. E. Driskell and E. Salas, "Group Decision Making under Stress," *Journal of Applied Psychology* 76 (1991), pp. 473–478.

30. Shaw, *Group Dynamics.*

31. Ibid.

32. D. C. Feldman, "The Development and Enforcement of Group Norms," *Academy of Management Review* 9 (1984), pp. 47–53.

33. A. Wahl, "Work Buds," *Canadian Business* 80, no. 9, pp. 56–57.

34. Shaw, *Group Dynamics*. See also N. Nicholson (ed.), *Encyclopedic Dictionary of Organizational Behavior* (Oxford, UK: Blackwell, 1995), p. 199.

35. Cohen, "What Makes Teams Work."

36. D. Druckman and J. A. Swets (eds.), *Enhancing Human Performance: Issues, Theories and Techniques,* National Research Council (Washington, DC: National Academy Press, 1988).

37. Ibid.

38. Shaw, *Group Dynamics*; Sethi, Smith, and Park, "How to Kill a Team's Creativity."

39. Shaw, *Group Dynamics*, p. 218; Sethi, Smith, and Park, "How to Kill a Team's Creativity."

40. D. M. Landers, M. O. Wilkinson, B. D. Hatfield, and H. Barber, "Causality and the Cohesion-Performance Relationship," *Journal of Sport Psychology* 4, no. 2 (1982), pp. 170–183; J. A. LePine, J. R. Hollenbeck, D. R. Ilgen, J. A. Colquitt, and A. Ellis, "Gender Composition, Situational Strength, and Team Decision-Making Accuracy: A Criterion Decomposition Approach," *Organizational Behavior and Human Decision Processes* 88, no. 1 (2002), pp. 445–475.

41. J. R. Hackman, "The Design of Work Teams," in J. W. Lorsch (ed.), *Handbook of Organizational Behavior* (Upper Saddle River, NJ: Prentice Hall, 1987), pp. 315–342.

42. Banker et al., "Impact of the Work Teams on Manufacturing Performance."

43. C. D. Cramton, "The Mutual Knowledge Problem and Its Consequences for Dispersed Collaboration," *Organization Science* 12 (2001), pp. 346–367; C. D. Cramton, "Finding Common Ground in Dispersed Collaboration," *Organizational Dynamics* 4 (2002), pp. 356–371; M. K. Ahuja and J. A. Galvin, "Socialization in Virtual Groups," *Journal of Management* 29, no. 2 (2003), pp. 161–186.

44. Cramton, "Finding Common Ground in Dispersed Collaboration"; Ahuja and Galvin, "Socialization in Virtual Groups."

45. B. E. Ashforth and F. Mael, "Social Identity Theory and the Organization," *Academy of Management Review* 14 (1989), pp. 20–39; Bettenhausen, "Five Years of Group Research."

46. J. S. Heinem and E. Jacobsen, "A Model of Task Group Development in Complex Organizations and a Strategy of Implementation," *Academy of Management Review* 1, no. 4 (1976), pp. 98–111; B. W. Tuckman and M. A. Jensen, "Stages of Small Group Development Revisited," *Group and Organization Studies* 2 (1977), pp. 419–427; R. L. Moreland and J. N. Levine, "Group Dynamics over Time: Development and Socialization in Small Groups," in J. M. McGrath (ed.), *The Social Psychology of Time: New Perspectives,* Sage Focus editions, vol. 19 (Newbury Park, CA: Sage, 1988), pp. 151–181; Sundstrom et al., "Work Teams"; Bettenhausen, "Five Years of Group Research"; A. Chang, P. Bordia, and J. Duck, "Punctuated Equilibrium and Linear Progression: Toward a New Understanding of Group Development," *Academy of Management Journal* 46, no. 1 (2003), pp. 106–117.

47. B. W. Tuckman, "Development Sequence in Small Groups," *Psychological Bulletin* 63 (1965), pp. 384–399; Tuckman and Jensen, "Stages of Small Group Development Revisited."

48. Sundstrom et al., "Work Teams," p. 127.

49. S. Convey, "Performance Measurement in Cross-Functional Teams," *CMA Magazine* 68, no. 8 (1994), pp. 13–15.

50. M. H. Safizadeh, "The Case of Workgroups in Manufacturing Operations," *California Management Review* 35, no. 4 (1991), pp. 61–82; A. Erez, J. A. Lepine, and H. Elms, "Effects of Rotated Leadership and Peer Evaluation on the Functioning and Effectiveness of Self-Managed Teams: A Quasi-Experiment," *Personnel Psychology* 55, no. 4 (2002), pp. 929–948; L. I. Glassop, "The Organizational Benefit of Teams," *Human Relations* 55, no. 2 (2002), pp. 225–249.

51. Kirkman and Shapiro, "The Impact of Cultural Values on Employee Resistance to Teams."

52. P. Baker, "Open Sesame!" *Works Management* 54, no. 8 (2001), p. 35.

53. K. Lovelace, D. L. Shapiro, and L. R. Weingart, "Maximizing Cross-Functional New Product Teams' Innovativeness and Constraint Adherence: A Conflict Communications Perspective," *Academy of Management Journal* 44 (2001), pp. 779–793.

54. A. R. Jassawalla, and H. C. Sashittal, "Building Collaborative Cross-Functional New Product Teams," *Academy of Management Executive* 13, no. 3 (1999), pp. 50–63; Bunderson and Sutcliffe, "Comparing Alternative Conceptualizations of Functional Diversity in Management Teams"; Sethi, Smith, and Park, "How to Kill a Team's Creativity."

55. J. M. Liedtka, "Collaborating across Lines of Business for Competitive Advantage," *Academy of Management Executive* 10, no. 2 (1996), pp. 20–38; Sethi, Smith, and Park, "How to Kill a Team's Creativity."

56. J. J. Distefano and M. L. Maznevski, "Creating Value with Diverse Teams in Global Management," *Organizational Dynamics* 29 (2000), pp. 45–63.

57. U. Vu, "A Variety of Options Gives Boost to Remote Work," *Canadian HR Reporter* 19, no. 14, pp. 15–16.

58. J. A. Cannon-Bowers and E. Salas, "Teamwork Competencies: The Interaction of Team Member Knowledge, Skills, and Attitudes," in H. F. O'Neil Jr. (ed.), *Workforce Readiness: Competencies and Assessment* (Mahwah, NJ:. Lawrence Erlbaum Associates, 1997), pp. 151–174; J. A. Cannon-Bowers and E. Salas, "A Framework for Developing Team Performance Measures in Training," in M. T. Brannick, E. Salas, and C. Prince (eds.), *Team Performance Assessment and Measurement: Theory, Methods, and Applications* (Mahwah, NJ: Lawrence Erlbaum Associates, 1997); J. A. Cannon-Bowers, S. I. Tannenbaum, E. Salas, and C. E. Volpe, "Defining Competencies and Establishing Team Training Requirements," in R. A. Guzzo, E. Salas and Associates (eds.), *Team Effectiveness and Decision Making in Organizations* (San Francisco: Jossey-Bass, 1995); E. Salas, T. L. Dickinson, S. A. Converse, and S. I. Tannenbaum, "Toward an Understanding of Team Performance and Training," in R. Swezey and E. Salas (eds.), *Teams: Their Training and Performance* (Norwood, NJ: Ablex, 1992), pp. 3–29; G. A. Okhuysen and K. M. Eisenhardt, "Integrating Knowledge in Groups: How Formal Interventions Enable Flexibility," *Organization Science* 13, no. 4 (2002), pp. 370–386.

59. Cannon-Bowers et al., "Defining Competencies and Establishing Team Training Requirements."

60. Cannon-Bowers and Salas, "Teamwork Competencies"; Cannon-Bowers and Salas, "A Framework for Developing Team Performance Measures in Training"; Cannon-Bowers et al., "Defining Competencies and Establishing Team Training Requirements"; Salas et al., "Toward an Understanding of Team Performance and Training."

61. S. Caudron, "Keeping Team Conflict Alive," *Training and Development* 52, no. 9 (1998), pp. 48–52.

62. A. C. Amason, W. A. Hochwater, K. R. Thompson, and A. W. Harrison, "Conflict: An Important Dimension in Successful Management Teams," *Organizational Dynamics* 24, no. 2 (1995), pp. 20–35; S. Schulz-Hardt, M. Jochims, and D. Frey, "Productive Conflict in Group Decision Making: Genuine and Contrived Dissent as Strategies to Counteract Biased Information Seeking," *Organizational Behavior and Human Decision Processes* 88, no. 2 (2002), pp. 563–586; K. A. Jehn, "A Multimethod Examination of the Benefits and Detriments of Intragroup Conflict," *Administrative Science Quarterly* 40 (1995), pp. 256–282.

63. Amason et al., "Conflict"; K. M. Eisenhardt, J. L. Kahwajy, and L. J. Bourgeois, III, "Conflict and Strategic Choice: How Top Management Teams Disagree," *California Management Review* 39, no. 2 (1997), pp. 42–62; K. A. Jehn and E. A. Mannix, "The Dynamic Nature of Conflict: A Longitudinal Study of Intragroup Conflict and Group Performance," *Academy of Management Journal* 44 (2001), pp. 238–251; T. L. Simons and R. S. Peterson, "Task Conflict and Relationship Conflict in Top Management Teams: The Pivotal Role of Intragroup Trust," *Journal of Applied Psychology* 85 (2000), pp. 102–111; Pelled et al., "Exploring the Black Box."

64. Jehn, "A Multimethod Examination of the Benefits and Detriments of Intragroup Conflict."

65. Amason et al., "Conflict"; Jehn, "A Multimethod Examination of the Benefits and Detriments of Intragroup Conflict."

66. Pelled et al., "Exploring the Black Box."

67. Pelled, "Demographic Diversity, Conflict, and Work Group Outcomes."

68. Jehn et al., "Why Differences Make a Difference."

69. Amason et al., "Conflict."

70. Eisenhardt et al., "Conflict and Strategic Choice."

71. Jehn et al., "Why Differences Make a Difference."

72. Jehn and Mannix, "The Dynamic Nature of Conflict."

73. D. R. Forsyth, *An Introduction to Group Dynamics*, (Monterey, CA: Brooks/Cole Publishing, 1983).

74. G. A. Neuman and J. Wright, "Team Effectiveness: Beyond Skills and Cognitive Ability," *Journal of Applied Psychology* 84 (1999), pp. 376–389; D. E. Hyatt and T. M. Ruddy, "An Examination of the Relationship between Work Group Characteristics and Performance: Once More into the Breech," *Personnel Psychology* 50 (1997), pp. 553–585; M. A. Campion, E. M. Papper, and G. J. Medsker, "Relations between Work Team Characteristics and Effectiveness: A Replication and Extension," *Personnel Psychology* 49 (1996), pp. 429–452; Cohen, "What Makes Teams Work."

75. J. Fitz-Enz, "Measuring Team Effectiveness," *HR Focus* 74, no. 8 (1997), p. 3.

76. J. R. Hackman (ed.), *Groups That Work (and Those That Don't): Creating Conditions for Effective Teamwork* (San Francisco: Jossey-Bass, 1990).

77. Hackman, *Groups That Work*.

78. Campion et al., "Relations between Work Team Characteristics and Effectiveness"; Hyatt and Ruddy, "An Examination of the Relationship between Work Group Characteristics and Performance."

79. R. Wageman and G. Baker, "Incentives and Cooperation: The Joint Effects of Task and Reward Interdependence on Group Performance," *Journal of Organizational Behavior* 18, no. 2 (1997), pp. 139–158.

80. Banker et al., "Impact of Work Teams on Manufacturing Performance"; M. Cottrill, "Give Your Teams Time and Training," *Academy of Management Executive* 11, no. 3 (1997), pp. 87–89.

81. Cohen, "What Makes Teams Work."

82. G. L. Hallam, "Seven Common Beliefs about Teams: Are They True?" *Leadership in Action* 17, no. 3 (1997), pp. 1–4.

83. G. Ahuja and M. Lampert, "Entrepreneurship in the Large Corporation: A Longitudinal Study of How Established Firms Create Breakthrough Inventions," *Strategic Management Journal* 22 (Special Issue) (2001), pp. 521–543.

CHAPTER 12

1. S. Bing, "Business as a Second Language," *Fortune*, 1998, pp. 57–58.

2. K. Krone, F. M. Jablin, and L. L. Putnam, "Communication Theory and Organizational Communication: Multiple Perspectives," in F. M. Japlin, L. L. Putnam, K. H. Roberts, and L. W. Porter (eds.), *Handbook of Organizational Communication: An Interdisciplinary Perspective* (Newbury Park, CA: Sage Publications, 1987).

3. H. C. Triandis, *Culture and Social Behavior* (New York: McGraw-Hill, 1994); B. A. Bechky, "Sharing Meaning across Occupational Communities: The Transformation of Understanding on a Production Floor," *Organization Science* 14, no. 3 (2003), p. 312; M. Becerra and A. K. Gupta, "Perceived Trustworthiness within the Organization: The Moderating Impact of Communication Frequency on Trustor and Trustee Effects," *Organization Science* 14, no. 1 (2003), pp. 32–44.

4. R. L. Daft and R. H. Lengel, "Information Richness: A New Approach to Managerial Behavior and Organization Design," in L. L. Cummings and B. Staw (eds.), *Research in Organizational Behavior*, vol. 6 (Greenwich, CT: JAI, 1984), pp. 191–223; R. L. Daft and R. H. Lengel, "Organizational Information Requirements, Media Richness and Structural Design," *Management Science* 32 (1986), pp. 554–572; K. Miller, *Organizational Communication: Approaches and Processes*, 2nd ed. (Belmont, CA: Wadsworth, 1999).

5. L. K. Trevino, R. L. Daft, and R. H. Lengel, "Understanding Managers' Media Concerns," in J. Fulk and C. Steinfeile (eds.), *Organizations and Communication Technology* (Newbury Park, CA: Sage Publications, 1990); Anonymous, "How to Create Communications Materials Employees Will Actually Use," *Harvard Business Review* 80, no. 1 (1990), p. 102.

6. B. B. Baltes, M. W. Dickson, M. P. Sherman, C. C. Bauer, and J. S. LaGanke, "Computer-Mediated Communication and Group Decision Making: A Meta-Analysis," *Organizational Behavior and Human Decision Processes* 87, no. 1 (2002), pp. 156–179.

7. J. Yates and W. J. Orlikowski, "Genres of Organizational Communication: A Structurational Approach to Studying Communication and Media," *Academy of Management Review* 17 (1992), pp. 299–326.

8. L. W. Porter, E. E. Lawler, III, and J. R. Hackman, *Behavior in Organizations* (New York: McGraw-Hill, 1975).

9. K. Davis, "The Care and Cultivation of the Corporate Grapevine," *Dun's Review* 102, no. 1 (1973), pp. 44–47.

10. C. Dellarocas, "The Digitization of Word of Mouth: Promise and Challenges of Online Feedback Mechanisms," *Management Science* 49, no. 10 (2003), pp. 1407–1424.

11. "BASF Launches SM/PO Venture," *Chemical Market Reporter* 262, no. 11 (2002), p. 23.

12. "He Said, She Said," *Communications* 46, no. 9 (2003), p. 11; H. Ibarra, "Homophily and Differential Returns: Sex Differences in Network Structure and Access in an Advertising Firm," *Administrative Science Quarterly* 37 (1992), pp. 422–447; H. Ibarra, "Personal Networks of Women and Minorities in Management: A Conceptual Framework," *Academy of Management Review* 18 (1993), pp. 56–87; H. Ibarra, "Race, Opportunity, and Diversity of Social Circles in Managerial Networks," *Academy of Management Journal* 38 (1995), pp. 673–703; K. A. Mollica, B. Gray, and L. K. Trevino, "Racial Homophily and Its Persistence in Newcomers' Social Networks," *Organization Science* 14, no. 2 (2003), pp. 123–136.

13. J. M. Beyer et al., "The Selective Perception of Managers Revisited," *Academy of Management Journal* 40 (1997), pp. 716–737.

14. A. Tversky and D. Kahneman, "Rational Choice and the Framing of Decisions," *Journal of Business* 59 (1986), pp. S251–278; I. Grugulis, "Nothing Serious? Candidates' Use of Humour in Management Training," *Human Relations* 55, no. 4 (2002), pp. 387–406.

15. C. M. Jones, "Shifting Sands: Women, Men, and Communication," *Journal of Communication* 49 (1999), pp. 148–155.

16. C. R. Rogers and F. J. Roethlisberger, "Barriers and Gateways to Communication," *Harvard Business Review* 69, no. 6 (1991), pp. 105–111; L. Perlow and S. Williams, "Is Silence Killing Your Company?" *Harvard Business Review* 81, no. 5 (2003), pp. 52–58.

17. R. Wilkinson, "Do You Speak Obscuranta?" *Supervision* 49, no. 9 (1988), pp. 3–5; C. Argyris, "Four Steps to Chaos," *Harvard Business Review* 81, no. 10 (2003), p. 140.

18. R. Harrison, *Beyond Words: An Introduction to Nonverbal Communication* (Upper Saddle River, NJ: Prentice Hall, 1974); A. Kristof-Brown, M. R. Barrick, and M. Franke, "Applicant Impression Management: Dispositional Influences and Consequences for Recruiter Perceptions of Fit and Similarity," *Journal of Management* 28, no. 1 (2002), pp. 27–46; H. A. Elfenbein and N. Ambady, "Predicting Workplace Outcomes from the Ability to Eavesdrop on Feelings," *Journal of Applied Psychology* 87, no. 5 (2002), pp. 963–971.
19. J. A. Mausehund, S. A. Timm, and A. S. King, "Diversity Training: Effects of an Intervention Treatment on Nonverbal Awareness," *Business Communication Quarterly* 58, no. 1 (1995), pp. 27–30.
20. J. H. Robinson, "Professional Communication in Korea: Playing Things by Eye," *IEEE Transactions on Professional Communication* 39, no. 3 (1996), pp. 129–134; G. E. Kersten, S. T. Koeszegi, and R. Vetschera, "The Effects of Culture in Computer-Mediated Negotiations," *Journal of Information Technology Theory and Application* 5, no. 2 (2003), pp. 1–28.
21. T. E. McNamara and K. Hayashi, "Culture and Management: Japan and the West towards a Transnational Corporate Culture," *Management Japan* 27, no. 2 (1994), pp. 3–13.
22. S. Okazaki and J. Alonso, "Right Messages for the Right Site: On-line Creative Strategies by Japanese Multinational Corporations," *Journal of Marketing Communications* 9, no. 4 (2002), pp. 221–240; M. Rosch and K. G. Segler, "Communication with Japanese," *Management International Review* 27, no. 4 (1987), pp. 56–67.
23. C. Gouttefarde, "Host National Culture Shock: What Management Can Do," *European Business Review* 92, no. 4 (1992), pp. 1–3.
24. H. Triandis, "Cross-Cultural Contributions to Theory in Social Psychology," in W. B. Gudykunst and Y. Y. Kim (eds.), *Reading on Communication with Strangers* (New York: McGraw-Hill, 1992), p. 75; R. S. Marshall and D. M. Boush, "Dynamic Decision-Making: A Cross-Cultural Comparison of U.S. and Peruvian Export Managers," *Journal of International Business Studies* 32, no. 4 (2001), pp. 873–893; T. R. Tyler and S. L. Blader, "Autonomous vs. Comparative Status: Must We Be Better Than Others to Feel Good about Ourselves?" *Organizational Behavior and Human Decision Processes* 89, no. 1 (2002), pp. 813–838; L. Huff and L. Kelley, "Levels of Organizational Trust in Individualist versus Collectivist Societies: A Seven-Nation Study," *Organization Science* 14, no. 1 (2003), pp. 81–90; A. C. Lewis and S. J. Sherman, "Hiring You Makes Me Look Bad: Social-Identity Based Reversal of the Ingroup Favoritism Effect," *Organizational Behavior and Human Decision Processes* 90, no. 2 (2003), pp. 262–276.
25. S. Carlson, "International Transmission of Information and the Business Firm," *Annals of the American Academy of Political and Social Science* 412 (1974), pp. 55–63; Marshall and Boush, "Dynamic Decision-Making"; Y. Luo, "Building Trust in Cross-Cultural Collaborations: Toward a Contingency Perspective," *Journal of Management* 28, no. 5 (2002), pp. 669–694.
26. J. Main, "How 21 Men Got Global in 35 Days," *Fortune*, 1989, pp. 71–79.
27. C. Peter, P. Scott, and J. Calvert, "Chinese Business Face: Communication Behaviors and Teaching Approaches," *Business Communication Quarterly* 66, no. 4 (2003), pp. 19–23; R. S. Burnert, "Ni Zao: Good Morning, China," *Business Horizons* 33, no. 6 (1990), pp. 65–71.
28. R. Alsop, "Playing Well with Others," *Wall Street Journal*, September 9, 2002, p. R1-1; Kristof-Brown, Barrick, and Franke, "Applicant Impression Management."
29. T. D. Lewis and G. H. Graham, "Six Ways to Improve Your Communication Skills," *Internal Auditor* (1988), p. 25.
30. G. M. Barton, "Manage Words Effectively," *Personnel Journal* 69, no. 1 (1990), pp. 32–40.
31. L. W. Porter and L. E. McKibbin, *Management Education and Development: Drift or Thrust into the 21st Century* (New York: McGraw-Hill, 1988).
32. S. L. Silk, "Making Your Speech Memorable," *Association Management* 46, no. 1 (1994), pp. L59–L62.
33. A. DeMeyer, "Tech Talk: How Managers Are Stimulating Global R&D Communication," *Sloan Management Review* 32, no. 3 (1991), pp. 49–58.
34. R. Fisher and W. Ury, *Getting to Yes* (London: Simon & Schuster, 1987); K. A. Wade-Benzoni et al., "Barriers to Resolution in Ideologically Based Negotiations: The Role of Values and Institutions," *Academy of Management Review* 27, no. 1 (2002), pp. 41–57.
35. Ibid.
36. Ibid., p. 54.
37. N. J. Adler, *International Dimensions of Organizational Behavior*, 2nd ed. (Boston: PWS-Kent, 1991), p. 185.
38. G. Fisher, *International Negotiations* (Chicago: Intercultural Press, 1980); J. L. Graham, "Brazilian, Japanese, and American Business Negotiations," *Journal of International Business Studies* 14, no. 1 (1983), pp. 47–61; J. L. Graham and N. M. Lam, "The Chinese Negotiation," *Harvard Business Review* 81, no. 10 (2003), pp. 82–91; J. K. Sebenius, "The Hidden Challenge of Cross-Border Negotiations," *Harvard Business Review* 80, no. 3 (2002), pp. 76–85; L. J. Kray, A. D. Galinsky, and L. Thompson, "Reversing the Gender Gap in Negotiations: An Exploration of Stereotype Regeneration," *Organizational Behavior and Human Decision Processes* 87, no. 2 (2002), pp. 386–409.
39. J. L. Graham and R. A. Herberger Jr., "Negotiators Abroad Don't Shoot from the Hip," *Harvard Business Review* 83, no. 4 (1983), pp. 160–168.
40. N. J. Adler and J. L. Graham, "Cross-Cultural Interaction: The International Comparison Fallacy?" *Journal of International Business Studies* 20, no. 3 (1989), pp. 515–537.
41. Fisher and Ury, *Getting to Yes*.
42. M. Lee, "10 Myths about Multicultural Customers," *Selling*, November 2003, pp. 10–12; K. Kumar, S. Noneth, and C. Yauger, "Cultural Approaches to the Process of Business Negotiation: Understanding Cross-Cultural Differences in Negotiating Behaviors," in C. L. Swanson (ed.), *International Research in the Business Disciplines* (Greenwich, CT: JAI Press, 1993), pp. 79–90; B. M. Hawrysh and J. L. Zaichkowsky, "Cultural Approaches to Negotiations: Understanding the Japanese," *International Marketing Review* 7, no. 2 (1990), pp. 28–42.
43. Kumar et al., "Cultural Approaches to the Process of Business Negotiations."
44. Graham and Herberger, "Negotiators Abroad Don't Shoot from the Hip."
45. Kumar et al., "Cultural Approaches to the Process of Business Negotiations."
46. N. Woliansky, "We Do (Do Not) Accept Your Offer," *Management Review* 75, no. 12 (1989), pp. 54–55; Kumar et al., "Cultural Approaches to the Process of Business Negotiations."
47. Kumar et al., "Cultural Approaches to the Process of Business Negotiations," p. 86.
48. Graham and Herberger, "Negotiators Abroad Don't Shoot from the Hip."
49. Adler and Graham, "Cross-Cultural Interaction"; C. Barnum and N. Wolniasky, "Why Americans Fail at Overseas Negotiations," *Management Review* 75, no. 10 (1989), pp. 55–57.
50. Kumar et al., "Cultural Approaches to the Process of Business Negotiations."

CHAPTER 13

1. S. A. Snell, M. A. Shadur, and P. M. Wright, "Human Resources Strategy: The Era of Our Ways," in M. A. Hitt, R. E. Freeman, and J. S. Harrison (eds.), *Handbook of Strategic Management* (Oxford, UK: Blackwell Publishing, 2001).
2. M. A. Hitt and R. D. Ireland, "The Essence of Strategic Leadership: Managing Human and Social Capital," *Journal of Leadership and Organization Studies* 9 (2002), pp. 3–14.
3. P. M. Wright, B. B. Dunford, and S. A. Snell, "Human Resources and the Resource-Based View of the Firm," *Journal of Management* 27 (2001), pp. 701–721.
4. M. W. McCall and M. M. Lombardo, *Off the Track: Why and How Successful Executives Get Derailed* (Greensboro, NC: Center for Creative Leadership, 1983).
5. D. Ulrich, *Human Resource Champions* (Boston: Harvard Business School Press, 1997).
6. R. W. Rowden, "Potential Roles of the Human Resource Management Professional in the Strategic Planning Process," *S.A.M. Advanced Management Journal* 64, no. 3 (1999), pp. 22–27.
7. M. Huselid, S. Jackson, and R. Schuler, "Technical and Strategic Human Resource Management Effectiveness as Determinants of Firm Performance," *Academy of Management Journal* 40 (1997), pp. 171–188; K. S. Law, D. K. Tse, and N. Zhou, "Does Human Resource Management Matter in a Transitional Economy? China as an Example," *Journal of International Business Studies* 34, no. 3 (2003), pp. 255–265; S. L. Rynes, K. G. Brown, and A. E. Colbert, "Seven Common Misconceptions about Human Resource Practices: Research Findings versus Practitioner Beliefs," *Academy of Management Executive* 16, no. 3 (2002), pp. 92–102; R. Batt, "Managing Customer Services: Human Resource Practices, Quit Rates, and Sales Growth," *Academy of Management Journal* 45, no. 3 (2002), pp. 587–597.
8. J. Pfeffer, *Competitive Advantage through People: Unleashing the Power of the Workforce* (Boston: Harvard Business School Press, 1994).
9. S. Bates, "Growing Pains Are Cited in Study of HR Outsourcing," *HRMagazine* 47, no. 8 (2002), p. 10; D. P. Lepak and S. A. Snell, "Examining the Human Resource Architecture: The Relationships among Human Capital, Employment, and Human Resource Configurations," *Journal of Management* 28, no. 4 (2002), pp. 517–543.
10. M. O'Daniel, "Online Assistance for Job Seekers," *New Strait Times*, November 11, 2003; L. Goff, "Job Surfing," *Computer-World* 30, no. 36 (1996), p. 81; M. K. McGee, "Job Hunting on the Internet," *InformationWeek* 576 (1996), p. 98.
11. D. Terpstra, "The Search for Effective Methods," *HR Focus* 73, no. 5 (1996), pp. 16–17.
12. J. S. Black, H. B. Gregersen, M. E. Mendenhall, and L. Stroh, *Global People through International Assignments* (Reading, MA: Addison-Wesley, 1999).
13. J. Conway, R. Jako, and D. Goodman, "A Meta-Analysis of Interrater and Internal Consistency Reliability of Selection Interviews," *Journal of Applied Psychology* 80, no. 5 (1995), pp. 565–579; M. McDaniel, D. Whetzel, F. Schmidt, and S. Maurer, "The Validity of Employment Interviews: A Comprehensive Review and Meta-Analysis," *Journal of Applied Psychology* 79, no. 4 (1994), pp. 599–616.
14. G. Dessler, *Human Resource Management*, 8th ed. (Upper Saddle River, NJ: Prentice Hall, 2000), Chapter 6.
15. L. Rudner, "Pre-Employment Testing and Employee Productivity," *Public Management* 21, no. 2 (1992), pp. 133–150; P. Lowry, "The Assessment Center: Effects of Varying Consensus Procedures," *Public Personnel Management* 21, no. 2 (1992), pp. 171–183; T. Payne, N. Anderson, and T. Smith, "Assessment Centres: Selection Systems and Cost-Effectiveness," *Personnel Review* 21, no. 4 (1992), pp. 48–56; D. J. Schleicher, D. V. Day, B. Mayes, and R. E. Riggio, "A New Frame for Frame-of-Reference Training: Enhancing the Construct Validity of Assessment Centers," *Journal of Applied Psychology* 87, no. 4 (2002), pp. 735–746; F. Lievens, "Trying to Understand the Different Pieces of the Construct Validity Puzzle of Assessment Centers: An Examination of Assessor and Assessee Effects," *Journal of Applied Psychology* 87, no. 4 (2002), pp. 675–686; W. Arthur Jr., E. A. Day, T. L. McNelly, and P. S. Edens, "A Meta-Analysis of the Criterion-Related Validity of Assessment Center Dimensions," *Personnel Psychology* 56, no. 1 (2003), pp. 125–154; D. J. Woehr and W. Arthur Jr., "The Construct-Related Validity of Assessment Center Ratings: A Review and Meta-Analysis of the Role of Methodological Factors," *Journal of Management* 29, no. 2 (2003), p. 231; K. Dayan, R. Kasten, and S. Fox, "Entry-Level Police Candidate Assessment Center: An Efficient Tool for a Hammer to Kill a Fly?" *Personnel Psychology* 55, no. 4 (2002), pp. 827–849.
16. R. Bentley, "Candidates Face Alternative Testing," *Computer Weekly*, November 18, 2003, p. 54; S. Adler, "Personality Tests for Salesforce Selection," *Review of Business* 16, no. 1 (1994), pp. 27–31.
17. M. McCullough, "Can Integrity Testing Improve Market Conduct?" *LIMRA's Marketfacts* 15, no. 2 (1996), pp. 15–16; H. J. Bernardin and D. Cooke, "Validity of an Honesty Test in Predicting Theft among Convenience Store Employees," *Academy of Management Journal* 36, no. 50 (1993), pp. 1097–1108.
18. B. Murphy, W. Barlow, and D. Hatch, "Employer-Mandated Physicals for Over-70 Employees Violate the ADEA," *Personnel Journal* 72, no. 6 (1993), p. 24; R. Ledman and D. Brown, "The Americans with Disabilities Act," *SAM Advanced Management Journal* 58, no. 2 (1993), pp. 17–20.
19. C. Fisher, "Organizational Socialization: An Integrative Review," in K. Rowland and J. Ferris (eds.), *Research in Personnel and Human Resource Management* 4 (1986), pp. 101–145.
20. T. J. Fogarty, "Socialization and Organizational Outcomes in Large Public Accounting Firms," *Journal of Managerial Issues* 12, no. 1 (2000), pp. 13–33; M. K. Ahuja and J. E. Galvin, "Socialization in Virtual Groups," *Journal of Management* 29, no. 2 (2003), p. 161; E. W. Morrison, "Newcomers' Relationships: The Role of Social Network Ties during Socialization," *Academy of Management Journal* 45, no. 6 (2002), pp. 1149–1160.
21. B. Jacobson and B. Kaye, "Service Means Success," *Training and Development* 45, no. 5 (1991), pp. 53–58; J. Brechlin and A. Rossett, "Orienting New Employees," *Training* 28, no. 4 (1991), pp. 45–51.
22. W. P. Anthony, P. L. Perrewé, and K. M. Kacmar, *Strategic Human Resource Management* (Fort Worth, TX: Harcourt Brace Jovanovich, 1993).
23. L. W. Porter and L. E. McKibbin, *Management Education and Development* (New York: McGraw-Hill, 1988); A. Kristof-Brown, M. R. Barrick, and M. Franke, "Applicant Impression Management: Dispositional Influences and Consequences for Recruiter Perceptions of Fit and Similarity," *Journal of Management* 28, no. 1 (2002), pp. 27–46.
24. J. De Kok, "The Impact of Firm-Provided Training on Production," *International Small Business Journal* 20, no. 3 (2002), pp. 271–295.
25. J. K. Eskildsen and J. J. Dahlgaard, "A Causal Model for Employee Satisfaction," *Total Quality Management* 11, no. 8 (2000), pp. 1081–1094.
26. M. Hammer and J. Champy, *Reengineering the Corporation* (New York: HarperCollins, 1993); D. A. Buchanan, "Demands, Instabilities, Manipulations, Careers: The Lived Experience of Driving Change," *Human Relations* 56, no. 6 (2003), p. 663.

27. T. Redman, E. Snape, and G. McElwee, "Appraising Employee Performance: A Vital Organizational Activity?" *Education and Training* 35, no. 2 (1993), pp. 3–10; R. Bretz, G. Milkovitch, and W. Read, "The Current State of Performance Appraisal Research and Practice," *Journal of Management* 18, no. 2 (1992), pp. 321–352.

28. R. Cardy and G. Dobbins, *Performance Appraisal* (Cincinnati, OH: South-Western Publishing, 1994).

29. L. Gomez-Mejia, "Evaluating Employee Performance: Does the Appraisal Instrument Make a Difference?" *Journal of Organizational Behavior Management* 9, no. 2 (1988), pp. 155–272.

30. C. Rarick and G. Baxter, "Behaviorally Anchored Rating Scales: An Effective Performance Appraisal Approach," *Advanced Management Journal* 51, no. 1 (1986), pp. 36–39; D. Naffziger, "BARS, RJPs, and Recruiting," *Personnel Administrator* 30, no. 8 (1985), pp. 85–96; M. Hosoda, E. F. Stone-Romero, and G. Coats, "The Effects of Physical Attractiveness on Job-Related Outcomes: A Meta-Analysis of Experimental Studies," *Personnel Psychology* 51, no. 2 (2003), p. 431; T. J. Watson, "Ethical Choice in Managerial Work: The Scope for Moral Choices in an Ethically Irrational World," *Human Relations* 56, no. 2 (2003), pp. 167–185.

31. K. Clark, "Judgment Day," *U.S. News & World Report* 134, no. 2 (2003), p. 31; D. Bohl, "Minisurvey: 360 Degree Appraisals Yield Superior Results," *Compensation and Benefits Review* 28, no. 5 (1996), pp. 16–19.

32. P. W. B. Atkins and R. E. Wood, "Self versus Others' Ratings as Predictors of Assessment Center Ratings: Validation Evidence for 360-Degree Feedback Programs," *Personnel Psychology* 55, no. 4 (2002), pp. 871–904.

33. J. Lawrie, "Steps toward an Objective Appraisal," *Supervisory Management* 34, no. 5 (1989), pp. 17–24.

34. "Changing with the Times," *IRS Employment Review*, February 21, 2003, pp. 14–17; J. Kanin-Lovers and M. Cameron, "Broadbanding—A Step Forward or a Step Backward?" *Journal of Compensation and Benefits* 9, no. 5 (1994), pp. 39–42.

35. L. Stroh, J. Brett, J. Baumann, and A. Reilly, "Agency Theory and Variable Pay Compensation Strategies," *Academy of Management Journal* 39, no. 3 (1996), pp. 751–767.

36. J. Herman, "Beating the Midlife Career Crisis," *Fortune*, 1993, pp. 52–62.

37. Personal communication with vice-president of human resources at Sony.

38. A. M. Chaker, "Luring Moms Back to Work," *Wall Street Journal*, December 30, 2003, pp. D1–D2; A. Leibowitz and J. Merman, "Explaining Changes in Married Mothers' Employment over Time," *Demography* 32, no. 3 (1995), pp. 365–378; S. Werner, "Recent Developments in International Management Research: A Review of 20 Top Management Journals," *Journal of Management* 28, no. 3 (2002), pp. 277–305.

39. J. S. Black and H. B. Gregersen, *So You're Going Overseas: A Handbook for Personal and Professional Success* (San Diego, CA: Global Business Publishers, 1999).

40. Foreign Affairs and International Trade Canada, www.infoexpert.gc.ca (accessed October 3, 2007); The Center for the Advancement of Working Women, www.miraikan.go.jp (accessed October 3, 2007); Government of Canada *Employment Equity Act*, 1995, c 44.

41. E. P. Gray, "The National Origin of BFOQ under Title VII," *Employee Relations Law Journal* 11, no. 2 (1985), pp. 311–321.

42. Canada Council for the Arts, "Cultural Diversity—The Cornerstone of Canadian Society," www.canadacouncil.ca (accessed October 3, 2007).

43. Ibid.

PART 3 INTEGRATIVE CASE

1. R. Crane, *European Business Culture* (Harlow, England: Financial Times/Prentice Hall, 2000).

2. K. Fader, *Russia* (San Diego, CA: Lucent Books, 1998).

3. R. Gesteland, *Cross-Cultural Business Behavior* (Copenhagen: Copenhagen Business School Press, 1999).

4. C. Mitchell, *Passport Russia* (San Rafael, CA: World Trade Press, 1998).

5. T. Morrison, W. Conaway, and G. Borden, *Kiss, Bow, or Shake Hands* (Holbrook, MA: Adams Media, 1994).

6. R. Munro, "Moscow's Top Hotels Greet the Good Times," *The Moscow Times*, May 21, 2002.

7. P. Newman, "Economic Terrorism in a Moscow Hotel." *Maclean's*, October 27, 1997.

8. W. Sears and A. Tamulionyte-Lentz, *Succeeding in Central and Eastern Europe* (Woburn, MA: Butterworth-Heinemann, 2001).

9. B. Smith, *The Collapse of the Soviet Union* (San Diego, CA: Lucent Press, 1994); O. Torchinsky, *Cultures of the World: Russia* (New York: Marshall Cavendish, 1997).

CHAPTER 14

1. R. E. Hoskisson and M. A. Hitt, *Downscoping: How to Tame the Diversified Firm* (New York: Oxford University Press, 1994).

2. G. Orwell, *1984: A Novel* (New York: New American Library, 1950); D. E. W. Marginson, "Management Control Systems and Their Effects on Strategy Formation at Middle-Management Levels: Evidence from a U.K. Organization," *Strategic Management Journal* 23, no. 11 (2002), pp. 1019–1031; M. Goold and A. Campbell, "Do You Have a Well-Designed Organization?" *Harvard Business Review* 80, no. 3 (2002), pp. 117–124; W. Nasrallah, R. Levitt, and P. Glynn, "Interaction Value Analysis: When Structured Communication Benefits Organizations," *Organization Science* 14, no. 5 (2003), pp. 541–557.

3. A. S. Tannenbaum (ed.), *Control in Organizations* (New York: McGraw-Hill, 1968); Marginson, "Management Control Systems and Their Effects"; Goold and Campbell, "Do You Have a Well-Designed Organization?"; Nasrallah, Levitt, and Glynn, "Interaction Value Analysis."

4. External Forces, Internal Strength: Royal Canadian Mint Annual Report 2006.

5. V. Govindarajan, "Impact of Participation in the Budgetary Process on Managerial Attitudes and Performance: Universalistic and Contingency Perspectives," *Decision Sciences* 7 (1986), pp. 496–516.

6. D. Drickhamer, "Europe's Best Plants: Medical Marvel," *Industry Week* 257, no. 3 (2002), pp. 47–49.

7. E. A. Locke, "The Ubiquity of the Technique of Goal Setting in Theories of and Approaches to Employee Motivation," *Academy of Management Review* 3 (1978), pp. 594–601; A. Drach-Zachavy and M. Erez, "Challenge versus Threat Effects on the Goal–Performance Relationship," *Organizational Behavior and Human Decision Processes* 88, no. 2 (2002), pp. 667–682.

8. R. N. Anthony and J. S. Reece, *Accounting Principles*, 7th ed. (Chicago: Richard D. Irwin, 1995).

9. Ibid.

10. J. Hope and R. Fraser, "Who Needs Budgets?" *Harvard Business Review* 81, no. 2 (2003), pp. 108–115.

11. F. D. Buggie, "Set the 'Fuzzy Front End' in Concrete," *Research Technology Management* 45, no. 4 (2002), pp. 11–14; Product Development Inc., "Product Innovation Guru

Dr. Robert G. Cooper and Nine Leading Companies Address Business Executives at the 1st Annual Stage-Gate® Leadership Summit," press release March 13, 2007, www.prod-dev.com (accessed June 14, 2007).

12. Marginson, "Management Control Systems and Their Effects"; M. Goold and J. J. Quinn, "The Paradox of Strategic Controls," *Strategic Management Journal* 77 (1990), pp. 43–57.
13. J. Hogan and B. Holland, "Using Theory to Evaluate Personality and Job-Performance Relations: A Socioanalytic Perspective," *Journal of Applied Psychology* 88, no. 1 (2003), p. 100; P. Lorange and D. C. Murphy, "Strategy and Human Resources: Concepts and Practice," *Human Resource Management* 22, nos. 1/2 (1983), pp. 111–135.
14. J. A. Alexander, "Adaptive Change in Corporate Control Practices," *Academy of Management Journal* 34 (1991), pp.162–193; V. Govindarajan and J. Fisher, "Strategy, Control Systems, and Resource Sharing: Effects on Business-Unit Performance," *Academy of Management Journal* 33 (1990), pp. 259–285.
15. A. Zuber, "McD Restructures to Beef Up Performance," *Nation's Restaurant News* 35, no. 44 (2001), pp. 1, 6.
16. Alexander, "Adaptive Change in Corporate Control Practices," p. 181.
17. G. Hamel and L. Valikangas, "The Quest for Resilience," *Harvard Business Review* 81, no. 9 (2003), pp. 52–63; Goold and Quinn, "The Paradox of Strategic Controls."
18. Goold and Quinn, "The Paradox of Strategic Controls," Figure 2, p. 55.
19. L. Strauss, "Come Fly with Me," *Barron's* 52, no. 33 (2002), p. T8.
20. Goold and Quinn, "The Paradox of Strategic Controls."
21. N. C. Churchill, "Budget Choice: Planning vs. Control," *Harvard Business Review* 62, no. 4 (1984), pp. 150–164.
22. R. Whiting, "Crystal-Ball Glance into Fiscal Future," *Information Week*, July 22, 2002, p. 37.
23. W. A. Van der Stede, "The Relationship between Two Consequences of Budgetary Controls: Budgetary Slack Creation and Managerial Short-Term Orientation," *Accounting, Organizations, and Society* 25 (2000), pp. 609–622.
24. D. Brown, "Using Competencies and Rewards to Enhance Business Performance and Customer Service at the Standard Life Assurance Company," *Compensation and Benefits Review* 33, no. 4 (2001), pp. 14–24.
25. J. R. Barker, "Tightening the Iron Cage: Concertive Control in Self-Managing Teams," *Administrative Science Quarterly* 38 (1993), pp. 408–437; Goold and Quinn, "The Paradox of Strategic Controls"; W. G. Ouchi, "A Conceptual Framework for the Design of Organizational Control Mechanisms," *Management Science* 25 (1979), pp. 833–848; W. G. Ouchi, "Markets, Bureaucracies, and Clans," *Administrative Science Quarterly* 25 (1980), pp. 129–141; R. E. Walton, "From Control to Commitment in the Workplace," *Harvard Business Review* 63, no. 2 (1985), pp. 76–84.
26. Barker, "Tightening the Iron Cage."
27. W. H. Newman, *Constructive Control: Design and Use of Control Systems* (Upper Saddle River, NJ: Prentice Hall, 1975).
28. P. Odell, "Wine.com Plans Big October E-Mailing," *Direct* 14, no. 11 (2002), p. 11; E. Gunn, "A Good Year," SmartBusinessMag.com, pp. 40–42.
29. R. N. Anthony, J. Dearden, and V. Govindarajan, *Management Control Systems*, 8th ed. (Burr Ridge, IL: Richard D. Irwin, 1995).
30. R. S. Kaplan and D. P. Norton, "The Balanced Scorecard—Measures That Drive Performance," *Harvard Business Review* 70, no. 1 (1992), pp. 71–80; A. Neely and M. Bourne, "Why Measurement Initiatives Fail," *Quality Focus* 4, no. 4 (2000), pp. 3–6.
31. Kaplan and Norton, "The Balanced Scorecard."
32. Kidwell, Ho, Blake, Wraith, Roubi, and Richardson, "New Management Techniques: An International Comparison," February 2002, www.nysscpa.org/cpajournal (accessed June 14, 2007).
33. E. M. Olson and S. F. Slater, "The Balanced Scorecard, Competitive Strategy, and Performance," *Business Horizons* 45, no. 3 (2002), pp. 3–6.
34. Neely and Bourne, "Why Quality Initiatives Fail."
35. G. F. Hanks, M. A. Freid, and J. Huber, "Shifting Gears at Borg-Warner Automotive," *Management Accounting* 75, no. 8 (1994), pp. 25–29.
36. G. A. Bigley and K. H. Roberts, "The Incident Command System: High-Reliability Organizing for Complex and Volatile Task Environments," *Academy of Management Journal* 44 (2001), pp. 1281–1299.
37. K. H. Roberts, "Managing High Reliability Organizations," *California Management Review* 34, no. 4 (1990), pp. 101–113.
38. D. M. Iadipaolo, "Monster or Monitor? Have Tracking Systems Gone Mad?" *Insurance and Technology* 17, no. 6 (1992), pp. 47–54.
39. M. A. Hitt, R. E. Hoskisson, R. A. Johnson, and D. D. Moesel, "The Market for Corporate Control and Firm Innovation," *Academy of Management Journal* 39 (1996), pp. 1084–1119.

CHAPTER 15

1. G. Hearn, "Managing Change Is Managing Meaning," *Management Communication Quarterly* 16 (2003), pp. 440–446; T. A. Stewart, "Gray Flannel Suit? Moi?" *Fortune* 137, no. 5 (1998), p. 76; F. M. van Ejnatten, "Chaos, Dialogue and the Dolphin's Strategy," *Journal of Organizational Change Management* 15 (2002), pp. 391+; Q. N. Huy, "Emotional Balancing of Organizational Continuity and Radical Change: The Contribution of Middle Managers," *Administrative Science Quarterly* 47, no. 1, (2002), pp. 31–69.
2. M. A. Hitt, R. D. Ireland, and R. E. Hoskisson, *Strategic Management: Competitiveness and Globalization* (Cincinnati, OH: South-Western Publishing Co., 2005).
3. P. F. Drucker, "The New Society of Organizations," *Harvard Business Review* 70, no. 5 (1992), pp. 95–104; C. K. Wagner, "Managing Change in Business: Views from the Ancient Past," *Business Horizons* 38 (1995), p. 812; G. Hamel and L. Valikangas, "The Quest for Resilience," *Harvard Business Review* 81, no. 9 (2003), pp. 52–63; H. Tsoukas and R. Chia, "On Organizational Becoming: Rethinking Organizational Change," *Organization Science* 13, no. 5 (2002), pp. 567–582.
4. J. Kotter, *Leading Change* (Boston: Harvard Business Press, 1998); M. Beer and N. Nohria, "Cracking the Code of Change," *Harvard Business Review*, May-June 2000, pp. 133–141.
5. K. E. Weik, "Enacted Sensemaking in Crisis Situations," *Journal of Management Studies* 25 (1998), pp. 305–318.
6. S. D. Sidle, "Best Laid Plans: Establishing Fairness Early Can Help Smooth Organizational Change," *Academy of Management Executive* 17, no. 1, pp. 127–128.
7. C. M. Christensen and M. Overdorf, "Meeting the Challenge of Disruptive Change," *Harvard Business Review* 78, no. 2 (2000), pp. 67–77; L. D. Schaeffer, "The Leadership Journey," *Harvard Business Review* 80, no. 10, pp. 42–48.
8. R. B. Reich, "Your Job Is Change," *Fast Company* 39 (2000), pp. 140–156; Hamel and Valikangas, "The Quest for Resilience."

9. M. W. McCall, *High Flyers: Developing the Next Generation of Leaders* (Boston: Harvard Business School Press, 1998); J. S. Black, A. J. Morrison, and H. B. Gregersen, *Global Explorers: The Next Generation of Leaders* (New York: Routledge, 1999).

10. Black, Morrison, and Gregersen, *Global Explorers*; M. L. McDonald and J. D. Westphal, "Getting by with the Advice of Friends: CEOs' Advice Networks and Firms' Strategic Responses to Poor Performance," *Administrative Science Quarterly* 48, no. 1, pp. 1–32.

11. B. Breen, "Forced to Face the Web," *Fast Company* 43, no. 2 (2001), pp. 162–167.

12. "Workplace Smoking Ban Would Help Kick Habit," *Occupational Health* 54, no. 9 (2002), p. 7; L. Doss, "Operators Feel Del. Smoke Ban's Heat, Fear Law Will Filter Business," *Nation's Restaurant News* 36, no. 23 (2002), pp. 8, 12; P. Frumpkin, "N.Y. County's Smoke Ban Sparks Downstate Furor," *Nation's Restaurant News* 36, no. 42 (2002), pp. 4, 6.

13. Statistics Canada, "A Portrait of Seniors in Canada," Catalogue no. 89-519-XIE, (2006).

14. J. Pfeffer, "Understanding Power in Organizations," *California Management Review* 34, no. 2 (1992), pp. 29–50.

15. N. Machiavelli, *The Prince* (trans. R. Prince) (New York: Cambridge University Press, 1988).

16. K. Lewin, "Frontiers in Group Dynamics," *Human Relations* 1, pp. 5–41.

17. M. L. Gick and K. J. Holyoak, "Analogical Problem Solving," *Cognitive Psychology* 12 (1980), pp. 306–355; M. L. Gick and K. J. Holyoak, "Schema Induction and Analogical Transfer," *Cognitive Psychology* 15 (1983), pp. 1–38; E. Laszlo, *Changing Visions: Human Cognitive Maps: Past, Present and Future* (Westport, CT: Praeger, 1996).

18. J. A. LePine, "Team Adaptation and Post-Change Performance: Effects of Team Composition in Terms of Members' Cognitive Ability and Personality," *Journal of Applied Psychology* 88, no. 1 (2003), pp. 27–39.

19. D. M. Macri, "A Grounded Theory for Resistance to Change in Small Organizations," *Journal of Organizational Change Management* 15 (2002), pp. 292–309.

20. T. L. Saaty and L. G. Vargas, "Uncertainty and Rank Order in the Analytic Hierarchy Process," *European Journal of Operational Research* 32, no. 1 (1987), pp. 108–118.

21. Lewin, "Frontiers in Group Dynamics"; McDonald and Westphal, "Getting by with the Advice of Friends."

22. Lewin, "Frontiers in Group Dynamics."

23. J. S. Black and H. B. Gregersen, *Leading Strategic Change* (Upper Saddle River, NJ: Prentice Hall, 2002).

24. L. L. Paglis and S. G. Green, "Leadership Self-Efficacy and Managers' Motivation for Leading Change," *Journal of Organizational Behavior* 23 (2002), pp. 215–235.

25. Gick and Holyoak, "Analogical Problem Solving"; Gick and Holyoak, "Schema Induction and Analogical Transfer"; W. Kim, "Exploring Competitive Futures Using Cognitive Mapping," *Long Range Planning* 29, no. 5 (1995), pp. 10–12.

26. F. Gavetti and D. Levinthal, "Looking Forward and Looking Backward: Cognitive and Experiential Search," *Administrative Science Quarterly* 45 (2000), pp. 113–137.

27. J. Brockner and E. T. Higgins, "Regulatory Focus Theory: Implications for the Study of Emotions at Work," *Organizational Behavior and Human Decision Processes* 86, no. 1 (2001), pp. 35–66.

28. M. J. Arean, "Changing the Way We Change," *Organization Development Journal* 20, no. 2 (2002), pp. 33–47; Macri, "A Grounded Theory for Resistance to Change in Small Organizations."

29. R. Cacioppe, "Using Team-Individual Reward and Recognition Strategies to Drive Organizational Success," *Leadership & Organization Development Journal* 20 (1999), pp. 322–331.

30. S. T. Fiske and S. E. Taylor, *Social Cognition* (2nd ed.) (Reading, MA: Addison-Wesley Publications, 1991).

31. N. Watson, "What's Wrong with This Printer?" *Fortune* 147, no. 3 (2003), pp. 120C–120H.

32. T. G. Donlan, "The 80–20 Rule," *Barron's* 83, no. 6 (2003), p. 39.

33. J. Covington and M. L. Chase, "Eight Steps to Sustainable Change," *Industrial Management* 44, no. 6 (2002), pp. 8–11.

34. N. Venkatraman, "IT-Enabled Business Transformation: From Automation to Business Scope Redefinition," *Sloan Management Review* 35, no. 2 (1994), pp. 73–87.

35. J. Evans, "Grand Cathay's Assets Take a Walk," *Asiamoney* 73, no. 9 (2002), p. 49.

36. A. D. Chandler, *Strategy and Structure: Chapters in the History of the Industrial Enterprise* (Cambridge, MA: M.I.T. Press, 1962); T. L. Amburgey and T. Dacin, "As the Left Foot Follows the Right? The Dynamics of Strategic and Structural Change," *Academy of Management Journal* 37 (1994), pp. 1427–1452; M. T. Hannan, L. Polos, and G. R. Carroll, "Cascading Organizational Change," *Organization Science* 14, no. 5 (2003), pp. 463–482.

37. D. A. Nadler and M. L. Tushman, "Beyond the Charismatic Leader: Leadership and Organizational Change," *California Management Review* 32, no. 2 (1990), pp. 77–97; Hannan, Polos, and Carroll, "Cascading Organizational Change."

38. "Nokia Restructures for More 'Mobility,'" *Electronic News* (North America) 49, no. 39 (2003).

39. D. L. Madison, R. W. Alien, L. W. Porter, P. A. Renwick et al., "Organizational Politics: An Exploration of Managers' Perceptions," *Human Relations* 33, no. 2 (1980), pp. 79–100; M. C. Kernan and P. J. Hanges, "Survivor Reactions to Reorganization: Antecedents and Consequences of Procedural, Interpersonal, and Informational Justice," *Journal of Applied Psychology* 87, no. 5 (2002), pp. 916–928.

40. D. Clark, "Inside Intel, It's All Copying," *Wall Street Journal*, October 28, 2002, p. B1.

41. S. Ghoshal and C. A. Bartlett, "Rebuilding Behavioral Context: A Blueprint for Corporate Renewal," *Sloan Management Review* 37, no. 2 (1989), pp. 23–36.

42. W. Weitzel and E. Johnson, "Decline in Organizations: A Literature Integration and Extension," *Administrative Science Quarterly* 34 (1989), pp. 91–109.

43. B. Dumaine, "Times Are Good? Create a Crisis," *Fortune*, 1993, pp. 123–130.

44. M. L. Tushman, W. H. Newman, and E. Romanelli, "Convergence and Upheaval: Managing the Unsteady Pace of Organizational Evolution," *California Management Review* 29, no. 1 (1986), pp. 29–44.

45. C. Piller, "So What if Amelio's File Is Closed? Apple Can Reboot," *Los Angeles Times*, July 10, 1997, pp. D1+; J. Carlton and L. Gomes, "Apple Computer Chief Amelio Is Ousted: Co-Founder Jobs to Assume Broader Role as Search for a Successor Begins," *Wall Street Journal*, July 10, 1997, p. A3.

46. F. Warner, "In a Word, Toyota Drives for Innovation," *Fast Company*, August 2002, pp. 36–38.

47. T. A. Stewart, "3M Fights Back," *Fortune*, 1996, pp. 94–99.

48. C. R. Leana, "Stability and Change as Simultaneous Experiences in Organizational Life," *Academy of Management Review* 25 (2000), pp. 753–762; Huy, "Emotional Balancing of Organizational Continuity and Radical Change."

49. V. Baxter and A. Margavio, "Assaultive Violence in the U.S. Post Office," *Work and Occupations* 23 (1996), pp. 277–296.

50. S. K. Piderit, "Rethinking Resistance and Recognizing Ambivalence: A Multidimensional View of Attitudes toward an Organizational Change," *Academy of Management Review* 25 (2000), pp. 783–795; V. J. Mabin, "Harnessing Resistance: Using the Theory of Constraints to Assist Change Management," *Journal of European Industrial Training* 25, nos. 2/3/4 (2001), p. 168; M. S. Feldman and B. T. Pentland, "Reconceptualizing Organizational Routines as a Source of Flexibility and Change," *Administrative Science Quarterly* 48, no. 1 (2003), pp. 94–118; Huy, "Emotional Balancing of Organizational Continuity and Radical Change"; R. Vince, "The Politics of Imagined Stability: A Psychodynamic Understanding of Change at Hyder plc," *Human Relations* 55, no. 10 (2002), pp. 1189–1208.

51. Piderit, "Rethinking Resistance and Recognizing Ambivalence"; Vince, "The Politics of Imagined Stability."

52. K. Lewin, *Field Theory in Social Science; Selected Theoretical Papers* (New York: Harper, 1951).

53. D. Wong-MingJi, "Dealing with the Dynamic Duo of Innovation and Inertia: The "In-" Theory of Organization Change," *Organization Development Journal* 20, no. 1 (2002), pp. 36–52.

54. B. K. Spiker and E. Lesser, "We Have Met the Enemy," *Journal of Business Strategy* 16, no. 2 (1995), pp. 17–21.

55. J. Kurtzman, "Is Your Company Off Course? Now You Can Find Out Why," *Fortune*, 135 (1997), pp. 58–60.

56. W. L. French, C. H. Bell Jr., and R. A. Zawicki, *Organizational Development and Transformation: Managing Effective Change*, 4th ed. (Burr Ridge, IL: Richard D. Irwin, 1994).

57. Ibid.

58. R. Beckhard, *Organization Development: Strategies and Models* (Reading, MA: Addison-Wesley, 1969); R. D. Smither, J. M. Houston, and S. D. McIntire, *Organization Development: Strategies for Changing Environments* (New York: HarperCollins, 1996); B. Pitman, "Leading for Value," *Harvard Business Review* 81, no. 4 (2003), pp. 41–46.

59. Smither et al., *Organization Development: Strategies for Changing Environments.*

60. Ibid.

61. Lewin, "Frontiers in Group Dynamics"; A. Clardy, "Learning to Change: A Guide for Organization Change Agents," *Personnel Psychology* 56, no. 3 (2003), pp. 785–788.

62. Smither et al., *Organization Development: Strategies for Changing Environments*; N. J. Foss, "Selective Intervention and Internal Hybrids: Interpreting and Learning from the Rise and Decline of the Oticon Spaghetti Organization," *Organization Science* 14, no. 3 (2003), pp. 331+.

63. W. L. French and C. H. Bell Jr., *Organization Development: Behavioral Science Interventions for Organizational Improvement*, 5th ed. (Upper Saddle River, NJ: Prentice Hall, 1995); M. J. Benner and M. E. Tushman, "Exploitation, Exploration, and Process Management: The Productivity Dilemma Revisited," *Academy of Management Review* 28, no. 2 (2003), pp. 238–256; M. J. Benner and M. Tushman, "Process Management and Technological Innovation: A Longitudinal Study of the Photography and Paint Industries," *Administrative Science Quarterly* 41, no. 4 (2002), pp. 676–706.

64. D. A. Garvin, "Leveraging Processes for Strategic Advantage," *Harvard Business Review* 73, no. 5 (1995), pp. 76–79; M. Hammer and J. Champy, *Reengineering the Corporation* (New York: HarperCollins, 1993).

65. D. Rigby, "Management Tools and Techniques: A Survey," *California Management Review* 43, no. 2 (2001), pp. 139–161.

66. Ibid.

67. G. Hall, J. Rosenthal, and J. Wade, "How to Make Reengineering Really Work," *Harvard Business Review* 71, no. 6 (1993), pp. 119–131.

68. J. B. White, "Next Big Thing: Reengineering Gurus Take Steps to Remodel Their Stalling Vehicles," *Wall Street Journal*, November 26, 1996, pp. A1, A10; Rigby, "Management Tools and Techniques"; D. Elmuti and Y. Kathawala, "Business Reengineering: Revolutionary Management Tool, or Fading Fad?" *Business Forum* 25, nos. 1/2 (2000), pp. 29–36.

69. Hall, Rosenthal, and Wade, "How to Make Reengineering Really Work"; Benner and Tushman, "Exploitation, Exploration, and Process Management."

70. Elmuti and Kathawala, "Business Reengineering"; Kernan and Hanges, "Survivor Reactions to Reorganization"; D. A. Buchanan, "Demands, Instabilities, Manipulations, Careers: The Lived Experience of Driving Change," *Human Relations* 56, no. 6 (2003), pp. 663–684.

71. White, "Next Big Thing"; Benner and Tushman, "Process Management and Technological Innovation"; Huy, "Emotional Balancing of Organizational Continuity and Radical Change"; A. E. Akgun, G. S. Lynn, and J. C. Byrne, "Organizational Learning: A Socio-Cognitive Framework," *Human Relations* 56, no. 7 (2003), pp. 839–868.

72. D. M. Rousseau, "Organizational Behavior in the New Organizational Era," *Annual Review of Psychology* 48 (1997), pp. 515–546; C. Argyris and D. A. Schoen, *Organizational Learning II: Theory, Method, and Practice* (Reading, MA: Addison-Wesley, 1996); D. A. Garvin, "Building a Learning Organization," *Harvard Business Review* 71, no. 4 (1993), pp. 78–91; E. C. Nevis, A. J. DiBella, and J. A. Gould, "Understanding Organizations as Learning Systems," *Sloan Management Review* 36, no. 2 (1995), pp. 73–85; F. A. Schein, "How Can Organizations Learn Faster? The Challenge of Entering the Green Room," *Sloan Management Review* 34, no. 2 (1993), pp. 85–92; P. M. Senge, "The Leader's New Work: Building Learning Organizations," *Sloan Management Review* 32, no. 1 (1990), pp. 7–23; P. M. Senge, *The Fifth Discipline* (New York: Doubleday, 1990); S. F. Slater, "Learning to Change," *Business Horizons* 38, no. 6 (1996), pp. 13–20.

73. A. D. Ellinger, A. E. Ellinger, Y. Bayin, and S. W. Howton, "The Relationship between the Learning Organization Concept and Firms' Financial Performance: An Empirical Assessment," *Human Resource Development Quarterly* 13, no. 1 (2002), pp. 5–21.

74. Garvin, "Building a Learning Organization," p. 80.

75. Nevis et al., "Understanding Organizations as Learning Systems."

76. Garvin, "Building a Learning Organization."

77. J. Levinson, "Benchmarking Compliance Performance," *Environmental Quality Management* 6, no. 4 (1997), pp. 49–60.

PART 4 INTEGRATIVE CASE

1. The P/E ratio is calculated by dividing the market price of a share by the earnings per share (EPS). In other words, if a company is reporting an EPS of Rs 2, and the stock is selling for Rs 20 per share, the P/E ratio is 10—because the buyer would be paying 10 times the earnings. [Rs 20 per share divided by Rs 2 per share earnings = 10 P/E.]

2. Summer was the peak demand season for colas, hence Coca-Cola was hesitant to disrupt the operations in any way.

Glossary

acquired needs theory a motivation theory that focuses on learned needs that become enduring predispositions for affiliation, power, and achievement 348

affirmative action programs hiring and training programs intended to correct past inequalities for certain categories of people based on gender, race and ethnicity, age, or religion 467

anchoring using an initial value received from prior experience or any external information source and giving it disproportionate weight in setting a final value 162

approved budget specifies what the manager is actually authorized to spend money on and how much 209

artifacts visible manifestations of a culture such as its art, clothing, food, architecture, and customs 117

assessment centres a work sampling technique in which candidates perform a number of exercises, each one designed to capture one or more key aspects of the job 454

assumptions beliefs about fundamental aspects of life 117

at-risk compensation pay that varies depending on specified conditions, including the profitability of the company; hitting particular budget, revenue, or cost savings targets for a unit; or meeting specified individual performance targets 463

balanced scorecard an integrated and "balanced" set of measures for four critical areas or perspectives: financial, customers, internal business, and innovation and learning 504

behavioural process orientation a key distinguishing feature of the OD approach to organizational change that focuses on new forms of behaviour and new relationships 553

behaviourally anchored rating scales (BARS) a performance appraisal system in which the rater places detailed employee characteristics on a rating scale 460

benchmarking the investigation of the best results among competitors and noncompetitors and the practices that lead to those results; identification, analysis, and comparison of the best practices of competitors against an organization's own practices 200, 557

bona fide occupational qualifications (BFOQ) qualifications that have a direct and material impact on job performance and outcomes 467

boundaryless organization an organization where barriers to effective integration are overcome by people empowered to work across boundaries 277

bounded rationality model (administrative man model) a descriptive model of decision making recognizing that people are limited in their capacity to fully assess a problem and usually rely on shortcuts and approximations to arrive at a decision they are comfortable with 156

brainstorming a process of generating many creative solutions without evaluating their merit 181

break-even point (B-E P) the amount of a product that must be sold to cover a firm's fixed and variable costs 496

broadband systems pay structures in which the range of pay is large and covers a wide variety of jobs 463

budgetary control a type of tactical control based on responsibility for meeting financial targets and evaluating how well those targets have been met 497

budgets used to quantify and allocate resources to specific activities 208

bureaucratic control an approach to tactical control that stresses adherence to rules and regulations and is imposed by others 500

cafeteria-style plans benefit plans in which employees have a set number of "benefit dollars" that they can use to purchase benefits that fit their particular needs 464

capital expenditure budget specifies the amount of money to be spent on specific items that have long-term use and require significant amounts of money to acquire 208

career paths sets and sequences of positions and experiences 464

cash cows products or SBUs that have relatively high market share in markets with unattractive futures 242

centralized organizations organizations that restrict decision making to fewer individuals, usually at the top of the organization 266

change agents individuals who are responsible for implementing change efforts; they can be either internal or external to the organization 553

charismatic leader someone who has influence over others based on individual inspirational qualities rather than formal power 326

code of ethical conduct a formal statement that outlines types of behaviour that are and are not acceptable 92

coercive power a type of position power based on a person's authority to administer punishments, either by withholding something that is desired or by giving out something that is not desired 307

cognitive specialization the extent to which people in different units within an organization think about different things or about similar things differently 258

cohesion the degree to which members are motivated to remain in the group 388

collaboration a part of negotiation in which parties work together to attack and solve a problem 434

collectivism the extent to which identity is a function of the group to which an individual belongs 121

command (supervisory) group a group whose members consist of a supervisor or manager and all those who report to that person 377

commitment (clan) control an approach to tactical control that emphasizes consensus and shared responsibility for meeting goals 500

committee a group that is either permanent or temporary (ad hoc) whose members meet only occasionally and otherwise report to different permanent supervisors in an organization's structure 380

communication the process of transferring information, meaning, and understanding from sender to receiver 414

communication networks identifiable patterns of communication within and between organizations, whether using formal or informal channels 423

compensatory justice if distributive and procedural justice fail, those hurt by the inequitable distribution of rewards are compensated 87

competitive advantage the ability of a firm to win consistently over the long term in a competitive situation 222

concentration of effect the extent to which consequences are focused on a few individuals or dispersed across many 89

concurrent control a type of operational control that evaluates the conversion of inputs to outputs while it is happening 501

conformity close adherence to the group's norms by individual members 387

confrontation a means of helping people perceive contrasts by providing an inescapable experience 533

conjunction fallacy the tendency for people to assume that co-occurring events are more likely to occur than if they were independent of each other or grouped with other events 162

content theories motivation theories that focus on what needs a person is trying to satisfy and what features of the work environment seem to satisfy those needs 344

context-driven competencies competencies that are specific to both the unique nature of the particular tasks and the particular composition of the team 398

contingency plans plans that identify key factors that could affect the desired results and specify what actions will be taken if key events change 198

contrast a means by which people perceive differences 533

control the regulation of activities and behaviours within organizations; adjustment or conformity to specifications or objectives 484

controlling regulating the work of those for whom a manager is responsible 23

core competency focusing on an interrelated set of activities that can deliver competitive advantage in the short term and into the future 238

core value a value that is widely shared and deeply held 130

corporate social responsibility the obligations that corporations owe to their stakeholders, such as shareholders, employees, customers, and citizens at large 80

cost leadership striving to be the lowest-cost producer of a product or provider of a service and yet charge only slightly less than industry average prices 229

critical incidents recording of specific incidents in which the employee's behaviour and performance were above or below expectations 462

cross-functional job rotation opportunities for employees to work in different functional areas and gain additional expertise 464

cross-functional teams employees from different departments, such as finance, marketing, operations, and human resources, who work together in problem solving 170

cultural context the degree to which a situation influences behaviour or perception of appropriateness 134

cultural distance the overall difference between two cultures' basic characteristics such as language, level of economic development, and traditions and customs 430

culture a learned set of assumptions, values, and behaviours that have been accepted as successful enough to be passed on to newcomers 113

customer segment a group of customers who have similar preferences or place similar value on product features 232

decentralized organizations organizations that tend to push decision-making authority down to the lowest level possible 266

decision making a process of specifying the nature of a particular problem or opportunity and selecting among available alternatives to solve a problem or capture an opportunity 151

decoding the act of interpreting a message 415

delphi technique a decision-making technique that never allows decision participants to meet face to face but identifies a problem and asks for solutions using a questionnaire 181

demographics the descriptive elements of the people in a society, such as average age, level of education, financial status, and so on 43

devil's advocate a group member whose role is to challenge the majority position 177

dialectical inquiry a process to improve decision making by assigning a group member (or members) the role of questioning the underlying assumptions associated with the formulation of a problem 180

differentiation a strategy for making a product or service different from those of competitors 229

directing the process of attempting to influence other people to attain organizational objectives 23

distributive justice the equitable distribution of rewards and punishment based on performance 87

dogs products or SBUs that have relatively low market share in unattractive markets 242

downward communication messages sent from higher organizational levels to lower levels 421

dual-career couples couples in which both partners work full time in professional, managerial, or administrative jobs 465

early wins early and consistent positive reinforcement of desired change 535

ease of recall making a judgment based upon the most recent events or the most vivid in our memory 161

effective leadership influence that assists a group or an organization to meet its goals and objectives and perform successfully 304

efficiency (activity) the ratio of amount of sales to total cost of inventory 495

efficiency perspective the concept that a manager's responsibility is to maximize profits for the owners of the business 99

80/20 rule a "rule" that suggests that 80 percent of the desired outcome is provided by 20 percent of the contributing factors 534

emotional intelligence an awareness of others' feelings and a sensitivity to one's own emotions and the ability to control them 312

empathy the ability to put yourself in someone else's place and to understand his or her feelings, situation, and motives 431

encoding the act of constructing a message 415

entry barriers obstacles that make it difficult for firms to get into a business 58

equity theory a motivation theory that focuses on individuals' comparisons of their circumstances with those of others and how such comparisons may motivate certain kinds of behaviour 352

escalation of commitment the tendency to exhibit greater levels of commitment to a decision as time passes and investments are made in the decision, even after significant evidence emerges indicating that the original decision was incorrect 162

ethical dilemmas having to make a choice between two competing but arguably valid options 83

ethical lapses decisions that are contrary to an individual's stated beliefs and the policies of the company 83

ethnocentrism the belief in the superiority and importance of one's own group 429

expatriate employees employees sent overseas on lengthy, but temporary, assignments 467

expectancy theory a motivation theory that focuses on the thought processes people use when they face particular choices among alternatives, especially alternative courses of action 354

expense budget includes all primary activities on which a unit or organization plans to spend money and the amount allocated to each for the upcoming year 208

expert power a type of personal power based on specialized knowledge not readily available to many people 307

external environment a set of forces and conditions outside the organization that can potentially influence its performance 42

externalities indirect or unintended consequences imposed on society that may not be understood or anticipated 100

extinction the absence of positive consequences for behaviour, lessening the likelihood of that behaviour being repeated in the future 361

feminine societies value activities focused on caring for others and enhancing the quality of life 122

flat organizational structure a structure that has fewer layers in its hierarchy than a tall organization 263

focus groups small groups involved in intense discussions of the positive and negative features of products or services 557

force field analysis uses the concept of equilibrium, a condition that occurs when the forces for change, the "driving forces," are balanced by forces opposing change, the "restraining forces," and results in a relatively steady state 548

formal communication channels routes that are authorized, planned, and regulated by the organization and that are directly connected to its official structure 422

formal group a group that is designated, created, and sanctioned by the organization to carry out its basic work and to fulfill its overall mission 380

formalization the official and defined structures and systems in decision making, communication, and control in an organization 262

formulation a process involving identifying a problem or opportunity, acquiring information, developing desired performance expectations, and diagnosing the causes and relationships among factors affecting the problem or opportunity 151

frames of reference existing sets of attitudes that provide quick ways of interpreting complex messages 426

gatekeepers individuals who are at the communication interface between separate organizations or between different units within an organization 433

general environment forces that typically influence the organization's external task environment and thus the organization itself 42

glass ceiling an invisible barrier that prevents women from promotion to the highest executive ranks 467

globalization the tendency to integrate activities on a coordinated, worldwide basis 284

goal-setting theory a theory that assumes human action is directed by conscious goals and intentions 357

Gresham's law of planning the tendency for managers to let programmed activities overshadow nonprogrammed activities 152

gross domestic product the total dollar value of final goods and services produced within a nation's borders 50

group a set of people, limited in number (usually from 3 to 20), who have some degree of mutual interaction and shared objectives 377

groupthink a mode of thinking in which the pursuit of agreement among members becomes so dominant that it overrides a realistic appraisal of alternative courses of action 175

heuristic a decision-making shortcut that can be based upon pre-set rules, memory, or past experiences 157

human resource policies and procedures a type of tactical control based on the organization's overall approach to using its human resources 499

hybrid a structure that combines one or more organizational structures to gain the advantages and reduce the disadvantages of any particular structure 274

in-group the group to which a person belongs 363

incentive plans systems that tie some compensation to performance 464

incremental budgeting approach where managers use the approved budget of the previous year and then present arguments for why the upcoming budget should be more or less 209

individualism the extent to which people base their identities on themselves and are expected to take care of themselves and their immediate families 121

informal communication channels routes that are not pre-specified by the organization but that develop through typical and customary activities of people at work 422

informal group a group whose members interact voluntarily 381

informal organization the unofficial but influential means of communication, decision making, and control that are part of the habitual way things get done in an organization 265

insensitivity to base rates the tendency to disregard information that suggests the likelihood of a particular outcome in the presence of other information 161

insensitivity to sample size the tendency to not consider sample size when using information taken from a sample within a given population 162

integration the extent to which various parts of an organization cooperate and interact with each other 259

interdependence the degree to which one unit or person depends on another to accomplish a task 259

interests in negotiation, a party's concerns and desires—in other words, what they want 434

intergroup conflict differences that occur between groups 401

internal environment key factors and forces inside the organization that affect how it operates 42

interventions sets of structured activities, or action steps, designed to improve organizations 553

intragroup conflict differences that occur within groups 401

intuitive decision making the primarily subconscious process of identifying a decision and selecting a preferred alternative 159

job analysis determination of the scope and depth of jobs and the requisite skills, abilities, and knowledge that people need to perform their jobs successfully 450

job characteristics model an approach that focuses on the motivational attributes of jobs through emphasizing three sets of variables: core job characteristics, critical psychological states, and outcomes 351

job design the structuring or restructuring of key job components 458

job enrichment increasing the complexity of a job to provide greater responsibility, accomplishment, and achievement 351

job posting an internal recruiting method whereby a job, its pay, level, description, and qualifications are posted or announced to all current employees 450

job sharing a situation in which two people share the same job by each working part time 459

justice approach an approach to ethical decision making that focuses on how equitably the costs and benefits of actions are distributed 87

lateral communication messages sent across essentially equivalent levels of an organization 421

legitimate power (formal authority) a type of position power granted to a person by the organization 306

leverage the ratio of total debt to total assets 495

liaisons individuals designated to act as a bridge or connection between different areas of a company 277

line of authority specifies who reports to whom 262

liquidity a measure of how well a unit can meet its short-term cash requirements 495

localization the tendency to differentiate activities country by country 284

LPC (least preferred co-worker) theory a contingency theory of leadership that identifies the types of situations in which task-oriented or person-oriented leaders would be most effective 319

magnitude of the consequences the anticipated level of impact of the outcome of a given action 88

management the process of assembling and using sets of resources in a goal-directed manner to accomplish tasks in an organizational setting 5

managerial ethics the study of morality and standards of business conduct 80

managerial grid a method for measuring the degree to which managers are task oriented and people oriented 317

masculine societies value activities focused on success, money, and possessions 122

Maslow's need hierarchy a theory that states people fulfill basic needs, such as physiological and safety needs, before making efforts to satisfy other needs, such as social and belongingness, esteem, and self-actualization needs 344

media richness different media are classified as rich or lean based on their capacity to facilitate shared meaning 418

medium the mode or form of transmission of a message 415

mental map habitual cognitive patterns 529

misconception of chance the expectation that small sets of randomly assembled objects or sequences should appear random 162

mission statement a statement that articulates the fundamental purpose of the organization and often contains several components 227

moral intensity the degree to which people see an issue as an ethical one 88

moral rights approach an approach to ethical decision making that focuses on examination of the moral standing of actions independent of their consequences 86

motivation the set of forces that energize, direct, and sustain behaviour 341

movement changing perceptions based on the level of certainty or uncertainty associated with the change 527

multiple advocacy a process to improve decision making by assigning several group members to represent the opinions of various constituencies that might have an interest in the decision 180

negative reinforcements undesirable consequences that, by being removed or avoided, increase the likelihood of a behaviour being repeated in the future 360

negotiation the process of conferring to arrive at an agreement between different parties, each with their own interests and preferences 433

network structures formal or informal relationships among units or organizations (e.g., along the firm's value chain) 275

networking a process of developing regular patterns of communication with particular individuals or groups to send and receive information 424

neutralizers of leadership aspects of the organization or work situation that can defeat the best efforts of leaders 324

niche strategy a limited scope or breadth of focus 232

noise potential interference with the transmission or decoding of a message 415

nominal group technique a process of having group members record their proposed solutions, summarize all proposed solutions, and independently rank solutions until a clearly favoured solution emerges 181

nonprogrammed decision a decision about a problem that is either poorly defined or novel 152

normative decision model a contingency model that prescribes standards to determine the extent to which subordinates should be allowed to participate in decision making 322

norms a group's shared standards that guide the behaviour of its individual members 385

objectives the end states or targets that company managers aim for 191

operational control the assessment and regulation of the specific activities and methods an organization uses to produce goods and services 501

operational plans plans that translate tactical plans into specific goals and actions for small units of the organization and focus on the near term 193

opportunity a chance to achieve a more desirable state than the current one 151

organizational charts an illustration of the relationships among units and lines of authority among supervisors and subordinates 257

organizational design the process of assessing the organization's strategy and environmental demands and then determining the appropriate organizational structures 257

organizational development (OD) an approach to organizational change that has a strong behavioural and people orientation, emphasizing planned, strategic, long-range efforts focusing on people and their interrelationships in organizations 552

organizational leadership an interpersonal process involving attempts to influence other people in attaining some goal 303

organizational learning exhibited by an organization that is skilled at creating, acquiring, and transferring knowledge, and at modifying its behaviour to reflect new knowledge and insights 555

organizational renewal a concept of organizational change that proposes a goal of flexibility and capability for continual change 553

organizational structure the sum of the ways an organization divides its labour into distinct tasks and then coordinates them 257

organizations interconnected sets of individuals and groups who attempt to accomplish common goals through differentiated functions and intended coordination 5

organizing systematically putting resources together 22

outsourcing the practice of taking a significant activity within the organization and contracting it out to an independent party 275

paternalism where a leader is regarded as the provider "father" who will take care of the subordinate in return for responsible behaviour and performance 331

path–goal theory of leadership a contingency theory of leadership that focuses on the leader's role in increasing subordinate satisfaction and effort by increasing personal payoffs for goal attainment and making the path to these payoffs easier 321

pay structure a range of pay for a particular position or classification of positions 463

people behaviours behaviours that focus on interaction, such as being friendly and supportive, showing trust and confidence, being concerned about others, and supplying recognition 313

perceptual distortion highlighting the positive features of the implicit favourite over the alternative 159

personal power power based on a person's individual characteristics 305

planning estimating future conditions and circumstances and making decisions about appropriate courses of action; a decision-making process that focuses on the future of an organization and how it will achieve its goals 22, 191

plans the means by which managers hope to hit the desired targets 191

portfolio analysis techniques designed to assist managers in assessing the attractiveness of a market 243

position power power based on an organizational structure 305

positions in negotiation, a party's stance regarding their interests 434

positive reinforcements desirable consequences that, by being given or applied, increase the likelihood of behaviour being repeated in the future 358

post-control a type of operational control that checks quality after production of goods or services outputs 501

power the capacity or ability to influence 305

power distance the extent to which people accept power and authority differences among people 121

pre-control a type of operational control that focuses on the quality, quantity, and characteristics of the inputs into the production process 501

presumed associations the assumption that two events are likely to co-occur based on the recollection of similar associations 161

primary activities activities that are directly involved in the creation of a product or service, getting it into the hands of the customer, and keeping it there 235

probability of effect the moral intensity of an issue rises and falls depending on how likely people think the consequences are 88

problem a gap between existing and desired performance 151

procedural justice ensuring that those affected by managerial decisions consent to the decision-making process and that the process is administered impartially 87

process costs the increasing costs of coordination as group size increases 382

process redesign (re-engineering) involves a fundamental redesign of business processes to achieve dramatic improvements 554

process technological changes alterations in how products are made or how enterprises are managed 46

process theories motivation theories that deal with the way different variables combine to influence the amount of effort people put forth 352

product technological changes changes that lead to new features and capabilities of existing products or to completely new products 45

profit centre a unit or product line in which the related expenses are deducted from the revenue generated 269

profitability the ratio of cost to benefit 495

programmed decision a routine response to a simple or regularly occurring problem 151

project/task force a temporary group put together by an organization for a particular purpose 378

proposed budget provides a plan for how much money is needed and is submitted to a superior or budget review committee 209

prospective rationality a belief that future courses of action are rational and correct 164

proximity the physical, psychological, and emotional closeness the decision maker feels to those affected by the decision 89

punishments undesirable consequences that are applied to decrease the likelihood of behaviour being repeated in the future 361

question marks products or SBUs that have relatively low market share in attractive markets 242

rational model (classical model) a seven-step model of decision making that represents the earliest attempt to model decision processes 153

re-engineering the fundamental rethinking and radical redesign of business processes to achieve dramatic improvements in critical, contemporary measures of performance 459

referent power a type of personal power gained when people are attracted to, or identify with, that person; this power is gained because people "refer" to that person 308

refreezing the process of reinforcing change so that it becomes established 528

regression to the mean overlooking the fact that extreme events or characteristics are exceptional cases that will likely revert back to historic averages over time 162

relationship (affective) conflict interpersonal differences among group members 399

retrievability a decision-making bias where judgments rely on the memory structures of an individual 161

retrospective decision model (implicit favourite model) a decision-making model that focuses on how decision makers attempt to rationalize their choices after they are made 159

reward power a type of position power based on a person's authority to give out rewards 307

rituals symbolic communication of an organization's culture 134

ROE (return on equity) an alternative term for ROI 495

ROI (return on investment) a measure of profitability obtained by dividing net income by the total amount of assets invested 495

role ambiguity a situation in which the expected behaviours for a group member are not clearly defined 385

role conflict a situation in which a member of a group faces two or more contrasting sets of expectations 385

satisficing the tendency for decision makers to accept the first alternative that meets their minimally acceptable requirements rather than pushing them further for an alternative that produces the best results 157

selective perception the process of screening out some parts of an intended message because they contradict our beliefs or desires 426

self-efficacy an individual's confidence about his or her abilities to mobilize motivation, cognitive resources, and courses of action needed to successfully execute a specific task within a given context 356

self-managing (autonomous) work-group a group that has no formally appointed supervisor but is similar to command groups in that the members coordinate their organizational work as if they all reported to the same formally appointed supervisor; members usually appoint their own informal team leader 394

short-term or long-term orientation societies that focus on immediate results and those that focus on developing relationships without expecting immediate results 123

situational leadership model a model that states that different types of appropriate leadership are "contingent" on some other variable, in this case "the situation" 318

social cognitive theory (SCT) a theory that focuses on how individuals think about, or "cognitively process," information obtained from their social environment 355

social consensus the extent to which members of a society agree that an act is either good or bad 88

social intelligence the ability to "read" other people and their intentions and adjust one's own behaviour in response 312

social loafing the phenomenon of reduced effort per person in large groups 382

societal values commonly shared desired end states 44

solution a process involving generating alternatives, selecting the preferred solution, and implementing the decided course of action 151

span of control the number of employees reporting to a given supervisor 262

specialization the extent to which tasks are divided into subtasks and performed by individuals with specialized skills 258

stakeholders individuals or groups who have an interest in and are affected by the actions of an organization 101

standard operating procedure (SOP) established procedure for action used for programmed decisions that specifies exactly what should be done 152

standards targets of performance 486

stars products that have relatively high market share in markets with attractive futures 242

status the standing or prestige that a person has in a group 385

stereotyping the tendency to oversimplify and generalize about groups of people 429

strategic control assessment and regulation of how the organization as a whole fits its external environment and meets its long-range objectives and goals 492

strategic objectives objectives that translate the strategic vision and mission of a firm into concrete and measurable goals 228

strategic partners organizations that work closely with a firm in the pursuit of mutually beneficial goals 59

strategic plans focus on the broad future of the organization and incorporate both external environmental demands and internal resources into managers' actions 192

strategic scope the scope of a firm's strategy or breadth of focus 232

strategic vision what an organization ultimately wants to be and do 226

strong versus weak cultural values the degree to which the cultural values are shared by organization members 128

structural changes changes that significantly affect the dynamics of economic activity 49

structured debate a process to improve problem formulation that includes the using a devil's advocate, multiple advocacy, and dialectical inquiry 180

structured interview an interview in which interviewers ask a standard set of questions of all candidates about qualifications and capabilities related to job performance 453

subculture where values are deeply held but not widely shared 128

subjectively expected utility (SEU) model a model of decision making that asserts that managers choose the alternative that they subjectively believe maximizes the desired outcome 154

substitutes alternative products or services that can substitute for existing products or services 58

substitutes for leadership alternative approaches that can at least partially substitute for the need for leadership or can sometimes overcome poor leadership 323

substitution whether or not the customer's need that you fulfill can be met by alternative means 224

supernormal returns the profits that are above the average for a comparable set of firms 225

supervisory structure a type of tactical control based on reporting levels in an organization 498

support activities activities that facilitate the creation of a product or service and its transfer to the customer 235

switching costs the amount of difficulty and expense involved when customers switch from one company to another 57

SWOT analysis an analysis that requires managers to consider their firm's Strengths, Weaknesses, Opportunities, and Threats for its continued operation 243

T-groups groups of individuals participating in organizational development sessions away from the workplace; also called basic-skills training groups 552

tactical control the assessment and regulation of the day-to-day functions of the organization and its major units in the implementation of its strategy 494

tactical plans plans that translate strategic plans into specific goals for specific parts of the organization 193

tall organizational structure a structure that has multiple layers or is high in terms of vertical differentiation 263

task behaviours behaviours that specify and identify the roles and tasks of leaders and their subordinates, such as planning, scheduling, setting standards, and devising procedures 313

task (substantive) conflict conflict that focuses on differences in ideas and courses of action in addressing the issues facing a group 399

task-contingent competencies competencies that are needed in teams that perform a specific and recurring set of tasks but have varying sets of members 399

task environment forces that have a high potential for affecting the organization on an immediate basis 42

task specialization specialization by what employees do 258

team a type of group that has additional characteristics: a high degree of interdependent, coordinated interaction and a strong sense of members' personal responsibility for achieving specified outcomes 377

team-contingent competencies competencies that are specific to the particular team, but applicable across a wide range of tasks 398

temporal immediacy a function of the interval between the time the action occurs and the onset of its consequences 89

Theory X managers assume the average human being has an inherent dislike for work and will avoid it if possible 120

Theory Y managers assume that work is as natural as play or rest 120

360-degree feedback a performance appraisal system in which information is gathered from supervisors, co-workers, subordinates, and sometimes suppliers and customers 461

traits relatively enduring characteristics of a person 310

transactional leadership leadership that focuses on motivating followers' self-interests by exchanging rewards for their compliance; emphasis is on having subordinates implement procedures correctly and make needed, but relatively routine, changes 328

transformational leadership leadership that motivates followers to ignore self-interests and work for the larger good of the organization to achieve significant accomplishments; emphasis is on articulating a vision that will convince subordinates to make major changes 328

transportable competencies competencies that can be used in any situation 398

two-factor theory a motivation theory that focuses on the presumed different effects of intrinsic job factors (motivation) and extrinsic situational factors (hygiene factors) 349

uncertainty the extent to which future input, throughput, and output factors cannot be forecast accurately 261

uncertainty avoidance the need for things to be clear rather than ambiguous 122

unfreezing undoing old patterns 527

unity of command the notion that an employee should have one and only one boss 262

universal approach an approach to ethical decision making where you choose a course of action that you believe can apply to all people under all situations 86

unstructured interview an interview in which interviewers have a general idea of the questions they might ask but do not have a standard set 453

upward communication messages sent from lower organizational levels to higher levels 421

utilitarian approach an approach to ethical decision making that focuses on the consequences of an action 84

valid selection technique a screening process that differentiates those who would be successful in a job from those who would not 453

value chain a set of key activities that directly produce or support the production of what a firm ultimately offers to customers 234

value proposition the ratio of what customers get from a firm to how much they pay relative to alternatives from competitors 233

values the enduring beliefs that specific conduct or end states are personally or socially preferred to others 117

virtual team a group composed of individuals who do not work together in close physical proximity 395

whistle-blower an employee who discloses illegal or unethical conduct on the part of others in the organization 95

work centrality the degree of general importance that working has in the life of an individual at a point in time 365

work simulation situations in which job candidates perform work they would do if hired or work that closely simulates the tasks they would perform 455

zero-based budgeting approach assumes that all allocations of funds must be justified from zero each year 209

Company Index

Name Index

Subject Index

C

T

U

V

W

X

Z

Credits

CHAPTER 1

p. 1 © Grant Faint/Getty Images, Inc.; p. 2 Courtesy of Home Depot Canada; p. 7 REUTERS/Mike Cassese/Landov; p. 8 © UNICEF/HQ07-1110/Shehzad Noorani; p. 12 EyeWire Collection/Getty Images, Inc.-Photodisc; p. 17 The Canadian Press (Steve White); p. 20 Keith Brofsky/Getty Images, Inc.-Photodisc.

CHAPTER 2

p. 40 Getty Images, Inc.; p. 41 REUTERS/Rebecca Cook/Landov; p. 47 Peter Steiner/CORBIS; p. 52 Wilson Chu/CORBIS/Bettmann; p. 61 REUTERS/Paul Darrow/Landov; p. 64 © Mark Peterson/CORBIS.

CHAPTER 3

p. 77 Kathy Willens/AP/Wide World Photos; p. 78 MaXx MB-03800809 © Vidler; p. 80 © Randi Baird '06 www.rbaird.com; p. 91 PA/The Canadian Press(Haydn West); p. 96 Courtesy of FAIR (fairwhistleblower.ca). Photograph by David Hutton; p. 97 REUTERS/Jim Young/Landov; p. 104 ABACA/The Canadian Press (Patrick Durand).

CHAPTER 4

p. 111 © Eric Bean/Getty Images, Inc.; p. 112 © Steve Murez/Getty Images, Inc.; p. 116 EyeWire Collection/Getty Images, Inc.; p. 118 Mark Wilson/Getty Images, Inc.; p. 125 Courtesy of Radical Entertainment; p. 136 Getty Images, Inc.

CHAPTER 5

p. 148 © Ron Chapple/Getty Images, Inc.; p. 149 REUTERS/Anthony P. Bolante/Landov; p. 158 Getty Images, Inc.-Liasion; p. 172 Photo Courtesy of The Computer History Museum;p. 176 Nokian Footwear Ltd.; p. 176 Nokia; p. 179 www.digitaljournal.com.

CHAPTER 6

p. 189 Stockbyte; p. 190 The Procter & Gamble Company; p. 194 Bellagio Hotel & Casino/MGM Mirage; p. 198 3M; p. 201 Spencer Grant/PhotoEdit; p. 204 Courtesy of Ginch Gonch; p. 212 Courtesy of David Powell.

CHAPTER 7

p. 219 © Stephen Umahtete/Index Stock Imagery, Inc.; p. 220 PETER JONES/Reuters/Landov; p. 225 Courtesy of the Cora Franchise Group; p. 227 KELLOGG'S FROSTED FLAKES, KELLOGG'S COCOA FROSTED FLAKES, KELOOGG'S CHOCO ZUCHARITAS AND KELLOGG'S ZUCHARITAS are trademarks of Kellogg Company. All rights reserved. Used with permission.; p. 244 AFT Photo/CORBIS/Bettmann.

CHAPTER 8

p. 255 © Digital Vision/Getty Images, Inc.; p. 256 © Tom & Dee Ann McCarthy/CORBIS; p. 260 Suncor Energy, Inc.; p. 286 Courtesy McCain Foods Limited.

CHAPTER 9

p. 300 © Justin Pumfrey/Getty Images, Inc.; p. 301 Cyril Jessop/Library and Archives Canada/PA-030212; p. 304 Toronto Star/The Candian Press(Ron Bull); p. 327 Rideau Hall; p. 329 Courtesy of Steven Fletcher, M.P.; p. 331 Courtesy of Sandra Lovelace Nicholas.

CHAPTER 10

p. 339 © Colin Hawkins/Getty Images, Inc.; p. 340 Winnipeg Free Press/The Canadian Press (Ken Gigliotti); p. 346 Courtesy of Assiniboine Credit Union; p. 348 Courtesy of the United Way/Centraide Ottawa, photograph by Jennifer Pershick.

CHAPTER 11

p. 374 © Jon Feingersh/Getty Images, Inc.; p. 376 Courtesy of Capital Health; p. 379 Courtesy of IBM; p. 385 Courtesy of the Forzani Group; p. 393 REUTERS/Andy Clark/Landov; p. 400 CORBIS Royalty Free.

CHAPTER 12

p. 412 © Daly & Newton/Getty Images, Inc.; p. 413 Barbara Filet/Getty Images, Inc.-Stone Allstock; p. 419 PA Photos/Landov; p. 420 The Candian Press (Steve White); p. 430 Getty Images, Inc.

CHAPTER 13

p. 444 © Jon Feingersh/Getty Images; p. 445 Richard Johnson, www.richardjohnson.ca; p. 451 Keith Brofsky/Getty Images, Inc.-Photodisc; p. 468 Photoluxstudio/Canada Council for the Arts; p. 470 Marriott International, Inc.

CHAPTER 14

p. 481 © White Packett; p. 482 © Ian Waldie/REUTERS/CORBIS; p. 487 The Ritz-Carlton Hotel Company, L.L.C.; p. 502 Courtesy of The Canadian Science Centre for Human and Animal Health.

CHAPTER 15

p. 516 © Robert Llewellyn/Imagestate; p. 517 © Royalty Free/CORBIS; p. 525 REUTERS/Mario Anzuoni/Landov; p. 537 Courtesy of Indigo Books & Music.